THE OXFORD HANDBOOK OF

RELIGIOUS CONVERSION

Edited by

LEWIS R. RAMBO

and

CHARLES E. FARHADIAN

OXFORD

UNIVERSITY PRESS

OXFORD

UNIVERSITY PRESS

Oxford University Press is a department of the University of Oxford.
It furthers the University's objective of excellence in research, scholarship,
and education by publishing worldwide.

Oxford   New York
Auckland   Cape Town   Dar es Salaam   Hong Kong   Karachi
Kuala Lumpur   Madrid   Melbourne   Mexico City   Nairobi
New Delhi   Shanghai   Taipei   Toronto

With offices in
Argentina   Austria   Brazil   Chile   Czech Republic   France   Greece
Guatemala   Hungary   Italy   Japan   Poland   Portugal   Singapore
South Korea   Switzerland   Thailand   Turkey   Ukraine   Vietnam

Oxford is a registered trademark of Oxford University Press
in the UK and certain other countries.

Published in the United States of America by
Oxford University Press
198 Madison Avenue, New York, NY 10016

© Oxford University Press 2014

The Oxford handbook of Religious Conversion / edited by Lewis R. Rambo and Charles E. Farhadian.
pages cm
Includes index.
ISBN 978-0-19-533852-2 (hardcover : alk. paper)—ISBN 978-0-19-971354-7 (ebook)
1. Conversion.   I. Rambo, Lewis R. (Lewis Ray), 1943– editor of compilation.
BL639.O94 2014
204'.2—dc23
2013024404

1 3 5 7 9 8 6 4 2
Printed in the United States of America
on acid-free paper

With love and profound gratitude this Handbook is dedicated to:

Judy Sha He
Anna C. Rambo
Vivian Y. Tan

Katherine L. Farhadian
Gabriel L. Farhadian
Gideon A. Farhadian

CONTENTS

Contributors   xi

Introduction   1
LEWIS R. RAMBO AND CHARLES E. FARHADIAN

PART I DISCIPLINARY PERSPECTIVES

1. History and Religious Conversion   25
   MARC DAVID BAER

2. Demographics of Religious Conversion   48
   TODD M. JOHNSON

3. Geographies of Religious Conversion   65
   LILY KONG AND SEETA NAIR

4. Anthropology of Religious Conversion   84
   HENRI GOOREN

5. The Role of Language in Religious Conversion   117
   PETER G. STROMBERG

6. Sociology of Religious Conversion   140
   FENGGANG YANG AND ANDREW ABEL

7. Conversion and the Historic Spread of Religions   164
   ROBERT L. MONTGOMERY

8. Migration and Conversion of Korean American Christians   190
   REBECCA Y. KIM

9. Psychology of Religious Conversion and Spiritual
   Transformation   209
   RAYMOND F. PALOUTZIAN

10. Religious Conversion and Cognitive Neuroscience   240
    KELLY BULKELEY

11. Dreaming and Religious Conversion   256
    KELLY BULKELEY

12. Deconversion   271
    HEINZ STREIB

13. Feminist Approaches to the Study of Religious Conversion   297
    ELIZA F. KENT

14. *Seeing* Religious Conversion Through the Arts   327
    DIANE APOSTOLOS-CAPPADONA

15. Religious Conversion as Narrative and Autobiography   343
    BRUCE HINDMARSH

16. Religious Conversion and Semiotic Analysis   369
    MASSIMO LEONE

17. Political Science and Religious Conversion   401
    TIMOTHY J. STEIGENGA

PART II RELIGIONS

18. Hinduism and Conversion   429
    ARVIND SHARMA

19. Conversion to Jain Identity   444
    ANDREA R. JAIN

20. Buddhist Conversion in the Contemporary World   465
    DAN SMYER YÜ

21. Conversion to Sikhism   488
    GURINDER SINGH MANN

22. Adherence and Conversion to Daoism   508
    LOUIS KOMJATHY

23. Conversion and Confucianism   538
    ANNA SUN

24. "Conversion" and the Resurgence of Indigenous Religion
in China 556
LIZHU FAN AND NA CHEN

25. Conversion to Judaism 578
ALAN F. SEGAL

26. Conversion to Christianity 598
DAVID W. KLING

27. Conversion to Islam in Theological and Historical Perspectives 632
MARCIA HERMANSEN

28. "Conversion" to Islam and the Construction of a Pious Self 667
KARIN VAN NIEUWKERK

29. Conversion to New Religious Movements 687
DOUGLAS E. COWAN

30. Disengagement and Apostasy in New Religious Movements 706
STUART A. WRIGHT

31. Legal and Political Issues and Religious Conversion 736
JAMES T. RICHARDSON

32. Conversion and Retention in Mormonism 756
SETH L. BRYANT, HENRI GOOREN, RICK PHILLIPS,
AND DAVID G. STEWART, JR.

Index 787

Contributors

Andrew Abel is Assistant Professor of Sociology at Hastings College, Hastings, Nebraska.

Diane Apostolos-Cappadona is Professor of Religious Art and Cultural History in the Catholic Studies and Women's & Gender Studies Programs at Georgetown University, Washington, DC.

Marc David Baer is Professor of International History, London School of Economics.

Seth L. Bryant is a US Navy Chaplain, endorsed by Community of Christ. He earned MA degrees in American religious history at Vanderbilt University and in religion in the Americas at the University of Florida.

Kelly Bulkeley, PhD, is a Visiting Scholar at the Graduate Theological Union in Berkeley, California.

Na Chen is Associate Professor of Communication at Fudan University, Shanghai, China.

Douglas E. Cowan is Professor of Religious Studies at Renison University College, the University of Waterloo in Waterloo, Canada.

Lizhu Fan is Professor of Sociology at Fudan University, Shanghai, China.

Charles E. Farhadian is Professor of World Religions and Christian Mission at Westmont College, Santa Barbara, California.

Henri Gooren is an Associate Professor of Anthropology at Oakland University in Rochester, Michigan.

Marcia Hermansen is Director of the Islamic World Studies program at Loyola University Chicago where she teaches courses in Islamic Studies and Religious Studies in the Theology Department.

Bruce Hindmarsh is the James M. Houston Professor of Spiritual Theology at Regent College in Vancouver, British Columbia.

Andrea R. Jain is Assistant Professor of Religious Studies at Indiana University-Purdue University Indianapolis, Indiana.

Todd M. Johnson is Associate Professor of Global Christianity and Director of the Center for the Study of Global Christianity at Gordon-Conwell Theological Seminary, Wenham, Massachusetts.

Eliza F. Kent is Associate Professor of Religion at Colgate University, Hamilton, New York.

Rebecca Y. Kim is the Frank R. Seaver Associate Professor of Sociology and the Director of Ethnic Studies at Pepperdine University, Malibu, California.

David W. Kling is Professor and Chair in the Department of Religious Studies at the University of Miami, Coral Gables, Florida.

Louis Komjathy is Assistant Professor of Theology and Religious Studies at the University of San Diego, San Diego, California, and Research Associate in the Institute of Religion, Science and Social Studies of Shandong University (PRC).

Lily Kong is a Professor of Geography at the National University of Singapore, Singapore.

Massimo Leone is Research Professor of Semiotics and Cultural Semiotics at the Department of Philosophy, University of Torino, Italy.

Gurinder Singh Mann is Professor of Sikh Studies and Director of Center for Sikh and Punjab Studies at the University of California, Santa Barbara.

Robert L. Montgomery, PhD, is an independent scholar in Asheville, North Carolina, who has published extensively in the sociology of missions.

Seeta Nair holds an MA degree in Geography from the National University of Singapore. She works collaboratively with Lily Kong at the National University of Singapore.

Karin van Nieuwkerk is Professor of Anthropology and Professor of Contemporary Islam in Europe and the Middle East at the Radboud University Nijmegen, The Netherlands.

Raymond F. Paloutzian is Professor Emeritus of Experimental and Social Psychology, Westmont College, Santa Barbara, California, and is editor of the *International Review for the Psychology of Religion.*

Rick Phillips is Associate Professor of Sociology at the University of North Florida in Jacksonville, Florida.

Lewis R. Rambo is Research Professor of Psychology and Religion at San Francisco Theological Seminary, San Anselmo, California, and the Graduate Theological Union, Berkeley, California. He has also been a Visiting Professor at Yonsei University, Seoul, Korea, and at Fudan University, Shanghai, China.

James T. Richardson is Foundation Professor of Sociology and Judicial Studies, Director, Grant Sawyer Center for Justice Studies and Judicial Studies Program at the University of Nevada, Reno, Nevada.

Alan F. Segal (1945–2011) was Professor of Religion and Ingeborg Rennert Professor of Jewish Studies at Barnard College, Columbia University in New York from 1980 to 2010.

Arvind Sharma is the Birks Professor of Comparative Religion in the Faculty of Religious Studies at McGill University in Montreal, Canada.

Timothy J. Steigenga is a Professor of Political Science and chair of the Social Sciences and Humanities at the Wilkes Honors College of Florida Atlantic University, Fort Lauderdale, Florida.

David G. Stewart, Jr., MD, is an orthopedic surgeon in Las Vegas, Nevada, and has conducted research and published extensively on the Church of Jesus Christ of Latter Day Saints missionary efforts in over thirty countries.

Heinz Streib is Professor for Religious Education and Ecumenical Theology at the University of Bielefeld, Germany.

Peter G. Stromberg is Professor of Anthropology at the University of Tulsa, Tulsa, Oklahoma.

Anna Sun is Associate Professor of Sociology and Asian Studies at Kenyon College, Gamblier, Ohio.

Fenggang Yang is Professor of Sociology and Director of the Center on Religion and Chinese Society at Purdue University, Indiana.

Dan Smyer Yü is a Research Group Leader at Max Planck Institute for the Study of Religious and Ethnic Diversity in Göttingen, Germany.

Stuart A. Wright is Professor of Sociology and Chair of the Department of Sociology, Social Work and Criminal Justice at Lamar University in Beaumont, Texas.

THE OXFORD HANDBOOK OF

RELIGIOUS CONVERSION

INTRODUCTION

LEWIS R. RAMBO AND CHARLES E. FARHADIAN

CONVERSION AND GLOBAL TRANSFORMATION

IN 1893 a Bengali Hindu monk, Swami Vivekananda, visited the United States and delivered a passionate speech at the meeting of the World Parliament of Religions in Chicago that praised the Vedic teaching on tolerance and universal acceptance. The audience was enraptured; his speech met with a standing ovation. Swami Vivekananda was the first major spokesperson for the Hindu tradition in the West, and he shared about Vedanta, the belief that God is within and everywhere, based on the insights of Swami Vivekananda's own guru, Ramakrishna (1836–86). Harvard philosopher William James proclaimed Vivekananda to be the "paragon of Vedantists." Leo Tolstoy claimed, "He is the most brilliant wise man."[1] Noble Prize recipient Rabindranth Tagore, a fellow Bengali Indian, declared, "If you want to know India, study Swami Vivekananda. In him everything is positive and nothing negative."[2] The impact of Swami Vivekananda's introduction of Vedanta philosophy and Hindu yoga in the West is incalculable, and some consider him the first Hindu missionary to the West. Public figures such as J. D. Salinger, Leo Tolstoy, Sarah Bernhardt, Aldous Huxley, Christopher Isherwood, and George Harrison embraced Vedanta philosophy. Following Vivekananda's stunning lecture at Harvard's Graduate Philosophical Club in 1896, "Eastern Philosophy" departments burgeoned at Ivy League colleges.[3] One aspect of Vedanta philosophy is the conclusion that behind the many religions and philosophies of the world is the One Absolute; this has become an immensely popular orientation in the West in both its popular and philosophical formulations.

Conversion occurs in all directions. Prior to Vivekananda's visit to the United States, another Indian had traveled West. In the late nineteenth century, a Brahmin Hindu woman, Pandita Ramabai (1858–1922), who was a brilliant poet, Sanskrit scholar, and activist, a polyglot who had memorized nearly twenty thousand Hindu sacred verses by the age of 12, traveled to Britain and the United States for education and converted to Christianity. Her conversion made her a pariah among some Indian intellectuals, but she was convinced that becoming a Christian should not entail a denial of Indian culture.

Pandita Ramabai declared that conversion to Christianity made her more cognizant of the inequality of women and the poor in Indian society, and she consequently worked tirelessly for women's social reform, starting the Mukti Mission for destitute women and children irrespective of their backgrounds. Her book, *The High-Caste Hindu Woman*, severely critiqued inequalities and injustices in Indian society. Pandita Ramabai's conversion hurt her reputation in India, yet years later she was touted by evangelicals, Anglicans, Catholics, Indian nationalists, and feminists as a major inspiration.

Conversion is never a neutral act. Pandita Ramabai and Swami Vivekananda each wrote influential works that advanced their distinctive ideas. Swami Vivekananda was well aware of Pandita Ramabai's conversion to Christianity, and he strategized to provide a countervailing force to her influence in the West.

The Swami would even unabashedly flatter women to realize his objective. With a view to recruiting a worker for propaganda against Pandita Ramabai, an Indian Christian woman in the United States trying to raise funds to help child widows of India, he asked Miss Sarela Ghosal, editor of the *Bharati*, to volunteer to preach Vedanta in the West. He wrote to her:

> If anyone like you go, England will be stirred, what to speak of America! If an Indian woman in Indian dress preach the religion which fell from the lips of the Rishis of India—I see a prophetic vision—there will rise a great wave which will inundate the whole Western world. Will there be no woman, in the land of Maitreyi, Khana, Lilavati, Savitri, and Ubhayabharati, who will venture to do this?[4]

Conversion establishes new boundaries; secondary identifications of ethnicity and nationalism often complicate new conversion identities shaped by religious communities that transcend geopolitical limitations.[5] The narratives of Swami Vivekananda and Pandita Ramabai illustrate the global reach of conversion and the controversies surrounding its occurrence.

Religious conversion comprises such monumental changes that previous ways of understanding the phenomenon seem inadequate. New ways of interpreting religious conversion are warranted because conversion encompasses religious, political, psychological, social, and cultural domains. Contemporary studies of religious conversion that are informed by Western notions of human beings, derived in large part from Western interests and Christianity, have to be enriched to include a broader array of religiously, culturally, socially, and psychologically relevant insights.

Religious conversion has inspired some of the greatest changes to the human condition. During what Karl Jaspers called the Axial Age (c. 800–200 B.C.E.), a period when some of the world's most significant intellectual shifts occurred, "the spiritual foundations of humanity were laid simultaneously and independently in China, India, Persia, Judea, and Greece. And these are the foundations upon which humanity still subsists today."[6] The unparalleled transformations that occurred during the Axial Age profoundly altered the world. Through the influence of Platonism, Mahavira, Buddha, King Ashoka, Confucius, Laozi Lao-tzu, Homer, Socrates, Elijah, Isaiah, Jeremiah, and the recording of the Upanishads, new ideas reshaped the world. Conversion marked the life of each major figure in this period. Mahavira left his Kshatriya Hindu family to start the Jain tradition; Shakyamuni Siddhartha Gautama, also raised in a Kshatriya Hindu family, became the Enlightened One—the Buddha—and promoted the "Middle Way" while sending missionaries to teach the path to enlightenment. Confucius and Lao-tzu, according to tradition, gained full insight and departed from their ordinary lives to promote their philosophies. King Ashoka, originally a Hindu, was known for his cruelty until his conversion to Buddhism, after which he promoted nonviolence and the expansion of Buddhist virtues throughout his kingdom and beyond the Indian subcontinent into other regions of Asia.

Centuries later, Saul, a Pharisaic Jew of the first-century Roman Empire, converted to become a servant of Jesus Christ after experiencing a vision of the resurrected Jesus.[7] Following his conversion, Saul was renamed Paul and then became the most influential early Christian missionary and the author of major portions of the New Testament. Sixth-century western Arabia was home to Prophet Muhammad, whom God called to leave polytheistic Meccan religions and submit to the One God, Allah, the Merciful, the Compassionate. In the fifteenth century, tradition notes that Guru Nanak, born into a Hindu family, was enlightened by God and realized that "there is no Hindu, no Muslim," compelling him to start the Sikh tradition. In nineteenth-century upstate New York, another prophet appeared, Joseph Smith, whose revelation declared the restoration of the Christian church and led to the founding of The Church of Jesus Christ of Latter-day Saints.

These famous religious leaders represent a small fraction of the massive numbers of people who have experienced religious conversion worldwide. The combined influence of countless religious converts over the centuries has led to massive social and cultural change in the history of the world. The conversion process will undoubtedly continue to transform the way human beings see themselves, the divine, the cosmos, and the natural environment. Reflecting on the massive social and cultural changes resulting from conversion, anthropologist Robert Hefner notes, "For many people, it would appear, incorporation into a broader social order brought not just technological and political transformations of traditional lifeways but far-reaching adjustments in the canons of divinity, identity, and social ethics as well."[8] Indeed, religious conversion has altered the course of the world as it has changed the trajectory of individual and corporate lifeways.

Every religion seeks to define the parameters of its tradition, often delineated by mandating orthodoxy and orthopraxy (i.e., the right beliefs and practices of the religious tradition). The early Buddhist Councils, for instance, sought to record and articulate the Buddhist nature of enlightenment. Disagreements over the details of scripture and monastic discipline eventually led to a split that gave rise to the Mahayana and Theravada Buddhist traditions. While early Buddhists generally accepted varying perspectives on the tradition, there was significant discussion about the nature of the Buddhist tradition itself and what marked a committed monk (*bhikkhu*). Entrance into the Buddhist tradition required knowledge of these qualities and conditions. Despite the fact that religions have always been self-monitoring, in part to decipher the tradition itself, and often give honorific titles to the more devout among the followers (e.g., guru, prophet, haji, saint), it has not been until the rise of modern scholarship that we have witnessed a more concentrated effort at understanding the complicated nature of religious conversion. That attempt has been a topic of intense study and debate for more than a century.

HISTORY OF THE STUDY OF CONVERSION

Religious conversion is a complex topic that elicits controversy, confusion, curiosity, fascination, skepticism, and enthusiasm. Everyone has an opinion about how and why people change within or to other religions or reject religion altogether. For many, conversion is a transcendent experience; for others, it comes at the cost of being shunned by the families and the religious communities that once nurtured them.

When discussing religious conversion, questions abound. Is religion expanding or contracting? Is secularization dominating the modern world or is religion expanding? The answer to these questions is yes! Both processes are at work in various parts of the world. Jürgen Habermas has called this a "post-secular" society, where both secularism and religion flourish.[9] Our world is marked by increasing fundamentalist radicalization and religion in general, as well as by secularization and the political use of religion to justify violence. Religion can also be the source of successful peace-making strategies and the source of forgiveness and human reconciliation between the human and the divine, between human beings, and between communities, such as through the work of peace and reconciliation commissions.[10]

What is occurring in the world today is complex and baffling. Some religious people celebrate the current proliferation and revitalization of religious options, but others are disconcerted by what they consider a return to primitive, pernicious ways of life and violent modes of behavior. Millions of people are embracing religion, while at the same time millions of others are departing from religion. In some cases, people leave one religion and find another religion; in other cases, people jettison religious beliefs and rituals in favor of a secular worldview or an assortment of ad hoc selections from a smorgasbord of religious options.

Conversion is a fascinating, complex, and contested topic. The idea and the phenomena associated with conversion have engaged people for centuries. How and why individuals and groups of people change religions or become passionately devoted to what was once merely a marginal concern, often elicits celebration among some and perplexity and outrage among others.

For most of history, religious change has been a domain of partisan advocacy and either quick dismissal or harsh criticism by others, especially those who see their family, friends, or co-religionists jettison their religion of origin. Converts and their new community of faith sometimes proclaim that a new convert is another confirmation of the truth of their religion. Judaism, Christianity, and Islam have tended to be the most demanding of the religions that have specific rules, rituals, and doctrines that provide guidelines for what are authentic and inauthentic modes of movement from a person's old allegiance to the new system of beliefs, practices, and community.

Theologians and historians have traced these vicissitudes within various traditions and locations. Since the end of the nineteenth century, various academic disciplines have proposed theories and methods to describe, understand, and interpret the nature of conversion processes. The origin of the field of psychology is deeply connected to this debate because it shaped the context of the early founders of psychology in general and of psychology of religion in particular.

Two of the most influential early scholars on religious conversion were Harvard professors: William James and A. D. Nock. William James's *Varieties of Religious Experience* (1902) has been at the center of the discussion related to conversion since the emergence of modern, critical scholarship on the nature of religious conversion. *Varieties of Religious Experience* has remained in print since it was first published and is still one of the most popular books on the topic. James described conversion in the following way:

> to be converted, to be regenerated, to receive grace, to experience religion, to gain
> an assurance, are so many phrases which denote the process, gradual or sudden, by
> which a self hitherto divided, and consciously wrong, inferior, and unhappy becomes
> unified and consciously right, superior, and happy in consequence of its firmer hold
> upon religious realities.[11]

James's typology of the healthy-minded and the sick soul has been cited in numerous articles and books for the last one hundred years. The healthy-minded person was "once born" (developing his or her religious orientation over time), whereas the "twice born" person often experienced excruciating guilt for his or her previous life of sin. Conversion for the sick soul was traumatic, dramatic, and compelling.

Arthur Darby Nock's book *Conversion* (1933) is the second most influential book on conversion. Conversion, for Nock, is a deliberate and definitive break with past religious beliefs and practices. Nock rejected any religious change that was less definitive, which he referred to as merely "adhesion." Nock asserts: "By conversion we mean the reorientation of the soul of an individual, his deliberate turning from indifference or from an earlier form of piety to another, a turning which implies a consciousness that a great change is involved, that the old was wrong and the new is right. It is seen at its fullest in the positive response of a man to the choice set before him by the prophetic religions."[12]

James's and Nock's perspectives reflect a subjectivist orientation deeply influenced by Protestant Pietistic understandings of religious conversion that privileges interior states and subjectivities. Influenced by James and Nock, early researchers focused on the psychological processes of change, turmoil, and resolution. Unpacking the inner experience of converts was viewed as crucial in the endeavor to comprehend the processes of conversion.

The focus of James and Nock on psychological processes of converts is still influential, but is being eclipsed by contemporary conversion studies which, while recognizing that some religious conversions fit James's and Nock's definitions, now view the majority of conversions as taking place gradually over a period of time and as less dramatic and radical. The emphasis today is on the process of constructing new identities within a context with, in some cases, starts, stops, diversions, and even reversals.

The work of James and of G. Stanley Hall, a pioneering American psychologist, was also important in the focus on what was, in their day, a widespread movement among Protestant Christians calling for, cultivating, and expecting conversions that were considered mandatory for the very salvation of people's souls. Historians of Puritans and various Protestant groups in the United States have tended to carefully explore the diaries, letters, and autobiographies of both ordinary and famous Puritans for an understanding of the process of religious transformation in the context of the perceived salvation of souls.

Within the last four decades, scholars have expanded their scope beyond Protestant and psychological approaches to conversion to see that there is a wider world of religious transformation. However, even though often ignored by earlier conversion scholars until recently, scholars, such as Thomas Walker Arnold's *The Preaching of Islam*, examined the complexities of Islamization and the submission (many Muslims prefer terms such as embracing or submitting to Allah instead of converting) of millions of people to Islam, now the second largest religion and some believe the fastest-growing religion in the world. Nehemiah Levtzion's *Conversion to Islam* (1979) has been a major stimulus in reshaping the contours of conversion studies. In addition, William Bulliet's *Conversion to Islam in the Medieval Period* (1979) has inspired both new theoretical and historical approaches to Islam as well as to the dynamics of religious change in various parts of the world (see chapters by Hermansen and van Nieuwkerk).

The contemporary field of conversion studies is the product of the confluence of a number of streams of scholarship in various parts of the world concerning multiple religious traditions. New theoretical and methodological developments have emerged, in part, because of the changing contours of contemporary global religions.

The unexpected growth and development of New Religious Movements, the resurgence of Islam, and the proliferation of various forms of charismatic-Pentecostal and vigorous forms of Roman Catholicism and Protestantism in many parts of the world have shattered the earlier expectation of the inevitable secularization of the world. There appears to be an ebb and flow of forces for sacralization and secularization that was unimagined thirty years ago.

During the last five decades, sociology has been the most prominent discipline examining the vicissitudes of New Religious Movements, first in the United States, then in Europe, and eventually in other parts of the world. The research of John Lofland and Rodney Stark is especially noteworthy. In their detailed studies of the Unification Church, Lofland and Stark shifted the discussion from notions of passive converts and of sudden and radical changes to an understanding of converting as a process over time in which active converts construct new ways of life in interaction with new religious communities, often ones with charismatic leaders and enthusiastic followers. Lofland and Stark's 1965 paper, "Becoming a World-Saver: A Theory of Conversion to a Deviant Perspective," began a new phase of conversion studies.[13] Indeed, James Richardson has argued persuasively that Lofland and Stark's paper was nothing less than a new paradigm for the study of conversion.[14]

Another historical stream of scholarship on conversion involved the work of anthropologists. Until the 1950s, early anthropologists tended to work primarily in remote areas and among small-scale societies, and their work was often not taken into consideration by historians, psychologists, and sociologists. The research of scholars like Robin Horton, however, served to broaden the field of knowledge. Horton, beginning in 1971, published three papers theorizing that Africans, in their encounter and engagement with Islam and Christianity, were attracted to or rejected these new religions based on their own sociocultural and religious predicaments. Horton proposed that conversion to a world religion involved an expansion of worldviews and religious rituals as people transitioned from indigenous religions that focused on their local, relatively limited microcosms to the broader world in which they were encountering expanding relationships with different groups and circumstances. Horton's "intellectualist" theory stimulated wide discussion that has, like Lofland and Stark's seminal 1965 article, shifted the direction of studies of conversion.[15]

Contemporary perspectives on conversion recognize that while a subjectivist orientation is a valuable way to understand religious change, there is a pressing need for the study of conversion to embrace a wider range of themes, disciplinary insights, and global forms. A more adequate approach widens the purview of discourse to consider the influence of sociocultural forces, cognitive scientific factors, psychological influences, identity formation, immigration, and intercultural contact in religious conversion.

Since the late twentieth and early twenty-first centuries, the field of conversion studies has explored a number of prominent themes. First, many early scholars of conversion emphasized the *discontinuities between a person's or a group's religious past and their new religion*. Today, students of conversion are more prone to see the continuities between the past and current religious/spiritual orientations. In other words, current scholarship works carefully with a wide continuum of points of continuity and discontinuity in order to understand religious conversion.

A second theme that has emerged in contemporary scholarship focuses on the *active agency of converts* in the conversion process. While not disregarding situations in which converts are coerced or induced to convert, most scholars today investigate the ways in which converts are actively engaged in a complex assessment and even negotiation with a new religious option. It should also be noted that religions and various advocates or missionaries of a religious tradition are flexible and creative as they encounter novel situations. They are, of course, seeking to embody long-standing traditions, but at the same time they are seeking to maximize their relevance and viability as they confront new challenges.

A third theme in the recent history of conversion studies involves the recognition of the *complexity and diversity of motivations* that engage converts in making the changes involved in conversion. Some scholars still insist that authentic conversion is motivated by only religious and spiritual concerns, but many scholars now acknowledge that motivations are multiple and change over time as a person experiences the converting process. Many scholars of conversion determine the authenticity of conversion based on the attributed or reported motivations for religious changes.

A fourth subject that has emerged in the recent history of conversion studies is the *importance of narratives*. While fraught with many difficulties (such as the reliability of converts' narratives of their own conversion story), the centrality of how people engage in discourse about their religious journeys is extremely important. In fact, many scholars of conversion today see the narrative itself as the constitutive process of how converts are "made." The language of conversion is, of course, not only personal but is intimately connected to the community of faith or religious tradition into which a person is moving (see the chapters by Stromberg and Hindmarsh).

A fifth theme in contemporary conversion studies is the recognition of the *significance of the human body*, the physical place and space in which conversion transpires and that sustains the conversion process. Most scholars now understand the centrality of ritual in conversion. How human beings orchestrate their actions is as important as, and some would argue more important than, the role of belief and other cognitive dimensions of conversion. Changes to the human body can crucially impact religious conversion. Few conversion scholars reject the significance of cognitive processes, but most contemporary scholars seek to give a fuller recognition to actions and behavior as expressed in the formation and sustaining power of rituals and other "material" dimensions of conversion.

A sixth trend in modern conversion studies exhibits a keen awareness of what James Richardson and Henri Gooren call *conversion careers*. In the past, conversion was seen as a radical, often sudden, and permanent change in a person or group. The empirical reality is that people are constantly on the move. People enter and leave various religious traditions and institutions, and many ultimately depart from organized religion. Millions of people are drifting away from religion and/or are actively rejecting religion. Hence, conversion studies must include both the resurgence of religion and spirituality and the dynamics of leaving religion. In the past, the topic of deconversion was not usually considered part of the literature of conversion studies, but that has recently changed. Movement into a new tradition or even the intensification of commitment within the same religious tradition may involve some degree of deconversion, apostasy, or disaffiliation as certain attitudes, beliefs, and practices are abandoned or curtailed in the process of adopting a new orientation.[16]

A seventh theme of contemporary scholarship on religious conversion is the *engagement of conversion analyses with historical material*. That is, theoretical work on religious conversion that emerged in the late twentieth and early twenty-first century is being applied not only to contemporary societies and movements but also to historical events and persons. By applying conversion research to historical conversion processes, new light can be shed on historical events. In addition, the rich, complex data of historical studies can critique, embellish, and expand the horizons of various conversion theories (see chapters by Jain and Yü).

The astonishing contemporary proliferation of books and articles on conversion indicates that conversion is moving from a specialized interest in various disciplines and religions to a field in which many issues converge. Given the remarkable globalization of perspectives, conversion serves as a topic that confronts not only religious and spiritual change but also how different societies and cultures encounter and interact with one another, in both colonial and postcolonial locations as well as in other contexts. Conversion studies examine how people and institutions are constantly in flux—adjusting, adapting, and resisting the various forces that are most visible in energetic proselytizing efforts but also actively pursuing new options. Another way to think about this proliferation of conversion studies is to recognize the ongoing fascination with how and why people and groups change in various circumstances.

While some may doubt that there is a field of "conversion studies," the editors and many of the contributors to this volume would propose that the dynamics of conversion processes is an important and growing enterprise in the contemporary academic scene that appeals not just to intellectuals but is of wide interest to all those fascinated by the vicissitudes of religious effervescence and also by the challenges of secularization.

Contemporary Issues in Conversion Studies

One of the most important and also most contentious issues in conversion studies is defining the term "conversion" itself. Perhaps the most straightforward, even if insufficient, way to understand conversion is as "change" or "transformation." The process of religious conversion—or "converting," the term we prefer—is dynamic and malleable. Likewise, "deconverting" is complex and variable. Each religion has its own normative definitions of the nature and purpose of converting and its own means of establishing who is "in" and who is "out" of its particular religious orientation and organization. These definitions change over time; if one focuses on the meaning of conversion or converting within Christian history, for example, variations of meanings are obvious (see chapter by Kling).[17] In addition, each academic discipline, with its own distinctive history, also argues for what is to be included and excluded in their definition of conversion. Each discipline usually has a specific interpretation of what constitutes the authentic causes of conversion and what does or does not fit its point of view of what constitutes conversion.

The authors of this handbook highlight new and emerging issues that are important, but often neglected, in conversion studies. For instance, Kent's chapter explores gender as a crucial variable in conversion processes. The role of signs and symbols is explicated in Leone's chapter. Bulkeley's chapter on dreams provides researchers with an overview and analysis of how dreams may be included in the study of conversion. Kim's chapter on migration points to the impact of the dislocation and relocation of people on their religious lives. Apostolos-Cappadona investigates the role of art in both the depiction of conversion and in eliciting or shaping conversion. Richardson's chapter surveys and critiques the often contentious use of legal systems in defining and controlling conversion. Political concerns about conversion are emphasized in Steigenga's chapter. Stromberg's chapter on language articulates both the ways in which language expresses conversion and how language is constitutive of the conversion experience.

A New Vision for the Future of Conversion Studies

The study of conversion is enjoying not only a rebirth of interest but also an astonishing transformation of meanings, methods, and paradigms. This handbook explores many of these developments and advocates for an interdisciplinary approach that is inclusive of various perspectives but also focuses on specific domains of research and theoretical critique.

Second, interdisciplinary approaches are crucial in order to explore the complexity and diversity of religious phenomena. Interdisciplinary and comparative studies of conversion do not, of course, obviate the importance of continuing to study carefully the particular, the local, and the distinctive phenomena of various religions in particular areas of the world.

Third, long-standing assumptions, methods, and theories can no longer be taken for granted. For instance, with new developments in cognitive neuroscience, we are more keenly aware than ever that the cognitive sciences can offer helpful theoretical insights and critiques of previous theories (see chapter by Bulkeley). Critique of virtually all approaches is the order of the day.

Fourth, the definition of conversion is undergoing serious reconsideration as new methods, new religions, new theories, and new paradigms are being examined. Indeed, some are even debating whether the word "conversion" should be applied to Islam, Christianity, Buddhism, Judaism, and other religions.

Defining Conversion

In this handbook, we have deliberately chosen to embrace a diversity of definitions of conversion. The reason is simple. Even though there are many different—and sometimes contradictory—definitions of conversion, we recognize that these multiple definitions are deployed by different religions and academic disciplines. From a normative point of view within a particular religious community, "conversion is what a group or a person says it is."[18] In other words, language is fashioned in the context of particular cultures at certain times in history and for distinct purposes.

We propose that conversion studies be reframed more broadly. While particular definitions may be appropriate to a certain religion at a specific time and place, there is no universal definition that we believe captures all aspects of religious conversion.

Marc Baer, a contributor to this handbook, provides a rich, nuanced definition of conversion that both articulates and embodies many of the aspirations of this handbook. While reflecting on Sunni Islam during the Ottoman Empire, Baer defines conversion as follows:

> I take an integrated approach to conversion, linking conversion of self, others, and space, and include the dimension of power and the context of war and conquest. This is one of the few works that examines the intricacies of religious change in its individual (personal) and social and political (public) aspects and places it in historical context. I argue that conversion is a decision or experience followed by a gradually unfolding, dynamic process through which an individual embarks on religious transformation. This can entail an intensification of belief and practice of one's own religion, moving from one level of observation to another, or exchanging the beliefs and practices in which one was raised for those of another religious tradition. In both cases, a person becomes someone else because his or her internal mind-set and/or external actions are transformed. In the case of intensification where one did not give other than cursory thought or attention to the theology of one's faith or engage in keeping wholeheartedly to its requirements, one devotes one's mind and body fully to understanding and embracing the religion. Whereas some scholars still posit an artificial distinction between 'exterior' and 'interior' conversion, I argue that conversion has an internal component entailing belief and an external component involving behavior, leading to the creation of a new self-identity and new way of life.[19]

The study of conversion and the converting process provides us with a fascinating window through which to understand more fully the dynamics of religion in the twenty-first century. Gannon avers that the study of conversion is a crucial "thematic site" in the study of the phenomena of religion and religious change.[20] In the following paragraphs, we highlight some of the requirements for conversion studies that will contribute to our understanding of the dynamics of religion in today's world.

Globalization of Conversion Studies

A crucial requirement for the enrichment of the field of conversion studies is to expand the horizons of what is included in the study of conversion. In the past, with some exceptions, the study of conversion focused primarily on conversion to Christianity and, more recently, New Religious Movements.[21] Even within the study of conversion to Christianity, the focus tended to be on evangelical and conservative forms of Christianity, giving short shrift to Roman Catholicism, Orthodox Christianity, and a wide range of historic Protestants such as the Anglican Communion, the Reformed Tradition, and the World Lutheran Federation.

Our approach to understanding conversion embodies several characteristics. First, we advocate taking into account the global forces that shape our contemporary world. Narrow approaches that seek to understand just the immediate context of conversion are no longer sufficient. The world is connected in ways that warrant innovative approaches to exploring the broad influences and global forces that impact converting processes.

An urgent requirement for conversion studies is the inclusion of as many religions as possible. Islam and Buddhism are especially important given their vast size (see chapters by Hermansen, van Nieuwkerk, Yü, and Montgomery). With more than 1.5 billion adherents, Islam has been virtually ignored in conversion studies until recently, and in the fields of psychology and sociology, few studies have been done.[22] Even anthropologists have devoted little time to the major religious traditions of the world, instead focusing on indigenous religions or so-called primal religions.[23] In addition, the study of conversion needs to be more geographically inclusive. Religious change in all areas of the world must come into the field of vision of scholars of conversion. In this regard, anthropologists and missiologists have already led the way.

Interdisciplinary Perspectives

Conversion studies should expand its horizons and include relevant disciplines in order to plumb the depths of human communities, cultures, experience, action, and consciousness. The topic of religious conversion requires the resources of various disciplines in order to understand the multiple factors and dimensions that intersect in religious and spiritual phenomena. Researchers have tended to focus on specific dimensions of religious change within their own disciplines, and no one discipline has yet created a comprehensive theory of conversion processes and patterns. We envision that future conversion studies will orchestrate the distinctive contributions of many disciplines, resulting in a genuinely multidisciplinary and, in some cases, an authentically interdisciplinary approach to the study of the phenomena of conversion. The task ahead is to find ways of creatively linking micro, meso, and macro studies of converting from many different perspectives.

Academic disciplines shape the questions, methods, and theories that influence the definitions of conversion. For instance, psychology and Protestant theology had a dominant influence in the study of conversion for most of the nineteenth and twentieth centuries. In addition, many express concern because the language of conversion is largely derived from Judaism and Christianity (see chapters by Fan and Chen, Komjathy, van Nieuwkerk, and Sun). In the 1970s, the field of sociology, especially in the study of New Religious Movements, began to exert an influence on the ways in which conversion was conceptualized and studied (see chapter by Yang and Abel). Anthropologists began to see the study of conversion as a topic worthy of investigation, in part because of its role in social, cultural, and political change, and in the last two decades a significant number of anthropological studies of conversion have been published (see chapter by Gooren).

Interdisciplinary work is, of course, extremely difficult. Scholars have worked hard to develop specialized knowledge and skills in their respective disciplines. Many are thus hesitant to incorporate (or even to consider) the work of colleagues in other disciplines. Disciplinary research traditions, assumptions, methods, and ideologies often constrain genuine consultation and collaboration, but the study of religious conversion needs to engage experts in various fields and afford them respect for the alternative perspectives each discipline may provide. This statement should not be read as advocating a form of interdisciplinary interaction requiring that each discipline jettison its distinctive contributions.[24] The importance of specialized disciplinary knowledge and perspectives is not in dispute. Rather, the issue is that specialized skills and knowledge carry with them concomitant limitations: "Each discipline has been developed to illuminate a different, particular facet of reality."[25] Scholars, therefore, must be encouraged to be open to perspectives that, while very different, offer valuable insights into the complex phenomena under examination (see chapters by Kent, Apostolos-Cappadona, Kong and Nair, and Hindmarsh).

In this case, scholars of converting processes must realize that various disciplines offer essential insights into the complex phenomena with which conversion studies contends.[26] For instance, qualitative and qualitative methodologies employed by each discipline can help illuminate the experience of converting. Through the work of the contributing authors, this handbook provides an example of the importance of intentional and systemic multidisciplinary and interdisciplinary research on conversion (see the chapters by Paloutzian and Steigenga).

Religious and Theological Perspectives on Conversion

It is imperative that scholars of conversion study the religious content, including the beliefs and practices, of the various persons and groups they are observing (see chapters by Mann and Jain). Such research is critical for understanding more fully the nature and depth of various religious traditions. For instance, researchers need to learn about the norms, expectations, metaphors of change, and patterns of relationships within the group, as well as the group's norms for who is considered a "real" convert. Without learning about a group's beliefs and practices, researchers may be misled to think the convert's description of his or her conversion is idiosyncratic. While each conversion has unique qualities, most conversions are shaped, to some degree at least, by the norms, practices, expectations, beliefs, and patterns of the religious group (see chapters by Stromberg and Hindmarsh).

The study of a particular religion in the exploration of conversion processes is also valuable since, with some exceptions, the language converts use is theological or religious. Virtually no convert discusses his or her conversion in terms familiar to the social sciences, for example, as a process in which they resolve emotional issues or enhance their upward social mobility. Some skeptical scholars reject the convert's language as merely a form of self-deception (which, of course, may be true in some cases), but this is a point of view different from the convert's. Converts usually convert because they believe their new religion is true, that it was ordained by God, or that it was a gift from God (or equivalent language used in various religions) (see chapters by Kling, Hindmarsh, and Stromberg).

Phenomenology of Conversion

Scholars also need to explore the nature of the conversion experience of particular individuals. Each person has distinctive concerns that they address in their journey of religious change. Each person, even those who strive to follow meticulously the rules and rituals of the group into which they are converting, has distinctive experiences of certain aspects of their conversion. The careful scholar can find new and often unexpected paths of interpretation when the authentic, complex reality of a person's experience of conversion is taken fully into account. For instance, see Bulkeley's chapter in this Handbook for an elucidation of the role of dreams in various religions.

In the past, phenomenology sought to find universal structures or themes related to various phenomena. In contrast, we suggest that scholars should also discover the unique and distinctive aspects of a particular person or group's experience of conversion.[27] Christian Smith's provocative article, "Why Christianity Works," reminds us that whatever forces and factors facilitate religious change, it is important to take into account the experiences people have within their religion.[28] Smith's focus is on Christianity, but the editors of this volume believe that similar essays could be written about each religion. Virtually all religions provide people with a range of experiences that are rarely mentioned in scholarly accounts or explanations of religion. The full range of human experience is cultivated in various religions and often plays a crucial role in the converting process.

Historical Perspectives on Conversion

Historians have often been interested in exploring the history of religions but have tended, until recently, to relegate conversion studies to church history or to the periphery rather than the center of the discussion. That approach has changed drastically in the last two decades. Hundreds of studies of conversions have been published by historians with expertise in a wide range of regions of the world. These studies add theoretical and historical richness to understanding the specific conditions and contours of conversion processes in many different places and periods.

It is important that particular conversions be placed within their appropriate historical contexts (see chapters by Baer, Hermansen, Hindmarsh, Kent, and Kling). While conversions are rooted in various theological traditions and have, at the same time, distinctive personal qualities, it is crucial to understand that conversion, even within the same theological tradition, is not the same over time. New themes, issues, rituals, and beliefs develop within traditions. There are, of course, certain theological beliefs that continue to be asserted over long periods of time, but the careful scholar recognizes that variations take place as the tradition confronts new challenges and constructs new insights.

In addition, different configurations of motivations play a different role at different times in the history of a particular religion at different stages of its history. Becoming a Baptist in eighteenth-century Pennsylvania is different from becoming a Baptist in twenty-first century Pennsylvania. In the former, it means a rejection of the religious status quo dominated by the Puritans in the early colonial period of the United States, while converting to the Baptist Church in the twenty-first century is, more than likely, a rather neutral act with few significant consequences in relation to the larger society. Historical studies also alert the scholar of conversion to the reasons behind the contours of the rhetoric of conversion at a particular time in history.[29] Baer's chapter in this handbook on the history of conversion provides an overview of the trajectories of religious change over time. Furthermore, it is important to highlight strategies that seek to sustain the identity of converts. These strategies for identity maintenance may include memorializing personal narratives or creating artistic works that serve as models of religious change (see chapters by Apostolos-Cappadona, Hindmarsh, and Stromberg).

Demographic Perspectives on Conversion

Johnson's chapter in this Handbook explains how the demographics of religious change affect the contours of the growth and decline of various religions in different times and places. Johnson addresses the impact of birth and death rates, the long-term consequences of religions that sustain and foster growth through both missionary activity and through the retention of those who are born into a family with certain religious loyalties, and the demographic consequences of conversions to a new religion.

Cognitive and Neuropsychological Perspectives on Conversion

One of the most recent and exciting developments is the study of the brain. With sophisticated new technologies such as Magnetic Resonance Imaging, scientists are able to examine in great detail the working of the human brain. Many neuroscientists see this work as definitively ruling out any supernatural explanations for religious beliefs and practices. For some, this field is the ultimate reduction of virtually everything to the science of the brain and its capacities. Others view the human brain as in a sense "wired" for God or for transcendence. As findings in this new field unfold, it is imperative that scholars of conversion pay attention to the field of neuroscience for potential clues to the nature of conversion. Bulkeley articulates a nuanced approach to the field of neuropsychology in order for conversion scholars to make the best use of this field in the future (see chapter by Bulkeley). Cognitive neuroscience offers a treasure trove of new understandings of the biological bases of human perception, experience, and meaning. It will be fascinating to see whether cognitive neuroscience will be viewed as descriptive or normative over the next two or three decades.

The importance of culture in shaping persons, communities, and religions must be given more weight in conversion studies. For instance, in the field of psychology, cultural and indigenous psychologists do not reject the goals of developing a sophisticated science, but they advocate locating psychology within the context of culture. Culture, rather than being a distraction to the goals of psychology, now becomes a central concern in the effort to develop a psychology that is profoundly connected to the human experience of living in various cultural communities, complete with their distinctive worldviews, assumptions, beliefs, religions, rituals, philosophies, modes of family relationships, forms of selfhood, and life-cycle trajectories (see chapter by Paloutzian).

As is evident in the research presented in this handbook, scholars are seeking not only to discover themes and patterns in conversion studies but also to provide critiques of the various methods, assumptions, and goals of those who study conversion.[30] An emerging consensus in conversion studies is a vivid awareness that human change in general and conversion in particular are dynamic processes. We do not, however, reject the importance of seeing some conversions as dramatic and sudden. Conversions include both long-term processes and, for many people, powerful conversion events. Few conversions, however, are total, complete, or irreversible. Human beings are always on the move. We are always negotiating our identity. We sometimes explore new options, and we often desire novelty and stimulation.[31]

HOW TO USE THIS HANDBOOK

This handbook is an invitation to a model of conversion studies that is global, interdisciplinary, multireligious, and inclusive of the personal, social, cultural, and political dimensions of the human predicament. Twelve of the chapters focus on conversion in various religious traditions, ranging from Hinduism to the Mormons (Church of Jesus Christ of Latter-day Saints). Each of these chapters explicates the ways in which believers enter the tradition and/or intensify and live out their involvement with specific disciplines, rituals, and integrity (see the chapter by Bryant et al.). Each chapter seeks to emphasize the distinctive methods deployed by various religions in their efforts to convert people, institutions, societies, and cultures (see the chapters by Komjathy and Sun).

As with any collection of diverse articles, the reader may approach this handbook in different ways. One approach is to begin by reading the chapters on various religions. Learning about the differences and similarities among the religions helps us to recognize the various religious paths within each tradition. The authors explore the religions not only in terms of how people can enter into or depart from a particular religion but also in terms of the modes of intensification and human transformation within a religion. Most religions seek to transform human beings. Many religions also inspire human beings to form communities of support, worship, and service. Moreover, many religions advocate the centrality of transforming human beings so that they can be in relationship with the divine, whether the divine is conceived as a personal God or as in harmony with the forces of the universe in a way that provides for human flourishing both individually and collectively.

Another approach is to read the chapters that approach conversion from the perspective of various academic disciplines in order to understand the aesthetic, gender, cultural, historical, personal, political, sociological, theological, and spiritual dimensions of how and why people convert. The chapters that focus on conversion in particular religions analyze the ways in which believers enter the tradition and/or become passionate or devoted to a religion that was previously of only marginal importance in their lives or of only perfunctory interest. The chapters on religions demonstrate that, while certain themes and patterns persist in a particular religion, the modes, motivations, and norms of conversion change over time and in various circumstances.

The section on religions illustrates how each religion deploys distinctive prescriptions and proscriptions in its effort to convert people, institutions, societies, and cultures. The authors of several of the chapters on religion also discuss the problematic issue of using the language of conversion to talk about change in these religions. Given the fact that conversion is a word derived primarily from Judaism and Christianity (see chapters by Segal and Kling), critical concerns are expressed about the viability and value of using the language and concepts derived from outside of a particular tradition. Some religions, such as Islam, explicitly reject the use of the word "conversion," using instead the language of return to the original state when humans were created by Allah or notions of submission to Allah and the disciplines of Islam in order to live a life in accord with the revelations received by Muhammad (see chapters by Hermansen and van Nieuwkerk). Fan and Chen (see their chapter) also question the use of the term "conversion," arguing that it is inappropriate in the widespread revitalization of folk or indigenous religions in the People's Republic of China.

The chapters on New Religious Movements examine the debates about the nature of conversion to and disengagement from these groups (see chapters by Cowan, Wright, and Richardson). These chapters also provide an assessment of the "brainwashing" theory of conversion and of the legal battles that have taken place in various parts of the world. These chapters make it clear that religious change often triggers political, religious, and cultural conflicts that have significant implications for some religious groups and for those who either join a New Religious Movement or who depart from these organizations by many avenues, in some cases through "deprogramming" (see chapter by Sharma for an example of conflicts regarding traditional religions).

It is our hope that after reading this handbook the reader will have a better understanding of how and why people change religions or why they depart from their religious beliefs and practices. Our world is changing at an astonishing pace, and the forces of religious experience, beliefs, and practices empower and inspire millions of people around the world. Other people, however, become disillusioned or are wounded in different ways by the vicissitudes of religious institutions, groups, and individuals (see chapter by Streib). In either case, the varieties of religious change exert enormous influence over individuals, communities, and the world.

As I (Rambo) was beginning to write this introduction to the *Oxford Handbook of Religious Conversion*, I went to a concert at the Seoul Arts Center in Korea. While I was relishing the beauty and energy of the orchestra, the thought came to me: "There are 32 members of this group. That is the same number of chapters in the Handbook." An editor is something like a conductor. Both select the musicians/scholars, both seek to give each musician/scholar the best possible venue for his or her gifts, and, when all is going well, all come together to create something new, stimulating, and even beautiful.

It is an honor for us to have worked with each of the authors of these 32 chapters. Each provides readers (like concert-goers) new insights into the nature of reality. We hope readers will find in these pages resources for navigating the dynamics of converting and deconverting that will inform and illuminate the understanding of these processes and also stimulate more questions to be explored in the future about the great human drama of religious transformation.

Notes

1. The quotations from James and Tolstoy were from the following: A. L. Bardach, "What did J. D. Salinger, Leo Tolstoy, and Sarah Bernhardt have in Common?" *Wall Street Journal*, Mar. 30, 2012.
2. Available online at http://awakeningindia.org.
3. See Bardach, "What did J. D. Salinger, Leo Tolstoy, and Sarah Bernhardt have in Common?"
4. Narasingha P. Sil, *Swami Vivekananda: A Reassessment* (London: Associated University Presses, 1997), 121.
5. Regarding the ways in which conversion creates boundaries, see David N. Gellner, "The Emergence of Conversion in a Hindu-Buddhist Polytropy: The Kathmandu Valley, Nepal, c. 1600–1995," *Comparative Studies in Society and History* 47, no. 4 (2005): 755–780.
6. Karl Jaspers, *The Way to Wisdom: An Introduction to Philosophy* (New Haven: Yale University Press, 2003), 98.
7. Scholars debate whether Saul/Paul "converted." Stendhal argued persuasively that Saul was "called," not converted. Stendhal was concerned that Saul's religious transformation not be interpreted through a Western, especially American Protestant, lens. See Krister Stendahl's *Paul among Jews and Gentiles, and Other Essays* (Philadelphia: Fortress Press, 1976) and Alan F. Segal's *Paul the Convert: The Apostolate and Apostasy of Saul the Pharisee* (New Haven: Yale University Press, 1990).
8. Robert W. Hefner, *Conversion to Christianity: Historical and Anthropological Perspectives on a Great Transformation* (Berkeley and Los Angeles: University of California Press, 1993), 3.
9. Jürgen Habermas, *An Awareness of What is Missing: Faith and Reason in a Post-Secular Age* (Malden, MA: Polity, 2010), 18.
10. Charles E. Farhadian and Robert A. Emmons, "The Psychology of Forgiveness and Religions," in *Forgiveness and Reconciliation: Psychological Pathways to Conflict Transformation and Peace Building*, ed. Ani Kalayjian and Raymond F. Paloutzian (New York: Springer, 2009), 55–70.
11. William James, *The Varieties of Religious Experience: A Study in Human Nature*, The Gifford Lectures on Natural Religion, given at Edinburgh 1901–02 (London: Longman, Green & Co., 1902). This edition 1920, Lecture 9, "Conversion," p. 189.
12. A. D. Nock, *Conversion: The Old and New in Religion from Alexander the Great to Augustine of Hippo* (New York: Oxford University Press, 1933), 7.

13. John Lofland and Rodney Stark, "Becoming a World-Saver: A Theory of Conversion to a Deviant Perspective," *American Sociological Review* 30 (1965): 862–875.

14. James T. Richardson, "The Active vs. Passive Convert: Paradigm Conflict in Conversion/ Recruitment Research," *Journal for the Scientific Study of Religion* 24, no. 2 (1985): 163–179.

15. Robin Horton's three essays on conversion have stimulated extensive debate and discussion. See "African Conversion," *Africa* 41, no. 2 (1971): 85–108; "On the Rationality of Conversion, Part 1," *Africa* 45, no. 3 (1975): 219–235; and "On the Rationality of Conversion, Part 2," *Africa* 45, no. 4 (1975): 373–399. See Deryck Schreuder and Geoffrey Oddie, "What is 'Conversion?' History, Christianity and Religious Change in Colonial Africa and South Asia," *Journal of Religious History* 15, no. 4 (1989): 496–518; and Lynette Olson's "The Applicability of the Horton Thesis of African Conversion to the Christian Conversion of Medieval Europe," *Sydney Studies in Religion* 2 (1999): 79–88.

16. There is a growing literature on the nature of apostasy, departures, rejection, etc., in relation to religion. For example, see Philip Zuckerman, *Faith No More: Why People Reject Religion* (New York: Oxford University Press, 2012) and Heinz Streib, Ralph W. Hood, Jr., Barbara Keller, Rosina-Martha Csöff, and Christopher F. Silver's *Deconversion* (Göttingen: Vandenhoeck & Ruprecht, 2009).

17. Marilyn J. Haran's *Luther on Conversion: The Early Years* (Ithaca, NY: Cornell University Press, 1983) provides a splendid overview of the different ways in which conversion was conceptualized before and during Martin Luther's life. See especially the introduction, pp. 15–54.

18. Lewis R. Rambo, *Understanding Religious Conversion* (New Haven: Yale University Press, 1993), 7 (see also pp. 2–3).

19. Marc David Baer, *Honored by the Glory of Islam: Conversion and Conquest in Ottoman Europe* (New York: Oxford University Press, 2008), 13.

20. Shane P. Gannon, "Conversion as a Thematic Site: Academic Representations of Ambedkar's Buddhist Turn," *Method & Theory in the Study of Religion* 23, no. 1 (2011): 1–28.

21. David M. Wulff, "A Century of Conversion in American Psychology of Religion," in *Konversion: Zur Aktualitat eines Jahrhundertthemas*, ed. Christian Henning and Erich Nestler (Frankfurt: Peter Lang, 2002), 43–73.

22. For important exceptions, see, for example, Ali Köse, *Conversion to Islam: A Study of Native British Converts* (London: Kegan Paul International, 1996); Ali Köse and Kate Miriam Loewenthal, "Conversion Motifs among British Converts to Islam," *International Journal for the Psychology of Religion* 10, no. 2 (2000): 101–110; Anna Mansson McGinty, *Becoming Muslim: Western Women's Conversion to Islam* (New York: Palgrave Macmillan, 2006); Carolyn Moxley Rouse, *Engaged Surrender: African American Women and Islam* (Berkeley and Los Angeles: University of California Press, 2004).

23. Exceptions include Andrew Buckser and Stephen D. Glazier, eds., *The Anthropology of Religious Conversion* (Lanham, MD: Rowman & Littlefield, 2003); McGinty, *Becoming Muslim*; Hefner, *Conversion to Christianity*; and Joel Robbins, "What is a Christian? Notes toward an Anthropology of Christianity," *Religion* 33, no. 3 (2003): 191–199.

24. Rick Szostak, "Modernism, Postmodernism, and Interdisicplinarity," *Issues in Integrative Studies* 25 (2007): 51. See also William H. Newell, "Decision-Making in Interdisciplinary Studies," in *Handbook of Decision Making*, ed. Göktug Morçöl (Boca Raton, FL: CRC/ Taylor & Francis, 2007), 245–264; Allen F. Repko, *Interdisciplinary Research: Process and Theory* (Los Angeles: Sage, 2008).

25. William H. Newell, "A Theory of Interdisciplinary Studies," *Issues in Integrative Studies* 19 (2001): 19.
26. For a more detailed discussion of this topic, see Lewis R. Rambo, "Theories of Conversion," *Social Compass* 46, no. 3 (1999): 259–271.
27. Lewis Rambo and Lawrence R. Reh, "The Phenomenology of Conversion," in *Handbook of Religious Conversion*, ed. H. Newton Malony and Samuel Southard (Birmingham, AL: Religious Education Press, 1992), 229–258.
28. Christian Smith, "Why Christianity Works: An Emotions-Focused Phenomenological Account," *Sociology of Religion* 68, no. 2 (2007): 165–178. Smith's paper has generated extensive debate in the scholarly community.
29. See, for example, James A. Sandos, *Converting California: Indians and Franciscans in the Missions* (New Haven: Yale University Press, 2004).
30. For more on this topic, see Edward L. Cleary, "Shopping Around: Questions about Latin American Conversions," *International Bulletin of Missionary Research* 28, no. 2 (2004): 50–54; Henri Gooren, *Religious Conversion and Disaffiliation: Tracing Patterns of Change in Faith Practices* (New York: Palgrave/Macmillan, 2010); McGinty, *Becoming Muslim*; Fenggang Yang, "Lost in the Market, Saved at McDonald's: Conversion to Christianity in Urban China," *Journal for the Scientific Study of Religion* 44, no. 4 (2005): 423–441.
31. For more on this topic, see Edward L. Cleary, "The Catholic Charismatic Renewal: Revitalization Movements and Conversion," in *Conversion of a Continent: Religious Change in Latin America*, ed. Timothy J. Steigenga and Edward L. Cleary (New Brunswick, NJ: Rutgers University Press, 2008), 153–173; Cleary, "Shopping Around."

BIBLIOGRAPHY

Arnold, Thomas Walker. *The Preaching of Islam: A History of the Propagation of the Muslim Faith*. LaHore: SH. Muhammad Ashraf Publisher, 1913.
Baer, Marc David. *Honored by the Glory of Islam: Conversion and Conquest in Ottoman Europe*. New York: Oxford University Press, 2008.
Buckser, Andrew, and Stephen D. Glazier, eds. *The Anthropology of Religious Conversion*. Lanham, MD: Rowman & Littlefield, 2003.
Bulliet, Richard W. *Conversion to Islam in the Medieval Period: An Essay in Quantitative History*. Cambridge, MA: Harvard University Press, 1979.
Cleary, Edward L. "The Catholic Charismatic Renewal: Revitalization Movements and Conversion." In *Conversion of a Continent: Religious Change in Latin America*, ed. Timothy J. Steigenga and Edward L. Cleary, 153–173. New Brunswick, NJ: Rutgers University Press, 2008.
——. "Shopping Around: Questions about Latin American Conversions." *International Bulletin of Missionary Research* 28, no. 2 (2004): 50–54.
Farhadian, Charles, and Robert A. Emmons. "The Psychology of Forgiveness and Religions." In *Forgiveness and Reconciliation: Psychological Pathways to Conflict Transformation and Peace Building*, ed. Ani Kalayjian and Raymond F. Paloutzian, 55–70. New York: Springer, 2009.
Gannon, Shane P. "Conversion as a Thematic Site: Academic Representations of Ambedkar's Buddhist Turn." *Method & Theory in the Study of Religion* 23, no. 1 (2011): 1–28.
Gellner, David N. "The Emergence of Conversion in a Hindu-Buddhist Polytropy: The Kathmandu Valley, Nepal, c. 1600–1995." *Comparative Studies in Society and History* 47, no. 4 (2005): 755–780.

Gooren, Henri. *Religious Conversion and Disaffiliation: Tracing Patterns of Change in Faith Practices*. New York: Palgrave/Macmillan, 2010.

Habermas, Jürgen. *An Awareness of What is Missing: Faith and Reason in a Post-Secular Age*. Malden, MA: Polity, 2010.

Haran, Marilyn J. *Luther on Conversion: The Early Years*. Ithaca, NY: Cornell University Press, 1983.

Hefner, Robert E., ed. *Conversion to Christianity: Historical and Anthropological Perspectives on a Great Transformation*. Berkeley and Los Angeles: University of California Press, 1993.

Heredia, Rudolf C. "Interrogations from the Margins: Conversion as Critique." *History and Sociology of South Asia* 5, no. 2 (July 2011): 83–102.

Horton, Robin. "African Conversion." *Africa* 41, no. 2 (1971): 85–108.

——. "On the Rationality of Conversion, Part 1." *Africa* 45, no. 3 (1975): 219–235.

——. "On the Rationality of Conversion, Part 2." *Africa* 45, no. 4 (1975): 373–399.

James, William. *The Varieties of Religious Experience: A Study in Human Nature*, The Gifford Lectures on Natural Religion, given at Edinburgh 1901–02. London: Longman, Green & Co., 1902.

Jaspers, Karl. *The Way to Wisdom: An Introduction to Philosophy*. New Haven: Yale University Press, 2003.

Köse, Ali. *Conversion to Islam: A Study of Native British Converts*. London: Kegan Paul International, 1996.

Köse, Ali, and Kate Miriam Loewenthal. "Conversion Motifs among British Converts to Islam." 10, no. 2 (2000): 101–110.

Levtzion, Nehemiah, ed. *Conversion to Islam*. New York: Holmes & Meier, 1979.

Lofland, John, and Rodney Stark. "Becoming a World-Saver: A Theory of Conversion to a Deviant Perspective." *American Sociological Review* 30 (1965): 862–875.

McGinty, Anna Mansson. *Becoming Muslim: Western Women's Conversion to Islam*. New York: Palgrave Macmillan, 2006.

Newell, William H. "Decision-Making in Interdisciplinary Studies." In *Handbook of Decision Making*, ed. Göktug Morçöl, 245–264. Boca Raton, FL: CRC/Taylor & Francis, 2007.

——. "A Theory of Interdisciplinary Studies." *Issues in Integrative Studies* 19 (2001): 1–25.

Nock, Arthur Darby. *Conversion: The Old and New in Religion from Alexander the Great to Augustine of Hippo*. New York: Oxford University Press, 1933.

Olson, Lynette. "The Applicability of the Horton Thesis of African Conversion to the Christian Conversion of Medieval Europe." *Sydney Studies in Religion* 2 (1999): 79–88.

Rambo, Lewis R. "Conversion: Toward a Holistic Model of Religious Change." *Pastoral Psychology* 38 (1989): 47–63.

——. "Current Research on Religious Conversion." *Religious Studies Review* 8, no. 2 (1982): 146–159.

——. "Theories of Conversion." *Social Compass* 46, no. 3 (1999): 259–271.

——. *Understanding Religious Conversion*. New Haven: Yale University Press, 1993.

Rambo, Lewis R., and Charles E. Farhadian. "Conversion." In *Encyclopedia of Religion*, Vol. 3, 2nd ed., ed. Lindsay Jones, 1969–1974. Detroit, MI: Thompson & Gale, 2005.

Rambo, Lewis R., and Lawrence A. Reh. "The Phenomenology of Conversion." In *Handbook of Religious Conversion*, ed. H. Newton Malony and Samuel Southard, 229–258. Birmingham, AL: Religious Education Press, 1992.

Repko, Allen F. *Interdisciplinary Research: Process and Theory*. Los Angeles: Sage, 2008.

Richardson, James T. "The Active vs. Passive Convert: Paradigm Conflict in Conversion/ Recruitment Research." *Journal for the Scientific Study of Religion* 24, no. 2 (1985): 163–179.

——, ed. *Conversion Careers: In and Out of the New Religions.* Sage Contemporary Social Science Issues. Vol. 47. Beverly Hills, CA: Sage Publications, 1978.

Robbins, Joel. "What is a Christian? Notes toward an Anthropology of Christianity." *Religion* 33, no. 3 (2003): 191–199.

Rouse, Carolyn Moxley. *Engaged Surrender: African American Women and Islam.* Berkeley and Los Angeles: University of California Press, 2004.

Sandos, James A. *Converting California: Indians and Franciscans in the Missions.* New Haven: Yale University Press, 2004.

Schreuder, Deryck, and Geoffrey Oddie. "What is 'Conversion?' History, Christianity and Religious Change in Colonial Africa and South Asia." *Journal of Religious History* 15, no. 4 (1989): 496–518.

Segal, Alan F. *Paul the Convert: The Apostolate and Apostasy of Saul the Pharisee.* New Haven: Yale University Press, 1990.

Sil, Narasingha P. *Swami Vivekananda: A Reassessment.* London: Associated University Presses, 1997.

Smith, Christian. "Why Christianity Works: An Emotions-Focused Phenomenological Account." *Sociology of Religion* 68, no. 2 (2007): 165–178.

Stendahl, Krister. *Paul among Jews and Gentiles, and Other Essays.* Philadelphia: Fortress Press, 1976.

Streib, Heinz, Ralph W. Hood, Jr., Barbara Keller, Rosina-Martha Csöff, and Christopher F. Silver, *Deconversion.* Göttigen: Vandenhoeck & Ruprecht, 2009.

Szostak, Rick. "Modernism, Postmodernism, and Interdisciplinarity." *Issues in Integrative Studies* 25 (2007): 32–83.

Wulff, David M. "A Century of Conversion in American Psychology of Religion." In *Konversion: Zur Aktualitat eines Jahrhundertthemas,* ed. Christian Henning and Erich Nestler, 43–73. Frankfurt: Peter Lang, 2002.

Yang, Fenggang. "Lost in the Market, Saved at McDonald's: Conversion to Christianity in Urban China." *Journal for the Scientific Study of Religion* 44, no. 4 (2005): 423–441.

Zuckerman, Philip. *Faith No More: Why People Reject Religion.* New York: Oxford University Press, 2012.

PART I

DISCIPLINARY PERSPECTIVES

CHAPTER 1

....

HISTORY AND RELIGIOUS
CONVERSION

....

MARC DAVID BAER

INTRODUCTION

....

UNTIL recently, historians have occasionally presented conversion as a gradual process but more often as a sudden and total change in belief. This view of conversion reflects contemporary scholarship in religious studies that typically depict conversion as an instantaneous transformation in which "a complete division is established in the twinkling of an eye between the old life and the new."[1] More recently, however, historians have doubted the totalizing experience of conversion. Again reflecting current trends in religious studies, they argue instead that religious conversion entails both an event or events and a gradually unfolding, dynamic, yet often incomplete process.[2] While the conversion may be set in motion by a single event (such as baptism or circumcision) that lasts but a single moment, the full process of converting may take years. Historians are most interested today in analyzing that ongoing, gradual process through which a person's or group's beliefs and practices change.

We can divide the way historians describe the conversion process into four categories: acculturation, adhesion or hybridity, syncretism, and transformation. Acculturation is when religious change accompanies the incorporation of a people and its territory into a conquering empire or socioeconomic system. Adhesion or hybridity is when the person or group adopts new beliefs and practices alongside the old. Syncretism occurs when the convert(s) reconcile or fuse old and new beliefs and practices to create a new religious synthesis. Transformation is when converts attempt to completely replace the old with the new. In the latter situation, a person or group may either turn to piety within the religion to which the person or group already adheres or may exchange the beliefs or practices in which the person or group was raised for those of another religion. The former may also be termed intensification or revitalized commitment, and the latter is also known as tradition transition.[3] Ultimately, whether conversion entails a process of acculturation, adhesion, syncretism, or transformation, it is also accompanied by the conversion of the landscape and sacred spaces. This chapter presents these four categories of conversion, offers historical examples of each, applies the term "conversion" to the transformation of space, and concludes with a final example illustrating these interrelated aspects of religious change.

ACCULTURATION

Many historians have written of conversion as acculturation. Acculturation is depicted as cultural change, incorporation or integration into the customs, habits, and language of a conquering civilization. Converts change their daily private and public routine; learn another sacred tongue or adopt religious terms from other languages into their language; dress differently; act and move according to a different choreography of ritual and prayer; consume certain food and drink and no longer consume others; and surround themselves with a new group of people as they separate from others, even family members, including spouses who do not follow the new piety or faith.[4]

Acculturation is the same as Christianization (or Islamization), or the incorporation of pagans (or Christians) into a Christian (or Islamic) state and the resulting transformation in their language, law, and tastes in food, drink, clothing, architecture, and art. Beginning in the fourth century, Christianization was identified with Romanization in western, northern, and central Europe as Celtic, Germanic, and Slavic peoples adopted Mediterranean Roman customs and lifestyles as well as the Christian religion that was identified with Roman imperial authority. Cultural change, imperial incorporation, and conversion went together.[5] When the territories of "uncivilized barbarians"—those not yet under Roman rule—were conquered and their inhabitants were transformed into Latin-speaking imperial subjects under Roman law, a way of life and system of belief merged. This was aided by the use of violence and strict measures enforcing Christianity and outlawing paganism. Similarly, centuries later Orthodox Christian missionaries sent from the third Rome, Moscow, sought to acculturate Buddhist, Muslim, and pagan peoples into the Russian Empire through Christianization.[6]

Acculturation to a religion with universal claims, in other words, is seen by those seeking the conversion of others, or proselytizers and those who support them, as part of the civilizing process.[7] Indigenous communities often adopt the predominant religion of the new empire into which they are incorporated. Acculturation has even been described as the "colonization of consciousness."[8] This is based on the view that power over the political leads to power over meaning and everyday activities. The colonial encounter allows imperial powers to draw colonized peoples into a world system (or at least a larger regional system), economy, and exchange. As will be explained below, this process is also often accompanied by resistance. Nevertheless, this leads to the incorporation of religion where values, ways of being, and perceptions of the universe, as well as ways of measuring time, dress, architecture, and language, are transformed. It is argued that religions of the colonized have often been replaced because local religions were narrower in focus, concentrating on local gods and lesser spirits and problems. The conversion to universal religions (such as Christianity) and belief in one Supreme Being accompanied the incorporation of smaller communities into a larger social and economic order.[9] When microcosm encountered macrocosm, a cosmological adjustment ensued in favor of the latter. This is as true for the spread of Christianity as for the spread of Islam. Pre-Islamic Arabs, for example, had local as well as supreme gods; incorporation into a larger imperial system allowed them to replace the former with the latter.

A similar process, which is also referred to as "conversion by assimilation," accompanied the spread of Buddhism, Confucianism-Taoism, and Islam in Eurasia.[10] Here I will focus on Islam. Historians of the Near East have used the term Islamization while their colleagues in the field of Roman history have used the term Romanization to describe incorporation into an empire and the ensuing acculturation. The English term Islamization comes from the Arabic verb *aslāma*, to submit, meaning both submitting to Islamic political rule and conversion to Islam. Islamization describes the political submission in Late Antiquity of much of the Near East to Islamic rule and the centuries-long process of conversion to Islam, adoption of the Arabic language, and choosing Muslim personal names rather than Arab, Persian, or biblical names.[11] As in Roman Europe, so too in the Near East did newly established towns and urban centers of trade and administration become the first centers of acculturation.[12] The population of Anatolia, which was predominantly Christian and Greek-speaking in the eleventh century, when it was largely ruled by the Byzantine Empire, had become predominantly Muslim and Turkish-speaking by the sixteenth century when the Ottoman Empire was the dominant political power.[13] Muslim writers considered Islamization an acculturating and civilizing process bringing urbanization and changes in law, language, and customs, and beliefs to the new Muslims.[14] Migrant Muslim religious adepts and merchants, such as those from the Hadramawt in Yemen, were a crucial element in the expansion of Islam across the Indian Ocean as they helped consolidate new Muslim polities—often later ruled by their descendants—across Asia.[15]

Scholars have also written about another major acculturation as an Islamization process, that is, the making of the Ottomans between roughly 1300 and 1650 by the transformation of Christian converts into the Ottoman elite. Similar to earlier eras in Islamic history, when Berbers, Circassians, or Turks were drafted as soldiers, taught Islam, and then helped spread Islamic rule from Morocco to Iraq, under the Ottomans boys were levied from Anatolia and southeastern Europe, circumcised, converted to Islam, and renamed. The levied boys were taken to the capital where they were trained in palace schools to be the leading statesmen, palace servants, and elite soldiers of the empire.[16] Not only boys were made into Ottomans in the palace; historians have also emphasized how converted Christian princesses and slaves became the leading women of the Ottoman royal family.[17] Reflecting the view that conversion equals acculturation, early modern Britons termed conversion to Islam "turning Turk."[18] Armenians, Catholics, and Orthodox Christians converted to Islam in Ottoman territories after being compelled to offer child levies, or after the loss of the institutions of their own religion, or due to acculturation to the customs, habits, languages, and ultimately the religion of the new rulers. Many other Christians from elsewhere in Europe were attracted to the empire, where they converted and served the sultan. The Ottoman Empire offered these converts opportunities for upward social mobility, even to positions of power. But how well absorbed were these converts? To answer this question, it is necessary to consider processes of adhesion and syncretism.

ADHESION AND SYNCRETISM

The fact that many of those bringing the faith to others had themselves only recently been Christianized or Islamized was no guarantee of transformation of the people they were converting. Converts to another religion cannot or do not always wish to completely reject or break away from former beliefs and practices but instead continue to engage in some of them privately and despite publicly changing religion.[19] There may be an adaptation or modification of the former and new ways of life, perhaps encouraged by the converter or mediator as a temporary means of ensuring religious transformation.[20]

For many Christians, like pagans in the Roman Empire before them, conversion to Islam in the Ottoman Empire did not entail a traumatic change from one religion to another but rather an adoption of a new religion alongside their former one, a practice known as "adhesion."[21] Adhesion is where there is "no definite crossing of religious frontiers"; it is "having one foot on each side" of a cultural fence because a person or group accepts "new worships as useful supplements and not as substitutes."[22] This process, where there is an absence of reconciliation, rejection, and renunciation between religions, can also be termed hybridity. As will be detailed below, in recent years historians have emphasized adhesion, hybridity, and continuities rather than discontinuities between religions and religious practices. Asking to what and from what people convert has caused them to understand that, more often than not, conversion was not a clean break in belief or practice. All traces of local or preexisting religions were not completely replaced by the new universalizing religions. The religions from which and to which people converted were themselves unstable works in progress with indeterminate boundaries. They were not closed, nor were they always well-defined and distinct. Scholars have investigated burial practices, for example, and have found that confessional separation of corpses came very late in Late Antiquity[23] and that pagan burial practices continued long after conversion to Christianity.[24]

The discussion of adhesion, hybridity, and continuities has allowed historians to lengthen the temporal span of conversion. Contrary to popular perception and, at times even the self-narratives or accounts of famous converts such as Constantine (272–337 C.E.) or Augustine (354–430 C.E.), scholars have focused on a long process of multiple conversions.[25] On the individual level, neither Constantine nor Augustine converted only one time. On the societal level, too, conversion did not lead immediately to a Christian society in the Roman Empire. Baptism did not make the Christian. Rather, post-baptismal societies had to be deliberately Christianized.[26] At first, some aspects of paganism were allowed to stay; the aim of those bringing Christianity to pagans was to tame, prune, tend, and train pagan holdovers until they yielded Christian fruit.[27] Syncretism emerged as a response. Temples were not destroyed, only the idols within them. The temples were cleansed and reconsecrated. The meaning of the sacrifice was altered. The same sacred spaces were reused, but allegiances were transferred. Tribal gods were transformed into patron saints; amulets became holy relics; the timbers from felled pagan sacred groves were made into Christian chapels; gold statues of snake gods were melted down to become the chalice. Old terms were recruited for new meanings: "possession by a spirit" became "the holy spirit"; "beneficence of the gods" became "salvation"; "military leader" became "lord"; "dependent on a lord" became "to believe"; and "luck bestowed by the gods" became "grace."[28]

Early modern and modern European missionaries took their established practices of acculturation, adhesion, and syncretism abroad. As a generalization, proselytizers translate the doctrine of their religion into the language of those they are attempting to convert, finding parallels, equivalences, and antecedents in their mode of expression and belief system, while at the same time the convert translates and assimilates the new ideas into his or her own language and idiom.[29] Translation creates the possibility of adhesion and syncretism.

When Catholic missionaries went to China, they couched Christianity in terms consonant with Confucian principles, just as missionaries had done in pagan northwestern Europe five centuries earlier. They found adhesion was an acceptable strategy for the convert coming from a religion characterized by its additive qualities and pantheon interchangeability, where one was allowed to juggle Christian and Confucian doctrine, symbol, and meanings.[30] Like the Jesuits in China, the Spanish in South America also utilized syncretistic approaches to conversion.[31] They sought Andean precedents for Catholicism, imagining a pre-Columbian evangelization and similarities between Andean and Spanish religion. But baptized and acculturated Andeans did not agree with the Spanish on the meaning of conversion. This was illustrated by the Andeans' clinging to non-Catholic burial practices and grounds. Taking the Spanish cue, they also sought to baptize their deceased ancestors, recognizing the ancestral past as part of the new Catholic order. For the Andeans, as for the Maya and Tarahumara in Mesoamerica, conversion did not require an exclusive affiliation to Catholicism.[32]

Catholic and Protestant missionaries in South and East Asia also ended up with more adhesion and syncretism among converts than they may have desired. The Portuguese faced resistance from Tamils[33] just as the Spanish faced Filipinos reluctant to give up their spirits and shamans.[34] Moreover, the Tagalog Christian texts could be understood in ways considerably at odds to Spanish expectations, such as when the term for "food taken on a journey" was used to convey "the host," and "long journey" stood in for "eternity." As a result, Tagalogs resisted the missionaries by converting conversion to something other than that which the Spanish intended. They confounded confession, submitting to Christianity without submission.[35] The Spanish attempted to replace indigenous myths and legends maintained in oral tradition with Catholic sermons, songs, and drama, but the Filipinos crafted beliefs that included an all-powerful deity and a pantheon of lesser gods.[36] In a similar way, for the Tamils Protestantism and Tamil religiosity were not at odds, for conversion to the former was often couched in terms of Brahman culture, including caste and gender segregation. Furthermore, among the Tamils Christian practices and appearances did not always match Christian beliefs.[37] Indians "understood Christianity through indigenous categories and selectively appropriated those aspects of it that corresponded to local values and scales of social worth."[38]

Historians have noticed similar trends in French and Spanish North America, where Catholic missionizing also brought about adhesion. Iroquois religion was not displaced; Catholicism and native religion were not blended to create something new. Rather, Catholicism and native religion became parallel, coexisting side by side and pursuing parallel tracks.[39] Indians were acculturated as they were brought within the Spanish mission system. They were taught the Spanish language and Spanish habits. They were baptized and renamed. They were compelled to give up their women-centered origin myths, marriage and sexual practices, and sexual politics.[40] Yet Catholicism complemented and supplemented but did not replace indigenous beliefs. Indian culture was not eradicated, because knowledge of tribal lore was kept alive and transmitted through oral tradition. In addition, the original Indian language was preserved. Christianity was added into the Indian knowledge base, but often no syncretism took place. Rather, Indians engaged in adhesion; Christianity and native beliefs were both perpetuated. In New Mexico, the Puebloans' Corn Mothers did not entirely go away. In California, the Diegueños, Luiseños, and Chumash added Christianity to native beliefs. According to a Luiseño chief, "Each religion must be understood on its own terms and should not be confused with another."[41] Most Indians simultaneously practiced two different and conflicting belief systems. The same bifurcation appeared in costume and architecture.

Adhesion may also occur among the self-missionized. In the 1970s the Urapmin of Papua New Guinea discarded Urapmin religious understanding and rituals but retained Urapmin social moral ideas without syncretizing them with Christian ones.[42] The Urapmin "adopted" Christianity. They did not assimilate the new paramount value into the old, nor did they transform their old paramount value in relation to the new; instead, they took on the new moral system on its own terms without integrating it with preexisting morality.[43] As a result, they simultaneously balance two distinct, contradictory paramount values side by side without subordinating one to the other.[44]

In Christian-ruled parts of the world, incorporation of foreign cultures was facilitated by adhesion and syncretism rather than wholesale acceptance of new beliefs and practices.[45] Like the spread of Christianity, a religion that emerged from a split between Jesus-following Jews and Jews who did not follow Jesus,[46] Islam arose in a similarly syncretistic fashion. Many aspects of the message Muhammad (570–632 C.E.) preached were couched in terms and concepts already familiar to the people of Arabia: monotheism, a final judgment, paradise and hell, prophecy and revelation, and piety.[47] A heavenly intermediary, later identified by tradition as the angel Gabriel, who had told Mary of the impending birth of the son of god, commanded Muhammad to recite, and that which was dictated to him became the Qur'an (Arabic: *iqra*, recite; *al-Qur'an*, the recitation).

Christians, some of whom were relatives of Muhammad, confirmed Muhammad's prophetic role, and some of the first believers took refuge in Christian Ethiopia.[48] The first people who followed what Muhammad revealed to them, who called themselves believers, prayed toward Jerusalem like the Jews, only later redirecting their prayers toward Mecca. Mecca possessed a central shrine of the gods, the Ka'aba, a cube-shaped building that housed the idols of tribal patron deities and was the site of a great annual pilgrimage and fair. Arabs held a shared belief in Allah, the supreme high god, the creator and sustainer of life. The Ka'aba in Mecca was cleansed of its idols and is still today the main pilgrimage center for Arabia. Allah became the single God yet, as is apparent in the Qur'an, new Muslims still had a hard time abandoning their previous gods and goddesses. By the end of the seventh century, however, after they had constructed the Dome of the Rock (691 C.E.) in Jerusalem over the foundations of the Israelites' temple overlooking the Church of the Holy Sepulchre, the believers had become full Muslims, distinct from other monotheists.[49]

Once established in the Near East, Islam spread through a process of adhesion and syncretism in southeastern Europe, Anatolia, China, Africa, and Central, South, and Southeast Asia. This was achieved by recourse to accommodation, the latitudinarian attitudes of those proselytizing the religion, and an emphasis on what was common to the local religions and Islam. The adoption of Christian sacred groves and springs and the appropriation of Christian festivals, saints, tombs, shrines and other sacred sites, miracles, and rituals increased Islam's appeal in southeastern Europe and Anatolia.[50] The popular Sufi order of the Bektashis had particular appeal in the Balkans. Hajji Bektash, its eponymous founder, was the "saint" of the Janissaries, the elite Ottoman infantry corps made up of converted Christians.

In China and Africa, syncretistic religious beliefs and practices were often the norm.[51] Traders as well as rulers lived complicated lives keeping two competing value systems in play. Arabs gave Islam a Chinese origin, linked Chinese mythology to Islamic history, claimed the father of monarchical China was a Muslim, and promoted the common origins of Islam and Confucianism as well as the similar aims of Buddhism and Islam.[52] Chinese Muslims used incense, Chinese texts, and local languages in worship, adorned their mosques with Chinese Qur'anic quotations, and wore Chinese funeral dress.[53] Over the course of centuries, Muslim Arabs were Sinicized, and some turned away from Islam. Conversion was not a one-way street. In Africa, people also kept two or more religious belief systems in play for centuries, as Islam was integrated into the religious, social, and cultural life of African societies, often without a clear break from the past.[54] Islamic rulers in West Africa, for example, who favored amulets and charms, simultaneously patronized Islamic and pre-Islamic religious experts, groves, and shrines and engaged in conflicting traditions, ceremonies, marriage customs, sexual practices, and dietary habits.[55] They made their subjects sprinkle dust on their own heads while bowing before their rulers in deference. Transformation to Islam took centuries.

Similar processes of adhesion and syncretism helped propel Islam across Central and South Asia. In Central Asia, Inner Asian and Islamic beliefs and rituals came together— even by identifying Muslim Sufis with shaman priests—to spread the religion.[56] South

Asia was particularly well-suited to syncretism.[57] Muslim proselytizers established centers of Islam on the sites of Buddhist and Hindu shrines and accommodated to prevailing beliefs and rituals. In South Asia a process of gradual, nearly imperceptible conversion occurred, which can be divided into three stages: inclusion, identification, and then displacement.[58] Inclusion is identical to adhesion. For example, Islamic superhuman agencies (Allah, Muhammad, minor spirits) became accepted in local Bengali cosmologies alongside local divinities (Krishna, Shiva, natural deities) already embedded therein. Identification is identical with syncretism; Islamic superhuman agencies ceased merely to coexist alongside Bengali agencies but actually merged with them (thus Allah was used interchangeably with Niranjan). Displacement is identical with transformation; the names of Islamic superhuman agencies replaced those of the divinities in local cosmologies.[59]

Islam was particularly successful in Southeast Asia, most notably in Indonesia. There it adapted successfully to Javanese religion, which had been forged by adopting competing elements of early deities, Buddhism, and Hinduism. Indeed, in different historical eras Buddhism and Hinduism in Java have been considered at least in dialogue with if not complementary to Islam. Javanese did not believe at first that they had to give exclusive allegiance to one belief system, to abandon older ideas in order to be Muslims.[60] Why should new beliefs supersede older ones? Why completely abandon belief in the Goddess of the Southern Ocean for Allah? Why not include the Islamic credo and a sunburst on gravestones? Why not believe that the king has supernatural powers and marries a goddess as well as believe in the unity of God? Why not accept books with supernatural powers deemed equivalent to the Qur'an? Javanese accepted both a transcendent God and the immanence of divinity. Indonesia was the site in the Islamic world where adhesion was longest lived, where Islam took the longest to displace the indigenous cosmology.

TRANSFORMATION AND TURN TO PIETY

One might get the impression that adhesion and syncretism are permanent states. However, these modes of religiosity are most often abandoned over time. In Bengal, for example, the displacement of local gods and spirits came about in modern times with the efforts of reformist pilgrims returned from Mecca. In Indonesia, adhesion was replaced by conversion in the nineteenth century in the wake of a revival movement, five centuries after the arrival of the Islamic religion. This type of conversion can be termed transformation. Transformation is "taking of a new way of life in place of the old" and a "deliberate turning from indifference or from an earlier form of piety to another, a turning which implies a consciousness that a great change is involved, that the old was wrong and the new is right."[61] Converts turn toward a new axis or set of ideals that motivates converts to transform themselves and their environment. They reject or denounce their past and former beliefs and practices, or their indifference (in the case of revivalists), labeling them wrong when compared with a different future on a new path that is conceived as being right. In the case of intensification, the person who formerly did not give more than cursory thought or attention to the theology of his or her faith or did not engage in or keep wholeheartedly to its requirements devotes his or her mind and body fully to understanding and embracing the religion.[62] Transformation thus entails a turn to piety within one's own religion or a change from one religion to another. These two aspects of conversion are beautifully portrayed in the film *The Mission*,[63] in which the slaver Mendoza becomes a sincere Jesuit missionary as the Guaraní Indians become Christian.

Converts to piety are especially zealous in leading, through their words and actions, less observant members of their own religion to become awakened and heed the religion's reformed tenets; now they devote themselves to what they consider a purified version of the faith. After all, "religious revivals grow by the conversion of new adherents."[64] When a ruler's aims and those of pietists converge, the most conducive environment is established for the conversion of members of the sovereign's religion and his subjects committed to other religions. As in Christendom, where "the missionary and the warrior traveled and worked together in the process of extending both Christ's kingdom and that of the king," pacifying foes and expanding the kingdom, the proselytizer in Islamic societies received "protection, endowments (often on a very grand scale)... the status that came with association with a king, the infectious example of a royal conversion," and "access to royal powers of coercion," all of which would spread the religion in areas of recent conquest and intensify it among subjects at home.[65]

Reflecting its syncretistic origins, Islam spread at first through acculturation. The same was true with Christianity. Many Christians accepted Christianity only as a form of adhesion, adding Christian beliefs and practices to pagan ones. To bring about what they considered true conversion, Christians sought to establish a more identifiable Christian society, to Christianize other Christians. Their efforts provide evidence that Christianization in such territories as Germany was a long, slow process, an ongoing effort to redefine behaviors and mores following the initial spread of the religion by syncretistic means.[66] Such practices were at odds with earlier efforts to reinterpret old gods to match the beliefs of the new faith and the compromises made by holy men.[67] Throughout much of the medieval period, conversion for Christians mainly meant taking up more intense forms of religious life.[68] Church leaders aimed to discipline the morals of the neophytes, enhance Christian observance, foster Christian ethics, and overhaul Christian institutions. Some of their methods included promoting saints' relic cults.

Reform or pious movements also arose in the Islamic world centuries after the initial Islamization, especially from the seventeenth century to the modern period, in order to move beyond adhesion or syncretism to transformation.[69] Most striking were pious reform, revival, and jihad movements throughout the Ottoman Empire,[70] Africa,[71] China,[72] Indonesia,[73] and Saudi Arabia.[74] Opposing long-accepted practices of adhesion or the adaptation of only some beliefs, which had accompanied the early spread of Islam, and attempting to make the religion their own, Muslims aimed to convert themselves and other Muslims to what they believed was the pure, original faith free of adhesion to earlier practices.[75] Jihad—moral self-transformation—and movements of repentance, renewal, and reform sought to reform lax Muslims, compelling them to live in accord with the beliefs and practices established in Muhammad's era and to abandon the regression to earlier forms of unbelief, those apparently idolatrous or polytheistic innovations that went against the beliefs and practices of Muhammad's time. In effect, the aim was to purge the Muslim faith of adhesion and those syncretistic elements that had originally been so influential in converting people to Islam.

A number of well-known twentieth-century conversions to Islam illustrate transformation and the turn to piety. Malcolm X's (1925–1965) multiple conversions from Christianity to a life of crime and then to Islam occurred in stages of ever-increasing piety. He became a member of the Nation of Islam in prison and then, after over a decade of building up the movement, learned of the moral failures of the movement's leader. He befriended a number of Sunni Muslims who convinced him to take the pilgrimage to Mecca. Thereafter he became a pious Sunni Muslim.[76] A similar journey from Christianity to a life of fast living to Islamic moral piety is recorded in a documentary about the life of NBA star Chris Jackson.[77] This journey is similar to the lives of other African-Americans whose conversion culminated in a reform phase in which they broke away from the sect of Islam that they had originally joined because they believed the sect's beliefs and practices drew them away from the original message revealed to Muhammad.[78] They then pursued lives as revitalized Sunni Muslims and established mosques in which to pray in accordance with their interpretation of the religion.

CONVERSION OF SACRED SPACE

The conversion of a people is incomplete without the conversion of space, place, and the landscape.[79] The processes of acculturation, adhesion and hybridity, syncretism, and transformation of converts are accompanied by a spatial dimension of religious change. If the ruler of a society converts, whether to piety or to a different religion altogether, he (rulers are usually male) converts holy spaces of other religions to his own, including the most grand and significant structures located in the capital and major cities of his state, or he constructs new edifices celebrating and announcing his personal decision. Female members of the royal family and male members of his retinue may do likewise. When the masses change religion, this occurs on a much wider scale, as all the new believers and those compelling their conversion demand spaces where the newfound faith can be articulated and demonstrated. Either way, we witness the ultimate transformation of sacred space as cityscapes reflect the revival movement or demographic change, and the sacred geography of the countryside is likewise transformed. Throughout lands conquered, colonized, and ruled by Muslims, for example, the conversion of sacred space and the establishment of Muslim institutions led to the conversion of the population, just as the conversion of the population led to the transformation of holy sites. Over

time, churches, synagogues, and fire temples were destroyed or appropriated and converted into regular and congregational mosques, shrines, and Sufi complexes to serve
the needs of and accommodate a population undergoing a radical change in religious
demography.[80]

The process of Islamization of Christians in the early Ottoman Empire, like the
Romanization of pagans in northwestern Europe, entailed the confiscation of the vast
majority of the lands, revenues, and buildings that had formerly been held by the conquered Christian people. Consequently, institutions of the new religion spread, often in
the same buildings and on the same lands that had previously belonged to the former
religion. Thus Constantinople's Hagia Sophia, the greatest cathedral in Christendom,
became Aya Sofya, the grandest Muslim mosque. These institutions and the newly
forming society absorbed the members of the formerly prevailing religion.

In late antique and medieval Europe, Christianization was also accompanied
by changes in the physical world as pagan sacred geography was transformed into
Christian sacred geography in city (especially temples and shrines) and countryside
(springs, wells, forests, and mountains).[81] Yet missionaries recognized that linking
Christian sacred geography to earlier sacred spaces and thus appropriating their power
required preserving sanctified local sites, whose foundations were left visible, and giving the objects and rituals practiced in them new meanings. In a famous letter, Pope
Gregory I (papacy 590–604 C.E.) writes:

> The idol temples...should by no means be destroyed, but only the idols in them.
> Take holy water and sprinkle it in these shrines, build altars and place relics in them.
> For if the shrines are well built, it is essential that they should be changed from the
> worship of devils to the service of the true God. When this people sees that their
> shrines are not destroyed they will be able to banish error from their hearts and be
> more ready to come to the places they are familiar with, but now recognizing and
> worshipping the true God.[82]

In colonial Mexico, Spanish Catholics converted Mayan tree deities with crosses to
crucifixes with faces; replaced human sacrifice with the sacrifice of Jesus; converted
open spaces for rituals to open church altars for liturgical processions; made dovecote
temples into dovecote churches; and made churches—aligned to solar patterns—resemble the sacred caves of the Indians.[83] The familiarity of the artwork within the churches,
which were built and decorated by Indians, was meant to ease conversion by using
local forms, such as depictions of Chichimec warriors fighting demons or native deities
alongside Catholic saints.

The transformed buildings and glorious new masterpieces, whether in Anatolia or
Southeastern Europe, Germany, or Mexico, become "theaters of conversion" that set
the stage for religious change.[84] The changed landscapes are readable to all passersby
as didactic instruments promoting conversion and communicating its reward: divine
favor. When a religious sanctuary or house of worship of one religion is modified to conform to the new religion of the convert, the preservation of the site's sanctity combined
with the adaptive use of the same sacred space by followers of the conquerors' religion

sends a message to those who formerly worshipped there. The sanctification of the same site means that the holy space serves another belief system. If those who venerate the familiar spot and have memories of praying there want to continue revering older deities, they ostensibly have to do so in another form. To facilitate conversion of others, the converters of a place choose to emphasize, accommodate, and even repackage those elements of belief and practices of their religion that most resemble those of the possessors of the former house of worship who offered rituals there. Visitors to the site may engage in similar rituals in the same place where they used to worship, but the agents of conversion aim for converts' hearts to eventually be changed.[85] This allows those whose buildings were taken over to comprehend the new religion within the framework of their own religion. Those who transform sacred spaces may expect some former accretions to continue for a while, trusting that after old locales and rituals are given new meaning the new practices will eventually lead to the new beliefs wiping away the old.

CONCLUSION

Conversion of the lived environment is one of the most durable and visible effects of conversion. Conversion of people is less stable. Converts may turn back to their original religion, convert again to yet another religion, or invent a religious understanding at variance with the understanding of those who mediated their conversion. Changes in individuals' or groups' religious beliefs and practices, over time, occur through processes of acculturation, adhesion or hybridity, syncretism, and transformation. All four processes are illustrated by a particular group of Jewish converts to Islam and their descendants in the Ottoman Empire and Turkey.

By the seventeenth century, large communities of Jews had been acculturated into Ottoman society.[86] One can even speak of Jewish and Muslim symbiosis.[87] Shared tastes, habits, and customs made it hard to distinguish Jew from Muslim, although the religious differences were clear. Many Jews also crossed the confessional boundary and became Muslims. The agents of conversion and converts can have radically different aims and understandings of religious change, however. Converts shape their religion in light of their own interpretation. Purification can never really succeed, for purification movements inevitably produce new hybrids.[88] The late seventeenth-century Kadızadeli Ottoman interpretation of Islam, for example, condemned any sign of the reconciliation or fusion of diverse beliefs and practices. Despite the aims of these religious reformers, however, one of the most long-lasting consequences of conversion may have been the creation of communities of descendants of seventeenth-century Christian and Jewish converts to Islam. These communities either maintained two sets of religious beliefs and practices or engaged in practices that syncretized elements of the original and adopted faiths following their ostensible conversion experience. An example of the former is the Hemshin of Eastern Anatolia;[89] the followers of Shabbatai Tzevi are an example of the latter.

Ottoman Sultan Mehmed IV (reign 1648–87) thought that he had converted the Jewish messianic claimant named Shabbatai Tzevi (1626–76), leader of the Shabbatean movement, into a Muslim. Tzevi was renamed Aziz Mehmed Efendi in 1666.[90] Aziz Mehmed Efendi's actions and those of his followers, however, demonstrate that the Shabbatean movement was not quenched. On the surface, the converted mystic appeared to engage in adhesion or hybridity. Despite being a Muslim after his conversion, however, Aziz Mehmed Efendi continued to practice Jewish mysticism, Kabbalah, alongside Islam. He encouraged his followers to retain a belief in his messianic calling and to practice the Kabbalistic rituals and prayers that he had taught them. Observers claimed that he and his converted followers visited synagogues in Istanbul and prayed in Hebrew. He was exiled to Albania in 1673. Before he died he married a Jewish woman from Salonica whose brother consolidated the first community of Aziz Mehmed Efendi's followers after his death.

Within this community, the radical failure of their messiah led not to disappointment but to rationalization, confirmation, acceptance of the paradox of the leader's conversion, renewed confidence, and the ecstasy of knowing that one cannot know the mysteries of God's chosen.[91] They readily accepted the messiah's explanations for his act, that conversion was a temporary punishment for Jews because they had not recognized the true God that he had discovered, and redoubled their belief by also converting to Islam. Having gone beyond the limits of Judaism and severing many social ties in the process, the followers of the messianic-mystic-turned-Muslim continued the movement centered on the former Shabbatai Tzevi with a new name and new practices, syncretizing Kabbalah and Sufism. Members of this group called themselves Ma'aminim (Hebrew, "believers"); Muslims called them Dönme (Turkish, "those who turn," "converts"). They continued to possess distinct beliefs and enact unique rituals, which neither Jews nor Muslims could claim as their own, into the twentieth century. Unlike Jews, the Ma'aminim ostensibly followed the requirements of Islam, including fasting at Ramadan and praying in mosques, one of which they built. Unlike Muslims, the Ma'aminim maintained the belief that the former Shabbatai Tzevi was the messiah, practiced Kabbalistic rituals, and recited prayers in Hebrew and Judeo-Spanish. They married only among themselves, maintained detailed genealogies, and buried their dead in distinct cemeteries.[92] For over two centuries they maintained their syncretistic religion.

Yet at the turn of the twentieth century some Ma'aminim became pious Muslims. The Ma'aminim began to drop the paramount values of their own syncretistic religion in favor of the paramount values of Islam. About the only trace of the group that remains today is the sole mosque they constructed during the period when their movement was most active. As the Muslim-ruled, religiously plural Ottoman Empire dissolved and was replaced by the officially secular Republic of Turkey, most Ma'aminim made their best efforts at transformation, first into Muslims and then into Turks. Illustrating the four processes of religious conversion explored in this essay—acculturation, adhesion or hybridity, syncretism, and transformation—the Ma'aminim changed over the course of two centuries from acculturated Jews to practitioners of Judaism and Islam to syncretists boasting their own religion to Muslims and finally to secular Turks.

NOTES

1. William James, *The Varieties of Religious Experience* (New York: Simon and Schuster, 2004), 162.
2. See Karl Frederick Morrison, *Understanding Conversion* (Charlottesville: University of Virginia Press, 1992); Karl Frederick Morrison, *Conversion and Text: The Cases of Augustine of Hippo, Herman-Judah, and Constantine Tsatso* (Charlottesville: University of Virginia Press, 1992); and Lewis Rambo, *Understanding Religious Conversion* (New Haven: Yale University Press, 1993).
3. Rambo, *Understanding Religious Conversion*, 13–14.
4. Marc David Baer, *Honored by the Glory of Islam: Conversion and Conquest in Ottoman Europe* (New York: Oxford University Press, 2008), 15; Marc David Baer, "Islamic Conversion Narratives of Women: Social Change and Gendered Religious Hierarchy in Early Modern Ottoman Istanbul," *Gender & History* 16, no. 2 (2004): 425–458.
5. This is the main thesis of Richard Fletcher, *The Barbarian Conversion: From Paganism to Christianity* (Berkeley and Los Angeles: University of California Press, 1997); see also Michael Maas, "'Delivered from Their Ancient Customs': Christianity and the Question of Cultural Change in Early Byzantine Ethnography," in *Conversion in Late Antiquity and the Early Middle Ages: Seeing and Believing*, ed. Kenneth Mills and Anthony Grafton (Rochester, NY: University of Rochester Press, 2003), 152–188.
6. As narrated by Michael Khodarkovsky, *Russia's Steppe Frontier: The Making of a Colonial Empire, 1500–1800* (Bloomington: Indiana University Press, 2002).
7. Robert Hefner, "World Building and the Rationality of Conversion," in *Conversion to Christianity: Historical and Anthropological Perspectives on a Great Transformation*, ed. Robert Hefner (Berkeley and Los Angeles: University of California Press, 1993), 3–44.
8. Jean Comaroff and John Comaroff, "Christianity and Colonialism in South Africa," *American Ethnologist* 13 (1986): 1–20.
9. Robin Horton, "African Conversion" *Africa* 41 (1971): 85–108; Robin Horton, "On the Rationality of Conversion: Part One," *Africa* 45 (1975): 219–235; Robin Horton, "On the Rationality of Conversion: Part Two," *Africa* 45 (1975): 373–399.
10. Jerry Bentley, *Old World Encounters: Cross-Cultural Contacts and Exchanges in Pre-Modern Times* (New York: Oxford University Press, 1993), 13.
11. Nehemia Levtzion, "Toward a Comparative Study of Islamization," in *Conversion to Islam*, ed. Nehemia Levtzion (New York: Holmes & Meier, 1979), 1–23; Richard Bulliet, "Conversion of Islam and the Emergence of a Muslim Society in Iran," in *Conversion to Islam*, ed. Nehemia Levtzion (New York: Holmes & Meier, 1979), 30–51.
12. Shaban, M. A. "Conversion to Early Islam," in *Conversion to Islam*, ed. Nehemia Levtzion (New York: Holmes & Meier, 1979), 24–29.
13. This process is documented in Spyros Vryonis, Jr., *The Decline of Medieval Hellenism in Asia Minor and the Process of Islamization from the Eleventh to the Fifteenth Century* (Berkeley and Los Angeles: University of California Press, 1971); and V. L. Ménage, "The Islamization of Anatolia," in *Conversion to Islam*, ed. Nehemia Levtzion (New York: Holmes & Meier, 1979), 52–67.
14. Natalie Zemon Davis, *Trickster Travels: A Sixteenth-Century Muslim between Worlds* (New York: Hill and Wang, 2006), 148–149.
15. For detailed accounts of the Hadrami, see Marshall Hodgson, *The Expansion of Islam in the Middle Periods*, vol. 2 of *The Venture of Islam: Conscience and History in a World*

Civilization, 3 vols. (Chicago: University of Chicago Press, 1974), 532–548; and Engseng Ho, *The Graves of Tarim: Genealogy and Mobility across the Indian Ocean* (Berkeley and Los Angeles: University of California Press, 2006).

16. Norman Itzkowitz, *Ottoman Empire and Islamic Tradition* (Chicago: University of Chicago Press, 1972), 37–63.

17. Leslie Pierce, *The Imperial Harem: Women and Sovereignty in the Ottoman Empire* (New York: Oxford, 1993).

18. Daniel Vitkus, *Turning Turk: English Theater and the Multicultural Mediterranean, 1570–1630* (New York: Palgrave Macmillan, 2003); and Nabil Matar, *Islam in Britain, 1558–1685* (New York: Cambridge University Press, 1998), 21–50.

19. [19]The most well-known examples of this phenomenon are the *Conversos* and *Moriscos*, Jews and Muslims compelled to become Catholics in medieval and early modern Spain. See Miriam Bodian, *Hebrews of the Portuguese Nation: Conversos and Community in Early Modern Amsterdam* (Bloomington, IN: Indiana University Press, 1999); Renée Levine Melammed, *Heretics or Daughters of Israel? The Crypto-Jewish Women of Castile* (New York: Oxford University Press, 2002); Miriam Bodian, *Dying in the Law of Moses: Crypto-Jewish Martyrdom in the Iberian World* (Bloomington, IN: Indiana University Press, 2007); and Elizabeth Perry, *The Handless Maiden: Moriscos and the Politics of Religion in Early Modern Spain* (Princeton: Princeton University Press, 2007).

20. Baer, *Honored by the Glory of Islam*, 15–16.

21. Matar, *Islam in Britain*, 16.

22. A. D. Nock, *Conversion: The Old and the New in Religion from Alexander the Great to Augustine of Hippo* (Baltimore: Johns Hopkins University Press, 1998), 7.

23. Eric Rebillard, "Conversion and Burial in the Late Roman Empire," in *Conversion in Late Antiquity and the Early Middle Ages: Seeing and Believing*, ed. Kenneth Mills and Anthony Grafton (Rochester, NY: University of Rochester Press, 2003), 61–83.

24. Fletcher, *Barbarian Conversion*, 508.

25. Peter Brown, *Augustine of Hippo: A Biography* (Berkeley and Los Angeles: University of California Press, 2000); Paula Fredricksen, "Paul and Augustine: Conversion Narratives, Orthodox Traditions, and the Retrospective Self," *Journal of Theological Studies* 37 (1986): 3–34; Morrison, *Conversion and Text*, 1–38; Raymond Van Dam, "The Many Conversions of the Emperor Constantine," in *Conversion in Late Antiquity and the Early Middle Ages: Seeing and Believing*, ed. Kenneth Mills and Anthony Grafton (Rochester, NY: University of Rochester Press, 2003), 127–151.

26. Richard Lim, "Converting the Un-Christianizable: The Baptism of Stage Performers in Late Antiquity," in *Conversion in Late Antiquity and the Early Middle Ages: Seeing and Believing*, ed. Kenneth Mills and Anthony Grafton (Rochester, NY: University of Rochester Press, 2003), 84–126.

27. Fletcher, *Barbarian Conversion*, 250.

28. Ibid., 228–284.

29. Baer, *Honored by the Glory of Islam*, 19.

30. David Jordan, "The Glyphomancy Factor: Observations on Chinese Conversion," in *Conversion to Christianity: Historical and Anthropological Perspectives on a Great Transformation*, ed. Robert Hefner (Berkeley and Los Angeles: University of California Press, 1993), 285–304; R. Po-chia Hsia, "Translating Christianity: Counter-Reformation Europe and the Catholic Mission in China, 1580–1780," in *Conversion: Old Worlds and New*, ed. Kenneth Mills and Anthony Grafton (Rochester, NY: University of Rochester

Press, 2003), 87–108; Liam Matthew Brockey, *Journey to the East: The Jesuit Mission to China, 1579–1724* (Cambridge, MA: Harvard University Press, 2007).

31. Peter Gose, "Converting the Ancestors: Indirect Rule, Settlement Consolidation, and the Struggle over Burial in Colonial Peru (1532–1614)," in *Conversion: Old Worlds and New*, ed. Kenneth Mills and Anthony Grafton (Rochester, NY: University of Rochester Press, 2003), 140–174.

32. Nancy Farriss argues that Maya religion and Christianity merged into a syncretistic cult of the saints. See Nancy Farriss, *Maya Society under Colonial Rule: The Collective Enterprise of Survival* (Princeton: Princeton University Press, 1984), 286–353. See also William Merrill, "Conversion and Colonialism in Northern Mexico: The Tarahumara Response to the Jesuit Mission Program, 1601–1767," in *Conversion to Christianity: Historical and Anthropological Perspectives on a Great Transformation*, ed. Robert Hefner (Berkeley and Los Angeles: University of California Press, 1993), 129–164.

33. Ines Županov, "Twisting a Pagan Tongue: Portuguese and Tamil in Sixteenth-Century Jesuit Translations," in *Conversion: Old Worlds and New*, ed. Kenneth Mills and Anthony Grafton (Rochester, NY: University of Rochester Press, 2003), 109–139.

34. Rafael Vicente, *Contracting Colonialism: Translation and Christian Conversion in Tagalog Society under Early Spanish Rule* (Durham, NC: Duke University Press, 1993).

35. Ibid., 135.

36. Carolyn Brewer, *Shamanism, Catholicism, and Gender Relations in Colonial Philippines, 1521–1685* (Burlington, VT: Ashgate, 2004).

37. Eliza Kent, *Converting Women: Gender and Protestant Christianity in Colonial South India* (New York: Oxford University Press, 2004).

38. Ibid., 239.

39. Allan Greer, "Conversion and Identity: Iroquois Christianity in Seventeenth-century New France," in *Conversion: Old Worlds and New*, ed. Kenneth Mills and Anthony Grafton (Rochester, NY: University of Rochester Press, 2003), 175–198; and Allan Greer, *Mohawk Saint: Catherine Tekakwitha and the Jesuits* (New York: Oxford University Press, 2006).

40. Ramón Guitérrez, *When Jesus Came, the Corn Mothers Went Away: Marriage, Sex, and Power in New Mexico, 1500–1846* (Stanford, CA: Stanford University Press, 1991).

41. James Sandos, *Converting California: Indians and Franciscans in the Missions* (New Haven: Yale University Press, 2004), 182.

42. Joel Robbins, *Becoming Sinners: Christianity and Moral Torment in a Papua New Guinea Society* (Berkeley and Los Angeles: University of California Press, 2004).

43. Ibid., 10–11.

44. Ibid., 327.

45. Bentley, *Old World Encounters*, 15–16.

46. "Judaism is not the 'mother' of Christianity; they are twins, joined at the hip." Daniel Boyarin, *Border Lines: The Partition of Judaeo-Christianity* (Philadelphia: University of Pennsylvania Press, 2004), 5.

47. Fred Donner, "Muhammad and the Caliphate: Political History of the Islamic Empire up to the Mongol Conquest," in *The Oxford History of Islam*, ed. John Esposito (New York: Oxford University Press, 1999), 6.

48. Jane Smith, "Islam and Christendom: Historical, Cultural, and Religious Interaction from the Seventh to the Fifteenth Centuries," in *The Oxford History of Islam*, ed. John Esposito (New York: Oxford University Press, 1999), 306.

49. Donner, "Muhammad and the Caliphate," 19. The Church of the Holy Sepulchre was built upon the site of a temple of Aphrodite by Emperor Constantine, whose conversion to Christianity has been of great scholarly controversy.

50. For extensive documentation, see F. W. Hasluck, *Christianity and Islam under the Sultans*, ed. Margaret Hasluck, 2 vols. (New York: Octagon Books, 1973); see also V. L. Ménage, "The Islamization of Anatolia," in *Conversion to Islam*, ed. Nehemia Levtzion (New York: Holmes & Meier, 1979), 52–67.

51. Rafael Israeli, "Islamization and Sinicization in Chinese Islam," in *Conversion to Islam*, ed. Nehemia Levtzion (New York: Holmes & Meier, 1979), 159–176; Murray Last, "Some Economic Aspects of Conversion in Hausaland (Nigeria)," in *Conversion to Islam*, ed. Nehemia Levtzion (New York: Holmes & Meier, 1979), 236–246; R. S. O'Fahey, "Islam, State, and Society in Dār Fūr," in *Conversion to Islam*, ed. Nehemia Levtzion (New York: Holmes & Meier, 1979), 189–206.

52. Ibid., 161–163.

53. Dru Gladney, "Central Asia and China: Transnationalism, Islamization, and Ethnicization," in *The Oxford History of Islam*, ed. John Esposito (New York: Oxford University Press, 1999), 449.

54. Nehemia Levtzion and Randall Pouwels, "Introduction: Patterns of Islamization and Varieties of Religious Experience among Muslims of Africa," in *The History of Islam in Africa*, ed. Nehemia Levtzion and Randall Pouwels (Athens: Ohio University Press, 2000), 8.

55. Nehemia Levtzion, "Islam in the Bilad al-Sudan to 1800," in *The History of Islam in Africa*, ed. Nehemia Levtzion and Randall Pouwels (Athens: Ohio University Press, 2000), 63–91.

56. The best account of this process is Devin DeWeese, *Islamization and Native Religion in the Golden Horde: Baba Tükles and Conversion to Islam in Historical and Epic Tradition* (University Park: Pennsylvania State University Press, 1994).

57. Peter Hardy, "Modern European and Muslim Explanations of Conversion to Islam in South Asia," in *Conversion to Islam*, ed. Nehemia Levtzion. New York: Holmes & Meier, 1979), 68–99.

58. Richard Eaton, *The Rise of Islam and the Bengal Frontier, 1204–1760* (Berkeley and Los Angeles: University of California Press, 1993), 268–290.

59. Ibid., 269.

60. M. C. Ricklefs, *Mystic Synthesis in Java: A History of Islamization from the Fourteenth to the Early Nineteenth Centuries* (Norwalk, CT: Eastbridge, 2006).

61. Nock, *Conversion*, 7.

62. Baer, *Honored by the Glory of Islam*, 15.

63. *The Mission*, dir. Roland Joffé, 125 min., Warner Brothers, 1986.

64. Christopher Clark, *The Politics of Conversion: Missionary Protestantism and the Jews in Prussia 1728–1941* (Oxford: Clarendon Press, 1995), 88.

65. James Muldoon, "Introduction: The Conversion of Europe," in *Varieties of Religious Conversion in the Middle Ages*, ed. James Muldoon (Gainesville: University Press of Florida, 1997), 5; Fletcher, *Barbarian Conversion*, 237, 242.

66. Julia Smith, "'Emending Evil Ways and Praising God's Omnipotence': Einhard and the Uses of Roman Martyrs," in *Conversion in Late Antiquity and the Early Middle Ages: Seeing and Believing*, ed. Kenneth Mills and Anthony Grafton (Rochester, NY: University of Rochester Press, 2003), 190.

67. Peter Brown, *Authority and the Sacred: Aspects of the Christianisation of the Roman World* (New York: Cambridge University Press, 1997).
68. John Van Engen, "Conversion and Conformity in the Early Fifteenth Century," in *Conversion: Old Worlds and New*, ed. Kenneth Mills and Anthony Grafton (Rochester, NY: University of Rochester Press, 2003), 30–65.
69. Levtzion, "Toward a Comparative Study of Islamization," 21.
70. Madeline Zilfi, *The Politics of Piety: The Ottoman Ulema in the Postclassical Age* (Minneapolis: Bibliotheca Islamica, 1988).
71. O'Fahey, "Islam, State, and Society"; Last, "Some Economic Aspects of Conversion in Hausaland (Nigeria)"; Levtzion, "Toward a Comparative Study of Islamization"; Donner, "Muhammad and the Caliphate," 49–52; Levtzion and Pouwels, "Patterns of Islamization."
72. Gladney, "Central Asia and China."
73. Ricklefs, *Mystic Synthesis in Java*.
74. John Voll, "Foundations for Renewal and Reform: Islamic Movements in the Eighteenth and Nineteenth Centuries," in *The Oxford History of Islam*, ed. John Esposito (New York: Oxford University Press, 1999), 516–518.
75. Humphrey Fisher, "Conversion Reconsidered: Some Historical Aspects of Religious Conversion in Black Africa," *Africa* 43 (1973): 27–40; Humphrey Fisher, "The Juggernaut's Apologia: Conversion to Islam in Black Africa," *Africa* 55, no. 2, (1985): 153–173; "Many Deep Baptisms: Reflections on Religious, Chiefly Muslim, Conversion in Black Africa," *Bulletin of the School of Oriental and African Studies* 57 (1994): 68–81.
76. Alex Haley, *Autobiography of Malcolm X* (New York: Penguin Books, 1973), 372–82; *Malcolm X*, dir. Spike Lee, 202 min., Warner Brothers, 1992.
77. *By the Dawn's Early Light: Chris Jackson's Journey to Islam*, dir. Zareena Grewal, 52 min., Cinema Guild, 2004.
78. Robert Dannin, *Black Pilgrimage to Islam* (New York: Oxford University Press, 2002).
79. Baer, *Honored by the Glory of Islam*, 18.
80. Eaton, *Rise of Islam and the Bengal Frontier*, 228–247; Jamsheed Choksy, *Conflict and Cooperation: Zoroastrian Subalterns and Muslim Elites in Medieval Iranian Society* (New York: Columbia University Press, 1997), 93–106; Ethel Sara Wolper, *Cities and Saints: Sufism and the Transformation of Urban Space in Medieval Anatolia* (University Park: Pennsylvania State University Press, 2003).
81. John Howe, "The Conversion of the Physical World: The Creation of a Christian Landscape," in *Varieties of Religious Conversion in the Middle Ages*, ed. James Muldoon (Gainesville: University Press of Florida, 1997), 63–79.
82. Ibid., 67.
83. Samuel Edgerton, *Theaters of Conversion: Religious Architecture and Indian Artisans in Colonial Mexico* (Albuquerque: University of New Mexico Press, 2001).
84. The phrase comes from Edgerton, *Theaters of Conversion*.
85. Howe, "Conversion of the Christian World," 67.
86. Stanford Shaw, *The Jews of the Ottoman Empire and Turkish Republic* (New York: New York University Press, 1991); Avigdor Levy, ed., *Jews, Turks, Ottomans: A Shared History, Fifteenth through the Twentieth Century* (Syracuse, NY: Syracuse University Press, 2003).
87. Bernard Lewis, *The Jews of Islam* (Princeton: Princeton University Press, 1984), 107–153.
88. Webb Keane, *Christian Moderns: Freedom and Fetish in the Mission Encounter* (Berkeley and Los Angeles: University of California Press, 2007), 79–80.
89. Hovann Simonian, *The Hemshin: A Handbook* (London: Routledge, 2006).

90. Baer, *Honored by the Glory of Islam*, 121–132.
91. Ibid., 256.
92. Marc David Baer, *The Dönme: Jewish Converts, Muslim Revolutionaries, and Secular Turks* (Stanford, CA: Stanford University Press, 2010), 1–21.

Bibliography

Books and Articles

Baer, Marc David. *The Dönme: Jewish Converts, Muslim Revolutionaries, and Secular Turks.* Stanford, CA: Stanford University Press, 2010.

——. *Honored by the Glory of Islam: Conversion and Conquest in Ottoman Europe.* New York: Oxford University Press, 2008.

——. "Islamic Conversion Narratives of Women: Social Change and Gendered Religious Hierarchy in Early Modern Ottoman Istanbul." *Gender & History* 16, no. 2 (2004): 425–458.

Bentley, Jerry. *Old World Encounters: Cross-Cultural Contacts and Exchanges in Pre-Modern Times.* New York: Oxford University Press, 1993.

Bodian, Miriam. *Hebrews of the Portuguese Nation: Conversos and Community in Early Modern Amsterdam.* Bloomington, IN: Indiana University Press, 1999.

——. *Dying in the Law of Moses: Crypto-Jewish Martyrdom in the Iberian World.* Bloomington, IN: Indiana University Press, 2007.

Boyarin, Daniel. *Border Lines: The Partition of Judaeo-Christianity.* Philadelphia: University of Pennsylvania Press, 2004.

Brewer, Carolyn. *Shamanism, Catholicism, and Gender Relations in Colonial Philippines, 1521–1685.* Burlington, VT: Ashgate, 2004.

Brockey, Liam Matthew. *Journey to the East: The Jesuit Mission to China, 1579–1724.* Cambridge, MA: Harvard University Press, 2007.

Brown, Peter. *Augustine of Hippo: A Biography.* Reprint, Berkeley and Los Angeles: University of California Press, 2000.

——. *Authority and the Sacred: Aspects of the Christianisation of the Roman World.* New York: Cambridge University Press, 1997.

Bulliet, Richard. "Conversion of Islam and the Emergence of a Muslim Society in Iran." In *Conversion to Islam*, ed. Nehemiah Levtzion, 30–51. New York: Holmes & Meier, 1979.

Choksy, Jamsheed. *Conflict and Cooperation: Zoroastrian Subalterns and Muslim Elites in Medieval Iranian Society.* New York: Columbia University Press, 1997.

Clark, Christopher. *The Politics of Conversion: Missionary Protestantism and the Jews in Prussia 1728–1941.* Oxford: Clarendon Press, 1995.

Comaroff, Jean, and John Comaroff. "Christianity and Colonialism in South Africa." *American Ethnologist* 13 (1986): 1–20.

Dannin, Robert. *Black Pilgrimage to Islam.* New York: Oxford University Press, 2002.

Davis, Natalie Zemon. *Trickster Travels: A Sixteenth-Century Muslim between Worlds.* New York: Hill and Wang, 2006.

DeWeese, Devin. *Islamization and Native Religion in the Golden Horde: Baba Tükles and Conversion to Islam in Historical and Epic Tradition.* University Park: Pennsylvania State University Press, 1994.

Donner, Fred. "Muhammad and the Caliphate: Political History of the Islamic Empire up to the Mongol Conquest." In *The Oxford History of Islam*, ed. John Esposito, 1–61. New York: Oxford University Press, 1999.

Eaton, Richard. *The Rise of Islam and the Bengal Frontier, 1204–1760*. Berkeley and Los Angeles: University of California Press, 1993.

Edgerton, Samuel. *Theaters of Conversion: Religious Architecture and Indian Artisans in Colonial Mexico*. Albuquerque: University of New Mexico Press, 2001.

Farriss, Nancy. *Maya Society under Colonial Rule: The Collective Enterprise of Survival*. Princeton: Princeton University Press, 1984.

Fisher, Humphrey. "Conversion Reconsidered: Some Historical Aspects of Religious Conversion in Black Africa." *Africa* 43 (1973): 27–40.

——. "The Juggernaut's Apologia: Conversion to Islam in Black Africa." *Africa* 55, no. 2 (1985): 153–173.

——. "Many Deep Baptisms: Reflections on Religious, Chiefly Muslim, Conversion in Black Africa." *Bulletin of the School of Oriental and African Studies* 57 (1994): 68–81.

Fletcher, Richard. *The Barbarian Conversion: From Paganism to Christianity*. Berkeley and Los Angeles: University of California Press, 1997.

Fredricksen, Paula. "Paul and Augustine: Conversion Narratives, Orthodox Traditions, and the Retrospective Self." *Journal of Theological Studies* 37 (1986): 3–34.

Gladney, Dru. "Central Asia and China: Transnationalism, Islamization, and Ethnicization." In *The Oxford History of Islam*, ed. John Esposito, 433–474. New York: Oxford University Press, 1999.

Gose, Peter. "Converting the Ancestors: Indirect Rule, Settlement Consolidation, and the Struggle over Burial in Colonial Peru (1532–1614)." In *Conversion: Old Worlds and New*, ed. Kenneth Mills and Anthony Grafton, 140–174. Rochester, NY: University of Rochester Press, 2003.

Greer, Allan. "Conversion and Identity: Iroquois Christianity in Seventeenth-Century New France." In *Conversion: Old Worlds and New*, ed. Kenneth Mills and Anthony Grafton, 175–198. Rochester, NY: University of Rochester Press, 2003.

——. *Mohawk Saint: Catherine Tekakwitha and the Jesuits*. New York: Oxford University Press, 2006.

Gutiérrez, Ramón. *When Jesus Came, the Corn Mothers Went Away: Marriage, Sex, and Power in New Mexico, 1500–1846*. Stanford, CA: Stanford University Press, 1991.

Hardy, Peter. "Modern European and Muslim Explanations of Conversion to Islam in South Asia." In *Conversion to Islam*, ed. Nehemia Levtzion, 68–99. New York: Holmes & Meier, 1979.

Hasluck, F. W. *Christianity and Islam under the Sultans*, ed. Margaret Hasluck, 2 vols. Reprint, New York: Octagon Books, 1973.

Hefner, Robert. *Hindu Javanese: Tengger Tradition and Islam*. Princeton: Princeton University Press, 1990.

——. "World Building and the Rationality of Conversion." In *Conversion to Christianity: Historical and Anthropological Perspectives on a Great Transformation*, ed. Robert Hefner, 3–44. Berkeley and Los Angeles: University of California Press, 1993.

Ho, Engseng. *The Graves of Tarim: Genealogy and Mobility across the Indian Ocean*. Berkeley and Los Angeles: University of California Press, 2006.

Hodgson, Marshall. *The Expansion of Islam in the Middle Periods*. Vol. 2 of *The Venture of Islam: Conscience and History in a World Civilization*. 3 vols. Chicago: University of Chicago Press, 1974.

Horton, Robin. "African Conversion." *Africa* 41(1971): 85–108.

———. "On the Rationality of Conversion: Part One." *Africa* 45 (1975): 219–235.

———. "On the Rationality of Conversion: Part Two." *Africa* 45 (1975): 373–399.

Howe, John. "The Conversion of the Physical World: The Creation of a Christian Landscape." In *Varieties of Religious Conversion in the Middle Ages*, ed. James Muldoon, 63–79. Gainesville: University Press of Florida, 1997.

Hsia, R. Po-chia. "Translating Christianity: Counter-Reformation Europe and the Catholic Mission in China, 1580–1780." In *Conversion: Old Worlds and New*, ed. Kenneth Mills and Anthony Grafton, 87–108. Rochester, NY: University of Rochester Press, 2003.

Israeli, Rafael. "Islamization and Sinicization in Chinese Islam." In *Conversion to Islam*, ed. Nehemia Levtzion, 159–176. New York: Holmes & Meier, 1979.

Itzkowitz, Norman. *Ottoman Empire and Islamic Tradition*. Chicago: University of Chicago Press, 1972.

James, William. *The Varieties of Religious Experience*. Reprint, New York: Simon and Schuster, 2004.

Jordan, David. "The Glyphomancy Factor: Observations on Chinese Conversion." In *Conversion to Christianity: Historical and Anthropological Perspectives on a Great Transformation*, ed. Robert Hefner, 285–304. Berkeley and Los Angeles: University of California Press, 1993.

Keane, Webb. *Christian Moderns: Freedom and Fetish in the Mission Encounter*. Berkeley and Los Angeles: University of California Press, 2007.

Kent, Eliza. *Converting Women: Gender and Protestant Christianity in Colonial South India*. New York: Oxford, 2004.

Khodarkovsky, Michael. *Russia's Steppe Frontier: The Making of a Colonial Empire, 1500–1800*. Bloomington: Indiana University Press, 2002.

Last, Murray. "Some Economic Aspects of Conversion in Hausaland (Nigeria)." In *Conversion to Islam*, ed. Nehemia Levtzion, 236–246. New York: Holmes & Meier, 1979.

Levtzion, Nehemia. "Islam in the Bilad al-Sudan to 1800." In *The History of Islam in Africa*, ed. Nehemia Levtzion and Randall Pouwels, 63–91. Athens: Ohio University Press, 2000.

———. "Toward a Comparative Study of Islamization." In *Conversion to Islam*, ed. Nehemia Levtzion, 1–23. New York: Holmes & Meier, 1979.

Levtzion, Nehemia, and Randall Pouwels. "Introduction: Patterns of Islamization and Varieties of Religious Experience among Muslims of Africa." In *The History of Islam in Africa*, ed. Nehemia Levtzion and Randall Pouwels, 1–18. Athens: Ohio University Press, 2000.

Levy, Avigdor, ed. *Jews, Turks, Ottomans: A Shared History, Fifteenth through the Twentieth Century*. Syracuse, NY: Syracuse University Press, 2003.

Lewis, Bernard. *The Jews of Islam*. Princeton: Princeton University Press, 1984.

Lim, Richard. "Converting the Un-Christianizable: The Baptism of Stage Performers in Late Antiquity." In *Conversion in Late Antiquity and the Early Middle Ages: Seeing and Believing*, ed. Kenneth Mills and Anthony Grafton, 84–126. Rochester, NY: University of Rochester Press, 2003.

Maas, Michael. "'Delivered from Their Ancient Customs': Christianity and the Question of Cultural Change in Early Byzantine Ethnography." In *Conversion in Late Antiquity and the Early Middle Ages: Seeing and Believing*, ed. Kenneth Mills and Anthony Grafton, 152–188. Rochester, NY: University of Rochester Press, 2003.

MacCormack, Sabine. *Religion in the Andes: Vision and Imagination in Early Colonial Peru*. Princeton: Princeton University Press, 1991.

Matar, Nabil. *Islam in Britain, 1558–1685*. New York: Cambridge University Press, 1998.

Melammed, Renée Levine. *Heretics or Daughters of Israel? The Crypto-Jewish Women of Castile.* New York: Oxford University Press, 2002.

Ménage, V. L. "The Islamization of Anatolia." In *Conversion to Islam*, ed. Nehemia Levtzion, 52–67. New York: Holmes & Meier, 1979.

Merrill, William. "Conversion and Colonialism in Northern Mexico: The Tarahumara Response to the Jesuit Mission Program, 1601–1767. In *Conversion to Christianity: Historical and Anthropological Perspectives on a Great Transformation*, ed. Robert Hefner, 129–164. Berkeley and Los Angeles: University of California Press, 1993.

Morrison, Karl Frederick. *Conversion and Text: The Cases of Augustine of Hippo, Herman-Judah, and Constantine Tsatsos.* Charlottesville: University of Virginia Press, 1992.

——. *Understanding Conversion.* Charlottesville, VA: University of Virginia Press, 1992.

Muldoon, James. 1997. "Introduction: The Conversion of Europe." In *Varieties of Religious Conversion in the Middle Ages*, ed. James Muldoon, 1–11. Gainesville: University Press of Florida.

Nock, A. D. *Conversion: The Old and the New in Religion from Alexander the Great to Augustine of Hippo.* New York: Oxford University Press. Reprint, Baltimore: Johns Hopkins University Press, 1998.

O'Fahey, R. S. "Islam, State, and Society in Dār Fūr." In *Conversion to Islam*, ed. Nehemia Levtzion, 189–206. New York: Holmes & Meier, 1979.

Peirce, Leslie. *The Imperial Harem: Women and Sovereignty in the Ottoman Empire.* New York: Oxford, 1993.

Perry, Elizabeth. *The Handless Maiden: Moriscos and the Politics of Religion in Early Modern Spain.* Princeton: Princeton University Press, 2007.

Rafael, Vicente. *Contracting Colonialism: Translation and Christian Conversion in Tagalog Society under Early Spanish Rule.* Durham, NC: Duke University Press, 1993.

Rambo, Lewis. *Understanding Religious Conversion.* New Haven: Yale University Press, 1993.

Rebillard, Eric. "Conversion and Burial in the Late Roman Empire." In *Conversion in Late Antiquity and the Early Middle Ages: Seeing and Believing*, ed. Kenneth Mills and Anthony Grafton, 61–83. Rochester, NY: University of Rochester Press, 2003.

Ricklefs, M. C. *Mystic Synthesis in Java: A History of Islamization from the Fourteenth to the Early Nineteenth Centuries.* Norwalk, CT: Eastbridge, 2006.

Robbins, Joel. *Becoming Sinners: Christianity and Moral Torment in a Papua New Guinea Society.* Berkeley and Los Angeles: University of California Press, 2004.

Sandos, James. *Converting California: Indians and Franciscans in the Missions.* New Haven: Yale University Press, 2004.

Shaban, M. A. "Conversion to Early Islam." In *Conversion to Islam*, ed. Nehemia Levtzion, 24–29. New York: Holmes & Meier, 1979.

Shaw, Stanford. *The Jews of the Ottoman Empire and Turkish Republic.* New York: New York University Press, 1991.

Simonian, Hovann. *The Hemshin: A Handbook.* London: Routledge, 2006.

Smith, Jane. "Islam and Christendom: Historical, Cultural, and Religious Interaction from the Seventh to the Fifteenth Centuries." In *The Oxford History of Islam*, ed. John Esposito, 305–346. New York: Oxford University Press, 1999.

Smith, Julia. "'Emending Evil Ways and Praising God's Omnipotence': Einhard and the Uses of Roman Martyrs." In *Conversion in Late Antiquity and the Early Middle Ages: Seeing and*

Believing, ed. Kenneth Mills and Anthony Grafton, 189–223. Rochester, NY: University of
Rochester Press, 2003.

Van Dam, Raymond. "The Many Conversions of the Emperor Constantine." In *Conversion
in Late Antiquity and the Early Middle Ages: Seeing and Believing*, ed. Kenneth Mills and
Anthony Grafton, 127–151. Rochester, NY: University of Rochester Press, 2003.

Van Engen, John. "Conversion and Conformity in the Early Fifteenth Century." In
Conversion: Old Worlds and New, ed. Kenneth Mills and Anthony Grafton, 30–65. Rochester,
NY: University of Rochester Press, 2003.

Vitkus, Daniel. *Turning Turk: English Theater and the Multicultural Mediterranean, 1570–1630*.
New York: Palgrave Macmillan, 2003.

Voll, John. "Foundations for Renewal and Reform: Islamic Movements in the Eighteenth
and Nineteenth Centuries." In *The Oxford History of Islam*, ed. John Esposito, 509–547.
New York: Oxford University Press, 1999.

Vyronis, Spyros, Jr. *The Decline of Medieval Hellenism in Asia Minor and the Process of
Islamization from the Eleventh to the Fifteenth Century*. Berkeley and Los Angeles: University
of California Press, 1971.

Wolper, Ethel Sara. *Cities and Saints: Sufism and the Transformation of Urban Space in Medieval
Anatolia*. University Park: Pennsylvania State University Press, 2003.

X, Malcolm. *The Autobiography of Malcolm X as told to Alex Haley*. New York: Penguin Books,
[1965] 1973.

Zilfi, Madeline. *The Politics of Piety: The Ottoman Ulema in the Postclassical Age*.
Minneapolis: Bibliotheca Islamica, 1988.

Županov, Ines. "Twisting a Pagan Tongue: Portuguese and Tamil in Sixteenth-century Jesuit
Translations." In *Conversion: Old Worlds and New*, ed. Kenneth Mills and Anthony Grafton,
109–139. Rochester, NY: University of Rochester Press, 2003.

Films

By the Dawn's Early Light: Chris Jackson's Journey to Islam. Directed by Zareena Grewal. 52 min.
Cinema Guild, 2004.

The Gospel According to the Papuans. Directed by Thomas Balmès, 52 min. Filmakers
Library, 1999.

Malcolm X. Directed by Spike Lee. 202 min. New York: Warner Brothers, 1992.

The Mission. Directed by Roland Joffé. 125 min. Warner Brothers, 1986.

....

CHAPTER 2

DEMOGRAPHICS OF RELIGIOUS CONVERSION

....

TODD M. JOHNSON

INTERNATIONAL religious demography is a burgeoning field of study. In the past twenty-five years, an enormous amount of data have been collected and analyzed. New sources of information include government censuses (half the countries in the world include a religion question), records kept by religious communities (membership rolls), and published works by individual scholars (such as monographs on new religious movements). These data have then been collated, analyzed, and published in a wide variety of ways, highlighting countries, regions, and—in more rare cases—the globe.

Despite this abundance of demographic material, writings about religion often have the appearance of sheer guesswork. Those brave enough to venture into this realm seem inexorably drawn to two extreme visions. At one pole are the writings of devout religionists that predict the onset of religious paradises ranging from pseudo-humanistic utopias (still based on religion) to Christian, Muslim, or Buddhist eschatological visions to New Age cosmic consciousness sans organized religion. At the other extreme are the writings of ultra-secularists who predict the inexorable decline and collapse of religion. The consistent bias in the latter predictions against the staying power of religion demonstrates that most of these writers do not take religion seriously or are interested in only its aberrations or extremes (e.g., fanaticism or fundamentalism). Notwithstanding differences in philosophical perspectives, however, what these two camps share is a deficiency of quantitative evidence to support their views.

PREDICTING THE DEMISE OR COLLAPSE OF RELIGION

....

Consistent with many of the classical theorists of sociology who argued, for example, that "religion had reached the pinnacle of its influence in the early modern period and could no longer be regarded as a formative institution for giving definition to late-modern patterns of development,"[1] social scientists continue to predict a decline in the prevalence of religion. They dismiss the role of religious communities during the last decade in Northern Ireland, the Middle East, and Latin America, as "a last-ditch effort by fundamentalists of one stripe or another to forestall the inevitable eclipse of religious hegemony in a world already well on the way toward deep structural secularization."[2]

This basic assumption has profoundly affected not only the field of sociology but also many interrelated fields for a long time.[3] "From Voltaire to Marx every Enlightenment thinker thought that religion would disappear in the 20th century because religion was fetishism, animistic superstition," writes Harvard's professor emeritus Daniel Bell.[4]

SECULARIZATION COMES UP SHORT

Rodney Stark and William Sims Bainbridge argue that "the vision of a religionless future is but illusion."[5] They recognize that secularization, a powerful trend in the present, is not a new phenomenon. Religious economies have always had to deal with secularizing influences. And with secularization come two counterbalancing factors: revival and religious innovation. Thus, in response to the perpetual nature of the secularizing influence of society, breakaway protest groups form to give a more dynamic otherworldliness to mainstream faith. Yet for all the evidence offered by Stark and Bainbridge for the enduring strength of religion, they present no statistical or numerical support for religious trends. For this one needs to return to the data sources.

DATA COLLECTIONS

Leaders in all religions are concerned about membership, but many do not keep direct records. In Muslim contexts, for example, the number of mosques or imams might be known, but not the number of worshipers. Instead, analysis of Muslim demographics must rely on secular data, particularly government statistics on population. If a country is 99 percent Muslim, such as Mauritania, then all statistics collected by the government on the total population apply directly to the religious community. These would include such information as birth and death rates, literacy rates, and health statistics. Thus, much is known about trends among Muslims in places where they are in the vast majority. Unfortunately, there are many significant countries where Muslims are a minority. Among them is India, one of the largest Muslim countries in the world, where Muslims make up less than 15 percent of the population.

For in-depth analysis, more data are needed. Fortunately, for the study of Christianity, the most detailed (but decentralized) data collection and analysis are undertaken each year by some 39,000 Christian denominations at a cost exceeding US $1.1 billion. Employing ten million printed questionnaires in 3,000 different languages, covering 180 major religious subjects and reporting on 2,000 socio-religious variables, the Christian "megacensus" provides an annual snapshot of the progress or decline of Christianity's diverse movements.

Since the twelfth century, the governments of the world have also been collecting information on religious populations. A question related to religion is now asked in the official national population censuses of over 120 countries. Until 1990 this number was slowly declining each decade as developing countries began dropping the question as too expensive and, apparently, uninteresting. By 2001, however, this trend appears to have reversed. Census data provide a detailed look at five- and ten-year trends that often extend back over one hundred years. Thus Britain, which produced the world's first national census of religious affiliation (the Compton Census in 1676) and later a religion question in the national census of 1851 (though none thereafter), reintroduced the religion question in Britain's 2000 census as the best way to get firm data on each and every non-Christian minority. In contrast, politicians in Russia recently drew the opposite conclusion and decided that a religion question would be too sensitive in the new census, even though they are retaining equally sensitive questions related to language and ethnicity. In Indonesia, where there has been a religion question in the census for decades, until recently there was no way for Sikhs to register their faith so they were simply counted as Hindus. In Nigeria, a religion question could help to settle competing claims by Christians and Muslims that they are in the majority, but successive governments have seen the issue as too controversial. These examples highlight the difficulty that governments face in counting religionists within their borders.

ANALYZING AND DEFINING

The starting point in any analysis of religious affiliation is Article 18 of the United Nations' Universal Declaration of Human Rights, published in 1948. It states, "Everyone has the right to freedom of thought, conscience and religion; this right includes freedom to change his religion or belief, and freedom, either alone or in community with others and in public or private, to manifest his religion or belief in teaching, practice, worship and observance."[6] The impact of Article 18 since its promulgation has been widespread. It has been incorporated, in whole or in part, into the state constitutions of a large number of countries around the world. Many countries instruct their census personnel to respect a person's declaration of religious affiliation. The result is a surprisingly robust assessment of the extent of religious profession in the world.

RESOLVING APPARENTLY
CONTRADICTORY DATA

As sizable quantities of data are amassed by religious and governmental sources, discrepancies between the respective data sets are not uncommon. In a particular country, the results from government censuses and information from religious organizations themselves can be strikingly different. For example, in Egypt, where the vast majority of the population is Muslim, elaborate government censuses taken every ten years for the last one hundred years reveal that some 6 percent of the population declare themselves as or profess to be Christians. However, church censuses point to a percentage figure two and a half times larger (15 percent). This discrepancy may be attributed, at least in part, to Muslim pressure on many Christians to record themselves as Muslims. Analysis of religious affiliation must reconcile the large collections of data arising from these two approaches.

GLOBAL RELIGIOUS RESURGENCE?

What, then, of the fate of religion? First, we can examine the question of whether there has been or is a global resurgence of religion. From the standpoint of the past one hundred years, the answer has to be a resounding "no." Table 2.1, "Percentage of the world's population belonging to no religion or religion, 1910–2010," shows the religious and nonreligious situation over the past century. In 1910 there were very few atheists and agnostics. By the year 2000, agnostics numbered in the hundreds of millions and represented

Table 2.1 Percentage of the World's Population Belonging to No Religion or Religion, 1910–2010

	1910	1950	1970	2000	2010
No religion	0.2	6.7	18.9	15.0	13.5
Agnostics	0.2	5.1	14.4	12.6	11.3
Atheists	0.0	1.6	4.5	2.4	2.2
Religion	99.8	93.3	81.1	85.0	86.5
Christians	34.8	34.4	33.4	33.0	33.5
Muslims	12.6	13.5	14.9	20.1	21.5
Hindus	12.6	12.3	12.6	13.1	13.4
Buddhists	7.9	7.1	6.3	6.0	5.8
Other religionists	31.9	26.0	13.9	12.8	12.3

Source: World Christian Database, July 2008.

15 percent of the world's population. Thus, over the twentieth century, religionists' share of the global population declined steadily in the context of modernization and secularization. In 1910, virtually 100 percent of the world's population was religious. By 2000, this had fallen to 85 percent.

Examining the data more closely, however, one can see that the raw percentage of nonreligious people peaked somewhere near the year 1970 at approximately 19 percent (81 percent being religious). Since then, the percentage of religionists has steadily risen and is expected to reach about 87 percent by 2010. The shift is largely due to the collapse of Communism in the former Soviet Union. While the number of atheists and agnostics continues to rise in the Western world, the current growth of religions of all kinds in China (where the vast majority of the nonreligious live today) bodes well for the demographic future of religion. Thus, when looking at the data for this time period (1970 to the present), it is evident that there has been a global religious resurgence in recent years.

A THREEFOLD DYNAMIC OF CHANGE IN RELIGIOUS AFFILIATIONS

All sources of data on religion—from the religions themselves, governments, and scholars—must be employed to understand the total context of religious affiliation. With this in mind, the dynamics of change in religious affiliation can be reduced to three sets of empirical population data that together enable us to enumerate the increase or decrease in adherents over time. In order to measure overall increase, these three sets can be written as follows: (1) births minus deaths, (2) converts minus defectors, and (3) immigrants minus emigrants. The first variable in each of these three sets (births, converts, immigrants) measures increase, and the second (deaths, defectors, emigrants) measures decrease (thus, the "minus" factors). All future projections of religious affiliation within any subset of the global population (normally a country or region) will be dependent on these dynamics.

Births

The primary mechanism of religious demographic change globally is births. Children are almost always counted as having the religion of their parents (this is the law in Norway and many other countries). In simple terms, if populations that are predominantly Muslim have, on average, more children than those that are predominantly Christian or Hindu, then over time—given no counterbalancing trends, such as conversion—Muslims will become an increasingly larger percentage of the world's population. This means that a religious population has a close statistical relationship to birth rates.

Deaths

At the same time, religious communities experience a constant decline through the deaths of members in their communities. While this often includes tragic, unanticipated deaths of younger members, it most frequently affects the elderly members. Thus, changes in healthcare and technology can positively impact religious communities if members live longer.

Births minus Deaths

The change over time in any given community is most simply expressed as the number of births into the community minus the number of deaths out of it. Many religious communities around the world experience little else in the dynamics of their growth or decline. This means that any attempt to understand religious affiliation must be based firmly on demographic projections of births and deaths. The impact of births and deaths on religious affiliation can change over time. For example, the recent Northern Ireland census revealed a closing of the gap between Protestants and Catholics over the past three decades. Protestants used to make up 65 percent of the population, but by 2001 this had dropped to 53 percent. Catholics, in the meantime, had grown from 35 percent to 44 percent of the population. This shift is due primarily to the higher birth rate among Catholic women. One would expect that, given time, Catholics would eventually claim over 50 percent of the population of Northern Ireland. But the census also revealed two counter-trends: the death rate among Protestants is falling, and the birth rate among Catholics is falling. Given these trends, forecasters believe that, barring any other changes, Protestants will remain in the majority in the coming decades.

Converts

Nonetheless, it is a common observation that individuals (or even whole villages or communities) change allegiance from one religion to another (or to no religion at all). Conversions in the twentieth century have been most pronounced in one general area: large numbers of tribal religionists who converted to Christianity, Islam, Hinduism, and Buddhism. In the African Sahel (semi-arid region south of the Sahara Desert), most countries are still experiencing a race between Islam and Christianity for those individuals and communities still adhering to tribal religions. Early in the twentieth century, it was assumed that within a generation all tribal religionists in Africa would become either Muslims or Christians. Although many conversions took place, a very large number had not converted by 2000. In the twenty-first century, then, one might project continued conversions to Christianity and Islam but be more modest about overall losses among tribal religionists.

Defectors

Conversion to a new religion, as was mentioned above, involves defection from a previous one. Thus, a convert to Islam, is, at the same time, a defector from another religion (such as a tribal religion). Among Christians in the twentieth century, defections have been found largely among Christians in the Western world who have decided to become nonreligious (agnostics) or atheists.

Converts minus Defectors

The net conversion rate in a population combines conversions and defections. Both conversions of tribal religionists and defections among Christians, however, had slowed considerably by the dawn of the twenty-first century. In fact, emerging twenty-first-century trends show that tribal religionist populations will remain relatively stable while world religions experience fewer defections, with corresponding decreases in the percentages of atheists and nonreligious.

Immigrants

Equally important at the national level is how the movement of people across national borders impacts religious affiliation. In the United States, the immigration of non-Christian Asians has resulted in accelerated growth in religions such as Islam, Hinduism, and Buddhism. In Europe, the spiritual influence of the large numbers of Muslim immigrants has extended into national political arenas, notably in France, Germany, Austria, and Italy, as well as into plans for European Union expansion. Turkey's desire for European Union membership has brought out the interesting contrast of an EU that is mainly "Christian" with one that could extend to countries not predominantly Christian.

Emigrants

In a reversal of nineteenth-century European colonization of Africa, Asia, and the Americas, the late twentieth century witnessed waves of emigration of people from these regions to the Western world. The impact on religious affiliation is significant. In the Central Asian countries of the former Soviet Union, for example, Christianity has declined significantly every year since 1990 due to the emigration of Russians, Germans, and Ukrainians.

Immigrants minus Emigrants

In the twenty-first century this trend could have significant impact on the religious composition of individual countries. Increasing religious pluralism is not always welcomed and may be seen as a political, cultural, national, or religious threat. Recent debates in Israel have been examining the difference between religious and secular Jews as it relates to immigration, especially the decade-long return to Israel of over one million Russians and other citizens of the former Soviet Union. The ultra-orthodox want to limit the "right of return" to religious Jews, whereas moderates want to welcome secular Jews in order to counter the rising numbers of Arabs (with their much higher birth rate). By 2100 it might be difficult to find a country in which 90 percent or more of its population belong to any one single world religion.

Current Trends in Religious Demography

Mapping religious affiliation has been greatly simplified with the recent availability of large data sets on demography and religious affiliation. Foundational demographic data for every country in the world are available for the years 1950–2100 through the United Nations Demographic Database. Data on religions for every country are available through the World Christian Database (*WCD*, developed for the *World Christian Encyclopedia*, 1st ed., 1982 and continuously updated each year).

Analyzing Christian Data

Christian data are more complete globally than data on other religions. These data are presented in Country Tables 2 in the *World Christian Encyclopedia* (*WCE*) (2nd ed.), Part 4 "Countries" for each of the world's then-238 countries. Statistics on 33,800 denominations are given for 1970 and 1995 and projected to 2000, 2005, 2010, and 2025 in *WCD*. Christian data can also be presented in the total context of other religions and demographic data. This is done in Country Tables 1 for each country in *WCE* Part 4. Here one finds a breakdown of the population into all of its constituent pieces—religious and nonreligious—for the years 1900, 1970, 1990, 1995, 2000, and 2025 (2005, 2010, and 2050 are added on *WCD*). The growth rates from 1990 to 2000 of all categories are presented here as well. Thus, if evidence exists that the Christian church is in decline in a particular country, then the percentage to be matched to that country at a future date will be lowered to an appropriate level. With adjustments made to religious and nonreligious populations in each country, a second stage of analysis is added. Now one can view the effects of demographic change and change in religious adherence.

EXAMINING ONE COUNTRY: THE
UNITED STATES

Table 2.2, "Religious adherents in the United States of America, 2000–2005," places eighteen categories of religious adherence (including atheists and nonreligious) into the context of change over a five-year period. For each of these categories, the total number of adherents is reported both for the year 2000 and for 2005. These are then divided by the total population to arrive at a percentage of the country's population. For example, Muslims in the United States grew from 4,322,000 (1.5 percent) in 2000 to 4,750,000 (1.6 percent) in 2005. Four additional columns have been added to look at annual change for each religion in the five-year period. The total rate is simply the average annual growth rate over the period. Thus, the nonreligious had an average annual increase of 854,800 over the five years. This total is then broken into two components that are labeled Natural and Conversion. Natural is the net demographic growth of the community. From our earlier analysis, this is births minus deaths, plus immigrants minus emigrants. Conversion is the net conversion growth incorporating conversions minus defections.

THE WHOLE WORLD, 1990–2000

Table 2.3, "Religious adherents in the world, 1990–2000," presents a similar demographic profile for the whole world over a ten-year period. Here, the columns have the same meaning as in table 2.2 except that there is no immigration or emigration in the Natural column (no one immigrates to or emigrates from Earth).

SIX DYNAMICS RELATED TO CHRISTIANITY

Although there is not enough comprehensive research on religions and conversion to construct a global table of the six dynamics described above for each of the world's religions, preliminary research on these trends within Christianity recently has been completed.[7] The results are presented in table 2.4, "Six dynamics of annual change in Christianity in Brazil, China, and UN areas, 2005–2010." The table sets out the United Nations population of the countries and areas in mid-2005 in column 2. It also sets out an estimate for the number of Christians in mid-2005 in column 3. In columns 4–6 the three positive factors in growth are presented (births, converts, and immigrants), adding up to a total annual increase in column 7. Columns 8–10 present the negative factors (deaths, defectors, and emigrants), adding up to a total annual decrease in column 11.

Table 2.2 Religious Adherents in the United States, 2000–2005

	Mid-2000	%	Mid-2005	%	Annual change, 2000–2005			Rate (%)
					Natural	Conversion	Total	
Christians	235,268,500	82.6	244,828,200	81.7	2,475,900	−564,000	1,911,900	0.80
Nonreligious (agnostics)	30,127,000	10.6	34,401,000	11.5	317,100	537,700	854,800	2.69
Jews	5,656,000	2.0	5,761,000	1.9	59,500	−38,500	21,000	0.37
Muslims	4,322,000	1.5	4,750,000	1.6	45,500	40,100	85,600	1.91
Buddhists	2,594,000	0.9	2,811,000	0.9	27,300	16,100	43,400	1.62
Neoreligionists	1,418,000	0.5	1,498,000	0.5	14,900	1,100	16,000	1.10
Ethnoreligionists	1,336,000	0.5	1,424,000	0.5	14,100	3,500	17,600	1.28
Hindus	1,238,000	0.4	1,338,000	0.4	13,000	7,000	20,000	1.57
Atheists	1,148,000	0.4	1,167,000	0.4	12,100	−8,300	3,800	0.33
Baha'is	552,000	0.2	593,000	0.2	5,800	2,400	8,200	1.44
Sikhs	239,000	0.1	270,000	0.1	2,500	3,700	6,200	2.47
Spiritists	142,000	0.0	149,000	0.0	1,500	−100	1,400	0.97
Chinese folk-religionists	80,300	0.0	86,700	0.0	800	500	1,300	1.55
Shintoists	57,500	0.0	60,600	0.0	600	0	600	1.06
Zoroastrians	16,200	0.0	17,000	0.0	200	0	200	0.97
Taoists	11,400	0.0	12,000	0.0	100	0	100	1.03
Jains	74,100	0.0	79,500	0.0	800	300	1,100	1.42
Other religionists	577,000	0.2	600,000	0.2	6,100	−1,500	4,600	0.78
US population	**284,857,000**	**100.0**	**299,846,000**	**100.0**	**2,998,000**	**0**	**2,998,000**	**1.03**

Source: World Christian Database, July 2008.

Table 2.3 Religious Adherents in the World, 1990–2000

Religion	1990	%	2000	%	Natural	Conversion	Total	Rate (%)
					Annual change, 1990–2000			
Christians	1,746,953,134	33.2	1,998,757,057	33.0	23,204,486	1,975,906	25,180,392	1.4
Muslims	953,797,445	18.2	1,185,923,292	19.6	22,168,049	1,044,536	23,212,585	2.2
Hindus	679,133,060	12.9	809,897,429	13.4	13,323,335	-246,898	13,076,437	1.8
Nonreligious (agnostics)	707,281,282	13.5	762,133,604	12.6	6,460,438	-975,206	5,485,232	0.8
Chinese folk-religionists	347,715,102	6.6	390,735,421	6.5	3,753,448	548,584	4,302,032	1.2
Buddhists	322,645,470	6.1	363,963,638	6.0	3,915,540	216,277	4,131,817	1.2
Ethnoreligionists	204,207,258	3.9	237,023,488	3.9	4,221,486	-939,863	3,281,623	1.5
Atheists	145,667,721	2.8	148,061,852	2.4	1,266,364	-1,026,951	239,413	0.2
Neoreligionists	92,912,326	1.8	104,066,537	1.7	1,027,937	87,484	1,115,421	1.1
Sikhs	19,341,080	0.4	17,001,604	0.3	369,564	-603,512	-233,948	-1.3
Jews	13,862,955	0.3	15,314,776	0.3	221,063	-75,881	145,182	1.0
Spiritists	10,101,675	0.2	12,240,548	0.2	137,749	76,138	213,887	1.9
Baha'is	5,670,187	0.1	7,056,204	0.1	120,636	17,965	138,602	2.2
Confucianists	5,870,040	0.1	6,354,510	0.1	58,801	-10,354	48,447	0.8
Jains	3,869,070	0.1	4,220,901	0.1	75,746	-40,563	35,183	0.9
Shintoists	3,081,790	0.1	2,769,879	0.1	9,549	-40,740	-31,191	-1.1
Taoists	2,402,090	0.1	2,649,539	0.0	25,338	-593	24,745	1.0
Zoroastrians	2,012,260	0.0	2,548,050	0.0	46,819	6,760	53,579	2.4
Other religionists	162,451	0.0	193,687	0.0	3,471	-347	3,124	1.8
Global population	**5,254,819,096**	**100.0**	**6,056,714,927**	**100.0**	**80,189,583**	**0**	**80,189,583**	**1.43**

Source: World Christian Database, April 2003.

Table 2.4 Six Dynamics in Annual Changes in Christianity in Brazil, China, and United Nations Areas, Mid-2005

Country or area	Population mid-2005	Christians mid-2005	Positive factors						Net Christian increase	Rate (%)	Negative factors						Net Christian decrease	Rate (%)	Net Christian growth	Rate (%)
			Christian births	Rate (%)	Christian converts	Rate (%)	Christian immigrants	Rate (%)			Christian deaths	Rate (%)	Christian defectors	Rate (%)	Christian emigrants	Rate (%)				
Brazil	186,830,759	170,597,790	3,372,554	1.98	1,609,444	0.94	0	0.00	4,981,998	2.92	1,114,391	0.65	1,231,565	0.72	500,000	0.29	2,845,956	1.67	2,136,042	1.25
China	1,297,614,979	109,576,362	1,518,348	1.39	2,310,502	2.11	0	0.00	3,828,849	3.49	817,741	0.75	347,581	0.32	150,000	0.14	1,315,322	1.20	2,513,528	2.29
Africa	922,010,528	431,223,266	17,802,794	4.13	3,437,294	0.80	120,040	0.03	21,360,129	4.95	6,907,027	1.60	1,594,916	0.37	1,242,635	0.29	9,744,578	2.26	11,615,551	2.69
Asia	3,938,019,815	345,240,246	6,786,198	1.97	3,952,455	1.14	39,150	0.01	10,777,803	3.12	2,418,065	0.70	1,340,763	0.39	614,340	0.18	4,373,168	1.27	6,404,635	1.86
Europe	731,086,770	582,373,715	5,988,883	1.03	2,872,132	0.49	2,575,140	0.44	11,436,155	1.96	6,880,933	1.18	4,111,870	0.71	127,745	0.02	11,120,548	1.91	315,607	0.05
Latin America	557,973,246	516,610,854	10,650,038	2.06	3,854,762	0.75	10,255	0.00	14,515,054	2.81	3,171,213	0.61	2,707,331	0.52	2,104,600	0.41	7,983,144	1.55	6,581,910	1.27
Northern America	332,244,951	270,635,170	3,775,620	1.40	1,374,825	0.51	1,212,737	0.45	6,363,182	2.35	2,254,146	0.83	1,759,260	0.65	10,250	0.00	4,023,655	1.49	2,289,527	0.85
Oceania	33,410,369	26,678,957	473,457	1.77	86,257	0.32	152,770	0.57	712,484	2.67	205,825	0.77	230,404	0.86	10,522	0.04	446,751	1.67	265,733	1.00
Global total	6,514,745,679	2,172,762,208	45,476,989	2.09	15,577,726	0.72	4,110,092	0.19	65,164,807	3.00	21,837,208	1.01	11,744,544	0.54	4,110,092	0.19	37,691,844	1.73	27,472,963	1.26

Source: *World Christian Database*, July 2008.

The total increase in column 7 is then added to the total decrease in column 11 (considered a negative number for this operation), which results in the net annual Christian growth in column 12.

Brazil and China

Christian growth patterns can be contrasted by comparing two of the world's largest countries, Brazil and China. Even though China's population is approximately seven times that of Brazil, Brazil has about one and a half times as many Christians as China. Here are comparisons for each of the six dynamics.

Positive Factors

Christian births. Brazilians have a much higher birth rate than the Chinese (1.98 percent p.a. vs. 1.39 percent p.a. [p.a. = per annum or per year]), so that over twice as many Christian births take place in Brazil as in China every year.

Christian converts. The conversion rate in China is twice that in Brazil (2.11 percent p.a. vs. 0.94 percent p.a.), resulting in almost one and a half times as many converts in China every year as in Brazil.

Christian immigrants. The number of Christian immigrants in each country is negligible.

Net Christian increase. The annual increase in Brazil is about 5 million new Christians, whereas the increase in China is about 3.8 million. Note that the rate in China is higher (3.49 percent p.a. vs. 2.92 percent p.a.).

Negative Factors

Christian deaths. The death rate among Chinese Christians is slightly higher than that of Brazilian Christians. Note that 1.1 million Brazilian Christians die every year whereas about 818,000 Chinese Christians die each year.

Christian defectors. The defection rate is much higher in Brazil than in China (0.72 percent p.a. vs. 0.32 percent p.a.). Consequently, 1.2 million Christians defect each year in Brazil (more than die), while about 350,000 a year defect in China.

Christian emigrants. Brazil loses 500,000 Christians every year through emigration, while 150,000 Chinese Christians leave China every year. Many of the Brazilians end up in the United States, while the Chinese join the diaspora around the world.

Net Christian decrease. Brazilian Christians experience a net decrease each year of about 2.8 million (1.67 percent of the total Christian community), while Chinese Christians lose 1.3 million (1.20 percent of the community).

Table 2.5 Percentage Share of Each of Six Dynamics in Annual Changes in Christianity, Mid-2005

	Positive factors			Negative factors		
	Christian births	Christian converts	Christian immigrants	Christian deaths	Christian defectors	Christian emigrants
Brazil	43	21	0	14	16	6
China	30	45	0	16	7	3
Africa	57	11	0	22	5	4
Asia	45	26	0	16	9	4
Europe	27	13	11	31	18	1
Latin America	47	17	0	14	12	9
North America	36	13	12	22	17	0
Oceania	41	7	13	18	20	1
Global total	44	15	4	21	11	4

Note: Totals may not add up to 100 percent due to rounding.
Source: World Christian Database, July 2008.

Net Christian growth. Both the Brazilian and Chinese communities gain over 2 million new members every year. In the Brazilian case, the net growth is about 1.25 percent, whereas among the Chinese it is almost double this (2.29 percent).

Another way to look at these data is to determine the proportion of each of the six dynamics that contribute to the growth or decline of Christianity in these two countries. The ratio of the six dynamics (in order of births, converts, immigrants, deaths, defectors, and emigrants) is presented in table 2.5, "Percentage share of each of the six dynamics in annual changes in Christianity, mid-2005." The table reveals significant differences between Brazil and China. In the first place, Christian births play a larger role in Brazil than China (45 percent vs. 30 percent), while conversions are twice as prevalent in China as in Brazil (45 percent vs. 21 percent). Another difference is found among losses, where the role of the defection rate in Brazil is over twice that of China (16 percent vs. 7 percent). One can see from this comparison that different countries are likely to have different proportions of the six dynamics as factors in the overall annual change of Christians.

UNITED NATIONS CONTINENTAL AREAS

Table 2.4, "Six dynamics in annual changes in Christianity in Brazil, China, and United Nations areas, mid-2005," shows the six dynamics for continental areas and the globe. In relation to continental areas, the following can be observed.

Positive Factors

Christian births. Even though only one out of five Christians in the world is African, two of every five Christian babies born annually are African. The Christian birth rate for Africa is twice the global average and more than twice that of any other area. The Christian birth rate for Europe is half of the global average and one-fourth of that in Africa. In addition, there are more Christian births in Asia every year than in Europe (6.8 million vs. 6 million).

Christian converts. The conversion rate is highest in Asia, where the non-Christian population is large. In Africa, the conversion rate has been slowing in the past two decades because most tribal religionists have already converted to Christianity or Islam. There are relatively few Muslims converting to Christianity in Africa. The rate of conversion to Christianity in Africa—which was much higher in the past—is today surprisingly low compared with Europe and North America.

Christian immigrants. Europe and North America receive three-fourths of all Christian immigrants. Most of these are from Africa and Latin America, with increasing numbers coming from Asia.

Net Christian increase. Not surprisingly, Africa and Asia have the highest rates of Christian increase. The Global South, with 61 percent of all Christians, claims 72 percent of the net Christian increase.

Negative Factors

Christian deaths. Given the numerous health challenges, ranging from infant mortality to AIDS, the death rate is highest among African Christians. At the same time, the relatively high death rate in Europe means that more Christians die every year there than are born (6.9 million vs. 6 million)—the only area where this is the case.

Christian defectors. Defection rates are highest in North America, Oceania, and Europe. The defection rate in Oceania means that more Christians defect each year than die (230,000 vs. 206,000).

Christian emigrants. Latin American Christians are on the move more than any other Christian community. At over 2 million emigrants per year, this means that for every ten Christians born in Latin America, two end up eventually leaving the area. Latin America accounts for half of all Christian emigrants globally.

Net Christian decrease. African Christians also have the highest net decrease, largely because of the high death rate, but Europe's net decrease is nearly as high as its net increase (11.1 million vs. 11.4 million).

Net Christian growth. Africa's Christian population is growing at three times the rate of North America's. One can also see that 90 percent of all Christian growth takes place in Africa, Asia, and Latin America.

Proportions of the Six Dynamics

Table 2.5 also reveals significant differences in the proportions of the six dynamics in each of the United Nations continental areas. The following findings can be observed in the table:

1. Most of the annual changes in Africa can be attributed to birth and death rates.
2. Conversion has the most significant role in annual changes among Christians in Asia.
3. The dynamics of change in Europe can be traced to Christian deaths and defections; these are the sources of a shrinking Christian population.
4. Emigration of the Latin American Christian population is a major factor in annual change.
5. In North America, the number of Christian immigrants is nearly as high as that of Christian converts.
6. In Oceania, defections play a leading role in annual decline—more than in any other area.

CONCLUSION

Annual changes in religious affiliation include at least six components, of which three are positive (births, conversions, immigration) and three negative (deaths, defections, emigration). Every religious (and nonreligious) community in the world experiences these dynamics. Preliminary research has revealed interesting trends, particularly among Christians; it is apparent that each religion is undergoing profound changes in the twenty-first century. Understanding underlying trends better will likely have important political, social, and religious implications.

NOTES

1. Roland Robertson and William R. Garrett, eds., *Religion and Global Order: Religion and the Political Order* (New York: Paragon House Publishers, 1991), 4:xiii.
2. Ibid.
3. See especially chapter 3, "Secularization, R.I.P.," in Rodney Stark and Roger Finke, *Acts of Faith: Explaining the Human Side of Religion* (Berkeley and Los Angeles: University of California Press, 2000).
4. John Naisbatt and Patricia Aburdene, *Megatrends 2000* (New York: William Morrow, 1990), 295.

5. Rodney Stark and William Bainbridge, eds., *The Future of Religion: Secularization, Revival and Cult Formation* (Berkeley and Los Angeles: University of California Press, 1985), 1.
6. Full text available online at http://www.un.org/Overview/rights.html.
7. For a global overview, see Todd M. Johnson and Kenneth R. Ross, *Atlas of Global Christianity* (Edinburgh: Edinburgh University Press, 2009), 64–65. Country-specific estimates are reported in Part III, 110–207.

Bibliography

Barrett, David B., George T. Kurian, and Todd M. Johnson. *World Christian Encyclopedia.* 2nd ed. New York: Oxford University Press, 2001.

Johnson, Todd M., and Kenneth R. Ross. *Atlas of Global Christianity.* Edinburgh: Edinburgh University Press, 2009.

Naisbatt, John, and Patricia Aburdene. *Megatrends 2000.* New York: William Morrow, 1990.

Robertson, Roland, and William R. Garrett, eds. *Religion and Global Order: Religion and the Political Order.* Vol. 4. New York: Paragon House Publishers, 1991.

Stark, Rodney, and William Bainbridge, eds. *The Future of Religion: Secularization, Revival and Cult Formation.* Berkeley and Los Angeles: University of California Press, 1985.

Stark, Rodney, and Roger Finke. *Acts of Faith: Explaining the Human Side of Religion.* Berkeley and Los Angeles: University of California Press, 2000.

CHAPTER 3

....

GEOGRAPHIES OF
RELIGIOUS CONVERSION

....

LILY KONG AND SEETA NAIR

INTRODUCTION

....

IN this chapter, we review the ways in which geographers have studied religious conversion, situating this within the larger discipline of human geography, and suggest the potential for geographers to pursue this area of research, potentially adopting new approaches to the study of religious conversion.

Beyond the academy, the geographical discipline continues to be imagined as one concerned with rocks and rivers, climate and weather, maps and atlases. Even within the academy, this view still holds for some scholars. There is also a tendency to imagine geography as the discipline that explains human behavior as causally determined by the physical environment; for example, colonial expansion occurred because of a need for more physical living space, or Jews imagine hell to be a burning place of intense heat while Eskimos imagine it to be a place of intense cold and darkness because their most negative experiences of the physical environment shape their perceptions. This environmental determinism characterized geographical thought in the era before the Second World War but has since faded into obscurity among geographers; nevertheless, it remains in the imagined discipline of geography for some beyond professional geography.

After the environmental determinism approach, scholars in the field of human geography have adopted more "possibilist" approaches, in which individual humans have agency in their use of the environment. Carl Sauer (1889–1975), a University of California at Berkeley cultural geographer, developed a perspective of humans as active agents in the production of landscapes that has become one of the most well-known reactions to environmental determinism. The subsequent "Berkeley tradition" of cultural geography was significantly involved in identifying distinctive cultural traits, mapping their diffusion, tracing the existence of culture regions (with distinctive cultural characteristics), and identifying the role of culture in shaping the landscape. It will become evident from the rest of this chapter that this remains the tradition within which geographical research on religious growth and change (including conversion) is located. Many of the other traditions of geography have not impacted the study of religious conversion, whether it is the spatial science of the 1960s, with its privileging of quantitative techniques, abstract modeling and techniques of locational analysis, or the radical and Marxist geography of the 1970s that sought to be more socially relevant, or the humanist tradition of the 1980s that emphasized qualitative understanding of human behavior, or the postmodern and poststructuralist voices since then.

The adoption of the "Berkeley tradition" has meant that the geographical study of religion has focused on the documentation of distribution patterns of religious groups;[1] examining the changes in such spatial distributions; and analyzing the strategies employed by religious groups to grow in spatial extent and member numbers.[2] These are admittedly somewhat traditional approaches to the geographical study of religion, but they remain a time-honored way in contemporary research agendas.

Of these areas of analyses, the last (analyzing the strategies of religious groups to grow in spatial and numerical extent) deals particularly with issues of religious conversion, since a key strategy for expansion is through conversion. Geographers researching this have thus examined how religious groups spread their influence; the strategies employed to attract new adherents; the factors aiding the influential growth of particular religious groups; and the resulting cultural, behavioral, and environmental changes that occur because of changes in religious beliefs.[3] In short, geographers are concerned with the spatial changes that occur as a result of different forces shaping a religion's distribution, plus the underlying reasons for and consequences of such changes.[4]

Having said that, the attention given by geographers to these various areas pertaining to conversion has been very uneven. For example, geographers have not given much attention to mapping patterns of conversion and rates of change. Nor have they carefully examined the factors and consequences of religious conversion on people and the environment. Rather, geographers interested in religion have generally focused on the role of religion in social relationships (e.g., identity formation or inter-religious conflict) and spatial changes (e.g., the establishment of religious infrastructure).

MAPPING SPATIAL CHANGE

Mapping spatial changes in religious affiliation can be complicated, because while some religions are monotheistic, others allow adherents to have "plural religious affiliations,"[5] and certain populations do indeed have multiple affiliations. Mapping the spatial extent of religions and changes in spatial patterns are not solely the domain of geographers. Historians, anthropologists, and religious studies scholars have also used the visual presentation of maps to illustrate religious distribution and diffusion.[6]

While maps provide great visual representation of social patterns, they are essentially static representations that often fail to capture the complexity and diversity of social phenomena or to take into account flows of processes and the absence of discrete boundaries in social relationships. Data collection on religious affiliation is also sparse and rarely undertaken by governments,[7] making the production of religious maps difficult and the production of maps depicting religious change a challenge. Further, there are different ways of collecting data on religions, and a key source of data is the population census where religious affiliation is captured, though not religious belief and practice, thus again presenting a simplistic visual picture of a complex interaction.[8]

Be that as it may, some basic mapping does offer a foundational set of data that presents a general sense of the spread and diversity of religions in the world. Figure 3.1 shows just one of the many maps produced by Warf and Vincent as they explore the spatial

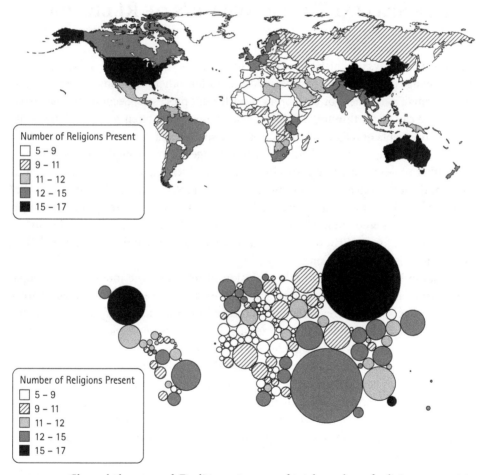

FIGURE 3.1 Choropleth map and Dorling cartogram of total number of religions present in each country in 2005

Source: Barney Warf and Peter Vincent, "Religious Diversity over the Globe: A Geographic Exploration," *Social & Cultural Geography* 8 (2007): 606.

extent of religious diversity in the contemporary world. Such maps allow for a quick, visual interpretation of the degree to which religious diversity varies spatially across the globe. In general, though, many religious atlases focus on the United States, like *The New Historical Atlas of Religion in America* and the *Atlas of American Religion: The Denominational Era 1776–1990*, perhaps because it is only there that such extensive data has been collected and allowed to be used. There is much benefit to making additional attempts at mapping religious change (beyond America), especially as technologies such as geographic information systems allow for the storage, manipulation, and visual presentation of large amounts of data.

MIGRATION, CONVERSION, AND CHANGES IN THE SPATIAL DISTRIBUTIONS OF RELIGIONS

There are three ways by which the spatial distribution of religious groups changes. First, spatial change occurs through processes of migration, where religious systems are diffused through permanent or temporary resettlement processes. Second, dramatic spatial change can occur through religious persecution, which often results in large-scale forced movements of religious groups from one spatial area to another. This is another form of migration, only forced. Third, spatial change occurs through religious conversion, either of nonbelievers into specific religions, which expands the spatial extent of religion, through conversion from one religion to another, which changes the spatial pattern of religion, or through conversion out of a religion into no religion, resulting in a reduction in adherent numbers and a contraction in the spatial extent of a religion.[9] In this section, the focus will be on different forms of migration and the ways in which they have led to religious conversions.

Migration is a major factor in the diffusion of religions. The movement of people across national and state boundaries, across cities, and between urban and rural areas has led to the spread of religions and increased the interaction of diverse religious groups. A geographer's role is to analyze such movements of people (whether permanent migration patterns such as the Jewish Diaspora or temporary movements such as tourism), their points of origin and destination, their motivations, the rate at which such movements take place, the influence of external circumstances that hinder or encourage such movements,[10] and the resulting impacts such flows have on the religious beliefs of different communities. In this section, we focus on the ways in which migration in various forms has led to significant religious conversions that have resulted in changes in the spatial distribution of religions.

The motivations for migration might be secular or religious. For example, migration often takes place because of secular reasons such as population pressures, changing environmental conditions, hope for better conditions elsewhere, trade, and political ambitions in the form of colonization. At the same time, religious motivations may prompt missionary work in distant lands, or migrations may occur when people attempt to escape religious persecution. Migrations result in the interactions of different religious traditions, with diverse impacts on the religious landscapes of many destinations.

Evidence shows that past migratory experiences have oftentimes led to the conversion of local populations, particularly when the original impetus for migration was colonization and/or missionary conversion. There is abundant evidence that historical migrations for conquest of land and colonization have shaped the religious landscapes of many places. In Europe, the geographic differentiation between areas that are predominantly inhabited by Roman Catholics or Protestants can be quite clearly delimited, in alignment with the changes inspired by the Protestant Reformation (early sixteenth century) and the Roman Catholic Church's own expansion plans, following the division between eastern and western forms of Christianity (figure 3.2).[11] The geographic differentiation was such that "Protestantism tended to flourish in parts of Europe dominated by Germanic languages and Roman Catholicism in areas dominated by Romance languages."[12] Later, beginning in the early 1800s, the migration of Protestant Christian populations from Europe to Latin America, North America, Australia, and New Zealand

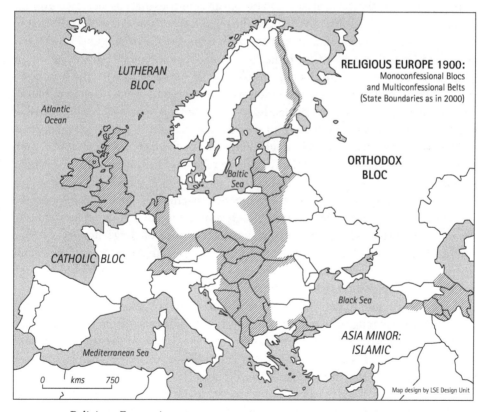

FIGURE 3.2 Religious Europe in 1990

Source: John Madeley, "A Framework for the Comparative Analysis of Church–State Relations in Europe," *West European Politics* 26 (2003): 28.

brought a variety of Protestant denominations to varied places around the world through contact with the local population, intermarriage with indigenous communities, and religious conversion.[13] Similarly, following colonial rule, Christian missionary success divided "non-Western" converts roughly into Protestants (mainly in British and Dutch colonial territories) and Catholics (mainly in French, Belgian, Spanish, and Portuguese colonial territories). This geographic distribution of religious conversion reflects political and colonial forces,[14] and the spatial pattern of religion in these lands remains observable today.

A modern "reversal" to the spread of Christian religious ideas is termed "Christianity with a Third World Face."[15] This is the phenomenon whereby Latin American, African, and Asian religious leaders and theologians travel to Europe and North America and spread among the Western nations their own interpretation and understanding of Christianity. In fact, Tyler states that "Christianity now has a non-white majority, and sub-Sahara Africa has been termed the most Christian continent on Earth."[16] The dynamics of this interaction are important to understand as unusual mixes of indigenous and cultural nuances intersect with previously Western-dominated interpretations of Christianity.

In a similar vein, the Asian diaspora to European countries that has increased over the last few decades has significantly changed the religious landscape of western European nations.[17] These Asian communities bring with them their own religious beliefs, traditions, and practices and establish their own religious centers, thereby changing the religious landscape and introducing complex social interactions with the host communities in myriad ways. These migration patterns have added a dimension of plurality to Western countries' religious landscape.[18] The interactions may have positive or negative repercussions, and the resulting landscape changes, issues of social cohesion and fragmentation, and various strategies employed by these communities are of interest to geographers and other scholars exploring religious change, as well as to political authorities.[19]

Returning the gaze to colonial rule, it is apparent that the migrations that it sponsored also aided the spread of religion, not through conversion but through relocation. For example, Hinduism and Islam spread through the relocation of a large number of Indian and Muslim slaves to Africa, the Caribbean, northern South America, and the Pacific Islands.[20] The increase in the Jewish presence in Palestine was also achieved through Zionist calls for migration and resettlement.[21]

Colonialism aside, trade routes were also important migratory routes that facilitated the spread of religion. For example, the caravan trade routes from the Middle East through Central Asia to North China, and across the Sahara to the Sudan facilitated the dissemination of Islamic teachings that led to the conversion of many communities.[22] Arabian and Persian merchants also brought Islam to Chinese coastal cities in the seventh century, lured by opportunities for trade and commerce.[23] Similarly, Indian merchants brought Hinduism to South East Asia beginning in approximately 500 B.C.E, with the most prominent and long-lasting impact felt in Bali, where it is the religion of the majority of Balinese today in Muslim-dominated Indonesia.[24] With trade routes, conversion therefore occurred "by the book," so to speak, rather than "by the sword," as religious ideas and teachings were spread by word of mouth rather than by force.

Apart from trade routes, another form of migration—"scholarly migration," or the movement of scholars within monastic orders—also encouraged the growth of Catholicism in Europe and the United States.[25] The relationship between education and religious conversion is seen in the numerous records of religious evangelism accompanying educational endeavors and in the scholarly works written to promote and aid missionary work.[26]

Religious Conversion: Proselytizing and Non-proselytizing Religions

Seeking religious converts is not a universal goal among all religions. Fundamentally, it is the proselytizing religions[27] that are more concerned with converting new adherents, unlike ethnic and tribal religions, for example, which typically do not actively seek converts.[28] Adherents of proselytizing religions believe that they have a fundamental obligation to bring new converts into their religion, and they place great significance on the rituals associated with the conversion process.

Within ethnic and tribal religions, religious conversion may take place slowly as the peoples of a community evolve their cultural practices and religious beliefs in a process termed "contact conversion."[29] Such conversion is characterized by a slow, gradual, and organic transition.[30] Examples include the many tribal folk groups in India that have slowly assimilated into the Hindu religious system of India's majority,[31] or the variety of African tribal communities that were relocated through the slave trade and then developed their own unique traditions and religious practices in Brazil.[32]

On the other hand, there are those religions (termed universal religions) with specific agendas to convert people to their faith.[33] Such activities are commonly associated with Christian missionary work or with the Muslim notion of da'wah, which have prescribed rituals such as baptism processes for Christianity that define the moment of conversion.[34] This defined moment is in contrast to, or perhaps marks the culmination of, the acculturation process described earlier. In his attempt to understand religious change, Roger B. Stump identifies three distinct processes at work: (1) the communication of new religious ideas (evangelism); (2) the conversion process, by which new adherents are convinced of the religious message; and (3) the confirmation act to distinguish believers from nonbelievers.[35] The deliberate and conscious effort to evangelize entails what Stanley Brunn calls the "packaging of religion," where religion and all its elemental facets may be commoditized, promoted, and "sold."[36]

FACTORS FACILITATING RELIGIOUS CONVERSION

In this section, we turn attention to the factors that encourage religious conversion. Those unfamiliar with the modern discipline of geography are likely to think immediately of how physical geography may facilitate or impede the spread of peoples and hence religion. Geographers have, however, long expressed caution about such environmentally deterministic views. Instead, they have focused on factors such as the availability and extent of personal contact, the similarity in religious teachings, the religion of kin, age, ethnic ties, use of a common language, socioeconomic circumstances, the presence of religious structures and institutions of the religion converted to, and the supporting or discouraging role of political authorities.

One of the most important factors that facilitate religious conversion among new adherents is personal contact.[37] These interactions encourage religious conversion through the opportunities for persuasion that they provide, especially if the religious message is transmitted through a charismatic person. Thus, for this personal contact to take place, evangelists and missionaries are often engaged in travel. In this respect, advances in transportation and communication have reduced distances and facilitated the flow of religious ideas and people.

Indeed, through technology, personal contact may be approximated (though not exactly replicated) without the need for travel, for example, through the use of religious broadcasting via electronic media such as the radio, television, and satellite and cable networks, all of which have been well utilized by enthusiastic Christian organizations, particularly in Asia, Africa, and the Soviet Union.[38] This mode of transmitting a religious message is particularly useful as it reaches far more people than traveling missionaries can and is able to connect with previously isolated communities or communities located in countries closed to missionaries. According to Stump, "religious broadcasting has the potential to effect substantial changes in religious distribution."[39] However, while this mode of communication is quite effective at increasing awareness of the religious messages sent, it does not commonly translate into actual conversion, as this medium lacks personal interaction and persuasion.[40] Only when opportunities for contact between believers and nonbelievers are rare does the successful conversion rate via religious broadcasting increase. Nonetheless, the use of new media has steadily increased over the years, especially by megachurches (particularly Evangelical and Pentecostal megachurches) in a bid to attract young members. The motivation is to appear relevant in the media age and to provide an experience of religious worship that is intimate with God, private and personal.[41] Whether the use of electronic media is the sole factor accounting for conversion to these denominations, reflected in high attendance rates at such religious institutions, has not been sufficiently explored.

A second factor is the similarity of religious teachings between the religion converted from and that converted to. This is evident in the numerous Protestant denominations that have adopted and adapted religious ideas from the same source—the Protestant Reformation. For example, the Black Christian Methodist Episcopal Church and the African Methodist Episcopal Zion Church in the United States separated from the other branches of the Methodist Church and brought along converts who were predominantly white adherents already familiar with Methodist teachings.[42]

The use of a common language is also a positive facilitator for religious conversion, though a necessary but insufficient condition. The use of Greek as the lingua franca of the eastern part of the Roman Empire was pivotal in encouraging the early spread of Christianity.[43] Additionally, the conversion from Catholicism to Protestantism among Hungarians in the sixteenth and seventeenth centuries was in part because Protestantism used Latin, "the official (and popular) mediator language of multiethnic Hungary."[44] Thus, the use of Greek in eastern Europe and Latin in western Europe shows Christianity's flexibility and determination in its initial spread. This language split brought about the subsequent divergence in religious understanding, and the Catholic Church later adopted Latin as its liturgical language to provide a common language for worship and practice. The importance of language cannot be underestimated.

Conversion also occurs because of kinship ties. For instance, religious expectations (particularly in Islam), or the wish to maintain family unity and religious harmony, may cause a spouse to change religious affiliation.[45] For example, the intermarriage of Muslim men with Chinese women was one factor in the numerical increase of minority Muslim communities in China.[46] On the other hand, a number of Christian communities in the United States, such as the Catholic Church, the Lutheran Church, and the Orthodox churches, initially sought to remain ethnically distinct, keeping religious ties and kinship ties within ethnic communities.[47] Aside from marriages, difference in denominational beliefs (such as within the different Protestant denominations) within a family could also lead to conversion by a more persuasive family member or by a strong need to unify the family.

Religious conversion may be perceived as bringing social and economic advantages, especially if the converting community is less well off than the religious community to be converted to. Furthermore, a sense of prestige accompanied by social and economic advantages may become associated with a particular religion when it is officially adopted by the ruling class, leading to its being readily taken up by the general population.[48] Additionally, economic factors may lure diverse religious groups, such as the attraction of economic opportunities that caused Jewish communities to establish themselves in eastern Europe during the Middle Ages and the adoption of Christianity in the Asian and African nations due to the material advantages and social status of Christians under European rule.[49] When such benefits are lacking, or suspicions of missionary endeavors continue unabated, then conversion efforts fail to produce any converts, at times, even experiencing complete disinterest.[50]

Beyond these factors, those seeking to convert others are likely to be more successful if they evidence sensitivity to local cultural traditions. If the conversion message is suitably tailored to complement indigenous beliefs, this can lead to successful conversion or to the development of a creolized or syncretic form of religious expression (a form of religion that has developed through influences from both native and foreign systems of religion).[51] Such syncretic creolized forms of religion may be found in Brazil and the Caribbean, which have a history of large immigration of African populations (because of the slave trade) who combined Roman Catholicism with their animistic beliefs and traditions, at times interchanging Roman Catholic saints with animistic supernatural beings.[52]

Another factor that aids religious conversion is the presence of active support structures and institutions of the religion seeking to attract converts, especially where they extend social support to potential converts. Such support includes the provision of educational services, health care, and charitable relief, and it is most notable among Christian churches. This is most apparent within migrant communities where religious institutions can play a direct social role in integrating immigrant communities into their new homes, helping them to develop social ties and developing a sense of belonging.[53] This can result in conversion for those not already in the religion or strengthen the commitment of those already in the religion.

The existence of religious structures and institutions is closely tied to the role of political authorities. In fact, the role of political authorities in supporting/discouraging religion(s) is a significant factor in the flourishing of a religion, as political agendas are pivotal in resolving tensions among different religious groups, allowing freedom of religious expression and the existence of religiously plural societies, and permitting the development of religious infrastructures that may be pivotal for the survival of religious groups.[54] By the same token, the lack of political support, or even the existence of political persecution, can drive religious groups underground, whereby personal expressions of religious adherence become more significant than overt communal expressions. Contemporary examples may be found in the practice of Tibetan Buddhism despite restrictions by the Chinese authorities or the persecution of the Baha'is in Iran. A historical example would be the imposition of specific religions by kings on their subjects. For example, the Lutheran church in Finland in the 1500s had the political support of the Swedish king (Finland was then under Swedish control), and he decided to impose Lutheranism on the Finns and to decree Lutheranism as the state religion.[55] Lutheranism is still dominant in Finland today, and the Lutheran church continues to be a religious and cultural authority to the people in Finland.[56]

At times, conversion may be due to political forces. For example, the conversions to Christianity that Muslims in Spain and Portugal had to undergo when their Muslim leaders were expelled by Christian armies were forced conversions; the power of the Christian armies allowed them to impose religious restrictions on their subjects.[57] Other examples of forced conversions include the imposition of Zoroastrianism by the rulers of Persia on their subjects and of Christianity on the people of the Roman Empire at the end of the fourth century.[58] The conversion of Lutheran and Calvinist peasants in Hungary to Catholicism during the seventeenth and eighteenth centuries to escape religious persecution is another example of conversions for political rather than religious reasons.[59]

IMPACTS OF RELIGIOUS CONVERSION

Besides examining the factors that encourage or discourage religious conversions, geographers have also contributed to an understanding of the impacts of religious conversions, which include changes social organization, social prestige, community stability, and economic activity. This section will explore briefly some of these impacts.

Some of the positive impacts of conversion include upward mobility in social circumstances, increased economic opportunities, and access to religious-affiliated institutional and social services (such as education, health care, and charity relief). For example, Christianity in India was mostly adopted by members of lower castes and tribal peoples for whom religious conversion offered a way out of their low social status and lack of economic opportunities.[60]

Religious conversion is often a personal journey, so it is impossible for two people to share the same spiritual epiphany at the same time and with the same intensity. When members of a community convert at different times and paces, social tensions may arise as different religious and social identities emerge within a once homogeneous community, and these tensions may have long-term effects on community stability.[61] For example, the introduction of Christianity to Jamaica during British colonial rule resulted in a fissure in society—"European Jamaica" and "African Jamaica"—which is still evident in contemporary Jamaica.[62] While early nineteenth-century Jamaica could be described as "rich in creole religious genesis," with the cult of Rastafarianism defining racial and religious identity, the subsequent conversion of segments of the population to the Anglo-Christian religion caused tensions in society.[63] Some of the issues that might arise within a religiously diverse community include the availability and appropriateness of religious schools, particularly public (or state) schools, the observance of religious holidays, dress codes and dietary concerns, and medical issues.[64] Research on tensions that arise from conversions are not the purview of geographers alone but are also of interest to historians, sociologists, and others.[65]

Social tensions may also emerge when evangelization is aggressively pursued, with successful conversions driving wedges into existing social relations.[66] Often, social pressures such as those described above result when a society initially has little religious diversity and thus has lower tolerance of change. Such tensions can result in religious wars that persist over time.[67] For example, atrocities toward human life and property between Protestants and Catholics during the Reformation occurred against a backdrop of intolerance and a struggle for religious supremacy.[68]

In contrast to the societies with a lack of religious diversity are nations or communities with a multiplicity of religions (or denominations). This is the case in the United States, for example, through immigration of myriad populations and the enthusiasm of "spiritual entrepreneurs" to grow their particular religion or denomination.[69] The assimilation and incorporation of immigrant religious groups, and the resulting religious conversion processes that took place within a number of these groups, has developed a markedly unique and vibrant religious landscape in the United States.

When religious conversion involves two quite different religions where the beliefs are at odds with each other, social tensions may result. This has happened, for example, in the case of those who convert to Christianity and then look back at traditional beliefs and practices as backward.[70]

A number of disputes have also arisen because of conversion practices, particularly those of Christian missionaries.[71] Christian missionary efforts at converting communities (often tribal communities) can often lead to the breakdown of traditional social ties, an unhealthy dependency on modern economic systems that the community members are ill-equipped to participate in, and susceptibility to imported diseases and illnesses. For example, a Christian missionary group has been criticized for their efforts at conversion in India because they reportedly destroyed India's social organization and culture, introduced foreign diseases to the indigenous people, and left the communities ill-equipped to deal with the socioeconomic pressures once they left their forests for the cities.[72]

Finally, the impact of conversion includes a change in the relationships between people and the physical (natural and urban) environment. This is particularly true for former animistic societies that held close and spiritual relationships with the natural environment. Upon conversion to the major religions, notably Christianity, reverence for sacred nature diminishes, and there is a shift in the way the communities then perceive and respond to the natural environment.[73] In fact, some argue that "Judaeo-Christian beliefs about the separation of humans and nature, and their presumption of difference and superiority over the latter" are the basis for this shift toward environmental neglect.[74] Furthermore, there are claims that the increased influence of Christianity in India following British colonization has had destructive effects on the environment; Rana P. B. Singh, for example, argues that the resulting weakening of "Hindu thinking about the man-nature-cosmos relationship is one of the basic causes for the present environmental crisis that India is facing today."[75] Of course, it is also the case that more syncretic belief systems may result from efforts at conversion, so that animistic beliefs are overlain by Christian beliefs in new ways. For example, some argue that Christmas actually has roots in the winter solstice and that the North American Thanksgiving tradition may be traced to an ancient indigenous celebration.[76]

A notable contrast is the Lutheran concept of "an artistic sense that is reflective of the need to nurture, rather than consume, God's kingdom on earth."[77] The Finnish adoption of Lutheranism in the 1500s (through conversion from Roman Catholicism) and the subsequent assimilation of Lutheranism with notions of secularism and individuality developed a people that focused on finding inner peace, who took responsibility for their own salvation and who respected the natural environment as a gift from God, in contrast to the harsh Protestantism that evolved in other parts of Europe. This religious understanding translated into an environmental ethos in Finland—"the need to nurture, rather than consume, God's kingdom on earth"—that promoted environmental stewardship, small-scale agricultural development, and even a reverence for nature in urban centers as new towns were built up that incorporated the natural topography in their urban planning.[78]

CONCLUDING REMARKS

The issues that geographers research in their efforts to better understand the individual and social changes due to religious conversion share many similarities with other disciplines in the humanities and social sciences, including especially the desire to understand the factors that encourage or inhibit religious conversion; the impacts of religious conversion, particularly the social and political conflicts and tensions that religious conversion may bring; and the adaptive practices and subsequent creolized religions that develop due to the interaction of social groups. Perhaps what distinguishes geographical research is the attention given to the spatial and environmental dimensions related to religious conversion, including the migratory processes that lead to conversion and hence to spatial change in the distribution of religions, the factors underlying conversion, and the impact of conversion on community, society, polity, and landscape.

Rarely has personal religious conversion, including the experience of conversion, been given much specific emphasis by geographers using the ethnographic tools that social and cultural geographers are familiar with. Instead of focusing simply on the spatial expansion and development of religious communities, more emphasis needs to be placed on understanding the experience of conversion. This effort can gain much from new theoretical ideas that have been adopted by geographers in more recent years. For example, non-representational theory, developed primarily through the work of Nigel Thrift, focuses not on the production of social relationships but on the performances or enactments of interactions, not only between humans but also between humans and non-humans.[79] In the concept of performance lies the potential for developing new geographical analyses of religious/sacred experience. Geographers can contribute to a better understanding of conversion by examining participation in the performance of ritual (such as through rhythm and comportment) and by considering how such (ritualistic) repetition can draw potential converts into a powerful experience of the sacred, resulting in a conversion decision. Such analysis may be just the response to calls for geographers to understand embodied experiences of religion and the sensuous geographies associated with sacred experience, in which emphasis is given to the ways in which place is experienced, not just through seeing but also through hearing, smell, touch, and taste.[80]

Religious conversion is a complex phenomenon, and it is the role of humanists and social scientists, including geographers, to attempt to understand both the impetus for conversion and its impacts upon social formation and landscape. Whereas the approach that geographers have taken to date has tended to keep very closely to the long-abiding and traditional interest in spatial distributions, as seen in their analyses of religious conversion and mapping spatial advances and contractions, some recent contributions attempt to understand the factors that promote and/or resist conversion as well as the impacts of conversion. All these, however, have generally adhered to quite dated views of what geographers can legitimately analyze or, rather, what they should eschew. In particular, existing analyses seem to adopt Levine's view that "the primary focus of the geography of religion lies not in the study of the individual religious experience, but, rather, centres on religion in an instituted social form."[81] As a result, existing geographies of conversion remain impoverished, and much potential remains for geographers to contribute useful insights.

NOTES

1. For example, see Michael Pacione, "The Geography of Religious Affiliation in Scotland," *Professional Geographer* 57 (2005): 235–255; Chris C. Park, "Religion and Geography," in *The Routledge Companion to the Study of Religion*, ed. John R. Hinnells (Abingdon, England: Routledge, 2005), 439–455; Barney Warf and Peter Vincent, "Religious Diversity over the Globe: A Geographic Exploration," *Social & Cultural Geography* 8 (2007): 597–613.
2. For example, David E. Sopher, *Geography of Religions* (Englewood Cliffs, NJ: Prentice-Hall, Inc., 1967); Wen Fei Wang et al., "Growth and Decline of Muslim Hui Enclaves in Beijing," *Eurasian Geography and Economics* 43 (2002): 104–122; Park, "Religion and Geography," 439–455.
3. Sopher, *Geography of Religions*; Rana P. B. Singh, "The Geography of Religion in India: Perspectives and Prospects," *National Geographical Journal of India* 38 (1992): 27–38; Chris C. Park, *Sacred Worlds: An Introduction to Geography and Religion* (London: Routledge, 1994); Wang et al., "Muslim Hui Enclaves in Beijing," 104–122; Ceri Peach and Richard Gale, "Muslims, Hindus, and Sikhs in the New Religious Landscape of England," *Geographical Review* 93 (2003): 469–490; Pacione, "Geography of Religious Affiliation in Scotland," 235–255; Park, "Religion and Geography," 439–455.
4. Roger W. Stump, *The Geography of Religion: Faith, Place, and Space* (Plymouth, England: Rowman & Littlefield Publishers, 2008), 63.
5. Sopher, *Geography of Religions*, 95.
6. For example, see Edwin Scott Gaustad, *Historical Atlas of Religion in America* (New York: Harper & Row Publishers, 1962); Edwin Scott Gaustad and Philip L. Barlow, *New Historical Atlas of Religion in America* (New York: Oxford University Press, 2001).
7. Warf and Vincent, "Religious Diversity over the Globe," 602.
8. Mark S. Brown, "Estimating the Size and Distribution of South Asian Religious Populations in Britain: Is There an Alternative to a Religion Question in the Census?" *International Journal of Population Geography* 6 (2000): 89.
9. Stump, *Geography of Religion*.
10. Park, "Religion and Geography," 443.
11. Sopher, *Geography of Religions*, 79–82; Hans Knippenberg, "The Political Geography of Religion: Historical State–Church Relations in Europe and Recent Challenges," *GeoJournal* 67 (2006): 254–256; Stump, *Geography of Religion*, 159–188.
12. This is, of course, an oversimplification of the evolution of Christianity and its continual impact on the religious landscape of the world. See Stump, *Geography of Religion*, 159–188, for a more detailed description and analysis of Christianity's historical evolution and contemporary patterns.

13. Sopher, *Geography of Religions*, 88.
14. Ibid., 70.
15. Stanley Brunn, "The Changing Map of World Religions," Keynote presentation at the International Conference: Religion at the Time of Change, Lodz, Poland, Sept. 11, 2004.
16. Charles Tyler, "Spreading the Word," *Geographical Magazine* 62 (1990): 14.
17. Peach and Gale, "New Religious Landscape of England"; Brunn, "The Changing Map of World Religions"; David Ley, "The Immigrant Church as an Urban Service Hub," *Urban Studies* 45 (2008): 2057–2074.
18. Knippenberg, "Historical State–Church Relations in Europe," 261.
19. Warf and Vincent, "Religious Diversity over the Globe," 598.
20. Park, "Religion and Geography," 445; Colin Clarke and David Howard, "Race and Religious Pluralism in Kingston, Jamaica," *Population Space and Place* 11 (2005): 119–136.
21. Hugh Clout, "Book Review: *Rothschild and Early Jewish Colonization in Palestine* by Ran Aaronsohn," *Journal of Historical Geography* 28 (2002): 306–307; Aron Golan, "Israeli Historical Geography and the Holocaust: Reconsidering the Research Agenda," *Journal of Historical Geography* 28 (2002): 554–565.
22. Park, "Religion and Geography," 449.
23. Wang et al., "Muslim Hui Enclaves in Beijing," 108.
24. Warf and Vincent, "Religious Diversity over the Globe," 600.
25. Sopher, *Geography of Religions*, 70.
26. Akhtar H. Siddiqi, "Muslim World: Its Dilemma of Development," in *Muslim World: Geography and Development*, ed. Mushtaqur Rahman (Lanham, MD: University Press of America, 1987): 17–22; Roger Stump, "Spatial Implications of Religious Broadcasting: Stability and Change in Patterns of Belief," in *Collapsing Space and Time: Geographic Aspects of Communication and Information*, ed. Stanley Brunn and Thomas R. Leinbach (London: Harper Collins, 1991): 354–375; Park, *Sacred Worlds*, 9; Wang et al., "Muslim Hui Enclaves in Beijing," 110; Jean René Bertrand, "State and Church in France: Regulation and Negotiation," *GeoJournal* 67 (2006): 301–305.
27. Proselytizing religions are religions whose membership is in theory open to individuals of any background and that spread in part through proselytizing, or efforts to attract converts into the faith.
28. Stump, *Geography of Religion*, 79.
29. Sopher, *Geography of Religions*, 7.
30. Park, "Religion and Geography," 439–440.
31. Sopher, *Geography of Religions*, 7.
32. Judith A. Carney and Robert A. Voeks, "Landscape Legacies of the African Diaspora in Brazil," *Progress in Human Geography* 27 (2003): 139–152.
33. Tyler, "Spreading the Word," 12; Park, "Religion and Geography," 440.
34. Sopher, *Geography of Religions*, 8; Park, "Religion and Geography," 439–440.
35. Stump, "Spatial Implications of Religious Broadcasting," 355.
36. Brunn, "The Changing Map of World Religions."
37. Sopher, *Geography of Religions*, 89–91; Stump, "Spatial Implications of Religious Broadcasting," 365; Alan Lester and David Lambert, "Missionary Politics and the Captive Audience: William Shrewsbury in the Caribbean and the Cape Colony," in *Colonial Lives across the British Empire*, ed. David Lambert and Alan Lester (Cambridge: Cambridge University Press, 2006), 88–112.
38. Stump, "Spatial Implications of Religious Broadcasting."

39. Ibid., 361.
40. Ibid., 364–367.
41. John Connell, "Hillsong: A Megachurch in the Sydney Suburbs," *Australian Geographer* 36 (2005): 316.
42. Park, *Sacred Worlds*, 117–120.
43. Sopher, *Geography of Religions*, 71.
44. Karoly Kocsis, "Spatial and Temporal Changes in the Relationship between Church and State in Hungary," *GeoJournal* 67 (2006): 360.
45. Roger Stump, "Regional Variations in Denominational Switching among White Protestants," *Professional Geographer* 39 (1987): 440; Wang et al., "Muslim Hui Enclaves in Beijing," 108.
46. Wang et al., "Muslim Hui Enclaves in Beijing," 108.
47. Sopher, *Geography of Religions*, 88.
48. Ibid., 90.
49. Ibid., 87, 91.
50. Lester and Lambert, "Missionary Politics," 100–103.
51. Tyler, "Spreading the Word," 14; Clark and Howard, "Race and Religious Pluralism in Kingston."
52. Stump, *Geography of Religion*, 184.
53. Ley, "Immigrant Church Urban Service Hub."
54. Peach and Gale, "New Religious Landscape of England," 479–486; Warf and Vincent, "Religious Diversity over the Globe," 600.
55. Ronald Bordessa, "The Iconic Self: Luther, Culture and Landscape in Finland," in *Sacred Places and Profane Spaces: Essays in the Geographies of Judaism, Christianity, and Islam*, ed. Jamie Scott and Paul Simpson-Housley (Westport, CT: Greenwood Press, 1991), 82–84; see also Kocsis, "Church and State in Hungary," for the Hungarian monarchy's alliance with the Catholic Church and the subsequent Christian development in Hungary.
56. Bordessa, "The Iconic Self," 83.
57. Knippenberg, "Historical State–Church Relations in Europe," 257.
58. Sopher, *Geography of Religions*, 102.
59. Kocsis, "Church and State in Hungary," 360.
60. Stump, *Geography of Religion*, 95.
61. Wang et al., "Muslim Hui Enclaves in Beijing"; Clark and Howard, "Race and Religious Pluralism in Kingston."
62. Clark and Howard, "Race and Religious Pluralism in Kingston," 120–121.
63. Ibid., 119.
64. Brunn, "The Changing Map of World Religions"; Lester and Lambert, "Missionary Politics," 92–93.
65. For example, see Robert J. Donia and John V. A. Fine, Jr., *Bosnia and Herzegovina: A Tradition Betrayed* (New York: Columbia University Press, 1994); John Wolffe, ed., *Religion in History: Conflict, Conversion and Coexistence* (Manchester, England: Manchester University Press, 2004); Merle Calvin Ricklefs, *Polarising Javanese Society: Islamic and Other Visions, c. 1830–1930* (Singapore: NUS Press, 2007); Steven A. Wernke, "Analogy or Erasure? Dialectics of Religious Transformation in the Early Doctrinas of the Colca Valley, Peru," *International Journal of Historical Archaeology* 11 (2007): 152–182.
66. It is also possible that conversion patterns are, to some degree, manifestations of pre-existing social tensions, thus making social tensions both cause and effect, depending on particular situations.

67. Tyler, "Spreading the Word"; Rafael Reuveny, "Fundamentalist Colonialism: The Geopolitics of the Israeli–Palestinian Conflict," *Political Geography* 22 (2003): 347–380; Lester and Lambert, "Missionary Politics."

68. Tyler, "Spreading the Word," 13.

69. Wilbur Zelinsky, "The Uniqueness of the American Religious Landscape," *Geographical Review* 91 (2001): 576.

70. Lester and Lambert, "Missionary Politics," 93, 98.

71. Tyler, "Spreading the Word."

72. Ibid., 19.

73. Sopher, *Geography of Religions*, 42.

74. Emma Mawdsley, "Hindu Nationalism, Neo-Traditionalism and Environmental Discourses in India," *Geoforum* 37 (2006): 382.

75. Rana P. B. Singh, "Ethical Values and Spirit of Sustainability in Indian Thought," in *Geographic and Planning Research Themes for the New Millennium*, ed. Allen Noble, Baleshwar Thakur, Anath Bandhu Mukerji, and Frank Costa (New Delhi: Vikas Publishing House, 2000), 454; see Mawdsley, "Hindu Nationalism," for a counterargument.

76. Sopher, *Geography of Religions*, 20–23.

77. Bordessa, "The Iconic Self," 88.

78. Ibid., 88–90.

79. Nigel Thrift, *Non-Representational Theory* (Abingdon, England: Routledge, 2008); see also John-David Dewsbury, "Witnessing Space: 'Knowledge without Contemplation,'" *Environment and Planning A* 35 (2003): 1907–1932.

80. Lily Kong, "Mapping 'New' Geographies of Religion: Politics and Poetics in Modernity," *Progress in Human Geography* 25 (2001): 211–233; Julian Holloway, "Make-Believe: Spiritual Practice, Embodiment, and Sacred Space," *Environment and Planning A* 35 (2003): 1961–1974.

81. Gregory J. Levine, "The Geography of Religion," *Transactions of the Institute of British Geographers* 11 (1986): 428–440.

BIBLIOGRAPHY

Bertrand, Jean René. "State and Church in France: Regulation and Negotiation." *GeoJournal* 67 (2006): 296–306.

Bordessa, Ronald. "The Iconic Self: Luther, Culture, and Landscape in Finland." In *Sacred Places and Profane Spaces: Essays in the Geographies of Judaism, Christianity, and Islam*, ed. Jamie Scott and Paul Simpson-Housley, 81–92. Westport, CT: Greenwood Press, 1991.

Brown, Mark S. "Estimating the Size and Distribution of South Asian Religious Populations in Britain: Is There an Alternative to a Religion Question in the Census?" *International Journal of Population Geography* 6 (2000): 87–109.

Brunn, Stanley. "The Changing Map of World Religions." Keynote presentation at the International Conference: Religion at the Time of Change, Lodz, Poland, Sept. 11, 2004.

Carney, Judith A., and Robert A. Voeks. "Landscape Legacies of the African Diaspora in Brazil." *Progress in Human Geography* 27 (2003): 139–152.

Clarke, Colin, and David Howard. "Race and Religious Pluralism in Kingston, Jamaica." *Population Space and Place* 11 (2005): 119–136.

Clout, Hugh. "Book Review: *Rothschild and Early Jewish Colonization in Palestine* by Ran Aaronsohn." *Journal of Historical Geography* 28 (2002): 306–307.

Connell, John. "Hillsong: A Megachurch in the Sydney Suburbs." *Australian Geographer* 36 (2005): 316.

Dewsbury, John-David. "Witnessing Space: 'Knowledge Without Contemplation.'" *Environment and Planning A* 35 (2003): 1907–1932.

Donia, Robert J., and John V. A. Fine, Jr. *Bosnia and Herzegovina: A Tradition Betrayed.* New York: Columbia University Press, 1994.

Gaustad, Edwin Scott. *Historical Atlas of Religion in America.* New York: Harper & Row Publishers, 1962.

Gaustad, Edwin Scott, and Philip L. Barlow. *New Historical Atlas of Religion in America.* New York: Oxford University Press, 2001.

Golan, Aron. "Israeli Historical Geography and the Holocaust: Reconsidering the Research Agenda." *Journal of Historical Geography* 28 (2002): 554–565.

Holloway, Julian. "Make-Believe: Spiritual Practice, Embodiment, and Sacred Space." *Environment and Planning A* 35 (2003): 1961–1974.

Knippenberg, Hans. "The Political Geography of Religion: Historical State–Church Relations in Europe and Recent Challenges." *GeoJournal* 67 (2006): 253–265.

Kocsis, Karoly. "Spatial and Temporal Changes in the Relationship between Church and State in Hungary." *GeoJournal* 67 (2006): 357–371.

Kong, Lily. "Mapping 'New' Geographies of Religion: Politics and Poetics in Modernity." *Progress in Human Geography* 25 (2001): 211–233.

Lester, Alan, and David Lambert. "Missionary Politics and the Captive Audience: William Shrewsbury in the Caribbean and the Cape Colony." In *Colonial Lives across the British Empire*, ed. David Lambert and Alan Lester, 88–112. Cambridge: Cambridge University Press, 2006.

Levine, Gregory J. "The Geography of Religion." *Transactions of the Institute of British Geographers* 11 (1986): 428–440.

Ley, David. "The Immigrant Church as an Urban Service Hub." *Urban Studies* 45 (2008): 2057–2074.

Madeley, John. "A Framework for the Comparative Analysis of Church–State Relations in Europe." *West European Politics* 26 (2003): 23–50.

Mawdsley, Emma. "Hindu Nationalism, Neo-Traditionalism and Environmental Discourses in India." *Geoforum* 37 (2006): 380–390.

Pacione, Michael. "The Geography of Religious Affiliation in Scotland." *Professional Geographer* 57 (2005): 235–255.

Park, Chris C. *Sacred Worlds: An Introduction to Geography and Religion.* London: Routledge, 1994.

———. "Religion and Geography." In *The Routledge Companion to the Study of Religion*, ed. John R. Hinnells, 439–455. Abingdon, England: Routledge, 2005.

Peach, Ceri, and Richard Gale. "Muslims, Hindus, and Sikhs in the New Religious Landscape of England." *Geographical Review* 93 (2003): 469–490.

Reuveny, Rafael. "Fundamentalist Colonialism: The Geopolitics of Israeli–Palestinian Conflict." *Political Geography* 22 (2003): 347–380.

Ricklefs, Merle Calvin. *Polarising Javanese Society: Islamic and Other Visions, c. 1830–1930.* Singapore: NUS Press, 2007.

Siddiqi, Akhtar H. "Muslim World: Its Dilemma of Development." In *Muslim World: Geography and Development*, ed. Mushtaqur Rahman, 17–22. Lanham, MD: University Press of America, 1987.

Singh, Rana P. B. "The Geography of Religion in India: Perspectives and Prospects." *National Geographical Journal of India* 38 (1992): 27–38.

——. "Ethical Values and Spirit of Sustainability in Indian Thought." In *Geographic and Planning Research Themes for the New Millennium*, ed. Allen Noble, Baleshwar Thakur, Anath Bandhu Mukerji, and Frank Costa, 445–458. New Delhi: Vikas Publishing House, 2000.

Sopher, David E. *Geography of Religions*. Englewood Cliffs, NJ: Prentice-Hall, Inc., 1967.

Stump, Roger. "Regional Variations in Denominational Switching among White Protestants." *Professional Geographer* 39 (1987): 438–449.

——. "Spatial Implications of Religious Broadcasting: Stability and Change in Patterns of Belief." In *Collapsing Space and Time: Geographic Aspects of Communication and Information*, ed. Stanley Brunn and Thomas R. Leinbach, 354–375. London: Harper Collins, 1991.

——. *The Geography of Religion: Faith, Place, and Space*. Plymouth, England: Rowman & Littlefield Publishers, 2008.

Thrift, Nigel. *Non-Representational Theory: Space, Politics, Affect*. Abingdon, England: Routledge, 2008.

Tyler, Charles. "Spreading the Word." *Geographical Magazine* 62 (1990): 12–19.

Wang, Wen Fei, Shang Yi Zhou, and Cindy C. Fan. "Growth and Decline of Muslim Hui Enclaves in Beijing." *Eurasian Geography and Economics* 43 (2002): 104–122.

Warf, Barney, and Peter Vincent. "Religious Diversity over the Globe: A Geographic Exploration." *Social & Cultural Geography* 8 (2007): 597–613.

Wernke, Steven A. "Analogy or Erasure? Dialectics of Religious Transformation in the Early Doctrinas of the Colca Valley, Peru." *International Journal of Historical Archaeology* 11 (2007): 152–182.

Wolffe, John, ed. *Religion in History: Conflict, Conversion and Coexistence*. Manchester, England: Manchester University Press, 2004.

Zelinsky, Wilbur. "The Uniqueness of the American Religious Landscape." *Geographical Review* 91 (2001): 565–585.

CHAPTER 4

....

ANTHROPOLOGY OF RELIGIOUS CONVERSION

....

HENRI GOOREN

INTRODUCTION

....

THIS chapter analyzes important approaches in anthropology that have dealt with religious change in general or religious conversion in particular. My central question is how do anthropologists identify and analyze the main factors in the conversion process of people changing their religion. I deal with the approaches more or less in chronological order, describing their main authors and main ideas, their conceptualization of religious change or conversion, and their methodologies. I also show how some approaches have built upon others and in turn influenced new approaches.

First, I analyze approaches to religious conversion that were developed by anthropologists who studied Native Americans converting to Christianity or to nativistic revitalization movements. Second, I discuss how Luther Gerlach and Virginia Hine presented their model of conversion to religious and social movements based on the Pentecostal and Black Power movements in the United States. Third, I consider how Robin Horton influenced many anthropologists with his "intellectualist" analysis of conversion to world religions in Africa, an approach that sparked heavy criticism.

Subsequent sections explore mission and modernity in Africa and Latin America, as well as Protestantism and modernity in Latin America. Next, I analyze two evangelical anthropologists who helped missionaries to spread the gospel. The intellectualist approach to conversion indirectly influenced a new generation working on the importance of language and discourse in conversion to evangelical Protestantism. Diane Austin-Broos and Simon Coleman developed the idea of "continuous conversion" in Pentecostalism. The latest approach that deals with conversion is the anthropology of Christianity inspired by the works of Joel Robbins and Fenella Cannell, who aim to develop that holy grail of the discipline: the anthropology of change.

My main conclusion is that anthropologists have consistently struggled to come to terms with religious conversion, but currently they are improving quickly. Most anthropologists have criticized modernity but have been unable to escape its gravitational pull. Another challenge for the future is developing comparative approaches to conversion to a host of religions in ways that include the indigenous understandings of the religions and explore their interactions with globalization processes. Anthropologists should capitalize on the main strengths of their discipline: their long-term perspective, their ethnographic approach, their theoretical flexibility, and their focus on the cultural context in understanding conversion cross-culturally.[1]

CONVERSION TO NATIVE AMERICAN REVITALIZATION MOVEMENTS

Anthony Wallace developed a model to explain periods of accelerated cultural change by looking at the crucial role of movements like Handsome Lake, Peyote, and Ghost Dance in North America. Wallace defined a revitalization movement as "a deliberate, organized, conscious effort by members of a society to construct a more satisfying culture."[2] He developed a concept that was linked to conversion that he termed the *mazeway*. "The mazeway is nature, society, culture, personality, and body image, as seen by one person."[3]

Wallace's universal model described the different phases all revitalization movements worldwide were supposed to go through: (1) steady state; (2) increased individual stress; (3) cultural distortion; (4) revitalization; and (5) the new steady state. The crucial phase was *revitalization*, which in turn was divided into six sub-phases: (a) *mazeway reformulation* through dreams or visions (which Wallace himself already noted was very similar to conversion);[4] (b) *communication* of the new vision to other people by the prophet and his disciples; (c) *organization* of the movement along the lines of Max Weber's "routinization of charisma"; (d) *adaptation* to mainstream society; (e) *cultural transformation* of the society as the new vision gains acceptance; and (f) *routinization* of the new vision.

Wallace concluded that the successful revitalization movement started by the prophet named Handsome Lake effectively changed Iroquois culture, agriculture, and religion. "By guiding the Seneca into an economic system which stressed private property and the profit motive, they confidently expected their ultimate acceptance of an ethical and moral, and eventually religious, code which emphasized the voice of conscience, sobriety, cleanliness, industry, and marital stability; in a word, a Protestant type of religion."[5]

Wallace reported that the new converts "retained an intense devotion to the prophet who gave them the strength to achieve salvation"[6] (i.e., the strength to give up drinking and witchcraft). Individual converts reported "a feeling of peace, confidence, and strength." This explained Handsome Lake's popularity and the appeal of his religion.

After Handsome Lake died in 1815, the Seneca lost their lands and suffered from internal divisions between a pagan and a Christian group, as described in the next section. To control factional strife, pagan group leaders redefined the old religion. They built upon the teachings of Handsome Lake because he had supported traditional religion but also "education, economic progress, and social harmony." This process "gradually produced between 1818 and 1845 a new religious institution—a church—devoted to the preservation and propagation of the prophet's message." For Wallace, historical, cultural, and political factors encouraged the institutionalization of Handsome Lake's religion into a church.[7]

Conversion to Christianity among Native Americans

Another important conversion model that emerged from the literature on Native American religion was developed by Robert Berkhofer, who analyzed three chronological conversion patterns in Native American communities between 1760 and 1860. The first he termed the *Community Reintegration Sequence*, in which early Christian missionaries converted only a minority, who were then pressured into apostasy by the indigenous majority. The "Pagan Party" majority often drove the missionaries out or even murdered them. The result was a reintegrated community. This pattern was typical during the period when the authority of the US federal government was still weak.[8]

Berkhofer's second conversion pattern was called the *Fragmented Community Sequence*. The missionaries eventually succeeded in converting a sizable minority or a small majority, which developed new social relationships. In practice, the Native American villages or bands were split into two groups, pagan and Christian, one of which was often required to relocate. Berkhofer points out that this sequence occurred about the time of the loss of political autonomy for the Native Americans.[9]

The third conversion pattern was called the *Fragmented Tribal Sequence*: "As more and more missionaries arrived and more Whites settled around the reservation, the coincidence between culture, social structure, and community broke down not only in one village as in the preceding sequences but in many towns in the tribe. To heal the divisions, attempts were made at political organization on the tribal level."[10] This tribal political organization was modeled after the dominant society, with a written constitution and elected officers in a government of divided powers.

Berkhofer's model was based on archival research that he deftly linked to sequential acculturation patterns. His model emphasized how entire Native American communities were affected by conversions rather than an analyzing the conversion process among individuals; the model also focused on the interaction between political and cultural factors in conversion.

CONVERSION AND COMMITMENT TO
RELIGIOUS AND SOCIAL MOVEMENTS

Like Berkhofer, US anthropologists Luther Gerlach and Virginia Hine developed a process model for conversion that in their case was based on their research of the Pentecostal and Black Power movements. Gerlach and Hine's model defined "commitment" as made up of four principal elements: strength of conviction, the capacity for risk-taking, personal charisma, and behavioral change.[11] They also identified seven stages in a person's conversion process: (1) initial contact with a participant; (2) focus of needs through demonstration; (3) re-education through group interaction; (4) decision and surrender; (5) the commitment event; (6) testifying to the experience; and (7) group support for cognitive and behavioral changes.[12]

The authors identified stages (3) and (5) as crucial for establishing a genuine (i.e., lasting) personal conversion experience. Re-education through group interaction illustrated the three main functions of the local Pentecostal group: providing a basis for cognitive reorientation by the potential convert, facilitating the development of in-group ties, and encouraging the formulations of expectations concerning the conversion experience.[13] Although they were vague on (4), the process of surrender, Gerlach and Hine deftly emphasized the importance of (5), the "commitment event"[14] or "bridge-burning act."[15] There had to be a public act to set the performer apart from mainstream society and to express the rupture with the former life, followed by (6), a testimony of the newly found cognitive and behavioral patterns. For Pentecostals, the commitment event was the Baptism of the Holy Spirit, manifested by speaking in tongues.

Although the seven stages of commitment were described from the point of view of the individual actor, they were tied to the religious organization. Gerlach and Hine concluded their study by identifying five key factors in the development of religious or social movements that they considered universal.

(1) Personal commitment, constructed along the lines sketched above in list of the seven factors.
(2) "Enthusiastic persuasion of friends, relatives, and neighbors to join in the small-scale effort."
(3) Articulation of beliefs and ideals appropriate to the contemporary period of national and world history.
(4) Building "flexible, non-bureaucratic cell-group organizations which can be created, altered, or dissolved at the desire of participants."
(5) An "expectation of and willingness to face opposition from those dedicated to the maintenance of the status quo."[16]

Like Wallace, Gerlach and Hine noted that the movements they studied thrived in the face of (limited) opposition.

Gerlach and Hine provided the first model of religious conversion that was based on extensive ethnographic research of two representative groups in US society: the Pentecostal and Black Power movements. They randomly selected local case studies of these movements in the midwestern United States, interviewed scores of leaders and members, and administered questionnaires.[17] Moreover, their book presented a wealth of ethnographic material from other movements and societies to support the claims of their general model.

Gerlach and Hine's model aimed to be applicable to all religious and social movements worldwide. However, not all social movements that developed in the 1970s could be analyzed adequately with their model. Their model's greatest strength is its ability to analyze religious movements that are still young, charismatic, and relatively less institutionalized. Their unique contribution was uniting individual and group factors into a single conversion model.[18]

CONVERSION TO MODERNITIES: THE RATIONALITY OF WORLD RELIGIONS

In the 1970s British anthropologist Robin Horton developed the "intellectualist" approach, which included the observation that most African traditional religions included the largely unelaborated concept of a Supreme Being. Religious life in the "standard situation"[19] was centered on the lesser spirits, which were local in nature. Horton's main thesis was that these local spirits become less important, and the supreme being more important, as the boundaries of the local microcosm weakened under the influence of *modernity*, marked by increased commerce and communication, penetration of the nation state, and migration to other locations: "As more and more people become involved in social life beyond the confines of their various microcosms, they begin to evolve a moral code for the governance of this wider life." The Supreme Being then moves from a position of "moral neutrality" to one of "moral concern."[20]

Horton maintained that Christianity and Islam became successful only when they coincided with "responses of the traditional cosmology to other, non-missionary, factors of the modern situation." This reduced Christianity and Islam to the role of catalysts, "stimulators and accelerators of changes which were 'in the air' anyway." Hence, world religions in Africa were successful because of encroaching modernity.[21]

Horton's intellectualist model has been vigorously criticized by other anthropologists for being deterministic and for its faulty assumptions on African traditional religions, Islam, and Christianity, which he presented as generic categories. Islamist Humphrey Fisher showed that Horton's assumptions of the "standard situation" of African traditional religion were faulty. Long-distance commerce and warfare preceded the modern situation and according to Horton's theory should have led to making the Supreme Being more important than the local spirits. Moreover, conversion to Islam in black

Africa was left out by Horton, who assumed it had "meager results."[22] By 1973, Fisher had developed a three-stage model of conversion to Islam in Africa: quarantine, mixing, and reform.[23] Syncretism of Islam and traditional religion spurred reform movements led by holy men and merchants bent on maintaining the purity of Islam. People who were mixing Islam had not gone through a true conversion but had merely experienced what Nock called *adhesion*.[24]

Horton countered Fisher with two articles. The first provided an overview of the ethnographic literature on African traditional religions, noting that only a very few had no concept of a Supreme Being. Horton's second article dealt with conversion to Islam in black Africa. After reviewing the historical material on nine reform movements, Horton saw a pattern.[25] When economic factors caused rulers to emphasize parochialism by restricting trade and raising taxes, a coalition of merchants, pastoralists, and holy men "intervened to redress the balance in favor of internationalism."[26]

Both Horton and Fisher depended heavily on historical records and their own fieldwork in Africa. They focused mostly on the highest levels of analysis: ethnic groups or social classes. How individuals converted was determined by these structural factors. Subsistence farmers would cling to local spirits, merchants would convert to Islam or Christianity, and pastoralists were usually in between, mixing traditional religion with the new world religion.

US anthropologist Robert Hefner appreciated Horton's model because it showed that "traditional religions are not necessarily less rational than world religions"[27] and "because it portrayed Africans as active players in religious change."[28] But Hefner severely criticized Horton for neglecting political and structural influences on conversion, including the role of Western colonialism, the unique emphasis on exclusivity in Islam and Christianity, and the lack of both literacy and authoritative institutions in most traditional religions.[29]

Quoting Weber, Hefner argued that the key feature distinguishing world religions was their "superior rationalization." "Traditional religions are piecemeal in their approach to problems of meaning, he believed, but world religions formulate comprehensive responses to the ethical, emotional, and intellectual challenges of human life."[30] Hefner correctly pointed out that rationalization of religion should not be confused with individual rationality, and he came up with a new definition of conversion: "At the very least—an analytic minimum—conversion implies the acceptance of a new locus of self-definition, a new, though not necessarily exclusive, reference point for one's identity."[31]

Hefner theorized an "elective affinity" between Christianity's individualizing message and "one of the modern era's key dispositions, social individualization." He noted that the Christian message is less appealing to peoples with "a view of the actor as socially embedded." Where the social order is in decline, however, "the individualism of the Christian message may be powerfully appealing, legitimating nonconformism and the organization of new forms of social relationship (cf. Martin 1990)."[32] I think Hefner followed Weber's view of Protestantism here, because his argument is problematic for Catholicism.[33]

None of the eleven fine articles in Hefner's 1993 work, *Conversion to Christianity*, presented a new anthropological model of conversion, but Peter Wood's afterword summarized their possible implications: "Christian belief makes little or no headway in circumstances, such as appear to be widespread among Amazonian and some Mexican Indians and among Australian Aborigines, where the universe is conceived as fundamentally fixed. The native religions in such cultures emphasize conceptual and ritual congruity" and are community rather than individually focused. Christian belief prospers "where there are vigorous traditions that encompass the addition to or alteration of religious affiliation," as in China and much of Africa. Christianity seems to do best in cultures that stress individualism and entrepreneurship, like many societies of Papua New Guinea.[34]

Dutch anthropologist Peter van der Veer argued consistently for the development of "multiple, different modernities"[35] as indigenous religions were faced with Western colonialism and Christian missionaries. Following Weber, van der Veer traced connections between Protestantism, with its emphasis on individual agency and inwardness, and the formation of the modern self.[36] Van der Veer pointed out that Christian missionaries were "simultaneously agents in spreading modernity and products of it." Conversion required self-examination, which was reinforced by the "constant scrutiny" of the Christian community.[37] Conversion to modernity was thus not only an interior state. A "genuine" conversion required "a performative act of communicating to others that one's sincerity is anchored in an interior state of self-questioning and self-accounting."[38] Van der Veer astutely noted the ambiguity of conversion, "in which some supernatural agents are seen as figments of imagination and thus as false forces, while others are seen as true and rightfully powerful.... The powerful speech of missionaries in condemning the false fetishes of others may, paradoxically, empower and re-enchant those practices and objects that are to be rejected, as Birgit Meyer has shown" (see next section).[39]

The Anthropology of Mission and Modernity in Africa

How were indigenous societies and religions affected by the introduction by missionaries of Christianity and Western education? German-Dutch anthropologist Birgit Meyer demonstrated what the Ewe of Ghana had to do following their conversion to Pietistic Presbyterianism in the mid-nineteenth century: "Baptism implied that a person had to choose a new Christian—preferably Biblical—name, to reject any 'connection with idol-worship', to refrain from participation in 'heathen ceremonies', and to take off all *dzo* ('medicine/magic') strings and amulets.... Every Sunday congregations had to attend church punctually and neatly dressed."[40] Meyer concluded, "Christian religion was attractive because it offered the material means to achieve a prosperous and relatively high position in colonial society."[41]

Analyzing the process of *diabolization* in Africa (i.e., the idea that the devil was the power behind traditional African religions), Meyer severely criticized Horton's intellectualist theory. The increasing emphasis on exorcism to cast out the devil of African traditional gods and spirits showed that in Africa there was no process of moving toward One High God. Instead, "The adoption of belief in the High God went hand in hand with the adoption of the image of the Devil, considered to be the Lord of the old gods and spirits and defining the boundary between Christianity and Ewe religion, though at the same time integrating the latter into Christian discourse."[42] Meyer concluded that Horton seriously underestimated the importance of the old gods and spirits for Africans. The spiritual warfare between God and Satan faithfully reflected the struggles Christian converts faced in their daily lives, balancing their obligations to their extended family, their nuclear family, and their church. "In talking about Satan and his demons they could even thematize hidden desires to return to the old, without actually doing so."[43] Pentecostalism (and Christianity in general) was attractive because "it is a new and strange religion opposed to African religion and culture."[44] People in Ghana converted to Pentecostalism "to make a complete break with the past."

Meyer's research confirmed "that Pentecostalism is especially appealing to people involved in modernization processes and longing for upward social mobility."[45] She argued that Pentecostalism in Ghana was very successful because it offered new forms rather than new content. Hence, it could "easily become localized and thus express a highly culturally-specific version of Christianity."[46] Pentecostalism offered "a ritual space and an imaginary language to deal with the demons which are cast out in the process of modernity's constitution, but which continue to haunt people"[47] —for example, in the form of obligations to the extended family.

Meyer also pointed out the "clear analogy" between the Pentecostal and Protestant "conceptualization of conversion in terms of a rupture with the past and modernity's self definition in terms of progress and continuous renewal."[48] She revealed the historical connections in Ghana between conversion to Protestantism and becoming modern in social, economic, and political respects.

British anthropologist Ruth Marshall-Fratani also developed a conversion approach that analyzed the success of Pentecostalism in Africa as a consequence of its ability to mediate between conflicting identities. "Conversion does not necessarily imply a rejection of other identities, but involves their assimilation within a complex of discourses and practices governing all aspects of social, cultural, economic, and political life which enable them to be mediated through and subsumed within a collective system of representations. One is always born-again first."[49] Marshall-Fratani also analyzed the connection between conversion to Pentecostalism and the construction of selfhood, writing, "It is not so much the individualism of Pentecostal conversion which leads to the creation of modern subjects, but the ways in which its projection on a global scale of images, discourses and ideas about renewal, change and salvation opens up new possibilities for local actors to incorporate these into their everyday lives."[50] This stresses the importance of transnational connections in the conversion process.

THE ANTHROPOLOGY OF MISSION AND MODERNITY IN LATIN AMERICA

Historical anthropologists and ethno-historians have analyzed the conversion to Roman Catholicism of the Latin American Indians. Spanish imperialism justified its actions by its Christian mission of converting the pagans to the Catholic faith.[51] Although the friars converted masses of Indians in a relatively short time by converting their leaders,[52] the effects of Christianization soon proved to be more superficial than they expected, which led to disillusionment.[53] US historian Christopher Vecsey gave this overview of the different ways Indians in Mexico responded to the friars' attempts to convert them:

> Some adopted a Christian worldview, identifying elements of Christianity as equivalent or complementary to analogous elements of the aboriginal religions. For most Indians of this sort, however, conversion did not rule out the observance of indigenous customs.... They were impressed with the claims of Christianity but did not understand them adequately, or understood them according to indigenous premise.... Some of these Indians separated and compartmentalized their native and Christian religious forms, participating in one, then the other, according to need and situation, and using the two systems of explanation alternatively.... Some Indians went through the motions of conversion but were indifferent to Christian theology and participated in Christian rituals only casually. Still others resisted Christianity more fully, either refusing baptism or acquiescing in the most minimal forms while continuing to engage actively in paganism, and in some instances working toward rebellion against their conquerors.... Finally, many Mexican Indians came, consciously and unconsciously, to join together elements of the aboriginal and Christian traditions into a syncretistic pattern of religious life, the controlling efforts of missionaries notwithstanding.[54]

A mixing of Catholicism and indigenous religions developed from the start of Spanish colonization.[55] However, the Spanish colonial administration and the Catholic Church forced the Indians to submit, resorting to torture and the death penalty.[56] The Indian gods and spirits were seen as demons and the pagans as Satan worshippers,[57] which justified bringing in the Inquisition. Severe punishments could not stop the syncretism, however, which became even more institutionalized with the development of indigenous fraternities or *cofradías*.[58]

The Roman Catholic Church supported a new lay movement beginning in the 1940s known as Catholic Action. In the predominantly Indian parts of Mexico, especially Guatemala, Indians started to convert from traditional (syncretized) Catholicism to Catholic Action in the 1960s. The first converts were ambitious young people who had no access to positions of power that were controlled by the appropriately named elders.

Guatemalan anthropologist Ricardo Falla analyzed the process of conversion from traditional to orthodox Catholicism in the early 1970s in the Quiché department of Guatemala.[59] Falla's definition of conversion is different from other anthropologists: "Conversion is a moment in a process of adaptation by an individual or a group to the environment, whether it be the world of nature, such as land, water, and all resources, the world of surrounding society, or both."[60] Hence, his conversion model stressed two main components: power[61] and liminality.[62]

Falla concluded that conversion to orthodox Catholicism was part of a general modernization process of opening up indigenous communities to the Guatemalan state and the outside world through better transportation (roads), improved communication (telephone lines), and a more open economy (trade). Successful traders retreated from the *cofradía* system and preferred to invest wealth in their business and (nuclear) family. Trading with outsiders gave them access to new information and new social networks; they were not dependent on the traditional authority structures of the village. Hence, they were able to break the traditional power of the elders and the *zahorines* ("witch doctors") by identifying them with the work of the devil. Falla theorized a similar process was driving the increasing number of conversions to Protestantism, although he did not study this phenomenon.[63]

THE ANTHROPOLOGY OF PROTESTANTISM AND MODERNITY IN LATIN AMERICA

In the 1950s and 1960s, anthropologists developed different modernization theories to explain the first converts to Protestantism in the same country where Protestant growth started early and was ultimately most successful: Guatemala. Manning Nash noted that in Cantel, almost 18 percent of artisans were Protestant, compared to 13.5 percent of farming families and 10 percent of factory workers.[64] June Nash emphasized the importance of economic changes and trade; Benson Saler explored the socially marginal position and the individual psychology of the first converts to Protestantism; and Ruben Reina stressed the role of class, status, and the geography of communities in the Petén frontier area.[65]

German-American anthropologist Emilio Willems identified three groups in Chile and Brazil that were especially receptive to Protestantism: newly arrived rural immigrants in the "impersonal and atomistic society of the city,"[66] recent immigrants to new agricultural frontier areas,[67] and isolated rural communities that contained many independent "rural middle class" farmers.[68] Willem's theoretical framework for conversion was structural and more influenced by Weber and Durkheim than by contemporary anthropologists. Echoing but not quoting from dominant models in the sociology of religion,[69] Willems also emphasized the role of anomie, stress, and alienation in conversion as part of a conversion to modernity approach.

Anthropologists were the first to note that dissatisfaction with the civil-religious cargo systems in the indigenous parts of Latin America formed a major motivation for conversion to Protestantism. By occupying ritual offices, called "cargos," in the *cofradías*, the wealthier members of the community sponsored fiestas and processions in honor of the saints. Hence, their wealth was transformed into prestige. "In a subsistence-oriented economy, prestige was a better investment than the accumulation of goods or property."[70] This leveling mechanism also reduced envy and thus witchcraft accusations. US anthropologist James Dow studied three Otomí villages in Mexico over a long period of time, finding that the young people rebelled against the financial requirements of the *cofradía* cargo system.[71] Young people wanted to pursue new possibilities for education and profit, and they did not want to turn the latter into prestige through a cargo office in the *cofradía*. To escape from these demands, many young people became Protestants. This phenomenon has been described by anthropologists as an important factor in conversion to Protestantism in Mexico,[72] Guatemala,[73] and Ecuador.[74]

However, Latin American anthropologists were the first to demonstrate that conversion to Protestantism by Indians was not always what it claimed to be: a complete break with the past. Mexican anthropologist Carlos Garma (2001) showed that Pentecostalism was attractive to Indians because of its similarities to Native American traditions, particularly in its faith healing, miracles, dreams and visions, charismatic religious leaders, and dramatic ritual performances. Various authors in a volume edited by Uruguayan-Dutch anthropologist Luis Samandú (1990) made the same point.

US anthropologist James Sexton is the clearest representative of the conversion to modernity approach in anthropology as applied to Guatemala. Based on fieldwork among Tzutuhil and Cakchiquel Indians in San Juan La Laguna and Panajachel, Sexton concluded that "Protestants living in a predominantly Catholic world appear to be more modern than their Catholic peers."[75] Most were in the process of becoming *Ladinos* (mestizo non-Indians), shedding their Indian language and dress for Spanish and Western clothes. However, Sexton's conceptualization of modernization was individual, based on indicators like migration, Ladino identity, child spacing, sobriety, exposure to print media, motivation, and personality (rejection of fatalism and traditional beliefs).[76] Sexton did not argue that religious values changed socioeconomic patterns of behavior, but he posited a mutual interaction between modernization and conversion to Protestantism at the level of the individual: "Protestant values and behavior reinforce exposure to print media, Ladino cultural adoptions, and increased wealth."[77]

In "Reconsidering Protestant Growth in Guatemala, 1900–1995" (Gooren 2001), I developed a structural model of Protestant church growth in Guatemala that included internal religious factors (appeal of the doctrine and evangelization activities), internal nonreligious factors (appeal of the organization and member retention), external religious factors (dissatisfaction with Catholicism and slow responses by the Catholic hierarchy), and external nonreligious factors (anomie and the urbanization process). Analyzing the available statistical material, I concluded that the explosion of Protestant growth between 1976 and 1986 was caused by a combination of factors: anomie was constantly high, many new churches were built, missionaries poured in after the 1976 earthquake and conducted evangelization activities, the civil war created higher urbanization rates, and popular Catholicism with its *cofradía* cargo offices had lost its domination.

In addition, the leadership of the Protestant, mostly Pentecostal, churches had changed from US missionaries to Guatemalans in the 1960s and early 1970s.

CHRISTIANITY IN CULTURE: CONVERSION IN EVANGELICAL ANTHROPOLOGY

Based on his life-long fieldwork in Oceania, Australian anthropologist Alan R. Tippett developed a four-stage process model of group conversion that aimed to be universal.[78] The initial stage of *Awareness* of the new message ended with a "Point of Realization" that marked the beginning of stage II, the period of *Decision*. During this stage there were four possible responses: total rejection, total acceptance, modified acceptance, and fission or division of the group. At the end of this stage, there was a "Point of Encounter," after which the (sub)group had to decide whether to accept the new message. If they accepted, the third stage, *Incorporation*, started. Following van Gennep (1960), Tippett distinguished three main acts in this period. First came an act of Separation (public testimony), next an act of Transition (instruction and training), and finally the act of Incorporation (baptism).[79] Tippett used his experiences as a missionary in the Solomon Islands to add the fourth stage, *Maturity*. To arrive here, the group first had to pass the "Point of Confirmation." The maturity period involved learning to live a life of holiness, or 'sanctification' as it is typically called in Methodism and Pentecostalism.[80]

US anthropologist Charles H. Kraft's *Christianity in Culture* (1979) defined Christian conversion as "a lifelong process, consisting of continuous divine–human interaction and a continuing series of human decisions."[81] The relevant stages during this process can be defined according to van Gennep's (1960) rites of *incorporation* and rites of *consolidation*.[82] The first rite of incorporation is baptism by immersion, but Kraft noted that most churches lacked further ritual stages except Sunday school or status as a missionary. Pentecostal success derived in part, he thought, from the powerful motivation of the "Baptism of the Holy Spirit" (or Second Baptism), when believers are filled with the Spirit and for the first time start speaking in tongues.[83] Kraft briefly mentioned but did not analyze the role of conversion in consolidation ceremonies like "the Lord's Supper, festivals, corporate worship services, retreats, conferences," but failed to mention evangelization activities like campaigns, tent meetings, street preaching, or public prayer.

Kraft's model developed five "constants" in the conversion process, which he claimed were biblical and universal. The conversion process started with (1) a conscious allegiance (faith commitment) to God, which led to (2) a dynamic interaction between God and human beings. As God was working with the converts, (3) a long-term process of growth or maturation followed. (4) This maturation process needed to take place in a Christian community, usually a church: "The people of God need other people of God to whom to relate to assure the direction and nature of their growth." The faith commitment should become the central point of reference to "make all decisions and around which they reorient all living." Kraft's final point was cultural: (5) "the human being's part of the conversion process is to be in keeping with the culture in which they are immersed."[84] Otherwise, a *cultural conversion* followed: a powerful (sub)culture imposes its own conversion model on other (sub)cultures in the name of Christ. The danger here was that people, say Africans, merely "convert to the culture of the witness without developing a saving relationship with God."

Kraft stressed the error of many missionaries who equated Christianity with Western culture and language, forcing Native Americans and Africans to give up their own culture in order to become Christians. Kraft argued that growth and maturation could only occur if converts within the context of other cultures are allowed to have direct interaction with God, without the imposition of an external cultural model by the witness.[85]

Hence, Kraft's conversion model was also a *process* model with three main stages. A change in allegiance (faith commitment to God) led to a change in worldview, which in turn led to a change in attitudes, habits, and behavior.[86] Christianity should change the worldview of all cultures—including the North American one that many missionaries cling to.

The conversion model of US anthropologist Paul Hiebert, summed up in his posthumously published *Transforming Worldviews* (2008), was similar to Kraft's. Hiebert also began by pointing out that conversion to Christ must encompass three levels: "behavior, beliefs, and the worldview that underlies these.... Conversion may include a change in beliefs and behavior, but if the worldview is not transformed, in the long run the gospel is subverted and the result is syncretistic Christo-paganism, which had the form of Christianity but not its essence." Under the influence of modernity, churches and missionaries defined conversion "primarily in terms of affirming a particular set of doctrines (orthodoxy) or practices (orthopraxy). Discipling of new converts was often haphazard and brief, often resulting in churches full of new, immature Christians."[87] Hiebert was very critical of this old model of Christian conversion.

For Hiebert, conversion was a life-long process that must include both personal transformation and corporate transformation. A local community of faith, a church, must set standards and define doctrinal boundaries.[88] His two main stages of conversion were (1) rejecting the old gods, turning around, and following Jesus, and (2) learning to know and serve Him more fully.[89] Hence, Hiebert distinguished three main levels of conversion:[90]

1. *Behavior and Ritual*: stop smoking and drinking, be baptized and attend church, memorize catechism and verses, put on clothes and be clean, pray and read the Bible.
2. *Beliefs and Belief Systems*: repent and confess sins, accept and follow Jesus, know the Bible.
3. *Worldview*: transform the old (cultural, religious, secular) worldview into a biblical worldview.[91]

Hiebert analyzed three ways in which worldviews could be transformed. First, we may examine our own worldview critically, for instance, when facing new problems that we cannot solve with traditional means. Second, when faced with alternative worldviews, we may be impressed by their power and consequences. Third, by creating new living rituals we "affirm our deepest beliefs, feelings, and morals" and our entry into a new community.[92]

CONVERSION DISCOURSE AND LANGUAGE

US anthropologist Susan Harding defined conversion as "a process of acquiring a specific religious language."[93] People learned this language through "witnessing": listening to testimonies from others and articulating their own about the power of the Holy Spirit. Harding gave a vivid example. After interviewing the Baptist Reverend Cantrell for hours, she was almost killed in a car accident on the way home: "I slammed on the brakes, sat stunned for a split second, and asked myself: 'What is God trying to tell me?' It was my voice, but not my language. I had been invaded by the fundamental Baptist tongue I was investigating."[94]

Harding concluded that "witnessing is an orthodox Protestant rite of conversion. If you are willing to be witnessed to, if you are seriously willing to listen to the gospel, you have begun to convert."[95] Harding noted that the conventional factors in conversion identified by social scientists were not the primary cause: "Crises, transitions, and upbringing as such do not lead you to convert; they may make you more likely to listen, and anything that makes you more likely to listen, including the work of ethnography, is actually what makes you susceptible."[96]

Harding distinguished three stages in getting saved among fundamental Baptists: (1) giving up and disavowing disbelief; (2) making born-again belief the "centering principle of your identity, your personal and public life, your view of human nature and history"; and finally (3) joining a particular narrative tradition "to which you willingly submit your past, present, and future *as a speaker*."[97] Her final conclusion was: "Listening to the gospel enables you to experience belief, as it were, vicariously. But generative belief, belief that indisputably transfigures you and your reality, belief that becomes you, comes only through speech. Among fundamentalist Baptists, speaking is believing."[98] Harding's argument concerning the significant role of language and discourse in conversion was strong, but it is limited to evangelical conversion and still cannot adequately explain why witnessing is only successful with some people and not with others.

US anthropologist Peter Stromberg looked more at the *function* of the conversion discourse. He aimed to demonstrate that conversion language "functions as a resource, which in enabling believers to come to terms with enduring problems of meaning in their lives, brings about the sense of having been transformed."[99] Stromberg's analysis tended toward psychology by echoing Freud in assuming that "an adherent finds meaning in ideological language because it allows him or her to communicate intentions that are in other contexts denied, meaningless. That is, the ideological language [of conversion] provides the resources to integrate denied intentions into a coherent set of intentions, an identity."[100] One informant expressed ambiguity over resisting or giving in to his father's authority; his other informant felt guilty over letting her parents down. Stromberg concluded that "change does not occur once and for all, but rather must be constantly recreated. Conflicts do not disappear subsequent to conversion, but rather come to be approached in a manner that makes their ongoing resolution possible."[101] This raised the danger of reducing conversion to a psychological coping mechanism.

US anthropologist Rita Smith Kipp combined structural and actor-oriented approaches in her study of the Karo, a Batak group in highland Sumatra. Kipp noted that their conversions after the anti-communist bloodbath of 1965 "appear to have been motivated by political pressures, ethnic pride, or the quest for education."[102] By using a practice approach, Kipp showed how "new structures (here an indigenous church) emerge as a consequence of individual agency (expedient conversions) and how these new structures then shape new forms of experience (in this case, religious life)."[103] This was achieved through the conversion narrative, the public declaration of a new identity, which was constantly modified over time as individual agency interacted with structural conditions.

The last anthropologist to develop a discourse-based model of conversion is Spanish anthropologist Manuela Cantón Delgado (1998). She defined conversion as "the global and radical acquisition of a new way of life, drastically separated from the earlier form of existence."[104] The conversion narrative was standardized in the specific ritual context of the religious group. It had three functions in public: socializing, didactic, and proselytizing.[105] Witnessing involved socializing people in the language and culture of evangelical Protestants, teaching this language and culture to others, and using this to try to convert them. Converts learned to organize their conversion testimony according to a "native sequential order" made up of five elements: self-presentation, description of the old Catholic life, dramatic events leading up to conversion and sustaining the new faith, description of the new evangelical life, and attacks from the devil: the life of the convert was constantly renewed by trials and tribulations.[106]

In Cantón's actor-oriented model, the main reasons for conversion are personal: a dissatisfaction with Catholicism, feelings of crisis and great personal suffering (economic, social, and family problems, often connected to alcoholism), and a need for spirituality and personal control. A special event—a serious illness, a fierce hangover—serves as a catalyst for conversion, which always constitutes a radical transformation in the believer's perspective. Neo-Pentecostal churches were successful in Guatemala in the 1990s because they offered empowerment and a strict religious ethic that could transform people's lives. But there were interesting differences based on social class. Poorer believers tended to see the problems in their lives and in Guatemala as trials by God and looked to millennial solutions (the Second Coming of Christ). By contrast, middle-class believers stressed the hand of the devil in personal and national problems. This view encouraged political participation and a more interventionist outlook on the secular world, which fitted nicely with the brief (and failed) presidency of neo-Pentecostal President Jorge Serrano.[107]

CONTINUOUS CONVERSION IN
PENTECOSTALISM

Australian anthropologist Diane Austin-Broos has studied Jamaican Pentecostalism since the early 1970s, noting that they created an egalitarian *communitas* (in Victor Turner's sense) through the liturgical order of Sunday worship service.[108] Austin-Broos[109] concluded that Pentecostalism in Jamaica appealed especially to three groups: (1) religiously committed men and women who did not qualify to become pastors; (2) poor farmers in isolated villages who wanted to show their superior Christian status to wealthier people in mainstream churches; (3) women affected by "displacement and individuation"[110] who found in Pentecostalism a religion that taught men to marry their partners.

Austin-Broos later reflected on how conversion "shapes aspirations and reorients social life."[111] She suggested seeing conversion as a passage rather than as syncretism or a break with the past. Converts express "new forms of relatedness"; conversion is "a type of passage that negotiates a place in the world. . . . It involves a process of continual embedding in forms of social practice and belief, in ritual dispositions and somatic experience."[112] Like Hefner, Austin-Broos singled out the unique characteristics of the world religions: "The world religions do assimilate, but they also create new diversity, in which numerous passages are possible."[113] The interaction between religious conversion and the functioning of the nation state is crucial to understanding religious change worldwide.

British anthropologist Simon Coleman conducted fieldwork in a Swedish Pentecostal Faith ministry, characterized by the prosperity gospel ("health-and-wealth"). Coleman argued for a broader definition of conversion, which he named *continuous conversion*: "[Continuous conversion] can imply that movement of the self toward charismatic conviction is an ongoing process; . . . it indicates a blurring of the boundaries of identity between religious affiliations; and it suggests that analysis of conversion practices should focus not only on the potential neophyte, but also on broader sets of social relations and ideological representations that include and influence the evangelizing believer."[114] Coleman noted that most Uppsala members were already active Christians before they joined, with most of them coming from other Pentecostal churches or from the Lutheran state church.[115]

Coleman concluded that conversion was "a set of ritualized practices that are key to Swedish charismatic identity on personal and collective levels. . . . My argument is that conversion as a multivalent idea and as a quality of action permeates the charismatic life, and under the right conditions it can help sustain that life, whether outsiders are persuaded to enter the body of Christ or not."[116] Through participation in the group, members were involved in a huge number of "conversionist" activities: evangelization, rituals, Bible courses, excursions, and so on. Coleman also made an interesting link between local conversion and feeling part of a global Christian movement.[117] He saw the conversion discourse and its associated practices in the worldwide prosperity gospel ministries as a revitalization mechanism in Pentecostalism and mainstream Protestantism in general.

In his study of Sicilian Pentecostals, Italian American anthropologist Salvatore Cucchiari considered conversion a creative "transformation of the self, marked by new awareness, new social being, and a new relationship to the sacred." Conversion is a continuous process of maturation or "spiritual insight."[118] "Once the conversion process stops, salvation is lost. But the continual making and remaking of the conversion experience can never be just an individual affair; it must be a collective one as well. The main vehicle and expression of collective conversion is the *culto*, or worship service, which in most Sicilian Pentecostal communities is held three times a week; the centerpiece of the *culto* is the preaching of the Word."[119] The final essential aspect of Sicilian Pentecostalism was "exorcistic healing" to drive out the demons of illness and immorality. The conversion process was under constant attack from demons, which made people fall back into their pre-conversion sins.

The interdisciplinary conversion career approach provides another way of looking at continuous conversion. Droogers, Gooren, and Houtepen defined the *conversion career* as "the member's passage, within his or her social and cultural context, through levels, types, and phases of church participation."[120] An essential part consists of a typology of religious activity. *Pre-affiliation* describes the worldview and social context of potential members of a group. *Affiliation* refers to formal church membership, which is not necessarily a central aspect of one's identity. *Conversion*, used here in the limited sense, refers to a (radical) personal change of worldview and identity. *Confession* is core membership, describing a high level of participation inside the new religious group and a strong missionary attitude toward nonmembers. Finally, *disaffiliation* refers to a lack of involvement in an organized religious group.[121]

The conversion career approach also distinguishes five main groups of factors influencing conversion: individual factors, social factors, institutional factors (related to the religious organization), cultural factors (including political and economic factors), and contingency factors. Contingency factors involve random meetings with missionaries, acutely felt crises, and other contingencies that bring individuals into the orbit of religious groups. Most converts call this Providence or divine intervention, which brings us to the anthropology of Christianity.

CONVERSION IN THE ANTHROPOLOGY OF CHRISTIANITY

US anthropologist Joel Robbins noted in 2003 that there exists no anthropology of Christianity similar to the anthropology of Islam, which he describes as "a self-conscious, comparative project...grappling with a common set of questions."[122]

He identified various cultural and theoretical reasons for this, including "the current anthropological suspicion of all comparative projects."[123]

The main obstacle to the anthropology of Christianity that Robbins identified is also theoretical: "cultural anthropology has generally been a science of continuity. Cultural anthropologists have for the most part either argued or implied that the things they study—symbols, meanings, logics, structures, power dynamics—have a fundamental and enduring quality and are not readily subject to change."[124] However, "most forms of Christianity provide their adherents some forms of disjunctive narrative by virtue of plotting conversion as a decisive break with a past self."[125] Hence, Christians are conditioned by their faith to aim for radical personal change. Anthropologists, using the tools of a science of continuity, are ill-equipped to understand this process. They tend to argue that "converts' fundamental ways of looking at the world have not really changed" and that "people actually convert for everyday, pragmatic reasons—in search of things like money and power."[126]

Robbins severely criticized Jean and John Comaroff (1991) for "sidelining" Christianity, and he analyzed how they achieved this. He listed all references to the Tswana ignoring, not fully understanding, resisting, or rejecting Christianity.[127] Women and people with marginal positions in Tswana society did engage deeply with Christianity, he argues, but "these people and their explorations never occupy the center of the Comaroffs' attention, and their engagement with the logic of Christianity is never described in detail."[128] The Comaroffs took their reasoning to its extreme by asserting that conversion "is not a significant analytic category in its own right."[129]

Robbins distinguished two main approaches used in anthropology to explain conversion. The *utilitarian* approach is connected to anthropology as the science of continuity. It "focuses on the worldly advantages, in terms of material goods, position, power, prestige, and so forth, that accrue to those who convert."[130] The *intellectualist* approach "argues that converts are attracted to the new religion because it renders meaningful new situations that defy the sense-making capacities of their traditional ways of understanding the world."[131] Robbins credited Horton as the founder of this approach, which argues that "conversion allows people to comprehend and live meaningfully in a changed world."[132] Robbins developed a two-stage model of religious conversion, arguing that the utilitarian approach better explains peoples' initial contacts with Christianity, while the intellectualist approach better analyzes how people gradually learn more about Christianity and become involved in its organizations.

Robbins's own ethnography analyzed why the Urapmin, a group of 390 people living in the western mountains of Papua New Guinea, collectively converted to Christianity following a revival in 1977.[133] In the early 1960s, Australian Baptist missionaries and their schools trained the first Urapmin leaders and pastors.[134] These young men were the first generation that was never brutally initiated into the traditional religion by the community's elders. The first stage of conversion for the Urapmin ended in the late 1960s, when Christian meanings themselves, "rather than ones drawn from traditional culture, begin to provide the motive for conversion."[135]

The revival of 1977 marked the successful second phase of conversion among the Urapmin, which included the building up of local church structures. Robbins noted that "Spirit possession was a new practice for the Urapmin in 1977, for they had no indigenous tradition of it."[136] Following the classic Pentecostal path, the Urapmin revival included miraculous healings, speaking in tongues, dreams, visions, and prophesying.

The revival's message was clear: the Urapmin were to abandon their old ancestral religion completely. They did exactly that, dismantling the system of sacred houses, using healing services to drive out the traditional territorial spirits that made people sick and removing (with great caution) the old bones of the ancestors to locations outside of the villages. After some time, the Urapmin noticed that they had more pigs and better harvests from their gardens. This new prosperity confirmed to them the rightness of their actions, and they started constructing the first church building.[137] Robbins did not offer details, but gradually more and more people became active Christians. After abandoning the bones of their ancestors for several years in forest caves, the Urapmin felt "there was no turning back from Christianity."[138]

Like Robbins, British anthropologist Fenella Cannell also wanted anthropologists to be open toward understanding Christianity in their ethnographies and be aware of their biases. She suggested that Christianity has functioned in some ways as "the repressed" of anthropology over the period of the formation of the discipline.[139] Cannell noted how "Christianity was the last major area of religious activity to be explored in ethnographic writing."[140] Early anthropology ignored Christianity, which was primarily identified with colonial administrations and the forced imposition of modernity.[141]

Cannell analyzed a connection similar to the one that Robbins established between Christianity and time, but her conclusion is puzzling: "The dominant Christian ideas of personal conversion depend on a break in time. Conversion changes the individual, and however much he might backslide, the event itself cannot be undone."[142] Although her endnote nuanced this slightly, it offered no sources to back up her claim. I would argue, however, that it is exactly the *precariousness* of conversion—the need for continuous conversion, the struggle with Satan, and the risk of backsliding into sin—that makes conversion such a pertinent category for both believers and anthropologists.

Conclusion: Escaping from the Past into the Future

This chapter supports the conclusion that anthropologists have struggled since the founding of the discipline to come to terms with religious conversion, but they are now improving quickly. The structural-functionalism paradigm guided anthropologists toward understanding the function of religion in keeping non-Western societies together. This was one of the main causes of the dominance of "continuity thinking" in anthropology.[143] It is also relevant that most anthropologists in the United States and

(Western) Europe have a secular worldview and hence are less inclined to study religious conversion.[144]

Most pre-globalization anthropologists had wanted to study non-Western religions without the Christian influences introduced by missionaries. Their uncomfortable relationship with Christian missionaries began in the nineteenth century.[145] Currently, some anthropologists in parts of the world like Papua New Guinea are still searching for the last Papua peoples who are as yet untouched by Catholic or Pentecostal missionaries.[146]

Talal Asad and Michael Lambek argued that anthropologists were heavily influenced by the Christian concepts of religion, which are dominant in Western societies. The most abstract theories of conversion, like Horton's, were Eurocentric because they projected Western notions of rationality onto non-Western tradition religions. Most approaches failed to properly theorize the indigenous understandings of religious change and conversion. Most were reductionist in that they ignored specific religious factors in conversion. And just like sociologists and psychologists, anthropologists analyzed the *consequences* of conversion more than the *causes*.[147]

Looking back at roughly fifty years of anthropological theorizing on religious change and conversion, I see three main analytical categories. First, there are two models that only claim a *limited applicability*: Berkhofer described the historical acculturation sequences of Native American groups and Harding explored witnessing as a conversion method in the case of evangelical Protestants. They made no claims for their models of a general worldwide applicability.

Second, at least four approaches aimed to develop *universal models* of conversion, although they rarely conceptualized how a person or group moved from one stage to the next. Tippett's group model of conversion and Wallace's concept of revitalization movements aimed to explain how entire groups converted. Tippett's model went from awareness to decision to incorporation to maturation, recognizing that at each stage the conversion could fail. Wallace aimed to show how revitalization movements could change cultures in a relatively short period of time. His emphasis on individual stress proved to be a recurring theme in the anthropology of conversion.[148] Wallace's six stages in the development of the revitalization movement were partly mirrored and partly expanded in Gerlach and Hine's group conversion model. But they added to the group model an individual model of conversion, stressing the constant interaction and feedback between individual concerns and actions and group structuring and reinforcement. Individual needs are focused and (re-)educated by the group, until the individual surrenders and makes a public testimony. The religious group then supports subsequent cognitive and behavioral changes. Religious content was absent in Gerlach and Hine's model but formed the basis for Kraft, who stressed the initial faith commitment to God and God's interaction with human beings in conversion. Kraft was also the first to stress conversion as a lifelong process of maturation, which required a Christian community to guide the convert into culturally relevant expressions of Christianity.

Third, almost all anthropological approaches to religious change used an implicit or explicit *modernity paradigm*. Horton, Falla, Hefner, and Robbins are the main representatives of this approach. Modernity, usually evaluated critically by the anthropologists, also forms the heart of the arguments in Wallace, Berkhofer, Austin-Broos, Meyer, Marshall-Fratani, Cannell, van der Veer, and all anthropologists studying Protestantism in Guatemala and Mexico. For all of their criticisms of modernity, most anthropologists have been unable to escape from its gravitational pull. Another challenge for the future is that of developing comparative approaches to conversion to a host of religions that include the indigenous understandings of conversion and exploring their interactions with globalization processes.

When studying conversion, anthropologists should capitalize on the main strengths of their discipline: their long-term perspective, their ethnographic approach, their theoretical flexibility,[149] and their focus on the cultural context; these will all aid in understanding conversion cross-culturally. This chapter has documented the contributions of anthropologists to analyzing the cultural contexts underlying conversion, for instance by paying attention to traditional religions, revitalization movements, multiple modernities, and the shift from Catholicism to Protestantism in Latin America. The conversion career approach is also useful in analyzing the cultural factor in conversion. In most parts of the world, religious organizations develop a "culture politics" to compete for members, and this typically includes a highly critical view of the mainstream culture, society, politics, and religions. Conversion may then become a vehicle for first cultural critique and later perhaps cultural change, not unlike a revitalization movement.[150]

The conversion career approach offers a systematic heuristic tool for understanding conversion processes all over the world.[151] It synthesizes a century of approaches to conversion in the social sciences and moves beyond simple mono-causal explanations. It combines conversion (i.e., religious demand) with the supply of religious organizations competing for members on the religious market. Using five different levels of religious participation, the comparative conversion career approach makes it possible to critically review and situate both stories of conversion and stories of disillusionment and backsliding.

Since conversion remains a topic that is both controversial and complex, it is very important for anthropologists and other scholars of religion to keep the following in mind in future research. First, delineate in detail the various levels of religious participation they utilize in their studies of religion. Second, systematize the variables impacting the various levels of conversion and disaffiliation. Third, recognize the importance of subjective religious experience in the conversion process. Fourth, systematically gauge the influence of gender on conversion for both male and female informants. Fifth, develop an even spread of informants from all levels of religious activity and all phases of the life cycle (adolescents, married couples, middle-aged people, and seniors). Sixth, endeavor to collect the most complete data possible at various locations in order to fill in the full comparative model of the conversion career.

NOTES

1. My sincere thanks to Peter Bertocci, James Dow, André Droogers, Charles E. Farhadian, Lewis Rambo, Suzanne Spencer-Wood, and Peter Versteeg for their extensive comments that helped to substantially improve this chapter.

2. Anthony F. C. Wallace, "Revitalization Movements," *American Anthropologist* 58, no. 2 (1956): 265.

3. Ibid., 266.

4. Ibid., 271.

5. Anthony F. C. Wallace, "Handsome Lake and the Great Revival in the West," *American Quarterly* 4, no. 2 (1952): 159.

6. Anthony F. C. Wallace, *The Death and Rebirth of the Seneca* (New York: Knopf, 1970), 301–302.

7. This paragraph is based on Wallace, who noted that Lewis Henry Morgan used the notes of the transcription for his ethnography *League of the Ho-De-No-Sau-Nee or Iroquois* (1851). Wallace, *Death and Rebirth of the Seneca*, 330–337.

8. Robert F. Berkhofer, Jr., "Protestants, Pagans, and Sequences among the North American Indians, 1760–1860," *Ethnohistory* 10, no. 3 (1963): 207–208.

9. Ibid., 209–210. The loss of Indian political autonomy in New York State occurred in the 1790s.

10. Ibid., 211.

11. Luther P. Gerlach and Virginia H. Hine, *People, Power, Change: Movements of Social Transformation* (Indianapolis: Bobbs-Merrill, 1970), 102–109.

12. Ibid., 110–137.

13. Ibid., 114.

14. Ibid., 119–135.

15. Ibid.

16. Ibid., 217–218. See also Luther P. Gerlach and Virginia H. Hine, "Five Factors Crucial to the Growth and Spread of a Modern Religious Movement," *Journal for the Scientific Study of Religion* 7, no. 1 (1968): 23–40; Gerlach and Hine, *People, Power, Change*, 199–201.

17. Gerlach and Hine *People, Power, Change*, 219–228. Separately, Gerlach and Hine also conducted short fieldwork visits to Haiti, Colombia, Mexico, and Jamaica.

18. One wonders why Gerlach and Hine's *People, Power, Change* has not inspired follow-up research. Perhaps the institutional focus of their model raised their appeal to sociologists while lowering it among anthropologists. They are mentioned in sociology of religion textbooks like Meredith McGuire's *Religion: The Social Context* (Belmont, CA: Wadsworth, 2002), but not in anthropology of religion textbooks like Richley Crapo's *Anthropology of Religion* (Boston: McGraw-Hill, 2003) or Michael Lambek's *A Reader in the Anthropology of Religion* (Malden, MA: Blackwell, 2002).

19. Robin Horton, "African Conversion," *Africa* 41, no. 2 (1971): 101 n. 1.

20. Ibid., 102.

21. Ibid., 104. Horton's thought experiments did not provide evidence for his claim that African traditional religions would have made the Supreme Being central even without the influence of Christianity or Islam. See Humphrey J. Fisher, "Conversion Reconsidered: Some Historical Aspects of Religious Conversion in Black Africa," *Africa* 43, no. 1 (1973): 29–30; Emefie Ikenga-Metuh, "The Shattered Microcosm: A Critical Survey of Explanations of Conversion in Africa," in *Religion, Development, and African Identity*, ed. Kirsten Holst Petersen (Uppsala: Scandinavian Institute of African Studies, 1987), 15–16.

22. Horton, "African Conversion," 104.

23. Fisher, "Conversion Reconsidered," 31 ff.

24. Ibid. The reference to adhesion is from Arthur Darby Nock, *Conversion: The Old and the New in Religion from Alexander the Great to Augustine of Hippo* (Oxford: Oxford University Press, 1969), 5–7.

25. Robin Horton, "On the Rationality of Conversion: Part II," *Africa* 45, no. 4 (1975): 382–387.
26. Ibid., 389–390.
27. Robert W. Hefner, "Introduction," in *Conversion to Christianity: Historical and Anthropological Perspectives on a Great Transformation*, ed. Robert W. Hefner (Berkeley and Los Angeles: University of California Press, 1993), 20.
28. Ibid., 22.
29. Ibid., 22–24.
30. Ibid., 7, citing Max Weber, *The Sociology of Religion* (Boston: Beacon, 1956) and Robert Bendix, *Max Weber: An Intellectual Portrait* (New York: Anchor, 1962), 87 ff. On religious rationalization, see also Hefner, "Introduction."
31. Hefner, "Introduction," 17.
32. Ibid., 32.
33. The individualism argument works for the Catholic Charismatic Renewal and Catholic Action, which stress individual conversion, but not for group-oriented popular Catholicism, liberation theology, or base communities.
34. Peter Wood, "Afterword: Boundaries and Horizons," in *Conversion to Christianity: Historical and Anthropological Perspectives on a Great Transformation*, ed. Robert W. Hefner (Berkeley and Los Angeles: University of California Press, 1993), 309, 319. On conversion to Christianity in New Guinea, see also Joel Robbins, *Becoming Sinners: Christianity and Moral Torment in a Papua New Guinea Society* (Berkeley and Los Angeles: University of California Press, 2004) and the section on Robbins in the main text.
35. Peter van der Veer, "Conversion and Coercion: The Politics of Sincerity and Authenticity," in *Cultures of Conversions*, ed. Wout J. van Bekkum, Jan N. Bremmer, and Arie Molendijk (Leuven, Belgium: Peeters, 2006), 3; see also S. N. Eisenstadt, "Multiple Modernities," *Daedalus* 129, no. 1 (2000): 1–29.
36. "Both Catholic and Protestant missionaries carry this new conception of the self, of bourgeois domesticity, of citizenship to the rest of the world." Peter van der Veer, "Introduction," in *Conversion to Modernities: The Globalization of Christianity*, ed. Peter van der Veer (New York: Routledge, 1996), 9.
37. Van der Veer, "Conversion and Coercion," 11.
38. Ibid. On agency and sincerity in conversion, compare Talal Asad, "Comments on Conversion," in *Conversion to Modernities: The Globalization of Christianity*, ed. Peter van der Veer (New York: Routledge, 1996), 263–273.
39. Van der Veer, "Conversion and Coercion," 11.
40. Birgit Meyer, *Translating the Devil: Religion and Modernity among the Ewe in Ghana* (Edinburgh: Edinburgh University Press, 1999), 9.
41. Ibid., 11.
42. Ibid., 109.
43. Ibid., 111.
44. Ibid., 139.
45. Ibid., 214.
46. Ibid., 215.
47. Ibid., 216.
48. Birgit Meyer, "'Make a Complete Break with the Past': Memory and Post-Colonial Modernity in Ghanaian Pentecostalist Discourse," *Journal of Religion in Africa* 28, no. 3 (1998): 317.

49. Ruth Marshall-Fratani, "Mediating the Global and Local in Nigerian Pentecostalism," in *Between Babel and Pentecost: Transnational Pentecostalism in Africa and Latin America*, ed. André Corten and Ruth Marshall-Fratani (London: Hurst, 2001), 86.

50. Ibid., 89.

51. Charles Gibson, *The Aztecs under Spanish Rule: A History of Indians in the Valley of Mexico, 1519–1810* (Stanford, CA: Stanford University Press, 1964), 98; J. Jorge Klor de Alva, "Aztec Spirituality and Nahuatized Christianity," in *South and Meso-American Native Spirituality*, ed. Gary H. Gossen (New York: Crossroad, 1993), 173–197; Robert M. Carmack, Janine L. Gasco, and Gary H. Gossen. *The Legacy of Mesoamerica: History and Culture of a Native American Civilization* (Upper Saddle River, NJ: Pearson/Prentice Hall, 2007), 182 ff.

52. See Adriaan C. van Oss, *Catholic Colonialism: A Parish History of Guatemala, 1524–1821* (Cambridge: Cambridge University Press, 1986), quoted in John D. Early, *The Maya and Catholicism: An Encounter of Worldviews* (Gainesville: University Press of Florida, 2006), 144–145.

53. Gibson, *The Aztecs under Spanish Rule*, 112; Klor de Alva, "Aztec Spirituality," 174; Early, *The Maya and Catholicism*, 173–174.

54. Christopher Vecsey, *On the Padres' Trail* (Notre Dame, IN: University of Notre Dame Press, 1996), 29–30.

55. Hence, some scholars argue that the Indians in Spanish colonial Latin America did not really *convert*, in the sense of embracing a new worldview and social identity (cf. Carmack, Gasco, and Gossen, *The Legacy of Mesoamerica*, 193); they merely changed their religious *affiliation* (Henri Gooren, *Religious Conversion and Disaffiliation: Tracing Patterns of Change in Faith Practices* [New York: Palgrave-Macmillan, 2010]) or *adhesion* (Nock, *Conversion*, 4–5, 7).

56. Gibson, *The Aztecs under Spanish Rule*, 117.

57. Western missionaries had a similar view of African traditional religions in the nineteenth century that African Pentecostals have continued until today, exorcising African spirits and deities (see Meyer, *Translating the Devil*, and in main text).

58. Gibson, *The Aztecs under Spanish Rule*, 127 ff.; Ruben E. Reina, *The Law of the Saints: A Pokomam Pueblo and Its Community Culture* (Indianapolis: Bobbs-Merrill, 1966); Ricardo Falla, *Quiché Rebelde: Religious Conversion, Politics, and Ethnic Identity in Guatemala* (Austin: University of Texas Press, [1978] 2001).

59. Falla, *Quiché Rebelde*.

60. Ibid., 253.

61. Ibid., 253–256.

62. Ibid., 164–167, 256–259.

63. Geographer Sheldon Annis concluded ten years later that the indigenous Protestants in San Antonio Aguascalientes, also located in the Guatemalan highlands, were predominantly traders and petty capitalists. Sheldon Annis, *God and Production in a Guatemalan Town* (Austin: University of Texas Press, 1987).

64. Manning Nash, *Machine Age Maya: The Industrialization of a Guatemalan Community* (Chicago: University of Chicago Press, 1967), 85. Redfield's study of Chan Kom in Yucatan, "a village that chose progress," emphasized the role of missionaries and kinship-based divisions in the spread of Protestantism. Chan Kom villagers were reportedly already practical, prudent, sober, honest, and obedient before converting. Robert Redfield, *A Village That Chose Progress: Chan Kom Revisited* (Chicago: University of Chicago Press, 1950), 156 ff.

65. June Nash, "Protestantism in an Indian Village in the Western Highlands of Guatemala," *Alpha Kappa Deltan* 30 (1960): 49–53; Benson Saler, "Religious Conversion and Self-Aggrandizement: A Guatemalan Case," *Practical Anthropology* 13 (1965): 107–114; Ruben E. Reina and Norman B. Schwartz, "The Structural Context of Religious Conversion in El Petén, Guatemala: Status, Community, and Multicommunity," *American Ethnologist* 9, no. 1 (1974): 157–191. Reina stressed political factors in conversion; Protestants in Chinautla supported the agrarian and literacy reforms of the Arbenz government in 1952 and were persecuted by local conservatives after the CIA-sponsored coup by Colonel Castillas Armas that disposed of Arbenz in 1954. The Chinautla *cofradías* were still influential in the 1960s. Reina, *The Law of the Saints*, 93–94.

66. Emilio Willems, *Followers of the New Faith: Culture Change and the Rise of Protestantism in Brazil and Chile* (Nashville, TN: Vanderbilt University Press, 1967).

67. Ibid., 78–80, 79, 90–92.

68. Ibid., 26–28, 91, 94–99.

69. For example, see John Lofland and Rodney Stark, "Becoming a World-Saver: A Theory of Conversion to a Deviant Perspective," *American Sociological Review* 30, no. 6 (1965): 862–875.

70. James W. Dow, "The Theology of Change: Evangelical Protestantism and the Collapse of Native Religion in a Peasant Area of Mexico," in *Explorations in Anthropology and Theology*, ed. Frank A. Salamone and Walter Randolph Adams (Lanham, MD: University Press of America, 1997), 119.

71. Dow, "The Theology of Change," 119–121.

72. Mary O'Connor, "Two Kinds of Religious Movements among the Mayo Indians of Sonora, Mexico," *Journal for the Scientific Study of Religion* 18, no. 3 (1979): 260–268; Dow, "The Theology of Change"; James W. Dow, "Protestantism in Mesoamerica: The Old within the New," in *Holy Saints and Fiery Preachers: The Anthropology of Protestantism in Mexico and Central America*, ed. James W. Dow and Alan R. Sandstrom (Westport, CT: Praeger, 2001), 1–23.

73. J. Nash, "Protestantism in an Indian Village"; Reina and Schwartz, "The Structural Context of Religious Conversion"; James D. Sexton, "Protestantism and Modernization in Two Guatemalan Towns," *American Ethnologist* 5, no. 2 (1978): 280–302; Falla, *Quiché Rebelde*; Annis, *God and Production*.

74. Blanca Muratorio, "Protestantism and Capitalism Revisited in the Rural Highlands of Ecuador," *Journal of Peasant Studies* 8, no. 1 (1980): 37–60.

75. Sexton, "Protestantism and Modernization," 297.

76. Ibid., 281.

77. Ibid., 297. O'Connor on the Mayo in Mexico and Lewellen for the Aymara in Peru came to similar conclusions on the connection between converting to Protestantism and modernization. O'Connor, "Two Kinds of Religious Movements"; Ted Lewellen, "Deviant Religion and Cultural Evolution," *Journal for the Scientific Study of Religion* 18, no. 3 (1979): 243–251.

78. Alan R. Tippett, "Conversion as a Dynamic Process in Christian Mission," *Missiology* 5, no. 2 (1977): 206.

79. Ibid., 211.

80. Ibid., 219–220.

81. Charles H. Kraft, *Christianity in Culture: A Study in Dynamic Biblical Theologizing in Cross-Cultural Perspective* (Maryknoll, NY: Orbis, 1979), 403.

82. Ibid., 331–332.

83. See also the section on Baptism in the Holy Spirit in Gerlach and Hine, *Five Factors,* 25–26.

84. Kraft, *Christianity in Culture,* 338.

85. Ibid., 341–343. Kraft stated in chapters 18 and beyond that cultures always change and that "God desires to participate with human beings in guiding culture change" (p. 345).

86. Ibid., 348–349. The worldview concept is analyzed extensively in Paul G. Hiebert, *Transforming Worldviews: An Anthropological Understanding of How People Change* (Grand Rapids, MI: Baker Academic, 2008), ch. 1.

87. Hiebert, *Transforming Worldviews,* 195.

88. Ibid., 11–12.

89. Ibid., 309.

90. Ibid., 316; quote is from figure 11.1.

91. Hiebert was open to diversity in Christianity; hence, he preferred the term "biblical."

92. Ibid., 319–324. Hiebert mentioned rituals of *transformation* (baptism, evangelistic crusades, retreats, and pilgrimages) and rituals of *intensification,* like Sunday worship services, Christmas, and Easter.

93. Susan F. Harding, "Convicted by the Holy Spirit: The Rhetoric of Fundamental Baptist Conversion," *American Ethnologist* 14, no. 1 (1987): 169.

94. Harding, "Convicted by the Holy Spirit," 169. The book version changed the word "invaded" into "inhabited." Susan F. Harding, *The Book of Jerry Falwell: Fundamentalist Language and Politics* (Princeton: Princeton University Press, 2000), 33.

95. Harding, "Convicted by the Holy Spirit," 178.

96. Ibid., 178.

97. Ibid., 179 (emphasis in original).

98. Ibid., 179.

99. Peter G. Stromberg, "Ideological Language in the Transformation of Identity," *American Anthropologist* 92, no. 1 (1990): 43.

100. Ibid., 53.

101. Ibid., 43.

102. Rita Smith Kipp, "Conversion by Affiliation: The History of the Karo Batak Protestant Church," *American Ethnologist* 22, no. 4 (1995): 868.

103. Ibid., 872.

104. Manuela Cantón Delgado, *Bautizados en fuego: Protestantes, discursos de conversión y política en Guatemala (1989–1993)* (Antigua, Guatemala: CIRMA, 1998), 130. This is my translation of "la adquisición global y radical de una nueva manera de vivir, drásticamente separada de la anterior forma de existencia."

105. Ibid., 134.

106. Ibid., 144–145.

107. Ibid., 272–274.

108. Diane J. Austin, "Born Again…and Again and Again: Communitas and Social Change among Jamaican Pentecostalists," *Journal of Anthropological Research* 37, no. 3 (1981): 226–246.

109. Diane J. Austin-Broos, *Jamaica Genesis: Religion and the Politics of Moral Orders* (Chicago: University of Chicago Press, 1997), 201–203.

110. Ibid., 203.

111. Diane J. Austin-Broos, "The Anthropology of Conversion: An Introduction," in *The Anthropology of Religious Conversion,* ed. Andrew Buckser and Stephen D. Glazier (Lanham, MD: Rowman and Littlefield, 2003), 1.

112. Ibid., 2.
113. Ibid., 5.
114. Simon Coleman, "Continuous Conversion? The Rhetoric, Practice, and Rhetorical Practice of Charismatic Protestant Conversion," in *The Anthropology of Religious Conversion*, ed. Andrew Buckser and Stephen D. Glazier (Lanham, MD: Rowman and Littlefield, 2003), 15–27.
115. Ibid., 19.
116. Ibid., 18.
117. Austin-Broos made the same observation for Jamaican Pentecostals with transnational, usually US, ties. Austin-Broos, *Jamaica Genesis*, 234, 236, 242.
118. Salvatore Cucchiari, "'Adapted for Heaven': Conversion and Culture in Western Sicily," *American Ethnologist* 15, no. 3 (1988): 418.
119. Ibid., 423.
120. André Droogers, Henri Gooren, and Anton Houtepen, "Conversion Careers and Culture Politics in Pentecostalism: A Comparative Study in Four Continents," Proposal submitted to the thematic program "The Future of the Religious Past" of the Netherlands Organization for Scientific Research (NWO), The Hague, 2003, 5–6; see also Gooren, *Religious Conversion and Disaffiliation*. Our use of conversion career is somewhat different from that of James Richardson, who coined the term. James T. Richardson, ed., *Conversion Careers: In and Out of the New Religions* (Beverly Hills, CA: SAGE, 1978).
121. Gooren, *Religious Conversion and Disaffiliation*, ch. 2. I return to the conversion career approach in the conclusion.
122. Joel Robbins, "What Is a Christian? Notes toward an Anthropology of Christianity," *Religion* 33 (2003): 191.
123. Ibid., 193.
124. Joel Robbins, "On the Paradoxes of Global Pentecostalism and the Perils of Continuity Thinking," *Religion* 33 (2003): 221.
125. Ibid., 224.
126. Joel Robbins, "Continuity Thinking and the Problem of Christian Culture," *Current Anthropology* 48, no. 1 (2007): 12.
127. Ibid., 7.
128. Ibid., 8.
129. Jean Comaroff and John Comaroff, *Of Revelation and Revolution: Christianity, Colonialism, and Consciousness in South Africa*, Vol. 1 (Chicago: University of Chicago Press, 1991), 250.
130. Robbins, *Becoming Sinners*, 85.
131. Ibid.
132. Ibid., 86.
133. Ibid., 1.
134. Ibid., 102–121.
135. Ibid., 115.
136. Ibid., 131.
137. Ibid., 147–151.
138. Ibid., 150.
139. Fenella Cannell, "The Anthropology of Christianity," in *The Anthropology of Christianity*, ed. Fenella Cannell (Durham, NC: Duke University Press, 2006), 4.
140. Ibid., 8.
141. Ibid., 12.

142. Ibid., 38.
143. See Robbins, "What Is a Christian?"; Robbins, "Continuity Thinking."
144. Charles Stewart, "Secularism as an Impediment to Anthropological Research," *Social Anthropology* 9, no. 3 (2001): 323. Claude E. Stipe, "Anthropologists versus Missionaries: The Influence of Presuppositions," *Current Anthropology* 21, no. 2 (1980): 167. Stipe also reported that "the majority of anthropologists are either atheistic or agnostic," based on "having been involved in the discipline for over 25 years" (p. 178). Based on my personal impressions from twenty years of experience as an anthropologist, this situation has not changed.
145. Sjaak van der Geest, "Missionaries," in *Encyclopedia of Cultural Anthropology*, ed. David Levinson and Melvin Ember (New York: Holt, 1996), 797–801; Stipe, "Anthropologists versus Missionaries"; Salamone and Adams, *Explorations in Anthropology and Theology*. Roger Keesing commented: "Anthropologists and missionaries have, at least in stereotype, been at odds with one another for many decades. The caricatured missionary is a strait-laced, repressed, and narrow-minded Bible thumper trying to get native women to cover their bosoms decently; the anthropologist is a bearded degenerate given to taking his clothes off and sampling wild rites." Roger M. Keesing, *Cultural Anthropology: A Contemporary Perspective*, 2nd ed. (New York: Holt, Rinehart, and Winston, 1981), 402.
146. Joel Robbins, personal communication, March 27, 2008. See also van der Veer, "Introduction," 9; Robbins, "Continuity Thinking," 6, 6 n. 3.
147. Gooren, *Religious Conversion and Disaffiliation*.
148. The psychology of conversion has James as a precursor of the anthropological emphasis on individual stress; the sociology of conversion has the classic model of Lofland and Stark. William James, *The Varieties of Religious Experience: A Study in Human Nature* (New York: New American Library, 1958); Lofland and Stark, "Becoming a World-Saver."
149. Lewis R. Rambo, "Anthropology and the Study of Conversion," in *The Anthropology of Religious Conversion*, ed. Andrew Buckser and Stephen D. Glazier (Lanham, MD: Rowman and Littlefield, 2003), 213.
150. Gooren, *Religious Conversion and Disaffiliation*, 67, 139.
151. Ibid.

Further Reading

Buckser, Andrew, and Stephen D. Glazier, eds. *The Anthropology of Religious Conversion*. Lanham, MD: Rowman and Littlefield, 2003. This is a recent collection of fifteen excellent articles on conversion written by prominent anthropologists like Austin-Broos, Coleman, Farhadian, and Glazier. It also contains a very useful overview of the anthropology of conversion by psychologist Lewis Rambo.
Hefner, Robert W., ed. *Conversion to Christianity: Historical and Anthropological Perspectives on a Great Transformation*. Berkeley and Los Angeles: University of California Press, 1993. This is a classic collection of ten excellent articles on conversion written by anthropologists. Particularly noteworthy are Hefner's Introduction and article and other contributions by Barker, Keyes, Pollock, Ranger, and Yengoyan.
Robbins, Joel. *Becoming Sinners: Christianity and Moral Torment in a Papua New Guinea Society*. Berkeley and Los Angeles: University of California Press, 2004. One of the best ethnographies written by anthropologists that deals with conversion, focusing on the Urapmin in the western highlands of Papua New Guinea.

van der Veer, Peter, ed. *Conversion to Modernities: The Globalization of Christianity*. New York: Routledge, 1996. Eleven articles on conversion written by prominent scholars like Keane, Meyer, van der Veer, and Viswanathan, with an afterword by Asad. Most authors develop a critical version of conversion to multiple modernities. Only half of the authors are anthropologists, but cross-cultural comparisons are essential to all contributions.

Bibliography

Annis, Sheldon. *God and Production in a Guatemalan Town*. Austin: University of Texas Press, 1987.

Asad, Talal. *Genealogies of Religion: Discipline and Reasons of Power in Christianity and Islam*. Baltimore: Johns Hopkins University Press, 1993.

——. "Comments on Conversion." In *Conversion to Modernities: The Globalization of Christianity*, ed. Peter van der Veer, 263–273. New York: Routledge, 1996.

——. *Formations of the Secular: Christianity, Islam, Modernity*. Stanford, CA: Stanford University Press, 2003.

Austin, Diane J. "Born Again . . . and Again and Again: Communitas and Social Change among Jamaican Pentecostalists." *Journal of Anthropological Research* 37, no. 3 (1981): 226–246.

Austin-Broos, Diane J. *Jamaica Genesis: Religion and the Politics of Moral Orders*. Chicago: University of Chicago Press, 1997.

——. "The Anthropology of Conversion: An Introduction." In *The Anthropology of Religious Conversion*, ed. Andrew Buckser and Stephen D. Glazier, 1–12. Lanham, MD: Rowman and Littlefield, 2003.

Bendix, Robert. *Max Weber: An Intellectual Portrait*. New York: Anchor, 1962.

Berkhofer, Robert F., Jr. "Protestants, Pagans, and Sequences among the North American Indians, 1760–1860." *Ethnohistory* 10, no. 3 (1963): 201–232.

Cannell, Fenella. "The Anthropology of Christianity." In *The Anthropology of Christianity*, ed. Fenella Cannell, 1–50. Durham, NC: Duke University Press, 2006.

Cantón Delgado, Manuela. *Bautizados en fuego: Protestantes, discursos de conversión y política en Guatemala (1989–1993)*. Antigua, Guatemala: CIRMA, 1998.

Carmack, Robert M., Janine L. Gasco, and Gary H. Gossen. *The Legacy of Mesoamerica: History and Culture of a Native American Civilization*. Upper Saddle River, NJ: Pearson/Prentice Hall, 2007.

Coleman, Simon. *The Globalisation of Charismatic Christianity: Spreading the Gospel of Prosperity*. Cambridge: Cambridge University Press, 2000.

——. "Continuous Conversion? The Rhetoric, Practice, and Rhetorical Practice of Charismatic Protestant Conversion." In *The Anthropology of Religious Conversion*, ed. Andrew Buckser and Stephen D. Glazier, 15–27. Lanham, MD: Rowman and Littlefield, 2003.

Comaroff, Jean, and John Comaroff. *Of Revelation and Revolution: Christianity, Colonialism, and Consciousness in South Africa*. Vol. 1. Chicago: University of Chicago Press, 1991.

Crapo, Richley. *Anthropology of Religion*. Boston: McGraw-Hill, 2003.

Cucchiari, Salvatore. "'Adapted for Heaven': Conversion and Culture in Western Sicily." *American Ethnologist* 15, no. 3 (1988): 417–441.

Dow, James W. "The Theology of Change: Evangelical Protestantism and the Collapse of Native Religion in a Peasant Area of Mexico." In *Explorations in Anthropology and Theology*, ed.

Frank A. Salamone and Walter Randolph Adams, 113–123. Lanham, MD: University Press of America, 1997.

———. "Protestantism in Mesoamerica: The Old within the New." In *Holy Saints and Fiery Preachers: The Anthropology of Protestantism in Mexico and Central America*, ed. James W. Dow and Alan R. Sandstrom, 1–23. Westport, CT: Praeger, 2001.

Droogers, André, Henri Gooren, and Anton Houtepen. "Conversion Careers and Culture Politics in Pentecostalism: A Comparative Study in Four Continents." Proposal submitted to the thematic program "The Future of the Religious Past" of the Netherlands Organization for Scientific Research (NWO), The Hague, 2003.

Early, John D. *The Maya and Catholicism: An Encounter of Worldviews*. Gainesville: University Press of Florida, 2006.

Eisenstadt, S. N. "Multiple Modernities." *Daedalus* 129, no. 1 (2000): 1–29.

Falla, Ricardo. *Quiché Rebelde: Religious Conversion, Politics, and Ethnic Identity in Guatemala*. Austin: University of Texas Press, 2001.

Fisher, Humphrey J. "Conversion Reconsidered: Some Historical Aspects of Religious Conversion in Black Africa." *Africa* 43, no. 1 (1973): 27–40.

———. "The Juggernaut's Apologia: Conversion to Islam in Black Africa." *Africa* 55, no. 2 (1985): 153–173.

Garma, Carlos. "Religious Affiliation in Indian Mexico." In *Holy Saints and Fiery Preachers: The Anthropology of Protestantism in Mexico and Central America*, ed. James W. Dow and Alan R. Sandstrom, 57–72. Westport, CT: Praeger, 2001.

Gerlach, Luther P., and Virginia H. Hine. "Five Factors Crucial to the Growth and Spread of a Modern Religious Movement." *Journal for the Scientific Study of Religion* 7, no. 1 (1968): 23–40.

———. *People, Power, Change: Movements of Social Transformation*. Indianapolis: Bobbs-Merril l, 1970.

Gibson, Charles. *The Aztecs under Spanish Rule: A History of Indians in the Valley of Mexico, 1519–1810*. Stanford, CA: Stanford University Press, 1964.

Gooren, Henri. "Reconsidering Protestant Growth in Guatemala, 1900–1995." In Holy Saints and Fiery Preachers: The Anthropology of Protestantism in Mexico and Central America, ed. James W. Dow and Alan R. Sandstrom (Westport, CT: Prager, 2001), 169–203.

———. "Conversion Narratives." In *Studying Global Pentecostalism: Theories and Methods*, ed. Allan Anderson, Michael Bergunder, André Droogers, and Cornelis van der Laan, 93–112. Berkeley and Los Angeles: University of California Press, 2010.

———. *Religious Conversion and Disaffiliation: Tracing Patterns of Change in Faith Practices*. New York: Palgrave-Macmillan, 2010.

Harding, Susan F. "Convicted by the Holy Spirit: The Rhetoric of Fundamental Baptist Conversion." *American Ethnologist* 14, no. 1 (1987): 167–181.

———. *The Book of Jerry Falwell: Fundamentalist Language and Politics*. Princeton: Princeton University Press, 2000.

Hefner, Robert W. "Introduction." In *Conversion to Christianity: Historical and Anthropological Perspectives on a Great Transformation*, ed. Robert W. Hefner, 3–44. Berkeley and Los Angeles: University of California Press, 1993.

———. "Of Faith and Commitment: Christian Conversion in Muslim Java." In *Conversion to Christianity: Historical and Anthropological Perspectives on a Great Transformation*, ed. Robert W. Hefner, 99–125. Berkeley and Los Angeles: University of California Press, 1993.

Hiebert, Paul G. *Transforming Worldviews: An Anthropological Understanding of How People Change*. Grand Rapids, MI: Baker Academic, 2008.

Hine, Virginia H. "Bridge Burners: Commitment and Participation in a Religious Movement." *Sociological Analysis* 31, no. 2 (1969): 61–66.

Horton, Robin. "African Conversion." *Africa* 41, no. 2 (1971): 85–108.

——. "On the Rationality of Conversion: Part I." *Africa* 45, no. 3 (1975): 219–235.

——. "On the Rationality of Conversion: Part II." *Africa* 45, no. 4 (1975): 373–399.

Ikenga-Metuh, Emefie. "The Shattered Microcosm: A Critical Survey of Explanations of Conversion in Africa." In *Religion, Development, and African Identity*, ed. Kirsten Holst Petersen, 11–27. Uppsala: Scandinavian Institute of African Studies, 1987.

James, William. *The Varieties of Religious Experience: A Study in Human Nature*. New York City: New American Library, 1958.

Keane, Webb. *Christian Moderns: Freedom and Fetish in the Mission Encounter*. Berkeley and Los Angeles: University of California Press, 2007.

Keesing, Roger M. *Cultural Anthropology: A Contemporary Perspective*. 2nd ed. New York: Holt, Rinehart, and Winston, 1981.

Kipp, Rita Smith. "Conversion by Affiliation: The History of the Karo Batak Protestant Church." *American Ethnologist* 22, no. 4 (1995): 868–882.

Klor de Alva, J. Jorge. "Aztec Spirituality and Nahuatized Christianity." In *South and Meso-American Native Spirituality*, ed. Gary H. Gossen, 173–197. New York: Crossroad, 1993.

Kraft, Charles H. *Christianity in Culture: A Study in Dynamic Biblical Theologizing in Cross-Cultural Perspective*. Maryknoll, NY: Orbis, 1979.

Lambek, Michael. *A Reader in the Anthropology of Religion*. Malden, MA: Blackwell, 2002.

——. "General Introduction." In *A Reader in the Anthropology of Religion*, ed. Michael Lambek, 1–16. Malden, MA: Blackwell, 2002.

Lewellen, Ted. "Deviant Religion and Cultural Evolution." *Journal for the Scientific Study of Religion* 18, no. 3 (1979): 243–251.

Linton, Ralph. "Nativistic Movements." *American Anthropologist* 45 (1943): 230–240.

Lofland, John, and Rodney Stark. "Becoming a World-Saver: A Theory of Conversion to a Deviant Perspective." *American Sociological Review* 30, no. 6 (1965): 862–875.

Marshall-Fratani, Ruth. "Mediating the Global and Local in Nigerian Pentecostalism." In *Between Babel and Pentecost: Transnational Pentecostalism in Africa and Latin America*, ed. André Corten and Ruth Marshall-Fratani, 80–105. London: Hurst, 2001.

Martin, David. *Tongues of Fire: The Explosion of Pentecostalism in Latin America*. Oxford: Blackwell, 1990.

McCleary, Timothy P. "An Ethnohistory of Pentecostalism among the Crow Indians of Montana." *Wicazo Sa Review* 15, no. 1 (2000): 117–135.

McGuire, Meredith. *Religion: The Social Context*. Belmont, CA: Wadsworth, 2002.

Meyer, Birgit. "'Make A Complete Break with the Past': Memory and Post-Colonial Modernity in Ghanaian Pentecostalist Discourse." *Journal of Religion in Africa* 28, no. 3 (1998): 316–349.

——. *Translating the Devil: Religion and Modernity among the Ewe in Ghana*. Edinburgh: Edinburgh University Press, 1999.

Morgan, Lewis Henry. *League of the Ho-De-No-Sau-Nee or Iroquois*. New York: Corinth, [1851] 1962.

Muratorio, Blanca. "Protestantism and Capitalism Revisited in the Rural Highlands of Ecuador." *Journal of Peasant Studies* 8, no. 1 (1980): 37–60.

Nash, June. "Protestantism in an Indian Village in the Western Highlands of Guatemala." *Alpha Kappa Deltan* 30 (1960): 49–53.

Nash, Manning. *Machine Age Maya: The Industrialization of a Guatemalan Community.* Chicago: University of Chicago Press, 1967.

Nock, Arthur Darby. *Conversion: The Old and the New in Religion from Alexander the Great to Augustine of Hippo.* Oxford: Oxford University Press, 1969.

O'Connor, Mary. "Two Kinds of Religious Movements among the Mayo Indians of Sonora, Mexico." *Journal for the Scientific Study of Religion* 18, no. 3 (1979): 260–268.

Rambo, Lewis R. "Anthropology and the Study of Conversion." In *The Anthropology of Religious Conversion,* ed. Andrew Buckser and Stephen D. Glazier, 211–222. Lanham, MD: Rowman and Littlefield, 2003.

Redfield, Robert. *A Village That Chose Progress: Chan Kom Revisited.* Chicago: University of Chicago Press, 1950.

Reina, Ruben E. *The Law of the Saints: A Pokomam Pueblo and Its Community Culture.* Indianapolis: Bobbs-Merrill, 1966.

Reina, Ruben E., and Norman B. Schwartz. "The Structural Context of Religious Conversion in El Petén, Guatemala: Status, Community, and Multicommunity." *American Ethnologist* 9, no. 1 (1974): 157–191.

Richardson, James T., ed. *Conversion Careers: In and Out of the New Religions.* Beverly Hills, CA: SAGE, 1978.

Robbins, Joel. "What Is a Christian? Notes toward an Anthropology of Christianity. *Religion* 33 (2003): 191–199.

——. "On the Paradoxes of Global Pentecostalism and the Perils of Continuity Thinking. *Religion* 33 (2003): 221–231.

——. *Becoming Sinners: Christianity and Moral Torment in a Papua New Guinea Society.* Berkeley and Los Angeles: University of California Press, 2004.

——. "Continuity Thinking and the Problem of Christian Culture." *Current Anthropology* 48, no. 1 (2007): 5–38.

Salamone, Frank A., and Walter Randolph Adams, eds. *Explorations in Anthropology and Theology.* Lanham, MD: University Press of America, 1997.

Saler, Benson. "Religious Conversion and Self-Aggrandizement: A Guatemalan Case." *Practical Anthropology* 13 (1965): 107–114.

Samandú, Luis E., ed. *Protestantismos y procesos sociales en Centroamérica.* San José, Costa Rica: CSUCA, 1990.

Sexton, James D. "Protestantism and Modernization in Two Guatemalan Towns." *American Ethnologist* 5, no. 2 (1978): 280–302.

Snow, David A., and Richard Machalek. "The Sociology of Conversion". *Annual Review of Sociology* 10 (1984): 167–190.

Stewart, Charles. "Secularism as an Impediment to Anthropological Research". *Social Anthropology* 9, no. 3 (2001): 323–328.

Stipe, Claude E. "Anthropologists versus Missionaries: The Influence of Presuppositions." *Current Anthropology* 21, no. 2 (1980): 165–179.

Stromberg, Peter G. "Ideological Language in the Transformation of Identity." *American Anthropologist* 92, no. 1 (1990): 42–56.

Tippett, Alan R. "Conversion as a Dynamic Process in Christian Mission." *Missiology* 5, no. 2 (1977): 203–221.

van der Geest, Sjaak. "Missionaries." In *Encyclopedia of Cultural Anthropology,* ed. David Levinson and Melvin Ember, 797–801. New York: Holt, 1996.

van der Veer, Peter. "Introduction." In *Conversion to Modernities: The Globalization of Christianity*, ed. Peter van der Veer, 1–21. New York: Routledge, 1996.

——. "Conversion and Coercion: The Politics of Sincerity and Authenticity." In *Cultures of Conversions*, ed. Wout J. van Bekkum, Jan N. Bremmer, and Arie Molendijk, 1–14. Leuven, Belgium: Peeters, 2006.

van Gennep, Arnold. *The Rites of Passage*. Chicago: University of Chicago Press, 1960.

van Oss, Adriaan C. *Catholic Colonialism: A Parish History of Guatemala, 1524–1821*. Cambridge: Cambridge University Press, 1986.

Vecsey, Christopher. *On the Padres' Trail*. Notre Dame, IN: University of Notre Dame Press, 1996.

Wallace, Anthony F. C. "Handsome Lake and the Great Revival in the West." *American Quarterly* 4, no. 2 (1952): 149–165.

—— "Revitalization Movements." *American Anthropologist* 58, no. 2 (1956): 264–281.

——. *The Death and Rebirth of the Seneca*. New York: Knopf, 1970.

Weber, Max. *The Sociology of Religion*. Boston: Beacon, 1956.

Willems, Emilio. *Followers of the New Faith: Culture Change and the Rise of Protestantism in Brazil and Chile*. Nashville: Vanderbilt University Press, 1967.

Wood, Peter. "Afterword: Boundaries and Horizons." In *Conversion to Christianity: Historical and Anthropological Perspectives on a Great Transformation*, ed. Robert W. Hefner, 305–321. Berkeley and Los Angeles: University of California Press, 1993.

CHAPTER 5

....

THE ROLE OF LANGUAGE
IN RELIGIOUS CONVERSION

....

PETER G. STROMBERG

OUR access to whatever we understand as the truth is mediated through language, and this generalization covers the ultimate truths about the cosmos. Indeed, it can be argued that the matters addressed in the world's religions are especially closely tied to the language in which these matters are formulated. As Kenneth Burke pointed out, the words used to describe the divine must ultimately be analogies based upon that which we encounter in this world; these words "are necessarily borrowed from the realm of our everyday experiences."[1] Unlike, say, water, typically the believer does not have free sensory access to all manifestations of the divinity; the divinity often cannot be touched and observed so that we may supplement what is said or written with what is sensed directly. Thus, the language in which religious doctrines are expressed has singular relevance for shaping such understandings.

For this reason, language has a close relationship to religious practice, and in all traditions with which I am familiar, language is manipulated in special ways in order to describe, invoke, supplicate, and understand divinity. I say "special ways" because religious language needs to be accommodated to the peculiar circumstances of speaking about the ultimate, and language can also be adapted to convey central religious ideas in subtle and compelling ways. To take a familiar example, religious speech is often laced with archaic formulations; such formulations may suggest that timeless truths are being uttered or may otherwise enhance the authority of the speech. Careful analysis of the way that language is used can reveal much about religious belief and practice, and often what we learn in this way reveals understandings that are not obvious from mere contemplation of official religious doctrines.

These observations hold for conversion as well; to study religious conversion through the language in which it is understood and realized offers rich possibilities for exploring such matters as the nature of religious change and the relationship between religion and identity. However, this topic also entails a slew of special challenges. Foremost among these challenges—and therefore a matter that must be at least briefly addressed here—is the fact that it is unclear what "religious conversion" is.[2] Although many thoughtful scholars have sought to pin conversion down, the effort to define conversion comprehensively and precisely still faces difficulties.

The most significant of these problems is that the term "conversion" is often used to refer to either or both of two processes that are empirically and conceptually separate (although often appearing together).[3] These are what might be called "experiences of personal transformation"[4] and "change in religious affiliation." Because joining a religious institution often entails coming into contact with a new and all-embracing view of the world, in practice denominational change often is associated with change in identity. As the authors of a preface to a recent collection of anthropological papers on conversion write: "To change one's religion is to change one's world, to voluntarily shift the basic presuppositions upon which both self and others are understood."[5] The point here is elegantly stated. However, to simply assert that a change in religion is to change foundational notions such as sense of self glides over one of the most important questions for students of conversion, that being, "Under what conditions is a change in religion a change in identity and worldview?" The association is not inevitable. When Henry the Eighth repudiated the Pope and created the new denomination of the Church of England, the men and women who suddenly found themselves members of a new religious institution did not all shift their basic presuppositions, nor did they simultaneously experience personal transformations.[6] It is worth spending a moment on the question of why these two different processes have so often been conflated in the concept of "conversion."

As noted, there are logical reasons to assume that personal transformation and denominational change will often be associated. Perhaps even more important, these processes have been strongly linked in parts of the Western tradition that have stressed religious individualism. Of particular importance here is the repeated manifestation, in the waves of the Reformation that began to occur around the sixteenth century in the Western Christian tradition, of an issue that contributed to the Puritans' name: the problem of the purification of God's church.[7] Speaking very broadly, the basic principle of Protestantism is that God's grace is mediated not through membership in any institution or group but rather through individuals who are the recipients of that grace. Max Weber famously pointed out that this principle creates psychological tension among believers who are then left to question whether they are in fact among the elect who have been blessed by the saving power of God's grace.[8] But there is also a sociological issue here that has been of enormous historical significance. If the group is not in itself a Godly institution, the question of separating any congregation into true and false members is likely to arise. What the Pietists were later to call the *Wiedergeburt* (born again) experience also emerged early on as a particularly convincing sign of the reception of grace among the Puritans[9] and other Protestant groups. Thus, questions of denominational affiliation and personal transformation have been strongly associated in parts of the Western Christian tradition for centuries. Again, however, this association is an artifact of a particular history and does not reflect a necessary connection between moving between religious institutions and experiences of personal transformation.

Our traditions of scholarship compound the complexities of this situation in that different disciplines have tended to understand conversion differently, depending upon their broader intellectual agendas.[10] If I grant myself the license to speak broadly, I can say (taking my examples from the social sciences) that anthropologists and historians have tended to study conversion in order to better understand processes of cultural continuity and change.[11] Given this set of interests, questions of denominational affiliation typically assume primary significance in these disciplines. On the other hand, in the psychology of religion, the focus has been upon questions of personal transformation. Interestingly, much of the work on religious conversion in sociology[12] struggles to come to terms with both religious change and personal transformation, but in doing so often implicitly assumes that these phenomena are necessarily associated. As a result of all this, we face a situation that is (sadly) too common in the social sciences and humanities—we try to talk to one another about conversion, but our discussion is hampered by the fact that we do not all mean the same thing when we use the term.

I will address this problem here by attempting to be as clear as I can about what I am talking about. Often those who adopt a linguistic approach to conversion resolve the issue by explicitly focusing on the conversion *narrative*. Here, the object of study is neither denominational change nor personal transformation, but rather the stories that people tell about these processes. This neatly avoids some of the conceptual problems I have raised, but not all of those who study the intersection of language and the conversion adopt this strategy. Thus, I will continue to use the term "conversion," but in analyzing the term I endeavor to distinguish personal transformation and denominational affiliation in order to avoid the murkiness that is generated when one is not clear about which one of these processes is under discussion.[13]

GENERIC FEATURES OF THE CONVERSION NARRATIVE

Interest in the language of the conversion manifested itself first among intellectual historians and literary critics in the years following the Second World War, although there are some isolated earlier works. These scholars[14] posed questions about the genre of the conversion narrative. They sought to explore the characteristic narrative features and stylistics of the conversion narrative, its theological, historical, and literary contexts, and often (at least implicitly) the relationship between conversion narratives and other genres, such as autobiography and the novel.[15] Since this time, so many studies of the history and development of conversion narratives have appeared that the current chapter can only scratch the surface of this work.

However, it is possible to offer some generalizations about the scholarship on conversion narratives in literary and intellectual history. In the first place, to study the conversion narrative as a genre is to call attention to the fact that the story has characteristic narrative conventions. The description of these conventions is important, but there is another implication here that has theoretical significance. We name and perhaps study the conversion experience because it seems to be a coherent process that occurs in similar ways in the lives of different people. Those who first named the conversion had no doubt about the cause of this coherent process: it represented the intervention of the divinity into the life of a believer who was transformed by that intervention. Today, those who study the conversion from a theological perspective still operate from this perspective, but roughly a century ago alternative understandings began to take shape. William James,[16] for example, while not ruling out the possibility that the coherence of the conversion experience reflected the hand of God, also took it for granted that the conversion could tell us something about the human mind. For him, and for the generations of psychologists who followed him, the conversion was a window through which psychological regularities might be glimpsed. To return now to the matter at hand, studying conversion stories as a genre raises another possibility as to the source of pattern in the conversion narrative: these could be culturally generated conventions, much like those that govern, say, the novel. The point concerns not only the relating of the conversion story; it can be extended to apply to the conversion experience itself. It may be that the trajectory of a person's experience—immersion in sin, exposure to the word of God, a period of doubt, a glorious moment of salvation—is conditioned by the expectations generated through familiarity with conversion narratives.

Most broadly, studies of the genre of conversion narratives can be understood as opening the door to a cultural understanding of the conversion. Consider, for example, Patricia Caldwell's study entitled *The Puritan Conversion Narrative*. Caldwell focuses her inquiry on the question of the differences between English and American Puritan conversion narratives of the early seventeenth century. She hopes thereby to gain a clearer view of the beginnings of a distinctive American literary voice. But in so doing, she also provides detailed evidence for how the language of the conversion narrative—and by extension the conversion itself—is shaped by culture.

Those who have studied the discursive characteristics of the early Protestant conversion narrative have provided a sophisticated set of analytic techniques for understanding the relationship between language and the conversion. Many of these insights are directed at matters that not even a beginning student of such narratives can miss. For example, there is the widespread occurrence of the passive voice, "And it came upon me that..." As Owen Watkins points out,[17] this is a means of testifying to the silent workings of the Divinity in the believer's mind and actions.[18] Or, consider the use of scriptural materials in building conversion narratives, a practice that took shape in the early period and has remained prominent.[19] Kenneth Burke alerts us to the import of such activity in his discussion of one of the two most important conversion narratives in Christian history. Speaking of St. Augustine, he writes:

> The great store of Biblical texts, learned verbatim and spouted forth at appropriate moments, were like attitudinally slanted names for situations. Each time a situation

arose, it presented itself to him in terms of some scriptural formula that in effect 'adopted a policy' with regard to it.[20]

The practice of weaving Bible passages into speech is so widespread that it is probably too easy to overlook the profound implication of this way of using language, for it is an ongoing means of linking the sacred and the profane, of construing the present in terms of the eternal.[21] In this sense, the conversion narrative itself can be understood as a ritual that does what rituals all over the world do; it brings an element of the divine into juxtaposition with the world of the here and now.

Indeed, it is interesting to contemplate—at least in the case of Puritan conversion narratives—the similarity between the order provided by narrative structure and the meaning and order brought to the life of the believer through the conversion. Reworking the flow of experience into a series of discrete episodes progressing toward an ending that makes sense of the whole is a powerful way of bringing meaning and coherence to the course of a life. Narrative does what God does, and this raises interesting questions, questions such as: To what extent can a group's understanding of the workings of the divinity be shaped by their experience of the workings of language, as in the capacity of language to render the flux of experience into a coherent story? Another question: Throughout history, rituals have been an important means of integrating persons and communities into the broader cosmos. Is it useful to think of the Western religious tradition as one in which this ritual function is increasingly accomplished though stories that are tailored to the idiosyncratic details of an individual biography? If such a line of thought is indeed worth pursuing, then in the broadest view we are thinking about how ritual language is used, in one cultural tradition, to link a concept of person (as unique individual) to the ultimate nature of the cosmos.

The questions I have just posed are directly addressed in a recent and comprehensive historiographical study of Protestant conversion narratives, Bruce Hindmarsh's *The Evangelical Conversion Narrative*. Hindmarsh focuses in particular on the period between 1730 and 1780, a period during which a similar set of narrative conventions proliferated across a number of different groups. Hindmarsh is both a historian and a careful scholar, so his study is weighted toward providing a detailed account of the characteristics, theological implications, and social contexts of early modern conversion narratives. This is a book more about the description of conversion narratives than about their social implications. At the same time, Hindmarsh is very aware of the range of theoretical issues raised in domains such as the relationship between language and identity, and he does not fail to address these issues when appropriate.

Thus, throughout his book Hindmarsh remains sensitive to questions of how issues of narrative genre and rhetoric have direct implications for broader matters such as morality and identity. For example, he looks at the rhetorical mechanisms whereby Methodist preaching of the mid-eighteenth century created a sense, among listeners, that they were being directly addressed as individuals (note the parallel to the discussion below of Harding[22]). At the same time, the regularities of the conversion genre provided a powerful basis for identification with a community. This illustrates a pervasive theme of Hindmarsh's analysis, the sense in which the early modern conversion narrative was a hybrid that marked the transition between emerging individualism and a Christian-based group identity more characteristic of earlier centuries: "It was precisely in the seventeenth and eighteenth centuries that the emerging modern identity could cross paths with the fading Christian moral hegemony. Evangelical conversion narrative appeared on the trailing edge of Christendom and the leading edge of modernity."[23]

Narrative Approaches in the Social Sciences

To summarize the previous section in general terms, historians and literary scholars have produced detailed descriptions of the development, variations, and social implications of the conversion narrative as it developed in Western Christianity after the Reformation. I would be happy to report that when psychologists and qualitative sociologists began to turn to the study of narrative in the 1980s, they were able to build upon this scholarship. Alas, it is not so. Many of the sophisticated analytic methods and insights that literary critics and historians have brought to bear in studying conversion narratives have still not breached the wall that often divides disciplines in our academic institutions. Rather, those who turned to narrative as a method for understanding the conversion seem to have been mostly influenced by seminal work in their own disciplines.

Among the earliest of the studies of the relationship between discourse and transformation is David A. Snow and Richard Machalek's well-known article, "The Convert as Social Type," which appeared in the journal *Sociological Theory* in 1983. Building upon the empirical foundation of Snow's dissertation research on the Nichiren Shoshu Buddhist movement, Snow and Machalek attempt to identify the properties that characterize the convert as a social type. They settle on the notion that the convert is one who has an experience in which his or her "universe of discourse" changes, a transformation that is reflected in his or her talk and reasoning.[24] They write, "To experience a radical and fundamental change in one's universe of discourse...entails the displacement of one universe of discourse by another and its attendant grammar or rules for putting things together."[25]

Snow and Machalek understand this displacement to take place in four primary areas. The first two of these are manifestations of narrative practices. What Snow and Machalek refer to as "biographical reconstruction" has to do with one's understanding of one's own life history. In the experience of personal transformation, "the past is not only shattered; the disjointed pieces are reassembled in accordance with the new universe of discourse and its grammar."[26] The second feature, "adoption of a master attribution scheme," refers to the fact that typically the new universe of discourse is appealing precisely because it seems to pull together the diverse memories and experiences of a personal history into a more coherent and embracing pattern.

Snow and Machalek identify a third property of the conversion as "suspension of analogical reasoning" and argue that the convert typically utilizes metaphors that emphasize the uniqueness of the new discourse (hence the claim that converts tend to avoid analogies when speaking about their faith). Snow and Machalek's generalization here seems incautious at best. To show that one type of metaphor dominates over another in the religious speech of converts would be extraordinarily difficult, and indeed this claim goes completely unsupported. Rather, the evidence cited in support of this claim consists of several examples of how Nichiren Shoshu converts assert that their new religious outlook is a unique path to truth; but this is a different matter from the notion that there is a consistent pattern of metaphor use throughout the religious speech of these converts.

Finally, these authors point to the "embracement of a master role" as a constituent element of the conversion. What is at stake here is the frequently observed fact that the convert assigns an overarching import to her new religious convictions, so that these convictions come to form the very core of her identity. As with the two features named at the outset, this generalization ultimately has to do with the narrative organization of the self, a topic that has been much studied in the years since Snow and Machalek's analysis first appeared.

The extent to which the Snow and Machalek approach constitutes a theory of conversion and language is not immediately apparent, but the connection is clarified by considering the theoretical underpinnings of Snow and Machalek's reasoning. Staples and Mauss[27] efficiently sketch these underpinnings, pointing out that in the symbolic interactionist framework within which this theory is formulated there is an assumed equivalence between idioms of communication and consciousness. As George Herbert Mead originally formulated the matter, human symbolic behavior is only possible against the background of a shared universe of meanings within which human action takes place. From this perspective, to change religion is to travel from one universe to another and thereby to transform one's consciousness.

Based upon this, Staples and Mauss suggest a refinement of Snow and Machalek's argument that brings the long-term effect of Snow and Machalek's contribution into clearer focus. Staples and Mauss argue that the change brought about in religious conversion is essentially a change in self-consciousness. It is a self-transformation, a change in the way that the convert views his or her core self.[28] Further, they assert that this transformation of self occurs "through language."[29] As Staples and Mauss then point out, what is at issue here is the difference between looking to language as a marker of the convert's status to looking at language as the means whereby transformation is accomplished.[30]

Staples and Mauss go on to argue—on the basis of fifteen open-ended interviews with evangelical Christians—that while biographical reconstruction does indeed seem to differentiate those who refer to themselves as converts, the other three proposed factors do not. Here, these authors indulge in a practice that is not infrequent in the social scientific study of conversion, that of offering sweeping generalizations about the nature of conversion on the basis of scanty evidence. Rather than engaging in back-and-forth sniping on the eternal features of the conversion, it would be better to acknowledge once and for all that experiences of self-transformation are culturally constituted and thus vary across different traditions.

In fact, for the most part, the theoretical groundwork laid by Staples and Mauss is a genuine advance in building such an approach, which looks to experiences of transformation as the accomplishments of agents who exploit the resources of language to bring about desired change. From this perspective, the features that Snow and Machalek originally isolated come to seem less like characteristics of conversion than rhetorical devices often used by converts. Re-shaping a life story around a master attribution scheme, for example, is a powerful means of persuading oneself and others that a genuine transformation has taken place.

More specifically, the features debated in both these articles are narrative devices. However, and somewhat surprisingly, there has been little follow-up of this point in the social scientific literature. While in recent decades it has often been acknowledged that conversion entails a shift in discursive patterns or symbolic universe, students of conversion have not shown much sustained interest in the details of the narrative and rhetorical strategies used by converts.[31] This holds true even in light of the recent explosive growth, especially in psychology and sociology, of the study of the narrative and identity. Unaccountably, the conversion has not been a prominent focus of concern in the hundreds of books and articles that have appeared on narrative and identity in the past several decades. Rather, the focus of concern in this realm has been the life story and its implications, with an emphasis on narrative as a powerful pan-human tool for the generation of meaning.

One strong exception to these generalizations is the work of anthropologist Susan Harding, in particular *The Book of Jerry Falwell*.[32] Harding provides a sophisticated and insightful analysis of the language of Baptist fundamentalists, including a compelling discussion of Biblical literalism.[33] Her discussion of the verbal performance of a preacher's conversion narrative isolates a number of rhetorical techniques whereby the listener is drawn into the narrative and is ultimately transformed through its telling. She examines such matters as how the preacher appropriates authority in the narrative and then uses that authority to define the social position of the listener. For example, consider the simple matter of using inclusive pronouns as a means of creating an identification between narrator and listener. I noted earlier that a prominent feature of the American Puritan conversion narrative (and, of course, this is true of other groups as well) was the creation of parallels between scriptural situations and those of the narrator. In the Baptist narrative Harding discusses, this technique is extended further; the preacher sets up and exploits a parallel between Scripture, his own conversion, and the impending conversion of his listener (thus making the latter rhetorically "inevitable").

Harding writes: "The speaker's language, now in the listener's voice, converts the listener's mind into a contested terrain, a divided self.... The Christian tongue locks into some kind of central, controlling, dominant place; it has gone beyond the point of inhabiting the listener's mind to occupy the listener's identity."[34] This summary is not Harding's finest moment. Perhaps this formulation reflects the impulse, fashionable among some ethnographers, to fully adopt the native point of view (manifested here as the miraculous power of the Word to convert). But in doing this, she strips these listeners of their agency and awards that power to "language." Her own analysis has illustrated in compelling ways the rhetorical mechanisms whereby the conversion narrative persuades. If language controls, if it occupies an identity, what need do we have of an analysis of how rhetorical features persuade a person, a person with memories, emotions, a temperament, convictions, and so on?

In a way, Harding's theoretical statement here (which, as noted, I find to be a poor formulation of her actual analysis) simply substitutes one form of essentialism for another. Throughout the literature on conversion, analysts have been overly willing to understand such terms as "conversion" and "identity" not as politically charged labels for processes we find in human history but rather as concrete entities with the capacity to function as historical actors. We gain nothing by conceiving "language" in similar terms.

If one takes a broader view of her accomplishment, however, Harding's work shows the potential power of the study of the rhetoric of the conversion narrative. But again, her book (although often cited) has not been much imitated by scholars studying conversion; social scientific work on the narrative features of the conversion remains both undeveloped and unconsolidated. The empirical and theoretical advances that have occurred in literary studies and narrative psychology have for the most part not been integrated into actual studies of the conversion. This is the bad news. The good news is that the ground is prepared for a fruitful harvest in the future. Students who have interests in this area have much to work with, and I hope that soon greater attention will be devoted to questions such as: How can we provide strong empirical evidence of the oft-asserted transformation of cultural outlook often associated with conversion? If we indeed succeed in showing in detail what this transformation entails, how are we to account for these changes? What can we learn by addressing the question of narrative coherence and discontinuity?[35] Can we begin to carefully map the generic features and rhetorical devices of the conversion narrative as it is manifested in different cultural traditions?[36]

CULTURE AND THE DISCOURSE OF CONVERSION

Up to this point, I have considered studies that for the most part focus on relatively broad aspects of language use, especially narrative organization. Through narrative, language is used to impart meaning to experiences by linking them into a causal order, describing and developing recurring themes in the trajectory of a life, and so on. But language also imparts meaning through a range of practices that operate on a less global level. Such matters as lexical choice, the nature of analogies and metaphors, evidentiality, language ideology, and a host of other factors can also be studied as they manifest themselves in different aspects of the conversion. Such features are perhaps especially interesting when scholars turn to the verbal performance of conversion narratives, for here one can also look at aspects of vocal and gestural performance. There is no clear line that divides these micro-level processes from those of narrative, but at least in the present context it is useful to separate out studies that go beyond the level of narrative organization to consider broader features of discourse.

In looking at scholarship on discourse and the conversion, I turn first to studies in anthropology; for one would expect that the close disciplinary relationship between anthropology and linguistics would have generated a number of analyses of this type. And indeed, there are some excellent studies along these lines. However, most anthropological work on conversion attends to the broader issues of how conversions and the colonial incursions they often represent may transform aspects of "cultural logic."[37] Most of this work is similar to the work in sociology discussed in the previous section; the focus of interest is the relationship between conversion and cultural transformation, broadly conceived, and the possibilities for linguistic analysis in this effort are not strongly exploited.

As noted, there are some exceptions to this generalization. Priest[38] considers lexical evidence in evaluating whether Aguaruna (of Peru) men and women can be said to have a sense of their sinfulness prior to conversion to Christianity, and more generally he attends carefully to the features of the Aguaruna conversion narrative. A more comprehensive approach in this vein is that of Comaroff and Comaroff.[39] This work is often cited on the basis of the questions it raises about conversion as an analytic category, but the analysis that raises those questions is—unfortunately—less often discussed. In particular, the Comaroffs study the implications of the contrasting *linguistic ideologies* among Non-Conformist British missionaries and the South African Tswana they sought to convert, an important approach that has been for the most part neglected.

All speech communities have their own linguistic ideologies, their own understandings of how language works.[40] That is, not only do such matters as conceptions of self and religious beliefs and practices vary across place and time, so too do understandings of the nature of language itself. One of the most important functions of language use— one which our own ideology of language tends to significantly underappreciate—is its capacity to constitute social situations. Westerners, on the basis of what some have called a "referential" linguistic ideology, tend to understand language as a system through which verbal signals designate aspects of a separately existing reality. While I have no doubt that a reality exists that would carry on just fine if all humans precipitously went up in smoke, I have considerable doubt that language simply labels that reality. Rather, our construal of the physical and social worlds is not only shaped by, but often constituted by, our language. My relationship to another person, to take a single example, does not exist apart from the speech I use to communicate with that person; rather, it is constituted in that speech. Anyone who doubts this might want to conduct a brief experiment. Try, for example, talking to your spouse or partner for five minutes using the style of speech that you would use with a small child or a professional colleague.

Because linguistic ideology is typically unarticulated and foundational, transformations in this sphere are likely to entail transformations in consciousness more generally.

One immediate implication of this fact is that a shift in language ideology can have impor-tant implications of a broadly political nature. For example, as the Comaroffs repeatedly note, the assumption among the group of British missionaries they studied—and it is probably safe to assume among most Christian missionaries—was that conversion to Christianity was the basis for acceptance of a Westernized way of life. This assumption was based on the conviction that acceptance of Christian discourse entails displacement of indigenous discourse[41] and (granted, the missionaries would not have conceptualized it in this way) of the linguistic ideology associated with indigenous discourse. In the case of the Tswana, that ideology was one "in which words shared in the reality of their ref-erents,"[42] one in which to speak something and to accomplish it are not understood as entirely separable processes. The referential ideology that has taken over in most regions of Western consciousness, on the other hand, stresses the division between reality and words that come to have meaning by corresponding to aspects of a separate reality. This view, not coincidentally, is part of a universalistic construal of the very nature of the cos-mos, a construal within which domination by one form of thought—the "correct" one—can be understood as a natural process. And, of course, among Westerners there has seldom been much doubt about who came closest to correct thought.

Although it is widely asserted that conversion is likely to carry with it a more or less total transformation of consciousness, the mechanisms of this transformation are rarely specified in any detail. In focusing on linguistic ideology, the Comaroffs' study exem-plifies one approach to understanding how this could occur. However, as they more or less acknowledge, there are some complications here. In particular, for evangelical Christians, the Word remains the one domain of discourse which is not governed by the basic assumptions of a referential ideology of language. Many conservative Christians today retain ideas reflected in some early Christian understandings of *Kerygma* (the notion that the saving efficacy of the word is carried not by the ideas to which it refers but rather by the magical efficacy of the words of the Gospel themselves). That is, there is a prominent aspect of linguistic ideology in some Western subcultures that looks much like that attributed to the Tswana. It implies no criticism of the Comaroffs' analysis to point out that there remain many interesting questions about conversion and language ideology that have yet to be addressed.

DISCOURSE AND TRANSFORMATION

Kenneth Burke's long essay on the conversion of St. Augustine in his *The Rhetoric of Religion*, originally written in the 1950s, remains a model for those who hope to study the discourse of the conversion narrative and its relationship to self-transformation. This difficult essay is made more challenging by the fact that, at the end of the day, Burke's goal is to use religious language to better understand language, not the conversion as such. Nevertheless, this analysis remains a rich source of insight and inspiration for any reader who tackles it.

Burke's starting point is the realization that language is our most basic tool for transcending experience. Burke assumes that it is because we relate to the world through language that we have an idea of transcendence, of standing apart from the stream of our experience. In this sense, language is our model for divinity: "What we say about *words*, in the empirical realm, will bear a notable likeness to what is said about *God*, in theology."[43] In looking at the personal transformation often associated with conversion, we must understand that we will be looking for the ways in which language creates bridges between situations or, in more Burkean terms, allows for a transformation of motives.

Burke's analysis of Augustine's account of his conversion in the *Confessions*, then, is a detailed, almost relentless search for the rhetorical tools which that master rhetorician used in achieving his own sought-after transformation. The complexity of this analysis defies summary, but I will try. Burke attends carefully to key words and even syllables that recur in Augustine's account and shows how these carriers of meaning are used to characterize Augustine's situation before conversion and eventually, through their rhetorical possibilities, are used to turn his consciousness and consequently his life around. Consider, for example, the function of the syllable "in," which carries some of the same meanings in Augustine's Latin prose as in English[44] : in particular, it can be used to designate something contained (innerness, inside, within, and so on), and it is a prefix of negation. The word thus can be used as a rhetorical agent of transformation, and it is used throughout the *Confessions* when Augustine takes up the subject of that which is within him and the need to turn that toward the path of Godliness: "The negative is in its very heart moralistic; it is the act of dissuasion reduced to one syllable—and Augustine invariably equates ethical improvement with innerness."[45]

Throughout the analysis, Burke sustains two overriding concerns. First, how does Augustine formulate and grasp divinity based upon analogies from the realm of language? Second, how does he use the capacity of language to embrace both who he was and who he becomes and also how that change occurs? Another group of related words that is prominent in Burke's analysis is, not surprisingly, the family of words based on "vert" (turn), and especially the contrast between the perversions of his early years and the conversion. Perhaps the best overall characterization of Burke's dazzling analysis shows us how much can be revealed through focusing on the poetics of the conversion narrative. Anyone who seeks inspiration in the quest to understand the language of the conversion narrative will want to return to this essay again and again; its riches are inexhaustible.

Once again, however, it is surprising and mildly depressing to note that Burke's approach has produced few imitations. Caldwell is attentive to poetics, as in her analysis of changing verb forms in the narrative of a Puritan woman who describes her more or less simultaneous conversion and trip to the New World[46] (Caldwell does not cite Burke, but her poetic analysis is undeniably Burkean.) Another example is her discussion of a narrative in which a woman testifies that a scriptural passage on deliverance came to her during childbirth, the passage both miraculously easing the pain of her labor and constituting a decisive moment in her conversion, rendering the experience (as Caldwell notes) a "double birth"—the child's physical birth and its mother's rebirth in Christ.

Interestingly, this moment of healing recalls one of the classic discussions of magic in the anthropological literature, Lévi-Strauss's analysis of the healing ritual of a Cuna (Central American) shaman.[47] Lévi-Strauss is also trying to understand how a sacred text might be effective in facilitating a difficult childbirth. He analyzes a lengthy transcript (collected by an earlier ethnographer) of the shaman's description of his journey to do battle with mythic figures from the Cuna pantheon, figures who are ultimately responsible for the woman's predicament. But, as both the original ethnographer and Lévi-Strauss point out, the shaman's quest is simultaneously a description of a journey into the woman's reproductive organs, and his dealings with the mythic figures also constitute an internal resolution of the difficulties she faces.

Here we encounter, once again, one of the most important processes for understanding the efficacy not only of religious language but of other symbolic practices through which human beings attempt to transcend their rootedness in an often intractable material world. The symbolism through which we represent a situation can be made to collapse into that situation, thereby effecting a momentary tangency between the transcendent and the mundane. The symbolism no longer describes the situation, it is the situation, and the potency of the symbolism—myth, scriptural passage, story—is thereby confirmed.[48] This is a particularly striking manifestation of what is sometimes termed the meta-pragmatic character of language, for it is a revelation of the always present yet seldom conceptualized capacity of language[49] to create the situations in which we dwell.[50]

Why should such a native meta-pragmatic event have the capacity to heal a medical or psychological problem? Lévi-Strauss himself provides a clearly worded answer that is worth quoting at length:

> The shaman provides the sick woman with a *language*, by means of which unexpressed, and otherwise inexpressible, psychic states can be immediately expressed. And it is the transition to this verbal expression—at the same time making it possible to undergo in an ordered and intelligible form a real experience that would otherwise be chaotic and inexpressible—which induces the release of the physiological process, that is, the reorganization, in a favorable direction, of the process to which the sick woman is subjected.[51]

This brings up the question that is in one sense the impetus to my own work on the conversion. In my *Language and Self-Transformation*, I begin from the assumption that the conversion narrative—in the form that I encountered it in an Evangelical Protestant Church—is typically a story of a journey from sin and confusion to salvation and certainty. That is, it is commonplace to observe that the experience of personal transformation[52] that is often a part of the Christian Protestant conversion narrative includes an account of healing from some sort of emotional or physical distress. What role does language play in facilitating this transformation?

It seemed to me that Burke's work was of particular importance for approaching this question, both in terms of the specific methods of analysis and in the broader attempt to understand the role of rhetoric in transforming motive. That is, the conversion narrative is often a story about how a believer transformed his or her motives from the destructive to the righteous. If we could understand more about how this happens, we would gain insight into both of the components of conversion, personal transformation and institutional affiliation. With regard to personal transformation, there is no doubt that many sorts of emotional and physical distress (perhaps especially substance abuse problems) have been resolved through conversion experiences. How does this happen? And with regard to the sociological question of institutional affiliation, perhaps better understanding the healing power of the conversion narrative will provide insight into how it helps to generate commitment to an institution.

Thus, for the purposes of the present chapter, the most important part of the analysis in *Language and Self-Transformation* is its study of the capacity of language to persuade both the performer of the conversion narrative and his or her listener that a personal transformation has been wrought by God. Of course, as a social scientist, I must bracket any judgment as to the ultimate mover behind the events I describe. My underlying assumption, one that is shared with a number of scholars both before and since this book,[53] is that said transformation is best understood as accomplished not in the original conversion event but rather in the ritual recounting of that event, the conversion narrative. The reasoning here is very simple: the analyst has no access to the original conversion event, and whatever it was that happened there, it cannot be observed. So, anyone who sets out to study religious experiences of personal transformation lands almost inevitably in the position of studying the conversion narrative, whether or not he or she acknowledges this.

This is not such a bad thing, however. As Erving Goffman noted, a re-telling is typically to some extent a re-living[54] (and all the more so for a life-changing event). He says of the narrator:

> In an important sense, even if his purpose is to present the cold facts as he sees them, the means he employs may be intrinsically theatrical, not because he necessarily exaggerates or follows a script, but because he may have to engage in something that is a dramatization—the use of such arts as he possesses to reproduce a scene, to *replay* it.[55]

No wonder that there is a rich tradition within Evangelical Christianity of considering the conversion narrative as itself a special means for the mediation of God's grace. As I have noted earlier, that narrative is often understood to be miraculously shaped by scriptural templates and is often assumed to have an evangelical efficacy of its own, to bring about the reception of grace as it recounts the reception of grace.

The student of the oral conversion narrative will likely find, as I did, that it swarms with rhetorical strategies, all the more so if one attends closely to the performance of the narrative. In my book, I pointed to several phenomena that can be catalogued and interpreted in an attempt to better understand the role of language (in the broadest sense) in transforming the motives that contribute to a life of sin to those that sustain a life of faith. Among the linguistic and para-linguistic features I considered were quoted speech, disfluencies and parapraxes (slips of the tongue), voice and rhythm changes, and lexical patterns.[56] Consistently, my hope was to understand how the capacity of language to carry and generate meaning allows utterances to bridge the old and the new, to embrace the believer's ambivalence.

I also considered aspects of linguistic ideology as they are reflected in the assumptions and persuasive strategies of the conversion narrative. My argument here is that because our popular linguistic ideology encourages us to understand language as working by corresponding to a separate reality, we are prone to understand many social and physical processes as things. An example here would be our very selves. Rather than seeing and acknowledging the aspects of our selves that are constituted in the language through which we conceptualize them, we are prone instead to think of the self on the model of an internal organ, something located within the body though notoriously difficult to locate.[57] Because we think of the self in this way, it can be surprising when a person has an immediate and visceral experience of how the self is constituted in language. Indeed, under the right circumstances such an experience can seem miraculous.

Think for example about the technique—already mentioned several times here—of construing an ongoing situation in terms of a biblical passage that seems to embrace it. If, as happened in the critical moment of Augustine's conversion, scriptural language seems to describe both the former phase of sinfulness and the current and future state of grace, then at that moment the passage constitutes self-understanding. In fact, from the perspective of the believer, it is misleading to speak of self-understanding. Rather, there is, figuratively speaking, no gap between the Word and the world here; the self and Scripture are one. My point here is that this miraculous confirmation of the Bible's sacredness and power is built upon the assumptions of a particular ideology of language.

Our language has such powerful capacities to express and shape our selves, our relationships, and our experience that we can find ourselves surprised and overwhelmed by what it has accomplished. *Language and Self-Transformation* is comprised of examples of how performances of conversion narratives express profound truths about the narrators, truths that may remain outside of conscious awareness. These insights are constituted in patterns of speech and narrative, and inevitably believers find a way to extend these patterns into the realm of the sacred. Not only do these patterns now have the significance of the eternal; they capture something at once momentous and nearly inarticulable about the believer. This is one more way that a conversion narrative may effect self-transformation by tapping into deep motivations and transforming them into something of religious significance.[58] And the healing that is wrought by such formulations becomes a deeply felt basis for commitment.

SUGGESTIONS FOR FUTURE WORK AND
FURTHER READING

Recent decades have seen enormous advances in the study of language behavior, and the resulting insights into language have given all social scientists a more powerful set of tools for investigating many different realms of social action. Certain areas of overlap between sociolinguistics and social life in general have received special attention, religion and concept of self being two of these. Thus, the ground is well prepared for those who hope to study the language of the conversion, and I hope that in the coming years these rich possibilities will be exploited.

I suggest that those who are interested in exploring these possibilities begin with, on the topic of language and person, Jane Hill and Judith Irvine's *Responsibility and Evidence in Oral Discourse* and Erving Goffman's *Frame Analysis*, especially chapter 13. On the topic of religious language, a good place to start is with Webb Keane's review article on religious language,[59] which also has an excellent bibliography. For a broader introduction to the extensive historical and literary scholarship on the Christian conversion narrative, we are now lucky to have Hindmarsh's *The Evangelical Conversion Narrative*. I wish I could recommend a similar work that covers the early history of the idea of conversion in traditions other than Christianity, but for the moment that book is waiting to be written. Finally, even half a century later, for both methodological and theoretical reasons, no student of language and the conversion can neglect Kenneth Burke's *The Rhetoric of Religion*.

NOTES

1. Kenneth Burke, *The Rhetoric of Religion: Studies in Logology* (Berkeley and Los Angeles: University of California Press, 1970), 7.
2. In addition to the problems I articulate in the text, what can we do with a phenomenon that looks for all the world like a conversion experience but is not considered to be such by its narrator? (For example, the believer affirms the doctrine of predestination and therefore denies the possibility of a turning point that changes one's state of salvation.) See James L. Peacock and Ruel W. Tyson, Jr., *Pilgrims of Paradox: Calvinism and Experience among the Primitive Baptists of the Blue Ridge* (Washington, DC: Smithsonian Institution Press, 1989).
3. Nock made a similar point when he distinguished conversion and adhesion. Comaroff and Comaroff also question the forced marriage of personal belief and denominational membership that is embedded in the social scientific conception of conversion. Arthur D. Nock, *Conversion: The Old and the New in Religion from Alexander the Great to Augustine of Hippo* (Baltimore: Johns Hopkins University Press, 1933); Jean Comaroff and John Comaroff, *Of Revelation and Revolution: Christianity, Colonialism, and Consciousness in South Africa*, 2 vols. (Chicago: University of Chicago Press, 1991), 249.
4. The association of religious change with identity change has a peculiarly American ring, and in my view scholars should be particularly careful about generalizing this association.

I suspect that we often underestimate the influence in our thought of the unique relationship between conversion and identity that took shape in parts of late nineteenth-century American Protestantism. The work of T. J. Jackson Lears is especially helpful for those who want to understand how ideas from the millenarian tradition within Protestantism and conceptions of personhood affiliated with emerging consumer capitalism converged to create the "therapeutic ethos" of contemporary Western (especially North American) culture. See, for example, "From Salvation to Self-Realization," in *The Culture of Consumption: Critical Essays in American History 1880–1980*, ed. Richard W. Fox and T. J. Jackson Lears (New York: Pantheon, 1983), 3–38. Without going into the matter in any depth, suffice it to say that contemporary ideas about personal identity and fulfillment, as well as the notion of the perfectibility of the self through therapeutic interventions, are by no means universally shared among all human beings. The sometimes taken-for-granted conception of religious conversion that understands it to be an experience of personal transformation can only grow in the fertile soil of a particular blend of ethnopsychological assumptions.

5. Andrew Buckser and Stephen D. Glazier, eds., *The Anthropology of Religious Conversion* (New York: Rowman and Littlefield, 2003), xi.

6. A particularly clear example of this point (and there are many, many examples) is contained in a recent article discussing the policies of the Russian empire in the early modern period. "In early modern Russia, conversion did not take place because non-Christians were interested in the Christian teachings. Instead, those natives who converted did so either because they were pressured by force and discrimination or because they were attracted by the numerous benefits that the government offered upon conversion. *Conversion in Russia was spiritual least of all; it generally involved only a nominal transfer of religious identity*" (emphasis added). Michael Khodarkovsky, " 'Not by Word Alone': Missionary Policies and Religious Conversion in Early Modern Russia, *Comparative Studies in Society and History* 38 (1996): 268–269.

7. Edmund S. Morgan, *Visible Saints: The History of a Puritan Idea* (New York: New York University Press, 1963).

8. Max Weber, *The Protestant Ethic and the Spirit of Capitalism* (New York: Charles Scribner's Sons, 1958).

9. Morgan, *Visible Saints*, 61 ff., offers evidence that the conversion narrative became the most important sign of the workings of God's grace in American churches sometime during the 1630s. See also Bruce Hindmarsh, *The Evangelical Conversion Narrative: Spiritual Autobiography in Early Modern England* (Oxford: Oxford University Press, 2005), 49.

10. An excellent example of how disciplinary boundaries can stand in the way of progress can be found in my own earlier work. In my *Language and Self-Transformation: A Study of the Christian Conversion Narrative* (Cambridge: Cambridge University Press, 1993), I state (p. 5) that I have been unable to find studies of the conversion narrative as a genre. This is because I was looking within the social sciences proper; this topic is abundantly covered by disciplines in the humanities. I make a small attempt to atone for my error in the present work.

11. See, for example, Nock, *Conversion: The Old and the New in Religion*; Arthur F. Glasser, "Conversion in Judaism," in *Handbook of Religious Conversion*, ed. Newton Malony and Samuel Southard (Birmingham, AL: Religious Education Press, 1992), 55–77; Robert W. Hefner, *Conversion to Christianity: Historical and Anthropological Perspectives on a Great Transformation* (Berkeley and Los Angeles: University of California Press, 1993); Buckser

and Glazier, *The Anthropology of Religious Conversion*; Howard Clark Kee, "From the Jesus Movement toward the Institutional Church," in *Conversion to Christianity: Historical and Anthropological Perspectives on a Great Transformation*, ed. Robert W. Hefner (Berkeley and Los Angeles: University of California Press, 1993), 47–64; Hindmarsh, *The Evangelical Conversion Narrative*; Comaroff and Comaroff, *Of Revelation and Revolution*.

12. For a brief discussion, see Rita Smith Kipp, "Conversion by Affiliation: The History of the Karo Batak Protestant Church," *American Ethnologist* 22 (1995): 868–882.

13. In so doing, I unfortunately have to neglect an interesting range of questions having to do with the relationship between these two social processes, a matter that will have to be taken up at another opportunity.

14. See Morgan, *Visible Saints*; Perry Miller, *The New England Mind: The Seventeenth Century* (Boston: Beacon Press, 1954); Norman Petit, *The Heart Prepared: Grace and Conversion in Puritan Spiritual Life* (New Haven: Yale University Press, 1966); Owen Watkins, *The Puritan Experience: Studies in Spiritual Autobiography* (New York: Schocken Books, 1972); Patricia Caldwell, *The Puritan Conversion Narrative: The Beginnings of American Expression* (Cambridge: Cambridge University Press, 1985).

15. The work I am discussing here is almost exclusively devoted to the Christian conversion narrative and, more broadly, it is fair to say that most of the available literature on this topic in general focuses heavily on Christianity. The present chapter comprises another example of this tendency, not because I regard the Christian conversion as any more worthy of attention than any other, but because to attempt to thoroughly discuss language and conversion in several different religious traditions would require not a chapter but a book. For what it is worth, I refer to some other traditions when I can do so without deviating from my central focus. Also for what it is worth, as an anthropologist I retain some doubts about whether the term "conversion" is useful in studying all religious traditions. Most scholars of conversion would likely acknowledge the diversity of conversion practices in different religious traditions but affirm that underlying this diversity is a single, definable entity that can be fairly labeled conversion. See Lewis R. Rambo, *Understanding Religious Conversion* (New Haven: Yale University Press, 1993), 1ff., for a clear statement of this position. I prefer to remain somewhat more agnostic on this issue, alert to the possibility that conversion is a concept so deeply rooted in the Judeo-Christian (and primarily Christian Protestant) tradition that it may not be appropriate for understanding seemingly similar processes in different traditions. For a recent argument that the concept does not travel well to Islam, see Marcia Hermansen, "Roads to Mecca: Conversion Narratives of European and Euro-American Muslims," *The Muslim World* 89 (1999): 56–89.

16. William James, *The Varieties of Religious Experience* (New York: New American Library, 1958).

17. Watkins, *The Puritan Experience*, 209.

18. Compare John W. Du Bois's discussion of divination in "Meaning Without Intention: Lessons from Divination," in *Responsibility and Evidence in Oral Discourse*, ed. Jane Hill and Judith Irvine (Cambridge: Cambridge University Press, 1993), 48–71, and his discussion of ritual speech in general in "Self-Evidence and Ritual Speech," in *Evidentiality: The Linguistic Coding of Epistemology*, ed. Wallace Chafe and Johanna Nichols (Norwood, NJ: Ablex, 1986), 313–336. Du Bois points out that the absence of the features that attribute responsibility for a statement is a prominent feature of many forms of ritual speech. Such issues of evidentiality are certainly of relevance for conversion narratives, yet I do not know of any studies that directly pursue this topic.

19. See Hindmarsh, *The Evangelical Conversion Narrative*, 204 ff., for a description of this practice among Scottish Presbyterians of a later period. See also Watkins, *The Puritan Experience*; Caldwell, *The Puritan Conversion Narrative*; Jeff Todd Titon, *Powerhouse for God: Speech, Chant, and Song in an Appalachian Baptist Church* (Austin: University of Texas Press, 1988); Peacock and Tyson, *Pilgrims of Paradox*.

20. Burke, *The Rhetoric of Religion*, 58.

21. One could write a separate chapter on magical practices centering on sacred language in conservative Protestant groups. One example is the practice of using randomly selected Bible verses in a form of divination that informs the believer about God's intentions; another is the belief that oral description of a situation may bring about its fulfillment (I refer to this idea repeatedly throughout this chapter). See Simon Coleman, "Continuous Conversion? The Rhetoric, Practice, and Rhetorical Practice of Charismatic Protestant Conversion," in *The Anthropology of Religious Conversion*, ed. Andrew Buckser and Stephen D. Glazier (New York: Rowman and Littlefield, 2003), 23.

22. Susan Friend Harding, *The Book of Jerry Falwell: Fundamentalist Language and Politics.* (Princeton: Princeton University Press, 2000).

23. Hindmarsh, *The Evangelical Conversion Narrative*, 340.

24. The phrase "universe of discourse" comes from George Herbert Mead, *Mind, Self, and Society: From the Standpoint of a Social Behaviorist* (Chicago: University of Chicago Press, 1934), 89.

25. David A. Snow and Richard Machalek, "The Convert as Social Type," in *Sociological Theory*, ed. Randall Collins (San Francisco: Jossey-Bass, 1983), 265.

26. Ibid., 266.

27. Clifford Staples and Armand L. Mauss, "Conversion or Commitment? A Reassessment of the Snow and Machalek Approach to the Study of Conversion," *Journal for the Scientific Study of Religion* 26 (1987): 133–147.

28. Without getting into the matter here, I should note that my formulation of this point does not imply that I assume that a person typically has a "core self" in the way that he or she typically has, say, a nose.

29. Staples and Mauss, "Conversion or Commitment," 137. Again I want to remind the reader that Staples and Mauss, along with many other authors, at least implicitly assume equivalence between religious conversion and religious experiences of self-transformation. As I have said, I do not accept this assumption.

30. Staples and Mauss, "Conversion or Commitment," 138.

31. Of course, there is variation in the literature, with some studies attending to such matters as narrative structure and typical metaphors (David A. Knight, Robert A. Woods, and Ines W. Jindra, "Gender Differences in the Communication of Christian Conversion Narratives," *Review of Religious Research* 47 [2005]: 113–134) and others not addressing these issues. For a recent example of an interesting study that would be improved by a more detailed analysis of rhetorical features of conversion narratives, see Chris M. Ponticelli, "Crafting Stories of Sexual Identity Reconstruction," *Social Psychology Quarterly* 62 (1999): 157–192.

32. Another recent work that directly considers narrative conventions and religious conversion is David Yamane, "Narrative and Religious Experience," *Sociology of Religion* 61 (2000): 171–189. However, Yamane's topic is really narrative and religious experience in general; he does not attempt to study the conversion per se in detail.

33. For another sophisticated analysis of the rhetoric of a religious group, not focused on issues of conversion, see Thomas J. Csordas, *Language, Charisma, and Creativity* (Berkeley and Los Angeles: University of California Press, 1997).

34. Harding, *The Book of Jerry Falwell*, 34.

35. See Jane H. Hill, "Finding Culture in Narrative," in *Finding Culture in Talk: A Collection of Methods*, ed. Naomi Quinn (New York: Palgrave Macmillan, 2005), 157–202.

36. Anna Mansson McGinty allows us to take a step in that direction by focusing on the conversion narratives of Swedish women who have converted to Islam. It would take further work, however, to start to sort out the extent to which her case studies reflect the conventions of Western personal transformation narratives and to what extent they reveal characteristic Islamic notions. Anna Mansson McGinty, *Becoming Muslim: Western Women's Conversions to Islam* (New York: Palgrave Macmillan, 2006).

37. See Hefner, *Conversion to Christianity*, 5; Buckser and Glazier, *The Anthropology of Religious Conversion*; Matthew Engelke, "Discontinuity and the Discourse of Conversion," *Journal of Religion in Africa* 34 (2004): 82–109.

38. Robert J. Priest, "'I Discovered My Sin!': Aguaruna Evangelical Conversion Narratives," in *The Anthropology of Religious Conversion*, ed. Andrew R. Buckser and Stephen D. Glazier (New York: Rowman and Littlefield, 2003), 95–108.

39. Comaroff and Comaroff, *Of Revelation and Revolution*.

40. Michael Silverstein, "Shifters, Linguistic Categories, and Cultural Description," in *Meaning in Anthropology*, ed. Keith Basso and Henry Selby (Albuquerque: University of New Mexico Press, 1976), 11–55; Kathryn A. Woolard and Bambi B. Schieffelin, "Language Ideology," *Annual Review of Anthropology* 23 (1994): 55–82.

41. The overall thrust of the analysis offered by the Comaroffs is to question this assumption and to point out that in the case they describe, acceptance of Christian belief and practice was likely to entail a synthesis with aspects of local religion.

42. Comaroff and Comaroff, *Of Revelation and Revolution*, 224.

43. Burke, *The Rhetoric of Religion*, 13–14.

44. I do not know Latin, but Burke did.

45. Burke, *The Rhetoric of Religion*, 53.

46. Caldwell, *The Puritan Conversion Narrative*, 27.

47. Claude Lévi-Strauss, *Structural Anthropology* (New York: Basic Books, 1963), 186–205.

48. See Titon, *Powerhouse for God*, for a discussion of this issue framed in terms of speech act theory.

49. As I have commented before, not all linguistic ideologies are like ours in diverting attention from the ways in which language constitutes our experience.

50. See Webb Keane, "Religious Language," *Annual Review of Anthropology* 26 (1997): 47–71; Silverstein, "Shifters, Linguistic Categories, and Cultural Description"; Richard Bauman and Charles L. Briggs, "Poetics and Performance as Critical Perspectives on Language and Social Life," *Annual Review of Anthropology* 19 (1990): 59–88; Michelle Z. Rosaldo, "The Things We Do with Words: Ilongot Speech Acts and Speech Act Theory in Philosophy," *Language in Society* 11 (1982): 203–237.

51. Lévi-Strauss, *Structural Anthropology*, 198.

52. It is worth emphasizing that experiences of personal transformation are themselves culturally constructed and are the product of a particular history. Although such experiences are highly elaborated in parts of the Western tradition, it does not follow that they are important in all times and places. At the same time, a focus on personal transformation cannot

be assumed to be unique to the Western tradition; consider, for example, the many strands of Buddhist thought that are oriented around this issue.

53. See Brian Taylor, "Recollection and Membership: Converts' Talk and the Ratiocination of Commonality," *Sociology* 12 (1978): 316–324; James A. Beckford, "Accounting for Conversion," *British Journal of Sociology* 29 (1978): 249–262; Yamane, "Narrative and Religious Experience." For a more general discussion of the position that religious experience is only available through the language in which it is formulated, see Wayne Proudfoot, *Religious Experience* (Berkeley and Los Angeles: University of California Press, 1985.

54. McGinty *Becoming Muslim*, 51, makes the same assumption for the Islamic conversion narratives she discusses.

55. Erving Goffman, *Frame Analysis: An Essay on the Organization of Experience* (Boston: Northeastern University Press, 1986), 503–504.

56. In this chapter I have only scratched the surface of the aspects of language use that could be considered in analyzing the conversion narrative. For example, I have said nothing about (and, as far as I know, no other scholar has said anything about) the entire question of entextualization of the conversion narrative: how is the conversion narrative divorced from its performance and rendered a meaningful segment of free-standing text? See Bauman and Briggs, "Poetics and Performance"; Keane, "Religious Language."

57. It would be understandable, in the current political and scholarly climate, if the reader were to assume that this statement means that I endorse another sort of essentialism, the often-encountered claim that the self is nothing other than the stories (or other linguistic processes) that constitute it. This would be an incorrect assumption; I believe that what we call selves emerge from certain kinds of physical beings who have a way of life based in culture, and both the culture and the beings are relevant.

58. See Ulrike Popp-Baier, "Narrating Embodied Aims: Self-transformation in Conversion Narratives—A Psychological Analysis," *Forum Sozialforschung/forum: Qualitative Social Research*, North America, 2 (Sept. 2, 2001).

59. Keane, "Religious Language."

BIBLIOGRAPHY

Bauman, Richard, and Charles L. Briggs. "Poetics and Performance as Critical Perspectives on Language and Social Life." *Annual Review of Anthropology* 19 (1990): 59–88.
Beckford, James A. "Accounting for Conversion." *British Journal of Sociology* 29 (1978): 249–262.
Buckser, Andrew, and Stephen D. Glazier, eds. *The Anthropology of Religious Conversion.* New York: Rowman and Littlefield, 2003.
Burke, Kenneth. *The Rhetoric of Religion: Studies in Logology.* Berkeley and Los Angeles: University of California Press, 1970.
Caldwell, Patricia. *The Puritan Conversion Narrative: The Beginnings of American Expression.* Cambridge: Cambridge University Press, 1985.
Coleman, Simon. "Continuous Conversion? The Rhetoric, Practice, and Rhetorical Practice of Charismatic Protestant Conversion." In *The Anthropology of Religious Conversion*, ed. Andrew Buckser and Stephen D. Glazier, 15–27. New York: Rowman and Littlefield, 2003.
Comaroff, Jean, and John Comaroff. *Of Revelation and Revolution: Christianity, Colonialism, and Consciousness in South Africa.* 2 vols. Chicago: University of Chicago Press, 1991.

Csordas, Thomas J. *Language, Charisma, and Creativity*. Berkeley and Los Angeles: University of California Press, 1997.

Du Bois, John W. "Self-Evidence and Ritual Speech." In *Evidentiality: The Linguistic Coding of Epistemology*, ed. Wallace Chafe and Johanna Nichols, 313–336. Norwood, NJ: Ablex, 1986.

——. "Meaning Without Intention: Lessons from Divination." In *Responsibility and Evidence in Oral Discourse*, ed. Jane Hill and Judith Irvine, 48–71. Cambridge: Cambridge University Press, 1993.

Engelke, Matthew. "Discontinuity and the Discourse of Conversion." *Journal of Religion in Africa* 34 (2004): 82–109.

Glasser, Arthur F. "Conversion in Judaism." In *Handbook of Religious Conversion*, ed. Newton Malony and Samuel Southard, 55–77. Birmingham, AL: Religious Education Press, 1992.

Goffman, Erving. *Frame Analysis: An Essay on the Organization of Experience*. Boston: Northeastern University Press, 1986.

Harding, Susan Friend. *The Book of Jerry Falwell: Fundamentalist Language and Politics*. Princeton: Princeton University Press, 2000.

Hefner, Robert W. *Conversion to Christianity: Historical and Anthropological Perspectives on a Great Transformation*. Berkeley and Los Angeles: University of California Press, 1993.

Hermansen, Marcia. "Roads to Mecca: Conversion Narratives of European and Euro-American Muslims." *The Muslim World* 89 (1999): 56–89.

Hill, Jane H. "Finding Culture in Narrative." In *Finding Culture in Talk: A Collection of Methods*, ed. Naomi Quinn, 157–202. New York: Palgrave Macmillan, 2005.

Hill, Jane H., and Judith Irvine, eds. *Responsibility and Evidence in Oral Discourse*. Cambridge: Cambridge University Press, 1992.

Hindmarsh, Bruce. *The Evangelical Conversion Narrative: Spiritual Autobiography in Early Modern England*. Oxford: Oxford University Press, 2005.

James, William. *The Varieties of Religious Experience*. New York: New American Library, 1958.

Keane, Webb. "Religious Language." *Annual Review of Anthropology* 26 (1997): 47–71.

Kee, Howard Clark. "From the Jesus Movement toward the Institutional Church." In *Conversion to Christianity: Historical and Anthropological Perspectives on a Great Transformation*, ed. Robert W. Hefner, 47–64. Berkeley and Los Angeles: University of California Press, 1993.

Khodarkovsky, Michael. " 'Not by Word Alone': Missionary Policies and Religious Conversion in Early Modern Russia. *Comparative Studies in Society and History* 38 (1996): 267–293.

Kipp, Rita Smith. "Conversion by Affiliation: The History of the Karo Batak Protestant Church." *American Ethnologist* 22 (1995): 868–882.

Knight, David A., Robert A. Woods, and Ines W. Jindra. "Gender Differences in the Communication of Christian Conversion Narratives." *Review of Religious Research* 47 (2005): 113–134.

Lears, T. J. Jackson. "From Salvation to Self-Realization." In *The Culture of Consumption: Critical Essays in American History 1880–1980*, ed. Richard W. Fox and T. J. Jackson Lears, 3–38. New York: Pantheon, 1983.

Lévi-Strauss, Claude. *Structural Anthropology*. New York: Basic Books, 1963.

McAdams, Dan P. *The Redemptive Self: Stories Americans Live By*. New York: Oxford University Press, 2006.

McGinty, Anna Mansson. *Becoming Muslim: Western Women's Conversions to Islam*. New York: Palgrave Macmillan, 2006.

Mead, George Herbert. *Mind, Self, and Society: From the Standpoint of a Social Behaviorist*. Chicago: University of Chicago Press, 1934.

Miller, Perry. *The New England Mind: The Seventeenth Century*. Boston: Beacon Press, 1954.

Morgan, Edmund S. *Visible Saints: The History of a Puritan Idea*. New York: New York University Press, 1963.

Nock, Arthur D. *Conversion: The Old and the New in Religion from Alexander the Great to Augustine of Hippo*. Baltimore: Johns Hopkins University Press, 1933.

Peacock, James L., and Ruel W. Tyson, Jr. *Pilgrims of Paradox: Calvinism and Experience among the Primitive Baptists of the Blue Ridge*. Washington, DC: Smithsonian Institution Press, 1989.

Petit, Norman. *The Heart Prepared: Grace and Conversion in Puritan Spiritual Life*. New Haven: Yale University Press, 1966.

Ponticelli, Chris M. "Crafting Stories of Sexual Identity Reconstruction." *Social Psychology Quarterly* 62 (1999): 157–192.

Popp-Baier, Ulrike. "Narrating Embodied Aims: Self-transformation in Conversion Narratives—A Psychological Analysis." *Forum Sozialforschung/forum: Qualitative Social Research*, North America, 2 (Sept. 2, 2001). http://www.qualitative-research.net/index.php/fqs/article.

Priest, Robert J. "'I Discovered My Sin!': Aguaruna Evangelical Conversion Narratives." In *The Anthropology of Religious Conversion*, ed. Andrew Buckser and Stephen D. Glazier, 95–108. New York: Rowman and Littlefield, 2003.

Proudfoot, Wayne. *Religious Experience*. Berkeley and Los Angeles: University of California Press, 1985.

Rambo, Lewis R. *Understanding Religious Conversion*. New Haven: Yale University Press, 1993.

Rosaldo, Michelle Z. "The Things We Do with Words: Ilongot Speech Acts and Speech Act Theory in Philosophy." *Language in Society* 11 (1982): 203–237.

Silverstein, Michael. "Shifters, Linguistic Categories, and Cultural Description." In *Meaning in Anthropology*, ed. Keith Basso and Henry Selby, 11–55. Albuquerque: University of New Mexico Press, 1976.

Snow, David A., and Richard Machalek. "The Convert as Social Type." In *Sociological Theory*, ed. Randall Collins, 259–289. San Francisco: Jossey-Bass, 1983.

Staples, Clifford, and Armand L. Mauss. "Conversion or Commitment? A Reassessment of the Snow and Machalek Approach to the Study of Conversion." *Journal for the Scientific Study of Religion* 26 (1987): 133–147.

Stromberg, Peter G. *Language and Self-Transformation. A Study of the Christian Conversion Narrative*. Cambridge: Cambridge University Press, 1993.

Taylor, Brian. "Recollection and Membership: Converts' Talk and the Ratiocination of Commonality." *Sociology* 12 (1978): 316–324.

Titon, Jeff Todd. *Powerhouse for God: Speech, Chant, and Song in an Appalachian Baptist Church*. Austin: University of Texas Press, 1988.

Watkins, Owen. *The Puritan Experience: Studies in Spiritual Autobiography*. New York: Schocken Books, 1972.

Weber, Max. *The Protestant Ethic and the Spirit of Capitalism*. New York: Charles Scribner's Sons, 1958.

Woolard, Kathryn A., and Bambi B. Schieffelin. "Language Ideology." *Annual Review of Anthropology* 23 (1994): 55–82.

Yamane, David. "Narrative and Religious Experience." *Sociology of Religion* 61 (2000): 171–189.

CHAPTER 6

....

SOCIOLOGY OF RELIGIOUS CONVERSION

....

FENGGANG YANG AND ANDREW ABEL

THE sociological study of religious conversion advanced appreciably from the 1960s to the 1980s.[1] Micro-level analysis predominated at that time, and the primary research questions concerned the kinds of individuals who convert and how these individuals are led to convert. In the 1990s and the early twenty-first century, the field broadened to include greater consideration of meso- and macro-level factors. Up to the 1980s, the secularization thesis, in its various incarnations, dominated the sociology of religion, and religious conversion was often regarded as a deviant behavior of some individuals against a presumed normative expectation of declining interest in religion under conditions of modernization.[2] Unfortunately, the secularization paradigm distracted researchers from addressing the continuing religious vitality characteristic of the world today.[3]

The widespread assumption that people become less religious as they become more modern has never fit conditions in the United States, which, despite being quite modern, nonetheless has maintained high rates of religious participation. As empirical evidence mounted against simplistic assumptions regarding modernity and religion, an alternative paradigm rose to explain religious vitality. R. Stephen Warner's "New Paradigm" posited a relationship between religious pluralism and competition between religious groups—competition that tends to increase the quality of the "product" offered.[4] In this view, the religious vitality in America's pluralist religious "marketplace" can be explained in contradistinction to those European nations in which national religions hold a near monopoly over religious life. The various theories and approaches within the New Paradigm, including the market theory and subcultural identities theory, have led to a flurry of research in the social scientific study of religion.[5]

Yet continuing vitality is not the whole picture. Another trend is the increased likelihood of individuals to change their religious orientations and affiliations, as between religious denominations, across major religions, or in or out of religion altogether. At the meso level[6] of religious institutions, recent congregational studies offer unique and important insights into conversion because people usually convert in and into congregations or, conversely, out of them.[7] Although the term "congregation" may suggest a Christian tone, the new congregational researchers employ the term broadly in relation to groups of any persuasion that gather regularly for religious practices.[8] Congregational studies typically treat congregations as communities of collective rituals and assume that a congregation, almost by definition, is made up of people who share a religious identity. Hence, ritual and subcultural identity practices play important roles in attracting and socializing new converts.

Since the 1960s, membership in mainline Christian denominations has declined, whereas conservative churches have attracted new members. Rational choice theorists have responded to this situation by arguing that the strictness of a church's doctrine affects recruitment and conversion. Theologically conservative and morally strict churches demand greater commitment from members in terms of time, tithing, and overall dedication. This not only reduces the potential for "free riders," it also attracts people willing to give more of themselves because they perceive even greater rewards, including the social benefits of a highly committed congregation and, spiritually, a sense of certainty of salvation.[9] For instance, Chinese converts in the United States and China have usually joined evangelical churches that are theologically conservative and morally strict rather than liberal churches, at least in part because many believe that evangelical churches provide greater assurance of salvation, clarity about moral values, and certainty amidst dramatic changes in society and personal life.[10] Yet this rational choice explanation has remained controversial, in part because it is possible for churches to be demanding in different ways. The contemporary worship styles favored by evangelical churches, for example, place fewer cultural demands upon potential converts than the ancient liturgical practices retained in such liberal, mainline denominations as the Episcopal Church.

At the macro level, to explain the phenomenon of large-scale conversion movements or "mass conversion," social and cultural contextual factors must be considered. By "mass conversion" we mean "the phenomenon of religious conversion happening to many individuals in a society within a relatively short period of time. These individuals converted voluntarily rather than being forced to do so by the king or the clan patriarch, as happened sometimes in medieval Europe and other premodern societies."[11] The growth of Christianity in Korea and China, for instance, or the rise of Pentecostalism in Latin America, indicates change at the level of collectivities and therefore demands sociological analysis of conversion as a sort of social movement. Indeed, the macro level has been a requisite focus of many recent studies that situate this religious change in the context of increasing globalization, cosmopolitanism, and transnationalism.[12] To ignore macro-level analysis is to omit precisely those variables that in many societies explain the most variance in conversion, and this entails a sharply reduced capacity to explore the ways that rates of conversion and the experience of conversion by individuals are affected by changing social contexts.

Such micro-, meso-, and macro-level analyses are not contradictory. Rather, each complements the others. Together they provide a more comprehensive and distinctly sociological understanding of religious conversion. In this chapter, we do not seek to review all of the sociological studies of conversion but will consider key work at each of these levels. Throughout the discussion, we emphasize cross-cultural comparisons and refer in particular to one of the most dramatic and instructive examples of conversion in recent years: the rise of Christianity among the Chinese.

CONVERSION AT THE MICRO LEVEL: FROM DEPRIVATION TO PERSONAL BONDS AND NETWORKS

The process model of conversion suggested by Lofland and Stark is arguably the first authentically sociological model of religious conversion in the sense that it moves beyond a psychological conception of conversion to consider personal bonds and social networks.[13] According to Lofland and Stark's model, religious conversion is not merely a psychological change in the convert but also a restructuring of the convert's social relationships. Some individuals may not even embrace the new theology for some time after joining a new religious group. Through participant observation and interviews with individuals associated with the Unification Church, then newly arrived in California, Lofland and Stark summarized the conversion process into seven stages or factors that they identified as "predisposing conditions" and "situational contingencies." Religious conversion occurs only when an individual has exhibited the predisposing conditions of tension or crisis, religious problem-solving perspective, and religious seeking. Among the predisposed individuals, whether one actually converts depends on situational contingencies, including being at a turning point in life, interacting with believers of the new religion, weakening of other social bonds, and increasing attachment to believers of the new religion.

This process model dominated theory construction and empirical testing for almost three decades, with detailed examination of the relevance of certain conditions and contingencies.[14] William Sims Bainbridge suggests that the process model achieved dominance in large part because it united strain theory and social influence theory.[15] Strain theory, more commonly known as deprivation theory, begins with the assumption that people turn toward religion when they lack something, either an "absolute" deprivation, such as bad health or poverty, or a "relative" deprivation, as when people in any condition subjectively feel the lack of something. Social influence theory has two variations: control theory and subculture theory. From this standpoint, religious conversion is treated as a change in group affiliation that necessitates learning new behaviors and norms. Bainbridge argued that combined use of these two approaches was a way forward in the study of conversion.

The process model was heavily applied in the study of conversion to New Religious Movements (NRM)[16] but was also applied to believers of mainstream religions, mostly to individual "returnees" or "switchers" within Protestantism, Catholicism, or Judaism.[17] In the award-winning *Vanishing Boundaries: The Religion of Mainline Protestant Baby Boomers*, based on a survey of some 500 respondents and 40 in-depth interviews with people who were confirmed in Presbyterian churches, Dean R. Hoge et al. (1992) examined the religious motivations of baby boomers and identified four "churched" and four "unchurched" types. They found that many Protestant youth drop out of church life when they are between sixteen and twenty-two years old but then many of these return later, especially when raising children. Many of the unchurched people still hold Christian worldviews and values, although they are more individualistic in religious matters.

It is important to point out that indications of affiliation and commitment often serve as effective proxy measures of conversion, in part because inner states of mind cannot be directly studied using empirical methods. Therefore, it has often been difficult for sociologists to distinguish between conversion and commitment, and this problem is compounded in traditions that emphasize practice over belief, such as Judaism or Buddhism. Barker and Currie demonstrate that a person's level of commitment may vary after a cognitively based conversion experience (i.e., a change in belief).[18] However, even though the individual's beliefs may remain the same, he or she may experience a shift in the felt intensity or frequency of participation.

For researchers who prefer to emphasize belief over practice, commitment is expected to vary, but this does not change one's basic religious orientation. Obviously, one year's unenthusiastic Easter service should not be taken to imply a whole congregation's loss of faith. For researchers who prefer to emphasize practice over belief, on the other hand, changes in intensity and participation are key markers of conversion. Although changes in belief may occur suddenly, other forms and patterns of conversion are best treated as processes shaped over time.[19]

CONVERSION AT THE MESO LEVEL: CONGREGATIONS, RITUALS, AND IDENTITIES

Although individuals may experience conversion in isolation, conversion typically occurs in congregations of some sort, often implying a change in a convert's identity. Ritual appears to link micro and meso factors. Many congregants in the United States— and in some religious organizations, all congregants—mostly limit their regular participation in congregational life to worship practices.[20] It is also common for congregants to spend time in informal socializing, or "fellowship" as it is sometimes called.[21] Worship and fellowship both involve ritual: *group ritual*, in the case of worship, and *interaction ritual*, in the case of fellowship. Thus, the micro-level affect and interaction so important to conversion are typically informed by the ritual activities organized by meso-level institutions.[22] Seen in this light, recent scholarship can be said to build upon Durkheim's insights into how social bonds are guided, structured, and/or created through rituals.[23]

Recent research on congregations has included massive survey projects.[24] One interesting finding from these studies is the extent to which activity in congregations centers on what can generally be called artistic production and ritual activity, including the production of music, skits or plays, and even dance. Congregations do, of course, run food banks, marriage counseling services, twelve-step programs, and soup kitchens. Congregations are sometimes involved in political activities, as well. What is surprising is just how small a part such programs and activities play in congregational life—many congregations provide none at all. The overwhelming majority of congregational time and resources go to conducting worship services, teaching members about the religion, and staging opportunities for social interaction. Most essentially, to paraphrase Mark Chaves, for most people in the United States conversion involves joining a group that meets each week to sing and hear a message.[25] Conversion thus typically involves a change in affiliation not just from one group to another, or from one set of beliefs to another, but to the ritual and interactional routines associated with these groups and their beliefs.

There is an ongoing need for sociologists to analyze the embodied aspects of religion and to consider the effects that physical presence in group activities has on conversion.[26] R. Stephen Warner describes the quasi-religious experience of Sacred Harp singing as a ritual means to community formation.[27] He employs Randall Collin's term "mutual entrainment"—the experience of shared focus and emotional response when participating in rituals—in reference to this form of group singing. The mutual entrainment that occurs when people enthusiastically sing together creates a visceral sensation of social solidarity. It is important to note that in such cases ritual does more than merely express relationships, identity, or ideology—ritual participates in creating such things.[28] Put another way, ritual creates and maintains an ideological and social milieu into which people convert.

There is no denying that religious practice involves the movements and affective responses of actual bodies in space and over time—whether an uncontrolled laughter in the context of the Toronto Blessing, an otherworldly sensation in the midst of Muslim prayers, or the quiet formalism of the Episcopal Eucharist. William H. McNeill's study of "keeping together in time," as in dance and military drill, suggests that rhythmic physical activity plays an important role in group dynamics, including religious congregations.[29] What McNeill calls "muscular bonding"—a process whereby social solidarity is created through repetitious and rhythmic physical activity—unites people in cohesive groups, with a resulting increase in efficiency in completing collective acts. This has important implications for the sociological study of conversion in the context of congregations, where hymn singing and ritual activities are also central to an experience of participation. For instance, some Chinese converts report that their initial interest in Christianity was sparked by experiencing the awe-inspiring congregational hymn singing, corporate prayers, and collective rituals of some congregations.[30]

Randall Collins posits a general social theory of ritual.[31] He argues that the emotional effervescence experienced in successful interaction rituals—a phenomenon similar to muscular bonding that he calls Emotional Energy—is the prime motivator behind all human behavior. Individuals choose to act in ways that will maximize their Emotional Energy. This theory implies that the level of Emotional Energy experienced by congregants would strongly relate to their level of participation in church activities and would consequently enhance conversion as well.

But religious rituals do not have to be emotionally stimulating to be efficacious. For example, although some Chinese Protestant worship services are (according to congregants) dull, potential converts may be attracted by other aspects of congregational life.[32] Chinese Christians employ a slightly different etiquette—that is to say, different interactional rituals—than is typical among Chinese; church members routinely break with the traditional protocols used by Chinese to make new acquaintances.[33] Such behavior among Chinese congregants catches the notice of recruits. Those who convert often report that it was personal qualities seen in the behavior of church members that attracted them to the church and to conversion. For instance, Chinese Christians routinely extend favors and gifts anonymously, to perfect strangers, persons of lower status, and with no expectation of return. It is common for such behavior to be interpreted as Christian Love and for converts to mention how well they were treated in their conversion accounts.[34]

It is well established that affective bonds are of particular salience to conversion in other groups as well, either in the form of existing friendships or even short-term acquaintances.[35] Religious leaders from a wide variety of traditions are clearly aware of this and instruct their congregants to create social ties through such techniques as "love bombing," "flirty fishing," and "favor fishing."[36] Dougherty finds that Baptist congregations are more likely to grow if they create a sense of belonging for recruits and congregants.[37] However, very strong bonds between congregants may hamper church growth for much the same reason; interested recruits are less likely to develop new social connections in "friendly" churches whose members' social lives are already full.[38]

It appears that conversion in a multi-ethnic context may involve alternative conversion experiences and identity transformations.[39] Gerardo Marti envisions a process by which recruits move from a sense of affinity, to an "identity reorganization," and finally to "ethnic transcendence," in which membership in multiethnic/multiracial congregations may suspend or supersede a previous identity.[40] In other words, the conversion process involves a change of identity from being white or black to being a white or black member of a certain congregation. Marti emphasizes that this transcendence is not merely a form of "color-blind" diversity. It is not that the previous racial identity is deliberately overlooked; rather, a new and shared religious identity emerges among congregants.[41] Despite the obvious salience of identity in the conversion experience, the role of identity is nonetheless difficult to interpret. It may be a key factor motivating an individual to join a particular congregation, yet at the same time it is likely to be an outcome of conversion and commitment.

Although the relationship between identity and religion is attractive to researchers, as witnessed by the large number of sociologists of religion who study identity, such studies have suffered from the imprecision of the identity concept and the inconsistency of its use in the sociological literature.[42] If the term is used as a near synonym to "group" (e.g., when "ethnic identity" is used in place of "ethnic group"), the concept of identity is relatively unproblematic; yet in the context of conversion studies, greater conceptual complexity is unavoidable because conversion to a religious identity presumably means more than just joining a group. It is possible to sidestep these problems by focusing on the means by which identity is expressed—the narratives people tell about themselves, for instance—although the relationship between what people say about themselves and what they actually are is never exact.[43] In general, we may say that (1) converts and potential converts more or less identify with certain groups, (2) religious groups often place great importance on such group affinities, and (3) conversion implies a change in identification to a new group.

Identity delineates community and membership in communities, which necessarily affects behavior and ideology. Converts, as they enter into religious communities, become active agents of their group's social and cultural orientation.[44] That is to say, they come to enact such roles as convert, congregant, or religious person. Conversion thus necessarily entails a process of socialization to a new religious identity and may even involve a lifelong "career" of religious adaptations.[45] Among Chinese immigrants, conversion may involve adaptation or assimilation within the context of a new culture.[46] For instance, Carolyn Chen finds that Taiwanese immigrants in either Buddhist or Christian groups are sometimes freed by their new religion from unwanted aspects of traditional culture.[47] This is most conspicuously the case for the women in her sample, who rely upon their newfound religious orientations to free themselves from burdensome traditional expectations for women. Her striking finding that members of such dramatically different religions as Buddhism and Christianity experience the same pragmatic benefits suggests that in some cases conversion may be a way of separating oneself from certain aspects of a previous group affiliation or identity.

Within the New Paradigm of the sociology of religion, the supply-side theory of the economic approach emphasizes the competitive strength of growing religious groups, from efficient polity and clergy to attractive theology and services and effective recruitment strategies.[48] Growing congregations are often those that are strict—those that demand greater dedication of individuals in terms of time and donations and, in turn, provide more communal goods and services and greater assurance of a world beyond.[49]

On the other hand, there is the phenomenon of "circulation of the saints," in which people move between different churches.[50] These "circulating saints" may or may not have experienced a spiritual conversion when they switch from one church to another. In our religiously pluralistic society, "stained-glass window shopping" has become increasingly common.[51] A set of beliefs may affect how a religious group fares in a religious marketplace, but so may a good program for families, engaging Bible study classes, or relaxing meditative practices.

CONVERSION AT THE MACRO LEVEL: THE IMPORTANCE OF SOCIAL AND CULTURAL CONTEXTS

Most of the sociological studies of religious conversion have focused on what Lofland and Stark (1965) called "situational contingencies," especially the path of conversion through personal bonds in small networks, whereas what they called "predisposing conditions" have been often neglected. This is unfortunate, as sociology is the prime discipline for examining institutional and social-structural processes. The problem is the common tendency (even among sociologists, alas) to consider conversion as an individualistic process or act, or something that occurs purely in the context of religious congregations. However, micro and meso approaches cannot adequately explain mass conversion events. A macro approach is needed to understand the "great transformation" of a tribe or nation to Christianity,[52] the spread of evangelical Protestantism in the underdeveloped societies,[53] or the rapid increase of evangelical Protestantism among Latinos and Chinese in the United States and other parts of the world.[54] At a time of increasing globalization, cosmopolitanism, and transnationalism, the contextual analysis of conversion becomes increasingly necessary to explain such developments as the growth of Christianity in the "Global South"[55] or the rise of Islam in Europe.[56]

To explain the large-scale Chinese conversion to evangelical Christianity among Chinese immigrants in the United States, Fenggang Yang has argued the importance of social and cultural contexts. Before the Second World War, in spite of intensive proselytizing efforts by American churches and individuals, only a tiny minority of Chinese immigrants in the United States converted to Christianity. However, post-1965 Chinese immigrants have established hundreds of Protestant churches for themselves, and the majority of church members are adult converts from non-Christian backgrounds.[57] Although not a traditional religion of China, Christianity has nonetheless emerged as the most practiced institutional religion among the Chinese in America.[58] Through examining testimonials of conversion, in-depth interviews with converts, and participant observation, Yang finds that the most important factors for the Christian conversion of Chinese immigrants are dramatic social and cultural changes in the process of coerced modernization—wars, social turmoil, political storms, and the collapse of Chinese traditional cultural systems. The experience of immigrant Chinese as a racial minority in the United States further intensifies the existential need for spiritual certainty; "Coming from such a society, Chinese immigrants are both free and bound to seek alternate meaning systems."[59]

The importance of social and cultural contexts can also be seen in the different responses to Christian evangelism at colleges in the United States. Although American evangelists are active on many university campuses and may particularly target international students, some groups, especially Chinese and Koreans, respond enthusiastically, whereas others do not.[60] Clearly, individualistic and institutional factors do not explain such differences. Rather, this conversion is overwhelmingly influenced by broader social and cultural developments. Focusing on Chinese-American college students, Brian Hall refurbishes the often neglected predisposing factors in the Lofland and Stark model.[61] The presence of "openness factors" causes the decline of barriers to joining another religion; the "receptivity factors" are those that make a religion attractive. Regarding the Chinese, openness to Christianity has increased because of the collapse of traditional culture in the process of rapid and coerced modernization, including industrialization, urbanization, and mass education that emphasizes modern sciences instead of Confucianism. Moreover, Buddhism has been a weak opponent because of its lack of proselytization and the widespread belief among mainland Chinese that Buddhism is out of touch with modernity. Christianity has grown more attractive because it is perceived by the Chinese as modern and liberating from stifling cultural traditions. In addition, and somewhat ironically given the previous association of Christianity with Western nations, many Chinese immigrant converts are interested in joining Chinese churches as a way of discovering and affirming what it means to be Chinese. Overseas Chinese are often drawn to Christian churches as a way to meet other Chinese and participate in traditional practices, such as celebrating the first month of a newborn's life, celebrating Chinese holidays, speaking Chinese, and enjoying membership in an organization that is run by fellow Chinese.[62]

Furthermore, contextual analysis explains Christian conversion in China.[63] The Christian population in mainland China is now approximating the population of France, and the conversion rate seems to be accelerating. Although micro- and meso-level factors are at work, they have to be situated in broader, macro-level contexts. The crucial contextual factors are the increasingly globalized market economy together with strict control by the Chinese Communist Party. Facing the challenge of modernization, some Chinese search internally in their cultural roots and find faith in a traditional religion such as Buddhism or Confucianism, whereas others search externally in other cultures, especially Western culture, and find faith in Christianity.[64] Converts claim that Christianity provides peace and certainty amid the wilds of market capitalism and that the Christian faith is liberating in a political atmosphere these converts characterize as stifling. To young and educated urban Chinese consciously seeking modernity and integration with the rest of the world, Christianity is attractive because it is seen as modern and cosmopolitan.

Although the previous literature on conversion reflects awareness of social context, it is necessary to reorient the sociology of conversion to take social context as the primary factor in many cases. Moreover, the importance of social context as a determinant of conversion implicitly links the seemingly individual experience of conversion, on the one hand, to group patterns of religious growth and decline, on the other. While the growth of Christianity among Chinese in China and America offers a particularly dramatic example of mass conversion, similar patterns can be seen in Europe and North America as religious conversion and apostasy rates rise and fall among various cultural groups. For instance, it is likely that secularization theorists' common assumption of modernity's increasing rationalism privileged cognitive aspects of religion not just for secular theorists but for some religious groups as well. It is in this sense that Joel Carpenter's characterization of fundamentalism representing both modern and anti-modern impulses intersects profoundly with studies of conversion. In Carpenter's conception, belief is particularly salient among fundamentalists.[65] Furthermore, it can be argued that the literalist Bible-*believing* orientation of Christian fundamentalism is comparable with Jewish and Muslim fundamentalisms precisely in regard to a shared ideological (i.e., cognitive) response to modernity. If so, then the separate formation of seemingly unrelated fundamentalist sects may be best conceived as different instances of a global mass conversion pattern.

Cultural change never occurs in a vacuum, and increased flows of traffic, ideas, and communication between nations sometimes brings religious people and potential converts together in unexpected ways and with unexpected consequences.[66] Whereas the highly developed nations of North American and Europe are important producers and exporters of religious innovation, the Global South is quite dynamic in its social patterns of religious adherence. Although the United States is more likely to give than receive both missionaries and religious culture, reverse flows do exist, such as the "holy hip hop music" from Ghana now popular in Atlanta. Also, the International Society for Krishna Consciousness (ISKCON), popularly known as "Hare Krishnas," has recently been supported by immigrant streams from India, whereas membership in the past was dominated by Caucasian "seekers."[67] This cross-national connection suggests the emergence of a transnational "religious economy" in which overseas evangelists may provide a receptive institution for subsequent migrants from the sending country. Interestingly, although one would expect that highly religious persons would be harder to convert, especially by cultural outsiders, this is apparently not always true. For instance, Eric Reinders reports that missionaries to China considered "earnest idolaters" easier to convert than persons indifferent to religion.[68]

Among transnational religious groups, Islam has received the most attention lately, especially among European social scientists. Although the rise in conversions to Islam in the wake of September 11, 2001, might at first glance appear relevant to a developing clash of civilizations, there is evidence that this is not the case, or at least not entirely the case. First, there has been marked growth in the numbers of converts to Islam in the West, even among ethnic whites.[69] Writing in *Africa Today*, de Montclos argues that in Africa, radical Islam often has more to do with protest against local ruling elites than anything else.[70] Similarly, in Brazil, interest in Islam appears relevant to local protest regarding racial issues faced by blacks.[71] Still, the timing of this increased interest in Islam around the world is disconcerting; the vicissitudes of local politics do not sufficiently explain this global pattern, nor do they account for the effects of recent American military adventures.

How do religious life and conversion differ under conditions of government repression? In regard to China, Fenggang Yang argues that the religious economy may be broken into three markets: red, black, and gray. The red market is composed of religious groups and activities that are allowed by the government; the black market includes religious groups and activities officially banned by the government; and the gray market comprises all religious groups and activities that are in the gray area—both legal and illegal at once or neither legal nor illegal in formal regulations. The existence of red, black, and gray markets has predictable results. Some people do not find satisfaction in the red market and yet are unwilling to risk black-market penalties; they may thus seek informal religious practices and spiritual alternatives, such as Mao worship or qigong. Indeed, in China today, while the officially sanctioned religions have been growing and underground sects continue to thrive, most Chinese resort to alternative spiritualities to meet their religious needs. An important reason that so many people have not formally converted to an institutionalized religion is the political and social cost under conditions of religious repression. Meanwhile, a major reason that underground sects thrive in rural and coastal urban areas is that the changed social structure has provided greater social space and perceived spiritual rewards for the converts. Again, social structural factors are necessary to the understanding of conversion in different religious markets of the same society.

CONCLUSION AND DISCUSSION

The sociology of conversion has changed considerably in the last few decades. In addition to the micro- and meso-level approaches, awareness of social, cultural, and even global contexts is now of inescapable importance. If the sociology of conversion up to the 1990s seems like a series of footnotes to Lofland and Stark (1965), the sociology of religion now has more on the table. The question is not which theory cuts the cleanest— rather, the magic is in the mix of micro-, meso-, and macro-level research. Conversion is a complex phenomenon and no single approach suffices.

In addition to these theoretical and contextual changes, the sociology of conversion has shifted in another important way: recent scholarship is more likely to emphasize behavioral, associational, and affective aspects of the conversion experience than earlier research. In other words, conversion is not just what you believe but what you do, who you do it with, and how you feel about doing it.

Several other areas of study are particularly in need of research. For instance, the strength of attachment theory remains to be assessed across different social and ethnic groups. Congregations are easily conceived of as "family surrogates" that are especially comforting to people without other group attachments, especially marriage attachments.[72] However, separate studies by Christiano and Gerstel and Sarkisian find stronger religious participation among married persons, and Christiano finds no meaningful difference with or without the presence of children.[73] However, the types of religious groups that best serve as a surrogate family and attract members on that basis have not been adequately studied. This is particularly at issue in the case of immigrant groups, assuming that many immigrants are at greater risk of social isolation and *anomie* after separation from their native cultures.[74]

However, it is clear that family can hamper conversion. David Smilde finds that Venezuelans may react quite negatively when family members increase their religious commitment.[75] Similarly, Chen and Sebastian and Parameswaran find that families are likely to very strongly oppose the religious conversion of family members to other religions.[76] These studies suggest a basic principle: family members seek to prevent conversion when they fear the new religion will threaten existing family practices and thus the means to family solidarity.

Another area that deserves greater attention is gender. Linda Woodhead points out that despite the great attention accorded gender in sociology, there has been far less attention paid to gender within the sociology of religion.[77] Yet, conversion differs by gender, and the patterns differ dramatically in different religious traditions. Davidman and Greil found that among orthodox Jews, males are more likely to enter the religion as "seekers," whereas women tend to mention the influence of family on their religious choices and behavior.[78] Knight et al. find a similar difference in the conversion stories of undergraduates at a Christian college: males tend to use "adventurous metaphors" to describe their religious decisions, whereas females are more likely to mention their relationships with others.[79] Several scholars argue that conversion sometimes serves as a limited means to the empowerment of women.[80] More comparative studies across different ethnic and religious boundaries are needed.

Lastly, we know little about how people lose religion or even whether it makes sense to consider de-conversion as a process distinct from conversion. Certainly, any change in religious status involves an experience of "role-exit,"[81] and this process deserves much greater attention (see Stuart Wright, this volume).

All such work should be integrated across different levels of analysis: micro, meso, and macro. Given the plethora of new developments in the sociology of religion, these are exciting days for those of us who study conversion.

NOTES

1. David A. Snow and Richard Machalek, "The Sociology of Conversion," *Annual Review of Sociology* 10 (1984): 167–190; William Sims Bainbridge, "The Sociology of Conversion," in *Handbook of Religious Conversion*, ed. H. Newton Malony and Samuel Southard (Birmingham, AL: Religious Education Press, 1992), 178–191.

2. See especially Peter Berger, *The Sacred Canopy: Elements of a Sociological Theory of Religion* (New York: Doubleday, 1967). Berger changed his view in the late 1990s; see his *The Desecularization of the World: Resurgent Religion and World Politics* (Washington, DC: Ethics and Public Policy Center, 1999).

3. See, for example, David Martin, *Tongues of Fire: The Explosion of Protestantism in Latin America* (Oxford: Basil Blackwell, 1990); Roger Finke and Rodney Stark, *The Churching of America, 1776–1990* (New Brunswick, NJ: Rutgers University Press, 1992); Jose Casanova, *Public Religions in the Modern World* (Chicago: University of Chicago Press, 1994); Grace Davie, *Religion in Britain since 1945: Believing Without Belonging* (Oxford: Blackwell, 1994); Fenggang Yang and Joseph B. Tamney, eds., *State, Market, and Religions in Chinese Societies* (Leiden, The Netherlands: Brill, 2005).

4. R. Stephen Warner, "Work in Progress toward a New Paradigm for the Sociological Study of Religion in the United States," *American Journal of Sociology* 98 (1993): 1044–1093.

5. See Laurence R. Iannaccone, "Why Strict Churches Are Strong," *American Journal of Sociology* 99 (1994): 1180–1211; Rodney Stark and Laurence R. Iannaccone, "A Supply-Side Reinterpretation of the 'Secularization' of Europe," *Journal for the Scientific Study of Religion* 33 (1994): 230–252; Roger Finke, "The Consequences of Religious Competition: Supply-Side Explanations for Religious Change," in *Rational Choice Theory and Religion: Summary and Assessment*, ed. L. A. Young (New York: Routledge, 1997), 45–64; Rodney Stark and Roger Finke, *Acts of Faith: Explaining the Human Side of Religion* (Berkeley and Los Angeles: University of California Press, 2000).

6. By "meso level" we mean simply that level of social organization between the state or society, on the one hand, and individuals and their families, on the other.

7. See especially James P. Wind and James W. Lewis, eds., *American Congregations*: vol. 1, *Portraits of Twelve Religious Communities* (Chicago: University of Chicago Press, 1994) and *American Congregations*: vol. 2, *New Perspectives in the Study of Congregations* (Chicago: University of Chicago Press, 1994); Cynthia Woolever and Deborah Bruce, *A Field Guide to U.S. Congregations: Who's Going Where and Why* (Louisville, KY: Westminster John Knox Press, 2002); Mark Chaves, *Congregations in America* (Cambridge, MA: Harvard University Press, 2004); Nancy Tatom Ammerman, *Pillars of Faith: American Congregations and their Partners* (Berkeley and Los Angeles: University of California Press, 2005).

8. See Nancy Tatom Ammerman, Jackson W. Carroll, Carl S. Dudley, and William McKinney, *Studying Congregations: A New Handbook* (Nashville, TN: Abingdon Press, 1998).

9. Stark and Finke, *Acts of Faith*; Iannaccone, "Why Strict Churches Are Strong," 1180–1211.

10. Fenggang Yang, *Chinese Christians in America* (University Park: Pennsylvania State University Press, 1999); Fenggang Yang, "Lost in the Market, Saved at McDonald's: Conversion to Christianity in Urban China," *Journal for the Scientific Study of Religion* 44 (2005): 423–441; Yuting Wang and Fenggang Yang, "More than Evangelical and Ethnic: The Ecological Factor in Chinese Conversion to Christianity in the United States," *Sociology of Religion* 67 (2006): 179–192.

11. Fenggang Yang and Joseph Tamney, "Exploring Mass Conversion to Christianity among the Chinese: An Introduction," *Sociology of Religion* 67 (2006): 125–129 (quotation is from p. 126).

12. Martin, *Tongues of Fire*; R. W. Hefner, *Conversion to Christianity: Historical and Anthropological Perspectives on a Great Transformation* (Berkeley and Los Angeles: University of California Press, 1993); Fenggang Yang, "Chinese Conversion to Evangelical Christianity: The Importance of Social and Cultural Contexts," *Sociology of Religion* 59 (1998): 237–257; Yang, *Chinese Christians in America*; Yang, "Lost in the Market"; Brian Hall, "Social and Cultural Contexts in Conversion to Christianity among Chinese American College Students," *Sociology of Religion* 67 (2006): 131–147; Philip Jenkins, *The Next Christendom: The Rise of Global Christianity* (New York: Oxford University Press, 2002); Philip Jenkins, *The New Faces of Christianity: Believing the Bible in the Global South* (New York: Oxford University Press, 2006); Philip Jenkins, *God's Continent: Christianity, Islam, and Europe's Religious Crisis* (New York: Oxford University Press, 2007); Wang and Yang, "More than Evangelical and Ethnic."

13. John Lofland and Rodney Stark, "Becoming a World-Saver: A Theory of Conversion to a Deviant Perspective," *American Sociological Review* 30 (1965): 862–875.

14. Snow and Machalek, "The Sociology of Conversion."

15. Bainbridge, "The Sociology of Conversion."

16. For example, see Lofland and Stark, "Becoming a World Saver"; Eileen Barker, *The Making of a Moonie: Choice or Brainwashing?* (New York: B. Blackwell, 1984); for reviews, see Arthur L. Greil and David R. Rudy, "Social Cocoons: Encapsulation and Identity Transformation Organizations," *Sociological Inquiry* 54 (1984): 260–278; Snow and Machalek, "The Sociology of Conversion"; Brock Kilbourne and James T. Richardson, "Paradigm Conflict, Types of Conversion, and Conversion Theories," *Sociological Analysis* 50 (1989): 1–21.

17. Lynn Davidman, *Tradition in a Rootless World: Women Turn to Orthodox Judaism* (Berkeley and Los Angeles: University of California Press, 1991); Debra R. Kaufman, *Rachel's Daughters: Newly Orthodox Jewish Women* (New Brunswick, NJ: Rutgers University Press, 1991); Mark C. Suchman, "Analyzing the Determinants of Everyday Conversion," *Sociological Analysis* 53S (1992): S15–S33; Lynn Davidman and Arthur L. Greil, "Gender and the Experience of Conversion: The Case of 'Returnees' to Modern Orthodox Judaism," *Sociology of Religion* 54 (1993): 83–100. See also Frank Newport, "The Religious Switcher in the United States," *American Sociological Review* 44 (1979): 528–552; Wade Clark Roof and Christopher Kirk Hadaway, "Denominational Switching in the Seventies: Going beyond Stark and Glock," *Journal for the Scientific Study of Religion* 18 (1979): 363–377; Dean R. Hoge, Kenneth McGuire, and Bernard F. Stratman, *Converts, Dropouts, Returnees: A Study of Religious Change among Catholics* (New York: Pilgrim Press, 1981); D. Paul Sullins, "Switching Close to Home: Volatility or Coherence in Protestant Affiliation Patterns?" *Social Forces* 72 (1993): 399–419; Marc Musick and John Wilson, "Religious Switching for Marriage Reasons," *Sociology of Religion* 56 (1995): 257–270.

18. Irwin R. Barker and Raymond F. Currie, "Do Converts Always Make the Most Committed Christians?" *Journal for the Scientific Study of Religion* 24 (1985): 305–313.

19. Henri Gooren, "Reassessing Conventional Approaches to Conversion: Toward a New Synthesis," *Journal for the Scientific Study of Religion* 46 (2007): 337–353; Lewis R. Rambo, *Understanding Religious Conversion* (New Haven: Yale University Press, 1993); David L. Preston, "Becoming a Zen Practitioner," *Sociological Analysis* 42 (1981): 47–55; James V. Downton, Jr., "An Evolutionary Theory of Spiritual Conversion and Commitment: The Case of Divine Light Mission," *Journal for the Scientific Study of Religion* 19 (1980): 381–396.

20. Such limited practice is rare among some groups—Christian congregations, for instance. However, other groups (e.g., those associated with Voodoo, Daoism, and NRMs) may limit their observances to a specific set of rituals, to the exclusion of volunteer work, social services, or even outreach. This phenomenon may be more strongly associated with the propitiation of ghosts and spirits as well as with very small congregations (as opposed to established churches or temples).

21. Chaves, *Congregations in America*; Ammerman, *Pillars of Faith*; Andrew Stuart Abel, "'It's the People Here': A Study of Ritual, Conversion, and Congregational Life among Chinese Christians," PhD diss., University of Massachusetts, Amherst, MA, 2008.

22. Barker, *The Making of a Moonie*; Snow and Machalek, "The Sociology of Conversion"; David A. Snow and Cynthia L. Phillips, "The Lofland-Stark Conversion Model: A Critical Reassessment," *Social Problems* 27 (1980): 430–447.

23. See Roy A. Rappaport, *Ritual and Religion in the Making of Humanity* (Cambridge: Cambridge University Press, 1999) and Randall Collins, *Interaction Ritual Chains* (Princeton: Princeton University Press, 2004).

24. These include Ammerman, *Pillars of Faith*; Chaves, *Congregations in America*; and Woolever and Bruce, *A Field Guide to American Congregations*.

25. Chaves, *Congregations in America*.

26. For relevant arguments, see R. Stephen Warner, "Presidential Address: Singing and Solidarity," *Journal for the Scientific Study of Religion* 47 (2008): 175–190, and Phillip A. Mellor, "Embodiment, Emotion, and Religious Experience: Religion, Culture, and the Charismatic Body," in *The SAGE Handbook of the Sociology of Religion*, ed. James A. Beckford and N. J. Demerath, III, 587–607 (Los Angeles: SAGE Publications, 2007).

27. Warner, "Presidential Address."

28. See also Rappaport, *Ritual and Religion*; Rambo, *Understanding Religious Conversion*; Collins, *Interaction Ritual Chains*; Abel, "It's the People Here"; David I. Kertzer, *Ritual, Politics, and Power* (New Haven: Yale University Press, 1988).

29. William H. McNeill, *Keeping Together in Time: Dance and Drill in Human History* (Cambridge, MA: Harvard University Press, 1995).

30. Yang, "Lost in the Market."

31. Collins, *Interaction Ritual Chains*.

32. Abel, "It's the People Here."

33. Strong familial loyalties among the Chinese tend to complicate relationships with non-family. In this context, protocols regarding social connections and exchanges of gifts and favors play an important part in building trust outside of families. See Thomas Gold, Doug Guthrie, and David Wank, eds., *Social Connections in China: Institutions, Culture, and the Changing Nature of Guanxi* (Cambridge: Cambridge University Press, 2002); Mayfair Mei-hui Yang, *Gifts, Favors, and Banquets: The Art of Social Relationships in China* (Ithaca, NY: Cornell University Press, 1994); Kwang-Kwo Hwang, "Face and Favor: The Chinese Power Game," *American Journal of Sociology* 2 (1987): 944–974; Yunxiang Yan, *The Flow of Gifts: Reciprocity and Social Networks in a Chinese Village* (Palo Alto, CA: Stanford University Press, 1996).

34. Andrew Abel, "Favor Fishing and Punch-Bowl Christians: Ritual and Conversion in a Chinese Protestant Church," *Sociology of Religion* 67 (2006): 161–178; Abel, "It's the People Here"; Kwai Hang Ng, "Seeking the Christian Tutelage: Agency and Culture in Chinese Immigrants' Conversion to Christianity," *Sociology of Religion* 63 (2002): 195–214.

35. Willem Kox, Wim Meeus, and Harm 't Hart, "Religious Conversion of Adolescents: Testing the Lofland and Stark Model of Religious Conversion," *Sociological Analysis* 52 (1991): 227–240; Kilbourne and Richardson, "Paradigm Conflict"; Barker, *The Making of a Moonie*; Snow and Machalek, "The Sociology of Conversion"; Snow and Phillips, "The Lofland-Stark Conversion Model"; Kelly H. Chong, *Deliverance and Submission: Evangelical Women and the Negotiation of Patriarchy in South Korea* (Cambridge, MA: Harvard University Press, 2008). Helen Rose Fuchs Ebaugh and Sharron Lee Vaughn, "Ideology and Recruitment in Religious Groups," *Review of Religious Research* 26 (1984): 148–157.

36. Abel, "Favor Fishing and Punch Bowl Christians"; Barker, *The Making of a Moonie*; Arthur G. McPhee, *Friendship Evangelism: The Caring Way to Share Your Faith* (Grand Rapids, MI: Zondervan, 1978).

37. Kevin D. Dougherty, "Institutional Influences on Growth in Southern Baptist Congregations," *Review of Religious Research* 46 (2004): 117–131.

38. Daniel V. A. Olson, "Church Friendships: Boon or Barrier to Church Growth?" *Journal for the Scientific Study of Religion* 28 (1989): 432–447.

39. Gerardo Marti, "Fluid Ethnicity and Ethnic Transcendence in Multiracial Churches," *Journal for the Scientific Study of Religion* 47 (2008): 11–16; Gerardo Marti, "Affinity, Identity, and Transcendence: The Experience of Religious Racial Integration in Diverse Congregations," *Journal for the Scientific Study of Religion* 48 (2009): 53–68; Russell Jeung, *Faithful Generations: Race and New Asian American Churches* (New Brunswick, NJ: Rutgers University Press, 2005).

40. Marti, "Affinity, Identity, and Transcendence."

41. Jeung, *Faithful Generations*; Nancy Tatom Ammerman and Arthur Emery Farnsley, *Congregation and Community* (New Brunswick, NJ: Rutgers University Press, 1997).

42. Arthur L. Greil and Lynn Davidman, "Religion and Identity," in *The SAGE Handbook of the Sociology of Religion*, ed. James A. Beckford and N. J. Demerath, III (Los Angeles: SAGE Publications, 2007), 549–565; Nancy Tatom Ammerman, "Religious Identities and Religious Institutions," in *Handbook of the Sociology of Religion*, ed. Michele Dillon (Cambridge: Cambridge University Press, 2003), 207–224.

43. Ammerman, "Religious Identities and Religious Institutions; Ammerman, Carroll, Dudley, and McKinney, *Studying Congregations*.

44. James T. Richardson, "The Active vs. Passive Convert: Paradigm Conflict in Conversion/Recruitment Research," *Journal for the Scientific Study of Religion* 24 (1985): 163–179.

45. Theodore E. Long and Jeffrey K. Hadden, "Religious Conversion and the Concept of Socialization: Integrating the Brainwashing and Drift Models," *Journal for the Scientific Study of Religion* 22 (1983): 1–14. Henri Gooren, "Reassessing Conventional Approaches to Conversion: Toward a New Synthesis," *Journal for the Scientific Study of Religion* 46 (2007): 337–353; James T. Richardson, ed., *Conversion Careers: In and Out of the New Religions* (Beverly Hills, CA: SAGE Publications, 1978).

46. Carolyn Chen, *Getting Saved in America: Taiwanese Immigration and Religious Experience* (Princeton: Princeton University Press, 2008); Ng, "Seeking the Christian Tutelage"; Yang, *Chinese Christians in America*.

47. Chen, *Getting Saved in America.*

48. Dean M. Kelley, *Why Conservative Churches are Growing* (New York: Harper Collins, 1972); Roger Finke and Rodney Stark, *The Churching of America, 1776–1990: Winners and Losers in Our Religious Economy* (New Brunswick, NJ: Rutgers University Press, 1992); Stark and Finke, *Acts of Faith.*

49. Iannaccone, "Why Strict Churches Are Strong."

50. Reginald W. Bibby and Merlin B. Brinkerhoff, "The Circulation of the Saints: A Study of People Who Join Conservative Churches," *Journal for the Scientific Study of Religion* 12 (1973): 273–283.

51. David Lyon, *Jesus in Disneyland: Religion in Postmodern Times* (Cambridge: Polity Press, 2000), 93.

52. Hefner, *Conversion to Christianity.*

53. Martin, *Tongues of Fire.*

54. Yang, "Chinese Conversion to Evangelical Christianity"; Yang, "Lost in the Market"; Yang and Tamney, "Exploring Mass Conversion to Christianity among the Chinese"; David Aikman, *Jesus in Beijing: How China Is Transforming China and Changing the Global Balance of Power* (Washington, DC: Regnery Publishing, 2003); Ryan Dunch, *Fuzhou Protestants*

and the Making of a Modern China, 1857–1927 (New Haven: Yale University Press, 2001); Tony Lambert, China's Christian Millions (Grand Rapids, MI: Monarch Books, 1999).

55. Jenkins, The Next Christendom; Jenkins, The New Faces of Christianity.
56. Jenkins, God's Continent; see also N. J. Demerath, III, Crossing the Gods: World Religions and Worldly Politics (New Brunswick, NJ: Rutgers University Press, 2001); James T. Duke and Barry L. Johnson, "The Stages of Religious Transformation: A Study of 200 Nations," Review of Religious Research 30 (1989): 209–224.
57. Ng, "Seeking the Christian Tutelage"; Yang, Chinese Christians in America.
58. See also Fenggang Yang, "Chinese Christian Transnationalism: Diverse Networks of a Houston Church," in Religions across Borders: Transnational Religious Networks, ed. Helen Rose Ebaugh and Janet S. Chafetz (Walnut Creek, CA: AltaMira Press, 2002), 129–148.
59. Yang, "Chinese Conversion to Evangelical Christianity," 253.
60. Hall, "Social and Cultural Contexts"; Rebecca Y. Kim, God's New Whiz Kids? Korean American Evangelicals on Campus (New York: New York University Press, 2006).
61. Hall, "Social and Cultural Contexts."
62. Yang, Chinese Christians in America; Abel, "It's the People Here."
63. Yang, "Lost in the Market."
64. Joseph B. Tamney and Linda Hsueh-Ling Chiang, Modernization, Globalization, and Confucianism in Chinese Societies (Westport, CT: Praeger Publishing, 2002).
65. Joel A. Carpenter, Revive Us Again: The Reawakening of American Fundamentalism (New York: Oxford University Press, 1997).
66. Robert Wuthnow and Stephen Offutt, "Transnational Religious Connections," Sociology of Religion 69 (2008): 209–232.
67. Travis Vande Berg and Fred Kniss, "ISKCON and Immigrants: The Rise, Decline, and Rise Again of a New Religious Movement," Sociological Quarterly 49 (2008): 79–104.
68. Eric Reinders, "The Economies of Temple Chanting and Conversion in China," International Bulletin of Missionary Research 31 (2007): 188–192.
69. Karin van Nieuwkerk, Women Embracing Islam: Gender and Conversion in the West (Austin: University of Texas Press, 2006).
70. Marc-Antoine Perouse de Montclos, "Conversion to Islam and Modernity in Nigeria: A View from the Underworld," Africa Today 54 (2008): 70–87.
71. Vitoria Peres De Oliveira and Cecilia L. Mariz, "Conversion to Islam in Contemporary Brazil," Exchange 35 (2006): 102–115.
72. Charles Y. Glock, Benjamin B. Ringer, and Earl R. Babbie, To Comfort and to Challenge: A Dilemma for the Contemporary Church (Berkeley and Los Angeles: University of California Press, 1967).
73. Kevin J. Christiano, "Church as a Family Surrogate: Another Look at Family Ties, Anomie, and Church Involvement," Journal for the Scientific Study of Religion 25 (1986): 339–354; Naomi Gerstel and Natalia Sarkisian, "Marriage: The Good, the Bad, and the Greedy," Contexts (2006): 16–21.
74. See Nanlai Cao, "The Church as a Surrogate Family for Working Class Immigrant Chinese Youth: An Ethnography of Segmented Assimilation," Sociology of Religion 66 (2005): 183–200.
75. David Smilde, "A Qualitative Comparative Analysis of Conversion to Venezuelan Evangelicalism: How Networks Matter," American Journal of Sociology 111 (2005): 757–796.

76. Chen, *Getting Saved in America*; Rodney Sebastian and Ashvin Parameswaran, "Conversion and the Family: Chinese Hare Krishnas," *Journal of Contemporary Religion* 22 (2007): 341–359.

77. Linda Woodhead, "Gender Differences in Religious Practice and Significance," in *The SAGE Handbook of the Sociology of Religion*, ed. James A. Beckford and N. J. Demerath, III (Los Angeles: SAGE Publications, 2007), 566–586.

78. Davidman and Greil, "Gender and the Experience of Conversion."

79. David A. Knight, Robert H. Woods, Jr., and Ines W. Jindra, "Gender Differences in the Communication of Christian Conversion Narratives," *Review of Religious Research* 47 (2005): 113–134.

80. Marc Baer, "Islamic Conversion Narratives of Women: Social Change and Gendered Religious Hierarchy in Early Modern Ottoman Istanbul," *Gender & History* 16 (2004): 425–458; van Nieuwkerk, *Women Embracing Islam*; Rodney Stark, "Reconstructing the Rise of Christianity: The Role of Women," *Sociology of Religion* 56 (1995): 229–244; Chen, *Getting Saved in America*; Chong, *Deliverance and Submission*.

81. Helen Rose Fuchs Ebaugh, *Becoming an Ex: The Process of Role Exit* (Chicago: University of Chicago Press, 1988).

BIBLIOGRAPHY

Abel, Andrew. "Favor Fishing and Punch-Bowl Christians: Ritual and Conversion in a Chinese Protestant Church." *Sociology of Religion* 67 (2006): 161–178.

——. " 'It's the People Here': A Study of Ritual, Conversion, and Congregational Life among Chinese Christians." PhD diss., University of Massachusetts, Amherst, MA, 2008.

Aikman, David. *Jesus in Beijing: How China is Transforming China and Changing the Global Balance of Power*. Washington, DC: Regnery Publishing, 2003.

Ammerman, Nancy Tatom. "Religious Identities and Religious Institutions." In *Handbook of the Sociology of Religion*, ed. Michele Dillon, 207–224. Cambridge: Cambridge University Press, 2003.

——. *Pillars of Faith: American Congregations and their Partners*. Berkeley and Los Angeles: University of California Press, 2005.

Ammerman, Nancy Tatom, and Arthur Emery Farnsley. *Congregation and Community*. New Brunswick, NJ: Rutgers University Press, 1997.

Ammerman, Nancy Tatom, Jackson W. Carroll, Carl S. Dudley, and William McKinney. *Studying Congregations: A New Handbook*. Nashville, TN: Abingdon Press, 1998.

Baer, Marc. "Islamic Conversion Narratives of Women: Social Change and Gendered Religious Hierarchy in Early Modern Ottoman Istanbul." *Gender & History* 16 (2004): 425–458.

Bainbridge, William Sims. "The Sociology of Conversion." In *Handbook of Religious Conversion*, ed. H. Newton Malony and Samuel Southard, 178–191. Birmingham, AL: Religious Education Press, 1992.

Barker, Eileen. *The Making of a Moonie: Choice or Brainwashing?* New York: B. Blackwell, 1984.

——. "Religious Movements: Cult and Anticult since Jonestown." *Annual Review of Sociology* 12 (1986): 329–346.

Barker, Irwin R., and Raymond F. Currie. "Do Converts Always Make the Most Committed Christians?" *Journal for the Scientific Study of Religion* 24 (1985): 305–313.

Beaman, Lori G. "The Myth of Pluralism, Diversity and Vigor: The Constitutional Privilege of Protestantism in the United States and Canada." *Journal for the Scientific Study of Religion* 43 (2003): 311–325.

Berger, Peter. *The Sacred Canopy: Elements of a Sociological Theory of Religion.* New York: Doubleday, 1967.

——. *The Desecularization of the World: Resurgent Religion and World Politics.* Washington, DC: Ethics and Public Policy Center, 1999.

Bibby, Reginald W., and Merlin B. Brinkerhoff. "The Circulation of the Saints: A Study of People Who Join Conservative Churches." *Journal for the Scientific Study of Religion* 12 (1973): 273–283.

Bruce, Steve. "The Supply-Side Model of Religion: The Nordic and Baltic States." *Journal for the Scientific Study of Religion* 39 (2000): 32–49.

Cao, Nanlai. "The Church as a Surrogate Family for Working Class Immigrant Chinese Youth: An Ethnography of Segmented Assimilation." *Sociology of Religion* 66 (2005): 183–200.

Carpenter, Joel A. *Revive Us Again: The Reawakening of American Fundamentalism.* New York: Oxford University Press, 1997.

Chao, Hsing-Kuang. "Conversion to Protestantism among Urban Immigrants in Taiwan." *Sociology of Religion* 67 (2006):193–204.

Chaves, Mark. *Congregations in America.* Cambridge, MA: Harvard University Press, 2004.

Chen, Carolyn. *Getting Saved in America: Taiwanese Immigration and Religious Experience.* Princeton: Princeton University Press, 2008.

Chong, Kelly H. *Deliverance and Submission: Evangelical Women and the Negotiation of Patriarchy in South Korea.* Cambridge, MA: Harvard University Press, 2008.

Christiano, Kevin J. "Church as a Family Surrogate: Another Look at Family Ties, Anomie, and Church Involvement." *Journal for the Scientific Study of Religion* 25 (1986): 339–354.

Collins, Randall. *Interaction Ritual Chains.* Princeton: Princeton University Press, 2004.

——. "The Classical Tradition in Sociology of Religion." In *The SAGE Handbook of the Sociology of Religion.* Los Angeles: SAGE Publications, 2007.

Davidman, Lynn. *Tradition in a Rootless World: Women Turn to Orthodox Judaism.* Berkeley and Los Angeles: University of California Press, 1991.

Davidman, Lynn, and Arthur L. Greil. "Gender and the Experience of Conversion: The Case of 'Returnees' to Modern Orthodox Judaism." *Sociology of Religion* 54 (1993): 83–100.

de Montclos, Marc-Antoine Perouse. "Conversion to Islam and Modernity in Nigeria: A View from the Underworld." *Africa Today* 54 (2008): 70–87.

De Oliveira, Vitoria Peres, and Cecilia L. Mariz. "Conversion to Islam in Contemporary Brazil." *Exchange* 35 (2006): 102–115.

Demerath, N. J., III. "Cultural Victory and Organizational Defeat in the Paradoxical Decline of Liberal Protestantism." *Journal for the Scientific Study of Religion* 34 (1995): 458–469.

——. *Crossing the Gods: World Religions and Worldly Politics.* New Brunswick, NJ: Rutgers University Press, 2001.

Demerath, N. J., III, and Arthur E. Farnsley, II. "Congregations Resurgent." In *The SAGE Handbook of the Sociology of Religion*, ed. James A. Beckford and N. J. Demerath, III, 193–204. Los Angeles: SAGE Publications, 2007.

Dougherty, Kevin D. "Institutional Influences on Growth in Southern Baptist Congregations." *Review of Religious Research* 46 (2004): 117–131.

Downton, James V., Jr. "An Evolutionary Theory of Spiritual Conversion and Commitment: The Case of Divine Light Mission." *Journal for the Scientific Study of Religion* 19 (1980): 381–396.

Duke, James T., and Barry L. Johnson. "The Stages of Religious Transformation: A Study of 200 Nations." *Review of Religious Research* 30 (1989): 209–224.

Dunch, Ryan. *Fuzhou Protestants and the Making of a Modern China, 1857–1927*. New Haven: Yale University Press, 2001.

Durkheim, Émile. *The Elementary Forms of Religious Life*. Trans. K. E. Fields. New York: Free Press, 1995.

Ebaugh, Helen Rose Fuchs. *Becoming an Ex: The Process of Role Exit*. Chicago: University of Chicago Press, 1988.

Ebaugh, Helen Rose Fuchs, and Sharron Lee Vaughn. 1984. "Ideology and Recruitment in Religious Groups." *Review of Religious Research* 26 (1984): 148–157.

Finke, Roger. "The Consequences of Religious Competition: Supply-Side Explanations for Religious Change." In *Rational Choice Theory and Religion: Summary and Assessment*, ed. L. A. Young, 45–64. New York: Routledge, 1997.

Finke, Roger, and Rodney Stark. *The Churching of America, 1776–1990: Winners and Losers in our Religious Economy*. New Brunswick, NJ: Rutgers University Press, 1992.

Gerstel, Naomi, and Natalia Sarkisian. "Marriage: The Good, the Bad, and the Greedy." *Contexts* (2006): 16–21.

Glock, Charles Y., Benjamin B. Ringer, and Earl R. Babbie. *To Comfort and to Challenge: A Dilemma for the Contemporary Church*. Berkeley and Los Angeles: University of California Press, 1967.

Gold, Thomas, Doug Guthrie, and David Wank, eds. *Social Connections in China: Institutions, Culture, and the Changing Nature of Guanxi*. Cambridge: Cambridge University Press, 2002.

Gooren, Henri. "The Religious Market Model and Conversion: Towards a New Approach." *Exchange* 35 (2006): 39–60.

———. "Reassessing Conventional Approaches to Conversion: Toward a New Synthesis." *Journal for the Scientific Study of Religion* 46 (2007): 337–353.

Granqvist, Pehr. "Attachment Theory and Religious Conversions: A Review and a Resolution of the Classic and Contemporary Paradigm Chasm." *Review of Religious Research* 45 (2003): 172–187.

Greil, Arthur L., and Lynn Davidman. "Religion and Identity." In *The SAGE Handbook of the Sociology of Religion*, ed. James A. Beckford and N. J. Demerath, III, 549–565. Los Angeles: SAGE Publications, 2007.

Greil, Arthur L., and David R. Rudy. "Social Cocoons: Encapsulation and Identity Transformation Organizations." *Sociological Inquiry* 54 (1984): 260–278.

Hall, Brian. "Social and Cultural Contexts in Conversion to Christianity among Chinese American College Students." *Sociology of Religion* 67 (2006): 131–147.

Hannigan, John A. "Social Movement Theory and the Sociology of Religion: Toward a New Synthesis." *Sociological Analysis* 52 (1991): 311–331.

Hefner, R. W. *Conversion to Christianity: Historical and Anthropological Perspectives on a Great Transformation*. Berkeley and Los Angeles: University of California Press, 1993.

Hoge, Dean R., Benton Johnson, and Donald A. Luidens. *Vanishing Boundaries: The Religion of Mainline Protestant Baby Boomers*. Louisville, KY: Westminster John Knox Press, 1992.

Hoge, Dean R., Kenneth McGuire, and Bernard F. Stratman. *Converts, Dropouts, Returnees: A Study of Religious Change among Catholics*. New York: Pilgrim Press, 1981.

Hwang, Kwang-Kwo. "Face and Favor: The Chinese Power Game." *American Journal of Sociology* 2 (1987): 944–974.

Iannaccone, Laurence R. "Why Strict Churches Are Strong." *American Journal of Sociology* 99 (1994): 1180–1211.

Iannaccone, Laurence R., Daniel V. A. Olson, and Rodney Stark. "Religious Resources and Church Growth." *Social Forces* 74 (1995): 705–731.

Jenkins, Philip. *The Next Christendom: The Rise of Global Christianity*. New York: Oxford University Press, 2002.

——. *The New Faces of Christianity: Believing the Bible in the Global South*. New York: Oxford University Press, 2006.

——. *God's Continent: Christianity, Islam, and Europe's Religious Crisis*. New York: Oxford University Press, 2007.

Jeung, Russell. *Faithful Generations: Race and New Asian American Churches*. New Brunswick, NJ: Rutgers University Press, 2005.

Kaplan, Steven. "Themes and Methods in the Study of Conversion in Ethiopia: A Review Essay." *Journal of Religion in Africa* 34 (2004): 373–392.

Kaufman, Debra R. *Rachel's Daughters: Newly Orthodox Jewish Women*. New Brunswick, NJ: Rutgers University Press, 1991.

Kelley, Dean M. *Why Conservative Churches Are Growing*. New York: HarperCollins, 1972.

Kertzer, David I. *Ritual, Politics, and Power*. New Haven: Yale University Press, 1988.

Kilbourne, Brock, and James T. Richardson. "Paradigm Conflict, Types of Conversion, and Conversion Theories." *Sociological Analysis* 50 (1989): 1–21.

Kim, Rebecca Y. *God's New Whiz Kids? Korean American Evangelicals on Campus*. New York: New York University Press, 2006.

Knight, David A., Robert H. Woods, Jr., and Ines W. Jindra. "Gender Differences in the Communication of Christian Conversion Narratives." *Review of Religious Research* 47 (2005): 113–134.

Kox, Willem, Wim Meeus, and Harm 't Hart. "Religious Conversion of Adolescents: Testing the Lofland and Stark Model of Religious Conversion." *Sociological Analysis* 52 (1991): 227–240.

Lambert, Tony. *China's Christian Millions*. Grand Rapids, MI: Monarch Books, 1999.

Lofland, John, and Rodney Stark. "Becoming a World-Saver: A Theory of Conversion to a Deviant Perspective." *American Sociological Review* 30 (1965): 862–875.

Long, Theodore E., and Jeffrey K. Hadden. "Religious Conversion and the Concept of Socialization: Integrating the Brainwashing and Drift Models." *Journal for the Scientific Study of Religion* 22 (1983): 1–14.

Lyon, David. *Jesus in Disneyland: Religion in Postmodern Times*. Cambridge: Polity Press, 2000.

Marti, Gerardo. "Fluid Ethnicity and Ethnic Transcendence in Multiracial Churches." *Journal for the Scientific Study of Religion* 47 (2008): 11–16.

——. "Affinity, Identity, and Transcendence: The Experience of Religious Racial Integration in Diverse Congregations." *Journal for the Scientific Study of Religion* 48 (2009): 53–68.

Martin, David. *Tongues of Fire: The Explosion of Protestantism in Latin America*. New York: Blackwell, 1990.

McNeill, William H. *Keeping Together in Time: Dance and Drill in Human History*. Cambridge, MA: Harvard University Press, 1995.

McPhee, Arthur G. *Friendship Evangelism: The Caring Way to Share Your Faith*. Grand Rapids, MI: Zondervan, 1978.

Mellor, Phillip A. "Embodiment, Emotion, and Religious Experience: Religion, Culture, and the Charismatic Body." In *The SAGE Handbook of the Sociology of Religion*, ed. James A. Beckford and N. J. Demerath, III, 587–607. Los Angeles: SAGE Publications, 2007.

Musick, Marc, and John Wilson. "Religious Switching for Marriage Reasons." *Sociology of Religion* 56 (1995): 257–270.

Newport, Frank. "The Religious Switcher in the United States." *American Sociological Review* 44 (1979): 528–552.

Ng, Kwai Hang. "Seeking the Christian Tutelage: Agency and Culture in Chinese Immigrants' Conversion to Christianity." *Sociology of Religion* 63 (2002): 195–214.

Olson, Daniel V. A. "Church Friendships: Boon or Barrier to Church Growth?" *Journal for the Scientific Study of Religion* 28 (1989): 432–447.

Preston, David L. "Becoming a Zen Practitioner." *Sociological Analysis* 42 (1981): 47–55.

Rambo, Lewis R. *Understanding Religious Conversion*. New Haven: Yale University Press, 1993.

———. 1999. "Theories of Conversion: Understanding and Interpreting Religious Change." *Social Compass* 46 (1999): 259–272.

Rappaport, Roy A. *Ritual and Religion in the Making of Humanity*. Cambridge: Cambridge University Press, 1999.

Reinders, Eric. "The Economies of Temple Chanting and Conversion in China." *International Bulletin of Missionary Research* 31 (2007): 188–192.

Richardson, James T., ed. *Conversion Careers: In and Out of the New Religions*. Beverly Hills, CA: SAGE Publications, 1978.

———. "The Active vs. Passive Convert: Paradigm Conflict in Conversion/Recruitment Research." *Journal for the Scientific Study of Religion* 24 (1985): 163–179.

Roof, Wade Clark, and Christopher Kirk Hadaway. "Denominational Switching in the Seventies: Going beyond Stark and Glock." *Journal for the Scientific Study of Religion* 18 (1979): 363–377.

Sebastian, Rodney, and Ashvin Parameswaran. "Conversion and the Family: Chinese Hare Krishnas." *Journal of Contemporary Religion* 22 (2007): 341–359.

Smilde, David. "A Qualitative Comparative Analysis of Conversion to Venezuelan Evangelicalism: How Networks Matter." *American Journal of Sociology* 111 (2005): 757–796.

Snow, David A., and Richard Machalek. "The Convert as a Social Type." *Sociological Theory* 1 (1983): 259–289.

———. "The Sociology of Conversion." *Annual Review of Sociology* 10 (1984): 167–190.

Snow, David A., and Cynthia L. Phillips. "The Lofland-Stark Conversion Model: A Critical Reassessment." *Social Problems* 27 (1980): 430–447.

Staples, Clifford L., and L. Mauss Armand. "Conversion or Commitment? A Reassessment of the Snow and Machalek Approach to the Study of Conversion." *Journal for the Scientific Study of Religion* 26 (1987): 133–147.

Stark, Rodney. "Reconstructing the Rise of Christianity: The Role of Women." *Sociology of Religion* 56 (1995): 229–244.

Stark, Rodney, and Roger Finke. *Acts of Faith: Explaining the Human Side of Religion*. Berkeley and Los Angeles: University of California Press, 2000.

Stark, Rodney, and Laurence R. Iannaccone. "A Supply-Side Reinterpretation of the 'Secularization' of Europe." *Journal for the Scientific Study of Religion* 33 (1994): 230–252.

Stark, Rodney, and William Sims Bainbridge. *A Theory of Religion*. New Brunswick, NJ: Rutgers University Press, 1996.

Suchman, Mark C. "Analyzing the Determinants of Everyday Conversion." *Sociological Analysis* 53S (1992): S15–S33.

Sullins, D. Paul. "Switching Close to Home: Volatility or Coherence in Protestant Affiliation Patterns?" *Social Forces* 72 (1993): 399–419.

Tamney, Joseph B., and Linda Hsueh-Ling Chiang. *Modernization, Globalization, and Confucianism in Chinese Societies*. Westport, CT: Praeger Publishing, 2002.

Thomas, George M. "Religions in Global Civil Society." *Sociology of Religion* 62 (2001): 515–533.

Tipton, Steven. *Getting Saved from the Sixties: Moral Meaning in Conversion and Cultural Change*. Berkeley and Los Angeles: University of California Press, 1982.

van Nieuwkerk, Karin. *Women Embracing Islam: Gender and Conversion in the West*. Austin: University of Texas Press, 2006.

Vande Berg, Travis, and Fred Kniss. "ISKCON and Immigrants: The Rise, Decline, and Rise Again of a New Religious Movement." *Sociological Quarterly* 49 (2008): 79–104.

Wang, Yuting, and Fenggang Yang. "More than Evangelical and Ethnic: The Ecological Factor in Chinese Conversion to Christianity in the United States." *Sociology of Religion* 67 (2006): 179–192.

Wang, Zhongxin. "A History of Chinese Churches in Boston." PhD diss., Boston University, School of Theology, 2000.

Warner, R. Stephen. "Work in Progress toward a New Paradigm for the Sociological Study of Religion in the United States." *American Journal of Sociology* 98 (1993): 1044–1093.

——. *A Church of Our Own: Disestablishment and Diversity in American Religion*. New Brunswick, NJ: Rutgers University Press, 2005.

——. "Presidential Address: Singing and Solidarity." *Journal for the Scientific Study of Religion* 47 (2008): 175–190.

Wind, James P., and James W. Lewis, eds. *American Congregations. Vol. 1, Portraits of Twelve Religious Communities*. Chicago: University of Chicago Press, 1994.

——. *American Congregations. Vol. 2, New Perspectives in the Study of Congregations*. Chicago: University of Chicago Press, 1994.

Woodhead, Linda. "Gender Differences in Religious Practice and Significance." In *The SAGE Handbook of the Sociology of Religion*, ed. James A. Beckford and N. J. Demerath, III, 566–586. Los Angeles: SAGE Publications, 2007.

Woolever, Cynthia, and Deborah Bruce. *A Field Guide to U.S. Congregations: Who's Going Where and Why*. Louisville, KY: Westminster John Knox Press, 2002.

Wuthnow, Robert, and Stephen Offutt. "Transnational Religious Connections." *Sociology of Religion* 69 (2008): 209–232.

Yan, Yunxiang. *The Flow of Gifts: Reciprocity and Social Networks in a Chinese Village*. Palo Alto, CA: Stanford University Press, 1996.

Yang, Fenggang. "Chinese Conversion to Evangelical Christianity: The Importance of Social and Cultural Contexts." *Sociology of Religion* 59 (1998): 237–257.

——. *Chinese Christians in America: Conversion, Assimilation, and Adhesive Identities*. University Park: Pennsylvania State University Press, 1999.

——. "Chinese Christian Transnationalism: Diverse Networks of a Houston Church." In *Religions Across Borders: Transnational Religious Networks*, ed. Helen Rose Ebaugh and Janet S. Chafetz, 129–148. Walnut Creek, CA: AltaMira Press, 2002.

——. "Between Secularist Ideology and Desecularizing Reality: The Birth and Growth of Religion in Communist China." *Sociology of Religion* 65 (2004): 101–119.

——. "Lost in the Market, Saved at McDonald's: Conversion to Christianity in Urban China." *Journal for the Scientific Study of Religion* 44 (2005): 423–441.

——. "Oligopoly Dynamics: Official Religions in China." In *The SAGE Handbook of the Sociology of Religion*, ed. James A. Beckford and N. J. Demerath, III, 635–653. Los Angeles: SAGE Publications, 2007.

Yang, Fenggang, and Joseph B. Tamney. "Exploring Mass Conversion to Christianity among the Chinese: An Introduction." *Sociology of Religion* 67 (2006): 125–129.

Yang, Mayfair Mei-hui. *Gifts, Favors, and Banquets: The Art of Social Relationships in China.* Ithaca, NY: Cornell University Press, 1994.

Zhang, Xuefeng. "How Religious Organizations Influence Chinese Conversion to Evangelical Protestantism in the United States." *Sociology of Religion* 67 (2006): 149–159.

CHAPTER 7

CONVERSION AND THE HISTORIC SPREAD OF RELIGIONS

ROBERT L. MONTGOMERY

A useful way of distinguishing different understandings of conversion is to examine it in connection with the spread of religions over time through propagation and conversion. Three religions in particular—Buddhism, Christianity, and Islam—have spread more widely than other religions, expanding to diverse sociocultural groups throughout the world in approximately two thousand three hundred years. This chapter considers conversion in light of the historic spread of these three religions. Their growth is viewed social scientifically as being the result of a set of three internal religious causes and four social causes. The ways in which these religions spread, and the causes of their expansion and transmission to succeeding generations, affect the various ways in which conversion may be understood, in particular as an experience with varying levels of volition.

THE DEFINITION OF CONVERSION IN THE SPREAD OF RELIGIONS

It is rather obvious that the spread of religions as a historical phenomenon could not have taken place without religious conversions. Although all religions can be considered as having the potential of spreading and all the major religions have spread to some degree, especially if expansion through migration is included, the three religions named above spread more widely through propagation and conversion to diverse sociocultural groups than other religions. Buddhism did not begin expanding widely until over two hundred years after the death of Buddha, dated by some as 544 B.C.E. and by others as

486 B.C.E.[1] The Emperor Ashoka (r. 273–232 B.C.E.) initiated the spread of Buddhism by sending out teachers of the *Dhamma* to neighboring countries and to Hellenic kingdoms to the west.[2] Christianity began spreading almost immediately after Jesus Christ commissioned his disciples in approximately 30 C.E., and Islam began spreading widely very soon after Muhammad died in 632 C.E.

I decided to seek social scientific reasons for the spread of these religions through their active propagation and the resulting conversion of numerous people from diverse populations.[3] These three religions were recognized in the nineteenth century by Max Muller and Thomas Arnold as "the missionary religions."[4] As I sought to explain the spread of these religions, I found that I had to incorporate at least a minimal concept of conversion, since religions cannot spread without people changing their religions and accepting new religious identities.

Religious identity is understood here to be one aspect of social identity, which is defined as "that *part* of the individuals' self-concept which derives from their knowledge of their membership of a social group (or groups) together with the value and emotional significance attached to that membership."[5] In other words, religious identity is only a part of one's total social identity and may be combined with a number of other aspects of a social identity, such as ethnic, national, gender, and occupational identities. The self-concept is a broader term than social identity since the latter only refers to group membership, whereas the self-concept includes various characteristics of the self that are not directly related to membership in a group. One of the insights of social identity theorist Henri Tajfel is that "an individual will tend to remain a member of a group and seek membership of new groups if these groups have some contribution to make to the positive aspects of his social identity; i.e., to those aspects of it from which he derives some satisfaction."[6] This means that people may change religious identities if by doing so they enhance, for example, their ethnic or gender identities, which they value or would like to value. Note that "value" and "emotional significance" are attached to the various aspects of social identity, in other words, to the various group memberships.

I decided that conversion associated with the spread of religions to numerous societies over the last approximately two millennia is most usefully defined in a broad but minimalist fashion as the acquiring of a religious identity not previously held. However, I came to see that this acquisition includes the possibility of various levels of volition. A high volitional level would be when a person makes a very conscious and deliberate commitment as an individual to be a follower of a religion not previously followed. A medium volitional level would be when a person simply decides to be identified with a religion new to him or her. A low volitional component would be when a person accepts a religious identity more or less as a matter of course, usually in concert with others who accept the same religious identity. This typically happens with subordinate people in close-knit groups or, once a religion is accepted, during the socialization process of young people. Of course, these descriptions of the acquisition of a religious identity are somewhat arbitrary. Actually, there is a continuum in the various levels of volition. Also, the higher levels of volition might be accompanied by deep emotions, including satisfaction and joy from having a new direction in life, but also other emotions such as awe and fear. The emotion may be obvious to others or felt primarily privately. The inner change of having a new direction and energy for life accompanying conversion is what Christians call "being born again." Although I could not discuss the inner life thoroughly in my historical and sociological, not social psychological, approach, I found that I had to consider motivational factors as a cause in the spread of the three religions.

Rather than trying to define conversion in the most complete way, which would include possible attendant emotions and various stages, I found it most useful for my purposes, as noted above, to define conversion in a minimalist fashion simply as the acceptance of a religious identity not previously held. After all, conversion to a religion may take place even when there is no particular consciousness of a prior religious identity or, especially in the modern world, when the prior identity was "having no religion." In tribal societies and in parts of large traditional societies there may be no consciousness of having a particular religious identity even though the people clearly have a religion or practice a variety of religions. In such societies there is simply a general pervasive religious consciousness because of the intertwining of religion with the social and political domains. Some come to identify with a particular religion mainly to contrast themselves with others from outside groups that they may be resisting. On the other hand, the acceptance of a particular religious identity may represent a very conscious change in religious identity. The histories the three most widely spreading religions show important variations in how conversions take place, but accepting a particular religious identity, whether for the first time or as an alternative to another religious identity, remains the basic criterion for all conversions associated with the spread of religions. This definition does not specify the level of volition, which may vary considerably. Variation in the level of volition becomes a way of comparing conversions in the spread and transmission of religions.

THE SPREAD OF RELIGIONS IN HISTORY

In order to understand the variations in the meaning of conversion that have accompanied the spread of religions and that go beyond simply the acquiring of a particular religious identity, it is necessary to review the historic spread of the three missionary religions that took place primarily over the last two millennia. The spread of religions, especially of Christianity, is rather well documented in numerous histories, but social scientists have paid surprisingly little attention to explaining why religions spread or why the most widely spreading religions have been the most successful in converting people. One of the few social scientists to examine the causes of the spread of religions is Rodney Stark, who examined the early spread of Christianity and the mission efforts under monotheism.[7] In my latest study of the causes for the spread of Buddhism, Christianity, and Islam, I identified a total of seven causes: three internal religious causes or the religious characteristics making these religions prone to spread (a single human mediating figure, their belief and morality systems, and their ability to gather and organize people) and four social causes—two macro (freedom of choice and inter-societal relationships) and two micro (social relationships and motivations)—that have either facilitated or blocked their spread.[8]

The spread of the three missionary religions over the last two thousand years provides the most numerous examples of conversion, particularly variations in how conversions have taken place. In brief, Buddhism, coming out of Hinduism, spread primarily throughout Asia, but in recent centuries Buddhism has spread to the West. Christianity and Islam, coming out of the biblical tradition of Judaism and more vigorous in spreading than Buddhism, expanded from the Middle East to much of the rest of the world. The present situation is far from static, but conversions to all three religions (and resistance to conversions) are continuing to take place around the world. We will examine how conversions have varied as these three religions crossed numerous social and political borders, not through a conventional historical review of the spread of these religions, but rather through relating conversion to the various causes for their spread.

CHARACTERISTICS OF THE THREE MISSIONARY RELIGIONS AFFECTING CONVERSION AND THE SPREAD OF RELIGIONS

The first of three religious characteristics influencing the spread of religions is found in a rather surprising fact ignored by most scholars of comparative religion. As different as these three religions are, they share the characteristic of presenting a single human being as a means of access to God and salvation and who is consequently a focus of personal adoration and loyalty. Christianity and Islam, in particular, inherit from Judaism the belief in a God who demands exclusive loyalty. This heightens the importance of the volitional element in conversion, or at least provides a basis for emphasizing deliberate and personal choice. But the two daughter religions go beyond Judaism in having central human figures who are the object of devotion.

In the Asian pattern that dominated the areas to which Buddhism spread, a single or exclusive loyalty was not demanded to the same extent. In a way not usually possible in Christian and Muslim areas, people could identify themselves as Buddhists and at the same time observe religious practices found in local religions that elevate other figures as sources of help. Nevertheless, the figure of the Buddha proved to have an attractive power that elevated him above the many gods worshipped in popular religion. Noting first that Buddhism in its original form did not attract large numbers, John Noss makes it clear what happened as Buddhism spread: "But the masses became interested. Not in the teaching, but *the man*. Original Buddhism would not have had so great an effect on the history of religion in the Orient, if the coldly rational philosophy of the sage of the Sakyas had not been mediated through a personality that could be adored."⁹ Other scholars recognize the centrality of Buddha, even though there are many bodhisattvas or secondary-level intermediaries. For example, Stephen Sharot states:

> Anthropologists appear to be in general agreement that the Buddha, gods, and spirits are all part of what Buddhists perceive as a single cosmological system.... All are agreed that Buddhists conceptualize the Buddha and his teaching as superior to the spirits.... Whereas Hindus have incorporated folk practices in a syncretistic fashion, Buddhists have incorporated them in stressing their separate and inferior status.¹⁰

And so the worship of the Buddha, who is above other deities, spread to many areas of Asia and is now spreading in the West. At the same time, although Christianity and Islam both incorporated a certain amount of popular religion that tended to be grounded in particular cultures and ethnic groups, both demanded an exclusive identification not demanded in Buddhism. Whatever may be said of the mixing of Buddhism with other religions, Buddhism, to a much greater extent than other Asian religions, continues to have committed followers in numerous societies across the world.

In addition to offering the powerful attraction of belief in a single mediating figure between humans and God (rather than simply the transcendent figure of God or multiple gods), a second, but closely related, religious content factor affecting the spread of the three missionary religions is the special emphasis they each give to the compassion of God for all people and the offer of salvation to every individual. The three missionary religions certainly cannot claim a consistently higher morality than other religions, but their belief and morality systems that emphasize salvation and compassion for every individual gave them an inner dynamic that produced (and still produces) a special moral energy among a diversity of people at different times. This "moral energy" is hard to define and may even be directed in ways that are destructive and exclusivist, but it is nevertheless based on followers' sense of having received special mercy "from above." All three of the most widely spreading religions have established extensive institutions and programs of humanitarian relief. The belief and moral systems, which are closely connected, have appealed to different segments of societies and sooner or later to leaders of societies who have facilitated their spread, as we shall see.

The third religious content characteristic that makes the three missionary religions prone to spread more widely than other religions is their ability to gather and organize people. I see this ability as represented in the sangha, the church, and the mosque, especially in the latter two religious bodies. These organizations have provided people with a clear means of identifying with these religions. These religions formed both strong locally based communities and international networks. Furthermore, the organizations have made serious efforts to spread their religions by sending out carriers of the faith (missionaries) who seek to convert people to these religions. Having strong organizations makes it possible for conversions to be directed toward "belonging" and receiving a clear religious identity.

In regard to the meaning of conversion in relation to the characteristics of religions, it is especially important that the three missionary religions each have a distinct individual human being, having special powers of mediation between humans and the Divine, to whom individuals are challenged to be loyal. People may thus become "followers," usually within a community of followers but sometimes as solitary "followers." The "followers" are often given a mission to carry the faith to others. As already noted, Christianity and Islam, in particular, received from their parent faith, Judaism, the view of faith as a response to God, who expected exclusive commitment and loyalty both to God and the community of believers. This means that these two religions especially had the basis for bringing a strong volitional component to the process of conversion. However, the volitional component in conversion was (is) weakened by two conditions: (1) As faith communities are formed, the transmission of the faith becomes part of the socialization process, so that acceptance of the identity of being a "follower" tends to become a matter of course or of routine for new generations. (2) Especially exacerbating this condition of a lowered volitional element in conversion is when the faith becomes established and supported by the coercive power of governments. As a monopolistic faith supported or even sponsored by the government, a religion may be accepted more or less passively with very little volitional action. When this happens, these missionary religions with their demand for a strong personal commitment become more or less like other religions that are part of the traditional culture of a society. Religious identity and ethnic or national identity become virtually synonymous. This matter will be examined in the next section that considers the social factors affecting the spread of the three missionary religions. In short, the three religions, especially Christianity and Islam, contain in themselves a strong basis for a high volitional aspect to conversion. However, there are important social factors that tend to reduce the volitional aspect of conversion.

MACRO SOCIAL FACTORS AFFECTING CONVERSION AND THE SPREAD OF THE MISSIONARY RELIGIONS

Two macro social factors either facilitated or blocked the spread of the three religions. As we shall see, these causes also affected the voluntary content of conversion associated with the spread of religions.

Opportunities for Choice

A basic factor affecting the spread of religions is the possibility of choice allowed by the structure of the societies to which the religions spread or the degree of influence on choices exercised by public authorities within societies. In certain rare times in the past, there have existed relatively high possibilities for making religious choices in certain societies. These were times when there was relative toleration by governments for the existence of a variety of religions and expressions of faith. One of these times was in the Roman Empire during the first three centuries of the first millennium C.E. The Roman Empire was awash with religions coming from the various kingdoms that had been overrun and incorporated into the Empire. These religions were allowed to exist and compete for the loyalty of people as long as the cult of the rulers and loyalty to the emperors was not seriously challenged. Previously, the Persian Achaemenid Empire had likewise been relatively tolerant of local religions. For example, Jews were encouraged to rebuild the temple in Jerusalem, as well as the walls of the city.

In addition, the powerful empires established by nomadic peoples that ruled over ethnically and religiously diverse populations, such as the Parthians, the Omayyads (the initial Islamic rulers in the east and the continuing rulers in Spain), and the Mongols were relatively tolerant of various religions. Another example of relative freedom of choice, often overlooked, was among the leaders, not the followers, in small societies; typically, tribal leaders could choose among a variety of religions or religious practices they encountered from nearby or surrounding societies. The populations of small societies, however, were more likely to accept as a matter of course the religious beliefs and practices accepted by the rulers or leaders of the societies into which they were socialized. In this way, the unity that is so important for small societies could be maintained.

Thus, Christianity in its first three hundred years spread in the midst of the religious diversity of the Roman Empire, forming numerous voluntary groups of followers of Jesus Christ. In addition, Buddhism, Christianity, and Islam all showed a propensity to spread to relatively small societies or tribes where the rulers, as "opinion leaders," often made the specific choice to convert to these religions as religions that would be a benefit to their people and, at the same time, enhance their own power. However, their followers tended to follow their leaders with a relatively low level of volition.

In many respects, these kinds of decisions by leaders took place on a large scale in the fourth century in Rome, where Constantine and those who followed him (not Julian, "the apostate") saw Christianity as enhancing their power in the Empire.[11] As the rulers made their decisions, the voluntary element became less important in conversion for the members at large. In the Roman Empire, the religious pluralism that had existed was eliminated; the social condition of a monopolistic religion represented a reversion to the typical pattern of most kingdoms and empires of the ancient world. Over time, all three of the missionary religions became "established religions" that were monopolistic in particular societies. Following conversions of the majorities in particular populations, the natural socialization within families and whole communities and societies became the primary way that faith was transmitted. This helped to strengthen the non-voluntary aspect of conversion. Although creating monopolistic religions helped to spread particular religions within the bounds of particular societies (thus being a very appealing action to religious leaders of the recognized religion), religious choices and thus conversions to other religions became limited under this kind of religious system. Acceptance of a religious identity soon became synonymous with acceptance of an ethnic or national identity, and religion became simply an aspect of culture. This became typical even for Christianity and Islam, religions that originally and in religiously pluralistic conditions require individual conversion. In the meantime, the principle of conversion with a high volitional aspect was maintained primarily by small groups of religious specialists, such as monks in Buddhism and Christianity, and imams and Sufis among Muslims.

Before leaving this section on the importance of the presence of choice in societies for conversion to take place, I will note the historic break from domination by monopolistic religions and the spread of freedom that took place in the West. After the establishment of Christianity as a state religion in the fourth century, the higher volitional aspect of faith was maintained primarily in the many orders of monks that developed within the Church and also among the "heretical" groups that arose in opposition to the dominant church. Oppositional or dissenting faith became a major movement in the sixteenth century with the Protestant Reformation, especially in the Radical wing of the Reformation represented by the Anabaptists. These latter groups, for example, only practiced "believer's baptism," which gives special emphasis to conversion as a personal commitment of faith resulting in being "born again."

Simultaneous with the movement in the eighteenth century in Europe stressing the importance of making a personal faith commitment and becoming "born again" (sometimes simply characterized as the "Evangelical Movement"), the Enlightenment began in Europe. Many in the Enlightenment, especially in France, emphasized freedom from the old religious authorities based on the challenge to the old knowledge by science. Although the Enlightenment in Europe was not entirely a movement in opposition to religion, it incorporated a movement against organized and established religion that has continued to the present and is most clearly represented in academia and among intellectuals in the West. This ensuing movement to the Enlightenment, sometimes called the "Secularization Movement," is often seen by European scholars as being anti-religious and as greatly weakening religions. However, many American scholars have come to see secularization as a process that benefits religion by creating religious diversity, competition, and more vital religiosity. Such opposite viewpoints can be seen, for example, in Steve Bruce,[12] on the one hand, and Rodney Stark and Roger Finke,[13] on the other. Although it could be said that irreligion rode the new wave of emphasis on human freedom and the autonomous individual, it is often forgotten by many scholars that religious people were in the forefront of the movement to separate religion from the coercive power of government, especially in North America. Colin Campbell writes:

> The secularists in America had to contend with a phenomenon almost unknown to their British counterparts of this period—a vigorous Christian anti-clerical movement. In fact, during the 1820s the Christian anti-clericals had more periodicals in circulation than the free-thinkers—a fact which made it that much harder for the real infidels to mobilize support and which may account for their excessive crudity of approach.... Thus, ironically enough, it was the same conditions which appeared to favor the growth of secularism in America which in fact worked against a strong and influential movement.[14]

Although secularism as an ideology was usually anti-religious in spirit, secularization as a process was far from being merely anti-religious. Christian Smith's book, *Secular*

Revolution: Power, Interests, and Conflict in the Secularization of American Public Life,[15] makes clear that although American public life was secularized to a great extent beginning about 1870 and extending through the 1930s, it did not prevent American religious life from continuing at a vigorous pace. For my purposes here, I note that the process of secularization, especially in North America, helped to give a strong personal voluntary content to the meaning of conversion. The groups emphasizing the need for individual conversion, which had been primarily dissenting groups in Europe, were at the forefront of the secularization movement in America when a major result of that movement is seen as the separation of church and state.

In addition to the structural factors affecting the possibilities of choice within societies, there remains another macro social factor that strongly affected the spread of religions and the meaning of conversion.

Intersocietal Relationships

Intersocietal relationships that inevitably developed as societies came in contact with one another may either help to transmit or to block the spread of religions. Typically, societies have tended to seek to dominate one another. For some time, I have theorized and argued that religions do not spread effectively when associated with domination or threat.[16] There is a conventional view that both Christianity and Islam primarily spread through coercion or in association with domination, but I believe this view is mistaken. At the same time, Buddhism is seen as a very peaceful religion. There is some validity to the association of militarism with Christianity and Islam and nonviolence with Buddhism. However, the question to consider here is whether coercion and domination "work" in the spread of religions. I believe that the evidence demonstrates that coercion and domination in intersocietal relationships in association with the attempted spread of religions, primarily Christianity and Islam, are not effective means for spreading religions. Furthermore, where there has not been a perception of coercion and domination, these religions have spread more effectively.

First, although Buddhism has never been accused of spreading primarily through coercion, it should not be forgotten that it became associated with governments and thereby monopolistic, especially in Southeast Asia, Tibet, Mongolia, and Japan. In these areas and others where Buddhism has received government sponsorship, it has the problem of all monopolistic religions, discussed in the previous section, of having large numbers of followers who are not particularly serious about their relationship to Buddhism. Monopolistic Christianity and Islam, of course, have the same problem.

However, Christianity and Islam are both accused of spreading through coercion and historically have been associated with conquering armies. During Christianity's first three hundred years, in contrast to its later history, the religion did not spread through the backing of any government and army but rather as a minority religious movement that attracted numerous individuals who chose to be Christian in spite of political and social opposition.[17] The result was that the volitional element remained high rather than low in conversion. This is seen both in the New Testament and the accounts of the early church. However, the pattern changed drastically in the fourth century. Christianity became associated with Roman coercive power, which gave Christianity official sanction and made becoming a Christian a matter of course for large numbers of people within the bounds of the Empire. This condition of Christianity being the official religion was to continue for some one thousand years in the Byzantine Empire. In the West, how- ever, Roman power was greatly reduced by the onslaught of the European tribes. Even in the East, the Byzantine Empire was not able to extend its domination over the tribes to the north or over the kingdoms to the east, especially the Persian Empire and later the Muslim lands. This meant that in the second great era of the spread of Christianity, when it spread northward throughout western and eastern Europe from the fourth to the eleventh centuries, it spread without association with the domination of the former powerful Roman or Byzantine empires. This fact is often overlooked by people who study the spread of Christianity. Nevertheless, as rulers and leaders of tribes accepted the Christian faith, they became "little Constantines" in the familiar pattern. This is the pattern in which the ruler made Christianity the official religion of the land. It was Theodosius, reigning from 378 to 395, rather than Constantine, reigning from 306 to 337, who enforced Christianity, but Constantine and "the Holy Roman Empire" became the "ideal" in succeeding centuries. The European kings were followed in their conversions by those they ruled, and the rulers subsequently established versions of Christianity as officially monopolistic state religions, as discussed in the previous section.

In the meantime, the Christianity of the Byzantine Empire that dominated Middle Eastern peoples created considerable opposition among these peoples, including non-Orthodox Christian groups such as the Monophysites and Nestorians. As the Byzantine Empire became officially Christian, the Persian Empire made it more diffi- cult for Christianity to spread. In fact, Samuel Moffett makes the point, "When Rome became Christian, its old enemy Persia became anti-Christian."[18] The Christianity of the Byzantine Empire failed to spread to the Persian Empire and eventually was rebuffed and conquered by Islamic Turks. Although Christianity had some success with tribes in Central Asia and in China and among Mongols, primarily through Nestorian mis- sionaries, it eventually failed to spread as successfully there as in the West. There was neither the sustained religious diversity of the pre-Christian Roman Empire in the empires of the East nor an abundance of leaders of small societies, as in Europe, who saw in Christianity a superior offering to what was already available to them in traditional Asian religions or newly offered in Islam.

Islam initially spread in association with a conquering army, but it showed consid- erable toleration for the "religions of the book" (Judaism and Christianity)—in fact, a greater toleration of the Middle Eastern and North African Christian populations than was given by the Christian rulers of the Byzantine Empire. In many respects, therefore, Islam came as a liberating power both from Byzantine and Persian Empires, the latter being ruled by the very oppressive Zoroastrian Sassanids. Some of the best evidence for the weakness of coercion in bringing about conversion, contrary to much conventional thought, was the failure of Islam to be accepted in large areas where Islamic governments ruled for centuries and applied laws against non-Muslims. These areas were the Iberian Peninsula, Sicily, Greece, the Balkans, and much of India. Furthermore, the greatest successes in the spread of Islam were with people who invaded and dominated Islamic societies, for example, the Turks and the Mongols. Also, Islam spread peacefully, through traders, to many African peoples and to large populations in Southeast Asia, so that the largest Islamic nation today is Indonesia. The volitional aspect of conversion remained high for Islam, at least among opinion leaders, but once made officially monopolistic, the volitional aspect of being a follower of Islam was lowered, as occurred with Christianity in Europe.

The issue of the influence of dominating intersocietal relationships on conversion came to the forefront again with the rise of imperialism and colonialism from the West after 1500. The beginning of Western exploration and colonization of foreign lands also saw the revival of the missionary movement that had carried Christianity throughout Europe. Following the conversion of Europe and the establishment of state churches, Christianity ceased spreading to a large extent. This marked "the great ebb" in Christian expansion between 1000 and 1500, and by the end of this medieval period Christianity faced a major crisis regarding its future.[19] As already seen, the development of Christian monopolies in Europe downplayed the phenomenon of conversion, but after 1500 the situation began to change in Europe as the former religious authorities began to be challenged more successfully. At the same time, Europeans increasingly came in contact with new peoples and their religions in the non-Western world. Exploration and conquest by Portugal and Spain was followed and exceeded by the colonialism of the northern European powers, which reached a high point in the nineteenth and first part of the twentieth century. The encounter of the "Christian powers" with the non-Western world placed a renewed emphasis on conversion, especially by Protestant missionaries, as the conscious individual choice of acquiring a new religious identity, but it also associated conversion with coercion and domination by the colonial powers.

As a result of this association, Christianity encountered strong resistance in large areas of the world, both in the ancient civilizations of the East and among the tribal peoples of Africa and the Americas. Countries dominated by Islam were already in opposition to Christianity due to enmities dating from the rise of Islam in opposition to the ancient empires of Byzantium and Persia. These enmities were exacerbated by the Crusades, conflicts in the Mediterranean, and then the decline of Muslim power in the Middle East in the face of Western colonialism. The old societies of Asia, with their well-established literary and religious traditions, largely opposed conversion to the Christianity that came to them in association with explorers and conquerors. A major exception to the general opposition to Christianity was from minority groups in Asian societies and from some other small-scale societies. In contrast to the majority populations in societies, many of the minority groups and small-scale societies such as those in India, China, Burma, Indonesia, Taiwan, and the Pacific Islands were receptive to Christianity. In the special case of Korea, the whole nation came under Japanese rule in the first half of the twentieth century, in contrast to the nations under the Western colonial domination that was associated with Christianity. Whereas in other countries nationalism caused anti-Christian attitudes to develop, Korea became receptive to Christianity because of the association of Christianity with patriotism.[20] The interior of Africa remained largely unexplored for some centuries, but as contacts increased in the nineteenth century the people remained generally resistant to Christianity, which was again associated with colonialism. Armies accompanied by Roman Catholic missionaries conquered Latin America and the Philippines, with the result that conversions of large numbers of people to Christianity took place. However, many of the indigenous peoples created distinctive forms of Christianity that have earned them the name "Christo-paganism" or "folk Catholicism." That is, they accepted the identity of Christian, but they incorporated much of their pre-Christian religion as a form of covert opposition to the imposed faith. Actually, this is a process that had earlier taken place to some extent in both the Roman Empire and among the European tribes. In contrast to these regions with mixed indigenous and Christian religions, the lands that did not perceive Christianity as being imposed upon them were much more likely to accept Christianity as presented to them. Of course, they also made various adaptations and innovations based on their cultures, but they were much less likely overtly to mix indigenous religions with Christianity, as happened in those lands where Christianity was imposed on the people such as Latin America and the Philippines. For example, in Korea, the Pacific Islands, and among the minority peoples of Asia, there is far less overt mixing of indigenous religions with Christianity.

The successful and unsuccessful efforts of evangelical missionaries who traveled throughout the world, especially beginning in the nineteenth century (and continuing today), brought a new emphasis on conversion. Unfortunately for Christian missions, the nineteenth century saw the increasing worldwide domination of Western powers, so that the Christian message was associated with domination in large sections of the world. Thus, Christianity was perceived by receiving countries as largely a "Western religion" or even "the white people's religion" that was officially sponsored by Western state governments. This largely remained the perception of non-Western people, but with the collapse of colonialism after World War II, this perception is changing. The result of this collapse and change of perception has been the explosive growth of Christianity in the non-Western world.[21]

Individuals throughout the world, especially in large societies, have increasingly been challenged by the possibility of making personal decisions to accept a new religion introduced to their societies. This often means breaking with family and community traditions, which are difficult decisions for these individuals. The dramatic results since the collapse of colonialism have demonstrated that Christianity spreads most effectively when it is not associated with domination and coercion. Africa and China have led the way in an explosive growth of Christianity, and Latin America has also seen the rapid growth of Pentecostalism. These trends emphasize the conversion experience that has a high volitional content. Religious diversity and increasing individualism around the world are now confronting people with the need to make choices. This is not to say, however, that postcolonial domination via cultural, economic, and political forces does not continue to create resistance to conversion in many non-Western societies.

I next briefly review the micro factors affecting the spread of religions that have been elevated by the macro shifts in world conditions discussed above.

MICRO SOCIAL FACTORS AFFECTING CONVERSION AND THE SPREAD OF RELIGIONS

Social Relationships

As already seen, macro social factors can increase or decrease the importance of micro social factors in the spread of religions. Most of the societies encountered by the first Western Christian missionaries were not societies like those in the West, in which individuals were generally accustomed to living more or less autonomously and making important decisions for themselves. In the West itself, individualism developed slowly but was given a great impetus by the Protestant Reformation, especially in its Radical and Dissenting forms. Individualism was accelerated by both Enlightenment thought and the Industrial Revolution. Even though the colonial age began about 1500, the Evangelical Movement did not arise until approximately two hundred years later, with its special emphasis on a personal decision to follow Jesus Christ and a continuing experiential relationship with Christ. Flowing from the Evangelical Movement of the eighteenth and nineteenth centuries was the worldwide missionary movement that has continued to the present. This movement found support from the new wealth of the Industrial Revolution.

In non-Western lands, as earlier in the West, populations often followed the "opinion leaders" in deciding which religion to follow or be identified with. These were people to whom they were related and whom they trusted personally in social networks, particularly in families, clans, and villages. Because of the difficulties of survival in most societies, social relationships were especially strong and were maintained through attachments to trusted persons. Among the followers in groups, either conversion or resistance to conversion took place, not on the basis of individual personal conviction concerning the content of religions but on the basis of what was most acceptable to the leaders of the group and to peers. At the same time, the spread of religions brought to light distinctions and fissures within groups among different group leaders, with some favoring and some opposing new religions. Group leaders made their decisions whether to accept or reject a new religion primarily based on how the religion would aid and strengthen their group, including their own leadership of the group or at least their part of the group.

However, in the last two centuries individualism as an economic, social, and political condition and as an ideal has spread around the world. There are increasing opportunities to choose from a variety of employments, as well as increasing demands for

individual rights. This has created social relationships that are more based on voluntary choices than simply on inherited family and traditional community relationships.
Nevertheless, because humans will always form social relationships, conversions or
change in religious identities will continue to follow the lines of the connections in
social relationships. John Lofland and Rodney Stark demonstrated the crucial importance of social relationships in bringing about conversions, and social networks
continued to be emphasized in succeeding studies.[22] The quality of the new social relationships offered by new religions that are being introduced is especially important
in influencing the acquiring of new religious identities. For example, in the spread of
Pentecostalism in Latin America, women have found some relief from the machismo
in Latin societies.[23]

Motivations

On the individual (micro) level, it is not only social relationships that are important in
conversion and the spread of religions, but motivations of individuals are increasingly
affecting the conversions that have been taking place around the world. That is, individuals increasingly make decisions regarding education, work, marriage, location, and the
election of leaders. Individuals like to rationalize and justify their decisions. Advertising
in the commercial world constantly appeals to people on the basis that some product is
"good for them." Previously, in many lands most people had very few such decisions to
make and therefore little reason to think about why they should decide on some course
of action or choose something to purchase. They largely acted as they were expected
to act and lived with what they had. Now, because of the increasing freedom of religion, it is possible to speak of "religious markets" in which various religions appeal for
people to decide to follow them and offer explanations of why people should make such
a decision.

Motivations that guide decisions are difficult to study because of their extremely complex and mixed nature. Adding to this difficulty is the fact that the motives of people
in the past or simply of people in other cultures must often be inferred. The three most
widely spreading religions offered to numerous peoples a means of lifting their literacy and educational levels and hence their level of knowledge. This certainly increased
self-esteem. The missionary religions had the least success when they encountered
people who already had literary traditions associated with an established religion. This
applies to the ancient societies of the Middle and Far East, with their traditional religions. On the other hand, the new religions offered minority groups an opportunity to
emphasize their distinctive identity in contrast to majority groups. Opinion leaders of
tribal societies were often motivated to encourage others to convert to missionary religions if leaders perceived those new religions as a means to enhance the identity and
status of the group vis-à-vis other societies. For the majority population of traditional
societies, whose main purpose was to survive, conforming to the behavior of others,
particularly those in authority, was typically the safest option.

It is not enough to consider only social influences as motivating conversions. The fact that the religious content of the three missionary religions is relevant to the motivations of individuals is often forgotten or neglected in scholarly studies. The evidence for the influence of religious content on the spread of the three religions has been discussed above and given in detail in my study.[24] Especially important is that from the beginning all three missionary religions offered an individual immanent savior who also provided continual access to the transcendent Divine and who attracted personal "followers." As the discussion above of the three immanent and knowable beings, Buddha, Jesus, and Muhammad, made clear, the three most widely spreading religions had the advantage of offering a historical person who could be envisioned and to whom people could give their loyalty and devotion. More than that, these figures gave access to the transcendent Divine and to spiritual power. Although other world religions offered great sages, teachers, and prophets, such as Confucius, Lao Zi, Mahavira, Zoroaster, Mani, and Moses, none of them reached the level accorded to Buddha, Jesus, and Muhammad. The three missionary religions could motivate people to choose them because of the potential source of divine or spiritual power that lay in each of these three special figures. The evidence from the history of the spread of these religions is that this is exactly what took place.

Interestingly, popular religion points to the human needs which the three founders met (and still meet) for many people. The study of popular religion in the world religions demonstrates that people seek help for their survival needs, such as healing and the provision of children, food, and general protection in a misery-filled and dangerous world.[25] In addition or along with seeking to fulfill material needs, they seek spiritual power. Typically they turn to individual figures, whether mythical or historic, as in the case of ancestors. The immanent savior-mediating figures of the three missionary religions do, in fact, offer these kinds of help for the daily lives of their followers. They can make this offer on the basis of their special status with the transcendent Divine. It is true, however, that various popular versions developed within the missionary religions that sought additional help from special "holy figures" who were presumed to have mediating powers. These additional mediating figures are numerous in Buddhism and some forms of Christianity, especially "older Christianity" (Orthodoxy and Roman Catholicism), but even Islam has its saints to whom appeals are made. These popular forms of religion are sometimes outside of the "official" forms of the religions. The desire for increased spirituality and its attendant powers are not only the basis for the creation of various forms of popular religion but also of various movements to create more spiritual or purer forms of established religions, some of which seek to return to the earliest forms of the religion and to greater devotion to the founders. Some movements to return to more spiritual forms of religions have tendencies toward dualism in distinguishing the spiritual and material, as in Docetism or later Manichaeism in Christianity. Docetism perceived Jesus Christ as God masquerading as a human. Manichaeism, based on the teachings of the "prophet" Mani, born 215–216 C.E. in Persia, was highly dualistic in elevating the spiritual against the physical and material. In medieval Europe the Bogomiles in the Balkans and the Cathars in France, both influenced by Manichaeism, plus the more orthodox Waldensians, Lollards, and Hussites, all represented movements to purify the established religion. These were in addition to the spiritual movements that stayed within the established religion, typically in the form of new "orders." These movements were followed by Reformations, both the Protestant Reformation and the Counter Reformation. The Protestant Reformation sought particularly to return to the biblical roots of Christianity, but the main Protestant movement was accompanied by the "Radical Reformation," which sought to go beyond the main Protestant movement in purifying Christianity. In the modern era, it may be said that Dispensationalism, initiated by John Nelson Darby (1800–1882), who founded the Plymouth Brethren Church in England, has sought to distinguish and establish spiritual churches from the "apostate" historic organized churches. Like other religious movements, it has also had a strong eschatological emphasis. In Islam, the Sufi movement, as well as the Shi'a movement, represented aspirations for greater spirituality within Islam and also included an eschatological element. Of course, the religious orders of Roman Catholicism were likewise movements seeking a more rigorous form of faith.

I am not seeking to make a judgment here regarding the truth claims of any of these movements, but I am making the point that these movements seeking new and more vigorous or spiritual forms of familiar and established religions contributed to the increase in the individual, volitional aspect of conversion. This is because they required individuals to make a decision to commit themselves to a "new way" that was in contrast to the "old way." They helped to lay the groundwork for the modern era in which individualism was raised to be a central feature of life. These movements have done much to make the modern content of "conversion" to be not simply the acquiring of a new religious identity, but an individual and personal volitional act or even a process or "career" based on what the individual sees, understands, and experiences in a new religion or religious movement that seeks to revive the traditional religion.[26]

A major historical event of the eighteenth century greatly accelerated what the religious movements before and during this period did to draw attention to conversion as a personal volitional act involving complex motivations. This was the establishment of a new nation based on immigrants from various religious backgrounds in North America, where they created a very fluid and diverse religious environment. It is not too much to say that everything was changed in the religious situation in North America. Although ideas related to human rights and political freedom had a great influence in the formation of the US government and its relationship to organized religion, it was the peculiar new social and religious conditions in the "New World" that made it possible for a new emphasis to be placed on individual conversion. These conditions were the mixing of ethnic and religious groups in the new land and the competition between religious groups for followers. Parts of the mix of religious groups were religious movements having roots in European Pietistic-evangelical movements. In the new land, people had opportunities to begin new lives in new locations away from their parents and relatives, so that the traditional lines of transmission of faith were changed. Socialization of coming generations always has and always will take place, but in the new conditions the major responsibility fell upon nuclear families together with the religious groups to which they belonged.

To aid in religious socialization, religious groups undertook various educational programs. A movement for public education gradually commenced, based on the values of people who deeply respected education, but the movement was also greatly aided by the fact that in modern societies families needed help in the socialization process. The movement was expressed in the development of public schools, often attached to churches, but in addition there was the Sunday School Movement in the churches themselves. Public schools in the United States were originally under the leadership of Protestants who sought to teach a "common Christianity," a phrase actually used by leaders of the National Educational Association before the early 1870s.[27] This approach of the majority Protestant society helped prompt the Roman Catholic Church to create an extensive parochial school system. However, beginning around 1870, the educational system in the United States became increasingly secular.[28] Because of the secularization of the educational system, as well as of many other aspects of life in America, over the last hundred or more years the religious socialization process has depended more heavily upon individual families and on the religious groups to which they belong. Since many families have tenuous or no relationship to religious groups, the rising generations become an open field for religious groups seeking converts. The result of the secularization of education and of public life generally means that individuals are faced with making their own decisions about religious attachments. In such a cultural ethos, conversion based on conscious choice has taken on increased importance.

The influence of informal and formal socialization on children is demonstrated in the important book on teenage religion by Christian Smith with Melinda Denton, followed by the book on religious and spiritual lives of emerging adults by Christian Smith with Patricia Snell.[29] These books show that in a religiously diverse society such as the United States, families and religious groups in order to perpetuate the faith must emphasize the volitional aspect of their religious faith as perhaps never before or at least since the days of the early church. Although children, when baptized or dedicated as babies, are usually accepted by churches on the basis of the faith of their parents, there is a provisional element in this acceptance in that children are expected to have their faith confirmed at a later time when they reach the "age of accountability." The churches that practice "believer's baptism" especially emphasize that their children need the experience of being converted. Even churches that practice infant baptism may teach that children who reach the "age of accountability" need to know that even though they cannot remember a conversion experience, they need to have experienced internal change over a period of time so that their public expression of faith will be personal and voluntary. Thus, it is in religiously diverse societies and in societies where religious socialization is primarily a family responsibility that the phenomenon of conversion based on an individual voluntary choice receives its strongest emphasis. Also, in religiously diverse societies such as the United States, conversion is maintained as a significant experience of many as they acquire or change religious identities. This is why in North America, in particular, conversion has become an important subject of study.[30] Since religious diversity is increasingly becoming a worldwide phenomenon, there is growing attention to what is involved in conversion from one religion to another religion, from no religion to a religion, and from a religion to no religion.

My purpose here is not to enter into a discussion of the meaning of conversion for individuals. My sociological approach is only one approach in the study of conversion, but I believe it contributes to understanding changes in how conversion is viewed. The major task of understanding the meaning of conversion for individuals belongs to social psychological and psychological analysis in concert with the various religious traditions, which have their distinctive interpretations of what conversion means. My purpose has been to show that, as religions have spread up to the present, although they have spread to groups and been transmitted within groups and families with relatively low levels of volition by many people, the issue of individual motives in conversion and what happens in conversion have increasingly become a matter of important study. I will only note that although motivations are quite varied and complex, in one way or another, the perceived "rewards" of accepting a religion are an important part of conversion to consider. Of course, the "rewards" of converting to a movement to reclaim the original form of the religion or to experience greater spiritual power may be rejection, suffering, and even death meted out to those who reject official and established religions. In these cases, the "rewards" are the intrinsic reward of knowing the "truth" and experiencing inner spiritual power. As religious freedom increases in the world, the evidence provided by the case of the United States discussed above is that the intrinsic rewards of conversion will continue to trump whatever extrinsic rewards may be offered by religions.

LOOKING TO THE FUTURE OF CONVERSION AND THE SPREAD OF RELIGIONS

Having reviewed the relationship of conversion to the factors in the spread of religions and having discussed how the three missionary religions actually spread, we have shown that religions expand both because of their religious content or characteristics that make them prone to spread and the macro and micro social factors that facilitate or block their growth. Conversion on the simplest level as acquisition of or change in a religious identity must take place for religions to spread. However, conversion can and has taken on deeper meanings in different conditions. The major variation in the meaning of conversion is in the emphasis on volition or personal choice.

Let me review the contexts of various meanings of conversion. The emphasis on volition in conversion is clear when faith is consciously chosen in response to the call and command of God. Ancient examples of this are found in the response of Abraham to God's call (Genesis 12). The people of Israel are challenged by the first of the Ten Commandments, "You shall have no other gods before me" (Exodus 20:2), to trust in the one God above all. Joshua challenged the people of Israel: "Choose this day whom you will serve, whether the gods your ancestors served in the region beyond the River or the gods of the Amorites in whose land you are living: but as for me and my household, we will serve the Lord" (Joshua 24:15). The volitional element is maintained most strongly in societies where people are aware of a contrast between religions, particularly where one religion claims access to the true God and its followers believe they have been chosen by this true God. Contrasting religions are most obvious in two situations: (1) in religiously diverse societies such as the ancient Roman Empire, the contemporary United States, and increasing numbers of societies around the world; (2) in the "religiously diverse field" that exists among, not within, small societies where these societies have contact with one another and encounter outsiders (occasionally or often) bringing new religions. However, the volitional element in conversion became less important in the spread of religion in cases where groups or large numbers of people accepted new religious identities on the basis of the decision of leaders and when particular religions become monopolistic in particular societies. A religious identity then becomes a taken-for-granted aspect of being a member of a particular ethnic or national group. In other words, the volitional aspect of conversion decreased in the societies in which Buddhism, Christianity, and Islam became monopolistic and closely allied to governments. In this respect, these missionary religions became like most other religions in which the religious identity of people becomes primarily an aspect of their ethnic, cultural, or national identities transmitted as part of ordinary socialization.

Monopolistic religions still exist where there has been a long tradition of such religions. In Buddhism, this is seen particularly in Southeast Asia and Japan. Europe still shows the effect of having state churches which were Orthodox, Roman Catholic, or Protestant. Nations with majority Muslim populations are usually very restrictive of other religions, thus creating a monopolistic Islam. The concept that a given territory or nation should have one religion is still accepted by many nations and their religious leaders. However, a worldwide trend moving away from monopolistic religions toward religious diversity appears to be taking place, with political leaders often making decisions favoring religious liberty.[31] Freedom of religion has become a worldwide ideal, even though it is not actually practiced in many countries.[32] In addition to the fact that governments increasingly claim to maintain freedom of religion, the worldwide economy is increasingly freeing people from conditions of dependency on their larger families in which they had been socialized. Previously, along with their beliefs and values, they received their religious identities from their families, usually their extended families. These religious identities were often shared with their villages and ethnic groups. Once individuals lose their dependence on the groups in which they were socialized, they then become free to make independent choices, which may include the choice to change their religious identities or reject a religious identity altogether.

These larger modern macro factors of growing religious freedom within societies and of economic advancement in many lands actually increase the importance of micro factors, in which individual relationships and motivations must be given greater weight in understanding conversion and the spread of religions. In these cases, people are less likely to maintain their religious identities as a matter of course simply to maintain the religious identity of their families or of the larger ethnic group or nation. Human social relationships have always been important, but in modern social conditions individuals have relative freedom to break and reconstitute their relationships. Geographical and social mobility especially encourage the formation of new social relationships. In the increasingly multiethnic societies of the world, people frequently marry across ethnic lines, which often means across religious lines.

One of the characteristics of the missionary religions that enabled them to spread was their ability to gather and organize people. This makes them ideally suited to attract people who are in new geographical or social locations (or both) and are looking for new relationships. The missionary religions are capable of becoming a "home away from home" for such people. Social networks have always been important, but because of the conditions in the modern world, they have to be more adaptable to change than previously. Social networks that are inflexible and are unable to replace people who die out will gradually cease to exist. Religious groups themselves have to be flexible social networks that are continually able to incorporate new people and make them feel they are a genuine part of the network.

The motivation to establish relationships with others is a basic motivation, but there are many other motivations that direct individuals to become identified with new religious groups and thus to change their religious identities. Social scientists are recognizing that human emotions or emotional energy is an extremely important component in human life.[33] The definition of identity given by the social identity theorist Henri Tajfel recognizes that people attach emotional content to the various aspects of their social identities.[34] Before, during, and after individual decisions to change religious identities, there are likely to be emotional elements. These vary with individuals, but it is affirmed in the definition by Tajfel that people make such decisions in the direction of what gives them emotional satisfaction. This view is consistent with that of the social scientists who hold that people make decisions that are rational to them, satisfaction being a rational goal for decisions. Stark and Finke state: "Within the limits of their information and understanding, restricted by available options, guided by preferences and tastes, humans attempt to make rational choices."[35] My assumption is that "emotional satisfaction" is an important reward that guides human choices. Of course, there may be suffering or discomfort in choosing a particular religion or religious path, but one of the strengths of religions is that they offer intrinsic or inner rewards, not simply extrinsic or outer rewards. An intrinsic reward, in fact, is specifically offered in the challenge of Christianity to deny the self, of Buddhism to eliminate all desires, and of Islam to obey God whatever the costs. The specific model set before the Christian is that of the "Pioneer of the faith" who, for "the *joy* set before him, endured the cross, despising the shame, and is set down at the right hand of God" (Hebrews 12:2). It is not surprising, then, that conversion should often have a strong emotional content. Some religious groups, such as Pentecostals, encourage the expression of emotion in their faith. Other groups, such as Presbyterians, encourage a decision of the will without much outward expression of emotion. The latter consider a deep and quiet emotion backing a determined will as an ideal for guiding behavior. Either way, emotion has an important place.

Thus, simply acquiring or changing religious identities is not a satisfactory or complete explanation of conversion for most people today. Such an explanation may be sufficient for describing changing denominational affiliation, but not for a life-changing decision. The volitional element in conversion has taken and continues to take on more importance. Along with the needs and rights of personal volition, the importance of emotion in human life adds to the significance of volition as a means of heightening emotion. People want to live lives of personal satisfaction.

The desire for a satisfying emotional life finds expression across the culture that has developed in American society and is spreading throughout the world. One major expression is the cult of romantic love that is found throughout the world and constantly expressed in the media. Romantic love is seen as a major source of happiness in life. The very use of the term "happiness" is a reminder that "the pursuit of happiness" is a strong cultural theme in the United States from its earliest days. In religious life, emotional expression was important in the revival movements that swept across America. The Pentecostal movement, with its special emphasis on emotion, took clear shape in the early twentieth century and has continually gained strength in both America and around the world.

Among sociologists, emotion has gained a new place of importance. Collins's book is an example of the movement to develop a sociology of emotions.[36] Smith gives a persuasive account of emotional aspects in the success of Christianity, summarizing: "I suggest that Christianity works in part because it meets many basic mental and emotional human needs and desires—for significance, security, love, ownership and confession of wrong, forgiveness, bearings for moral living, and belonging." He believes that sociologists of religion "have much more work to do regarding the role of emotions in religious life."[37] As conversion increasingly incorporates a volitional element, it will also be increasingly important to incorporate how emotions are involved. At the very least, people choose a religious identity (experience conversion) because they see in the chosen religion a source of satisfaction and joy in their lives. This satisfaction and joy must be intrinsic and lasting and not simply extrinsic and temporary. However, this is just to begin to plumb the emotions that are involved in conversion.

With increasing options for individuals to make religious choices, it is understandable that conversion has come to be analyzed more completely than previously. As an example, Henri Gooren, studying primarily contemporary conversion, shows that it may be understood as a dynamic and complex process or "conversion career" consisting of preaffiliation, affiliation, conversion, confession, and disaffiliation.[38] This understanding of conversion makes the term "recruitment" perhaps a more useful term for tracing how religions spread. However, recruitment, like the term "conversion," may also involve various levels of volition, ranging from very conscious and deliberate choice to matter-of-fact assent. One way or another, it is helpful to recognize that conversion, especially in the modern setting, may be best understood as involving a process of change. This is particularly true for those being socialized to a religion. A process may be arrested at certain stages and then later continued.

CONCLUSION

A useful way of understanding the various meanings of the term "conversion" is to review the spread of the three missionary religions, Buddhism, Christianity, and Islam. These religions could not have spread without conversions taking place, but the meaning of these conversions has varied over time and in various conditions. A minimalist definition of conversion is to accept or change religious identities. Such a definition allows one to trace the spread of religions and examine the causes of their spread, but it does not do justice to how conversion may vary as a human religious experience.

A useful barometer for variation in the meaning of conversion is the strength of volition involved, from more or less passive acceptance of a religion to an active individual and personal choice to become a follower. In the somewhat longer more than two thousand year history of the spread of religions (a short time in human history), it appears that in conditions of religious diversity the volitional element in conversion tends to be high, but when religions become allied to governments and thereby monopolistic the volitional element is low for most people. The transmission of faith over generations also raises the question as to how much volition is involved. In the context of religiously diversity and individualistic societies, as now exist in much of the world, a strong challenge is made to nuclear families to transmit the faith clearly to their children. At the same time, because of the many cross-cutting relationships of individuals to diverse social groups that compete for attention in modern life, religious groups are also strongly challenged to make their faith known effectively to members and potential members. In the context of growing religious freedom and increasing interest in human rights, religious groups can hardly escape the need to emphasize personal volition in religious faith. Thus, personal volition in conversion, with all the attendant emotions, is likely to retain an important and increasing role in the world. This means that both the experiential and intellectual content of religions (and of no religion) will also receive increasing attention as people seek to know as much as possible about the religions to which they are being asked to convert.

NOTES

1. Frank E. Reynolds and Charles Hallisey, "The Buddha," in *Buddhism and Asian History*, ed. Joseph Kitagawa and Mark D. Cummings (New York: Macmillan Publishing Company, 1989), 31, 32.

2. Romila Thapar, "Asoka Buddhism," in *Sociology and Religion*, ed. Norman Birnbaum and Gertrude Lenzer (Englewood Cliffs, NJ: Prentice-Hall, Inc., 1969), 309.

3. Robert L. Montgomery, "The Spread of Religions and Macrosocial Relations," *Sociological Analysis* (now *Sociology of Religion*) 52, no. 1 (Spring 1991): 37–53; *The Diffusion of Religions: A Sociological Perspective* (Lanham, MD: University Press of America, 1996); *The Lopsided Spread of Christianity: Toward an Understanding of the Diffusion of Religions* (Westport, CT: Praeger, 2002); *The Spread of Religions: A Social Scientific Theory Based on the Spread of Buddhism, Christianity, and Islam* (Hackensack, NJ: Long Dash Publishing, 2007).

4. Thomas Arnold, *The Spread of Islam in the World: A History of Peaceful Preaching* (New Delhi: Goodword Books, 2006), 1.

5. Henri Tajfel, ed., *Social Identity and Intergroup Relations* (Cambridge: Cambridge University Press, 1982), 2.

6. Henri Tajfel, *Human Groups and Social Categories* (Cambridge: Cambridge University Press, 1981), 256.

7. Rodney Stark, *The Rise of Christianity* (San Francisco, CA: Harper, 1997); *One True God: Historical Consequences of Monotheism* (Princeton: Princeton University Press, 2001).

8. Montgomery, *The Spread of Religions.*

9. John B. Noss, *Man's Religions* (New York: Macmillan Company, 1949), 172.

10. Stephen Sharot, *A Comparative Sociology of World Religions* (New York: New York University Press, 2001).

11. H. A. Drake, *Constantine and the Bishops: The Politics of Intolerance* (Baltimore: Johns Hopkins Press, 2000).

12. Steve Bruce, *God is Dead: Secularization in the West* (Oxford: Blackwell Publishing, 2002).

13. Rodney Stark and Roger Finke, *Acts of Faith: Explaining the Human Side of Religion* (Berkeley and Los Angeles: University of California Press, 2000).

14. Colin Campbell, *Toward a Sociology of Irreligion* (New Haven: Yale University Press, 1972), 59, 61.

15. Christian Smith, ed., *The Secular Revolution: Power, Interests, and Conflict in the Secularization of American Life* (Berkeley and Los Angeles: University of California Press, 2003).

16. Montgomery, "The Spread of Religions and Macro Relations"; *The Diffusion of Religions.*

17. David G. Horrell, "Becoming a Christian: Solidifying Christian Identity and Conduct," in *Handbook of Early Christianity: Social Science Approaches*, ed. Anthony J. Blasi, Jean Duhaime, and Paul-Andre Turcotte (Walnut Creek, CA: AltaMira Press, 2002), 309–335; Jack T. Sanders, "Establishing Social Distance between Christians and Both Jews and Pagans," in *Handbook of Early Christianity: Social Science Approaches*, ed. Anthony J. Blasi, Jean Duhaime, and Paul-Andre Turcotte (Walnut Creek, CA: AltaMira Press, 2002), 361–382.

18. Samuel Hugh Moffett, *A History of Christianity in Asia*: vol. 1, *Beginnings to 1500* (San Francisco: HarperCollins Publishers, 1992), 137.

19. Kenneth Scott Latourette, *A History of the Expansion of Christianity: Three Centuries of Advance, 1500 AD—1800*, Vol. 3 (New York: Harper & Brothers Publishers, 1939), 1.

20. Montgomery, *The Diffusion of Religions*; Danielle Kane and Jung Mee Park, "The Puzzle of Korean Christianity: Geopolitical Networks and Religious Conversions in Early Twentieth-Century East Asia," *American Journal of Sociology* 115, no. 2 (Sept. 2009): 365–404.

21. Philip Jenkins, *The Next Christendom: The Coming of Global Christianity* (New York: Oxford University Press, 2002).

22. John Lofland and Rodney Stark, "Becoming a World-saver: A Theory of Conversion to a Deviant Perspective," *American Sociological Review* 30, no. 6 (Dec. 1965): 862–875; Stark and Finke, *Acts of Faith*.

23. Kurt Bowen, *Evangelicalism and Apostasy: The Evolution and Impact of Evangelicals in Modern Mexico* (Montreal: McGill-Queen's University Press 1996).

24. Montgomery, *The Spread of Religions*.

25. Stephen Sharot, *A Comparative Sociology of World Religions* (New York: New York University Press, 2001).

26. Henri Gooren, *Religious Conversion and Disaffiliation: Tracing Patterns of Change in Faith Practices* (New York: Palgrave Macmillan, 2010).

27. Kraig Beyerlein, "Educational Elites and the Movement to Secularize Public Education," in *The Secular Revolution: Power, Interests, and Conflict in the Secularization of American Public Life*, ed. Christian Smith (Berkeley and Los Angeles: University of California Press, 2003), 160.

28. Christian Smith, ed., *The Secular Revolution: Power, Interests, and Conflict in the Secularization of American Life* (Berkeley and Los Angeles: University of California Press, 2003).

29. Christian Smith, with Melinda Linquist Denton, *Soul Searching: The Religious and Spiritual Lives of American Teenagers* (New York: Oxford University Press, 2005); Smith with Patricia Snell, *Souls in Transition: The Religious and Spiritual Lives of Emerging Adults* (New York: Oxford University Press, 2009).

30. William James, *The Varieties of Human Experience: A Study in Human Nature* (New York: Modern Library, 1929). H. Newton Malony and Samuel Southard, eds., *Handbook of Religious Conversion* (Birmingham, AL: Religious Education Press, 1992); Lewis Rambo, *Understanding Religious Conversion* (New Haven: Yale University Press, 1993); Gooren, *Religious Conversion and Disaffiliation*.

31. Anthony Gill, *The Political Origins of Religious Liberty* (New York: Cambridge University Press, 2008).

32. Brian Grim and Roger Finke, "International Religion Indexes: Government Regulation, Government Favoritism, and Social Regulation of Religion," *Interdisciplinary Journal of Research on Religion* 2, Article 1 (2006): 1–40.

33. Randall Collins, *Interactive Ritual Chains* (Princeton: Princeton University Press, 2004).

34. Tajfel, *Human Groups and Social Categories*, 255, 256; Tajfel, *Social Identity and Intergroup Relations*, 2.

35. Stark and Finke, *Acts of Faith*, 38.

36. Collins, *Interactive Ritual Chains*.

37. Christian Smith, "Why Christianity Works: An Emotions-Focused Phenomenological Account," *Sociology of Religion* 68, no. 2 (2007): 165–178, at 177.

38. Gooren, *Religious Conversion and Disaffiliation*.

BIBLIOGRAPHY

Arnold, Thomas. *The Spread of Islam in the World: A History of Peaceful Preaching*. New Delhi: Goodword Books, 2006.

Beyerlein, Kraig. "Educational Elites and the Movement to Secularize Public Education." In *The Secular Revolution: Power, Interests, and Conflict in the Secularization of American Public Life*, ed. Christian Smith, 160–196. Berkeley and Los Angeles: University of California Press, 2003.

Bowen, Kurt. *Evangelicalism and Apostasy: The Evolution and Impact of Evangelicals in Modern Mexico*. Montreal: McGill-Queen's University Press 1996.

Bruce, Steve. *God is Dead: Secularization in the West*. Oxford: Blackwell Publishing, 2002.

Campbell, Colin. *Toward a Sociology of Irreligion*. New Haven: Yale University Press, 1972.

Collins, Randall. *Interactive Ritual Chains*. Princeton: Princeton University Press, 2004.

Drake, H. A. *Constantine and the Bishops: The Politics of Intolerance*. Baltimore: Johns Hopkins Press, 2000.

Gill, Anthony. *The Political Origins of Religious Liberty*. New York: Cambridge University Press, 2008.

Gooren, Henri. *Religious Conversion and Disaffiliation: Tracing Patterns of Change in Faith Practices*. New York: Palgrave Macmillan, 2010.

Grim, Brian, and Roger Finke. "International Religion Indexes: Government Regulation, Government Favoritism, and Social Regulation of Religion." *Interdisciplinary Journal of Research on Religion* 2 (2006): Article 1. http://www.religjournal.com.

Horrell, David G. "Becoming a Christian: Solidifying Christian Identity and Conduct." In *Handbook of Early Christianity: Social Science Approaches*, ed. Anthony J. Blasi, Jean Duhaime, and Paul-Andre Turcotte, 309–335. Walnut Creek, CA: AltaMira Press, 2002.

James, William. *The Varieties of Human Experience: A Study in Human Nature*. New York: Modern Library, 1929.

Jenkins, Philip. *The Next Christendom: The Coming of Global Christianity*. New York: Oxford University Press, 2002.

Kane, Danielle, and Jung Mee Park. "The Puzzle of Korean Christianity: Geopolitical Networks and Religious Conversions in Early Twentieth-Century East Asia." *American Journal of Sociology* 115, no. 2 (Sept. 2009): 365–404.

Latourette, Kenneth Scott. *A History of the Expansion of Christianity: Three Centuries of Advance, 1500 ad–1800*. Vol. 3. New York: Harper & Brothers Publishers, 1939.

Lofland, John, and Rodney Stark. "Becoming a World-saver: A Theory of Conversion to a Deviant Perspective." *American Sociological Review* 30, no. 6 (Dec. 1965): 862–875.

Malony, H. Newton, and Samuel Southard, eds. *Handbook of Religious Conversion*. Birmingham, AL: Religious Education Press, 1992.

Moffett, Samuel Hugh. *A History of Christianity in Asia: vol. 1, Beginnings to 1500*. San Francisco: HarperCollins Publishers, 1992.

Montgomery, Robert L. "The Spread of Religions and Macrosocial Relations." *Sociological Analysis* (now *Sociology of Religion*) 52, no. 1 (Spring 1991): 37–53.

——. *The Diffusion of Religions: A Sociological Perspective*. Lanham, MD: University Press of America, 1996.

——. *The Lopsided Spread of Christianity: Toward an Understanding of the Diffusion of Religions*. Westport, CT: Praeger, 2002.

——. *The Spread of Religions: A Social Scientific Theory Based on the Spread of Buddhism, Christianity, and Islam*. Hackensack, NJ: Long Dash Publishing, 2007.

Noss, John B. *Man's Religions*. New York: Macmillan Company, 1949.

Rambo, Lewis. *Understanding Religious Conversion*. New Haven: Yale University Press, 1993.

Reynolds, Frank E., and Charles Hallisey. "The Buddha." In *Buddhism and Asian History*, ed. Joseph Kitagawa and Mark D. Cummings, 29–49. New York: Macmillan Publishing Company, 1989.

Sanders, Jack T. "Establishing Social Distance between Christians and Both Jews and Pagans." In *Handbook of Early Christianity: Social Science Approaches*, ed. Anthony J. Blasi, Jean Duhaime, and Paul-Andre Turcotte, 361–382. Walnut Creek, CA: AltaMira Press, 2002.

Sharot, Stephen. *A Comparative Sociology of World Religions*. New York: New York University Press, 2001.

Smith, Christian, ed. *The Secular Revolution: Power, Interests, and Conflict in the Secularization of American Life*. Berkeley and Los Angeles: University of California Press, 2003.

——. "Why Christianity Works: An Emotions-Focused Phenomenological Account." *Sociology of Religion* 68, no. 2 (Summer 2007): 165–178.

Smith, Christian, with Melinda Linquist Denton. *Soul Searching: The Religious and Spiritual Lives of American Teenagers*. New York: Oxford University Press, 2005.

Smith, Christian, with Patricia Snell. *Souls in Transition: The Religious and Spiritual Lives of Emerging Adults*. New York: Oxford University Press, 2009.

Stark, Rodney. *The Rise of Christianity*. San Francisco, CA: Harper, 1997.

——. *One True God: Historical Consequences of Monotheism*. Princeton: Princeton University Press, 2001.

Stark, Rodney, and Roger Finke. *Acts of Faith*. Berkeley and Los Angeles: University of California Press, 2000.

Tajfel, Henri. *Human Groups and Social Categories*. Cambridge: Cambridge University Press, 1981.

——, ed. *Social Identity and Intergroup Relations*. Cambridge: Cambridge University Press, 1982.

Thapar, Romila. "Asoka Buddhism." In *Sociology and Religion*, ed. Norman Birnbaum and Gertrude Lenzer, 303–309. Englewood Cliffs, NJ: Prentice-Hall, Inc., 1969.

CHAPTER 8

....

MIGRATION AND CONVERSION OF KOREAN AMERICAN CHRISTIANS

....

REBECCA Y. KIM

INTRODUCTION

....

ALTHOUGH new immigrants are initially preoccupied with their economic situation, one of their primary early concerns is establishing a transplanted version of
their old religious organization in the new country. For many immigrants, rebuilding their old church, synagogue, temple, or mosque is a way of establishing their
ethnic identity, community, and settling in the new land. This intimate connection
between migration and religion is clearly evident in the Korean American Christian
community.

Nearly 30 percent of the 49 million or so South Koreans are Christian.[1] In the United
States, however, 70 to 80 percent of the million-plus Koreans are Christian and are
affiliated with an ethnic church.[2] A common saying in the Asian American community is that the Chinese start restaurants upon arrival while the Koreans start churches.
Wherever there are a group of Korean Americans, one can expect a Korean church
nearby. This chapter examines this interesting nexus between migration and religion
among Korean Americans. After a review of the historical connection between immigration and the Korean church in the United States, it considers the migration and
conversion experiences of Korean Americans. In particular, it examines why and how
Koreans are more religiously engaged as Christians in the United States than they are in
South Korea.

KOREAN IMMIGRATION AND THE
ETHNIC CHURCH

It is hard to find a Korean immigrant who is not involved in a church. The majority of Koreans regularly attend one of the 4,000 or so Korean churches every Sunday in the United States.[3] Church is the most important institution in the Korean American community. In Southern California, where many Koreans concentrate, an association of Korean Protestant churches has 1,359 congregations that represent 39 denominations.[4] A 2007 study by a Christian group for developing Asian American leadership counted 7,000 Protestant Asian congregations in the United States, 4,000 of which were Korean.[5] The significance of the Christian faith and the church in the lives of Korean Americans is evident in each of the three major waves of Korean immigration to the United States.

The First Wave (1903–1950)

The story of Korean immigration in America begins with the arrival of 102 Koreans in Honolulu, Hawaii, on January 13, 1903.[6] Between 1903 and 1905, more than 7,226 Koreans arrived in Hawaii to work in its sugar plantations. Many of these early Korean immigrants are believed to have been peasants or semi-skilled urbanites from fairly developed metropolitan and port cities in Korea that were also the sites of massive Christian conversions.[7] A significant number of Korean emigrants were also mobilized by Protestant missionaries to journey to the United States. Recruiters for American companies turned to Protestant missionaries in Korea for assistance in persuading Koreans in the missionaries' care to migrate to the islands of Hawaii. Consequently, Protestant Christians were among the first Koreans to migrate to the United States.[8] Roughly 40 to 60 percent of the Koreans who arrived in the United States before 1905 were Christian, and Korean churches were quickly formed upon their arrival.[9] While Christians made up a significant portion of the migrant population to the United States at this time, Christians made up only 1 percent of the population in Korea.[10]

Within the first few months of settlement, Korean laborers formed the Hawaii Methodist Church in 1903 and the Hawaii Korean Anglican Church in 1905. By 1904, there were seven Korean Christian chapels in Hawaii. From the very start, these early churches became important clearinghouses of social services and information as the umbrella organization for the Korean American community.[11] Beyond religious services, churches provided a forum for Korean Americans to discuss a wide range of issues, including their economic concerns, status as an ethnic racial minority, and their desire to see Korea free from Japanese colonial oppression. The church became a place of comfort and meaning in a new land.

Since one out of ten Korean immigrants were female during this first wave of immigration, the sex ratio among Korean laborers was not as skewed as was the case for the Chinese and Japanese laborers at this time. With the arrival of a little over a thousand Korean women who entered as picture brides, women made up 21 percent of the adult Korean population in the United States by 1920.[12] The presence of Korean women facilitated the development of families and the formation of Korean churches in the United States.

With the passage of the Immigration Act of 1924 prohibiting the entrance of Asian immigrants (also known as the Oriental Exclusion Act), no official immigration took place from Korea to the United States between 1924 and 1950. As strangers in a foreign land and cut off from home, particularly with the Japanese annexation of Korea, immigrants in the early wave were isolated. Laws limited Koreans' engagement with the broader society. Korean immigrant men could not freely marry US citizens. According to the Cable Act of 1922, women who married foreign men who were "aliens" and ineligible for naturalization would lose their US citizenship. Until the passage of the McCarran Walter Act in 1952, individuals born in Korea were not allowed to become naturalized US citizens.

Unable to fully engage themselves as US citizens and troubled over the Japanese colonization of Korea, Korean Americans actively involved themselves in homeland politics and advocated Korea's independence from Japan. In this process, Korean Christian churches became important sites for Korean immigrants' political activism and nationalism.[13] The separation of church and state found in mainstream America was not evident in the early Korean church in the United States. Homeland politics commonly intermingled with religion.[14]

In addition to being the locus of political activity, Korean churches operated as the main community centers that addressed the various survival needs of their congregants. Located close to where the Korean immigrants resided, the churches provided multiple services and programs to ease Korean immigrants' settlement in the new country, including job placement, counseling, legal aid, language classes, interpretation, and translation.[15] Moreover, the churches served as a "home away from home" where fellow Korean exiles could find emotional and social support. At the ethnic church, immigrants could speak their native language, exchange stories from back home, seek the advice and assistance of fellow co-ethnic church members, and support each other through the difficulties of working at the sugar plantations. The Korean church thus functioned as the educational, cultural, political, and social service centers for Koreans. With pastors serving as community leaders, as well as spiritual counselors, churches also became the representative of the Korean community to the rest of US society.

The Second Wave (1951–1964)

Impelled by the Korean War, the second wave of Korean immigrants in the United States consisted mostly of wives of US servicemen (6,423), orphaned adoptees (5,348), and a few refugees, professionals, and students.[16] The stories of the Korean wives of American GIs and war orphans are not well-documented in the history of Korean America.[17] The experiences of these two silenced groups are considered to be secondary within and outside of the Korean American community, and the two groups did not provide a fertile basis for the development of ethnic churches.[18]

Very little is also documented about the estimated 5,000 students who came to the United States between 1950 and 1965. But, it is known that US missionaries had an active role in recruiting these Korean students to study in the United States in the hopes that they would propagate Christianity. "At the time of the political and economic upheaval in the divided Korea, many (male) Koreans made decisions to put their souls in the hands of U.S. missionaries in exchange for a ticket to the 'land flowing with milk and honey.'"[19] Survival and faith were interlinked.

The Third Wave (post-1965)

During the ideological competition of the Cold War, racist immigration laws that favored European immigration and excluded Asian immigration became somewhat of an embarrassment to the US government. This, along with the need for skilled labor, led to the passage of the Hart-Cellar Act of 1965, which abolished the national origins quota system and aimed to unify families and also draw skilled laborers into the United States. Enacted in 1968, nations outside of the Western hemisphere were permitted to send up to 20,000 emigrants per year, and immediate relatives of US citizens were not subject to numerical limitations. The family reunification provisions, however, were actually intended to facilitate the immigration of Europeans, who had the most relatives in the United States. Despite the original intention of the provisions, immigration from Asia increased dramatically while immigration from Europe unexpectedly fell in the 1970s.[20]

Changes in immigration law along with the forced modernization programs under the dictatorial regime of General Park Chung Hee of Korea drove many Koreans to emigrate in the 1960s. General Park, who later became president of South Korea (1961–1979), pushed Korea away from its traditional role as an agricultural nation and moved the country toward world capitalism and export-oriented industrialization. Successful industrialization and economic development, however, went hand-in-hand with social dislocation and polarization of the rich and the poor. Park's regime favored large business conglomerates (*chaebols*) and the elite segment of Korean society at the expense of the lower and middle strata. The rural population became impoverished, smaller businesses were weakened, white-collar workers became frustrated, and various civil rights were violated. In this context, many Koreans with the means to emigrate, namely middle-class Koreans, left for the United States in search of better lives.

From 1970 to 1980, the Korean population in the United States increased by 412 percent, and Korea has consistently been on the list of the top ten immigrant-sending countries since the 1980s.[21] The Korean American population increased from 69,150 in 1970 to 1,076,872 in the year 2000. Koreans are currently the fifth largest Asian group in the

United States, behind the Chinese, Filipinos, Vietnamese, and South Asians. According to the 2000 US census, Koreans made up 0.39 percent of the US population and 10.8 percent of the non-Hispanic Asian and Pacific Islander population.

Korean immigration to the United States dropped in the 1990s, however, as Korea advanced socioeconomically and as stories of the 1992 Los Angeles riots and the struggles of Korean immigrants became more commonplace. The number of Korean immigrants fell from an average of 35,000 per year in the late 1980s to less than 15,000 per year in the mid-1990s. This shift, along with natural population growth, contributed to the declining foreign-born Korean population in America. In 1990, 82.2 percent of the Korean population in the United States was foreign born. Estimates drawn from the 1998 and 2000 Current Population Surveys, however, show that foreign-born Koreans now make-up approximately 52.4 percent of the population. Meanwhile, the second generation makes up 21.9 percent, and the third and later generations make up 25.7 percent of the Korean population.[22]

While the numbers of Korean immigrants have declined, Korean churches in the United States continue to be dominated by the first generation. Leadership positions in the Korean American faith communities are monopolized by the first generation and are handed down to the new immigrants from Korea. And as in the previous migration waves, the recent waves of Korean immigrants consist of a large number of Christians. Surveys conducted in the 1980s show that almost three-quarters of the Korean immigrant population in America identified themselves as Christians and attended mostly Protestant churches.[23] In some cities, the numbers are higher. A 1997–98 survey conducted by Pyong Gap Min reported that 79 percent of Korean immigrants in Queens, New York, identified themselves as Christians, and 83 percent of them reported that they attended an (ethnic) church once a week or more.[24] The church participation rate of Korean Christians, most of whom are Presbyterians, is much higher than that of other Christian groups in the United States. The Racial and Ethnic Panel of Presbyterians study shows that 28 percent of white, 34 percent of African American, and 49 percent of Latino Presbyterians attend Sunday worship services every week, compared to 78 percent of Korean Presbyterians.[25] Korean Presbyterians also donate more money to church, spend more time at church, and take part in more church activities than their non-Korean counterparts. While Korean immigrants tend not to stay in one church for long and do "church hop," they will likely take part in an ethnic church for most of their lives and do so extensively.[26] The Korean churches in the United States also have more than one service each week and provide various opportunities for its members to take part in the church. Where there is a settlement of Koreans, there will be a Korean church nearby where they will be actively engaged.

Defying the stereotype that Asians are mostly Buddhists, the Korean immigrant community in the United States is thus largely a Protestant Christian population that faithfully attends church. What then makes this the case? What contributes to Korean Americans' religious conversion and vitality in America?

KOREAN AMERICANS' CHRISTIAN
CONVERSION AND RELIGIOUS VITALITY

Selective Migration

Part of the reason why Korean immigrants are drawn to the Christian faith and church in the United States is because they were Christians before their arrival. While over one-quarter of the population in South Korea can be counted as Christian, approximately half of the Koreans who left during the post-1965 immigration wave were estimated to be Christian.[27] This is not surprising considering that Christianity in Korea is strong among the urban middle class, the group that is most likely to take part in contemporary immigration to the United States. Christians are also more likely to migrate than Buddhists or other Koreans with no religion.[28]

The Korean American community's religious vitality is also due to the abundance of Korean immigrant pastors in the United States. There are pastors that come directly to the United States to work at Korean immigrant churches. The US government issues "R-1 Religious Worker Visas" not only for members of the clergy but also for other key employees of religious organizations, such as choir directors. There are also Koreans who come to the United States as seminary students who stay on in the country as religious workers upon graduation. At Fuller Theological Seminary located in Southern California, Koreans make up over 25 percent of the student body. Directors of Protestant seminaries commonly note that they are staying afloat in part because of the large Korean student population. The significant cadre of Korean Christian religious professionals fuels the growth of Korean churches in the United States.[29] If they cannot lead an existing church, the religious professionals can start a new church and expand the Korean Christian religious community. Establishing a church with a significant number of followers is a legitimate way for Korean immigrants to gain permanent residence in the country.

Reviving the Spirit

Crisis, deprivation, weakened social bonds, and being at a turning point in one's life are some of the major predisposing factors for conversion.[30] Given this, immigrants who are dislocated and faced with the difficult task of adjusting to a myriad of new changes in a foreign land can find psychic relief and meaning through faith and church. Due to the uncertainties of sojourning or migrating to a foreign country, migration and settlement can be a "theologizing experience."[31] "Loneliness, the romanticizing of memories, the guilt for imagined desertion of parents and other relatives, and the search for community and identity in a world of strangers [brought] . . . formidable psychic challenges" to the new immigrants.[32] In this situation, religion and its organizations can become important sources of spiritual comfort, community, and meaning. Religion can help immigrants to understand, interpret, and confront the challenges of becoming American. This is certainly the case for Korean immigrants.

Korean immigrants often turn to a conservative Protestant faith because it provides them with an absolute belief system and a clear moral standard in an otherwise volatile existence as not only immigrants but also as a racial minority in a new land.[33] They may be strangers, misunderstood and a marginalized in the broader society, but within the church community they can be accepted, understood, and uplifted. For many Korean immigrants, "the religious need (meaning), the social need (belonging), and the psychological need (comfort) for attending the Korean church are inseparable from each other; they are functionally intertwined under the complex conditions of uprooting, existential marginality, and sociocultural adaptation for rerooting."[34]

With these existential and spiritual factors in place, it is important to note that the Korean church is the most well-established social, cultural, and educational center in the Korean American community. No other voluntary organization can compete with the church in offering practical social services and a sense of community and belonging for Korean immigrants.

Social Capital

Immigrants need information and practical assistance as they settle and incorporate into a new country. Ethnic churches certainly fill this need. In their study of Korean Christian churches in Houston, Texas, Victoria Kwon and her colleagues found that ethnic churches provide "aid in buying a vehicle, and finding housing…baby-sitter referrals, social security information, and translating services; making airport pick-ups; visitations for new babies and hospitalized members; registering children for school; applying for citizenship; dealing with the courts."[35] Pastors and other religious elders provide their church members counseling and information on finding housing, employment, and the best schools for their children. One can get practical advice on where to buy the best *kimchi* (a popular Korean side-dish) and how to pay a traffic ticket. And, if they need financial capital to start a business or send their children to college, they can join credit associations, *kyes*, through their church contacts.[36] Korean churches also provide Korean language programs for the children in addition to marriage seminars, family conferences, daycare, and classes on how to be better parents (e.g., Father's School, Mother's School). Not surprisingly, church offers many fellowship opportunities. In addition to formal religious gatherings, there are picnics, retreats, sports events, holiday celebrations, and more. Those who are single can also find their future partners within the church. Koreans who are not part of a Korean church miss out on multiple social opportunities.

Ethnic entrepreneurs whose businesses cater to the co-ethnic community find the ethnic church to be a particularly valuable place for conducting business and gaining a reliable clientele base. In a study of the New York Korean community, Ilsoo Kim[37] found that some Korean entrepreneurs even hold memberships in several Korean churches to expand their networks for business purposes. Those who receive services from these business entrepreneurs also benefit; they can be assured that they will be treated fairly by the businesses since news of dishonesty or improper business can spread quickly within a tight ethnic religious community. Those seeking employment can also get news of potential employment from businesspeople within the ethnic church.

The multiple social services and community support that the ethnic churches provide are particularly important given the lack of formal social service agencies for Korean immigrants. Because their meetings tend to be less extensive and frequent, nonreligious ethnic organizations are also less effective than churches in fostering co-ethnic networks. The proactive outreach strategies of the Korean Protestant churches, relative to other alternative religious and/or ethnic organizations, further contribute to the high levels of church participation among Korean Americans. Buddhist monks are not at the local Korean grocery stores and other Korean businesses or the major airports looking for converts, but Korean Protestants are.

Status Revival

Due to language limitations, cultural unfamiliarity, and other disadvantages, many contemporary Korean immigrants cannot maintain the professional, administrative, and managerial positions that they once had in Korea. In this situation, the ethnic church helps alleviate immigrants' status depreciation and deprivation by giving them recognition and opportunities to take on leadership positions within the church.[38] Besides positions as elders and deacons, there are various committees, such as the committees for education, fellowship, finance, and publications that members can lead. They can be the directors of the choir, children's Bible schools, or language school. Multiple positions exist to satisfy members' needs for social status and recognition. While the broader US public may not recognize and/or respect middle-class Korean immigrants' past social status and achievement as college graduates or professionals in Korea, fellow co-ethnics will. And they can find each other at the Korean church.

Constructing Identity and Culture

The Korean church offers the plausibility structure, the stable social relationships, that help preserve and reconstruct not only Koreans' religious identity but also their ethnic identity. The Korean church provides the social arena for Korean immigrants to regularly gather, speak Korean, eat Korean food, celebrate Korean holidays, exchange news from Korea, and practice traditional Korean culture and norms. With familiar faces, smells, and sounds surrounding them, Korean immigrants can share as well as pass on parts of their culture to the next generation. Korean churches organize various social activities that help build ethnic networks; they have Korean language programs, daycare, and other children's programs that facilitate the transmission of Korean culture to the later generations. After the main Sunday worship service, Korean churches serve Korean food, full lunches and refreshments, with time for fellowship. At these and other gatherings, Korean immigrants can celebrate birthdays for the children and the elderly members in the traditional Korean fashion with Korean food. Korean churches also celebrate Korean holidays like Chuseok, the Korean equivalent to Thanksgiving.[39] Outside of the family, Korean churches are a major, if not the major, source of co-ethnic cultural interaction.

Conversion after Religious Engagement?

Because of the various social, practical, and cultural benefits that individuals can obtain from attending an immigrant church, some may be initially drawn to the church for largely nonreligious reasons. Individuals can be first drawn to the church for the various resources and ethnic support that it can offer. Religious commitment to a church can precede serious religious seeking and conversion. An elder of a Korean church explains the worldly factors that contributed to his conversion: "I came here as a student and I had no friends except one or two Korean students like myself. I felt very lonely. I never went to church back in Korea, nor was I a believer. But I began to attend the [Korean] church shortly after my arrival here. Yes, I admit, I went to church to see other Koreans... to talk to them, to hang around with them."[40] Thus, the initial impetus for church involvement can be a desire for co-ethnic support and fellowship versus genuine religious seeking. Other studies of immigrant congregations also show that religious engagement often precedes existential questioning and conversion.[41]

Once Koreans enter through the church doors, the small fellowship or cell groups that exist within Korean immigrant churches function as important vehicles of conversion. In response to the geographic dispersion of their members, many Korean churches in the United States have "cell group" ministries. Church members are divided into various groups based on where they live. These small groups function as an important network that helps members to obtain various practical social services. But they also have the expected religious function. They help members to understand the norms and expectations regarding the Christian faith and religious engagement. Members directly and indirectly learn how they should view, practice, and advance their faith within the intimate cell group structure.

The desire for meaning, identity, and support so important in leading the first generation to the ethnic church and to eventual conversion also motivate the second generation's religious engagement. For the second generation, however, the ethnic church is not simply about preservation of traditional culture. Ethnic churches also provide the social arena for Korean Americans, particularly the later generation, to forge emergent identities of their own as both Koreans and Americans.

THE SECOND GENERATION

Studies of second-generation Korean American Christians show that the second generation is constructing their own faith communities and spaces of worship.[42] Besides the various young adult ministries or "de facto" congregations that run parallel to the first-generation-based immigrant church, there are emerging churches for the second generation. These new churches provide religious community in a language, setting, and subculture that resonates with the distinct worldviews and experiences of second-generation Korean Americans. In her study of the growing second-generation Korean American churches in the Los Angeles area, Sharon Kim[43] finds that these churches create a "hybrid" second-generation spirituality by appropriating and fusing together elements of Korean Protestantism and various expressions of American Evangelicalism. In their quest to invent an independent second-generation spirituality, these new churches adopt what they perceive to be essential beliefs, symbols, and practices from diverse sources and re-anchor them in their newly formed churches. They are not carbon copies of the first-generation church or the popular mainstream evangelical churches. They are carving out their own emergent ethnic religious community.[44] In the Los Angeles area, where many Korean Americans reside, there are over fifty independent second-generation Korean American churches.[45]

These new congregations are attuned to the unique cultural upbringings and needs of the second generation. The new churches fill the void and longing for a more intimate and supportive family among the second generation. Second-generation churches provide for the English-speaking population a sense of an integrative community in which individuals who would otherwise be isolated in impersonal environments become part of a family network of "brothers" and "sisters."[46] At these churches, they find a supportive community of like-minded individuals who have had a similar set of life experiences. Besides friends, the second generation can meet co-ethnic singles at the new church. Since the majority of the second-generation church population is single young professionals or college students in their twenties and thirties, the second generation can fulfill many of their parents' wishes and find a co-ethnic Christian spouse through the church. While far more integrated into the broader community than their parents, similar desires for comfort, commonality, and majority group status contribute to the second generations' participation in the emerging second-generation church.

One of the interesting developments in the new second-generation churches is that the churches seek to be open to and inclusive of other ethnic groups even as they help construct a unique Korean American Christian identity and community. As the emerging second-generation churches are constructing new expressions of a spirituality and religious community that incorporates their varied ethnic, racial, and generational selves, they are trying to reach and welcome "all peoples" into their churches. In her study of second-generation Korean American churches in Los Angeles, Sharon Kim found that over 30 percent of the members are non-Korean Americans. While the majority of these non-Korean Americans are other Asian Americans (about 25 percent), 10 percent are non-Asians. With all of the services held in English and with pastors trained in American seminaries and raised in the United States, the second-generation churches can draw a broader audience. Introduced to the church by their peers at college campuses or the workplace, non-Korean Americans are coming to the second-generation church, drawn together by class homogeneity and generational similarity as people in their twenties and thirties growing up in an increasingly diverse America.

Thus, the new generations of Korean American churches are more than ethnic enclaves. Koreans are not just converting Koreans. The process of migration and conversion is not just about immigrants and their children becoming more or less religious upon immigration. They also shape and color the broader religious landscape. On this note, it is important to consider Korean immigrants who come to the country primarily for religious reasons, as missionaries to save Americans' souls.

KOREAN MISSIONARIES IN AMERICA

Using a broad definition of missionaries as people from one region that move to another and bring about religious change, we can include various new immigrants, including Koreans, that are de-Europeanizing the Christian faith simply by their presence in the United States. Sociologist R. Stephen Warner writes, "What many people have not heard, however, and need to hear, is that the great majority of the newcomers are Christian....New immigrants represent not the de-Christianization of American society but the de-Europeanization of American Christianity."[47] As immigrants acculturate and become incorporated into the greater American communities, the United States will enter into a "wholly new phase of religious synthesis and hybridization."[48] Immigrants are introducing new faiths, but they are also "Asianizing" and "Latinoizing" the American Christian community. Some estimate that foreign-born Latin Americans make-up almost 40 percent of the United States' Roman Catholic population.[49] Latin, Asian, and African Catholics and Protestants also tend to be more Pentecostal, evangelical, and conservative compared to the average American Catholic or Protestant.

Immigrant churches in the United States are "sending" versus simply gathering places of worship. As Judy Han finds in her study of an evangelical Korean congregation in the United States, immigrant churches are just as concerned about "sending" their fellow ethnics out into the community and the world for missions as they are about being places of gathering.[50] According to the 2003 survey conducted by the Korean American Coalition and Korean Churches for Community Development, Korean churches in Southern California support missionaries in 85 different countries. Of the 149 churches surveyed, the mean number of missionaries was 7.37 with a maximum of 120. Spending on "missionary support" (13.31 percent) ranked third after spending on salaries/compensation and building facility maintenance.[51] These figures are notable considering that there are numerous Korean American churches in the United States and that many Koreans faithfully tithe.[52]

Besides Korean immigrants who come to the United States for economic and other nonreligious reasons and then play a role in shaping the American religious landscape, there are Koreans who come to the country specifically as missionaries. There are Korean immigrants that fall under the classic definition of missionaries as individuals that are sent from one place to another to convert or proselytize. These Korean missionaries include those who worked as missionaries in other nations who later move to the United States. Korean pastors suspect that the expectation that missionaries "bury their bones" in their country of mission—to be faithful to their mission until death—encourages Korean missionaries, particularly those working in poor countries, to move to a country like the United States later on in their career instead of returning to Korea. Their move to the United States is also fueled by the ease of immigration and desirability of settlement, particularly as they age and have concerns for their children's education and their health.

Korean missionaries in the United States include those who work within the Korean community. For example, Korea-Campus Crusade for Christ sends missionaries to US college campuses to help Korean students studying abroad as well as other Korean American students. Korean missionaries, however, also include those that work outside of the Korean community. Some work with the broader homeless population, regardless of race, and others work in particular minority communities, for example, in Native American communities. Korean missionaries may further work as professional clergy within and outside of the Korean community. This is part of a broader trend in the United States. For example, in 2005, one in six priests in the Catholic Church in America came from Asia, Africa, South America, or Europe.[53] Besides these religious professionals, there are a growing number of lay or "tentmaker" missionaries.

Inspired by the Apostle Paul, who supported himself while preaching and teaching in Corinth (Acts 18:3) by making tents, a "tentmaker" is a self-supporting missionary.[54] Unlike most missionaries who are financially supported by missionary agencies and/or churches, lay missionaries work in the secular marketplace to support their mission work.[55] One of the largest and first lay missionary organizations in South Korea is the University Bible Fellowship (UBF). UBF is a lay international campus ministry from South Korea that focuses on preaching the gospel to the "native" college population outside of the Korean Diaspora. According to Korea UBF's 2007 statistics, UBF missionaries are in 88 nations and 287 chapters. There are over six hundred Korean missionaries in 75 UBF chapters in Canada and the United States. With approximately a hundred "native" non-Koreans who are active leaders in the ministry, US and Canada UBF have had some success in converting non-Koreans and building disciples among the "native" population. Korea Research Institute for Mission's 2000 as well as 2006 surveys place UBF as the second largest missionary-sending organization in South Korea in terms of numbers of missionaries sent.[56]

CONCLUSION

Since the first group of Korean migrants settled in Hawaii, faith and church have been central for the Korean American community. The church is the heart of the Korean American community. Faith and church provide significant meaning systems and provide Korean Americans the plausibility structure to forge their own spiritual and ethnic space. It functions as an essential social emotional support system for new and old immigrants alike. Given the evangelical zeal of many Protestant Korean Christians, it is not surprising that some within the community would now seek to and even succeed in converting and drawing individuals from outside of the Korean Diaspora into their churches. This kind of interactive process paints a richer, fuller picture of the ongoing migration and conversion experience in the United States than is often depicted.

NOTES

1. Louis Lugo and Brian J. Grim, "Presidential Election in South Korea Highlights Influence of Christian Community," *The Pew Forum on Religion and Public Life Publications*, Dec. 12, 2007, http://pewforum.org/docs/?DocID=269.
2. Won Moo Hurh and Kwang Chung Kim, "Religious Participation of Korean Immigrants in the United States," *Journal for the Scientific Study of Religion* 29 (1990): 19–34; Jung Ha Kim, "Cartography of Korean American Protestant Faith Communities in the United States," in *Religions in Asian America: Building Faith Communities*, ed. Pyong Gap Min and Jung Ha Kim (Walnut Creek, CA: AltaMira Press, 2002), 185–214; Pyong Gap Min, "Immigrants' Religion and Ethnicity: A Comparison of Indian Hindu and Korean Christian Immigrants in the United States," *Bulletin of the Royal Institute of Inter-Faith Studies* 2 (2000): 122–140.
3. Connie K. Kang, "Southern California's Korean Christians Put a Premium on Evangelism," *Los Angeles Times*, Nov. 8, 2008, section B-3; Sharon Kim, *A Faith of Our Own: Second Generation Spirituality in Korean American Churches* (New Brunswick, NJ: Rutgers University Press, 2010); Pyong Gap Min, *Asian Americans: Contemporary Trends and Issues*, 2nd ed. (Newbury Park, CA: Pine Forge Press, 2005).
4. Kang, "Southern California's Korean Christians Put a Premium on Evangelism."
5. Ibid.
6. Hawaii officially became a US territory on Feb. 22, 1900, and it became the fiftieth state of the Union on Aug. 21, 1959; Nancy Abelmann and John Lie, *Blue Dreams: Korean Americans and the Los Angeles Riots* (Cambridge, MA: Harvard University Press, 1995); Bong-Young Choy, *Koreans in America* (Chicago: Nelson-Hall, 1979); Hurh and Kim, "Religious Participation of Korean Immigrants in the United States," 19–34; Kyeyoung Park, *The Korean American Dream: Immigrants and Small Businesses in New York City* (Ithaca, NY: Cornell University Press, 1997).
7. Sucheng Chan, *Asian Americans: An Interpretive History* (New York: Twayne Publishers, 1991); Hurh and Kim, "Religious Participation of Korean Immigrants in the United States," 19–34; J. Kim, "Cartography of Korean American Protestant Faith Communities in the United States," 185–214.

8. David K. Yoo and Ruth Chung, *Religion and Spirituality in Korean America* (Urbana: University of Illinois Press, 2008), 3.
9. Ilsoo Kim, *New Urban Immigrants: The Korean Community in New York* (Princeton: Princeton University Press, 1981); J. Kim, "Cartography of Korean American Protestant Faith Communities in the United States," 185–214.
10. James H. Grayson, "A Quarter-Millennium of Christianity in Korea," in *Christianity in Korea*, ed. Robert E. Buswell, Jr. and Timothy S. Lee (Honolulu: University of Hawaii Press, 2006), 7–25.
11. Yoo and Chung, *Religion and Spirituality in Korean America.*
12. Ho-Young Kwon, Kwang Chung Kim, and R. Stephen Warner, *Korean Americans and Their Religions: Pilgrims and Missionaries from a Different Shore* (University Park: Pennsylvania State University Press, 2001).
13. Today's Korean churches in America, however, are not known for their political activism.
14. The story of Syngman Rhee, the first president of the Republic of Korea after Korea gained independence from Japan in 1945, captures this well. Before he became the president of Korea, Rhee immigrated as a laborer to Hawaii in 1905. He formed the Korean Independence Church of Hawaii and was a pastor for Korean Americans during the 1920s.
15. J. Kim, "Cartography of Korean American Protestant Faith Communities in the United States," 185–214.
16. Won Moo Hurh and Kwang Chung Kim, *Korean Immigrants in America: A Structural Analysis of Ethnic Confinement and Adhesive Adaptation* (Madison, NJ: Fairleigh Dickenson University Press, 1984).
17. Ji-Yeon Yuh, *Beyond the Shadow of Camptown: Korean Military Brides in America* (New York: New York University Press, 2004).
18. J. Kim, "Cartography of Korean American Protestant Faith Communities in the United States," 185–214. Many of the Korean wives of American GIs, however, played a significant role in sponsoring their relatives from Korea to bring them to the United States after the passage of the Immigration Act of 1965.
19. J. Kim, "Cartography of Korean American Protestant Faith Communities in the United States," 195.
20. R. Stephen Warner and Judith G. Wittner, *Gatherings in Diaspora: Religious Communities and the New Immigration* (Philadelphia: Temple University Press, 1998).
21. U.S. Immigration and Naturalization Service (USINS), *Statistical Yearbook of the Immigration and Naturalization Service* (Washington, DC: U.S. Government Printing Office, 1997).
22. John Logan, Dierdre Oakley, Polly Smith, Jacob Stowell, and Brian Stults, "Separating the Children," Lewis Mumford Center report, May 4, 2001, http://mumford.albany.edu/census/Under18Pop/U18Preport/page1.html.
23. Hurh and Kim, *Korean Immigrants in America*; Hurh and Kim, "Religious Participation of Korean Immigrants in the United States," 19–34.
24. Min, "Immigrants' Religion and Ethnicity," 122–140.
25. Kwang Chung Kim and Shin Kim, "The Ethnic Roles of Korean Immigrant Churches in the United States," in *Korean Americans and Their Religions: Pilgrims and Missionaries from a Different Shore*, eds. Ho-Youn Kwon, Kwang Chung Kim, and R. Stephen Warner (University Park: Pennsylvania State University Press, 2001), 82.
26. Ibid., 71–94.

27. Hurh and Kim, *Korean Immigrants in America*; Hurh and Kim, "Religious Participation of Korean Immigrants in the United States," 19–34.

28. Kelly Chong, *Deliverance and Submission: Evangelical Women and the Negotiation of Patriarchy in South Korea* (Cambridge, MA: Harvard University Press, 2008); Min, "Immigrants' Religion and Ethnicity," 122–140.

29. Min, *Asian Americans*.

30. William Sims Bainbridge, "The Sociology of Conversion," in *Handbook of Religious Conversion*, ed. H. Newton Malony and Samuel Southard (Birmingham, AL: Religious Education Press, 1992), 178–191; John Lofland and Rodney Stark, "Becoming a World-Saver: A Theory of Conversion to a Deviant Perspective," *American Sociological Review* 30 (1965): 862–875; David A. Snow and Richard Machalek, "The Convert as a Social Type," *Sociological Theory* 1 (1984): 259–289.

31. Timothy L. Smith, "Religion and Ethnicity in America," *American Historical Review* 83 (1978): 1155–1185.

32. Ibid., 174.

33. Kim and Kim, "The Ethnic Roles of Korean Immigrant Churches in the United States," 71–94; Fenggang Yang, *Chinese Christians in America: Conversion, Assimilation, and Adhesive Identities* (University Park: Pennsylvania State University Press, 1999).

34. Hurh and Kim, "Religious Participation of Korean Immigrants in the United States," 31.

35. Victoria Hyonchu Kwon, Helen Rose Ebaugh, and Jacqueline Hagan, "The Structure and Functions of Cell Group Ministry in a Korean Christian Church," *Journal for the Scientific Study of Religion* 36 (1997): 247–256.

36. Park, *The Korean American Dream*.

37. I. Kim, *New Urban Immigrants*.

38. Hurh and Kim, *Korean Immigrants in America*; I. Kim, *New Urban Immigrants*; Pyong Gap Min, "The Structure and Social Functions of Korean Immigrant Churches in the United States," *International Migration Review* 26 (1992): 1370–1394.

39. Min, *Asian Americans*.

40. Helen Rose Ebaugh and Janet Saltzman Chafetz, eds., *Religion and the New Immigrants: Continuities and Adaptations in Immigrant Congregations* (Walnut Creek, CA: AltaMira Press, 2000), 334.

41. Carolyn Chen, *Getting Saved in America: Taiwanese Immigration and Religious Experience* (Princeton: Princeton University Press, 2008).

42. Karen Chai, "Competing for the Second Generation: English-Language Ministry at a Korean Protestant Church," in *Gatherings in Diaspora: Religious Communities and the New Immigration*, ed. R. Stephen Warner and Judith G. Wittner (Philadelphia: Temple University Press, 1998), 295–331; Elaine Howard Ecklund, *Korean American Evangelicals: New Models for Civic Life* (New York: Oxford University Press, 2006); Rebecca Kim, *God's New Whiz Kids? Korean American Evangelicals on Campus* (New York: New York University Press, 2006); S. Kim, *A Faith of Our Own*.

43. S. Kim, *A Faith of Our Own*.

44. R. Kim, *God's New Whiz Kids?*

45. S. Kim, *A Faith of Our Own*.

46. Ibid.

47. R. Stephen Warner, "Coming to America: Immigrants and the Faith They Bring." *Christian Century*, Feb. 10, 2004, 1.

48. Philip Jenkins, *The Next Christendom: The Coming of Global Christianity* (Oxford: Oxford University Press, 2007), 249.
49. Guillermina Jasso, Douglas S. Massey, Mark R. Rosenzweig, and James P. Smith, "Exploring the Religious Preferences of Recent Immigrants in the United States: Evidence from the New Immigrant Survey Pilot," in *Religion and Immigration: Christian, Jewish, and Muslim*, ed. Yvonne Yazbeck Haddad, Jane I. Smith, and John L. Esposito (Lanham, MD: Rowman and Littlefield, 2003), 217–253; Peggy Levitt, *God Needs No Passport: Immigrants and the Changing American Religious Landscape* (New York: New Press, 2007).
50. Judy Ju Hui Han, "Missionary Destinations and Diasporic Destiny: Spatiality of Korean/ American Evangelicalism and Cell Church," Institute for the Study of Social Change, ISSC Fellows Working Papers, 2005.
51. Eui-Young Yu, "Sample Survey of Korean Churches in Southern California," Korean American Coalition, Sept. 17, 2003, PowerPoint presentation (Table 22), http://www.author-stream.com/Presentation/Valeria-53269-Survey-churches-Sample-Korean-Southern-California-2003-149-of-churc-Education-ppt-powerpoint/ (accessed December 17, 2008)
52. Kang, "Korean Churches Growing Rapidly in Southern California," section B-2; Kang, "Southern California's Korean Christians Put a Premium on Evangelism.
53. Brooks E. Holifield, *God's Ambassadors: A History of the Christian Clergy in America* (Grand Rapids, MI: Eerdmans Publishing Company, 2007), 315.
54. Christy J. Wilson, *Today's Tentmakers* (Eugene, OR: Wipf and Stock Publishers, 1979).
55. Some who call themselves lay missionaries or tentmakers, however, may get partial support from churches or missionary agencies.
56. Steve Sang-Cheol Moon, "The Protestant Missionary Movement in Korea: Current Growth and Development," *International Bulletin of Missionary Research* 32 (2008): 59–64.

BIBLIOGRAPHY

Abelmann, Nancy, and John Lie. *Blue Dreams: Korean Americans and the Los Angeles Riots.* Cambridge, MA: Harvard University Press, 1995.
Bainbridge, William Sims. "The Sociology of Conversion." In *Handbook of Religious Conversion*, ed. H. Newton Malony and Samuel Southard, 178–191. Birmingham, AL: Religious Education Press, 1992.
Chai, Karen. "Competing for the Second Generation: English-Language Ministry at a Korean Protestant Church." In *Gatherings in Diaspora: Religious Communities and the New Immigration*, ed. R. Stephen Warner and Judith G. Wittner, 295–331. Philadelphia: Temple University Press, 1998.
Chan, Sucheng. *Asian Americans: An Interpretive History.* New York: Twayne Publishers, 1991.
Chen, Carolyn. *Getting Saved in America: Taiwanese Immigration and Religious Experience.* Princeton: Princeton University Press, 2008.
Chong, Kelly. *Deliverance and Submission: Evangelical Women and the Negotiation of Patriarchy in South Korea.* Cambridge, MA: Harvard University Press, 2008.
Choy, Bong-Youn. *Koreans in America.* Chicago: Nelson-Hall, 1979.
Ebaugh, Helen Rose, and Janet Saltzman Chafetz, eds. *Religion and the New Immigrants: Continuities and Adaptations in Immigrant Congregations.* Walnut Creek, CA: AltaMira Press, 2000.

Ecklund, Elaine Howard. *Korean American Evangelicals: New Models for Civic Life*. New York: Oxford University Press, 2006.

Foley, Michael W., and Dean R. Hoge. *Religion and the New Immigrants: How Faith Communities Form Our Newest Citizens*. New York: Oxford University Press, 2007.

Garces-Foley, Kathleen. *Crossing the Ethnic Divide: The Multiethnic Church on a Mission*. New York: Oxford University Press, 2007.

Grayson, James H. "A Quarter-Millennium of Christianity in Korea." In *Christianity in Korea*, ed. Robert E. Buswell, Jr. and Timothy S. Lee, 7–25. Honolulu: University of Hawaii Press, 2006.

Han, Judy Ju Hui. "Missionary Destinations and Diasporic Destiny: Spatiality of Korean/American Evangelicalism and Cell Church." Institute for the Study of Social Change, ISSC Fellows Working Papers, 2005.

Holifield, Brooks E. *God's Ambassadors: A History of the Christian Clergy in America*. Grand Rapids, MI: Eerdmans Publishing Company, 2007.

Hurh, Won Moo, and Kwang Chung Kim. *Korean Immigrants in America: A Structural Analysis of Ethnic Confinement and Adhesive Adaptation*. Madison, NJ: Fairleigh Dickenson University Press, 1984.

——. "Religious Participation of Korean Immigrants in the United States." *Journal for the Scientific Study of Religion* 29 (1990): 19–34.

Jasso, Guillermina, Douglas S. Massey, Mark R. Rosenzweig, and James P. Smith. "Exploring the Religious Preferences of Recent Immigrants in the United States: Evidence from the New Immigrant Survey Pilot." In *Religion and Immigration: Christian, Jewish, and Muslim*, ed. Yvonne Yazbeck Haddad, Jane I. Smith, and John L. Esposito, 217–253. Lanham, MD: Rowman and Littlefield, 2003.

Jenkins, Philip. *The Next Christendom: The Coming of Global Christianity*. Oxford: Oxford University Press, 2007.

Jeung, Russell. *Faithful Generations: Race and New Asian American Churches*. New Brunswick, NJ: Rutgers University Press, 2005.

Kang, Connie K. "Korean Churches Growing Rapidly in Southern California." *Los Angeles Times*, Nov. 1, 2008, section B-2.

——. "Southern California's Korean Christians Put a Premium on Evangelism." *Los Angeles Times*, Nov. 8, 2008, section B-3.

Kim, Ilsoo. *New Urban Immigrants: The Korean Community in New York*. Princeton: Princeton University Press, 1981.

Kim, Jung Ha. "Cartography of Korean American Protestant Faith Communities in the United States." In *Religions in Asian America: Building Faith Communities*, ed. Pyong Gap Min and Jung Ha Kim, 185–214. Walnut Creek, CA: AltaMira Press, 2002.

Kim, Kwang Chung, and Shin Kim. "The Ethnic Roles of Korean Immigrant Churches in the United States." In *Korean Americans and Their Religions: Pilgrims and Missionaries from a Different Shore*, ed. Ho-Youn Kwon, Kwang Chung Kim, and R. Stephen Warner, 71–94. University Park: Pennsylvania State University Press, 2001.

Kim, Rebecca. *God's New Whiz Kids? Korean American Evangelicals on Campus*. New York: New York University Press, 2006.

Kim, Sharon. *A Faith of Our Own: Second Generation Spirituality in Korean American Churches*. New Brunswick: Rutgers University Press, 2010.

Kim, Won Moo, and Kwang Chung Kim. "Religious Participation of Korean Immigrants in the United States." *Journal for the Scientific Study of Religion* 29 (1990): 19–34.

Kniss, Fred, and Paul D. Numrich. *Sacred Assemblies and Civic Engagement: How Religion Matters for America's Newest Immigrants*. New Brunswick, NJ: Rutgers University Press, 2007.

Kwon, Ho-Youn, Kwang Chung Kim, and R. Stephen Warner. *Korean Americans and Their Religions: Pilgrims and Missionaries from a Different Shore*. University Park: Pennsylvania State University Press, 2001.

Kwon, Victoria Hyonchu, Helen Rose Ebaugh, and Jacqueline Hagan. "The Structure and Functions of Cell Group Ministry in a Korean Christian Church." *Journal for the Scientific Study of Religion* 36 (1997): 247–256.

Levitt, Peggy. *God Needs No Passport: Immigrants and the Changing American Religious Landscape*. New York: New Press, 2007.

Lofland, John, and Rodney Stark. "Becoming a World-Saver: A Theory of Conversion to a Deviant Perspective." *American Sociological Review* 30 (1965): 862–875.

Logan, John, Dierdre Oakley, Polly Smith, Jacob Stowell, and Brian Stults. "Separating the Children." Lewis Mumford Center report, May 4, 2001. http://mumford.albany.edu/census/Under18Pop/U18Preport/page1.html.

Lugo, Luis, and Brian J. Grim. "Presidential Election in South Korea Highlights Influence of Christian Community." *The Pew Forum on Religion and Public Life Publications*, Dec. 12, 2007. http://pewforum.org/docs/?DocID=269.

Min, Pyong Gap. "The Structure and Social Functions of Korean Immigrant Churches in the United States." *International Migration Review* 26 (1992): 1370–1394.

——. "Immigrants' Religion and Ethnicity: A Comparison of Indian Hindu and Korean Christian Immigrants in the United States." *Bulletin of the Royal Institute of Inter-Faith Studies* 2 (2000): 122–140.

——. *Asian Americans: Contemporary Trends and Issues*. 2nd ed. Newbury Park, CA: Pine Forge Press, 2005.

Min, Pyong Gap, and Jung Ha Kim. *Religions in Asian America: Building Faith Communities*. Walnut Creek, CA: AltaMira Press, 2002.

Moon, Steve Sang-Cheol. "The Protestant Missionary Movement in Korea: Current Growth and Development." *International Bulletin of Missionary Research* 32 (2008): 59–64.

Park, Kyeyoung. *The Korean American Dream: Immigrants and Small Businesses in New York City*. Ithaca, NY: Cornell University Press, 1997.

Smith, Timothy L. "Religion and Ethnicity in America." *American Historical Review* 83 (1978): 1155–1185.

Snow, David A., and Richard Machalek. "The Convert as a Social Type." *Sociological Theory* 1 (1984): 259–289.

U.S. Immigration and Naturalization Service (USINS). *Statistical Yearbook of the Immigration and Naturalization Service*. Washington, DC: U.S. Government Printing Office, 1997.

Warner, R. Stephen. "Coming to America: Immigrants and the Faith They Bring." *Christian Century*, Feb. 10, 2004.

Warner, R. Stephen, and Judith G. Wittner. *Gatherings in Diaspora: Religious Communities and the New Immigration*. Philadelphia: Temple University Press, 1998.

Wilson, Christy J. *Today's Tentmakers*. Eugene, OR: Wipf and Stock Publishers, 1979.

Yang, Fenggang. *Chinese Christians in America: Conversion, Assimilation, and Adhesive Identities*. University Park: Pennsylvania State University Press, 1999.

Yoo, David K., and Ruth Chung. *Religion and Spirituality in Korean America*. Urbana: University of Illinois Press, 2008.

Yu, Eui-Young. "Sample Survey of Korean Churches in Southern California," Korean American Coalition, Sept. 17, 2003, PowerPoint presentation (Table 22). http://www.authorstream.com/Presentation/Valeria-53269-Survey-churches-Sample-Korean-Southern-California-2003-149-of-churc-Education-ppt-powerpoint/.

Yuh, Ji-Yeon. *Beyond the Shadow of Camptown: Korean Military Brides in America.* New York: New York University Press, 2004.

CHAPTER 9

PSYCHOLOGY OF RELIGIOUS CONVERSION AND SPIRITUAL TRANSFORMATION*

RAYMOND F. PALOUTZIAN

SOME research topics stand the test of time; the psychology of religious conversion has done so. Why is this so, when many areas of research are popular for a while until another "hot" topic emerges to take their place? I think the answer is that psychological research on the processes that mediate religious conversion, and its more recent superset, spiritual transformation, goes to the core of what it means to be a human. One way to illustrate this point is to pose the questions: What is a human being? Is it possible for human beings to change? Whoever holds the keys to answering these questions holds the keys to engaging human lives at their core and perhaps controlling or freeing those lives with the power that such possession implies. This issue, a timeless and cross-disciplinary question, has existed in its pre-psychological form (i.e., understood and bounded within particular religious contexts) possibly as far back as whenever religiousness first appeared on the human scene. However, the psychological manifestation of this question and a scientific approach to answering it are recent, barely more than one hundred years old. But unlike its religious precursors, this approach is based on the assumption that valid knowledge about religious conversion and spiritual transformation can in principle be created or discovered by standard scientific means and that it is possible to construct a theory broad enough to account for the data in all their varied forms. Such knowledge is independent of the ontological reality or unreality of specific religious metaphysical truth claims.

I highlight that the psychology of religious conversion's data and theory are a complement to the knowledge gained in other fields of study. People do not convert in a historical or contextual vacuum; and cultures, social movements, groups, and social strata do not convert or produce individual converts apart from the behavior of individuals. Understanding conversion processes requires that we take into account not only individual factors or social-cultural factors, but the complex interactions among them. However, gaining such knowledge can be difficult because research in various disciplines does not necessarily develop along parallel paths or at uniform rates. Psychological research on conversion has occurred primarily during two broad phases, one approximately a hundred years ago as Psychology was establishing itself as a discipline and one during the last third of the twentieth century and continuing to the present. Therefore, in order to convey its place in psychology in particular and its contribution to scholarship on religious conversion as a whole, we need to examine the following:

1. The paths that the early psychological researchers in this area took and the context in which they worked;
2. The gaps that remained in the data and theory as that era came to an end;
3. How researchers in the more recent period, by employing the model of religion as a meaning system[1] within the multilevel interdisciplinary paradigm,[2] may be able to integrate diverse types of research on religious conversion and spiritual transformation through a common language;
4. How, in its modern manifestation, psychological research on religious conversion and spiritual transformation has expanded far beyond the scope of the early researchers and has bequeathed a great potential to us.

CONVERSION RESEARCH IN THE ROOTS OF PSYCHOLOGY

Research on religious conversion was the first and primary topic studied by the early psychologists of religion. Like its companion disciplines in which research on religious conversion is done, psychology has a particular approach, set of methods and assumptions, and one or more theories that scholars use to guide their research. This includes guiding the questions that are posed, the subjects who are studied, the sorts of data that are examined, and the definitions of religious conversion for psychological purposes. Similarly, psychological researchers work in contexts that may include assumptions of which they are not aware, implicit or explicit biases, limitations of knowledge and resources, or guidelines for which conversions are of interest and how to study them. These are foundational issues. As we look at who the early researchers were and how they did their work in light of the above issues, we gain an appreciation of the intriguing start they gave us.

FOUNDATIONS

Psychology. Psychology is defined as the scientific study of mental and behavioral processes. As in all sciences, we strive to create knowledge based on valid theory, and the path toward this requires that we create hypotheses and test them against empirical data. The data may be experimental, correlational, quantitative, or qualitative,[3] but they are the evidence for evaluating claims about the processes that operate within the human mind to mediate what people do. Because psychology's goal encompasses all that humans do, it is a field of breathtaking sweep and myriad subdisciplines.[4] Psychological knowledge ranges from the micro to the macro in level of analysis. As one illustration of this, the *Handbook of the Psychology of Religion and Spirituality*[5] includes chapters with a focus as pinpointed as the neuropsychology of religious experience and as global as a meaning system analysis of religious terrorism. Scientific research on religious conversion is within its orbit. But to execute this research we need to define conversion, conceptually and operationally.

Conversion. A variety of ways of defining religious conversion for psychological purposes have been offered. It initially seemed to be seen as an event, a specific moment when someone came to a point of faith. Claims of this type of conversion could be accepted as especially valid if the person experienced a crisis that was relieved by a dramatic conversion. A consequence was that the literature sometimes used the phrase "conversion experience" to describe the phenomenon. The conversion of Saul of Tarsus into Paul the Apostle as recorded in the Book of Acts, Chapter 9, could be taken as the gold standard, or prototype, of the true conversion.[6] Other definitions have included a heightening of religious intensity within one's already-held tradition, a change from one tradition to another, or a change from one subgroup (e.g., denomination) to another within a broader tradition.[7] More recently and usefully, however, religious conversion has been understood at a psychological level as a complex process involving many contextual, personal, and other variables.[8] I have found it useful to blend notions of religious conversion with notions of spiritual transformation, thus:

> [Conversion is defined as] a more distinct process by which a person goes from believing, adhering to, and/or practicing one set of religious teachings or spiritual values to believing, adhering to, and/or practicing a different set. The transformative process in conversion may take variable amounts of time, ranging from a few moments to several years, but it is the distinctiveness of the change that is its central identifying element.[9] In contrast to someone arriving at a point of belief through the process of socialization and other developmental mechanisms, the convert can identify a time before which the religion was not accepted and after which it was accepted.[10]

EARLY RESEARCHERS

Starbuck. One of the first books ever written with a title including the phrase "The Psychology of…" was *The Psychology of Religion* by Edwin Starbuck, a young professor at Stanford University. Published in 1899, its topic was religious conversion. This followed shortly after the publication of two journal articles on conversion, one by James Leuba in 1896 and one by Starbuck in 1897.[11] Starbuck had been a student of William James at Harvard University and of G. Stanley Hall at Clark University. Leuba had been a student of Hall at Clark. Both Starbuck and Leuba used methods acquired under Hall, reflecting an approach that came to be associated with the Clark School of Religious Psychology. The historical context of this is important to appreciate, because the end of the nineteenth century is a long time ago in the history of psychology. At that time it had been only about twenty years since Wilhelm Wundt established the first formal experimental psychology laboratory at the University of Leipzig, Sigmund Freud had not yet launched psychoanalysis with the publication of *The Interpretation of Dreams* (1900), John B. Watson had not yet established behaviorism (1913), and the Gestalt school of psychology was yet to emerge at the hands of Kaffka, Kohler, and Lewin (1920s and 1930s). Almost none of the major subdisciplines of modern psychology existed at that time.[12] Nevertheless, at the beginning of psychology as an identifiable field of study, the psychology of religious conversion drew research attention from the field's leaders, such as James and Hall, two of the founding figures of the American Psychological Association.

Starbuck's research methods foreshadowed those that would evolve as psychology developed sophistication in statistics, experimental design, and research methods. He collected answers to questionnaire items asking about religious conversion (in the context of Protestant Christianity)—when it occurred, how it occurred, what mental or emotional states were involved at the time, prior to it, or following it, and the nature of the changes in attitude, affect, and behavior over long periods of time following the conversion. Starbuck was thus able to get fairly close-up accounts of individual cases, at least as close as one could get on paper, and was also able to tabulate (and therefore plot on a graph) the frequency and percentage of converts who reported various emotional, behavioral, and attitudinal states before and after their conversion. This was a marvelous achievement for its time.

Starbuck concluded that conversion was preceded by a negative psychological state that might include a mixture of anxiety, depression, guilt, aimlessness, doubt, unhappiness, and related feelings. If this state was sufficiently intense, a person would be motivated, maybe driven, to seek a solution to the crisis. Conversion provided that solution, the problem was thus solved, and positive feelings such as happiness, peace, joy, and a sense of being "new" or "reborn" would ensue. For Starbuck, this included a giving up of one's old self while acquiring a new self that included a sense of completeness, wholeness, and personal peace.

James. William James published his classic *The Varieties of Religious Experience* in 1902 based on the renowned Gifford Lectures he gave at the University of Edinburgh. His approach diverged from that of Starbuck, yet some of his conclusions were parallel. James used an interpretive-analytic approach to study the intense religious experiences of individuals. His raw data were a series of first-person verbatim accounts of extreme religious or mystical experiences. He examined these in order to get as close as possible to the phenomenology itself—its elements, vividness, divergence from the ordinary, and meanings. By studying such extreme or exemplar cases, James thought that he could learn about the most basic, elemental experiences that occur in the conversion process. James concluded that there is religion of the healthy-minded and religion of the sick soul. The intense conversion experience belongs to the sick soul. James saw this sort of conversion as a consequence of the same negative pre-conversion states that Starbuck described, including a divided self that became unified through conversion. However, James put his emphasis on this "negative" type in particular; he showed less concern with conversions that might be more gradual, rational, or deliberative.

Other leading contemporaries. Other psychologists who were part of the Clark School or whose work was influenced by James also published books and articles on religious conversion. G. Stanley Hall himself wrote about religious conversion off and on over much of his career. He included material on adolescent conversion in his two-volume magnum opus *Adolescence*,[13] gave public lectures on it, and included articles on conversion in the journal that he established, *The American Journal of Religious Psychology and Education*, founded in 1904 and published intermittently until 1915. In 1917 he published the landmark, *Jesus, the Christ, in light of Psychology*. The students Hall mentored are among the most important contributions he made to the field. Leuba wrote *The Psychological Study of Religion: Its Origins, Function, and Future* (1912) and *The Psychological Study of Mysticism* (1925), among other books and articles on the topic. These books were ahead of their time as far as general psychological knowledge is concerned.

Two additional contemporaries, Albert Coe[14] and James Pratt,[15] round out the list of key authors on the psychology of conversion during this early period. Both of them, like Starbuck, James, and Leuba, regarded the psychological process at the heart of religious conversion as the unification of a divided self. On that point there was general consensus. However, there were variations. For example, Coe concluded that gradual conversion was as important for achieving the higher levels of spiritual growth, as was the intense moment of the change itself. Therefore, for Coe, the conversion "event" is only one moment in a longer growth process. This idea is further extended by Pratt, who regarded gradual conversion as more important in the process of development of wholeness in adulthood.

Freud and Jung: Depth Psychology. The depth psychological approach to understanding religious conversion differed from the others prevalent at the time in two fundamental ways. First, James, Hall, and the others conducted conversion research with nonclinical populations and used standard empirical methods. The Clark School used questionnaires, and James used written first-person accounts of vivid, dramatic, or extreme mental experiences that the person considered spiritual or religious. Those doing questionnaire research began with preset response categories to which subjects responded, and they tabulated those responses. James began with the written versions of raw experiences and interpreted them in light of the psychological and physiological knowledge of the time. In contrast to these techniques, those employing depth-psychological methods studied clinical cases, often patients showing signs of neurosis, hysteria, or other psychiatric syndromes. Their methods included dream analysis, interpreting a patient's free associations during psychotherapy, and detecting the symbolic meaning imbedded in something the patient would say, do, or produce. Such methods of interpretation, they believed, revealed more of the "true" nature of their (unconscious) motivations than they could consciously identify or verbalize. Thus, the depth psychologists used a distinctly clinical method of research.

Second, the theoretical difference is evidenced by the almost exclusive emphasis by Freud[16] and Jung[17] on the unconscious mind as the "real" root of the motivations for conversion. By the 1920s Freud's psychoanalytic theory had been well established, and in 1927, with the publication of *The Future of an Illusion*, he clarified how his theory applied to interpreting people's attraction to religion. For Freud, human motivation was based in unconscious, irrational needs that were symbolically met by accepting belief in a God who is always protective, always forgiving, and who promises eternal life. When the convert comes to believe such ideas, the most primitive, deeply rooted anxieties (e.g., perceived lack of safety in a dangerous world, guilt over actual or unconsciously desired misdeeds, or uncertainties associated with death) are relieved. The person is then comforted by the faith that an all-powerful God is protector, forgiver, and life sustainer. This conclusion seems to follow straightforwardly from Freud's fundamental theoretical assumption that the human unconscious is the location from which irrational, self-serving motivations find their expression.

Jung was an early follower of Freud but split off from Freud's inner circle in 1909 to establish his own approach to understanding the unconscious and people's tendency toward religion. Whereas Freud's view assumes "negative" motivations in the unconscious, Jung's view places more "positive" motivations there. For example, Jung thought that the human mind contained built-in universal ideas or thought-forms that motivated a person to seek and find their real-world counterparts; e.g., the built-in universal idea "mother" motivated an infant to seek and find its real mother. One of the main notions was that of the *archetype*. An archetype was considered an unconscious psychic reality. Thus, for Jung, God was an archetype (whether or not it was a literal, ontological reality), and humans came with the unconscious tendency to search for and find God. For both Freud and Jung, therefore, conversion to a god belief and acceptance of the beliefs implied by that were motivated by powerful, but unknown, unconscious forces. For Freud, people accepted religion because of built-in human weaknesses, whereas for Jung, this occurred because of a built-in need to psychically find a match for the unconscious god archetype. Thus it could be said that for Freud, conversion served human needs, whereas for Jung, conversion fulfilled them.

ASSESSMENT

Although religious conversion was among the first topics studied by psychologists in a scientific way, scholarship on the topic declined after the mid-1930s, and little was done until the mid-1960s. Then, in 1967, Scroggs and Douglas[18] helped stimulate research by publishing a paper that summarized the knowledge then available on seven issues in conversion research. Their names for each issue are self-explanatory and reveal the concerns that came with the topic: the definition issue, the psychopathology issue, the convertible type issue, the ripe age issue, the voluntaristic issue, the science-versus-religion issue, and the appropriate conceptual scheme issue. Their stimulus and the trend of young people at that time to join New Religious Movements, most thoroughly studied by sociologists, led to conversion research being prominent once again in the psychology of religion. Since then the amount of research on conversion and transformation has increased to the point where it is a thriving area. This is evident in the last section of this chapter.

A mix of limitations of the early period seems relevant to understanding how the field could wane after a few decades. First, the research was influenced by the particular religious context in which it was conducted—specifically, the Protestant United States at the turn of the century. The overall field of the psychology of religion was a product of both England and the United States, but conversion research was primarily American. The Protestant emphasis on evangelism, with an intense conversion experience regarded as the marker of a valid acquisition of religious (i.e., Christian) faith, meant that (a) the scholars themselves were influenced by and therefore prone to study it, and (b) this was the primary religious population and phenomenon that was available for study. Taken in context, why their research focused on this particular type of conversion is understandable. Second, this meant that the research could not easily include conversions to other religions or spiritualities. Third, a corollary is that the nature of the conversion accessible for study was restricted to those who emphasized individualistic acceptance of a doctrine, public confession, and being able to identify the moment of change. Thus, accessibility to conversions of other types, such as ones that took different amounts of time, were to non-Christian beliefs or practices, or happened in other languages was not realistic. Fourth, the consequence of this combined set of limitations is that religious conversion had a restricted meaning; circumstances did not allow it to have the broader meaning that is being accommodated in the contemporary period of research.

Nevertheless, psychologists did not do a good job of integrating the empirical research on the causes and consequences of conversion with the theoretical ideas available to try to account for them.[19] We should regard this not as a disappointment, however, but only an observation. All of psychology once suffered from a lack of theoretical synthesis, so it should not be a surprise that the psychology of religious conversion looks the same.

TRANSITIONS TO PRESENT RESEARCH

One-shot studies. A primary reason for the lack of synthesis in the case of the psychology of religious conversion is that most of the psychological research done on conversion is in the context of one-shot studies whose ideas were not expanded and applied to future studies. Each piece of past and present research on conversion often cited in reviews has largely been conceptualized and conducted within the preferred orientation of its author. For example, Batson, Schoenrade, and Ventis[20] summarize their model of conversion within a cognitive-illumination model, Beit-Hallahmi and Nevo[21] report their findings by employing the concept of authoritarianism and degree of identification with parents, Galanter[22] uses a psychiatric model and explains converts' commitment to new religious movements by invoking the concept of a "relief effect," James[23] invokes medical and clinical imagery when referring to a healthy mind versus a sick soul, I[24] rely on the cognitive principle of closure to explain how converts come to perceive increased meaning in life, Ullman[25] adapts some predictions from psychoanalytic theory to account for how converts had imperfect relations with parents, and Starbuck[26] invokes the concept of spiritual growth to describe an apparent enhancement in converts seeing their religion as an umbrella to their lives as a whole over time. This research has seldom been part of a larger research program, and none of it, to my knowledge, has been part of a systematic research program on religious conversion.

Attachment. The one (recent) exception is by Granqvist and Kirkpatrick,[27] who report the results of a combined sequence of studies on conversion conceptualized within attachment theory. Attachment theorists propose that attachments of a child to its caregiver develop during the formative years and that these vary in type and quality. Within this theory, the character of the bond between caregiver and offspring is central to whether a person relates to others in a secure versus insecure way and gravitates toward holding a God-belief during adulthood and, if so, what form it takes. Specifically, type and strength of attachment determines whether the person is later prone to conversion.

Three types of attachment experiences are proposed—secure, insecure, and avoidant. Each type results in an "internal working model"—a mental model of interpersonal relationships—that the person later uses as a guide for his or her interactions with the world, including relationships with God. Those who have had secure attachments are least likely to become religious converts, and if they are raised with a religious belief they are more likely to sustain than change it. Those who have had insecure or avoidant attachment relationships are more likely to undergo a religious conversion. The implications seem to be that children raised securely tend to retain a sense of security during adulthood, so that there is relatively little in the way of security and safety needs to be met by a new relationship with God. But children raised insecurely have a need for a safe haven in times of danger, and this need is met by accepting a loving God who is always there to protect and sustain them. A theoretical implication is that people with insecure childhood attachments are more likely to convert to religion or god belief as part of a compensatory process. See Granqvist and Kirkpatrick (2004) for further elaboration. Their research program is a good example for the rest of us.

From event to process. As psychologists have continued to better understand religious conversion,[28] our knowledge about what constitutes a conversion has become more sophisticated and intellectually sound. What at one time was talked about as an *event*, often occurring at a single point in time that the convert could identify even if the process leading up to it was gradual,[29] is now understood as a far more complicated *process* that involves many contextual, cultural, group process, personality, situational, and other variables.[30] The conversion of Paul is no longer taken as the gold standard.[31] There are nevertheless popular stereotypes of conversion, most notably the occasional newsworthy account of the "radical convert" (i.e., someone who undergoes a change in all aspects of life meaning, belief, and behavior, such as a Christian who becomes a Muslim, or an atheist who strives to become an ultra-Orthodox Jew). The phrase *quantum change* has been used to talk about some of these total changes, which are sometimes based on an "epiphany" experience.[32] However, radical conversions in which a person has a complete transformation of all aspects of life and belief and behavior are statistically rare. Importantly, a convert's perceptions and those of close others that all aspects of the convert's personality have transformed after conversion may be filtered through retrospective bias.[33] The vast majority of conversions are changes from one variation of the religion of one's culture or upbringing to another variation of it (e.g., someone changing from being a Protestant to a Catholic in the United States or Western Europe, which are traditionally Christianized cultures) or are changes of lesser to greater intensity of one's religious commitment within the same tradition as one's upbringing. These instances include what some consider the most "spiritual" conversions.[34] A person who is a non-devout Protestant, Catholic, Jew, or Muslim who later becomes a devout believer in and follower of that same religion is the most common example of this.

A meaning system approach is better able to account for the myriad variations of conversions, or spiritual transformations, than any of the single-process theoretical approaches of the past. But what is it, both in terms of understanding religious conversion in particular and in terms of psychology as a whole, that we would like the meaning system model to do for us, theoretically and empirically, that has not been accomplished before?

TASKS AHEAD—HOW RESEARCH CAN PROCEED

The Need for a Meaning-System Model

Psychology is about meaning, and the psychology of religious conversion is about how a person comes to perceive meaning of a particular sort. Although the concept of meaning applies much more broadly than only to religion or conversion, scholars have recently proposed that the concept of religion as a meaning system provides a common language capable of connecting diverse areas of research.[35] The crux of this argument is that the model of religion as a meaning system is the most powerful idea that psychologists have created to understand at all levels of analysis how human religiousness functions and how conversions and spiritual transformations happen. The model gets us closer to understanding the full range of elements of the conversion process than any theory from the past. And because its language is capable of stretching across disciplinary boundaries, it can facilitate scholarship within an overarching multilevel interdisciplinary paradigm[36] that is likely to guide future research. The concept of religion as a meaning system allows for a language that cuts across all topics to evolve synthetically. It is a language that is at the heart of each process studied, whether it is conversion in response to visual or auditory stimuli, emotionally triggered reactions or thoughts, or culturally normative cues, expectations, or rules. All is meaning-laden, meaning-implicating language, with the result that conversion research from the micro to the macro levels of analysis can therefore fit within a multilevel interdisciplinary paradigm, enabling us to proceed with our research in a more integrative way. Furthermore, the notion of meaning systems applies to allied scholarly disciplines and is therefore interdisciplinary and inclusive.[37]

What specific version(s) of psychological processes might constitute the central idea of a multilevel interdisciplinary paradigm? Current evidence suggests that a comprehensive evolutionary metatheory framework (i.e., a large conceptual umbrella under which theories about a more focused range of phenomena may fit) serves this purpose because it allows for ideas from psychology overall and psychology of religion to be integrated with the most powerful ideas that have helped to integrate much of the rest of the sciences.[38] Within that, current evidence seems to be pointing to a combination of social psychology, cognitive psychology, and neuroscience, broadly construed to include everything from cultural to neural processes.[39] This hybrid field might become a new central core area through which research and theory about religious conversion and its superset, spiritual transformation, connect with other areas of knowledge. There are a number of implications of this for understanding religious conversion and spiritual transformation. I will summarize some of them at the end of this chapter.

Three Goals

Three goals are intrinsic to the scholarly efforts to understand religious conversion and spiritual transformation. None of them has been reached. Because of this, research and theory on religious conversion and spiritual transformation can help fulfill three ideals.

First, the most lofty goal, the broadest concern, is to create a complete psychological theory of human functioning—all human functioning, not only human religiousness or conversions. This is because, whatever else religiousness is, it is human behavior (broadly understood to include beliefs, feelings, cognitions, motivations, etc.) that is

mediated and constituted by the same psychological processes that mediate and constitute any other sort of human behavior. Thus a theory that explains human religiousness and conversion to it actually explains all of human behavior. This is a far-reaching
goal with many implications, but it is nevertheless the long-term ideal accomplishment
that would come from this line of research. Obviously, we have much more interesting
research to do to achieve that goal.

Second, a mid-range goal, a path that helps accomplish the first goal, is the promotion of the psychology of religion in general psychology. This means that we need to
further explore the degree to which religiousness is or is not psychologically unique,[40]
fine-tune our understanding of where this area is primarily an applied topic versus a
substantively basic topic, and clarify the ways that it shows something about human
functioning that is not shown elsewhere. The result ought to be that parts of the psychology of religion and knowledge about religious conversion are found to be non-unique,
with the implication that those aspects of religiousness are regulated by the same processes that regulate other human behaviors, while other parts are found to be unique,
with the implication that those aspects are regulated by processes not found elsewhere.
Thus, both the overlap and the distinctiveness of psychological processes that regulate
human religiousness will become a standard and integrated part of general psychological knowledge.

The third goal, lesser in scope but essential to progress toward goals one and two
above, is to create a theory based on data-evidence that explains the psychological processes that mediate religious conversion and the larger category of which it is a part,
spiritual transformation. The classical grand theories (e.g., of Freud and Jung) were
(and still are) interesting and ingenious ideas, but as originally stated they did not lead
to empirical research sufficient to test and support them. Analogously, the many questionnaire studies in which people indicated their religious beliefs, which were then correlated with almost every other psychological variable available, were not considered
relevant to the theories then available and thus little theoretical relevance was attached
to them.[41]

Of lesser prevalence in psychological circles was the occasional proposal for one or
another version of a religious psychology, such as a "Muslim Psychology" or a "Christian
Psychology." In these cases, the notion of what processes might regulate or constitute
a religious conversion might be decided in advance of psychological thinking or data
collection due to a doctrine taught by that religion (e.g., Only God makes 'real' conversions happen, which the convert declares by essential beliefs and practices). Given such
reasoning, the answer to a psychological question is not tested against empirical evidence but is instead tested against the presumed meaning of a scripture deemed sacred
and authoritative by its believers. Of course, this does not reflect scientific psychological
thinking. Efforts to account for the psychological processes in religious conversion by
such efforts (i.e., by basing an explanation on supernatural attributions to account for
how psychological processes work) have not worked.

In contrast, however, a psychological approach does include efforts within a religious
tradition to understand how that particular religion, with its various metaphors, rituals,

expectations, and ideologies (theologies) may shape or elicit certain kinds of religious/ spiritual experiences. Thought of in these terms, a particular "religious psychology" is a special case of a cultural psychological approach.[42] Analyses from this emerging field of psychology can add to our knowledge of how a particular religious culture affects people's experiences, desires, goals, sense of meaning, and other human qualities.

The task ahead, therefore, is to start afresh with new research that adopts a comprehensive language capable of connecting the many meanings implied by conversion, across the many levels of analysis at which they can be tested and across all cultural variations. This will enable us to learn what religious conversion and spiritual transformation mean psychologically,[43] what they have to do with identity change, and how they interact with the full menu of factors in Rambo's[44] descriptive model. The overall implications embrace research from the micro to the macro levels and either suggest or are consistent with a social cognitive neuroscience of conversion and spiritual transformation. Also, this seems to be the core of what is aimed at in the emerging blended area referred to as the cognitive science of religion.[45]

MEANING SYSTEMS, RELIGIOUS CONVERSION, AND SPIRITUAL TRANSFORMATION

The Question of Meaning

Questions of meaning are infinite. Whether we are thinking about a kiss, an IQ score, a Euro or a US dollar, teaching anything, or all of life—in all instances of a person having an idea or thought about anything, the question of what it means is automatically invoked. Questions of meaning are typically construed as theological or philosophical, but they are also and are perhaps fundamentally psychological questions. When we ask what something means, we are asking what it stands for, what it implies or leads to, how it relates to something else, what its representations and connections are in the human mind.[46] These are not questions about meaning detected or whether it could be verified; they are questions about how the human mind makes meaning—how we attribute a meaning to a stimulus. Meaning, like value, is always in relation to something else. Thus, to create a theory of the psychological processes in religiousness, conversion, and spiritual transformation that captures the heart and soul of what it is about, we need to answer the question of meaning's meaning in religion, because religion is essentially about meaning. Such meanings include thoughts, feelings, emotional motivations or reactions, cues to the treatment of others, behavioral scripts—no thought, emotion, or action is immune from the possible implications of meaning processes. By extension, then, whether we are talking about a "religious experience"[47] or an "experience deemed religious,"[48] religious development,[49] religious actions and social attitudes,[50] the neurological processes involved in experiences deemed religious,[51] coping,[52] religious processes in physical and mental health,[53] how spiritual transformation affects a workplace culture,[54] forgiveness in world religions as practiced on the ground,[55] or the role of religion in international terrorism and peace efforts,[56] we are invoking questions about meaning.

I can present only a brief summary of what a meaning system is and its general processes. There are different versions of it,[57] but they share a common core. An excellent diagram of meaning assessment and reconstruction processes is presented by Park[58] in the context of coping. Mine is a social psychological way of construing a meaning system and applying it to conversion and spiritual transformation.[59]

A meaning system is a structure within a human cognitive system that includes attitudes and beliefs, values, focused goal orientations, general overall purposes, self-definition, and some locus of ultimate concern. Each element affects the others, so that when pressure is imposed on one component of the system (e.g., a person who holds one set of religious beliefs is introduced to beliefs of a different religion and is encouraged to convert), the beliefs that are under pressure confront information already in the other elements of the system and, if changed in the direction of the pressure, may become inconsistent with them. If the initial beliefs are resistant enough, the ties among the elements of the system sustain belief and repel the pressure to change. But if resistance capabilities have not developed, the pressure on the beliefs might be strong enough to dent or topple other elements of the system. Thus, a meaning system can be modified in one or more aspect(s). Any modification constitutes some amount of transformation of the meaning system. When the degree of change reaches a certain threshold, we call it religious conversion. If the whole system is replaced by a completely different one, then we consider it a dramatic spiritual transformation, the relatively rare example of the radical convert.

Using this brief portrait of how the model of religion as a meaning system helps us understand religious conversions and spiritual transformations, it is easy to extrapolate and apply this model to all aspects of religiousness from the micro (neuropsychology of experiences deemed religious) to the macro (religious motivation to or justification for violence and terrorism). It may be possible that an extrapolation of this model might serve some of the needs of scholars in areas beyond psychology who need a compelling model to fit their data. The model summarized above is psychological and its elements are social-cognitive constructions, but the general notion that any system at any level of analysis has its meaning elements allows scholars in other disciplines to expand the idea presented above to identify meaning elements within a neurological system, a social system, a culture, or a political system within a particular historical context.[60]

Transformation of a Meaning System

The above summary of what a meaning system is and how its elements may interact leads to some understanding of the processes that can result in a change in the system.

These changes would be those that constitute some level of a religious conversion (for meaning systems deemed religious) or some degree of spiritual transformation (for meaning systems seen in broader or generic terms that may not be specifically religious).[61] For a person to convert from one religion or spirituality to another, at least the following elements are part of the process.

1. The person must need or want something; this may or may not be conscious or explicit. Examples include pleasure, rights, purpose, perception of justice, basic survival needs, reduction of unpleasant mental or emotional states such as guilt, anxiety, or loneliness, or continuity between major life domains.

2. The person must doubt (broadly conceptualized as cognitive disbelief, vague unease, emotional aversion, or other) that the need(s) can or will be met or that the problem(s) will be solved within the current frame of reference. Examples include a perception of conflict between two statements in scripture, a belief that a scientific notion and the teaching of one's religion are incompatible, hypocrisy observed in one's religious leaders, or one's own failure to live up to an ideal taught by one's religion. In all cases, there is a discrepancy between the "is" and "ought"[62] in the person's own life or in the perceived religious life of others. It is this discrepancy that feeds a generic doubt, or unease, with the status quo.

3. There must be contextual resources that make conversion possible.[63] For example, even if a person is on a personal quest for meaning, finding meaning in religious ways does not occur by random chance. There must also be some agency (whether formally organized or not, of any size, etc.) that the person can potentially encounter; individual or group contact must be possible via any medium, as well as the potential for social support, materials, or communication of information relevant to the to-be-converted-to system or entity.

4. The above resources must be noticed, encountered, and appropriated. The more that goes into the system through the input side, the greater the probability of change in one or more elements within the system, and the more likely we are to see identifiable changes on the output side in the form of psychological functioning or belief or behavior that is different than it was before.

5. Prohibitions and other barriers must be either set aside or satisfied. For example, if one's ethnic, religious, or cultural group forbids a person within it to accept some alternative to what has been inculcated in the person, a would-be convert is likely to face resistance if he or she indicates a desire to change. In some instances the barrier to leaving one's parent group is extreme, at the threat of death. Occasionally this has meant the literal killing of the person or, slightly less extreme, the symbolic death of the convert, such as when the person is "cut off" from all aspects of the family, never to be spoken of again because the person converted to a religion regarded as fundamentally incompatible with and anathema to the religion of the family. Many lesser barriers exist; the degree to which they are permeable varies with the tolerance level of the parent group or culture. The dilemmas that these circumstances can create for a person who wants to

change religions has the potential to be extreme and can cause distress, loneliness, and feelings of grief and loss. At the same time, the person may also feel elated by the feelings of release, comfort, satisfaction, and joy experienced in the wake of the final decision to follow the new religion. In either case, the person must disregard the barriers to a degree that will enable him or her to make the change (or, for example, psychologically set them aside as no longer important) and/or must satisfy them in some way, if possible in a way that is acceptable to the former group or culture.

6. The change must be implemented; something new must be believed or something actually done differently than before. Acceptance of a new set of doctrines as revealed truth, changing one's opinion about whether Jesus was the messiah or Muhammad was the final prophet and the corresponding change in learning and following what they said, are examples of this, as are altering where one attends religious services, what one does to practice the faith, what one listens to as sacred music, whether one teaches a known religion or other spirituality to one's children, and so forth. Similarly, changing from a religion to "none" is equally as important a transformation of a meaning system as changing from no religion to one or from one to another. This has been confirmed by recent research on deconversion.[64] If a person becomes an atheist or an agnostic after having been a religious believer, the person may have come to that point due to doubts (again broadly construed), may need to confront, disregard, or accommodate prohibitions or barriers to denying there is a God, and will show evidence of the reality of the transformation by identifiable differences between what the person said and did before and after the transformation.[65]

In sum, the above implies that there are *inputs, intermediate processes,* and *outputs* involved in the process of religious conversion or spiritual transformation. The list of inputs is functionally infinite, but the principle that they are forces that enter the system that are sufficient to prompt a modification (of any size) in one or more elements of the system is the same regardless of the specific input. The intermediate processes are the elements of a meaning system as I have presented[66] and summarized above. Other variations are possible. The outputs are the changes that ought to emerge from the modification of the system. The greater the internal change, the more we ought to be able to identify differences in the outputs.

Conversion of Identity in Culture

The argument summarized above, that inputs, intermediate processes, and outputs are all involved in the process of religious conversion or spiritual transformation, applies broadly. First, meaning system analysis is far-reaching because it conceptually crosses all boundaries, religious, cultural, or otherwise, so that it is capable of accounting for conversions of all types to all religions at all times under all circumstances. This is a much bigger idea than summarizing conversion as only a cultural process, personality process, social influence process, cognitive reconstruction, or change in a brain state. A meaning model can stretch across levels of analysis to account for conversion. Therefore, this approach to religious conversion immediately broadens its explanatory reach to include other forms of spiritual transformation, all of which have meaning reconstruction at the heart of the process. This includes deconversion. Second, this approach speaks to not only the questions about how religious conversion occurs but also to the entire field of psychology. A theory that can explain conversion can go the distance and be expanded to explain the rest of human functioning. That degree of total understanding of how humans work is the end goal, the lofty ideal, and understanding religious conversion and spiritual transformation is a very interesting and important step along the way.

New Conversion Research Directions

The combination of (a) conceptualizing religion as a meaning system, (b) doing research in view of the multilevel interdisciplinary paradigm, and (c) recent expansions in the populations studied, phenomena brought under the view of conversion/transformation ideas, and tools available to us for conducting conversion research at levels not seriously considered before, has the potential to yield expanded and integrative theoretical frameworks for understanding the type of human change called religious conversion or spiritual transformation. If we accomplish this, psychology will have come a long way toward a fuller scientific account of the functioning of human beings. A look at these recent expansions gives us clues for future research.

Expanded Populations

For most of the twentieth century, studies of religious conversion were conducted on Western, Christianized populations, and one of the obvious criticisms of the research focused on the limited samples on which data were collected—most often Protestants. An understandable and valid criticism was, therefore, "What about Buddhists, Jews, Muslims, or believers in a New Religious Movement (NRM) or other alternative spirituality?" This is an elementary sort of criticism, because anyone starting a study on a topic is usually able to study only those subjects who are reasonably accessible.[67] Thus, because most psychologists are in the West, most studies of conversion would be expected to be done on conversion-oriented groups in the West. Until recently, these were primarily Protestant Christians. On the other hand, it is an important point because the discipline of psychology as a whole is far more comprehensive than the psychology of Western Protestants. If a valid, globally applicable psychology of religious conversion is to emerge, then extending the reach of research to all populations, religions, cultures, and languages is essential.

Fortunately, some research steps in this direction have been made. Beit-Hallahmi and Nevo[68] studied Israeli Jews who converted to Orthodox Judaism and found them to score higher on the Authoritarianism scale than a control group. Interestingly, they used the term "Born Again" (a phrase usually used in a Christian conversion context) to refer to the dynamics of this identity change in Jews in Israel. Pirutinsky (2009) examined the relation between conversion and attachment insecurity among Orthodox Jews. Kose and Loewenthal[69] explored the psychological factors involved in British converts to Islam. Lakhdar et al.[70] studied the motives behind why French adolescents and adults converted to Islam, and Maslim and Bjorck explored reasons for conversion to Islam among US women.[71] Bockian, Glenwick, and Bernstein[72] applied a "stages of change" model to Jewish conversion. Jindra[73] explored religious stage development in samples of Jehovah's Witnesses and Unitarian Universalists. Hunsberger and Altemeyer[74] explored the reasons behind why people who were raised in a religion might decide to become an atheist (i.e., deconvert) as an adult, certainly one type of spiritual transformation. Streib, Hood, Keller, Csöff, and Silver[75] explored the process of deconversion in the United States and Germany, and Nanimi and Murken were successful in exploring the fit between a convert to an NRM in Germany and the convert's familial antecedents.[76] Although the world is much bigger than that which is reflected in the above set of psychological studies, this number of studies on expanded samples in a short amount of time is an indication of the degree to which the psychology of religious conversion is beginning to mature. And the more this trend continues, the more we will also see studies of different phenomena.

Expanded Phenomena and Techniques

Just as the convert populations that were studied were limited, the phenomena about which psychological questions were asked and the tools used to answer the questions were also limited. The two dominant research questions focused on (a) what the conversion experience was like phenomenologically and whether its character might be related to specific beliefs that were acquired, and (b) why someone would be motivated to (or susceptible to) convert. The two dominant research techniques were the interview (to tap the phenomenology of the experience) and the questionnaire (to get answers to more objectified information such as the content of the convert's new belief). These questions and techniques are powerful and will continue to be widely used.

Also, we now have additional analytic techniques that add a level of statistical precision and power of data analysis that did not prevail in the past. New techniques of content analysis and qualitative research methods that yield data that can then be available for quantitative statistical analysis promise in-depth exploration of the internal meaning of a conversion experience in terms of both content and implications and also promise hypothesis testing of psychological ideas about the processes mediating those contents and meanings. Jindra[77] combined both qualitative and quantitative techniques in her research on NRM conversions, and Streib et al.[78] used both techniques in their research on deconversion in the United States and Germany. The blending of both sorts of tools will yield knowledge that is more extensive than that which can come from use of only one method alone.

One new technique that is especially rich in potential is brain- (or neuro-) imaging. Although conversion research properly emphasizes the study of transformative process at the level of the whole person, we nevertheless have a keen interest in knowing what is going on in the brain. Given that neuroimaging studies have now been conducted on religious mental states such as prayer and meditation,[79] it is likely that we will see a study that documents the neurological changes that mediate religious conversions and spiritual transformations, along with the various steps and stages that comprise them. An extension of research at this level can give us knowledge about the neurocognition of conversion and transformation experiences[80] and about how the mind/brain constructs meaning(s) out of bits and pieces of information.[81]

Advances in the techniques of cross-cultural research will allow us to develop a synthetic knowledge pool of conversions across languages and cultures. We now know that, for example, it is insufficient to translate the wording of a questionnaire that was created in one language (e.g., English) into another language and assume that the scores obtained on the translated version of the questionnaire mean that same thing that they do in the original language. This is because even the "same" words in different languages do not necessarily carry the same meaning, or the same weight of a meaning. Thus, it is not sufficient to merely translate a questionnaire item with the words "belief in god" in it, to which respondents can give a 1-7 rating of agreement, into another language, partly because the words themselves may not convey the same meaning and partly because the numerical weights do not automatically carry over to the other language. This means that in order to translate tools correctly, one must translate the meanings of the tool accurately, not merely the words in the tool—and this is a useful research practice only if the construct to be assessed has any meaning in the other language. Such refinements in techniques and in considerations about the meaning of what one is studying will prevail in future research and enrich the accuracy and reliability of cross-cultural knowledge about religious conversion and much else.

Expanded Integrative Theory

If we step back and view the whole map of theories and their evidence, we may be able to conceptualize a process that overlays them and under which each one operates in interactive fashion with the others. I think there is a model that does this and it is captured best by the notion of religion as a meaning system and of conversion as a change in or of a meaning system. While Rambo[82] gave us the comprehensive descriptive map of all the variables, personal and social motives, cognitive processes, and circumstantial and contextual factors that would have to be accounted for in a complete theory of conversion, the meaning system model offers a tool with which we can conceptualize the processes that are operating in conversion, in a language that can be common to all aspects from the micro to macro levels. The consequence is that a meaning system analysis can foster the integration of the data and the extant approaches into a more encompassing theory that can fit within a larger evolutionary metatheory (see Kirkpatrick 2005) that has served to integrate knowledge from a broad band of the sciences.

IMPLICATIONS: UNIQUE AND NON-UNIQUE

There are some important implications of a meaning system analysis. Some of them are unique to this particular approach, and some of them apply equally well to other approaches. Space allows only brief comments about each implication.

1. Given the advances in the research base that supports a meaning system approach,[83] we can now be more insistent that the ideas we keep have a data foundation and that the data we collect address theory more directly than previously. It is no longer necessary or useful to hold on to ideas without sufficient data support or to continue to collect more numerical data without theoretical relevance.
2. The model of religion as a meaning system can be tested empirically. Research on it can be done both quantitatively and qualitatively.[84]
3. The concepts can be extrapolated from the micro to the macro levels; thus, research from the neurology of religion and conversion to the sociology and cultural understanding of religion and conversion can eventually be integrated.
4. Psychology of religious conversion is placed squarely in the midst of the psychology of human change. Much of psychology is about change—personality change, developmental psychology, clinical treatment, attitude change and persuasion, learning, coping—thus, research on conversion can become synthesized with these other areas.
5. Knowledge of the experience of conversion increases our understanding of human consciousness generally. Much research in cognitive science (from the neurobiological, psychological, and computer science approaches) in recent years has increased our knowledge about human consciousness, and the emerging area of the cognitive science of religion can contribute to this with the application of a meaning system approach to religion.[85]
6. A meaning system approach neither requires nor promotes reductionism. Just because it is possible to explain the psychological processes that are involved in religious conversion does not mean that such explanations "explain away" other factors that may possibly be operating but that cannot be explored scientifically. This means that, like other psychological approaches that fit properly with a modern philosophy of science, understanding the psychological meaning-implications of something does not equal absolute knowledge about

all possible meanings of it. Thus, one may hold either theological or purely naturalistic presuppositions about the process of conversion and at the same time hold to the same far-reaching psychological understanding of it.

7. Of fundamental importance to humans, knowledge of this approach can free people to identify the meanings inherent in their already existing beliefs and practices and can also offer people confronted with information on the input side of the transformation process sufficient to challenge their system the intellectual tools needed to free them from automatic responses. This allows people experiencing new input to step back, look closely at the processes that are occurring, and choose the response that they wish to occur. Knowledge of the meaning-making process can help people make their own new meaning.

Finally, a meaning system analysis gives us a fresh view of where truth may be found. Psychologically speaking, truth is in the meaning system of the beholder.[86]

NOTES

* Portions of this chapter are based on a talk presented at the conference "La Conversion religieuse, Colloque International," Université de Lausanne, Switzerland, May 15–16, 2008, and published in Pierre-Yves Brandt and Claude-Alexandre Fournier, eds., *La Conversion religieuse: Analyses psychologiques, anthropologiques et sociologiques* (Geneva: Labor et Fides, 2009). I thank Ann Taves for helpful critiques of an earlier draft, the Psychology Faculty at Westmont College, the Katholieke Universiteit Leuven, Belgium, and the Center for Advanced Study in the Behavioral Sciences at Stanford University, for providing excellent facilities and resources, plus a cordial social environment, for writing this chapter. Correspondence can be addressed to Raymond F. Paloutzian, Department of Psychology, Westmont College, Santa Barbara, California 93108-1099 USA (email: paloutz@westmont.edu).

1. Crystal L. Park, "Religion and Meaning," in *Handbook of the Psychology of Religion and Spirituality*, ed. Raymond F. Paloutzian and Crystal L. Park (New York: Guilford Press, 2005), 295–314; Crystal L. Park and Susan Folkman, "Meaning in the Context of Stress and Coping," *Review of General Psychology* 1 (1997): 115–144; Israela Silberman, "Religion as a Meaning-System: Implications for the New Millennium," *Journal of Social Issues* 61 (2005): 641–664; Raymond F. Paloutzian, "Religious Conversion and Spiritual Transformation: A Meaning-System Analysis," in *Handbook of the Psychology of Religion and Spirituality*, ed. Raymond F. Paloutzian and Crystal L. Park (New York: Guilford Press, 2005), 331–347; and Paloutzian, Raymond F. and Crystal L. Park. "Recent Progress and Core Issues in the Science of the Psychology of Religion and Spirituality." In *Handbook of the Psychology of Religion and Spirituality*, 2nd ed. Ed. Raymond F. Paloutzian and Crystal L. Park, 3–22. New York: Guilford Press, 2013.

2. Robert A. Emmons and Raymond F. Paloutzian, "The Psychology of Religion," *Annual Review of Psychology* 54 (2003): 377–402; Raymond F. Paloutzian and Crystal L. Park,

"Integrative Themes in the Current Science of the Psychology of Religion," in *Handbook of the Psychology of Religion and Spirituality*, ed. Raymond F. Paloutzian and Crystal L. Park (New York: Guilford, 2005), 3–20; and Paloutzian, Raymond F. and Crystal L. Park. "Recent Progress and Core Issues in the Science of the Psychology of Religion and Spirituality." In *Handbook of the Psychology of Religion and Spirituality*, 2nd ed. Ed. Raymond F. Paloutzian and Crystal L. Park, 3–22. New York: Guilford Press, 2013.

3. Ralph W. Hood, Jr. and Jacob A. Belzen, "Research Methods in the Psychology of Religion," in *Handbook of the Psychology of Religion and Spirituality*, ed. Raymond F. Paloutzian and Crystal L. Park (New York: Guilford, 2005), 62–79.

4. American Psychological Association: see http://www.apa.org for its fifty-four divisions.

5. Paloutzian and Park, "Integrative Themes in the Current Science of the Psychology of Religion." See also Paloutzian, Raymond F. and Crystal L. Park. "Recent Progress and Core Issues in the Science of the Psychology of Religion and Spirituality." In *Handbook of the Psychology of Religion and Spirituality*, 2nd ed. ed. Raymond F. Paloutzian and Crystal L. Park, 3–22. New York: Guilford Press, 2013.

6. James T. Richardson, "The Active vs. Passive Convert: Paradigm Conflict in Conversion/Recruitment Research," *Journal for the Scientific Study of Religion* 24 (1985): 119–236.

7. Raymond F. Paloutzian, James T. Richardson, and Lewis R. Rambo, "Religious Conversion and Personality Change," *Journal of Personality* 67 (1999): 1047–1079.

8. Lewis R. Rambo, *Understanding Religious Conversion* (New Haven: Yale, 1993).

9. Benjamin Beit-Hallahmi and Michael Argyle, *The Psychology of Religious Behaviour, Belief, and Experience* (London: Routledge, 1997); Raymond F. Paloutzian, *Invitation to the Psychology of Religion*, 2nd ed. (Boston: Allyn & Bacon, 1996); Paloutzian, Richardson, and Rambo, "Religious Conversion and Personality Change"; Rambo, *Understanding Religious Conversion*; Ralph W. Hood, Jr., Peter C. Hill, and Bernard Spilka, *The Psychology of Religion: An Empirical Approach*, 4th ed. (New York: Guilford, 2009).

10. Paloutzian, "Religious Conversion and Spiritual Transformation," 331. See also Paloutzian, Raymond F., S. Murkin, H. Steib, and Sussan Rößler-Namini. "Conversion, Deconversion, and Spiritual Transformation: A Multilevel Interdisciplinary View." In *Handbook of the Psychology of Religion and Spirituality*, 2nd ed. Ed. Raymond F. Paloutzian and Crystal L. Park, 399–421. New York: Guilford Press, 2013.

11. Edwin D. Starbuck, "A Study of Conversion," *American Journal of Psychology* 8 (1897): 268–308; Leuba, "A Study in the Psychology of Religious Phenomena."

12. Until the mid-1930s, introduction to psychology courses were taught reflecting one particular "school" of psychology (e.g., functionalism, psychoanalysis, behaviorism, or Gestalt psychology). The first eclectic introduction to psychology was not published until 1937 (Floyd Ruch, *Psychology and Life* [Glenview, IL: Scott, Foresman, 1937]); it reflected the precursors of the subdisciplines of modern psychology—developmental, personality, social, physiological, learning, perception, abnormal, clinical, and so forth.

13. G. Stanley Hall, *Adolescence: Its Psychology and Its Relations to Physiology, Anthropology, Sociology, Sex, Crime, Religion, and Education*, 2 vols. (New York: D. Appleton, 1904).

14. George A. Coe, *The Psychology of Religion* (Chicago: University of Chicago Press, 1916).

15. James B. Pratt, *The Psychology of Religious Belief* (New York: Macmillan, 1907); id., *The Religious Consciousness* (New York: Macmillan, 1920).

16. Sigmund Freud, *The Future of an Illusion*, trans. J. Strachey (New York: Norton, 1961).

17. Carl G. Jung, *Psychology and Religion* (New Haven: Yale, 1938).

18. James R. Scroggs and William G. T. Douglas, "Issues in the Psychology of Religious Conversion," *Journal of Religion and Health* 6 (1967): 204–216.
19. James E. Dittes, "Psychology of Religion," in *The Handbook of Social Psychology*, Vol. 5, ed. Gardner Lindzey and Elliott Aronson, 2nd ed. (Reading, MA: Addison-Wesley, 1969), 602–659; Paloutzian and Park, "Integrative Themes in the Current Science of the Psychology of Religion."
20. C. Daniel Batson, Patricia Scheonrade, and W. Larry Ventis, *Religion and the Individual: A Social Psychological Perspective* (London: Oxford, 1993).
21. Benjamin Beit-Hallahmi and Baruch Nevo, "'Born again' Jews in Israel: The Dynamics of an Identity Change," *International Journal of Psychology* 22 (1987): 75–81.
22. Marc Galanter, *Cults: Faith, Healing, and Coercion* (New York: Oxford, 1989).
23. William James, *The Varieties of Religious Experience* (New York: New American Library, 1958).
24. Raymond F. Paloutzian, "Purpose in Life and Value Changes following Conversion," *Journal of Personality and Social Psychology* 41 (1981): 1153–1160.
25. Chana Ullman, "Cognitive and Emotional Antecedents of Religious Conversion," *Journal of Personality and Social Psychology* 43 (1982): 183–192; id., *The Transformed Self: The Psychology of Religious Conversion* (New York: Plenum, 1989).
26. Edwin D. Starbuck, *The Psychology of Religion* (London: Walter Scott, 1899).
27. Pehr Granqvist, and Lee A. Kirkpatrick, "Religious Conversion and Perceived Childhood Attachment: A Meta-Analysis," *International Journal for the Psychology of Religion* 14 (2004): 223–250; Lee A. Kirkpatrick, *Attachment, Evolution, and the Psychology of Religion* (New York: Guilford, 2005).
28. Benjamin Beit-Hallahmi, *Prolegomena to the Psychological Study of Religion* (Lewisburg, PA: Bucknell University Press, 1989); Paloutzian, "Religious Conversion and Spiritual Transformation"; Paloutzian, Richardson, and Rambo, "Religious Conversion and Personality Change."
29. Geoffrey E. W. Scobie, *Psychology of Religion* (New York: Halsted/Wiley, 1975).
30. Rambo, *Understanding Religious Conversion.*
31. Richardson, "The Active vs. Passive Convert."
32. William R. Miller and Janet C'deBaca, "Quantum Change: Toward a Psychology of Transformation," in *Can Personality Change?* ed. Todd F. Heatherton and Joel L. Weinberger (Washington, DC: American Psychological Association. 1994), 253–280.
33. Peter Halama and Mária Lačná, "Personality Change Following Religious Conversion: Perceptions of Converts and their Close Acquaintances," *Mental Health, Religion & Culture* 14 (2011): 757–768.
34. Brian J. Zinnbauer and Kenneth I. Pargament, "Spiritual Conversion: A Study of Religious Change among College Students," *Journal for the Scientific Study of Religion* 37 (1998): 161–180.
35. Park, "Religion and Meaning"; Park and Folkman "Meaning in the Context of Stress and Coping"; Silberman, "Religion as a Meaning-System."
36. Emmons and Paloutzian, "The Psychology of Religion." The multilevel interdisciplinary paradigm is an idea that promotes research that connects the various levels of analysis within psychology (e.g., from the molecular neuropsychological level to the molar social psychological level) and facilitates research that cross-fertilizes psychological research with that in surrounding disciplines. See Paloutzian, Raymond F. and Crystal L. Park. "Recent Progress and Core Issues in the Science of the Psychology of Religion and Spirituality." In

Handbook of the Psychology of Religion and Spirituality, 2nd ed. Ed. Raymond F. Paloutzian and Crystal L. Park, 3–22. New York: Guilford Press, 2013.

37. Crystal L. Park and Raymond F. Paloutzian, "One Step Toward Integration and an Expansive Future," in *Handbook of the Psychology of Religion and Spirituality*, ed. Raymond F. Paloutzian and Crystal L. Park (New York: Guilford, 2005), 550–564.

38. Kirkpatrick, *Attachment, Evolution, and the Psychology of Religion*.

39. Ann Taves, *Religious Experience Reconsidered: A Building Block Approach to the Study of Religion and Other Special Things* (Princeton: Princeton University Press, 2009).

40. See Roy F. Baumeister, ed., *Psychological Inquiry: An International Journal of Peer Commentary and Review* 12, no. 3 (2002): whole issue; Dittes, "The Psychology of Religion"; and Paloutzian and Park, "Integrative Themes in the Current Science of the Psychology of Religion," for discussions of the uniqueness issue.

41. Bruce Hunsberger, "Empirical Work in the Psychology of Religion," *Canadian Psychology* 32 (1991): 497–504.

42. Adam B. Cohen, "Many Forms of Culture," *American Psychologist* 64 (2009): 194–204.

43. See Raymond F. Paloutzian, "Psychology, Religion, and the Human Sciences," in *Oxford Handbook of Religion and Science*, ed. Philip Clayton (Oxford: Oxford University Press, 2006), 236–252, for a historical and conceptual presentation of the meanings of religious conversion and spirituality; see Brian J. Zinnbauer and Kenneth I. Pargament, "Religiousness and Spirituality," in *Handbook of the Psychology of Religion and Spirituality*, ed. Raymond F. Paloutzian and Crystal L. Park (New York: Guilford, 2005), 21–42, for an analysis of the psychological research on the meaning of these two constructs. See also D. Oman, "Defining Religion and Spirituality, in *Handbook of the Psychology of Religion and Spirituality*, 2nd ed., Ed. Raymond F. Paloutzian and Crystal Park, 23–47.

44. Rambo, *Understanding Religious Conversion*.

45. Taves, *Religious Experience Reconsidered*.

46. Roy F. Baumeister, *Meanings of Life* (New York: The Guilford, 1991); Park, "Religion and Meaning"; Paul T. P. Wong and Prem S. Fry, eds., *The Human Quest for Meaning: A Handbook of Psychological Research and Clinical Applications* (Mahwah, NJ: Erlbaum, 1998); Silberman, "Religion as a Meaning-System."

47. Ralph W. Hood, Jr., "Mystical, Spiritual, and Religious Experiences," in *Handbook of the Psychology of Religion and Spirituality*, ed. Raymond F. Paloutzian and Crystal L. Park (New York: Guilford, 2005), 348–364.

48. Taves, *Religious Experience Reconsidered*.

49. Chris J. Boyatzis, "Religious and Spiritual Development in Childhood," in *Handbook of the Psychology of Religion and Spirituality*, ed. Raymond F. Paloutzian and Crystal L. Park (New York: Guilford, 2005), 123–143; Michael R. Levenson, Carolyn M. Aldwin, and Michelle D'Mello, "Religious Development from Adolescence to Middle Adulthood," in *Handbook of the Psychology of Religion and Spirituality*, ed. Raymond F. Paloutzian and Crystal L. Park (New York: Guilford Press, 2005), 144–161; Susan H. McFadden, "Points of Connection: Gerontology and the Psychology of Religion," in *Handbook of the Psychology of Religion and Spirituality*, ed. Raymond F. Paloutzian and Crystal L. Park (New York: Guilford, 2005), 162–176.

50. Michael J. Donahue and Michael E. Nielsen, "Religion, Attitudes, and Social Behavior," in *Handbook of the Psychology of Religion and Spirituality*, ed. Raymond F. Paloutzian and Crystal L. Park (New York: Guilford, 2005), 274–291; Bernard Spilka, "Religious Practice,

Ritual, and Prayer," in *Handbook of the Psychology of Religion and Spirituality*, ed. Raymond F. Paloutzian and Crystal L. Park (New York: Guilford Press, 2005), 365–377.

51. Andrew B. Newberg and Stephanie K. Newberg, "The Neuropsychology of Religious and Spiritual Experience," in *Handbook of the Psychology of Religion and Spirituality*, ed. Raymond F. Paloutzian and Crystal L. Park (New York: Guilford, 2005), 199–215.

52. Park, "Religion and Meaning."

53. Lisa Miller and Brien S. Kelley, "Relationships of Religiosity and Spirituality with Mental Health and Psychopathology," in *Handbook of the Psychology of Religion and Spirituality*, ed. Raymond F. Paloutzian and Crystal L. Park (New York: Guilford, 2005), 460–478; Doug Oman and Carl E. Thoresen, "Do Religion and Spirituality Influence Health?" in *Handbook of the Psychology of Religion and Spirituality*, ed. Raymond F. Paloutzian and Crystal L. Park (New York: Guilford, 2005), 435–459.

54. Raymond F. Paloutzian and Deborah A. Lowe, "Spiritual Transformation and Engagement in Workplace Culture," in *Psychology of Religion and Workplace Spirituality*, ed. Peter C. Hill and Bryan Dik (Charlotte, NC: Information Age Publishing, forthcoming).

55. Charles Farhadian and Robert A. Emmons, "The Psychology of Forgiveness in the World Religions," in *Forgiveness and Reconciliation: Psychological Pathways for Conflict Transformation and Peace Building*, ed. Ani Kalayjian and Raymond F. Paloutzian (New York: Springer, 2009), 55–70.

56. J. Harold Ellens, ed., *The Destructive Power of Religion: Violence in Judaism, Christianity, and Islam*, Vols. 1–4 (Westport, CT: Praeger, 2004); Israela Silberman, "Religious Violence, Terrorism, and Peace: A Meaning-System Analysis," in *Handbook of the Psychology of Religion and Spirituality*, ed. Raymond F. Paloutzian and Crystal L. Park (New York: Guilford, 2005), 529–549.

57. Park, "Religion and Meaning"; Park and Folkman "Meaning in the Context of Stress and Coping"; Silberman, "Religion as a Meaning-system"; Paloutzian, "Religious Conversion and Spiritual Transformation." See also Paloutzian, Raymond F., S. Murkin, H. Steib, and Sussan Rößler-Namini. "Conversion, Deconversion, and Spiritual Transformation: A Multilevel Interdisciplinary View." In *Handbook of the Psychology of Religion and Spirituality*, 2nd ed. Ed. Raymond F. Paloutzian and Crystal L. Park, 399–421. New York: Guilford Press, 2013.

58. Park and Folkman "Meaning in the Context of Stress and Coping."

59. Paloutzian, "Religious Conversion and Spiritual Transformation." See also Paloutzian, Raymond F., S. Murkin, H. Steib, and Sussan Rößler-Namini. "Conversion, Deconversion, and Spiritual Transformation: A Multilevel Interdisciplinary View." In *Handbook of the Psychology of Religion and Spirituality*, 2nd ed. Ed. Raymond F. Paloutzian and Crystal L. Park, 399–421. New York: Guilford Press, 2013.

60. Jacob A. Belzen, *Towards Cultural Psychology of Religion: Principles, Approaches, and Applications* (New York: Springer, 2009).

61. See note 43.

62. Peter C. Hill, "Spiritual Transformation: Forming the Habitual Center of Personal Energy," *Research in the Social Scientific Study of Religion* 13 (2002): 87–108. See also Paloutzian, Raymond F., S. Murkin, H. Steib, and Sussan Rößler-Namini. "Conversion, Deconversion, and Spiritual Transformation: A Multilevel Interdisciplinary View." In *Handbook of the Psychology of Religion and Spirituality*, 2nd ed. Ed. Raymond F. Paloutzian and Crystal L. Park, 399–421. New York: Guilford Press, 2013.

63. Rambo, *Understanding Religious Conversion*.

64. Heinz Streib et al., *Deconversion: Qualitative and Quantitative Results from Cross-Cultural Research in Germany and the United States*, Research in Contemporary Religion, vol. 4 (Göttingham, Germany: Vandenhoeck & Ruprecht, 2009).

65. See Bruce E. Hunsberger and Bob Altemeyer, *Atheists: A Groundbreaking Study of America's Nonbelievers* (Amherst, NY: Prometheus Books, 2006), for research on changes to atheism, and Streib et al., *Deconversion*, for research on deconversion.

66. Paloutzian, "Religious Conversion and Spiritual Transformation." See also Paloutzian, Raymond F., S. Murkin, H. Steib, and Sussan Rößler-Namini. "Conversion, Deconversion, and Spiritual Transformation: A Multilevel Interdisciplinary View." In *Handbook of the Psychology of Religion and Spirituality*, 2nd ed. Ed. Raymond F. Paloutzian and Crystal L. Park, 399–421. New York: Guilford Press, 2013.

67. Lewis Rambo (personal communication) has also pointed out that "accessibility" is related to the sociology of knowledge. That is, for a time in the history of psychology, colleges and universities were populated by Protestants—not just because they were the dominant part of the population of the United States, but also because many groups (Jews, Blacks, etc.) were systematically excluded from many educational institutions. Also, one could argue that Roman Catholics were in their own enclave—in part because of the prejudice and patterns of exclusion imposed by the White Protestant majority and also because, pre-Vatican II, Roman Catholics had their own parochial school systems and were highly concentrated in ethnic communities in urban areas of the United States. Finally, for much of the history of psychology, research was conducted almost exclusively on undergraduates who were captive audiences in schools that offered psychology courses. In addition, in terms of the psychology of religion, these courses were often very limited in where they were taught—Protestant liberal arts colleges and, in some rare cases, theological seminaries. Needless to say, much of the work was also biased in terms of gender issues.

68. Beit-Hallahmi and Nevo, "'Born Again' Jews in Israel."

69. Ali Köse, "Religious Conversion: Is It an Adolescent Phenomenon? The Case of Native British Converts to Islam," *International Journal for the Psychology of Religion* 6 (1996): 253–262; Ali Köse and Kate Miriam Loewenthal, "Conversion Motifs among British Converts to Islam," *International Journal for the Psychology of Religion* 10 (2000): 101–110.

70. Mounia Lakhdar et al., "Conversion to Islam among French Adolescents and Adults: A Systematic Inventory of Motives," *International Journal for the Psychology of Religion* 17, no. 1 (2007): 1–15.

71. Audrey A. Maslim and Jeffrey P. Bjorck, "Reasons for Conversion to Islam among Women in the United States," *Psychology of Religion and Spirituality* 1, no. 2 (2009): 97–111.

72. Martha J. Bockian, David S. Glenwick, and David P. Bernstein, "The Applicability of the Stages of Change Model to Jewish Conversion," *International Journal for the Psychology of Religion* 15 (2005): 35–50.

73. Ines W. Jindra, "Religious Stage Development among Converts to Different Religious Groups," *International Journal for the Psychology of Religion* 18 (2008): 195–215.

74. Hunsberger and Altemeyer, *Atheists*.

75. Streib et al., *Deconversion*.

76. Sebastian Murken and Sussan Namini, "Childhood Familial Experiences as Antecedents of Adult Membership in New Religious Movements: A Literature Review," *Nova Religio* 10 (2007): 17–37; Sussan Namini and Sebastian Murken, "Familial Antecedents and the Choice of a New Religious Movement: Which Person in Which Religious Group?" *Nova*

Religio 11 (2008): 83–103; Sussan Namini et al., "How is Well-being Related to Membership in New Religious Movements? An Application of Person-Environment Fit Theory," *Applied Psychology: An International Review* (forthcoming); Sussan Namini and Sebastian Murken, "Self-chosen Involvement in New Religious Movements (NRMs): Well-being and Mental Health from a Longitudinal Perspective," *Mental Health, Religion & Culture* (forthcoming).

77. Jindra, "Religious Stage Development among Converts to Different Religious Groups."
78. Streib et al., *Deconversion.*
79. Newberg and Newberg, "The Neuropsychology of Religious and Spiritual Experience."
80. Bulkeley, this volume; Raymond F. Paloutzian, Erica L. Swenson, and Patrick McNamara, "Religious Conversion, Spiritual Transformation, and the Neurocognition of Meaning Making," in *The Neurology of Religious Experience*, ed. Patrick McNamara (Stamford, CT: Praeger, 2006), 151–169.
81. Crystal L. Park and Patrick McNamara, "Religion, Meaning, and the Brain," in *Where God and Science Meet: How Brain and Evolutionary Studies Alter Our Understanding of Religion*, ed. Patrick McNamara, The Psychology of Religious Experience, vol. 3 (Westport, CT: Praeger, 2006), 67–89.
82. Rambo, *Understanding Religious Conversion.*
83. Park, "Religion and Meaning."
84. Jozef Corveleyn and Patrick Luyten, "Psychodynamic Psychologies and Religion: Past, Present, and Future," in *Handbook of the Psychology of Religion and Spirituality*, ed. Raymond F. Paloutzian and Crystal L. Park (New York: Guilford, 2005), 80–100; Hood and Belzen, "Research Methods in the Psychology of Religion."
85. Taves, *Religious Experience Reconsidered.*
86. Paloutzian, "Psychology, Religion, and the Human Sciences."

FURTHER READING

Granqvist, Pehr, and Lee A. Kirkpatrick. "Religious Conversion and Perceived Childhood Attachment: A Meta-analysis." *International Journal for the Psychology of Religion*, 14 (2004): 223–250.

James, William. *The Varieties of Religious Experience.* New York: New American Library, 1958. This is a classic, full of first-person accounts of intense religious and spiritual experiences, and has been in print without interruption since it was first published in 1902.

Paloutzian, Raymond F. "Religious Conversion and Spiritual Transformation: A Meaning-System Analysis." In *Handbook of the Psychology of Religion and Spirituality*, ed. Raymond F. Paloutzian and Crystal L. Park, 331–347. New York: Guilford Press, 2005. This chapter integrates the research on conversion within the meaning system model.

Paloutzian, Raymond F., James T. Richardson, and Lewis R. Rambo. "Religious Conversion and Personality Change." *Journal of Personality*, 67 (1999): 1047–1079. This review focuses on the question, "Does religious conversion cause a change in personality?" with findings that answer it at the levels of basic traits, mid-level goals and strivings, and self-identity and worldview.

Rambo, Lewis R. *Understanding Religious Conversion.* New Haven: Yale University Press, 1993. This book presents a comprehensive, descriptive stage model of conversion

comprised of myriad facets of the process—personal, contextual, background, circumstantial, and chance.

Streib, Heinz, Ralph W. Hood, Jr., Barbara Keller, Rosina-Martha Csöff, and Christopher
F. Silver. *Deconversion: Qualitative and Quantitative Results from Cross-Cultural Research
in Germany and the United States.* Research in Contemporary Religion, vol. 4. Göttingham,
Germany: Vandenhoeck & Ruprecht, 2009. This is the first comprehensive, cross-cultural
empirical study of deconversion; especially important, it combines qualitative and quantitative research methods.

Bibliography

Batson, C. Daniel, Patricia Scheonrade, and W. Larry Ventis. *Religion and the Individual: A Social
Psychological Perspective.* London: Oxford, 1993.

Baumeister, Roy F. *Meanings of Life.* New York: The Guilford, 1991.

Baumeister, Roy F., ed. *Psychological Inquiry: An International Journal of Peer Commentary and
Review* 12, no. 3 (2002): whole issue.

Beit-Hallahmi, Benjamin. *Prolegomena to the Psychological Study of Religion.* Lewisburg,
PA: Bucknell University Press, 1989.

Beit-Hallahmi, Benjamin, and Michael Argyle. *The Psychology of Religious Behaviour, Belief,
and Experience.* London: Routledge, 1997.

Beit-Hallahmi, Benjamin, and Baruch Nevo. "'Born again' Jews in Israel: The Dynamics of an
Identity Change." *International Journal of Psychology* 22 (1987): 75–81.

Belzen, Jacob A. *Towards Cultural Psychology of Religion: Principles, Approaches, and
Applications.* New York: Springer, 2009.

Bockian, Martha J., David S. Glenwick, and David P. Bernstein. "The Applicability of the Stages
of Change Model to Jewish Conversion." *International Journal for the Psychology of Religion*
15 (2005): 35–50.

Boyatzis, Chris J. "Religious and Spiritual Development in Childhood." In *Handbook of the
Psychology of Religion and Spirituality*, ed. Raymond F. Paloutzian and Crystal L. Park, 123–
143. New York: Guilford, 2005.

Brandt, Pierre-Yves, and Claude-Alexandre Fournier, eds. *La Conversion religieuse: Analyses
psychologiques, anthropologiques et sociologiques.* Geneva: Labor et Fides, 2009.

Coe, George A. *The Psychology of Religion.* Chicago: University of Chicago Press, 1916.

Cohen, Adam B. "Many Forms of Culture." *American Psychologist* 64 (2009): 194–204.

Corveleyn, Jozef, and Patrick Luyten. "Psychodynamic Psychologies and Religion: Past, Present,
and Future." In *Handbook of the Psychology of Religion and Spirituality*, ed. Raymond F.
Paloutzian and Crystal L. Park, 80–100. New York: Guilford, 2005.

Dittes, James E. "Psychology of Religion." In *The Handbook of Social Psychology*, Vol. 5, ed.
Gardner Lindzey and Elliott Aronson, 602–659. 2nd ed. Reading, MA: Addison-Wesley, 1969.

Donahue, Michael J., and Michael E. Nielsen. "Religion, Attitudes, and Social Behavior." In
Handbook of the Psychology of Religion and Spirituality, ed. Raymond F. Paloutzian and
Crystal L. Park, 274–291. New York: Guilford, 2005.

Ellens, J. Harold, ed. *The Destructive Power of Religion: Violence in Judaism, Christianity, and
Islam.* Vols. 1–4. Westport, CT: Praeger, 2004.

Emmons, Robert A., and Raymond F. Paloutzian. "The Psychology of Religion." *Annual Review
of Psychology* 54 (2003): 377–402.

Farhadian, Charles, and Robert A. Emmons. "The Psychology of Forgiveness in the World Religions." In *Forgiveness and Reconciliation: Psychological Pathways for Conflict Transformation and Peace Building*, ed. Ani Kalayjian and Raymond F. Paloutzian, 55–70. New York: Springer, 2009.

Freud, Sigmund. *The Future of an Illusion*. Trans. J. Strachey. New York: Norton, 1961.

Galanter, Marc. *Cults: Faith, Healing, and Coercion*. New York: Oxford, 1989.

Granqvist, Pehr, and Lee A. Kirkpatrick. "Religious Conversion and Perceived Childhood Attachment: A Meta-Analysis." *International Journal for the Psychology of Religion* 14 (2004): 223–250.

Halama, Peter, and Mária Lačná. "Personality Change Following Religious Conversion: Perceptions of Converts and their Close Acquaintances." *Mental Health, Religion & Culture* 14 (2011): 757–768.

Hall, G. Stanley. *Adolescence: Its Psychology and Its Relations to Physiology, Anthropology, Sociology, Sex, Crime, Religion, and Education*. 2 vols. New York: D. Appleton, 1904.

Hill, Peter C. "Spiritual Transformation: Forming the Habitual Center of Personal Energy." *Research in the Social Scientific Study of Religion* 13 (2002): 87–108.

Hood, Ralph W., Jr. "Mystical, Spiritual, and Religious Experiences." In *Handbook of the Psychology of Religion and Spirituality*, ed. Raymond F. Paloutzian and Crystal L. Park, 348–364. New York: Guilford, 2005.

Hood, Ralph W., Jr., and Jacob A. Belzen. "Research Methods in the Psychology of Religion." In *Handbook of the Psychology of Religion and Spirituality*, ed. Raymond F. Paloutzian and Crystal L. Park, 62–79. New York: Guilford, 2005.

Hood, Ralph W., Jr., Peter C. Hill, and Bernard Spilka. *The Psychology of Religion: An Empirical Approach*. 4th ed. New York: Guilford, 2009.

Hunsberger, Bruce. "Empirical Work in the Psychology of Religion." *Canadian Psychology* 32 (1991): 497–504.

Hunsberger, Bruce E., and Bob Altemeyer. *Atheists: A Groundbreaking Study of America's Nonbelievers*. Amherst, NY: Prometheus Books, 2006.

James, William. *The Varieties of Religious Experience*. New York: New American Library, 1958.

Jindra, Ines W. "Religious Stage Development among Converts to Different Religious Groups." *International Journal for the Psychology of Religion* 18 (2008): 195–215.

Jung, Carl G. *Psychology and Religion*. New Haven: Yale, 1938.

Kirkpatrick, Lee A. *Attachment, Evolution, and the Psychology of Religion*. New York: Guilford, 2005.

Köse, Ali. "Religious Conversion: Is It an Adolescent Phenomenon? The Case of Native British Converts to Islam." *International Journal for the Psychology of Religion* 6 (1996): 253–262.

Köse, Ali, and Kate Miriam Loewenthal. "Conversion Motifs among British Converts to Islam." *International Journal for the Psychology of Religion* 10 (2000): 101–110.

Lakhdar, Mounia, Genevieve Vinsonneau, Michael J. Apter, and Etienne Mullet. "Conversion to Islam among French Adolescents and Adults: A Systematic Inventory of Motives." *International Journal for the Psychology of Religion* 17, no. 1 (2007): 1–15.

Leuba, James H. "A Study in the Psychology of Religious Phenomenon." *American Journal of Psychology* 5 (1896): 309–335.

——. *A Psychological Study of Religion: Its Origin, Function, and Future*. New York: Macmillan, 1912.

Levenson, Michael R., Carolyn M. Aldwin, and Michelle D'Mello. "Religious Development from Adolescence to Middle Adulthood." In *Handbook of the Psychology of Religion and*

Spirituality, ed. Raymond F. Paloutzian and Crystal L. Park, 144–161. New York: Guilford Press, 2005.

Maslim, Audrey A., and Jeffrey P. Bjorck. "Reasons for Conversion to Islam among Women in the United States." *Psychology of Religion and Spirituality* 1, no. 2 (2009): 97–111.

McFadden, Susan H. "Points of Connection: Gerontology and the Psychology of Religion." In *Handbook of the Psychology of Religion and Spirituality*, ed. Raymond F. Paloutzian and Crystal L. Park, 162–176. New York: Guilford, 2005.

Miller, Lisa, and Brien S. Kelley. "Relationships of Religiosity and Spirituality with Mental Health and Psychopathology." In *Handbook of the Psychology of Religion and Spirituality*, ed. Raymond F. Paloutzian and Crystal L. Park, 460–478. New York: Guilford, 2005.

Miller, William R., and Janet C'deBaca. "Quantum Change: Toward a Psychology of Transformation." In *Can Personality Change?* ed. Todd F. Heatherton and Joel L. Weinberger, 253–280. Washington, DC: American Psychological Association. 1994.

Murken, Sebastian, and Sussan Namini. "Childhood Familial Experiences as Antecedents of Adult Membership in New Religious Movements: A Literature Review." *Nova Religio* 10 (2007): 17–37.

Namini, Sussan, and Sebastian Murken. "Familial Antecedents and the Choice of a New Religious Movement: Which Person in Which Religious Group?" *Nova Religio* 11 (2008): 83–103.

Namini, Sussan, and Sebastian Murken. "Self-chosen Involvement in New Religious Movements (NRMs): Well-being and Mental Health from a Longitudinal Perspective." *Mental Health, Religion & Culture* 12 (2009): 561–585.

Namini, Sussan, Claudia Appel, Ralph Jürgensen, and Sebastian Murken. "How is Well-being Related to Membership in New Religious Movements? An Application of Person-Environment Fit Theory." *Applied Psychology: An International Review* 59 (2010): 181–201.

Newberg, Andrew B., and Stephanie K. Newberg. "The Neuropsychology of Religious and Spiritual Experience." In *Handbook of the Psychology of Religion and Spirituality*, ed. Raymond F. Paloutzian and Crystal L. Park, 199–215. New York: Guilford, 2005.

Oman, Doug. "Defining Religion and Spirituality." In *Handbook of the Psychology of Religion and Spirituality*, 2nd ed. Ed. Raymond F. Paloutzian and Crystal L. Park, 23–47. New York: Guilford, 2013.

Oman, Doug, and Carl E. Thoresen. "Do Religion and Spirituality Influence Health?" In *Handbook of the Psychology of Religion and Spirituality*, ed. Raymond F. Paloutzian and Crystal L. Park, 435–459. New York: Guilford, 2005.

Paloutzian, Raymond F. *Invitation to the Psychology of Religion*. 2nd ed. Boston: Allyn & Bacon, 1996.

——. "Psychology, Religion, and the Human Sciences." In *Oxford Handbook of Religion and Science*, ed. Philip Clayton, 236–252. Oxford: Oxford, 2006.

——. "Purpose in Life and Value Changes following Conversion." *Journal of Personality and Social Psychology* 41 (1981): 1153–1160.

——. "Religious Conversion and Spiritual Transformation: A Meaning-System Analysis." In *Handbook of the Psychology of Religion and Spirituality*, ed. Raymond F. Paloutzian and Crystal L. Park, 331–347. New York: Guilford Press, 2005.

Paloutzian, Raymond F., and Deborah A. Lowe. "Spiritual Transformation and Engagement in Workplace Culture." In *Psychology of Religion and Workplace Spirituality*, ed. Peter C. Hill and Bryan Dik, 179–199. Charlotte, NC: Information Age Publishing, 2012).

Paloutzian, Raymond F., and Crystal L. Park. "Integrative Themes in the Current Science of the Psychology of Religion." In *Handbook of the Psychology of Religion and Spirituality*, ed. Raymond F. Paloutzian and Crystal L. Park, 3–20. New York: Guilford, 2005.

——. "Recent Progress and Core Issues in the Science of the Psychology of Religion and Spirituality." In *Handbook of the Psychology of Religion and Spirituality*, 2nd ed. Ed. Raymond F. Paloutzian and Crystal L. Park, 3–22. New York: Guilford Press, 2013.

Paloutzian, Raymond F., James T. Richardson, and Lewis R. Rambo. "Religious Conversion and Personality Change." *Journal of Personality* 67 (1999): 1047–1079.

Paloutzian, Raymond F., Erica L. Swenson, and Patrick McNamara. "Religious Conversion, Spiritual Transformation, and the Neurocognition of Meaning Making." In *The Neurology of Religious Experience*, ed. Patrick McNamara, 151–169. Stamford, CT: Praeger, 2006.

Paloutzian, Raymond F., S. Murkin, H. Steib, and Sussan Rößler-Namini. "Conversion, Deconversion, and Spiritual Transformation: A Multilevel Interdisciplinary View." In *Handbook of the Psychology of Religion and Spirituality*, 2nd ed. Ed. Raymond F. Paloutzian and Crystal L. Park, 399–421. New York: Guilford Press, 2013.

Park, Crystal L. "Religion and Meaning." In *Handbook of the Psychology of Religion and Spirituality*, ed. Raymond F. Paloutzian and Crystal L. Park, 295–314. New York: Guilford Press, 2005.

Park, Crystal L,. and Susan Folkman. "Meaning in the Context of Stress and Coping." *Review of General Psychology* 1 (1997): 115–144.

Park, Crystal L., and Patrick McNamara. "Religion, Meaning, and the Brain." In *Where God and Science Meet: How Brain and Evolutionary Studies Alter Our Understanding of Religion*, ed. Patrick McNamara, 67–89. The Psychology of Religious Experience, vol. 3. Westport, CT: Praeger, 2006.

Park, Crystal L., and Raymond F. Paloutzian. "One Step Toward Integration and an Expansive Future." In *Handbook of the Psychology of Religion and Spirituality*, ed. Raymond F. Paloutzian and Crystal L. Park, 550–564. New York: Guilford, 2005.

Pirutinsky, Steven. "Conversion and Attachment Insecurity among Orthodox Jews." *International Journal for the Psychology of Religion* 19 (2009): 200–206.

Pratt, James B. *The Psychology of Religious Belief*. New York: Macmillan, 1907.

——. *The Religious Consciousness*. New York: Macmillan, 1920.

Rambo, Lewis R. *Understanding Religious Conversion*. New Haven: Yale, 1993.

Richardson, James T. "The Active vs. Passive Convert: Paradigm Conflict in Conversion/ Recruitment Research." *Journal for the Scientific Study of Religion* 24 (1985): 119–236.

Ruch, Floyd. *Psychology and Life*. Glenview, IL: Scott, Foresman, 1937.

Scobie, Geoffrey E. W. *Psychology of Religion*. New York: Halsted/Wiley, 1975.

Scroggs, James R., and William G. T. Douglas. "Issues in the Psychology of Religious Conversion." *Journal of Religion and Health* 6 (1967): 204–216.

Silberman, Israela. "Religion as a Meaning-System: Implications for the New Millennium." *Journal of Social Issues* 61 (2005): 641–664.

——. "Religious Violence, Terrorism, and Peace: A Meaning-System Analysis." In *Handbook of the Psychology of Religion and Spirituality*, ed. Raymond F. Paloutzian and Crystal L. Park, 529–549. New York: Guilford, 2005.

Spilka, Bernard. "Religious Practice, Ritual, and Prayer." In *Handbook of the Psychology of Religion and Spirituality*, ed. Raymond F. Paloutzian and Crystal L. Park, 365–377. New York: Guilford Press, 2005.

Starbuck, Edwin D. *The Psychology of Religion*. London: Walter Scott, 1899.

———. "A Study of Conversion." *American Journal of Psychology* 8 (1897): 268–308.

Streib, Heinz, Ralph W. Hood, Jr., Barbara Keller, Rosina-Martha Csöff, and Christopher F. Silver. *Deconversion: Qualitative and Quantitative Results from Cross-Cultural Research in Germany and the United States. Research in Contemporary Religion*, vol. 4. Göttingham, Germany: Vandenhoeck & Ruprecht, 2009.

Taves, Ann. *Religious Experience Reconsidered: A Building Block Approach to the Study of Religion and Other Special Things*. Princeton: Princeton University Press, 2009.

Ullman, Chana. "Cognitive and Emotional Antecedents of Religious Conversion." *Journal of Personality and Social Psychology* 43 (1982): 183–192.

———. *The Transformed Self: The Psychology of Religious Conversion*. New York: Plenum, 1989.

Wong, Paul T. P., and Prem S. Fry, eds. *The Human Quest for Meaning: A Handbook of Psychological Research and Clinical Applications*. Mahwah, NJ: Erlbaum, 1998.

Zinnbauer, Brian J., and Kenneth I. Pargament. "Religiousness and Spirituality." In *Handbook of the Psychology of Religion and Spirituality*, ed. Raymond F. Paloutzian and Crystal L. Park, 21–42. New York: Guilford, 2005.

———. "Spiritual Conversion: A Study of Religious Change among College Students." *Journal for the Scientific Study of Religion* 37 (1998): 161–180.

CHAPTER 10

....

RELIGIOUS CONVERSION AND COGNITIVE NEUROSCIENCE

....

KELLY BULKELEY

INTRODUCTION

....

RECENT advances in the neuroscientific study of brain/mind functioning have stimulated fresh thinking and vigorous debate on a wide range of topics, from ethics and gender to child-rearing and religion.[1] Thanks to powerful new technologies and increased
funding from governmental and commercial sources, we now know far more about the
workings of the human brain/mind system than ever before. Much of the research to
date has focused on finding a cure for degenerative brain conditions like Alzheimer's and
Parkinson's diseases. Less attention has been given to the neuroscientific dimensions of
psychospiritual phenomena like religion. Unfortunately for the present purposes, we
have no neuroscientific research directly addressing the topic of this handbook, namely,
religious conversion. As a result, this chapter will necessarily adopt a constructive and
forward-looking approach. Rather than analyzing previous studies (which do not exist),
I will survey the current state of cognitive neuroscience for areas of ongoing research
that relate to important aspects of conversion processes. Even though few neuroscientists recognize it, their work has genuine significance for the study of transformative
religious experiences. This chapter aims to map out the most likely future paths that
researchers will follow in seeking a better understanding of how changes in brain/mind
functioning correlate with changes in a person's religious and/or spiritual orientation.

The chapter starts with a section devoted to the philosophical, conceptual, and methodological issues that confront anyone wanting to explore the relationship between
religion and neuroscience. Leading researchers take varying stances on these issues,
and I will briefly present the main arguments related to each question and highlight
their pragmatic consequences. The second section describes several topics of active

neuroscientific research with relevance to conversion, including recent investigations into brain development, neuroplasticity, visual processing, and meditation. Although my own views will become obvious, readers will hopefully find enough information here to pursue their own exploration of the various topics. The conclusion to the chapter will push the discussion one step further than is usually taken. After reflecting on the neuroscience of religious conversion, neuroscience is considered as a tool for converting people to, or away from, religion.

PRINCIPLES AND PRACTICES

Definitions of Religious Conversion and Cognitive Neuroscience

Like most of the contributors to this handbook, my understanding of religious conversion has been guided by the work of Lewis Rambo. While acknowledging earlier researchers like William James and G. Stanley Hall, who focused on dramatic, singular experiences, Rambo has argued for more attention to the long-term psychological and sociological processes at work in both sudden and gradual cases of conversion.[2] This chapter follows Rambo, along with James and Hall, in seeking a theoretical integration of the multiple factors of brain/mind functioning, personal circumstance, cultural context, and theological history that come together in any given conversion experience.

"Religion," as I will use the term, is an imperfect but useful shorthand for an awareness of powers that transcend human control or understanding and yet have a formative influence on, and active presence within, human life. Most cultural traditions represent these trans-human powers in the form of gods, spirits, ancestors, mythic beings, and forces of nature. Religions tend to venerate certain places, objects, and/or texts because of their capacity to bring people closer to these powers, and special practices (e.g., pilgrimage, sacrifice, dance, music, prayer, meditation) are performed to enhance their beneficent influence on people's lives. Although human existence may be filled with pain and misfortune, religions teach various methods for overcoming that suffering, either in this life or in another one to come, by means of harmonizing one's thoughts, feelings, and behavior with transcendent forces. One important way that religions achieve this is by creating and sustaining a personal sense of connection to a community. Religious traditions have developed a variety of systems to bind (*religare*) people together over the span of multiple generations, preserving ancestral wisdom and preparing the group for future challenges and opportunities. I use the term "spirituality" as a general synonym for religion, with the added connotation of emphasizing the personal experiential qualities shared by religious traditions and nonreligious philosophies of life.

"Cognitive neuroscience" (hereinafter CN) is a broad term that includes many different disciplines devoted to the study of the human brain/mind system. The core of CN is the neural functioning of the brain and its relationship with the conscious experience of the mind. Technological improvements in imaging tools such as positron emission tomography (PET), functional magnetic resonance imaging (fMRI), and single positron emission computed tomography (SPECT) have enabled a more precise mapping of the activation levels of various regions of the brain during many different mental states. The imaging research has combined with several other methods of investigation, all of which come under the general heading of cognitive neuroscience: EEG studies of the electrophysiological features of brain activities;[3] chemical analyses of the dozens of neurotransmitters flowing through the brain and influencing synaptic efficiency;[4] anatomical studies of the cognitive losses resulting from damage or disease to the brain;[5] experiments on the neural systems of other animals;[6] genetic inquiry into the heritable features of brain/mind development;[7] and computer-based efforts to create systems of artificial intelligence.[8] In addition to these disciplines, CN also draws upon philosophy, anthropology, and linguistics insofar as these fields also provide resources for understanding the nature and functioning of the mind.

Reading the Cognitive Neuroscience Literature

Religious studies scholars who take an interest in CN are immediately confronted by a vast and constantly expanding technical literature. Although this may seem discouraging, it actually teaches an important lesson: there is no monolithic consensus among CN researchers on how the brain/mind system works. Instead, there are many competing theories trying to account for as much of the increasingly voluminous research data as possible. The rapid pace of new discoveries has made it difficult if not impossible for any single model to establish theoretical supremacy. What is taken as an adequate explanation today will likely be superseded by new evidence and better models tomorrow. For this reason, those who want to explore the relevance of CN to religious conversion need to remain open to the continuous unfolding of brain/mind research (rather than fixing on one theory alone), following the developments in specific areas over time and taking multiple theoretical perspectives into account. The most successful investigations will be those that focus on carefully circumscribed phenomena with clear points of convergence with CN; overly broad approaches are always vulnerable to refutation by more specialized forms of research. A prior familiarity with major twentieth-century figures in the psychology of religion (e.g., James, Freud, Jung) will be helpful, since they anticipated many of the key areas of interest in CN and foresaw many of the possible paths toward integrated understanding. Religious studies scholars are further advised to read secondary-source CN summaries with caution, as useful guides to the research literature but not as definitive statements of a putative CN consensus. When in doubt, go to the primary sources.

The basic methodological approach I am describing is analogous to learning a new language. With enough time and effort, a degree of fluency and dialogical competence may be achieved, giving "outside" researchers the ability to understand and form judgments about the significance of CN research, at least as it relates to their home fields of study.

The Mind/Body Problem

Much of the excitement and controversy surrounding CN stems from its relevance to the mind/body problem in the Western philosophical tradition. As Kandel et al. put it, "We are dealing here with biology's deepest riddle: the neural representation of consciousness and self-awareness."[9] The most extreme arguments present CN as the final solution to this problem: the mind is nothing but the physical properties of brain functioning.[10] Others see the mind and the brain as mutually interdependent in ways that are not adequately explained by a strictly reductionistic materialism.[11] Closely related to this philosophical debate is the question of determinism vs. free will, with CN evidence used by some researchers to argue that free will is an illusion and our mental lives are more predetermined than we consciously realize. Other researchers point to the dynamic complexity and creative freedom of the human brain/mind system as incompatible with a strongly deterministic view. Scholars in religious studies (henceforth RS) should be aware of the extent to which the philosophical convictions of CN researchers shape the significance they and others draw from their findings. To be clear, this is not a recommendation to read only those texts that seem "friendly" to one's personal views or to avoid research that takes a critical line against religion. Although I favor a more interactive and pluralist response to these questions, the mind-to-brain reductionist approach has many intelligent and eloquent advocates, and their research data are almost always valuable, even if one may question their interpretations of those data. The point here is for readers to recognize the practical consequences of using different philosophical perspectives to evaluate the meaning and relevance of CN research and to factor those consequences into the analysis of past studies and the planning of future investigations.

Conceptual Polarities and Methodological Challenges in Cognitive Neuroscience

In studying the neuroscientific dimensions of conversion, readers should also strive to clarify where CN researchers stand on some important conceptual and methodological questions. The choices they make about how to answer these questions directly influence the production of their research findings and their subsequent theoretical extrapolations from those data. Below is a brief list of some of the issues that RS readers should keep in mind as they explore the CN literature.

Modularity or holism. Is the mind best characterized as a "Swiss army knife" of specialized cognitive tools? A great deal of scientific progress has been made using the modular approach.[12] However, some researchers see this perspective as too limited in its explanations of the psychological complexity of conscious life.[13] The question then becomes: if not a modular approach, then what is a better way to account for the global, synthetic, whole-is-greater-than-the-sum-of-its-parts functioning of the brain?

The limits of brain imaging. Since imaging technologies can only be applied to a fairly narrow range of human activities (typically those that can be performed while sitting still in a controlled laboratory context), how far can we generalize from the findings in this area of research? Future technological advances will surely expand the list of what can be studied via brain scans, but questions will still remain concerning which kinds of human experiences cannot be replicated in a lab setting and what limitations are consequently imposed on general psychological theories based only or primarily on brain scans.

The value of introspection. Is it legitimate to use first-person reports of inner psychological experience as CN evidence? Some researchers say no, rejecting introspection as inherently unreliable and unverifiable. Other researchers take the opposite stance and argue that it is not scientifically legitimate to ignore first-person reports when trying to understand the nature of the mind.[14] A pragmatic compromise is to acknowledge the innate subjectivity of introspection and yet still generate valid empirical insights by using systematic methods of identifying the consistent themes and recurrent patterns across numerous reports from multiple research participants.

Newtonian or quantum physics. Can brain/mind processes be comprehensively explained in terms of Newtonian physics, or do the insights of quantum physics need to be included? One line of CN thought says that whatever subatomic phenomena may be at work in the brain, they are washed out by its ordinary Newtonian physical functioning, with no significant impact on the macro-processes of the mind. An alternative approach insists that quantum phenomena and other probabilistic, nonlinear processes do indeed influence neural activities, which means that CN cannot explain the workings of the brain with Newtonian concepts alone.[15] Most CN research today proceeds in general disregard of this question, but that is likely to change with future discoveries in the still-young science of quantum physics.

Conceptual Polarities and Methodological Challenges in Religious Studies

A growing number of researchers in RS have used recent findings in brain/mind science to study various aspects of religious belief and practice. Like their CN counterparts, these RS researchers have also made choices about their conceptual frameworks and methods of inquiry that impact their findings. For someone wanting to study religious conversion, just as much critical scrutiny should be given to the RS sources as to the CN literature. Here are a few of the issues to keep in mind:

Sui generis or ascriptive models of religion. Is there anything irreducibly distinctive about religious life, or can all its features and qualities be explained in terms of other causal factors (e.g., psychological, sociological, historical)? Mircea Eliade is regularly taken as the strongest representative of the former approach, while Karl Marx and Émile Durkheim were early practitioners of the latter. Many RS scholars today reject the mystifying effects of sui generis models and argue that the best connections to CN depend on using an "ascriptive" approach by which religious concepts are explained in relation to ordinary cognitive processes.[16] Others in the RS field question the sufficiency of ascriptive explanations that fail to account for the dynamic and creative qualities of religious phenomena like mysticism, prophecy, and other altered states of consciousness.[17] This is a major divide in the discipline, which is best summed up as a battle of prepositions: the ascriptive model seeks to be a scientific study of religion, while the latter-day sui generis advocates want to study science and religion.

Universalism or pluralism. Is there a core truth or set of truths held by every religion? Phrased in more individual terms, does every religious experience point to the same perennial truth? Or are different religious traditions and experiences genuinely different, leading humans in a variety of developmentally and spiritually unique directions? A person's answer to these questions very likely goes to the heart of his or her ultimate worldview and should be respected as such. But in terms of practical scholarly consequences, a provisional pluralism seems to be the wisest course to follow, since it avoids explanatory overreach and promotes an open view to the appearance of new data.

Insider or outsider perspectives. Can a person who does not have personal familiarity with a religious tradition ever be able to give an accurate description of its essential nature? Alternatively, can a religious insider ever take a truly objective perspective on his or her faith tradition? Both sides of this methodological polarity have strong arguments. In practical research terms, however, there must be at least some acknowledgment of the validity of outsider, third-person perspectives if CN is to have a viable role in religious studies.

Ordinary or extraordinary experiences. Should the study of religion focus on the ordinary features of daily human existence, or should special attention be given to extraordinary experiences that occur relatively rarely but have a significant impact on people's religious lives? Pascal Boyer has argued for the "ordinary" approach, as did Sigmund Freud many years ago in *Civilization and its Discontents.*[18] William James's *The Varieties of Religious Experience* is the best example of the "extraordinary" approach. In principle, there is no reason to exclude either method. Nevertheless, a tendency toward the former in RS is a natural consequence of the fact that more CN research is available on the analysis of "ordinary" brain/mind functioning. Much less data is available on the kinds of extraordinary religious experiences studied by James and others, though that will probably change as new research technologies become more widely used.

TOPICS OF ONGOING RESEARCH

Introduction and Limitations

In this section, the CN literature will be surveyed through the specific and admittedly narrow lens of the study of religious conversion. This will not be a survey of brain/mind science in general; good sources for that purpose are listed in the bibliography. Rather, I will concentrate on those areas of current CN research that relate most closely to the psychospiritual dynamics of religious conversion. These topics offer some excellent opportunities for interdisciplinary research between RS and CN. Whatever answers you gave to the philosophical and methodological questions in the preceding section, you will likely find a great deal of highly relevant data in these brain/mind research areas. The space limitations of this chapter mean the descriptions will try to convey as much information as possible in quite brief terms, so readers are encouraged to investigate the sources listed below for more detailed accounts.

BRAIN DEVELOPMENT

The past several decades of research on brain development has shown very clearly the evolutionary roots of human consciousness in the mammalian central nervous system. The human species occupies a "cognitive niche" in the global environment in that our unusually large and densely interconnected cerebral cortexes have given us an advantage over other species by expanding our capacities for memory, learning, forethought, and social communication. Through a process called *neurogenesis,* the brain of a human fetus grows a total of approximately 200 billion neurons while still in the womb. These neurons are then "pruned" back by spontaneous bursts of internal brain activation so that about half the original number forms the synaptic circuits the child has at birth, while the other 100 billion or so neurons are not used and simply die off.

The significance of this line of research for conversion appears when CN looks for evidence of neurogenesis occurring after birth. It turns out there is another major burst of new neural growth in adolescence, an especially common time of life for religious conversion, as RS researchers from G. Stanley Hall onward have shown.[19] According to Schwartz and Begley, "the teen brain, it seems, reprises one of the most momentous acts of infancy, the overproduction and then pruning of neuronal branches."[20] Even more intriguingly, the surge in neurogenesis during adolescence seems to take place with special intensity in the frontal and parietal lobes of the brain. The frontal lobe is generally associated with the "executive functions" of the mind, including self-control, judgment, and emotional regulation, while the parietal lobe is involved in the coordination of different streams of perceptual information. These are relatively "high-level" cognitive processes whose emergence in the adolescent brain goes a long way toward shaping the mature mental life of the individual. The pruning and reorganization of these new neural outgrowths is different from what occurs during pre-natal development, since the fetus receives very limited stimulation from outside the womb. Adolescents, by contrast, are typically immersed in complex social worlds where they are continually influenced by external factors such as families, friends, neighbors, cultural symbols, and religious traditions. Although there is no research directly on this point, a plausible and empirically testable hypothesis would be that religious traditions provide cognitive templates for reorganizing the mind during adolescent neurogenesis. The religious teachings that become the governing principles of a new convert's life focus on the regulation of precisely those psychological functions of self-control and information management that CN has associated with the frontal and parietal lobes. Conversion, in this view, would be an especially dramatic pruning of adolescent neurogenesis into a framework provided by the newly adopted religion.

Another important factor in brain development, *plasticity*, has direct relevance for conversion studies. Genetic programming plays a big role in the cerebral localization of many important neural systems, but genes do not specify the exact wiring of every neural circuit. Much of the brain's actual growth and functioning depend on its always unpredictable interactions with the environment (both social and natural), and for that reason the brain of a newborn human retains a tremendous capacity for structural change and flexible adaptation. For example, children who are born with severe deficiencies in the left hemisphere of their brains, where language abilities are usually centered, are somehow able to shift the neural underpinnings of their language abilities to their brains' right hemispheres. This kind of radical plasticity was once thought to be limited to early childhood, with neural circuits fixed immutably in place once adulthood was reached. Recent research has shown, however, that a considerable degree of plasticity is also evident in the adult brain. Azari and Seitz looked at stroke patients who had suffered damage to their primary motor cortex, with severe paralysis to one hand.[21] Four weeks after the stroke, they had recovered most of their hand functioning, and PET scans showed that their brains had developed a compensatory neural pathway from "higher" centers of the brain to the spinal cord, allowing for the reestablishment of volitional control of the hand. No one yet knows how far the brain's plasticity extends, but Azari and Seitz also found that in other stroke cases the individual's brains engaged in "cross-modal" plasticity, in which neural resources from one system (e.g., visual) were recruited to compensate for damage in an entirely different system (e.g., motor).

The general import of this research is to underscore the dynamic malleability of the brain, a point that provides a new opportunity for the study of religious conversion. The phenomenon of conversion is predicated on the capacity of humans to change the way they perceive and experience the world. According to CN research on neuroplasticity, a fundamental capacity for change remains with us throughout our lives and extends across many areas of brain/mind functioning.

Not all brains develop and grow in a healthy fashion, however. One particular type of brain dysfunction, temporal lobe epilepsy (TLE), bears an intriguing connection to religious experience. Indeed, TLE has long been of interest to those seeking a brain-based theory of religion.[22] Epilepsy involves varying degrees of neural hyperactivation and physical seizure, sometimes only affecting small cortical regions and other times sweeping across the whole brain. In a surprising number of TLE cases, the affected individuals describe the seizures as profound spiritual experiences and direct communions with the divine. According to Ramachandran and Blakeslee,

> These brief temporal lobe storms can sometimes permanently alter the patient's personality so that even between seizures he is different from other people. No one knows why this happens, but it's as though the repeated electrical bursts inside the patient's brain (the frequent passage of massive volleys of nerve impulses within the limbic system) permanently 'facilitate' certain pathways or may even open new channels, much as water from a storm might pour downhill, opening new rivulets, furrows and passages along the hillside. This process, called kindling, might permanently alter—and sometimes enrich—the patient's inner emotional life.[23]

RS scholars who study conversion are well advised to become familiar with the CN literature on epilepsy and follow its future course as new investigations are pursued and new empirical data generated. How one interprets the phenomenon of epileptic spirituality, whether as proof of the brain-based pathology of religion or as evidence of the mind's capacity for higher consciousness, depends once again on one's philosophical and methodological assumptions. Although a rare disorder like temporal lobe epilepsy should not be taken as a general model for religion, it does provide a valuable window into the neurological dimensions of intense religious experiences, including sudden conversions to a new faith.

Vision and Meditation

The brain/mind processes involved in sensory perception have received extensive attention from CN researchers in recent years. A remarkable amount is now known about visual perception in particular,[24] and we may identify at least two possible implications for the study of religious conversion.

First, the numerous unconscious inferences the brain/mind system makes in transforming sensory input into conscious experience has the unfortunate consequence of producing a species-wide vulnerability to visual illusions and misapprehensions.[25] As magicians and conjurors have long known, we are easily deceived by our automatic assumptions about the reality of things we seem to be seeing. In cases of conversion, where a person's motivation derives to some degree from "visions" of miraculous events or divine beings, CN findings can legitimately be brought to bear to analyze the neural substrate of such unusual and perhaps faulty visual perceptions.

Second, seeing (along with all other forms of perception) turns out to be a constructive process rather than a passive reproduction of external reality. What people see depends fundamentally on what their minds are interested in seeing and what their brains are capable of representing. In this regard, CN finds an unexpected harmony with postmodern philosophy from Nietzsche onward—reality is not a given but is actively created by the human psyche. This insight can and should be investigated further in relation to religious conversions where people undergo a basic reordering of the assumptions and expectations that frame their perceptions of the world. Indeed, in cases where a conversion prompts a dramatic and lasting improvement in mood, energy, and motivation, CN researchers may find new evidence regarding the latent potentials of future brain/mind development.

Furthermore, CN can illuminate the effectiveness of religious practices that either stimulate the visual processing system or try to shut it down. This leads to the topic of meditation, which several CN researchers have investigated.[26] The felicitous fact that meditators and people in prayer are usually sitting still for long periods of time makes them ideal subjects for current-generation brain-scanning technologies. Practitioners of Buddhist, Hindu, and Christian contemplative traditions have participated in these studies, which typically involve the individual meditating in a hospital or university setting while attached to neuroimaging machines and under the supervision of the laboratory staff. Although artificial and questionably relevant to other forms of religious experience, this research paradigm has produced important results that all RS scholars, not just those studying conversion, should take into account.

CN has found that meditation and other contemplative practices alter the brain's functioning in measurable, material, and predictable ways. According to CN, meditation works. Several implications flow from that basic finding. One is that at least some aspects of religion are not generated by pathological brain functioning. Current CN research refutes the idea that religion qua religion stems from faulty brain/mind processes. The best available scientific evidence indicates that people who engage in religiously motivated contemplative practices have normal, healthy brains. Perhaps other forms of religion can be more directly tied to neuropathology, but in the case of meditation and prayer the CN literature supports a pragmatic appreciation of the effectiveness of religious practices in shaping the healthy interaction of brain and mind.

Another important implication regards the variety of changes that meditation and prayer have been shown to make on the brain/mind system. Best known, perhaps, are the findings of Newberg and D'Aquili showing that Buddhist meditators and Franciscan nuns in prayer both showed more activation in the prefrontal cortex, seat of the "executive functions" (responsible for focused attention and protection against distraction, mentioned above) and less activation in the brain regions responsible for sensory perception and bodily orientation (prompting feelings of selflessness and fusion with all of reality). However, that is not the only brain pattern associated with meditation. A different set of findings comes from Hans Lou and colleagues, who used PET scans to study yoga teachers performing the relaxation technique known as yoga nidra. They found increased activation in precisely those brain regions one would predict would be stimulated by this multifaceted type of meditation: the visual cortex in the posterior part of the brain was activated during a period of intense visualization; the brain regions devoted to bodily awareness and control were more active during a reflection on the weight of the limbs; and the prefrontal cortex showed a markedly decreased activation as the "executive" control of the mind yielded to the flow of bodily sensations.

Despite the lack of space to go into these or any other CN studies in more detail, an important point may still be made: different contemplative practices produce different patterns of brain activation. A type of meditation that concentrates on stripping the mind of all external awareness can successfully alter the brain's neural functioning in the bodily orientation area, while a type of meditation that centers on a particular visionary image, symbol, or icon can "light up" the visual processing system in another part of the brain. This may seem obvious, but it runs counter to the universalist claim of Newberg and D'Aquili that CN research is proving that all religious experiences can be explained as approximations on the path toward "absolute unitary being." Some traditions may seek that as their spiritual goal, but others clearly do not, and Newberg and D'Aquili's sweeping conclusions do not square with the multiplicity of CN data (nor with the RS literature on comparative religions). As noted above, a provisional pluralism seems at present to be a better approach for understanding the varieties of contemplative practices.

In light of this, RS scholars studying conversion should be heartened by the prospect of growing CN knowledge about religion's capacity to change the brain/mind system. At the same time, a healthy skepticism is warranted toward overly ambitious, prematurely universalistic theories of how the brain gives rise to religion. As new studies are performed with better technologies on a wider variety of religious and spiritual practitioners, the inadequacy of one-size-fits-all explanatory frameworks will become increasingly apparent.

Conclusion

This chapter has surveyed only a few of the areas where CN research offers useful resources for the study of religious conversion. Many other lines of inquiry and potential connection with CN can and should be considered by RS scholars, including the topics of memory,[27] addiction, social intelligence,[28] empathy, the placebo effect,[29] music,[30] trauma, brainwashing, perceptual binding,[31] wonder,[32] and dreaming.[33] The same conceptual and methodological issues raised in the first section of this chapter apply to these topics as well.

A final word may be said about the contemporary use of CN to convert people to or away from religion. As an example of the former, Tenzin Gyatso, the fourteenth Dalai Lama of Tibetan Buddhism, has shown great enthusiasm for the work of Western neuroscientists, whose results he takes as proof of the effectiveness of core Buddhist teachings.[34] The Dalai Lama clearly regards CN as a valuable ally in persuading people of the truth of his faith, and the growth of Buddhism in North America and Europe testifies to his success. At the same time, several Christian theologians have drawn upon CN to highlight what they believe are the central insights of their faith.[35] In their view, CN provides additional evidence in favor of Christianity's basic understanding of human nature, with helpful implications for pastoral ministry.

On the other end of the spectrum, rationalist scourges of religion like Richard Dawkins use the findings of brain/mind science not simply to explain people's religious faith but to eliminate it, replacing it with a sober trust in science.[36] These "ultra-Darwinian" skeptics employ CN as one of their weapons against religious moral codes and explanations of natural phenomena. Dawkins makes clear his deconversion goal in the preface to *The God Delusion*, where he says, "If this book works as I intend, religious readers who open it will be atheists when they put it down."[37] To judge by the popular reception of Dawkins's writings and those of his comrades-in-arms, the deconverting effect of this approach may be considerable.

So, does CN support religion or refute it? The answer is both and neither. The vast research literature in CN provides data that seem very favorable to religion, along with data that seem very dismissive of religion. If we take into account all the available evidence, we must conclude that neither explanatory approach is adequate. Herein lies the greatest challenge for the future study of religious conversion and brain/mind science: to develop an interdisciplinary, self-reflexive method of integrating multiple sources of CN evidence without being limited by the ideological presuppositions of those who are either "for" or "against" religion.

NOTES

1. Michael S., Gazzaniga, ed., *The Cognitive Neurosciences*, 3rd ed. (Cambridge, MA: MIT Press, 2004); Eric R. Kandel, James H. Schwartz, and Thomas M. Jessel, eds., *Principles of Neural Science*, 4th ed. (New York: McGraw-Hill, 2000); Richard F. Thompson, *The Brain: A Neuroscience Primer* (New York: Worth, 2000).
2. Lewis Rambo, *Understanding Religious Conversion* (New Haven: Yale University Press, 1993).
3. James F. Pagel, *The Limits of Dream: A Scientific Exploration of the Mind/Brain Interface* (Amsterdam: Elsevier, 2008).
4. Joseph LeDoux, *Synaptic Self: How Our Brains Become Who We Are* (New York: Penguin, 2003).
5. Oliver Sacks, *The Man Who Mistook His Wife for a Hat, and Other Clinical Tales* (New York: Touchstone, 1998); Mark Solms, *The Neuropsychology of Dreams: A Clinico-Anatomical Study* (Mahwah, NJ: Lawrence Erlbaum, 1997).
6. Jeffrey M. Schwartz, and Sharon Begley, *The Mind and the Brain: Neuroplasticity and the Power of Mental Force* (New York: ReganBooks, 2002).
7. Kandel, Schwartz, and Jessel, *Principles of Neural Science.*
8. Mark Graves, *Mind, Brain and the Elusive Soul* (Farnham, England: Ashgate, 2008).
9. Kandel, Schwartz, and Jessel, *Principles of Neural Science*, 16.
10. Daniel Dennett, *Breaking the Spell: Religion as a Natural Phenomenon* (New York: Viking, 2006).
11. James W. Jones, "Brain, Mind, and Spirit: A Clinician's Perspective, or Why I Am Not Afraid of Dualism," in *Soul, Psyche, Brain: New Directions in the Study of Religion and*

Brain-Mind Science, ed. Kelly Bulkeley (New York: Palgrave Macmillan, 2005); V. S. Ramachandran and Sandra Blakeslee, *Phantoms in the Brain: Probing the Mysteries of the Mind* (New York: Quill, 1998); Edward F. Kelly et al., *Irreducible Mind: Toward a Psychology for the 21st Century* (Lanham, MD: Rowman & Littlefield, 2007).

12. J. H. Barkow, L. Cosmides, and J. Tooby, eds., *The Adapted Mind: Evolutionary Psychology and the Evolution of Culture* (New York: Oxford University Press, 1992); Minsky, Marvin, *The Society of Mind* (New York: Simon and Schuster, 1988); Kandel, Schwartz, and Jessel, *Principles of Neural Science*.

13. Pagel, *The Limits of Dream*; Ramachandran and Blakeslee, *Phantoms in the Mind*; Schwartz and Begley, *The Mind and the Brain*; Kelly et al., *Irreducible Mind*.

14. Alan Wallace, *Contemplative Science: Where Buddhism and Neuroscience Converge* (New York: Columbia University Press, 2006).

15. D. Kahn, "From Chaos to Self-Organization: The Brain, Dreaming, and Religious Experience," in *Soul, Psyche, Brain: New Directions in the Study of Religion and Brain-mind Science*, ed. K. Bulkeley (New York: Palgrave Macmillan, 2005), 138–158; Walter J. Freeman, *How Brains Make Up Their Minds* (New York: Columbia University Press, 2000); Schwartz and Begley, *The Mind and the Brain*; Anne L. C. Runehov, *Sacred or Neural? The Potential of Neuroscience to Explain Religious Experience* (Gottingen: Vandenhoeck & Ruprecht, 2007).

16. Ann Taves, "Ascription, Attribution, and Cognition in the Study of Experiences Deemed Religious," *Religion* 20 (2008): 1–16; Pascal Boyer, *Religion Explained: The Evolutionary Origins of Religious Thought* (New York: Basic Books, 2001); Ilkka Pyysiainen, *How Religion Works: Towards a New Cognitive Science of Religion* (Leiden: Brill, 2001).

17. William B. Parsons, *The Enigma of the Oceanic Feeling: Revisioning the Psychoanalytic Theory of Mysticism* (Oxford: Oxford University Press, 1999); Jeffrey J. Kripal, *The Serpent's Gift: Gnostic Reflections on the Study of Religion* (Chicago: University of Chicago Press, 2007); G. William Barnard, *Exploring Unseen Worlds: William James and the Philosophy of Mysticism* (Albany: State University of New York Press, 1997).

18. Boyer, *Religion Explained*.

19. David Wulff, *Psychology of Religion: Classic and Contemporary* (New York: John Wiley & Sons, 1997).

20. Schwartz and Begley, *The Mind and the Brain*, 129.

21. Nina P. Azari and Rudiger J. Seitz, "Brain Plasticity and Recovery from Stroke," *American Scientist* 88 (2000): 426–431.

22. Wilder Penfield and Theodore Rasmussen, *The Cerebral Cortex of Man: A Clinical Study of Localization of Function* (New York: Macmillan, 1950); Michael Persinger, *Neuropsychological Bases of God Beliefs* (New York: Praeger, 1987).

23. Ramachandran and Blakeslee, *Phantoms in the Brain*, 180.

24. Christof Koch, *The Quest for Consciousness: A Neurobiological Approach* (Englewood, CO: Roberts and Company, 2004).

25. Steven Pinker, *How the Mind Works* (New York: W. W. Norton, 1997).

26. Hans C. Lou et al., "A 15O-H2O PET Study of Meditation and the Resting State of Normal Consciousness," *Human Brain Mapping* 7 (1999): 98–105; Sara W. Lazar et al., "Functional Brain Mapping of the Relaxation Response and Meditation," *NeuroReport* 11, no. 7 (2000): 1581–1585; Andrew Newberg, Eugene D'Aquili, and Vince Rause, *Why God Won't Go Away: Brain Science and the Biology of Belief* (New York: Ballantine, 2001); Richard J. Davidson et al., "Alterations in Brain and Immune Function Produced by Mindfulness Meditation," *Psychosomatic Medicine* 65 (2003): 564–570; James H. Austin, *Zen and the Brain*

(Cambridge, MA: MIT Press, 1998); Herbert Benson and Marg Stark, *Timeless Healing: The Power and Biology of Belief* (New York: Fireside, 1996); Jonathan Shear, "Experimental Studies of Meditation and Consciousness," in *Religion and Psychology: Mapping the Terrain*, ed. Diane Jonte-Pace and William B. Parsons (London: Routledge, 2001), 280–294; Nina Azari et al., "Neural Correlates of Religious Experience," *European Journal of Neuroscience* 13 (2001):1649–1652.

27. Harvey Whitehouse, *Modes of Religiosity: A Cognitive Theory of Religious Transmission* (Walnut Creek, CA: Altamira Press, 2004).

28. Boyer, *Religion Explained*.

29. Carol Hart, "The Mysterious Placebo Effect," *Modern Drug Discovery* 2, no. 4 (1999): 30–40; Anne Harrington, *The Placebo Effect: An Interdisciplinary Exploration* (Cambridge, MA: Harvard University Press, 1997).

30. Patrik N. Juslin and John A. Sloboda, eds., *Music and Emotion: Theory and Research* (Oxford: Oxford University Press, 2001).

31. Koch, *The Quest for Consciousness*.

32. Kelly Bulkeley, *The Wondering Brain: Thinking about Religion with and beyond Cognitive Neuroscience* (New York: Routledge, 2005); Robert C. Fuller, *Wonder: From Emotion to Spirituality* (Chapel Hill: University of North Carolina Press, 2006).

33. Kelly Bulkeley, *Dreaming in the World's Religions: A Comparative History* (New York: New York University Press, 2008); Davis, this volume.

34. The Dalai Lama, *Sleeping, Dreaming, and Dying* (Boston: Wisdom Publications, 1997).

35. James B. Ashbrook and Carol Rausch Albright, *The Humanizing Brain: Where Religion and Neuroscience Meet* (Cleveland, OH: Pilgrim Press, 1997); David Hogue, *Remembering the Future, Imagining the Past: Story, Ritual, and the Human Brain* (Cleveland, OH: Pilgrim Press, 2003); Nancey Murphy, *Bodies and Souls, or Spirited Bodies?* (Cambridge: Cambridge University Press, 2006); Fraser Watts, *Theology and Psychology* (Burlington, VT: Ashgate, 2002).

36. Richard Dawkins, *The God Delusion* (New York: Houghton Mifflin, 2006); Sam Harris, *Letter to a Christian Nation* (New York: Knopf, 2006).

37. Dawkins, *The God Delusion*, 5.

BIBLIOGRAPHY

Ashbrook, James B., and Carol Rausch Albright. *The Humanizing Brain: Where Religion and Neuroscience Meet*. Cleveland, OH: Pilgrim Press, 1997.

Austin, James H. *Zen and the Brain*. Cambridge, MA: MIT Press, 1998.

Azari, Nina P., and Rudiger J. Seitz. "Brain Plasticity and Recovery from Stroke." *American Scientist* 88 (2000): 426–431.

Azari, Nina, Nickel Janpeter, Gilbert Wunderlich, Michael Niedeggen, and Harald Hefter. "Neural Correlates of Religious Experience." *European Journal of Neuroscience* 13 (2001):1649–1652.

Barkow, J. H., L. Cosmides, and J. Tooby, eds. *The Adapted Mind: Evolutionary Psychology and the Evolution of Culture*. New York: Oxford University Press, 1992.

Barnard, G. William. *Exploring Unseen Worlds: William James and the Philosophy of Mysticism*. Albany: State University of New York Press, 1997.

Benson, Herbert, and Marg Stark. *Timeless Healing: The Power and Biology of Belief.* New York: Fireside, 1996.

Boyer, Pascal. *Religion Explained: The Evolutionary Origins of Religious Thought.* New York: Basic Books, 2001.

Bulkeley, Kelly. *Dreaming in the World's Religions: A Comparative History.* New York: New York University Press, 2008.

———. *The Wondering Brain: Thinking about Religion with and beyond Cognitive Neuroscience.* New York: Routledge, 2005.

Davidson, Richard J., Jon Kabat-Zinn, Jessica Schumacher, Melissa Rosenkranz, Daniel Muller, Saki F. Santorelli, Ferris Urbanowski, Anne Harrington, Katherine Bonus, and John F. Sheridan. "Alterations in Brain and Immune Function Produced by Mindfulness Meditation." *Psychosomatic Medicine* 65 (2003): 564–570.

Dawkins, Richard. *The God Delusion.* New York: Houghton Mifflin, 2006.

Dennett, Daniel. *Breaking the Spell: Religion as a Natural Phenomenon.* New York: Viking, 2006.

Freeman, Walter J. *How Brains Make Up Their Minds.* New York: Columbia University Press, 2000.

Fuller, Robert C. *Wonder: From Emotion to Spirituality.* Chapel Hill: University of North Carolina Press, 2006.

Gazzaniga, Michael S., ed. *The Cognitive Neurosciences.* 3rd ed. Cambridge, MA: MIT Press, 2004.

Graves, Mark. *Mind, Brain and the Elusive Soul.* Farnham, England: Ashgate, 2008.

Harrington, Anne. *The Placebo Effect: An Interdisciplinary Exploration.* Cambridge, MA: Harvard University Press, 1997.

Harris, Sam. *Letter to a Christian Nation.* New York: Knopf, 2006.

Hart, Carol. "The Mysterious Placebo Effect." *Modern Drug Discovery* 2, no. 4 (1999): 30–40.

Hogue, David. *Remembering the Future, Imagining the Past: Story, Ritual, and the Human Brain.* Cleveland, OH: Pilgrim Press, 2003.

Jones, James W. "Brain, Mind, and Spirit: A Clinician's Perspective, or Why I Am Not Afraid of Dualism." In *Soul, Psyche, Brain: New Directions in the Study of Religion and Brain-Mind Science,* ed. Kelly Bulkeley, 36–60. New York: Palgrave Macmillan, 2005.

Juslin, Patrik N., and John A. Sloboda, eds. *Music and Emotion: Theory and Research.* Oxford: Oxford University Press, 2001.

Kahn, D. "From Chaos to Self-Organization: The Brain, Dreaming, and Religious Experience." In *Soul, Psyche, Brain: New Directions in the Study of Religion and Brain-mind Science,* ed. K. Bulkeley, 138–158. New York: Palgrave Macmillan, 2005.

Kandel, Eric R., James H. Schwartz, and Thomas M. Jessel, eds. *Principles of Neural Science.* 4th ed. New York: McGraw-Hill, 2000.

Kelly, Edward F., Emily Williams Kelly, Adam Crabtree, Alan Gauld, Michael Grosso, Bruce Greyson. *Irreducible Mind: Toward a Psychology for the 21st Century.* Lanham, MD: Rowman & Littlefield, 2007.

Koch, Christof. *The Quest for Consciousness: A Neurobiological Approach.* Englewood, CO: Roberts and Company, 2004.

Kripal, Jeffrey J. *The Serpent's Gift: Gnostic Reflections on the Study of Religion.* Chicago: University of Chicago Press, 2007.

Lama, The Dalai. *Sleeping, Dreaming, and Dying.* Boston: Wisdom Publications, 1997.

Lazar, Sara W., George Bush, Randy L. Gollub, Gregory L. Fricchione, Gurucharan Khalsa, and Herbert Benson. "Functional Brain Mapping of the Relaxation Response and Meditation." *NeuroReport 11*, no. 7 (2000): 1581–1585.

LeDoux, Joseph. *Synaptic Self: How Our Brains Become Who We Are*. New York: Penguin, 2003.

Lou, Hans C., Troels W. Kjaer, Lars Friberg, Gordon Wildschiodtz, Soren Holm, and Markus Nowak. "A 15O-H2O PET Study of Meditation and the Resting State of Normal Consciousness." *Human Brain Mapping 7* (1999): 98–105.

Minsky, Marvin. *The Society of Mind*. New York: Simon and Schuster, 1988.

Murphy, Nancey. *Bodies and Souls, or Spirited Bodies?* Cambridge: Cambridge University Press, 2006.

Newberg, Andrew, Eugene D'Aquili, and Vince Rause. *Why God Won't Go Away: Brain Science and the Biology of Belief*. New York: Ballantine, 2001.

Pagel, James F. *The Limits of Dream: A Scientific Exploration of the Mind/Brain Interface*. Amsterdam: Elsevier, 2008.

Parsons, William B. *The Enigma of the Oceanic Feeling: Revisioning the Psychoanalytic Theory of Mysticism*. Oxford: Oxford University Press, 1999.

Penfield, Wilder, and Theodore Rasmussen. *The Cerebral Cortex of Man: A Clinical Study of Localization of Function*. New York: Macmillan, 1950.

Persinger, Michael. *Neuropsychological Bases of God Beliefs*. New York: Praeger, 1987.

Pinker, Steven. *How the Mind Works*. New York: W. W. Norton, 1997.

Pyysiainen, Ilkka. *How Religion Works: Towards a New Cognitive Science of Religion*. Leiden: Brill, 2001.

Ramachandran, V. S., and Sandra Blakeslee. *Phantoms in the Brain: Probing the Mysteries of the Mind*. New York: Quill, 1998.

Rambo, Lewis. *Understanding Religious Conversion*. New Haven: Yale University Press, 1993.

Runehov, Anne L. C. *Sacred or Neural? The Potential of Neuroscience to Explain Religious Experience*. Gottingen: Vandenhoeck & Ruprecht, 2007.

Sacks, Oliver. *The Man Who Mistook His Wife for a Hat, and Other Clinical Tales*. New York: Touchstone, 1998.

Schwartz, Jeffrey M., and Sharon Begley. *The Mind and the Brain: Neuroplasticity and the Power of Mental Force*. New York: ReganBooks, 2002.

Shear, Jonathan. "Experimental Studies of Meditation and Consciousness." In *Religion and Psychology: Mapping the Terrain*, ed. Diane Jonte-Pace and William B. Parsons, 280–294. London: Routledge, 2001.

Solms, Mark. *The Neuropsychology of Dreams: A Clinico-Anatomical Study*. Mahwah, NJ: Lawrence Erlbaum, 1997.

Taves, Ann. "Ascription, Attribution, and Cognition in the Study of Experiences Deemed Religious." *Religion 20* (2008): 1–16.

Thompson, Richard F. *The Brain: A Neuroscience Primer*. New York: Worth, 2000.

Wallace, Alan. *Contemplative Science: Where Buddhism and Neuroscience Converge*. New York: Columbia University Press, 2006.

Watts, Fraser. *Theology and Psychology*. Burlington, VT: Ashgate, 2002.

Whitehouse, Harvey. *Modes of Religiosity: A Cognitive Theory of Religious Transmission*. Walnut Creek, CA: Altamira Press, 2004.

Wulff, David. *Psychology of Religion: Classic and Contemporary*. New York: John Wiley & Sons, 1997.

CHAPTER 11

··

DREAMING AND RELIGIOUS CONVERSION

··

KELLY BULKELEY

INTRODUCTION

SINCE the pioneering psychological investigations of Sigmund Freud (1856–1939) and Carl Jung (1875–1961), the study of dreams has expanded in many new directions, encompassing the work of scholars in anthropology, neuroscience, cognitive linguistics, history, film studies, and religious studies, among other disciplines. Many questions remain unanswered and debates continue on fundamental issues, but it is fair to say that most researchers agree on the general idea that dreams are a widely distributed, pan-species feature of human life in which we find meaningfully structured expressions of the brain-mind system's activities during sleep. When people are going through a major transition or crisis in waking life—a natural disaster, wartime violence, cultural dislocation, personal problems like divorce or job loss—dreams become especially salient in their efforts to make meaning of their situation and find a way toward healing and new growth.

The universality of dreaming and the transformative effects of certain dream experiences point directly to the relevance of this topic for the study of religious conversion. Recurrent features in dream content can illuminate shared themes in conversion experiences across historical and cultural boundaries, enabling a more nuanced and empirically grounded comparison of conversions in different contexts. Dream research also provides new ways of understanding individual cases of religious conversion by highlighting the multilayered interaction of personal, cultural, and spiritual forces at work in conversion dreams. If one of the goals of conversion studies is to understand the dynamic complexity of people's experiences when they go through a major change of religious outlook, then a familiarity with contemporary dream research can be a valuable means of identifying the different strands of meaning woven into those transformative experiences.

Unfortunately, the study of dreams has a dubious reputation in mainstream academics. The long historical connection with practices of popular divination like astrology and crystal-gazing make it hard for modern scholars to take dream interpretation seriously. In some quarters psychoanalysis is considered a dangerous pseudo-science, and thus the connection with Freud's and Jung's research casts additional doubt on academic efforts to study dreams. Added to this is the widespread misconception that modern scientists have proven that dreams are random nonsense produced by a sleep-addled brain. In fact, abundant evidence has emerged in recent decades to show this idea is false, yet it often appears in popular media stories about dreams, and many people in academia assume it is the properly scientific view of the subject.

Nevertheless, embedded in all this skepticism are legitimate questions about how a phenomenon as personal and ephemeral as dreaming can be the subject of serious academic investigation. The first section of this chapter addresses those questions and other issues of dream research methodology and builds a case for a constructive, evidence-based approach to the interpretation of conversion-related dreams that can be employed by scholars from any disciplinary perspective. The goal in this section will be to establish a set of principles to support the interdisciplinary study of dreams relating to religious conversion.

The second part of the chapter applies those principles to examples drawn from different cultures and traditions. Here, the goal is to give readers a sense of the multiplicity of possible interpretive paths they may choose to follow. The analyses are brief and suggestive rather than exhaustive, opening up new lines of inquiry rather than arguing for specific claims, theories, or explanations. The work of Patricia M. Davis (2005) on Anglo-Saxon dreams and visions in the seventh and eighth centuries B.C.E. is presented as an exemplary approach to studying conversion dreams in a more detailed historical context.

METHODOLOGICAL ISSUES

The critical questions most often raised about the academic legitimacy of dream research are helpful insofar as they clarify the boundaries of what can and cannot be said based on empirical evidence. A fair degree of skepticism is healthy and indeed necessary in the study of dreams, but total skepticism is not warranted in light of several decades of scientific investigation. These questions do have answers, and the answers give us a better idea of how to proceed in our work.

Here are seven specific methodological concerns that can be raised against any form of dream research:

1. A dream report is not the same as a dream experience. There seems to be an unbridgeable gap between the immediate experience of a dream and the later recollection of it. Dreaming is ineffable, beyond the capacity of waking language

to convey. The multimodal sensory qualities of dream experience seem to defy any attempt at a complete description.

2. Every dream report is deeply conditioned by factors of language, history, and religion, making it impossible to tell where the "real" dream ends and the cultural framework begins. These cultural factors also indelibly influence the types of dreams that are and are not recalled; when and where and with whom dreams are shared; and what constitutes a valid interpretation.

3. Dream reports cannot be independently verified. We have no choice but to take the dreamer's word for it. More problematically, it is clear that dreamers often have personal incentives to edit, embellish, revise, or even fabricate their reports.

4. It is even more difficult to establish the authenticity and reliability of the source of any dream presented in a historical text, as well as to account for factors of literary form, editorial transmission, and audience expectations (all of which becomes further complicated if the dream text has been translated from one language to another).

5. Dreams are by nature so bizarre, jumbled, disordered, and chaotic that no reasonable sense can be made of them.

6. If there is any meaningful content to dreams, it can only derive from the personal associations of the dreamer. Without the dreamer's input about the memory sources of the dream and their connections to current waking life events, no valid interpretation can be made.

7. Any attempt to infer symbolic or metaphorical meanings in dreams is like imagining shapes in the clouds. Such meanings may be imposed on the dreams, but they do not reflect anything intrinsic to the dreams themselves.

The most reasonable response to the first question is simply to agree. The gap between dream experience and dream report cannot be eliminated, not even by sleep laboratory technology (although science fiction movies like *Dreamscape* (1985) and *Inception* (2010) suggest a technological bridge may one day be possible). The key methodological question then becomes: Does the dream report bear no relation whatsoever to the dream experience? To answer in the affirmative seems excessively skeptical and dismissive of people's abilities to convey accurately at least some aspects of their dream experiences. Once dream reports are recognized as legitimate yet partial representations of dream experience, the methodological focus turns to finding ways of accounting for the limits and clarifying the areas of most accurate insight into the dream-as-dreamt.

The same line of reasoning applies to the second question regarding cultural influences on the recall, sharing, and interpretation of dreams. Any answer must begin by acknowledging the power of these influences, but it does not follow that dream reports are entirely determined by them or that access is forever denied to the authentically individual aspects of dreaming experience.

The third question, about lack of verifiability, is endemic to any field of research depending on introspective data and first-person reports of subjective experience. Some scientists dismiss introspection as entirely unreliable, but once again that stems from an extreme skepticism that would, if applied across the academic spectrum, eliminate large swaths of the humanities and social sciences. This may seem the properly tough-minded attitude to take, but in my view it represents a disappointing timidity and scholarly cowardice. Antonio Damasio puts the point well: "Whether one likes it or not, all the contents in our minds are subjective, and the power of science comes from its ability to verify objectively the consistency of many individual subjectivities."[1] The best methods in dream research seek this exact aim, to verify objectively the consistency of many individual dream reports, and they do so by gathering large amounts of data in which the patterns of consistency can be most easily identified.

The questions of textual history and translation are most effectively answered by a critical literary analysis that does the scholarly work of identifying these factors and assessing their influence on the authenticity of a given dream report. It may be impossible to determine if a dream report in a historical text accurately represents an actual person's dream experience, but it can be ascertained with a high degree of confidence that the author and presumed audience shared a cultural understanding of what such dream experiences were like. Although more partial and limited than other sources of data, historical evidence expands our knowledge of how dreaming involves the dynamic interaction of personal and collective systems of meaning-making.

The fifth question goes to the center of the rationalist prejudice against dream research, which ironically fails to account for the preponderance of present-day scientific evidence showing the psychological structure and personal meaningfulness of dreaming. Brain functioning during sleep is certainly different than in waking, but its activities are not entirely random or arbitrary; on the contrary, the brain functions differently in sleep, in ways that seem to correspond with general features of dreaming (e.g., higher activation of brain centers for visual imagination, emotion, and instinctual response in REM sleep). The content of dreams certainly includes many strange and irrational elements, but it just as certainly includes many realistic elements that are continuous with people's waking lives and faithfully represent familiar settings, characters, and activities. Evidence in favor of the "continuity hypothesis" of dreaming, most clearly formulated by G. William Domhoff,[2] continues to accumulate, showing beyond any reasonable doubt that dream content accurately reflects people's most significant emotional concerns in waking life. Not all dream content is meaningfully structured in this way, but much of it is, to the point where the rationalist prejudice can no longer rationally be sustained.

The sixth of these methodological questions grants the possibility of the meaningfulness of dreams but denies that it can ever extend beyond the sphere of the dreamer's personal associations. Freud was not the first to insist on the importance of the dreamer's input about his or her current life circumstances and reflections on what the dream might mean; this interpretive principle can be found in many ancient cultural traditions as well. The value of personal associations is not in doubt, so the real question is whether a valid interpretation of a dream can be made using information other than, or in addition to, personal associations. Here, the answer depends on how much additional information is available and what kind of interpretation is being attempted. For example, information about the dreamer's family upbringing and cultural background would be helpful if the interpretation focused on interpersonal dynamics. Information about cognitive science and brain functioning would be helpful if the interpretation focused on the connection of thought and emotion. Some examples of how to balance these factors are presented below.

Finally, the skepticism about symbolic interpretation can be restated as a question about the status of discontinuous dream content. As already noted, a surprisingly high proportion of dream content is continuous with the dreamer's waking life. The remaining discontinuous content can be regarded in two ways: as meaningless noise or as indirect, metaphorical expressions of the dreamer's concerns (the continuous content may also have metaphorical in addition to literal meanings). A good case for regarding at least some dream content as metaphorical has been made by George Lakoff, a cognitive linguist who has identified the metaphorical processes underlying virtually all aspects of mental life. Lakoff argues that dreaming depends on these same metaphorical processes at work during sleep. This supports the efforts of interpreters trying to make accurate inferences about a dream's meaning based on a broad knowledge of typical metaphors in the dreamer's culture and elsewhere. Of course, caution is necessary lest interpreters impose inappropriate metaphorical meanings on the dreams they are studying. But Lakoff's work makes it clear that dream interpretation can reasonably identify metaphorical meanings that are accurate expressions of psychological reality and not simply shapes in the clouds.

To run the gauntlet of skeptical questioning about dream research methodology is necessary if one wants to include dream data in high-quality scholarship on religious conversion. As long as these principles and limitations are kept in mind, researchers may proceed to investigate the multiple roles of dream experience in religious conversions throughout history and in traditions all over the world.

INTERPRETIVE PATHWAYS

Dream reports can be extremely short, or epically long. The dreamer may be the only character, or a whole troop of people, animals, and creatures may be involved. The infinite variability of dreaming experience can be a source of delight to dreamers, but it poses major challenges to researchers. How does one know where to begin? What's the best way to orient oneself and decide where to look for possible meanings?

One of the most useful tools devised by psychologist C. G. Jung was a four-part template for analyzing dream reports at the very outset of the interpretation process. He saw dreams as symbolically equivalent to theatrical plays and dramatic performances, so he took ideas from the world of theater to divide each dream into four elements:

1. *Locale*: The place and time of the dream and a list of the characters.
2. *Exposition*: The situation at the start of the dream, the beginning of the plot.

3. *Peripateia*: How the plot develops, where it goes, what changes.
4. *Lysis*: The result, solution, closure; how it ends.

Jung said, "Most dreams show this dramatic structure," although he emphasized that some dreams do not have a clear-cut lysis or conclusion, which can be a sign of an unresolved conflict.[3] In the dream examples below I use this four-part dramatic schema as Jung did, as an opening gambit, a map-making exercise that helps in the initial assessment of a dream's content and possible meanings.

Constantine: The Cross of Light

Accordingly he [Constantine] called on him [God] with earnest prayer and supplications that he would reveal to him who he was, and stretch forth his right hand to help him in his present difficulties. And while he was thus praying with fervent entreaty, a most marvelous sign appeared to him from heaven, the account of which it might have been hard to believe had it been related by any other person. But since the victorious emperor himself long afterwards declared it to the writer of this history, when he was honored with his acquaintance and society, and confirmed his statement by an oath, who could hesitate to accredit the relation, especially since the testimony of after-time has established its truth? He said that about noon, when the day was already beginning to decline, he saw with his own eyes the trophy of a cross of light in the heavens, above the sun, and bearing the inscription, CONQUER BY THIS. At this sight he himself was struck with amazement, and his whole army also, which followed him on this expedition, and witnessed the miracle. He said, moreover, that he doubted within himself what the import of this apparition could be. And while he continued to ponder and reason on its meaning, night suddenly came on; then in his sleep the Christ of God appeared to him with the same sign which he had seen in the heavens, and commanded him to make a likeness of that sign which he had seen in the heavens, and to use it as a safeguard in all engagements with his enemies. At dawn of day he arose, and communicated the marvel to his friends: and then, calling together the workers in gold and precious stones, he sat in the midst of them, and described to them the figure of the sign he had seen, bidding them represent it in gold and precious stones. And this representation I myself have had an opportunity of seeing.[4]

Locale: The setting of the dream is the same as Constantine's waking vision, some place outside looking up at the heavens. The only other character in the dream is Christ.
Exposition: Constantine sees the same sign in his dream as he did in his vision.
Peripateia: Christ tells him to make a tangible representation of the sign and to use it as a sign for his troops in battle.
Lysis: The dream ends with Christ's admonition.
   This is a significant dream in the history of Christianity because it came just before Constantine (d. 337 C.E.) led his forces into the battle of the Milvian Bridge (October 28,

312) against Maxentius, his rival for control of the Roman Empire. When Constantine won the battle he converted fully to Christianity, and his subsequent military victories enabled him to establish his new faith as the official religion of the empire.

Dreams that come on the eve of a battle have been reported throughout history (e.g., 2 Maccabeus 15:11–17; Qur'an 8:42–43). Of course, military leaders have some incentive to fabricate such dreams to rally the spirits of their soldiers. But psychological research indicates that dreams do indeed respond creatively to times of stress, fear, and uncertainty.[5] Thus, it is plausible that Constantine could have actually dreamed such a dream, reassuring him in the face of mortal danger and giving him hope for the future.

In this case, the dream elaborates on a waking vision. The emblem itself, a cross of light, clearly referred to the Christian cross, but it also had a solar aspect that connected it to traditional Roman religion. This kind of creative synthesis is a signature feature of conversion dreams. It shows the power of the dreaming imagination to generate symbols and metaphors that bridge people's traditional religious beliefs and their newly adopted faith. Constantine's vision gave him the divine support he was seeking, but it took the dream visit from Christ to confirm the vision's significance and instruct him in its proper application. The dream gave Constantine a direct call to action, with Christ serving as the mediator showing Constantine how to put God's plan for him into effect.

Jerome: A Follower of Cicero

> Suddenly I was caught up in the spirit and dragged before the judgment seat of the Judge; and here the light was so bright, and those who stood around were so radiant, that I cast myself upon the ground and did not dare to look up. Asked who and what I was I replied: "I am a Christian." But he who presided said: "Thou liest, thou art a follower of Cicero and not of Christ. For where thy treasure is, there will thy heart be also." Instantly I became dumb, and amid the strokes of the lash—for he had ordered me to be scourged—I was tortured more severely still by the fire of conscience.... At last the bystanders, falling down before the knees of Him who presided, prayed that He would have pity on my youth, and that He would give me space to repent of my error. He might still, they urged, torture me, should I ever again read the works of Gentiles.... Accordingly I made an oath and called upon His name, saying: "Lord, if ever again I possess worldly books, or if ever again I read such, I have denied Thee." Dismissed, then, on taking this oath, I returned to the upper world, and, to the surprise of all, I opened upon my eyes so drenched with tears that my distress served to convince even the credulous. And that this was no sleep nor idle dream, such as those by which we are often mocked, I call to witness the tribunal before which I lay, and the terrible judgment which I feared.... I profess that my shoulders were black and blue, that I felt the bruises long after I awoke from my sleep, and that thenceforth I read the books of God with a zeal greater than I had previously given to the books of men.[6]

Locale: The setting is the Judgment seat of God. The characters include God and a group of bystanders who seem to be angels.

Exposition: Jerome is interrogated about his faith.

Peripateia: His claim to being a Christian is rejected, and he is tortured. The bystanders beg God to be merciful.

Lysis: Jerome takes an oath to reject the writings of his pagan past.

A conversion to a new tradition is, by definition, a conversion away from another tradition. For many converts this tension becomes a source of extreme discomfort and confusion as they try to create a new religious identity. In such circumstances, dreaming offers an arena in which the individual can explore the tension, clarify the competing demands, and seek a path forward. Jerome's situation was emblematic of many well-educated Romans of late Antiquity who struggled to make sense of their new Christian faith in relation to the cultural heritage of classical Greco-Roman civilization.

Jerome's narrative anticipates the kind of skeptical response we discussed in the previous section. He recognizes that other people might not believe he really had this dream, and he knows they might suspect he made it up to serve his evangelical purposes. To alleviate that suspicion he offers three arguments. First, he swears an oath with God as his witness; there is no higher authority to whom he can appeal as a warrant of his truthfulness. Second, he cites the fact that his shoulders were bruised upon awakening. Researchers today call this a "carry-over effect," an aspect of dreaming experience that carries over into the waking state after the dream has ended. Usually such effects are emotional (e.g., feeling elated after a dream of flying), but occasionally they have physical dimensions (e.g., a seminal emission after a sexual dream). In Jerome's case the carry-over effects embody his torments in the dream, enhancing the realism of the experience. His third argument for the veracity of his dream is its pragmatic impact on his life—it changed his behavior for the better, prompting him to read the Bible as avidly as he used to read pagan texts. Many dream interpreters point to this level of pragmatic consequence as the best test of a dream's veracity: Does it inspire the individual to behave better, to act more creatively, to pursue the good and the true more effectively?

A deeper study of this remarkable dream would explore Jerome's upbringing and the reasons for his attachment to Cicero and other classical philosophers. What attracted him to the ideas of those thinkers in the first place? What did he learn from them, and what questions did they answer for him? The key bridging term in Jerome's conversion experience is the book. He does not change his devotion to reading, but rather switches from one kind of book to another. Understanding the role of literature in Jerome's life would certainly help with the evaluation of his religious conversion. So would a greater familiarity with his theology of divine judgment and mercy. His dream portrays God as stern, demanding, and punitive, with a penetrating insight into Jerome's inner psychic world. Jerome needs the intercession of the angelic bystanders to persuade the wrathful deity to grant him a reprieve. It would be interesting to consider how much this dream experience anticipates Jerome's later theological teachings about what it means to be a true Christian.

Victoria: A Clearing in the Forest

> On the night before she [Victoria] was to be baptized she dreamt that she had been driven from her father's house and sent to wander in the bush. She saw herself as a lame person walking through a dense forest in eastern Nigeria where she encountered numerous snakes but had nothing to eat except berries and water. Then one day a light appeared and guided her to a clearing which abounded with her favorite foods. Her lameness disappeared, and while she was drinking water from a clear pool she saw an image of God, who told her to renounce all of her medicines and follow the rules of the True Church as strictly as possible. She was baptized the next day, when she recounted the dream to the assembled congregation, which received it enthusiastically.[7]

Locale: The setting is a forest near Victoria's father's house. The characters include snakes and an image of God.

Exposition: She is cast out of her father's house and finds herself physically disabled.

Peripateia: She wanders the forest, with little food and threatened by snakes. Then she sees a light, her lameness disappears, and she comes to a fountain where an image of God speaks to her.

Lysis: She is instructed by God to renounce the healing traditions of her local culture.

Victoria was a 30-year-old woman preparing to be baptized as a new member of the True Church of God, a syncretistic religious community in Nigeria combining biblical worship and theology with traditional African spiritual practices. She had already made the decision to convert, so this dream was an experiential affirmation of her choice rather than an impetus to make the change. Like Jerome's dream, Victoria's casts her in a situation of conflict between the old and the new, the past and the future. She finds herself wandering alone in the forest, a circumstance of both literal and metaphorical danger, particularly for a single woman. She has left her father's house behind and has set out on her own. She knows what she has left, but she does not yet know where she is going.

The dream portrays her as physically impaired in a way that makes it hard for her to continue moving through the forest independently. Whenever a dream changes some aspect of waking reality, it can be a metaphorical indication of unconscious insight and truth. In this case, being "lame" seems to indicate Victoria's inability to make it through the forest safely, without any other source of guidance. Snakes are, of course, the classic biblical symbol of evil and temptation, but in an African context they are also genuine sources of physical threat and danger. Victoria may have succeeded in her determination to leave her old culture behind, but she is incapable of finding safety and nourishment by herself.

Then she comes upon a place where everything changes for the better. The dense forest opens into a clearing. Her hunger is sated by an abundance of food. A pool of clear water slakes her thirst, and a voice instructs her to abandon the old healing practices of her culture and embrace the teachings of the True Church. Water in dreams has many symbolic dimensions (emotions, the unconscious, the origins of life), and in this case it seems to refer (at least at one level) to the baptismal water with which Victoria will be cleansed the next day. The water heals her lameness and enables her to continue her spiritual journey through life. She is baptized in the dream before she is baptized in waking life. An inner conversion prefigures the outer conversion.

There may be more significance to these elements in the dream (forest, snakes, water) depending on Victoria's Nigerian background, her relationship with her father, and the theology of the True Church, and more ethnographic detail about these elements would surely enrich our understanding of Victoria's conversion. It would also be interesting to explore the long-term impact of her dream on her personal faith and the spiritual community of the True Church. Many indigenous cultures in Africa and elsewhere have lively traditions of collective dream-sharing that play a direct role in people's spiritual development. A dream of conversion is very likely to lead to other dreams that convey religious guidance and existential wisdom through the course of a person's life.

Lady Sarafina: The Glowing Buddha

> Yet we continue to live despite all our suffering. I was greatly worried that my expectations for the future world would also be disappointed, and my only hope was the dream I remembered from the thirteenth night of the Tenth month of the third year of Tenki. Then I had dreamed that Amida Buddha was standing in the far end of our garden. I could not see him clearly, for a layer of mist seemed to separate us, but when I peered through the mist I saw that he was about six foot tall and that the lotus pedestal on which he stood was about four feet off the ground. He glowed with a golden light, and one of his hands was stretched out, while the other formed a magical sign. He was invisible to everyone but me. I had been greatly impressed but at the same time frightened and did not dare move near my blinds to get a clearer view of him. He had said, 'I shall leave now, but later I shall return to fetch you.' And it was only I who could hear his voice. Thereafter it was on this dream alone that I set my hopes for salvation.[8]

Locale: The setting is Lady Sarafina's garden, and the only character is a glowing image of the Buddha. Other people are implied but not explicitly present.

Exposition: She encounters the image of the Buddha, seen through a mist.

Peripateia: The Buddha speaks to her, promising to return later.

Lysis: She receives the message, which only she can hear.

This dream was reported in a diary by a Japanese woman, known only as "Lady Sarafina," who worked as a servant in the court of a minor ruler in the eleventh century C.E. Her diary describes a life of family turmoil, personal suffering, and spiritual longing, with this dream providing a precious beacon of hope in an otherwise sorrowful existence.

As with the other dreams discussed so far, Sarafina is blessed with a divine revelation that gives her religious comfort at a time of worldly distress. Her dream does not change her from one faith to another, but it does make a powerful and lasting impact on her spiritual outlook on life, reinvigorating her connection to the Buddhist teachings of her culture. Unlike Victoria's sojourn through an unknown forest, Sarafina encounters her savior in the familiar space of her garden; even though she has little freedom or mobility in her life, she can still find the Buddha close to home. There is a tension between proximity and distance in her dream; the Buddha is present in her garden, visible and audible only to her, yet he floats above the ground she stands on, and a mist separates them. The dream does not erase her spiritual yearning, nor does it tempt her with a promise of mystical union. She remains who she is and where she is, but now she knows something that no one else knows. Now she has a deeply personal, long-lasting, and experientially validated faith in her future salvation.

Apparently Sarafina did not share this dream with anyone else at the time. People often keep spiritually powerful dreams to themselves, either out of respect for the deity's revelation or out of fear of being ridiculed by those who have not had such an experience and who can only think of it in pathological terms. For scholars of conversion, this suggests that a considerable number of people may be carrying private memories of extremely vivid and profoundly meaningful dreams that directly contributed to the formation of their religious perspectives. To learn about these experiences one must develop a high degree of trust, empathy, and willingness to embrace the mysteries of faith.

Matteo Ricci: An Unknown Man on the Roads

> Close to the city of Jiangxi, he [Father Ricci] was quite pensive all day about things to be done, and an unknown man appeared to him in a dream, who said to him on the roads: "And you go about with the intention of extinguishing the ancient religion of this realm and replacing it with a new one?" The father who at this time took great care not to disclose to anyone his intention of disseminating our holy law, said: "Oh, you must be God or the Devil to know this." He replies: "I am not the devil, but God." The father immediately prostrated himself at his feet, since he had met the one whom he had desired to meet for lamenting, and said, "Lord, since you know my intention, why do you not help me?" And he began to weep at his feet. Then the Lord began to console him and said to him he would be favorable to him at the courts.[9]

Locale: The roads of China, where Ricci is currently traveling. The other character turns out to be God.

Exposition: An unknown man appears to him.

Peripateia: The man challenges his missionary intentions, and Ricci wonders if he is God or the Devil.

Lysis: Ricci and God discuss how to make his mission a success.

Matteo Ricci (1552–1610) was an Italian Jesuit priest and one of the first Christian missionaries to travel to China. He had this dream in June 1595, after a disappointing setback in his effort to visit an important capital city. Here we have a dream not of a person's conversion, but of a person who tries to convert others. The pattern is similar to the other dreams we have considered. The individual receives a personal revelation at a time of uncertainty, with a reassuring message of future guidance and protection. The unknown man's first words put Ricci on the defensive, demanding an honest account of his actual intentions in China. Like Jerome's dream, this one casts the conversion process in stark, either/or terms, calling on Ricci to be true to the full consequences of his missionary work.

The uncertainty about the unknown man's identity reflects a perennial concern in Christianity regarding the potential to be deceived in dreams. Ricci's question—Are you God or the Devil?—indicates a healthy theological caution about the provenance of revelatory dreams. He does not explain why he comes to accept the unknown man is indeed God; it seems to be an intuitive recognition that in this specific dream he is not being misled by the Devil. Once Ricci reaches this moment of acceptance, God's behavior changes from ambiguous challenger to consoling ally.

Ricci's dream highlights an important but perhaps underappreciated aspect of the study of conversion: What are the psychological, social, and religious dynamics of working as a missionary trying to persuade people to abandon their native traditions? What are the obligations to be honest and truthful about one's intentions? What are the implications for one's own religious faith and connection with the divine?

Steve Lyon: Not Converting to Islam

> In my dream, I was drinking tea in the local tea shop called, rather grandly, the "hotel" by the villagers. The hotel is small and has only three walls. Customers sit in *charpais*, smoke hookahs or water pipes (locally called *chillum*), and drink the milky tea freshly prepared while they wait. In my dream, I was sitting on a *charpai* drinking tea when suddenly I fell into a trance, and a white glow emanated from around my body. In the trance I began to recite the Qur'an in Arabic. I remained in the trance until I completed the Qur'an and then woke up from my trance with no knowledge of what I had done and no sudden ability to speak Arabic.[10]

Locale: The dream is set in the rural Punjab village where Lyon was doing anthropological fieldwork on Pakistani Muslims in the late 1990s. No other characters are mentioned.

Exposition: He is sitting in the tea shop, enjoying its wares.

Peripateia: He falls into a trance and recites the Qur'an.

Lysis: He awakens from the trance with total amnesia about what he had just done.

Here we have a case of resisting conversion in a dream. Lyon is a professional anthropologist who teaches at the University of Durham in the United Kingdom. He described this dream in the course of his foreword to Iain Edgar's book *The Dream in Islam: From Qur'anic Tradition to Jihadist Inspiration.* Lyon says that during his three years of fieldwork he was repeatedly asked to convert to Islam, and he found it necessary to "develop coping strategies for politely resisting conversion." This dream came after two especially intense appeals from his informants to adopt the Islamic faith, and he said, "I interpreted this, rightly in my view, as a response to continual attempts to persuade me to become a Muslim." He told the dream to a relatively secular friend in the village, noting that "I do not normally tell my dreams to people, but this one happened to be rather vivid and seemed to speak to my situation explicitly." [11] Upon hearing the dream, his friend became nervous and told Lyon to keep the dream secret, because it was clearly a sign from God, and if he let other local people know he would receive even more unwelcome attention.

It is easy to agree with Lyon that the dream accurately reflected his waking life experiences as the constant target of conversion efforts. Lyon said he never actually wavered in his personal and professional detachment from the Muslim people he was studying. That may be why no other characters appear in the dream—he's a solitary figure in this cultural setting, an outsider who seeks to understand the religious wisdom of the insiders. The "hotel" seems to function as a community center, and Lyon is comfortable there, even though he is not interacting with anyone else.

The split of consciousness in the dream suggests another dimension of meaning, one that goes a step beyond Lyon's waking assessment of his dream. The "trance" represents another mode of awareness and being, another realm of knowledge that seems entirely alien to his waking consciousness. Yet within that trance state, he behaves as a Muslim— he is a Muslim for that period of time in the dream. Then he leaves the trance, detaches himself from that Islamic mode of consciousness, and returns to his identity as Western anthropologist. As his friend instantly knew, such a dream would be interpreted by all the locals as a de facto conversion. Even if Lyon's waking identity disagreed with that interpretation, the theological clarity and experiential vividness of the dream would be treated as a divine warrant of his Muslim identity. In this view, his dream does not simply reflect the efforts of people to convert him; they mark the success of those efforts, at least at the level of dream experience, which Islam (but not Lyon) treats as an epistemologically valid source of knowledge.

This raises the intriguing question of whether people can convert to a new religion and not know it—that is, not consciously understand or accept the degree to which a religious conversion has occurred in their lives. If there are situations like this where conversion is contested and a matter of debate, then dreams may be a useful resource for researchers seeking to discern the variable levels of religious belief, practice, and experience.

Each of these brief case studies could be expanded and amplified in ways that enhance our understanding of the religious dynamics at work in the dreamer's waking life. To conclude this chapter, let me point to an article that illustrates the further potential of this area of investigation. Patricia M. Davis's 2005 study of dreams and visions among the Anglo-Saxons in the seventh and eighth centuries offers an admirable example of historically informed and psychologically sensitive insights into conversion dreams. She argues that dreams served as powerful agents of change for the Anglo-Saxons as their local culture absorbed the teachings of the earliest Christian missionaries. Their dreams and night-visions combined pagan and Christian themes, enabling people to integrate their traditional beliefs with the new religious ideas. Davis draws on multiple sources of ecclesiastical history, hagiography, and cultural analysis to identify eight recurrent types of dreams that reflected the conversion process.

First are conception dreams relating to the birth of a child who will have a special religious destiny. Second are vocation dreams, signaling a new intensity of commitment in the dreamer's life toward a particular life path or religious identity. Third are dreams that inspire people to create poems or songs that convey a deep personal sense of divine presence and guidance. Fourth are dreams, and often nightmares, of temptation and consolation that afflict people trying to maintain an ascetic or monastic discipline. Fifth are otherworldly journeys that lead beyond this earthly realm to reveal astonishing visions of heaven and hell. Sixth are prophecies of death and destruction, with divine warnings of impending apocalypse. Seventh are visions of the death of a saint, either just before or just after the *Gloriosus Obitus* (glorious death). Eighth are dreams of saints' relics and their secret locations.

These eight categories may or may not apply to other cultural or historical contexts. Davis developed the categories after a careful assessment of both the historical sources and modern dream research. Other researchers working in other settings should not copy her work but rather take it as a model for developing their own integrated frameworks of analysis. As Davis points out, some of her categories (conception dreams, artistically inspiring dreams, and otherworldly dreams) can be found in other places and times. The potential for comparative research is especially strong here, although scholars should always be careful to account for subtle differences at the same time as they identify cross-cultural similarities. Every dream is a fresh creation of a unique dreamer's imagination, emerging out of the idiosyncratic, multidimensional details of that dreamer's lived experience. When dreams are studied with caution and humility they may, as Freud once said, provide a royal road to a deeper knowledge of the human psyche as it develops and grows through life.

NOTES

1. Antonio Damasio, *The Feeling of What Happens: Body and Emotion in the Making of Consciousness* (San Diego, CA: Harvest Books, 1999), 83.
2. See G. William Domhoff, *The Scientific Study of Dreams: Neural Networks, Cognitive Development, and Content Analysis* (Washington, DC: American Psychological Association, 2003).
3. Carl G. Jung, *Children's Dreams: Notes from the Seminar Given in 1936–1940*, trans. Ernst Falzeder and Tony Woolfson (Princeton: Princeton University Press, 2008), 30–31.
4. Eusebius, *Life of Constantine*, Book 1, chapters 28–30.
5. See Rosalind Cartwright and Lynn Lamberg, *Crisis Dreaming: Using Your Dreams to Solve Your Problems* (New York: Harper Collins, 1992).
6. Morton Kelsey, God, Dreams, and Revelation: A Christian Interpretation of Dreams (Minneapolis, MN: Augsburg Publishing, 1981), 136–137.
7. Richard T. Curley, "Dreams of Power: Social Process in a West African Religious Movement," *Africa: Journal of the International African Institute* 53, no. 3 (1983): 27–28.
8. Ivan Morris, trans., *As I Crossed a Bridge of Dreams* (London: Penguin Books, 1971), 107.

9. R. Po-Chia Hsia, "Dreams and Conversion: A Comparative Analysis of Catholic and Buddhist Dreams in Ming and Qing China. Part One," *Journal of Religious History* 29, no. 3 (2005): 224.
10. Iain R. Edgar, *The Dream in Islam: From Qur'anic Tradition to Jihadist Inspiration* (London: Berghahn Books, 2011), xiv–xv.
11. Ibid., xv–xvi.

Bibliography

Bulkeley, Kelly. *Dreaming in the World's Religions: A Comparative History.* New York: New York University Press, 2008.

Cartwright, Rosalind, and Lynn Lamberg. *Crisis Dreaming: Using Your Dreams to Solve Your Problems.* New York: Harper Collins, 1992.

Curley, Richard T. "Dreams of Power: Social Process in a West African Religious Movement." *Africa: Journal of the International African Institute* 53, no. 3 (1983): 20–37.

Damasio, Antonio. *The Feeling of What Happens: Body and Emotion in the Making of Consciousness.* San Diego, CA: Harvest Books, 1999.

Davis, Patricia M. "Dreams and Visions in the Anglo-Saxon Conversion to Christianity." *Dreaming* 15, no. 2 (2005): 75–88.

Domhoff, G. William. *The Scientific Study of Dreams: Neural Networks, Cognitive Development, and Content Analysis.* Washington, DC: American Psychological Association, 2003.

Edgar, Iain R. *The Dream in Islam: From Qur'anic Tradition to Jihadist Inspiration.* London: Berghahn Books, 2011.

Eusebius. *The Life of Constantine.* Available: http://www.fordham.edu/halsall/basis/vita-constantine.asp (November 17, 2011).

Hsia, R. Po-Chia. "Dreams and Conversion: A Comparative Analysis of Catholic and Buddhist Dreams in Ming and Qing China. Part One." *Journal of Religious History* 29, no. 3 (2005): 223–240.

Jung, Carl G. *Children's Dreams: Notes from the Seminar Given in 1936–1940.* Trans. Ernst Falzeder and Tony Woolfson. Princeton: Princeton University Press, 2008.

Kelsey, Morton. *God, Dreams, and Revelation: A Christian Interpretation of Dreams.* Minneapolis, MN: Augsburg Publishing, 1981.

Lakoff, George. "How Metaphor Structures Dreams: The Theory of Conceptual Metaphor Applied to Dream Analysis." *Dreaming* 3, no. 2 (1993): 77–98.

Morris, Ivan, trans. *As I Crossed a Bridge of Dreams.* London: Penguin Books, 1971.

CHAPTER 12

....

DECONVERSION

....

HEINZ STREIB

INCLUDING a chapter on deconversion in a handbook on conversion is not only appropriate but also necessary. It is no longer possible to ignore the fact that a growing number of people choose to convert more than once in their lifetime; multiple conversions are unavoidable in cultures in which religion is no longer a single tradition in a mono-religious environment but plural in a pluralistic environment. Multiple conversions, however, involve deconversion(s) as well as conversions. While some researchers use the term "conversion" for both the disaffiliation and the reaffiliation, I focus on "deconversion" in order to include disaffiliations without reaffiliation, in response to the growing attention to atheists and apostates, especially in the United States.[1] Disaffiliation processes constitute an independent field of study that deserves special scientific attention. Here, the term "deconversion" may serve as a reminder of the depth and intensity of biographical change and the new orientation of one's life that eventually is associated with disaffiliation and is not confined to conversion alone. In this chapter, I start by discussing how to conceptualize deconversion, then discuss recent quantitative and qualitative research, and finally draw conclusions and suggest directions for future research.

CONCEPTUALIZING "DECONVERSION"

....

For a conceptualization of deconversion, three basic elements are necessary: criteria for a definition, a typology of deconversion trajectories, and a model of the religious field that is the context. As a point of departure for a conceptualization of deconversion, John D. Barbour's work is significant.[2] Barbour presents an analysis of published autobiographies of leading theologians, philosophers, and other writers who have engaged in deconversion. He interprets the rise of and interest in deconversion as being due to the increasing individualism and religious pluralism in modernity. Using the term deconversion in a broad sense to mean loss or deprivation of religious faith, he identifies four criteria of deconversion that come together in most deconversions: (1) intellectual doubt or denial in regard to the truth of a system of beliefs; (2) moral criticism, including the rejection of the entire way of life of a religious group; (3) emotional suffering that consists of grief, guilt, loneliness, and despair; and finally, (4) disaffiliation from the community.

A comparison of Barbour's definition with Charles Y. Glock's five dimensions of religion[3] reveals that Barbour's list of deconversion criteria does not explicitly include the *experiential* dimension. It may, however, be important to attend to the loss of sometimes very specific religious experiences as a feature of deconversion. Therefore, we include the experiential dimension in our list of elements of deconversion and thus propose a set of five characteristics: (1) loss of specific religious experiences; (2) intellectual doubt, denial, or disagreement with specific beliefs; (3) moral criticism; (4) emotional suffering; and (5) disaffiliation from the community.[4]

Using these five characteristics to conceptualize deconversion prevents the reduction of deconversion to termination of membership in a religious organization. Conversely, disaffiliation from the community does not exclusively mean the termination of membership; for example, it can consist of total withdrawal from participation without formally terminating the membership. This is especially important in regard to religions without formal membership, such as Islam. The polythetic conceptualization of deconversion using these five criteria aims at a multi-perspective interpretation of deconversion and can be used to identify biographical accounts as deconversion stories. These characteristics have also been used in empirical research.[5]

Aside from this set of core characteristics for defining deconversion, a conceptualization of deconversion should also identify the potential deconversion avenues and eventually construct a typology. Already, simple observation reveals that deconversion can be a change from one religious organization to another, which thus takes place within the zone of organized religion, but it can be also an exit from the religious field altogether. But there may be even more options. I suggest (Streib et al.[6]) a set of six possible deconversion trajectories: (1) *secularizing exit*: termination of (concern with) religious belief and praxis and, in addition, disaffiliation from organized religion; (2) *oppositional exit*: adopting a different system of beliefs and engaging in different ritualistic practices, while affiliating with a higher-tension, more oppositional religious organization,[7] such as conversion into a fundamentalist group; (3) *religious switching*: migration to a religious organization with a similar system of beliefs and rituals and with no, or only marginal, difference in terms of integration; (4) *integrating exit*: adopting a different system of beliefs and engaging in different ritualistic practices, while affiliating with an integrated or more accommodated religious organization; (5) *privatizing exit*: disaffiliating from a religious organization, eventually including termination of membership, but continuation of private religious belief and private religious praxis; and (6) *heretical exit*: disaffiliating from a religious organization, eventually including termination of membership, and individual heretical appropriation of new belief system(s) or engagement in different religious praxis but without new organizational affiliation.[8]

Deconversion can be viewed as migration within and out of the religious field. The religious field can be understood, with reference to Pierre Bourdieu,[9] as an arena in which a variety of religious actors with different degrees of organization and different commodities interact with clients in order to keep or acquire their attraction and affiliation. With reference to Weber's classical distinction, Bourdieu profiles three ideal types of actors or competitors in the religious field besides the lay people: priests, prophets, and magicians. Aside from—or instead of—magicians, we may, with reference to Ernst Troeltsch's work,[10] define *mystics* as the third group of actors in the religious field. While all three, priest, prophet, and magician/mystic, are actors in the religious field, there is a clear distinction between them in regard to the structure and degree of organization, which are classically defined as church, sect, and private office. Taking this just one step further, I divide the religious field into two segments: one segment with clear organizational structures (church, sect) and another segment without organizational structures, which I call the unorganized segment of the religious field. In sum, the variety of deconversion trajectories can be drawn as migration movements within and out of the religious field. Figure 12.1 presents this ideal type of the religious field, including the deconversion migrations.

According to my conceptualization, deconversion is an intense biographical change that includes individual and social aspects. Among the constitutive criteria for the definition of deconversion, the experiential, motivational, intellectual-ideological, and moral-critical aspects are individual aspects that call for psychological investigation. Changes or termination of membership and the entire variety of migrations within and

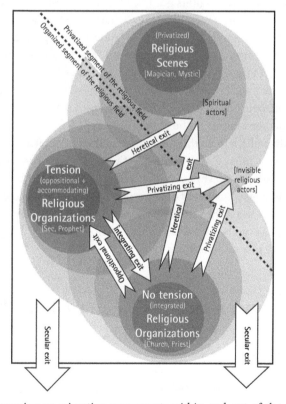

FIGURE 12.1 Deconversion as migration movements within and out of the religious field

out of the religious field are social aspects which call for sociological investigation that must take into account ongoing changes in the religious landscape.

EMPIRICAL STUDIES OF DECONVERSION

Proceeding from conceptualization to empirical research on deconversion, it should be kept in mind that, in contrast to a century-long tradition of research about *conversion*, research about *deconversion* is relatively young and began as a rather unsystematic and occasional enterprise. A more detailed description of extant research on deconversion can be found elsewhere,[11] but here it may suffice to briefly mention three developments. (1) Large-scale surveys have, on occasion, included items in their questionnaires concerning the respondents' and their parents' religious affiliations and participation when the respondents were in late childhood.[12] This information allows for inferences about deconversion, although based on a limited understanding of deconversion. (2) The discussion in the 1980s about new religious movements and public concern about cults triggered some interest in research, mostly interview studies, about apostates or defectors from controversial new religious groups.[13] (3) A series of studies of church-leavers and secular apostates in Europe and the United States indicates a shift of research focus in the 1990s to mainstream religions and the religious landscape as a whole.[14] This focus of research continues today, with a special interest in atheist and agnostic milieus that appear to be something new, especially in the United States.[15]

In the following sections I restrict attention to the most recent studies. I focus on specific sets of questions, the first of which is the following: Are there any reliable data about the frequency of deconversions in the religious field? What do we know about the reasons why people disaffiliate from their religious tradition? What are the aims and directions of deconversion moves? These are questions that are primarily appropriate for national and international surveys. Another set of questions regards the psychological predispositions and consequences of deconversion: Is deconversion related to personality? What do we know about the well-being, growth, or religious development of deconverts? These questions can be answered using psychological methods and instruments, especially qualitative research methods.

DECONVERSION IN LIGHT OF RECENT SURVEY DATA

For the questions concerning the frequency and the directions of deconversions and religious migrations, quite recent data are available, including the results of the Pew

Forum on Religion & Public Life (2009) and the data from the International Social Survey Programme (ISSP), Religion III.[16] I present a summary of these recent survey results about change of religious affiliation in table 12.4. But first I describe and discuss the results of these two surveys in some detail.

Results of the Pew Forum on Religion & Public Life

The Pew study used a sample of 2,867 US citizens who were selected from Pew's Religious Landscape Survey conducted in 2007 among a sample of more than 35,000 US citizens; after the initial survey, disaffiliates and new affiliates were re-contacted for a detailed interview. This recent study reveals new and interesting data about the high number of people who have changed their religious affiliation or denomination once or even more than once. The Pew Report's most striking results are the statistics that 44 percent of the respondents do not currently belong to their childhood faith and that most changes of religious affiliation occur before the age of 24. The Pew data focus on migration within the field of organized religion, giving special attention to religious switching within the field of Protestant denominations in the United States. The Pew results document that 15 percent of American citizens have engaged in denominational switching. If these denominational switchers are set aside, the Pew study counts almost 30 percent who have changed religious affiliation in some way—that is, have migrated between, exited from, or newly affiliated with Catholic, Protestant, Jewish, or other organized religions.[17]

One of the questions in the study of religious disaffiliation regards the assessment of multiple changes.[18] Here, the new Pew data fill a gap and reveal striking results. Counting all of the disaffiliation paths, the Pew data identify more than 50 percent who report that they have changed their religious affiliation more than once. Within the group of Protestants, the multiple changers/switchers amount to 70 percent.

Another interesting piece of information regards the age of the person when they first disaffiliate. Here, the most noteworthy group is that of the disaffiliates with no reaffiliation: approximately 79 percent (former Catholics) or 85 percent (former Protestants) of this type of exiters report that disaffiliation from their childhood faith occurred before the age of 24. If we include all respondents under the age of 35 years, the Pew results reveal that between 97 percent (former Catholics) and 96 percent (former Protestants) of non-reaffiliates left their childhood faith before the age of 35.

When asked for the reasons why they left their childhood faith, respondents in the Pew study reported, as key motives, that their spiritual needs had not been fulfilled, that they had stopped believing in the religion's teachings, or simply that they had gradually drifted away from their former religion. Attending to the answers to open questions about disaffiliation motives, the loss of belief in the former religion or in any religion stand out, along with dissatisfaction with institutions, practices, and people.

The Pew data also allow for detailed portraits of denominational groups in regard to their adherents' religious involvement over the course of their life cycles, because the study assessed the frequency of church attendance, participation in youth groups, and strength of belief in God as a child, as a teen, and as an adult. This results in a very detailed profile for each of the disaffiliation or reaffiliation paths. The Pew study pays special attention to Catholics and Protestants and dedicates a special section to the switchers within the Protestant denominations.

The most common deconversion motives according to the Pew study appear to be, in my terms, intellectual doubt and moral criticism and, to a lesser degree, the loss of religious experiences.[19] Thus, in the framework of my conceptualization of "deconversion," I assume that most disaffiliates in the Pew research have engaged in deconversion, with exceptions perhaps in the groups of Protestant denomination switchers who, as the Pew Report notes, "are much less likely to cite beliefs as the main reason for leaving their former religious group" (2009, 7).

Results from the International Social Survey Programme (ISSP), Religion III

The other source of recent information about disaffiliation and deconversion is the ISSP 2008, Religion III survey, for which data was collected in the spring and summer of 2008. This survey presents data for the US population but also allows for a cross-cultural comparison. For such a cross-cultural comparison I refer to the situation in Germany, which can be understood as somewhere near the middle of the European nations in regard to level of religiosity.

For the assessment of deconversion, I have used three ISSP variables: change from pre-adolescent religious affiliation, change of belief in God, and self-identification as a religious or spiritual person. The first variable is my own construction on the basis of two ISSP variables: religious affiliation in pre-adolescence and present religious affiliation. Table 12.1 presents values and frequencies for this new variable. The second variable is taken directly from the ISSP databases. Table 12.2 presents the items and frequencies of change in belief in God. The third variable is also taken directly from the ISSP data, namely from the ISSP's first-time inclusion of a set of four questions related to self-identification as a religious or spiritual person (see table 12.3 for items and frequencies). I have included this variable in the calculation in order to fine-tune the deconversion trajectories, namely to distinguish between heretical and privatizing exiters and also between religious and spiritual switchers.

In an intermediary step, I have related the first and third variables, which allows for attending to spiritual/religious self-identification in relation to disaffiliation. Figure 12.2 presents the results of a cross-tabulation of the constructed variable on affiliation changes (table 12.1) with the question about self-identification as a spiritual person (table 12.3). For this cross-tabulation, I have selected three groups: (1) people without change of affiliation or denomination; (2) people who deconvert/convert within the field segment of organized religion; and (3) people who exit the field segment of organized religion. Between the first and the second group there are only small differences. Almost 50 percent of the people in the United States who remain within the field of organized religion self-identify as "equally religious and spiritual" whether they change affiliation or not. There is, however, a considerable increase in self-identification as "spiritual, but not religious" among people who change affiliation.

Table 12.1 Disaffiliation from Pre-Adolescent Religious Affiliation

	ISSP 2008 United States (%) (N = 1,348)	ISSP 2008 Germany (%) (N = 1,669)
No change (current religious affiliation same as in pre-adolescence)	67.7	59.4
Change of religious affiliation (current different from pre-adolescent)	12.4	5.0
New religious affiliation; none in pre-adolescence	3.9	1.6
Termination of pre-adolescent religious affiliation (no current)	11.4	14.0
No religious affiliation, neither current nor pre-adolescent	4.6	19.9
Total	100.0	100.0

Table 12.2 Change in Belief in God

Which best describes your beliefs about God	ISSP 2008 United States (%) (N = 1,323)	ISSP 2008 Germany (%) (N = 1,482)
I don't believe in God and never have.	4.2	28.3
I don't believe in God now, but I used to.	5.4	15.2
I believe in God now, but I didn't used to.	7.3	8.5
I believe in God now and I always have.	83.1	47.9
Total	100.0	100.0

Table 12.3 Religious/Spiritual Self-Identification (ISSP 2008, Religion III)

What best describes you	United States (%) (N = 1,298)	Germany (%) (N = 1,452)
I follow a religion and consider myself to be a spiritual person interested in the sacred or the supernatural.	40.7	9.8
I follow a religion, but don't consider myself to be a spiritual person interested in the sacred or the supernatural.	23.4	30.9
I don't follow a religion, but consider myself to be a spiritual person interested in the sacred or the supernatural.	24.0	11.5
I don't follow a religion and don't consider myself to be a spiritual person interested in the sacred or the supernatural.	11.9	47.9
Total	100.0	100.0

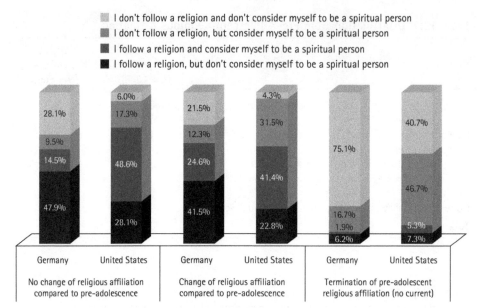

FIGURE 12.2 Spiritual/religious self-identification and change of religious affiliation in Germany and the United States in 2008

The surprising difference comes with the respondents who have terminated their pre-adolescent religious affiliation and have left the organized segment of the religious field. This group, as would be expected, self-identify in large part as not following a religion (United States: 87.4 percent; Germany: 91.8 percent), if we combine the two answers in which the respondent indicates he or she follows no religion. However, 46.7 percent of those who have emigrated from the organized segment of the religious field in the United States self-identify as "spiritual" persons. We see significant cross-cultural differences here, for the portion of "spiritual" disaffiliates in this group is only 16.7 percent in Germany. Taken together, these results shed some light on the disaffiliates who leave organized religion. Not all of them simply dwell in secularity and have exchanged belief for unbelief; in fact, one in two exiters from organized religion in the United States and one in six exiters from organized religion in Germany consider themselves "spiritual" persons although they do not follow a "religion."

We may draw the following conclusion from the ISSP results discussed so far: the high (United States) and considerable (Germany) proportions of "spiritual, but not religious" self-identifications in the group of disaffiliates suggest that a further differentiation of the deconversion trajectories is needed. There is more than one type of exiter from the field of organized religion. This differentiation is done in the next and final step of variable construction that I perform using the ISSP data.[20]

The cross-tabulation of all three variables allows for an assessment of the deconversion trajectories as defined in the first part of this chapter. To give some examples, disaffiliation from a religious organization without reaffiliation with another religious

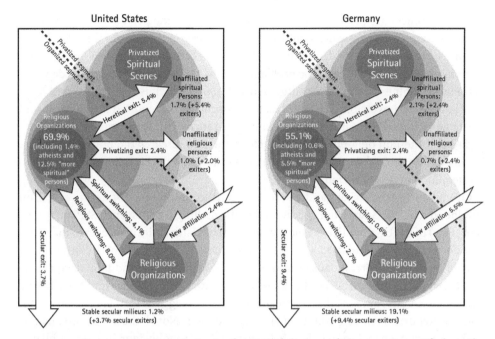

FIGURE 12.3 Deconversion trajectories in the United States and Germany quantified on the basis of the ISSP 2008 Religion III Survey

organization can be distinguished into three different kinds of exits: (a) secular exit, which involves not only disaffiliation but also loss of belief in God and self-identification as neither a religious nor a spiritual person, (b) privatizing exit, which, aside from disaffiliation, involves the continuation of belief in God and self-identification as a religious person, and (c) heretical exit, which involves disaffiliation, continuation of religion or religious quest, and a spiritual but not religious preference. Further, change from one religious affiliation or denomination to another is divided into spiritual switching and religious switching.[21] The percentages of the deconversion trajectories in the religious fields, based on the ISSP data, are presented in Figure 12.3.[22]

CONCLUSIONS DRAWN FROM THE QUANTITATIVE RESULTS RELATED TO DECONVERSION

As the synopsis of frequencies in table 12.4 shows,[23] the Pew results and my calculation of the ISSP results largely correspond for the US landscape, although there are some differences.

The differences are particularly significant in regard to the percentage of Protestant denomination switchers, which could not be quantified on the basis of the ISSP. This is the unique result of the Pew data, which included very careful and detailed investigation of denominational migrations. The problem with the Pew's detailed analysis of denominational switching is an understanding of disaffiliation which is slightly different from how I define deconversion. The Pew data focus primarily on reported membership and are rather detailed for particular denominations; furthermore, as explicitly stated in regard to Protestant denominational switchers, the Pew research did not seriously take intellectual doubt and denial into account as a criterion, but this criterion is central to my definition of deconversion.

Overall correspondences can be seen in regard to the number of deconverts from childhood religion. Apart from denominational switching, 27.7 percent (ISSP) or 29 percent (Pew) of the US population report major changes later in life in respect to their religious orientation in childhood. Going into more detail, the number of deconverts who remain unaffiliated corresponds even more precisely in the Pew and ISSP data: 11 percent (Pew) or 11.4 percent (ISSP) did not reaffiliate with a new religious tradition. Taking a closer look at the milieu of the disaffiliated population suggests further differentiation. The Pew Report concluded from the Landscape survey: "Not all those who are unaffiliated lack spiritual beliefs or religious behaviors; in fact, roughly four-in-ten unaffiliated individuals say religion is at least somewhat important in their lives" (2009, 8). In the ISSP data (see figure 12.2), I have identified for the United States 7.3 percent religious, 5.3 percent religious and spiritual, and 46.7 percent spiritual persons who are not affiliated with a religious organization; thus this group may be even somewhat larger. Six in ten of the unaffiliated respondents, according to the ISSP data, believe in God or search

Table 12.4 Changing Religious Affiliation: Synopsis of Recent Survey Results for United States and Germany

	Pew 2008 United States (%) (N = 2,867)	ISSP 2008 United States (%) (N = 1,348)	ISSP 2008 Germany (%) (N = 1,669)
Do not currently belong to childhood religion	29	27.7	20.6
Raised in a religious tradition, now unaffiliated	11	11.4	14.0
Raised unaffiliated, now affiliated	4	3.9	1.6
Change of childhood religious affiliation	5	12.4	5.0
Other change in religious affiliation (Pew)	9		
Switching between Protestant denominations	15		
Same faith as in childhood	56	67.7	59.4
Changed faith at some point	9		
Have not changed affiliation	47		
Never affiliated with any religious tradition		4.6	19.9
Total	100.0	100.0	100.0

for or practice religion or spirituality one way or another. This, again, casts new light on the population of deconverts who do not affiliate anew; not all of them have lost their faith or have given up concern with religion and spirituality.

Concluding the discussion of recent quantitative contributions to deconversion research, I would like to emphasize that, instead of simply repeating and summarizing numbers and statistics, my attempt has been to incorporate these data and results in my pre-defined typological model of deconversion. This indicates that purely quantitative survey data such as the ISSP allow for the differential reconstruction of a variety of options—but only if there is a pre-defined conceptual model that accounts for this variety of options, in our case: the variety of deconversion trajectories within and out of the religious field.

DECONVERSION IN LIGHT OF PSYCHOMETRIC AND BIOGRAPHICAL RESEARCH: THE BIELEFELD-BASED STUDY ON DECONVERSION

Is deconversion related to personality? What do we know about the psychological well-being and growth of people who deconvert? How is deconversion related to faith development? These questions cannot be answered on the basis of the surveys discussed so far, because answers to these questions require research using psychometric scales or qualitative methods.

Concerning these questions, I present the research results of the Bielefeld-based Cross-cultural Study of Deconversion.[24] This research was conducted in the years 2002 to 2005 in the United States and in Germany and included a total of 129 deconverts in the two countries. Narrative interviews and faith development interviews were conducted with 99 of these deconverts.[25] Aside from these qualitative instruments, an extensive questionnaire was answered by all deconverts; in addition, in-tradition members also answered the questionnaire ("In-tradition members" is the term used in the Bielefeld-based deconversion study for members of the religious group from which the deconverts have disaffiliated), the goal being to interview ten in-tradition members per deconvert. Thus, the quantitative database includes questionnaire data from 1,067 in-tradition members and 129 deconverts. The measures included in the questionnaire assess spiritual/religious self-identification, personality traits, psychological well-being and growth, religious fundamentalism, right-wing authoritarianism, and religious styles.[26] In addition to the 99 faith development interviews of deconverts, 177 faith development interviews with in-tradition members were conducted. As can be seen from this brief characterization of the data, this research on deconversion is based on an innovative design triangulating quantitative and qualitative data, and the study is aimed at comparing deconverts and in-tradition members.

Using the biographical information from the interviews, the deconversion trajectories of the 99 cases could be identified. All types of deconversion trajectories are represented:[27] 29 secular exiters, 24 privatizing exiters, 9 heretical exiters, 13 religious switchers, 16 integrating exiters, and 8 oppositional exiters. Using the quantitative data, the deconverts could be profiled and contrasted to the in-tradition members, allowing many aspects such as personality, well-being, and faith development to be addressed that could not be answered by previous research.

DECONVERSION AND PERSONALITY

The relation of deconversion to personality is indicated by the mean differences between in-tradition members and deconverts as presented in table 12.5. Here, *openness to experience* is the subscale that indicates significant differences for deconverts in both the United States and Germany, with the greatest difference in the United States. *Openness to experience* also emerged as one of the key characteristics of deconversion in a series of other calculations, including linear regression analysis, in which it emerged as one of the most effective predictors of deconversion.

Another interesting result reflects a cross-cultural difference between Germany and the United States. In contrast to the deconverts in the United States, for the German subjects all Big Five subscales display significant differences between in-tradition members and deconverts, and all of these except *openness to experience* are negative. This

Table 12.5 Significant Differences on the "Big Five" Personality Subscales between Deconverts and In-Tradition Members in the United States and Germany

	Germany				United States			
	In-tradition members (N = 368)		Deconverts (N = 53)		In-tradition members (N = 658)		Deconverts (N = 66)	
	Mean	SD	Mean	SD	Mean	SD	Mean	SD
Openness to experience	*41.22*	*5.82*	**46.00**	5.75	*38.63*	*6.24*	**46.91**	6.00
Extraversion	*40.57*	*5.75*	*38.23*	7.52	*42.08*	*7.30*	42.08	7.30
Agreeableness	46.34	4.82	**44.15**	5.57	42.20	5.81	44.29	5.07
Conscientiousness	45.26	6.03	**41.30**	7.23	43.55	6.07	42.74	6.06
Emotional stability	*41.66*	*7.07*	*35.43*	10.15	*39.28*	*7.61*	41.26	6.65

Note: Significant difference between deconverts and in-tradition members for specified country (*p* <.01) are in **bold**; significant differences between countries (*p* <.01) are in *italics*.

involves, primarily, *emotional stability*. What do these results indicate? Deconversion in Germany appears to be associated with some kind of mild crisis. Confirmation for this characteristic of German deconverts comes from a closer inspection of the results of the *psychological well-being and growth* scale that attends specifically to the consequences of deconversion.

DECONVERSION AND PSYCHOLOGICAL WELL-BEING AND GROWTH

As table 12.6 shows, the consequences of deconversion, as indicated by all six sub-scales of Ryff's Psychological Well-Being and Growth Scale, are completely different in Germany than in the United States. While in the United States we see significant gains in *autonomy* and *personal growth* and no significant differences in the rest of the subscales as a result of deconversion, the opposite is the case for German deconverts: *environmental mastery, positive relations with others, purpose in life,* and *self-acceptance* are all significantly lower for deconverts compared to in-tradition members.

The conclusion is this: many US deconverts are able to associate personal gains with their deconversion, but a higher percentage of German deconverts report losses rather than gains and indicate some kind of mild crisis associated with deconversion. In the United States, by comparison, deconversion is associated more strongly with

Table 12.6 Significant Differences on the Subscales of Ryff's Psychological Well-Being and Growth Scale between Deconverts and In-Tradition Members in the United States and Germany

| | Germany | | | | United States | | | |
| | In-tradition members ($N = 367$) | | Deconverts ($N = 53$) | | In-tradition members ($N = 660$) | | Deconverts ($N = 66$) | |
	Mean	SD	Mean	SD	Mean	SD	Mean	SD
Autonomy	31.66	4.47	*32.60*	4.97	32.20	4.76	*35.56*	4.32
Environmental mastery	*33.61*	4.59	*29.66*	6.74	*32.16*	4.87	*32.55*	4.58
Personal growth	35.05	4.18	36.47	4.14	34.38	4.56	**38.08**	4.46
Positive relations with others	*34.98*	4.26	**31.98**	6.19	*34.05*	5.53	34.03	5.36
Purpose in life	35.09	4.09	*32.28*	5.06	*34.30*	4.90	*35.12*	4.35
Self-acceptance	34.27	4.52	*31.09*	7.34	33.46	5.10	*35.02*	4.67

Note: Significant difference between deconverts and in-tradition for specified country ($p < .01$) are in **bold**; significant differences between countries ($p < .01$) are in *italics*.

openness fueled by a quest for personal growth and autonomy. In this sense, many of the American deconverts seem to be involved in what might be referred to as explorations of self-realization within a generalized "spiritual" context. This suggests the necessity of taking a closer look at religious/spiritual self-identification.

DECONVERSION AND RELIGIOUS/SPIRITUAL SELF-IDENTIFICATION

The questionnaire included four questions that probe for spiritual and religious self-identification. Questions and results are presented in figure 12.4.

Less striking are the results for the in-tradition members in both cultures; the big difference is found in the results for the deconverts in both cultures. More than one-third (36.5 percent) of the German deconverts and almost two-thirds (63.6 percent) of the US deconverts identify as "more spiritual than religious." In the United States, a great majority (80.3 percent) of deconverts are hesitant to identify with "being religious" one way or the other; among the German deconverts, reservations against a religious self-identification are indicated by 57.7 percent.

These results are based on samples which included only respondents who are, or have been, active members in religious communities. Therefore, results for religiosity and for spirituality are very high and must not be read as being representative of the population as a whole (for that purpose, refer to the results of the 2008 ISSP study as presented in figure 12.2). However, both the ISSP and the Bielefeld-based deconversion study indicate

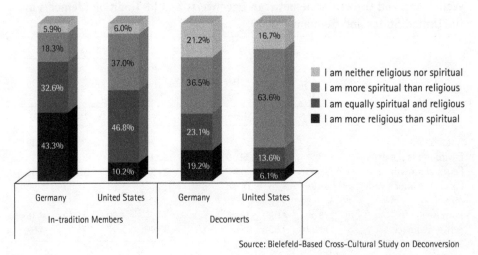

Source: Bielefeld-Based Cross-Cultural Study on Deconversion

FIGURE 12.4 Spiritual/religious self-identification and deconversion in Germany and the United States

that deconverts have an extraordinary increase in spiritual self-identification. The number of self-identified "more spiritual" deconverts in the United States is almost twice as high as that of the in-tradition members. In both the United States and Germany, deconversion is associated with a reluctance to identify with religion combined with a preference for identifying with "spirituality."

DECONVERSION, FAITH DEVELOPMENT, AND RELIGIOUS SCHEMATA

Deconversion is also associated with changes in religious styles, whether we assess these using faith development interview ratings or using the Religious Schema Scale (RSS).[28] There are differences between in-tradition members and deconverts in both the US and the German samples.

As detailed elsewhere,[29] the faith development interview ratings reveal significant mean differences between deconverts and in-tradition members of 0.32 in Germany and 0.51 in the United States. This means that, on average, deconverts score one-third or one-half a faith stage higher than in-tradition members. The movement in faith development scores is mainly between synthetic-conventional faith (stage 3) and individuative-reflective faith (stage 4). The relation of deconversion and faith development can also be shown by a cross-tabulation of the rounded faith stage assignments with deconversion. Results indicate that between 70 percent (Germany) and 80 percent (United States) of the in-tradition members are at stage 3, while half of the *deconverts* in both countries are at stage 4. This is evidence that people may prefer an individuative-reflective religious style when they deconvert.

When religious style is assessed by our new instrument, the Religious Schema Scale,[30] there is a significant decrease in the scores on the RSS subscale of *truth of texts and teachings* for deconverts in both countries, as table 12.7 shows. This reflects deconverts' reluctance to insist on the truth of their own religion and also their openness to the truth of other religions, which is indicated by their higher means on the RSS subscale of *xenosophia/inter-religious dialog*[31] in both countries (even though this is significant only for the US respondents).

In sum, deconverts have a considerably larger share in individuative-reflective style than in synthetic-conventional style, as well as higher scores on the RSS subscales of *fairness, tolerance and rational choice*, and *xenosophia/inter-religious dialog* and lower scores on the subscale of *truth of text and teachings*. This suggests that changes in faith development, religious styles, and religious schemata are characteristics of deconversion.

Table 12.7 Differences on the Faith Development Interview Scores and the Subscales of the Religious Schema Scale between Deconverts and In-Tradition Members in the United States and Germany

	Germany				United States			
	In-tradition members		Deconverts		In-tradition members		Deconverts	
	Mean	SD	Mean	SD	Mean	SD	Mean	SD
Truth of texts and teachings	**17.17**[a]	4.38	**14.41**[b]	5.31	**17.35**[c]	4.14	**11.42**[d]	4.38
Fairness, tolerance	20.98[a]	2.21	20.42[e]	1.81	**19.57**[f]	2.49	**21.00**[g]	2.80
Xenosophia	15.73[h]	4.10	16.54[g]	4.60	**16.51**[i]	2.95	**18.32**[g]	3.32

[a] N = 226; [b] N = 27; [c] N = 532; [d] N = 26; [e] N = 28; [f] N = 535; [g] N = 28; [h] N = 225; [i] N = 536; **bold** = significant difference (p <.01) between in-tradition members and deconverts.

A TYPOLOGY OF DECONVERSION NARRATIVES

Last, but definitely not least, since narrative interviews with 99 deconverts constitute the core of the Bielefeld-based study on deconversion, I present the typology that has emerged from the analysis of narrative and faith development interviews and from triangulation with the questionnaire data. Four types of deconversion narratives can be identified.

The first type is called *pursuit of autonomy.* This type of deconversion narrative is characterized by a rather long-term gradual process of stepping out from the previously taken-for-granted religious environment into which one was born or brought by one's parents as a child. It is a search for individuation and the critical development of new perspectives which, rather as a rule than as an exception, lead to secular and heretical exits. It is generally associated with the prevalence of the individuative-reflective religious style and with low scores on the *truth of text and teachings* subscale of the Religious Schema Scale. Scores on *psychological well-being* appear to be high for US deconverts of this type but, in contrast, moderate or low for German deconverts. Religious persons who were either born into a faith tradition or were brought by their parents to a community at a very young age tend to leave their traditions during adolescence or early adulthood and to step out away from the family and religious group, orienting toward an open and sometimes insecure future and insisting on their independence and autonomy.

The second type of deconversion narrative, *debarred from paradise,* is characterized by an emotionally deep attachment to a religious tradition that is supposed to heal early trauma and protect from personal loss—a rather deep affiliation that does not normally develop before adolescence or early adulthood. Thus, for the conversion part of their story, many of these cases are mid-life converts with all the expectations and affection of a once-in-a-lifetime decision. Characteristics of the disaffiliation process in this type of deconvert are disappointment of high expectations, abandonment of earlier hopes, withdrawal of affection for religious leaders, and the wish to give testimony of these traumatic experiences. It is an open question as to which direction the disaffiliation for those *debarred from paradise* may go—whether into secularity, private religious practice, or heretical search—but one thing is almost certainly excluded: new affiliation with a religious organization. Thus, this type of deconvert is very likely to leave the segment of organized religion, and this type is also the most intense and dramatic type of deconversion. With only rare exceptions, this type of deconvert is characterized by very low scores on the *religious fundamentalism* scale, indicating very strong rejection of the former belief system, and by high scores in faith development, including individuative-reflective and conjunctive styles.

The third type of deconversion is called *finding a new frame of reference*. This type of deconvert is characterized by searching and finding more intensity, guidance, and structure in one's religious life. This type very likely consists of disaffiliates from the mainline churches in which the deconverts grew up. These deconversion trajectories are therefore mostly oppositional exits and involve converting to a higher tension group. Deconversion here involves a conversion experience that can be seen as conversion or reconversion. As the German cases in particular indicate, this is a very intense personal experience that leads to a new kind of personal religiosity, such as an intense personal relation to Jesus. Before the (re-) conversion, there may be a kind of moratorium that may involve orientations such as atheism, interest in other world religions, depression, or perhaps the taking of drugs. Thus, the new religiosity is portrayed as a complete change of life and morality.

The fourth type of deconversion narrative, *life-long quests—late revisions*, is characterized by leaving a religious environment once or multiple times because it does not meet one's needs and expectations. This is the type of seeker whose religious quest typically emerged in adolescence and young adulthood and led to conversion at a relatively early age, typically into a religious tradition with higher tension. So far, deconverts of this type have parallels with the second type that later is "debarred from paradise." Deconverts of this type are not "debarred," however, but mostly leave of their own free will to look for something better. There may even be a series of deconversions that usually are integrating exits but may also be private or heretical exits. Some deconverts of this type are on a lifelong journey pursuing an individual project such as coming to terms with a traumatic childhood, finding the most "fitting" mystical or spiritual environment, or attaining the inner peace that they desire.

CONCLUSION

The results of the recent studies discussed in this chapter—the Pew disaffiliation study, the ISSP Religion III, and the Bielefeld-based deconversion study—can be seen as complementing each other, differences notwithstanding. Two of these studies have the potential of cross-cultural comparison, putting deconversion in the United States in a larger perspective and opening up a global view. The great contribution and advantage of the ISSP and Pew results is that they are based on large samples that are representative of the population of an entire nation. This allows questions to be answered in relation to the frequency of deconversion, for example, and about migration streams within and out of the religious field. This comprises the first theme for my conclusion.

In the study of deconversion, a polythetic definition of deconversion and a conceptually predefined typology of deconversion trajectories in the religious field may count as advancement. I do not insist that my conceptualization and typology is the only one which can be imagined and thus should be accepted without critique. But any nomothetic approach depends on the quality of conceptualization. For the study of deconversion, such conceptualization is necessary, not just to help prevent oversimplifications such as the identification of deconversion with termination of membership. The model of the religious field that includes the segment of unorganized religion also helps to interpret empirical results that indicate that deconversion is not simply "falling from the faith," a move into mere unbelief, atheism, or secularism. On the contrary, many deconversions—certainly the majority of deconversions in the United States—can be understood as migrations within the boundaries of the religious field when we include the unorganized segment.

There is a special group of deconverts which is easily overlooked: the considerable number of deconverts who migrate into the unorganized segment of the religious field. This is supported by the results of ISSP and the Bielefeld-based deconversion study, but only because they have paid special attention to "spiritual" self-identification: in both cultures, the United States and Germany, deconversion is associated with a reluctance to identify as "being religious" and with a clear preference to self-identify as a "spiritual person." In sociological terms, these are indications that deconverts do not tend to associate with religious organizations that require self-identification as being "religious" but instead prefer affiliations which allow self-identifications of being "spiritual" or being "neither," if such organizations are available. The latter appears to be the case in the United States, but not in Germany.

The lack of religious organizations that allow members to self-identify as spiritual may be one of the reasons why there are more secular exits in Germany than in the United States. The difference between Germany and the United States in this regard is large. As figure 12.3 reveals, the net loss of members in the religious field in the United States—or, viewed from the other side, the net increase in the secular realm—appears rather small (1.2 percent of the population) and has almost no net increase, when we compare the 3.7 percent secular exiters with the 2.4 percent converts who enter the religious field. This is completely different in Germany, where we have not only 19.1 percent permanently secular people, but also an increase of 9.4 percent in the secular milieus (this is, in part, due to the subsample of East Germany, which is very likely one of the most secular regions of the globe). Deconversion in the United States seems to be more different from deconversion in Europe than expected.

The difference between the religious fields in the United States and Germany may help to explain the difference in empirical results in the Bielefeld-based study of deconversion regarding personality factors and well-being, which indicate a mild crisis associated with deconversion. The options for social association and integration—the likelihood of finding a new religious community that responds to one's spiritual quest or simply to one's religious crisis—makes a difference. German deconverts appear to have fewer options and thus to be more likely to be left alone without a religious community after deconversion than deconverts in the United States.

The second theme of this conclusion is the creation of a summary portrait of deconversion from an analysis of the psychometric scales and biographies. Deconversion appears to be a step into freedom, autonomy, and personal growth. The comparison of deconverts and in-tradition members in the Bielefeld-based study on deconversion, as shown above, indicates this, especially for deconverts in the United States. The interpretation of the biographical material has resulted in the emergence of the "pursuit of autonomy" type of deconvert, which the "life-long quests—late revision" deconversion narrative type resembles.

Yet, upon reconsidering the pre-defined deconversion criteria (which have been key in defining what can count as deconversion), there is something new emerging from the research using the psychometric scales and from the analysis of the biographical material. The deconversion criteria, as defined with reference to Barbour's work,[32] reflect a crisis and focus on negations that are associated with the disaffiliation process. The results of the Bielefeld-based study on deconversion shed light on the fact that a crisis can be a turning point to something even better. This can be demonstrated in some detail by a review of the deconversion criteria one by one. Loss of religious experience corresponds to *openness to experience* on the Big Five subscale, which has emerged from empirical analysis as one of the key characteristics of deconversion. Intellectual doubt and denial may indicate the cognitive crisis that precedes faith stage transition and structural conversion in classical faith development theory;[33] in any case, a change in religious style appears to be another key characteristic of deconversion, as the data from the Bielefeld-based study on deconversion indicate. The crisis of deconversion could very well lead to a new cognitive structure, to a new interpretation of heaven and earth with a preference for new religious schemata. Moral criticism could signal the advent of the sense of *autonomy* which appears from the data to be another key characteristic of deconversion. Emotional suffering can be exchanged for a sense of *personal growth*. This is especially relevant for the type of deconvert who is or feels "debarred from paradise." But even here, when interpreting the biographical accounts of these cases, we have seen, with some exceptions, instances of post-traumatic growth. Finally, disaffiliation from the community indicates a loss and deconverts struggle with the compensation for this loss. And indeed, *positive relations with others* in the Ryff Scale are lower for German deconverts and indifferent for the US deconverts. On the other hand, however, there are gains in regard to a sense of connectedness (apart from the lucky ones who immediately find a new community); a kind of new identity appears to emerge which is associated with the self-identification as "spiritual person." This self-identification as "spiritual" has also emerged as a key characteristic of deconversion. Perhaps the formation of "spiritual scenes"—which, to be sure, are largely unorganized—is a new development, especially in the United States, and one that may help deconverts feel at home.

In sum, exceptions notwithstanding, the portrait of deconversion, as I see it emerging from the psychometric and biographical analyses, is that of an active deconvert resembling the "active convert" as profiled by James T. Richardson,[34] a profile which has been a major turning point in conversion research.

I conclude with a note on methodology for the study of deconversion. For a detailed portrait of deconversion, a mixed-method approach that includes psychometric scales and semi-structured or open-ended interviews is best. The construction of the typology of deconversion narratives in the Bielefeld deconversion study would not have been possible without the thorough interpretation of narrative and faith development interviews and the triangulation of all sorts of data in the case studies.

Notes

1. See Heinz Streib and Constantin Klein, "Atheists, Agnostics, and Apostates," in *APA Handbook of Psychology, Religion and Spirituality*, ed. Kenneth Ira Pargament, Julie Juola Exline, and James W. Jones (Washington, DC: American Psychological Association, forthcoming).
2. John D. Barbour, *Versions of Deconversion: Autobiography and the Loss of Faith* (Charlottesville: University Press of Virginia, 1994).
3. Charles Y. Glock, "On the Study of Religious Commitment," in *Kirche und Gesellschaft: Einführung in die Religionssoziologie*, ed. Joachim Matthes (Reinbek, Germany: Rowohlt, 1969), 98–110.
4. Heinz Streib and Barbara Keller, "The Variety of Deconversion Experiences: Contours of a Concept in Respect to Empirical Research," *Archive for the Psychology of Religion / Archiv für Religionspychologie* 26, no. 1 (2004): 181–200.
5. Heinz Streib et al., *Deconversion: Qualitative and Quantitative Results from Cross-Cultural Research in Germany and the United States of America*, Research in Contemporary Religion, 5 (Göttingen, Germany: Vandenhoeck & Ruprecht, 2009).
6. Ibid.
7. With reference to Bromley's distinction of religious groups as subversive, contestant, and allegiant religious organizations, but modifying Bromley's typology in a way that attends primarily to the degree of tension with or integration in society, Streib et al. (*Deconversion*) distinguish between oppositional, accommodating, and integrated religious organizations. See David G. Bromley, "The Social Construction of Contested Exit Roles: Defectors, Whistleblowers, and Apostates," in *The Politics of Religious Apostasy: The Role of Apostates in the Transformation of Religious Movements*, ed. David G. Bromley (Westport, CT: Praeger, 1998), 19–48.

8. *Privatizing exit* and *heretical exit* correspond largely to what Luckmann called "invisible religion." Thomas Luckmann, *The Invisible Religion: The Problem of Religion in Modern Society* (New York: Macmillan 1967).

9. Pierre Bourdieu, "Genesis and Structure of the Religious Field," *Comparative Social Research* 13 (1991): 1–44; Pierre Bourdieu, "Legitimation and Structured Interest in Weber's Sociology of Religion," in *Max Weber: Rationality and Modernity*, ed. Scott Lash and Sam Whimster (London: Allen & Unwin, 1987), 119–136.

10. Ernst Troeltsch, "Das stoisch-christliche Naturrecht und das moderne profane Naturrecht," *Verhandlungen des Ersten Deutschen Soziologentages vom 19–22. Oktober 1910 in Frankfurt a.M.*, Schriften der Deutschen Gesellschaft für Soziologie, Erste Serie (Tübingen, Germany: Mohr [Paul Siebeck], 1911), 166–214; Ernst Troeltsch, *The Social Teaching of the Christian Churches*, Vol. 2 (London: George Allen & Unwin, 1956).

11. See chapter 2 of Streib et al., *Deconversion*, for a more detailed summary of extant research on deconversion prior to 2007.

12. Here I refer especially to the International Social Survey Programme (ISSP) that includes longitudinal data on religion from 1991, 1998, and 2008. Such data for the United States are integrated in the General Social Survey (GSS 1972–2008).

13. Examples of this kind of study are L. Norman Skonovd, *Apostasy: The Process of Defection from Religious Totalism* (Ann Arbor, MI: University Microfilms, 1981); Saul V. Levine, *Radical Departures: Desperate Detours to Growing Up* (New York: Harcourt Brace Jovanovich, 1984); Janet L. Jacobs, *Divine Disenchantment: Deconverting from New Religions* (Bloomington: Indiana University Press, 1989); Stuart A. Wright, *Leaving Cults: The Dynamics of Defection* (Washington, DC: Society for the Scientific Study of Religion, 1987). Somewhat later, but still belonging in this category, the Enquete Commission on "So-called Sects and Psycho-Groups" of the 13th German Parliament initiated some qualitative studies in which I participated. See Heinz Streib, "Sub-project on 'Biographies in Christian Fundamentalist Milieus and Organizations,'" in *Final Report of the Enquête Commission on "So-called Sects and Psychogroups,"* ed. Deutscher Bundestag, Referat Öffentlichkeitsarbeit (Bonn: Deutscher Bundestag, 1999), 402–414; Heinz Streib, *Biographies in Christian Fundamentalist Milieus and Organizations: Report to the Enquete Commission of the 13th German Parliament on "So-called Sects and Psychogroups,"* trans. Ella Brehm, CIRRuS Research Reports, No. 1 (Bielefeld: University of Bielefeld, 2000), http://repositories.ub.uni-bielefeld.de/biprints/volltexte/2009/2134.

14. As examples of these studies, see Bob Altemeyer and Bruce Hunsberger, *Amazing Conversions: Why Some Turn to Faith and Others Abandon Religion* (New York: Prometheus, 1997); for a study in the United States, see Bruce Hunsberger, "Swimming Against the Current: Exceptional Cases of Apostates and Converts," in *Joining and Leaving Religion: Research Perspectives*, ed. Leslie J. Francis and Yaacov J. Katz (Leominster, England: Gracewing, 2000), 233–248; for research on church-leavers in the United Kingdom, see Philip Richter and Leslie J. Francis, *Gone But Not Forgotten: Church Leaving and Returning* (London: Darton, Longman, Todd, 1998); for a study in New Zealand, see Alan Jamieson, *A Churchless Faith: Faith Journeys beyond the Churches* (London: Society for Promoting Christian Knowledge, 2002).

15. For America, again, Bob Altemeyer and Bruce Hunsberger's study stands out; see *Atheists: A Groundbreaking Study of America's Nonbelievers* (Amherst, NY: Prometheus Books, 2006); see also Barry A. Kosmin and Ariela Keysar, "Secularism and Secularity:

Contemporary International Perspectives," 2007, http://prog.trincoll.edu/ISSSC/Book/Chapters.asp.

16. For my calculations, I have used the data from the *International Social Survey Programme* (*ISSP*), *Religion III*, released Feb. 14, 2011. Country-specific data sets for the United States have already been included in the database of the *General Social Survey* (GSS 1972–2008), and the data for Germany is included in the *Allgemeine Bevölkerungsumfrage der Sozialwissenschaften* (ALLBUS 2008).

17. In the presentation of the Pew study, 9 percent was labeled "other changes in religious affiliation." The report explains: "This group consists of converts from a variety of different backgrounds, including converts to Catholicism and converts from or to religions other than Catholicism or Protestantism. Because this is such a disparate group, it is not analyzed in most of this report." Pew Forum on Religion and Public Life, "Faith in Flux: Changes in Religious Affiliation in the U.S.," 2009, 1 n.

18. Previous results concerning the frequency of multiple changes are outdated. They date back as long ago as 1988 (e.g., the GSS) and report 23.8 percent with one previous preference, 9.1 percent with two, 2.2 percent with three, and 0.6 percent with four or more previous preferences. Most other previous studies, however, only allow a comparison of the present religious affiliation with the affiliation in childhood and thus do not account for the religious migrations that may have occurred between childhood and the present. Likewise, a person who, after a tour through different religions, reaffiliated with her or his childhood faith could not be identified as a deconvert.

19. This portrait emerges from the Pew Report, even though it may be noted that the motives could be grouped together more systematically. For a more systematic portrait of deconversion motives, I would suggest either a conceptual approach using the deconversion criteria as defined by Streib and Keller ("Variety of Deconversion Experiences"), or a purely statistical procedure such as a factor analysis. Unfortunately, the data base of the Pew research on disaffiliation had not been released before this manuscript was completed. So, I can only discuss here what is presented in the Pew Report ("Faith in Flux").

20. Figure 2 corresponds to results from the Bielefeld-based cross-cultural study on deconversion (Heinz Streib, "More Spiritual than Religious: Changes in the Religious Field Require New Approaches," in *Lived Religion: Conceptual, Empirical and Practical-Theological Approaches*, ed. Heinz Streib, Astrid Dinter, and Kerstin Söderblom (Leiden: Brill, 2008), 53–67; Streib et. al., *Deconversion*). These results, even without the distinction between the various deconversion trajectories, indicated high percentages of deconverts who self-identify as "more spiritual than religious," namely 63.6 percent for the United States and 36.5 percent for Germany (see figure 12.4). For an explanation of the difference between the deconversion study and the ISSP, we may refer to the different ways of asking the spirituality question, to the different assessments of deconversion or disaffiliation, to the different amounts of time since the disaffiliation took place, and to the different samples in respect to representativeness and number of deconverts.

21. Unfortunately, the ISSP data sets do not allow the reconstruction of the distinction between church and sect or, in the terms of the deconversion study, the distinction between integrated and oppositional religious organizations. The data set for Germany lacks any information which would allow for such an assessment, and the data set for the United States has information only about a (limited) variety of Protestant denominations which perhaps could be divided into integrated and oppositional (e.g., by expert rating), but even then

it would only cover a rather limited field segment of (Protestant) denominations in the United States.

22. The results from my ISSP calculations can be used to assess the quantity of disaffiliation/reaffiliation migrations in the religious landscape with more precision. Thus, this assessment of deconversion trajectories was entered in table 12.4 and used for the comparison with the Pew results. This calculation from the ISSP data sets allows what could not be accomplished on the basis of the data of the Bielefeld-based study of deconversion, namely, the quantification of the deconversion trajectories on the basis of a large-scale survey representative of the populations in the United States and in Germany.

23. I have slightly rearranged the table offered in the Pew Report ("Faith in Flux," 1). Further, it should be noted that the values from the *ISSP* for the United States and for Germany are recalculations based on my own construction of a variable for the deconversion trajectories, which is the basis for the values in figure 12.3.

24. Streib et al., *Deconversion.*

25. Methods and instruments used for the qualitative part of the Bielefeld-based Cross-cultural Study on Deconversion: (1) The *narrative interview* was the core instrument of the study focusing on the deconversion process, religious socialization in the past, and consequences for the present. These interviews were transcribed and evaluated in a computer-assisted procedure. Cases selected according to the emerging typology were elaborated into case studies. Quantifiable results were entered into an SPSS database; (2) The *faith development interviews* were conducted and evaluated according to James W. Fowler, Heinz Streib, and Barbara Keller, *Manual for Faith Development Research,* 3rd ed. (Bielefeld: Research Center for Biographical Studies in Contemporary Religion, 2004), http://wwwhomes. uni-bielefeld.de/religionsforschung/. Evaluation of this semi-structured interview is interpretative, but it was done in a computer-assisted procedure. These results were also entered into SPSS.

26. The questionnaire included not only demographics but also a set of four items to assess the spiritual/religious self-identification (see figure 12.4). Scales included in the questionnaire were: the Big Five Personality Factor Instrument (Costa and McCrae, 1985; McCrae and Costa, 1987) in its NEO-FFI version probing for extraversion, openness to experience, agreeableness, conscientiousness, and neuroticism (which was reverse-coded into emotional stability); C. Ryff's scale on Psychological Well-Being and Growth (Ryff and Singer, 1996), which assesses six characteristics related to personal growth and well-being (Ryff, 1989; Ryff and Singer, 1998a, 1998b): autonomy, environmental mastery, personal growth, positive relations with others, and purpose in life; the Religious Fundamentalism Scale (Altemeyer and Hunsberger, 1992); the Right Wing Authoritarianism Scale (Altemeyer, 1981); and finally 78 new items designed for the assessment of religious styles, which became the basis for the Religious Schema Scale (Streib, Hood, and Klein, 2010).

27. The distribution of deconversion trajectories in the Bielefeld-based study of deconversion does not exactly correspond to the distribution as calculated for this chapter on the basis of the ISSP data (and presented in figure 12.3), because the sampling strategy applied methods of theoretical sampling and did not start with a sample representative of the population.

28. Heinz Streib, Ralph W. Hood, and Constantin Klein, "The Religious Schema Scale: Construction and Initial Validation of a Quantitative Measure for Religious Styles," *International Journal for the Psychology of Religion* 20, no. 3 (2010): 151–172.

29. Heinz Streib, "More Spiritual than Religious: Changes in the Religious Field Require New Approaches," in *Lived Religion: Conceptual, Empirical and Practical-Theological*

Approaches, ed. Heinz Streib, Astrid Dinter, and Kerstin Söderblom (Leiden: Brill, 2008), 53–67; Streib et al., *Deconversion*.

30. Streib, Hood, and Klein, "Religious Schema Scale."
31. Xenosophia, it should be explained, is the wisdom (*sophia*) of the strange or alien (*xenos*); it is thus the opposite of xenophobia and exceeds the attitude of tolerance to include the appreciation of the alien and strange as a source of creativity and inspiration. See Yoshiro Nakamura, *Xenosophie:Bausteine für eine Theorie der Fremdheit* (Darmstadt, Germany: Wissenschaftliche Buchgesellschaft, 2000).
32. Barbour, *Versions of Deconversion*.
33. James W. Fowler, *Stages of Faith: The Psychology of Human Development and the Quest for Meaning* (San Francisco, CA: Harper & Row, 1981).
34. James T. Richardson, ed., *Conversion Careers: In and Out of the New Religions* (Beverly Hills, CA: Sage Publications, 1978); James T. Richardson, "Psychological and Psychiatric Studies on New Religious Movements," in *Advances in the Psychology of Religion*, ed. L. B. Brown (Oxford: Pergamon Press, 1985), 209–223; James T. Richardson, "The Active vs. Passive Convert: Paradigm Conflict in Conversion/Recruitment Research," *Journal for the Scientific Study of Religion* 24, no. 2 (1985): 163–179; James T. Richardson, "Clinical and Personality Assessment of Participants in New Religions," *International Journal for the Psychology of Religion* 5, no. 3 (1995): 145–170.

BIBLIOGRAPHY

ALLBUS. *Allgemeine Bevölkerungsumfrage der Sozialwissenschaften (Data File)*. Köln: GESIS, 2008.

Altemeyer, Bob. *Right-Wing Authoritarianism*. Winnipeg: University of Manitoba Press, 1981.

Altemeyer, Bob, and Bruce Hunsberger. *Amazing Conversions: Why Some Turn to Faith and Others Abandon Religion*. New York: Prometheus, 1997.

——. *Atheists: A Groundbreaking Study of America's Nonbelievers*. Amherst, NY: Prometheus Books, 2006.

——. "Authoritarianism, Religious Fundamentalism, Quest and Prejudice." *International Journal for the Psychology of Religion* 2, no. 2 (1992): 113–133.

Barbour, John D. *Versions of Deconversion: Autobiography and the Loss of Faith*. Charlottesville: University Press of Virginia, 1994.

Bourdieu, Pierre. "Genesis and Structure of the Religious Field." *Comparative Social Research* 13 (1991): 1–44.

——. "Legitimation and Structured Interest in Weber's Sociology of Religion." In *Max Weber: Rationality and Modernity*, ed. Scott Lash and Sam Whimster, 119–136. London: Allen & Unwin, 1987.

Bromley, David G. "The Social Construction of Contested Exit Roles: Defectors, Whistleblowers, and Apostates." In *The Politics of Religious Apostasy: The Role of Apostates in the Transformation of Religious Movements*, ed. David G. Bromley, 19–48. Westport, CT: Praeger, 1998.

Costa, Paul T., and Robert R. McCrae. *Revised NEO Personality Inventory (NEO PI-R) and NEO Five-Factor-Inventory (NEO-FFI). Professional Manual*. Odessa, FL: Psychological Assessment Resources, 1985.

Fowler, James W. *Stages of Faith: The Psychology of Human Development and the Quest for Meaning*. San Francisco, CA: Harper & Row, 1981.

Fowler, James W., Heinz Streib, and Barbara Keller. *Manual for Faith Development Research.* 3rd ed., Bielefeld: Research Center for Biographical Studies in Contemporary Religion, Bielefeld, 2004. http://wwwhomes.uni-bielefeld.de/religionsforschung/.

General Social Survey 1972–2008 (Data File). Chicago: National Opinion Research Center, The Roper Center for Public Opinion Research, University of Connecticut, 2009.

Glock, Charles Y. "On the Study of Religious Commitment." In *Kirche und Gesellschaft: Einführung in die Religionssoziologie,* ed. Joachim Matthes, 98–110. Reinbek, Germany: Rowohlt, 1969.

Hunsberger, Bruce. "Swimming Against the Current: Exceptional Cases of Apostates and Converts." In *Joining and Leaving Religion: Research Perspectives,* ed. Leslie J. Francis and Yaacov J. Katz, 233–248. Leominster, England: Gracewing, 2000.

Jacobs, Janet L. *Divine Disenchantment: Deconverting from New Religions.* Bloomington: Indiana University Press, 1989.

Jamieson, Alan. *A Churchless Faith: Faith Journeys beyond the Churches.* London: Society for Promoting Christian Knowledge, 2002.

Kosmin, Barry A., and Ariela Keysar. "Secularism and Secularity: Contemporary International Perspectives." 2007. http://prog.trincoll.edu/ISSSC/Book/Chapters.asp.

Levine, Saul V. *Radical Departures: Desperate Detours to Growing Up.* New York: Harcourt Brace Jovanovich, 1984.

Luckmann, Thomas. *The Invisible Religion: The Problem of Religion in Modern Society.* New York: Macmillan 1967.

McCrae, Robert R., and Paul T. Costa. "Validation of the Five-Factor Model of Personality across Instruments and Observers." *Journal of Personality and Social Psychology* 52 (1987): 81–90.

Nakamura, Yoshiro. *Xenosophie: Bausteine für eine Theorie der Fremdheit.* Darmstadt, Germany: Wissenschaftliche Buchgesellschaft, 2000.

Pew Forum on Religion and Public Life. "Faith in Flux: Changes in Religious Affiliation in the U.S." 2009. http://pewforum.org/.

Richardson, James T., "The Active vs. Passive Convert: Paradigm Conflict in Conversion/ Recruitment Research." *Journal for the Scientific Study of Religion* 24, no. 2 (1985): 163–179.

——. "Clinical and Personality Assessment of Participants in New Religions." *International Journal for the Psychology of Religion* 5, no. 3 (1995): 145–170.

——. "Psychological and Psychiatric Studies on New Religious Movements." In *Advances in the Psychology of Religion,* ed. L. B. Brown, 209–223. Oxford: Pergamon Press, 1985.

Richardson, James T., ed. *Conversion Careers: In and Out of the New Religions.* Beverly Hills, CA: Sage Publications, 1978.

Richter, Philip, and Leslie J. Francis. *Gone But Not Forgotten: Church Leaving and Returning.* London: Darton, Longman, Todd, 1998.

Ryff, Carol D. "Happiness Is Everything, Or Is It? Explorations on the Meaning of Psychological Well-Being." *Journal of Personality and Social Psychology* 57, no. 6 (1989): 1069–1081.

Ryff, Carol D., and Burton H. Singer. "The Contours of Positive Human Health." *Psychological Inquiry* 9, no. 1 (1998a): 1–28.

——. "Psychological Well-Being: Meaning, Measurement, and Implications for Psychotherapy Research." *Psychotherapy and Psychosomatics* 65, no. 1 (1996): 14–23.

——. "The Role of Purpose in Life and Growth in Positive Human Health." In *The Human Quest for Meaning: Handbook of Psychological Research and Clinical Applications,* ed. Paul T. P. Wong and Prem S. Fry, 213–235. Mahwah, NJ: Lawrence Erlbaum Associates, 1998b.

Skonovd, L. Norman. *Apostasy: The Process of Defection from Religious Totalism.* Ann Arbor, MI: University Microfilms, 1981.

Streib, Heinz. *Biographies in Christian Fundamentalist Milieus and Organizations: Report to the Enquete Commission of the 13th German Parliament on "So-called Sects and Psychogroups."* Trans. Ella Brehm, CIRRuS Research Reports, No. 1, Bielefeld: University of Bielefeld, 2000. http://repositories.ub.uni-bielefeld.de/biprints/volltexte/2009/2134.

——. "More Spiritual than Religious: Changes in the Religious Field Require New Approaches." In *Lived Religion: Conceptual, Empirical and Practical-Theological Approaches*, ed. Heinz Streib, Astrid Dinter, and Kerstin Söderblom, 53–67. Leiden: Brill, 2008.

——. "Sub-project on 'Biographies in Christian Fundamentalist Milieus and Organizations.'" In *Final Report of the Enquête Commission on "So-called Sects and Psychogroups,"* ed. Deutscher Bundestag, Referat Öffentlichkeitsarbeit, 402–414. Bonn: Deutscher Bundestag, 1999.

Streib, Heinz, and Barbara Keller. "The Variety of Deconversion Experiences: Contours of a Concept in Respect to Empirical Research." *Archive for the Psychology of Religion / Archiv für Religionspychologie* 26, no. 1 (2004): 181–200.

Streib, Heinz, and Constantin Klein. "Atheists, Agnostics, and Apostates." In *APA Handbook of Psychology, Religion and Spirituality*, ed. Kenneth Ira Pargament, Julie Juola Exline, and James W. Jones. Washington, DC: American Psychological Association, 2013.

Streib, Heinz, Ralph W. Hood, and Constantin Klein. "The Religious Schema Scale: Construction and Initial Validation of a Quantitative Measure for Religious Styles." *International Journal for the Psychology of Religion* 20, no. 3 (2010): 151–172.

Streib, Heinz, Ralph W. Hood, Barbara Keller, Rosina-Martha Csöff, and Christopher Silver. *Deconversion: Qualitative and Quantitative Results from Cross-Cultural Research in Germany and the United States of America.* Research in Contemporary Religion, 5. Göttingen: Vandenhoeck & Ruprecht, 2009.

Troeltsch, Ernst. "Das stoisch-christliche Naturrecht und das moderne profane Naturrecht." *Verhandlungen des Ersten Deutschen Soziologentages vom 19–22. Oktober 1910 in Frankfurt a.M.* Schriften der Deutschen Gesellschaft für Soziologie, Erste Serie, 166–214. Tübingen, Germany: Mohr (Paul Siebeck), 1911.

——. *The Social Teaching of the Christian Churches.* Vol. 2. London: George Allen & Unwin, 1956.

Wright, Stuart A. *Leaving Cults: The Dynamics of Defection.* Washington, DC: Society for the Scientific Study of Religion, 1987.

CHAPTER 13

....

FEMINIST APPROACHES TO THE STUDY OF RELIGIOUS CONVERSION

....

ELIZA F. KENT

CHANGES in the social organization of gender are frequently central to the constitution of new identities and communities through religious conversion, whether the conversion takes place via the embrace of a new religious tradition or via the intensification of religiosity while remaining within the same tradition. Similarly, the methods of evangelism, the psychological and social conditions predisposing one to conversion and the manifold effects of conversion are also thoroughly imbricated with changing social norms and expectations related to gender. And yet, until recently, scholarship on conversion has largely neglected gender as a category of analysis.

One reason for this is that in many religious traditions women have been excluded from public and/or professional areas of religious life and so have not been readily visible to researchers. In many religious traditions women can only act publicly in gender-segregated spaces, and even there, their activities have not been granted much importance or value. For example, the extent to which male voices and concerns dominated the archives of the English Society for the Propagation for the Gospel (and the Society itself in its heyday) was such that historian Jeffrey Cox worked in them for months before he realized that the mission was predominantly female.[1] Second, to the extent that these sexist biases extend into the academy, scholars have often considered men's experiences to be the norm and thus have not questioned whether the patterns they see among men apply equally to women. As Lewis Rambo observes in his 1991 examination of a wide spectrum of theories of conversion, "there are very few studies of women's conversion experiences to offset the assumed generic (but almost always male) research to date."[2] Consider William James's classic, *The Varieties of Religious Experience*, published in 1902. In the two chapters on conversion, he cites the personal testimony of thirty-five individuals spanning a range of social types: artists, writers, social activists, clergy, and ordinary "men-on-the-street." But of these only one is clearly identified as a woman.[3] Twenty-three are men, and the gender of eleven is not specified. The salience of "gender" as a specific category of analysis has only arisen with the recognition that women's experience may well be different from men's experience.

From this fundamental recognition, feminist thought has evolved in complex ways and continues to be enriched and extended by new questions and debates up to the present day.[4] Much early feminist scholarship began with the task of making women and their contributions visible against centuries of marginalization and obfuscation.[5] More recent feminist research, however, has broadened the focus from "women" to "gender," where gender refers to the norms, conventions, processes, and practices through which people come to understand, implicitly and more rarely explicitly, what it means to be a "man" or a "woman" and what is expected of the relationships between and among men and women.[6] The meanings attached to perceived differences between the sexes are shaped by and shape in turn innumerable dimensions of social life. The sexual division of labor, the assignment of roles within the family, kinship relationships, the organization of domestic and public space, and norms that govern how one should speak, dress, and walk are all arenas within which masculinity and femininity are constituted.

All these arenas of social life are also transformed by the process of conversion. The inclusion of gender as a central analytic category in the study of religious change thus opens up vast new areas of inquiry. In the following sections, I attempt to show how trends within gender and feminist studies in religion have brought new questions and approaches to the study of religious change.

HISTORICAL STUDIES OF WOMEN AND CONVERSION: AFRICA AND INDIA

From a historical point of view, one could argue that the first pioneers to pay careful attention to the specificity of women's experience of conversion were Christian missionaries who noted clear patterns in the way that the men and women to whom they had been "sent" were either attracted to or repulsed by the gospel. Male and female missionaries in India, for example, initially perceived Indian women to be more resistant than Indian men to the spiritual and social transformations that conversion to Christianity entailed. Missionary observers felt that men exposed to Christianity through mission-sponsored schools, for example, might have been eager to embrace Christianity, but their wives remained "staunch," even "bigoted," Hindus.[7] The perception that uneducated Hindu women presented an obstacle to the widespread acceptance of Christianity in India was, in fact, an important rationale for the creation of the so-called *zenana* missions, meant to reach women secluded in their homes by strict rules governing modesty. Named after the Hindi-Urdu word for the women's compartments in a traditional north Indian home, missionaries had high ambitions for what *zenana* missions could accomplish. It was hoped that converting Indian women as wives would not only make it easier for their husbands to live openly as Christians but also that newly Christian Indian women would bring their nurturing influence to bear on the next generation in their capacity as mothers. "Reaching women," however, meant developing new methods of evangelism. These built on ideas about women's nature that Indians and Westerners shared in common, namely, that women are more emotional and less intellectual and that they have a natural propensity for domestic endeavors like home-making and child-rearing.

Many supporters of the *zenana* missions saw distinct differences in the ways in which men and women came to an understanding of what they regarded as religious truth. In the 1850s, Protestant missions in India were pouring resources into bazaar preaching and mission-based schools, both evangelistic methods that depended on intellectual persuasion and on making a case in the public sphere for Christianity against Hinduism, Islam, and Sikhism. Such methods, it was thought, would not work on secluded Indian women with poorly developed intellectual capacities. At the second decennial Missionary Conference held in Calcutta in 1883, which brought together Protestant missionaries from many denominations and regions of India, speaker after speaker stood up to extol the virtues of the *zenana* missions. One representative, Miss Greenfield of the Society for the Promotion of Female Education in the East, eloquently expressed the matter in this way:

> "Higher education," we are told "was to slay Hinduism through its brain"—though it has not done so yet! My sisters, you and I in all our woman's weakness and conscious insufficiency are here in India to strike the death-blow, not at the monster's *head* but at his HEART, and by God's help we shall drain out his lifeblood yet! For I believe that the heart of Hinduism is not in the mystic teaching of the Vedas or Sharsters [*sic*], not in the finer spun philosophy of its modern exponents, not even in the bigoted devotion of its religious leaders; but enshrined in its homes, in the family life and hereditary customs of the people; fed, preserved, and perpetuated by the wives and mothers of India.... Let us in our Master's name lay our hand on the hand that rocks the cradle, and tune the lips that sing the lullabies. Let us win the mothers of India for Christ, and the day will not be long deferred when India's sons also shall be brought to the Redeemer's feet.[8]

As Greenfield suggests, a crucial assumption of the *zenana* missions was that religious sentiments were not only espoused in the scriptural and philosophical dimensions of a tradition but were also embedded in the practices of everyday life. If conversion was to really work, unconscious thoughts and feelings implanted by mothers at an early age would have to change.[9] The *zenana* missions, thus, sought to instill new virtues and new ideas in their pupils, the present and future mothers of India, by combining literacy training with Bible lessons and needlework. They positioned themselves in the home so that the lessons of the Bible could be applied pragmatically. Although the voices of converts are not well represented in missionary archives, some evidence suggests that Indian women converts themselves embraced the role of edifying mother and saw their conversion fundamentally within the context of their ability to bring others to Jesus, especially members of their family.[10]

If it is true that women missionaries (and the supporters of women's missionary societies) were the first to attend carefully to the differences in women's experiences of conversion, it is not surprising that the first scholarly studies to direct attention to these
differences focused on women's missionary societies. Patricia Hill's *The World Their
Household*, published in 1985, was one of the first English-language books to analyze
the social conditions that gave rise to women's involvement in foreign missions between
1870 and 1920.[11] In the United States and the United Kingdom, women's missions drew
their personnel mostly from the unmarried graduates of women's colleges and normal
schools, women who belonged to the first generation that was able to contemplate a life
of professional service rather than marriage and motherhood. Faced with a shortage of
suitable employment opportunities at home, they looked to domestic and foreign missions for positions consistent with the ambitions cultivated in these schools—to bring
women's nurturing and edifying talents to the world.[12] Such women were socially more
conservative than their equally activist counterparts in the movement for women's suf-
frage. They sought to bring their morally improving influence to society not through the
vote, but by expanding the boundaries of the domestic realm so as to make "the world
their household."

Confirming many of Hill's findings about the social location and political orientation of women missionaries, Jane Hunter's *The Gospel of Gentility: American Women
Missionaries in Turn-of-the-Century China* (1989) focuses attention on the extent to
which women missionaries supported the imperial project that provided the material
conditions for their work. They were, she finds, "empire seekers" in a fashion similar to
American and English merchants and soldiers, who depended on the social networks
and institutional infrastructure of British colonialism and thereby found an outlet for
their prodigious productive energy.[13] Hunter addresses a recurring question in scholarship on missionary women in colonial societies: did they contribute to the racist and
exploitative project of colonialism, or did they help to mitigate its negative impact,
reaching across racial barriers in alliances with native women? Clearly, white women
in the colonies—whether Christian evangelists or not—exhibited both complicity with
and resistance to the structures of imperial power. What is more interesting are the
ways in which religion in general, and conversion in particular, played a part in this. It is
hard to avoid the rhetoric of imperialism in the written portraits of missionary women
that nineteenth-century young women and girls eagerly consumed. In the writings of
many women missionaries, evangelism was often viewed as a battle for souls against an
invisible, but implacable, demonic adversary, such that political conflict could be read
as the material manifestation of spiritual conflict. While such rhetoric can be seen as
an endorsement of European imperialism, it is important to recognize the ways that
it energized women in a powerful new way. Through books, tracts, guest speakers in
churches, and fund-raising campaigns of all sorts, the missionary enterprise involved
British and American women in a heroic mission of cosmic proportions, whether as
missionaries themselves or as financial supporters back home pooling their "widows'
mites" to fund the former.

Hunter, like Hill and myself, also documents how the increasing independence and influence of white women in the colonies was built, in some ways, on the creation of a subordinate class of dependents among native women. And yet, Hunter argues that Christianity, and particularly the American-style Protestantism brought by US missionaries, also created new niches in which Chinese women thrived. For one, Christian women missionaries inspired their students to envision a meaningful life beyond the confines of marriage. Hunter recognizes considerable mutual benefit in the encounter between American missionary women and Chinese women, drawing on the testimony of women who looked back with pride on their experiences as an "experiment in international sisterhood." Hunter writes,

> Both students and teachers had ventured beyond strict conventions and away from easy traditions. Both were poised on a cultural interface, both engaged in creating feasible lives for themselves from an amalgam of feminine expectation, religious conviction, national affiliation and newfound opportunity.... The frontier where East met West offered them escape from home hierarchies. In remarkably similar ways, both Chinese women and their foreign mentors found mission institutions useful oases beyond the deserts of conventional familial expectation. Both Chinese and American women discovered that the margins of others' societies could encourage collective pride, nationalist consciousness, and female autonomy discouraged at the center of their own.[14]

One could argue that such possibilities for radical self-transformation are what make religious conversion so compelling for women and so threatening at the same time.

After years of neglect by historians, there is now a growing body of scholarship that attends to the importance of women as agents of conversion.[15] Given the lack of missionary sources that depict convert women's experiences, women at the receiving end of evangelism have been less frequently the focus of attention in historical studies. Interestingly, converts themselves are at the center of contemporary studies on conversion, as I will discuss shortly.

CHANGING ROLES OF MEN AND WOMEN IN AFRICA: CONVERSION TO CHRISTIANITY

It is important to remember that "gender" does not signify only "women." Rather, it refers to the norms, conventions, processes, and practices through which people come to understand, implicitly and more rarely explicitly, what it means to be a "man" or "woman" and what is expected of the relationships between and among men and women. Anthropologists Jean and John Comaroff's two-volume study of conversion in southern Africa, *Of Revelation and Revolution* (1991, 1997) has had an enormous impact on the study of conversion in colonized societies, in part because it makes plain how traditional gender roles for men and women were reshaped when Africans entered into relationships with the British evangelical Christian mission. In their delineation of "African worlds," for example, the Comaroffs detail how the early nineteenth-century Tswana household was organized around gender. Polygamous families maintained several discrete houses where each wife and her children lived, and each wife had her own field to till. Public spaces were those where men bound by agnatic ties (kinship ties created through the father) gathered: the front yard, the ward's meeting place, and the royal court. Private spaces—the hut and the enclosed back yard—were presided over by women. The relationship between a man and his agnatic relatives was fraught with conflict and competition, which was only partly moderated by naturalizing privilege according to age. In contrast, the relationship between a man and his maternal relatives (mother's brother, mother, siblings, etc.) was constructed as a refuge of harmony and mutual support. Besides this fundamental division between matrilateral and patrilateral kin, another gendered tension existed at the level of property. Strict rules governed the treatment of two very different kinds of property: land and agricultural produce, which were controlled by women, and cattle, which was controlled by men (though passed through women as bride price). Whereas owning cattle was highly valued, the agricultural produce that women produced through their labor was not.[16] Given this understanding of Tswana social structure, it is not surprising that the first converts from among the Tswana people were women of all ranks and junior males, who had the least to gain from the prevailing distribution of resources according to age. And yet, as Protestant missionaries in southern Africa began intervening in Tswana society, things became more complex.

Missionaries saw the gendered division of labor among the Tswana as perhaps the most deeply problematic aspect of their lives, even the most barbaric. That "tender" women should have to engage in hard physical labor while men eschewed the ennobling work of tilling the soil seemed to them a perverse reversal of the correct order of things.[17] Offering their own lives as examples for new converts, and encouraging those converts who lived within the ambit of their control to adopt productive practices they regarded as more civilized, missionaries set about encouraging men to engage in agriculture of the "proper" sort, that is, based on heavy tilling and irrigation. Interestingly, the Comaroffs argue that when Tswana women began to discern the implications of this "gospel of agriculture," they started sabotaging the missionaries' gardens and stealing their fruit. They continued to defend their near monopoly over agricultural production for several decades.[18] In addition to bringing about changes in productive relationships that were closely linked to gender differences, missionaries encouraged Tswana converts to change how they organized their homes and how they dressed and adorned their bodies. Such changes had an impact on the way that people came to see the meaning of both masculinity and femininity, as these were articulated in many different domains of social life.

Whereas in India missionaries had to struggle initially to attract women, and in southern Africa women were ambivalent toward the Protestant mission, in Tanzania women were the ones who flocked to the church in great numbers. This suggests that here too gender played a role in shaping how people responded to proselytization efforts. Historian Dorothy Hodgson's book, *The Church of Women: Gendered Encounters between Maasai and Missionaries* (2005), examines Roman Catholic churches founded by missionaries from the Congregation of the Holy Spirit (also known as Spiritans) working among the Maasai in eastern Africa from the 1950s to the present day in order to explain how the priests ended up creating a church composed almost entirely of women in spite of all their efforts to recruit men. As in India, the Spiritans tried a number of different methods of evangelism to attract adherents: mission-sponsored schools that sought to remake the "uncivilized" Maasai into proper modern subjects; group conversion of individuals organized into homesteads (*boma*) so as to inculturate Christianity by communicating the central message of the gospel through Maasai concepts and customs; and individual instruction classes. As Hodgson writes, "Maasai women were restricted from attending school, tolerated but not encouraged to attend homestead instruction and services, and dissuaded from holding formal leadership positions in the church. Despite these gendered evangelization strategies and objectives, however, significantly more Maasai women than men have sought instruction and baptism in the Catholic Church."[19] Through analysis of both ethnographic and historical data, Hodgson explains this paradoxical situation by illuminating how conversion to Christianity not only created new areas for women's exercise of social and moral power but also reclaimed old ones by building on women's traditional religious practices. Known mostly as nomadic pastoralists, the Maasai actually pursued a variety of livelihoods, including agro-pastoralism, farming, and hunting and gathering. Wealth, however, was mostly bound up with the ownership of cattle. Until the mid-nineteenth century, a complementary division of property and labor according to gender prevailed. Cattle were tended by both men and women, but the livestock and the products of livestock were divided according to gender. Women controlled the production and distribution of hides and milk (the primary food staple), while men were responsible for the distribution of meat, a highly prestigious food eaten mostly on ritual occasions.[20] The early nineteenth century, though, saw Maasai lifeworlds disrupted by disease epidemics and the consolidation of European colonization in Tanzania, first by the Germans and then by the British. State-sponsored campaigns to sedentarize the Maasai and integrate them into the modern colony (and later the nation) tended to reinforce patriarchal elements within Maasai society, for example, by replacing women's trade in milk and hides through barter with a cash-based market in cattle dominated by men. Hodgson argues that the scope of women's material power was greatly diminished as a result. But, unlike many scholars of conversion in Africa and elsewhere, Hodgson does not regard material or instrumental explanations for conversion as sufficient.

Hodgson demonstrates how involvement in the church allowed women to create an "alternative female community beyond the control of Maasai men," arguing that spirituality and morality constituted significant domains of power for women.[21] Church services offered important social spaces for women, where they gathered to dance, talk, laugh, joke, and eat with each other. The services also provided women with opportunities to take on formal and informal leadership roles. Even when men occupied formal positions such as "secretary" or "chairperson," Hodgson observed that members of the congregation typically directed questions to informal female leaders who commanded respect based not on office but on seniority and the depth of their piety. Significantly, Catholicism was inculturated into Maasai society in such a way that converts could continue to conceive of God as female or androgynous through the retention of the word Eng'ai to describe the supreme deity. Hodgson's interview with a middle-aged widow and catechist-in-training provides a glimpse of the confidence that women gained through both the moral power of the church and its feminine image of God. Hodgson writes that "she liked what she learned in instruction, especially about the rights of widows, 'so when [a widow] asks for something, she should be listened to. And Eng'ai will help her; She is with her every hour. And once I heard this I realized that I no longer had to get remarried to help myself, since Eng'ai can help me and loves me even more than I love myself."[22] Women sometimes attributed the confidence they gained from church to the "wisdom" they acquired there through formal instruction and from what they learned informally from other women. Indeed, churches functioned for Maasai women much the way schools did for Maasai men, generating multifaceted material and immaterial benefits: a sense of belonging, confidence, pragmatic knowledge, and also more profound insight into living well in the powerful, protective presence of Eng'ai.

While the social, political, and environmental changes of the nineteenth and twentieth century eroded those traditional domains of moral and material power that Maasai women had previously controlled, making Christianity attractive to women for diverse reasons, it enhanced the power of men. However, these changes simultaneously exacerbated existing divisions among Maasai men. They created rifts first between junior men and the councils of elders who cooperated with colonial rulers, and second between "traditionalists" who sought to maintain the specificity of Maasai ethnicity through staunch adherence to Maasai customs and religion and "modernists" who wore Western dress, spoke Swahili, and sought to assimilate to an emerging national culture. Some elders who cared little for peer pressure joined the church, but the majority of male converts were younger men of the modernist stripe, who sought the cultural and educational opportunities gained through conversion. For the most part, though, Maasai men—in contrast to Maasai women—perceived a stark conflict between Christianity and Maasai culture and articulated their disinterest in Christianity in terms of not wanting to give up their Maasai identity. Some even attributed this to a basic difference in the *iltauja* (the "spirit," "heart," or seat of spirituality and emotion) of men and women. Whereas women's *iltauja* were more flexible—more open both to Eng'ai and to new experiences—men's were inherently more rigid.[23] Local theories about gender clearly contributed to Maasai understanding of men's lack of interest in Christianity and women's ready embrace of it.

Psychological Bases for Gender Differences in Conversion: Conversion Narratives

The pursuit of a natural basis for gender differences in religious conversion is by no means confined to Tanzania. Several scholars interested in the gendered dimensions of conversion have profited from analysis of the oral and written narratives through which converts describe their experiences, finding in them evidence of innate cognitive or psychological differences between men and women. In 1981, historian Barbara Epstein examined accounts of religious conversion drawn from evangelical publications from the period 1800 to 1830 and found men and women had divergent theological understandings of sin, God, and redemption.[24] Literary scholar Virginia Brereton closely analyzed the formal and verbal structures of women's conversion narratives drawn from the nineteenth and twentieth centuries in her book, *From Sin to Salvation: Stories of Women's Conversions, 1800–to the present*.[25] More recently, a team of scholars has applied linguist Deborah Tannen's theories of gender differences in language use to forty conversion narratives elicited from college students at a Christian liberal arts college. They found significant gender differences in self-presentation, specifically in the use of metaphors to describe the conversion experience. For example, while men presented themselves as clever, women tended to present themselves as foolish; while men used metaphors that compared the experience to an adventure, women described conversion through metaphors that evoked peace or comfort.[26]

This is an area that deserves further exploration, but one early study is particularly useful for the purpose of tracing the impact of varieties of feminist theory on the study of conversion. Susan Juster's article, " 'In a Different Voice': Male and Female Narratives of Religious Conversion in Post-Revolutionary America," illustrates the widespread influence of feminist psychology in the 1980s and 1990s sparked by the 1982 publication of Carol Gilligan's *In a Different Voice: Psychological Theory and Women's Development*. Building on the work of psychoanalyst Nancy Chodorow, Gilligan and others argued that men's personalities and moral psychologies were deeply influenced by the fact that as small children they had to break the strong attachment they had to their mothers in order to identify with their fathers in the process of maturation. This tended to make men more individualistic and their sense of morality more rules-oriented. Conversely, girl children did not need to sever the strong maternal bond created in infancy quite so violently in order to mature, and as a consequence their psychology was more other-oriented and their sense of right and wrong organized around relationships. In her study, Susan Juster applies this framework to two hundred conversion narratives drawn from US evangelical magazines published between 1800 and 1830. For evangelical Protestants at this time, conversion meant "the awakening of the sinner to the true nature of his or her depraved state and the final regeneration of the soul through a process of self-abasement and unconditional surrender to the will of a gracious God."[27] Juster argues that both men and women struggled mightily with the surrender of personal autonomy central to this understanding of conversion, especially when people's narratives are viewed in the historical context of the recent emergence of the new nation from the Revolutionary War. Yet men and women in antebellum America experienced the trauma of submission to God quite differently. Looking back at their unregenerate state, men saw themselves struggling not against God as a person, but against the apparently irrational injustice of Calvinist soteriological theology, according to which one attained election through God's grace alone rather than through personal effort. The drama of women's conversion narratives, on the other hand, hinged on women's rebellion against and final submission to an autocratic father-God. Far from focusing on the justice or injustice of Calvinist theology in the abstract, women converts transformed God "into an 'other' endowed with human qualities and capable of expressing human affection and sympathy."[28] While men in the course of conversion grappled with doctrines contrary to reason, women defied an unjust father who arbitrarily, it seemed, preferred some of his "children" over others.[29]

Gilligan's work has often been misunderstood as an essentialist theory of gender that posits innate, eternal, unchanging gender characteristics. But in fact, to the extent that it recognizes the impact of different family structures on child development, it promotes awareness of wide variations depending on culture. Indeed, cross-cultural psychology is an exciting sub-field that promises to deliver new insights as culturally sensitive theories of psychology are applied to the experience of conversion in different times and places.

THE DIVERSITY OF WOMEN'S EXPERIENCE: WOMEN'S CONVERSION TO ISLAM IN THE WEST

Just as attention to the specificity of women's experience of conversion led to the recognition that men's experiences could not adequately serve as the default or generic representation of human experience, so the evolution of feminist thought led to an awareness that white women's experience was also distinctive and not generalizable to that of all women everywhere. In the 1980s, gender studies/women's studies took a self-critical turn that sought to break out of a perceived ethnocentric focus on white women.[30] This brought about a heightened awareness of the way that gender is intertwined with and mutually shaped by class, caste, social status, race, ethnicity, age, sexual orientation, and religion.[31] Feminist anthropologists and sociologists demonstrated with particular clarity how groups that embrace another religion are themselves stratified and fissured internally, with different gender expectations in each niche.[32]

Some of the most exciting recent work in this vein examines conversion to Islam in the United States and in Western Europe. In a historical moment of heightened

Islamophobia in the West due to the September 11th terrorist attacks and the ensuing so-called War on Terror, many find it surprising that any European or American
would convert to Islam. Given the widespread perception of Islam as oppressive toward
women, the evidence suggesting that more women than men are embracing Islam may
be even more startling. The prevalence of Islam in the United States and other Western
nations is difficult to measure and is the subject of some controversy. Some studies, however, reveal thought-provoking trends. The British Muslims Monthly Survey of 2002
asserts that, in Britain, women converts outnumber men by two to one, while estimates
in the United States range from a ratio of 4:1 to 2:3 women to men.[33] There have been a
number of waves of conversion to Islam in the West, and the motivations for and consequences of conversion for women have varied enormously, demonstrating that the same
religion can have markedly different appeals.

In the 1960s and 1970s, many African Americans were attracted to the Nation of Islam
because of the ways it wove Black Nationalism with Islam, providing a community
context for aspirations toward economic self-sufficiency and ethnic pride. For African
American converts to the Nation of Islam, conversion served as a rebuke to the long
history of racism in the United States, experienced on both an individual and collective
level. For these converts, Christianity was complicit in the creation of a subjugated, passive, self-blaming "slave" mentality. Thus, conversion provided an opportunity to shed
a crippling Christian identity and acquire what Aminah Beverly McCloud has termed
"somebodiness."[34] After the death of the founder, Elijah Muhammad, in 1975, many
American Muslims followed his son, Warith Deen Muhammad, into a more orthodox
Sunni expression of Islam, although the Nation of Islam continues under the leadership
of Louis Farakkhan. Even if the stridency of Black Nationalist rhetoric has diminished
in African American Sunni Islam, for many African Americans conversion still constitutes a dramatic rejection of mainstream US values and culture.

In her 2004 book, *Engaged Surrender,* anthropologist Carolyn Moxley Rouse examines the way gender, class, race, and religious identities intersect in complex ways for
Sunni African American women spanning two generations, those who first entered
Islam under the aegis of the Nation of Islam and those who converted after the shift
toward more orthodox Islam. Rouse observes that women who converted to Islam during the Nation of Islam era framed their conversion in terms of "social justice, redis-
tribution of wealth, or reversing racism and self-hatred," whereas these themes appear
muted or nonexistent in the conversion narratives of more recent converts, whose
choices seem motivated by a desire to "perfect the performance of [their] faith."[35] If
the organizing telos of African American Sunni Islam is not radical social change, but
rather spiritual liberation and the regeneration of society through the influence of pious
Muslims, then where, asks Rouse, do feminist visions of gender justice fit into this for
African American women?

Rouse argues that an implicit feminism guides the embodiment of Islam by most
contemporary African American women. This is especially apparent within the
realm of conjugality. As I will describe in more detail shortly, many contemporary

women—including African American Muslim women—have turned to conservative religions that endorse a patriarchal form of gender complementarity. In part this comes from a general disenchantment with the stubbornly partial liberation of women in secular, modern democracies. While the modern women's movement did achieve greater access for women to education, the labor market, and the political process, it has not altered women's primary responsibility for maintaining the household and raising children. One finds among some African American women a search for freedom from the contemporary woman's "double day" through a return to traditional gender roles. But Rouse's interviews indicate that even when African American Muslim women aspire to live according to the patriarchal division of labor envisioned by the Prophet, where husbands provide for and protect women and children and women maintain a comfortable home life, these aspirations are complicated by the conditions of racism that have made dignified full employment difficult for many black men to achieve. Some African American men, for their part, seek self-esteem in the context of US racism by asserting themselves within the household and the community and by stressing their role as rulers as much as protectors of women.[36] Rouse describes how debates over wearing the *hijab* (veil, head covering) can become an occasion for conflict between husbands and wives that requires close Quranic exegesis. A common rejoinder to the pressure to assume a more conservative form of veiling, which tends to compromise women's professional lives, is that submission in Islam is to *Allah*, not to the men in their lives. For example, when the husband of Alia, a young married college student and mother, suggested that she wear the *niqab* (face veil) because "her eyes are so big that she appears to be making eye contact with men even when she is not," Alia argued that the *niqab* was a matter of personal choice, rather than religious obligation, and moreover, "she must practice her faith for Allah and not her husband."[37]

Rouse finds that African American Muslim women place more importance on their own direct readings of the Quran and the *hadith* (collected accounts of the Prophet Muhammad's life) than on Islamic law (*shariah*) as a basis for determining how to properly embody Islam in practice. This is consistent with the relative insignificance of *shariah* among African American Muslims more generally, who seek an indigenous Islam that is adapted to features of US society. Because the *shariah* developed over centuries, largely in the medieval Middle East and South Asia, African American Muslims regard it as "tainted" in some ways by other Muslim cultures. Similarly, even the *hadith* is viewed by some women with skepticism due to its absorption of cultural norms from other Muslim societies in the process of transmission. However, the Quran too contains passages that can be interpreted as endorsing women's subordination.

The conflict between women's own firm acknowledgment of gender equality and some of the male supremacist language of the Quran takes shape as ambivalence, which gets resolved in various ways. Rouse's study is remarkable for the patience with which the author investigates how converts grapple with the inevitable tension between their own views of the world, based on common sense and personal experience, and their community's understanding of genuine piety. As she rightly notes, ambivalence is not the opposite of faith: "ambivalence is part of faith, and it is within this ambivalent space that followers transform and adapt their religion to meet personal challenges."[38] Women's conflicted feelings surrounding gender expectations that do not conform to their sense of women's integrity is dealt with in various ways, beginning with intense exegesis undertaken in conversation with other women, both through "sisters' meetings" and the writings of African America feminist Muslims like Amina Wadud and Aminah B. McCloud.[39] Rouse also provides evidence that some women respond to patriarchal demands with silence and acquiescence, an important acknowledgement that, indeed, women do not always resist what feminists regard as the self-limiting aspects of religion.[40] Finally, sometimes conflict over gender expectations cannot be resolved, as the high divorce rate among African American Muslim couples testifies. In one striking example, Rouse describes the challenges met by Nadia, a teacher and mother of four. Nadia's first husband entered the faith through the Nation of Islam and still carried many patriarchal assumptions long after he and Nadia became Sunnis. Not only was he unfaithful, he also quit a lucrative job as a contractor "because he said he didn't want to [be] bothered with those devils [i.e., white people]."[41] Compelled to become both the family breadwinner and the homemaker, "Nadia was forced to confront the fact that her personal reality did not correspond with her Islamic exegesis, feminism, or race consciousness. As a result, she acted according to her faith and common sense, and left her husband."[42] Although Nadia does not regret her decision and is happily remarried—thanks in part to the fact that divorce is permitted and not particularly stigmatized within either Islamic or US law—her narrative of this first marriage conveys the difficulties faced by African American women in conforming to the idealization of submission in the discourse surrounding Islamic womanhood.

While Rouse's monograph attends to the differences among African American women Muslims in the United States, Karen van Nieuwkerk's edited volume, *Women Embracing Islam*, brings together analyses of conversion among a wide range of European and American women, providing a fascinating basis for considering how race and nationality affect one's experience of conversion. One of the volume's findings is that regardless of nationality or race, Western women share a fascination for the perceived "Otherness" of Islam, but they draw on very different elements of Islamic discourse in their construction of an ideological platform for criticizing Western society, depending on their individual biographies, race, and social location.[43] As described above, for African American women, conversion to Islam represents a rebuke to the long history of racism in the United States. For white American women, on the other hand, Sufism, the mystical dimension of Islam, has been the main avenue for entering Islam. Offering solace and affirmation in its symbolic celebration of the feminine as sacred, Sufism has held special appeal for white women disturbed by what they see as the triumph of masculine values in the American public sphere.[44] Across the Atlantic, German converts from the former East (German Democratic Republic) find in Islam a way to articulate their disappointment with the consequences of German unification. For them, converting to Islam is a means of becoming part of a new "imagined community" and withdrawing from "being German."[45]

In both Europe and the United States, one finds considerable evidence that women converts to Islam discover in it a more dignified embodiment of femininity. The very same modesty requirements—most visibly the veil—that many non-Muslims view as emblematic of women's repression under Islam are regarded by converts in a very different light. In highly secularized and culturally liberal nations like the Netherlands and Germany, white women converts describe their adoption of modest dress and the *hijab* as their rejection of a culture in which women are made into sex objects.[46] Monika Wohlrab-Sahr quotes a woman who explained her choice to swim in a Berlin lake fully clothed and wearing a headscarf next to people swimming in the nude by saying, "If they dare...so do I."[47] "Daring" here signifies the moral courage to jettison normative gender expectations in pursuit of a higher ideal. In similar fashion, the *hijab* for African American Muslim women represents "decolonization of the Third World body" and a new female aesthetic that challenges the racist beauty standards of American mass culture. One of Rouse's informants compared the simplicity of Islamic requirements with the arduous labor necessary to maintain straight hair in pursuit of a beauty norm based on whiteness. She says, "We have bought into a system that says [straight] hair is beautiful.... [We] go buy perms, which are temporary. We go and fry, dye, lay it to side, we put everything in it that we can so we be someone we are not. Then Allah told us that we should just put a scarf on. I was really grateful for the scarf."[48] It seems that for many women the modesty expectations of Islam are experienced not as a burden, but as a means of liberation from alienating aesthetic norms that are themselves experienced as burdensome. In contrast, the *hijab* enables women to feel more themselves and more at home.

Such generalizing statements, however, should be taken with caution. If there is one clear finding of the research on conversion to Islam among women in contemporary United States and Europe, it is that converts are attracted to different aspects of a tradition depending on their individual biographies and their personal needs. As van Nieuwkerk argues, we should not essentialize any tradition, expecting that it will speak in the same way to all actual or potential converts.[49]

Agency and Structure in the Study of Conversion: Conservative Religion and Patriarchal Pro-familialism

In the past ten years, the question of women's agency—both its limits and its extent—has been of major concern to feminist scholars. These questions arise with particular acuteness in the context of religious conversion in the contemporary moment, as women in liberal democratic societies flock to conservative religious communities whether Jewish, Christian, or Muslim. Such women are mostly educated and involved in the public employment sector, so they presumably enjoy some measure of personal freedom. Why would women with choices choose to involve themselves in religious communities that often place strict limits on their individual freedom and autonomy, relegating them (to use the language of traditional feminism) to the home and valuing them only to the extent that they successfully fulfill traditional roles for women by being good wives and mothers? Or, to put the question a different way, given that religious discourse often appears to demean women, representing them as physically and mentally weak, morally corrupt and corrupting, or only valuable for their reproductive labor as mothers, why is it that women would so enthusiastically embrace a discourse that appears to marginalize them?

In the contemporary world, changes wrought by industrialization, modernization, and increasing specialization in labor have transformed the context of women's—and men's—lives. Moreover, in some quarters, secularization has undermined the authority of traditional religious sources that mandate distinctly different roles for men and women in the family and in society at large. Many religious communities have responded to these wider societal changes by relaxing rules governing gender roles, for example, by now allowing men and women to sit together in religious services and permitting women to serve as rabbis or ordained priests.[50] One might think that secularization would steadily continue to advance in this way, liberalizing options for women more and more. And yet, what one sees is that some women are embracing traditional gender roles—largely through a return to more conservative religion. As Lynn Davidman writes in her study of women converting to Orthodox Judaism, "In the current climate of loose gender definitions and multiplications of options for family life, converts are often strongly attracted to a religious community's legitimation of reconstructed 'traditional' gender roles as the basis for marriage and family life."[51]

Women's embrace of more traditional gender roles may be connected to a broader trend, namely the resurgence of conservative religion in the twentieth and twenty-first centuries. Much nineteenth- and early twentieth-century research on religion suggested that the forces of modernization—industrialization, bureaucratization, the rise of scientific authority, and the rationalization of the state—would lead inevitably to the secularization of the world. At best, religion would cease to make demands on citizens' participation in public life and would retreat to a private sphere to lend meaning to people's lives. And yet, this "secularization hypothesis" has been challenged by the rise of so-called fundamentalist groups, representing virtually every religious tradition in nations around the world, who advance an intensified form of religiosity. I agree with those who argue that "fundamentalist" is a misleading term, since most pious adherents grant authority to the "fundamentals" of a religion, whether they claim that the Torah is the revealed word of God or that Muhammad is the final prophet. What distinguishes the resurgent forms of religion that have troubled secular observers and fascinated scholars is adherents' desire to let religion govern much more of their life than is typical in the "privatized" religion of secular societies, shaping choices about clothing, sexuality, language use, media consumption, and much else beyond the content of the relatively mild metaphysical beliefs held by the ideal post-Enlightenment citizen.[52]

Another component of the secularization hypothesis that is relevant to the study of conversion, especially in the developed world, is the observation that with the expansion of choices comes a relativization of any particular choice. Sociologist Peter Berger has been the most eloquent in articulating this thesis, that with the rise of competing worldviews in an increasingly interconnected and secularized world, the overarching "canopy" of orthodoxy no longer enjoys the same stature as unquestioned Truth. We are now consumers of cosmologies in a marketplace of religions. But in such a context, argues Berger, any religion that is so chosen—either by conversion or by a conscious reaffirmation of the tradition one is born into—is at a sort of epistemological disadvantage insofar as it is inevitably just one among many possible points of view.[53] In such a context, the fact that some women are choosing to embrace a more conservative form of religion, even when other more liberal alternatives are available to them, requires explanation. In converting to conservative forms of religion, are women simply seeking to maximize their interests with the least conflict? Are they exercising agency by putting patriarchal ideology in service of their own needs? Or are they being forcefully inserted into oppressive structures that render them more docile wives and compliant workers? Systematic examination of the diverse conditions under which women around the world are coming to embrace conservative forms of religion reveals striking continuities, suggesting that women are choosing intensified religious commitment from among several imperfect solutions to the predicaments in which they find themselves.

In her review of sociological literature on women's involvement in Pentecostalism in developing countries, Bernice Martin offers a sharp indictment of sociologists whose secular biases caused them to ignore the benefits for women in conservative religion. She argues that secularist sociologists too often dismiss the women's involvement as a form of false consciousness, depicting conservative religious women as deluded by patriarchal religious ideology and unaware of their own oppression or its sources. Indeed, throughout the 1980s many scholars collapsed a wide variety of forms of resurgent religion under the rubric of "fundamentalism," thereby eliding crucial distinctions. Among these distinctions were the ways women were actually empowered through their involvement in churches whose language was laden with patriarchal rhetoric. And yet, this same patriarchal rhetoric masked the fact that women flocked to these churches because they helped women to "domesticate" men, reigning in the selfishness and abusive behavior that patriarchal liberal capitalism had unleashed.[54] Writing of Pentecostalism, Martin observes, "Above all, women have used the Pentecostal religious discourse to rewrite the moral mandate on which sexual relations and family life rest."[55] Comparable forms of this phenomenon have been studied in the United States (Griffith), Sicily (Cucchiari), Latin America (Brusco), and South Korea (Chong). The dynamics of conversion play out differently within each particular national or religious context as inherited cultural norms, religious values, political history, economic changes, family structure, ethnic or racial hierarchies, and so forth interact with gender norms to create unique sex and gender systems. Let me consider three cases.

Numerous scholars, including Murray Danzger, Lynn Davidman, and Debra Kaufman, have turned their attention to newly Orthodox men and women in the

United States. Jewish by birth, newly Orthodox Jews typically have been raised in relatively secular homes that, if they were religious at all, were religious in a relatively casual way. As adults they have returned to Judaism and have been re-socialized into an all-encompassing way of life that strives to adhere fully to Jewish law. Jews from secular backgrounds who have become more religiously observant are called *ba'alei* and *ba'a lot teshuvah* (lit. "masters of return"), where *teshuvah* is a multivalent word that can mean both "return" and "repentance," as when all Jews are called to return to a more faithful adherence to Torah during the season of repentance, Yom Kippur.

Many of the women who embrace conservative forms of Judaism express disillusionment or disappointment with secular modernity; life in secular societies feels "empty," "soul-less," and morally adrift because "everything is up in the air."[56] To the extent that the moral ambiguities of secularism are experienced as a feeling of being "lost," converting to orthodox Judaism feels like "coming home."[57] Indeed, many of the women who have embraced conservative forms of Judaism in recent decades have gone through elaborate conversion careers, long spiritual journeys that have taken them along sometimes circuitous paths. Debra Kaufman notes that many newly Orthodox women had been involved with a range of religious movements, from quasi-religious therapeutic communities to newly implanted varieties of Asian religions and revitalized forms of evangelical Christianity.[58] Scholars have interpreted the spiritual ferment of the 1960s and 1970s as responses to the deepening normative ambiguity of these tumultuous decades, in which gender norms were questioned along with many other established social conventions. Yet, combined with the intense individualism of late capitalist US society, the critique of traditional gender roles had an unexpected consequence for some women who had considered themselves feminists. The relaxation of normative gender roles created a situation of profound uncertainty for women economically dependent on men who were themselves now "liberated" from the traditional male role as family provider and protector. In such a context, some women turned away from this toward what Kaufman and others term a "patriarchal pro-familialism" that affirms traditional gender roles for both men and women and locates the heterosexual, nuclear family firmly at the center of communal life. As Kaufman writes, the stories of newly orthodox women, "and those of other 'born again' women, reveal more than the antipathy of an antifeminist religious Right. Their voices are the voices of women trying to cope with what they perceive to be the inequities and imbalances of postindustrial living and liberal patriarchal culture."[59] This backlash reaction to the norms (or norm-lessness) of secular society can be seen with particular clarity in women's interest in stricter norms governing sexuality in Orthodox Judaism.

Not unlike the Muslim converts considered earlier, these women have experienced "liberated sexuality" in the secular world as exploitative or personally demeaning. They gratefully embrace the emphasis on modesty and sexual morality as a safer route, one that affirms and respects their femininity. Far from finding the expectation of monogamy and chastity constricting, newly orthodox women speak of the enhanced pleasure surrounding sexuality when it is made sacred by being regulated by *mitzvoth* (Jewish religious law). Women report that embedding sexuality in the periodicities of women's

menstrual cycle and the cycles of the religious week such that stretches of enforced celibacy alternate with periods of sexual activity helps to retain excitement in the marital
sexual relationship. Ennobled by religious meaning, sexuality becomes more satisfying,
even empowering.[60]

In addition, newly Orthodox women reject what they perceive as the leveling effects of
feminism in contemporary society, such that genuine and valuable differences between
men and women are effaced. Kaufman notes that *ba'al teshuvah* view feminism as an
ideology that achieves gender equality by making women behave like men—competitive, individualistic, aggressive, etc.—with the result that the whole world is organized
according to male values. In Orthodox Judaism they find a celebration of their wom-
anly nature, especially in their enhanced capacity to be in touch with the spiritual. For
example, women speak highly about the rules that excuse women from the time-bound
prayers that orthodox men are enjoined to observe. Long-standing feminist interpretations have argued that this "exemption" in fact disenfranchises women by excluding them from Torah study and life in the synagogue, where the most highly valued
forms of Jewish ritual and practice take place. In conjunction with other similar rules
that allocate distinct responsibilities for men and women, this exemption structures a
whole gender-segregated way of life in which women lack access to public liturgy and
Torah study. The latter is particularly consequential since it is the study and application
of Jewish law that organizes the community's lifeworld; thus, women's exclusion from
Torah study means they have no legitimate way of challenging discriminatory or harm-
ful rulings, such as the rule that a woman can only obtain a divorce after gaining a *get*, or
agreement, from her husband, while a husband can freely divorce and remarry without
his wife's permission.[61] Yet, newly orthodox women see the roles assigned to women
and the gender-segregation that organizes daily life in conservative Jewish communities
very differently than feminists do. To them, the exemption from time-bound rituals testifies to their innately superior spiritual discipline, and gender-segregation affirms their
distinctive natural capacities as women. As one woman articulated it:

> Each week I bring divine presence into this household by preparing for Shabbos,
> I *make* Shabbos. When I separate and burn a portion of the *challah* (Sabbath bread),
> when I light the candles to welcome the Shabbos queen, I am like a high priest-
> ess.... Through my actions, my understanding, my feminine sensibilities, light and
> understanding are brought into the world. We women take care of the goodness in
> the world; we nurture and protect it.[62]

Such sentiments are reminiscent of the attractions that the feminine symbolism pervasive in Sufism has for women converts to Islam. The women Kaufman interviewed
celebrated the way feminine values such as nurturing and charity were sanctified by the
community and upheld as the primary virtues of Jewish life, not just for women but for
men as well.

Lynn Davidman, another scholar of *ba'al teshuvah*, provides some clues as to why
women would be attracted to more conservative forms of religion with their more traditional gender roles. "Many of these movements define a role for men that emphasizes

the importance of their participation in family life. Thus, women members are benefited by the community's emphasis on the nuclear family because it provides legitimation of and clear instructions for men's greater involvement in the home."[63] Scholars have observed similar patterns in women embracing conservative forms of Christianity—the patriarchal pro-familialism of conservative religion attracts women disillusioned by the supposed gains for women in modern societies. The coexistence of patriarchal social forms and capitalist economic structures can create intolerable double-binds and contradictions from which church life becomes a refuge.[64]

In one of the pioneering studies in this area, Elizabeth Brusco argues that women's conversion to Pentecostal or evangelical Christianity in Columbia takes place in a context in which men's and women's value spheres have become highly antagonistic. In Columbia, men perform their masculinity for other men through excessive drinking, aggression, and womanizing. Their sense of well-being rests on achieving a solid sense of "machismo" in competition with other men in public arenas, not through attachment to their family. Women's well-being, on the other hand, is bound up with the household. Due to economic changes accompanying the transition from collective agricultural production to wage labor, economic production has become more individualistic and women more dependent on wage-earning men. Given the state's staunch support of the Roman Catholic Church and the suspicions leveled at Pentecostals, becoming a *creyente* (a believer and a reader of the Bible) takes enormous courage and exacts considerable social costs. Yet evangelical Christianity is increasingly attractive to Columbians. Brusco argues that, in part, this is because evangelicalism effectively reconciles women's and men's divergent value systems by domesticating men. This is not simply a change at the level of ideology; it also brings a measurable improvement in household living standards. "Quite simply," writes Brusco, "no longer is 20 to 40 percent of the household budget consumed by the husband in the form of alcohol."[65] One can clearly see why, in this context, women would embrace a religion that exhorts men to curtail their self-interest and assume the role of bread-winner. But given the inherent dangers in the "machismo" lifestyle—violence, sexually transmitted disease, instability—Columbian men too have good reasons to convert.[66] The asceticism demanded of Pentecostals regulates consumption patterns, in part by banning many of the extra-domestic expenses formerly indulged in by men: drinking, smoking, gambling, and prostitution. Even more importantly, with conversion the private realm is revalued, becoming the center of the family's life for both men and women, as reflected in an interesting study cited by Brusco. This survey conducted among Catholic and Pentecostal Columbians revealed that the first consumer item purchased by Catholics is a radio, which facilitates contact with the outside world, while that first purchased by Pentecostals is a dining room table.[67] Brusco finds the transformation of Pentecostal households in Columbia so dramatic that she views evangelical Protestantism in Columbia as a form of female collective action more powerful than feminism. Feminism has fought for, and to some extent achieved, women's equal access to education, the labor force, the political process, and so on, but men's roles have not changed to accommodate these sweeping social changes.

Evangelical Protestantism, on the other hand, has been effective in raising the living standards of women by bringing about a transformation in men's consciousness as much as in women's.[68]

Although the religious history of South Korea is quite different from that of Columbia, Kelly Chong's recent study of evangelical Protestantism in South Korea is set in a similar context where rapid economic modernization has transformed gender relations, intensifying women's dependency on men whose primary interests do not reside in caring for them.[69] Here too one sees an explosion of Protestant churches and women's active involvement in fostering and spreading what appears to be a conservative form of religious patriarchy. If anything, Korea's economic transformation has been even more dramatic than Columbia's. In the thirty-five years between 1960 and 1995, the country's total GNP grew from US$1.9 to US$ 451.7 billion.[70] This astonishing economic "miracle" brought manifold changes to Korean society, including the achievement of universal literacy, the widespread incorporation of women into the workforce, and legal changes that guarantee women's equality before the law in the Constitution. However, these accomplishments were accompanied by an intensification, or reinvention as Chong puts it, of neo-Confucian social mores that privileged elders over juniors and men over women. While more women worked as wage-earners than previously, they were relegated to dead-end blue-collar and pink-collar jobs, as evidenced by the fact that Korea has one of the greatest gender-based pay disparities in the world. Faced with limits on professional mobility, college-educated women often opt out of paid work after marriage, hoping to realize their ambitions for a better life within the household as enlightened housewives.[71] And yet, as Chong describes, even in the home women encounter frustration because the patriarchal expectations of wifely virtue have not diminished. Wives are overwhelmingly responsible not only for child-rearing and their children's education but also for caring for in-laws and promoting the family's social standing in a highly status-conscious society. Husbands often do not share their wives' expectations surrounding conjugal intimacy, but rather advance a Confucian sense of loyalty to their natal family. As one convert said, "My husband is the most traditionally Confucian [yugyojoek] man. When we first got married, he said to me that his parents were like his limbs, irreplaceable and with him forever, but I was like clothing, disposable and interchangeable."[72] Caught between expectations generated by education and modernization and the limits imposed within the workplace and the home, many Korean women experience anguish, resentment, and deep anger, which sometimes boils over into illness. Women describe their ailments as the result of *han,* "a kind of pent-up and repressed set of emotions stemming from accumulated anger, resentment, and bitterness rooted in years of suffering and victimization by injustice and oppression."[73] These powerful emotions can find physical expression in a diseased condition aptly known as "fire disease" (*hwabyeong*).

Korean churches provide such women with a source of "spiritual healing" through emotionally intense prayer practice, which teaches them to "open up" to God (and one another) about their suppressed emotions over conflicts with husbands and mothers-in-law, pouring out in tearful prayer their sorrow and grief, frustration and rage.[74] In addition, frequent church attendance creates an extra-domestic space for building female community. In a fashion reminiscent of Hodgson's findings about Catholic Spiritan women in Tanzania, Chong writes, "Running parallel to personal growth in the spiritual realm, achievements through church work can result in experiences of new forms of personal power and alterations in self-conception and identity that can have consider-able ramifications for the ways women negotiate their environment and interpersonal relations."[75] Similar to R. Marie Griffith's research on evangelical women in the United States, Chong reports that acquiescence to the doctrine of submission to patriarchal authority (both human and divine) is taught as a means of coping with conflict, by com-pelling from husbands and in-laws the respect and affection deserved by a dutiful wife. Whereas Brusco reports that such accommodation of patriarchal ideology is a practical strategy with significant benefits for Pentecostal Columbian women, rivaling Western feminism in its capacity for "revolutionary" transformation of women's lives, Chong's view of the liberatory potential of the strategic use of the Christian-Confucian ideology of feminine submission is decidedly more cautious. While Chong acknowledges that women may garner some practical "bargaining power" in a rather constrained situation, she draws attention to the ways that the ideology involves the women in a coercive pro-cess of re-domestication of their gender consciousness. Preachers and leaders of "fam-ily seminars" for evangelical husbands and wives place the blame for domestic conflict squarely on the shoulders of women who are too "smarty," "haughty," and impatient, counseling them to seek wholeness through the cultivation of the virtues of humility, forgiveness, and forbearance.[76]

These examples illustrate that women in a variety of cultural contexts have found increased satisfaction, security, and overall well-being in religious communities that support a patriarchal vision of the heterosexual nuclear family organized around gender complementarity. This phenomenon could be read as a general indictment of feminism. Indeed, it could be interpreted as eloquent testimony to feminism's failure to meet the needs of modern women. In my view, however, such an assessment would be prema-ture. There is not just one uniform variety of patriarchy; rather, male domination takes a wide range of forms, depending on the culture, economy, and prevailing family struc-ture. It seems some women are finding it easier to negotiate for themselves and their children from within a framework of patriarchal pro-familialism than within the highly individualistic forms of patriarchy made possible by the modernization process toward liberal, capitalistic societies. In an environment where income-earning opportunities for women are limited—either because of a transition from a trade-barter to a market, cash-based economy because of pervasive discrimination in employment, or because of restrictions on women's time due to their responsibility for raising children and car-ing for the elderly—women are more dependent on male income than before, putting them in a vulnerable position. Liberal feminists have long argued that to remedy this situation, what is needed is a change in values so that domestic labor is more equita-bly distributed and/or compensated by the state and laws against discrimination against women do not just exist on paper but are rigorously enforced. It seems that when such changes are slow to take place (as in the United States), inadequate to women's perceived needs (West Germany, the Netherlands, and the United States), or stymied by other cultural norms (South Korea), or nonexistent (Columbia), some women are finding an attractive alternative in a more family-centered patriarchy, endorsed by new interpretations of Christianity, Islam, or Judaism.

CONCLUSION: FUTURE RESEARCH ON GENDER AND CONVERSION

Incorporating gender as a primary category of analysis in the study of religious conversion makes visible a great many facets of this complex phenomenon. One of the most important contributions of feminist scholarship on conversion has been to demonstrate incontrovertibly that religious conversion entails not merely a change of worldview or ethos, but a change in lifeworld. Such scholarship challenges Protestant and Enlightenment biases about religion that privilege belief over other dimensions of religiosity. At stake in conversion are not only ideas about the sacred or the source of salvation, but habits and customs ranging from how one eats and dresses to how one organizes domestic space. To paraphrase Miss Greenfield, the missionary cited at the beginning of this chapter, the "heart" of religion is not necessarily in mystic teachings or the "finer spun philosophy" of learned adherents, but rather is "enshrined in ... homes, in the family life and hereditary customs of [a] people." Attention to these domestic practices has been a common thread in much recent work on gender and conversion. One promising direction for future research would be to observe and analyze these lifestyle changes more carefully and systematically. How long does it take before a convert's embodied practice of the faith matches community expectations? What is at stake in negotiations over that process? Are some changes more consequential than others, for example, those related to sexuality, clothing, or the organization of time by prayer or ritual? What relationship obtains between lifestyle changes and cognitive, discursive, or more internal changes? In her study of conversion to Islam, Karen van Nieuwkerk gives a sense of why this is important: "Conversion does not stop at the moment of embracing Islam, and it is not solely a mental activity of accepting a new belief. It requires embodiment of new social and religious practices. Within this process of embodiment and learning new practices, new ideas and insights are created that can generate new discourses and receptivity to other voices of Islamic discourse."[77] Careful attention to the dynamic interplay between embodied practices and the verbal discourses that support and explain them should be the focus of more study, because this interplay gets at how religious ideas are mapped onto the body and how embodied practices in turn shape discourse. Conversion, where the convert is asked to—suddenly or gradually—adopt a new set of practices, provides an ideal context for examining this phenomenon, which obviously takes place in all religious traditions.

Another promising direction in feminist studies of conversion is to focus more on the specificity of men's conversion. How do men respond to the challenges and opportunities of embodying a new religious tradition? How does growing a beard or abstaining from alcohol for the sake of Islam alter the relationship a male convert has with other men? How do the newly orthodox husbands of the women that Debra Kaufman interviewed feel about the periods of sexual abstinence required by Jewish law? It is striking that scholarship on the manifold lifestyle changes associated with conversion has tended to take the point of view of women, as if they were the only ones called upon to make dramatic changes in their lives. More ethnographic research needs to be done with male informants and by male researchers who are sensitive to the significance of gender. Such research could also help answer some of the questions left unaddressed in the growing body of research on contemporary women's involvement in conservative religion. An unspoken implication of the research on patriarchal pro-familialism in conservative Christianity, Judaism, and Islam is that men allow themselves to be "domesticated" in exchange for an affirmation of male authority over women, at least at the level of religious discourse. Is this really attractive to men, and if so, why? What motivates their return to a discourse of strict gender complementarity that their fathers and uncles presumably jettisoned in the 1970s?

Finally, another area of research where attention to gender differences promises to deliver new insights is the phenomenology of conversion. Do men and women experience conversion differently? What precipitates conversion? What does it feel like? Should different methods be used for arriving at a sense of the inner experience of conversion of men and women? Psychologists are well positioned to inquire into these questions; indeed, exciting work is already underway. But psychologists need to be aware not only of gender differences but of cultural differences as well. One of the lessons of the last thirty years of feminist scholarship is that while gender is an enormously significant factor in shaping human identity and experience, it is itself inextricably bound up with other factors such as race, class, ethnicity, sexuality, and so on. To arrive at a more truthful understanding of what the complex, multifaceted experience of conversion really entails for people of all genders, scholars need to have the observational and analytical skills of the psychologist and sociologist, the cultural and linguistic skills of the anthropologist and the historian of religion, and the empathy and imagination of the literary scholar.

NOTES

1. Jeffrey Cox, "Independent English Women in Delhi and Lahore, 1860–1947," in *Religion and Irreligion in Victorian Society*, ed. R. J. Helmstadter (London: Routledge, 1992), 170.
2. Lewis R. Rambo, *Understanding Religious Conversion* (New Haven: Yale University Press, 1993), 175.
3. William James, *The Varieties of Religious Experience* (New York: Penguin Books, 1985), 249.
4. For histories of feminist thought, the feminist movement, and their interrelationship, see, for example, Estelle Freedman, *No Turning Back: The History of Feminism and the Future of*

Women (New York: Ballantine Books, 2002); Sue Morgan, ed., *The Feminist History Reader* (New York: Routledge, 2006).

5. See, for example, Renate Bridenthal and Claudia Koonz, eds., *Becoming Visible: Women in European History*, 1st ed. (Boston: Houghton Mifflin, 1977); Shirley Ardener, ed., *Perceiving Women* (New York: Wiley, 1975).

6. Influential scholarship in this vein includes Judith Butler, *Gender Trouble: Feminism and the Subversion of Identity* (New York: Routledge, 1990); Judith Lorber, "'Night to His Day': The Social Construction of Gender," in *Race, Gender and Class in the United States*, ed. Paula S. Rothenberg, 54–64, 6th ed. (New York: Worth Publishers, 2004); Joan Wallach Scott, *Gender and the Politics of History* (New York: Columbia University Press, 1988); Denise Riley, *Am I that Name? Feminism and the Category of "Women" in History* (Minneapolis: University of Minnesota Press, 1988). A significant impetus for the theorization of gender in the 1990s was the deconstruction of the notion of a shared, universal "womanhood" initiated by feminist women of color in the 1980s. See bell hooks, *Ain't I a Woman? Black Women and Feminism* (Boston: South End Press, 1981); Cherríe Moraga and Gloria E. Anzaldúa, eds., *This Bridge Called My Back: Writings by Radical Women of Color*, 2nd ed. (New York: Kitchen Table, Women of Color Press, 1983). Feminist scholarship continues to challenge the tendency to naturalize gender through the emergence of transgender studies, which examines societies with more complex, non-binary gender system and analyzes the lives of individuals who eschew the binary gender system that prevails in most Western societies. See Serena Nanda, *Neither Man nor Woman: The Hijras of India* (Belmont, CA: Wadsworth Publishing, 1990); Susan Stryker and Stephen Whittle, *The Transgender Studies Reader* (New York: Routledge, 2006).

7. Mrs. E. R. (Emma Raymond) Pitman, *Indian Zenana Missions: Their Need, Origin, Objects, Agents, Modes of Working, and Results* (London: John Snow & Co., n.d.), 25.

8. Miss Greenfield, "Paper on Zenana Education," in *Report of the Second Decennial Missionary Conference Held in Calcutta, 1882–1883* (Calcutta, 1883), 210–211.

9. Greenfield's intuition about the nature of religious conversion, that it is not merely an intellectual transformation but has to do with habits of the heart and body, is something that scholars of religion, in my view, have still not sufficiently investigated.

10. Eliza F. Kent, "Tamil Bible Women of the Zenana Missions of Colonial South India," *History of Religions* 39, no. 2 (1999): 117–149.

11. Patricia R. Hill, *The World Their Household: The American Woman's Foreign Mission Movement and Cultural Transformation, 1870–1920* (Ann Arbor: University of Michigan Press, 1985).

12. Hill, *The World Their Household*, 40; Eliza F. Kent, *Converting Women: Gender and Protestant Christianity in Colonial South India* (New York: Oxford University Press, 2004), 92.

13. Jane Hunter, *The Gospel of Gentility: American Women Missionaries in Turn-of-the-Century China* (New Haven: Yale University Press, 1984).

14. Ibid., 255.

15. See, for example, Fiona Bowie, Deborah Kirkwood, and Shirley Ardener, eds., *Women and Missions: Past and Present: Anthropological and Historical Perceptions* (Providence, RI: Berg Press, 1993); Naipur Chaudhuri and Margaret Strobel, eds., *Western Women and Imperialism: Complicity and Resistance* (Bloomington: Indiana University Press, 1992); Leslie Flemming, ed., *Women's Work for Women: Women Missionaries and Social Change in Asia* (Boulder, CO: Westview Press, 1989): Patricia Grimshaw, *Paths of Duty: American*

Missionary Wives in Nineteenth-Century Hawaii (Honolulu: University of Hawaii, 1989); Mary Taylor Huber and Nancy C. Lutkehaus, eds., *Gendered Missions: Women and Men in Missionary Discourse and Practice* (Ann Arbor: University of Michigan Press, 1999); Dana L. Robert, *American Women in Mission A Social History of Their Thought and Practice* (Macon, GA: Mercer University Press, 1997); Karen K. Seat, *'Providence Has Freed Our Hands': Women's Missions and the American Encounter with Japan* (Syracuse, NY: Syracuse University Press, 2008).

16. John L. Comaroff and Jean Comaroff, *Of Revelation and Revolution: Christianity, Colonialism and Consciousness in South Africa*, Vol. 1 (Chicago: University of Chicago Press, 1991), 132–140.

17. Ibid., 129–131.

18. Ibid., 136–137.

19. Dorothy L. Hodgson, *The Church of Women: Gendered Encounters between Maasai and Missionaries* (Bloomington: Indiana University Press, 2005), 1.

20. Ibid., 9–10.

21. Ibid., 187.

22. Ibid., 186.

23. Ibid., 214–215.

24. Barbara Leslie Epstein, *The Politics of Domesticity: Women, Evangelicalism, and Temperance in Nineteenth-Century America* (Middletown, CT: Wesleyan University Press, 1981).

25. Virginia L. Brereton, *From Sin to Salvation: Stories of Women's Conversion, 1800 to the Present* (Bloomington: Indiana University Press, 1991).

26. David A. Knight, Robert H Woods, Jr., Ines W. Jindra, "Gender Differences in the Communication of Christian Conversion Narratives," *Review of Religious Research* 47, no. 2 (Dec. 2005): 113–134.

27. Susan Juster, "'In a Different Voice': Male and Female Narratives of Religious Conversion in Post-Revolutionary America," *American Quarterly* 41, no. 1 (March 1989): 34.

28. Ibid., 42.

29. Ibid., 49.

30. As mentioned previously, landmark texts include hooks, *Ain't I a Woman?* and the edited volume, *This Bridge Called My Back*.

31. Kimberlé Williams Crenshaw, "Mapping the Margins: Intersectionality, Identity Politics, and Violence against Women of Color," *Stanford Law Review* 43, no. 6 (1991): 1241–1299; Leslie McCall, "The Complexity of Intersectionality," *Signs* 30, no. 3 (2005): 1771–1802; Patricia Hill Collins, "It's All in the Family: Intersections of Gender, Race, and Nation" *Hypatia* 13, no. 3 (1998): 62–82.

32. See, for example, my work on caste and class differences among Indian converts to Protestant Christianity in colonial Tamil Nadu and Lynn Davidman's attention to class differences among newly Orthodox Jewish women in the contemporary United States: Eliza F. Kent, *Converting Women: Gender and Protestant Christianity in Colonial South India* (New York: Oxford University Press, 2004); Lynn Davidman, *Tradition in a Rootless World: Women Turn to Orthodox Judaism* (Berkeley and Los Angeles: University of California, 1991).

33. Haifaa Jawad, "Female Conversion to Islam: The Sufi Paradigm," in *Women Embracing Islam: Gender and Conversion in the West*, ed. Karin van Nieuwkerk (Austin: University of Texas Press, 2006), 154; Karin van Nieuwkerk, "Gender and Conversion to Islam in the West," in van Nieuwkerk, *Women Embracing Islam*, 1.

34. Aminah Beverly McCloud, "African American Muslim Women," in *The Muslims of America*, ed. Yvonne Haddad (New York: Oxford University Press, 1991).

35. Carolyn Moxley Rouse, *Engaged Surrender: African American Women and Islam* (Berkeley and Los Angeles: University of California Press, 2004), 28.

36. In a powerful essay, Gwendolyn Zoharah Simmons, a scholar of Islam who was in the Nation of Islam for five years, writes of the community's complex gender dynamics, which in her view severely discriminated against women. "African American Islam as an Expression of Converts' Religious Faith and Nationalist Dreams and Ambitions," in van Nieuwkerk, *Women Embracing Islam*, 182–191. See also Monika Wohlrab-Sahr, "Symbolizing Distance: Conversion to Islam in Germany and the United States," in van Nieuwkerk, *Women Embracing Islam*, 83–84.

37. Rouse, *Engaged Surrender*, 27–28.

38. Ibid., 178.

39. Ibid., 76–78.

40. Ibid., 172–173. For a lucid discussion of the difficulties feminists have had in conceptualizing women's efforts to attain spiritual perfection through self-limitation, see Saba Mahmood, "Feminist Theory, Embodiment, and the Docile Agent: Some Reflections on the Egyptian Islamic Revival," *Cultural Anthropology* 6, no. 2 (2001): 202–236.

41. Rouse, *Engaged Surrender*, 55.

42. Ibid., 55.

43. van Nieuwkerk, "Gender and Conversion to Islam in the West," 6–7.

44. Jawad, "Female Conversion to Islam: The Sufi Paradigm," 162–169; Yvonne Yazback Haddad, *A Century of Islam in America: The Muslim World Today*, Occasional Paper No. 4 (Washington, DC: American Institute for Islamic Affairs, 1986). The gulf between white American and African American converts to Islam is illustrated by Monika Wohlrab-Sahr's anecdote about attending two Muslim conferences on the same weekend in the San Francisco Bay Area in 1996: a nearly all-white Sufi conference in San Francisco, and an all-black gathering of followers of Warith Deen Muhammad in Berkeley. Wohlrab-Sahr, "Symbolizing Distance," 89.

45. Wohlrab-Sahr, "Symbolizing Distance," 86.

46. Karin van Nieuwkerk, "Gender, Conversion and Islam: A Comparison of Online and Offline Conversion Narratives," in van Nieuwkerk, *Women Embracing Islam*, 103.

47. Ibid., 73.

48. Rouse, *Engaged Surrender*, 63–64.

49. van Nieuwkerk, 11–12.

50. Lynn Davidman, *Tradition in a Rootless World: Women Turn to Orthodox Judaism* (Berkeley and Los Angeles: University of California, 1991), 42.

51. Ibid., 42.

52. Bruce Lincoln, "Conflict," in *Critical Terms for Religious Studies*, ed. Mark C. Taylor (Chicago: University of Chicago Press, 1998).

53. Peter L. Berger, *The Sacred Canopy: Elements of a Sociological Theory of Religion* (New York: Anchor Books, 1990).

54. Bernice Martin, "The Pentecostal Gender Paradox: A Cautionary Tale for the Sociology of Religion," in *The Blackwell Companion to Sociology of Religion*, ed. Richard K. Fenn (Oxford, England: Blackwell Publishers, 2001), 54.

55. Ibid., 54.

56. Davidman, *Tradition in a Rootless World*, 90–102.

57. Debra Renee Kaufman, *Rachel's Daughters: Newly Orthodox Jewish Women* (New Brunswick, NJ: Rutgers University Press, 1991), 33.
58. Kaufman, *Rachel's Daughters*, 15–35.
59. Ibid., 157.
60. Ibid., 75–85.
61. Ibid., 67–70.
62. Ibid., 41.
63. Davidman, *Tradition in a Rootless World*, 43.
64. Kaufman, *Rachel's Daughters*, 86–112; Kelly H. Chong, *Deliverance and Submission: Evangelical Women and the Negotiation of Patriarchy in South Korea*, Harvard East Asian Monographs (Cambridge, MA: Harvard University Press, 2008).
65. Elizabeth E. Brusco, *The Reformation of Machismo: Evangelical Conversion and Gender in Columbia* (Austin: University of Texas, 1995), 5.
66. Ibid., 114–115.
67. Ibid., 124.
68. Ibid., 138.
69. Kelly Chong, *Deliverance and Submission: Evangelical Women and the Negotiation of Patriarchy in South Korea* (Cambridge, MA: Harvard University Press, 2008).
70. Ibid., 55–56.
71. Ibid., 64–75.
72. Ibid., 51.
73. Ibid., 93.
74. Ibid., 97.
75. Ibid., 133.
76. Ibid., 149.
77. van Nieuwkerk, "Gender and Conversion to Islam in the West," 11.

BIBLIOGRAPHY

Ammerman, Nancy. *Bible Believers: Fundamentalists in the Modern World*. New Brunswick, NJ: Rutgers University Press, 1987.
Ardener, Shirley, ed. *Perceiving Women*. New York: Wiley, 1975.
Berger, Peter L. *The Sacred Canopy: Elements of a Sociological Theory of Religion*. New York: Anchor Books, 1990.
Bowie, Fiona, Deborah Kirkwood, and Shirley Ardener, eds. *Women and Missions: Past and Present: Anthropological and Historical Perceptions*. Providence, RI: Berg Press, 1993.
Brereton, Virginia L. *From Sin to Salvation: Stories of Women's Conversion, 1800 to the Present*. Bloomington: Indiana University Press, 1991.
Bridenthal, Renate, and Claudia Koonz, eds. *Becoming Visible: Women in European History*. Boston: Houghton Mifflin, 1977.
Brusco, Elizabeth E. *The Reformation of Machismo: Evangelical Conversion and Gender in Columbia*. Austin: University of Texas, 1995.
Butler, Judith. *Gender Trouble: Feminism and the Subversion of Identity*. New York: Routledge, 1990.
Chakravarty, Uma. *Rewriting History: The Life and Times of Pandita Ramabai*. New Delhi, Kali for Women, 1998.

Chaudhuri, Naipur, and Margaret Strobel, eds. *Western Women and Imperialism: Complicity and Resistance*. Bloomington: Indiana University Press, 1992.

Chen, Carolyn. *Getting Saved in America: Taiwanese Immigration and Religious Experience*. Princeton: Princeton University Press, 2008.

Chong, Kelly H. *Deliverance and Submission: Evangelical Women and the Negotiation of Patriarchy in South Korea*. Harvard East Asian Monographs. Cambridge, MA: Harvard University Press, 2008.

Collins, Patricia Hill. "It's All in the Family: Intersections of Gender, Race, and Nation." *Hypatia* 13, no. 3 (1998): 62–82.

Comaroff, John L., and Jean Comaroff. *Of Revelation and Revolution: Christianity, Colonialism and Consciousness in South Africa*. Vol. 1. Chicago: University of Chicago Press, 1991.

——. *Of Revelation and Revolution: The Dialectics of Modernity on a South African Frontier*. Vol. 2. Chicago: University of Chicago Press, 1997.

Cox, Jeffrey. "Independent English Women in Delhi and Lahore, 1860–1947." In *Religion and Irreligion in Victorian Society*, ed. R. J. Helmstadter, 166–184. London: Routledge, 1992.

Crenshaw, Kimberlé Williams. "Mapping the Margins: Intersectionality, Identity Politics, and Violence against Women of Color." *Stanford Law Review* 43, no. 6 (1991): 1241–1299.

Cucchiari, Salvatore. "Between Shame and Sanctification: Patriarchy and its Transformation in Sicilian Pentecostalism." *American Ethnologist* 18 (1991): 687–707.

Danzger, Murray Herbert. *Returning to Tradition: The Contemporary Revival of Orthodox Judaism*. New Haven: Yale University Press, 1989.

Davidman, Lynn. *Tradition in a Rootless World: Women Turn to Orthodox Judaism*. Berkeley and Los Angeles: University of California, 1991.

Epstein, Barbara Leslie. *The Politics of Domesticity: Women, Evangelicalism, and Temperance in Nineteenth-Century America*. Middletown, CT: Wesleyan University Press, 1981.

Flemming, Leslie A. "A New Humanity: American Missionaries' Ideals for Women in North India, 1870–1930." In *Western Women and Imperialism: Complicity and Resistance*, ed. Nupur Chauduri and Margaret Strobel, 191–206. Bloomington: Indiana University Press, 1992.

Flemming, Leslie, ed. *Women's Work for Women: Women Missionaries and Social Change in Asia*. Boulder, CO: Westview Press, 1989.

Freedman, Estelle. *No Turning Back: The History of Feminism and the Future of Women*. New York: Ballantine Books, 2002.

Gilligan, Carol. *In a Different Voice: Psychological Theory and Women's Development*. Cambridge, MA: Harvard University Press, 1993.

Greenfield, Miss. "Paper on Zenana Education." In *Report of the Second Decennial Missionary Conference Held in Calcutta, 1882–1883*. Calcutta, 1883.

Griffith, R. Marie. *God's Daughters: Evangelical Women and the Power of Submission*. Berkeley and Los Angeles: University of California, 2001.

Grimshaw, Patricia. *Paths of Duty: American Missionary Wives in Nineteenth-Century Hawaii*. Honolulu: University of Hawaii, 1989.

Haddad, Yvonne Yazbeck. *A Century of Islam in America: The Muslim World Today*. Occasional Paper No. 4. Washington, DC: American Institute for Islamic Affairs, 1986.

Haddad, Yvonne Yazbeck, Jane I. Smith, and Kathleen M. Moore, eds. *Muslim Women in America: The Challenge of Islamic Identity Today*. New York: Oxford University Press, 2006.

Hill, Patricia R. *The World Their Household: The American Woman's Foreign Mission Movement and Cultural Transformation, 1870–1920*. Ann Arbor: University of Michigan Press, 1985.

Hodgson, Dorothy L. *The Church of Women: Gendered Encounters between Maasai and Missionaries*. Bloomington: Indiana University Press, 2005.

hooks, bell. *Ain't I a Woman? Black Women and Feminism*. Boston: South End Press, 1981.

Huber, Mary Taylor, and Nancy C. Lutkehaus, eds. *Gendered Missions: Women and Men in Missionary Discourse and Practice*. Ann Arbor: University of Michigan Press, 1999.

Hunter, Jane. *The Gospel of Gentility: American Women Missionaries in Turn-of-the-Century China*. New Haven: Yale University Press, 1984.

James, William. *The Varieties of Religious Experience*. New York: Penguin Books, [1901] 1985.

Jawad, Haifaa. "Female Conversion to Islam: The Sufi Paradigm." In *Women Embracing Islam: Gender and Conversion in the West*, ed. Karin van Nieuwkerk, 153–171. Austin: University of Texas Press, 2006.

Juster, Susan. "'In a Different Voice': Male and Female Narratives of Religious Conversion in Post-Revolutionary America." *American Quarterly* 41, no. 1 (March 1989): 34–62.

Kaufman, Debra Renee. *Rachel's Daughters: Newly Orthodox Jewish Women*. New Brunswick, NJ: Rutgers University Press, 1991.

Kent, Eliza F. *Converting Women: Gender and Protestant Christianity in Colonial South India*. New York: Oxford University Press, 2004.

———. "Tamil Bible Women of the Zenana Missions of Colonial South India." *History of Religions* 39, no. 2 (1999): 117–149.

Knight, David A., Robert H Woods, Jr., and Ines W. Jindra. "Gender Differences in the Communication of Christian Conversion Narratives." *Review of Religious Research* 47, no. 2 (Dec. 2005): 113–134.

Lincoln, Bruce. "Conflict." In *Critical Terms for Religious Studies*, ed. Mark C. Taylor, 55–69. Chicago: University of Chicago Press, 1998.

Lorber, Judith. "'Night to His Day': The Social Construction of Gender." In *Race, Gender and Class in the United States*, ed. Paula S. Rothenberg, 54–64. 6th ed. New York: Worth Publishers, 2004.

Mahmood, Saba. "Feminist Theory, Embodiment, and the Docile Agent: Some Reflections on the Egyptian Islamic Revival." *Cultural Anthropology* 6, no. 2 (2001): 202–236.

Martin, Bernice. "The Pentecostal Gender Paradox: A Cautionary Tale for the Sociology of Religion." In *The Blackwell Companion to Sociology of Religion*, ed. Richard K. Fenn, 52–66. Oxford, England: Blackwell Publishers, 2001.

McCall, Leslie. "The Complexity of Intersectionality." *Signs* 30, no. 3 (2005): 1771–1802.

McCloud, Aminah Beverly. "African American Muslim Women." In *The Muslims of America*, ed. Yvonne Yazbeck Haddad, 177–187. New York: Oxford University Press, 1991.

Moraga, Cherríe, and Gloria E. Anzaldúa, eds. *This Bridge Called My Back: Writings by Radical Women of Color*. 2nd ed. New York: Kitchen Table, Women of Color Press, 1983.

Morgan, Sue, ed. *The Feminist History Reader*. New York: Routledge, 2006.

Nanda, Serena. *Neither Man nor Woman: The Hijras of India*. Belmont, CA: Wadsworth Publishing, 1990.

Pitman, Mrs. E. R. (Emma Raymond). *Indian Zenana Missions: Their Need, Origin, Objects, Agents, Modes of Working, and Results, Outline Missionary Series*. London: John Snow, n.d.

Ramabai Saraswati, Pandita. *Pandita Ramabai Through Her Own Words: Selected Works*. Compiled and edited, with translations by Meera Kosambi. New Delhi: Oxford University Press, 2000.

Rambo, Lewis R. *Understanding Religious Conversion*. New Haven: Yale University Press, 1993.

Riley, Denise. *Am I that Name? Feminism and the Category of "Women" in History.* Minneapolis: University of Minnesota Press, 1988.

Robert, Dana L. *American Women in Mission: A Social History of Their Thought and Practice.* Macon, GA: Mercer University Press, 1997.

Rouse, Carolyn Moxley. *Engaged Surrender: African American Women and Islam.* Berkeley and Los Angeles: University of California Press, 2004.

Scott, Joan Wallach. *Gender and the Politics of History.* New York: Columbia University Press, 1988.

Seat, Karen K. *'Providence Has Freed Our Hands': Women's Missions and the American Encounter with Japan.* Syracuse, NY: Syracuse University Press, 2008.

Simmons, Gwendolyn Zoharah. "African American Islam as an Expression of Converts' Religious Faith and Nationalist Dreams and Ambitions." In *Women Embracing Islam: Gender and Conversion in the West*, ed. Karin van Nieuwkerk,182–191. Austin: University of Texas Press, 2006.

Stryker, Susan, and Stephen Whittle. *The Transgender Studies Reader.* New York: Routledge, 2006.

Taylor, Mark C., ed. *Critical Terms for Religious Studies.* Chicago: University of Chicago Press, 1998.

van Nieuwkerk, Karin. "Gender and Conversion to Islam in the West." In *Women Embracing Islam: Gender and Conversion in the West*, ed. Karin van Nieuwkerk, 1–16. Austin: University of Texas Press, 2006.

——. "Gender, Conversion and Islam: A Comparison of Online and Offline Conversion Narratives." In *Women Embracing Islam: Gender and Conversion in the West*, ed. Karin van Nieuwkerk, 95–119. Austin: University of Texas Press, 2006.

van Nieuwkerk, Karin, ed. *Women Embracing Islam: Gender and Conversion in the West.* Austin: University of Texas Press, 2006.

Wohlrab-Sahr, Monika. "Symbolizing Distance: Conversion to Islam in Germany and the United States." In *Women Embracing Islam: Gender and Conversion in the West*, ed. Karin van Nieuwkerk, 71–92. Austin: University of Texas Press, 2006.

CHAPTER 14

....

SEEING RELIGIOUS CONVERSION THROUGH THE ARTS

....

DIANE APOSTOLOS-CAPPADONA

SINCE the beginning of human experience, there has been a connection—if not a series of connections—between religion and art. Mircea Eliade argued that the elemental dimension of human experience is as *homo religiosus*, while for Ernst Cassirer the primary communicative nature of the human is the ability to create and communicate through symbols as *homo symbolicus*. I would advocate that it is the merging of *homo religiosus* with *homo symbolicus* that provides *homo aestheticus* with the ability to answer the epistemological question; we come to know through the visualization of concepts, ideas, and truth, through the imaging energies of the imagination. As human beings we come to know through our natural and primary aesthetic sensibilities—sight, sound, movement—through icon, image, and illustration, through myth and story, through dance and ritual. Central to this process is the human recognition of the sacred and the holy as well as of the profane and the secular.

All world religions have a perspective(s) on images, and these perspectives range from the aniconic to the iconic to the iconoclastic. Images are inexorably intertwined with religious experience and in tonalities from modes of veneration and devotion to phenomena of ritual and pedagogy. Defined by a multiplicity of characteristics including function, placement, patronage, iconography, and artistic intentionality, religious images are identifiable by human responses encompassing embodied immanence, mystical transcendence, devotional or spiritual communion, visual thinking, and invisible immediacy.

Given the multiple social, cultural, political, and religious shifts that began in the late nineteenth century and became most pronounced in the 1960s, however, religion and art as both independent and interdependent realities have taken on new definitions, natures, and expressions. As art turned from the representational to the abstract and religion from the intellectual to the experiential, the Western, especially the American, audience made a crucial "turn" beyond what might be defined as an amorphous religious pluralism to the incorporation of the principles, practices, and images of Eastern religions. Thereby, the popular imagination and scholarly attention have been attracted to what became known as "the spiritual" and, in particular, "the spiritual in art."

While not a new phenomenon, religious conversion, or the turn from one religious identity to another, has captured the religious landscape. Conversion may be an overt and total rejection of the faith tradition an individual was born and socialized into for a totally "other" faith or the quieter transformation of one's religious identity by the incorporation of pluralistic practices such as "Christian yoga" or "Protestant icons." Although the twentieth century is known as "the secular century," it was curiously highlighted by extraordinary religious metamorphoses, globalized spirituality, and works of art that appeared secular on initial contact but proved to be deeply religious in both foundation and influence. Human beings are fundamentally curious, especially about other people, and the idea, if not the act, of changing one's religion remains a fascination and a conundrum, particularly as religious faith is understood as grounded in family, societal identity, cultural traditions, and ingrained customs.

ON THE POWER OF
IMAGES: A PROLEGOMENON

Robert Frost once wrote, "It's God. / I'd have known Him from Blake's picture anywhere."[1] The evidence of his eyes, then, was affirmed by familiar images of God. Such images were recognizable to Frost's readers from the works of art on museum walls or in books, in photographs, on television, in movies, in newspapers and magazines, in illustrated books and Bibles, and on the Internet. Fundamentally, the images Frost knew were those images with which he grew up and was surrounded by in adulthood and by which he had been socialized as a member of his social, political, cultural, and religious communities. Such images would have been readily recognized by his readers. So the American poet recognized God not from a spiritual experience or biblical reference but from works of art created by William Blake.

In an often-quoted passage, Anne Graham Lotz writes about the significance of her childhood experience of seeing the movie *The King of Kings*:

> The first encounter with God that I can remember took place on Good Friday when I was a young girl of seven or eight years of age. I had watched Cecil B. DeMille's classic movie, King of Kings, on television. Even today, I can remember being overcome by an incredible awareness of my sin, along with an overwhelming realization that Jesus died just for me. Personally. Specifically. The encounter was so real that I whispered to God that I was sorry for my sin and I tremblingly asked Him to forgive me. It was a life-defining, life-directing, life-determining moment. Because during that very first encounter, I not only became a child of God, I fell in love ... with Jesus.[2]

As I have written elsewhere, "Images have power: power to please, power to shock, power to educate, power to convert, power to transform."[3] The power of images extends beyond the visual arts to the larger arena of the arts, from film to music to drama to dance. Fundamentally, this power is predicated upon the act of *seeing*—an activity that encompasses and coordinates the fullness of being human. Historically, artists, critics, philosophers, and even art historians have emphasized the centrality of *seeing* as intrinsic to the process of the making and the experiencing of art and as distinctive to the relationship between art and the spiritual. For example, even the Marxist critic John Berger in his writings on art has accentuated the significance of *seeing* as both a fundamental human activity and as primary to any text:

> Seeing comes before words. The child looks and recognizes before it can speak.... Soon after we can see, we are aware that we can also be seen. The eye of the other combines with our own eye to make it fully credible that we are part of the visible world.... The reciprocal nature of vision is more important than that of spoken dialogue.[4]

Expanding the boundaries of the arts, images embody the shared memories that are the foundation of community identity. The process of conversion encompasses the transformation of an individual from within the constructs of one's original community into those of a new community and thereby into a new realm of images and symbols. So, in this present discussion I will be guided by two central and interrelated questions: "What are the commonalities or distinctions between art and conversion, both as a process of individual faith experience and as topics for academic study?" and "What is the role of the arts in the process of conversion?"

On Conversion: A Brief Excursus

According to the *Oxford English Dictionary*, the English word "conversion" is derived from the Latin *conversio* meaning "turning around," and in concept from the Greek *metanoia* signifying "going the other way." Traditionally, when used by Western scholars the term "conversion" implies more than a change in position or character but rather the change from one religious posture to confirmation in another. In Protestant references, however, conversion is the turn of a sinner to God once he/she recognizes his/her fundamental sinful nature and need for grace. More often than not, conversion has been analyzed or discussed from the perspective of Western Christianity and references further Christianity's missionary enterprise to evangelize the world. Therefore, a valid question for conversion studies, especially in terms of the arts, is the relationship between the fact of conversion and the Christian hegemonic legacy, as well as the historical reality, that conversion may most properly be considered as essential to colonial imperialism.

The drama of the proscribed "moment of conversion," whether of an adult in the Early Christian world, such as Paul or Augustine, or of a child in nineteenth-century

American Protestantism, such as the 12-year-old Henry Ward Beecher, is characterized as an "unasked for" moment of grace of God's unconditional love, a recognition of individual unworthiness, and a transformation of individual identity. For example, the person that Augustine was before and after his conversion experience resulted in distinctively different personalities, and so the drama of his moment of change became the heart of his autobiographical narrative and, eventually, the keystone for imaging his singular moment of conversion.

To undergo a conversion is to redefine one's religion; to change one's religion, as the adage goes, is to change one's world. Each of us lives in several worlds, from the large geological entity to the smaller referential frames of society, religion, and personal relationships. Central to the patterns of behavior, action, and individual personae by which we become members of each of our worlds is a socialization process within which images and imaging play a primary role. Each of these worlds is a combination of real and imaginary constructs, and as we enter into those worlds our "way of seeing" is our primary mode of acceptance and interpretation. As Berger advises, "Although every image embodies a way of seeing, our perception or appreciation of an image depends upon our own way of seeing."[5] Our own way of seeing is, of course, a communicator of ideas and ideals and of the perception of the self. We are shaped, formed, affected, and influenced by all that is incorporated within those worlds of images of which we are a part.

As seeing is fundamental to the epistemological process, we recognize it as central to the connection between culture and the self as it is between the self and the world. Along with the other parts of its definition and function, religion constitutes a theory of the world—its creation, its purpose, our place within it, and how we *see* that world, ourselves, and others. Although scholars of religion as diverse as Mircea Eliade and Victor Turner discuss the commonalities between the conversion experience with that of the initiate, the reality of how the convert experiences, comes to know, and *sees* either the path to conversion or the world after conversion is at the heart of the matter. While one might argue that the time and place of conversion are a personal matter, questions concerning the emotional and cognitive changes that are involved in the conversion process and how the process of *seeing* is affected are central to the human dimension of conversion and its relationship to and through art, thereby creating a rich cultural matrix of conversion.

ON CONVERSION THROUGH THE ARTS

The famous painting by the Zen monk Mu-ch'i in the Ryoko-in temple in the Daitoku-ji Zen temple complex in Kyoto is a small work in which nothing but six persimmons are painted. From the perspective of Zen, this painting surpasses any standard Buddhist depictions of Buddha. Zen paintings directly show the true Buddha, which is prior to and free from any form; this is the Formless Self, or the True Self, as it is called in Zen.

It is in this direct indication of the Formless Self that the uniqueness of the Zen cultural experience resides. The seven characteristics of Zen aesthetics evidenced in the *Six Persimmons* are asymmetry, simplicity, austerity, naturalness, profound subtlety, freedom from attachment, and tranquility. Meditation upon this image should result in a recognition of these characteristics as the unity of the aesthetic, moral, and spiritual dimensions of human existence. Either prolonged or momentary, this experience of *seeing* should result in *satorī*, or enlightenment.

In the *Nātyaśastras*, a Hindu text on the arts, one of Bharata's themes is the relationship between dance and painting. "He who is not a dancer cannot be a painter, he who is not a painter cannot be a dancer. He who cannot see has no body, he who has no body cannot feel."[6] Once again the human embodiment of the aesthetic dimensions is interpreted as an integration of the arts and spirituality—as a making, *seeing*, and experiencing through images.

Images, whether they are visual, verbal, aural, or tactile, have power simply because they make us *feel*. We need merely to remember that an anesthetic inhibits or prevents our ability to have feeling. One of the singular characteristics of being human is the ability to have feelings; our word "aesthetic" comes from the same Greek root for *aisthetikos* connoting a coming to know through the senses (plural emphasized). Similarly, the Hindu understanding of the aesthetic is premised, according to Bharata, on the *rasas*, which have a series of levels to be achieved by both artist/performer and viewer/audience. The *rasas* are like the gastric juices which allow the human to perceive, to smell, to savor, to taste, to select, to chew, and to digest food; full bodily processes are engaged with the visual and tactile senses as we see and touch foods and place them in our mouths. We chew, we swallow, we digest, we excrete, and we retain—we are different before, during, and after this process and at its highest moments are raised to a level of universal oneness.

The arts—whether visual, oral, or performative—can be characterized by believers as forms of spiritual communication either as meditation, contemplation, or prayer, given the common attribute of the suspension of time and space as we know them, and by artists as an experience of the infusion of light or of "joy." The fundamental nature of art can be defined as a ritual for both the artist and the believer. While all the arts can be identified as tangible expressions of the fact or experience of revelation, the more modern arts, especially in terms of abstraction, may be categorized as camouflaging the Sacred.[7] For some religious traditions, especially those from the East or those described as pluralistic fusions of East and West, there is a fundamental indivisibility of art, life, and spirituality. Traditionally, even in the West, there was a tendency until the ascent of Christianity that the artist was not simply divinely inspired but also a shaman, a characterization embraced with great enthusiasm by many modern artists from Picasso to the Abstract Expressionists. If we coordinate these principles with my proposition that to be human is to be *homo aestheticus*, then we can consider how art impinges upon, narrates, and supports conversion.

For the magisterial historian of religions, Mircea Eliade, artists succeed in circumventing fate. They are able to suspend our traditional perceptions of time and space by the act of making, an act in which we share through participating in the environment of that artwork. During the moments of artistic creation, artists fulfill the fundamental human instinct for transcendence. The craving to be freed from the limitations of one's humanness is satisfied by the experience of passing over into the Other. Momentarily tasting transcendence, artists break the boundaries of individuality and experience universality. They are freed not only from the limitations of human individuality and fallibility but also from human frailty, and, precisely the most powerful form of that frailty, which is death. Artistic creation suspends Time (with a capital "T"). The arts reflect Eliade's recognition of the "possibility of being religiously moved by the image and the symbol."[8]

Eliade was nurtured in a world which was Eastern Orthodox in religious orientation. This worldview senses the aesthetic dimensions of religion, intuits a sacramental understanding of matter, and places an aesthetic and spiritual importance on light. In order to understand that perspective and its implications for his own perceptions of reality (as in his personal being and his scholarly and creative work), Eliade had to travel outside of himself to encounter and know himself—a form of conversion brought about through art. He recounted his recognition of the role of the icon in Eastern Orthodox spirituality as follows:

> The second discovery, the second part of the lesson I learned, is the meaning of symbols. In Romania, I hadn't been particularly attracted to religion; to my eyes, all those icons in the churches seemed merely to clutter them up. I didn't exactly regard the icons as idols, of course, but still.... Well, in India I happened to live for a time in a Bengali village, and I saw the women and girls touching and decorating a lingam, a phallic symbol, or, more precisely, an anatomically very accurate stone phallus; and naturally, the married women at least could not be unaware of what it was, of its physiological function. So I came to understand the possibility of seeing the symbol in the lingam. The lingam was the mystery of life, of creativity, of the fertility that is manifested at every cosmic level. And that manifestation of life was Siva, not the anatomical member we know. So this possibility of being religiously moved by the image and the symbol—that opened up a whole world of spiritual values to me. I said to myself: it is clear that in looking at an icon the believer does not perceive simply the figure of a woman holding a child; he is seeing the Virgin Mary and therefore the Mother of God and Sophia, Divine Wisdom. This discovery of the importance of religious symbolism in traditional cultures—well, you can imagine its importance in my training as a historian of religions.[9]

Among the aesthetic systems of world religions is the icon of Eastern Orthodoxy. The icon is distinguished from the idol. Worshiping an icon is not an idolatrous activity, for the devout pray through the icon to the sacred presence manifested therein. In that sense, the icon is a threshold, a window to a sacramental encounter. It is a centering point for meditation and contemplation that leads toward the possibility of a spiritual encounter that is fundamentally grounded in an aesthetic experience.

A work of art is able to *presence* mystery in a new way which manifests a religious interpretation. This sense of mystery, which is both terrifying and fascinating, leads one forward on a path as difficult and as experiential as a religious ritual. The resulting aesthetic experience of art leads to the possibility of a transformed consciousness and new sense of self. Neither the perceiver nor the artist is reborn in the sense of physical new life, but rather in that sense of a transformed spiritual consciousness. This is a result of the new life experience of time-space relations that occurs as a result of the aesthetic experience. This is a parallel to that moment when an initiate enters totally into the ritual experience and is no longer who he or she was nor who he or she will be, but becomes everyone—a return to that universal and primordial moment. Eliade advises:

> To be like a child means to be newborn, to be reborn to a new spiritual life; in short, to be an initiate. Unlike all other modes of being, the spiritual life has nothing to do with the law of becoming, for it does not develop within time. The "newborn" is not a suckling child who will grow up only to grow old one day. He is *puer aeternus*. He will remain a child *in aeternum*: he will partake of the atemporal beatitude of the Spirit, and not of the flux of history. The second life—the life of the initiate—does not repeat the first, human, historical life: its mode of being is qualitatively different.[10]

Artists, then, for Eliade, have made an attempt by the destruction of traditional modes of being and the creation of a unique elemental style to *presence* the mysteriousness and fascination of the Sacred. Experiencing this art becomes the way one enters into a ritual which seeks to create for the participant a new sense of self. The experience of art becomes the melding of aesthetic and religious modes-of-being, culminating in a ritualization which allows one to recover the holiness that is extant in the world and in human life.

On an Iconography of Conversion

Paraphrasing the magisterial art historian Ernst Gombrich, I can affirm that "theories date rapidly, but works of art, like diamonds, are forever."[11] One of the fundamental and keystone dimensions of the arts is their experiential and intuitive roles in both human existence and culture. Since the human sense of sight is central to both the nature of being human and of being religious, we find a common ground in which the conversion experience can take root and flourish. Each world religion develops its own narratives, images, and symbols; however, the connections in Early Christianity may offer the most direct example of these symbolic fusions as Jesus as the Christ was described and recognized as "the illuminator," that is, the one who brought the light, thereby linking not simply daily experience with religious values but also connecting the Classical with the Early Christian world through the metaphors of light and sight.

Building upon the Hebrew Scriptural tradition that no one sees God and lives, the promise of the beatific vision became a significant Christian concept codified ultimately by Dante in his lengthy tale of religious longing, doubting, questioning, and affirmation, *The Divine Comedy*. The arts are predicated upon images—still, moving, animate or inanimate, as confirmed by Pope St. Gregory I (also known as Gregory the Great) who defended the importance of images as Christian pedagogy in his now-classic "Letter to Bishop Serenus" and, further, as the necessary equal of written texts when he dispatched Augustine to Canterbury with an icon of Christ, a processional cross, and a Bible to convert the Anglo-Saxons. This pope recognized that those who were not textually literate would be visually literate! A similar idea was expressed by St. John of Damascus, who advised that anyone who wished to know about Christianity need only to enter a church and look everywhere to see the story of the faith played out in the icons on the walls, the ceiling, and the iconostasis.

How an image functions, how images garner meaning, and the history, if any, of this "power of images" are crucial to understanding the role of the arts in the process of conversion. In the first overt discussion of the transformative power and reception theory of images, art historian David Freedberg provided the first cross-cultural and socioeconomic analysis of images which were both secular and sacred. Combined with his earlier studies on the history and meaning of iconoclasm, that is, the "smashing" or destruction of images, Freedberg emphasized the unspoken-of and little-examined ability of images to communicate more than social, religious, and political ideas.

Images, he countered, are capable of inspiring both fear and delight in those who encounter them. The fear, we may expect, is the most natural cause of iconoclasm, especially religiously inspired iconoclasm. While the delight inspires, soothes, or elevates the viewer, the fear elicits anxiety and disobedience. The communicative attributes of images include the fundamental elements of art, whether painting, sculpture, dance, or cinema, that is, color, form, scale, movement, and placement. Individuals respond to images sometimes simultaneously, others independently on at least two levels—the intuitive or affective dimension as known or expressed through the senses and the rational or effective dimension which brings about intellectual transformations:

> People are sexually aroused by pictures and sculptures; they break pictures and sculptures; they mutilate them, kiss them, cry before them, and go on journeys to them; they are calmed by them; and incited to revolt. They give thanks by means of them, expect to be elevated by them, and are moved to the highest levels of empathy and fear. They have always responded in these ways; they still do. They do so in societies we call primitive and in modern societies in East and West, in Africa, America, Asia, and Europe.[12]

The arts, especially the visual arts, communicate religious ideals and theological meaning through both the intuitive and the rational dimensions of human perception. Color and scale are the central modalities for intuitive expression and response, while composition and form signify the patterns of visual communication that are directed and responded to by rationality. The fundamental modality for these forms of artistic communication is the act of *seeing*. Historically, and regardless of class or geographic location, children learn to *see* before they are taught to read or write. The process of *seeing*, like the more primal tactile sense, is foundational to human development, and the singular place of the senses cannot be ignored. The human quest for meaning—social, political, or religious—is predicated upon the communication accessed through images. Human beings come to the arts—dance, cinema, painting, sculpture, photography— with a set of socialized experiences of *seeing*, especially of our individual and communal *seeing* of meaning through signs and symbols.

Traditionally, art historians and iconographers distinguish iconography as having religious subject matter(e.g., Christian or Buddhist iconography); having a chronologi- cal character(e.g., International Gothic iconography or Southern Baroque iconogra- phy); or as having a geographic limitation(e.g., Japanese Zen iconography or Australian Aboriginal iconography). These multiple approaches to iconography are dependent upon the ability of the artist to express multiple meanings and upon the audience's abil- ity to "read" the signs and symbols encoded in works of art. Composed of animals, flora, vegetables, inanimate objects, colors, numbers, shapes, costumes, and so forth, signs and symbols have a variety of interpretations predicated as much upon regional and his- torical attitudes as upon cultural and theological transformations. While not inscribed in stone but rather on the shifting sands of cultural advance and human development, iconography responds to social and religious attitudes toward gender and race as well to developments in painting and sculpting techniques.

Thematically, religious art may be said to be dependent upon the narratives of a religious tradition. In the specific case of religious conversion, regardless of the par- ticular religions involved, three visual thematic approaches to conversion can be identi- fied: first, the presentation of the religious pedagogy that has led to or leads to conversion (iconography as theology of conversion); second, the illustration of the conversion nar- ratives of significant individuals within a faith tradition or of the general presentation of the conversion experience (an iconography of conversion); and finally, art that is in and of itself elemental to the conversion experience (conversion iconography).

Cognizant of the art historical (and theological) distinctions between iconography and iconology—the former being an interpretation of the meaning of the symbolism within a work of art while the latter is a larger reading of that same symbolism within the socio-political-cultural-religious climate in which the work was created—we need to consider whether we can realistically discuss an iconography (or an iconology) of con- version. While a visual history of conversion is more than possible, we must recognize both its limitations and its benefits. First is, of course, the logical limitation of religious tradition. In other words, a careful analysis of the visual imagery of conversion within Catholicism, for example, is both possible and informative to a particular and a general discussion of conversion, while a cross-religions approach may end up being a form of visual "fruit salad." As this is a new iconographic theme, it might also be best to restrict the visual field to a particular historical period and geographic locale.

While conversion is an element in the life of every world religion, and within every world religion is embedded an attitude toward art, it may be the case that not every world religion has developed an iconography of conversion. Without doubt, Christianity, especially Western Christianity, has artistically fashioned, perhaps unconsciously or perhaps intentionally, an iconography of conversion which might be identified as a carefully wrought chronology of conversion. Whether the practice of an iconography of conversion is appropriate to all world religions, or whether it is singularly Christian, is for now a moot point. A rapid survey of conversion in Western Christian art can provide us with several crucial building blocks for the larger pluralistic religious iconography of conversion, from the basic signs and symbols for the conversion experience to the artistic and theological modes for selecting those conversion experiences that are rendered as significant for communal pedagogy and role models.

The cohesive visual trail of conversion narratives in Western Christian art is our best source for what an iconography of conversion would look like. The selected imagery discussed below reflects highlights of significant historical conversion moments in Christian history and offers iconographic models for an entrée into this topic, especially as a presentation of the multiple answers to the questions of where does conversion occur—in private or public spaces, sacred or secular places—and whether conversion is a private internal event or a public external event.

One of the earliest and most dramatic discussions of conversion in Christianity is that of Saul of Tarsus, whose moment of "unasked for" grace resulted in his temporary blindness and in the changing of his name to Paul. According to the Book of Acts, this persecutor of early Christians was dispatched to continue his campaign in Damascus, but on the way he was struck down by the shock of a bright and glowing light and a voice that was identified later as that of the Risen Christ. Paul was "blind" for three days, undoubtedly a metaphor for his inability to see spiritual truth and for his rebirth after three days "in a tomb."

This scriptural description of the sudden and overwhelming experience of an unexpected flash of revelation combined with the radical reversal of previous beliefs and allegiances, and the recognition of his unworthiness to receive God's grace, became the Pauline paradigm of conversion. Recalling the early Christian idea of Christ as the illuminator who brings the light of faith, presaging the Christian metaphor for God as a glowing white light, this dramatic event is highlighted in the Christian hegemony of conversion iconography by the image of the newly named "Paul" lying on the ground as his horse stumbles or flees in fright. While artistic representations of Paul are legion, from Early Christian art to the present, the most moving depictions of his conversion experience are those by Michelangelo (1542–50, Cappella Paolina, CittàVaticani) and Caravaggio (1601, Cappella Cerasi, Santa Maria del Popolo, Roma).

Traditionally, the conversion of the Emperor Constantine has garnered great attention in the visual litany of Christian conversion iconography. There are two versions of his experience of conversion, one compiled by his contemporaneous biographer (and bishop) Eusebius and the second in the writing of Lactantius. With the eyes of history and as Christianity has evolved, depictions of Constantine's conversion have combined the central elements of both authors. According to Eusebius, the Emperor reported two visions. The first was of a cross of light in the sky with the now-famous inscription IHS, or *In hoc signovinces* (Latin for "By this sign conquer"). In the second vision, he was instructed to have the Chi-Rho inscribed on the Labarum and the shields of his soldiers. Lactantius related the Emperor's dream on the night before his fateful battle with

Maxentius. In his sleep state, Constantine saw that placing the Chi-Rho on his troops and his standard would result in a God-given victory. Given the significance of dreams in both the Classical and Christian worlds as incorporating divine messages, this imperial dream narrative became a model not only for visualizing the light of conversion but also for the divine mission of Christian rulers on the eve of battle (see, for example, medieval images of Charlemagne).

The coordination of the privacy of the dream sequence and the public realm of the entry onto the battlefield becomes significant in the iconography of Constantine's conversion. In particular, Pierodella Francesca's mural cycle of *The Legend of the True Cross* (1452–59, San Francesco, Arezzo) emphasizes the dream sequence by the inclusion of the episode of "The Dream of Constantine." The visions the Emperor Constantine encountered in his dreams on the night before the great battle of the Milvian Bridge (and later on the eve before the finding of the True Cross by his mother, the Empress Helena) are characterized by the angelic messenger and the glowing light from heaven as divine intervention in a battle critical to the future of Christianity.

Alternatively, Gian Lorenzo Bernini depicts a very public vision of the Emperor on horseback in a very public and ecclesiastical setting (1654–70, ScalaReggia, San Pietro, CittàVaticani). His horse rearing in fright at the glowing light in the sky (similar to the posture of Saul/Paul's horse as painted by Caravaggio), Constantine reacts in embodied amazement at the wonder he has just seen. All of his senses are brought to a holistic experience with his body and his mind as he responds aesthetically to this vision and its promise.

Painted by an unknown twelfth-century Umbrian artist, the crucifix over the altar of the Church of San Damiano was integral to the conversion of Francis of Assisi. According to tradition, during a dramatic moment of prayer in the abandoned church Francis heard a voice coming from the crucifix. The awe-struck young man was challenged to rebuild the church, a challenge he first took literally to be the Church of San Damiano. As Francis's mission progressed, however, he understood that the voice of Christ was calling out to him to rebuild THE Church. Many artists, most prominently Giotto (fourteenth century, San Francesco, Assisi), have depicted Francis kneeling before the "speaking crucifix."

Francis's interaction with art extends beyond its significant role in his conversion. The iconic motif serves as a model for others of the extraordinary influence both the saint and his teachings had on medieval and Renaissance artists who developed devotional and humanistic themes including the Nativity crèche and the Stations of the Cross, as well as the presentations of human emotions, as in Giotto's *Lamentation* (1303–5, Cappella Scrovegni, Padova). The latter, in particular, supported the viewer's reaction and highlighted a participative response—aspects of an emerging Christian humanism that played important roles in the conversion process.

Although best known as a society painter of well-dressed, beautiful women in elegant settings, James Jacques Tissot experienced a conversion moment which he described as "a vision" in the Église Saint-Sulpice, Paris, in 1885. From that moment forward, the focus of his art moved away from the secular to the sacred. He traveled to Egypt, Palestine, and Syria to *see* the places and settings where Jesus lived, taught, and walked—and to paint a visual narrative of the New Testament. Initially exhibited in Paris in 1894, Tissot's 350 watercolors were on view in London, Manhattan, Brooklyn, Boston, Philadelphia, and Chicago before becoming immortalized as illustrations in the so-called *Tissot Bible,*which was printed in multiple editions in French and English.

Highly popular from both the American tour and published editions of the *Tissot Bible*, his (or the artist's) original images were ultimately purchased by public subscription for the Brooklyn Institute of Arts and Sciences (now the Brooklyn Museum of Art) in 1900. Created as a result of his own conversion, these images of the life of Christ were influential not simply on the hearts and minds of his contemporaries but also on later generations of Americans, including D. W. Griffith, Cecil B. DeMille, and other film-makers (see especially Tissot's*What the Saviour Saw from the Cross*, c.1890, Brooklyn Museum of Art, Brooklyn). We need to consider the influence of cinema as more than an entertainment medium; DeMille's *The King of Kings* has been identified as the most-watched religious film of the twentieth century and as the vehicle of many conversions.

This does not detract, of course, from the significant role of both traditional Christian art and of the spirituality of modern art. The Protestant theologian Paul Tillich offered multiple insights in his lectures, sermons, and writings on the significance of art as a source of religious sustenance and spiritual meaning to him. Throughout his life, Tillich frequently described the fact and spiritual significance of his *seeing* Botticelli's *Madonna and Child with Singing Angels* (1477, Berlin-Dahlem Museum, Berlin). Clearly, the impact of this "moment of beauty" provided that form of enduring sustenance for Tillich of a moment of conversion, and perhaps, for Tillich, this *aesthetic* experience was his grace-filled moment:

> But at the end of the war I still had never seen the original paintings in all their glory. Going to Berlin, I hurried to the Kaiser Friedrich Museum. There on the wall was a picture that had comforted me in battle: *Madonna with Singing Angels*, painted by Sandro Botticelli in the fifteenth century.
>
> Gazing up at it, I felt a state approaching ecstasy. In the beauty of the painting there was Beauty itself. It shone through the colors of the paint as the light of day shines through the stained-glass windows of a medieval church.
>
> As I stood there, bathed in the beauty its painter had envisioned so long ago, something of the divine source of all things came through to me. I turned away shaken.
>
> That moment has affected my whole life, given me the keys for the interpretation of human existence, brought vital joy and spiritual truth. I compare it with what is usually called revelation in the language of religion.[13]

Even more extraordinary, perhaps, as Tillich was both a great theological mind and a Protestant, was his reflection on the critical importance of Expressionist art to his own theology:

Nolde—*The Pentecost*. And I must confess that some of my writings are derived from just this picture, as I always learn more from pictures than from theological books.[14]

In this very rapid survey of selected visual highlights of what an iconography of conversion could look like through the lens of Christian art, we have witnessed all three of my suggested approaches to images: as religious pedagogy, as illustration of conversion narratives, and as an element of the conversion process. Further, we have discussed art as visual narrative (Paul), prophecy (Constantine), instrument and influence (Francis), visual theology (Tissot), and evocative imagery (Tillich). The often misidentified Christian hegemony of conversion exposes a series of themes, motifs, styles, and approaches applicable to the art of world religions and to my central questions: "What are the commonalities or distinctions between art and conversion, both as a process of individual faith experience and as topics for academic study?" and "What is the role of the arts in the process of conversion?"

NOTES

1. Kathleen Rainer, *William Blake* (London: Thames and Hudson, 1970), 185.
2. Ann Graham Lotz, e-mail message to author, December 18, 2008.
3. Diane Apostolos-Cappadona, "The Image of Woman in Contemporary Religious Film," in *New Image of Religious Film*, ed. John R. May (Kansas City, MO: Sheed & Ward, 1997), 113.
4. John Berger, *Ways of Seeing* (Baltimore: Penguin Books, 1972), 1, 9.
5. Ibid., 10.
6. Bharata Muni, *The Nātyaśastra: A Treatise on Ancient Indian Dramaturgy and Histrionics* (New Delhi: Asiatic Society for Bibliotheca Indica, 1950), 272.
7. The concept of "the camouflage of the Sacred" comes from Mircea Eliade, *Symbolism, the Sacred, and the Arts*, ed. Diane Apostolos-Cappadona (New York: Continuum, 1992), 32–52.
8. Mircea Eliade, *Ordeal by Labyrinth* (Chicago: University of Chicago Press, 1982), 55.
9. Ibid.
10. Mircea Eliade, *No Souvenirs: Journal, 1957–69* (New York: Harper and Row, 1977), 22.
11. Ernst Gombrich, "Zebra Crossings," *New York Review of Books*, May 4, 1972, 38.
12. David Freedberg, *The Power of Images: Studies in the History and Theory of Response* (Chicago: University of Chicago Press, 1989), 1.
13. Paul Tillich, *On Art and Architecture*, ed. Jane Daggett Dillenberger and John Dillenberger (New York: Continuum, 1987), 235.
14. Ibid., 151.

BIBLIOGRAPHY

Adams, Doug. *Transcendence with the Human Body in Art: George Segal, Stephen DeStaebler, Jasper Johns, and Christo*. New York: Continuum, 1991.
Adams, Doug, and Diane Apostolos-Cappadona, eds. *Art as Religious Studies*. Eugene, OR: Wipf & Stock, 2002.

Apostolos-Cappadona, Diane. "Art." In *Encyclopedia of Women and World Religions*, ed. Serenity Young, 61–65. New York: Macmillan, 1999.

———. "Iconography." In *The Routledge Companion to Religion and Film*, ed. John C. Lyden, 440–464. London: Routledge, 2009.

———. "The Image of Woman in Contemporary Religious Film." In *New Image of Religious Film*, ed. John R. May, 111–127. Kansas City, MO: Sheed & Ward, 1997.

———. "[Christian] Painting," "[Christian] Sculpture," and "[Christian] Symbol." In *Christianity: A Complete Guide*, ed. John Bowden, 881–886, 1099–1114, 1160–1171. London: Continuum, 2005.

Apostolos-Cappadona, Diane, ed. *Art, Creativity, and the Sacred: An Anthology in Religion and Art*. New York: Continuum, 1995.

Bailey, Gauvin A. *Art on the Jesuit Missions in Asia and Latin America, 1542–1773*. Toronto: University of Toronto Press, 1999.

Berger, John. *Ways of Seeing*. Baltimore: Penguin Books, 1972.

Blair, Sheila S., and Jonathan M. Bloom. *Islamic Arts*. London: Phaidon, 1997.

Bowden, Hugh. "Constantine's Conversion." In *Christianity: A Complete Guide*, ed. John Bowden, 279–281. London: Continuum, 2005.

Bremmer, Jan N., Wout J. Van Bekkum, and Arie L. Molendijk, eds. *Cultures of Conversion*. Leuven: Peeters, 2006.

Brown, Frank Burch. *Good Taste, Bad Taste, and Christian Taste: Aesthetics in Religious Life*. New York: Oxford University Press, 2000.

Buckser, Andrew, and Stephen D. Glazier, eds. *The Anthropology of Religious Conversion*. Lanham, MD: Rowman & Littlefield, 2003.

Coomaraswami, Ananda K. *The Dance of Shiva: Fourteen Indian Essays*. Rev. ed., New York: Pantheon, 1957.

Cort, John E. "Art, Religion, and Material Culture: Some Reflections on Method." *Journal of the American Academy of Religion* 64, no. 3 (1996): 613–632.

Crumlin, Rosemary. *Images of Religion in Australian Art*. Kensington, NSW: Bay Books, 1988.

Crumlin, Rosemary, ed. *Aboriginal Art and Spirituality*. North Blackburn, Victoria: Collins Dove, 1991.

———. *Beyond Belief: Modern Art and the Religious Imagination*. Melbourne: National Gallery of Victoria, 1998.

Dillenberger, Jane. *Image and Spirit in Sacred and Secular Art*. New York: Continuum, 1990.

Dillenberger, John. *A Theology of Artistic Sensibilities: The Visual Arts and the Church*. New York: Continuum, 1986.

Dixon, John W. *Images of Truth: Religion and the Art of Seeing*. Atlanta, GA: Scholars Press, 1996.

Elkins, James. *Pictures and Tears: A History of People Who Have Cried in Front of Paintings*. New York: Routledge, 2001.

Eliade, Mircea. *No Souvenirs: Journal, 1957–69*. New York: Harper and Row, 1977.

———. *Ordeal by Labyrinth*. Chicago: University of Chicago Press, 1982.

———. *Symbolism, the Sacred, and the Arts*, ed. Diane Apostolos-Cappadona. New York: Continuum, 1992.

Freedberg, David. *The Power of Images: Studies in the History and Theory of Response*. Chicago: University Chicago Press, 1989.

Gombrich, Ernst. "Zebra Crossings." *New York Review of Books*, May 4, 1972, 38.

Grabar, Oleg. *The Formation of Islamic Art*. New Haven: Yale University Press, 1973.

Hackett, Rosalind I. J. *Art and Religion in Africa*. London: Palgrave, 1996.

Hisamatsu, Shin'ichi. *Zen and the Fine Arts*. Tokyo: Kodansha, 1982.

Jensen, Robin M. *Face to Face: Portraits of the Divine in Early Christianity*. Philadelphia: Augsburg Fortress, 2004.

Khodarkovsky, Michael. "'Not by Word Alone': Missionary Policies and Religious Conversion in Early Modern Russia." *Comparative Studies in Society and History* 38, no. 2 (1996): 267–293.

Kramrisch, Stella. *The Art of India: Traditions of Indian Sculpture, Painting and Architecture*. London: Phaidon Press, 1965.

Leeuw, Gerardus van der. *Sacred and Profane Beauty: The Holy in Art*. New York: AAR/Oxford University Press, 2005.

Lotz, Ann Graham. "You can be sure you will go to heaven when you die." http://www.anngrahamlotz.com.

McDannell, Colleen. *Material Christianity: Religion and Popular Culture in America*. New Haven: Yale University Press, 1995.

Malraux, André. *The Voices of Silence*. Garden City, NY: Doubleday, 1953.

Mann, Vivian. *Jewish Texts on the Visual Arts*. Cambridge: Cambridge University Press, 2000.

Maritain, Jacques. *Creative Intuition in Art and Poetry*. Princeton: Princeton University Press, 1978.

Martland, Thomas R. *Religion as Art*. Albany: SUNY Press, 1981.

Mathews, Thomas F. *The Clash of Gods: A Reinterpretation of Early Christian Art*. Princeton: Princeton University Press, 1993.

Moore, Albert C. *Arts in the Religions of the Pacific*. London: Palgrave, 1997.

Morgan, David. *Religious Visual Culture in Theory and Practice*. Berkeley and Los Angeles: University of California Press, 2005.

——. *Visual Piety: A History and Theory of Popular Religious Images*. Berkeley and Los Angeles: University of California Press, 1998.

Muni, Bharata. *The Nāṭyaśastra: A Treatise on Ancient Indian Dramaturgy and Histrionics*. New Delhi: Asiastic Society for Bibliotheca Indica, 1950.

Panofsky, Erwin. *Studies in Iconology: Humanistic Themes in the Art of the Renaissance*. New York: Harper and Row, 1972.

Percy, Martyn. "Conversion." In *Christianity: A Complete Guide*, ed. John Bowden, 282–285. London: Continuum, 2005.

Plate, S. Brent, ed. *Religion, Art, and Visual Culture: A Cross-Cultural Reader*. New York: Palgrave-Macmillan, 2002.

Rainer, Kathleen. *William Blake*. London: Thames and Hudson, 1970.

Rambo, Lewis R. *Understanding Religious Conversion*. New Haven: Yale University Press, 1993.

Rambo, Lewis R., and Charles E. Farhadian. "Conversion." In *Encyclopedia of Religion*, ed. Lindsey Jones. 2nd ed., Detroit: Macmillan, 2005.

Suzuki, Daisetz T. *Zen and Japanese Culture*. Princeton: Princeton University Press, 1970.

Thompson, Robert Farris. *African Art in Motion*. Berkeley and Los Angeles: University of California Press, 1974.

Tillich, Paul. *On Art and Architecture*. Ed. Jane Daggett Dillenberger and John Dillenberger. New York: Continuum, 1987.

Tuchman, Maurice, Judi Freeman, and Carel Blotkamp, eds. *The Spiritual in Art: Abstract Painting, 1890–1985*. Los Angeles: Los Angeles County Museum of Art, 1986.

Wolterstorff, Nicholas. *Art in Action: Toward a Christian Aesthetic*. Grand Rapids, MI: Eerdmans, 1980.

Wuthnow, Robert. *All in Sync: How Music and Art Are Revitalizing American Religion.* Berkeley and Los Angeles: University of California Press, 2003.
——. *Creative Spirituality: The Way of the Artist.* Berkeley and Los Angeles: University of California Press, 2001.
Zimmer, Heinrich. *Myths and Symbols in Indian Art and Culture.* Princeton: Princeton University Press, 1974.

CHAPTER 15

....

RELIGIOUS CONVERSION
AS NARRATIVE AND
AUTOBIOGRAPHY

....

BRUCE HINDMARSH

We bring our years to an end, as it were a tale that is told.
—Psalm 90:9 (Book of Common Prayer)

SAMPSON Staniforth (1720–1799) was a 25-year-old soldier in the English army who was converted in a Methodist revival that began among the soldiers after the Battle of Dettingen in 1743. He claimed that his conversion was from a state of complete irreligion to serious Christian commitment. He described the critical turning point in his own words:

> From twelve at night till two it was my turn to stand sentinel at a dangerous post....As soon as I was alone, I kneeled down, and determined not to rise, but to continue crying and wrestling with God, till He had mercy on me. How long I was in that agony I cannot tell: but as I looked up to heaven, I saw the clouds open exceeding bright, and I saw Jesus hanging on the cross. At the same moment these words were applied to my heart, "Thy sins are forgiven thee." My chains fell off; my heart was free. All guilt was gone, and my soul was filled with unutterable peace. I loved God and all mankind, and the fear of death and hell was vanished away. I was filled with wonder and astonishment.[1]

Staniforth was discharged from the army in 1748 and became a Methodist lay preacher under John Wesley. This quotation is an excerpt from an account he wrote for Wesley's *Arminian Magazine* in 1783, when he was 62 years of age.

At the beginning of this account, Staniforth made quite clear that this conversion experience was the defining moment of his life, and he structured his entire narrative around it, announcing, in his first paragraph, "I shall, first, speak of my life from the time of my birth, till I was about twenty-five years old: and, Secondly, from the time that God called me, to the present time."[2] Everything that preceded his conversion was prologue; everything that followed was epilogue. Staniforth's evangelical conversion was not therefore an experience on the periphery of his life; conversion went to the heart of his identity, and he proclaimed this in a new ordering of his life's story, one that still made sense of his life some thirty-seven years later. He did not just have a conversion experience; he had a conversion narrative.

Something similar can be seen in other religious conversion narratives, such as Muhammad Asad's spiritual autobiography, *Road to Mecca* (1954), which looked back some twenty-eight years to tell the story of his growing alienation from Western culture and his conversion to Islam in 1926. A statesman and journalist, Asad narrates his conversion as a journey (geographically and spiritually) from one world to another, until he was finally able to declare in the presence of two witnesses "that there is no God but God, and that Muhammad is His Messenger."[3] Or, again, the Chinese spiritual autobiography from the late Ming period, written by the Buddhist master Te-ch'ing (1546–1623) a year before his death, recounted the events which had led him to achieve spiritual illumination almost half a century earlier. As with Staniforth and Asad, Te-ch'ing's religious experience marked his life decisively and shaped his whole identity: "From that time on I was clear both internally and externally, and sounds and sights no longer posed obstacles. All the former doubts and confusions were now gone."[4]

In this chapter, I hope to show how the study of religious conversion may be approached by paying particular attention to the way in which the experience of conversion is narrated by the converts themselves. In the cases of Staniforth, Asad, and Te-ch'ing, we are able to distinguish clearly the life lived in the past by the convert and the life lived in the present by the narrator, separated as these two are by a gap of decades. And in the sharply etched pattern of life pre-conversion and post-conversion, we are also able to see that the narrators are doing something more than simply reporting data; they are telling a story. Religious conversion often comes to us thus as *narrative* and *autobiography*, inviting further exploration of these forms of expression.

While religious conversion has been richly studied from theological perspectives, on the one hand, and social scientific perspectives, on the other, students of religious conversion have not drawn as fully on the perspectives opened up by literary critics over the last half century in the fields of narrative and autobiographical theory.[5] In what follows, I draw upon research in these fields and seek to show how this research offers insight into the religious conversion of figures such as Sampson Staniforth, Muhammad Asad, and Te-ch'ing. Most of the scholarship devoted to the study of narrative and autobiography in the past century has been done from a Western perspective in which Christianity has figured prominently, and some have argued indeed that autobiography is particularly (if not exclusively) Western and modern since, from the seventeenth century to the present, autobiographical practice has expanded beyond anything seen earlier or outside the Western context. In this, of course, religious beliefs have mattered greatly. Although more work remains to be done to compare the narrative traditions of self-biography among different religions and cultures, we may expect that personal conversion narratives will figure more prominently in religious traditions and cultures that place especial value on the individual as compared with those that regard individual identity as less important or illusory.

Because of the preponderance of autobiography in the modern West and the development of scholarship, the survey of narrative and autobiographical theory in this chapter is necessarily framed primarily in terms of the Christian and post-Christian Western world. But what Geoffrey Galt Harpham writes of St. Augustine's conversion to Christianity in the garden at Milan is true also of countless other figures such as Asad and Te-ch'ing: "The conversion that organizes the entire narrative around itself" anticipates a second conversion, "the conversion of life into textual self-representation."[6] I will attend closely to these two poles of religious conversion—conversion as lived experience and conversion as narrated in words—in the survey that follows.

Narrative Theory and Criticism

When we ask a person why they converted to a particular religious community, we are not surprised to receive a narrative in response, and, indeed, a narrative often serves as a satisfying form of explanation. It is a natural progression for religious conversion to lead to conversion narrative.

In the attempt to understand narrative, several theorists have turned back to Aristotle's *Poetics* and to his classic analysis of the role of plot in Greek tragedy.[7] Aristotle identifies the plot (*mythos*) as the first principle or soul of tragedy, and the most important characteristic of a plot, according to Aristotle, is its quality of being whole (*holos*) or complete (*teleios*). "A whole," says Aristotle, "is that which has a beginning, middle, and end." And well-constructed plots, he continues, "should neither begin nor end at arbitrary points," since this would be to destroy any sense of wholeness.[8] What Aristotle deplored was a merely "episodic" plot governed by no overarching principle and without any larger probability or necessity.[9] Time itself, in its unbroken succession of moments, does not provide this overarching principle or pause in its restless march for endings or beginnings. It is a human act to lift narrative from time, story from chronology, and plot from events.

The key idea from Aristotle that was taken up by narrative theorists in the 1960s is the distinction between the temporal succession of events in "real time" and the careful *emplotting* of those events in narrative by a storyteller.[10] Although Aristotle was analyzing poetry ("the kinds of things that *might* occur") rather than history ("actual events"), and therefore the universal rather than the particular, he allowed that a poet may indeed find in actual events the material of true poetry: "There is nothing to prevent some actual events being probable as well as possible, and it is through probability that the poet makes his material from them."[11] Of the many things that happened to Sampson Staniforth in 1743, it was his midnight vision of the crucified Christ that he selected when he wrote his autobiography years later, and he *emplotted* this according to Aristotle's narrative syntax of beginning, middle, and end. This vision was the turning point in his story that moved from his beginning in irreligion to his end as a servant of God. In narrative terms, he displayed starkly all the syntax of stories as situation—transformation—new situation. Among the countless events of his life, that is, he found something that could be raised to the level of religious *poesis*, a particular witness to universal truths. I will say more below about the special significance of conversion as a leitmotif for narrative more generally, but the close relationship between conversion and narrative should be clear already. If narrative in its classical form is defined as a plot with a beginning, middle, and end—with sufficient magnitude, as Aristotle said, to allow for transformation—then all narratives are, in one sense, conversion narratives.

Aristotle provides us thus with a classical analysis of narrative, but it remains to describe in outline some of the main trends in the study of narrative since the 1960s, when such study revived significantly. James Phelan, whose expert analysis of these trends I draw upon in the survey that follows, makes the claim: "We are living in the age of the Narrative Turn, an era when narrative is widely celebrated and studied for its ubiquity and importance."[12] The renewed attention to narrative theory and criticism may be considered in terms of three principal preoccupations: formal, ideological, and ethical.

Narrative as a Formal System

I referred to Aristotle's sequence of beginning—middle—end as a kind of narrative *syntax* inherent in plots, and the word "syntax" is, of course, a linguistic term. One influential model for the study of narrative has derived from structural linguistics, where the aim has been to discern the formal system of stories, much as grammar provides the rules of a language. Before there can be individual utterances, there must be a formal system for the selection of words ("choose a noun for a subject") and for the arrangement of words ("combine a subject and predicate to make a sentence"). When I was a child, popular booklets called "Mad Libs" provided stories in which certain words or phrases were replaced with blanks with specific instructions such as, "Provide a noun here," or, "Choose an adjective here," and so on. In a group of friends, the person with the book would call out for suggestions and then scribble in the (often outrageous) words offered to fill in the blanks. When done, he or she would read out the story with the words provided, usually to uproarious laughter. This narrative game was based on what structuralists would call *paradigmatic* rules of selection. Writing in a noun where a verb was called for would not work. A second type of book that has been popular with children from time to time contains "choose your own ending" stories. Here, the reader is offered the choice that the character in the story is faced with at a particular moment in the plot. Do you want Elizabeth Bennet to go on and snub Mr. Darcy? If yes, then turn to page 65 to continue the story; if no, then continue on page 44. In this second type of book the rules are what structuralists call *syntagmatic*, since they have to do with the syntax or combination of narrative elements.

Are there conventions like these that provide the deep structure for the selection and arrangement of the elements of narrative, a *narratology*, that explain all stories? Is there a more or less fixed code for characters: a hero, a villain, a helper, or a lover, and so on? And are there conventions for the basic types of events the characters will encounter: a test, a journey, a discovery, a battle, and other recurrent patterns? And then are there rules that govern how these events are stitched together for certain character roles, such as the requirement that the hero must kill the monster before he wins the hand of the maiden? If there are narrative conventions such as these operating in stories generally, then the question arises whether conversion narrative may itself be read in light of these codes.

If the examples I have just given seem to recall fairy tales and myths, that is because it is folk tales that have received the greatest attention in this sort of structuralist narratology.[13] And the criticism has been that such stories are exceptional rather than typical for their adherence to rules and codes. It is this encoding, in part, that distinguishes them as folk tales. Most stories are in fact much more flexible than this. The theoretical analysis of narrative in terms of rules has, nevertheless, sustained an effort to determine whether there are some general narrative patterns at work in all human storytelling, even if some of these vary from culture to culture.[14] Northrop Frye's important work of criticism, *The Great Code* (1981), argues that in the case of Western art and literature, it is the Christian Bible that has decisively shaped the imaginative tradition well into the modern period, with its dominant narrative pattern of original prosperity, descent into humiliation, and return, and its characteristic imagery. If this is a "great code" for literature from Dante to Milton, it is evident that it is also a "code" for conversion narratives from Augustine to Luther to Bunyan and beyond.

John Bunyan (1628–1688) is a good case in point, since his *Grace Abounding* is a classic Protestant conversion narrative from the mid-seventeenth century that ought to be read in tandem with his famous imaginative allegory, *The Pilgrim's Progress*. Although one work is history and one is fiction, both drew upon the "great code" provided in the Bible, as read by Reformed Protestants for several generations: both were conversion narratives. Somewhat differently constructed cultural codes have been at work in the non-Western world and have contributed to the narrative form of religious autobiographies in, for example, traditional China in the sixteenth and seventeenth centuries around the same time as Bunyan.[15] Here, as in the case of the Buddhist Te-ch'ing, the climax of spiritual autobiography comes most often with a moment of enlightenment in the midst of a journey narrative. The emergence of this pattern among Neo-Confucians leads one critic to allude to Bunyan in a chapter analyzing these narratives that is entitled, "The Confucian's Progress."[16] As in seventeenth-century England, the appearance of conversion narrative was preceded by a religious culture of self-examination and diary-keeping and by the experience of increased travel and mobility. But in traditional China the "great code" was provided by the religious teachings of Buddhism, Taoism, and Confucianism rather than Christianity, and the climax of the narrative was framed more in terms of enlightenment than forgiveness of sins.[17]

Although conversion narratives can be formulaic in their adherence to a structure derived from theology, more often there is a creative interaction with religious codes. An Elizabethan sonnet has a very constrained form: fourteen lines of iambic pentameter, divided into three quatrains and concluding couplet and rhyming *abab, cdcd, efef, gg*. Yet these limitations are full of potential for introducing diverse problems, bringing them to a crisis, and resolving them in the final couplet. Likewise, a theologically patterned understanding of conversion offers a narrative structure that has often been exploited as a creative means of literary self-discovery. Sometimes it is in the interstices of the structure that individuality and personality are communicated. As Linda Peterson has observed, "To write an autobiography, one must in some way violate the generic tradition or deviate from it and, in so doing, discover the self."[18] One can see this, for example, in the early pages of the autobiography of the Puritan Richard Baxter, when he worried that his own spiritual experience was unlike that reported in funeral sermons of great ministers. He worried that he was merely socialized as a Christian, rather than truly regenerate. The breakthrough came for him when he realized that God's ways with his people were various, and that what really mattered was that one possessed presently the signs of genuine spirituality: "I understood at last," he wrote, "that God breaketh not all men's hearts alike."[19]

The literary analysis offered in formalist narrative criticism opens up several lines of enquiry for students of religious conversion who seek to understand a particular account of conversion as not just raw data but as a narrative. To take just one example, we might attend to the differences between chronological story-time and the order and timing of events in the narration. Narratologists are keen to note how narrative time speeds up and slows down, interrupts the movement of the events in the story, or tells them in a different order (such as happens with the classic technique of "flashbacks"). In addition to "real time" narration, there may be *prolepses*, where the future is anticipated, or *analepses*, where the past is recalled. Thus, when the converted slave trader John Newton wrote in his autobiography, *An Authentic Narrative* (1764), that "the Lord's time was not yet come," he was not only quoting the Gospel of John and creating an analogue between his life and the life of Christ, but he was also narrating a particular event in the narrative in terms of his future conversion that had "not yet come." The poet William Cowper penned his private religious memoir in 1767, and in the early pages he reported the story of a sheepdog he observed that wrested a sheep from the flock, forced it to the edge of a precipice, and stared down the trembling sheep until it submitted and edged slowly away back to the flock. Later, when Cowper narrated his own attempted suicide that would lead to his madness, incarceration, and, in due course, his religious conversion, he reminded the reader of the story of the dog and the sheep, saying that he was now at the edge of the precipice. This is a "hook and eye" narrative pattern, where the author leaves an "eyehole" early in the narrative and later reaches back to "hook" and pull forward the thought. The result for the reader is an analogical interpretation of Cowper's suicide attempt as a spiritual precipice that had been narrowly avoided. As these examples demonstrate, attention to the narrative level of a conversion account makes us aware of how we as readers move with the narrator back and forth along the storyline. The story, narrated in these ways, creates syntax by linking memory and expectation and the "sense of an ending" that is more than chronological. The reader (or listener) is lifted from the temporal plane of annalistic report to the narrative plane of unfolding progression, where one event leads to another. The narrator clearly writes retrospectively from the point of view of the end. In the case of religious converts, this "sense of an ending," as Frank Kermode calls it, is unmistakable.

We also, as it were, move in closer or withdraw farther from the action in the course of a narrative, depending on whether we are immersed in the story through, say, reported dialogue (He said, "…" Then I said, "…") or are removed at a distance, more remote from the action, through, say, narrative summary or ellipsis ("over the next three years, things went on much the same"). In theoretical terms that go back to Plato, the more distant we are from the action, the more the narrative is *diegetic* (telling); the more immersed we are in the action, the more the narrative is *mimetic* (showing). Although a conversion narrative may be told ingenuously and with artless sincerity, these elements of craft in storytelling may still often be identified and can help the reader to reflect a second time on the narrative and appreciate the way in which it expresses the larger self-understanding and religious identity of the narrator, who has raised the events of his or her life from mere chronology to the meaningfulness of a story in the very act of narrating.[20] The experience of religious conversion has led, that is, to creative re-reading of one's own life in these new terms, a second conversion of life into text.

Narrative as Political Ideology

This act of narrating one's life does not, however, occur in isolation. There is always a relationship between the world of the text and the world outside the text. In the post-1960s era literary and narrative theorists reacted against structuralist preoccupations by stressing the relationship between texts and society and the embeddedness of authors and readers in their historical contexts. As the Russian theorist Mikhail Bakhtin emphasized, every utterance is dialogical: "It responds to something, objects to something, affirms something, anticipates possible responses and objections, seeks support, and so on.… [It] is only a moment in the continuous process of verbal communication." Again, "Language acquires life and historically evolves precisely here, in concrete verbal communication, and not in the abstract system of language forms, nor in the individual psyche of speakers."[21]

This awareness of language as social and contextual, rather than simply structural and grammatical, has refocused the attention of critics away from the purely formal character of narratives, or the literary intentions of the author, to the political and ideological forces at work in such stories. In particular, there has been a renewed interest in the way attitudes toward gender, sexuality, race, and class are reinforced in the production and reception of literature. A critic might therefore read a narrative against the grain to expose motivations of which the author was unaware.[22] Such critique may show, for example, the way in which patriarchy, colonialism, or capitalism is woven into the narrative or the way the narrative seeks to discipline its readers. For some theorists influenced by the "masters of suspicion" (Marx, Freud, and Nietzsche), even the subjectivity of authors is regarded as not so much their own as it is inscribed on them as their language has been interpellated by the dominant ideologies of their society. The agential self is not essential, or prior to language, but the product of it. The narrative becomes not the expression of an individual point of view, but a site that registers the push and pull of social values as embodied in institutions and power structures. This, for example, is the way that Felicity Nussbaum interprets William Cowper's conversion narrative, not as the expression of a liberal humanist self but as a register of various unresolved cultural tensions.[23]

This movement away from formal criticism to ideological criticism has been largely shaped by the neo-Marxist or neo-Nietzschean agenda to critique, resist, and replace dominant discourses or "regimes of truth," since narratives or "metanarratives" are key elements in the nexus between knowledge and power. Although conversion narratives, like other narratives, may be studied to explore or challenge assumptions about race, class, gender, and sexuality, and readers ought to be active evaluators and not merely passive receivers of texts, we must not forget to acknowledge that the narrator wants us to see, above all, that the convert is a subject named, identified, and even interpellated by religion. There is a certain amount of bathos in such a statement, since this is so obviously the ethos of such texts, but the regnant assumptions in the academy require that we remind ourselves from time to time that people do act for religious reasons and that not all religious motivation is epiphenomenal. Since the late-twentieth century, it has become clear even to the casual observer that religion is not in decline in the world. There are signs that literary theorists are beginning to take this better into account. The literary critic Stanley Fish wrote famously, "When Jacques Derrida died I was called by a reporter who wanted [to] know what would succeed high theory and the triumvirate of race, gender, and class as the center of intellectual energy in the academy. I answered like a shot: religion."[24]

In order to avoid the Charybdis of skepticism and the Scylla of naivety in the reading of conversion narratives, one might consider the proposal of narrative theorist Paul Ricoeur of a hermeneutic that balances trust and suspicion in the movement from initial naivety, through critique, to a post-critical second naivety.[25] One ought at least to read with the grain before reading against the grain.[26] The religion in conversion narratives such as those of Staniforth, Asad, and Te-ch'ing is clearly essential to their stories and to the identity of the converts. However, our awareness that these stories are produced and received under concrete historical conditions ought ideally to help us gain a more rounded picture of the religion of the converts. In my own field of eighteenth-century studies, Phyllis Mack has carefully explored the gendered and class-based identities of religious converts in Methodism and uses this to enrich rather than supplant our understanding of their religious experiences in her book, *Heart Religion in the British Enlightenment: Gender and Emotion in Early Methodism* (2008). It was precisely by attending to gender and to narrative (in print and manuscript) that Mack was able to show, for example, the tensions involved for male converts such as Staniforth between their public lives as preachers and their private lives as husbands and fathers. This was the context in which they were working out the whole of their religious faith.[27]

Narrative as Ethical Rhetoric

Awareness of the link between the textual world (formal) and the social world (ideological and political) has led some theorists to return to a classical or neo-Aristotelian understanding of narrative as rhetorical in a multi-layered way, giving attention to the whole communication triangle, with all its nuances, of the author, the text, and the audience. The rhetorical approach recognizes that stories are told for a purpose with certain ends in view. Rhetoric focuses on narrative communication as an act of persuasion; the author seeks to influence audiences toward certain ethical ends. By emphasizing the agency of the author in making choices, the narrative is viewed not simply as a structured text to be decoded or a site that registers the ideologies of its production, but as communication. The rhetorical turn is also therefore an ethical turn in criticism, since a narrative invites serious questions about the nature of the good implied in the story told and the way it is told.

The ethical questions raised by a story may be framed in terms of the characters and their actions within the story (an "ethics of the told"), or of the narrator telling the story and the audience listening to it (an "ethics of the telling"). If an author seems to be asking us to sympathize with a morally reprehensible character, then we may find ourselves making ethical judgments at both levels; we trust neither the character nor the author. In fact, within narrative fiction the possible levels of ethical analysis correspond to many more levels of agency than this, since the real flesh-and-blood author may be distinguished, first, from the implied author or authorial persona in the text. (An author may well present a better image of himself or herself in the text than he or she displays in real life, or there may at least be some slippage between the two.) Then, further, the author may adopt one or more of several possible points of view in telling the story: the first-person observer, first-person protagonist, third-person omniscient, third-person limited, etc. When reading a story from the point of view of Huck Finn, for example, I as reader will find myself evaluating his character as an actor in the story and as a storyteller, as well as evaluating Mark Twain as a writer in terms of what seem to be his larger aims and attitudes in *The Adventures of Huckleberry Finn*. How would I distinguish Huck Finn's racial attitudes from those of the author, and what do I think myself about the issues of race in Southern ante-bellum society? The same sort of issues could be raised in Daniel Defoe's *Robinson Crusoe*, where Crusoe is the first-person narrator of a story that has been taken as a kind of conversion narrative.[28]

With historical narrative, such as narratives of conversion, things are a little more straightforward, since history writing typically does not have recourse to sustained internal focalization (telling the story from a character's internal point of view), and there is an implied compact with the reader that the story will fit with empirical facts. Yet the telling of the story will involve some art in the selection, arrangement, highlighting, and explanation of events, and thus far a conversion narrative will overlap considerably with the art involved in a fictional narrative genre such as the realistic novel; it will also raise similar questions about rhetorical choices and ethical aims. One of the ethical questions in such historical writing will always have to do with fidelity, since a tacit compact between writer and reader is that there is an identity between the representation in the text and the actuality of events. Another telling (even by myself of my own story) may well be different, since it will involve a new point of view, and yet there will always be the expectation of fidelity to real events, even if these events are internal mental events. With autobiography there is also a kind of contract with the reader that the author intends to understand and interpret his or her own life sincerely. This might be understood as a kind of minimal "ethics of the telling" for conversion narrative. One ought to be a reliable narrator, and one cannot invent characters or fabricate events just because this might make for a better story—or, if so, the reader expects to know whether this sort of embellishment is present.

There is also, however, an "ethics of the told." Conversion narratives clearly make or imply strong standards of goodness and what constitutes human flourishing or detracts from it. Recognizing that narrative has such a moral trajectory allows the student of conversion narrative to enter more directly into ethical dialogue with the text. The alienation from Western values in Asad's narrative that was part of his conversion to Islam calls for the reader to agree or disagree (sympathize or react negatively) and to offer his or her own justification or counter-narrative. It is perhaps to be expected, therefore, that conversion narratives in particular will provoke strong reactions in readers, since these narratives (like all narratives) ask the reader to sympathize with the protagonist and to feel what he or she feels, and conversion narratives by their very nature deal with ultimate questions and present a narrative apologia for the particular beliefs embraced by the convert over against others left behind. As Wayne Booth writes, "In most works of any significance, we are made to admire or detest, to love or hate, or simply to approve or disapprove of at least one central character, and our interest in reading from page to page, like our judgment upon the book after reconsideration, is inseparable from this emotional involvement."[29] Elsewhere Booth says, similarly, "Narratives . . . both depend on and implant or reinforce patterns of desire. . . . We find ourselves to some degree shaped into those patterns."[30] Booth's concern here is principally with narrative fiction, where the reader's vicarious hopes and fears for the protagonist are tempered by the knowledge that the story is fiction. This distancing from real life is diminished in conversion narrative which, though it takes the form of narrative, presents itself as history. I will discuss further the ethics of narrative, below, after examining the particular case of narrative as autobiography, but the rhetorical and ethical turn in narrative theory seems to be the most promising development for helping readers to elucidate the religious significance of conversion texts.

AUTOBIOGRAPHICAL THEORY AND CRITICISM

Autobiography is that special case of narrative literature in which, as Philippe Lejeune puts it, the author, narrator, and protagonist are one and the same: they share the same proper name. If an autobiography is a printed book, and if we take the title page to be part of the book, then it is the assertion of authorship on this title page that forms a sort of "autobiographical pact" with the reader, identifying the real flesh-and-blood author as the storyteller and the subject of the story.[31] This is fundamentally different from a "fictional pact" that says or implies, "Let us suppose…"

   St. Augustine was perhaps the first autobiographical theorist. At the close of the fourth century, he wrote his *Confessions*, a remarkably precocious spiritual autobiography. Augustine's autobiography was unlike any of the models provided by ancient biographers, such as Plutarch, whose "lives" were by and large the *res gestae* or "great deeds" of famous men. The *Confessions* was in a literal sense *sui generis*—of its own kind, unique. Augustine also reflected seriously upon what he was doing by writing a spiritual autobiography. In Books 10 and 11 he turned from his narrative to consider the nature of time, change, memory, and identity. He wondered what the relationship was between himself in the present and himself in the past as a child and a young man and an adult. These are the classic questions of autobiographical theory, and Augustine found it hard going. He knew it had something to do with the memory, but he was exasperated and wrote, "Who is to carry the research beyond this point?…O Lord, I am working hard in this field, and the field of my labours is my own self. I have become a problem to myself."[32] Anyone who has pondered long over the nature of autobiography will have some sympathy with Augustine, and many modern theorists have returned to his reflections to stimulate their own thinking about the nature of both narrative and autobiography.[33]

   Literary historians and theorists have discussed issues similar to those raised by Augustine and have recognized with him that autobiography has a hermeneutical significance transcending its appearance as a factual narrative about oneself. James Olney asks three simple questions that are central to autobiographical theory: "What do we mean by the self, or himself (*autos*)? What do we mean by life (*bios*)? What significance do we impute to the act of writing (*graphe*)—what is the significance and the effect of transforming life, or *a* life into a text?"[34] Like Augustine, Olney is asking about the relationship between oneself as author, oneself as subject, and oneself as portrayed in a literary text.

   This division of autobiography into these parts also serves as a useful outline for the progress of autobiographical theory and criticism since the mid-twentieth century. From their initial preoccupation with the *bios* and life achievement, the focus of critics turned to the *autos* and questions of identity and, more recently, to the *graphe* and the way that textual performances inscribe and display ideology.[35] As we shall see below, some of the issues that have surfaced in this survey of narrative theory have likewise animated the serious study of autobiography over the past half century because these fields have developed and interacted with each other.[36]

Autobiography as History

The word "autobiography" was coined in 1797, and the first use of the word in a book title was in 1832, but in the West the tradition of self-biography and memoir as a more general phenomenon goes back at least to the Renaissance. There are earlier examples, such as Augustine, but before the year 1500 there were relatively few instances of autobiography in Europe compared with what would appear later, in the early modern period. After 1500 a number of notable Renaissance examples appeared, such as the celebrated *Life* of the artist Benvenuto Cellini, and then after 1600 the phenomenon became truly widespread as autobiographical practice became popular as a central feature of the "modern" way of life.[37] Although it has often been remarked that autobiography is uniquely Western and that self-writing first became popular in the English-speaking world, this assertion ought to be qualified since, as we have already noted, autobiography flourished for a period in seventeenth-century China, just as it did in eleventh-century Japan and elsewhere. There may be unique social conditions for the rise of autobiography, but this does not mean the form is uniquely Western.[38]

The earliest forms of self-writing did not use the term "autobiography," and the increasing use of this new term in the nineteenth century probably reflects the beginning of the theoretical and critical interest in life-writing that would lead Wilhelm Dilthey in 1883 to claim that autobiography is "the highest and most instructive form in which the understanding of life confronts us."[39] In the late nineteenth century, a heightened interest in the eminent individual first led to a critical appreciation for the genre as such. The first major student of autobiography was Dilthey's pupil and son-in-law Georg Misch, who wrote his thorough *Geschichte der Autobiographie* (1907), a work of nearly 3,000 pages translated into English as, *A History of Autobiography in Antiquity* (1951). At Misch's death, the work had reached as far as the Renaissance; his students added another 1,000 pages posthumously to bring the story up to the nineteenth century.

The preoccupation of this first wave of criticism, epitomized by Misch, was with autobiography as the representative life of a great man in the tradition of the *res gestae* ("great deeds"). Autobiography was celebrated as the highest mode of history, as public figures offered exemplary narratives. Thus, Misch claimed that it was the self-assertion of political will as the author related to the public that was normative in the history of autobiography. Autobiographies were representative of their period not because they registered social conditions, as such, but because their authors were themselves outstanding public figures who sat atop corporate social hierarchies or represented their times by their participation in important historical events and by their public achievements. It was in this spirit that Cellini began his *Life*, saying, "Everyone who has to his credit what are or seem great achievements, if he cares for truth and goodness, ought to write the story of his own life in his own hand."[40] The autobiography of a "great man" thus summarized the achievement of a culture. Interest in conversion narratives in this tradition was limited to those of great public figures or literary artists, such as Augustine.

This first wave of scholarship heralded a fascination with autobiography that would continue unabated throughout the twentieth century, but the controlling idea of autobiography as the life of a "great man" was limiting in several ways. Not only did this paradigm exclude non-Western biographical traditions, but it also failed adequately to identify and appreciate autobiographical examples from the West that did not fit the "ascent of man" narrative, among which were many forms of spiritual autobiography, including conversion narratives of various kinds. For example, the autobiographical form appealed to many women spiritual writers in the late Middle Ages who wrote in the vernacular, from Catherine of Siena in Italy to Margery Kempe in England. There was an especially strong tradition of female spiritual autobiography that developed among Cistercian nuns and beguines in Flemish and north German areas in the thirteenth and fourteenth centuries, among whom were Beatrice of Nazareth, Hadewijch, Mechthild of Magdeburg, and Marguerite Porete.[41] These women wrote, however, not from the center of political power but from the margins, and autobiography was one of the few forms available to them for self-expression. The authority of works such as the *Revelations* of Margaret Ebner or the *Revelations* of Julian of Norwich was intimately connected to the authors' personal religious and visionary experience. These were not narratives of proselyte conversions from one religion to another, but they were conversion narratives insofar as they recounted stories of religious transformation. A critical preoccupation with the lives of "great men" passes over such writings in silence.

Indeed, the religious impulse in autobiography significantly challenges the notion of self-fashioning in the autobiographical tradition of the high Renaissance, which so largely informed the first wave of autobiographical study. One may choose to write an autobiography not only for the sort of vainglorious reasons that Cellini offers but also for hortatory and doxological motives. To confess, to testify, to glorify God, to express gratitude for spiritual blessing, to strengthen and encourage other believers, to understand one's own spiritual experiences better—these explicitly religious motivations have often been present in autobiography, and an appreciation of these motives opens up a much wider and richer field of autobiography than the constrained political ideal of the "great man." The Hebrew tradition of anti-heroic biography evident in the Deuteronomic History, which brought Hebrew kings under the judgment of the Torah, was epitomized in King David, who, though a public figure and "great man," was presented in the second book of Samuel and the Psalter as also a weak and a sinful man. This anti-heroic tradition in Judaism continues in the Christian accounts of the disciples of Jesus, such as Peter.

There is thus a tradition of spiritual biography and autobiography that runs alongside the *res gestae* tradition, sometimes overlapping it and sometimes departing from it. The spiritual impulse could lead to "great" passages of literary autobiography, as in the case of Petrarch or Dante; it could be expressed in heroic conversion narratives that stand as foundation legends for whole societies, such as St. Patrick's *Confession* or the royal conversion narratives of Clovis of the Franks in the fifth century, Ethelbert of Kent in the sixth century, and Edwin of Northumbria in the seventh century; or, it could be expressed more privately and contritely in the confessional diaries and letters of a medieval nun or a parish priest. Augustine's precedent in autobiographical conversion narrative did require a certain sense of individual agency that was often lacking in other times and places, but the impulse to that "second conversion" that turns spiritual experience into words is surely perennial.

Autobiography as Self-Identity

A second wave of autobiographical theory and criticism emerged in the last third of the twentieth century as the focus shifted from the simple *bios* of great lives to the craft and agency of the *autos*, the self. More attention was paid to the distinctiveness of autobiography as a literary genre and to its hermeneutical significance as a parable of identity. Whereas the concept of autobiography as the history of culture through eminent representatives authorized a limited canon of texts and raised few philosophical questions about self-narration, this new wave of study was more interested in the process by which people from all walks of life might shape a narrative identity out of the disparate and amorphous experiences of their own subjectivity. The "truth" of autobiography was therefore seen to be a little more like art than history.[42] Georges Gusdorf's landmark essay, "Conditions and Limits of Autobiography" (1956), argued that the significance of autobiography lies in the complex questions it raises about self-identity, as it answers the question, Who am I?[43] This complexity is its "anthropological prerogative" as a genre:

> It is one of the means to self-knowledge thanks to the fact that it recomposes and interprets a life in its totality. An examination of consciousness limited to the present moment will give me only a fragmentary cutting from my personal being without the guarantee that it will continue. In recounting my history I take the longest path, but this path that goes round my life leads me the more surely from me to myself.[44]

The shift in that last phrase from the personal pronoun to the reflexive pronoun is significant: this is the shift from the *bios* to the *autos*, from the life lived in the past to the present self-understanding of the subject. Gusdorf concludes that autobiography "obliges me to situate what I am in the perspective of what I have been."[45] At one level an autobiography simply promises to retrace the history of a life, but at a deeper level it is always an apologetic for the individual. Autobiography is one of the ways to answer the question of what my life *means*: I am the sort of person about which this story can be told.[46] This second reading of experience, doubling back on one's life to tell it again, led James Olney, the leading theorist of this wave of criticism, to describe autobiography in 1972 as a metaphor of the self or "correlative of being."[47]

This renewed attention to the form of autobiography and its importance for identity has led both to typological studies, analyzing kinds of autobiography among which conversion narrative figured as one type, and to studies that seek to demonstrate the close relationship between autobiographical practice and modernity since, as we have noted, it is in modern Western societies that autobiography appears to have flourished most notably.[48] There has also been a growth in historical and literary scholarship devoted to particular traditions of religious autobiography and conversion narrative, such as, for example, studies of medieval women's autobiography and examinations of the Puritan conversion narrative. The canon has therefore become less exclusive, and more autobiographical conversion texts likewise have become available for students and scholars.[49]

Given the importance of conversion as not just one experience among others for religious communities but as a central identity-giving experience with lifelong implications, students of conversion have much to gain from considering the work of this second wave of autobiographical theorists. As Gusdorf claimed, "Autobiography is a second reading of experience, and it is truer than the first because it adds to experience itself consciousness of it."[50] Whether this second conversion of life into text is indeed "truer," as Gusdorf asserts, it is certainly crucial to the enduring significance of religious experience. If conversion narrative functions as what anthropologists call an "encapsulation ritual" (like baptism or fetish burning) that helps to cement a convert into his or her new community by taking on the language and appropriating the narrative of that community, then there is much to gain by exploring the links between autobiography, narrative form, and self-identity. Within religious communities themselves, spiritual leaders have been quick to appreciate the pastoral and catechetical importance of guiding converts through the process of biographical reconstruction, or retelling their own story in the light of their conversion.[51] Muhammad Asad might well have become and remained a devout Muslim without writing his autobiography, but it is clear nonetheless that the narrative recounted in *Road to Mecca* was essential to his religious identity and vocation. His autobiography does not, that is, simply recount his past; it also tells us who he is now. As Augustine realized long ago, memory is one of the deepest parts of a human person, and it is there that religious conversion may take root most profoundly as this experience is prayerfully mulled over and re-examined all one's life. Conversion and conversion narrative are both likewise religious events.

Autobiography as Ideology

As theory of autobiography and critical commentary has followed wider trends in critical theory, a third wave of scholarship can be discerned in which, as Sidonie Smith and Julie Watson observe, emphasis upon the concept of "self" has been superseded by that of "subjectivity."[52] Here again, as we observed in the case of narrative theory, the underlying assumption is that the author has been manipulated by wider ideological forces, and it is these that constitute the subject. The autonomous individual or agential self is a fiction, a display, a false consciousness. Autobiography is instead a textual performance that need not presume an autonomous self. The unified individual displayed in the text is not speaking but is "spoken by" the language, a product of discursive regimes that elide knowledge and power. Clearly, then, if individual agency has all but disappeared in the linguistic turn, with the text an artifact of ideology and the subject immanent in the language, then we may say that from the *bios* (the life lived in the past) to the *autos* (the self in the present) we have now arrived at a preoccupation solely with the *graphe* (the words spoken or written) as a register of these cultural forces. Michael Sprinkler can therefore make the claim, "The origin and end of autobiography converge in the very act of writing...for no autobiography can take place except within the boundaries of a writing where concepts of subject, self, and author collapse into the act of producing a text."[53] The task of criticism from this perspective is chiefly to expose and critique the contested power relations that are inscribed in the text with respect to race, gender and sexuality, and class. Criticism speaks truth to power.

Contemporary criticism is keen to appreciate the complexity of the relation between the author as subject and object in an autobiography. Just as when I wash my own hands I shift back and forth between being agent and patient, subject and object, a dozen times before I leave the sink—or I am both at the same time—so also we may see the subject of an autobiography as more fragmented and mobile than the humanist literary tradition has implied. Viewing the text thus as a performance also undermines to some degree the stability and autonomy of the text as a work of art, and it heightens the attention of the critic to its social location. Accordingly, the contemporary avant-garde feminist, postcolonial, and postmodern interventions in autobiographical theory and criticism have opened up a diversity of approaches that are increasingly difficult to map, in part because the principle most privileged at present seems to be diversity itself.[54]

For students of conversion in particular, the critical ethos that valorizes diversity contributes to the recovery and appreciation of autobiographical voices from the margins of cultural power, whether these be the voices of women converts, converts from nations in the Global South, or converts who are poor or illiterate. It likewise fosters a critical appropriation of a wider variety of autobiographical forms, including everyday speech and writing, digital communications, and visual media. And, finally, it calls into question the trope of autonomous selfhood that has been so dominant in the modern West for many generations. Religious converts who narrate their experience generally do so with an appreciation that their own sense of agency is only ever partial and that they have become who they are only because of and through other people, and, ultimately, through an agency more divine than human. The sense of personal agency in most conversion narratives is therefore contingent (as co-agency) rather than autonomous. Margaret Austin was a single mother who wrote about her spiritual experience in a manuscript letter to Charles Wesley in 1740, and she captured perfectly this sense of contingent agency by quoting the Epistle to the Hebrews at the close of her own narrative: "I see there is a great work to be wrought still in my soul: but he that has begun the work will surely finish; he that is the author will be the finisher."[55]

CONCLUSION

It is to these questions of agency that we turn in conclusion, since a central issue in both narrative and autobiographical theory is the extent to which the self (in our case the "religious convert") is constructed or discovered. Is the act of narrating a conversion story the creation of a fiction or the reporting of facts? Or is it some kind of hybrid art that involves elements of both?

The Hebrew scholar and portraitist V. Philips Long has wrestled with these questions in the context of biblical narrative and offers the helpful analogy of portrait painting, since in portraiture there is an interest both in the sitter (the historical personage portrayed) and in the interpretation of the subject by the painter. It is a false dichotomy to separate the two.[56] The referential character of portraiture never entirely disappears, even in non-representational forms such as cubism. Likewise, even highly representational works, such as those of the British academicians, involve enormous craft and interpretation.[57] According to this analogy, autobiography is a kind of self-portraiture, subject to these same constraints and open to these same possibilities. Rembrandt's "autobiography," in this sense, was contained in a remarkable oeuvre of more than ninety self-portraits painted over more than four decades between the beginning of his career in the 1620s and his death in 1669. John Wesley's autobiography, on the other hand, was given in a serialized journal of over a million words (some of which recounted his conversion and many more that recounted the conversion of others) produced over a similarly long period in the eighteenth century. In both figures we see a shifting and revised sense of themselves. While in portraiture it is impossible to convey much of a narrative since a picture captures only a cross-section or point in time, verbal art (and film) allows the possibility of narrative and opens up a correspondingly wider field of self-interpretation. Rembrandt's profusion of self-portraits seem almost to provide a narrative in the way that an animator creates movement through a rapid succession of still images, but the syntax that connects the pictures, one with another, is missing. Narrative seems to belong, above all, to the provenance of words.

And narrative is also, as we have already observed, the provenance of the ethical. The philosopher Charles Taylor, who studied under Paul Ricoeur, argues in his *Sources of the Self* (1992) that when we make statements of strong evaluation, we make an implicit appeal to the "incomparably higher" or "the good." But this also implies a narrative understanding of ourselves, since we always have an implicit sense of where we are, relative to that good:

> In order to make sense of our lives, in order to have an identity, we need an orientation to the good, which means some sense of qualitative discrimination, of the incomparably higher. Now we see that this sense of the good has to be woven into my understanding of my life as an unfolding story. But this is to state another basic condition of making sense of ourselves, that we grasp our lives in a *narrative*. . . . Our lives exist also in this space of questions, which only a coherent narrative can answer. In

order to have a sense of who we are, we have to have a notion of how we have become, and of where we are going.[58]

The "wholeness" that was essential to plot for Aristotle corresponds, therefore, to our sense of wholeness in an ethical sense, since the temporal syntax of stories that Aristotle described as beginning—middle—end is also a moral structure, as the narrator discerns the progress of the protagonist from an original situation through a moral transformation to a final situation. The trajectory of desire and the establishment of character (what Aristotle called *ethos*) in such a movement is predicated on a sense of "the good," which the narrator invites the audience to share for the duration of the story. We follow the line of a narrative in the hopes that there will be some satisfaction in reaching the end, and in so doing we are ethically influenced. The plot works upon us as rhetoric in "the total patterning of the reader's desires and satisfactions."[59] To the extent that the good envisioned in the story is ultimate or transcendent, to that extent will the story have a religious dimension and be a kind of conversion narrative.

In place of an extreme neo-Nietzschean skepticism of the narrative identity displayed in these stories as arbitrary fictions—a kind of "will to narrative"—we may argue instead that life itself is "a story in search of a narrator."[60] Paul Ricoeur challenges the commonplace dichotomy that "stories are told and not lived; life is lived and not told." There is a mixture of doing and undergoing, acting and suffering, that gives every life a kind of "pre-narrative capacity."[61] This is why Aristotle referred to narrative as *mimetic*, or an imitation of human action. We understand any meaningful human action in the same way we understand stories: both involve interpretation and the sort of "syntax" we identified earlier, by which we find actions (imagined or real) to be meaningful. To be human is, as Augustine reflected, to live with a sense of memory (past), expectation (future), and awareness (present), so that we live (not just tell) our lives as a kind of story, though this narrative identity may change over time. Carolyn Heilbrun writes of women's unwritten lives, saying, "The woman may write her own life in advance of living it, unconsciously, and without recognizing or naming the process."[62] This describes well, I think, the idea of life as itself possessing a "pre-narrative capacity." In our actions we are often writing a kind of story, fulfilling an implicit narrative and achieving in life a kind of mimesis of stories we value. A religious conversion may, in this sense, be a personal imitation of oft-heard conversion narratives. In response to testimonies of the faithful, the potential convert acts out in real life the deeds that make his or her life that kind of story. Life's experiences may be repeated in stories, but so also stories may be repeated in life's experiences.

For religious thinkers such as Augustine, this pre-narrative capacity in a human life is also capacity for religious conversion. This understanding was integral to his anthropology. Narrative capacity was an aspect of the divine image in the human person: "The heart is restless until it finds its rest in thee, O God," is how he famously put it at the beginning of the *Confessions*.[63] Drawing on the Platonic distinction between potency and act, Augustine believed, in common with the early church fathers, that human beings were created in God's image and intended for God's likeness.[64] Irenaeus likewise described the human person as created, like an infant, with the potential for growth into divine perfection.[65] Some such sense of human beings as objects of salvation, perfectibility, or enlightenment undergirds conversion narratives beyond the Christian tradition as well. This is why Charles Taylor can say that "the full definition of someone's identity thus usually involves not only his stand or moral and spiritual matters but also some reference to a defining community."[66]

Conversion thus has explanatory power as a theoretical category in its own right in ethics and anthropology, as in narrative and autobiographical theory. If we view the self as an interlocutor, alternately agent and patient, then identity appears to be both discovered and constructed in language.[67] This moves beyond the extreme skepticism of some ideological critics to allow for readings of self-identity in which suspicion is balanced by trust in human community and power relations are not always seen as conflictual. Moreover, the recognition that self-understanding is inherently moral and intrinsically narratival invites religious questions. As soon as we identify a good, we understand ourselves with reference to this good as nearer or further from it, and this puts us in a kind of moral space and on a journey that can be narrated. This also points toward, or opens us up to, a transcendent ground for our lives. It suggests, in fact, that conversion is not accidentally a suitable subject of study for autobiographical and narrative critics. If the human person is inherently a being with the capacity for moral and religious conversion—and this seems to be something that can be argued empirically as well as theologically—then we should expect narrative frameworks for human life. From the Platonic doctrine of ascent and natural *eros* to Augustine's restless desire, an anthropology that recognizes the human person as a potential convert implicitly places every human being in a story. Religious traditions that recognize likewise that the human person finds his or her fulfillment in a transcendent end will be able to ground a narrative and its moral discourse in terms of well-articulated ends. Whereas such higher and transcendent ends are, as Charles Taylor claims, often occluded in modern secular discourse, religious communities can often provide a more adequate grounding for moral narrative than naturalism. As Taylor writes, "High standards need strong sources." And, "great as the power of naturalist sources might be, the potential of a certain theistic perspective is incomparably greater."[68]

One of the great challenges therefore for scholars of religious conversion is not merely to draw upon narrative and autobiographical theories to interpret their subjects but also to demonstrate the explanatory potential of religious conversion and belief for our understanding of the human person as inveterate storyteller and self-biographer. To the question of why human beings tell stories, and especially stories about themselves, Christians such as Sampson Staniforth, Muslims such as Muhammad Asad, and Buddhists such as Te-ch'ing, will, in the end, give their own answers.

NOTES

1. *The Arminian Magazine* 6 (1783): 72.
2. Ibid., 13.
3. Muhammad Asad, *The Road to Mecca* (New York: Simon and Schuster, 1954). See also Marcia Hermansen, "Roads to Mecca: Conversion Narratives of European and Euro-American Muslims," *The Muslim World* 89, no. 1 (1999): 56–89.
4. Pei-yi Wu, *The Confucian's Progress: Autobiographical Writings in Traditional China* (Princeton: Princeton University Press, 1990), 153.
5. Both of these fields have developed to the point where they have their own historiographies, handbooks, bibliographies, specialist journals, and professional societies. For the study of narrative there is, for example, *The Routledge Encyclopedia of Narrative Theory*, ed. David Herman, Manfred Jahn, and Marie-Laure Ryan (New York: Routledge, 2005), and *A Companion to Narrative Theory*, ed. James Phelan and Peter J. Rabinowitz (Oxford: Blackwell Publishing, 2005), as well as the journals *Narrative Inquiry* (1991–present) and *Narrative* (1993–present), the latter of which is published by the International Society for the Study of Narrative (founded 1984). In the field of autobiography, there is the handbook by Sidonie Smith and Julia Watson, *Reading Autobiography: A Guide for Interpreting Life Narratives* (Minneapolis: University of Minnesota Press, 2001), as well as the journals *Auto/Biography: An International and Interdisciplinary Journal* (1992–2006) and *Auto/Biography Studies* (1985–present), the latter of which is published by the AutoBiography Society.
6. Geoffrey Galt Harpham, "Conversion and the Language of Autobiography," in *Studies in Autobiography*, ed. James Olney (New York: Oxford University Press, 1988), 42.
7. The use of Aristotle's *Poetics* was evident in the early and now classic works on narrative from the 1960s: Wayne C. Booth, *The Rhetoric of Fiction*, (1962; new ed., Chicago: University of Chicago Press, 1983); Robert E. Scholes and Robert L. Kellogg, *The Nature of Narrative* (1966; new ed., New York: Oxford University Press, 2006), and Frank Kermode, *The Sense of an Ending: Studies in the Theory of Fiction* (1967; new ed., New York: Oxford University Press, 2000). The *Poetics* of Aristotle is foundational also for Paul Ricoeur, *Time and Narrative*, Vol. 1 (Chicago: University of Chicago Press, 1984), 31–51.
8. Aristotle also adds that a tragic plot must have sufficient "magnitude" to allow for this transformation from the beginning, through the middle, to the end.
9. Aristotle, *Poetics*, ed. and trans. Stephen Halliwell, Loeb Classical Library (Cambridge, MA: Harvard University Press, 1995), 55, 63.
10. For Aristotle, emplotment is a function of "thought" (*dianoia*) in the handling of events to create the impression or effects of pity, terror, significance, or necessity (ibid., 97).
11. Ibid., 63.
12. James Phelan, "Narrative Theory, 1966–2000: A Narrative," in *The Nature of Narrative*, rev. and enl. ed., ed. Robert E. Scholes, James Phelan, and Robert L. Kellogg (New York: Oxford University Press, 2006), 283–336 (quotation, p. 285). See also Monika Fludernik on the "narrative turn" in media studies, law, medicine, psychology, economics, and the social sciences more generally in "Histories of Narrative Theory (II): From Structuralism to the Present," in *A Companion to Narrative Theory*, ed. James Phelan and Peter J. Rabinowitz (Oxford: Blackwell, 2005), 46–48.
13. For example, Vladimir Propp, *Morphology of the Folktale* (first published in 1928), trans. C. K. Scott Moncrieff and Terence Kilmartin (New York: Modern Library, 1992).

14. Gérard Genette, *Narrative Discourse: An Essay in Method* (first published in 1972), trans. Jane E. Lewin (Ithaca, NY: Cornell University Press, 1980).

15. See, for example, Wu, *Confucian's Progress*.

16. Ibid., 93. This also provides the author with the title for the book itself.

17. Whereas Bunyan was one of the progenitors of the still flourishing genre of modern spiritual autobiography in the West, the genre of spiritual autobiography that appeared in sixteenth- and seventeenth-century China has almost entirely disappeared, and very little autobiography that was not strictly annalistic or impersonal would surface again until the twentieth century (ibid., 235–236).

18. Linda Peterson, "Newman's *Apologia* and English Spiritual Autobiography," *Proceedings of the Modern Languages Association* 100 (1985): 304; cf. Karl J. Weintraub, "Autobiography and Historical Consciousness," *Critical Inquiry* 1 (1975), who writes, "The individual will always find room for his idiosyncrasies in the interstitial spaces of the basic components of his model" (833–834).

19. Richard Baxter, *Reliquiae Baxterianae* (London, 1696), 3.

20. In addition to formal narratology, which draws heavily on linguistic models, the field of cognitive narratology emphasizes the structures inherent in the mental processes that operate for the narrators of and listeners to stories. The mind seems to function in a way that particular scripts (recurring patterns of action) are associated with more broadly framed domains of experiences. These mental processes are involved in recognizing and reconstructing the time and space and particular context of a story world and then running scripts within it—action sequences, dialogues, characterizations, etc. Narrative structures do not then simply exist in the words spoken or written; they are integral to the mental processes by which we draw on our own experience to frame up and recognize patterns. We are wired for narrative. See Phelan, "Narrative Theory," 290–292.

21. Quoted in "V. N. Voloshinov: 'Language, Speech, and Utterance' and 'Verbal interaction,'" in *Bakhtinian Thought: An Introductory Reader*, ed. Simon Dentith (London: Routledge, 1994), 137.

22. Fludernik, "Histories of Narrative Theory (II)," 45.

23. Felicity A. Nussbaum, "Private Subjects in William Cowper's 'Memoir,'" in *The Age of Johnson*, Vol. 1, ed. Paul Korshin (New York: AMS Press, 1987), 307–326.

24. Stanley Fish, "One University under God?" *The Chronicle of Higher Education* (January 7, 2005), http://chronicle.com/jobs/news/2005/01/2005010701c.htm.

25. Paul Ricoeur, *The Rule of Metaphor*, trans. R. Czerney (Toronto: University of Toronto Press, 1977), 318.

26. Cf. Wayne C. Booth: "Only readers who have known the thrill of joining authors in their full engagement, their full achievement, their full cleansing or purification, leaving abstract critical questions to one side until the poem has been fully experienced—only such fully hooked readers ever discover how that joining changes one's life." This "fully hooked" reading of the text is, for Booth, the beginning of criticism. Wayne C. Booth, "Resurrection of the Implied Author: Why Bother?" in *A Companion to Narrative Theory*, ed. James Phelan and Peter J. Rabinowitz (Oxford: Blackwell, 2005), 86.

27. This enriched reading of Methodist conversion is in marked contrast to the ideological criticism of Felicity Nussbaum, *The Autobiographical Subject: Gender and Ideology in Eighteenth-Century England* (Baltimore: Johns Hopkins, 1989), which takes a more typically neo-Marxist line that sees John Wesley's own autobiographical writing as constituting

a bourgeois identity of self-mastery that he naturalized for his followers, with the result that "this class-identified self serves the interests of emerging capital" (p. 102).

28. G. A. Starr, *Defoe and Spiritual Autobiography* (Princeton: Princeton University Press, 1965).

29. Wayne C. Booth, *The Rhetoric of Fiction*, 2nd ed. (Chicago: University of Chicago Press, 1983), 130.

30. Wayne C. Booth, *The Company We Keep: An Ethics of Fiction* (Berkeley and Los Angeles: University of California Press, 1988), 272. With respect to narrative, Booth says, likewise, "The most powerful effect on my own ethos, at least during my reading, is the concentration of my desires and fears and expectations, leading with as much concentration as possible toward some further, some *future* fulfilment: I am made to want something that I do not yet have enough of" (ibid., 201). In this sense, all narratives are didactic and make claims on readers.

31. Philippe Lejeune, *On Autobiography*, ed. Paul John Eakin, trans. Katherine Leary (Minneapolis: University of Minnesota Press, 1989), 3–30.

32. Augustine, *Confessions*, trans. R. S. Pine-Coffin (London: Penguin Classics, 1961), 222.

33. See, especially, Paul Ricoeur, "The Aporias of the Experience of Time: Book 11 of Augustine's *Confessions*," Chap. 1 of *Time and Narrative*, Vol. 1, trans. Kathleen Mclaughlin and David Pellauer (Chicago: University of Chicago Press, 1984), 5–30.

34. James Olney, "Autobiography and the Cultural Moment: A Thematic, Historical, and Bibliographical Introduction," in *Autobiography: Essays Theoretical and Critical*, ed. James Olney (Princeton: Princeton University Press, 1980), 6. This tripartite analysis of autobiography originated with Georg Misch, whose pioneering contribution to the field is discussed below.

35. This periodization of the field corresponds to the three waves of theorizing recounted in the excellent survey in Smith and Watson, *Reading Autobiography*, 111–164.

36. The way in which the study of autobiography has reflected wider critical theory in the twentieth century is the subject of Charles Berryman, "Critical Mirrors: Theories of Autobiography," *Mosaic* 32, no.1 (March 1999): 71–84.

37. Autobiography as a characteristic modern practice, formally related to individualism, is the subject of Michael Mascuch, *Origins of the Individualist Self* (Cambridge: Polity Press, 1997).

38. The importance of English-speaking countries in the rise of autobiography is asserted in William Matthews, *British Autobiography: An Annotated Bibliography* (Berkeley and Los Angeles: University of California Press, 1955), and Wayne Shumaker, *English Autobiography: Its Emergence, Materials and Form* (Berkeley and Los Angeles: University of California Press, 1954). On the challenge to Western exceptionalism in autobiography and the parallel critique of the Western "ascent of man" narrative, see Peter Burke, "Representations of the Self from Petrarch to Descartes," in *Rewriting the Self: Histories from the Renaissance to the Present*, ed. Roy Porter (London: Routledge, 1977), 17–28.

39. Cited in Berryman, "Critical Mirrors," 73.

40. Benvenuto Cellini, *Autobiography*, trans. George Bull (London: Penguin, 1956), 15.

41. Elizabeth Spearing, ed., *Medieval Writings on Female Spirituality* (London: Penguin Classics, 2002). See also Caroline Walker Bynum, "Religious Women in the Later Middle Ages," in *Christian Spirituality: High Middle Ages and Reformation*, ed. Jill Raitt, with Bernard McGinn and John Meyendorff (New York: Crossroad, 1987), 121–139.

42. This issue was raised by Roy Pascal, in particular, in *Design and Truth in Autobiography* (Cambridge, MA: Harvard University Press, 1960).

43. Although written first in 1956, Gusdorf's essay was translated into English by James Olney in 1980, in Olney, ed., *Autobiography*, 28–48.

44. Ibid., 38.

45. Ibid.

46. Cf. Paul Ricoeur on "narrative identity": "That which we call subjectivity is neither an incoherent succession of occurrences nor an immutable substance incapable of becoming. It is exactly the kind of identity which the narrative composition alone, by means of its dynamism, can create." Paul Ricoeur, "Life: A Story in Search of a Narrator," in *Facts and Values: Philosophical Reflections from Western and Non-Western Perspectives*, ed. M. C. Doeser and J. N. Kraay (Dordrecht: Martinus Nijhoff Publishers, 1986), 131.

47. Among James Olney's many works on autobiography, see especially *Metaphors of Self: The Meaning of Autobiography* (Princeton: Princeton University Press, 1972) and *Memory and Narrative: The Weave of Life Writing* (Chicago: University of Chicago Press, 1998). Olney also edited the important collection of essays, *Autobiography: Essays Theoretical and Critical* (Princeton: Princeton University Press, 1980).

48. For the former, see, for example, Susanna Egan, *Patterns of Experience in Autobiography* (Chapel Hill: University of North Carolina Press, 1984), and for the latter, Robert Elbaz, *The Changing Nature of the Self: A Critical Study of Autobiographical Discourse* (London: Croom Helm, 1988). See also, on these themes, Karl Joachim Weintraub, *The Value of the Individual: Self and Circumstance in Autobiography* (Chicago: University of Chicago, 1978) and William Spengemann, *The Forms of Autobiography: Episodes in the History of a Literary Genre* (New Haven: Yale University Press, 1980).

49. See, e.g., Hugh T. Kerr and John M. Mulder, eds., *Famous Conversions* (Grand Rapids, MI: Eerdmans, 1983) and Amy Mandelker and Elizabeth Powers, eds., *Pilgrim Souls: An Anthology of Spiritual Autobiographies* (New York: Simon & Schuster, 1999).

50. Gusdorf, "Conditions and Limits," 38.

51. See, for example, Jonathan Edwards, *Religious Affections*, ed. John E. Smith, Vol. 2 of *The Works of Jonathan Edwards* (New Haven: Yale University Press, 1959), where he observes, "A scheme of what is necessary, and according to a rule already received…has a vast (though to many a very insensible) influence in forming persons' notions of the steps and method of their own experiences. I know very well what their way is, for I have had much opportunity to observe it" (p. 162).

52. Smith and Watson, *Reading Autobiography*, 129.

53. Michael Sprinkler, "Fictions of the Self: The End of Autobiography." This is the final sentence in the collection of essays edited by James Olney, *Autobiography: Essays Theoretical and Critical*, 342.

54. See, however, the superb survey in Smith and Watson, *Reading Autobiography*, 129–163.

55. Margaret Austin to Charles Wesley, May, 19, 1740, autograph letter, John Rylands University Library, Manchester.

56. Cf. Linda Peterson, who describes autobiography as "essentially hermeneutic, a category that supersedes the label fiction or nonfiction" ("Newman and Autobiography," 311).

57. Iain Provan, V. Philips Long, and Tremper Longman III, *A Biblical History of Israel* (Louisville, KY: Westminster John Knox Press, 2003), 82, and V. Philips Long, *The Art of Biblical History* (Grand Rapids, MI: Zondervan, 1994), 106–107.

58. Charles Taylor, *Sources of the Self* (Cambridge: Cambridge University Press, 1992), 47.

59. Booth, *Company We Keep*, 206.

60. This phrase is from the title of Paul Ricoeur's article "Life: A Story in Search of a Narrator," 121–132.
61. Ibid., 127.
62. Carolyn Heilbrun, *Writing a Woman's Life* (New York: Norton, 1988), 11.
63. Augustine, *Confessions*, 1.1.
64. See Lars Thunberg, "The Human Person as Image of God, 1: Eastern Christianity," and Bernard McGinn, "The Human Person as Image of God, 2: Western Christianity," in *Christian Spirituality: Origins to the Twelfth Century*, ed. Bernard McGinn, John Meyendorff, and Jean Leclercq (New York: Crossroad, 1989), 291–330.
65. Irenaeus, *Against Heresies*, 4. 38.
66. Taylor, *Sources of the Self*, 36.
67. Ibid., 29; cf. Booth's central metaphor of authors and friends in *Company We Keep* as this is worked out in interaction with Taylor, 268–273.
68. Taylor, *Sources of the Self*, 516, 518.

BIBLIOGRAPHY

Aristotle. *Poetics*. Ed. and trans. Stephen Halliwell. Loeb Classical Library. Cambridge, MA: Harvard University Press, 1995.

Asad, Muhammad. *The Road to Mecca*. New York: Simon and Schuster, 1954.

Augustine. *Confessions*. Trans. R. S. Pine-Coffin. London: Penguin Classics, 1961.

Austin, Margaret, to Charles Wesley, May 19, 1740. Autograph letter. John Rylands University Library, Manchester, England.

Baxter, Richard. *Reliquiae Baxterianae*. London, 1696.

Berryman, Charles. "Critical Mirrors: Theories of Autobiography." *Mosaic* 32, no.1 (March 1999): 71–84.

Booth, Wayne C. *The Company We Keep: An Ethics of Fiction*. Berkeley and Los Angeles: University of California Press, 1988.

——. "Resurrection of the Implied Author: Why Bother?" In *A Companion to Narrative Theory*, ed. James Phelan and Peter J. Rabinowitz, 75–88. Oxford: Blackwell, 2005.

——. *The Rhetoric of Fiction*. New ed. Chicago: University of Chicago Press, 1983.

Burke, Peter. "Representations of the Self from Petrarch to Descartes." In *Rewriting the Self: Histories from the Renaissance to the Present*, ed. Roy Porter, 17–28. London: Routledge, 1997.

Bynum, Caroline Walker. "Religious Women in the Later Middle Ages." In *Christian Spirituality: High Middle Ages and Reformation*, ed. Jill Raitt, with Bernard McGinn and John Meyendorff, 121–139. New York: Crossroad, 1987.

Cellini, Benvenuto. *Autobiography*. Trans. George Bull. London: Penguin, 1956.

Dentith, Simon, ed. *Bakhtinian Thought: An Introductory Reader*. London: Routledge, 1994.

Edwards, Jonathan. *Religious Affections*. Ed. John E. Smith. *The Works of Jonathan Edwards*. Vol. 2. New Haven: Yale University Press, 1959.

Egan, Susanna. *Patterns of Experience in Autobiography*. Chapel Hill: University of North Carolina Press, 1984.

Elbaz, Robert. *The Changing Nature of the Self: A Critical Study of Autobiographical Discourse*. London: Croom Helm, 1988.

Fish, Stanley. "One University under God?" *The Chronicle of Higher Education* (January 7, 2005). Online. Available: http://chronicle.com/jobs/news/2005/01/2005010701c.htm.

Fludernik, Monika. "Histories of Narrative Theory (II): From Structuralism to the Present." In *A Companion to Narrative Theory*, ed. James Phelan and Peter J. Rabinowitz, 36–59. Oxford: Blackwell, 2005.

Genette, Gérard. *Narrative Discourse: An Essay in Method*. Trans. Jane E. Lewin. Ithaca, NY: Cornell University Press, 1980.

Gusdorf, Georges. "Conditions and Limits of Autobiography." In *Autobiography: Essays Theoretical and Critical*, ed. James Olney, 28–48. Princeton: Princeton University Press, 1980.

Harpham, Geoffrey Galt. "Conversion and the Language of Autobiography." In *Studies in Autobiography*, ed. James Olney, 42–50. New York: Oxford University Press, 1988.

Heilbrun, Carolyn. *Writing a Woman's Life*. New York: Norton, 1988.

Herman, David, Manfred Jahn, and Marie-Laure Ryan, eds. *The Routledge Encyclopedia of Narrative Theory*. New York: Routledge, 2005.

Hermansen, Marcia. "Roads to Mecca: Conversion Narratives of European and Euro-American Muslims," *The Muslim World* 89, no. 1 (1999): 56–89.

Irenaeus. *Against Heresies*. Trans. Alexander Roberts and William Rambaut. N.p.: Ante-Nicene Fathers, 1885.

Kermode, Frank. *The Sense of an Ending: Studies in the Theory of Fiction*. New ed. New York: Oxford University Press, 2000.

Kerr, Hugh T., and John M. Mulder, eds. *Famous Conversions*. Grand Rapids, MI: Eerdmans, 1983.

Lejeune, Philippe. *On Autobiography*. Ed. Paul John Eakin. Trans. Katherine Leary. Minneapolis: University of Minnesota Press, 1989.

Long, V. Phillips. *The Art of Biblical History*. Grand Rapids, MI: Zondervan, 1994.

Mandelker, Amy, and Elizabeth Powers, eds. *Pilgrim Souls: An Anthology of Spiritual Autobiographies*. New York: Simon & Schuster, 1999.

Mascuch, Michael. *Origins of the Individualist Self*. Cambridge: Polity Press, 1997.

Matthews, William. *British Autobiography: An Annotated Bibliography*. Berkeley and Los Angeles: University of California Press, 1955.

McGinn, Bernard. "The Human Person as Image of God, 2: Western Christianity" In *Christian Spirituality: Origins to the Twelfth Century*, ed. Bernard McGinn, John Meyendorff, and Jean Leclercq, 312–330. New York: Crossroad, 1989.

Nussbaum, Felicity A. *The Autobiographical Subject: Gender and Ideology in Eighteenth-Century England*. Baltimore: Johns Hopkins, 1989.

——. "Private Subjects in William Cowper's 'Memoir.'" In *The Age of Johnson*, Vol. 1, ed. Paul Korshin, 307–326. New York: AMS Press, 1987.

Olney, James, ed. "Autobiography and the Cultural Moment: A Thematic, Historical, and Bibliographical Introduction." In *Autobiography: Essays Theoretical and Critical*, ed. James Olney, 3–28. Princeton: Princeton University Press, 1980.

——. *Autobiography: Essays Theoretical and Critical*. Princeton: Princeton University Press, 1980.

——. *Memory and Narrative: The Weave of Life Writing*. Chicago: University of Chicago Press, 1998.

——. *Metaphors of Self: The Meaning of Autobiography*. Princeton: Princeton University Press, 1972.

Pascal, Roy. *Design and Truth in Autobiography*. Cambridge, MA: Harvard University Press, 1960.

Peterson, Linda. "Newman's *Apologia* and English Spiritual Autobiography." *Proceedings of the Modern Languages Association* 100 (1985): 300–314.

Phelan, James. "Narrative Theory, 1966–2000: A Narrative." In *The Nature of Narrative*, New ed., ed. Robert E. Scholes, James Phelan, and Robert L. Kellogg, 283–336. New York: Oxford University Press, 2006.

Phelan, James, and Peter J. Rabinowitz, eds. *A Companion to Narrative Theory*. Oxford: Blackwell Publishing, 2005.

Propp, Vladimir. *Morphology of the Folktale*. Trans. C. K. Scott Moncrieff and Terence Kilmartin. New York: Modern Library, 1992.

Provan, Iain, V. Philips Long, and Tremper Longman III. *A Biblical History of Israel*. Louisville, KY: Westminster John Knox Press, 2003.

Ricoeur, Paul. "Life: A Story in Search of a Narrator." In *Facts and Values: Philosophical Reflections from Western and Non-Western Perspectives*, ed. M. C. Doeser and J. N. Kraay, 121–132. Dordrecht: Martinus Nijhoff Publishers, 1986.

——. *The Rule of Metaphor*. Trans. R. Czerney. Toronto: University of Toronto Press, 1977.

——. *Time and Narrative*. 3 vols. Chicago: University of Chicago Press, 1984–1988.

Scholes, Robert E., James Phelan, and Robert L. Kellogg. *The Nature of Narrative*. New ed. New York: Oxford University Press, 2006.

Shumaker, Wayne. *English Autobiography: Its Emergence, Materials and Form*. Berkeley and Los Angeles: University of California Press, 1954.

Smith, Sidonie, and Julia Watson, *Reading Autobiography: A Guide for Interpreting Life Narratives*. Minneapolis: University of Minnesota Press, 2001.

Spearing, Elizabeth, ed. *Medieval Writings on Female Spirituality*. London: Penguin Classics, 2002.

Spengemann, William. *The Forms of Autobiography: Episodes in the History of a Literary Genre*. New Haven: Yale University Press, 1980.

Sprinkler, Michael. "Fictions of the Self: The End of Autobiography." In *Autobiography: Essays Theoretical and Critical*, ed. James Olney, 321–342. Princeton: Princeton University Press, 1980.

Staniforth, Sampson. ["Memoir."] *The Arminian Magazine* 6 (1783).

Starr, G. A. *Defoe and Spiritual Autobiography*. Princeton: Princeton University Press, 1965.

Taylor, Charles. *Sources of the Self*. Cambridge: Cambridge University Press, 1992.

Thunberg, Lars. "The Human Person as Image of God, 1: Eastern Christianity." In *Christian Spirituality: Origins to the Twelfth Century*, ed. Bernard McGinn, John Meyendorff, and Jean Leclercq, 291–312. New York: Crossroad, 1989.

Weintraub, Karl J. "Autobiography and Historical Consciousness." *Critical Inquiry* 1 (1975): 821–848.

——. *The Value of the Individual: Self and Circumstance in Autobiography*. Chicago: University of Chicago, 1978.

Wu, Pei-yi. *The Confucian's Progress: Autobiographical Writings in Traditional China*. Princeton: Princeton University Press, 1990.

CHAPTER 16

RELIGIOUS CONVERSION AND SEMIOTIC ANALYSIS

MASSIMO LEONE

THE FOCUS OF SEMIOTICS

ACCORDING to Umberto Eco's witty definition, semiotics is the discipline that studies everything that can be used to lie.[1] As a consequence, if religious conversion[2] was exclusively signaled by, for instance, a sudden change in the structure of the convert's genome—a phenomenon that no human being can intentionally determine—conversion would not be a matter for semiotic inquiry but one for biological investigation,[3] for no human being would be able to intentionally "fake" conversion, that is, no one would be able to produce a certain series of signs in order for them to be interpreted as signs of conversion. Conversion would be an entirely unintentional phenomenon.

On the contrary, conversion can be "faked" in all religions, since in every religious tradition conversion is signified or communicated through signs[4] that can be intentionally produced: words, gestures, behaviors, rituals, and so on. According to contemporary semiotics, a subtle but fundamental conceptual difference obtains between "signification" and "communication."[5] "Signification" designates the phenomenon through which a perceptible element of reality can be referred by someone to a non-perceptible element of reality (e.g., when a smoke column signifies to a forest ranger the presence of a fire that she cannot perceive because such fire is, for instance, hidden by woods or hills). This reference may or may not be ascribed to an agency.[6] On the contrary, "communication" designates the phenomenon through which someone assumes that an agency has determined the fact that a perceptible element of reality is referred to a non-perceptible element of it (e.g., when the forest ranger formulates the hypothesis that smoke is actually being used by someone who got lost in the woods, as a sign of her presence and therefore as a call for help). As the simple examples above suggest, distinction between signification and communication depends on the way the recipient of a sign relates it to an agency and, therefore, to an intentionality.

This distinction between signification and communication is paramount in conversion phenomena. First of all, the distinction is fundamental in the process of conversion, especially as this process is experienced and represented by the convert herself. For instance, when Augustine narrates the process of his conversion, he reports that he interpreted the refrain *tolle et lege,* "take and read," repeated by the singsong voice of a child in a nearby house, not as signification (a string of words that had been uttered without the intention to communicate something to him) but as miraculous communication, as a divine injunction to take the Bible and read it, as a supernatural message addressed to him with pragmatic consequences on his acts, thoughts, and emotions. As it will be pointed out in this chapter, from the point of view of semiotics, conversion often consists in the process through which someone becomes a convert by interpreting certain signification phenomena as phenomena of communication determined by a transcendent agency and addressed to the convert herself. Distinction between signification and communication is fundamental also in the way the process of conversion is experienced and represented from an external point of view, even though the internal point of view is also, to a certain extent, an external one; the convert looks at her own conversion as if from the outside, so being able to develop an awareness of it that is a meta-language that has the ability to represent her conversion—and, therefore, the ability to represent herself as a convert—both to herself and to others.[7] From an external point of view, the behavior of a convert is interpreted by someone else, for example, a family member, a former coreligionist, a new coreligionist, an advocate, and so on. For the convert, the process of conversion consists in a switch from signification to communication (that is, the discovery of a transcendent agency beyond a signifying reality, the establishment of a communication channel between the convert and a transcendent dimension). For those who interpret the behavior of a convert from an external point of view, however, such behavior will be considered as a sign of conversion insofar as, and only insofar as, this behavior is interpreted as a signification phenomenon and not as a phenomenon of communication. For instance, when an advocate interprets the behavior of a convert as communication determined by the convert's agency in order to please the advocate and convince her of the truthfulness of the convert's conversion, such behavior is likely to be considered as a lie, as faked conversion; on the contrary, when the advocate interprets the convert's behavior not as communication addressed to the missionary herself but as unintentional signification of the new relation between the convert and a transcendent dimension, such behavior is likely to be considered as a sign of true conversion.[8]

In some dramatic historical circumstances, when entire religious communities have been forced to convert to a different faith, for example, Iberian Jews after 1492,[9] or Japanese Christians after 1637,[10] most of such conversions were likely to be "fake" according to the current, mainstream understanding of the word "conversion." Many converts strove to privately maintain their "true" faith while publicly displaying all the signs of "fake" conversion, while institutions like the Inquisition were created in order to develop methods able to ascertain the truthfulness of those signs.[11]

Semiotics is not a postmodern version of the early modern Catholic inquisition. It is not interested in elaborating a method in order to distinguish between "true" and "fake" signs of conversion. Nor does saying that semiotics is interested in how conversion can be "faked" mean that, according to semiotics, every conversion is a forgery. On the contrary, stressing that conversion can be "faked" and studying the cultural conditions through which this "fakery" can take place means that, according to semiotics, knowledge about how to produce the signs of conversion is something that can be taught, learned, and transmitted from generation to generation but also reformed, transformed, and deformed.

In other words, semiotics is interested in exploring the ways in which the signs of conversion are fabricated or constructed by a person in accordance with a certain religious culture and tradition. If these qualities can be fabricated, there is the possibility that some people will be fakes, fabricators, or outright liars, as well as there is the possibility that other people will be "true" converts and will use those same signs in order to exteriorize, signify, and communicate their truthful inner mutation;[12] moreover, there is the possibility that some people who have converted to a faith intentionally suppress those signs in order for their conversion to remain an exclusively private matter.

Stressing that conversion can be "faked" means emphasizing that every conversion, even a genuine one, can appear as such only insofar it is signified and communicated through a cultural code that, at a certain time and in a certain space, is more or less homogeneously shared by a religious community.[13] This means that every conversion, even those that a religious tradition commonly represents as brought about by direct, immediate communication between an individual convert and a transcendent dimension—such as the conversion of Saul/Paul of Tarsus as it is commonly represented by the Christian tradition[14] —inevitably involves that institutive dimension of sociality that semioticians designate as "language."[15] Semiotics is interested in understanding the cultural conditions thanks to which conversion can be "faked" because these are also the cultural conditions thanks to which "true" conversion can be signified and communicated.

Indeed, what does it mean to "fake" conversion? Conversion is successfully "faked" when the convert produces a series of signs whose interpretation will move most external observers to abduce[16] that such signs signify a remarkable change in the religious life of the convert. For example, in order to "fake" conversion to Islam (but also in order to express one's truthful adhesion to this faith) one commonly must commit through a ritual that entails a complex orchestration of systems of signs: the utterance of a verbal message known as the *Shahada*[17] (*La illaha ill Allah, Muhammadur Rasul Allah*),[18] better if such utterance takes place in a "semiotic theater" commonly involving the presence of a witness who already adheres to Islam, that of an Islamic moral authority, the religious architecture of a mosque, the written message of a conversion certificate, and so on. However, in order to "fake" conversion one must not only produce the signs of a customary commitment ritual but also display a consequent behavior that, to most observers, will be interpreted as a sign of conversion: the convert abides by the religious laws of her new religious community, commonly with greater intensity than older insiders.[19] For example, the Islamic convert will commonly restrain herself from drinking alcohol but will also display intransigence toward those who, in the same religious community, do not behave with the same rigor.

Furthermore, in order to "fake" conversion one must signify and communicate not only a converting present (the process of religious commitment) and a converting future (the consequences of such commitment), but also a converting past: the convert will have to "rewrite" the story of her life from the point of view of conversion in order to communicate it as a further sign of her conversion. For instance, the Islamic convert will narrate her autobiography by recasting many elements of it as traces of a transcendent agency leading the convert toward her conversion.

In summary, conversion is successfully "faked" when the convert demonstrates having interiorized the cultural code through which a religious community (1) distinguishes between insiders and outsiders and (2) determines the processes through which outsiders can become and be recognized as insiders and vice versa. "Faking" religious conversion, therefore, means having acquired an insider's competence about the thresholds that both give shape and delimit a religious culture.

Conversion among Sociality, Individuality, and Transcendence

According to semiotics, conversion is never the expression of a contact between a pure individuality[20] and a pure transcendence[21] but a compromise between such contact and a context. The primary purpose of semiotics, then, is to study, describe, analyze, and interpret the expressive patterns and the patterns of meaning through which such compromise takes place, thereby enabling the convert to signify and communicate her contact with transcendence to both herself and to other human beings. Semiotics, thus, does conceive every conversion as a forgery, but only insofar as it conceives the human predicament itself as a forgery, as something that, for the fact itself of taking place within a social context, must take place according to a pattern that is shared with other individuals.

Does this mean that semiotics denies or downplays both the theological and the individual dimensions of conversion?

As regards theology, semiotics does not deny that conversion involves a genuinely theological dimension. It does not deny that, in genuine conversion, a new contact takes place between the convert and a transcendent dimension. Neither does semiotics deny that such a transcendent dimension might be the primary agency behind the commitment of the convert and the consequences in her behavior. Semiotics simply suggests that, as soon as transcendence manifests itself in the world, encounters a human being, and becomes the agent[22] of her conversion, such manifestation, such encounter, and such agency take place according to patterns that are intelligible to human beings insofar as human beings have shaped them in a constant dialectic with transcendence. Semiotics primarily focuses on the human side of this dialectic, but does not deny that a transcendent side exists; it rather suggests that this side can only be imagined as the imperceptible signified of a perceptible signifier,[23] and that both the signifier and its semiosic[24] relation with the signified are, to a certain extent, subject to human investigation.

As regards individuality, it is true that, by stressing the role of language in conversion, semiotics implicitly downplays the individual dimension of conversion. This is particularly evident if one considers the assumptions of semiotics that (1) individual language does not exist[25] and (2) monologue does not exist.[26] The first assumption implies that every conversion is signified and communicated through patterns of expression and meaning that are shared with a religious community; the second assumption implies that the social dimension of conversion manifests itself not only when conversion is signified and communicated to a religious community but also when it is signified and communicated to the convert herself in her "internal forum."[27] In fact, according to the way in which semiotics currently interprets Bakhtin,[28] such an internal forum would mostly work as an interiorization of the external one[29], so that the convert would construe her religious conversion according to the way in which a given cultural context pushes her to do so.[30]

However, stressing the sociality of the language of conversion (that through which conversion is signified and communicated) does not imply that such language does not change through time and space. Change is a great conundrum in semiotics and in structuralism in general; if conversion is a socially shared language and does not rely on individual expressions, how can this language change through time and space? A tentative answer could be the following: saying that conversion is a language stresses not only its sociality; it also emphasizes its creativity. From Saussure on,[31] and especially after Benveniste,[32] language has been conceived by semioticians mostly as a dialectic phenomenon that involves a constant interaction between a social dimension (language as *langue*, as a socially shared deposit of patterns of expression and meaning) and an individual dimension (language as *parole*, as a fundamental instance through which human beings express both their subjectivity and their creativity). This is particularly evident in those structures designated by semiotics as "enunciation," which are the semiotic mechanisms that enable the passage from *langue* to *parole*, from language as dimension of shared sociality to language as dimension of creative individuality.

According to semioticians, human beings draw their patterns of expression and meaning from a socially shared deposit (otherwise they would be unable to signify and communicate with other human beings), but they do so by rearranging those patterns in a way that is, in many circumstances, not only subjective but also creative (otherwise they would be unable to respond to a constantly changing environment). Moreover, sometimes some individual creations of language are so effective that they are more or less rapidly adopted by a whole semiotic community, thus contributing in changing the social deposit of language forms. Semiotics sees this dialectics at work in every signification and communication process, including conversion; when converts want to signify and communicate their contact with transcendence, most of them adopt patterns of expression and meaning learned from a particular religious tradition.

However, sometimes converts are able to rearrange these patterns in a way that deeply affects the religious tradition itself. For example, Augustine narrated his conversion by adopting many of the language forms through which both the Christian and the classical traditions had commonly represented radical spiritual changes. At the same time, Augustine, who was one of the most talented rhetoricians of all times, remodeled these forms in such a way that, after him, few converts to Christianity were able to signify and communicate their conversion (both to themselves and to others) without making reference to the patterns of expression and meaning created by Augustine.[33] Semiotics, therefore, does not deny the individuality of conversion; on the contrary, semiotics affirms that many conversions are "creative" but that this creativity takes place as a dialectic between the social and the individual dimensions of language.

Semiotics as a New Perspective on Conversion

In order to understand the position of semiotics within the complex research area of conversion studies, it is important to stress that semiotics is probably better defined as "a field of interests," like medicine, than as "a discipline" *tout court*, like sociology or psychology. Indeed, semiotics is characterized less by a common scientific literature, object, or method of inquiry than by a common point of view; signification offers a perspective from which new light is cast on subjects traditionally studied by other disciplines. Every element of reality can therefore become an object for semiotic investigation, insofar as the element is looked at from the point of view of how it signifies and communicates its meaning. As a consequence, religion—and conversion in particular—can be observed, described, analyzed, and interpreted as a semiotic phenomenon. However, the results of all these activities are likely to be different according to the specific semiotic theory that is adopted in order to carry them out.

Thus far, three major trends have characterized the history of semiotics. The first originated from the linguistic research of the Swiss linguist Ferdinand de Saussure (1857–1913), the second from the philosophical inquiry of the US philosopher Charles S. Peirce (1839–1914), and the third from the original work on history and literature of the Russian semiotician Jurij M. Lotman (1922–1993). These three trends developed in complex ways that cannot be easily summarized here. However, what is important in this context is to point out how they contributed to semiotic research on religious phenomena in general and on conversion in particular.

Saussure's Approach to Semiotics and Conversion

In Saussure's approach to semiotics, signs are mostly conceived as static entities, composed by a signifier and a signified. In general, languages are considered as systems of signs where patterns of expression are associated with patterns of meaning; knowledge of nonverbal languages (such as the language of conversion, for instance) is predominantly modeled upon knowledge of verbal language. Signifiers and their signified are usually comprehended not extrinsically, in relation to a supposed external referent of language, but rather intrinsically, through the internal logic of language itself; such logic is construed as fundamentally based on difference among opposite elements; in Saussure as well as in the vast trend of scholarship that stemmed from his research (basically, the whole structuralist and post-structuralist agenda), signification exists as a byproduct of difference.[34] Saussure's approach to semiotics is quite effective in dealing with some aspects of conversion: (1) the study of how religious cultures tend to express conversion through a sort of code by associating a set of possible spiritual changes to a set of possible expressive devices;[35] and (2) the semiotic analysis of texts that narrate conversion.

The first point has already been briefly dealt with above. As regards the second point, Saussure's insights on verbal language and other systems of signs led to the development of a new trend in the study of (both verbal and nonverbal) narration. The Franco-Lithuanian semiotician Algirdas J. Greimas, in particular, combined Saussure's linguistics—mostly read through the glossematics[36] of the Danish linguist and semiotician Louis Hjelmslev[37] —with some elements of Noam Chomsky's theory of language,[38] Vladimir Propp's survey of narrative structures in Russian folktales,[39] George Dumézil's monumental inquiry about the Indo-European civilization,[40] and some tenets of Claude Lévi-Strauss's structuralist anthropology[41] in order to elaborate first a new structuralist comprehension of meaning,[42] then a complex method meant to analyze narrative texts as structural machines where sense is produced through the articulation of patterns of differences among opposite elements (mainly at the semantic level).[43]

From the mid-1970s on, this line of investigation had a considerable impact on research in the field of religious studies: scholars like Pierre Geoltrain and his research group at the École Pratique des Hautes Études in Paris,[44] Louis Panier and his research group at the Catholic University of Lyon,[45] and Daniel Patte and his research group at Vanderbilt University[46] sought to apply the semiotic method created by Greimas and his school to the narrative analysis of religious texts, and of the biblical discourse in particular. Other scholars, like Michel de Certeau (École des Hautes Études en Sciences Sociales of Paris, University of California San Diego, other universities),[47] Louis Marin (École des Hautes Études en Sciences Sociales of Paris, Johns Hopkins University, and other universities),[48] and Giovanni Pozzi (University of Fribourg, CH)[49] maintained a fecund dialogue with Greimas's structuralist semiotics, combining it with other methods in order to cast new light on the Christian discourse. Other scholars then adopted a semiotic approach (often blurred with other methods) in order to decipher the meaning of nonverbal texts produced and diffused in Christian civilization (mainly paintings and other forms or visual communication). These scholars include Daniel Arasse (École des Hautes Études en Sciences Sociales of Paris),[50] Omar Calabrese (University of Siena),[51] and Victor I. Stoichita (University of Fribourg, CH).[52]

Greimas's method is too complex and elaborate to be effectively summarized here. In this context suffice it to say that for Greimas and his school a narrative text (but also any kind of signifying object, narrativity being for Greimas the general dynamics through which meaning is created and shared) can be decomposed[53] through an inverted pyramidal structure known as the "semiotic path," where the patterns of meaning that characterize the text are arranged and analyzed from the most abstract and deep to the more concrete and superficial, each layer in the pyramid being both a "conversion" (according to the semantic meaning of the term)[54] and an enrichment of the previous layer. The most deep and abstract layer in the semiotic path is, according to the Greimasian method, that in which an abstract value[55] becomes meaningful (i.e., it becomes matter for signification and communication) through its difference with an opposite value. For instance, in most (religious) conversion narratives, "belief" is likely to be the main value, but it can become part of a narrative only insofar it is placed in significant relation with an opposite value, disbelief. The so-called "semiotic square," a logic diagram elaborated by Aristotle and other ancient philosophers, is adapted by Greimas and his school in order to articulate and visualize the possible semantic relations between a value and its counterparts (see figure 16.1).

Such a static arrangement of semantic relations starts to become a dynamic narrative when it is "converted" into a more superficial, and more concrete, layer of the semiotic path, denominated by Greimas and his school as "fundamental narrative grammar." This section of the pyramid seeks to account for a common characteristic of narrative texts; although what they ultimately signify and communicate is the triumph of a value over its counterparts (in the case of a conversion narrative, the triumph of belief over disbelief), such signification can take place only insofar as values are embodied in a story. Greimas and his school interpret this narrative embodiment as a tension between a subject, which is deprived of a value, and an object, which embodies that same value. Four main steps articulate the narrative tension between the subject and the object of value: contract, competence, performance, and sanction. In contract, a "sender" pushes a subject to eliminate this tension by acquiring the object of value; in competence, the subject develops the ability to acquire the object of value, often through the help of some positive agents and against the hostility of some negative agents; in performance, the subject acquires the object of value, often by defeating an antagonist, or anti-subject that also yearns to acquire the same object; and in sanction, a "receiver," often the one that had pushed the subject to acquire the object of value, assesses that said object has been acquired and that all narrative tension has been eliminated from the story.

FIGURE 16.1 The semiotic square of belief and disbelief

As an illustration of this abstract scheme, think about the way in which many early modern Catholic narratives recount the religious conversion of Therese of Avila.[56] God (the "sender") destines her to pious life at her birth, and yet Therese (the subject) chooses the cloister (the "object of value") only after struggling against the devil (the anti-subject), which pushes her, on the contrary, toward mundane life. On the one hand, some helpers encourage her toward spiritual perfection (her parents, one of her uncles, devotional books that she reads, etc.), but on the other hand, some opponents push her toward the opposite choice of dissipation of her spiritual gifts (older friends, a vain cousin, profane books she reads, etc.); it is only through entering the convent and acquiring full awareness of her spiritual destiny ("competence") that Therese breaks her ties with the mundane world and is, therefore, positively sanctioned by God with the blessing of ecstasy. Understanding, through Greimas's method of semiotic analysis, the structure and dynamic of values that underlie this narrative is important for grasping its persuasive and, therefore, cultural influence. Through this narrative, readers of Therese's *Life* observe, like in a theatrical representation, the triumph of belief over disbelief, of pious life over mundane existence, and of God over his enemy.

According to Greimas, the narrative sequence of contract-competence-performance-sanction is abstract enough to account for every semiotic phenomenon and, therefore, to seize the way in which conversion is signified and communicated not only through texts destined for an external audience but also in the convert's "internal forum." Conversion stories frequently entail a narrative sequence in which an external agent (be it transcendent or immanent) induces a subject to perceive herself as separated from belief in a certain object (usually a set of religious tenets) and to engage in a quest that consists in acquiring the religious competence necessary to ultimately transform the initial situation of disjunction and crisis into one of conjunction and commitment, followed by the sanction of the advocating agent.[57]

Nevertheless, this narrative sequence is not a story; in order to become such, it has to be "converted" and enriched through a series of semantic patterns that Greimas and his school describe and analyze at a more superficial, and less abstract, layer of the semiotic path, denominated as "production of discourse." Here the Greimasian method seeks to formalize what is another common characteristic of texts: although their meaning stems from a social system of semantic oppositions and narrative forms, such meaning can be created and shared only insofar as this social system is transformed into an individual message, according to a dialectics that Saussure first identified in verbal language as a relation between *langue* (the social dimension of language) and *parole* (the individual dimension of language). The series of semio-linguistic mechanisms that mediate between the social and the individual dimension of meaning are defined by Greimas and his school as "enunciation," a field of inquiry which has greatly benefited from the insights of the French linguist Émile Benveniste.[58] According to the Greimasian elaboration of Benveniste's ideas, enunciation is what enables the passage from the deep semantic level of a text (the network of values and their anthropomorphic "conversion") to produce discourse, which Greimas and his school consider as a sort of "theater." Three elements characterize the "scene" where the deep semantics of a text is "staged" into a story: space, time, and actors.

Regarding the first element, space, stories not only choose between opposite kinds of space[59] (for instance, a space that is close to the source of enunciation vs. one that is distant from it) but also arrange a series of homologies[60] between the space of a story and its deeper semantic layers. For instance, the four steps of the fundamental narrative grammar—contract, competence, performance, and sanction—are usually staged in spaces whose characteristics reflect those of these narrative phases.[61] Accordingly, the semiotic analysis of conversion phenomena, processes, and texts can reveal how a religious culture, in a certain phase of its development, tends to produce and diffuse conversion narratives in which different steps of conversion are staged in different spaces, according to a more or less precise cultural code that it is the semiotician's task to identify. For instance, the "conversion contract" can be staged in an open religious context or in a religious enclave, through free interaction with other subjects or through encapsulation, according to a centripetal or centrifugal "choreography of the soul";[62] similarly, "conversion performance" takes place through specific rituals of separation, transition, and incorporation where space plays a fundamental role as a metaphor of disjunction/conjunction between the subject and the object of value.[63]

Regarding the element of time, once again the production of the "discursive scene" coincides, according to Greimas and his school, with a choice between opposite patterns;[64] time is not an original element of the semiotic path (the deeper and more abstract layers of it being logical, not chronological), but rather a discursive effect, a construction of language. First, conversion can be represented as simultaneous or as non-simultaneous to the source of enunciation. In the first case, conversion is narrated as a remote event, situated either in the past or in the future, while in the second case conversion is narrated as if it were happening here and now, at the same moment when the enunciate that narrates conversion is enunciated. So, for instance, many converts narrate their conversion (either to an external audience or to their "internal forum") by adopting a sort of "squinting temporality," so that, on the one hand, conversion is a phenomenon situated in the past and narrated as a story, but on the other hand, it is a phenomenon that never ceases to deconstruct and reconstruct the point of view from which it is narrated as a story. As a consequence, conversion is often narrated through the production of a paradoxical discourse wherein past, present, and future interlace in a complex temporal weaving.

A further dynamic in the construction of discursive temporality is what Greimas and his school define as "aspectualization."[65] This layer of the semiotic path seeks to account for the way in which stories usually distinguish not only between different temporal dimensions (simultaneity and non-simultaneity; past, present, and future) but also between different temporal aspects. It is as if the story contained an abstract observer who chooses to emphasize a particular aspect of the temporal structure, for example, the instantaneity of it instead of its duration or the initial part of a process instead of its climax or ending.

Understanding the temporal structure through which a conversion story is staged allows the semiotician to distinguish, for instance, between cultural contexts that tend to represent conversion as an event (according to the fundamental model of Saul/Paul of Tarsus) and those that, on the contrary, tend to represent conversion as a process (according to the equally fundamental model of Augustine of Hippo). This also allows the semiotician to develop a typology of conversion stories, depending on the amount of emphasis placed on each phase of conversion (contract, competence, performance, or sanction).

Actors are the last element that, according to Greimas's approach to semiotics, composes the discursive scene of a text. Indeed, the anthropomorphic roles that appear in the fundamental narrative grammar—the subject, the object, the agent that intervenes in the contract ("sender"), the agent that intervenes in the sanction ("receiver")—are not actors yet but mere "narrative macro-functions" (technically called "actants"). Through enunciation,[66] actants are "converted" and enriched into a more superficial and concrete layer of the semiotic path, giving rise to patterns of meaning that resemble more what common sense defines as "the protagonists of a story." Here, too, meaning emerges as a byproduct of choices within a matrix of possibilities, within a system of differences.

Enunciation must first opt for either a personal or an impersonal narration of conversion. In the first case, the actor that embodies the subject of conversion will appear as the one who produces the discourse that narrates the conversion; in verbal language this effect of meaning is achieved mainly through the adoption of the first and the second person (I/you) of verbal morphology[67] (as, for example, in Augustine's *Confessions*). In the second case, however, the actor that impersonates the subject of conversion will appear as different from the one who is responsible for the narration of the conversion; in verbal language, this effect of meaning is achieved when the third person of verbal morphology (he) is preferred[68] (as, for example, in Pedro Ribadeneyra's account of Ignatius of Loyola's conversion). Once again, when converts narrate their conversion to their "internal forum," they often produce paradoxical narratives, where conversion is "put on stage" by a discourse in which converts are both internal protagonists and external observers of their own conversion.

Analyzing how conversion narratives organize the actors of discourse in a more or less subjective/objective way is fundamental for understanding how these same actors can work as what semiotics defines as "simulacra."[69] When conversion is narrated by adopting the first person of a verb, for example, the actors of discourse bring about a double identification between the subject of conversion (the convert) and its narrator (the narrating "I") and between the receiver of narration (the "you" to which the "I" is implicitly or explicitly addressed) and the receiver of the text that contains such narration (the reader of a conversion story, the observer of a conversion image, etc.). So, for instance, most readers of Augustine's *Confessions*, which adopts a personal structure of actors and simulacra, will have the impression that the bishop of Hippo is right in front of them, sharing their same time and space, narrating the story of his conversion directly to them. The cognitive, pragmatic, and emotional effect of a discourse adopting an impersonal structure of actors (the third person of a verb, for instance) would be radically different; readers would not have the impression of receiving the narration of conversion directly from the voice of the convert.

Understanding how discursive structures produce an effect of either proximity or distance between the convert and those to whom conversion is narrated is paramount in order to account for the persuasive potential of conversion stories. In many religious cultures, conversion and narration are considered as forming a virtuous circle; conversions are narrated through stories that, in their turn, promote the development of new conversions, which are subsequently narrated through new stories, and so on and so forth, in an infinite chain that is imagined as never ending until the last human being has been converted.[70] However, all conversion stories do not have the same rhetorical potential, and the way in which the structures of their discourse are arranged is one of the main reasons for their efficacy or lack thereof.[71]

Enunciation must opt not only for a more or less personal/impersonal structure of actors, but also for a certain model of relation between narrative macro-functions (actants) and actors. Three models are possible at this layer of the semiotic path: (1) a single actant is embodied by a single actor; (2) a single actant is embodied by more than one actor; (3) more than one actant are embodied by a single actor. In relation (1), a single narrative macro-function (the subject, the object, the agent behind the contract, the one responsible for the sanction) is impersonated by a single actor on the discursive scene.

As an illustration, think about the ways in which Catholic early modern narratives represent religious conversion in hagiographies devoted to Saint Francis Xavier, the mighty "converter of Asia."[72] First, there is the conversion of Francis Xavier himself. Influenced by the spiritual episteme of early modernity, texts represent the future saint's "inner forum" as a theater where opposite values and, as a result, opposite narrative actants, compete over domain within the young missionary's soul. This is clearly the third arrangement mentioned above: to a single narrative actor (Francis Xavier) correspond several narrative forces. Second, there is the conversion of Indian villages, where Francis Xavier, according to tradition, christened thousands of people at a time. This is evidently the second arrangement mentioned above: to a multitude of actors (the many converts baptized by Francis Xavier) corresponds a single actant, a single narrative force. Finally, there is the conversion of Japanese individuals. This is without a doubt the first arrangement mentioned above, since hagiographic texts that recount Francis Xavier's missionary accomplishments neither attribute to Japanese people the same psychological complexity that they attribute to the future saint's "inner forum," nor do they conflate Japanese individualities into macro-actants, as in the conversion of Indian villages. Articulating this typology has not only a taxonomic interest but also an ideological one. For example, it reveals the emergence—in the aftermath of the Protestant Reformation—of the idea of multifaceted religious consciousness in early modern Europe, its somewhat Orientalistic[73] denial in the "conversion of the East," and the exception represented by the Japanese, which the sources often consider as halfway between the inner complexity of "white Europeans" and the psychological simplicity of "brown Asians" (the Japanese assuming the pigmentocratic intermediate position of "white Asians").

Such an arrangement, characteristic of most folktales, rarely occurs in conversion narratives. In fact, one of the most typical features of these texts is precisely their tendency to present the convert as an actor that embodies many different actants (the third arrangement mentioned above) to the point that the convert is often simultaneously the subject of conversion and the anti-subject of it.[74] The second type of arrangement typically occurs in stories of collective conversion, where the opposite phenomenon takes place: the subject of conversion is "distributed" through several actors and is usually deprived of any individual subjectivity.

According to Greimas and his school, the last layer of the semiotic path contains the most superficial and concrete patterns of meaning, those that "convert" and enrich the semantic plane[75] of a text sufficiently for it to be manifested through semiosis with an expressive plane.[76] At this layer, meaning is generated through figurative discourse, a semiotic mechanism that signifies the more abstract patterns of meaning described above by associating these patterns with a series of "figures."[77] In the Greimasian method, the term "figures" designates elements of "the real world"[78] adopted as signifiers in the semantic structure of a text.

It is exactly at this layer of the semiotic path that some elements of reality can become "symbols of conversion," that is, figures[79] where the whole semantics of a conversion narrative is concentrated with extraordinary density.[80] The fig tree under which Augustine threw himself after hearing the phrase *tolle et lege*; the horse that, according to a vast literary and iconographic tradition, unsaddled Saul of Tarsus at the moment of his conversion; the ointment that Mary Magdalene poured on Jesus' body after her contrition— these are all objects of the real world that are absorbed into conversion narratives and loaded with a huge semantic value (mostly deriving from the fact that they summarize a whole semiotic path).[81] Structural semiotics is meant to (1) analyze the relation between the figurative discourse of a conversion narrative and the semiotic path behind it, and (2) study how figures of conversion "migrate" from narrative to narrative, and with what effects:[82] for instance, when the Italian poet Petrarch adopts the Augustinian figure of the fig tree in order to evoke the turning point of his own spiritual life, he empowers his own conversion narrative through a figure that condenses the whole semantics of Augustine's conversion.[83]

The Greimasian method is a rich repository of semio-linguistic tools that can be used to analyze how different "morphologies of conversion"[84] take shape, are signified, and are communicated. However, over the last three decades this method has been shown to have many limits. These are the most relevant: (1) a certain inefficacy in dealing with the philosophical problem of time, fundamental also in the comprehension of conversion and its narratives;[85] (2) a certain inefficacy in dealing with the materiality of signification, paramount for the study of the "semiotic ideologies" and the "economies of representation" that underlie some conversion phenomena;[86] (3) a certain inefficacy in dealing with meanings that do not emerge from patterns of binary differences (e.g., black vs. white) but from positions within a continuum; the need to develop a method to account for non-discrete[87] forms of meaning is primary in relation to conversion narratives, which often do not embody an opposition between belief and disbelief but rather signify a movement between two positions within a continuum;[88] (4) a certain inefficacy in tackling the problem of how the Greimasian method might be inaccurate and, therefore, need reformulation, when applied to "non-Western" cultures; the analysis of "non-Western" conversion narratives could therefore require extensive re-elaboration of the whole project of structuralist semiotics.[89]

The other two major branches of semiotics, the one stemming from Peirce's philosophical inquiry and the one developed from Lotman's work as a semiotician of history and literature, probably have not given rise to methods for textual micro-analysis as well articulated as the one developed by Greimas and his school. Nevertheless, Peirce's and Lotman's semiotic "schools" seem to be, in many respects, complementary to the structuralist project, offering helpful insights precisely related to those areas of the semiotic project in which the Greimasian method is rarely effective.

Peirce's Approach to Semiotics and Conversion

The approach to semiotics of Charles S. Peirce is extremely complex and cannot be easily summarized.[90] However, the most important points of Peirce's legacy in relation to the study of conversion phenomena are: (1) a dynamic conception of signs and signification; (2) the possibility of elaborating a typology of signs; and (3) the foundation of semiotics as a new logic, characterized by a form of reasoning called "abduction."

As regards the first point, while Saussure would conceive the sign as a mostly static entity, deprived of any significant relation with extralinguistic referents and their materiality, Peirce conceives the sign as a relation between a "representamen," or the signifying part of the sign, and an object, or the ontological referent of the representamen, always mediated through a further sign called the "interpretant." Such a conception of the sign presents two advantages. First, although the referent is never signified directly, but always asymptotically,[91] through the mediation of a further sign, Peirce's approach to semiotics does not totally exclude the relevance of ontology for semiosis. As a consequence, Peirce's model of the sign may be more suitable than the one elaborated by Saussure in accounting, for example, for how the encounter of an advocate and a potential convert must be read as an encounter of different semiotic ideologies that attribute different value to the relation between the materiality of signifying objects and their meaning.[92] The adoption of Peirce's model of the sign by linguistic and semiotic anthropology has brought about, for instance, interesting insights related to the anthropology of conversion contexts.[93] The second advantage of Peirce's model of the sign is that his model entails the idea of "unlimited semiosis"; a sign can signify only when "interpreted" by another sign, and that sign in its turn can signify only when "interpreted" by a further sign, and so on and so forth through a potentially infinite process that comes to an end only because human beings develop "an interpretative habitus" compelling them to stop this chain when their interpretation of a sign is suitable for dealing pragmatically with a given context.

The idea of "unlimited semiosis" is useful to account for (a) the endless chain of signs and interpretants that constitute the conversion process;[94] (b) the effects of meaning and persuasion that are triggered by the more or less wide circulation of conversion stories within a religious community (or even outside of it), each one of these stories being a sign "interpreted" by a further conversion and vice versa.

As regards Peirce's typology of signs, its philosophical framework is too complex to be easily evoked here; however, the most influential aspect of such a typology is a distinction between indexes, that is, signs where a relation of physical contiguity obtains between the "representamen" and the object (for instance, smoke as an index of fire); icons, that is, signs where a relation of resemblance obtains between the "representamen" and the object (for instance, the portrait of a man as an icon of his face); and symbols, that is, signs where a conventional relation obtains between the representamen and the object (e.g., the word "dog" as a symbol of a certain animal species in English). Semioticians have realized that signs rarely fall exclusively in one of these types and more commonly appear to signify at the same time as indexes, icons, and symbols, one of the three semiotic dynamics being predominant over the other two. Also, they have realized that it is difficult, if not impossible, to account for the meaning of isolate signs, for signs rarely appear separated from other signs and more commonly signify within the complex semiotic fabric of texts.

Nevertheless, Peirce's typology is useful in order to elaborate a general typology of conversion signs, one that distinguishes between indexical signs of conversion (the convert signifies her conversion through the physical proximity between her body and certain people and spaces and also through certain marks of conversion on the body, such as circumcision in the case of male converts to Judaism, for example), iconic signs of conversion (the convert modifies her aspect and behavior in order to resemble an ideal type of believer within a certain religious community), and symbolic signs of conversion (the convert changes her name in order to signal her affiliation with a new faith).[95]

Finally, Peirce is credited with the "invention" of a new form of logical inference known as "abduction." In his works before 1900, Peirce mostly referred to abduction as to the way of using a known rule in order to explain an observation. However, later on he used the term "abduction" in order to designate the creation of new rules in order to explain new observations, claiming that abduction is the only way in which new knowledge is produced. Peirce's theory of abductive reasoning is closely connected with his semiotics; it is through the interpretation of signs, indeed, that abduction brings about a sort of "leap" between old knowledge and new insights. According to Peter L. Berger, three religious options are currently available in the contemporary religious scene:[96] (1) deductive religiosity, based on some source of authority; here, "conversion is regulated by norms that delineate specific requirements for change in belief, behavior, and feeling"; (2) reductive religiosity, according to which the philosophical and theological orientation is epistemologically superior to all other orientations; here, "conversion is seen as a coping mechanism in religious garb"; and (3) inductive religiosity, which encourages "a phenomenological approach to conversion, allowing for diversity and complexity."[97] On the basis of Peirce's approach to semiotics, the existence of a fourth option can be pointed out: abductive religiosity. In abductive religiosity, conversion is not understood according to a binary logic, that is, as a rigid relation between a set of causes and a set of effects, but rather according to a triadic logic, where the relation between the signs of conversion (its effects) and its ontological ground (its causes) are never direct but always mediated by a (potentially infinite) chain of interpretants.[98]

This explicative model has two advantages: (1) although conversion processes can be categorized within more or less articulated typologies, by suggesting that each conversion phenomenon follows an individual path, an original way of building up the chain of interpretants leading from disbelief to belief, explanations based on abductive religiosity preserve the uniqueness of conversion phenomena; (2) by introducing the process of unlimited semiosis in the explanation of conversion phenomena, reasoning based on abductive religiosity admits the possibility that conversion might stem from an encounter between finitude and infinitude, between the limitedness of "representamens" and the unlimitedness of the ontology to which they refer; human beings therefore become the interpretants that connect finitude and infinitude through language and semiosis. In other words, abductive religiosity would suggest that language is the dimension of the human predicament where a gracious infinitude becomes available to human beings, although always in the incomplete way in which finite means can signify infinitude.

Lotman's Approach to Semiotics and Conversion

The third major branch of contemporary semiotics, the so-called "School of Tartu,"[99] stems less from philosophical inquiry and more from the application of the structuralist framework to the study of history, folklore, and literature.[100] In this context, only those aspects of this semiotic school that appear useful to the study of conversion phenomena can be singled out. The main ambition of Lotman and his followers is to develop a semiotics of cultures, that is, a semiotics that takes as objects of its analyses not only micro-phenomena like isolated signs, fragments of discourse, or texts, but also macro-realities like civilizations and cultures. Indeed, on the one hand, Lotman and his school realize, maybe more than the two branches of semiotics described above, that the way in which texts signify can be accounted for only if they are considered as elements within a wider semiotic network where they circulate and acquire their meaning; on the other hand, Lotman formulates the hypothesis that cultures too may function as texts where identity is defined through mechanisms that are substantially linguistic.

In order to understand cultures as semiotic phenomena, Lotman introduces the concept of "semiosphere," modeled upon the biological concept of "biosphere."[101] As the biosphere is the part of the Earth within which life occurs, the semiosphere defines the limits within which a given society seeks to transform the chaos of "nature" into the cosmos of culture. According to Lotman, verbal language plays a fundamental role in such transformation and is therefore called the "primary modeling system";[102] however, other systems (called "secondary modeling systems") are able to confer a certain structure of intelligibility to reality, although they do so by adopting verbal language as a model. The ultimate goal of Lotman and his school is to elaborate a typology of cultures, that is, a comprehension of how different societies conceive the limits of the semiosphere, determine the mechanisms through which texts and other particles of meaning are created, diffused, or destroyed within the semiosphere, and regulate the transition between the outside and the inside of the semiosphere (mainly through processes that translate what is perceived as unintelligible into particles of meaning). Lotman's approach presents many advantages for the study of conversion phenomena: (1) it allows scholars to reinterpret the anthropology of religious conversion from a semiotic point of view; (2) it conceives religious cultures as dynamic phenomena whose limits are not defined once and for all but are continuously shaped by complex dialectics with other systems of belief; and (3) it understands conversion phenomena as translation processes[103] that allow individual and groups to step from the outside of a semiosphere into its interior by adopting the semiotic "ethos"[104] that characterizes a given religious community.[105]

Conclusions

Semiotics is a vast field of interests where problems, methods, and insights characteristic of several disciplines converge to shape a new perspective on the human predicament. Although a rich literature has been produced about the application of semiotics to the analysis of phenomena of religious signification and communication, the adoption of semiotics as a framework for the study of conversion is still a recent but promising trend. This short chapter has sought to point out the most important insights the major branches of semiotic investigation have brought about so far in the field of conversion studies, as well as the most relevant advantages the semiotic mindset could offer to future scholars for the study of this fascinating religious phenomenon.

In his *Understanding Religious Conversion*, Lewis R. Rambo lamented that "what has been described thus far [about conversion] is very much like sighted people entering through separate doors into a dark room—one barely large enough to contain the elephant—and each trying to describe the beast discovered with only a penlight to see by,"[106] invoking "the electrical switch on the wall that will illuminate the whole animal." Unfortunately, semiotics is not that switch. More modestly, semiotics offers guidance in recognizing "the elephant" from the signs of it that emerge from the darkness.

Notes

1. Umberto Eco, *Trattato di semiotica generale* (Milan: Bompiani, 1975).
2. From this point on, the term "conversion" will be used to refer to "religious conversion."

3. However, a branch (or rather a certain interpretation of) semiotics, called "biosemiotics," seeks to blur the frontier between phenomena of human communication and analogous phenomena involving non-human agents (such as bacterial communication or genetic processes); see Marcello Barbieri, ed., *Introduction to Biosemiotics: The New Biological Synthesis* (Dordrecht: Springer, 2007).

4. There are many different definitions of sign. The purpose of semiotics might be thought of as exactly that of elaborating a suitable definition of sign. However, a classical definition, especially in the Peircean branch of semiotics, is the one offered by Peirce himself (one of the many): "A sign, or *representamen*, is something which stands to somebody for something in some respect or capacity" (A Fragment, *Collected Papers* 2.228, c. 1897).

5. Ugo Volli, *Manuale di Semiotica* (Rome: GLF Editori Laterza, 2003); Massimo Leone, "Agency, Communication, and Revelation," in "Actants, Actors, Agents—the Meaning of Action and the Action of Meaning: From Theories to Territories," ed. Massimo Leone, monographic issue of *Lexia*, new series, 3–4 (Dec. 2009).

6. An agency can be defined as the source of the intention that determines an action; see Leone, "Actants, Actors, Agents."

7. Massimo Leone, "Le mutazioni del cuore: esperienza, narrazione e narratività della conversione religiosa," in *Narrazione ed esperienza: Per una semiotica della vita quotidiana*, proceedings of the 34th Congress of the Italian Association for Semiotic Studies held in Arcavacata di Rende, Nov. 2006, *E/C*, online journal of the Italian Association for Semiotic Studies, vol. 20 (2007), http://www.ec-aiss.it/archivio/tipologico/atti.php.

8. Keith P. Luria, "The Politics of Protestant Conversion to Catholicism in Seventeenth-Century France," in *Conversion to Modernities: The Globalization of Christianity*, ed. Peter van der Veer (London: Routledge, 1996), 28. The human inability to determine the relation between the behavior of a convert and a transcendent dimension has represented a dramatic conundrum not only for advocates of all time, space, and faith, but also for converts themselves (when I behave as a convert, do I do so because my behavior, independently from my own agency and intentions, signifies that I have been really transformed by communication with a transcendent dimension, or because through this behavior I intend to convince myself—as well as those who observe it—that I have been really transformed?) If the convert's behavior is a theatre through which a new relation with transcendence is represented, who is behind the scenes, transcendence or the convert's agency? On the relation between agency and conversion, see Talal Asad, "Comments on Conversion," in *Conversion to Modernities: The Globalization of Christianity*, ed. Peter Van der Veer (London: Routledge, 1996).

9. Alisa Mehuyas Ginio, ed., *Jews, Christians and Muslims in the Mediterranean World after 1492* (London: Cass, 1992); Massimo Leone, *Saints and Signs: A Semiotic Reading of Conversion in Early Modern Catholicism* (Berlin: Walter de Gruyter, 2010), 481–489.

10. Charles Ralph Boxer, *The Christian Century in Japan: 1549–1650* (Manchester: Carcanet, 1993); Leone, *Saints and Signs*, 355–66.

11. Henry Charles Lea, *A History of the Inquisition of Spain*, 4 vols. (New York: Macmillan Company, 1906–07); torture was, therefore, the attempt to find in the converts' tormented bodies more "truthful" signs of secret "heresy" and fake conversion than those displayed by the converts' behavior.

12. There are levels of assessment among various religious groups that evaluate the authenticity, sincerity, completeness, etc., of a conversion. On one level, "faking" is sometimes rather easy to discern. Are there, for example, external rewards or enticements to the conversion?

The problem for most people is to find out whether the person is sincere, but, after that is determined ... to what degree is the person sufficiently changed in order to be considered an authentic convert? ... Should a good enough conversion count as the real thing?

13. Roland Robertson, *Meaning and Change: Explorations in the Cultural Sociology of Modern Societies* (New York: New York University Press, 1978).

14. Massimo Leone, *Religious Conversion and Identity: The Semiotic Analysis of Texts* (London: Routledge, 2004); Massimo Leone, "La Conversion de Saint Paul comme Pathosformel théologique," in *L'Humanisme dans tous ses états ou la spiritualité plurielle*, Festschrift in honor of Raymond Baustert, ed. Marion Colas-Blaise et al. (Tübingen: Gunter Narr Verlag, forthcoming).

15. Unlike most linguists, semioticians characteristically conceive language as not exclusively "verbal language," but rather as "language faculty," the human ability to produce and receive meaning by associating some expressive patterns with some semantic patterns (even though expressive patterns are, for example, nonverbal behavior); see Vicente Rafael, *Contracting Colonialism: Translation and Christian Conversion in Tagalog Society under Early Spanish Rule* (Durham, NC: Duke University Press, 1993), which claims that conversion (changing one thing into something else) is synonymous with translation (changing one language into another); see Lewis R. Rambo, *Understanding Religious Conversion* (New Haven: Yale University Press, 1993), 108, on the role of rhetoric in the interaction that leads to conversion; see Thomas Fawcett, *The Symbolic Language of Religion* (Minneapolis, MN: Augsburg, 1971), 171–172, for a definition of conversion as a phenomenon involving a symbolic language.

16. For the meaning of the word "abduction" and its derivates, see below.

17. From the Arabic verb *šahida*, "to testify."

18. Commonly translated into English as: "There is no God but Allah, Muhammad is the Messenger of Allah."

19. The paradox that many converts face is that they frequently appear as different from the older members of the religious community to which they adhere because of the same intensity by which they seek to eliminate any difference between themselves and such older members. At the same time, should they try to eliminate this difference of intensity, they would probably appear as not believable as converts, for in most religious cultures a greater intensity of commitment and religious behavior is a fundamental sign through which converts manifest themselves as such; see Andrew Buckser, "Social Conversion and Group Definition in Jewish Copenhagen," in *The Anthropology of Religious Conversion*, ed. Andrew Buckser and Stephen D. Glazier (Lanham, MD: Rowman & Littlefield Publishers, 2003).

20. By "individuality" here is meant an intentional agency anchored to a single body, to a single corporeal unity.

21. By "transcendence" here is meant a dimension that human beings consider as endowed with a hierarchically ontological superior status in relation to the dimension in which they believe to be conducting their existence.

22. Or co-agent, according to the different theologies of conversion; see Massimo Leone, "Prefazione," in id., "Actants, Actors, Agents"; id., "Agency, Communication, and Revelation," in id., "Actants, Actors, Agents."

23. According to structural semiotics, the "signifier" is the part of a sign that does not mean itself, but that to which it refers to, that is, the "signified." Vice versa, also according to structural semiotics, the "signified" is the part of a sign that does not mean by itself, but

through that which refers to it, that is, the "signifier." For instance, the word "cat," as uttered by a certain speaker, is a signifier that does not mean the phonetic sounds that compose it, but that to which they refer, that is, a certain idea of cats. Vice versa, this idea does not mean by itself, as a sort of mystical image, but through the phonetic sounds that refer to it. As a consequence, the word "cat" is the signifier of a certain idea of cats, which is, in turn, the signified of that word.

24. Semiosis is the dynamics that brings about signification through correlation between a pattern of meaning and an expressive pattern.

25. Ludwig Wittgenstein, *Philosophische Untersuchungen: Philosophical Investigations*, English trans. Gertrude E. M. Anscombe, 3rd ed. (Malden, MA: Blackwell Publishing, 2001), sections 244–271.

26. Mikhail Mikhailovich Bakhtin, *The Dialogic Imagination: Four Essays*, trans. Caryl Emerson and Michael Holquist (Austin: University of Texas Press, 1981). Such a "social" conception of conversion is probably influenced by my Roman Catholic religious background, which maybe leads me to stress the communitarian dimension of religious phenomena more than their individual nature. In order to expose my bias in my approach to conversion, it is useful to provide answers to the short questionnaire designed by Lewis R. Rambo (*Understanding Religious Conversion*, 93): (1) Am I religious or not?—My conception of the world is certainly influenced by a Roman Catholic religious background; at the same time, I tend to value communication between differences more than between identities; I am fascinated by otherness. (2) Am I religious in a way that is the same as—or similar to—that of the person I am assessing?—In studying conversion, I have a tendency to focus primarily on conversions to Christianity. (3) If I am not religious, what is my personal response to the nature of the religious conversion I am studying?—My intellectual background and the institutional framework in which I work define me as a "secular scholar"; nevertheless, although I am interested more in the social context in which conversion takes place than in the theological nature or in the psychological mechanisms of it, my personal response to most conversion phenomena is one of sympathy; I like the idea that human beings can freely shape their communication with transcendence and I dislike every attempt to thwart such freedom. (4) Am I repulsed or attracted?—I am definitely attracted by every form of conversion, although I tend to limit this attraction to conversions that I repute as "genuine." (5) What is my fundamental agenda in studying such phenomena?—I am not sure that my fundamental agenda is entirely clear to me; I am certainly fascinated by the way in which human beings can radically change in order to pursue a more perfect equilibrium with both the immanent and the transcendent dimensions of their lives.

27. The "internal forum" of an individual is the psychological arena in which the dynamics of her intimate existence takes place, before it is externalized through semiotic expressions. As a result, the concept of "internal forum" seeks to render the idea that the intimate existence of human beings is often a tumultuous struggle of various and sometimes conflicting tendencies, which compete against each other like advocates in a forum behind the curtains of the apparent unity of the human predicament.

28. In Bakhtin's thought, semiotics mostly highlights the idea that the internal language of an individual's inner forum reproduces the dialogical, polyphonic structure of the social arenas of discourse.

29. Ibid., 158: "These [conversion] stories as they are retold orally and composed as autobiographies become the paradigms by which people interpret their own lives"; on the charismatic preacher as self-listener, see also Simon Coleman, "Continuous Conversion: The

Rhetoric, Practice, and Rhetorical Practice of Charismatic Protestant Conversion," in *The Anthropology of Religious Conversion*, ed. Andrew Buckser and Stephen D. Glazier (Lanham, MD: Rowman & Littlefield Publishers, 2003).

30. Brian Stanley, "Conversion to Christianity: The Colonization of the Mind?" *International Review of Mission* 92, no. 366 (July 2003): 315–331.

31. Ferdinand de Saussure, *Cours de linguistique générale*, ed. Tullio de Mauro (Paris: Payot, 1972).

32. Émile Benveniste, *Problèmes de linguistique générale I* (Paris: Gallimard, 1966); *Problèmes de linguistique générale II* (Paris: Gallimard, 1971).

33. See Anne Hunsaker Hawkins, *Archetypes of Conversion: The Autobiographies of Augustine, Bunyan, and Merton* (Lewisburg, PA: Bucknell University Press, 1985) on the "archetype" of Augustine's conversion, which includes the tendency to express one's religious transformation through the construction of a narrative verbal account. However, this tendency does not characterize all the Christian denominations in the same way. For instance, testimonies are not a part of the way in which Church of Christ believers conceive conversion. The Church of Christ stresses behavior, proper beliefs (derived from careful study of the Bible, especially the New Testament), and little personal or emotional expression. One reads the Bible, studies, does what is right, and follows the guidelines to believe, repent, confess to Jesus Christ, and be baptized (as an adult by total immersion), and then goes to church regularly, abstains from alcohol and extramarital sex, and so on (personal communication, Lewis Rambo). See Charles Lloyd Cohen, *God's Caress: The Psychology of Puritan Religious Experience* (New York: Oxford University Press, 1986) on archetypical patterns in Puritan conversion narratives; compare to Paula Fredriksen, "Paul and Augustine: Conversion Narratives, Orthodox Traditions, and the Retrospective Self," *Journal of Theological Studies*, new series, 37 (1986): 3–34. In other Christian denominations, such as among many Evangelicals, for instance, people like C. S. Lewis replace Augustine in playing a paradigmatic or mentor role in the conversion process.

34. Saussure, *Cours de linguistique générale*.

35. For example, especially from the second half of the sixteenth century forward, tears became a fundamental signifier of attrition, contrition, and radical spiritual change in Roman Catholic religious culture, so that many (both verbal and nonverbal) texts produced and diffused in this culture would signify the acme of conversion through the representation of such a bodily expressive element; Sheila Page Bayne, *Tears and Weeping: An Aspect of Emotional Climate Reflected in Seventeenth-Century French Literature* (Tübingen: G. Naar, 1981); "Le Rôle des larmes dans le discours de la conversion," in *La Conversion au XVII siècle*, ed. Roger Duchene (Marseille: Centre Méridional de Rencontres sur le XVIIe siècle, 1983); Leone, *Saints and Signs*, 195–197.

36. A formalized study of language.

37. Louis Hjelmslev, *Omkring sprogteoriens grundlæggelse* (Copenhagen: Ejnar Munksgaard, 1943).

38. Noam Chomsky, *Aspects of the Theory of Syntax* (Cambridge, MA: MIT Press, 1965).

39. Vladimir Yakovlevich Propp, *Morphologies of the Folktale*, trans. Laurence Scott (Bloomington: Research Center, Indiana University, 1958).

40. Georges Dumézil, *Mythe et épopée: L'Idéologie des trois functions dans les épopées des peuples indo-européens* (Paris: Gallimard, 1968).

41. Claude Lévi-Strauss, *Anthropologie structurale* (Paris: Plon, 1958).

42. Algirdas Julien Greimas, *Sémantique structurale: Recherche et méthode* (Paris: Larousse, 1966).

43. Algirdas Julien Greimas, *Du sens* (Paris: Seuil, 1970); id., *Maupassant: La Sémiotique du texte, exercices pratiques* (Paris: Seuil, 1975); id. *Du sens II: Essais sémiotiques* (Paris: Seuil, 1983).

44. Jean Delorme and Pierre Geoltrain, "Le Discours religieux," in *Sémiotique: L'École de Paris*, ed. Jean-Claude Coquet (Paris: Hachette, 1982).

45. Louis Panier, *Écriture, foi, révélation: Le Statut de l'Écriture dans la révélation* (Lyon: Profac, 1973); *La Vie Éternelle: Une Figure dans la 1ère Épître de Saint Jean* (Paris: Groupe de recherches sémiolinguistiques, 1983); *Récit et commentaires de la tentation de Jésus au désert: Approche sémiotique du discours interprétatif: Étude* (Paris: Cerf, 1984); *La Naissance du fils de Dieu: Sémiotique et théologie discursive—lecture de Luc 1–2* (Paris: Cerf, 1991); ed., *Le Temps de la lecture: Exégèse biblique et sémiotique—recueil d'hommages pour Jean Delorme* (Paris: Cerf, 1993); ed., *Récits et figures dans la Bible: Colloque d'Urbino* (Lyon: Profac–Cadir, 1999); ed., *Les Lettres dans la Bible et dans la littérature: Actes du Colloque de Lyon, 3–5 juillet 1996* (Paris: Cerf, 1999).

46. Daniel Patte, *What Is Structural Exegesis?* (Philadelphia: Fortress Press, 1976); *Carré sémiotique et syntaxe narrative: Exegèse structurale de Marc, ch. 5* (Besancon: Groupe de recherches semio-linguistiques, 1981); *Paul's Faith and the Power of the Gospel: A Structural Introduction to the Pauline Letters* (Philadelphia: Fortress Press, 1983); *The Religious Dimensions of Biblical Texts: Greimas's Structural Semiotics and Biblical Exegesis* (Atlanta, GA: Scholars Press, 1990); *Structural Exegesis for New Testament Critics* (Minneapolis: Fortress Press, 1990); Daniel Patte and Gay Volney, "Religious Studies," in *Encyclopedic Dictionary of Semiotics*, ed. Thomas A. Sebeok (Berlin: Mouton de Gruyter, 1986).

47. Michel de Certeau, *L'Écriture de l'histoire* (Paris: Gallimard, 1975); *La Fable mystique, 1- XVI–XVII siècle* (Paris: Gallimard, 1982); *La Possession de Loudun* (Paris: Gallimard, 1989); *Il Parlare angelico* (Florence: Olschki, 1989); *L'Étranger ou l'union dans la différence* (Paris: Desclée de Brouwer, 1991); *La Faiblesse de croire* (Paris: Seuil, 2003).

48. Louis Marin, *Études sémiologiques, écritures, peintures* (Paris: Klincksieck, 1972); id., *Lectures traversières* (especially the essay "Échographies: Les Traversées d'une conversion") (Paris: Albin Michel, 1992); id., *De la représentation* (Paris: Gallimard-Seuil, 1994); id., *Sublime Poussin* (Paris: Seuil, 1995); id., *Philippe de Champaigne ou la présence cachée* (Paris: Hazan, 1995); id., *L'Écriture de soi: Ignace de Loyola, Montaigne, Stendhal, Roland Barthes* (Paris: PUF, 1999).

49. Giovanni Pozzi, *La rosa in mano al professore* (Fribourg: Éditions Universitaires, 1974); *La parola dipinta* (Milan: Adelphi, 1981); *Rose e gigli per Maria: Un'antifona dipinta* (Bellinzona: Casagrande, 1987); *Sull'orlo del visibile parlare* (Milan: Adelphi, 1993); *Alternatim* (Milan: Adelphi, 1996); *Grammatica e retorica dei santi* (Milan: Vita e pensiero, 1997).

50. Daniel Arasse, *Le Détail: Pour une histoire rapprochée de la peinture* (Paris: Flammarion, 1992); *L'Ambition de Vermeer* (Paris: A. Biro, 1993); *Le Sujet dans le tableau: Essais d'iconographie analytique* (Paris: Flammarion, 1997); *L'Annonciation italienne: Une histoire de perspective* (Paris: Hazan, 1999); *On n'y voit rien: Descriptions: essai* (Paris: Denoël, 2001).

51. Omar Calabrese, *Semiotica della pittura* (Milan: il Saggiatore, 1980); id., *L'intertestualità in pittura: Una lettura degli Ambasciatori di Holbein* (Urbino: Centro internazionale di semiotica e linguistica, 1984); id., *Il linguaggio dell'arte* (Milan: Bompiani, 1985); id., *La*

macchina della pittura: Pratiche teoriche della rappresentazione figurativa fra Rinascimento e Barocco (Rome: Laterza, 1985); id., *L'età neobarocca* (Rome-Bari: Laterza, 1987); id., *Lezioni di semisimbolico: Come la semiotica analizza le opere d'arte* (Siena: Protagon Editori Toscani, 1999); id., "Semiotic Aspects of Art History: Semiotics of the Fine Arts," in *Semiotik: Ein Handbuch zu den zeichentheoretischen Grundlagen von Natur und Kultur*, ed. Roland Posner, Klaus Robering, and Thomas A. Sebeok (Berlin: Walter de Gruyter, 2003).

52. Victor I. Stoichita, *Visionary Experience in the Golden Age of Spanish Art* (London: Reaktion Books, 1995); id., *L'Instauration du tableau: Métapeinture à l'aube des temps modernes* (Geneva: Droz, 1999); id., *Brève histoire de l'ombre* (Geneva: Droz, 2000).

53. Meaning that it can be broken down in its constitutive elements.

54. In order to avoid confusion, every time that the word "conversion" and its derivates are used as a technical term related to Greimas's approach to semiotics, the word will be put inside quotation marks.

55. In structural linguistics and semiotics, the value of something essentially stems from its being opposed to something else. As a consequence, "value" is an abstract measure of the relation that a certain element holds with other elements that are potentially alternative to it. For instance, the value of an idea like "freedom," as embodied in an epic tale, stems from its being emphasized in relation to alternative ideas, such as the contrary idea of "captivity" or the contradictory idea of "lack of freedom." After all, Greimas's approach to semiotics is nothing but a method meant to describe the ways in which these abstract relations and the values that they bring about are expressed through various semiotic means.

56. Leone, *Saints and Signs*, 481–530.

57. This paragraph implicitly seeks to suggest a parallel between the fundamental narrative grammar as sketched by Greimas's approach to semiotics and the converting process as summarized by Lewis R. Rambo, *Understanding Religious Conversion*. The main difference between the two models consists in the fact that, for Greimas, narrative tension is always determined by an external agent (this is why the step of "contract" precedes those of "competence" and "performance"), whereas Rambo seems to suggest an understanding of conversion where the autonomy of the subject is emphasized more than the influence of external agents (unlike Greimas, though, Rambo does not claim that his model is rigid; he admits that "there is sometimes a spiraling effect—a going back and forth between stages"). It is probable that different ways of organizing conversion models reflect different conceptions of the interplay of divine and human agency in conversion.

58. Jean-Claude Coquet, *Le Discours et son sujet* (Paris: Klincksieck, 1984); Joseph Courtès, *L'Énonciation comme acte sémiotique* (Limoges: PULIM, 1998); Giovanni Manetti, *La teoria dell'enunciazione: L'origine del concetto e alcuni più recenti sviluppi* (Siena: Protagon, 1998); Ayako Ono, *La Notion d'énonciation chez Émile Benveniste* (Limoges: Lambert-Lucas, 2007).

59. As usual, meaning in structuralist semiotics is conceived as emerging from opposition among different elements.

60. "Homology" here is meant as "formal parallelism" between two different dimensions of language.

61. Algirdas J. Greimas, "Pour une sémiotique topologique," in *Sémiotique et sciences sociales* (Paris: Seuil, 1976); Sandra Cavicchioli, ed., "La semiotica dello spazio," monographic issue of *Versus—Quaderni di studi semiotici* 73/74 (1996). The Greimasian school defines as "utopian" the space where the subject eliminates the disjunction between herself and the object of value and "paratopian" as the space where the competence for such a conjunction is acquired.

62. Lewis R. Rambo, *Understanding Religious Conversion* (New Haven: Yale University Press, 1993), 106.

63. Theodore W. Jennings, "On Ritual Knowledge," *Journal of Religion*, 62 (1982): 113–127.

64. Denis Bertrand and Jacques Fontanille, eds., *Régimes sémiotiques de la temporalité: La Flèche brisée du temps* (Paris: PUF, 2006).

65. Jacques Fontanille, *Les Espaces subjectifs: Introduction à la sémiotique de l'observateur (discours-peinture-cinéma)* (Paris: Hachette, 1989).

66. Here, the word "enunciation" is used in order to designate the series of semio-linguistic operations that bring about the passage from *langue* (the repository of virtual semio-linguistic forms) to *parole* (the realization of one of these forms in discourse).

67. This is true at least in the Indo-European languages.

68. This is true at least in the Indo-European languages.

69. Umberto Eco, *Lector in fabula: La cooperazione interpretativa nei testi narrativi* (Milan: Bompiani, 1979); a "simulacrum" is something whose main function is that of symbolically replacing something else, especially as regards the symbolical substitution of intentional agencies.

70. See Rambo, *Understanding Religious Conversion*, 158: "These [conversion] stories typically generate stories of that process which may then stimulate conversion in others"; see also Susan Harding, "Convicted by the Holy Spirit—The Rhetoric of Fundamental Baptist Conversion," *American Ethnologist* 14, no. 1 (1987): 167–182, 167: "Witnessing, and conversion talk more generally (testifying, evangelizing, gospel preaching, spreading the Word), is rhetorical in the sense that it is an *argument* about the transformation of self that lost souls must undergo, and a *method* of bringing about that change in those who listen to it" (emphasis in the original).

71. One of the interesting achievements of structural semiotics has been that of re-evaluating the insights of ancient rhetoric through a new formalization so as to use the insights in order to analyze the persuasive efficacy of texts; Groupe μ (J. Dubois, F. Edeline, J. M. Klinkenberg, P. Minguet, F. Pire, and H. Trinon), *Rhétorique générale* (Paris: Larousse, 1970); Groupe μ (F. Edeline, J. M. Klinkenberg, and P. Minguet), *Traité du signe visuel* (Paris: Seuil, 1992); μ is the initial letter of the word for "metaphor" in ancient Greek, chosen as a "brand" by this group of Belgian scholars.

72. Leone, *Saints and Signs*, 321–480.

73. By "Orientalism" here is meant, mainly with reference to Edward Said's famous homonymous book, the tendency to produce a stereotypical, distorted, and somehow degrading imaginary of non-European sociocultural contexts, especially in relation to the so-called "East."

74. This relation between actants and actors is typical of the modern psychological novel, many semiotic structures of which have appeared, perhaps for the first time, in conversion narratives.

75. That is, Greimas's re-conceptualization of Saussure's "signified."

76. That is, Greimas's re-conceptualization of Saussure's "signifier."

77. Jacques Fontanille, *Modes du sensible et syntaxe figurative* (Limoges: PULIM, 1999).

78. For Greimas and his school, "the real world" is defined as a macro-semiotics composed of an expressive plane (objects of reality as they appear) and of a semantic plane (meanings attributed to such objects in a given culture). According to this perspective, the figurative discourse of a text is shaped by transposing some elements of the expressive plane of the macro-semiotics of the world into the semantic plane of the text.

79. In Greimas's semiotic lexicon, a "figure" is an element of the semantic plane of the macro-semiotic structure of the "natural world" that becomes an element of the expressive plane of the micro-semiotic structure of a text. For instance, a horse is part of the semantic plane of the macro-semiotic structure of the "natural world," since it is singled out and differentiated, through language, from other elements that, for instance, share with horses the same semantic field (dogs, cats, donkeys, etc.). Whenever a text uses this semantic unit as an element of the expressive plane of its micro-semiotic structure, according to Greimas's approach to semiotics it turns it into a figure. In simpler words, the "natural" semantic unit is transformed into a semiotic device in order to convey other meanings.

80. See Massimo Leone, *Religious Conversion and Identity: The Semiotic Analysis of Texts* (London: Routledge, 2004); John Weir Perry, *Roots of Renewal in Myth and Madness* (San Francisco: Jossey-Bass, 1976); and William G. McLoughlin, *Revivals, Awakenings, and Reform* (Chicago: University of Chicago Press, 1978); see also Rambo, *Understanding Religious Conversion*, 42, points 3.1.1 and 3.1.2.

81. Ralph Metzner, *Opening to Inner Light: The Transformation of Human Nature and Consciousness* (Los Angeles: Jeremy P. Tarcher, 1986).

82. Such migration of figures is technically called "intertextuality"; Allen Graham, *Intertextuality* (London: Routledge, 2000); Massimo Leone, "L'Inépuisable," in *L'Intertextualité*, ed. Robert Gauthier and Pierre Marillaud (Toulouse: Presses de l'Université, 2004).

83. Leone, *Religious Conversion and Identity*.

84. Edmund S. Morgan, *Visible Saints: The History of a Puritan Idea* (Ithaca, NY: Cornell University Press, 1963), 66–73, 90–92.

85. In Greimas's approach to semiotics, time is less a philosophical problem than a textual effect; Paul Ricoeur, who maintained an intense, critical, and fecund dialogue with Greimas, was the one who most effectively pointed out this shortcoming of his method (a shortcoming that, to a certain extent, affects the whole structuralist project); Algirdas Julien Greimas and Paul Ricoeur, *Tra semiotica ed ermeneutica*, ed. Franscesco Marsciani (Rome: Meltemi, 2000).

86. Webb Keane, *Christian Moderns: Freedom and Fetish in the Mission Encounter* (Berkeley and Los Angeles: University of California Press, 2007). A lack of attention to the materiality of the signifier is evident in Saussure, whose definition of sign tends to deprive it of its relation with the referent and its materiality; it is even more evident in Hjelmslev, whose glossematics tends to transform language dynamics into purely formal mechanisms; and it is certainly evident in Greimas, whose semiotic method exclusively deals with the immanence of texts, putting the problem of their material manifestation into brackets. The last works of Greimas and the most recent trends in his school try to remedy this difficulty by intensifying an already fertile dialogue with Merleau-Ponty's phenomenology; Algirdas J. Greimas, *De l'imperfection* (Périguex: P. Fanlac, 1987); Jacques Fontanille, *Soma et Séma: Figures du corps* (Paris: Maisonneuve & Larose, 2004).

87. This is according to the mathematical meaning of the term "discrete."

88. Greimas sought to tackle the problem of meaning as a non-discrete phenomenon in his last works, which gave rise to two of the most interesting trends in contemporary structuralist (or post-structuralist) semiotics: the semiotics of passions and the semiotics of tensions. The semiotics of passions tries to explain the emotional dimension of narratives (see Harding, "Convicted by the Holy Spirit"), which had been neglected in previous works of Greimas and his school, and admits the possibility of conceiving meaning as emerging from a tension between values rather than from an opposition between them; Algirdas

Julien Greimas and Jacques Fontanille, *Sémiotique des passions: Des états de choses aux états d'âme* (Paris: Seuil, 1991); Isabella Pezzini, *Le passioni del lettore: Saggi di semiotica del testo* (Milan: Bompiani, 1998); id, ed., *Semiotica delle passioni: Saggi di analisi semantica e testuale* (Bologna: Esculapio, 1991); id., ed., *Semiotic Efficacity and the Effectiveness of the Text: From Effects to Affects* (Turnhout: Brepols, 2000); see also Ugo Volli, *Figure del desiderio: Corpo, testo, mancanza* (Milan: Raffaele Cortina, 2002). The semiotics of tensions pushes this theoretical intuition to the greatest extent, claiming that all semantic phenomena actually stem from a tension between two opposite forces; Jacques Fontanille and Claude Zilberberg, *Tension et signification* (Sprimont: Mardaga, 1998); Claude Zilberberg, *Éléments de grammaire tensive* (Limoges: PULIM, 2006).

89. Contemporary semioticians seek to face this challenge by blending the semiotic method with qualitative sociology, ethnology, or anthropology; Silvana Miceli, *In nome del segno: Introduzione alla semiotica della cultura* (Palermo: Sellerio, 2005); Maurizio Del Ninno, ed., *Etnosemiotica* (Rome: Meltemi, 2007); Francesco Marsciani, *Tracciati di etnosemiotica* (Milan: Franco Angeli, 2007); Massimo Leone, "Invisible Frontiers in Contemporary Cities: An Ethno-Semiotic Approach," *International Journal of Interdisciplinary Social Sciences* 4, no. 11 (2010): 59–74.

90. Charles Sanders Sebastian Peirce, *Collected Papers*, 8 vols. (Cambridge, MA: Harvard University Press, 1931–35); *Writings of Charles S. Peirce: A Chronological Edition*, 6 vols. (Bloomington: Indiana University Press, 1982–2000).

91. That is, in a way that approaches fullness without ever attaining it.

92. Webb Keane, "Materialism, Missionaries, and Modern Subjects in Colonial Indonesia," in *Conversion to Modernities: The Globalization of Christianity*, ed. Peter van der Veer (London: Routledge, 1996).

93. Webb Keane, *Christian Moderns: Freedom and Fetish in the Mission Encounter* (Berkeley and Los Angeles: University of California Press, 2007).

94. The Peircian notion of habitus would, therefore, be related to that of "impression point," as outlined by Peter G. Stromberg, "The Impression Point: Synthesis of Symbol and Self," *Ethos: Journal of the Society for Psychological Anthropology* 13 (1985): 56–74.

95. Roger S. Bagnall, "Religious Conversion and Onomastic Change in Early Byzantine Egypt," *Bulletin of the American Society of Papyrologists* 19 (1982): 105–124; Greg H. R. Horsley, "Name Changes as an Indication of Religious Conversion in Antiquity," *Numen* 34 (1987): 1–17; Massimo Leone, "Conversion and Controversy," in *Controversies and Subjectivity*, ed. Pietro Barrotta and Marcelo Dascal (Amsterdam: John Benjamins, 2005).

96. Peter L. Berger, *The Heretical Imperative* (Garden City, NY: Doubleday, 1979).

97. Rambo, *Understanding Religious Conversion*, 30.

98. In Peirce's triadic model of sign, the interpretant is what mediates between the representamen and the object.

99. Founded and animated by Jurij M. Lotman at the University of Tartu, in today's Estonia.

100. Iurij Michajlovich Lotman, *Analysis of the Poetic Text*, trans. D. Barton Johnson (Ann Arbor, MI: Ardis, 1976); id., *The Structure of the Artistic Text*, trans. Ronald Vroon (Ann Arbor: University of Michigan, 1977); id., *The Semiotic of Russian Culture*, ed. Ann Shukman (Ann Arbor: University of Michigan, 1984); id., *Universe of the Mind: A Semiotic Theory of Culture*, trans. Ann Shukman (Bloomington: Indiana University Press, 1990); Iurij Michajlovich Lotman, Lidiia Ia. Ginsburg, and Boris A. Uspenskii, eds., *The Semiotics of Russian Cultural History* (Ithaca, NY: Cornell University Press, 1985).

101. Massimo Leone, "La sfera e il linguaggio: Topologie della cultura," in *Forme e formalizzazione*, proceedings of the XVI congress of the Italian Society for the Philosophy of Language, ed. Elisabetta Gola and Gian Pietro Storari (Cagliari: CUEC, 2010).

102. See Rambo, *Understanding Religious Conversion*, 9: "An individual's core sense of reality is rooted in language, which is the central vehicle for the transmission of cultural perceptions and values."

103. See the concept of "translation" in Steven Kaplan, "The Africanization of Missionary Christianity—History and Typology," *Journal of Religion in Africa* 16 (1986): 166–186; see also Paolo Fabbri, "L'intraducibilità da una fede a un'altra," in id., *Elogio di Babele* (Rome: Meltemi, 2000) as an attempt to study a conversion phenomenon as a case of semiotic translation.

104. "Ethos" here is meant as spiritual, religious, and ethical style of a certain community of believers. See Rambo, *Understanding Religious Conversion*, 172: "I would argue that traditions convey models of conversion and exert more direct influence than the formal theology of the intellectuals"; one of the purposes of semiotics is to describe, analyze, and understand such traditions as systems of meaning.

105. Peter Torop, *La traduzione totale*, trans. Bruno Osimo (Modena: Guaraldi Logos, 2000). See also Margaret Jolly, "Devils, Holy Spirits, and the Swollen God: Translation, Conversion and Colonial Power in the Marist Mission, Vanuatu, 1887–934," in *Conversion to Modernities: The Globalization of Christianity*, ed. Peter van der Veer (London: Routledge, 1996), 234–235: "Missionary linguists typically did not grant the semiotic equality of languages.... Translatability became an index of the spread of God's Word."

106. Rambo, *Understanding Religious Conversion*, 16.

BIBLIOGRAPHY

Arasse, Daniel. *Le Détail: Pour une histoire rapprochée de la peinture*. Paris: Flammarion, 1992.
——. *L'Ambition de Vermeer*. Paris: A. Biro, 1993.
——. *Le Sujet dans le tableau: Essais d'iconographie analytique*. Paris: Flammarion, 1997.
——. *L'Annonciation italienne: Une histoire de perspective*. Paris: Hazan, 1999.
——. *On n'y voit rien: Descriptions: Essai*. Paris: Denoël, 2001.
Asad, Talal. "Comments on Conversion." In *Conversion to Modernities: The Globalization of Christianity*, ed. Peter Van der Veer, 263–274. London: Routledge, 1996.
Bagnall, Roger S. "Religious Conversion and Onomastic Change in Early Byzantine Egypt." *Bulletin of the American Society of Papyrologists* 19 (1982): 105–124.
Bakhtin, Mikhail Mikhailovich. *The Dialogic Imagination: Four Essays*. Trans. Caryl Emerson and Michael Holquist. Austin: University of Texas Press, 1981.
Barbieri, Marcello, ed. *Introduction to Biosemiotics: The New Biological Synthesis*. Dordrecht: Springer, 2007.
Bayne, Sheila Page. *Tears and Weeping: An Aspect of Emotional Climate Reflected in Seventeenth-Century French Literature*. Tübingen: G. Naar, 1981.
——. "Le Rôle des larmes dans le discours de la conversion." In *La Conversion au XVII siècle*, ed. Roger Duchene, 249–262. Marseille: Centre Méridional de Rencontres sur le XVIIe siècle, 1983.
Benveniste, Émile. *Problèmes de linguistique générale I*. Paris: Gallimard, 1966.
——. *Problèmes de linguistique générale II*. Paris: Gallimard, 1971.

Berger, Peter L. *The Heretical Imperative*. Garden City, NY: Doubleday, 1979.

Bertrand, Denis, and Jacques Fontanille, eds. *Régimes sémiotiques de la temporalité: La Flèche brisée du temps*. Paris: PUF, 2006.

Boxer, Charles Ralph. *The Christian Century in Japan: 1549–1650*. Manchester: Carcanet, 1993.

Buckser, Andrew. "Social Conversion and Group Definition in Jewish Copenhagen." In *The Anthropology of Religious Conversion*, ed. Andrew Buckser and Stephen D. Glazier, 69–84. Lanham, MD: Rowman & Littlefield Publishers, 2003.

Calabrese, Omar. *Semiotica della pittura*. Milan: il Saggiatore, 1980.

——. *L'intertestualità in pittura: Una lettura degli Ambasciatori di Holbein*. Urbino: Centro internazionale di semiotica e linguistica, 1984.

——. *Il linguaggio dell'arte*. Milan: Bompiani, 1985.

——. *La macchina della pittura: Pratiche teoriche della rappresentazione figurativa fra Rinascimento e Barocco*. Rome: Laterza, 1985.

——. *L'età neobarocca*. Rome-Bari: Laterza, 1987.

——. *Lezioni di semisimbolico: Come la semiotica analizza le opere d'arte*. Siena: Protagon Editori Toscani, 1999.

——. "Semiotic Aspects of Art History: Semiotics of the Fine Arts." In *Semiotik: Ein Handbuch zu den zeichentheoretischen Grundlagen von Natur und Kultur*, ed. Roland Posner, Klaus Robering, and Thomas A. Sebeok, 3: 3212–3233. Berlin: Walter de Gruyter, 2003.

Cavicchioli, Sandra, ed. "La semiotica dello spazio." Monographic issue of *Versus—Quaderni di studi semiotici* 73/74 (1996).

Chomsky, Noam. *Aspects of the Theory of Syntax*. Cambridge, MA: MIT Press, 1965.

Cohen, Charles Lloyd. *God's Caress: The Psychology of Puritan Religious Experience*. New York: Oxford University Press, 1986.

Coleman, Simon. "Continuous Conversion? The Rhetoric, Practice, and Rhetorical Practice of Charismatic Protestant Conversion." In *The Anthropology of Religious Conversion*, ed. Andrew Buckser and Stephen D. Glazier, 15–28. Lanham, MD: Rowman & Littlefield Publishers, 2003.

Coquet, Jean-Claude. *Le Discours et son sujet*. Paris: Klincksieck, 1984.

Courtès, Joseph. *L'Énonciation comme acte sémiotique*. Limoges: PULIM, 1998.

de Certeau, Michel. *L'Écriture de l'histoire*. Paris: Gallimard, 1975.

——. *La Fable mystique, 1- XVI–XVII siècle*. Paris: Gallimard, 1982.

——. *La Possession de Loudun*. Paris: Gallimard, 1989.

——. *Il Parlare angelico*. Florence: Olschki, 1989.

——. *L'Étranger ou l'union dans la différence*. Paris: Desclée de Brouwer, 1991.

——. *La Faiblesse de croire*. Paris: Seuil, 2003.

Del Ninno, Maurizio, ed. *Etnosemiotica*. Rome: Meltemi, 2007.

Delorme, Jean, and Geoltrain, Pierre. "Le Discours religieux." In *Sémiotique: L'École de Paris*, ed. Jean-Claude Coquet, 103–126. Paris: Hachette, 1982.

Dumézil, Georges. *Mythe et épopée: L'Idéologie des trois functions dans les épopées des peuples indo-européens*. Paris: Gallimard, 1968.

Eco, Umberto. *Trattato di semiotica generale*. Milan: Bompiani, 1975.

——. *Lector in fabula: La cooperazione interpretativa nei testi narrativi*. Milan: Bompiani, 1979.

Fabbri, Paolo. "L'intraducibilità da una fede a un'altra." In id., *Elogio di Babele*, 81–98. Rome: Meltemi, 2000.

Fawcett, Thomas. *The Symbolic Language of Religion*. Minneapolis, MN: Augsburg, 1971.

.,-.

Fontanille, Jacques. *Les Espaces subjectifs: Introduction à la sémiotique de l'observateur (discours-peinture-cinéma)*. Paris: Hachette, 1989.

———. *Modes du sensible et syntaxe figurative*. Limoges: PULIM, 1999.

———. *Soma et Séma: Figures du corps*. Paris: Maisonneuve & Larose, 2004.

Fontanille, Jacques, and Claude Zilberberg. *Tension et signification*. Sprimont: Mardaga, 1998.

Fredriksen, Paula. "Paul and Augustine: Conversion narratives, orthodox traditions, and the retrospective self." *Journal of Theological Studies*, new series, 37 (1986): 3–34.

Graham, Allen. *Intertextuality*. London: Routledge, 2000.

Greimas, Algirdas Julien. *Sémantique structurale: Recherche et méthode*. Paris: Larousse, 1966.

———. *Du sens*. Paris: Seuil, 1970.

———. *Maupassant: La Sémiotique du texte, exercices pratiques*. Paris: Seuil, 1975.

———. "Pour une sémiotique topologique." In id., *Sémiotique et sciences sociales*, 129–158. Paris: Seuil, 1976.

———. *Du sens II: Essais sémiotiques*. Paris: Seuil, 1983.

———. *De l'imperfection*. Périguex: P. Fanlac, 1987.

Greimas, Algirdas Julien, and Jacques Fontanille. *Sémiotique des passions: Des états de choses aux états d'âme*. Paris: Seuil, 1991.

Greimas, Algirdas Julien, and Paul Ricoeur. *Tra semiotica ed ermeneutica*. Ed. Franscesco Marsciani. Rome: Meltemi, 2000.

Groupe μ (J. Dubois, F. Edeline, J. M. Klinkenberg, P. Minguet, F. Pire, and H. Trinon). *Rhétorique générale*. Paris: Larousse, 1970.

Groupe μ (F. Edeline, J. M. Klinkenberg, and P. Minguet). *Traité du signe visuel*. Paris: Seuil, 1992.

Harding, Susan. "Convicted by the Holy Spirit—The Rhetoric of Fundamental Baptist Conversion." *American Ethnologist* 14, no. 1 (1987): 167–182.

Hjelmslev, Louis. *Omkring sprogteoriens grundlæggelse*. Copenhagen: Ejnar Munksgaard, 1943.

Horsley, Greg H. R. "Name Changes as an Indication of Religious Conversion in Antiquity." *Numen* 34 (1987): 1–17.

Hunsaker Hawkins, Anne. *Archetypes of Conversion: The Autobiographies of Augustine, Bunyan, and Merton*. Lewisburg, PA: Bucknell University Press, 1985.

Jennings, Theodore W. "On Ritual Knowledge." *Journal of Religion*, 62 (1982): 113–127.

Jolly, Margaret. "Devils, Holy Spirits, and the Swollen God: Translation, Conversion and Colonial Power in the Marist Mission, Vanuatu, 1887–934." In *Conversion to Modernities: The Globalization of Christianity*, ed. Peter van der Veer, 231–262. London: Routledge, 1996.

Kaplan, Steven. "The Africanization of Missionary Christianity—History and Typology." *Journal of Religion in Africa* 16 (1986): 166–186.

Keane, Webb. "Materialism, Missionaries, and Modern Subjects in Colonial Indonesia." In *Conversion to Modernities: The Globalization of Christianity*, ed. Peter van der Veer, 137–170. London: Routledge, 1996.

———. *Christian Moderns: Freedom and Fetish in the Mission Encounter*. Berkeley and Los Angeles: University of California Press, 2007.

Lea, Henry Charles. *A History of the Inquisition of Spain*. 4 vols. New York: Macmillan Company, 1906–1907.

Leone, Massimo. *Religious Conversion and Identity: The Semiotic Analysis of Texts*. London: Routledge, 2004.

———. "L'Inépuisable." In *L'Intertextualité*, ed. Robert Gauthier and Pierre Marillaud, 249–262. Toulouse: Presses de l'Université, 2004.

——. "Conversion and Controversy." In *Controversies and Subjectivity*, ed. Pietro Barrotta and Marcelo Dascal, 91–114. Amsterdam: John Benjamins, 2005.

——. "Le mutazioni del cuore: esperienza, narrazione e narratività della conversione religiosa." In *Narrazione ed esperienza: Per una semiotica della vita quotidiana*. Proceedings of the 34th Congress of the Italian Association for Semiotic Studies held in Arcavacata di Rende, Nov. 2006. *E/C*, online journal of the Italian Association for Semiotic Studies, vol. 20 (2007). http://www.ec-aiss.it/archivio/tipologico/atti.php.

——. "Prefazione." In "Actants, Actors, Agents—the Meaning of Action and the Action of Meaning: From Theories to Territories," ed. Massimo Leone, 11–28. Monographic issue of *Lexia*, new series, 3–4 (Dec. 2009).

——. "Agency, Communication, and Revelation." In "Actants, Actors, Agents—the Meaning of Action and the Action of Meaning: From Theories to Territories," ed. Massimo Leone, 77–94. Monographic issue of *Lexia*, new series, 3–4 (Dec. 2009).

——, ed. "Actants, Actors, Agents—the Meaning of Action and the Action of Meaning: From Theories to Territories." Monographic issue of *Lexia*, new series, 3–4 (Dec. 2009).

——. "Remarks for a Semiotics of the Veil." *Chinese Semiotic Studies* 4, no. 2 (2010): 258–278.

——. *Saints and Signs: A Semiotic Reading of Conversion in Early Modern Catholicism*. Berlin: Walter de Gruyter, 2010.

——. "Invisible Frontiers in Contemporary Cities: An Ethno-Semiotic Approach." *International Journal of Interdisciplinary Social Sciences* 4, no. 11 (2010): 59–74.

——. "La sfera e il linguaggio: Topologie della cultura." In *Forme e formalizzazione*, proceedings of the XVI congress of the Italian Society for the Philosophy of Language, ed. Elisabetta Gola and Gian Pietro Storari, 67–74. Cagliari: CUEC, 2010.

——. "La Conversion de Saint Paul comme Pathosformel théologique." In *L'Humanisme dans tous ses états ou la spiritualité plurielle*, Festschrift in honor of Raymond Baustert, ed. Marion Colas-Blaise et al. Tübingen: Gunter Narr Verlag, forthcoming.

Lévi-Strauss, Claude. *Anthropologie structurale*. Paris: Plon, 1958.

Lotman, Iurij Michajlovich. *Analysis of the Poetic Text*. Trans. D. Barton Johnson. Ann Arbor, MI: Ardis, 1976.

——. *The Structure of the Artistic Text*. Trans. Ronald Vroon. Ann Arbor: University of Michigan, 1977.

——. *The Semiotic of Russian Culture*. Ed. Ann Shukman. Ann Arbor: University of Michigan, 1984.

——. *Universe of the Mind: A Semiotic Theory of Culture*. Trans. Ann Shukman. Bloomington: Indiana University Press, 1990.

Lotman, Iurij Michajlovich, Lidiia Ia. Ginsburg, and Boris A. Uspenskii, eds. *The Semiotics of Russian Cultural History*. Ithaca, NY: Cornell University Press, 1985.

Luria, Keith P. "The Politics of Protestant Conversion to Catholicism in Seventeenth-Century France." In *Conversion to Modernities: The Globalization of Christianity*, ed. Peter van der Veer, 23–46. London: Routledge, 1996.

Manetti, Giovanni. *La teoria dell'enunciazione: L'origine del concetto e alcuni più recenti sviluppi*. Siena: Protagon, 1998.

Marin, Louis. *Études sémiologiques, écritures, peintures*. Paris: Klincksieck, 1972.

——. *Lectures traversières*. Paris: Albin Michel, 1992.

——. *De la représentation*. Paris: Gallimard-Seuil, 1994.

——. *Philippe de Champaigne ou la présence cachée*. Paris: Hazan, 1995.

——. *Sublime Poussin*. Paris: Seuil, 1995.

——. L'Écriture de soi: Ignace de Loyola, Montaigne, Stendhal, Roland Barthes. Paris: PUF, 1999.

Marsciani, Francesco. Tracciati di etnosemiotica. Milan: Franco Angeli, 2007.

McLoughlin, William G. Revivals, Awakenings, and Reform. Chicago: University of Chicago Press, 1978.

Mehuyas Ginio, Alisa, ed. Jews, Christians and Muslims in the Mediterranean World after 1492. London: Cass, 1992.

Metzner, Ralph. Opening to Inner Light: The Transformation of Human Nature and Consciousness. Los Angeles: Jeremy P. Tarcher, 1986.

Miceli, Silvana. In nome del segno: Introduzione alla semiotica della cultura. Palermo: Sellerio, 2005.

Morgan, Edmund S. Visible Saints: The History of a Puritan Idea. Ithaca, NY: Cornell University Press, 1963.

Ono, Ayako. La Notion d'énonciation chez Émile Benveniste. Limoges: Lambert-Lucas, 2007.

Panier, Louis. Écriture, foi, révélation: Le Statut de l'Écriture dans la révélation. Lyon: Profac, 1973.

——. La Vie Éternelle: Une Figure dans la 1ère Épître de Saint Jean. Paris: Groupe de recherches sémiolinguistiques, 1983.

——. Récit et commentaires de la tentation de Jésus au désert: Approche sémiotique du discours interprétatif: étude. Paris: Cerf, 1984.

——. La Naissance du fils de Dieu: Sémiotique et théologie discursive—lecture de Luc 1–2. Paris: Cerf, 1991.

——, ed. Le Temps de la lecture: Exégèse biblique et sémiotique—recueil d'hommages pour Jean Delorme. Paris: Cerf, 1993.

——, ed. Les Lettres dans la Bible et dans la littérature: Actes du Colloque de Lyon, 3–5 juillet 1996. Paris: Cerf, 1999.

——, ed. Récits et figures dans la Bible: Colloque d'Urbino. Lyon: Profac–Cadir, 1999.

Patte, Daniel. What Is Structural Exegesis? Philadelphia: Fortress Press, 1976.

——. Carré sémiotique et syntaxe narrative: Exégèse structurale de Marc, ch. 5. Besancon: Groupe de recherches semio-linguistiques, 1981.

——. Paul's Faith and the Power of the Gospel: A Structural Introduction to the Pauline Letters. Philadelphia: Fortress Press, 1983.

——. The Religious Dimensions of Biblical Texts: Greimas's Structural Semiotics and Biblical Exegesis. Atlanta, GA: Scholars Press, 1990.

——. Structural Exegesis for New Testament Critics. Minneapolis: Fortress Press, 1990.

Patte, Daniel, and Gay Volney. "Religious studies." In Encyclopedic Dictionary of Semiotics, ed. Thomas A. Sebeok, 3: 797–807. Berlin: Mouton de Gruyter, 1986.

Peirce, Charles Sanders Sebastian. Collected Papers, 8 vols. Cambridge, MA: Harvard University Press, 1931–1935.

——. Writings of Charles S. Peirce: A Chronological Edition, 6 vols. Bloomington: Indiana University Press, 1982–2000.

Perry, John Weir. Roots of Renewal in Myth and Madness. San Francisco: Jossey-Bass, 1976.

Pezzini, Isabella. Le passioni del lettore: Saggi di semiotica del testo. Milan: Bompiani, 1998.

——, ed. Semiotica delle passioni: Saggi di analisi semantica e testuale. Bologne: Esculapio, 1991.

——, ed. Semiotic Efficacity and the Effectiveness of the Text: From Effects to Affects. Turnhout: Brepols, 2000.

Pozzi, Giovanni. La rosa in mano al professore. Fribourg: Éditions Universitaires, 1974.

——. La parola dipinta. Milan: Adelphi, 1981.

——. Rose e gigli per Maria: Un'antifona dipinta. Bellinzona: Casagrande, 1987.

——. Sull'orlo del visibile parlare. Milan: Adelphi, 1993.

——. *Alternatim*. Milan: Adelphi, 1996.

——. *Grammatica e retorica dei santi*. Milan: Vita e pensiero, 1997.

Propp, Vladimir Yakovlevich. *Morphologies of the Folktale*. Trans. Laurence Scott. Bloomington: Research Center, Indiana University, 1958.

Rafael, Vicente. *Contracting Colonialism: Translation and Christian Conversion in Tagalog Society under Early Spanish Rule*. Durham, NC: Duke University Press, 1993.

Rambo, Lewis R. *Understanding Religious Conversion*. New Haven: Yale University Press, 1993.

Robertson, Roland. *Meaning and Change: Explorations in the Cultural Sociology of Modern Societies*. New York: New York University Press, 1978.

Saussure, Ferdinand de. *Cours de linguistique générale*. Ed. Tullio de Mauro. Paris: Payot, 1972.

Stanley, Brian. "Conversion to Christianity: The Colonization of the Mind?" *International Review of Mission* 92, no. 366 (July 2003): 315–331.

Stoichita, Victor I. *Visionary Experience in the Golden Age of Spanish Art*. London: Reaktion Books, 1995.

——. *L'Instauration du tableau: Métapeinture à l'aube des temps modernes*. Geneva: Droz, 1999.

——. *Brève histoire de l'ombre*. Geneva: Droz, 2000.

Stromberg, Peter G. "The Impression Point: Synthesis of Symbol and Self." *Ethos: Journal of the Society for Psychological Anthropology* 13 (1985): 56–74.

Tippett, Alan R. "Conversion as a Dynamic Process in Christian Mission." *Missiology* 2 (1977): 203–221.

Torop, Peeter. *La traduzione totale*. Trans. Bruno Osimo. Modena: Guaraldi Logos, 2000.

Volli, Ugo. *Figure del desiderio: Corpo, testo, mancanza*. Milan: Raffaele Cortina, 2002.

——. *Manuale di Semiotica*. Rome: GLF Editori Laterza, 2003.

Wittgenstein, Ludwig. *Philosophische Untersuchungen: Philosophical Investigations*. English trans. Gertrude E. M. Anscombe. 3rd ed. Malden, MA: Blackwell Publishing, 2001.

Zilberberg, Claude. *Éléments de grammaire tensive*. Limoges: PULIM, 2006.

CHAPTER 17

POLITICAL SCIENCE AND RELIGIOUS CONVERSION

TIMOTHY J. STEIGENGA

FORTY years ago, asking about religious conversion and politics would likely have drawn primarily blank stares from a room full of political scientists. For most political scientists, the impact of religion on politics was considered either a foregone conclusion (i.e., Catholicism correlates with authoritarianism) or largely irrelevant due to ongoing processes of modernization and secularization.[1] Today, religion plays a critical role across the subfields of the discipline. In the subfields of American and Comparative Politics, Kenneth Wald, Ted Jelen, Clyde Wilcox, Ronald Inglehart, Robert Putnam, Anthony Gill, Robert Wuthnow, and a host of other political scientists have integrated religion as a critical element in studies of civic participation, political mobilization, and public attitudes.[2] In the field of International Relations, Samuel Huntington's *Clash of Civilizations* has reinvigorated debate over the future of religion in intergroup conflict or cooperation.[3]

Although political science recently has come up to speed in understanding the importance of religion as an independent variable explaining political outcomes, the discipline has paid scant attention to the process or meaning of religious conversion. Although political scientists have made valiant attempts to capture and categorize the impact of religious change on politics, they have, for the most part, assiduously avoided the fact that religious conversion is the complex process that frequently drives larger processes of religious change. Issues of church and state, modernity and secularism, religion and social movements, and fundamentalism and religious conflict have spurred hundreds of studies, but far less attention has been paid to questions related to how the process of conversion impacts individual and collective beliefs and actions. The dual goals of this chapter are to provide a brief overview of the recent headway that has been made in the study of politics and religious change and to point to areas where the study of conversion can enrich (and likely complicate) our methods and conclusions. In other words, I seek to outline where we have been in the study of religion and politics, where we are now, and how we might move forward by incorporating new methods and concepts drawn from the study of religious conversion into our political analyses.

Religious conversion has a rich history of study in the disciplines of sociology, anthropology, and the interdisciplinary field of religious studies.[4] Within this literature, there is a general consensus that conversion involves a process of significant personal change in beliefs, values, and, to some degree, personal identity and worldview.[5] However, questions about how to measure these changes (self-identification, degree of commitment, beliefs and convictions, demonstration events, and discourse or rhetorical indicators), which level of analysis to utilize (individual, societal, cultural, network location, or market analysis), and the role of personal agency versus external contextual factors remain matters of significant dispute and debate within the fields of sociology, anthropology, psychology, and religious studies.[6] Bringing political science scholarship and empirical case studies into dialogue with this existing literature on religious conversion helps to establish a set of guidelines for studying conversion that can direct further scholarship and generate improved methods and hypotheses for studying the political impact of religious change. In particular, I argue that the explicit and implicit models of conversion assumed in political science research conceive of religious conversion as a single discrete event, fundamentally mischaracterizing the nature of conversion. Conversion is a multiply determined and evolving phenomenon that demands a more complex and multifaceted research methodology than is currently employed in most political science research. Because of this complexity, political scientists would be well served by reevaluating the categories and concepts utilized for measuring the political and social effects of religious conversion. While these propositions may seem self-evident to scholars of religious studies, anthropologists, and sociologists, they remain far outside of the mainstream of political science research on religion and politics.

THE EVOLVING STUDY OF RELIGION AND POLITICS

Any analysis of the "politics" of religious conversion must begin with a larger discussion of the evolution of the study of religion and politics in general. As noted earlier, this is because the relationship between religion and politics has only slowly and haltingly made its way onto the agenda of mainstream political science. Political scientist Ronald Inglehart sheds some light on this tendency. According to Inglehart, "contemporary social scientists tend to underestimate the historical importance of religion, both because they are social scientists, habituated to viewing the world from a secular and scientific viewpoint, and because they are contemporary and live in societies in which the functions of religion have diminished drastically."[7] As Inglehart points out, political scientists trained in the secularized societies of Europe and the United States operated for years in an intellectual and social climate that made them uncomfortable with religious explanations for political behavior. At best, religion was considered to be ana-lytically separate from politics. At worst, religion was perceived as simple, irrelevant, or irrational.

Trends within the discipline mirrored these tendencies. Early modernization theo-rists predicted that the salience of religion and ethnicity would fade as culture, ideas, and economic practices were transported from "modern" to "traditional" societies.[8] Partly as a backlash against these predictions in the face of contradictory evidence, the theoretical pendulum soon swung in the other direction. For very different reasons, modernization theorists and dependency theorists embraced different versions of the "secularization thesis" and thus concluded that the significance of religion would inevi-tably decline in developing countries.

How Political Science "Found Religion"

The late 1970s and early 1980s brought a renewed interest in the study of cultural and religious politics, as events in the United States, the Middle East, and Latin America forced analysts to reevaluate the secularization thesis and reexamine the significance of religious variables in explaining political outcomes. In the United States, the rise of Jerry Falwell's Moral Majority (1979–1989) caught many political commentators off guard. Upset over Supreme Court losses on abortion and school prayer, conservative evangeli-cal Protestants in the United States began to organize around issues they perceived as threats to "traditional values."[9] Televangelist Pat Robertson's 1988 presidential bid served to galvanize this conservative religio-political movement. While conventional wisdom at the time held that Robertson's loss and the scandals associated with televangelists Jimmy Swaggart and Jim Bakker would mark the end of the influence of the religious right, most political scientists (and campaign managers) now frame this constituency as a permanent part of the American political system. As David Leege argues and recent US elections have demonstrated, religion has played, and will continue to play, a crucial role in electoral alignments in the United States.[10]

In a very different context, the Islamic revolution in Iran and the ensuing recogni-tion of the spreading influence of a more militant and political Islam also forced ana-lysts to reconsider the importance of religious motivations in political life. According to Ali Banuazizi's study of the Islamic revolution in Iran, the "traditional" traits associated with Islamic fundamentalists, such as "a lack of personal efficacy, passivity, fatalism, pre-occupation with personal and family affairs, and a sense of isolation from the outside world," did not limit the political efficacy of the Shiite Islamic movement.[11] Banuazizi's findings have been supported and extended in multiple studies of Islamic and Christian millenarian religio-political movements in different national contexts, echoing the conclusion that secularization is certainly not the predominant trend in developed or developing societies.[12] Across the Middle East and Asia, revolutionary Islamic groups have challenged secular power. In Israel, tensions between the most orthodox tradition-alists and other Jewish groups have led to open conflicts and have thwarted multiple movements toward peace accords. In India, ascending waves of Hindu nationalism led to the 1992 destruction of the Babri Masjib mosque and subsequent riots targeting Muslim and Christian minorities. In Latin America, followers of liberation theology formed social movements and challenged political authorities from Brazil to Central America.[13]

More recently, analysts such as Mark Juergensmeyer, Samuel Huntington, and Bassam Tibi have highlighted the patterns of behavior and ideology among disparate nationalist religious groups willing to use violence to achieve their religio-political goals. Evaluating religio-political movements from Hamas in the Palestinian territories, to US Christian militia movements, to Aum Shinrikyo in Japan, these authors predict that conflicts driven by religious fundamentalism are clearly on the upswing and likely to multiply in the future.[14] For the most part, these authors assume that religious fundamentalism, in its multiple forms, is likely to undermine or to directly compete with democratic governance around the world. Claims such as these have moved the study of religion and culture back into the mainstream of political science.

What Have We Learned?

Two broad insights can be gleaned from the recent literature on religion and politics. First, religious variables persist as important motivations in political life. While debates over secularization continue, the notion that secularization is an inevitable law of history has been largely abandoned. Religion has not faded away in the developed or the developing world. To the contrary, much of the world is experiencing what one author has termed a "global religious revival."[15]

This is not to say that theories of secularization have been put fully to rest. To a significant degree, differing perspectives on secularization frame the primary approaches political scientists have taken to understand the interactions between religion and politics. On the one hand, some proponents of the religious economy approach argue that the secularization thesis should be scrapped altogether, pointing to empirical evidence (even among European countries) that does not necessarily reflect downward trends in religiosity.[16] Correspondingly, these scholars propose a focus on religious suppliers and their institutional interests as a fruitful area for comparative research on the political outcomes of religious politics.[17]

On the other hand, numerous scholars continue to explain the rise of fundamentalism and attendant religious activism in terms of reactions to modernization and secularization.[18] They argue that combinations of material insecurity, encroaching foreign values, urbanization, or other forms of displacement generate social anomie and a greater openness to religious alternatives. For the most part, this is a familiar account and one that tends to emphasize the "content" of religious beliefs, institutions, and practices as the driving factors behind the political trajectory of religious movements.

Straddling these two approaches, authors such as Pippa Norris and Ronald Inglehart have endeavored to salvage portions of the secularization theory, arguing that secularization is related to rising levels of human security. In other words, there is a correlation between levels of personal safety, having basic needs met, physical and economic security, and greater secularity. Despite this correlation, the overall trend is toward less secularization in the developing world due to high levels of insecurity and demographic trends. Thus the world is becoming less secular due to population growth in developing (insecure) areas, while its most secure and developed nations (with the exception of the United States) are following the path charted by earlier secularization theorists.[19] Norris and Inglehart offer a bridge between supply-side approaches to understanding religious politics and those that are focused on the role of personal security and ideational factors.

The second broad finding arising from the literature on religion and politics is that religion represents more than a mere epiphenomenon, obfuscating political or economic factors previously assumed to be more "true" explanations of political outcomes. While religion is clearly not the only variable explaining most political beliefs or behaviors, it cannot be ignored if we wish to improve our understanding of political outcomes. This argument in no way implies that religious variables are necessarily prior to political or economic variables or that causality does not run in both directions.[20] But it has become the conventional wisdom in political science that religious beliefs, religious practices, and religious affiliation may be considered independent variables in their own right. At the same time, the institutional constraints and interests of religious actors, individual religious preferences, and state regulation of religious actors all condition and help to explain the outcomes of religious politics. A brief review of recent studies in American and comparative politics highlight some of the key findings on politics and religious change.

Highlighting Insights from the Literature on Politics and Religious Change

If there is one thing on which most political analysts agree, it is that the United States remains a unique case in terms of religion and politics. In part due to its outlier status as one of the most modern and yet most religious states in the world, the United States has been the subject of myriad studies producing significant findings on the links between religion and politics. Wald, Owen, and Hill demonstrate that church attendance can "maximize behavioral contagion and thus disseminate common political outlooks."[21] In other words, those who attend church frequently may be more likely to pick up the political cues provided by their religious leaders and peers.[22] At the same time, denominational affiliation has also been found to have a significant effect on political affiliations and activities. In their far-reaching volume explaining the role of civic skills in political participation in the United States (*Voice and Equality*), Sidney Verba et al. suggest that denominational affiliation with Catholicism explains lower levels of political participation among Latinos.[23] Other authors have outlined the relationships between denominational affiliation and political partisanship,[24] political conservatism, and support of the Moral Majority platform.[25] Specifically, members of Pentecostal churches have been found to hold more conservative political beliefs than other Protestants.[26] Political scientist Ted Jelen found that doctrinal orthodoxy (defined as adherence to the truth claims of orthodox Christianity) had a conservatizing effect on seven of nine public policy issues he evaluated in his study.[27]

On the other hand, some scholars have questioned the focus on affiliation and beliefs, pointing to the role of social capital and associational participation in religious institutions as the driving factors behind political engagement.[28] For these authors, it is relationships, networks of information, and the possibility of recruitment offered through religious participation that explain variance across ethnic and sociocultural groups belonging to the same religion or denomination.

David E. Campbell provides a compelling argument that reconciles these competing explanations, at least in the case of white evangelical Protestants. According to Campbell, in the case of "strict churches" (such as white evangelical churches),[29] the cost of high participation in church activities limits members' constant availability for political causes but "thickens social networks that can be used sporadically for rapid and intensive political mobilization."[30] In other words, evangelicals may tend to be less politically active than non-evangelicals on average, but their networks make them available for short-term mobilization around key issues, a trend that was not lost on campaign strategists during the 2000 and 2004 US presidential elections.

In sum, studies of religion and politics in the United States illustrate that religious vitality is strong while also suggesting that beliefs and intensity may be better explanatory variables than institutional affiliation for understanding political orientation and outcomes. Furthermore, religious networks play a key role in explaining political mobilization. Notably lacking in this literature, however, is an emphasis on the act, process, or meaning of religious conversion or how these factors may interact with variables posited as driving political outcomes. For example, do the same networks that lead to conversion also play a role in political mobilization? Do the beliefs posited as driving political orientations cross pre- and post-conversion time periods for individuals? As I argue below, a more specific focus on conversion can help us to answer these questions and begin to untangle the knotty problem of directionality in the relations between religion and politics.

Religion and Politics Worldwide

The intensified focus on religion in comparative and international politics has been extremely fruitful, producing numerous cross-national generalizations and new hypotheses. A number of studies have revealed the key role of religion as an explanatory variable for understanding political mobilization, policy disputes, identity politics, and other important political outcomes. In *Religion and Politics in Comparative Perspective*, Ted Jelen and Clyde Wilcox divide the role of religion into two broad categories: the "priestly" or accommodating role of religion and the "prophetic" or oppositional role of religious politics.[31] For the most part, their case studies suggest that there is very little ongoing empirical support for what Peter Berger termed the "sacred canopy" model of religion and politics, where religion provides a sense of widely shared values that create social consensus on political issues.[32] Even in cases such as Iran and Ireland, where single religious traditions remain dominant, competing elements within those traditions lead to political differences that make the purely "priestly" role of religion problematic. The more prominent trend in modern religious politics seems to be that the closer a religious tradition comes to exercising state power, the more theological and social differences tend to erode the political unity of the movement.[33] In contexts of pluralistic religious competition, political outcomes vary from healthy democratic contestation (as in the majority of Western European cases) to divisive and potentially violent battles over the appropriate role of religion in politics (as in the case of the religious right in the United States or Hindu nationalists in India).

As noted earlier, perspectives on secularization tend to drive the focus on factors offered for these tendencies within religious politics. Many authors focus on the content of religious beliefs and practices to explain political outcomes. For example, Maria Toyoda and Aji Tanaka note the key distinctions between the universalistic and monotheistic nature of Islam, Judaism, and Christianity and the syncretism of the Japanese Buddhist and Shinto religious traditions. In the case of Japan, they argue that the syncretism of Buddhist and Shinto traditions effectively mutes political conflict along religious lines. On the other hand, monotheistic traditions such as Christianity or Islam have greater immunity to syncretism and greater propensity for religiously motivated political conflict.[34]

Turning to those monotheistic traditions, Jelen and Wilcox posit that "intramural" conflicts between religious groups, such as Pentecostal/Catholic competition in Latin America or issues of state protections and subsidies in Western Europe, are more easily played out within the bounds of democratic politics. Conflicts between fundamentally different religious traditions, each with their own universalist and exclusivist claims, however, are likely to elicit outright political conflict that may destabilize democratic politics (as in India) or handcuff policy initiatives (as in the case of immigration policy in Western Europe or peace accords in Israel).[35]

These conflicts become particularly acute when religious majorities or secular states make use of state legal powers (or extra-legal means) to deny rights or services to particular religious groups. From local or national authorities who implement *sharia* laws against religious conversion (as in Malaysia or Afghanistan) to ostensible "freedom of religion" legislation that actually has the opposite effect (such as the recent moves by Indian states to require converters out of Hinduism to register or risk civil penalties), we see political factors dictating the boundaries of religious choices. At the same time, elements of the George W. Bush administration's "faith-based initiative" have internationalized these tensions through directing aid to Christian organizations in primarily Muslim areas of the world. Whether by design or through contacts and knowledge of the rules and regulations, Christian organizations have recently received significant portions of United States Agency for International Development (USAID) and private

funding in Indonesia, Afghanistan, Pakistan, and Iraq, dwarfing the amount of aid allot-
ted to Muslim organizations.[36] It should come as no surprise that tensions over the rights
and regulations related to proselytism, conversion, and the links between religious organizations and geopolitical actors have become major topics of debate for policymakers,
NGO activists, and religious leaders engaged in interfaith dialogues.[37]

Some of the most influential studies on religion and politics focus specifically on
the politics of fundamentalist religious movements, arguing that fundamentalist religious nationalism leaves little room for political tolerance or popular sovereignty and is
likely to lead to increased clashes within and between secular and democratic states and
religio-political movements.[38] In broad strokes (generally aimed at Islamic fundamentalism but also applied to the growth of Pentecostalism in Latin America and Asia), the
argument is that conservative, anti-democratic, and illiberal politics emerge from fundamentalist groups that feel threatened by modernization, secularization, globalization,
or the privatization of religion.[39]

As Anthony Gill has pointed out, however, this line of argument over-predicts both
the growth of fundamentalist religious movements and their political trajectories.[40]
After all, if the impact of modernization is the driving force behind the growth of fundamentalism, how do we account for those who choose other religious, cultural, or
political options in the face of unwelcome or feared changes? Furthermore, the politics
of fundamentalism may not be quite as monolithically frightening as many accounts
would have us believe. Militant fundamentalists are generally minorities within their
faith tradition and are frequently counterbalanced by co-religionists who generally
accept and play by the rules of democratic politics.[41]

For Gill and other proponents of the religious economy approach, the explanation
for disparate reactions to broad processes of modernization and globalization lies
within the foundational interests of religious actors, religious institutions, and the other
political institutions (states, interest groups, parties, etc.) with whom they interact.
Predictions and findings utilizing the religious economy approach focus on the impact
of government regulation of religion on religious participation (offering an alternative
explanation for secularization), strategic choices in church–state relationships (such as
Gill's analysis of national Catholic episcopacies' choices to support or oppose authoritarian regimes in Latin America), and product specialization among religious producers (such as Andrew Chesnut's work on the "pneumacentric" elements of Pentecostalism
and African diaspora religions in Latin America and the Caribbean).[42]

Both the religious economy approach and broader approaches working within the
secularization school rely upon implicit assumptions about religious conversion in
order to reach their respective conclusions about the relations between religion and politics. Market theorists generally explain conversion in terms of exogenous constraints
upon utility-maximizing religious consumers with set preferences. Thus, conversion is
about rationally pursuing spiritual satisfaction while balancing other resources.[43] Most
of the work focusing on the political impact of religious beliefs, intensity, and fundamentalism, however, implicitly accepts some version of the "anomie" perspective on
religious conversion. For these authors, it is assumed that conversion represents an

adaptive response to varying external structures and processes. A brief overview of these two perspectives can assist us in understanding what is assumed in most political analyses of religious change, why those assumptions lead to different predictions, and how they might be reconciled.

EXPLICIT AND IMPLICIT MODELS OF RELIGIOUS CONVERSION

The religious market approach is not well received by many scholars in the field of religious studies precisely because it models religious institutions as primarily utility-maximizing firms and converts as religious consumers. Despite charges of reductionism leveled by some scholars, this approach is noteworthy because, unlike other approaches, it lays out an explicit theory of conversion. Focusing on individual choices in a pluralistic religious market, Laurence Iannaccone explains conversion to "strict" (and in many cases fundamentalist) religions in terms of the role that exclusivity, commitment, and participation play in deterring free-riders—those who would benefit from the religious institution without adding significantly to (and sometimes even reducing) its resources.[44] Thus, we can understand conversion, particularly the kind of conversion that has concerned most political analysts (to fundamentalist or strict religions), in terms of the interactions between institutional interests and rational religious consumers. Furthermore, Iannaccone predicts that individuals with low levels of religious capital (the skills, networks, and other factors associated with religious production and consumption) will be the most likely to convert.[45] Because the focus is on the supply side of the equation (and the constraints on actors' choices and resources), the model assumes that demand for religious goods is constant across time and space.

Depending on the unit of analysis (utility-maximizing individuals, churches, or states), authors in the religious economy school emphasize the production and consumption of religious goods. In the context of Latin America, for example, the Catholic Church is analogous to a "lazy monopoly" which has recently faced challenges from other religious providers.[46] Thus, the rational-actor perspective can be utilized both to explain Pentecostal growth, correlated with market openings where states deregulated their religious markets, and to theorize about and predict the actions of state authorities and the institutional Catholic Church.[47]

Despite critics' claims, most rational actor theorists do not purport to explain the specific intellectual or emotional processes involved in religious conversion. Rather, the utility-maximization assumption is considered valid based on whether it effectively predicts religious behavior. Imperfect information and other constraints on rational decision-making aside, market theorists suggest that the ultimate proof of their assumptions is in the empirical pudding.[48] Are pluralist religious markets the most religiously vibrant? Does religious regulation provide a better explanation of trends toward secularism than other factors? The data on these questions remain mixed, suggesting that, at a minimum, the "inelastic demand" assumption should be dropped, opening the door to an examination of the ways that culture, context, and nonreligious alternatives both impact demand for religious goods and condition religious choices.[49]

Market as Analogy

Andrew Chesnut's recent work is one example of a less strict market approach that sets out to explain the recent growth not only of Pentecostalism but also of Afro-diasporan religions, and the Charismatic Renewal in the Catholic Church.[50] While Chesnut maintains that he is still working with the assumptions of the religious economy model, he has actually opened up a larger set of questions about the way local context interacts with religious supply to increase the attractiveness of new religions to potential converts. In other words, if we are allowed to assume that demand for religious goods is higher in some areas than in others, it opens the possibility for an evaluation of both sides of the market (supply and demand), new areas of product specialization and marketing strategies by religious "firms," and the religious preferences of individuals.[51] Therefore, the different intensity of religious demand should be studied cross-nationally as well as cross-regionally and cross-locally. Demand shifts and who responds to them are not foregone conclusions. Understanding who converts and when will depend on local contexts, network connections, and the preference order of potential religious consumers.

The key to this approach is that it opens the door to integrating the content of religion into a model of religious conversion. Thus, the spiritual, supernatural, experiential, and doctrinal elements of religious options are posited as factors attracting converts, alongside institutional and resource constraints and trade-offs in religious capital. It is worth noting that crude versions of these arguments have also drawn criticism for either reifying cultural primitivism or ignoring critical differences in local culture.[52] In other words, the pneumatic elements of Pentecostalism and African diaspora religions that Chesnut posits as attracting converts may hold very different meanings for indigenous Pentecostals in Chiapas and black Brazilians in the slums of Rio de Janeiro. The fact that these religious groups are gaining converts in both places requires a deeper explanation than a broad generalization about cultural affinity. If religious demand is to be introduced into our explanations for conversion, we must follow the lead of supply-side theorists and be as careful as possible in delineating our assumptions, hypotheses, and variables posited as impacting religious choices.

The Implicit "Modernization" Hypothesis

Most studies focused on the politics of resurgent fundamentalism or other aspects related to the content of religious movements implicitly subscribe to various extensions of Durkheim's "anomie" thesis of religious conversion. The specifics vary from case to case, but the common theme posited across cases is that the drastic changes associated with modernization (urbanization, changing land tenure patterns, the loss of traditional community) cause a sense of moral uncertainty and a loss of security in terms of relationships and norms of behavior.[53] In the face of these crises, individuals may join new religious organizations or revitalize their commitment to their current faith.

As noted earlier, the predicted political trajectory of this implied conversion model varies significantly across cases and authors. Samuel Huntington, Mark Juergensmeyer, and a host of other authors have sounded alarms about the challenges of militant religious fundamentalism for democracy in the Middle East, Africa, and Asia. In Latin America, a number of authors have focused on the otherworldly and millennialist elements of Pentecostal Protestantism, arguing that it represents little more than a comforting replication of corporatist norms and values.[54]

Still others have interpreted the rapid growth of Pentecostalism in Latin America, Africa, and Asia as an adaptive strategy that may actually promote capitalist values.[55] According to this interpretation, conversion opens "social spaces" for people who have been dislocated by rapid economic and political changes in their countries. The results of conversion are then associated with the promotion of development and even democracy in the developing world.[56]

Across these divergent cases and projections, two factors stand out. First, the same broad explanatory factor—modernization—is posited as the driving force behind religious conversion and the ensuing political changes. Second, these changes are framed in sweeping either/or terms about their impact on democracy, development, and political change. In other words, religious change is viewed broadly either as a dangerous challenge to democracy and development or as a motor for economic growth and democracy building. In each case, more explicit attention to the process and content of religious conversion is likely to improve both theory building and our political predictions

WHAT POLITICAL SCIENTISTS CAN LEARN FROM CONVERSION STUDIES

For the most part, political science has adopted the "Pauline Paradigm" of conversion: the notion that conversion is a sudden, dramatic, and all-encompassing event. For a discipline that increasingly measures variables and tests hypotheses through quantitative methods and survey research, this is a normal and understandable disciplinary trend. However, the fluidity of the religious marketplace worldwide has given rise to multiple and diverse challenges to this approach in conversion studies. A number of authors working on religion in Latin America and Africa have argued that such traditional conceptions of conversion do not fully apply to the emerging religious field.[57] Some authors have referred to "passages" or "minimal conversions" rather than clear-cut conversions to understand this phenomenon in Brazil.[58] According to these authors, as some churches move closer to secular norms, their parishioners are able to relax the tensions between the sacred and the secular enough to make conversion a less radical and complete event. Furthermore, these authors suggest that some cultures are suffi-ciently syncretistic that transit between religious groups is a natural and non-dramatic occurrence for many converts. From elite Indians who practice elements of Buddhism but remain formally Hindu to Mayan converts in Guatemala who combine the practice of *costumbre*[59] with their newfound Pentecostal faith, the formal lines drawn between religious groups in theory are far more obscure in practice. Taken together, these studies and cases force us to take a closer look at what we mean by conversion. If conversion is not always characterized by a dramatic change in religious beliefs and values, how can we define and utilize the concept in comparative study?

Conversion as a Continuum

The first step in addressing this dilemma is to accept that conversion should be under-stood as a process and continuum rather than as a single event.[60] Conceiving of con-version as a continuum allows us to pinpoint dual membership, passage, minimal conversion, re-conversion, or even apostasy as levels within this continuum. In other words, we can adopt what Henri Gooren calls a "conversion careers" approach in which we look at levels of conversion as well as the movement across these levels over time. Such an approach demands that we gather network, life cycle, and life histories of con-verts (and non-converts) in order to distinguish the multiple causal factors involved in conversion. In contrast to previous models of conversion, the conversion career approach may be understood as "the member's passage, within his or her social and cul-tural context, through levels, types, and phases of church participation."[61] While various authors have provided more complex schema, Gooren's synthesis establishes a func-tional model for following and comparing different stages of conversion (pre-affiliation, affiliation, conversion, confession, and disaffiliation).

Introducing the Role of Networks in Conversion

It is also crucial that we begin disaggregating questions of how many people convert from questions about specifically who converts. Teasing out these questions requires that we bring social networks into the analysis. As we noted earlier, sweeping assump-tions linking the cultural, material, or other types of "crises" of modernization tend to over-predict conversion. For example, based on his research in Venezuela, David Smilde argues that the personal problems that Pentecostalism helps converts to address are widespread among Venezuela's poor and thus do not provide a sufficient explanation for conversion. Smilde found instead that networks played an important role. People who were living away from their families or with a Pentecostal were more likely to con-vert than those who were not. The presence of nearby Catholic family members acted as a deterrent to conversion, but individuals who moved away from their families were more likely to have the freedom to innovate. Smilde also points out that some people actively construct the network positions that eventually lead to their conversion.[62] In other words, instrumental action on the part of individuals leads them toward or away from conversion.

Taken together, the two insights summarized here suggest that researchers should beware of reifying the instrumental nature of conversion as a path to resolving life crises. Conversion is not the only avenue explored by people in crisis. The material and psychological impacts of modernization and globalization are much more widespread than religious conversion. Who converts and who does not, who joins political movements or links their political and religious worldviews, what role pre-conversion networks and social capital play in post-conversion mobilization, and who pursues nonreligious alternatives in response to the same objective conditions are all questions that should inform our political analyses.

Conceiving of conversion as a process also keeps us from becoming overly deterministic about the variables contributing to conversion. While social conformity, networks, and crises may condition conversion, these are not the sole determining factors. On the other hand, purely instrumental approaches may give too much credit to the convert's "other" preferences (financial gain, personal safety, crisis management, or political issues). That which appears instrumental or purely preference-based to the outside observer may actually have multiple contextual and network determinants that are not immediately evident. One way for researchers to investigate these different levels of analysis is to take a more critical approach to the role of conversion narratives and discourse in the study of conversion.

Studying Conversion Narratives

Conversion is defined, in part, by the new discourse repeated in the conversion narrative; pitting past against present and future, good against evil, old against new are part of adopting a new religious identity (not only adopting it, but actively reshaping and re-embracing it in the retelling). The conversion narrative can thus make conversion appear purely tactical, precisely because the discourse is framed in terms of what was wrong and bad about the past. Conversion almost always has "practical" explanations: fighting addiction, bottoming out, facing a medical crisis, or other psychological or material factors. A common characteristic of conversionist religious groups is that converts must learn to interpret these factors in a manner consistent with the group's norms and discursive style.[63]

This is not to say that conversion narratives should be discounted as disingenuous or programmed, but rather that researchers must pay attention to the convert's stage in their conversion career, always remaining cognizant of the fact that narratives are socially constructed and retrospectively reinterpreted over time. This is a particularly critical point for understanding the politics of religious conversion. While the inherent limits of cross-sectional survey research mean that we cannot necessarily capture the entire lifespan of religious adherents in our research, we can be sensitive to the fact that religious and political variables interact across time, may be mutually reinforcing, and are impacted by the context in which the data is collected.

A careful analysis of conversion narratives demonstrates an ongoing process of continuity and rupture with the former life for many converts. In their studies of Pentecostalism, Patricia Birman and Joel Robbins each argue that the spiritual forces of previous religious practice remain very much alive in the worldviews and narratives of converts, despite the fact that they are now demonized within the Pentecostal dualist worldviews.[64] For Pentecostals, fighting against the "real" world of local spirits allows them, as Joel Robbins puts it, "to turn their new religion immediately to addressing local issues in locally comprehensible terms."[65]

These studies provide us with practical methodological lessons for studying conversion. Tracking and measuring religious change requires a methodology that can capture the multiplicity of causal factors and gradations of conversion. Qualitative interviews and survey data collected by most political scientists must be complemented with participant observation in order to capture the complexities of conversion careers. Non-converts must be interviewed as well. Without this control group we may be missing half of the story. Overlooking this group has led some researchers to over-predict the causal nature of precipitant events (drug use, stress, and other emotional/psychological crises) in the conversion process.[66]

Researchers should also approach conversion narratives carefully because, although such narratives are an empirical indicator of conversion, they are socially constructed and are influenced by the discourse of the new group to which the convert has affiliated. They are also affected by the context of the interview itself. If the conversion narrative is not considered carefully, we may lose sight of the fundamental tension in conversion discourses between the processes of choosing (individual agency) and being chosen (by religious authorities and institutions).

REFRAMING QUESTIONS ABOUT CONVERSION AND POLITICS

As the first sections of this chapter have demonstrated, the debate over the impact of religious change in the field of political science has been framed largely in terms of big questions about democracy, church–state conflict or cooperation, resistance, and accommodation. The studies asking questions within that framework, however, have varied widely and led to inconclusive results. This is because most political scientists have either glossed over the complexity of religious conversion or adopted an implicit model of conversion without fully examining the assumptions. Religious conversion is primarily a personal and religious decision that takes place over time. While such individual decisions may add up to a larger process of religious, social, and political change, the most important political effects of these changes have to do with the manner in which new religiously held values enter the public sphere, inform public discourse, and combine to resolve or exacerbate local cultural, social, individual, or familial tensions. These are not the kind of political effects that fall neatly into categories of left/right, democratic/authoritarian, or resistance/accommodation utilized in most political analyses.

While this is by no means a comprehensive list, the following guidelines can hopefully assist us in disaggregating some of the complicated relationships between religious conversion and politics and in setting agendas for future research. First, we must untangle and specifically define the religious variables we posit as having political effects. As I have argued elsewhere, the act of conversion or belonging to a given religious affiliation is simply not a good predictor of political attitudes and activities.[67] We are much better served by focusing on the specific religious beliefs and practices associated with the religious groups under study and how those beliefs and practices interact over time with specific local and national contexts. For example, strong tendencies toward millennialism and charismaticism among both Pentecostal Protestants and charismatic Catholics are associated with political quietism in closed and authoritarian political contexts. At the same time, the identical set of religious beliefs and practices can have a positive impact on voting frequency if political participation is encouraged as both a right and a duty for citizens.[68]

This insight applies to the study of other religious traditions as well. While the events of September 2001 and subsequent reactions and counter-reactions have brought the violent role of extremist Islamists to the foreground, the experiments in Muslim political inclusion and exclusion that are ongoing in Kuwait, Lebanon, Jordan, Turkey, and Algeria provide further evidence of the interactive nature of religious beliefs and contexts. The role of religion in the 2011 "Arab Spring" will provide a fertile ground for careful analysis of the content and process of religious as well as political actions.

Second, as these examples illustrate, the religious impact on politics obviously involves institutions and identities as well as beliefs and practices. But we should not take such identities or institutional labels for granted in our research. By identifying the stages and networks involved in conversion, we open our research agenda to analyze the networks that lead individuals both toward and away from religious conversion. This raises questions about the role of networks in forming both political and religious identities, the resources such networks provide to political projects, and whether ethnic, cultural, or political variables precede and drive religious choices in certain national or local contexts.

Third, acknowledging the model of conversion that informs our research can help us to bridge supply- and demand-driven research agendas on religion and politics. On this front, it is time to find common ground for further analysis. While economic supply-side approaches have produced significant and testable propositions about secularization, state regulation, and the actions of religious institutions, the empirical claims of this approach continue to be disputed. If the model is not fully predictive, it is worth opening the door to carefully defined demand-side variables. For their part, theorists on the demand side of the equation should recognize the "modernization" model of conversion implicit in their theories and ask some serious questions about whether such "grand theorizing" is sufficient to explain the plethora of religious (and secular) political responses to modernization and globalization.

A fourth and related point is that sweeping generalizations connecting religious change to claims about democracy, world conflict, or capitalist development should be viewed with suspicion. While it was precisely these claims that brought religion back into the forefront of political science, it is too much to expect a series of individual religious choices to necessarily add up to a coherent, direct, and sweeping force for economic or political change. As Jeffrey Rubin argued recently, we may better understand the effects of social and religious movements if we investigate the manner in which they introduce alternative rationalities, discourses, and narratives into public spaces, rather than forcing our "square peg" research subject into the "round hole" of standard political categories.[69]

David Smilde provides us with one such nuanced approach in his study of evangelical political participation in Venezuela.[70] Smilde argues that evangelical "publics" in Venezuela are purposely constructed relational contexts which extend network ties and introduce a "moralized" discourse into the public sphere. The same could be argued for television and radio evangelism throughout the region. This discourse, and political responses to it (such as Hugo Chavez' adoption of evangelical images and phrases), make up a rich area for further study. This sort of political participation does not fall neatly into the bounds of traditional political categories, but it remains important and demands careful analysis.

Finally, the most influential and insightful studies of religion and politics have learned from anthropology to accept and respect the validity of both religious and political experiences. This is perhaps the most difficult and yet rewarding aspect of studying religion and politics. It means that we respect religious experiences and beliefs that may be very different from our own. It means that we must accept and try not to prejudge practices with which we may not be familiar or comfortable. It means we must come to some understanding of the context in which religious organizations and individuals operate. It requires, as Daniel Levine has pointed out, that we "see that religious phenomena have a logic and dynamic of their own, that people who belong to religious groups find satisfaction in the very act of participation, just as they may in organizing and carrying out the group's specific activities."[71]

Conversion is a process that takes place over time, interacts with institutional religion, networks, and cultural contexts, and does not necessarily proceed in a linear or chronological fashion. If political science is to expand our view of religious politics and make strides in understanding the political impact of religious conversions, we must undertake not only a re-conceptualization of our implicit and explicit models of conversion but also of the methods and subjects studied as its effects. Integrating insights from conversion studies can help us to avoid the pitfalls of overgeneralization, understand the multiple lines of causality involved in conversion, and utilize methods that better capture the complexity of the interactions between religion and politics.

NOTES

I would like to acknowledge the invaluable assistance of Sandra Lazo de la Vega, who served as a research assistant and intern while working on portions of this chapter. I would also like to thank David Smilde and Daniel Levine for providing critical feedback on earlier versions of the chapter.

1. See Walt Rostow, *The Stages of Economic Growth: A Non-Communist Manifesto* (Cambridge: Cambridge University Press, 1960); N. J. Smelser, *Social Change in the Industrial Revolution* (London: Routledge, 1958); Samuel S. Huntington, *Political Order in Changing Societies* (New Haven: Yale University Press, 1968).

2. See Ted Jelen, *The Political Mobilization of Religious Beliefs* (New York: Praeger, 1991); Ronald Inglehart, *Culture Shift in Advanced Industrial Society* (Princeton: Princeton University Press, 1990); Kenneth D. Wald and Allison Calhoun-Brown, *Religion and Politics in the United States* (Lanham, MD: Rowman & Littlefield, 2006); Ted Jelen, "Research in Religion and Political Behavior: Looking Both Ways after Two Decades of Research" *American Politics Quarterly* 26 (1998): 110–113; Ted Jelen and Clyde Wilcox, *Public Attitudes toward Church and State* (Armonk, NY: M. E. Sharpe, 1994); David Leege, "Religion and Politics in Theoretical Perspective," in *Rediscovering the Religious Factor in American Politics,* David Leege and Lyman A. Kellstedt (Armonk, NY: M. E. Sharpe, 1993), 3–25; Robert D. Putnam and David E. Campbell, *American Grace: How Religion Divides and Unites Us* (New York: Simon & Schuster, 2010); Anthony Gill, "Religion and Comparative Politics," *Annual Review of Political Science* 4 (2001): 117–138; Robert Wuthnow, *The Restructuring of American Religion: Society and Faith Since World War II* (Princeton: Princeton University Press, 1988).

3. Samuel P. Huntington, *The Clash of Civilizations and the Remaking of the World Order* (New York: Simon and Schuster, 1996).

4. For comprehensive reviews of this literature, see David A. Snow and Richard Machalek, "The Sociology of Conversion," *Annual Review of Sociology* 10 (1984):167–190; James Richardson, ed., *Conversion Careers: In and Out of the New Religions* (Beverly Hills, CA: Sage, 1978); Lewis R. Rambo, *Understanding Religious Conversion* (New Haven: Yale University Press, 1993); Henri Gooren, "Towards a New Model of Conversion Careers: The Impact of Personality and Situational Factors," *Exchange* 34 (2005): 149–166; Henri Gooren, "Towards a New Model of Religious Conversion Careers: The Impact of Social and Institutional Factors," in *Conversion in Modern Times,* ed. Wout J. van Bekkum, Jan N. Bremmer, and Arie Molendijk (Leuven: Peeters, 2006), 25–39.

5. Snow and Machalek, "The Sociology of Conversion," 170.

6. Ibid., 168–174; Gooren, "Towards a New Model of Religious Conversion Careers."

7. Ronald Inglehart, "The Renaissance of Political Culture," *American Political Science Review* 82 (Dec. 1988): 1221.

8. See Rostow, *The Stages of Economic Growth*; Smelser, *Social Change in the Industrial Revolution*.

9. For an analysis of the rise of the religious right in the United States, see Michael Lienesch, *Redeeming America: Piety and Politics in the New Christian Right* (Chapel Hill: University of North Carolina Press, 1993).

10. David Leege, "Coalitions, Cues, Strategic Politics, and the Staying Power of the Religious Right, or Why Political Scientists Ought to Pay More Attention to Cultural Politics," *PS: Political Science and Politics* 25 (June 1992): 198–204.

11. See Ali Banuazizi, "Social-Psychological Approaches to Political Development," in *Understanding Political Development*, ed. Myron Weiner and Samuel Huntington (New York: Harpers Collins, 1987), 281–316.

12. Richard T. Antoun and Mary Elaine, *Hegland's Religious Resurgence: Contemporary Cases in Islam, Christianity, and Judaism* (Syracuse, NY: Syracuse University Press, 1987) emphasizes the theme that millenarian religious movements are adaptable and may serve multiple purposes, acting both to legitimize the status quo and bolster movements for political dissent. Also see Jose Casanova, *Public Religions in the Modern World* (Chicago: University of Chicago Press, 1994). In addition, see the impressive four-volume Fundamentalism series edited by Martin E. Marty and R. Scott Appleby under the auspices of the Fundamentalism Project, sponsored by the American Academy of Arts and Sciences: Vol. 1, *Fundamentalisms Observed* (1992); Vol. 2, *Fundamentalisms and Society: Reclaiming the Sciences, the Family, and Education* (1993); Vol. 3, *Fundamentalisms and the State* (1993); and Vol. 4, *Accounting for Fundamentalisms: The Dynamic Character of Movements* (1994) (all volumes were published by the University of Chicago Press). Also see Bronislaw Misztal and Anson Shupe, eds., *Religion and Politics in Comparative Perspective: Revival of Religious Fundamentalism in East and West* (Westport, CT: Praeger, 1994). For a further critique of the secularization thesis, see Roger Finke, "An Unsecular America," in *Religion and Modernization: Sociologists and Historians Debate the Secularization Thesis*, ed. Steve Bruce (Oxford: Clarendon Press, 1992) 145–169.

13. Daniel Levine, *Religion and Politics in Latin America: The Catholic Church in Venezuela and Colombia* (Princeton: Princeton University Press, 1981); Thomas C. Bruneau, *The Church in Brazil: The Politics of Religion* (Austin: University of Texas Press, 1982); Brian Smith, *The Church and Politics in Chile: Challenges to Modern Catholicism* (Princeton: Princeton University Press, 1982); Scott Mainwaring, *The Catholic Church and Politics in Brazil, 1916–1985* (Stanford, CA: Stanford University Press, 1985).

14. See Mark Juergensmeyer, *Terror in the Mind of God: The Rise of Religious Violence* (Berkeley and Los Angeles: University of California Press, 2000). Also see Mark Juergensmeyer, "The Global Rise of Religious Nationalism," in *Religions/Globalizations: Theories and Cases*, ed. Dwight N. Hopkins, Lois Ann Lorentzen, Eduardo Mendieta, and David Batstone (Durham, NC: Duke University Press, 2001), 66–83; Huntington, *The Clash of Civilizations*; Bassam Tibi, *The Challenge of Fundamentalism: Political Islam and the New World Disorder* (Berkeley and Los Angeles: University of California Press, 1998).

15. Jeff Haynes, *Religion in Third World Politics* (Boulder, CO: Lynne Rienner Publishers, 1994), 10.

16. Rodney Stark and Lawrence Iannaccone, "A Supply-Side Reinterpretation of the 'Secularization' of Europe," *Journal for the Scientific Study of Religion* 33 (1994): 230–252; Andrew M. Greely, "The Persistence of Religion," *Cross Currents* 45 (Spring 1995): 24–41.

17. See Gill, "Religion and Comparative Politics."

18. See Martin E. Marty and R. Scott Appleby, *Fundamentalisms Observed* (Chicago: University of Chicago Press, 1991). Also see David Martin, *Tongues of Fire: The Explosion of Protestantism in Latin America* (Oxford: Basil Blackwell, 1990); Emilio Willems, *Followers of the New Faith: Culture Change and the Rise of Protestantism in Brazil and Chile* (Nashville, TN: Vanderbilt University Press, 1967).

19. See Pippa Norris and Ronald Inglehart, *Sacred and Secular: Religion and Politics Worldwide* (Cambridge: Cambridge University Press, 2004).

20. See, for example, Stephen A. Kent, *From Slogans to Mantras: Social Protest and Religious Conversion in the Late Vietnam War Era* (Syracuse, NY: Syracuse University Press, 2002). Kent argues that conversion to New Religious Movements represented a continuation of converts' previous political motivations.

21. Kenneth D. Wald, D. E. Owen, and S. D. Hill, Jr., "Churches as Political Communities," *American Political Science Review* 82 (June 1988): 531–548 (quote is from p. 546).

22. Ibid., 546.

23. Sidney Verba, Kay Lehman Schlozman, and Henry Brady, *Voice and Equality: Civic Voluntarism in American Politics* (Cambridge, MA: Harvard University Press, 1995).

24. David Knoke, *Change and Continuity in American Politics* (Baltimore, MD: Johns Hopkins University Press, 1976).

25. See Lyman Kellstedt, "The Falwell Issue Agenda: Sources of Support among White Protestant Evangelicals," in *Research in the Social Scientific Study of Religion*, ed. M. Lynn and D. Moberg (Greenwich, CT: JAI Press, 1990), 109–132.

26. See Ted Jelen, *The Political Mobilization of Religious Beliefs* (New York: Praeger, 1991); Clyde Wilcox, "Religion and Politics among White Evangelicals: The Impact of Religious Variables on Political Attitudes," *Review of Religious Research* 32 (1990): 27–41.

27. See Jelen, *The Political Mobilization of Religious Beliefs*.

28. See Michael A. Jones-Correa and David L. Leal, "Political Participation: Does Religion Matter?" *Political Research Quarterly* 54, no. 4 (2001): 751–770. Also see Robert Putnam, "The Prosperous Community: Social Capital and Public Life," *The American Prospect* 13 (Spring 1993): 35–42.

29. Laurence R. Iannaccone, "Why Strict Churches Are Strong," *American Journal of Sociology* 99 (1994):1180–1211.

30. David E. Campbell, "Acts of Faith: Churches and Political Engagement," *Political Behavior* 26, no. 2 (2004): 155–180 (quote is from p. 156).

31. Ted Gerard Jelen and Clyde Wilcox, eds., *Religion and Politics in Comparative Perspective: The One, the Few, and the Many* (Cambridge: Cambridge University Press, 2002).

32. Peter Berger, *The Sacred Canopy: Elements of a Sociological Theory of Religion* (Garden City, NY: Anchor, 1969).

33. Jelen and Wilcox, *Religion and Politics*.

34. Maria A. Toyoda and Aji Tanaka, "Religion and Politics in Japan," in Jelen and Wilcox, *Religion and Politics*.

35. Jelen and Wilcox, *Religion and Politics*.

36. Susan Milligan, "Together, but Worlds Apart: Christian Aid Groups Raise Suspicion in Strongholds of Islam," *The Boston Globe*, Oct. 10, 2006.

37. See A. Rashied Omar, "The Right to Religious Conversion: Between Apostasy and Proselytization," Kroc Institute Occasional Paper #27, OP: 1, 2006.

38. Huntington, *The Clash of Civilizations*; Juergensmeyer, *Terror in the Mind of God*; Gilles Kepel, *The Revenge of God: The Resurgence of Islam, Christianity, and Judaism in the Modern World* (University Park: Pennsylvania State University Press, 1994).

39. See Jeffrey Haynes, "Islamic Militancy in East Africa," *Third World Quarterly* 26, no. 8 (2005): 1321–1339.
40. Gill, "Religion and Comparative Politics," 126–130.
41. See Bruce B. Lawrence, *Shattering the Myth: Islam beyond Violence* (Princeton: Princeton University Press, 1998); John L. Esposito and John O. Voll, *Islam and Democracy* (New York: Oxford University Press, 1996); Vali Nasr, "Military Rule, Islamism, and Democracy in Pakistan," *Middle East Journal* 58 (Spring 2004): 195–209, for examples of arguments for a more nuanced picture of fundamentalist Islam.
42. Roger Finke and Rodney Stark, *The Churching of America, 1776–1990* (New Brunswick, NJ: Rutgers University Press, 1992); Rodney Stark and James C. McCann, "Market Forces and Catholic Commitment: Exploring the New Paradigm," *Journal for the Scientific Study of Religion* 32 (1993): 113; Anthony Gill, *Rendering unto Caesar* (Chicago: University of Chicago Press, 1998); Anthony Gill, "The Economics of Evangelization," in *Religious Freedom and Evangelization in Latin America: The Challenge of Religious Pluralism*, ed. Paul E. Sigmund (Maryknoll, NY: Orbis Books, 1999), 70–86; Andrew Chesnut, "Specialized Spirits: Conversion and the Products of Pneumacentric Religion in Latin America's Free Market of Faith," in *Conversion of a Continent: Contemporary Religious Change in Latin America*, ed. Timothy Steigenga and Edward Cleary (New Brunswick, NJ: Rutgers University Press, 2007), 53–71.
43. For a concise explanation and defense of this perspective, see Gill, *Rendering unto Caesar*, 193–202. Also see Finke and Stark, *The Churching of America*; Stark and McCann, "Market Forces and Catholic Commitment," 113.
44. Iannaccone "Why Strict Churches are Strong."
45. Ibid. Also see Gill, *Rendering unto Caesar*, 198–199.
46. See Gill, *Rendering unto Caesar*; Andrew Chesnut, *Competitive Spirits: Latin America's New Religious Economy* (Oxford: Oxford University Press, 2003).
47. See Gill, *Rendering unto Caesar*; Gill, "The Economics of Evangelization," 70–86.
48. Gill, *Rendering unto Caesar*, 199.
49. See Norris and Inglehart for an overview of the conflicting evidence on the predictions of market models. Also see Mark Chaves and Philip S. Gorski, "Religious Pluralism and Religious Participation," *Annual Review of Sociology* 27 (2001): 261–281.
50. Chesnut terms his approach a "heterodox market" analysis. Chesnut, "Specialized Spirits," 53–71.
51. Ibid.
52. Joel Robbins, "The Globalization of Charismatic and Pentecostal Christianity," *Annual Review of Anthropology* 33 (2004): 126.
53. See Peter Berger, *The Desecularization of the World: Resurgent Religion and World Politics* (Grand Rapids, MI: Eerdmans, 1999).
54. Christian Lalive d'Epinay, *Haven of the Masses: A Study of the Pentecostal Movement in Chile* (London: Lutterworth, 1969); Jean-Pierre Bastian, "The Metamorphosis of Latin American Protestant Groups: A Sociohistorical Perspective," *Latin American Research Review* 28 (1993): 33–62.
55. Amy Sherman, *The Soul of Development: Biblical Christianity and Economic Transformation in Guatemala* (New York: Oxford University Press, 1997), 163–165; Emilio Willems, *Followers of the New Faith: Culture Change and the Rise of Protestantism in Brazil and Chile* (Nashville, TN: Vanderbilt University Press, 1967); Martin, *Tongues of Fire*; Sheldon Annis, *God and Production in a Guatemalan Town* (Austin: University of Texas Press, 1987).

56. Martin, *Tongues of Fire*, 235, 289. Martin compares the spread of Pentecostal Protestantism in Latin America to the previous growth of Puritanism and Anglo-American Methodism in England and the United States, drawing out similarities in terms of social function.

57. Alejandro Frigerio, "Analyzing Conversion in Latin America: Theoretical Questions, Methodological Dilemmas, and Comparative Data from Argentina and Brazil," in *Conversion of a Continent: Contemporary Religious Change in Latin America*, ed. Timothy Steigenga and Edward Cleary (New Brunswick, NJ: Rutgers University Press, 2007), 33–51. See also Sidney Greenfield and Andre Droogers, *Reinventing Religions: Syncretism and Transformation in Africa and the Americas* (New York: Rowman and Littlefield, 2000).

58. Patricia Birman, "Cultos de possessão e pentecostalismo no Brasil: Passagens," *Religião e Sociedade* 17 (1996): 90–109.

59. *Costumbre* describes "the body of locally prescribed religious belief, ritual, dress, language and lifeways" of being Mayan. See Virginia Garrard-Burnett, "'God Was Already Here When Columbus Arrived': Inculturation Theology and the Mayan Movement in Guatemala" in *Conversion of a Continent: Contemporary Religious Change in Latin America*, ed. Timothy Steigenga and Edward Cleary (New Brunswick, NJ: Rutgers University Press, 2007), 148.

60. Henri Gooren, "Conversion Careers in Latin America: Entering and Leaving Church among Pentecostals, Catholics, and Mormons," in *Conversion of a Continent: Contemporary Religious Change in Latin America*, ed. Timothy Steigenga and Edward Cleary (New Brunswick, NJ: Rutgers University Press, 2007), 52–71.

61. André Droogers, Henri Gooren, and Anton Houtepen, *Conversion Careers and Culture Politics in Pentecostalism: A Comparative Study in Four Continents*, proposal submitted to the thematic program "The Future of the Religious Past" of the Netherlands Organization for Scientific Research (NWO), 2003.

62. See David Smilde, *Reason to Believe: Cultural Agency in Latin American Evangelicalism* (Berkeley and Los Angeles: University of California Press, 2007). See also David Smilde, "Works of the Flesh, Fruit of the Spirit: Religious Action Frames and Meaning Networks in Venezuelan Evangelicalism," PhD diss., University of Chicago, 2000, chapters 3 and 4.

63. Snow and Machalek, "The Sociology of Conversion," 175–178.

64. Patricia Birman, "Conversion from Afro-Brazilian Religions to Neo-Pentecostalism: Opening New Horizons of the Possible," in *Conversion of a Continent: Contemporary Religious Change in Latin America*, ed. Timothy Steigenga and Edward Cleary (New Brunswick, NJ: Rutgers University Press, 2007), 115–132.

65. Robbins, "The Globalization of Charismatic and Pentecostal Christianity," 129.

66. See Snow and Machalek, "The Sociology of Conversion," for examples of this research.

67. Timothy Steigenga, *The Politics of the Spirit: The Political Implications of Pentecostalized Religion in Costa Rica and Guatemala* (Lanham, MD: Lexington Books, 2001).

68. Ibid.

69. Jeffrey Rubin, "Meanings and Mobilizations: A Cultural Politics Approach to Social Movements and States," *Latin American Research Review* 39, no. 3 (2004). See also Jeffrey W. Rubin, "In the Streets or in the Institutions?" *LASA Forum* 37 (2006): 26–29. For an example of such a dialectical or oppositional approach, see Jean and John Comaroff, *Of Revelation and Revolution: Christianity, Colonialism, and Consciousness in South Africa* (Chicago: University of Chicago Press, 1991).

70. David Smilde, "Rational Analysis of Religious Conversion and Social Change: Networks and Publics in Latin American Evangelicalism," in *Conversion of a Continent: Contemporary*

Religious Change in Latin America, ed. Timothy Steigenga and Edward Cleary (New Brunswick, NJ: Rutgers University Press, 2007), 93–114.

71. Daniel H. Levine, ed., *Religion and Political Conflict in Latin America* (Chapel Hill: University of North Carolina Press, 1986), 17.

Bibliography

Annis, Sheldon. *God and Production in a Guatemalan Town*. Austin: University of Texas Press, 1987.

Antoun, Richard T., and Mary Elaine, *Hegland's Religious Resurgence: Contemporary Cases in Islam, Christianity, and Judaism*. Syracuse, NY: Syracuse University Press, 1987.

Banuazizi, Ali. "Social-Psychological Approaches to Political Development." In *Understanding Political Development*, ed. Myron Weiner and Samuel Huntington, 281–316. New York: Harpers Collins, 1987.

Bastian, Jean-Pierre. "The Metamorphosis of Latin American Protestant Groups: A Sociohistorical Perspective." *Latin American Research Review* 28 (1993): 33–62.

Berger, Peter. *The Desecularization of the World: Resurgent Religion and World Politics*. Grand Rapids, MI: Eerdmans, 1999.

——.*The Sacred Canopy: Elements of a Sociological Theory of Religion*. Garden City, NY: Anchor, 1969.

Birman, Patricia. "Conversion from Afro-Brazilian Religions to Neo-Pentecostalism: Opening New Horizons of the Possible." In *Conversion of a Continent: Contemporary Religious Change in Latin America*, ed. Timothy Steigenga and Edward Cleary, 115–132. New Brunswick, NJ: Rutgers University Press, 2007.

——. "Cultos de possessão e pentecostalismo no Brasil: Passagens." *Religião e Sociedade* 17 (1996): 90–109.

Bruneau, Thomas C. *The Church in Brazil: The Politics of Religion*. Austin: University of Texas Press, 1982.

Campbell, David E. "Acts of Faith: Churches and Political Engagement." *Political Behavior* 26, no. 2 (2004): 155–180.

Casanova, Jose. *Public Religions in the Modern World*. Chicago: University of Chicago Press, 1994.

Chesnut, Andrew. "Specialized Spirits: Conversion and the Products of Pneumacentric Religion in Latin America's Free Market of Faith." In *Conversion of a Continent: Contemporary Religious Change in Latin America*, ed. Timothy Steigenga and Edward Cleary, 53–71. New Brunswick, NJ: Rutgers University Press, 2007.

Comaroff, Jean, and John Comaroff. *Of Revelation and Revolution: Christianity, Colonialism, and Consciousness in South Africa*. Chicago: University of Chicago Press, 1991.

Droogers, André, Henri Gooren, and Anton Houtepen. *Conversion Careers and Culture Politics in Pentecostalism: A Comparative Study in Four Continents*. Proposal submitted to the thematic program "The Future of the Religious Past" of the Netherlands Organization for Scientific Research (NWO), 2003.

Esposito, John L., and John O. Voll. *Islam and Democracy*. New York: Oxford University Press, 1996.

Finke, Roger. "An Unsecular America." In *Religion and Modernization: Sociologists and Historians Debate the Secularization Thesis*, ed. Steve Bruce, 145–169. Oxford: Clarendon Press, 1992.

Finke, Roger, and Rodney Stark. *The Churching of America, 1776–1990*. New Brunswick, NJ: Rutgers University Press, 1992.

Frigerio, Alejandro. "Analyzing Conversion in Latin America: Theoretical Questions, Methodological Dilemmas, and Comparative Data from Argentina and Brazil." In *Conversion of a Continent: Contemporary Religious Change in Latin America*, ed. Timothy Steigenga and Edward Cleary, 33–51. New Brunswick, NJ: Rutgers University Press, 2007.

Garrard-Burnett, Virginia. "'God Was Already Here When Columbus Arrived': Inculturation Theology and the Mayan Movement in Guatemala." In *Conversion of a Continent: Contemporary Religious Change in Latin America*, ed. Timothy Steigenga and Edward Cleary, 218–238. New Brunswick, NJ: Rutgers University Press, 2007.

Gill, Anthony. "The Economics of Evangelization." In *Religious Freedom and Evangelization in Latin America: The Challenge of Religious Pluralism*, ed. Paul E. Sigmund, 70–86. Maryknoll, NY: Orbis Books, 1999.

——. "Religion and Comparative Politics." *Annual Review of Political Science* 4 (2001): 117–138.

——. *Rendering unto Caesar*. Chicago: University of Chicago Press, 1998.

Gooren, Henri. "Conversion Careers in Latin America: Entering and Leaving Church among Pentecostals, Catholics, and Mormons." In *Conversion of a Continent: Contemporary Religious Change in Latin America*, ed. Timothy Steigenga and Edward Cleary, 52–71. New Brunswick, NJ: Rutgers University Press, 2007.

——. "Towards a New Model of Religious Conversion Careers: The Impact of Social and Institutional Factors." In *Conversion in Modern Times*, ed. Wout J. van Bekkum, Jan N. Bremmer, and Arie Molendijk, 25–39. Leuven: Peeters, 2006.

Greely, Andrew M. "The Persistence of Religion." *Cross Currents* 45 (Spring 1995): 24–41.

Haynes, Jeffrey. "Islamic Militancy in East Africa." *Third World Quarterly* 26, no. 8 (2005): 1321–1339.

——. *Religion in Third World Politics*. Boulder, CO: Lynne Rienner Publishers, 1994.

Huntington, Samuel S. *Political Order in Changing Societies*. New Haven: Yale University Press, 1968.

——. *The Clash of Civilizations and the Remaking of the World Order*. New York: Simon and Schuster, 1996.

Iannaccone, Laurence R. "Why Strict Churches Are Strong." *American Journal of Sociology* 99 (1994):1180–1211.

Inglehart, Ronald. *Culture Shift in Advanced Industrial Society*. Princeton: Princeton University Press, 1990.

——. "The Renaissance of Political Culture." *American Political Science Review* 82 (Dec. 1988): 1221.

Jelen, Ted. "Research in Religion and Political Behavior: Looking Both Ways after Two Decades of Research." *American Politics Quarterly* 26 (1998): 110–113.

——. *The Political Mobilization of Religious Beliefs*. New York: Praeger, 1991.

Jelen, Ted, and Clyde Wilcox. *Public Attitudes toward Church and State*. Armonk, NY: M. E. Sharpe, 1994.

——, eds. *Religion and Politics in Comparative Perspective: The One, the Few, and the Many*. Cambridge: Cambridge University Press, 2002.

Jones-Correa, Michael A., and David L. Leal, "Political Participation: Does Religion Matter?" *Political Research Quarterly* 54, no. 4 (2001): 751–770.

Juergensmeyer, Mark. "The Global Rise of Religious Nationalism." In *Religions/ Globalizations: Theories and Cases*, ed. Dwight N. Hopkins, Lois Ann Lorentzen, Eduardo Mendieta, and David Batstone, 66–83. Durham, NC: Duke University Press, 2001.

———. *Terror in the Mind of God: The Rise of Religious Violence*. Berkeley and Los Angeles: University of California Press, 2000.

Kellstedt, Lyman. "The Falwell Issue Agenda: Sources of Support among White Protestant Evangelicals." In *Research in the Social Scientific Study of Religion*, ed. M. Lynn and D. Moberg, 109–132. Greenwich, CT: JAI Press, 1990.

Kepel, Gilles. *The Revenge of God: The Resurgence of Islam, Christianity, and Judaism in the Modern World*. University Park: Pennsylvania State University Press, 1994.

Knoke, David. *Change and Continuity in American Politics*. Baltimore, MD: Johns Hopkins University Press, 1976.

Lalive d'Epinay, Christian. *Haven of the Masses: A Study of the Pentecostal Movement in Chile*. London: Lutterworth, 1969.

Lawrence, Bruce B. *Shattering the Myth: Islam beyond Violence*. Princeton: Princeton University Press, 1998.

Leege, David. "Coalitions, Cues, Strategic Politics, and the Staying Power of the Religious Right, or Why Political Scientists Ought to Pay More Attention to Cultural Politics." *PS: Political Science and Politics* 25 (June 1992): 198–204.

———. "Religion and Politics in Theoretical Perspective." In *Rediscovering the Religious Factor in American Politics*, ed. David Leege and Lyman A. Kellstedt, 3–25. Armonk, NY: M. E. Sharpe, 1993.

Levine, Daniel H. ed., *Religion and Political Conflict in Latin America*. Chapel Hill, NC: University of North Carolina Press, 1986.

———. *Religion and Politics in Latin America: The Catholic Church in Venezuela and Colombia*. Princeton: Princeton University Press, 1981.

Lienesch, Michael. *Redeeming America: Piety and Politics in the New Christian Right*. Chapel Hill: University of North Carolina Press, 1993.

Mainwaring, Scott. *The Catholic Church and Politics in Brazil, 1916–1985*. Stanford, CA: Stanford University Press, 1985.

Martin, David. *Tongues of Fire: The Explosion of Protestantism in Latin America*. Oxford: Basil Blackwell, 1990.

Marty, Martin E., and R. Scott Appleby. *Fundamentalisms Observed*. Chicago: University of Chicago Press,1991.

Milligan, Susan. "Together, but Worlds Apart: Christian Aid Groups Raise Suspicion in Strongholds of Islam." *The Boston Globe*, Oct. 10, 2006.

Misztal, Bronislaw, and Anson Shupe, eds., *Religion and Politics in Comparative Perspective: Revival of Religious Fundamentalism in East and West*. Westport, CT: Praeger, 1994.

Nasr, Vali. "Military Rule, Islamism, and Democracy in Pakistan." *Middle East Journal* 58 (Spring 2004): 195–209.

Norris, Pippa, and Ronald Inglehart. *Sacred and Secular: Religion and Politics Worldwide*. Cambridge: Cambridge University Press, 2004.

Omar, A. Rashied. "The Right to Religious Conversion: Between Apostasy and Proselytization." Kroc Institute Occasional Paper #27, OP: 1, 2006.

Putnam, Robert. "The Prosperous Community: Social Capital and Public Life." *The American Prospect* 13 (Spring 1993): 35–42.

Putnam, Robert D., and David E. Campbell. *American Grace: How Religion Divides and Unites Us.* New York: Simon & Schuster, 2010.

Robbins, Joel. "The Globalization of Charismatic and Pentecostal Christianity." *Annual Review of Anthropology* 33 (2004): 117–143.

Rostow, Walt. *The Stages of Economic Growth: A Non-Communist Manifesto.* Cambridge: Cambridge University Press, 1960.

Rubin, Jeffrey. "In the Streets or in the Institutions?" *LASA Forum* 37 (2006): 26–29.

Sherman, Amy. *The Soul of Development: Biblical Christianity and Economic Transformation in Guatemala.* New York: Oxford University Press, 1997.

——. "Meanings and Mobilizations: A Cultural Politics Approach to Social Movements and States." *Latin American Research Review* 39, no. 3 (2004): 106–142.

Smelser, Neil J. *Social Change in the Industrial Revolution.* London: Routledge, 1958.

Smilde, David. "Rational Analysis of Religious Conversion and Social Change: Networks and Publics in Latin American Evangelicalism." In *Conversion of a Continent: Contemporary Religious Change in Latin America*, ed. Timothy Steigenga and Edward Cleary, 93–114. New Brunswick, NJ: Rutgers University Press, 2007.

——. *Reason to Believe: Cultural Agency in Latin American Evangelicalism.* Berkeley and Los Angeles: University of California Press, 2007.

——. "Works of the Flesh, Fruit of the Spirit: Religious Action Frames and Meaning Networks in Venezuelan Evangelicalism." PhD diss., University of Chicago, 2000.

Smith, Brian. *The Church and Politics in Chile: Challenges to Modern Catholicism.* Princeton: Princeton University Press, 1982.

Snow, David A., and Richard Machalek. "The Sociology of Conversion." *Annual Review of Sociology* 10 (1984):167–190.

Stark, Rodney, and Lawrence Iannaccone, "A Supply-Side Reinterpretation of the 'Secularization' of Europe." *Journal for the Scientific Study of Religion* 33 (1994): 230–252.

Stark, Rodney, and James C. McCann. "Market Forces and Catholic Commitment: Exploring the New Paradigm." *Journal for the Scientific Study of Religion* 32 (1993): 111–124.

Steigenga, Timothy. *The Politics of the Spirit: The Political Implications of Pentecostalized Religion in Costa Rica and Guatemala.* Lanham, MD: Lexington Books, 2001.

Tibi, Bassam. *The Challenge of Fundamentalism: Political Islam and the New World Disorder.* Berkeley and Los Angeles: University of California Press, 1998.

Toyoda, Maria A., and Aji Tanaka. "Religion and Politics in Japan." In *Religion and Politics in Comparative Perspective: The One, the Few, and the Many*, ed. Ted Jelen and Clyde Wilcox, 269–288. Cambridge: Cambridge University Press, 2002.

Verba, Sidney, Kay Lehman Schlozman, and Henry Brady. *Voice and Equality: Civic Voluntarism in American Politics.* Cambridge, MA: Harvard University Press, 1995.

Wald, Kenneth D., and Allison Calhoun-Brown. *Religion and Politics in the United States.* Lanham, MD: Rowman & Littlefield, 2006.

Wald, Kenneth D., D. E. Owen, and S. D. Hill, Jr. "Churches as Political Communities." *American Political Science Review* 82 (June 1988): 531–548.

Wilcox, Clyde. "Religion and Politics among White Evangelicals: The Impact of Religious Variables on Political Attitudes." *Review of Religious Research* 32 (1990): 27–41.

Willems, Emilio. *Followers of the New Faith: Culture Change and the Rise of Protestantism in Brazil and Chile.* Nashville, TN: Vanderbilt University Press, 1967.

Wuthnow, Robert. *The Restructuring of American Religion: Society and Faith Since World War II.* Princeton: Princeton University Press, 1988.

PART II

RELIGIONS

....

CHAPTER 18

HINDUISM AND CONVERSION

....

ARVIND SHARMA

A standard classification of religions of the world divides religions into those that are missionary and those that are non-missionary. This concept goes back at least as far December 3, 1873, when Max Müller articulated it in a lecture given at Westminster Abbey.[1] The classification rests on the fact of whether a religion seeks converts or does not do so. By this criterion, the three major religions that fell into the category of missionary religions when this classification was first proposed were Buddhism, Christianity, and Islam. The religions that were categorized as non-missionary religions were Judaism, Zoroastrianism, and Hinduism. Perhaps the Primal Religions (otherwise called tribal religions),[2] Confucianism,[3] and Taoism[4] could also be placed in this category.

HINDUISM AND THE CONCEPT OF A MISSIONARY RELIGION

....

Hinduism is classified as a non-missionary religion, and this provides a clear indication of its attitude toward religious conversion. This statement, while substantially correct, requires clarifications and caveats. The above categorization classifies the world religions as either missionary or non-missionary. This distinction is based on whether a religion proselytizes or not and, as such, could be restated as a distinction between proselytizing and non-proselytizing religions. This new terminology is helpful because it possesses certain advantages:

(1) It is possible for a religion to possess a sense of "mission" without it necessarily getting involved in the process of "conversion" in the formal religious sense. It

could be a religion's mission to stop conversion rather than to carry it out. This could distinguish it from other religions that do not promote conversion but that do not oppose it, either. In fact, in terms of this distinction, Hinduism could be described as a missionary religion but not a proselytizing one, on account of its views about conversion (presented later in this chapter).

(2) To describe a missionary religion as a proselytizing one places the emphasis where it belongs, because many of the so-called non-missionary religions do "accept" converts while they may not seek them. This is true of Judaism, for instance. Moreover, Judaism does possess a sense of mission: to be a light among the nations. So, Judaism could also be called a missionary but not a proselytizing religion.[5]

(3) A distinction may have to be drawn between those non-proselytizing religions that do accept converts and those that do not do so. Zoroastrianism as practiced in India comes close to being a religion of the latter type. Thus, non-proselytizing religions may accept or reject converts who seek admission into a religion on their own. This may provide a clearer vector of distinction among the religions than the terms missionary and non-missionary.

(4) Sometimes a distinction is drawn between "proselytization" and "conversion" along the following lines, as the National Christian Council notes: "Conversion has been confused with proselytism, but there is a difference. The proselyte may have no inner change of life, hence he has no conversion. He is one who has passed from one religion to another, changing some external features of his life, manners, and customs. But these may not correspond to any spiritual illumination, reconciliation, and peace."[6]

Hinduism, then, is a non-proselytizing religion that accepts converts. But this statement also needs to be hedged with certain caveats:

(1) A non-proselytizing religion may come to cover a sizable area even if it is not supposed to "spread" the way proselytizing religions do. Hinduism, which is often associated with India, did spread beyond India to an extent that cannot be explained by migration alone. Bali, in Indonesia, remains Hindu to this day.[7] Hinduism, then, is an example of a non-proselytizing religion that also spread considerably far from its origins. One factor in this has been the fact that acceptance of Hinduism does not involve rejection of one's previous religion. Interestingly, this is a feature that Buddhism shares to a certain extent with Hinduism which, unlike Hinduism, is classified as a proselytizing religion.

(2) Another point that needs to be borne in mind here has been made by Sarvepalli Radhakrishnan, as follows:

In a sense, Hinduism may be regarded as the first example in the world of a missionary religion. Only its missionary spirit is different from that associated with the proselytizing creeds. It did not regard it as its mission to convert humanity to any one opinion. For what counts is conduct and not belief. Worshippers of different gods and followers of different rites were taken into the Hindu fold. Kṛṣṇa, according to the *Bhagavadgītā*, accepts as his own, not only oppressed classes, women and śūdras, but even those of unclean descent (*pāpayonayaḥ*), like the Kirātas and the Huṇas. The ancient practice of vrātyastoma, described fully in the *Tāṇḍya Brāhmaṇa*, shows that not only individuals but whole tribes were absorbed into Hinduism.[8]

(3)   The Arya Samaj, a major nineteenth-century reform movement within Hinduism, developed the concept of *śuddhi*, or purification, to allow for the readmission to Hinduism of Hindus who had been weaned away from the religion in India by Islam and Christianity.[9] This apparently involves conversion to Hinduism, from a certain point of view, but to the Hindu it constitutes the reversion of those who had been, in Hinduism's understanding, diverted away from the parent religion, so what is involved is not "conversion" but "reversion," or homecoming.

(4)   Although conversion to Hinduism on anyone's part does not normally require the abandonment of one's previous affiliation so much as acceptance of the new, there are now sects within Hinduism that insist that conversion to their sects involves the severing of such previous ties.[10]

(5)   While it is true that Hinduism's attitude toward conversions could be conveyed by describing it as a non-proselytizing religion which accepts but does not seek converts, some Hindu leaders are reluctant even to accept converts who on their own wish to become Hindus. The following conversation between the late Śrī Chandraśehara Bhāratī Swami and an American tourist in 1953 illustrates this point well:

"Why must it be," impatiently demanded an earnest American tourist, "that you will not convert other peoples to Hinduism? You have such a beautiful religion, and yet you keep so many struggling souls out of it. If you say 'yes' I will be the first to become a Hindu!"

"But why," came the counter-question, "do you want to change your religion? What is wrong with Christianity?"

Taken aback, but not daunted, the tourist said, "I cannot say what is wrong, but it has not given me satisfaction."

"Indeed, it is unfortunate," was the reply, "but tell me honestly whether you have given it a real chance. Have you fully understood the religion of Christ and lived according to it? Have you been a true Christian and yet found the religion wanting?"

"I am afraid I cannot say that, Sir."

"Then we advise you to go and be a true Christian first; live truly by the word of the Lord, and if even then you feel unfulfilled, it will be time to consider what should be done."

To put the puzzled American at his ease the sage explained:

"It is no freak that you were born a Christian. God ordained it that way because by the *samskāra* acquired through your actions (karma) in previous births your soul has taken a pattern which will find its richest fulfillment in the Christian way of life. Therefore your salvation lies there and not in some other religion. What you must change is not your faith but your life."

"Then, Sir," exclaimed the American, beaming with exhilaration, "your religion consists in making a Christian a better Christian, a Muslim a better Muslim and a Buddhist a better Buddhist. This day I have discovered yet another grand aspect of Hinduism, and I bow to you for having shown me this. Thank you indeed."[11]

With these clarifications and caveats, Hinduism's attitude to conversions may be summarized by describing it as a non-proselytizing religion.

REASONS UNDERLYING THE HINDU AVERSION TO RELIGIOUS CONVERSION

The question which then remains to be addressed is the following: Why is Hinduism unenthusiastic about the idea of religious conversion? A number of factors seem to be involved. The first is a historical factor: Hinduism as a religion has a very thick association with the landmass of the Indian subcontinent, which gives it a pronounced ethnic character, and ethnic religions in general tend to be non-proselytizing. Shinto and the Primal Religions come to mind. Another way in which this factor affects Hinduism's attitude to conversion is that, as the European Indologist, Sir Charles Eliot once wrote, "Hinduism has not been made but has grown. It is a jungle, not a building. It is the living example of a great national paganism such as might have existed in Europe if Christianity had not become the state religion of the Roman Empire, if there had remained an incongruous jumble of old local superstitions, Greek philosophy, and Oriental cults such as the worship of Sarapis or Mithras."[12] It is worth noting that joining a cult involves *initiation* into it rather than a conversion from one religion to another. Hinduism is not limited to India, however, as Louis Renou comments:

> To confine Hinduism to the circumference of India, however, would be to bypass the missionary character of this religion in the past. In the so-called Hinduization of southeast Asia, Indian religious influences combined with indigenous elements and in the course of time were assimilated by Buddhism, Islam or some form of national religion. In this way Hinduism has had a profound influence, especially in Cambodia, ancient Champa and Bali. One should also recall that there are Hindus in Ceylon (among the Dravidian population), in Nepal, in Pakistan (an inestimable number) and in Indian settlements scattered all over the world.[13]

A significant cultural factor is the fact that Hinduism is as much a culture as a religion, or alternatively, that the distinction between religion and culture is alien to it. Thus, it may spread as a culture but does not proselytize as a religion.[14] Proselytizing religions, on the other hand, typically cut across cultural boundaries. The sociological factor related to Hinduism's lack of enthusiasm for proselytizing is concerned with the so-called caste system. The caste system is a highly debated topic, but there is broad agreement that a key element of it consists of the fact that it is based on birth. At one time it was even claimed that in order to be a Hindu one must belong to a caste, and since one is born into a caste one could not become a Hindu but only be one (or cease to be one). Thus, Donald Eugene Smith notes, "The conversion of a Hindu to Christianity or Islam has invariably led to excommunication from his caste and frequently to expulsion from the joint family to which he belonged. Hinduism allows the greatest latitude in religious and philosophical beliefs, but actions which threaten its social solidarity by transferring the individual to a different religious community will be vigorously resisted. The general Hindu attitude places the value of social cohesion far above that of individual freedom."[15] There are elements of overstatement in this proposition, but it does contain an important grain of truth. The karmic factor is also relevant, because one is born into a particular religion (as into a particular caste) because of one's karma, and while it may be possible to change the present situation, such a karmic view encourages a certain conservatism in the matter.[16]

Hinduism tends to promote the view that all religions are valid as ways of approaching the ultimate reality and for obtaining salvation or liberation. So, according to this soteriology, why change one's religion or ask anyone else to do so? In response to claims that if all religions are valid, why not allow conversion, since the new way is as effective as the old, Hinduism responds by saying: But why change it in the first place? In this respect, the position of Ramakrishna has been paradigmatic for modern Hinduism and is succinctly described by Eric J. Sharpe as follows:

> Ramakrishna (1834–1886) had, in his attempts to explore every available means for the attainment of spiritual insight, experimented with what he took to be the *sādhanas* of Islam and Christianity; he had seen visions of Jesus and of Muhammad, and had claimed that the differences between the spiritual disciplines were of no real significance; the Bengali, Urdu and English languages have different words to describe water, he once said, but the substance itself is one, not three. In the same way competing and apparently contradictory views of religion refer to one attainable spiritual vision of reality. All *sādhanas* lead finally to the same goal, and the only ultimate heresy is to fail to realize that fact. Conversion, or the attempt to convert, is a waste of time, an exchanging of one path up the mist-shrouded mountain for another; indeed, it may be worse, since there are sound cultural reasons for remaining within one's own ancestral fold. So while Ramakrishna could say that "every man should follow his own religion. A Christian should follow Christianity, a Muslim should follow Islam, and so on," he could immediately add: "For the Hindus the ancient path, the path of the Aryan Rishis, is the best."[17]

There is also a communal factor in Hinduism's reluctance to proselytize. Religious conversion often leads to tension in a community because it involves the assertion of an individual's right to change his or her own religion without regard to the religion of those around him or her. This may work reasonably well in atomized modern societies, but most traditional societies take the situatedness of a person quite seriously, and conversion in such situations could be quite disruptive. Another factor is moral. The proselytizing religions, in their enthusiasm to win converts, may employ what might be considered unethical means, such as bribery or deception. A stronger case for conversion can be made when a person does so of his or her own free will rather than being induced to do so. And the final factor is related to peace; proselytization leads to conflict among religions as each tries to steal the others' adherents.[18]

Although all these factors play a role in establishing or confirming Hinduism as a non-proselytizing religion, the soteriological argument is a very important component of Hinduism and provides the ideological basis of its position.

HINDU REACTION TO PROSELYTIZATION

Hinduism as a non-proselytizing religion has been at the receiving end of two major proselytizing religions: Islam and Christianity. What is more, it came under pressure from them at a time when they were enjoying political ascendancy. Thus, Islam was politically ascendant in India from ca. 1200 to 1800[19] and Christianity from ca. 1800 to 1947.[20] As a result, about one-fourth of the population had converted to Islam by the time India became independent in 1947 and somewhere between 2 and 3 percent had converted to Christianity.

The manner in which Hinduism reacted to this pressure is significant. One reaction was to borrow the methods of the opponent and itself become a proselytizing religion, even if this impulse of conversion was often restricted to accepting back into the fold those who had been lost to it. Evidence of this attitude goes back to medieval times, but its articulation in modern times has been more explicit. As Gauri Viswanathan explains:

> Although Hinduism traditionally claimed that, unlike Christianity and Islam, it was not a proselytizing religion and that Hindus were born not made, the Ārya Samāj introduced practices that unsettled those claims. A practice akin to the baptismal rites of conversion, the ritual purification act of *śuddhi* initiated non-Hindus to the religion. Though claiming earlier scriptural antecedents, *śuddhi* was intended to help Hindus reclaim converts to Christianity. The ritual is an example of how Hinduism adapted to the new challenges set by colonialism by borrowing some of the very features—such as conversion—that it had earlier repudiated, claiming Hinduism's privileged status on the basis of birth. Reconversion rituals have been a fundamental part of modern Hinduism's attempt to reclaim and sustain its majoritarian status.[21]

The more prominent reaction, however, was to oppose conversions either way—either to Islam or Christianity, or to Hinduism. This latter trend is a marked feature of modern Hindu thought, and the two religious figures who have probably been most influential in shaping this attitude are Ramakṛṣṇa Paramahaṁsa (1836–1886)[22] and Mahatma

Gandhi (1869–1948). The following dialogue between C. F. Andrews and Gandhi goes to the core of the matter:

C. F. Andrews: "What would you say to a man who after considerable thought and prayer said that he could not have his peace and salvation except by becoming a Christian?"

GANDHIJI: "I would say if a non-Christian (say a Hindu) came to a Christian and made that statement, he should ask him to become a good Hindu rather than find goodness in change of faith."

C. F. ANDREWS: "I cannot in this go the whole length with you, though you know my own position. I discarded the position that there is no salvation except through Christ long ago. But supposing the Oxford Group Movement people changed the life of your son, and he felt like being converted, what would you say?"

GANDHIJI: "I would say that the Oxford Group may change the lives of as many as they like, but not their religion. They can draw their attention to the best in their respective religions and change their lives by asking them to live according to them. There came to me a man, the son of brahmana parents, who said his reading of your book had led him to embrace Christianity. I asked him if he thought that the religion of his forefathers was wrong. He said, 'No.' Then I said: 'Is there any difficulty about your accepting the Bible as one of the great religious books of the world and Christ as one of the great teachers?' I said to him that you had never through your books asked Indians to take up the Bible and embrace Christianity, and that he had misread your book—unless of course your position is like that of the late M. Mahomed Ali's, viz. that 'a believing Mussulman [Muslim], however bad his life, is better than a good Hindu.'"

C. F. ANDREWS: "I do not accept M. Mahomed Ali's position at all. But I do say that if a person really needs a change of faith I should not stand in his way."

GANDHIJI: "But don't you see that you do not even give him a chance? You do not even cross-examine him. Supposing a Christian came to me and said he was captivated by a reading of the Bhagawata and so wanted to declare himself a Hindu, I should say to him: 'No. What the bhagawata offers the Bible also offers. You have not yet made the attempt to find it out. Make the attempt and be a good Christian.'"

C. F. ANDREWS: "I don't know. If someone earnestly says that he will become a good Christian, I should say, 'You may become one', though you know that I have in my own life strongly dissuaded ardent enthusiasts who came to me. I said to them, 'Certainly not on my account will you do anything of the kind'. But human nature does require a concrete faith."

GANDHIJI: "If a person wants to believe in the Bible let him say so, but why should he discard his own religion? This proselytization will mean no peace in the world. Religion is a very personal matter. We should by living the life according to our lights share the best with one another, thus adding to the sum total of human effort to reach God."

"Consider," continued Gandhiji, "whether you are going to accept the position of mutual toleration or of equality of all religions. My position is that all the great religions are fundamentally equal. We must have innate respect for other religions as we have for our own. Mind you, not mutual toleration, but equal respect."[23]

Mahatma Gandhi's overall position in the matter is ably summarized by Donald Eugene Smith, as follows:

> Gandhi once wrote that the different religions were branches of the same majestic tree; all faiths were "equally true, though being received and interpreted through human instruments equally imperfect." This great truth should preclude even the thought that another individual embrace one's own faith. "Accepting this position, we can only pray, if we are Hindus, not that a Christian should become a Hindu, or if we are Mussalmans, not that a Hindu or a Christian should become a Mussalman, nor should we even secretly pray that any one should be converted, but our inmost prayer should be that a Hindu should be a better Hindu, a Muslim a better Muslim and a Christian a better Christian." Gandhi felt so strongly about this question that on another occasion he wrote: "If I had power and could legislate, I should stop all proselytizing." Gandhi did agree, however, that if an individual found that he could realize God better through embracing a different religion, he should have complete freedom to do so.[24]

LIMITATIONS OF THE HINDU VIEW ON CONVERSION

The Hindu view on conversion is subject to several limitations. The blanket opposition to conversion that Hinduism sometimes exhibits does not discriminate sufficiently between a sincere desire on the part of a religion to share one's beliefs with another and a perverse desire to bring everyone within one's fold. If one feels that one has found the answer to the cosmic riddle, then it is only natural that one would wish to communicate this to others. Similarly, at the other end, one could have an authentic conversion experience the way Paul had on the road to Damascus. The fact that Hinduism became exposed to Christianity under the shadow of imperialism may justify a "hermeneutics of suspicion" in relation to conversion, but it should not blind one to the possibility of conversion as an authentic religious experience.

Hinduism tends to view "conversion" in purely spiritual terms, but often in real life it may be a response to social and economic conditions experienced by a disadvantaged group, as exemplified by the conversion of former untouchables or Dalits to Buddhism in significant numbers under the leadership of Dr. B. R. Ambedkar. If an individual or a group genuinely feels that it can only achieve its full potential, whether material or spiritual, outside Hinduism, then this sentiment should perhaps be respected.

THE POLITICS OF CONVERSION IN INDIA

The politics of conversion in India needs to be analyzed.[25] Hinduism itself is essentially a non-proselytizing religion and therefore does not go in for conversions. However, conversion from Hinduism to other proselytizing religions, such as Islam and Christianity, has occurred from time to time. Indian Christians continue to believe that St. Thomas made converts in India soon after the appearance of Christianity, and Indian Muslims believe that conversions to Islam took place on India's southern coast soon after the appearance of Islam through the agency of Arab traders. These accounts may have a legendary component to them but are significant for the fact that they refer to conversions occurring outside the context of the political subjugation of the Hindus. This sets them apart qualitatively from conversion in India to Islam during the period of Islamic political ascendancy and to Christianity during the period of Christian political ascendancy. The political situation changed with the arrival of Indian independence in 1947; the new government had the opportunity to define its stance toward conversion when the constituent assembly met to frame the constitution of India. This was done in the form of Article 25(1) of the Indian Constitution, according to which "all persons are equally entitled to freedom of conscience and the right freely to profess, practice and propagate religion."[26] This freedom was, however, "subject to public order, morality and health and to other provisions of this Part."[27]

This would seem to settle the matter, as the Indian Constitution guarantees the right to propagate religion. However, as Donald Eugene Smith notes, "Despite the clarity of the constitutional provision, there is in India a continuing debate on whether the propagation of religion should be permitted, and, if so, on what terms."[28]

This debate has been continually fueled by a Hindu sense of grievance at being taken advantage of, as a non-proselytizing religion, by the proselytizing religions which are sometimes dubbed predatory religions, and also by a sense of grievance on the part of the proselytizing religions of Christianity and Islam at not being allowed to exercise their constitutional right to rescue the underprivileged from the clutches of the Hindu caste system. These tensions have typically been negotiated not at the federal but rather at the state level. An early manifestation of this tension led to the appointment of the Christian Missionary Activities Inquiry Committee, headed by Dr. M. B. Niyogi and hence known as the Niyogi Committee, which submitted its report in 1956. Its recommendations, which were not implemented, included legislation that would have entirely eliminated the propagation of religion.

The electoral successes of some of the political parties with close ties to Hindu sentiment led to enactment of what are called freedom of religion acts in some states of India, such as Orissa, Gujarat, and Rajasthan, which, while not banning conversion, make it subject to several safeguards to ensure that it is not brought about by threat or inducement. This raises the question of whether the right to propagate should be unchecked or whether it can or should be made subject to legislation to ensure that no unfair practices are involved.

The recent religious eruption in Orissa is a useful case study of this contentious issue. The sequence of events was set in motion by the murder of an octogenarian Hindu religious figure, Swami Lakshmanananda (or Laxmanananda) Saraswati, who was gunned down on August 23, 2008, by thirty masked men. The Swami was a Viswa Hindu Parishad (VHP) saint (or religious figure) who had arrived from the Himalayas in 1966 to challenge Christian missionary activity in the area and set up an ashram in 1967. He was in the forefront of the VHP's *ghar vapasi* (homecoming) movement, which consisted of reconverting tribals and Dalits (former untouchables) who had been converted by Christian missionaries. His murder was allegedly perpetrated by the Maoists of the region. Out of the 22 members of the district committee of Maoists, however, 70 percent are Christians. Although claiming no responsibility for the killing, the Maoists did accuse the Swami of spreading social unrest.

On Christmas Day in 2007, according to an article in *India Today International*, "clashes between VHP [Viswa Hindu Parishad] supporters and Hindus had erupted when some Christians tried to set up a gate in front of a temple in Brahmanigaon village. When Saraswati visited the site he was allegedly attacked. Around 800 houses were damaged in the violence that followed and 580 families were displaced. It left five dead."[29] However, the journalist continues:

> This time, there is an air of mystery around the controversial swami's killing. Despite being a high-risk security threat, on the night he was killed, his bodyguard was on leave while four unarmed constables attached to his security had gone to a nearby market. Despite the fact that there were as many as eight attempts on his life, the...administration ignored his security. The swami was the Hindutva icon in the state, spearheading a crusade supporting implementation of the ban on cow slaughter, spreading Hindu teachings among tribal youth and opposing forced conversion. Curiously, just three days before his assassination, the swami had received threatening letters and even though the police were informed, security around him was not tightened. His killing resulted in the mass upsurge of fanatics who presumed that Christians had a hand in his death.[30]

The opposition to "forced conversion" on the part of the Swami should be noted. Soumyajit Pattnaik of *Hindustan Times* reported on August 26, 2008, that "the Swami was spearheading the re-conversion movement in Orissa to bring back converted Christians to the Hindu fold. He confronted missionaries and Church leaders in the process. He also led movements against cow slaughter and ran Vanavasi Kalyan Ashrams to educate tribal children."[31]

The conflict arose in a context of conversion, resistance to conversion, reconversion, and resistance to reconversion. Satyen Moharpatra reported in the *Hindustan Times* on September 3, 2008:

> The Catholic Bishops' Conference of India (CBCI) have been stating that members of their faith had been forcibly converted and made to attack the very churches they used to pray in. Mishra [Orissa home secretary T. K. Mishra] told HT on the phone

from Bhubaneswar that "forced conversion is unlawful under the Orissa Freedom of Religion Act". He said any priest performing a conversion is supposed to inform the district magistrate or collector concerned. The state can intervene only if it finds that "any threat, compulsion or inducement" has been used, Mishra said.[32]

There is also an ethnic dimension to the issue, due to the tension between the Pana Christians (52 percent) and the Kundha tribals (17 percent) in Kandhamal district. In order to understand these tensions one needs to realize that the Indian Constitution provides for affirmative action benefits for former Hindu untouchable castes and tribes. The Panas are former untouchables who have converted to Christianity; by doing so, they can no longer benefit from scheduled caste reservations open only to former Hindu untouchables. They are therefore demanding scheduled tribe status, whose benefits are open to all tribals irrespective of religion. This move is being resisted by the Kandh Adivasis, or tribals, who are backed by Hindu organizations although some of the tribals are Christians. Mohuya Chaudhuri reports, "And caught in this volatile cocktail of caste and communal conflict are the poor villagers who have nowhere to go. Those who are outnumbered in their own villages choose the easiest option—that of conversion to the majority."[33]

The issue of conversion and reconversion, however, is a vital element in the situation. It has been noted by observers that people in several areas of the state of Orissa have been embracing Christianity since the days of the British Raj, but such conversion was not considered a problem until the counter movement to either stop the conversions or to reconvert Christians was started by the Hindus. Hence, religious conversion is a major cause of conflict in the area.

Pradip Nina Thomas, an Australia-based author and teacher who has made a special study of the emergence of Christian fundamentalism in Tamil Nadu, remarks on the current situation as follows:

> The situation in Orissa does not augur well for inter-faith relationships in the country. While there is certainly a case to be made to rein in the Sangh Parivar, especially the VHP and the Bajrang Dal, I think it offers an opportunity for the Christian hierarchy to dwell on the consequences of what some might term "militant" forms of Christian mission.
>
> A number of conservative para-Church organizations and new churches are involved in a "numbers" game and conversion and contribute to undoing the good work done by Roman Catholics and Protestants in the areas of health, education and development. When there is a backlash, all Christians, irrespective of whether they are involved in militant forms of mission or not, become fair game for Hindu militants.[34]

Proselytization is thus fueling interfaith rivalry in a way which does not bode well for cordial interfaith relations.

CONCLUSION

In conclusion, it is important to assess the contribution the Hindu attitude to religious conversion makes to the general discussion of religious conversion. This contribution can be identified at two levels.

At one level, the Hindu attitude toward religious conversion helps clarify an ambiguity surrounding the process of religious conversion in terms of human rights discourse. Conversion involves changing one's religion, and Article 18 of the Universal Declaration of Human Rights specifically refers to this right to change one's religion. This right, however, does not distinguish sufficiently between *my* right to change my religion and *somebody else's* right to ask me to change my religion. The distinction is important, because the two rights are not symmetrical; my right to change my religion is more self-evident than someone else's right to ask me to change my religion. If one is committed to religious freedom, then one's right to change one's religion should perhaps be unrestricted, but someone else's right to ask someone else to change his or her religion, after a point, could compromise the other person's own right to unhindered religious freedom; aggressive proselytizing could be construed as an hindrance. How these two sets of rights are to be adjusted thus needs to be specifically addressed in human rights discourse, and this is one contribution the Hindu perspective on conversion can make to the field in general.

The other contribution is more far-reaching. Conversion has to do with the question of how the various religions of the world relate to one another, and the conversion model allows followers of one religion to convert to another. In this respect, Hinduism offers another model for interaction among religions, one that does away with religious conversion altogether as an ingredient in their interaction. According to this model, religions should not be concerned with changing the religion of others but, instead, with helping each other make a Hindu a better Hindu, a Christian a better Christian, a Muslim a better Muslim, and so on. Mahatma Gandhi was an uncompromising advocate of this model.[35] In light of his position, some modern Hindu scholars distinguish between *horizontal* conversion involving moving from "one formal faith to another" and *vertical* conversion involving moving "from the lower to the higher conception of God"[36] and/or moving from a lower to a higher level of moral behavior. Donald Eugene Smith correctly notes that this Hindu view does not preclude spiritual teaching across religious boundaries because, "once conversion of the conventional type is eliminated... there is wide scope for sharing the religious insights among the various world faiths."[37] P. J. Mehta expressed his views along these lines to Christian missionaries as follows: "By all means discuss your faith with us, share your views and your experiences with us, but... India would like to suggest that the true missionary is one who... helps the other to live his own faith more perfectly,"[38] rather than asking one to change one's faith. This is in keeping with the prevailing ethos of modern Hinduism that the goal of interfaith action is not to convert people to one's own faith but to help them live their own faith more fully.

NOTES

1. Max Müller, *Chips from a German Workshop* (London: Longmans, Green & Co., 1875), 4: 253.

2. Arvind Sharma, *A Primal Perspective on the Philosophy of Religion* (Amsterdam: Springer, 2006), 174–175.

3. A. C. Graham, "Confucianism," in *The Concise Encyclopedia of Living Faiths*, ed. R. C. Zaehner (Boston: Beacon Press, 1967), 383.

4. Werner Eichhorn, "Taoism," in *The Concise Encyclopedia of Living Faiths*, ed. Zaehner, 401.

5. Alan Segal, "The Jewish Tradition," in *World Religions: Western Traditions*, ed. Willard Oxtoby (Toronto: Oxford University Press, 1996), 80.

6. Quoted in Donald Eugene Smith, *India as a Secular State* (Princeton: Princeton University Press, 1963), 174.

7. Louis Renou, ed., *Hinduism* (New York: George Braziller, 1962), 16.

8. S. Radhakrishnan, *The Hindu View of Life* (London: George Allen & Unwin, 1927), 37–38.

9. S. F. Seunarine, *Reconversion to Hinduism Through Śuddi* (Bangalore: Christian Institute for the Study of Religion and Society, 1977).

10. See Satguru Sivaya Subramuniyaswami, *How to Become a Hindu: A Guide for Seekers and Born Hindus* (Kauai, HI: Himalayan Academy, 2000).

11. T. M. P. Mahadevan, *Outlines of Hinduism* (Bombay: Chetana, 1971), 294–295.

12. Quoted in A. C. Bouquet, *Hinduism* (London: Hutchinson University Library, 1969), 17.

13. Renou, *Hinduism*, 16.

14. Julius Lipner, *Hindus: Their Religious Beliefs and Practices* (London: Routledge, 1994), 7.

15. Smith, *India as a Secular State*, 165.

16. Mahadevan, *Outlines of Hinduism*, 295.

17. Eric J. Sharpe, *Comparative Religion: A History* (London: Duckworth, 1985), 254–255.

18. Mahatma Gandhi, *Hindu Dharma* (Ahmedabad: Navajivan Publishing House, 1950), 231, 232.

19. S. M. Ikram, *Muslim Civilization in India*, ed. Ainslie T. Embree (New York: Columbia University Press, 1964), 232–233.

20. But see Gauri Viswanathan, "Colonialism and Construction of Hinduism," in *The Blackwell Companion to Hinduism*, ed. Gavin Flood (Oxford: Blackwell Publishing, 2003), 33, 39.

21. Ibid., 36.

22. For a discussion of his position, see Arvind Sharma, *The Concept of Universal Religion in Modern Hindu Thought* (London: Macmillan Press, 1998), ch. 5.

23. Gandhi, *Hindu Dharma*, 230–232.

24. Smith, *India as a Secular State*, 168–169.

25. For more on this theme, see Joe Arun, "Conversion and the Rise of Hindu Fundamentalism: A Case Study of Tamil Nadu, South India," Institute of Dialogue with Cultures and Religions, http://www.idcrdialogue.com/publiations.php; Chad Bauman, *Christian Identity and Dalit Religion in Hindu India, 1868–1947* (Grand Rapids, MI: Eerdmans Publishers, 2008); Kevin Boyle and Juliet Sheen, eds., *Freedom of Religion and Belief: A World Report* (New York: Routledge, 1997); Sebastian Kim, *In Search of Identity* (New Delhi: Oxford University Press, 2005); Smita Narula, "Overlooked Danger: The Security and Rights Implications of Hindu Nationalism in India," *Harvard Human Rights Journal* 16 (2003): 41–68; Biswamoy Pati, *Identity, Hegemony, Resistance: Towards a Social History of Conversions in Orissa, 1800–2000* (Gurgoan: Three Essays Collective, 2003);

Kumkum Sangari, "Gender Lines: Personal Laws, Uniform Law, Conversion," *Social Scientist* 27, no. 5/6 (1999): 11–61.

26. Smith, *India as a Secular State*, 135.
27. Ibid.
28. Ibid., 163.
29. Farzand Ahmed, "For God's Sake," *India Today International*, Sept. 22, 2008.
30. Ibid.
31. Soumyajit Pattnaik, "Why Communal Fire Spread across Orissa," *Hindustan Times*, Aug. 26, 2008, http://www.hindustantimes.com/StoryPage/StoryPage.aspx?sectionName=&id=10f82f11-3511-469d-95fd-f731ac211ac7&&Headline=Why+communal+fire+spread+across+Orissa.
32. Satyen Mohapatra, "No Complaints of Forcible Conversions," *Hindustan Times*, Sept. 3, 2008, http://www.hindustantimes.com/StoryPage/StoryPage.aspx?sectionName=&id=dc89fff6-4fec-4361-8ec6-b2df63bb2e24&&Headline=%e2%80%98No+complaints+of+forcible+conversions%e2%80%99.
33. Mohuya Chaudhuri, "Kandhmal Becoming Laboratory of Hate," NDTV, Sept. 2, 2008, http://www.ndtv.com/convergence/ndtv/story.aspx?id=NEWEN20080063877.
34. Cited in Mohuya Chaudhuri, "Religious Divide Deepens in Kandhmal," NDTV, Sept. 2, 2008, http://www.ndtv.com/convergence/ndtv/story.aspx?id=NEWEN20080063875&ch=633562671223307500.
35. Gandhi, *Hindu Dharma*, 230–232.
36. Mahadevan, *Outlines of Hinduism*, 20.
37. Smith, *India as a Secular State*, 169.
38. Ibid.

BIBLIOGRAPHY

Ahmed, Farzand. "For God's Sake." *India Today International*, Sept. 22, 2008.

Arun, Joe. "Conversion and the Rise of Hindu Fundamentalism: A Case Study of Tamil Nadu, South India." Institute of Dialogue with Cultures and Religions. http://www.idcrdialogue.com/publications.php.

Bauman, Chad. *Christian Identity and Dalit Religion in Hindu India, 1868–1947*. Grand Rapids, MI: Eerdmans Publishers, 2008.

Bouquet, A. C. *Hinduism*. London: Hutchinson University Library, 1969.

Boyle, Kevin, and Juliet Sheen, eds. *Freedom of Religion and Belief: A World Report*. New York: Routledge, 1997.

Chaudhuri, Mohuya. "Kandhmal Becoming Laboratory of Hate." NDTV, Sept. 2, 2008. http://www.ndtv.com/convergence/ndtv/story.aspx? id=NEWEN20080063877.

———. "Religious Divide Deepens in Kandhmal." NDTV, Sept. 2, 2008. http://www.ndtv.com/convergence/ndtv/story.aspx?id=NEWEN20080063875&ch=633562671223307500.

Eichhorn, Werner. "Taoism." In *The Concise Encyclopedia of Living Faiths*, ed. R. C. Zaehner, 385–401. Boston: Beacon Press, 1967.

Gandhi, Mahatma. *Hindu Dharma*. Ahmedabad: Navajivan Publishing House, 1950.

Graham, A. C. "Confucianism." In *The Concise Encyclopedia of Living Faith*, ed. R. C. Zaehner, 365–384. Boston: Beacon Press, 1967.

Ikram, S. M. *Muslim Civilization in India*, ed. Ainslie T. Embree. New York: Columbia University Press, 1964.

Kim, Sebastian. *In Search of Identity*. New Delhi: Oxford University Press, 2005.

Lipner, Julius. *Hindus: Their Religious Beliefs and Practices*. London: Routledge, 1994.

Mahadevan, T. M. P. *Outlines of Hinduism*. Bombay: Chetana, 1971.

Mohapatra, Satyen. "No Complaints of Forcible Conversions." *Hindustan Times*, Sept. 3, 2008. http://www.hindustantimes.com/StoryPage/StoryPage.aspx?sectionName=&id=dc89fff6-4fec-4361-8ec6-b2df63bb2e24&&Headline=%e2%80%98No+complaints+of+forcible+conversions%e2%80%99.

Müller, F. Max. *Chips from a German Workshop*. London: Longmans, Green & Co., 1875.

Narula, Smita. "Overlooked Danger: The Security and Rights Implications of Hindu Nationalism in India." *Harvard Human Rights Journal* 16 (2003): 41–68.

Oxtoby, Willard, ed. *World Religions: Western Traditions*. Toronto: Oxford University Press, 1996.

Pati, Biswamoy. *Identity, Hegemony, Resistance: Towards a Social History of Conversions in Orissa, 1800–2000*. Gurgoan: Three Essays Collective, 2003.

Pattnaik, Soumyajit. "Why Communal Fire Spread across Orissa." *Hindustan Times*, Aug. 26, 2008. http://www.hindustantimes.com/StoryPage/StoryPage.aspx?sectionName=&id=10f82f11-3511-469d-95fd-f731ac211ac7&&Headline=Why+communal+fire+spread+across+Orissa (accessed Oct. 8, 2008).

Radhakrishnan, Sarvepalli. *The Hindu View of Life*. London: George Allen & Unwin, 1927.

Renou, Louis, ed. *Hinduism*. New York: George Braziller, 1962.

Sangari, Kumkum. "Gender Lines: Personal Laws, Uniform Law, Conversion." *Social Scientist* 27, no. 5/6 (1999): 17–61.

Segal, Alan. "The Jewish Tradition." In *World Religions: Western Traditions*, ed. Willard Oxtoby, 12–150. Toronto: Oxford University Press, 1996.

Seunarine, S. F. *Reconversion to Hinduism through Śuddhi*. Bangalore: Christian Institute for the Study of Religion and Society, 1977.

Sharma, Arvind. *The Concept of Universal Religion in Modern Hindu Thought*. London: Macmillan Press, 1998.

——. *A Primal Perspective on the Philosophy of Religion*. Amsterdam: Springer, 2006.

Sharpe, Eric J. *Comparative Religion: A History*. London: Duckworth, 1985.

Smith, Donald Eugene. *India as a Secular State*. Princeton: Princeton University Press, 1963.

Subramuniyaswami, Satguru Sivaya. *How to Become a Hindu: A Guide for Seekers and Born Hindus*. Kauai, HI: Himalayan Academy, 2000.

Viswanathan, Gauri. "Colonialism and the Construction of Hinduism." In *The Blackwell Companion to Hinduism*, ed. Gavin Flood, 22–44. Oxford: Blackwell Publishing, 2003.

Zaehner, R. C., ed. *The Concise Encyclopedia of Living Faiths*. Boston: Beacon Press, 1967.

CHAPTER 19

CONVERSION TO JAIN IDENTITY

ANDREA R. JAIN

INTRODUCTION

THROUGHOUT Jain history, Jains have attracted converts by adapting to profound social shifts and participating in emergent religious markets. In fact, their ability to attract converts to the Jain tradition has depended on social processes and transformations that resulted in contexts conducive to religious conversion.[1] The likelihood of conversion to a Jain identity is enhanced by the fact that, even though Jains have not developed a doctrine of conversion that serves to legitimate and encourage proselytizing endeavors, they remain motivated to attract converts. Because Jain communities are made up of both lay and monastic individuals, and monastics depend on the laity for sustenance since they have taken vows of renunciation, Jains must sustain a large enough laity in order to support the monastics who embody the Jain ascetic ideal and transmit Jain teachings.

Conversion itself is "religious change."[2] That change depends on an advantageous social context and motivation for proselytization as well as on successful processes of socialization into a new Jain religious identity.[3] I will demonstrate how conversion to a Jain identity involves a conglomeration of changes with regard to social and religious variables such as social identity, socioeconomic status, lifestyle, and ritual incorporation.

Lewis R. Rambo argues that conversion usually requires rituals that both deconstruct and reconstruct identity.[4] In line with Émile Durkheim's social theory that ritual consolidates social identity, participation in Jain rituals, such as temple worship or *dana* (ritual giving to monastics), is essential for the construction of Jain identities among converts. With regard to rituals that serve to deconstruct previous identities, conversions sometimes require dramatic shifts in ritual life.[5] Jain converts usually do not undergo dramatic rituals that aim to deconstruct previous identities, but they do often undergo a dramatic shift in lifestyle, primarily through the adoption of vegetarianism. The absence of dramatic deconstructive rituals and the prevalence of reconstructive ones along with submission to certain lifestyle mandates enhance the likelihood of attracting adherents in the contexts where conversions to Jain identities occur.[6] Such contexts are characterized by religious eclecticism or plurality whereby individuals participate in rituals and other practices that they share with individuals who have different religious self-identities.

Michael Carrithers describes the South Asian socio-religious world as a place of "spiritual cosmopolitanism."[7] According to Carrithers, such cosmopolitanism is characterized by "eclecticism and fluidity of South Asian religious life…the sense in which people turn toward many sources for their spiritual sustenance, hope, relief, or defense."[8] In a similar but ultimately different way than Carrithers, Phyllis Granoff uses the category of "ritual eclecticism" to describe the ritual fluidity of South Asia: "The group of insiders explicitly acknowledges that others have rituals, and then enjoins or permits the practice of those rituals along with the rituals specific to the group itself."[9] For example, a Hindu may participate in a ritual organized around the worship of a *jina* (literally, "conqueror," a reference to one of the twenty-four liberated beings and great teachers of the Jain tradition).

It is important to understand the eclectic ritual culture of South Asia in order to avoid confusing moments of religious eclecticism with conversion to a Jain identity. As I will demonstrate below, religious eclecticism and conversion are different, but at the same time, Jain responses to religious eclecticism are important to Jain conversion even in contemporary cases. Historically, Jains attracted converts by making it easy to gain the perceived socioeconomic, religious, or ideological benefits of a Jain identity while also retaining the freedom to participate in Hindu, Buddhist, or tribal practices or movements important to one's familial or regional identity or one's ethical or social agenda. Although participation in an eclectic religious culture does not always lead to conversion, I will demonstrate that Jain adaptation to such cultural contexts often enabled Jain conversion by allowing individuals to construct new identities without abandoning important non-Jain practices or movements that functioned to meet different needs.

When the Jain tradition emerged circa the fifth century B.C.E as a new religious movement in the Ganges basin, it owed its existence to a particular social context that featured the growth of an ascetic culture. That culture emphasized the need to abandon the world and limit all social and physical action. Despite the Jain emphasis on withdrawal from the social and material worlds, Jains succeeded in attracting converts in the following one thousand years because of their adaptation to the shifting social contexts they encountered. They accommodated regional deities, participated in mainstream literary traditions, built temples, and acquired socioeconomic power, all of which enhanced their ability to attract converts, socialize the converts into Jain identities, and support Jain monastics who in turn attracted more converts. Jains continued to attract converts as they adapted to social changes in the medieval period. That period featured the rapid growth and popularity of *bhakti* (a devotional movement oriented around passionate reciprocal love between a devotee and a god) and *tantra* (a ritual and textual movement aimed toward the mystical experience of non-duality that requires the practitioner to transcend normative social rules and categories). Jains responded by building Jain temples in which Jain and non-Jain deities were objects of devotion and by providing Jain interpretations of the ideas and practices of *tantra*.

Today there are about 4.2 million Jains living in India and an estimated 100,000 living outside of India.[10] Contemporary Jains attract converts from Indian tribal communities by offering socioeconomic support and institutionalized programs for social reform. On a global scale, Jains adapt to a new contemporary social context that features a global religious market and certain popular ethical movements based on calls for social activism. Before discussing contemporary cases of Jain conversion, I will briefly review ancient and medieval examples. Tracing the historical trajectory of conversion to a Jain identity reveals the historical significance of Jain conversion and the importance of social context in determining Jain strategies for attracting converts.

EARLY CONVERSIONS

The Jain tradition emerged as a new religious movement in a social context that cultivated religious change. That context was the north Indian ascetic movement along the Ganges basin that arose in the seventh century B.C.E.[11] At that time, ascetics participated in movements that differed from the orthodox ritual culture established by *brahmans*, the Hindu socio-religious elites. The Jain movement was a radical one because it required a total break from *brahmanic* orthodox ritual and conversion to a new orientation toward the material world (*ajiva*) and the soul (*jiva*) based on unique conceptions of violence and physical action as taught by Vardhamana Mahavira (henceforth Mahavira).

Scholars estimate that Mahavira, the Great Hero (*maha-vira*) and historical founder of the Jain tradition, lived circa the fifth century B.C.E.[12] Mahavira taught that the material world is characterized by suffering caused by action in the world. The world is real, and the soul is absolutely distinct from it. The goal is to purify the soul from accumulated karma, a material substance that attaches to the soul as a consequence of violence, which he equated with all action in the world. One rids the soul of karma and therefore purifies it by means of *ahimsa* or "nonviolence." Mahavira is well known for exemplifying an ascetic ideal whereby one must "conquer" the body through processes of withdrawal, both of the senses and from society, in order to attain advanced spiritual states. Thus he prescribed *ahimsa* as a non-activist, nonviolent behavioral mandate.

After achieving *kevalajnana* or an enlightened state of omniscience, Mahavira became a countercultural charismatic religious teacher who attracted adherents to his movement. His closest disciples consisted of twelve men called the *ganadharas*. The *ganadharas* were *brahmans* who converted from Hindu orthodoxy. Thus processes of conversion were paramount to the establishment of the earliest Jain community. The disciples adopted ascetic rituals and devotional relationships, all of which functioned to construct new Jain identities. Lay people were also attracted to Mahavira and his new movement. The social context consisted of a culture of devotion to advanced monastic figures, and Mahavira and his disciples would have been especially attractive because of what would have been perceived as their heroic asceticism.[13]

Following Mahavira's death, the Jain community continued to grow between the sixth century B.C.E. and the sixth century C.E. As articulated by Paul Dundas, "The trajectory of Jain history over the first millennium or so reflects the transformation of this community into a civilisational religion with an elaborate social and cultural infrastructure into which large numbers of adherents were integrated."[14] So the Jain tradition grew in northern India, and this was especially the case in centers of commerce because Jains were highly concentrated in the merchant class.[15] It continued to grow following the fall of the Mauryan Empire in the third century B.C.E.

Many Jains were successful in commerce, and the post-Mauryan society was characterized by increased economic development and the concomitant growth of the merchant class, which in turn provided the lay support necessary for the survival and growth of the monastic community.[16] Monastic teachers replicated the proselytizing endeavors of Mahavira by transmitting Jain teachings to potential converts. In exchange for teachings and for beneficial *punya* or "merit," monastics received offerings of food and shelter.[17] Like Mahavira and his disciples, such monastics would have been perceived as heroic in their ascetic endeavors and thus capable of ensuring merit in exchange for offerings. In fact, many South Asian religious traditions maintain that the more an object of devotion represents the ascetic ideal, the more worthy it is of worship and the more merit one accumulates through its worship. Thus, when the worshiper makes offerings to the Jain monastic, she receives merit, which then results in worldly benefits for the worshiper. Such ritual exchanges would have constructed Jain identities for lay participants.

Other practices that would have attracted non-Jains to the Jain tradition include the use of vernacular languages and popular myths in literary endeavors. The northern Indian city of Mathura had a wealthy Jain laity by the second century B.C.E. Since Mathura was religiously dominated by Vaishnavism (the worship of Vishnu), especially in the form of devotion to Krishna (an *avatar* or incarnation of Vishnu), it is not surprising that Jains included Krishna in their own narrative traditions. In fact, Jains constructed their own Krishna mythology, in which Krishna is the cousin of Nemi, the twenty-second *jina*. They wrote Jain renditions of popular Vaishnava myths, including the *Mahabharata* and the *Ramayana*, with a reorientation of such myths toward Jain teachings, especially a Jain interpretation of *ahimsa*.

In addition, lay and monastic Jains were a part of the thriving *bhakti* movement in Mathura and participated in image worship in Jain temples.[18] This process probably satisfied Jains who were attracted to Jain ritual worship as well as the worship of Krishna; they simultaneously absorbed and subordinated both Krishna and Vaishnavism to the Jain tradition.[19] Such active participation in the religious eclecticism of northern India, which featured a growing *bhakti* movement, also explains how Jains attracted adherents who then constructed and sustained Jain temples and provided lay support for the growing monastic community.

Although some have argued that Jain *bhakti* is simply a borrowing from Hindu traditions and is thus marginal to Jain identity, scholars on conversion must acknowledge that *bhakti* was not simply a borrowing but an important part of the construction of Jain identity.[20] Devotion to the *jinas* as well as to living monastics was a central ritual practice from the beginning of the tradition, and Jains continued to participate in the *bhakti* movement as it developed throughout the first half of the first millennium C.E.

The Jain tradition also spread to the Tamil region in the south of India, where it depended on adaptation to a particular social context that privileged the Tamil literary and *bhakti* traditions. Jains acclimated to the predominantly Shaiva (oriented around the worship of Shiva) religious culture by producing Jain versions of Tamil poetry, epics, and ethical texts.[21] There was a long-term ideological exchange between the Jain and Shaiva schools.[22] Jain participation in the religious eclecticism of the region as well as Jains' high socioeconomic status contributed to their success as they gained the support of powerful kings and wealthy merchants.[23] Since socioeconomic power was necessary to build temples for ritual worship and provide support for monastics, financial and political factors were necessary for the spread of the Jain tradition in the south. The Jain tradition continued to attract adherents until it reached its peak in the south between the fifth and seventh centuries C.E., when Jains politically dominated certain regions of Tamil Nadu.

MEDIEVAL PERIOD CONVERSIONS

Jains in the medieval period (ca. 500 C.E. to 1500 C.E.) continued to attract converts by participating in eclectic religious cultures. As Granoff points out, Haribhadra, an important eighth-century Jain thinker, permitted lay Jains to worship "the gods of others," including the Buddha, Vishnu, and Shiva.[24] Jain ritual practice also included devotion to *yakshas*, powerful spirits who were popular as objects of devotion because of their abilities to punish and reward.[25] Furthermore, Jains participated in the worship of goddesses in order to compete with the Vaishnava and Shaiva *bhakti* movements for the laity's attention.[26] Adaptation to the growing and thriving *bhakti* movements provided a social context in which Jain conversion was possible, since converts could construct new identities while not having to endure a radical break from such popular practices.

Some Jains participated in other growing religious trends. For instance, Haribhadra shows a "cosmopolitan" interest in the yoga ideas and techniques of *tantra*.[27] Christopher Key Chapple argues that Haribhadra places yoga in an "orthodox Jain framework" in an attempt to expand his audience.[28] Haribhadra appropriates certain popular yoga elements, such as Patanjali's eight limbs of yoga and goddess worship, into his own form of Jain yoga in an attempt to "co-opt" its lure.[29] Such practical innovations enabled Jains to participate in the eclectic religious culture and consequently maintain the Jain tradition's popularity among competing religious sects. Their participation in growing movements demonstrates that Jains actively adapted to shifting social contexts in order to address emerging desires and demands of adherents and potential converts.

And they were successful. In Rajasthan, Jain groups emerged beginning in the twelfth century, and today Jains in that region trace their lineage to the conversion of Rajasthani Hindus to Jain identities. The actual processes through which Jain conversion occurred is difficult to confirm historically, but there are definite themes that stand out in the narrative traditions. It is a common theme, which actually goes as far back as Mahavira's conversion of the *ganadharas*, that proselytizing monastics were the primary agents in attracting converts, often with the help of miracle and healing demonstrations.[30] Jains in Rajasthan argue that their Jain identities result from the conversions of their ancestors by miracle-working monastics. Lawrence A. Babb elaborates upon this point:

> It is not enough for a convert-to-be to be overawed by an ascetic's miraculous power; a vital ingredient is a transformation in the convert-to-be's outlook. Whether or not it is made explicit in the narrative, the assumption is that this is accomplished by means of the ascetic's *updes*, his teachings. The ascetic is usually said to "awaken" (*pratibodh dena*) the convert. The convert thereby becomes "influenced" (*prabhavit*) by the ascetic's teachings. He then comes to "accept" (*angikar karna*) the Jain *dharm* (Jainism).[31]

There are numerous accounts of new Jain sects and castes emerging from such proselytizing endeavors. Although these narratives are not historical, they demonstrate the affirmative Jain attitude toward conversion and the significance of social strategies necessary for that process. Such narratives point to the influence of Jain monastics who were perceived as heroic. The consequent culture of devotion to such monastics would have instigated the construction of Jain identities for converts.

CONTEMPORARY CONVERSIONS

The thirteenth century featured mass conversions of Digambara Jains to Shaivism in southern India. Then, from the sixteenth to the nineteenth centuries, Jain numbers decreased in the north as many Shvetambara Jains became Vaishnava.[32] In the twentieth and twenty-first centuries, however, Jains developed new and creative ways to attract adherents. The prevalence of conversions to Jain identities in this period can be located in two social contexts: Jain missionary and socioeconomic activities among Hindu tribal populations in India and the global religious market in which Jains construct and disseminate Jain ideas and practices by linking them to popular ethical movements.

First I will discuss conversions among the tribal populations in Gujarat and Rajasthan. When discussing Jain influence on tribal populations, complex questions arise about whether religious identities actually change or not. The Raika people of the Jodhpur and Pali districts of Gujarat provide one example that demonstrates the complexity of conversion to a Jain identity. The Raika are a vegetarian semi-nomadic pastoral people who live in northern Gujarat and Rajasthan. They worship Hindu deities. They also worship *jinas*. The laity living and working in this region do not differentiate between Hindu and Jain self-identities.[33] This appears to be a case in which religious practice comes to include rituals that previously belonged to an outside religious tradition, but there is no shift from one religious identity to another.

Some Raikas, however, have formally acknowledged religious change by taking initiation into Jain monastic traditions. One Raika, Shanti Suri (1889–1943), is particularly worth mentioning. Shanti Suri is famous for his miraculous interventions on behalf of his devotees' safety, his healing abilities, his promotion of vegetarianism, and his support for Jain worship spaces.[34] Raikas continue to believe that his soul, like those of other highly esteemed monastics from the past, is still present and can intervene on their behalf.[35]

Despite his profound influence, however, there remain remnants of tensions that arose as a consequence of the encounter between Jain and Raika ideologies and practices in the figure of Shanti Suri. For instance, Shanti Suri advised Raikas not to sell their animals to butchers lest they participate in the murder of those animals and thus violate the Jain vow of *ahimsa*. Raikas, however, did not always follow this advice since much of their economic stability depended on selling animals for their meat.[36] In such cases, there does not appear to be a perceived conflict between economic activity and religious ideals, and the change from one identity to another was more complete for some Raikas than for others.

The case of Shanti Suri also brings up the issue of socioeconomic variables for religious participation and conversion. Although Shanti Suri became a Jain under the influence of a Jain monastic uncle, his *dadaguru* (guru's guru) became a Jain after being employed by a Jain merchant.[37] And, in fact, there are many circumstances in which Raikas depend economically on Jains. In Raika districts, Jains open stores, provide banking services including loans, and hire Raikas as domestic servants or as labor in their shops.[38] Thus the financial success of Jains has led to the financial dependence of Raikas on Jains. Jains have also had the financial resources to build Jain temples and provide shelter for Jain monastics.[39] As a consequence of Jain presence and influence, Raikas do not differentiate between Hindu and Jain ritual practice, and many Raikas who choose a life of renunciation choose initiation into a Jain monastic order.[40] The case of the Raikas demonstrates how Jain financial success and power enhances their influence in processes of socialization through ritual and economic activity. This has resulted in increased participation in Jain ritual and some complete conversions to Jain identities.

Another case demonstrates how Jains have more aggressively and self-consciously sought converts from tribal groups. Jains are actively proselytizing in the Vadodara and Panchmahal districts of Gujarat in an attempt to convert tribal populations. According to one account, two hundred thousand members of the Adivasi tribal communities converted to Jain identities between 1993 and 1999 as a consequence of Jain proselytizing endeavors.[41]

The proselytizing movement is believed to have begun as a Jain "de-addiction and vegetarian movement" by a Jain monastic, Vijay Indradinna Suri (b. 1924) who himself is from the tribal community in Gujarat.[42] That movement became, quoting Purushottam K. Jain, "a Jain missionary movement."[43] One government worker in the area, Narsinh Rathwa, stated that the tribal people regard the Jain tradition as "a reform movement."[44] Some indigenous ethnic minority communities show unease with the conversions and claim that Jains use their money and power to lure Adivasis to convert.[45]

Socioeconomic factors have definitely made Jain conversions possible in this context. Jains had the financial resources to exercise significant social influence through building and maintaining key resources, primarily through two organizations: the Parmar Kshatriya Jain Seva Samaj and the Vijay Vallabh Mission Trust of Ludhiana. Members of these organizations actively proselytize among the Adivasis and are believed to have reduced alcoholism, built numerous temples, and even established a Jain colony in the Adivasi region.[46]

Contemporary Jains are not only concerned with conversions among Indian tribal populations; they also work to attract converts globally. A new set of conversion strategies that has been intimately linked to the context of globalization emerged in the twentieth century. That context features the pluralization of the global religious market, in which individuals do not simply choose from a limited set of religious systems within a particular cultural point of reference but from an eclectic set of transnational ideological and religious systems, including the scientific one.

What Peter L. Berger refers to as "modern consciousness" results from a combination of socio-historical forces.[47] Modern technology increases the individual's ability to choose commodities, lifestyles, and means of communication as well as religious identities. This new ability to self-consciously construct one's position vis-à-vis the world depends largely on the freedom in physical mobility that results from technological developments. Mobility allows individuals to travel and adopt disparate ideologies and practices. It also makes it possible for proselytizing teachers to travel and disseminate their religious ideas and practices all over the world and to attract converts.

Dramatic technological developments and the concomitant increase in physical mobility are only the beginning of processes resulting in the pluralization that characterizes the contemporary global situation. Developments in technology bring about changes in the division of labor and thus economic institutions. As argued by Berger, however, modernity has complicated social institutional networks, and this has major implications for areas beyond technology and economics.[48] Berger argues, "Where there used to be one or two institutions, there are now fifty. Institutions, however, can best be understood as programs for human activity. Thus, what happens is that where there used to be one or two programs in a particular area of human life, there now are fifty."[49]

Consumer culture emerges as a consequence of technological and economic changes and the concomitant increase in choice that results from pluralization. The result in the global religious market is that individuals choose religious ideas and practices in a similar way that they choose commodities, that is, according to individual desires and needs.

Marketing strategies aimed at a global audience thus enter into religious culture, including that of many Jains. For instance, at a recent JAINA (Jain Association in North America, an umbrella organization for Jain societies) convention in Cincinnati, Ohio, a presenter proposed that Jains use the "McDonald plan" whereby an institution attracts young people during their most formative ages and gets them "hooked" lest they be drawn to other religious ideas and practices in the global market.[50] Such attempts to get young people "hooked" on the Jain tradition occur mostly within diaspora communities where there are efforts to establish firm Jain identities in children who are born to Jain parents but are continuously exposed to competing religions. In this case, Jains construct marketing strategies to convince Jain children to remain adherents to the Jain tradition into their adulthood rather than convert into competing religious identities.

Jains, however, also invoke marketing strategies aimed at attracting converts to Jain identities from a global audience of people born to non-Jain parents. Most often, strategies to get people of non-Jain background "hooked" involve attempts to link Jain ideas and practices to ethical movements that call for social activism and that are popular in the global religious market, such as antiwar/peace, animal rights, ecological, and modern yoga movements. Contemporary Jain magazines, newsletters, blogs, *pathsalas* (religious schools), monastic teachers, and regional organizations associate Jain ideas and practices with those of such movements as they increasingly experience global popularity.

Before I provide some examples of this phenomenon, I want to address the question of how the ideologies underlying such proselytizing activities compare to orthodox Jain ideas. Certainly not all Jains share the concerns of such movements. In fact, the Jain virtue of *ahimsa* is traditionally about purification and withdrawal from the social and natural worlds, hence the ascetic ideal embodied by figures like Mahavira. It is not traditionally about social activism for the improvement of the world. Although some Jains throughout history have been motivated by *ahimsa* to pursue such socially ethical agendas, on the level of ideology, a Jain may be concerned with worldly affairs, but performing rituals or participating in social activism for the sake of bringing about worldly benefits has nothing to do with the spiritual path toward release from the cycle of rebirth. In other words, there is a radical distinction between actions done for worldly benefits and actions (or more precisely, non-actions or ascetic withdrawal) done for spiritual release.[51]

Certain contemporary Jains, however, frequently reconstruct Jain identity and *ahimsa* as transnational religious products that feature an ethical injunction concerned with activism in the world and on behalf of the world. More specifically, Jains call for health-oriented behaviors and the protection of environment and animal life. Such concerns translate well in a global culture where marketing oneself not as a religion but as a "healthy" or "environmentally friendly" "philosophy" or "way of life" is attractive to large segments of consumers. Many Jains have become so concerned with their reconstruction of Jain virtues as oriented around a healthy, animal-friendly, or environmental ethic that their promotion of the tradition focuses upon those issues.

Jains concerned with adapting to contemporary global culture respond to transnational movements, and thus the phenomenon cannot be located in any region or state. Many Jains in North America, for instance, have been active in the attempt to market Jain ideas and practices as compatible with certain transnational ethical movements. In fact, the JAINA 2010 annual convention had "ecology" as its theme. Furthermore, Jains from India and Europe have also participated in this effort. Jains in Europe, for instance, have formed Jain organizations and publications in order to inform a global audience about the benefits of Jain ideas and practices to transnational movements.

Consider *Jain Spirit Magazine*. The magazine was published in London between 2000 and 2006 and addressed a global audience with articles about Jain activists with vegetarian and environmental agendas. The founding editor of the magazine was Atul Shah, a British Jain entrepreneur who uses his expertise in business and media to create global awareness of Jain ideas and practices.[52] In a recent blog, Shah laments the lack of widespread knowledge about the Jain tradition and its relationship to ecology and other transnational ethical concerns:

> Yesterday, I had to give a talk on Science and Jainism, and I spoke about the modern concepts of sustainability, holistic thinking, living with a light footprint, vegetarian diet as a green diet for the planet, and global warming. In all these areas, the Jain philosophical and practical contribution is immense. The beauty is that this lifestyle is not just a theory but is lived in practice right now, this very era. And the Jain approach to eco-friendly living is thousands of years old—it was not developed when we were threatened by global warming—it was seen by our eminent scientist Mahavir as the 'right way to live—ahimsa'.
>
> What I find shocking is that in spite of the huge access to information and knowledge that we have, the world is so blind and ignorant about Jain philosophy and culture.[53]

There are additional Jain organizations that are concerned with such agendas. These include Jain organizations in India, such as the Dakshin Bharat Jain Sabha (South Indian Jain Society), that aim to disseminate Jain ideas and practices, which they link to social activism in India as well as transnational movements.

Jain participation in these movements has steadily increased since the beginning of the second half of the twentieth century, largely because Jain monastic teachers have participated in them. In fact, not only has monastic support increased the popularity of such movements among Jains, their charismatic leadership is often the catalyst for religious conversion to Jain identity. Some monastic teachers have focused on marketing the Jain tradition as a system compatible with growing transnational campaigns for contemplative and health-oriented practices.

Such teachers have participated in the development and popularization of Jain systems of modern yoga, a transnational health and fitness discipline believed to be compatible with modern biomedicine. Their global proselytizing endeavors have often required radical breaks from orthodox rules for Jain monastics. For instance, two Jain Shvetambara monks separately abandoned their monastic vows in order to travel to the United States in the 1970s to attract converts to Jain identities. According to Jain orthodoxy, Jain monastics are not allowed to travel by means of mechanical transportation but can only travel by foot. They are also not allowed to leave India. Chitrabhanu (b.

1922) and Sushil Kumar (1926–1994) were two countercultural Jain monks who opposed those rules and left India in pursuit of converts.

Chitrabhanu was a Shvetambara Jain monk who, in 1970, became the first Jain to leave his monastic order and travel to the United States. Accounts of his departure from India demonstrate that his choice was controversial. According to Chitrabhanu himself, a crowd of protestors gathered and called out to him, begging for him not to leave India and break the Jain tradition against monastics traveling abroad.[54] They blocked the roads leading to and the entrance to the airport. The police commissioner intervened. After deceiving the protestors by taking Chitrabhanu to the airport via an alternative route, the police commissioner secretly entered the airport through a back entrance and escorted Chitrabhanu directly to the airplane.

Upon his arrival in the United States, Chitrabhanu initially struggled to attract disciples. He spent his first month at a Holiday Inn, eating only bread and salad (the only vegetarian options). After a small group of Jain-American students raised money to support him, he settled in New York and gradually began receiving attention from Jain Americans interested in the guidance he could provide to the Jain American community, non-Jain Americans interested in the insights of Indian religions, and the media. The *New York Times* even published an article on Chitrabhanu's activities in 1973 entitled, "Iconoclastic Jain Leader Is Likened to Pope John."[55]

Chitrabhanu teaches a "nonsectarian" Jain doctrine. He focuses on the benefits of meditation and thus can be located within the transnational modern yoga movement that promotes contemplative practice and/or postural techniques as means to a healthy lifestyle. Most importantly from his perspective, he prescribes a vegan diet based on an ethical mandate against the torture and slaughter of animals by the food production industry. Although a sex scandal involving Chitrabhanu erupted in 1981 and caused major controversy among his disciples, his Jain Meditation International Center in New York City survived, and he and his disciples continue to teach there and at other religious centers to the present day.[56] According to one close disciple, Chitrabhanu has attracted several converts to the Jain tradition.[57] Disciples, however, do not always consider themselves converts to Jain identities.[58] Rather, they adopt many of what are considered Chitrabhanu's universal teachings on nonviolence and meditation.[59]

Sushil Kumar, a Shvetambara monk, also did away with the orthodox rules prohibiting monastics from traveling by means of mechanical transportation and went to the United States in 1975 to attract converts. Unlike Chitrabhanu, he held on to his monastic identity, despite criticism by some Jains who argued that he could not possibly maintain that identity since he broke monastic rules. Like Chitrabhanu, Kumar often referred to his teachings as a "nonsectarian" message. He synthesized Jain ideas with Hindu yoga practices and established a temple and retreat center in Blairstown, New Jersey, where he taught what he called "Arhum Yoga" to his students.[60]

Both Chitrabhanu and Kumar were reformers and innovators with regard to marketing the Jain tradition, and they have experienced some success in their separate attempts. Especially in the 1980s and 1990s, they were popular Jain teachers in the United States. They attracted converts from Euro-American backgrounds and were often honorary guests at Jain and inter-religious events. But despite that success, they were unsuccessful in attracting large numbers of permanent converts who have self-identified as Jains.

By compromising the strict Jain monastic prohibitions against mechanical travel and prolonged engagement with the laity, Chitrabhanu and Kumar crossed the boundary between ascetic and worldly values according to Jain orthodoxy, but they both considered their choices to be legitimate acts of adaptation to the social context in which they proselytized. Another monastic teacher, Mahaprajna of the Jain Terapanth, did not consider such acts of adaptation appropriate for a Jain monastic but wanted to adapt nonetheless.[61] Thus he took different steps toward what he and his disciples have called "moving with the times." First of all, in 1975, Mahaprajna introduced *preksha dhyana* (henceforth *preksha*), literally, "concentration of perception," but most often translated by the tradition itself as "insight meditation and yoga."[62] He prescribed *preksha* as a universal system that would resolve contemporary global problems, including violence and widespread unhealthy lifestyles, which he linked to modernization and industrialization. This innovation was in line with global trends in the 1970s: first, the popularization of Satya Narayan Goenka's *vipassana* ("insight meditation" prescribed as a universal form of Buddhist meditation) within and beyond India; second, the turn by Indian yogis, often motivated by nationalism, to yoga as a tool for "re-forming the physical body" in the battle to reclaim India from colonialism;[63] and third, the global popularization of yoga as a health and fitness practice, especially in India, the United States, and Europe.

Like the teachings of Sushil Kumar and Chitrabhanu, *preksha* was particularly innovative because, in contrast to the orthodox Jain ascetic ideal, it involved an affirmation of the body and included a system of diet and exercise aimed not at spiritual release from the world, but physical and psychological enhancement and thus the improvement of life in the world. *Preksha* is a medicalized yoga similar to other transnational forms of modern yoga that were popularized in India, the United States, and Europe beginning in the 1960s and 1970s. Such systems do not focus on transcendent spiritual goals but on immanent goals and posture practice.[64]

Representatives were needed to disseminate *preksha* to Jain and non-Jain people throughout India and the world. There was a global demand for yoga, and Jains sought to respond to that demand and consequently attract converts. Thus, beginning in 1980, the Terapanth introduced a new order of proselytizing monastics, the *samanis*.[65] The *samanis* make up an order of intermediary monastics who live a life of asceticism but are not fully initiated into the monastic order. They are charged with the mission to travel throughout India and abroad in order to bring about the global dissemination of the Jain tradition, and they seek to do this through the dissemination of *preksha*. The *samanis* consider their efforts to be philanthropic in nature. They maintain that *preksha* is a means to improve the world on a global scale.

Few people outside of India have actually converted to Jain identities as a result of the *samanis'* proselytizing endeavors. Some people have, however, and they have been influential in the global dissemination of Jain ideas and practices. Two Jain converts from Berlin, Germany, Karuna Jain and Aparigraha Jain, provide insight into the socially contextual construction of Jain self-identity for contemporary converts.

Karuna first encountered the Jain tradition through the teaching endeavors of *samanis* who had traveled to Berlin to teach *preksha*. She responded immediately to the perceived benefits of *preksha*. After she and her husband, Aparigraha, traveled to India and met Mahaprajna himself, they became Jains. Like the Jain proselytizing teachers described above, Karuna and Aparigraha construct their Jain identities in a way that responds to the social context in which they live. According to Aparigraha:

> The 'Love & Peace' message of the Hippies is possibly a positive definition of Lord Mahavir's ahimsa. 'All You Need Is Love' (The Beatles) was a global message for this planet in the seventies of the 20th century. Perhaps I already was a Jain without knowing it at that time.[66]

Jain identity in this case is intimately tied to the Jain virtue of *ahimsa*, but as a reconstructed virtue rather than that conceptualized by Jain orthodoxy. In this context, it is an ethical injunction to bring about global peace in the contemporary world.

Jain ritual and other forms of religious practice, including yoga, devotion to a guru, and vegetarianism, ground Karuna and Aparigraha's Jain identities. They feel so committed to the Terapanth interpretation of the Jain tradition that they have dedicated their lives to attracting others to the tradition. They publish an online magazine in English and German called *HereNow4U* in which they include Jain news and responses to certain popular transnational interests and concerns such as yoga, vegetarianism, animal rights, and ecology. In their efforts to disseminate Jain ideas and practices, they are constructing a transnational Jain tradition that is attractive and accessible to a global audience in which such concerns are popular.

Although Karuna and Aparigraha represent a small group of Europeans and Americans who have fully converted to the Jain tradition, others have been influenced by Jain ideas and practices as part of their personal religious eclecticism but have not actually undergone conversion. They adopt Jain ideas insofar as they believe such ideas address certain contemporary global concerns and offer meaningful solutions. In addition to *ahimsa*, another Jain idea that has had far-reaching influence on non-Jains is *anekantavada* (the doctrine of manypointedness). In classical Jain philosophy, *anekantavada* is a position maintaining the non-absolute truth of all knowledge claims. It is a polemical tool for debunking Hindu and Buddhist arguments, which Jains consider limited philosophical approaches.[67] Yet contemporary European and American non-Jains as well as Jains engaged with global movements reconstruct *anekantavada* in a postmodern direction and use it in support of such global agendas as religious pluralism and tolerance, ecology, and world peace.[68] They argue that *anekantavada* has the potential to function, not as a polemical tool, but as a tool for peaceful coexistence between individuals, religious institutions, and nations that hold opposing or different views.

There are numerous examples of non-Jains reconstructing Jain ideas and practices in support of transnational movements. Proselytizing teachers encourage such activities and, in fact, do not emphasize conversion to Jain identity but promote Jain ideas and practices as supplemental to their work toward transnational agendas. In other words, the movements are prioritized over religious identity. Jains who are actively involved in interfaith activities and who produce publications that aim to spread global awareness about the Jain tradition and its contemporary ethical injunctions emphasize its attractiveness, not as a religion into which one should convert, but as a "way of life" or "philosophy" that supports certain socially ethical agendas.

Another issue that prevents complete conversion of non-Jains to Jain identities is the fact that even though Jain ideas and practices may be attractive to certain non-Jains, the dualist ontology, ascetic soteriology, and view of history as defined by Jain orthodoxy are not widely attractive. In fact, many non-Indian people who are familiar with Buddhist and Hindu traditions are not familiar with Jain traditions because attention to the details of the Jain social, ritual, and communal practices are often marginalized in scholarly analyses. Jains have often been associated with "extreme" asceticism both within and beyond South Asia.[69]

If few people outside of India know about the Jain tradition, and those who are familiar with it tend to hold a stereotypical picture of Jains as "extreme" ascetics, then it is not surprising that there are few converts to Jain identity outside of India. And all this is true despite the fact that my analysis of the Jain tradition throughout this chapter demonstrates that the tradition is characterized by a social-historical vitality and thus a high degree of plurality. Different Jains hold different intentions, priorities, and motivations, hence the context-specificity of the construction and practice of the Jain tradition. Yet even non-Jains who are familiar with Jain involvement and contributions to the activist, ethical, and social contemporary movements discussed above prefer to adopt only certain ideas and practices and leave complete conversion behind, since that would entail acceptance of the Jain orthodox ontological, historical, and soteriological views, which in many ways contrast with a socially activist agenda.

CONCLUSION

In a historical context characterized by dramatic social change and new religious movements, the Jain tradition emerged with the proselytizing endeavors of a charismatic ascetic teacher. But the Jain tradition did not become a stagnant, insulated community following the death of that teacher. Rather, it became a vital tradition that participated in processes of adaptation, appropriation, syncretism, and competition, all for the sake of keeping its adherents and attracting new ones.

Contemporary proselytizing endeavors by Jain monastic teachers and the Jain laity have succeeded in informing a global audience about the Jain tradition. This is evident in the fact that the president of the United States, Barack Obama, acknowledged the significance of the Diwali holiday to Jains in a public speech on October 14, 2009. Obama's reference to the Jain tradition in this speech was an important event for Jains insofar as it signaled increased global awareness of their religion. Yet, despite this increased recognition and awareness of their religion, Jains have not been successful in attracting many converts. This is largely attributable to Jain orthodoxy, which draws a sharp distinction between worldly and spiritual action. Many people are drawn to Jain ideas and practices because of the association of those ideas and practices with transnational movements that call for social activism. Thus the distinction between worldly and spiritual action is irreconcilable for those people concerned with global transformation through activism.

After reviewing cases of conversion to the Jain tradition, it becomes evident that whether or not they have always succeeded in attracting converts, Jains have an affirmative view of conversion and have actively responded to shifting social contexts in attempts to attract converts. Jains construct religious practices and ideas appropriate to particular religious markets. They offer potential converts merit gained by devotion to monastic teachers, rituals to popular deities believed to deliver benefits to their devotees, programs for social reform, and yoga classes. The Jain tradition is a socially vital one, and its adherents have historically taken steps toward constructing Jain identities for converts.

NOTES

1. Although such distinguishing categories as "Jain" and "Hindu" that we rely on today to talk about South Asian religions have been far more fluid and unstable throughout South Asian history, it would be correct to state that the category of "Jain" is at least useful for identifying those individuals over the past twenty-five hundred years or so who have shared membership in a particular social group and a dualist ontological assessment of the world, which was tied to a particular understanding of history and resulted in the construction of a particular ascetic soteriology as well as behavioral (including ritual) mandates. When I use the categories of "Jain identity" or "Jain tradition," I mean those individuals, ideas, or practices that fit within these parameters.
2. Lewis R. Rambo and Charles E. Farhadian, "Conversion," in *Encyclopedia of Religion*, 2nd ed., Vol. 3, ed. Lindsay Jones (Detroit: Macmillan Reference USA, 2005), 1969.
3. Sociologists have argued that conversion is linked to socialization. See, for example, Theodore E. Long and Jeffrey K. Hadden, "Religious Conversion and the Concept of Socialization: Integrating the Brainwashing and Drift Models," *Journal for the Scientific Study of Religion* 22 (1983): 1–14.
4. Lewis R. Rambo, *Understanding Religious Conversion* (New Haven: Yale University Press, 1993), 116.
5. Ibid., 117.
6. A different analysis of conversion applies to those who become fully initiated monastics. Monastic initiation ceremonies involve a number of deconstructive rituals. For instance, initiates pull the hair from their heads as an act of renunciation of previous identities, and this functions to deconstruct those identities.
7. Michael B. Carrithers, "On Polytropy: Or the Natural Condition of Spiritual Cosmopolitanism in India: The Digambara Jain Case," *Modern Asian Studies* 34, no. 4 (2000): 831–861.
8. Ibid., 824.

9. Phyllis Granoff, "Other People's Rituals: Ritual Eclecticism in Early Medieval Indian Religions," *Journal of Indian Philosophy* 28 (2000): 401.

10. For data on Jains in India, see Government of India Census Data 2001, http://www.censusindia.gov.in/Census_Data_2001/India_at_glance/religion.aspx. For data outside of India, see Paul Dundas, *The Jains* (New York: Routledge, 2002), 271.

11. Throughout this chapter, I use the category of "ascetic," by which I mean the following: "A voluntary, sustained, and at least partially systematic program of self-discipline and self-denial in which immediate, sensual, or profane gratifications are renounced in order to attain a higher spiritual state or a more thorough absorption in the sacred." Walter O. Kaelber, "Asceticism," *Encyclopedia of Religion*, 2nd ed., Vol. 3, ed. Lindsay Jones (Detroit: Macmillan Reference USA, 2005), 526. This definition implies the dichotomy that exists between "sacred" and "profane" according to the analysis of Émile Durkheim. Durkheim argues that the sacred is antagonistic to the profane. Émile Durkheim, *The Elementary Forms of Religious Life*, trans. Carol Cosman (New York: Oxford University Press, 2001), 236. He further argues that the distinction between the sacred and profane can only be defined by their heterogeneity (Durkheim, *Elementary Forms*, 38). In the Jain tradition, this heterogeneity is most explicitly expressed in the duality of soul (sacred) and matter (profane) as well as in the distinction between monastic (*shramana*) and laity (*shravaka*).

12. Whereas scholars maintain that Mahavira is the historical founder of the Jain tradition, Jain doctrine on history considers him the most recent of the twenty-four *jinas*.

13. Paul Dundas, "Conversion to Jainism: Historical Perspectives," in *Religious Conversion in India: Modes, Motivations, and Meanings*, ed. Rowena Robinson and Sathianathan Clarke (Oxford: Oxford University Press, 2003), 130.

14. Ibid., 126.

15. Smita Sahgal, "Spread of Jinism in North India between circa 200 BC and circa AD 300," in *Jainism and Prakrit in Ancient and Medieval India: Essays for Prof. Jagdish Chandra Jain*, ed. N. N. Bhattacharyya (New Delhi: Manohar, 1994), 216. Some speculate that Jains became concentrated in merchant classes because this occupation made it possible to avoid the violence associated with other occupations, particularly agriculture.

16. Sahgal, "Spread of Jinism," 210.

17. *Punya* is a form of karma, but it is advantageous karma insofar as it results in worldly benefits such as wealth or health. Such karma is distinct from worldly disadvantageous karma, *papa*, which may result in undesirable circumstances such as ill health or poverty.

18. John E. Cort, "Bhakti in the Early Jain Tradition: Understanding Devotional Religion in South Asia," *History of Religions* 42, no. 1 (August 2002): 69. "*Bhakti*" refers to the emotionally charged devotional religiosity that became increasingly popular in medieval India and is the most abundant expression of South Asian religiosity today.

19. Sahgal, "Spread of Jinism," 228. See also Padmanabh S. Jaini, *Jaina Path of Purification* (New Delhi: Motilal Banarsidass, 2004), 306.

20. John Cort demonstrates that the common assumption in scholarship on the Jain tradition that *bhakti* is a borrowing from the Hindu tradition is incorrect. Cort, "Bhakti in the Early Jain Tradition," 59–86.

21. Indira Viswanathan Peterson, "Sramanas against the Tamil Way: Jains as Others," in *Open Boundaries: Jain Communities and Cultures in Indian History*, ed. John E. Cort (New York: SUNY, 1998), 166–167.

22. Richard H. Davis, "The Story of the Disappearing Jains: Retelling the Saiva-Jain Encounter in Medieval South India," in *Open Boundaries: Jain Communities and Cultures in Indian History*, ed. John E. Cort (New York: SUNY Press, 1998), 214.

23. Peterson, "Sramanas against the Tamil Way," 166.

24. Granoff, "Other People's Rituals," 401. For a detailed study on Haribhadra's religious inclusivism, see Christopher Key Chapple, *Reconciling Yogas: Haribhadra's Collection of Views on Yoga*, with a new translation of Haribhadra's *Yogadrstisamuccaya* by Christopher Key Chapple and John Thomas Casey (New York: SUNY, 2003). Haribhadra is believed to have converted to a Jain identity himself, having been born into a *brahman* family but taking initiation into a Jain monastic order. Chapple, *Reconciling Yogas*, 1.

25. Sahgal, "Spread of Jinism," 215.

26. Padmanabh S. Jaini, "Is There a Popular Jainism?" in *The Assembly of Listeners: Jains in Society*, ed. Michael Carrithers and Caroline Humphrey (New York: Cambridge University Press, 1991), 196.

27. Christopher Key Chapple, "Haribhadra's Analysis of Patanjala and Kula Yoga in the Yogadrstisamuccaya," in *Open Boundaries: Jain Communities and Cultures in Indian History*, ed. John E. Cort, 15–30 (New York: SUNY Press, 1998), 15.

28. Ibid., 20.

29. Ibid., 26. Cort also demonstrates how Jains incorporated tantric rituals, including *vidyas*, verbal invocations of goddesses. John E. Cort, "Medieval Jaina Goddess Traditions," *Numen* 34, no. 2 (1987): 237. Likewise, Dundas and Cort demonstrate how Shaiva transferences to Jain thought occurred, particularly in the development of a Jain system of *mantra* and the attendant rituals for the sake of gaining magical powers. John E. Cort, "Worship of Bell-Ears the Great Hero, a Jain Tantric Deity," in *Tantra in Practice*, ed. David Gordon White (Princeton: Princeton University Press, 2000), 417; Paul Dundas, "Becoming Gautama," in *Open Boundaries: Jain Communities and Cultures in Indian History*, ed. John E. Cort (New York: SUNY Press), 1998; and Paul Dundas, "The Jain Monk Jinapati Suri Gets the Better of a Nath Yogi," in *Tantra in Practice*, ed. David Gordon White, 231–238 (Princeton: Princeton University Press, 2000), 232.

30. Lawrence A. Babb, *Absent Lord: Ascetics and Kings in a Jain Ritual Culture*, (Berkeley and Los Angeles: University of California Press, 1996), 168.

31. Ibid., 168.

32. Dundas, "Conversion to Jainism," 142.

33. Vinay Kumar Srivastava, *Religious Renunciation of a Pastoral People* (Delhi: Oxford University Press, 1997), 128.

34. Ibid., 163.

35. Ibid., 163–165.

36. Ibid., 165.

37. Ibid., 164–165.

38. Ibid., 127.

39. Ibid., 128.

40. Ibid., 128–129.

41. Syed Khalique Ahmed, "Jainism Got Two Lakh Converts in 6 Yrs, Quietly," *Indian Express*, Mar. 8, 1999, http://www.indianexpress.com/ie/daily/19990308/ige08013.html.

42. Ibid.

43. Ibid.

44. Ibid.

45. Ibid.
46. Ibid.
47. Peter L. Berger, *The Heretical Imperative: Contemporary Possibilities of Religious Affirmation* (New York: Doubleday, 1979), 8.
48. Ibid.,15.
49. Ibid. Berger maintains that not all such pluralization means increased choice, but much of it does. As an example of increased pluralization without increased choice, Berger describes the contemporary citizen who has to pay five different sets of taxes as opposed to the subject of a traditional ruler who only has to pay one. On the other hand, increased choice is a consequence of the pluralization of "sexual lifestyles." Berger, *Heretical Imperative*, 15–16.
50. Yashwant K. Malaiya, "Jainism for Future Generations," paper presented at the annual meeting of the JAINA Convention, Cincinnati, OH, 2003.
51. In contrast to appeals to Indian ascetic and mystical traditions for constructing ethical systems, some scholars have argued that ascetic ideologies actually lack a socially construed ethics because of their emphasis on non-action and social withdrawal. See Albert Schweitzer, *Indian Thought and Its Development*, trans. Charles E. B. Russell (Gloucester, MA: Peter Smith, 1977). For more on the ethics, or non-ethics, of Indian asceticism and mysticism, see Andrea R. Jain and Jeffrey J. Kripal, "Quietism and Karma: Non-Action as Non-Ethics in Jain Asceticism," Symposium: Apology for Quietism, Part 2, *Common Knowledge* 15, no. 2 (Spring 2009): 197–207; and Jeffrey J. Kripal, "Debating the Mystical as the Ethical: An Indological Map," in *Crossing Boundaries: Essays on the Ethical Status of Mysticism*, ed. G. William Barnard and Jeffrey J. Kripal (New York: Seven Bridges Press/ Chatham House, 2002).
52. *Diverse Ethics*, "About Us," http://www.diverseethics.com/info/about-us.
53. Atul Shah, "Day 5—Science and Jainism," *Diverse Ethics*, http://www.diverseethics.com/ category/masala/paryushan-blog.
54. This account is based on a personal communication with Chitrabhanu, Whitmore Lake, MI, October 10, 2010.
55. George Dugan, "Iconoclastic Jain Leader Is Likened to Pope John," *New York Times*, Dec. 18, 1973.
56. On the sex scandal involving Chitrabhanu, see Carrie Schneider, *American Yoga: The Paths and Practices of America's Greatest Yoga Masters*, photography by Andy Ryan (New York: Silver Lining Books, 2003), 39; for more on the Jain Meditation International Center, see Jain Meditation International Center, http://www.jainmeditation.org.
57. Yashoda Jordan, email message to author, Sept. 13, 2010.
58. Personal communications with many of Chitrabhanu's disciples at the Lighthouse Center in Whitmore Lake, MI, Oct. 10, 2010.
59. Ibid.
60. The center, Siddhachalam Jain Tirth, established by Sushil in 1983 in Blairstown, NJ, is still active today.
61. The author completed the research presented here on *preksha dhyana* and the Jain Terapanth as part of her dissertation project. Andrea R. Jain. "Health, Well-Being, and the Ascetic Ideal: Modern Yoga in the Jain Terapanth," PhD diss., Rice University, Apr. 2010. See also Andrea R. Jain, "The Dual-Ideal of the Ascetic and Healthy Body: Modern Yoga, the Jain Terapanth, and the Context of Late Capitalism," *Nova Religio* 15, no. 3 (Feb. 2012): 29-50..

62. Members of the Terapanth most often translate the full title of *preksha dhyana* as "preksha meditation," but since the category of "yoga" includes *dhyana* or "meditation," and *preksha* involves more than just meditation, I use "yoga" in the current chapter.
63. Sarah Strauss, *Positioning Yoga: Balancing Acts across Cultures* (New York: Berg, 2005), 7.
64. The category "posture practice" comes from Mark Singleton, *Yoga Body: The Origins of Modern Posture Practice* (Oxford: Oxford University Press, 2010).
65. *Samani* is the feminine of *saman*. *Saman* is derived from the Sanskrit word *shramana*, which means "striver," and is used as an epithet for world-renouncers. It is used in the sense of one who "strives" for release from the cycle of rebirth. Although four *samanas* or male *saman* were initiated in 1986, almost all *saman* are *samanis* or female *saman*. The first initiation of semi-monastics in 1980 included six *samanis*. Today, there are one hundred and three. Of the four *samana* initiated in 1986, only two remain *samana*. The other two have undergone full initiation into the monastic order, and there have been no additional initiations of *samana* since 1986.
66. *HereNow4U*, "True Story—Jains Without Knowing It," http://www.herenow4u.net/index.php?id=63596a.
67. Dundas, *The Jains*, 199; and John E. Cort, "'Intellectual Ahimsa' Revisited: Jain Tolerance and Intolerance of Others, *Philosophy East and West* 50, no. 3 (July 2000): 331–333.
68. For a variety of examples, see John Cort, "'Intellectual Ahimsa' Revisited," 330.
69. Dundas, *The Jains*, 1–3.

BIBLIOGRAPHY

Ahmed, Syed Khalique. "Jainism Got Two Lakh Converts in 6 Yrs, Quietly." *Indian Express*, Mar. 8, 1999. http://www.indianexpress.com/ie/daily/19990308/ige08013.html.

Babb, Lawrence A. *Absent Lord: Ascetics and Kings in a Jain Ritual Culture*. Berkeley and Los Angeles: University of California Press, 1996.

Berger, Peter L. *The Heretical Imperative: Contemporary Possibilities of Religious Affirmation*. New York: Doubleday, 1979.

Carrithers, Michael B. "Jainism and Buddhism as Enduring Historical Streams." *Journal of the Anthropological Society of Oxford* 221, no. 2 (1990): 141–163.

——. "On Polytropy: Or the Natural Condition of Spiritual Cosmopolitanism in India: The Digambara Jain Case." *Modern Asian Studies* 34, no. 4 (2000): 831–861.

Chapple, Christopher Key. "Haribhadra's Analysis of Patanjali and Kula Yoga in the Yogadrstisamuccaya." In *Open Boundaries: Jain Communities and Cultures in Indian History*, ed. John E. Cort, 15–30. New York: SUNY Press, 1998.

——. *Reconciling Yogas: Haribhadra's Collection of Views on Yoga*, with a new translation of Haribhadra's *Yogadrstisamuccaya* by Christopher Key Chapple and John Thomas Casey. New York: SUNY, 2003.

Cort, John E. "Bhakti in the Early Jain Tradition: Understanding Devotional Religion in South Asia." *History of Religions* 42, no. 1 (August 2002): 59–86.

——. "'Intellectual Ahimsa' Revisited: Jain Tolerance and Intolerance of Others." *Philosophy East and West* 50, no. 3 (July 2000): 331–333.

——. "Medieval Jaina Goddess Traditions." *Numen* 34, no. 2 (1987): 235–255.

——. "Worship of Bell-Ears the Great Hero, a Jain Tantric Deity." In *Tantra in Practice*, ed. David Gordon White, 417–433. Princeton: Princeton University Press, 2000.

Davis, Richard H. "The Story of the Disappearing Jains: Retelling the Saiva-Jain Encounter in Medieval South India." In *Open Boundaries: Jain Communities and Cultures in Indian History*, ed. John E. Cort, 213–224. New York: SUNY Press, 1998.

Diverse Ethics. "About Us." http://www.diverseethics.com/info/about-us.

Dugan, George. "Iconoclastic Jain Leader Is Likened to Pope John." *New York Times*, Dec. 18, 1973.

Dundas, Paul. "Becoming Gautama: Mantra and History in Svetambara Jainism." In *Open Boundaries: Jain Communities and Cultures in Indian History*, ed. John E. Cort, 31–52. New York: SUNY Press, 1998.

——. "Conversion to Jainism: Historical Perspectives." In *Religious Conversion in India: Modes, Motivations, and Meanings*, ed. Rowena Robinson and Sathianathan Clarke, 125–148. Oxford: Oxford University Press, 2003.

——. "Haribhadra's Lalitavistara and the Legend of Siddharsi's Conversion to Buddhism." In *Jainism and Early Buddhism: Essays in Honor of Padmanabh S. Jaini*, ed. Olle Qvarnstrom, 151–166. Fremont, CA: Asian Humanities Press, 2003.

——. "The Jain Monk Jinapati Suri Gets the Better of a Nath Yogi." In *Tantra in Practice*, ed. David Gordon White, 231–238. Princeton: Princeton University Press, 2000.

——. *The Jains*. New York: Routledge, 2002.

Durkheim, Émile. *The Elementary Forms of Religious Life*, trans. Carol Cosman. New York: Oxford University Press, 2001.

Featherstone, Mike. *Consumer Culture and Postmodernism*. 2nd ed. London: Sage, 1991.

Granoff, Phyllis. "Other People's Rituals: Ritual Eclecticism in Early Medieval Indian Religions." *Journal of Indian Philosophy* 28 (2000): 399–424.

HereNow4U. "True Story—Jains Without Knowing It." http://www.herenow4u.net/index.php?id=63596a.

Jain, Andrea R. "Health, Well-Being, and the Ascetic Ideal: Modern Yoga in the Jain Terapanth." PhD diss., Rice University, Apr. 2010.

——. "The Dual-Ideal of the Ascetic and Healthy Body: Modern Yoga, the Jain Terapanth, and the Context of Late Capitalism." *Nova Religio* 15, no. 3 (Feb. 2012): 29–50.

Jain, Andrea R., and Jeffrey J. Kripal. "Quietism and Karma: Non-Action as Non-Ethics in Jain Asceticism." Symposium: Apology for Quietism, Part 2, *Common Knowledge* 15, no. 2 (Spring 2009): 197–207.

Jain Meditation International Center. http://www.jainmeditation.org.

Jaini, Padmanabh S. "Is There a Popular Jainism?" In *The Assembly of Listeners: Jains in Society*, ed. Michael Carrithers and Caroline Humphrey, 187–200. New York: Cambridge University Press, 1991.

——. *Jaina Path of Purification*. New Delhi: Motilal Banarsidass, 2004.

Jinabhadra. *Ganadharavada*, ed. and trans. E. A. Solomon. Ahmedabad: Gujarat Vidya Sabha, 1966.

Kaelber, Walter O. "Asceticism." *Encyclopedia of Religion*, 2nd ed., Vol. 3, ed. Lindsay Jones, 526–530. Detroit: Macmillan Reference USA, 2005.

Kripal, Jeffrey J. "Debating the Mystical as the Ethical: An Indological Map." In *Crossing Boundaries: Essays on the Ethical Status of Mysticism*, ed. G. William Barnard and Jeffrey J. Kripal, 15–69. New York: Seven Bridges Press/Chatham House, 2002.

Long, Theodore E., and Jeffrey K. Hadden. "Religious Conversion and the Concept of Socialization: Integrating the Brainwashing and Drift Models." *Journal for the Scientific Study of Religion* 22 (1983): 1–14.

Malaiya, Yashwant K. "Jainism for Future Generations." Paper presented at the annual meeting of the JAINA Convention, Cincinnati, OH, 2003.

Peterson, Indira Viswanathan. "Sramanas against the Tamil Way: Jains as Others." In *Open Boundaries: Jain Communities and Cultures in Indian History*, ed. John E. Cort, 163–186. New York: SUNY, 1998.

The Pluralism Project at Harvard University. "Authority without Monks." http://pluralism.org/resources/tradition/essays/jain8.php.

Rambo, Lewis R. *Understanding Religious Conversion*. New Haven: Yale University Press, 1993.

Rambo, Lewis R., and Charles E. Farhadian. "Conversion." *Encyclopedia of Religion*, 2nd ed., Vol. 3, ed. Lindsay Jones, 1969–1974. Detroit: Macmillan Reference USA, 2005.

Sahgal, Smita. "Spread of Jainism in North India between circa 200 BC and circa AD 300." In *Jainism and Prakrit in Ancient and Medieval India: Essays for Prof. Jagdish Chandra Jain*, ed. N. N. Bhattacharyya, 205–232. New Delhi: Manohar, 1994.

Schneider, Carrie. *American Yoga: The Paths and Practices of America's Greatest Yoga Masters*, photography by Andy Ryan. New York: Silver Lining Books, 2003.

Schweitzer, Albert. *Indian Thought and its Development*, trans. Charles E. B. Russell. Gloucester, MA: Peter Smith, 1977.

Shah, Atul. "Jain Fast—Day 5." *Jain Festive Journey*, Sept. 8, 2010. http://www.diverseethics.com/category/masala/paryushan-blog.

Singleton, Mark. *Yoga Body: The Origins of Modern Posture Practice*. Oxford: Oxford University Press, 2010.

Srivastava, Vinay Kumar. *Religious Renunciation of a Pastoral People*. Delhi: Oxford University Press, 1997.

Strauss, Sarah. *Positioning Yoga: Balancing Acts across Cultures*. New York: Berg, 2005.

Turner, Bryan S. "The Body in Western Society: Social Theory and its Perspectives." In *Religion and the Body*, ed. Sarah Coakley, 15–41. New York: Cambridge University Press, 1997.

....

CHAPTER 20

BUDDHIST CONVERSION IN THE CONTEMPORARY WORLD

....

DAN SMYER YÜ

THIS chapter is written from the perspective of contemporary Buddhist studies in an effort to examine conversion processes in the modern Buddhist context. Its focus is not on textual or historical cases of Buddhist conversion, as these are readily available in various venues. Instead, it prioritizes the current state of Buddhism beyond Asia and accentuates both Buddhist and Buddhological discourses on the localization of the historical Buddha's teachings. By drawing cases particularly from the sociocultural context of the West, this chapter attempts to highlight two patterns of the contemporary Buddhist conversion process. First, the majority of the world's Buddhist conversions in the last three decades did not take place due to the missionary efforts of Asian Dharma masters, unlike Christian missionaries' evangelical attempts since the eighteenth century. Instead, Buddhist conversion is mostly the result of local cultural elites' efforts to disseminate Buddhist messages. Second, Buddhist conversion, in a concurrent rather than linear, fashion, involves deversion, syncretization, and transference. All these facets and dimensions occur in the type of globalization that Peter Berger[1] and Roland Robertson[2] have identified in relation to the global migration of religious values and spiritual practices in the contemporary world.

REORIENTING CONVERSION STUDIES IN THE BUDDHIST CONTEXT

....

The study of religious conversion has primarily been shaped and advanced by the study of the spread of Christianity. Scholars from Western theological institutions and the divinity schools of prominent universities have devoted much of their effort to empirical research and advancing new theories on religious conversion. The traditional theological approach to Christian conversion is often centered upon the sudden and dramatic aspect of individual conversion stories. This approach is event-oriented, focusing on cases resembling the experience of St. Paul as narrated in the New Testament. When this type of conversion is discerned as a sudden transformation, it is regarded as "a timeless point of decision."[3] This "timelessness" signifies what Rosemary Haughton calls the "death of the natural man" and the "birth of the whole human being, the perfection of man."[4] In this context, the birth exclusively refers to the resurrection of Jesus or what Reinhold Niebuhr[5] calls the "new selfhood," with Christ embodied. The "decision" is not the personal decision of the convert but "a decision of God for him."[6] This traditional approach to the study of conversion reflects a distinct trait of Christian theology, that is, that God is externally invoked, independent of the convert concerned.

This traditional approach to conversion studies is not relevant to the Buddhist context. Theologically speaking, becoming a Buddhist is both a rational and a spiritual choice, one made by the individual with a relatively high degree of idealization. Theologically speaking, unlike the paradigm of Christian conversion centered upon the duality of the new and the old, or the saved and the unsaved, becoming a Buddhist de-emphasizes these dualistic splits but heads straight toward an inward awakening from one's ignorance about the causes and nature of suffering in the sentient realm. No matter what Buddhist tradition the convert is initiated into, whether Theravada, Mahayana, or Tantric, he or she inwardly discovers the seed of Buddhist enlightenment, or *tathagatagarbha* in Sanskrit, that is often translated as Buddha Nature.[7] Thus, one who becomes a Buddhist embraces nothing new but awakens the seed of enlightenment that was formerly dormant. The Buddha metaphorically elaborated that Buddha Nature is like pure gold bullion dropped in filthy and odious waste; a poverty-ridden person sleeplessly contemplating his poverty without knowing treasures are buried under his house; and a monstrous-looking pregnant woman who does not know her forthcoming child will be the one who turns the Dharma Wheel.[8] Thus, conversion is not a "timeless point of decision" but a point in time marking the beginning of a long inner process guided by the teachings of the Buddha in which the convert may discover his or her inner spiritual treasure that is qualitatively the same as that of the Buddha.

In this respect, John E. Smith's etymological explication of religious conversion[9] and Lewis R. Rambo's[10] approach to religious conversion are more fitting to the understanding of Buddhist conversion in the contemporary world than the traditional approach to conversion. In Smith's etymological reading, "conversion" is derived from Latin "conversus," meaning "to revolve," "to reverse," "to turn round," or "to turn toward for guidance, direction and assistance."[11] Thus, conversion conveys a sense of motion, change, or "a quest to be at home in a world experienced as turbulent or constraining or, in some particular way, as wanting in value."[12] Thich Nhat Hanh, the prominent global Vietnamese Dharma master, often metaphorically refers to Buddhist liberation from suffering as a process of "coming home."[13] This Buddhist quest for spiritual homecoming entails embracing a higher awareness that reveals itself only when one moves closer and closer to Buddha Nature, the overarching basis of Buddhist enlightenment existing in each and every sentient being.

Buddhist conversion, in this backdrop, was expressed clearly in the Buddha's first sermon in which he propounded the Four Noble Truths, namely, suffering (*dukkha*), cause of suffering (*samudaya*), cessation of suffering (*nirodha*), and path to the cessation of suffering (*marga*). These claimed truths are not static statements but are fundamental formulae initiating a spiritual homecoming process. Indeed, "coming home" spiritually, in this Buddhist sense, is a process. For instance, the fourth truth is the last stage toward Buddhist liberation as one fully embraces the path of the Buddha by cultivating Buddha Nature within; thus, one may eventually reach the same spiritual state as the historical Buddha. This unique Buddhist idea of spiritual equality sets Buddhist soteriology apart from other world religions, especially Christianity, Islam, and other traditions that rely on a divinity higher than and independent from humans and other sentient beings. In other words, qualitatively, the essence of the Buddha is also the essence of sentient beings except that the latter are in an unawakened state. And, the awakening process is a series of turning points, not just one single point of change.

Rambo emphatically remarks, "Conversion is very rarely an overnight, all-in-an-instant wholesale transformation that is now and forever."[14] Its central meaning, according to Rambo, is a change or a process over time.[15] This reflects the reality of Buddhist conversion. The majority of Buddhists the world over do not reach a sudden enlightenment such as was experienced by Hui Neng, the Sixth Patriarch of the Chinese Ch'an (Zen) tradition. Instead, most undergo a life-long process of gradual conversion or a series of ever deeper soteriological and existential realizations over time. This process entails various phases and stages, and sometimes an amalgamation of multiple occurrences.

The seven-stage model of conversion developed by Rambo and Farhadian is pertinent to the study of Buddhist conversion. Based on their empirical findings mostly in contemporary Christian settings, these seven stages are context, crisis, quest, encounter, interaction, committing, and consequences.[16] According to them, these stages are understood in a temporal sequence reflecting the process rather than the event-centered religious conversion. When this model is used in contemporary Buddhist settings, instead of treating these seven factors as temporal stages, it is helpful to see them as facets or different sides of the same conversion process. Some, if not all, of these facets could very likely take place simultaneously. One particular characteristic of contemporary religious conversion, as Rambo notes, is apostasy which, occurring especially in the stages of encounter and interaction, denotes "the repudiation of a religious tradition or its beliefs by previous members."[17] Apostasy is an important point of Buddhist conversion in the contemporary world. It is also what André Godin terms "deversion" or "abandonment of religious faith or membership of religious groups."[18] The last portion of this chapter particularly addresses this facet of Buddhist conversion.

FROM MISSION TO CONVERSION—WHO ARE THE BUDDHIST MISSIONARIES?

Western scholars who insist that Buddhism is a missionary religion often cite this passage from the Pali canon:

> Go ye now, O bhikkhus, and wander for the gain of the many, for the welfare of the many, out of compassion for the world, for the good, for the gain, and for the welfare of gods and men. Let not two of you go the same way.[19]

These scholars, when elaborating their argument on Buddhism as a missionary religion, tend to look for textual evidence from the canons of different Buddhist traditions. Linda Learman, in her recent work, also cites Mahayana texts such as the *Lotus Sutra* to make the point that textual evidence "all strongly suggests purposeful outreach to believers and nonbelievers alike."[20] In reality, the spread of Buddhism has been mostly the work of local cultural elites who either are influential in their communities or possess resources, such as the historical Buddha's chief lay disciple Anathapindika and the Buddhist Indian King Asoka of the third century B.C., not Buddhist missionaries similar to their Christian counterparts. However, this sociocultural reality of the regional and global expansion of Buddhism has not been well researched and continues to be argued against by those who cite textual sources from Buddhist canons as historical evidence.

Whether or not Buddhism is properly identified as a missionary religion, it is currently undergoing "explosive growth" worldwide.[21] At the end of the twentieth century, researchers connected with Peter Jennings's *ABC Nightly News* "estimated the Buddhist population [in the United States] to be between four and six million individuals...making American Buddhism a religious movement significantly larger than many Protestant denominations."[22] This estimate is consistent with Pew Research Center's survey about the current state of Buddhism as the fourth largest religion in the United States.[23] Furthermore, according to the survey, 53 percent of American Buddhists are European-Americans (ibid.). In other words, Asian immigrants and descendants are no longer the primary Buddhist population in the United States. The current status of Buddhism shows that Buddhism is rapidly growing roots in the United States. Other correlated statistics also affirm the growing trend of Buddhism among Westerners. Ninety percent of Buddhist organizations in America were founded in the last three decades of the twentieth century. In North America, during the period of 1900 to 1970, only 100 PhDs in Buddhist studies were awarded; however, between 1971 and 2000 over 1,000 doctoral degrees were granted to those researching different aspects of Buddhism.[24] Many Buddhologists are also Buddhist practitioners. In addition, Buddhism is rapidly growing elsewhere in the world. Australia, for instance, in a ten-year span (1996–2006) doubled its Buddhist population, from 199,812 to 418,849, excluding cases involving immigration.[25]

In the mid-1960s, in the context of the Catholic Church's ecumenical spirit, the Second Vatican Council regarded Buddhism as "a radiant faith" or "a path by which men, in a devout and confident spirit, can either reach a state of absolute freedom or attain supreme enlightenment by their own efforts."[26] However, toward the end of the twentieth century, Cardinal Joseph Ratzinger, the future Pope Benedict XVI, "issued a position paper forbidding Eastern-inspired meditation practices for Catholics."[27] Obviously, Buddhist conversion is not a simple process of changing from non-faith to Buddhist faith; instead, it draws adherents from other religions, such as Catholicism. The question is: who are the ones responsible for this unprecedented growth of Buddhism worldwide?

Asian Immigrant Buddhists

In her article "Who is A Buddhist? Charting the Landscape of Buddhist America," Jan Nattier discerns two types of Buddhists in America, namely, Asian immigrant Buddhists and European American Buddhists.[28] She refers to the former as "Baggage" Buddhists, meaning that this group of Buddhists came to America as immigrants with Buddhism as their hereditary religion. The primary Asian immigrant Buddhists were Chinese and Japanese. Both Buddhist traditions, upon arriving in America, were self-enclosed, mostly serving Buddhists within their own ethnic enclaves. Temples were built within immigrant communities, and there was no missionary outreach effort toward non-Buddhists. Immigrant Buddhism, stigmatized by the Christian majority, was despised by members of the majority culture as a heathen religion, a superstition, or idol worship. The experiences of North American immigrant Buddhists were similar to their counterparts in Brazil, Australia, and South Africa. Their religion remained inscrutable to the mainstream of these countries for a long period of time. Thus, Asian immigrant Buddhists suffered from cultural stigma and low social status. They were in no position to broadcast Buddhism to non-Buddhists on a large scale.

Asian Dharma Masters

The 1960s and 1970s changed the contours of Buddhism. As a result, Buddhism is no longer regionally limited to Asia but has become a global religion on par with other world religions. This recent global migration of Buddhism is largely a result of a variety of geopolitical events, regional conflicts, and post–Cold War economic globalization. The Vietnam War brought Thich Nhat Hanh to the West. The exile of the Dalai Lama moved Tibetan Buddhism to North America and Europe. Meanwhile, in the ongoing immigration traffic between East Asia and the United States, the late Ven. Xuanhua from Taiwan landed in San Francisco in the 1960s. Among these prominent Asian Dharma masters, some came to the West accidentally due to political turmoil in their home regions, while others came with a missionary deliberation—that is, with their Buddhist vows to plant the seed of Buddha Dharma beyond Asia, especially in the West.

The Global Presence of the Dalai Lama

When the 14th Dalai Lama left his homeland for India in 1959, he was not filled with Buddhist missionary zeal to convert non-Tibetans into Buddhists. He went to Dharamsala, India, as a refugee because communist China was not only annexing Tibet to China but was also implementing a series of socialist reforms toward the traditional Tibetan governing system and Buddhist institutions. Many Tibetans resisted but were quickly quelled by Chinese communist troops. The city of Lhasa, "a place of gods," fell into the hands of modern atheists. The Dalai Lama and his entourage fled to the Potala Palace. Upon arriving in Dharamsala, his immediate agenda was to maintain his exiled government in refugee status. The United States and Great Britain offered aid and also involved young Tibetan refugees in their cause to fight communism. Western resources, particularly from the United States, were directed not at the promotion of Tibetan Buddhism but to the advancement of the United States' own geopolitical interests in the name of the Tibetan humanitarian crisis. Many Tibetans from Kham (eastern Tibet) were recruited by US clandestine services to conduct guerrilla warfare in China. John Kenneth Knaus, a former CIA political officer who trained Tibetan guerrillas, remarked that Tibetans were the "orphans of the Cold War,"[29] meaning that their geopolitical utilitarian value was placed higher than their humanitarian needs. Thus, for the first three decades of his exile, the Dalai Lama did not teach Buddhism on a global scale but did everything he could to sustain his exiled government by working with his Western allies.

Thich Nhat Hanh's Peace Activism in the West

Thich Nhat Hanh, a globally renowned Vietnamese monk, first traveled to the United States in the 1960s. His mission was not, originally, to spread Buddhism, but to stop the Vietnam War. While in Vietnam, he had engaged in peace activism, founding the School of Youth for Social Services, a relief organization dedicated to rebuilding war-torn villages in Vietnam. In the United States, his mission was to promote this peace activism by building allies with American peace and civil rights activists such as Martin Luther King, Jr., who later nominated him for the Nobel Peace Prize. Thus, Thich Nhat Hanh was a part of the "monks' war"[30] against the Vietnam War during his initial years in the West. He attended various public peace rallies, speaking and dialoguing with American peace activists. His perspective on peace was not directly drawn from Buddhist doctrines but was articulated in modern terms such as "co-responsibility," "inter-being," and "universal ecology." Unlike Christian missionaries, Thich Nhat Hanh mostly worked alone with just a few Vietnamese monastic assistants when he came to the West. However, his well-received published works on peace and environmental activism laid a foundation for his later cause of promoting Buddhism in the West.

Taiwanese Dharma Masters' Global Missionary Efforts

The late Ven. Xuanhua was the first Taiwanese Dharma master to explicitly make a vow of spreading Buddhism in the West. He came to the United States alone, bringing a small bronze Buddha statue, in the late 1950s and settled in San Francisco's Chinatown. According to his disciples' narrative, he lived in abject conditions. "Because the Master started out living in a damp and windowless basement that resembled a grave, he called himself 'The Monk in the Grave.'"[31] However, three decades later these living conditions changed and Ven. Xuanhua had established dozens of Buddhist Dharma centers, such as the City of Ten Thousand Buddhas in Talmage, California. His mission was clearly to propagate Buddhism in the West. The charismatic nature of his earlier years in the United States drew Euro-American disciples into his community. In 1968, after a Dharma talk on the campus of the University of Washington in Seattle, five young Euro-Americans took monastic discipleship with him. For the next two decades, Ven. Xuanhua was successful not only in drawing adherents from the Euro-American population, but he also began to make frequent appearances in the American mainstream as he became a public figure known to many American politicians, including former California Governor Pete Wilson and former President George Bush. However, toward the mid-1990s, many of his Euro-American students began to leave his *sangha*. Among his initial five Euro-American monastic disciples, only one remained his disciple and is now a prominent Dharma master. The current demographic composition of Ven. Xuanhua's lay and monastic communities appears mostly Asian, consisting of predominantly Chinese Americans and Asian immigrants from Taiwan, mainland China, and Vietnam. The cultural outlook of Ven. Xuanhua's teachings emphasizes traditional Chinese values such as Confucianism, the parental position of Chinese Dharma teachers, collective regimentation, and strict spatial separation of men and women. These cultural practices have perhaps become hindrances to his Buddhist mission in the West, as they run counter to Western democratic and individual-oriented cultural values.

Master Xingyun, the founder of Fo Guang Shan or the Buddha's Light International Association (BLIA), based in Taiwan, often proclaims, "I am a global person."[32] Although the global mission of his Buddhism started nearly ten years later than that of Ven. Xuanhua, he has established one hundred and fifty Dharma centers and temples worldwide, dwarfing Ven. Xuanhua's achievement. Among these one hundred and fifty establishments, fifty-seven are in Taiwan, but ninety-five are in North and South America, Africa, and Southeast Asia.[33] His first temple in the United States was built in Los Angeles and named "Hsi-Lai," which means "coming to the West." In subsequent years, he built a fully-accredited Buddhist university in the Los Angeles area named after the temple. The first/current president of the university is Lewis Lancaster, who is Professor Emeritus and the founding chairperson of the University of California Berkeley's Buddhist Studies Program. Xingyun has publicly described his missionary intent as his "response to the history of Christian missionary activity in China."[34] He has posed the rhetorical question, "Catholics and Protestants have built churches all round the world, so why can't Foguangshan?"[35] Speaking culturally and religiously, Xingyun's assessment is that, "Although America is not a Buddhist country, Americans have the character and spirit of humanistic Buddhism and the Mahayana bodhisattva path."[36]

The "missionary" strategy toward Americans, in this case, does not resemble that of Christian missionaries who tend to emphasize the teachings of Christianity as being the only path to salvation. Instead, Xingyun encourages his monastic and lay adherents to establish "links of affinity," or *jie-yuan* in Chinese, with local populations. This missionary method is similar to Ven. Xuanhua's outreach effort to make his Buddhist establishment known in mainstream America by developing intentional, positive rapport with American politicians. According to Chandler, a "link of affinity," in the context of BLIA's missionary activities, "relies upon and augments the spontaneous creative energy that arises through direct interaction among people."[37] Xingyun is more resourceful than Xuanhua. His links of affinity includes March Fong Eu, California Secretary of State, former presidents Reagan and Bush, and former Vice President Al Gore. These links with the American elite population resulted from Xingyun's rationale, "If those of high status and power support it [Buddhism], it will develop even faster."[38] However, BLIA's US chapter lowered its public profile after Al Gore's presidential fund-raising activity, hosted on the grounds of Hsi-Lai Temple in Los Angeles in 1999, was subject to inquiry by US law enforcement as being possibly in violation of laws pertaining to the legal framework of presidential fund-raising activities.[39]

The success of Xingyun's Buddhist mission in Asia is indisputable; however, his missionary track record in countries whose residents are predominantly European descendants is not as spectacular as his Buddhist architectural establishments there might suggest. His mission in South Africa became stagnant. Most South African monastic converts returned to lay life and are now engaged in livelihoods that have little to do with Buddhist practice.[40] BLIA's chapter in Australia had a similar outcome.[41] In North America, the name of Master Xingyun is popular in Buddhist communities and known to many politicians; however, the actual number of Euro-American converts remains low. BLIA continues to appear ethnically Chinese. The majority of BLIA's monastic and lay populations are Asian Americans and recent Chinese immigrants from Taiwan, Hong Kong, and mainland China. This phenomenon is identical to Xuanhua's establishment, where Chinese cultural values and practices tend to preclude more flexible forms of Buddhist practice in North America.

Convert Dharma Teachers

Prince Gotama, before achieving Buddhahood, was a seeker and a wanderer. After leaving home at the age of 29, he spent seven years seeking the ultimate liberation from suffering. His spiritual conversion was a personal process but was extensively linked with contemporary Hindu religious teachers and sacred natural sites traditionally reserved for spiritual recluses. After emerging from his ascetic life, he attained a unique path of spiritual enlightenment which was later known as Buddhism. The Buddha's teachings frequently targeted cultural and political elites of his time. Bimbisara, the King of Maghada, donated Veluvana Bamboo Grove as a monastic ground for the Buddha. The Buddha's first five disciples, Sariputta, Mahamoggallana, Mahakasyapa, Ananda, and Anuruddha, all came from Brahmin and royal families. Throughout his forty-five years of teaching the Dharma, the Buddha had extensive contact with diverse populations ranging from untouchables to individuals of noble origins. However, the actual spread of his teachings relied on generous support from the elite population of his time in terms of patronage of his growing *sangha*, sponsorship of large gatherings for his Dharma talks, and documentation and dissemination of his teachings.

This archetypal Buddhist conversion and promulgation has repeated itself in the modern world since the turn of the twentieth century. It is not an exaggeration to say that the establishment of Buddhism beyond Asia is mostly the work of local cultural elites. Although tremendously indebted to their Asian masters, non-Asian Buddhist elite converts nevertheless deserve much credit for spreading Buddhism in their home countries. During the latter half of the nineteenth and the early twentieth centuries, when Buddhism was considered outside Asia as an outlandish oriental wisdom source, a handful of Western spiritual seekers and academics were already following the routes of their home nations' colonial and commercial ventures into Asia, committing themselves to bringing Eastern philosophical and religious systems back to the West and addressing their misrepresentation. Max Müller, the renowned German philologist based at Oxford University, devoted over thirty years to translating and compiling the 50-volume *The Sacred Books of the East*. The Theosophical Society, founded by H. P. Blavatsky, Henry Steel Olcott, and William Quan Judge in the late nineteenth century, initiated Western popular interest in Buddhism. This organization supported a new generation of seekers in the early twentieth century, many of whom also made pilgrimages to Asia, including Alexandra David-Neel, the first Western woman to live in Tibet and author of personal accounts of Tibetan Buddhism, and Walter Yeeling Evans-Wentz, the translator and editor of *The Tibetan Book of the Dead* by Karma Lingpa (*Karma-glin-pa*), a fourteenth-century Tibetan Buddhist saint.

Since the latter half of the twentieth century, non-Asian Buddhist seekers have increased in number and have refined their understanding of Buddhism. Before the Dalai Lama began actively offering Buddhist teachings worldwide in the late 1980s, there was already a handful of Westerners in Dharamsala who were studying with Tibetan teachers, including the Dalai Lama himself. Upon becoming an ordained monk at Dharamsala, the young Robert Thurman, now Jey Tsong Kappa Professor of Indo-Tibetan Studies at Columbia University, took discipleship with the Dalai Lama in 1967. A few years later he returned to lay life and earned his PhD in Sanskrit from Harvard in 1972. His monastic years decisively shaped his current livelihood through Buddhist studies. As both a Buddhologist and a Buddhist practitioner, Thurman has published extensively on Buddhism, influencing generations of college students as well as the general public. Like Thurman, José Cabezón, the Dalai Lama Professor of Tibetan Buddhism and Cultural Studies at University of California Santa Barbara, and B. Allan

Wallace, President of Santa Barbara Institute of Consciousness Studies, were both once ordained monks under the guidance of the Dalai Lama in Dharamsala. Currently, through their active scholarship in Buddhist philosophy and Buddhist dialogue with modern science, they continue to introduce Tibetan Buddhism to the West.

Other Buddhist traditions, such as those of Mahayana and Theravada, have produced influential convert teachers. Unlike his compatriot Robert Thurman, whose Buddhist conversion began with his taking monastic discipleship with the Dalai Lama but who now propagates Buddhist teachings to the greater English-speaking world as a lay professor of Buddhist studies, Rev. Heng Sure (Christopher Clowery) did not begin as a monastic disciple, although later he became one of the initial five monastic disciples of the late Dharma Master Xuanhua, the founder of the City of Ten Thousand Buddhas in northern California. Rev. Sure began as a doctoral student in Buddhist studies at the University of California at Berkeley in the early 1970s but later chose to be ordained as a monk by Dharma Master Xuanhua. His career change, or rather his formal Buddhist conversion, became a legend among University of California Berkeley's renowned Buddhist Studies Group. However, his absence in Berkeley was only temporary as he returned in the 1990s with a dual purpose. While fulfilling the role of abbot of Berkeley Buddhist Monastery, he also returned to the academic world as a doctoral student at the Graduate Theological Union. Resembling other convert teachers in North America, his doctoral degree earned from the GTU adds more credibility to his monastic mastership and enables him to reach out to more lay people.

Jack Kornfield, one of the founders of the Insight Meditation Society and Spirit Rock Meditation Center, entered Theravada Buddhist training as an ordained monk. He received extensive training in *vipassana* (insight meditation) techniques from teachers in Burma, Sri Lanka, and India in the 1960s and 1970s. Like many other ordained Westerners, he eventually returned to lay life, earning his PhD in clinical psychology and taking the path of being a lay Dharma teacher.[42] Through his many publications, he has reached far more potential Western converts than he could have as a monk.

The impact of convert Dharma teachers on the general public of their home countries is far more expansive than the impact of their Asian masters. However, the majority of these convert teachers do not refer to themselves as "missionaries" due to the term's pejorative association with evangelical and colonial versions of Christianity. If all Christian connotations were removed from the word, this group of Buddhist convert teachers obviously expresses their Buddhist mission in various capacities. By publicizing the narratives of their personal spiritual searches, using their social networks, and taking advantage of modern means of communication, this group of highly educated native convert Buddhist teachers has cultivated a diverse body of Buddhists in non-Asian cultural settings. Among contemporary convert Buddhists in the West, there are "green," "engaged," "feminist," "environmental," and "Protestant" Buddhists. This sociocultural reality of globalized Buddhism in the twenty-first century confirms that contemporary Buddhist conversion has multilayered meanings pertinent to the psychological, sociocultural, pre-Buddhist conditions of individual converts. However, one common thread which links all these facets of Buddhist conversion is what Rambo and Farhadian[43] refer

to as the "context" that has shaped a distinct transpersonal psychology of Buddhist converts, especially in non-Asian cultural environments.

MODERN BUDDHISM: DEVERSION, SYNCRETIZATION, AND TRANSFERENCE

Globalized Buddhism, in the twenty-first century, is drastically different from its
traditional counterparts throughout Asia. It is notably lay-oriented rather than
monastic-centered. This manifestation of Buddhism worldwide, in non-Asian sociocultural settings, is not a coincidence but is a confirmed developmental trend, especially in
the West.[44] As most convert Dharma teachers conduct their teachings as lay persons, it
is inevitable that their Buddhist communities have been founded with an emphasis on
lay adherents. Going deeper, if one examines this unique global Buddhist phenomenon
with Rambo's macro-contextual lens,[45] it could also be said that the lay-orientation of
convert Dharma teachers is a product of the macro-context in which they live and teach.
This macro-context is the distinct secular Western values of modern science, rationalism, egalitarianism, individualism, and anti-hierarchy. These cultural values have been
deeply ingrained in the collective psychology of the West. This macro-context of the
West has thus shaped the transpersonal characteristic of Western Buddhist converts.
Culturally, it establishes a critical position in relation to traditional Buddhist practices
in Asia, and thus distances itself from the monastic-based Buddhism of Asian masters,
which is alleged by Western converts as being "a tableau of resilient hierarchy, authoritarianism, patriarchy (edging into misogyny), dogmatism, ritualism, social conservatism and superstition."[46]

Given this cultural backdrop, it is evident that the conversion process of Buddhism
in non-Asian locales is a process that many Western scholars refer to as "modern
Buddhism" in the making. The emphasis is obviously on "modern," which is not a temporal marker of the new vs. the old but a qualitative gauge that distinguishes itself from
the rest of the world. As Theodor Adorno remarked, "Modernity is a qualitative, not
a chronological category."[47] It penetrates into the present and the future of what are
deemed non-modern societies and cultural constituencies, reorienting their existing
operating systems toward both superstructural and infrastructural modernization—a
full physical and moral conformity to modern values and life styles. Thus, modernity
is a "universal point of reference"[48] that is allegedly free from any social, cultural, and
historical conditions and yet creates conditions for the transition from backwardness to
progress.

But, as a premodern and regional religion, why is Buddhism being chosen for modernization in a global scene? Is this a conscious choice of potential and actual Buddhist
converts? One thing which stands out in the global market of religion and spirituality
is the widespread collective imagination of Buddhism as a viable path toward ultimate

spiritual liberation. In her assessment of this global imagination of a premodern religion, Marilyn Ivy points out that Buddhism is both historical and transhistorical:

> (1) Buddhism as object of modern fantasy and longing, bearing the nostalgic freight of the premodern and the non-Western; (2) Buddhism as a transhistorical religion comprising transcendent technologies of liberation, thus intrinsically empty of historical signification or cultural baggage: the way it is, when- and wherever.[49]

This transhistorical quality of Buddhism is fully embraced by non-Asian convert teachers and their adherents, while its historical and culturally specific "baggage" is being selectively filtered out. Although Buddhism is a premodern religion, it nevertheless possesses qualities that are a universal point of reference in both a religious and a spiritual sense. Like modernity, the transhistorical aspect of Buddhism could be placed in or adopted by any historically and culturally specific milieu. This contradictory modern classification of a premodern religion and the selective process of alleged transhistorical conversion reflect the very nature of globalized Buddhism, that is, the actuality of the conversion process is two-way traffic. On one side, an increasing number of non-Asians are converting to Buddhism, and, on the other side, the new converts also transform the religion that they have embraced. This is what many scholars call the "localization" or "indigenization" of Buddhism, involving not only Buddhist spirituality and doctrines but also differences of cultural and political values and racial/ethnic appearances. This complex interplay between Buddhist traditions and local values and sociocultural dynamics suggests deversion, syncretization, and transference as inherent components of modern Buddhist conversion.

Deversion

Deversion is a distinct characteristic of Buddhist conversion in the contemporary world. The process of becoming Buddhist is not a simple, unidirectional move from a nonreligious background; it involves a complex interplay, rejection, and negotiation between Buddhism as the new faith and pre-existing religious beliefs and practices. These pre-existing religious elements do not have to be formally associated with an organized religious environment; instead, they manifest themselves as the ethos of a given culture, such as the culture of Protestantism in America. The interest in Buddhism in modern societies of the West, as we have seen, grew dramatically between the 1960s and 1970s, a time when the younger generations were experiencing disenchantment with their society's social and moral systems. Buddhism in the non-Asian, non-traditional, context has been presented "as rational and scientific, grounded on reason and individual experience."[50] The historical Buddha has been emphasized as a spiritual seeker in narratives published since in the twentieth century, such as Thich Nhat Hanh's *Old Path White Clouds: Walking in the Footsteps of the Buddha* and Herman Hesse's Nobel Prize-winning *Siddhartha*.

The emphasis on the human quality of the historical Buddha has been essential in attracting new adherents. Since the 1960s, Buddhism has attracted most of its converts from among "free-spirited bohemian intellectuals"[51] and youth who have lost confidence in the moral provisions of their home societies, especially in monotheistic religious settings where tolerance of differences and alternative viewpoints are minimized and where the externality of the divinity is emphasized over individual experiences and/ or freely chosen spiritual practices.

On a material level, in the 1960s and 1970s the West was experiencing rampant consumerism, the destructive power of technology, and a collective sense of meaninglessness. Many individuals turned to psychedelic drugs or eastern belief systems such as Buddhism. Situated in this historical background, Buddhist conversion inevitably manifested itself as a deversion process—deversion from existing conventional values and pre-existing belief systems such as Christianity. It bore New Age traits—self-as-divine, a holistic worldview, and no authority higher than the individual self.[52] These modern cultural constituents have contributed to the complexity of Buddhist conversion on non-Asian soil.

Syncretization: Engaging Buddhism with Social Activism

The localization of Buddhism beyond Asia is a matter of adaptation, a process that "emphasizes how an original is being altered, modified, fitted for a different use; maybe even decentered, drawn out of an earlier orbit by the gravitational pull of an alien body."[53] Buddhism in the West is a telling example of this type of sociocultural-religious adaptation. It has been predominantly a lay movement led by lay convert teachers. In the last three or four decades, the adaptations experienced by Buddhists in the West are cultural and political rather than doctrinal. A collectively felt sense of alienation, meaninglessness, awareness of worldwide environmental degradation, and regional conflicts due to modern technology and the excessive consumption of resources, is manifestly expressed in the dynamics of the Buddhist conversion process. On the one hand, modern new converts desire the original teachings of the historical Buddha based on his rational choice and individual experimentation. On the other hand, they are most eager to apply Buddhist teachings in their collective actions to remedy social injustice and global issues that threaten the commonwealth of humankind. Peter Matthiessen, the renowned social activist and writer, narrated his process of conversion to Zen Buddhism as follows:

> I love zazen, but somehow sitting on that black cushion and straining toward the absolute while in the relative world, where there was so much misery and poverty, didn't make sense. I don't think Americans were ever really geared for sitting only, and I think there was always a schism between American students and Japanese teachers for this reason.[54]

Socially engaged Buddhism is a predominant trend among Western Buddhists and is referred to as a "New Vehicle," or *Navayana* in Sanskrit, to mark its distinction from traditional Buddhist forms in Asia.[55] The initial idea of engaged Buddhism came from Thich Nhat Hanh in his Vietnam-era peace activism, but it has flourished among postwar North Americans. In both scholarly and Buddhist circles, Thich Nhat Hanh is given credit for advocating engaged Buddhism as "a new paradigm of Buddhist liberation."[56] The imperative of engaged Buddhism is action that is collective in nature. Thich Nhat Hanh bases engagement on the Buddhist concept of the interdependence of all sentient beings and the "co-responsibility" of all social members.[57] The co-responsibility of all social members is to heal their collective wounds. Thich Nhat Hanh elaborated his Buddhist view on the relation between the individual and society: "Our individual consciousness is a product of our society, ancestors, education, and many other factors.... Your personal healing will be the healing of the whole nation, your children, and their children."[58] The Buddhist Peace Fellowship (BPF), based in California, is the emblem of engaged Buddhism in the West. With its 4,000 members from different Buddhist lineages, BPF has "shaped the American engaged Buddhist identity" and "forged a language of social engagement."[59]

The orientation toward social engagement in modern Buddhism marks its distinction from its traditional counterpart through the ideas and practices of "gender equality, anti-ritual, anti-hierarchy." This political stance has become the moral basis for modern Buddhists in the West to distance themselves from traditional monastic authorities that are alleged to perform "socially-integrative and regime-legitimizing functions."[60] Thus, Western values of equality, inclusiveness, and collective self-rule are the institutional principles of modern Buddhism in the West.[61] Meanwhile, methods and philosophies of Western social activism have also been syncretized into the practices of modern Buddhist converts. Through the combination of all these macro-contextual elements, Buddhist converts in the West have successfully built prominent modern Buddhist institutions such as the American Zen Teachers Association, the Insight Meditation Society, and Spirit Rock Meditation Center. With the notable exceptions of Thich Nhat Hanh and the Dalai Lama, permanent Asian masters are absent at these lay-oriented Dharma centers, evidencing the successful toppling of traditional Asian monastic authorities. Both of these charismatic Asian masters are dearly loved but are not in proximity to these modern Buddhist facilities on a daily basis. This is a unique expression of the modern North American Buddhist conversion process.

Transference

Since the early 1990s, Buddhists and Buddhologists in non-Asian settings, especially in the West, have been pushing for a global Buddhism distinct from its traditional counterpart in Asia. After nearly two decades of attempts to define this form of Buddhism in both academic conferences and Buddhist publications, the consensus has rested on the aforementioned "modern Buddhism" that is characterized by the qualities of diversity, egalitarianism, social engagement, and transhistoricity. If these attributes are temporarily bracketed, the picture of modern Buddhists looks racially white, economically middle- and upper-class, and culturally highly educated. During a Buddhist studies conference held in Berkeley in the mid-1990s, the late Zen scholar and practitioner Rick Fields acknowledged the emerging phenomenon of "American Buddhism" but also remarked that its core is "mainly white Buddhists who are busy doing the defining. Nor is it surprising that they are defining it in their own *image*. This *image* has been in large part formed by the countercultural movement of the sixties, the dramatic rigors of Zen practice galvanized the most zealous white Buddhists."[62]

The rapid global dissemination of Buddhism and the impressive spread of Dharma centers and temples beyond Asia are evidence of the growth of modern Buddhism. However, comparatively speaking, the cultural legitimacy and institutional establishments of Asian Buddhist traditions outside India were a natural outgrowth of the translation of the entire canon of Buddha's teachings and of a long period of relentless practicing; whereas modern, Western Buddhism is still waiting for the completed translation of Buddhist canon into the various regional languages and for a formidable body of fresh commentaries by qualified Western Buddhist teachers. In this sense, it is slightly premature to qualify modern Buddhism as the New Vehicle as it offers few hermeneutical results from its adherents' practices of Dharma except their own cultural values. Thus, the image of modern Buddhism does not quite correspond to the traditional ways of Dharma teachings in the forms of devotional acts, monastically centeredness, and extensive training in the exegesis of *sutra* (Buddha's teachings), *sastra* (commentaries on the teachings), and *vinaya* (precepts). This discrepancy can be taken as a deficiency of modern Buddhism from their traditionally trained Asian masters but can be also viewed neutrally as a sign toward a new form of Buddhism. It deserves more discernment.

What are modern Western Buddhists experiencing in their conversion process at this point in time? It is obvious that modern Buddhists are undergoing the stages that Rambo calls "encounter" and "interaction." One facet is the previously discussed deversion process. Another, from the perspective of psychoanalysis, is transference, as defined in Webster's *New College Dictionary* as "a reproduction of emotions relating to repressed experiences, especially of childhood, and the substitution of another person...for the original object of the repressed impulses." The roots of modern Buddhism, as commonly agreed among scholars, are found in the counterculture movement of the 1960s—an expression of a series of socioculturally specific repressions embedded in individual psyches. What stood out among the repressed experiences of modern Westerners were the collective imagination of a pristine spirituality that could be identified inward, not with an omnipotent external divinity; the distrust of authority and preference for individual choices free from patriarchal dominance; and a sexual intimacy defined by horizontal affinity without vertical norms defined by religious and secular institutions. The manifestations of these collectively repressed experiences generated countercultural movements of all sorts starting in the 1950s and 1960s, such as neo-paganism, feminism, returning to nature; however, in essence, all these social movements dealt with one thing—power.

When this collective psychological complex of modern Westerners and the transhistorical quality of Buddhism encountered and interacted with each other, their relationship quickly evolved to resemble that of a sage and student or of a psychoanalyst and a patient. Thus, the transhistorical or the transcendental aspect of Buddhism becomes a point of transference. It opens a new gateway for the new convert's personal healings and the collective goals of social changes envisioned by his or her comrades. However, when one formally takes refuge in the Buddha's teachings, the conversion process does not end. The process continues on in a dual fashion. On one side, the convert undergoes a long learning process about the Buddha's teachings undertaken on a routine basis with his or her teacher and community. On the other side, the currents of the convert's repressed experiences continue to remain unconscious but search for a new breaking point. In the West, the traditional monastic structure has obviously been targeted as the breaking point. In other words, repressed emotions and desires for power have adapted to a fresh setting.

In his study on modern Buddhism, Andrew Kennedy comments, "Western interest in Buddhism is an unconscious retreat into an alternative enlightenment," and "Western individualism...remains the ideological superstructure of global capitalism: an obsession with social identity that effectively eliminates navigational reflections back to biographical self-identity."[63] Ally Ostrowski, another critical scholar, equates the global mobility of Western convert teachers and seekers with "the power and wealth of their countries."[64] Fields alleges the existence of racism in modern Western Buddhism whose communities appear mostly white, saying, "Racism at its deepest level is the power to define, which is always the paramount power in a racist society."[65] This defining power has transformed Buddhism beyond Asia into a predominantly lay movement replacing the traditional authority of Asian masters with modern democratic convert masters of European descent; however, this has not yet created a Buddhism without authority; instead, a new modern authority has replaced the old and continues to transfer its culturally specific repressions onto Buddhism. The institutional comfort zone of modern Western Buddhism often features a rotating lay abbotship and collective governing process. Does this form of self-governing bring the corruption and abuse of authority to an end?

Richard Baker was the first Euro-American abbot of San Francisco Zen Center, serving in that position between 1971 and 1984. During his tenure, the Zen center grew into an organization with assets worth $25 million and an annual income of $4 million from its Tassajara Bakery and Greens Restaurant.[66] Baker's intimate association with politicians such as former California governor Jerry Brown was publicly known. He was often chauffeured in a BMW. His involuntary resignation in 1981 was due to his sexual affair with the wife of one of his close friends. Another example of the abuse of authority is Osel Tendzin, born Thomas F. Rich in New Jersey, who was the Dharma heir of the late Chögyam Trungpa, a renowned Tibetan tantric master and founder of Shambhala Center. He contracted HIV but continued to have sexual relations with his students, and one of them died of AIDS.[67] Osel Tendzin himself passed away in 1990.

Jack Kornfield once conducted a survey titled "Sex Life of the Gurus," in which he found, "Only fifteen of the teachers declared themselves celibate. Thirty-four out of fifty-four—63 percent—said that they had engaged in sex with one or more students."[68] What often shakes the foundation of modern Buddhist organizations is sex and power, and, as James W. Coleman puts it, "It was often sex that set off the explosion."[69]

In the forefront of social activism, engaged Buddhists have become a critical force influencing the contours of Western conventional politics. However, they continue to face a crude question: how are Buddhists engaged in social action? Critical remarks of engaged Buddhism often occur in public, such as the criticism that "its social action agenda has suffered from purely conventional thinking, polarizing the oppressor and oppressed, and that its actions have no distinctly Buddhist analysis or strategy behind them."[70] Meanwhile, a conventional theological question continues to challenge engaged Buddhists' dismissive stance toward monastic-based Buddhist practices in Asia: Do the historical Buddha's teachings not count as socially engaged since they were mostly the result of his solitary meditation and wandering in ancient India?

Viewed not from a moral but from a psychoanalytical perspective, the power and sex scandals, as well as social activism in the name of Buddhism, are indicators that transference, as an integral part of modern Buddhist conversion, also transforms traditional Buddhism at least in form if not in content. Modern Buddhist understanding of Asian monastic authority apparently is a result of transference, that is, the negative modes of Western authority (i.e., church and state) have evidently been projected onto Asian Dharma masters and their monastic institutions.

SUMMARY

This chapter primarily focuses on Buddhist conversion experiences in the West, where global Buddhism or modern Buddhism is being shaped. The rationale of this focus is that the emergence of modern Buddhism is a dynamically multidimensional case of religious conversion in terms of its inter-religious, transpersonal, transcultural nature. Traditionally, conversion, understood as transformation, has often been centered upon personal spiritual and psychological changes; however, in the context of contemporary globalization of religions, modern Buddhist conversion clearly involves the collective psychology of contemporary Western societies and demonstrates that collectively witnessed social injustice and environmental degradation are challenging the limitations of the traditional exegesis of the Buddhist concept of suffering. The unprecedented growth of modern Buddhism indicates that modern Buddhist conversion travels a two-way path: Asian masters have bred non-Asian Dharma teachers, and, in turn, these modern Buddhist teachers and their cultural constituencies have taken the initiative to transform traditional versions of Buddhism to meet their own social and political needs.

From both the Asian perspective and from the critical position of scholars of Buddhist studies, modern Buddhism may have permanently changed the heretofore traditional ways of practicing Buddhism. Although the demographics of modern Buddhism appear racially white, it nevertheless is not a unique case of "racialization" in the midst of a conversion process. Historically, Buddhism was Sinicized, Tibetanized, Koreanized, and Japanized after it had entered these culturally specific regions. The images and the teachings of the historical Buddha and local sociocultural ethos were intimately intertwined, mutually mirroring each other. Buddhists in all these regions continue to claim the authenticity of their versions of Buddhism. In the same manner, modern Buddhists in the West are making a similar claim.

However, unlike Buddhism in the histories of Asian nations, the localization of Buddhism in the modern West is also simultaneously a globalization of Buddhism with a modern twist that emphasizes a rational and scientific understanding of the historical Buddha's teaching. This simultaneous localization and globalization of modern Buddhism is expressed in its contribution to Buddhist revitalizations in those Asian countries such as China and Vietnam where religions have been suppressed by state violence and ideology. For instance, Thich Nhat Hanh's writings on peacemaking have been translated from European languages into Vietnamese and Chinese. So also has been Sogyal Rinpoche's *The Tibetan Book of Living and Dying*. The importation of these modern Buddhist bestsellers into Asian countries has contributed to the current revitalization of Buddhism there, also with the same modern turn toward a scientific representation of Buddhism. Currently under-researched, this emerging religious conversion phenomenon in contemporary Asia awaits more scholarly attention.

NOTES

1. Peter Berger, "Introduction: The Cultural Dynamics of Globalization," in *Many Globalizations: Cultural Diversity in the Contemporary World*, ed. Peter L. Berger and Samuel P. Huntington (Oxford: Oxford University Press, 2002).
2. Roland Robertson, "Social Theory, Cultural Relativity and the Problem of Globality," in *Culture, Globalization and the World-System: Contemporary Conditions for the Representation of Identity*, ed. Anthony D. King (Minneapolis: University of Minnesota Press, 1997), 69–90.
3. Rosemary Haughton, "Formation and Transformation," in *Conversion: Perspectives on Personal and Social Transformation*, ed. Walter E. Conn (New York: Alba House, 1978), 23.
4. Ibid., 24.
5. Reinhold Niebuhr, "Grace as Power in, and as Mercy towards, Man," in *Conversion: Perspectives on Personal and Social Transformation*, ed. Walter E. Conn (New York: Alba House, 1978), 29.
6. Karl Barth, "The Awakening to Conversion," in *Conversion: Perspectives on Personal and Social Transformation*, ed. Walter E. Conn (New York: Alba House, 1978), 47.
7. Sallie B. King, *Buddha Nature* (Albany: State University of New York Press, 1991).
8. William H. Grosnick, "The Thathagatagarbha Sutra," in *Buddhism in Practice*, ed. Donald S. Lopez, Jr. (Princeton: Princeton University Press, 2007), 101.
9. John E. Smith, "The Concept of Conversion," in *Conversion: Perspectives on Personal and Social Transformation*, ed. Walter E. Conn (New York: Alba House, 1978), 51–60.

10. Lewis R. Rambo, "Anthropology and the Study of Conversion," in *The Anthropology of Religious Conversion*, ed. Andrew Buckser and Stephen D. Glazier (New York: Rowman & Littlefield Publishers, 2003), 211–222.

11. Smith, "The Concept of Conversion," 51.

12. Diane Austin-Broos, "The Anthropology of Conversion: An Introduction," in *The Anthropology of Religious Conversion*, ed. Andrew Buckser and Stephen D. Glazier (New York: Rowman & Littlefield Publishers, 2003). 2.

13. Thich Nhat Hanh, *Peace Is Every Step: The Path of Mindfulness in Everyday Life* (New York: Bantam Books, 1991).

14. Lewis R. Rambo, *Understanding Religious Conversion* (New Haven: Yale University Press, 1993). 1.

15. Ibid., 3.

16. Lewis R. Rambo and Charles E. Farhadian, "Converting: Stages of Religious Change," in *Religious Conversion: Contemporary Practices and Controversies*, ed. Christopher Lamb and M. Darrol Bryant (New York: Cassell, 1999), 23–34.

17. Rambo, *Understanding Religious Conversion*, 13.

18. André Godin, *The Psychological Dynamics of Religious Experience* (Birmingham, AL: Religious Education Press, 1985), 73.

19. T. W. Rhys Davids and Herman Oldenberg, *Vinaya Texts* (New York: Charles Scribner's Sons, 1899), 112.

20. Linda Learman, "Introduction," in *Missionaries in the Era of Globalization*, ed. Linda Learman (Honolulu: University of Hawaii Press, 2005), 8.

21. Martin Baumann, "Working in the Right Spirit: The Application of Buddhist Right Livelihood in the Friends of the Western Buddhist Order," *Journal of Buddhist Ethics* 5 (1998): 122.

22. Charles Prebish, "Introduction," in *The Faces of Buddhism in America*, ed. Charles S. Prebish and Kenneth K. Tanaka (Berkeley and Los Angeles: University of California Press, 1998), 1.

23. Pew Research Center, "53 percent—American Buddhists," http://pewresearch.org/databank/dailynumber/?NumberID=485.

24. Victor Sogen Hori, Richard P. Hayes, and James Mark Shields, "Introduction," in *Teaching Buddhism in the West: From the Wheel to the Web*, ed. Victor Sogen Hori, Richard P. Hayes, and James Mark Shields (London: Routledge Curzon, 2002), xii.

25. Michelle Barker, "Investments in Religious Capital: An Explorative Case Study of Australian Buddhists," *Journal of Global Buddhism* 8 (2007): 68.

26. Lawrence Sutin, *All is Change: The Two-Thousand-Year Journey of Buddhism to the West* (New York: Little, Brown and Company, 2006), 283.

27. Ibid., 290.

28. Jan Nattier, "Who Is a Buddhist? Charting the Landscape of Buddhist America," in *The Faces of Buddhism in America*, ed. Charles S. Prebish and Kenneth K. Tanaka (Berkeley and Los Angeles: University of California Press, 1998), 188.

29. John Kenneth Knaus, *Orphans of the Cold War: America and the Tibetan Struggle for Survival* (New York: Public Affairs, 1999).

30. Patricia Hunt-Perry and Lyn Fine, *All Buddhism Is Engaged: Thich Nhat Hanh and the Order of Interbeing*, in *Engaged Buddhism in the West*, ed. Christopher S. Queen (Boston: Wisdom Publications, 2000), 2.

31. City of Ten Thousand Buddhas (CTTB), http://www.cttbusa.org/.

32. Steven Chandler, *Establishing a Pure Land on Earth: The Foguang Buddhist Perspective on Modernization and Globalization* (Honolulu: University of Hawaii Press, 2004), 1.

33. Steven Chandler, "Spreading Buddha's Light: The Internationalization of Foguang Shan," in *Missionaries in the Era of Globalization*, ed. Linda Learman (Honolulu: University of Hawaii Press, 2005), 165.

34. Chandler, *Establishing a Pure Land on Earth*, 270.

35. Ibid., 270.

36. Ibid., 284.

37. Chandler, "Spreading Buddha's Light," 171.

38. Chandler, *Establishing a Pure Land on Earth*, 284.

39. Chandler, "Spreading Buddha's Light," 171.

40. Chandler, *Establishing a Pure Land on Earth*.

41. Ibid.

42. David Bubna-Litic, "The Emergence of Secular Insight Practice in Australia," *Journal of Global Buddhism* 8 (2007): 159.

43. Rambo and Farhadian, "Converting: Stages of Religious Change."

44. Bubna-Litic, "The Emergence of Secular Insight Practice in Australia,"165.

45. Rambo, *Understanding Religious Conversion*.

46. Bubna-Litic. "The Emergence of Secular Insight Practice in Australia," 160.

47. Theodor W. Adorno, *Minima Moralia: Reflections from Damaged Life*, trans. E. F. Jephcott (London: Verso, 1974).

48. Marilyn Ivy, "Modernity," in *Critical Terms for the Study of Buddhism*, ed. Donald Lopez, Jr. (Chicago: University of Chicago Press, 2005), 315.

49. Ibid., 313.

50. Martin Baumann and Charles S. Prebish, "Introduction: Paying Homage to the Buddha in the West," in *Westward Dharma: Buddhism beyond Asia*, ed. Charles S. Prebish and Martin Baumann (Berkeley and Los Angeles: University of California Press, 2002), 3.

51. James William Coleman, *The New Buddhism: The Western Transformation of an Ancient Tradition* (Oxford: Oxford University Press, 2001), 85.

52. Glynis Parker, "The Conversion of South Africans to Buddhism," PhD diss., University of South Africa, 2007, 61.

53. Eve Kosofsky Sedgwick, "Pedagogy," in *Critical Terms for the Study of Buddhism*, ed. Donald Lopez, Jr. (Chicago: University of Chicago Press, 2005), 165.

54. Peter Muryo Matthiessen, "The Coming of Age of American Zen," in *Buddhism in America*, ed. Brian D. Hotchkiss (Rutland, VT: Charles E. Tuttle, 1998), 398.

55. Christopher S. Queen, "Introduction: A New Buddhism," in *Engaged Buddhism in the West*, ed. Christopher S. Queen (Boston: Wisdom Publications, 2000), 2.

56. Ibid., 1.

57. Hunt-Perry and Fine, *All Buddhism is Engaged*, 12.

58. Ibid., 17.

59. Judith Simmer-Brown, "Speaking Truth to Power: The Buddhist Peace Fellowship," in *Engaged Buddhism in the West*, ed. Christopher S. Queen (Boston: Wisdom Publications, 2000), 68.

60. Bubna-Litic, "The Emergence of Secular Insight Practice in Australia,"160.

61. Ibid., 160.

62. Rick Fields, "Divided Dharma: White Buddhists, Ethnic Buddhists, and Racism," in *The Faces of Buddhism in America*, ed. Charles S. Prebish and Kenneth K. Tanaka (Berkeley and Los Angeles: University of California Press, 1998), 200, emphasis added.

63. Andrew Kennedy, "Reflections on Buddhism in Leeds: Identity, Practice and Experience,"
     Contemporary Buddhism 5, no. 2 (2004): 147, 148.
64. Ally Ostrowski, "Buddha Browsing: American Buddhism and the Internet," *Contemporary
     Buddhism* 7, no. 1 (2006): 92.
65. Fields, "Divided Dharma," 200.
66. Sutin, *All is Change*, 327.
67. Jeffery Paine, *Re-enchantment: Tibetan Buddhism Comes to the West* (New York: W. W.
     Norton & Co., 2004), 103.
68. Sutin, *All is Change*, 302.
69. Coleman, *The New Buddhism*, 86.
70. Simmer-Brown, "Speaking Truth to Power," 2.

FURTHER READING

Bubna-Litic, David. "The Emergence of Secular Insight Practice in Australia." *Journal of Global
     Buddhism* 8 (2007): 157–173.
Chandler, Steven. *Establishing a Pure Land on Earth: The Foguang Buddhist Perspective on
     Modernization and Globalization*. Honolulu: University of Hawaii Press, 2004.
Coleman, James William. *The New Buddhism: The Western Transformation of an Ancient
     Tradition*. Oxford: Oxford University Press, 2001.
Hori, Victor Sogen, Richard P. Hayes, and James Mark Shields, eds. *Teaching Buddhism in the
     West: From the Wheel to the Web*. London: Routledge Curzon, 2002.
Learman, Linda, ed. *Missionaries in the Era of Globalization*. Honolulu: University of Hawaii
     Press, 2005.
Prebish, Charles S., and Martin Baumann, eds. *Westward Dharma: Buddhism beyond Asia*.
     Berkeley and Los Angeles: University of California Press, 2002.
Queen, Christopher S., ed. *Engaged Buddhism in the West*. Boston: Wisdom Publications, 2000.
Smyer Yü, Dan. *The Spread of Tibetan Buddhism in China: Charisma, Money, Enlightenment*.
     London: Routledge, 2011.

BIBLIOGRAPHY

Adorno, Theodor W. *Minima Moralia: Reflections from Damaged Life*, trans. E. F. Jephcott.
     London: Verso, 1974.
Austin-Broos, Diane. "The Anthropology of Conversion: An Introduction." In *The
     Anthropology of Religious Conversion*, ed. Andrew Buckser and Stephen D. Glazier, 1–12.
     New York: Rowman & Littlefield Publishers, 2003.
Barker, M. "Investments in Religious Capital: An Explorative Case Study of Australian
     Buddhists." *Journal of Global Buddhism* 8 (2007): 65–80.
Barth, Karl. "The Awakening to Conversion." In *Conversion: Perspectives on Personal and Social
     Transformation*, ed. Walter E. Conn, 35–39. New York: Alba House, 1978.
Baumann, Martin. "Working in the Right Spirit: The Application of Buddhist Right
     Livelihood in the Friends of the Western Buddhist Order." *Journal of Buddhist Ethics* 5
     (1998): 120–143.

Baumann, Martin, and Charles S. Prebish. "Introduction: Paying Homage to the Buddha in the West." In *Westward Dharma: Buddhism beyond Asia*, ed. Charles S. Prebish and Martin Baumann, 1–13. Berkeley and Los Angeles: University of California Press, 2002.

Berger, Peter. "Introduction: The Cultural Dynamics of Globalization." In *Many Globalizations: Cultural Diversity in the Contemporary World*, ed. Peter L. Berger and Samuel P. Huntington, 1–16. Oxford: Oxford University Press, 2002.

Bubna-Litic, David. "The Emergence of Secular Insight Practice in Australia." *Journal of Global Buddhism* 8 (2007): 157–173.

Chandler, Steven. *Establishing a Pure Land on Earth: The Foguang Buddhist Perspective on Modernization and Globalization*. Honolulu: University of Hawaii Press, 2004.

——. "Spreading Buddha's Light: The Internationalization of Foguang Shan." In *Missionaries in the Era of Globalization*, ed. Linda Learman, 162–185. Honolulu: University of Hawaii Press, 2005.

City of Ten Thousand Buddhas (CTTB). http://www.cttbusa.org/.

Coleman, James William. *The New Buddhism: The Western Transformation of an Ancient Tradition*. Oxford: Oxford University Press, 2001.

Davids, T. W. Rhys, and Herman Oldenberg. *Vinaya Texts*. New York: Charles Scribner's Sons, 1899.

Fields, Rick. "Divided Dharma: White Buddhists, Ethnic Buddhists, and Racism." In *The Faces of Buddhism in America*, ed. Charles S. Prebish and Kenneth K. Tanaka, 196–206. Berkeley and Los Angeles: University of California Press, 1998.

Godin, André. *The Psychological Dynamics of Religious Experience*. Birmingham, AL: Religious Education Press, 1985.

Grosnick, William H. "The *Thathagatagarbha Sutra*." In *Buddhism in Practice*, ed. Donald S. Lopez, Jr., 92–106. Princeton: Princeton University Press, 2007.

Haughton, Rosemary. 1978. "Formation and Transformation." In *Conversion: Perspectives on Personal and Social Transformation*, ed. Walter E. Conn, 23–26. New York: Alba House.

Hesse, Herman. *Siddhartha*. New York: New Directions, 1951.

Hori, Victor Sogen, Richard P. Hayes, and James Mark Shields. "Introduction." In *Teaching Buddhism in the West: From the Wheel to the Web*, ed. Victor Sogen Hori, Richard P. Hayes, and James Mark Shields, viii–xxv. London: Routledge Curzon, 2002.

Hunt-Perry, Patricia, and Lyn Fine. "All Buddhism is Engaged: Thich Nhat Hanh and the Order of Interbeing." In *Engaged Buddhism in the West*, ed. Christopher S. Queen, 35–66. Boston: Wisdom Publications, 2000.

Ivy, Marilyn. "Modernity." In *Critical Terms for the Study of Buddhism*, ed. Donald Lopez, Jr., 311–331. Chicago: University of Chicago Press, 2005.

Kennedy, Andrew. "Reflections on Buddhism in Leeds: Identity, Practice and Experience." *Contemporary Buddhism* 5, no. 2 (2004): 143–156.

King, Sallie B. *Buddha Nature*. Albany: State University of New York Press, 1991.

Knaus, John Kenneth. *Orphans of the Cold War: America and the Tibetan Struggle for Survival*. New York: Public Affairs, 1999.

Learman, Linda. "Introduction." In *Missionaries in the Era of Globalization*, ed. Linda Learman, 1–21. Honolulu: University of Hawaii Press, 2005.

Matthiessen, Peter Muryo. "The Coming of Age of American Zen." In *Buddhism in America*, ed. Brian D. Hotchkiss, 396–406. Rutland, VT: Charles E. Tuttle, 1998.

Nattier, Jan. "Who Is a Buddhist? Charting the Landscape of Buddhist America." In *The Faces of Buddhism in America*, ed. Charles S. Prebish and Kenneth K. Tanaka, 183–195. Berkeley and Los Angeles: University of California Press, 1998.

Niebuhr, Reinhold. "Grace as Power in, and as Mercy towards, Man." In *Conversion: Perspectives on Personal and Social Transformation*, ed. Walter E. Conn, 27–34. New York: Alba House, 1978.

Ostrowski, Ally. "Buddha Browsing: American Buddhism and the Internet." *Contemporary Buddhism* 7, no. 1 (2006): 91–103.

Paine, Jeffery. *Re-enchantment: Tibetan Buddhism Comes to the West*. New York: W. W. Norton & Co., 2004.

Parker, Glynis. "The Conversion of South Africans to Buddhism." PhD diss., University of South Africa, 2007.

Pew Research Center. "53 percent–American Buddhists." http://pewresearch.org/databank/dailynumber/?NumberID=485.

Prebish, Charles. "Introduction." In *The Faces of Buddhism in America*, ed. Charles S. Prebish and Kenneth K. Tanaka, 1–10. Berkeley and Los Angeles: University of California Press, 1998.

Queen, Christopher S. "Introduction: A New Buddhism." In *Engaged Buddhism in the West*, ed. Christopher S. Queen, 1–31. Boston: Wisdom Publications, 2000.

Rambo, Lewis R. "Anthropology and the Study of Conversion." In *The Anthropology of Religious Conversion*, ed. Andrew Buckser and Stephen D. Glazier, 211–222. New York: Rowman & Littlefield Publishers, 2003.

——. *Understanding Religious Conversion*. New Haven: Yale University Press, 1993.

Rambo, Lewis R., and Charles E. Farhadian. "Converting: Stages of Religious Change." In *Religious Conversion: Contemporary Practices and Controversies*, ed. Christopher Lamb and M. Darrol Bryant, 23–34. New York: Cassell, 1999.

Robertson, Roland. "Social Theory, Cultural Relativity and the Problem of Globality." In *Culture, Globalization and the World-System: Contemporary Conditions for the Representation of Identity*, ed. Anthony D. King, 69–90. Minneapolis: University of Minnesota Press, 1997.

Sedgwick, Eve Kosofsky. "Pedagogy." In *Critical Terms for the Study of Buddhism*, ed. Donald Lopez, Jr., 162–187. Chicago: University of Chicago Press, 2005.

Simmer-Brown, Judith. "Speaking Truth to Power: The Buddhist Peace Fellowship." In *Engaged Buddhism in the West*, ed. Christopher S. Queen, 67–96. Boston: Wisdom Publications, 2000.

Smith, John E. "The Concept of Conversion." In *Conversion: Perspectives on Personal and Social Transformation*, ed. Walter E. Conn, 51–61. New York: Alba House, 1978.

Sutin, Lawrence. *All is Change: The Two-Thousand-Year Journey of Buddhism to the West*. New York: Little, Brown and Company, 2006.

Thich Nhat Hanh. *Old Path White Clouds: Walking in the Footsteps of the Buddha*. Berkeley and Los Angeles: Parallax, 1991.

——. *Peace Is Every Step: The Path of Mindfulness in Everyday Life*. New York: Bantam Books, 1991.

CHAPTER 21

....

CONVERSION TO SIKHISM

....

GURINDER SINGH MANN

INTRODUCTION

THE history of the Sikh community begins with Nanak (1469–1539), a religious leader and poet whose life story unfolded in Punjab, a Muslim majority area presently split between India and Pakistan. Born into an upper-caste, educated, and affluent land-owning family, Nanak grew up in Talwandi, a village founded by a Hindu Rajput convert to Islam that was in close proximity to Lahore, the cultural and political center of the region.[1] Around 1500, while working for Daulat Khan Lodhi, an influential district chief at Sultanpur and a cousin of Sikandar Lodhi (1469–1517), the emperor at Delhi, Nanak underwent a powerful experience of "being taken to the divine court" (*dargah*), which resulted in his perception of being the bearer of a divine mission.[2] Subsequent years of Nanak's life included extensive travels, establishment of a new town named Kartarpur ("Creator's town"), and the gathering of a community (*Panth*) there, beginning in the early 1520s. The people who joined the new group were known as Sikhs and/or Nau Dhariks ("the bearers of divine teachings/name"). Nanak positioned himself as their Baba (leader) and before his death he appointed a successor to oversee the continuation of his legacy.[3]

The community that originally formed around Baba Nanak in the early sixteenth century currently numbers twenty-five million adherents, and their places of worship (*gurdwara*, "the house of the Guru") have moved well beyond the Punjab to various parts of the global landscape.[4] The question of how the Sikhs evolved over the past half millennium into the largest community of the smaller major religious traditions of the world has not yet been adequately addressed in the scholarly literature. The Sikhs consider themselves a non-proselytizing community and tend to believe that people simply joined over time as they became aware of the uniqueness of the founder's teachings (*gurmat*).[5] The Sikh code of belief and practice (*Rahit Maryada*), an influential document whose drafting took over two decades of collective communal reflection and was first published in 1950, does not even mention the issue of conversion to Sikhism.[6] The scholarly consensus of the past generation, particularly those writing in English, tended to situate the pre-1900 Sikh community within the larger Hindu ethos, and a specific discussion of conversion to Sikhism understandably did not carry much relevance within this context.[7]

Interestingly, the issue of religious conversion in Sikh history has been revisited due to the involvement of scholars in the comparative study of this theme. Doris R. Jakobsh and Louis E. Fenech, two researchers based in North America, deserve credit for opening this area of discussion.[8] Their respective work on conversion in the Sikh tradition, however, is informed by three shared assumptions: Nanak was a mystic affiliated with the Sant movement and displayed very little interest in building an intentional community; his successors were responsible for the creation of institutions and the growth of the community; and it was only during the colonial period in the last quarter of the nineteenth century that Sikhs understood themselves as a distinct religious community and became concerned with issues such as conversion. As we will see later in the chapter, all three of these assumptions are problematic, resulting in the need for alternative ways to understand the phenomenon of conversion in the Sikh community.[9]

The goals I have set for myself in this exploratory essay are rather modest. Using primary Sikh and Punjabi sources, I will focus on a select number of developments over the course of five centuries of Sikh history. In the process, I will attempt to address issues such as: Who joined the Sikh community and why? What ceremonial and/or ritual mechanisms were used to bring new people into the fold? How did the Sikhs relate to members of their earlier religious communities? And, what contribution did the first-generation converts make to the Sikh community? The answers to these questions understandably vary depending on the time period under examination, and this essay will chart the evolution of the Sikh community from the foundation of the community in early sixteenth-century Punjab to recent developments in twentieth-century diasporic Sikh communities. This is therefore an effort to focus on a hitherto unaddressed dimension of Sikh history: How did less than a hundred families that gathered at Kartarpur in the 1520s develop into a community that has its places of worship scattered all around the globe at the turn of the twenty-first century? Given that the Sikh community has emerged relatively recently and as a result the data pertaining to its expansion is firm, one hopes that this discussion may be useful for those interested in the cross-cultural understanding of religious conversion.

FOUNDING OF THE COMMUNITY UNDER BABA NANAK

In order to understand the context in which Nanak founded the Sikh community, we can begin with four observations regarding the overall profile of medieval Punjab. First, Islam was introduced into the southern Punjab in the opening decades of the eighth century.[10] By the sixteenth century, Muslims were the majority in the region, and an elaborate network of mosques and mausoleums marked the landscape. Local converts constituted the majority of this Muslim community, and as for the mechanisms of conversion, the sources of the period emphasize the recitation of the Islamic confession of faith (*shahada*), the performance of the circumcision (*indri vaddani*), and the ingestion of cow-meat (*bhas khana*).[11]

Second, Punjabi Hindu society of the time was constructed along sectarian lines centered on the worship of Vishnu (Vaishnava), Shiva (Shaiva), Devi (Shakta), and some local deities. It seems fair to assume that people moved from one group to another depending upon factors such as the presence of a particular temple in their village. There are references to the Nath Yogis, an influential Shaivite group, expanding their numbers and deploying an initiation ceremony that involved the piercing of ears and a vow of celibacy. While Punjabi Hindu society was relatively well established, there was also a small but vibrant Jain community in the Punjab. Buddhist communities, however, had largely disappeared by the turn of the tenth century.[12]

Third, there was a large group of erstwhile nomads known as Jats who had begun the process of sedentarization around the thirteenth century in the central Punjab. We know relatively little about their early history, but their turn to settled agriculture was facilitated by the fertile soil of the Punjab and their use of the Persian water wheel. Scholars tend to place these Jats, these nomads, in the lower echelons of Hindu caste society, but there is no evidence to support this association. These people had their own beliefs centered on the worship of deities such as Sakhi Sarvar and Gugga, and they followed their own independent social customs such as widow marriage and reverence for clan leaders (*vaderas*). During this phase of their history they were keen on building a steady relationship with settled society.[13]

And finally, it should be noted that Punjabi, the language of the region, does not have a word for conversion. The three verbs generally used to express this phenomenon are *hona* (to become, *uh Sikh ho gia* [he became a Sikh]), *banana* (to make, *main Sikh ban gia* [I became a Sikh]), and *sajana* (to turn into, *unaha mainu Sikh saja dita* [They turned me into a Sikh]). Against this backdrop, there was a great deal of exchange between various religious communities, including competition to increase their respective numbers and instances of intra- as well as inter-community strife. We have records of violence in Lahore between Shias and Hindus, at Thaneser between Hindu ascetics (*sanyasis*), and at Batala involving the Nath Yogis and Muslim ascetics (*faqirs*).[14] Having emerged within this multilayered religious environment in the early sixteenth century, the Sikhs would come to predominate both the political and religious landscape of the Punjab by 1800. How they built their community is the key issue to which we now turn.

An examination of Baba Nanak's beliefs about his own position in society and the social constituency of the community he founded at Kartarpur provide a helpful point of departure. First, it is worth noting that he saw his life's activity in direct response to the divinely ordained mission of spreading the name of the Creator (Kartar), and the Sovereign (Sahib/Patishah) of the universe. As mentioned earlier, Nanak had a powerful personal experience that resulted in his understanding himself as a bard (*dhadhi*) and a public herald (*tabal baz*) of divine wisdom. In the subsequent two decades after his revelatory experience, he traveled and encountered the leaders and followers of Muslim, Hindu, and Jain communities. In the process, he developed and refined ideas regarding his own mission. In his compositions, Nanak critiques the society of his times. In regard to Hindu beliefs and practices, he condemns the polytheism of Hindu gods and goddesses and the religiously sanctioned caste hierarchy (*Guru Granth*, 1153). As for the Jains, Nanak condemns their atheism and nonviolence and makes it a point to specifically critique the practice of non-bathing for fear of hurting any small living creature (*Guru Granth*, 149–150). As for the Muslims, he shares their overall conception of God but is critical of what he viewed as their hypocritical religious practices and the political corruption of their leadership (*Guru Granth*, 24). With the invasion of Babur in the early 1520s, Nanak brought his travels to a close and founded Kartarpur as a community devoted to the divine teachings (*sikhia*). For the remainder of his life, he invested all of his energies in building the required institutions to ensure the future growth of this fledgling new group of Sikhs.[15]

The life history and personal example of Baba Nanak, coupled with his compositions (*bani*), provided a blueprint for the beliefs and practices of the new community. The residents at Kartarpur gathered at the time of sunrise and sunset for congregational prayers at Baba Nanak's house and sang the praises of the sole creator and sovereign of the universe as enshrined in his compositions. After these sessions of devotional singing (*kirtan*), Baba Nanak would provide guidance before the group shared a common meal (*langar*) and departed for their daily work in the fields. The community life was framed by the notion of a sovereign God whose divine command (*hukam*) governs all of creation. The position of Baba Nanak as the founder of Kartarpur would have been to provide guidance to its inhabitants in matters both religious (*din*) and secular (*dunia*).

Janam Sakhi Babe Nanak Ji ki ("The Life Story of Baba Nanak," hereinafter *Janam Sakhi*) came into circulation less than fifty years after Baba Nanak's death and is now popularly known as *Puratan Janam Sakhi* ("The Old Life Story of Baba Nanak"). This text sheds an interesting light on Baba Nanak's activity at Kartarpur that is directly relevant to our discussion.[16] For instance, this text leaves no doubt that there was an active effort to attract families to the community at Kartarpur. A large number of people from different religious and socioeconomic strata visited the town, and Baba Nanak was available to receive them and address their concerns. In the process, these individuals witnessed the orientation of life at Kartarpur.

The *Janam Sakhi* also reports that after the establishment of Kartarpur, Baba Nanak undertook four extensive trips to distant places in the Indian subcontinent. These travels were clearly geared toward bringing new people to the Sikh fold. Saido and Siho Gheo (both Jats), his companions during the first two journeys, are reported to have administered nectar (*pahul*) to the new initiates. While the details of this ceremony are not clearly delineated, its mention is significant in and of itself. The impression created is that there was growing interest in the message of Baba Nanak among individuals and large communities. After these individuals took nectar they are referred to as Sikhs and/or Nau Dhariks. In addition to these early references to the administration of nectar, and the attendant new religious labeling, there are also references to Baba Nanak establishing seats of authority (*manjis*) in order to provide local leadership to large congregations of Sikhs in near and distant places.

What these aforementioned developments suggest is that Baba Nanak was directly and indirectly involved in expanding the community, both in Kartarpur and in other places. The process of bringing people into the Sikh community was not restricted to the person of Baba Nanak. During Baba Nanak's lifetime, Sikhs themselves began to assume this role of attracting new followers to the fold. The following episodes in the *Janam Sakhi* offer additional details by way of stories about the varied responses of individuals and communities to the teachings of Baba Nanak. In one episode, a Bhalla Khatri (trader) resides in a village named Khadur established by Khaira Jats (agriculturalists). Most of the Khatri's friends are followers of the Goddess, and their religious leader is a Khatri named Lehina Trehan. We are then told that one morning Lehina Trehan happens to overhear the recitation of Baba Nanak's *Jap* ("Repeat") by a neighboring Sikh. Deeply moved, he expresses a strong desire to meet its author and accompanies the Bhalla Sikh to Kartarpur. Upon meeting Baba Nanak, he discards his ankle bells (*devi de ghungru*), joins the Sikh community, and begins to live a life of hard work and service. It is clear that Baba Nanak's message was often disseminated through his followers, and one of the reasons they were so successful in sharing their message was that Baba Nanak's compositions were written in the vernacular spoken language of Punjabi. In other words, people could understand his message directly in a language that was familiar to them. His compositions, however, were recorded in a new script called Gurmukhi ("of the Sikhs") that the Sikhs were expected to learn once they entered the community. The adoption of Punjabi and the organization of a new script to commit it to writing also served to distinguish the Sikhs from the Muslims who considered Arabic as their sacred language, and the Hindus who considered Sanskrit written in Devanagari as the sacred vehicle of their wisdom.

In another story, a Khatri Sikh named Bhagirath meets Mansukh, a rich Khatri from Lahore. Mansukh is so impressed with Bhagirath's personal loyalty to Baba Nanak that he decides to come to Kartarpur. The meeting with Baba Nanak is so inspiring to Mansukh that he suspends his business activity in Lahore and stays at Kartarpur. He memorizes Baba Nanak's compositions and prepares written copies of them intended for circulation among Sikh families. After three years, he returns to Lahore and makes a business trip to the south, in all likelihood to the region of Sindh. There he lives in a Hindu enclave and the local residents observe him reciting Baba Nanak's compositions. They are so disturbed by his unwillingness to perform Hindu prayers that they take him to their chief, Shivnabh, and initiate a complaint against him for disregarding their practices while staying in their quarters. The conversation that follows between Shivnabh and Mansukh creates a deep desire in the heart of the chief to meet Baba Nanak, who eventually visits the area. As a result of Baba Nanak's visit, a Sikh community is formally established and Shivnabh is assigned the responsibility to oversee its welfare in that area.

Based on these early accounts, we can make a few basic observations. While the founder was central to the life of the community, his compositions and other devout

Sikhs were deeply involved in aiding its expansion. In the *Janam Sakhi* we see time and again that people joined the new community after meeting Baba Nanak, listening to the recitation of his compositions, and/or interacting with his Sikhs. The transition to the new community involved discarding the previous beliefs and practices. Lehina Trehan, for example, discards his Shakta beliefs and practices, while Mansukh abandons his Vaishnava background; the Jats Saido and Siho Gheo leave behind their reverence for Sakhi Sarvar, a folk deity popular among the Jats. It is clear that these new entrants believed that Baba Nanak's path was superior to what they had previously followed and that, having made this break themselves, they were expected to help bring their immediate and extended family into the Sikh fold.

Within this framework, Baba Nanak's selection of the location of Kartarpur also comes into sharper relief. We know that the family of Baba Nanak's wife, Sulakhani, lived and worked in the immediate vicinity of Kartarpur and that this may have been instrumental in shaping his decision to move there. In addition to the personal dimensions of this decision, Baba Nanak would have also taken note of the objective qualities of the area. We know that the fertile swaths of land and water sources in the vicinity would have attracted the most powerful Jat tribes to Kartarpur. As mentioned earlier, these people were actively searching for ways to integrate into settled society, and Kartarpur offered them a unique opportunity to continue working with the land while becoming integral and respected members of this new community. Far from being relegated to the position of followers, these Jats would have held significant positions of leadership. The location of Kartarpur was also ideal because it was literally on the path of pilgrims going to Shakta and Shaiva places of worship in the Punjab hills and Kashmir. While on their journey, religious pilgrims and the spiritually inclined would have had the opportunity to have a first-hand experience of Baba Nanak's experiment at Kartarpur, if they had any interest.

A visionary of considerable foresight, Baba Nanak could not have been oblivious to the location of Kartarpur and its implications for both the short- and long-term viability of his community. He would have recognized that it was easier to reach the Jats, who predominated in this area, than those who already belonged to established Hindu and Muslim societies. The evidence at our disposal supports the position that the Jats constituted the largest segment of the early Sikh community, and it is worth noting that the early accounts include Lehina Trehan, a Khatri, and Buddha Randhawa, a Jat, as the finalists in the list of candidates to succeed Baba Nanak. We are told that, unlike Buddha Randhawa, Lehina Trehan offered unquestioning loyalty to his leader and that that quality may have been the determining factor given the crucial transition of authority within the new community at this point in its history. By the time of Baba Nanak's death in 1539, the community had reached a level of significant expansion wherein internal dissension was possible. The *Janam Sakhi* reports that at the time of the elevation of Lehina Trehan, renamed Angad, to the office of the Guru (1539–1551), Baba Nanak's son, Sri Chand, refused to accept this appointment and, as a result, Guru Angad had to relocate to his village of Khadur. We are also told of Buddha Randhawa's crucial role in establishing Guru Angad among his fellow Jats at Khadur.[17]

DESIGNATING THE COMMUNITY AS THE KHALSA PANTH

The nine leaders who succeeded Baba Nanak over the subsequent century and a half were understood to share in his light (*joti*), and accordingly they oversaw the expansion of the Sikh Panth. After Baba Nanak, personal leadership can be divided into two phases: from Guru Angad (1539–1551) to Guru Arjan (Guru 1581–1606), with the Sikh center in the Punjab plains, and from Guru Hargobind (Guru 1606–1644) to Guru Gobind Singh (Guru 1675–1708), with the center shifting to the Punjab hills. These geographical shifts were due both to internal divisions within the community as well as external pressures from the Mughals and Rajputs. Far from its origins in the central Punjab, the subsequent movement of the Gurus resulted in the establishment of cities and the construction of religious and civic buildings that by the end of the Guru period (1500–1708) resulted in a Sikh sacred geography spread across the Punjab and beyond.

Baba Nanak's four successors who provided leadership to the community during the first phase expanded upon the traditions created at Kartarpur as they continued to build new cities. It is important to note that in comparison to Baba Nanak, none of these early leaders traveled as extensively as the founder had. Contemporary accounts report how Guru Angad distributed the *langar* of the divine word at his court (*Guru Granth*, 967) to those who came from Khadur as well as distant places. His wife, Mata Khivi, oversaw the distribution of "the rice pudding and butter that taste like nectar in the *langar*" (*Guru Granth*, 967). At Goindval, Guru Amardas (Guru 1551–1574) confidently declared that the Sikh path was the way of liberation and urged the *sheikhs* and *brahmins* to join the community (*Guru Granth*, 646; *Guru Granth*, 849).

By the turn of the seventeenth century, Guru Arjan, who was based at Ramdaspur (present-day Amritsar), sang of the Sikhs with their own sacred text, places, and ceremonies representing a path distinct from those of Muslims and Hindus (*Guru Granth*, 885, 1136). He also mentions of his lofty palaces and army and claims that the Sikhs were present throughout the region (*Guru Granth*, 622, 1141). The growing strength of the community manifested itself in the construction of *Darbar Sahib* ("The Divine Court"), an impressive accomplishment at the center of a large body of water following the contemporary architectural model of a water palace (*jal mahal*).

During this time, the ceremony of *pahul* mentioned in the *Janam Sakhi* developed along three distinct lines. In the presence of the Guru, the *pahul* represented the water that was touched by his toe (*charan pahul*); in large congregations where the Guru was not present, the ceremony involved the touching of the toe of the local leaders (the holders of the *manji*, or seat of authority, who came to be called the *masand*); and in small and distant congregations, we have references to *pahul* created from the touching of a new entrant's toe and the congregation that he joined drinking it.[18] While an initiation ceremony centered around the submission of the new initiate to the Guru's and/or masand's personal authority followed the general norms of initiation at the time, the practice of drinking *pahul* by the community members at the time of the entry of every new member was a distinct and unique departure from established initiation ceremonies. Such an innovation seems to have been marked by humility and the spirit of warm welcome toward those who decided to join the Sikh community; it would have also underscored the disavowal of purity and pollution taboos operative within caste society.

By 1600, manuscripts recording scriptural writings contain terse statements obligating each and every Sikh family to do the following: participate in congregational worship; be generous toward the needy, suffering, and poor; help with the marriage of an unmarried Sikh; assist a non-Sikh to join the Sikh fold; and pray for the welfare of all, with no ill will for anyone.[19] The encouragement to bring new entrants into the community seemingly bore good results. While the Jats continued to constitute a majority of the Sikh community—both Kartarpur and Khadur were Jat towns—the Khatri population expanded in step. Built by Guru Amardas and Ramdas, respectively, Goindval and Amritsar developed as trading centers with significant Khatri Sikh as well as non-Sikh populations. The Khatri Sikhs spread to larger cities such as Lahore and traveled along trading routes, carrying the Sikh teachings to the distant places. We have references to growing Sikh populations in the cardinal directions of the subcontinent—Dhaka and Patna in the east, Balakh and Kabul in the west, Kashmir in the north, and Burhanpur in the south. Thus, less than a century after Guru Nanak's revelation, it is clear that Sikh numbers had grown considerably, and some of the distant Khatri congregations would emerge as sources of significant financial help to sustain the activities at the Sikh center.

Any effort to understand the growing strength of the community must take into account the role played by the Mughal administration of the time. The liberal regime of Emperor Akbar (1556–1604) provided a conducive environment for the expansion of the Sikh community. Although Akbar's liberal religious agenda was denounced by Islamic clerics (*ulema*), his reign witnessed a relatively stable period of economic growth and religious non-persecution. Soon after his elevation to the throne, Jehangir (1604–1626) took notice of the expanding Sikh community and felt the need to curtail its growing influence. Regarding the Sikhs, he wrote in his memoir that "a large number of simple-minded Hindus and even some ignorant and silly Muslims" had joined this group and that he had ordered "an end to this shop of falsehood" unless it could be brought into "the fold of Islam."[20] Less than seventy years after Baba Nanak's death, the Sikh community had acquired the numbers, resources, and significance needed to evoke a response from the Mughal emperor. In response to Jehangir's demands, Guru Arjan saw fit to die for his faith, and with his execution in Lahore, the first phase of personal leadership came to a close.

The successors of Guru Arjan stood in opposition to the Mughals and, as a result, his son and immediate successor, Guru Hargobind, was forced to leave Amritsar and move to the Punjab hills. In the difficult period that followed, Sikh efforts at reassertion under the leadership of Guru Tegh Bahadur (Guru 1664–1675), the first Guru after Baba Nanak to travel extensively and forge direct contacts with far-flung Sikh congregations, resulted in his execution/martyrdom in Delhi under the orders of Aurangzeb (1658–1707). The internal dissension that emerged after the death of Guru Arjan became more intense in the subsequent decades and affected the hierarchy of authority within the community in significant ways. In addition to the schismatic groups, many Sikh masands declared their autonomy and brought individuals into the Sikh fold under the umbrella of their own personal authority.[21]

In response to mounting external pressure and internal fissures, Guru Gobind Singh initiated developments that addressed the issue of personal authority within the community in a radical way. In the late 1690s, he renamed the Sikh community the Khalsa Panth (literally "the pure"; in Mughal revenue terminology this term referred to lands directly under the control of the emperor [khalisa]). The primary implication of the new name was that the Khalsa Panth only accepted the authority of the Vahiguru, the commonly used epithet for God at this point in Sikh history. Even Guru Gobind Singh submitted himself to and became a member of the Khalsa Panth. From this point forward, the terms Khalsa Panth and Sikh Panth have been used interchangeably. In Guru Gobind Singh's vision for the future of the community, there was no place for personal authority, including his own, and he invited erstwhile masands and the schismatic groups to be part of this egalitarian community.

Baba Nanak's concerns with issues related to the matters of the world took a pronounced turn when the Khalsa/Sikh Panth was declared duty-bound to create a sovereign rule (Khalsa Raj) in which the weak were to be protected and evil ones punished.[22] The langar (common meal) of the early days was to be extended to become the rule of deg (cauldron) and tegh (sword), and there was no ambivalence regarding the divine sanction of the Khalsa Panth to rule over the Punjab. Having failed to administer divine justice, the Hindu and Muslim chiefs were declared to have forfeited their moral right to continue in their positions. The execution/martyrdom of Guru Tegh Bahadur by the Mughals in Delhi, and the opposition of the neighboring Hindu Rajput chiefs in the 1690s, were indicative of this overall moral collapse. As a result, it was thought that the Sikh community was destined to take control of the political reins and bring justice to the region.[23]

In order to fulfill the destiny of the Khalsa Panth, a new ceremony called the nectar of the double-edged sword (khande di pahul) was initiated. This involved the stirring of water with a double-edged sword while a set of Sikh sacred compositions was recited over it.[24] The double-edged sword, symbolizing divine grace and justice, dissolved the sacred utterings of the Gurus and thus turned the water into nectar. It was seen to instill courage and strength in those who took it. The salutation after partaking the nectar, Vahiguru ji ka khalsa, Vahiguru ji ki fateh (The Khalsa of Vahiguru will be victorious), declared that the Sikhs would only submit to Vahiguru and that they were dedicated to the establishment of divine rule. As per this new ceremony, the Sikhs were to carry on with their earlier code of belief and practice, but as markers of their expanded identity they were to add Singh ("lion") to their names, keep their hair uncut, and carry weaponry on them. Popularly referred to as the 5K's, Sikhs were enjoined to keep and maintain unshorn hair (kes and kangha), carry a protective bracelet and a weapon (kara and kirpan), and wear britches (kaccha).

The projected vision of Sikh sovereignty squarely challenged the local Rajput chiefs in the Punjab hills and posed a threat to the Mughal authority in Delhi. In the face of resurgent Sikh power, the Rajputs invited Mughals to join forces with them to confront this common threat, and after a long siege of Anandpur they were able to oust the Sikhs in 1704. Ensuing battles resulted in the death of several hundred Sikhs and of the Guru's four sons—Ajit Singh and Jujhar Singh died fighting and Zoravar Singh and Fateh Singh were arrested and executed by the Mughals—and of the Guru's mother, Mata Gujari, who died of shock. Before he could return to Anandpur, the Guru died in south India after an assassination attempt in late 1708. Building on the developments of the 1690s, Guru Gobind Singh formally terminated the office of the human Guru and replaced his authority with that of the scriptural text (*Guru Granth*) and of the community (*Guru Panth*) before his death.

During this phase of personal authority, significant developments occurred in rela-tion to the numbers and composition of the Sikh community. By the 1600s, the Sikhs had moved from Kartarpur on the left bank of the River Ravi to spread across the central Punjab and spill beyond the River Beas. In the seventeenth century, they spread across the Beas and Satluj rivers and built a large following in the southern Punjab. The primary Sikh constituency remained rural, with the Jat tribes joining in large numbers. With the travels of Guru Tegh Bahadur and Guru Gobind Singh, the stretch of Sikh geography expanded to include Patna, the city of Gobind's birth in the east, and Nander, the place of his passing away, in south India.

As for the future expansion of the community, Guru Gobind Singh gave instructions that while no coercion was to be used to bring a person into the Sikh fold, those who identified with the mission of establishing the Khalsa Raj, a sovereign rule of the Sikhs, were welcome to join.[25] There are other references pertaining to the consolidation of the community in the prescriptive manuals of behavior known as the *Rahitnama* from this period. In these texts it states that Sikhs should marry their daughters to other Sikhs and that if a Sikh wishes to marry a non-Sikh, then he or she should be encouraged to join the community before the marriage itself.[26] The impression that the Khalsa Panth is non-proselytizing is thus correct only to the extent that there is no collective effort from this point on to bring people into the Sikh community. However, there are no obstruc-tions placed in the way of a person who wishes to join the community; as in the time of Baba Nanak, anyone can become a Sikh regardless of age, gender, caste, etc. Anyone can join as long as s/he follows the teachings enshrined in the scriptural *Guru Granth* and is willing to identify with the Sikh's mission of ensuring justice and welfare for all.

With the termination of the line of human gurus, the role of initiation ceremonies underwent significant change. The earlier ceremony of *charan pahul* had largely been phased out during Guru Gobind Singh's tenure. And in the new and changed circum-stances of the community after his death, the symbolic content of the ceremony of *charan pahul* vis-à-vis the issue of personal authority and public submission had no rel-evance. Guru Gobind Singh had created the *khande di pahul* ceremony to inspire Sikhs to become the instruments of divine justice, and we have reports that he himself under-took it as well, but over time it turned into an initiation ceremony replacing *charan pahul*, and it has become, for some, a prerequisite for joining the Sikh fold as it involves a public commitment to the vision of the Khalsa Raj.

Less than a century after Guru Gobind Singh's death, the dream of the Khalsa Raj was realized with the establishment of a Sikh kingdom at Lahore under the leadership of Ranjit Singh (1780–1839). During the eighteenth century, the Punjab was a battlefield in which the Sikhs fought the Mughals, Afghans, and Iranians for political supremacy. With the capture of Lahore in 1799, Ranjit Singh was able to integrate the Punjab under the banner of the Khalsa Raj. This backdrop of Sikh political ascendance created the context in which the Sikhs generated the belief that the region of the central Punjab is the Sikh sacred land and that Guru Gobind Singh had assigned them the responsibility to rule over it.[27] Circumstances on the ground also helped attract new members to the Sikh community. The increasing Sikh dominance must be understood on three levels. First, the villages of the central Punjab with a large number of Sikh Jats became overwhelmingly Sikh as ancillary groups such as carpenters, blacksmiths, and leatherworkers all joined the Sikh community. Second, during Ranjit Singh's reign, more Hindu Khatris joined the Sikh fold, and those Khatri families that did not become Sikh began the tradition of making their eldest son a Sikh with an eye towards ensuring his employment in the Sikh kingdom. Finally, in their position as the ruling elite of the region, the Sikhs changed the landscape of the Punjab. While all religious communities received grants from Sikh rulers, the Sikh community benefited tremendously. In addition to the Darbar Sahib, which received expensive marble inlay work with gold plating (*Guru Granth*, 17) during Ranjit Singh's tenure, village gurdwaras, or places of worship, with provisions for teaching Sikh children were built throughout the Punjab. Additionally, gurdwaras were constructed at sites associated with the lives of Baba Nanak, his nine successors, and Sikh historical events. At the end of this phase, we see a considerable increase in Sikh numbers, and the impact of this expansion on the landscape of the region was profound.

During this period, the Sikhs' perception of themselves as a community was transformed significantly. At the turn of the eighteenth century, Sikh numbers were relatively small and their dominance was restricted to the area around Anandpur in the Punjab hills. They were thus nothing more than an aggravating irritant, a mote in the eyes of their Muslim and Hindu counterparts.[28] However, by the end of the century, with the establishment of Sikh power radiating outwards from the Punjab to Afghanistan and Kashmir, the Sikhs began to perceive themselves as "Mount Sumer," the axis of the world. Within this new scheme, though the Sikhs were still in a demographic minority, they referred to the Muslims and Hindus as particles of "rye."[29] Despite their political domination of the Punjab and its surrounding areas, no effort was made to forcibly convert Hindus or Muslims to increase the Sikh ranks. The very rationale for the establishment of the Khalsa Raj was to protect the weak, and forcing people to convert would have undermined the responsibility of the Sikhs to ensure justice and welfare for all. People joined the community voluntarily, but even at the peak of Sikh political power their numbers never exceeded 10 percent of the total population. In terms of social constituency, the overwhelming majority of Sikhs remained the Jats and the ancillary groups associated with agriculture. These Jats had at best a tenuous relationship with the Hindu segments of Punjabi society, and once they joined the Islamic or the Sikh fold they made no attempt to maintain their earlier tribal ties. As for those who had come from the lowest rungs of Hindu society, there could not be much interest in sustaining the memory of their painful past.

Unlike the Jats and other rural segments of the Sikh society, the Khatris and Aroras, two trading groups, largely maintained their relationship with Hindu caste society. This implied the continued tradition of marriages between Sikh and Hindu Khatris and their participation in each other's religious traditions and social customs. It is interesting to note that toward the end of the eighteenth century, segments of the Sikh Khatri leadership began to see these linkages as problematic and argued for the need to reform their traditions by eliminating Hindu religious and social practices.[30] On the basis of the data at our disposal, it is fair to say that the numbers of the Khatri and Arora segment of Sikh society never reached more than 8 percent of the total Sikh population and, as a result, their continued relationship with Hindu society was not an issue of much significance within the larger Sikh community.

By the 1840s then, the Sikh community had a sizable constituency and the landscape of the Punjab reflected its predominance. Even non-Sikhs (e.g., the Muslims, Hindus, and Europeans associated with Ranjit Singh's court) approximated Sikh appearance due to their uncut hair and turbans. Ranjit Singh's personal beliefs were firmly rooted in the Sikh tradition; he listened to prayers from the *Guru Granth* as part of his daily morning routine, undertook pilgrimages to Sikh gurdwaras, and ensured that the requisite resources were available to build impressive and commemorative structures at locations significant in Sikh history. The respect and affection Ranjit Singh enjoyed was not limited to the Sikh community; when he died, newspapers from Australia to England felt obligated to inform their readers of his death.[31]

In the modern period, with the demise of Sikh sovereignty and the assertion of British power in the region, the Punjab was incorporated into the colonial order. In addition to the changes brought by print media, census operations, and Western education, the arrival of Christian missionaries in the Punjab marked a new phase in the religious history of the region. Although only a minuscule number of people converted to Christianity during the second half of the nineteenth century, the entry of a new religious tradition into the region was significant.[32] Furthermore, against the backdrop of religious enumeration in the British census and the importance of communal numbers, Punjabi Hindu leadership came up with an ingenious idea of declaring the Sikhs to be part of the Hindu fold, which would support the Hindu case for being the majority religious community in the Punjab. The Hindu leadership's argument of their close relationship with the Sikhs, however, was only applicable to the situation prevalent among the Khatri and Arora Sikhs, not to the rest of the community that constituted 90 percent or so of the Sikh population.[33]

The defeat of the Khalsa army in 1849 at the hands of the British raised existential questions that needed to be answered by Sikh leadership and the community. How could the Sikhs have lost the Khalsa Raj and the sovereignty conferred upon them by Guru Gobind Singh? With the British incorporation of the Punjab into the all-India empire, the Sikh community was removed from its status as the ruling elite and became a relatively helpless minority in the new scheme of things. With the counting of the heads becoming the sole criterion for representation in the political sphere, the Sikhs did not see much of a future for themselves, as they were a perpetual minority within the larger Hindu and Muslim populations. This issue continued to haunt the Sikh community and proved to be its undoing in the negotiations leading up to the partition of the Punjab and the creation of India and Pakistan in 1947. The Sikhs could not make a viable case for a homeland and had no option but to put their lot with India in 1947. The heartland of the Sikh community was cut in half when Punjab was divided into West Punjab and East Punjab. Sikh history was carved into two as the important religious, political, social, and economic resources of the community were divided between Pakistan and India. Dislocated after 1947, the Sikhs were involved in a long struggle to create a Punjabi-speaking state (*Punjabi Suba*) and to ensure that they would be in a majority, however slight. In 1966, a truncated state was approved by the Indian government in which the Sikhs constituted 60 percent of the population.[34]

This development finally brought a sense of relief to Sikh leadership, although internal dissension and the continuous interference of the federal government did not permit them to realize the Khalsa Raj they had dreamed of. Ensuing political disagreements among Sikh leaders and between Sikh leadership and the federal government resulted in a group of Sikhs, under the guidance of Jarnail Singh Bhindrawale (1946–1984), posing a full-blown armed challenge to the authority of the Indian government. In 1984, this conflict ultimately resulted in a massive Indian army action code-named Operation Bluestar centered on the Darbar Sahib, Amritsar. Depending on the source, between five hundred to three thousand people lost their lives in that battle, including Bhindranwale. A memorial dedicated to the Sikh martyrs who perished during Operation Bluestar is currently being built in the Darbar Sahib precinct, and it is clear that the state government in Chandigarh, under the leadership of Parkash Singh Badal (b. 1927), and the federal government in New Delhi, with Manmohan Singh (b. 1932) as the prime minister, will no longer be able to delay this memorial.[35]

Between the loss of political power in 1849, the creation of a Sikh majority state in 1966, and Operation Bluestar in 1984, Sikh communal thinking has remained focused on cultivating internal solidarity and resisting efforts of encroachment upon its territory by other communities.[36] Around 1900, two key manifestations of this were represented by the approaches of two significant figures, Khem Singh Bedi (1832–1905), a Khatri Sikh leader based in British Punjab, and Teja Singh Bhasour (1867–1933), a Jat ideologue whose life's activity unfolded in the Sikh princely states with nominal British interference. While Bedi emphasized the need for the *khande di pahul* ceremony for all Sikhs and the importance of maintaining ties with Hindu society, Teja Singh Bhasour underlined the separate nature of the Sikh community by focusing on the *khande di pahul* ceremony as a means to realize Sikh religio-political supremacy. Bhasour was staunchly opposed to any negotiations with non-Sikhs. Although there have been various shades of opinions and leaders, modern Sikh politics has essentially remained centered on these two positions. As the time of this writing, Parkash Singh Badal represents the literal continuation of Khem Singh Bedi's thinking, and those commemorating Operation Bluestar are the products of the ideology that Teja Singh Bhasour preached.

As mentioned earlier, *Rahit Maryada*, the most influential statement of Sikh beliefs and practices, does not contain any reference to conversion to Sikhism. Yet it is interesting to point out that many influential Sikh leaders of the past century undertook extensive travels to administer the *khande di pahul*. These include Khem Singh Bedi and Teja Singh Bhasour, as well as Fateh Singh (1911–1972), the Sikh leader instrumental in the movement for the *Punjabi Suba*, and Jarnail Singh Bhindranwale. Currently, the large public ceremonies administering *khande di pahul* are regularly enacted at historic gurdwaras on festival days. There may well be no stated endorsement of proselytization in normative Sikh literature, but it is fair to claim that this activity is part of Sikh religious life, and those who are involved in it are assigned a high degree of respect in Sikh society.

To sum up, the Sikh community has come a long way from its early days when the lonely figure of Nanak, the first Sikh ("the bearer of divine wisdom" or *sikhia*) traversed the Punjabi landscape in the early 1500s and reflected on how best to translate the content of his divine mission into reality. His vision of creating a new community dedicated to living in harmony with the divine order, the natural world, and human society has unfolded with reasonable success during the first half millennium of Sikh history. Although a small minority within the larger South Asian context, the Sikhs have become synonymous with the land of the Punjab and wield an influence disproportionate to their numbers.

At the time of this writing, the Sikhs are also in the process of raising their profile as a global community. In an interesting turn of events, in the late 1960s a Punjabi Sikh traveled to North America and unwittingly began the process of introducing a small number of mainstream Americans to the Sikh tradition. Harbhajan Singh Puri (1929–2004), a mid-level official in the Indian civil services, came to Toronto in the fall of 1968 and reinvented himself as a yoga teacher at Los Angeles in early 1969. In addition to learning yoga, his young students soon became interested in his Sikh beliefs, and two of them partook in the *khande di pahul* in April 1970. More students followed this path, and by the end of the year, their leader, now known as Harbhajan Singh Yogi, took eighty-four of them to Darbar Sahib, Amritsar. The Sikh leadership was delighted by this development. They welcomed Yogi, bestowed titles upon him, and were deeply impressed by the devotion of these young American men and women. The Yogi's entourage interpreted this warmth as an unequivocal acceptance of their group by the top tier of Sikh religious and political leadership. Known as the American Sikhs, the position of this small group of people within the larger Sikh community is still in the process of sorting itself out.[37] With the passing of Yogi, the American Sikhs are in a state of transition, and perhaps the future of this group will prove to be a test case for the promises and challenges of joining the Sikh community in the times ahead.

NOTES

1. For a general introduction, see J. S. Grewal, *History of the Sikhs* (London: Cambridge University Press, 1989); W. H. McLeod, *Sikhism* (New York: Penguin, 1997); Gurinder Singh Mann, *Sikhism* (Saddle River Road, NJ: Prentice Hall, 2004).

2. For Nanak's description of this experience, see his composition opening with the verse "I was an employed bard, God gave me the assignment" (*Guru Granth*, 150). The text of the *Guru Granth* has standard pagination, so the references used here are valid irrespective of the edition one uses.

3. My usage of "Baba" is based on the simple fact that this is Nanak's favorite description of himself and appears over forty times in his compositions. The terms Sikh and Nau Dharik appear in *Janam Sakhi Babe Nanak ki*, the first story of Nanak's life that appeared within fifty years or so after his death. See Vir Singh, ed., *Puratan Janam Sakhi* (Amritsar: Khalsa Samachar, [1926] 1986); Rattan Singh Jaggi, ed., *Puratan Janam Sakhi* (Patiala: Gurmat Prakashan, 2010); and Gurinder Singh Mann and Ami P. Shah, eds. and trans., *Janam Sakhi Babe Nanak Ji ki* (forthcoming).

4. The global distribution of Sikhs in approximately 2001 was as follows:
   Punjab area 15.99 million
   Other Indian states   3.32 million
   Other countries   2.00 million
   Total   21.31 million
My conversations with people tabulating the 2011 census support the current Sikh population as being 25 million, of whom 25 to 30 percent now live outside the Punjab area.

5. For a study based on this assumption, see Harbans Singh, *The Heritage of the Sikhs* (New Delhi: Manohar Publications, 1983).

6. For an English version of this text, see *Sikh Rahit Maryada* (Amritsar: Shiromani Gurdwara Parbandhak Committee, 1997).

7. The impression in circulation is that early Sikh identities were "fluid," and it was only in the late 1800s that the "boundaries" between the Sikhs and the Hindus were "constructed." For the most detailed statement of this point of view, see Harjot Oberoi, *Construction of Religious Boundaries* (New Delhi: Oxford University Press, 1994). The thrust of this study is applicable only to the urban Sikhs, a group that has never comprised more than 8 percent or so of the total Sikh population.

8. Doris R. Jakobsh, "Conversion in the Sikh Tradition," in *Religious Conversion: Contemporary Practices and Controversies*, ed. Christopher Lamb and M. Darrol Bryant (New York: Cassell, 1999), 166–174; and Louis E. Fenech, "Conversion in Sikh Tradition," in *Religious Conversion in India: Modes, Motivations, and Meanings*, ed. Rowenna Robinson and Sathianathan Clarke (New Delhi: Oxford University Press, 2003), 149–180.

9. Their scholarship is essentially built on W. H. McLeod, *Guru Nanak and the Sikh Religion* (Oxford: Clarendon Press, 1968), which in my view represents a mechanical application of the categories created in the area of Gospel Studies to Sikh literature. For the details of my critique of the book, see "Guru Nanak's Life and Legacy: An Appraisal," in *Punjab Reconsidered*, ed. Anshu Malhotra and Farina Mir (New Delhi: Oxford University Press, 2012), 116–160.

10. Yohanan Friedmann, ed., *Islam in Asia* (Jerusalem: The Hebrew University, 1984), 23–37.

11. *Parachi Patshahi Dasvin ki*, ed. Piara Singh Padam (Patiala: Kalam Mandi, [1708] 1988), 73.

12. This information is culled from the writings of Baba Nanak and *Janam Sakhi Babe Nanak ki*.

13. For information on the Jats, see Ainslie T. Embree, *Alberuni's India* (New York: Norton Library, 1971), 401; Gursharan Kaur Jaggi, ed., *Varan Bhai Gurdas* (Patiala: Punjabi University, 1987), *Var* 8:12; various sections from *Dabistan-i-Mazahib*, in *Sikh History from Persian Sources*, trans. Irfan Habib (New Delhi: Tulika, 2001), 74; Joseph Davey Cunningham, *A History of the Sikhs* (New Delhi: S. Chand, [1848] 1985), 299–300; K. R. Qanungo, *History of the Jats* (Delhi: Delhi Originals, [1925] 2003); M. C. Pradhan, *The Political System of the Jats of Northern India* (New Delhi: Oxford University Press, 1966); Irfan Habib, "The Jats of Punjab and Sind," in *Essays in Honor of Ganda Singh*, ed. Harbans Singh and N. Gerald Barrier (Patiala: Punjabi University, 1976), 92–103; and Nonica Datta, *Forming an Identity: A Social History of the Jats* (New Delhi: Oxford University Press, 1999). *Alberuni's India* characterizes the Jats as untouchables, and *Dabistan-i-Mazahib* incorporates them in the caste structure as the Vaishayas. The Jat hostility to authority even at the risk of damaging themselves and their tribe/clans is part of the local folklore (*Jat mahian sansar qabila galade*, "The Jats, the bulls, and the crocodiles destroy their own").

14. Irfan Habib, ed., *Medieval India* (New Delhi: Oxford University Press, 1999), 144; Henry Beveridge, ed., *The Akbar Nama of Abu-L-Fazl* (Delhi: Low Price Publications, 1998), 2:144, 422–424; Sujan Rai Bhandari, *Khulasat-ut-Tavarikh*, trans. Ranjit Singh Gill (Patiala: Punjabi University, 1972), 436.

15. Baba Nanak also calls the community at Kartarpur the Gurmukh Panth (The community of the Gurmukhs/Sikhs). It may be useful to point out that the Nanak Panth (The community of Nanak/his personal followers), a favorite term in current scholarship used to describe the early Sikh community, does not appear in the writings of Baba Nanak and his successors. For scholarly usage of these terms, see W. H. McLeod, *Who Is a Sikh?* (Oxford: Clarendon Press, 1989), 7–22; Oberoi, *The Construction of Religious Boundaries*, 24, 76–78, 89, 211, 395, 420; Jakobsh, "Conversion in the Sikh Tradition," 167; Fenech, "Conversion in Sikh Tradition," 157. The term begins to appear in the literature of the early seventeenth-century schismatic groups such as the Minas and Handalis. See Kirpal Singh et al., eds., *Janam Sakhi Miharban* (Amritsar: Khalsa College, [pre-1618] 1962, 1969); Gurbachan Kaur, ed., *Janam Sakhi Bhai Bala* (Patiala: Bhasha Vibahg, [1650] 1987).

16. See note 3.

17. Kulwinder Singh Bajwa, *Mahim Prakash Vartak* (Amritsar: Singh Brothers, [1810s] 2004), 51–52, 56–57.

18. *Varan Bhai Gurdas*, 1:3, 23; 4:17; 6:12; 7:13; 9:10; 10:4, 9; 11:6, 7,11; 12:19; 16:19; 23:2, 3, 4, 9; 24:22; 25:2, 12, 18; 37:28; 39:4; 40:22; *Dabistan-i-Mazahib*, 78, 84.

19. The five prohibitions were no stealing, no adultery, no slander, no gambling, and no consumption of liquor and meat. This entry is recorded in early scriptural manuscripts such as the *Bahoval Pothi* and the manuscript associated with Bhai Painda compiled around 1600.

20. Habib, *Sikh History from Persian Sources*, 57.

21. For literature on these groups, see Pritam Singh and Joginder Singh Ahluwalia, *Sikhan da Chhota Mel: Itihas te Sarvekhanh* (San Leandro, CA: Punjab Educational and Cultural Foundation, 2009), 84–97; Varinder Kaur, "Parchi Baba Handal: Sampadan te Itihasik Visleshanh," M. Phil. thesis, Guru Nanak Dev University, Amritsar, 1989; and Hardip Singh Syan, *Sikh Militancy in the Seventeenth Century: Religious Violence in Mughal and Early Modern India* (London: IB Tauris, forthcoming).

22. Piara Singh Padam, ed., *Rahitname* (Amritsar: Singh Brothers, 1995), 59–60; 147–149.

23. Kulwant Singh, ed., *Makke Madine di Goshati* (Patiala: Punjabi University, 1988), 190–191.

24. The primary sources of information for this period are Ami P. Shah, "In Praise of the Guru: A Translation and Study of Sainapati's *Sri Gursobha*," PhD diss., University of California, Santa Barbara, 2010; Sainapati, *Sri Gur Sobha*, ed. Ganda Singh (Patiala: Punjabi University, [1701–1708] 1967); and, for a general study of the period, Gurinder Singh Mann, "Sources for the Study of Guru Gobind Singh's Life and Times," *Journal of Punjab Studies* 15, nos. 1–2 (2008): 229–284.
25. *Hukaname*, ed. Ganda Singh (Patiala: Punjabi University, 1985), 179.
26. See note 23.
27. Ratan Singh Bhangu, *Sri Gur Panth Parkash* (Amritsar: Singh Brother, 2004), 36–38.
28. W. H. McLeod, ed., *Chaupa Singh Rahitnama* (Otago: University of Otago, 1987), 92.
29. *Sudharam Marag Granth*, MS 90280, Panjab University, folio 37b.
30. Grewal, *Baba Dayal Ji*; John C. B. Webster, *The Nirankari Sikhs* (Batala: The Christian Institute of Sikh Studies, 1979); Kirpal Singh Kasel, *Tawarikh Sant Khalsa* (Delhi: Arsi Publications, 2006), 309–320.
31. See "Death of Runjeet Sing," *The Freeman Journal* (Dublin, Ireland), Monday, Sept. 23, 1839; "Death of Runjeet Sing," *The Sydney Herald* (Sydney, Australia), Wednesday, Nov. 13, 1839; and "Death and Funeral Ceremonies of Runjeet Sing," *The Essex Standard* (Colchester, England), Friday, Feb. 28, 1840. I am grateful to Harpreet Singh of the University of Dunedin, New Zealand, for sending these interesting news stories to me.
32. For the development of the community, see John C. B. Webster, *The Christian Community and Change in Nineteenth Century North India* (Delhi: The Macmillan Company, 1976).
33. While the Khatri and Arora Sikhs intermarried with their urban Hindu counterparts, this practice was not followed by the overwhelming majority of the Sikh community, especially among Jats. How this general perception of the relationship between the Sikh and Hindu communities evolved and became popular in academic literature would be an interesting exercise. For instance, the primary responsibility for the ousting of the Sikhs from Anandpur falls on the shoulders of the Rajputs in the Punjab hills. In his *Zafarnama*, Guru Gobind Singh asks Emperor Aurangzeb how he could order an attack on the Sikhs who, like him, are the "breakers of the icons" at the behest of those who "worship the icons." For the text, see Christopher Shackle, "Zafarnama," *Journal of Punjab Studies* 15, nos. 1–2 (2008): 161–180. The theological differences between the Hindus and the Sikhs are clearly underlined here. Sikh literature of the period claims that Guru Tegh Bahadur's sacrifice was meant to protect "the religious symbols of the Kashmiri Brahmins" a group persecuted by the Mughals. In late nineteenth-century Hindu thinking, however, this position developed further and the Khalsa Panth was seen as the militant arm of the Hindus. Since the issue of the suppression of the Hindu community was no longer relevant in the British Punjab of the 1880s, some Hindu thinkers argued that the Sikhs should simply return to their mother community. This sentiment can be found in publications such as Narian Singh Bawa, *Sikh Hindu Hain* (Amritsar: Matbaknuni, 1899); Gurmukh Singh, *Vaidak Sanatan Gurmat Martand* (Nankana Sahib: Author, 1913); Munshi Ram Sharma, *Gurmat Divakar* (Ferozepur: Author, 1923)..
34. For details, see the relevant sections in Grewal, *History of the Sikhs*.
35. See the *Tribune* (Chandigarh), June 6, 2012, http://www.tribuneindia.com/2012/20120606/main7.htm.
36. See Kahn Singh Nabha, *Ham Hindu Nahin* (Lahore: Bhai Mayia Singh, 1898), 109 (the revised edition published in 1921 is in current circulation); Teja Singh Bhasour, *Khalsa Rahit Parkash* (Bhasour: Panch Khalsa Diwan, 1907); Lal Singh Sangrur (1881–1975), *Na*

Ham Hindu na Musalman (Bhasour: Panch Khalsa Diwan, 1921). The three important ideologues of this group were Dhillon, Brar, and Bhandal Jats, respectively, but in order to mark their equality within the Sikh community, they only used the names of their places of residence rather than the Jat clans to which they belonged.

37. For details, see *The History of Sikh Dharma of the Western Hemisphere* (Espanola, NM: Sikh Dharma International, 1995). In my conversations with Yogi in the late 1990s, the issue of creating the requisite infrastructure to ensure the sustainability of the group came up several times and he seemed very keen to work out these issues before his death. It seems that he was not entirely successful in accomplishing this goal; issues regarding the succession of authority are still in the process of being worked out.

BIBLIOGRAPHY

Bajwa, Kulwinder Singh, ed. *Mahim Prakash Vartak*. Amritsar: Singh Brothers, [1810s] 2004.

Barrier, N. Gerald, and Verne A. Dusenbery, eds. *The Sikh Diaspora: Migration and the Experience beyond Punjab*. Columbia, MO: South Asia Books, 1989.

Bawa, Narian Singh. *Sikh Hindu Hain*. Amritsar: Matbaknuni, 1899.

Beveridge, Henry, ed. *The Akbar Nama of Abu-L-Fazl*. Delhi: Low Price Publications, 1998.

Bhandari, Sujan Rai. *Khulasat-ut-Tavarikh*, trans. Ranjit Singh Gill. Patiala: Punjabi University, [1696] 1972.

Bhangu, Ratan Singh. *Sri Gur Panth Parkash*. Amritsar: Singh Brother, [pre-1814] 2004.

Bhasour, Teja Singh Bhasour. *Khalsa Rahit Parkash*. Bhasour: Panch Khalsa Diwan, 1907.

Cole, William Owen, and Piara Singh Sambhi. *The Sikhs: Their Religious Beliefs and Practices*. Brighton: Sussex Academic Press, 1995.

Cunningham, Joseph Davey. *A History of the Sikhs*. New Delhi: S. Chand, [1848] 1985.

Datta, Nonica. *Forming an Identity: A Social History of the Jats*. New Delhi: Oxford University Press, 1999.

Elsberg, Constance Waeber. *Graceful Women: Gender and Identity in an American Sikh Community*. Knoxville: University of Tennessee Press, 2003.

Embree, Ainslie T. *Alberuni's India*. New York: Norton Library, [1020s] 1971.

———. *Utopias in Conflict: Religious Nationalism in Modern India*. Berkeley and Los Angeles: University of California Press, 1990.

Fenech, Louis E. "Conversion in Sikh Tradition." In *Religious Conversion in India: Modes, Motivations, and Meanings*, ed. Rowenna Robinson and Sathianathan Clarke, 149–180. New Delhi: Oxford University Press, 2003.

Friedmann, Yohanan, ed. *Islam in Asia*. Jerusalem: The Hebrew University, 1984.

Grewal, J. S., ed. *Baba Dayal Ji*. Chandigarh: Man Singh Nirankari, 2003.

———. *History of the Sikhs*. London: Cambridge University Press, 1989.

———. *The Sikhs of the Punjab*. New York: Cambridge University Press, 1990.

Grewal, J. S., and Irfan Habib, ed. *Sikh History from Persian Sources*. New Delhi: Tulika, 2001.

Guru Granth. Complete text with English translation is available at http://www.srigranth.org/about.html.

Habib, Irfan. "The Jats of Punjab and Sind." In *Essays in Honor of Ganda Singh*, ed. Harbans Singh and N. Gerald Barrier, 92–103. Patiala: Punjabi University, 1976.

———, ed. *Medieval India*. New Delhi: Oxford University Press, 1999.

The History of Sikh Dharma of the Western Hemisphere. Espanola, NM: Sikh Dharma International, 1995.

Jaggi, Gursharan Kaur, ed. *Varan Bhai Gurdas*. Patiala: Punjabi University, 1987.

Jaggi, Rattan Singh, ed. *Puratan Janam Sakhi*. Patiala: Gurmat Prakashan, 2010.

Jakobsh, Doris R. "Conversion in the Sikh Tradition." In *Religious Conversion: Contemporary Practices and Controversies*, ed. Christopher Lamb and M. Darrol Bryant, 166–174. New York: Cassell, 1999.

Kasel, Kirpal Singh. *Tawarikh Sant Khalsa*. Delhi: Arsi Publications, 2006.

Kaur, Gurbachan, ed. *Janam Sakhi Bhai Bala*. Patiala: Bhasha Vibahg, [1650] 1987.

Kaur, Varinder. "Parchi Baba Handal: Sampadan te Itihasik Visleshanh." M. Phil. thesis, Guru Nanak Dev University, Amritsar, 1989.

Mahmood, Cynthia. *Fighting for Faith and Nation: Dialogues with Sikh Militants*. Philadelphia: University of Pennsylvania Press, 1997.

Mann, Gurinder Singh. "Guru Nanak's Life and Legacy: An Appraisal." In *Punjab Reconsidered*, ed. Anshu Malhotra and Farina Mir, 116–160. New Delhi, Oxford University Press, 2012.

——. *Sikhism*. Saddle River Road, NJ: Prentice Hall, 2004.

——. "Sources for the Study of Guru Gobind Singh's Life and Times." *Journal of Punjab Studies* 15, nos. 1–2 (2008): 229–284.

Mann, Gurinder Singh, and Ami P. Shah, eds. and trans. *The Life Story of Baba Nanak* (forthcoming).

McLeod, W. H., trans. *The B-40 Janam-Sakhi*. Amritsar: Guru Nanak Dev University, 1980.

——, ed. *Chaupa Singh Rahitnama*. Otago: University of Otago, 1987.

——. *Sikhism*. New York: Penguin Books, 1997.

——. *Who Is a Sikh?* Oxford: Clarendon Press, 1989.

Nabha, Kahn Singh. *Ham Hindu Nahin*. Lahore: Bhai Mayia Singh, 1898.

Oberoi, Harjot. *The Construction of Religious Boundaries: Culture, Identity and Diversity in the Sikh Tradition*. New Delhi: Oxford University Press, 1994.

Padam, Piara Singh, ed. *Parachi Patshahi Dasvin ki*. Patiala: Kalam Mandi, [1708] 1988.

——, ed. *Rahitname*. Amritsar: Singh Brothers, 1995.

Pradhan, M. C. *The Political System of the Jats of Northern India*. New Delhi: Oxford University Press, 1966.

Qanungo, Kalika Ranjan. *History of the Jats*. Delhi: Delhi Originals, [1925] 2003.

Sainapati. *Sri Gur Sobha*, ed. Ganda Singh. Patiala: Punjabi University, [1701–1708] 1967.

Sangrur, Lal Singh. *Na Ham Hindu na Musalman*. Bhasour: Panch Khalsa Diwan, 1921.

Shackle, Christopher. "Zafarnama." *Journal of Punjab Studies* 15, nos. 1–2 (2008): 161–180.

Shah, Ami P. "In Praise of the Guru: A Translation and Study of Sainapati's *Sri Gursobha*." PhD diss., University of California, Santa Barbara, 2010.

Sharma, Munshi Ram. *Gurmat Divakar*. Ferozepur: Author, 1923.

Sikh Rahit Maryada. Amritsar: Shiromani Gurdwara Parbandhak Committee, 1997.

Singh, Ganda, ed. *Hukaname*. Patiala: Punjabi University, 1985.

Singh, Gurmukh. *Vaidak Sanatan Gurmat Martand*. Nankana Sahib: Author, 1913.

Singh, Harbans. *The Heritage of the Sikhs*. New Delhi: Manohar Publications, 1983.

Singh, Kirpal, et al., eds. *Janam Sakhi Miharban*. Amritsar: Khalsa College, [pre-1618] 1962, 1969.

Singh, Kulwant, ed. *Makke Madine di Goshati*. Patiala: Punjabi University, 1988.

Singh, Pritam, and Joginder Singh Ahluwalia. *Sikhan da Chhota Mel: Itihas te Sarvekhanh*. San Leandro, CA: Punjab Educational and Cultural Foundation, 2009.

Singh, Vir, ed., *Puratan Janam Sakhi*. Amritsar: Khalsa Samachar, [1926] 1986.

Syan, Hardip Singh. *Sikh Militancy in the Seventeenth Century: Religious Violence in Mughal and Early Modern India.* London: IB Tauris, 2013.

Tatla, Drashan Singh. *The Sikh Diaspora: The Search for Statehood.* Seattle: University of Washington Press, 1999.

Webster, John C. B. *The Christian Community and Change in Nineteenth Century North India.* Delhi: Macmillan Company, 1976.

——. *The Nirankari Sikhs.* Batala: The Christian Institute of Sikh Studies, 1979.

CHAPTER 22

....

ADHERENCE AND CONVERSION TO DAOISM

....

LOUIS KOMJATHY

"CONVERSION" is not a word that readily comes to mind when one thinks of Daoism, but conversion, adherence, and religious identity are central aspects of the religious tradition. Historically speaking, Daoists have organized and continue to structure their tradition along a number of distinct lines, with the most prominent being initiation, ordination, and lineage affiliation (spiritual genealogies). In addition, one finds the consistent occurrence of revelations and mystical experiences as well as a strong emphasis on self-cultivation throughout Daoist history. The latter characteristics are potentially subversive: new movements and lineages have been established through personal revelations, mystical experiences, and personal practice. This means that Daoist ways to affiliation include conversion through both human and divine inspiration. Some individuals have converted to Daoism through standardized ritual procedures (e.g., ordination rites), others through personal instruction under a recognized religious leader, and still others through encounters with immortals and Perfected (*zhenren*).[1] In addition, as discussed below, there is a larger pattern in earlier Chinese history of entire communities and "non-Chinese" ethnic groups converting to Daoism for cultural, economic, and political reasons.

Daoist conversion, like religious conversion more generally, is thus a complex and multifaceted topic. It includes demographics, such as age, ethnicity, gender,[2] socioeconomic background, and levels of education, plus the psychology of potential adherents and the socio-political and economic dimensions of affiliation. These various dimensions of religious conversion bring our attention to other, equally challenging interpretative issues. For example, is there a hierarchy of motivations? Is it more "authentic" to convert based on personal affinity with doctrine and practice rather than economic distress or socio-political expediency? This may sound like a normative question, but it can be profitably approached by investigating adherent views on the subject. Unfortunately, the ways in which Daoists have established and maintained religious affiliation have not been thoroughly studied. One fundamental question that awaits future research focuses on requirements for conversion and corresponding commitments. As discussed below, some insights may be found in Daoist precept texts and monastic manuals.

The present chapter presents a tentative and pioneering inquiry into Daoist adherence, affiliation, and conversion. I present, synthesize, and analyze disparate scholarship in an attempt to present a more complete account of historical examples and patterns of Daoist conversion. In addition to discussing "conversion" as a comparative category and as a cultural phenomenon in China, I investigate Daoist views on the subject and the ways in which Daoists have set parameters for religious affiliation and inclusion. This is followed by an examination of domestic conversion, by people of both Chinese ("Han") ethnic identity and ethnic minorities, to Daoism in Chinese history. In this respect, one interesting topic is the relationship among ethnic, cultural, and religious identity. On one level, the ideal form of Daoist identity is one in which the adherent is ethnically and culturally Chinese. However, there is also some sense in which "barbarians" and "foreigners" can become Chinese and Daoist by being enculturated. The final section presents information on foreign conversion to Daoism. This includes brief discussions of Daoist conversion in Hong Kong, Korea, Japan, and in the modern West. Here, I suggest that Daoism has become a global religious tradition.

CONVERSION AS A COMPARATIVE CATEGORY

Etymologically speaking, the English term "conversion" relates to two Greek terms: *epistrophe*, which can mean "conversion" or "turning around," and *metanoia*, which can mean "repentance" or "turning around," with emphasis placed on the inner transformation of the convert.[3] "The term *conversion* was employed initially within Judeo-Christian circles to describe a believer's self-identification with a religious [Abrahamic] tradition either through faith in God and/or through commitment to new beliefs, rituals, and a religious community."[4] Considered cross-culturally, "conversion" may be employed as a comparative category to refer to changes in religious identity, affiliation, and participation (see below), although there are nonreligious forms of "conversion" as well. We may also make a distinction between adherent and academic perspectives on the matter. This includes a larger theoretical and interpretative spectrum, which Rambo and Farhadian divide as follows: personalistic theories (psychoanalytic, archetypical, attachment, and attribution); social/cultural theories (multicultural, postcolonial, identity, intellectualist, narrative, and globalization); religious/spiritual theories (theological and translation); as well as convergence theories (process, feminist, and Christianization, and Islamization).[5] Each reveals a certain dimension of the phenomenon of conversion from a specific interpretative perspective. Reflecting on such theories from another perspective, one might categorize them as anthropological, comparative, philosophical, psychological, sociological, and theological.

In studying the process of religious conversion in specific religious traditions, I would suggest that we begin with a phenomenological approach. Phenomenologically speaking, religious conversion involves a change in religious affiliation, which includes dimensions of personal and social identity and forms of social participation. In the case of converting to a new religious tradition, there frequently is a corresponding commitment to a new worldview, set of concerns and values, practices, and way of life. This may entail apostasy (from the Greek, "defection" or "revolt"), the formal abandonment or renunciation of former beliefs. Outside of the contemporary global context, wherein one finds individuals who claim multiple religious identities, one cannot be an adherent of two religious traditions with mutually exclusive soteriologies and theologies (e.g., Judaism and Zen Buddhism ["Jubus"]).[6] Globalization, multiculturalism, and religious pluralism lead to distinctive patterns of modification, adaptation, and appropriation. That is, there are types of conversion and of religious identity and affiliation that only occur through the encounter with radically alterior worldviews and constructions of reality.

The proposed phenomenological and comparative "definition" of conversion requires some additional clarification. There is a tendency to conflate conversion with evangelism, missionization, and proselytization. While there may be overlap in certain religious movements, a distinction must be made. Proselytization is the practice of religious adherents actively attempting to convert non-adherents to their religious tradition. In the case of Christianity, proselytism is often referred to as evangelism, the process of bringing the "word of God" to non-Christians and preparing the way for eternal and universal salvation. Among contemporary American evangelical Christians, this often goes by the name of "bearing witness to Christ" or "spreading the good news." As undertaken by adherents, proselytization presumes the superiority and salvific power of their own beliefs. Similarly, missionization is an intentional, organized, and large-scale process of colonizing other peoples and cultures in the attempt to increase the degree of adherence to the missionary's religion. (Of course, missionaries tend to frame their activities in more humanitarian and altruistic terms.) There is thus overlap between proselytization and missionization. However, "missions" are usually supported by a larger institution. While most proselytizers work to change individuals, missionaries usually attempt to establish viable institutions within which proselytization may occur. One might say that proselytization is psychological and social, while missionization is institutional. The former may occur inside or outside of the adherent's own culture, while the latter usually involves one ethnic group entering a different cultural context to missionize another ethnic group. Historically speaking, proselytizing and missionary activity is most prominent among Buddhists, Christians, and Muslims. In the modern world, the tendency is well represented in more recent Christian groups such as the Church of Jesus Christ of Latter-day Saints (LDS; "Mormons"), Jehovah's Witnesses, and Seventh Day Adventists. Invariably, there is a soteriological worldview that envisions global transformation and perhaps homogenization. Of committed missionary sensibilities and projects, one may thus ask the following questions: Do they presume a world purified of difference and restructured according to their own constructs? Can their religious imaginations include alternative possibilities? Is there an underlying soteriology and teleology that is utopian and contains the potentiality of genocide, whether cultural or physical? Connecting these views to conversion, we may make a distinction between "voluntary" or "self-directed conversion" and "forced" or "coerced conversion." Much of proselytizing and missionary activity falls into the latter category, with problematic ethical and political dimensions that are either ignored or subordinated to supposed "higher callings." There is often a corresponding installation of fear and/or threat and the exercise of violence. Proselytization and missionization are thus often connected with colonialism and imperialism. Such tendencies are almost entirely absent among Daoists, and this chapter will explore some of the reasons why this is the case.

In the case of China, the primary missionary religions have been Buddhism and Christianity, both Catholic religious orders and Protestant denominations. That is, missionization principally happened within the context of foreigners entering China in an attempt to convert the indigenous populations. Buddhist missionaries, principally from Central Asia, first entered China in the second century C.E. The initial indigenous response was dismissal and rejection. It took a few centuries for Buddhists to establish their tradition in mainland China in the form of translated sutras and viable institutions, including ethnic Chinese converts. However, it was not until Sinification (the process of making something Chinese) occurred that Buddhism became more accepted and acceptable.[7] The transformation of Buddhism into a Chinese religion resulted in a variety of indigenous Chinese schools, which became the dominant forms of Mahayana Buddhism throughout East Asia. Similarly, missionaries from Catholic religious orders, first the Jesuits and then the Dominicans, began entering China in the sixteenth century.[8] Christianity was even less palatable than Buddhism, especially due to its claims of exclusivity and its authoritarian power structure. The latter in particular challenged a parallel indigenous framework with the emperor as autocrat. In both cases, foreign religious traditions faced enormous challenges from the indigenous population and established cultural norms, especially among the cultural and political elites.

As far as current research has determined, Daoists never made a formal and sustained attempt to convert non-Chinese people to Daoism; instead, relevant research suggests that minority groups within China actively sought affiliation with the tradition (see below). Generally speaking, individuals converted to Daoism; Daoists did not strive to convert individuals or communities to their tradition. Moreover, historically speaking, most people who converted to Daoism were ethnic Chinese and living within China.[9] Unlike their Buddhist counterparts, Daoists did not engage in missionary activity in other East Asian countries. Even in the modern world, where Daoism has become a global, transnational, and multiethnic religion, instances of conversion are voluntary and self-directed. This chapter attempts to provide a preliminary exploration of the patterns and motivations behind such conversion.

DAOIST IDENTITY, AFFILIATION, AND CONVERSION

The religious tradition that is Daoism is intimately connected with traditional Chinese culture. Many of the defining characteristics of Daoism are distinctively Chinese, although certain Daoist values and concerns have challenged dominant Chinese views. Daoism thus must be recognized as an indigenous Chinese religion and as an important dimension of Chinese history, culture, and society. However, unlike some modern European and Chinese scholars, I see no evidence that Daoism can be considered the "essence" or "spirit" of China. It is also a mistake to deny the possibility and reality of the transformation of Daoism into a "trans-Chinese" religious tradition, which is clearly occurring in the modern world. The latter makes inquiry into Daoist conversion much more complex.

Examining the deep connection between Daoism and Chinese culture provides some insights into the near absence of Daoist missionary activity, especially in the form of "coerced conversion." Throughout Chinese history, the ethnic majority and ruling elite considered Chinese culture to be the pinnacle of human civilization. Generally speaking, before the modern period of Chinese history and the complex patterns of cultural exchange between the indigenous Chinese population and Western colonialists and missionaries, to be cultured and civilized was to be Chinese. This was so much the case that non-Chinese peoples had to become Chinese (through enculturation) in order to gain recognition. Chinese culture and history is thus characterized by a distinct form of ethnocentricism, or Sinocentrism to be more specific.

The Chinese sense of cultural and ethnic superiority was expressed in many ways, and one can find endless examples. Here three will suffice to provide some glimpses into dominant cultural mindsets, views that were influential on and accepted by Daoists. The first is the indigenous Chinese name for China: Zhongguo (Central Kingdom). Those living within the borders of China were part of the center, and this center was characterized by a series of contracting and expanding concentric circles. The Chinese emperor, imperial house, and capital represented the center of the center. The further away from the center, the less cultured and civilized one was. The civility of all other "kingdoms," or countries in modern terms, was directly proportional to their proximity to China. Thus, Japan and Korea, kingdoms that early on in their histories accepted Chinese culture as superior, were considered among the most cultured and civilized. Another symbolic expression of Sinocentrism is the Great Wall, the earliest sections of which were constructed by the Qin, an ancient state located in the central and southwest part (Shaanxi to Sichuan) of what we now refer to as China. After unifying the other so-called "warring states" in 221 B.C.E., the Qin made two responses concerning walls: they destroyed earlier wall fortifications between states, and they connected sections of walls on the northern frontier.[10] The former action expressed the unity of the Central Kingdom, while the latter sealed the realm from the possibility of foreign invasion, specifically from the Xiongnu, a nomadic tribe in the north. While it is true that the Great Wall served as a political demarcation and military fortification, it also tells us something significant on a metaphorical level: the inside would be kept in, while the outside would be kept out. The inside ("Chinese") was seen as superior; it deserved respect and protection. The outside ("foreign") was inferior; it was dangerous and required either opposition or enculturation. This inside/outside mentality and social ordering would continue throughout Chinese history, and it played a major role in Daoist views of the Daoist religious affiliation.

Finally, the so-called Rites Controversy (roughly 1615 to 1721) provides yet another window into indigenous Chinese attitudes toward things foreign. During the early moments of Catholic, specifically Jesuit, missionary activity in China, this controversy centered on the nature and correct categorization of Chinese rituals, specifically whether or not they were religious ("idolatrous") and therefore incompatible with Catholicism.[11] The Jesuits, who themselves became Sinified in many ways, argued for the compatibility, while the Dominicans took the opposite position. In the eighteenth century, Pope Clement XI (1649–1721; r. 1700–1721) and Pope Benedict XIV (1685–1758; r. 1740–1758) sided with the Dominicans and condemned Chinese rituals. This remained the position of the Catholic Church until 1939. The papal condemnation led to a corresponding indigenous Chinese response: the Kangxi Emperor (1654–1722; r. 1661–1722) issued a decree that proscribed Christianity, a decree which was not lifted until 1846. From the perspective of the pope, his power extended beyond national and political borders; from the perspective of the emperor, nothing inside of China was exempt from imperial authority (and the outside was, of course, irrelevant).[12] This general stance is perhaps best represented by the Chinese emperor sitting on his throne and receiving ministers and guests for an imperial audience, and by the Silk Road along which foreign merchants brought foreign goods in and took Chinese goods out.

I have provided some examples of Sinocentrism so that readers may understand dimensions of Chinese culture that have informed Daoist approaches towards religious affiliation and conversion. Why have Daoists not been active missionaries? One answer is that Daoists, as members of Chinese culture and society, already resided at the center of the world and within the most advanced civilization. There was no reason to leave China's borders. Moreover, Daoism, as an indigenous Chinese religion and as part of Chinese culture, was inherently superior. Although Daoists' views of their own religious tradition have yet to be thoroughly studied, certain patterns are clearly relevant for the study of adherence and conversion. One of the most peculiar and indicative is the infamous *huahu* ("conversion of the barbarians") theory.[13] This theory represents a Daoist nativistic response to the introduction and increasing power of Buddhism in Chinese society. It was first expressed in a nascent form toward the end of the Later Han dynasty (25–220 C.E.) and became more fully developed in the Six Dynasties period (220–589 C.E.). Briefly stated, this Daoist theory, drawing on the mythological biography of Laozi (Master Lao) in the *Shiji* (Records of the Historian), which tells us that Laozi left China through the western frontiers, argued that the historical Buddha was, in fact, Laozi and that Buddhism was a simplified form of Daoism appropriate for "barbarians" (read: Indians and Central Asians). According to the *huahu* theory, Laozi attempted to explain the complex philosophy and soteriology of Daoism to non-Chinese peoples, but they were unable to understand due to their ethnic/cultural inferiority and intellectual deficiencies. Laozi, as the Buddha, then created Buddhism as a means of moral rectification.[14] The theory was codified in the *Huahu jing* (Scripture on the Conversion of the Barbarians; partially lost; DH 76),[15] which contains historical layers from the fourth to eighth centuries, and the Yuan dynasty (1279–1368) *Laojun bashiyi hua tushuo* (Illustrated Explanations of Lord Lao's Eighty-one Transformations),[16] an illustrated recounting of Lord Lao's various incarnations through which he attempted to assist humanity. Part of the motivation behind this theory involved attempts to gain cultural capital and imperial patronage, and Buddhists, as one would expect, issued passionate responses.

This dimension of religio-cultural exchange came to a head in the Buddho-Daoist debates of 520 and 580 and of 1258 and 1281, all of which eventually led to various proscriptions against Daoism.[17] The enduring presence and continuous modification of the *huahu* theory in Daoism provides specific insights into issues of conversion and missionization. Daoists viewed Daoism as inherently superior, partly because it was indigenous to China and produced by Chinese sages.[18] If one accepts the logic of the *huahu* theory, Daoism *as Daoism* could not be exported because only Chinese people were capable of understanding it. It was intricately tied to being Chinese. This view continues into the modern world in many forms, present among both Daoists and scholars of Daoism; one must be Chinese in order to be a Daoist. If one is not ethnically Chinese, one must "become Chinese" by learning the language, understanding the culture, and perhaps taking on its mannerisms.

However, active or coerced conversion and proselytism also go against foundational Daoist values and principles. For example, the so-called Nine Practices (*jiuxing*) of the early Tianshi (Celestial Masters) movement, which derive from the *Daode jing* (Scripture on the Dao and Inner Power), read as follows:

> Practice non-action.
> Practice softness and weakness.
> Practice guarding the feminine. Do not initiate actions.
> Practice being nameless.
> Practice clarity and stillness.
> Practice being adept.
> Practice being desireless.
> Practice knowing how to stop and be content.
> Practice yielding and withdrawing.[19]

Here and in the corresponding passages in the *Daode jing*,[20] emphasis is placed on living in a state of open receptivity. Daoists who embraced and applied these principles—they formed an ethical cornerstone of one of the earliest Daoist religious communities—endeavored to embody specific existential qualities: effortless activity, flexibility and yielding, egolessness, contemplative presence, voluntary simplicity, and so forth.

These and similar values, values that have had a pervasive and continuous influence in the tradition, inhibit the habituated human tendency to elevate self above others and to persuade others about one's philosophical and religious positions.[21] The Daoist tendency to be carefree or unconcerned has often led non-Daoists to categorize Daoists as lacking compassion, but such is the perspective of enculturated modes of perceiving. A Daoist perspective would see the classical and foundational existential approach as a transpersonal, or Dao-centered, way of being, beyond the limitations of ordinary human perception. In terms of converting others, such values translate into a distinctive lack of interest. Beyond the necessity of patronage and support, Daoists have seen conversion to the tradition as a matter of personal affinity and fate. Patterns of conversion in Daoism are largely voluntary and based on personal affinity.

Although much of the present discussion is conjectural and requires additional research, I would also suggest that other defining characteristics of the tradition have influenced Daoist ways of relating to others in terms of their religious beliefs. First, Daoism is a place-specific religious tradition; places matter to Daoists. In this way, Daoism more closely resembles traditions such as ancient Judaism, Shinto, and Native American religions. Most of the events in Daoist religious history have a corresponding geographical dimension that Daoists regard as significant and that the religious community remembers. This includes the mythological transmission of the *Daode jing* from Laozi to Yinxi at Hangu Pass; Lord Lao's revelations given to Zhang Daoling on Mount Heming; and Wang Chongyang's training of his disciples in the Kunyu mountains. The place-specific aspect of Daoism is perhaps most clearly expressed in the system of the grotto-heavens (*dongtian*).[22] The standardized system of grotto-heavens consists of ten major and thirty-six minor sites. These are hidden passageways into a sacred landscape where the numinous presence of the Dao is more fully present. Each and every one of these sacred sites, or mystical terrestrial spaces, if you will, is in China. Traditionally speaking, to be outside of China is to be remote from the sacred as accessible in landscapes.[23] In terms of place-significant sacred sites, sacred sites to which the majority of Daoists might consider making pilgrimages, none are outside of mainland China. From such a perspective, it is difficult to imagine the significance or necessity of "non-Chinese" converts to Daoism.

A second dimension of the tradition that inhibits active proselytizing and coerced conversion is the non-eschatological or non-apocalyptic dimension of Daoism. This includes a fundamental lack of concern with "salvation." It was only under the influence of Buddhism that Daoists began creating soteriological systems based on notions of universal salvation and messianic intervention in human history. The most representative and influential movement in this respect is Lingbao (Numinous Treasure).[24] It seems likely that religious tendencies toward mass conversion and homogenization are rooted in a specific teleology, and perhaps a world-consuming one at that. In the case of Buddhist-inspired Daoist eschatologies, they invariably focused on Chinese rulers, on China itself, and on the Chinese people. Perhaps the most famous example in Daoist history was the early Taiping (Great Peace), sometimes inaccurately referred to as the Yellow Turban Rebellion.[25] It is, moreover, no coincidence that this notion of Great

Peace and a messianic figure melded quite easily with the Christian apocalyptic movement known as Taiping during the years of 1850 and 1864.[26]

Issues of conversion also relate to identity. On the one hand, conversion focuses one's attention on religious affiliation, including types of participation and levels of commitment. This is the anthropological and sociological dimension of conversion. However, viewed from a theological perspective, conversion and religious identity are often determined by certain types of religious experiences. In the case of Daoism, we find the entire spectrum of ways to affiliation, from ordination and lineage affiliation to revelation and mystical experiences. Initiation, ordination, and lineage (spiritual genealogies) have been central defining characteristics of Daoism from its earliest stages of development. For example, the early Celestial Masters organized their communities hierarchically, with the Celestial Master at the top, followed by libationers (*jijiu*), and then by community members more generally.[27] There were corresponding degrees of commitment and requirements for participation, often appearing in the form of precept texts.[28] Similarly, the importance of formal religious standing is expressed in the late medieval and late imperial Daoist ordination systems.[29]

However, this institutional and ecclesiastical dimension of Daoist religious affiliation is challenged by other features of the tradition. First, individuals engaging in eremitic and ascetic training, most often in the mountains and away from imperial court politics, have been recognized as Daoists by Daoists.[30] This includes alternative ways of understanding and expressing religious identity: from a greater emphasis on cultivation and refinement to master–disciple relationships that do not easily fit into standardized or official presentations. Daoist sources that substantiate these claims include received hagiographies.[31]

Similarly, conventional accounts of Daoist religious history often neglect or gloss over the centrality of revelations and mystical experiences in the lives of specific Daoists and in the formation of specific communities and movements. The later lineages or schools of organized Daoism were most often formed through a revelation/transmission from specific deities or immortals to the recognized founder. To name a few, these include revelations from Lord Lao to Zhang Daoling (fl. 140 C.E.) and the subsequent formation of the Tianshi (Celestial Masters) movement; the mystical encounters of Yang Xi (330–386?) and the Xu brothers with various deities and Perfected and the subsequent establishment of the Shangqing (Highest Clarity) movement; and Wang Chongyang's (1113–1170) mystical experiences with immortals, traditionally identified as Zhongli Quan and Lü Dongbin, and the subsequent formation of the Quanzhen (Complete Perfection) movement. That is, these Daoists, some of the most important figures in Daoist history, became Daoists through divine, not human, means. Although such examples prove challenging to social scientific and materialist accounts of religious identity, affiliation, and conversion, they nonetheless problematize certain constructions of institutional locatedness. The importance of revelation and mystical experience in the Daoist tradition suggests that the inspiration for and motivation behind "conversion" may come from non-human sources. This might lead a scholar with theological leanings to redefine the Daoist religious community to include divine beings, similar to what Daoists themselves would do.

Before discussing specific examples of conversion to Daoism, I would like to make one additional point. Following the introduction and subsequent Sinification of Buddhism in China, especially during and after the Period of Disunion (220–581), Daoists increasingly accepted and developed certain aspects of Buddhism. For present purposes, one of the most significant modifications to a foundational Daoist worldview involved the notion of reincarnation (*lunhui*). This account of human existence involved a corresponding soteriology based on karma (*yinyuan*). The extent to which Daoists at various moments of Chinese history believed in reincarnation is an important question and one that deserves further research; however, it is clear that a Buddhist-inspired worldview based on reincarnation became increasingly convincing to Daoists over time and has occupied a central place in the tradition. In the case of contemporary Daoism, this is expressed in an emphasis on "former incarnations" (*sushi*) and "predestined affinities" (*yuanfen*). Taken seriously in terms of the study of conversion, reincarnation has a number of potentially disturbing consequences. For example, it is possible that members of religious traditions in a previous existence have been reborn into other religious traditions. Imagine an apparent Roman Catholic who converts to Daoism. From a reincarnation-based perspective, this is not an example of conversion at all because the supposed "Daoist convert" has, in fact, returned to her actual religious tradition.

DOMESTIC CONVERSION TO DAOISM

The study of conversion to Daoism and of Daoist views concerning conversion is complicated not only by the lack of research on the topic but also by the relative dearth of attention to the demographics of the religious tradition. In particular, because specialists so frequently identify Daoism as "China's indigenous higher religion," little research has been done on the ethnic backgrounds of adherents and converts. Pioneering research has, of course, been conducted by Michel Strickmann and his intellectual heir, Terry Kleeman, but there are major gaps in our understanding. For example, possible relevant topics include Tangut and Jurchen conversion to Quanzhen (Complete Perfection) Daoism during the Song-Jin period (tenth to thirteenth centuries) and Manchu conversion to the Longmen (Dragon Gate) lineage of that same monastic order during the Qing dynasty (1644–1911). In this section, I investigate domestic conversion to Daoism by both ethnic Han ("Chinese") and minority groups[32] and offer some tentative suggestions about the motivations behind such conversions.

Tianshi dao (Way of the Celestial Masters) was one of the earliest forms of organized Daoism, and the success of this movement proved seminal in the development of Daoism as an organized religious tradition. The Celestial Masters are so named because of a revelation that Zhang Daoling (Zhang Ling; fl. 140s C.E.) received from Lord Lao, the deified form of Laozi, in 142 C.E. In addition to being directed to establish a regional Daoist community in the land of Shu and Ba (present-day Sichuan), Zhang Daoling was appointed as the first Celestial Master, Lord Lao's terrestrial representative. Pejoratively

referred to the "Five Pecks of Rice" sect, this movement embraced a patrilineal organizational structure, with the position of Celestial Master passing from father to son.
For present purposes, it is noteworthy that the Celestial Masters movement created an
autonomous theocracy that remained independent of imperial control until Cao Cao
(155–220), the nominal founder of the Wei dynasty (220–265), conquered it in 215. After
the initial revelations and subsequent organization, especially under the third Celestial
Master, Zhang Lu (d. 216), the Celestial Masters movement gained regional control
and large numbers of followers. This culminated in the Daoist millennial kingdom of
Hanzhong.[33] According to extant historical sources, several tens of thousands of households became members of the community.[34] The community was organized hierarchically into "parishes" (zhi), twenty-four administrative centers. Each parish was overseen
by a libationer (jijiu), who served as the community leader and local representative of
the Celestial Master. Both men and women filled these positions.[35]

Various motivations for adherence and conversion to the early Celestial Masters may
be identified. In addition to providing protection from violence, the Celestial Masters
instituted a system of grain distribution. They collected and stored grain from the various parishes as a requirement for membership. This grain was then distributed throughout the region, with the abundance and surplus of one area relieving shortages in
another. There were also millennial dimensions of the movement. The Celestial Masters
envisioned a world purified of moral degradation and social injustice. The social and
political upheaval of the coming end times would be replaced with a utopia, a Celestial
Masters' kingdom, characterized by Great Peace (taiping). Members of the Celestial
Masters' community would serve as the "seed people" (zhongmin), who would repopu-
late a purified world.

> The Masters of the Three Offices will select seed people and take those who have
> matched their qi (heqi) [through our communal rites]. There will be 18,000. How
> many have there been until today? The great quota is not yet full. You should admon-
> ish yourself and rectify your heart-mind.[36]

The promise of a life free of turmoil and strife and of a society free of violence and chaos
was at least one major influence on this particular pattern of Daoist conversion.

Primarily due to the research of Terry Kleeman, we also now know that the early
Celestial Masters attracted large numbers of non-Chinese converts. In particular, the Ba
(also identified in some sources as Man and Zong), an ethnic minority living in the eastern part of Sichuan at the time of the Celestial Masters, became a distinctive segment
of that Daoist religious community. First documented in Chinese history around 700
B.C.E., the Ba people were hunter-gatherers most well-known for their military prowess
and their service as mercenaries for their neighbors.[37] In the formative moments of the
Celestial Masters movement, there were large numbers of Ba living in Sichuan. Their
socio-political life was characterized by an adversarial relationship with local representatives of the Chinese state, who sought to integrate the wealth and power of the unas-
similated Ba tribes into the Chinese administrative framework and thereby provoked

repeated rebellions. "When the [Celestial Masters'] Daoist message of deliverance spread through the region, the Ba flocked to its banner, with Ba kings, marquises, and other local elites leading groups numbering in the thousands to adopt the new faith and join the apocalyptic kingdom of Hanzhong."[38] There are, in turn, various accounts of mass conversions among the Ba to the Celestial Masters movement. Local leaders converted with their entire communities, and one group in particular under Li Hu, a Ba tribal leader and grandfather of the founder of the Dacheng state (see below), consisted of more than 500 families, amounting to perhaps 2,500 individuals. Some Ba converts migrated to Hanzhong to participate directly in Zhang Lu's millennial kingdom, while others maintained a base of support in Sichuan.[39] In addition to the above-mentioned motivations for conversion to the Celestial Masters more generally, it seems that the Ba were attracted to Daoist claims about prophylactic and mantic techniques for controlling demonic forces.[40] These various details not only reveal a pattern of conversion among non-Chinese peoples but also demonstrate a religious openness among the early Celestial Masters. As Kleeman notes, "We must conclude, I believe, that the earliest Celestial Masters community was truly multiethnic, accepting people from a variety of ethnic backgrounds as equal members of the new faith."[41]

Equally interesting and perhaps even more surprising, the Ba eventually established their own millennial kingdom called Dacheng (Great Perfection).[42] This could be seen as the culmination of early Ba conversion to the Celestial Masters. In 215, the famous Chinese general Cao Cao attacked the Hanzhong community and defeated Zhang Lu and the Celestial Masters' army. Following this, Cao Cao divided the Daoist community and forcibly transferred its members throughout present-day Shaanxi and Gansu. Several tens of thousands of families, possibly as many as two hundred to three hundred thousand individuals, were relocated to the Chang'an area. This group probably included Li Hu and other Ba tribesmen, who passed through the Chang'an area on their way to Gansu.[43] At the end of the third century, a large number of Ba refugees were driven south by civil unrest, natural disasters, and famine. Members of the Li family, descendants of the Ba tribal leader Li Hu, eventually resettled in eastern Sichuan. In 306, with the support of Fan Changsheng, Li Xiong, the grandson of Li Hu, established the kingdom of Dacheng,[44] of which the total population was probably over one million people. The Ba rulers of this Daoist utopian kingdom attempted to incorporate Daoist principles and the early Celestial Masters' theocratic model into their own administrative system.[45] For about fifty years, Dacheng, in a fashion parallel to the earlier Hanzhong kingdom, consisted of Chinese and non-Chinese Daoists living in harmony and equality and enjoying the limited government and lenient punishments associated with Daoist rule. Here we have an example in Chinese history of "non-Chinese" Daoists, members of the Ba ethnic minority, endeavoring to create and preserve a Celestial Masters Daoist community.

The Yao, also distinguished as Miao-Yao and Hmong-Mien, is another minority ethnic group with large numbers of members who converted to Daoism.[46] Traditionally speaking, Yao tribal culture was characterized by slash-and-burn agriculture, upland habitation, and widespread migratory patterns.[47] People of Yao ethnic identity have lived in the southern Chinese provinces of Fujian, Hunan, Guangdong, Guangxi, and

Yunnan. They eventually migrated to Vietnam, Laos, and Thailand, probably in the thirteenth century, where they continue to form a segment of those societies. The Yao have their own non-Sinitic (possibly Sino-Tibetan) language, but, similar to pre-modern Japanese, Korean, and Vietnamese, they utilize Chinese script as the primary form of written language. Extant sources and current research suggest that large numbers of Yao most likely began converting to Daoism during the Southern Song dynasty (1127–1279). With the defeat of the Northern Song by the Jurchens, the Song imperial court and masses of northern Chinese migrated to Hangzhou in Zhejiang province. There they came in direct contact with the Yao and other indigenous peoples living in southern China.[48] In this context, Daoism, specifically as expressed by Daoist ritual masters and communities in the newly codified "orthodox rites of Celestial Heart" (*tianxin zhengfa*),[49] formed part of the dominant Chinese state, wherein it served as a means by which to assimilate and "civilize" non-Chinese peoples (i.e., Sinification).[50] According to Michel Strickmann's state-centered perspective,

> T'ien-hsin cheng-fa [Tianxin zhengfa] priests worked as ambulant missionaries, bringing their exorcistic and therapeutic rituals directly into the homes of the common people. There is evidence that they received official support.... Several magistrates who were initiated into the movement...made use of T'ien-hsin rites in the course of their official duties: pacifying their district, reducing epidemics, and guaranteeing the harvest.[51]

In terms of the Yao's own motivations for conversion, little research has been done to date. Many accounts, following a fairly conventional anthropological and sociological perspective wherein the Yao are seen as passive recipients rather than active agents, fail to consider the Yao's own views on Daoism and their own process of "Yaoicization" of Daoism. That is, the Yao did not simply become Sinicized or Daoicized.

One of the most interesting and distinctive characteristics of "Yao Daoism," especially as expressed among contemporary Yao communities in Laos, Thailand, and Vietnam,[52] is its social organization. The Yao maintain a universal Daoist priesthood, with every member passing through successive levels of ordination with corresponding Daoist spirit registers (*lu*). Social standing within Yao society is based on one's position in the religious community. The Yao situation is particularly noteworthy because identity formation and social standing are directly correlated to Daoist religious adherence and affiliation. To be a respected and senior member of Yao society is to be a higher-level Daoist ordinand. Here we see a context of conversion and adaptation wherein certain Yao communities have become "more Daoist" than their indigenous Chinese counterparts. While the Yao have, of course, adapted and modified Daoist beliefs and practices to their own cultural concerns, "it is still remarkable that they have maintained a non-Chinese society over an extended period of time based upon the strictures and beliefs of a distinctively Chinese religion."[53]

The final example of domestic conversion to Daoism that I would like to present involves the Quanzhen (Complete Perfection) movement. Composed of the nominal founder Wang Chongyang (1113–1170) and his first-generation disciples, Quanzhen began as a small eremitic community in eastern Shandong that eventually transformed into a regional religious movement and subsequent monastic order.[54] One dimension of conversion centers on the lives of the first-generation adepts and on the relationship between Wang and his disciples. Quanzhen sources tell us that Wang Chongyang only became fully committed to a Daoist religious path after a series of mystical experiences, specifically with immortals or spirit beings. That is, from a Quanzhen perspective, Quanzhen originates in the founder's encounter with and instruction under immortals and in his subsequent commitment to Daoist ascetic and alchemical training. As a spiritual teacher, Wang Chongyang is remembered as strict and demanding, with very high expectations concerning committed and sustained practice. Requiring abstinence from the Four Hindrances (alcohol, sex, wealth, and anger) and dedicated self-cultivation for lineage affiliation, Wang exercised discernment concerning potential adherents:

> Because he frequently manifested his divine extraordinariness (*shenyi*), people of the east [Shandong] followed him. He forged and purified those who were authentic and reliable, and excluded and purged those who were hollow and false. Refining them a hundred times, he punished and angrily insulted them. The unworthy fled.[55]

Among Wang's "methods of refinement" concerning potential converts, perhaps the most famous is his "dividing pears" (*fenli*). According to the preface to the *Fenli shihua ji* (Anthology of Ten Conversions through Dividing Pears; DZ 1155), Wang sent poems accompanied with a divided pear (*fenli*) to Ma Danyang and Sun Buer every ten days. The purpose of this gesture was to convince the couple to divorce, with the Chinese phrase "divided pear" also being a pun on *fenli* ("separation" or "division"). While Wang Chongyang's personal dedication and conviction probably played some role in Ma's eventual conversion, it seems that it was other anomalous experiences that were especially influential. According to the *Jinlian ji* (Record of the Golden Lotus; DZ 173, 5.9b), "[Wang Chongyang] would send out his spirit and enter their [Ma and Sun's] dreams in various kinds of transformative manifestations (*bianxian*). He frightened them through [visions of] the Earth Prison (*diyu*) and enticed them through [visions of] the Celestial Hall (*tiantang*)."[56] Similarly, a stele inscription preserved in the *Ganshui lu* (Record of Ganshui; DZ 973, 1.2b–10a) contains the following account:

> [Wang Chongyang] was locked in the Hermitage of Complete Perfection for one hundred days transforming himself. Sometimes he ate and sometimes he refrained from eating.... [One night] Master Ma was sleeping on the second floor of his private residence. The doors and windows were all locked. Perfected [Chongyang] arrived during the night to have a face-to-face conversation. Ma did not know where he came from. [Later] a person wanted to draw his [Wang's] spirit. [However,] his left eye revolved to the right, while his right eye revolved to the left. At various moments he appeared as old and young, fat and skinny, yellow and vermilion, as well as azure and white. His form and appearance had no stability.[57]

Among Wang's early formal disciples and lay supporters, there were a variety of motivations for conversion. One aspect was the movement's local connections: many of Wang's early disciples were prominent members of eastern Shandong's, specifically Muping's, aristocracy and social elite. A more influential element was the leader's personal charisma and level of spiritual cultivation. However, if we follow standard hagiographical accounts, many people converted due to the numinous abilities (Skt.: *siddhi*; Chn.: *shentong*) of Wang and his direct disciples. This included the ability to send out a yang-spirit, formed through alchemical praxis that could enter people's dreams and manifest in distant places. There were spiritual and mystical, in addition to socio-political, dimensions of religious conversion to Quanzhen.

In addition to formal disciples, those who embraced a renunciant and monastic life, we know that large numbers of people in Shandong became lay followers and supporters. During the years of 1168 and 1169, Wang and his disciples established five religious associations throughout the Shandong peninsula. Although it is generally unclear who initiated such establishments, how many people participated, what types of activities occurred, and what, if any, lasting influence they had on the later development of Quanzhen as a formal monastic order, these meeting halls provided a communal context for the early Quanzhen adepts, a place for potential adherents to become familiar with Quanzhen views and practices, and an opportunity for lay participation and involvement. With respect to the number of lay adherents and patrons, there is some fragmentary information. One source informs us that the Pingdeng hui (Association of Equal Rank) may have had as many as one thousand members.[58] In the formative phase of the movement, lay members of Quanzhen probably numbered in the thousands. By establishing these associations, Wang created a context where those with less resolve and fortitude could gain basic instruction and spiritual benefits. The associations also were places were charitable deeds and communal ritual was carried out[59] and where basic forms of meditation, emphasizing clarity (*qing*) and stillness (*jing*), were taught. There is also substantial evidence that the Quanzhen incorporation and modification of the "cult of Lü Dongbin" contributed to the increased institutional success of the movement; in addition to religious motivations, there were socioeconomic factors involved in singling out Lü for veneration and inclusion in an emerging Quanzhen pantheon.[60] Thus, the motivations for lay conversion, adherence, and patronage were diverse, and that diversity only increased after Chinnggis Qan (Genghis Kahn; ca. 1162–1227; r. 1206–1227) granted imperial recognition to Qiu Changchun, the third patriarch and national leader, and the Quanzhen monastic order in 1223.

FOREIGN CONVERSION TO DAOISM

The formation and growth of a global Daoist community is largely the result of socio-political developments in the early to middle twentieth century, specifically the Chinese Communist revolution and rise of the secular nation-state of the People's Republic of China (PRC) in 1949. In this way, the globalization of Daoism parallels that of Tibetan Buddhism. In the case of Daoism, again paralleling the dissemination of other Asian religions throughout the world, this has occurred through Chinese immigrant teachers, their foreign converts who become disciples and eventual spiritual heirs, as well as foreigners who trained in China and Taiwan and subsequently established communities in their home countries. Jan Nattier has noted a similar pattern in American Buddhism, which she categorizes in terms of "import Buddhism" (demand-driven transmission), "export Buddhism" (supply-driven transmission), and "baggage Buddhism" (non-missionary immigrant adherents).[61]

When discussing the globalization of Daoism, specifically with respect to foreign conversion, it is vital to identify defining characteristics. One key consideration involves employing an informed, accurate, and sophisticated understanding of the religious tradition that is Daoism. This is especially important in the case of Daoism, as there is much confusion among non-specialists, including many self-identified Daoist adherents and teachers.[62] Most prominent is the mistaken belief that there is a non-religious pre-modern form of Daoism. In terms of the emergence of a "trans-Chinese" Daoism, or at least the presence of Daoists and Daoist communities outside of mainland China, I would suggest that a significant aspect involves cultural adaptation, assimilation, and modification. Here, Daoism becomes a transnational, multicultural, and multiethnic religious tradition. Paralleling the emergence of new schools of Buddhism in medieval China (e.g., Chan and Tiantai), we are witnessing a corresponding transformation of Daoism throughout the contemporary world. In addition, it is not enough to note the presence or influence of certain "Daoist ideas" on foreign cultures.[63] I suggest that additional conditions must be met. On the most basic level, these include the following: (1) the presence of ordained clergy members, namely, Daoist monastics or priests, (2) the formation and development of a community of adherents, and (3) commitment to Daoist doctrines and practices on the part of adherents, including some understanding of Daoist scriptures. That is, religious affiliation presupposes religious literacy, commitment, and communal involvement. The extent to which Daoism as an intact religion, one which would be recognizable to and recognized by Chinese Daoists, is present in countries beyond the traditional Chinese cultural sphere of influence is directly connected to the establishment of viable institutions. The relative youth of Daoism as a global religion is evidenced by the almost complete absence of Daoist temples, monasteries, and sacred sites outside of mainland China, Hong Kong, and Taiwan.

Prior to the twentieth century, Daoism was largely contained within the boundaries of China. As far as current research goes, and it should be mentioned that much work remains to be done, Daoism was never established as a viable religious tradition in the larger Chinese cultural sphere, which includes Japan, Korea, and northern Vietnam. Within Japan and Korea in particular, Chinese schools of Buddhism and Confucianism were much more influential. Our understanding of foreign conversion to Daoism is complicated by the dearth of research on this important topic. Here, I provide some information on Hong Kong, Korea, and Japan. This is followed by a brief discussion of contemporary global Daoism.

The establishment of Daoist communities and institutions in Hong Kong was largely an extension of popular spirit-writing cults and charitable societies in southern China during the late Qing dynasty (1644–1911).[64] Many of the former specifically focused on mediumistic activity related to Lü Dongbin ("Ancestor Lü"), a famous Tang dynasty immortal and wonder-worker identified as the patriarch of certain internal alchemy lineages. For some reason, these groups often identified themselves as Longmen (Dragon Gate), a lineage of the Quanzhen (Complete Perfection) monastic order. However, if one believes the internal histories of certain southern families, it seems that there were also formal Longmen temples in southern China whose affiliates eventually migrated to Hong Kong. According to the *Luofu zhinan* (Guide to Luofu), ordained Longmen priests first established temples in Guangdong in the late seventeenth century,[65] but the actual relationship between these temples and the Daoist temples in Hong Kong remains unclear.[66] In any case, major Daoist temples and organizations were established in Hong Kong from the late nineteenth through the middle of the twentieth century.[67]

These organizations include both ordained, married clergy as well as a much larger lay community. Hong Kong Daoism has developed its own unique characteristics and forms of ritual activities, including newer forms of Daoist liturgical practice. It seems that the dissemination and growth of Daoism among southern Chinese groups who would eventually migrate to Hong Kong was largely due to two major factors. First, in the case of Lüzu cultic activity and temples, individuals were given insights into an unpredictable future through spirit-writing sessions. In addition, many people reported supernatural and healing experiences. Such events no doubt proved appealing to potential converts. Second, in the case of charitable societies, people were given assistance in times of need. Combined together, one finds a context where popular devotionalism and social solidarity flourished. Such patterns of community involvement continue in the contemporary Hong Kong Daoist emphasis on services for departed ancestors.

Although conversion to Confucianism and Buddhism was most common throughout East Asia, we do have some evidence of a Daoist presence in these countries during different moments of Chinese history. Among the larger Chinese cultural sphere, namely, Japan, Korea, and northern Vietnam,[68] Korea received the greatest degree of transmission and acceptance of Daoism. Current research indicates that Daoism was first introduced into Korea when Emperor Gaozu (r. 618–626) of the Tang dynasty sent Chinese Daoist priests and a statue of a Celestial Worthy to the kingdom of Koguryŏ in 624 and had priests read the *Daode jing* before the Korean king and court.[69] The first Daoist temple, named Bokwŏn kung (Palace of the Auspicious Source) was built at the beginning of the twelfth century under the Koryŏ dynasty (918–1392). It housed statues of the Sanqing (Three Purities) and was tended to by more than ten white-robed Korean Daoist priests.[70]

It appears that some form of institutionalized Daoism, however small, existed in Korea until the Chosŏn dynasty (1392–1910), which adopted Confucianism as state ideology. The then-extant fifteen officially recognized sites for Daoist offerings and rites that had been established during the Koryŏ dynasty were almost all abolished.[71] Early Korean involvement with Daoist beliefs and practices primarily centered on the court; Daoist priests performed rituals to protect the state on behalf of the court and royal family. With the decline of Daoist state ritual under the Chosŏn dynasty, Korean intellectuals became more interested in nourishing life (*yangsheng*) and internal alchemy (*neidan*) practices. Around the fifteenth or sixteenth century, such interest grew into the formation of a specifically Korean *neidan* school, namely the Haedong sŏnp'a (Korean Immortal Lineage).[72] Although the motivations behind and degree of Korean conversion during this period is currently unknown, Daoist internal alchemy practice became one dimension of Korean religious culture. For example, the contemporary group Kuksŏn to (Way of National Immortals) practices a form of *neidan*-inspired breathing techniques.[73] There is also Sundo (Way of the Immortals), a more recent group founded by Hyunmoon Kim (dates unknown). The movement is present in the United States among groups associated with Hyunmoon Kim[74] as well as with Hyunoong Sunim (dates unknown) of the Sixth Patriarch Zen Center.[75] Both groups are principally rooted in Korean Son (Zen) Buddhism, but Zen meditation is combined with *daoyin* and internal alchemy practice.

In contrast to Korea, Daoism as an intact religious tradition, with ordained clergy and temples, never gained a foothold in Japanese society. Recalling the earlier four dimensions of Daoist transmission and adherence, Japan historically lacked an ordained Daoist clergy, a formal Daoist community, and any viable Daoist institutions. Similarly, as far as current research indicates, no Daoist *jiao* offering or *zhai* purification rituals were ever performed in Japan. It is primarily in the areas of doctrine and practices that one finds Daoist influence on Japanese culture, religion, and society.[76] One major early Japanese folk custom associated with Daoism was the Kōshin cult.[77] First introduced in the ninth century and practiced even in contemporary Japan, the Kōshin cult is based on the belief that the body is inhabited by the Three Death-bringers (*sanshi*). Once in every sixty-day cycle, on the *kōshin* (Chn.: *gengshen*; 57th) day, these biospiritual parasites or worms ascend to the heavens to report a person's transgressions and to receive instructions for punishments, such as sickness, bad fortune, and early death. In order to prevent them from leaving and making their detrimental report, on the eve of the corresponding day people take ritual precautions and attempt to stay awake. The belief is that three such vigils on the Kōshin night will severely weaken the worms. If they are prevented from leaving seven times, they will perish. The individual will, in turn, become free of sickness and bad fortune, and his or her lifespan and happiness will increase.[78] The example of the Kōshin cult reveals one aspect of Daoist influence on Japanese culture; noticeable is a Japanese concern for health, longevity, and good fortune. This example also shows that Daoist conversion and adherence among Japanese people was small to non-existent, but that Daoist beliefs and practices occupied some place in Japanese culture. In addition, it seems that Daoist elements were incorporated in Shinto (Way of the Kami) and Shugendo (Way of Cultivation and Experiential Confirmation),[79] with the latter also associated with the Yamabushi mountain hermits.

With respect to the larger Chinese cultural sphere, specifically conversion to Daoism outside of mainland China, we may thus conclude that large-scale conversion and adherence was non-existent outside of Hong Kong and Taiwan. Korea had the greatest number of "non-Chinese" converts and adherents, but they still represented a very small segment of the larger Korean population. Nonetheless, there were ordained Korean Daoist priests who inhabited Korean Daoist temples until the Chosŏn dynasty. In contrast, Japanese society lacked formal Daoist converts or adherents; Daoist influence on Japanese culture was largely in the form of specific beliefs and practices.

As mentioned, the formation and growth of a global Daoist community, a transnational, multiethnic, and multicultural community, is largely the result of socio-political developments in the early to middle twentieth century, specifically the Chinese Communist revolution and rise of the secular nation-state of the People's Republic of China (PRC) in 1949. That is, modern political events in mainland China have led to the globalization of Daoism. There are now a variety of national Daoist organizations, including the Belgian Taoist Association (http://www.taoiststudies.org), Brazilian Taoist Association (http://www.taoismo.org.br), British Taoist Association (http://www.tao-ists.co.uk), French Taoist Association (http://www.aftao.org), Singapore Taoist Mission (http://www.taoism.org.sg), Swiss Taoist Association (http://www.ataos.populus.ch), and so forth. The matter is complicated by a number of factors, not the least of which is that the contemporary designation of a national "Daoist association" (*daojiao xiehui*) technically indicates elected leaders who represent the entire tradition in a given country. For most of these organizations, such conditions are not met. In the case of the United States, a number of individuals, most of whom have no formal standing in the Daoist religious tradition, have attempted to form such a nominal organization without the requisite community outreach. We also have yet to see the establishment of Daoist temples and monasteries inhabited by a distinctively Daoist community in the West.

In the remaining pages, I will focus on Daoist adherence and conversion in North America, as this is the area with which I am most familiar.[80] Such a study faces a variety of challenges. One of the most representative issues involves popular constructions of Daoism. I will not address these in detail here.[81] Briefly stated, there is a fundamental ignorance about the religious tradition that is Daoism. This is so much the case that many self-identified American "Daoists" deny that Daoism is a religious tradition. Most of these individuals are part of a New Religious Movement (NRM) best categorized as "Popular Western Taoism" (PWT), with "Taoism" pronounced with a hard "t" sound.[82] In the present context, such individuals are neither converts nor adherents. They are best understood, following Thomas Tweed's interpretative framework,[83] as sympathizers. Here I will focus on insights gleaned from my ethnographic research on Daoism in North America, including my involvement with a variety of communities as a participant-observer. I will concentrate on individuals and communities who fulfill three necessary requirements: (1) they accept the historical fact of Daoism as an indigenous Chinese religion; (2) they have some formal connection with that tradition, either through lineage, ordination, or training; and (3) they understand Daoist adherence as a religious path.[84] Needless to say, these conditions are almost completely absent among members of the larger American population who claim some interest or affiliation with Daoism. In this respect, the current state of American Daoism is comparable to that of Zen Buddhism in the 1960s and 1970s.

In studying Daoism in North America, one encounters the whole spectrum of transmission, adaptation, and appropriation. The American Daoist community is largely composed of Chinese immigrant teachers, Chinese immigrants, ethnic Chinese adherents, and Euro-American converts. The latter include a few ordained Daoist priests with formal lineage affiliation, some of whom studied and received ordination in China.[85] The majority of potential converts to Daoism in the United States are interested in health and longevity techniques or "Daoist philosophy." Again, the matter is complicated by the misidentification of such things as Qigong (Ch'i-kung), Taiji quan (T'ai-chi ch'üan), Traditional Chinese Medicine (TCM), the *Yijing* (Classic of Changes), and yin-yang cosmology as "Daoist." Few individuals actually think of themselves as "converting to Daoism." Rather, Daoism is conceptualized as a "way of life" or a "philosophy of living."

In the case of individuals who actually consider themselves as "Daoist converts" and "Daoist adherents," there are various motivations. Some individuals began an active search for "alternative spirituality" and "personal healing" after a catastrophic illness or injury. Their interest in Daoism developed out of personal trauma, and in Daoism they found healing and rejuvenation. Similarly, one finds many people who want to recover or maintain optimal health. These types of converts represent the largest segment of the American Daoist community, and there is much overlap with the larger phenomenon of American health and fitness movements. Other converts had distinctive mystical experiences that eventually led them to seek out and find Daoist teachers and communities. These mystical experiences include both unitive and relational types of experiences. Some individuals have had feelings of oneness with nature and the cosmos, which they later identified as "union with the Dao." Others have encountered specific Daoist gods and immortals through visionary and auditory experiences. This latter group is among the most fascinating, as most individuals did not know anything about Daoism when the event occurred. I have elsewhere referred to this as "trans-tradition mystical experience."[86] One example is a woman who woke up in the middle of the night to see a spirit-being standing at the base of her bed. The being had the appearance of a refined Chinese gentleman who was dressed in traditional robes and carried a fly whisk. There was a corresponding subtle communication that the woman needed to change her life. Somewhat bewildered, the woman spent many years searching for an explanation. She eventually ended up at a branch of the Hong Kong-based Ching Chung Taoist Association (Ching Chung Koon) in Australia. After she described her experience, the resident monks showed her a picture of Lü Dongbin and asked if he was the being whom she encountered. It was indeed. From that moment forward, she became a devout lay Daoist. Similar mystical experiences have led others to seek out formal training as Daoist priests. When I discussed such events with contemporary Daoist monastics in mainland China, they often categorized them as instances of "predestined affinity" (*yuanfen*) or as evidence that such people were Daoists in a former existence (*sushi*). Still other converts find an affinity with some aspect of Daoism. Common interests include

Daoist reverence for body and place, Daoist literature, and Daoist philosophy. As one would expect in a country characterized by individualism, the motivations behind Daoist conversion and adherence are quite diverse. They often differ significantly from earlier patterns in Chinese history that have been described above.

WAYS TO AFFILIATION

The history of Daoist conversion and adherence reveals complex and multifaceted patterns. Although additional research needs to be done, among indigenous Chinese converts those patterns of conversion have centered on personal affinity and social solidarity, as well as eschatological and soteriological promises. They have involved charismatic teachers and leaders, regional communities, mystical experiences, revelations, and so forth. Conversion is, in turn, connected with religious affiliation and identity. In the case of Daoism, adherence has most frequently centered on initiation, ordination, and lineage affiliation. As Daoist monastic manuals, precept texts, and ritual texts indicate, the ethical requirements, expectations, and types of adherence become increasingly strict as one progresses through the levels of Daoist commitment and participation. This is perhaps most clearly expressed in the late medieval Daoist ordination system.

In the case of "non-Chinese" and foreign converts, the Daoist religious tradition has been intricately tied to larger Chinese cultural values and perspectives. As the above discussion indicates, Daoism became one agent in a larger pattern of Sinification throughout East Asia, from the Ba and Yao within the geographical borders of China to people of Korean and Japanese descent in their own countries. Major influences on and motivations behind conversion included eschatological and soteriological aspirations, socioeconomic prosperity, personal health and fortune, and Sinitic cultural hegemony. Interesting in terms of demographics and the categorization of Daoism as the "indigenous higher religion of China," it seems that the earliest Daoist religious communities were multicultural and multiethnic. Research on the ways in which "non-Chinese" traditions were incorporated into Daoism and the ways in which Daoism became transformed by non-Chinese converts and adherents is a promising and important topic.

With the contemporary globalization of Daoism, the traditional connection between Daoism and Chinese culture becomes more tenuous. Contemporary Daoism, paralleling earlier Chinese adaptations of Buddhism, is being transmitted, adapted, and appropriated in varying degrees throughout the modern world. The emergence of an international Daoist community, a community that is transnational, multiethnic, and multicultural, begs the question of what it means to be a Daoist. How have Daoists understood the requirements and expectations of conversion and affiliation? How have Daoists set parameters for participation in their tradition? Here the issue of recognizability and family resemblance is central, including the germane historical question concerning origins and influences. It also requires researchers to reflect on the difficult topic of who participates in and represents the Daoist community. In the case of modern Daoism, self-identification proves insufficient because of modern constructions with roots in colonialist, missionary, and Orientalist legacies.

Notes

1. Immortals (*xianren*), also translated as "transcendents," and the Perfected (*zhenren*) are the primary religious ideals in organized Daoism, especially within the context of external alchemy (*waidan*) and internal alchemy (*neidan*). From this perspective, Immortals and Perfected are individuals who have completed a process of self-divinization.

2. The present discussion does not address gender issues in Daoist conversion. The most famous example of female conversion to Daoism involves two Tang dynasty princesses, but female religious leaders and community members have occupied a central place and made major contributions to the tradition. See Charles Benn, *The Cavern Mystery Transmission: A Taoist Ordination Rite of A.D. 711* (Honolulu: University of Hawaii Press, 1991); Catherine Despeux and Livia Kohn, *Women in Daoism* (Cambridge, MA: Three Pines Press, 2003); Suzanne Cahill, *Divine Traces of the Daoist Sisterhood: Records of the Assembled Transcendents of the Fortified Walled City* (Cambridge, MA: Three Pines Press, 2006).

3. Lewis Rambo and Charles E. Farhadian, "Conversion," in *Encyclopedia of Religion*, rev. ed., ed. Lindsay Jones, 3: 1969–1974 (Detroit: Macmillan Reference, 2005).

4. Ibid.

5. In their entry in the revised *Encyclopedia of Religion*, Rambo and Farhadian provide brief summaries of each approach utilized in "conversion studies." For additional clarification, see Andrew Buckser and Stephen Glazier, eds., *The Anthropology of Conversion* (Lanham, MD: Rowman & Littlefield Publishers, 2003); Donald Gelpi, *The Conversion Experience* (New York: Paulist Press, 1998); Christopher Lamb and M. Darol Bryant, eds., *Religious Conversion: Contemporary Practices and Controversies* (London: Continuum, 1999); H. Newton Malony and Samuel Southard, eds., *Handbook of Religious Conversion* (Birmingham, AL: Religious Education Press, 1992); Lewis Rambo, *Understanding Religious Conversion* (New Haven: Yale University Press, 1993); Lewis Rambo, "Theories of Conversion," *Social Compass* 46, no. 3 (1999): 259–271; Chana Ullman, *The Transformed Self: The Psychology of Religious Conversion* (New York: Springer, 1989).

6. I use "soteriology" and "theology" as comparative categories. "Soteriology" refers to actualization, liberation, perfection, realization, salvation, or however religious adherents define the ultimate goal of a religious system. "Theology" refers to "discourse on the sacred," with "sacred" being a place-holder for that which a given individual or community identifies as ultimately real. Primary cross-cultural theologies include animistic, monistic, monotheistic, panenhenic, panentheistic, pantheistic, and polytheistic. We also need to make a distinction among descriptive, historical, and normative theological discourse.

7. See Arthur Wright, *Buddhism in Chinese History* (Stanford, CA: Stanford University Press, 1959); Kenneth Ch'en, *Buddhism in China* (Princeton: Princeton University Press, 1972); Robert H. Sharf, *Coming to Terms with Chinese Buddhism* (Honolulu: University of Hawaii Press, 2002).

8. David E. Mungello, *Curious Land: Jesuit Accommodation and the Origins of Sinology* (Honolulu: University of Hawaii Press, 1989); David E. Mungello, *The Great Encounter of China and the West, 1500–1800* (Lanham, MD: Rowman & Littlefield Publishers, 2005); Norman Girardot, *The Victorian Translation of China: James Legge's Oriental Pilgrimage* (Berkeley and Los Angeles: University of California Press, 2002); Eric Reinders, *Borrowed Gods and Foreign Bodies: Christian Missionaries Imagine Chinese Religion* (Berkeley and Los Angeles: University of California Press, 2004); Matthew Brockey, *Journey to the East: The Jesuit Mission to China, 1579–1724* (Cambridge, MA: Harvard University Press, 2007).

9. To what extent this can be considered "conversion" and the ways in which particular Chinese "converts" understood their religious identity deserve further research.

10. See Denis Twitchett and Michael Loewe, eds., *The Cambridge History of China*: vol. 1, *The Ch'in and Han Empires* (Cambridge: Cambridge University Press, 1986); Michael Loewe and Edward Shaughnessy, eds., *The Cambridge History of Ancient China: From the Origins of Civilization to 221 BC* (Cambridge: Cambridge University Press, 1999).

11. See David E. Mungello, ed., *The Chinese Rites Controversy: Its History and Meaning* (Nettetal, Germany: Steyler Verlag, 1995); Mungello, *The Great Encounter of China and the West*.

12. Interestingly, this even included the promotion of gods in the celestial bureaucracy. See Valerie Hansen, *Changing Gods in Medieval China, 1127–1276* (Princeton: Princeton University Press, 1990); James Watson, "Standardizing the Gods: The Promotion of T'ien-hou ('Empress of Heaven') along the South China Coast," in *Popular Culture in Late Imperial China*, ed. David Johnson et al. (Berkeley and Los Angeles: University of California Press, 1985), 292–324.

13. See Livia Kohn, *Laughing at the Tao: Debates among Buddhists and Taoists in Medieval China* (Princeton: Princeton University Press, 1995); Livia Kohn, *God of the Dao: Lord Lao in History and Myth* (Ann Arbor: Center for Chinese Studies, University of Michigan, 1998), 275–289.

14. The history and defining characteristics of the *huahu* theory are much more complex than this brief summary indicates. For some readily available discussions, see Erik Zürcher, *The Buddhist Conquest of China* (Leiden: Brill, 1959), 288–320.

15. DH refers to the Dunhuang manuscripts, while DZ refers to the Ming-dynasty *Daozang* (Daoist Canon). Catalogue numbers for Daoist textual collections follow Louis Komjathy, *Title Index to Daoist Collections* (Cambridge, MA: Three Pines Press, 2002), with DZ numbers paralleling those of Kristofer Schipper et al. Unless otherwise indicated, all translations are my own.

16. See Florian Reiter, *Leben und Wirken Lao-Tzu's in Schrift und Bild: Lao-chün pa-shih-i-hua t'u-shuo* (Würzburg: Königshausen & Neumann, 1990).

17. On the Buddho-Daoist debates, see Kohn, *Laughing at the Tao*. Although opposition and contention was one form of interaction between Buddhists and Daoists, it was clearly not the only one. For additional insights on this complex historical issue, see Zürcher, *Buddhist Conquest*; Erik Zürcher, "Buddhist Influence on Early Taoism," *T'oung Pao* 66 (1980): 84–147; Stephen Bokenkamp, *Ancestors and Anxiety: Daoism and the Birth of Rebirth in China* (Berkeley and Los Angeles: University of California Press, 2007); Christine Mollier, *Buddhism and Taoism Face to Face: Scripture, Ritual, and Iconographic Exchange in Medieval China* (Honolulu: University of Hawaii Press, 2008).

18. Compare Terry Kleeman, "Ethnic Identity and Daoist Identity in Traditional China," in *Daoist Identity: History, Lineage, and Ritual*, ed. Livia Kohn and Harold Roth (Honolulu: University of Hawaii Press, 2002), 31.

19. *Laojun jinglü*, DZ 786, 1a.

20. See Louis Komjathy, *Handbooks for Daoist Practice*, Vol. 5 (Hong Kong: Yuen Yuen Institute, 2008).

21. For a classical and seminal Daoist perspective on the importance of "nonknowing" (*wuzhi*) and philosophical openness, see chapter 2 of the fourth-century B.C.E. *Zhuangzi* (Book of Master Zhuang).

22. See Franciscus Verellen, "The Beyond Within: Grotto-Heavens (*Dongtian*) in Taoist Ritual and Cosmology," *Cahiers d'Extrême-Asie* 8 (1995): 265–290; Thomas Hahn, "Daoist Sacred Sites," in *Daoism Handbook*, ed. Livia Kohn (Leiden: Brill, 2000), 683–708.

23. There is, of course, another Daoist reading of places in which any natural place is a manifestation of the Dao and thus Daoist temples and altars can be built anywhere.

24. See Stephen Bokenkamp, *Early Daoist Scriptures* (Berkeley and Los Angeles: University of California Press, 1997).

25. Barbara Hendrischke, *The Scripture on Great Peace: The Taiping jing and the Beginnings of Daoism* (Berkeley and Los Angeles: University of California Press, 2007).

26. See Jonathan D. Spence, *God's Chinese Son* (New York: Norton, 1996).

27. See Terry Kleeman, *Great Perfection: Religion and Ethnicity in a Chinese Millennial Kingdom* (Honolulu: University of Hawaii Press, 1998), 61–85; Barbara Hendrischke, "Early Daoist Movements," in *Daoism Handbook*, ed. Livia Kohn (Leiden: Brill, 2000), 134–164.

28. See Livia Kohn, *Cosmos and Community: The Ethical Dimension of Daoism* (Cambridge, MA: Three Pines Press, 2004).

29. See Livia Kohn, *Monastic Life in Medieval Daoism* (Honolulu: University of Hawaii Press, 2003); Kohn, *Cosmos and Community*.

30. See Aat Vervoorn, *Men of the Cliffs and Caves: The Development of the Chinese Eremitic Tradition to the End of the Han Dynasty* (Hong Kong: Chinese University Press, 1990); Alan Berkowitz, *Patterns of Disengagement: The Practice and Portrayal of Reclusion in Early Medieval China* (Stanford, CA: Stanford University Press, 2000).

31. See Stephan Peter Bumbacher, *Fragments of the Daoxue zhuan* (Frankfurt: Peter Lang, 2000); Robert Ford Campany, *To Live as Long as Heaven and Earth: A Translation and Study of Ge Hong's Traditions of Divine Transcendents* (Berkeley and Los Angeles: University of California Press, 2002).

32. Throughout Chinese history, various minority groups (Di, Hu, Man, Yi, etc.), often identified by the ethnic majority and ruling elite as "barbarians," were seen as outside of the dominant culture, as "others." In modern Communist China, there has been a tendency to read over this history and to imagine a unified China wherein the category "Chinese" includes minority groups such as these, including Tibetans. Today, the Chinese government officially recognizes fifty-five minority ethnic groups ("non-Chinese peoples") who speak over 150 distinct languages and worship a variety of spirits and gods.

33. Kleeman, *Great Perfection*.

34. Ibid., 68.

35. See Bokenkamp, *Early Daoist Scriptures*, 29–77; Kleeman, *Great Perfection*, 61–85; Hendrischke, "Early Daoist Movements."

36. *Nüqing guilü*, DZ 790, 5.1a; adapted from Kleeman, *Great Perfection*, 74.

37. Kleeman, *Great Perfection*, 25–46.

38. Kleeman, "Ethnic Identity and Daoist Identity," 25.

39. Ibid., 26.

40. Ibid., 27–28; see also Kleeman, *Great Perfection*, 74–76.

41. Kleeman, "Ethnic Identity and Daoist Identity," 28.

42. Kleeman, *Great Perfection*.

43. Ibid., 77.

44. Ibid., 80–84, 98; Kleeman, "Ethnic Identity and Religious Identity," 29–30.

45. Kleeman, *Great Perfection*, 84–85.

46. On the Yao, see Michel Strickmann, "The Tao among the Yao: Taoism and the Sinification of the South," in *Rekishi ni okeru minshu to bunka* (Tokyo: Kokusho kankōkai, 1982), 23–30; Jacques Lemoine, *Yao Ceremonial Paintings* (Bangkok: White Lotus, 1982); Jess Pourret, *The Yao: The Mien and Mun Yao in China, Vietnam, Laos and Thailand* (Bangkok: River Books, 2002); Eli Alberts, *A History of Daoism and the Yao People of South China* (Youngstown, NY: Cambria Press, 2006). See also the website of Barend ter Haar, http://website.leidenuniv.nl/~haarbjter/yao.htm.

47. Alberts, *A History of Daoism*, 1.

48. Lemoine, *Yao Ceremonial Paintings*, 22; Alberts, *A History of Daoism*, 125.

49. Tianxin was one of a number of new Daoist ritual lineages that became prominent during the later Song dynasty. See Judith Boltz, *A Survey of Taoist Literature: Tenth to Seventeenth Centuries* (Berkeley and Los Angeles: University of California, Institute of East Asian Studies, 1987).

50. For a brief overview, see Alberts, *A History of Daoism*, 14–16, 118–121.

51. Strickmann, "The Tao among the Yao," 26, 28.

52. See Lemoine, *Yao Ceremonial Paintings*; Pourret, *The Yao*; Alberts, *A History of Daoism*.

53. Kleeman, "Ethnic Identity and Daoist Identity," 33.

54. The present discussion is based on Louis Komjathy, *Cultivating Perfection: Mysticism and Self-transformation in Early Quanzhen Daoism* (Leiden: Brill, 2007).

55. *Ganshui lu*, DZ 973, 1.10b; Komjathy, *Cultivating Perfection*, 45.

56. In the *Panxi ji* (DZ 1159, 3.3a), Qiu Changchun writes, "[Wang Chongyang] sent out his spirit and entered dreams, and people became frightened."

57. *Ganshui lu*, DZ 973, 1.5a; cf. *Jinlian xiangzhuan*, DZ 174, 21b; translated in Komjathy, *Cultivating Perfection*, 224.

58. *Lishi tongjian xubian*, DZ 297, 1.6a; Hachiya Kunio, *Kindai dōkyō no kenkyū—O Chōyō to Ba Tanyō* (Tokyo: Tōkyō daigaku Tōyō bunka kenkyūjo hōkoku, 1992), 132; Stephen Eskildsen, *The Teachings and Practices of the Early Quanzhen Taoist Masters* (Albany: State University of New York Press, 2004), 10.

59. See Eskildsen, *Teachings and Practices*, 155–193.

60. See Paul Katz, *Images of the Immortal: The Cult of Lü Dongbin at the Palace of Eternal Joy* (Honolulu: University of Hawaii Press, 1999).

61. Jan, Nattier, "Who Is a Buddhist? Charting the Landscape of Buddhist America," in *The Faces of Buddhism in America*, ed. Charles Prebish and Kenneth Tanaka (Berkeley and Los Angeles: University of California Press, 1998), 188–190.

62. For reliable general accounts of Daoism, see Livia Kohn, ed., *Daoism Handbook* (Leiden: Brill, 2000); Livia Kohn, *Daoism and Chinese Culture* (Cambridge, MA: Three Pines Press, 2001); James Miller, *Daoism: A Short Introduction* (Oxford: Oneworld, 2003); Russell Kirkland, *Taoism: The Enduring Tradition* (London: Routledge, 2004); Fabrizio Pregadio, ed., *The Encyclopedia of Taoism* (London: Routledge, 2008); Komjathy, *Handbooks for Daoist Practice*.

63. Compare J. J. Clarke, *The Tao of the West* (London: Routledge, 2000).

64. See Mori Yuria, "Identity and Lineage: The *Taiyi jinhua zongzhi* and the Spirit-writing Cult of Patriarch Lü in Qing China," in *Daoist Identity: History, Lineage, and Ritual*, ed. Livia Kohn and Harold Roth (Honolulu: University of Hawaii Press, 2002), 165–184; Shiga Ichiko, "Manifestations of Lüzu in Modern Guangdong and Hong Kong: The Rise and Growth of Spirit-writing Cults," in Kohn and Roth, *Daoist Identity*, 185–209; Bartholomew P. M. Tsui, *Taoist Tradition and Change: The Story of the Complete Perfection Sect in Hong Kong* (Hong Kong: Hong Kong Christian Study Center on Chinese Religion and Culture, 1991).

65. Tsui, *Taoist Tradition and Change*, 66–70.

66. See Shiga, "Manifestations of Lüzu."

67. See Tsui, *Taoist Tradition and Change*; You Zian, ed., *Daofeng bainian: Xianggang daojiao yu daoguan* (Hong Kong: Fung Ying Seen Foon, 2002); Li Zhitian et al., eds., *Xianggang daotang keyi lishi yu chuancheng* (Hong Kong: Zhonghua shuju, 2007). Hong Kong Daoism is understudied at present, especially in terms of Western language publications. Much more attention has been given to Taiwanese Daoism due to its nominal connection with the early Celestial Masters and its relative accessibility in the modern period.

68. Research on Daoism in Vietnam, apart from the above-mentioned Yao ethnic group, has yet to be conducted in a systematic way. One group that exhibits some Daoist characteristics is Caodai, a modern syncretistic and monotheistic movement. For an adherent perspective, see H. D. Bui and Ngasha Beck, *Caodai: Faith of Unity* (Fayetteville, AR: Emerald Wave. 2000); see also http://www.caodai.org. Members of Caodai see it as a synthesis of Buddhism, Christianity, Confucianism, and Daoism. In terms of the present discussion, the history and characteristics of Daoism in Vietnam are intriguing.

69. Jung Jae-seo, "Daoism in Korea," in *Daoism Handbook*, ed. Livia Kohn (Leiden: Brill, 2000), 794; Miura Kunio, "Taoism in the Korean Peninsula," in *Encyclopedia of Taoism*, ed. Fabrizio Pregadio (London: Routledge, 2008), 190.

70. Miura, "Daoism in the Korean Peninsula," 190.

71. Jung, "Daoism in Korea," 798.

72. Ibid., 799; Miura, "Daoism in the Korean Peninsula," 192.

73. Miura, "Daoism in the Korean Peninsula," 192; cf. Jung, "Daoism in Korea," 802.

74. See http://www.sundo.org.

75. See http://www.zenhall.org.

76. See Masuo Shin'ichiro, "Daoism in Japan," in *Daoism Handbook*, ed. Livia Kohn (Leiden: Brill, 2000), 821–842; Sakade Yoshinobu, "Taoism in Japan," in *Encyclopedia of Taoism*, ed. Fabrizio Pregadio (London: Routledge, 2008), 192–196.

77. See Livia Kohn, "Kōshin: A Taoist Cult in Japan," *Japanese Religions* 18, no. 2 (1993): 113–139 (Part 1); 20, no. 1 (1995): 34–55 (Part 2); 20, no. 2 (1995): 123–142 (Part 3).

78. Masuo, "Daoism in Japan," 835.

79. Ibid., 827–831.

80. See Louis Komjathy, "Tracing the Contours of Daoism in North America," *Nova Religio* 8, no. 2 (Nov. 2004): 5–27; Louis Komjathy, "Qigong in America," in *Daoist Body Cultivation*, ed. Livia Kohn (Cambridge, MA: Three Pines Press, 2006), 203–235. Other relevant resources may be found on the website of the Center for Daoist Studies (http://www.daoistcenter.org).

81. See Komjathy, "Qigong in America."

82. See Komjathy, *Handbooks for Daoist Practice*.

83. Thomas A. Tweed, *The American Encounter with Buddhism, 1844–1912: Victorian Culture and the Limits of Dissent* (Bloomington: Indiana University Press, 1992), 39–47.

84. Almost everything on the Internet and in popular publications expresses Western colonialist and Orientalist appropriations. Some representative examples of PWT include the Church of the Latter-Day Dude (Dudeism), Reform Taoist Congregation (Western Reform Taoism), Tao Bums, Wandering Daoists, and various other "Tao Groups." One issue here involves family resemblances and recognizability. In the case of PWT, rhetoric most often supersedes reality, including the use of a "rhetoric of tradition."

85. Although their claims of lineage affiliation deserve further study, some such individuals include Alex Anatole, Wesley Chaplin, Bill Helm, Jerry Alan Johnson, Michael Rinaldini, Scott Rodell, and Brock Silvers.

86. Komjathy, *Cultivating Perfection*.

BIBLIOGRAPHY

Alberts, Eli. *A History of Daoism and the Yao People of South China*. Youngstown, NY: Cambria Press, 2006.

Benn, Charles. *The Cavern Mystery Transmission: A Taoist Ordination Rite of A.D. 711*. Honolulu: University of Hawaii Press, 1991.

Berkowitz, Alan. *Patterns of Disengagement: The Practice and Portrayal of Reclusion in Early Medieval China*. Stanford, CA: Stanford University Press, 2000.

Bokenkamp, Stephen. *Ancestors and Anxiety: Daoism and the Birth of Rebirth in China*. Berkeley and Los Angeles: University of California Press, 2007.

——. *Early Daoist Scriptures*. Berkeley and Los Angeles: University of California Press, 1997.

Boltz, Judith. *A Survey of Taoist Literature: Tenth to Seventeenth Centuries*. Berkeley and Los Angeles: University of California, Institute of East Asian Studies, 1987.

Brockey, Matthew. *Journey to the East: The Jesuit Mission to China, 1579–1724*. Cambridge, MA: Harvard University Press, 2007.

Buckser, Andrew, and Stephen Glazier, eds. *The Anthropology of Conversion*. Lanham, MD: Rowman & Littlefield Publishers, 2003.

Bui, H. D., and Ngasha Beck. *Caodai: Faith of Unity*. Fayetteville, AR: Emerald Wave. 2000.

Bumbacher, Stephan Pete. *Fragments of the Daoxue zhuan*. Frankfurt: Peter Lang, 2000.

Cahill, Suzanne. *Divine Traces of the Daoist Sisterhood: Records of the Assembled Transcendents of the Fortified Walled City*. Cambridge, MA: Three Pines Press, 2006.

Campany, Robert Ford. *To Live as Long as Heaven and Earth: A Translation and Study of Ge Hong's Traditions of Divine Transcendents*. Berkeley and Los Angeles: University of California Press, 2002.

Ch'en, Kenneth. *Buddhism in China*. Princeton: Princeton University Press, 1972.

Clarke, J. J. *The Tao of the West*. London: Routledge, 2000.

Despeux, Catherine, and Livia Kohn. *Women in Daoism*. Cambridge, MA: Three Pines Press, 2003.

Eskildsen, Stephen. *The Teachings and Practices of the Early Quanzhen Taoist Masters*. Albany: State University of New York Press, 2004.

Gelpi, Donald. *The Conversion Experience*. New York: Paulist Press, 1998.

Girardot, Norman. *The Victorian Translation of China: James Legge's Oriental Pilgrimage*. Berkeley and Los Angeles: University of California Press, 2002.

Hachiya Kunio. *Kindai dōkyō no kenkyū—O Chōyō to Ba Tanyō*. Tokyo: Tōkyō daigaku Tōyō bunka kenkyūjo hōkoku, 1992.

——. *Kin Gen jidai no dōkyō: Shichijin kenkyū.* Tokyo: Tōkyō daigaku Tōyō bunka kenkyūjo hōkoku, 1998.

Hahn, Thomas. "Daoist Sacred Sites." In *Daoism Handbook*, ed. Livia Kohn, 683–708. Leiden: Brill, 2000.

Hansen, Valerie. *Changing Gods in Medieval China, 1127–1276.* Princeton: Princeton University Press, 1990.

Hendrischke, Barbara. "Early Daoist Movements." In *Daoism Handbook*, ed. Livia Kohn, 134–164. Leiden: Brill, 2000.

——. *The Scripture on Great Peace: The Taiping jing and the Beginnings of Daoism.* Berkeley and Los Angeles: University of California Press, 2007.

Jung Jae-seo. "Daoism in Korea." In *Daoism Handbook*, ed. Livia Kohn, 792–820. Leiden: Brill, 2000.

Katz, Paul. *Images of the Immortal: The Cult of Lü Dongbin at the Palace of Eternal Joy.* Honolulu: University of Hawaii Press, 1999.

Kirkland, Russell. *Taoism: The Enduring Tradition.* London: Routledge, 2004.

Kleeman, Terry. "Ethnic Identity and Daoist Identity in Traditional China." In *Daoist Identity: History, Lineage, and Ritual*, ed. Livia Kohn and Harold Roth, 23–38. Honolulu: University of Hawaii Press.

——. *Great Perfection: Religion and Ethnicity in a Chinese Millennial Kingdom.* Honolulu: University of Hawaii Press, 1998.

Kohn, Livia. *Cosmos and Community: The Ethical Dimension of Daoism.* Cambridge, MA: Three Pines Press, 2004.

——. *Daoism and Chinese Culture.* Cambridge, MA: Three Pines Press, 2001.

—— ed. *Daoism Handbook.* Leiden: Brill, 2000.

——. *God of the Dao: Lord Lao in History and Myth.* Ann Arbor, MI: Center for Chinese Studies, University of Michigan, 1998.

——. "Kōshin: A Taoist Cult in Japan." *Japanese Religions* 18, no. 2 (1993): 113–139 (Part 1); 20, no. 1 (1995): 34–55 (Part 2); 20, no. 2 (1995): 123–142 (Part 3).

——. *Laughing at the Tao: Debates among Buddhists and Taoists in Medieval China.* Princeton: Princeton University Press, 1995.

——. *Monastic Life in Medieval Daoism.* Honolulu: University of Hawaii Press, 2003.

Kohn, Livia, and Harold Roth, eds. *Daoist Identity: History, Lineage, and Ritual.* Honolulu: University of Hawaii Press, 2002.

Komjathy, Louis. *Cultivating Perfection: Mysticism and Self-transformation in Early Quanzhen Daoism.* Leiden: Brill, 2007.

——. *Handbooks for Daoist Practice.* Hong Kong: Yuen Yuen Institute, 2008.

——. "Qigong in America." In *Daoist Body Cultivation*, ed. Livia Kohn, 203–235. Cambridge, MA: Three Pines Press, 2006.

——. *Title Index to Daoist Collections.* Cambridge, MA: Three Pines Press, 2002.

——. "Tracing the Contours of Daoism in North America." *Nova Religio* 8, no. 2 (Nov. 2004): 5–27.

Lamb, Christopher, and M. Darol Bryant, eds. *Religious Conversion: Contemporary Practices and Controversies.* London: Continuum, 1999.

Lemoine, Jacques. *Yao Ceremonial Paintings.* Bangkok: White Lotus, 1982.

Li Zhitian et al., eds. *Xianggang daotang keyi lishi yu chuancheng.* Hong Kong: Zhonghua shuju, 2007.

Loewe, Michael, and Edward Shaughnessy, eds. *The Cambridge History of Ancient China: From the Origins of Civilization to 221 BC.* Cambridge: Cambridge University Press, 1999.

Malony, H. Newton, and Samuel Southard, eds. *Handbook of Religious Conversion*. Birmingham, AL: Religious Education Press, 1992.

Masuo Shin'ichiro. "Daoism in Japan." In *Daoism Handbook,* ed. Livia Kohn, 821–842. Leiden: Brill, 2000.

Miller, James. *Daoism: A Short Introduction*. Oxford: Oneworld, 2003.

Miura Kunio. "Taoism in the Korean Peninsula." In *Encyclopedia of Taoism*, ed. Fabrizio Pregadio, 190–192. London: Routledge, 2008.

Mollier, Christine. *Buddhism and Taoism Face to Face: Scripture, Ritual, and Iconographic Exchange in Medieval China*. Honolulu: University of Hawaii Press, 2008.

Mori Yuria. "Identity and Lineage: The *Taiyi jinhua zongzhi* and the Spirit-writing Cult of Patriarch Lü in Qing China." In *Daoist Identity: History, Lineage, and Ritual,* ed. Livia Kohn and Harold Roth, 165–184. Honolulu: University of Hawaii Press, 2002.

Mungello, David E., ed. *The Chinese Rites Controversy: Its History and Meaning*. Nettetal, Germany: Steyler Verlag, 1995.

——. *Curious Land: Jesuit Accommodation and the Origins of Sinology*. Honolulu: University of Hawaii Press, 1989.

——. *The Great Encounter of China and the West, 1500–1800*. Lanham, MD: Rowman & Littlefield Publishers, 2005.

Nattier, Jan. "Who Is a Buddhist? Charting the Landscape of Buddhist America." In *The Faces of Buddhism in America*, ed. Charles Prebish and Kenneth Tanaka, 183–195. Berkeley and Los Angeles: University of California Press, 1998.

Pourret, Jess. *The Yao: The Mien and Mun Yao in China, Vietnam, Laos and Thailand*. Bangkok: River Books, 2002.

Pregadio, Fabrizio, ed. *The Encyclopedia of Taoism*. London: Routledge, 2008.

Rambo, Lewis. "Theories of Conversion." *Social Compass* 46, no. 3 (1999): 259–271.

——. *Understanding Religious Conversion*. New Haven: Yale University Press, 1993.

Rambo, Lewis, and Charles E. Farhadian. "Conversion." In *Encyclopedia of Religion*, ed. Lindsay Jones, 3: 1969–1974. Rev. ed. Detroit, MI: Macmillan Reference, 2005.

Reinders, Eric. *Borrowed Gods and Foreign Bodies: Christian Missionaries Imagine Chinese Religion*. Berkeley and Los Angeles: University of California Press, 2004.

Reiter, Florian. *Leben und Wirken Lao-Tzu's in Schrift und Bild. Lao-chün pa-shih-i-hua t'u-shuo*. Würzburg: Königshausen & Neumann, 1990.

Sakade Yoshinobu. "Taoism in Japan." In *Encyclopedia of Taoism*, ed. Fabrizio Pregadio, 192–196. London: Routledge, 2008.

Schipper, Kristofer, and Franciscus Verellen, eds. *The Taoist Canon: A Historical Companion to the Daozang*. Chicago: University of Chicago Press, 2004.

Sharf, Robert H. *Coming to Terms with Chinese Buddhism*. Honolulu: University of Hawaii Press, 2002.

Shiga Ichiko. "Manifestations of Lüzu in Modern Guangdong and Hong Kong: The Rise and Growth of Spirit-writing Cults." In *Daoist Identity: History, Lineage, and Ritual,* ed. Livia Kohn and Harold Roth, 185–209. Honolulu: University of Hawaii Press, 2002.

Spence, Jonathan D. *God's Chinese Son*. New York: Norton, 1996.

Strickmann, Michel. "The Tao among the Yao: Taoism and the Sinification of the South." In *Rekishi ni okeru minshu to bunka*, ed. Sakai Tadao, 23–30. Tokyo: Kokusho kankōkai, 1982.

Tsui, Bartholomew P. M. *Taoist Tradition and Change: The Story of the Complete Perfection Sect in Hong Kong*. Hong Kong: Hong Kong Christian Study Center on Chinese Religion and Culture, 1991.

Tweed, Thomas A. *The American Encounter with Buddhism, 1844–1912: Victorian Culture and the Limits of Dissent.* Bloomington: Indiana University Press, 1992.

Twitchett, Denis, and Michael Loewe, eds. *The Cambridge History of China,* Vol. 1: *The Ch'in and Han Empires.* Cambridge: Cambridge University Press, 1986.

Ullman, Chana. *The Transformed Self: The Psychology of Religious Conversion.* New York: Springer, 1989.

Verellen, Franciscus. "The Beyond Within: Grotto-Heavens (Dongtian) in Taoist Ritual and Cosmology." *Cahiers d'Extrême-Asie* 8 (1995): 265–290.

Vervoorn, Aat. *Men of the Cliffs and Caves: The Development of the Chinese Eremitic Tradition to the End of the Han Dynasty.* Hong Kong: Chinese University Press, 1990.

Watson, James. "Standardizing the Gods: The Promotion of T'ien-hou ('Empress of Heaven') along the South China Coast." In *Popular Culture in Late Imperial China,* ed. David Johnson et al., 292–324. Berkeley and Los Angeles: University of California Press, 1985.

Wright, Arthur. *Buddhism in Chinese History.* Stanford, CA: Stanford University Press, 1959.

You Zian, ed. *Daofeng bainian: Xianggang daojiao yu daoguan.* Hong Kong: Fung Ying Seen Foon, 2002.

Zürcher, Erik. *The Buddhist Conquest of China.* Leiden: Brill, 1959.

——. "Buddhist Influence on Early Taoism." *T'oung Pao* 66 (1980): 84–147.

CHAPTER 23

CONVERSION AND CONFUCIANISM

ANNA SUN

INTRODUCTION: UNDERSTANDING CONFUCIANISM THROUGH THE LENS OF CONVERSION

WHAT do we mean by religious conversion?[1] Very often the idea of conversion brings to mind passionate experiences of religious awakenings and radical transformations of individual lives, as well as large-scale transformations of societies—both peaceful transitions and fervent clashes—throughout history. In her introduction to the edited volume *The Anthropology of Religious Conversion*, Diane Austin-Broos describes conversion as a fundamental change in one's worldview: "To change one's religion is to change one's world, to voluntarily shift the basic presuppositions upon which both self and others are understood."[2] And William James famously formulates the experience of conversion in the following way:

> To be converted, to be regenerated, to receive grace, to experience religion, to gain an assurance, are so many phrases which denote the process, gradual or sudden, by which a self hitherto divided, and consciously wrong and inferior, becomes unified and consciously superior and happy, in consequence of its firmer hold upon religious realities. This at least is what conversion signifies in general terms, whether or not we believe that a direct divine operation is needed to bring such a moral change about.[3]

However, in the case of Confucianism, the process of becoming a Confucian is in most cases not an impassioned engagement but a gradual process that involves ritual practices, academic education, and moral self-cultivation, as well as participation in certain Confucian social institutions. Historically, to become a Confucian in China is not about the renunciation of other religious beliefs or the exclusion of other religious practices but rather a deepening of one's bonds in a given community and tradition and a consolidation of one's different social and cultural identities.

Moreover, to be a Confucian has meant very different things in different historical periods and in different cultural contexts in China. Indeed, to be a Confucian is to have one of the most fluid religious identities. The traditional concept of conversion cannot be applied in a straightforward way to Confucianism, for the process of *becoming* a Confucian has had radically different forms over the course of Chinese history.

Although here I speak of being a Confucian as a religious identity, I am not addressing directly the question of whether Confucianism is a religion.[4] In this chapter I am assuming the following three premises without further arguments: (1) Confucianism is seen as one of the major world religions today, both in popular imagination and in academic work (notwithstanding the fact that its religious nature has been constantly contested by scholars); (2) the definition of religion, like the definition of many important concepts, is produced by consensus of communities of practitioners and scholars, and it is a historical product rather than an ahistorical, normative concept; (3) because of the non-static nature of both the definition of religion and the ideas and practices associated with Confucianism, it is entirely plausible for Confucianism to be seen or understood as a religion by both practitioners and scholars in a given social and historical context, and not as a religion in a different context.

In his discussion of conversion to Buddhism in India, Torkel Brekke makes a distinction between two basic modes of understanding religious conversions: the "Pauline paradigm" (following J. T. Richardson), which uses the conversion of St. Paul as the paradigm case, emphasizing the power of an external force (e.g., the voice of Jesus) over the converted person, versus the so-called "activist paradigm," which stresses the choices made by rational individuals in the conversion process.[5]

If we follow these two basic definitions of religious conversion, we may formulate a conversion process as follows:

> One converts to X.

This formula can be easily understood when we discuss the case of someone converting to Catholicism or Islam:

> One converts to Catholicism.
> or
> One converts to Islam.

We know what the act of "converting" refers to, regardless of whether we know what "Catholicism" or "Islam" entails. Such acts of conversion are common occurrences in our contemporary social life as well as throughout history, and although social scientists might disagree on how to best analyze them from sociological or psychological perspectives, they would all agree that such religious conversions are social facts that can be examined, for there are doctrinal rules and procedures regulating the conversion process, such as the *Catechism of the Catholic Church* and the Catholic *Rite of Christian Initiation of Adults* (RCIA). In addition, there are tangible, historically rooted, and standardized ritual ceremonies that formalize the conversion process, sanctifying a person's new identity as a convert and marking his/her acceptance into a new religious community.[6]

Yet the situation is very different in the case of Confucianism. Let us consider the following formulation:

One converts to Confucianism.

What does the phrase "one converts to Confucianism" mean, exactly? The truth is that very few people have ever uttered these words to describe their experiences in relation to Confucianism. Historically, no Chinese person has described his or her affiliation with Confucianism in terms that can be translated as "conversion," even though terms that mean "conversion" are often used in relation to Buddhism, such as *guiyi* (converting to Buddhism). Furthermore, although there are voluminous studies of Chinese converts to Catholicism, Protestantism, or Islam, we do not know of cases of Catholics, Protestants, or Muslims who have been "converted to Confucianism."

There are two main difficulties in describing Confucianism in the traditional language of conversion. The first lies in the fact that there are no definitive conversion rites in Confucianism, such as baptism in Catholicism and Protestantism. In traditional China, one becomes a Confucian through a process that involves undergoing a Confucian education and living a certain form of life. Although one also participates in Confucian rituals, there is no official conversion rite to signify one's acceptance into this particular religious tradition. In other words, there is no formal religious ceremony marking one's transformation from being a non-Confucian into being a Confucian; the process is a much more gradual one, and most people who are considered Confucians might not be able to identify the precise moment at which they became Confucians. Indeed, there is no membership record in Confucianism, as opposed to Christianity.

The second difficulty comes from the fact that there are no official religious organizations in Confucianism, such as churches or mosques, nor is there an official priesthood or clergy. As a result, there is no religious authority in charge of the acceptance of new members, nor religious authority to administer official certificates of conversions, as in many other traditions. In fact, it is difficult to speak of membership in Confucianism in general, since the foundation of Confucianism is not religious institutions but diverse and interconnected social and education systems.

In his influential book *Religion in Chinese Society,* C. K. Yang makes the distinction between what he calls "institutional religion" and "diffused religion."[7] For instance, in the case of institutional religions, we find temples or churches with their own clergy and clear institutional structure; in the case of diffused religion, the religious activities are conducted in more secular settings, such as the family. Joseph Adler argues that Confucianism is a diffused religion according to Yang's definition: "This is one of the reasons why it is so difficult to speak of Confucianism as 'a religion': this

terminology implicitly reifies the phenomenon as a distinct 'thing', yet as diffused religion Confucianism does not exist separately and apart from the secular social settings
in which it is practiced."[8] This is particularly true of Confucian rituals; they can be performed on the ground of Confucius temples, in front of the ancestral tablets in one's
household, as well as at the graveside of one's deceased family members.[9]

Due to the unique nature of Confucianism, instead of using the formulation of "One
converts to X," I propose the following modified formula:

One *becomes* a *Confucian.*

Here the emphases are on both *"become"* and *"Confucian,"* for there are many different
ways of *becoming* a Confucian and many different ways of *being* a Confucian. Indeed,
the term Confucian has meant a wide range of things throughout the course of Chinese
history.

In the rest of this chapter, I focus on these two key aspects of Confucianism, providing
both historical background and theoretical considerations that are based on historical
materials, ethnographic fieldwork, and survey data.

HISTORICAL CONSIDERATIONS

Although Confucius (ca. 551–ca. 479 B.C.E.) states that he prefers not to address matters
related to gods and spirits (*Analects*, 7.21), there are many discussions about the proper
performance of rituals in the *Analects*; the importance of ritual practice to Confucius
cannot be underestimated. Confucius speaks of *tian* (literally meaning the sky, the
heaven above, or a personal deity) fifty-one times in the *Analects* and, as P. J. Ivanhoe
suggests, Confucius seems to believe that Heaven has a concrete plan for human beings
and that he has been chosen to play a special role in the realization of this plan toward a
peaceful, just, and harmonious society.[10]

Although Confucius was highly regarded as a teacher and sage prior to the Han
dynasty, the so-called "cult of Confucius" did not start until the Han dynasty (206
BCE–220 C.E.). The worship of Confucius through rituals performed by the emperor
or his surrogates can be dated to the late sixth or seventh century. Thomas Wilson notes
that, starting in the Tang dynasty (618–907), a liturgy for the worship of Confucius was
constructed based on ancient canonical texts on rituals, and these codes for sacrifices
were used throughout imperial China, with modifications along the way. For instance,
the Tang codes required the first offering be presented by the crown prince and the second and the third by the two top officials of the Directorate of Education; in the Ming
dynasty (1368–1644), the ritual sacrifices were supervised by senior officials from the
Court of Imperial Sacrifices, the Directorate of Education, and the Ministry of Rites.[11]
Such formal and official ritual performances are often referred to by scholars as the
"state cult of Confucius." These ritual practices were carried out by the royal court of

different dynasties, and temples devoted to the veneration of Confucius flourished in major cities until the republican revolution in 1911 put an end to imperial China as well as to the imperial worship of Confucius.

Besides such state or public performances of rituals, another important component of Confucian ritual practices is the personal worship of ancestral spirits. Although this practice existed in China long before the rise of Confucianism,[12] ancestral rites have long been appropriated by the disciples of Confucius as an essential ritual. The Jesuit missionaries in China were forced to deal with the issue of such rituals in the seventeenth century, which became known as the so-called "Chinese Rites Controversy." The "Chinese Rites Controversy" highlighted the diffused nature of Confucian ritual practice. As Liam Matthew Brockey puts it, the Jesuits considered Confucianism, especially the worship of Confucius, "the sect of the literati," and they saw "the yearly participation of Christian literati in rituals at Confucian temples as a solemn expression of remembrance for a revered master."[13] Their accommodation policy came from their realization that they needed the support and protection of the dominant social and political elites, who were "by profession, committed Confucians."[14]

However, the Franciscan and Dominican missionaries objected to Chinese converts' participation in certain Confucian rites. Brockey notes, "These missionaries especially objected to seeing Christian literati participate in Confucian ceremonies and ordinary Christians keep tablets inscribed with their ancestors' names in their homes. In the friars' opinion, both were intolerable manifestations of idolatry and not, as the Jesuits claimed, merely political and social customs."[15] Their response to the Jesuits' accommodation policy was "roaming the streets of Peking, preaching that 'the king was wrong and Confucius was in hell.'"[16]

The controversy also underscores another unique feature of Confucianism, which is how closely related the centrality and development of Confucianism is to the rise of the civil examination system in imperial China. The Emperor Yang of the Sui dynasty (581–618) established the first civil service examinations in 605, using tests of literary subjects to select officials for the court. Throughout imperial China, the examinations were expanded, standardized, and methodically institutionalized, with earlier literary subjects replaced by the increasingly rigorous Confucian canon. National exams were held every three years, and there were also local-level as well as court-level exams. This was the social structure through which political, social, and cultural elites were educated, selected, and reproduced.

According to Benjamin Elman, the civil service examination system in imperial China (which ended in 1904 in an attempt at modernization) was the institutional link that connected several important aspects of Chinese political, social, and cultural life. First, the imperial dynasties used the rigorous civil service examinations to select officials to fill the most important positions within the dynastic government; second, the gentry-literati elites utilized the examinations to gain political positions and economic assets; third, classical studies, which formed the core content of the examinations, flourished because of the examinations, yet it was also reconstructed through the complex interactions between imperial bureaucracy and elite gentry-literati groups.[17]

The civil examination is also the bridge between Confucius worship and officially rec-ognized Confucians. In *Sages and Saints,* Chin-shing Huang makes the important point that, unlike Christian churches where everyone is welcome to enter, Confucius temples in imperial China were a sacred space reserved for imperial courtiers, scholar-officials, and Confucian students (*rusheng*), people who had either passed through the civil examination system or were about to enter it. Newly appointed local officials were often required to pay respect to Confucius in the local Confucius temple before they could begin their official duty, and the Confucius temples were also the sites where Confucian students celebrated their success in the civil examination exams by offering their thanks-giving to Confucius. Such rituals marked their transformation into officialdom—and, indeed, their new identity as full-fledged Confucians.[18] This is indeed a unique feature of membership in Confucianism; it only existed in imperial China, and it had little to do with a formal process of conversion but had everything to do with one's acceptance into the learned world of Confucian social and political elites.

In 1895, Kang You-wei, a leading reform-minded scholar-official who had come up through the civil examination system, campaigned for the establishment of "Confucian religion" or "Confucianity," modeled after Christianity, as the national religion of China in the spirit of modernization. The "Association of Confucian Religion" was founded in 1912, shortly after the founding of the Republic of China in 1911. This was the famous yet short-lived "Confucianity Movement." It became evident very soon that there was not enough political support for reinventing Confucianism as a national religion; in the late 1920s the government ordered the association to change its name to "Association of Confucian Learning," which did not have any religious connotation. However, some followers of the movement continued to spread their understanding of Confucianism as a religion in places such as Taiwan and Hong Kong long after the association was dissolved.[19]

When the People's Republic of China was founded in 1949, the state realized that it needed an official religious policy to control the large segment of China's population that was religious. The "Five Major Religions" classification was established in the 1950s, and it includes Catholicism, Protestantism, Buddhism, Daoism, and Islam but not Confucianism. Confucianism as a philosophy and ethical system was demonized dur-ing the Cultural Revolution (1966–1976), and Confucian rituals such as ancestral rites either disappeared or went underground in that turbulent time.

THE CONTEMPORARY REVIVAL OF CONFUCIAN RITUALS IN CHINA

Beginning in the 1980s, there has been a renaissance of scholarly interests in the reli-gious nature of Confucianism, including fierce intellectual debates,[20] and there has also been a renewed interest in Confucian rituals. Indeed, in the first decade of the

twenty-first century, there has been a noticeable revival of rituals traditionally associated with Confucianism in China. The revival has taken both the "official religion" form
and the "personal religion" form. The official form includes state-sponsored ritual performances in Confucius temples around the country.[21] Personal worship takes the form
of the worship of ancestral spirits at gravesites, before household ancestral shrines, or in
ancestral temples, as well as the personal worship of Confucius in Confucius temples,
which is a notable departure from the convention in imperial China, which dictated
only Confucian scholar-officials and students could enter Confucius temples.

Most people who worship in Confucius temples these days are young men and women
about to take an important exam, such as the annual national college entrance exam or
a graduate school entrance exam; they burn incense in Confucius temples and pray to
Confucius for blessings. Although there are also people who pray for blessings for success in job interviews or promotions, the general purpose of worshiping in Confucius
temples is for blessings in one's educational life.

In terms of ancestral rites, according to a recent survey of Chinese religious practices,
an astonishingly high percentage of people have been making annual trips in recent
years to their ancestral hometowns to perform rituals at the graveside of their deceased
family members. In 2007, 67 percent of people surveyed reported that they had performed "ancestral rites on the gravesite of a deceased family member in the past year."[22]
When people venerate their ancestors' spirits at a gravesite, they ask for their protection
and blessing for the year, and it is believed by many that the ancestor's blessing will guarantee good fortune in one's personal affairs.

This annual trip usually takes place in early April, on the day of the Qing Ming
Festival, which is the 15th day after the spring equinox. The ancestral rite is often called
saomu (grave-sweeping), since the main rituals involve the cleaning of graves and the
displaying of sacrifices. The sacrificial objects vary greatly in different regions; they
often consist of paper goods that are made to resemble luxury products, as well as real
food, drinks, and flowers. The demands for the paper goods are so high that in some cities there are now commercial streets devoted to sacrificial goods.

Since the graves are generally located in people's ancestral hometowns, often far from
where they now live, many people need to make a special trip in order to do the rites. The
high percentage of people who have done so "in the past year" indeed speaks volumes of
the significance of this ritual in people's lives today. These annual visits to the graves have
become so pervasive that the Chinese government has declared the Qing Ming Festival
to be an official national holiday as of 2008 so that people can officially take the day off
from their work for the sake of observing the rituals.

THEORETICAL CONSIDERATIONS

Given the complex history and reality of Confucianism, how do we find a theoretical model that can encompass the many different ways through which one becomes a

Confucian? Lewis Rambo has offered a very useful typology of conversion in his study, *Understanding Religious Conversion* (1993):

Apostasy, or *defection*: the repudiation of a religious tradition or its beliefs by previous members.

Intensification: the revitalized commitment to a faith with which the convert has had previous affiliation, formal or informal.

Affiliation: the movement of an individual or group from no or minimal religious commitment to full involvement with an institution or community of faith.

Institutional Transition: the change of an individual or group from one community to another within a major tradition (such as denominational switching).

Tradition Transition: the movement of an individual or a group from one major religious tradition to another.[23]

The case of Confucianism seems to lie between the modes of *Intensification* and *Affiliation*, for the process of becoming a Confucian can be seen as an intensification of one's previous bonds with the Confucian tradition through ritual practices (especially ancestral rites) as well as self-cultivation through education and spiritual exercises. And it is also an official affiliation in the case of the Confucian elites in imperial China, who were entitled to participate in the formal rites venerating Confucius in Confucius temples, a privilege that was reserved for members of the imperial court and scholar-officials who were selected through national civil examinations.

In contemporary China, however, with the absence of the imperial "state cult of Confucius" or the officiating process of one's status as a Confucian through the imperial civil service examination, how do we identify who the Confucians are, and how do we differentiate the varied ways through which they become Confucians? Furthermore, how do we convey the rich inclusiveness of religious ritual life in the Chinese context, where, unlike in monotheistic traditions such as Christianity and Islam, a person can carry out diverse ritual practices from different religious traditions in one's life— Confucian, Buddhist, Daoist, and so on—without seeing them as contradictory?

I propose the following three criteria to define whether someone is behaving as a Confucian in terms of his/her participation in Confucian practice. I am not using these criteria to define whether someone is a Confucian, which suggests an exclusive religious identity that is not suitable in the discussion of Confucianism. Rather these criteria define when someone is a Confucian, meaning the occasions during which one behaves as a Confucian. The first one is what I term the "Minimal Criterion: Confucius Worship":

The Minimal Criterion: Confucius Worship.
One is a Confucian when one practices any of the following rituals that take place in a Confucius temple:
(a) Burning incense;
(b) Praying to the statue or the tablet of Confucius;

(c) Writing prayers on prayer cards that hang on the trees or special shelves within the temple;

(d) Any other rituals that take place in a Confucius temple.

This refers to the people who participate in Confucius worship in Confucius temples. The Minimalist Criterion ensures the undeniable religious dimension of Confucianism; these are religious rituals performed in a sacred space.

The next criterion is what I call the "Inclusive Criterion: Ancestral Rituals":

The Inclusive Criterion: Ancestral Rituals
One is a Confucian when one practices any of the following rituals:

(a) Any ritual practices in an ancestral temple;

(b) Any ritual practices on the gravesite of one's deceased ancestors/family members.

These sets of practices refer to people who participate in either Confucius worship or ancestral worship. As the name suggests, this is a more inclusive criterion than merely Confucius worship, for it includes all the religious rituals that are commonly seen as Confucian.

The last criterion is what I call the "Extended Criterion: Cultural Confucianism":

The Extended Criterion: Cultural Confucianism
One is a Confucian when one does any of the following:

(a) Practicing filial piety and other Confucian virtues;

(b) Practicing Confucian spiritual exercises in order to live a more Confucian life, such as reading the Confucian classics and meditating.

(c) Practicing other Confucian social rituals, such as family rituals (*jiali*).[24]

This refers to people who may or may not participate in Confucian religious rituals such as ancestral worship or Confucius worship but who are "culturally Confucian" because of their practices of Confucian virtues and spiritual exercises that aim at cultivating one's mind and body, and/or their practices of Confucian social rituals such as the proper way to interact with one's family members and friends.

For instance, if someone takes the virtue of filial piety—one of the most fundamental Confucian virtues—seriously in one's life by behaving in a certain way toward one's parents, one can be seen as a "Cultural Confucian" under this measure. This also includes people who are involved in the study of classical texts in the Confucian canon, such as the *Analects* and the *Mencius*, as well as more popular Confucian texts such as *The Classics of Filial Piety* (*xiaojing*) or *The Book of Three-Character Verse* (*sanzi jing*), in order to use Confucian ideas as the guiding ethical principles in their life (and often also as the foundation of the education of their child/children). The relationship between the three criteria can be seen in figure 23.1.

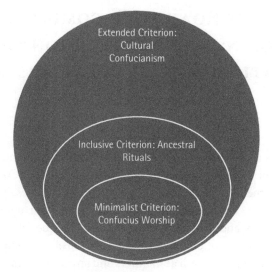

FIGURE 23.1 Three criteria of Confucian practice

There is an additional aspect of Confucianism that might be called "Political Confucianism," a term promoted by the contemporary scholar and Confucian activist Jiang Qing. This refers to the idea that Confucianism should serve as the foundation of Chinese politics and culture and that Confucian political philosophy should be the guiding force in China's transformation from a socialist state to a new form of political system. This has become an influential way of understanding Confucianism in China among intellectuals who are increasingly nationalistic in their cultural and political outlook; Jiang Qing and Kang Xiaoguang are two leading voices in this reformulation of Confucian politics.[25] Indeed, today Confucianism is being considered as a viable alternative to Western liberal democracy,[26] even though the official discourse of Confucianism is still full of ambiguities.[27]

As Prasenjit Duara has suggested, there is a long-standing "transmutation (or traffic) of religious ideas into political ideas," especially in the case of Confucianism, which has a long, entangled history with dynastic rulers, political reformers, and the creation of a modern "national citizenry" in China.[28] So it should not come as a surprise that "Political Confucianism" is experiencing a new wave of revival in China, and it remains to be seen whether it will make use of the religious aspects of Confucianism in the legitimation of its authority.

The Road to Becoming a Confucian: Self-Cultivation through Education, Spiritual Exercises, and Social Rituals

Since one becomes a Confucian not through a radical transformation of one's fundamental beliefs or worldview, but rather through steady practice of Confucian rituals and an ongoing commitment to the Confucian way of life, the idea of self-cultivation is central to the process. One becomes a true Confucian, a *junzi* (virtuous person), through intense self-cultivation, and the Confucians see the techniques of the cultivation of the self as involving all aspects of one's being: intellect, sensibility, imagination, temperament, and relation to others, as well as manners and any other physical manifestation of one's self.

In Pierre Hadot's articulation, the main aspects of spiritual exercise in Hellenistic philosophy are strikingly similar to the components of self-cultivation in the Confucian tradition:

1. Learning to Live: Learning the art of living though a transformation of one's inner self.
2. Learning to Dialogue: Learning to have genuine dialogues with others as well as with oneself.
3. Learning to Die: Training for death through contemplation of the nature of life and death.
4. Learning How to Read: learning "how to pause, liberate ourselves from our worries, return into ourselves, and leave aside our search for subtlety and originality, in order to meditate calmly, ruminate, and let the texts speak to us."[29]

For Confucians such as Confucius, it is through observing *li* (social rules and rituals) that one cultivates virtuous desires, and one must be guided by teachers and helped by virtuous friends along the way. This is why the internalization and mastery of *li* is essentially a social process that includes both education and spiritual exercise.[30] Confucius calls this process "restraining oneself with social rules and rituals" (*Analects*, 6.27, 9.11), "establishing oneself through social rules and rituals" (*Analects*, 8.8, 20.3), and "self-disciplining by submitting oneself to social rules and rituals (*keji fuli*)" (*Analects*, 12.1). Confucius says that at age 70 he is able to "follow all the desires of his heart without breaking any rules," because all the rules have become constitutive of his self (*Analects*, 2.4).

Self-cultivation through education and spiritual exercise remains a central concern in Confucianism throughout Chinese history. Partly due to the influence of

Daoism and Buddhism, the Neo-Confucian philosophers in the Song Dynasty (960–1279) and Ming Dynasty (1368–1644) developed elaborated theories of Confucian self-cultivation as well as rich techniques, making use of ideas and methods from Zen Buddhism.[31]

It was Zhu Xi (1130–1200), a leading Neo-Confucian philosopher, who first advanced the idea of the "Four Books," which included the *Analects*, the *Mencius*, the *Great Learning*, and the *Doctrine of the Mean*, texts Confucius considered to be the most significant parts of Confucian canon. Through the Four Books, Zhu Xi advocated the idea of self-cultivation through both philosophical and spiritual exercises such as contemplation and reading, pointing to an "inward" shift toward inner sources of personal morality.

However, this does not mean that social rituals such as family rituals are no longer important. Commenting on Zhu Xi's manual on family rituals, Patricia Ebrey remarks:

> Although the main focus of Zhu Xi's work was the theory and practice of self-cultivation, the defining and shaping of the self always took place in a social context, and the study of rites remained a major concern of his, as it has been earlier for the Confucius of the *Analects*, in which humanness and rites were twin themes. . . . As a practical matter for the local elite, Zhu gave family ritual priority over the royal and state rituals that occupied so much of the Zhou texts [ancient ritual texts]. . . . Subsequently, Zhu's prescriptions became models for the cultural and social elite, adapted widely in premodern East Asia.[32]

In other words, even for Neo-Confucians like Zhu Xi, who emphasized the kind of contemplative practices of meditation and reading that were not unlike the intense contemplative practices of prayers and sacred reading (*lectio divina*) found in Catholic monastic life, the religious and social rituals of everyday life were still indispensable.

These aspects of Confucian self-cultivation—education in the Confucian canon, various forms of spiritual exercises, emphasis on social rituals—can be felt clearly in the contemporary revival of Confucian practices. The "Reading of the Classics" movement was first started in the 1990s as a grassroots movement designed to teach children Confucian classics through reading and memorization, and it has now spread widely throughout China, with classes offered in private schools and its impact felt in state-run educational institutions.

There are also efforts to bring back classical Confucian social rituals, to relearn the proper ways of behaving in the Confucian tradition. Such social rituals include the veneration of one's parents through proper etiquette at formal occasions, such as weddings, as well as at informal occasions, paying respect to one's teachers with deferential manners in the classroom, and the general Confucian way of conduct of treating people as well as oneself with dignity and reverence.

BECOMING A CONFUCIAN IN THE
GLOBAL WORLD

What makes one a Confucian in today's world? Among the different criteria we have discussed, which ones are the most fundamental, most essential to becoming Confucian today? Is someone who worships Confucius in a Confucius temple more of a Confucian than someone who practices filial piety toward his or her parents, or someone who reads the *Analects* as his or her spiritual manual for life? And does it matter whether one is Chinese if one wants to become a Confucian?

To answer these questions is to confront the internal tensions in Confucianism in the contemporary world; they are not necessarily causes of conflicts, but often sources of renewal and innovation. Confucianism is often seen as a conservative force, for historically it has placed great emphasis on preserving canonical texts, maintaining ritual traditions, defending existing social hierarchies, and protecting a uniquely Chinese social, cultural, and political identity.

Yet we also know that the Confucian canon has been remade over and again by countless generations of scholars who have transformed it through extensive commentaries over two thousand years of intense hermeneutic practices. And numerous Confucian scholars and politicians have acted as agents of change, such as becoming some of the earliest Catholic converts in China or serving as leading political reformers in the twentieth century. And rituals such as Confucius worship ceremonies have gone through a striking alteration, changing from ceremonies conducted by imperial courts for nearly 1,500 years to ritual performances staged by the state in today's China.

Indeed, the once-forbidden Confucius temples are now open to anyone who wishes to enter, and the revival of traditional rituals of burning incense in Confucius temples as well as the newly invented ritual practice of praying to Confucius through prayer cards have changed the dynamic of the sacred space. Such creative actions often produce what Hacking calls the "looping effect of human kinds," which refers to the often intense interactions between people and the ways in which they are classified. Hacking states: "*Author* and *brother* are kinds of people, as are *child viewer* and *Zulu*. People of these kinds can become aware that they are classified as such. They can make tacit or even explicit choices, adapt or adopt ways of living so as to fit or get away from the very classification that may be applied to them."[33] And people's social actions in the end affect the classification scheme as well, which is constantly modified and redefined through institutional processes.

If we view the revival of Confucian rituals in this light, it becomes clear that this revival may indeed have transformative effects on the way Confucianism is classified and understood in contemporary Chinese society, as well as on the way we understand what constitutes being a Confucian. For instance, the revival, renewal, and invention of ritual actions related to Confucius worship and ancestral worship in recent years in China have already had an impact on the legitimation of Confucianism as a religion, and it is not inconceivable that Confucianism might be recognized by the state in the future as one of the major religions in China, which would have many significant religious, political, and social consequences.

And, one does not need to be a Chinese person to be a Confucian. Indeed, Confucianism has been thriving outside of China for hundreds of years, especially in Korea, Japan, and Vietnam, with South Korea being the country that has perhaps best preserved Confucian ritual practice in the contemporary world.[34] Scholars have long referred to "Confucian East Asia," and now there is also the so-called "Boston Confucianism" represented by Tu Weiming, Robert Neville, and John Berthrong, scholars as well as followers of Confucianism.[35] Through endorsing ongoing Confucian–Christian dialogues, the Boston Confucians have been emphasizing the profound relevance of Confucian ideas and spiritual exercises to the Western world.

The truth is that, like any living religious tradition, Confucianism is ever-changing and ever-evolving, and its future is cast through its transformation in the present. Its current metamorphosis might not be particularly dramatic, yet there are already signs pointing to new developments, indicating adjustment and regeneration. As a result, there will always be new ways of becoming a Confucian, and the search for a Confucian life that is transcendent and virtuous will never cease.

NOTES

1. My thanks go first to the editors of this volume, Lewis R. Rambo and Charles E. Farhadian, for their unfailing support and patience. I also wish to thank my colleagues in the "Empirical Study of Religion in China" project, particularly Rodney Stark, Byron Johnson, F. Carson Mencken, and Fenggang Yang, for their inspiration and support. I am also grateful to the John Templeton Foundation for funding our project. And my deep thanks go to Yang Xiao, my excellent first reader, as always. A modified version of this chapter has appeared in my book *Confucianism as a World Religion: Contested Histories and Contemporary Realities*.

2. Diane Austin-Broos. "The Anthropology of Conversion: An Introduction," in *The Anthropology of Religious Conversion*, ed. Andrew Buckser and Stephen Glazier (Lanham, MD: Rowman & Littlefield, 2003), 11.

3. William James, *The Varieties of Religious Experience* (New York: Penguin Classics, 1982), 189.

4. In this chapter, I do not address the larger issue of how Confucianism became a religion (or world religion), which is a question that cannot be answered without an account of the historical development of the very concept of "religion" as well as of the historical processes through which Confucianism has become one of the major world religions since the end of the nineteenth century. For a detailed historical analysis of the making of Confucianism as a world religion, see my dissertation, "Confusions over Confucianism: Controversies over the Religious Nature of Confucianism, 1870–2007," PhD diss., Princeton University, 2008.

5. Torkel Brekke, "Conversion in Buddhism?" in *Religious Conversions in India: Modes, Motivations, and Meanings*, ed. Rowena Robinson and Sathianathan Clarke (New Delhi: Oxford University Press, 2003), 183.

6. See, for instance, David Yamane and Sarah MacMillen, *Real Stories of Christian Initiation: Lessons for and from the RCIA* (Collegeville, MN: Liturgical Press, 2006); Anna Mansson-McGinty, *Becoming Muslim: Western Women's Conversions to Islam* (New York: Palgrave Macmillan, 2006).

7. C. K. Yang, *Religion in Chinese Society: A Study of Contemporary Social Functions of Religion and Some of Their Historical Factors* (Berkeley and Los Angeles: University of California Press, 1967).

8. Joseph A. Adler, "Confucianism as Religion/Religious Tradition/Neither: Still Hazy after All These Years," paper presented at annual meeting of the American Academy of Religion, 2006, 10.

9. For details about rituals performed in Confucius temples, see Anna Sun, "The Revival of Confucian Rites in Contemporary Mainland China and Taiwan," in *Confucianism and Spiritual Traditions in Modern China and Beyond*, ed. Fenggang Yang and Joseph Tamney (Leiden: Brill, 2012), 309–328.

10. P. J. Ivanhoe, "Heaven as a Source for Ethical Warrant in Early Confucianism," *Dao: A Journal of Comparative Philosophy* 6, no. 3 (2007): 211–220.

11. Thomas Wilson, ed., *On Sacred Grounds: Culture, Society, Politics, and the Formation of the Cult of Confucius* (Cambridge, MA: Harvard University Asia Center, 2002).

12. Mu-chou Poo, *In Search of Personal Welfare: A View of Ancient Chinese Religion* (Albany: State University of New York Press, 1998); Lothar Von Falkenhausen, *Chinese Society in the Age of Confucius (1000–250 BCE): The Archaeological Evidence* (Los Angeles: Cotsen Institute of Archaeology, UCLA, 2006).

13. Liam Matthew Brockey, *Journey to the East: The Jesuit Mission to China, 1579–1724* (Cambridge, MA: Belknap Press of Harvard University Press, 2007), 106–107.

14. Ibid., 107.

15. Ibid., 105.

16. Ibid., 107.

17. Benjamin Elman, *A Cultural History of Civil Examinations in Late Imperial China* (Berkeley and Los Angeles: University of California Press, 2000), xxiv.

18. Chin-shing Huang, *Sages and Saints: Collected Essays on History and Religion (shengxian yu shengtu)* (Taipei, Taiwan: Asian Culture Press, 2001), 143–144.

19. Hsi-Yuan Chen, "Confucianism Encounters Religion: The Formation of Religious Discourse and the Confucian Movement in China," PhD diss., Harvard University, 1999.

20. Sun, "Fate of Confucianism"; John Makeham, *Lost Soul: "Confucianism" in Contemporary Chinese Academic Discourse* (Cambridge, MA: Harvard University Asia Center, 2007).

21. Sebastien Billious and Joel Thoraval. "*Lijiao*: The Reinvention of Confucian Ceremonies at the Start of the New Century," *China Perspectives* 4 (2009).

22. Horizon, "The Spiritual Life Study of Chinese Residents" (Beijing, China: HorizonKey, 2007), cited with the permission of Horizon.

23. Lewis R. Rambo, *Understanding Religious Conversion* (New Haven: Yale University Press, 1993), 13.

24. I intentionally use the term "social rituals" rather than "civil rituals" for the reason that the term "civil rituals" was used by the Jesuits during the Chinese Rites Controversy to refer to rituals that they considered nonreligious, such as the veneration of Confucius and ancestors, but that are seen as religious rites in this analysis.

25. Qing Jiang, *Zhengzhi Ruxue* (Political Confucianism) (Beijing: Sanlian Shudian 2004); Xiaoguang Kang, Benevolent Government (Ren Zheng): The Third Path of China's Political Development (Singapore: World Scientific Publishing, 2005).

26. Daniel A. Bell, *China's New Confucianism: Politics and Everyday Life in a Changing Society* (Princeton: Princeton University Press, 2008).

27. Sebastien Billioud and Joel Thoraval, "*Jiaohua*: The Confucian Revival Today as an Educative Project," *China Perspectives* 4 (2007): 4–20; Sebastien Billioud and Joel Thoraval, "*Anshen Liming* or the Religious Dimension of Confucianism." *China Perspectives* 3 (2008): 4–22.

28. Prasenjit Duara, "Religion and Citizenship in China and the Diaspora," in *Chinese Religiosities: Afflictions of Modernity and State Formation*, ed. Mayfair Yang (Berkeley and Los Angeles: University of California Press, 2008), 43.

29. Pierre Hadot, *Philosophy as a Way of Life: Spiritual Exercises from Socrates to Foucault* (Oxford: Blackwell, 1995), 82–109.

30. Weiming Tu, *Humanity and Self-Cultivation* (Berkeley and Los Angeles: University of California Press, 1979); Weiming Tu, *Confucian Thought: Selfhood as Creative Transformation* (Albany: State University of New York Press, 1985); Robert Eno, *The Confucian Creation of Heaven: Philosophy and the Defense of Ritual Mastery* (Albany: State University of New York Press, 1990).

31. P. J. Ivanhoe, *Confucian Moral Self Cultivation* (Indianapolis: Hackett, 2000).

32. Patricia B. Ebrey, ed. and trans., *Chu Hsi's Family Rituals* (Albany: State University of New York Press, 1991), 3–4.

33. Ian Hacking, "Why Ask What?," in *The Social Construction of What?* (Cambridge, MA: Harvard University Press, 1999), 33–34.

34. Benjamin Elman, J. B. Duncan, and H. Ooms, eds., *Rethinking Confucianism: Past and Present in China, Japan, Korea, and Vietnam*, Asian Pacific Monograph Series (Los Angeles: UCLA, 2002); and Martina Deuchler, *The Confucian Transformation of Korea* (Cambridge, MA: Harvard University Press, 1995).

35. Robert Neville, *Boston Confucianism: Portable Tradition in the Late-Modern World* (Albany: State University of New York Press, 2000).

BIBLIOGRAPHY

Adler, Joseph A. "Confucianism as Religion/Religious Tradition/Neither: Still Hazy after All These Years." Paper presented at the annual meeting of the American Academy of Religion, 2006.

Austin-Broos, Diane. "The Anthropology of Conversion: An Introduction." In *The Anthropology of Religious Conversion*, ed. Andrew Buckser and Stephen Glazier, 1–14. Lanham, MD: Rowman & Littlefield, 2003.

Bell, Daniel A. *China's New Confucianism: Politics and Everyday Life in a Changing Society.* Princeton: Princeton University Press, 2008.

Billioud, Sebastien. "Confucianism, 'Cultural Tradition,' and Official Discourse in China at the Start of the New Century." *China Perspectives* 3 (2007): 50–65.

Billioud, Sebastien, and Joel Thoraval. "*Anshen Liming* or the Religious Dimension of Confucianism." *China Perspectives* 3 (2008): 4–22.

——. "*Jiaohua*: The Confucian Revival Today as an Educative Project." *China Perspectives* 4 (2007): 4–20.

——. "*Lijiao*: The Return of Ceremonies Honouring Confucius in Mainland China." *China Perspectives* 4 (2009): 82–100.

Brekke, Torkel. "Conversion in Buddhism?" In *Religious Conversions in India: Modes, Motivations, and Meanings*, ed. Rowena Robinson and Sathianathan Clarke, 181–191. New Delhi: Oxford University Press, 2003.

Brockey, Liam Matthew. *Journey to the East: The Jesuit Mission to China, 1579–1724.* Cambridge, MA: Belknap Press of Harvard University Press, 2007.

Chen, Hsi-Yuan. "Confucianism Encounters Religion: The Formation of Religious Discourse and the Confucian Movement in China." PhD diss., Harvard University, 1999.

Deuchler, Martina. *The Confucian Transformation of Korea*. Cambridge, MA: Harvard University Press, 1995.

Duara, Prasenjit. "Religion and Citizenship in China and the Diaspora." In *Chinese Religiosities: Afflictions of Modernity and State Formation*, ed. Mayfair Yang, 43–64. Berkeley and Los Angeles: University of California Press, 2008.

Ebrey, Patricia B., ed. and trans. *Chu Hsi's Family Rituals*. Albany: State University of New York Press, 1991.

Elman, Benjamin. *A Cultural History of Civil Examinations in Late Imperial China*. Berkeley and Los Angeles: University of California Press, 2000.

Elman, Benjamin, J. B. Duncan, and H. Ooms, eds. *Rethinking Confucianism: Past and Present in China, Japan, Korea, and Vietnam*. Asian Pacific Monograph Series. Los Angeles: UCLA, 2002.

Eno, Robert. *The Confucian Creation of Heaven: Philosophy and the Defense of Ritual Mastery*. Albany: State University of New York Press, 1990.

Hacking, Ian. *The Social Construction of What?* Cambridge, MA: Harvard University Press, 1999.

Hadot, Pierre. *Philosophy as a Way of Life: Spiritual Exercises from Socrates to Foucault*. Oxford: Blackwell, 1995.

Horizon. "The Spiritual Life Study of Chinese Residents." Beijing, China: HorizonKey, 2007.

Huang, Chin-shing. *Sages and Saints: Collected Essays on History and Religion (shengxian yu shengtu)*. Taipei, Taiwan: Asian Culture Press, 2001.

Ivanhoe, P. J. *Confucian Moral Self Cultivation*. Indianapolis: Hackett, 2000.

——. "Heaven as a Source for Ethical Warrant in Early Confucianism." *Dao: A Journal of Comparative Philosophy* 6, no. 3 (2007): 211–220.

James, William. *The Varieties of Religious Experience*. New York: Penguin Classics, 1982.

Jiang, Qing. *Zhengzhi Ruxue* (Political Confucianism). Beijing: Sanlian Shudian 2004.

Kang, Xiaoguang. *Benevolent Government (Ren Zheng): The Third Path of China's Political Development*. Singapore: World Scientific Publishing, 2005.

Makeham, John. *Lost Soul: "Confucianism" in Contemporary Chinese Academic Discourse*. Cambridge, MA: Harvard University Asia Center, 2007.

Mansson-McGinty, Anna. *Becoming Muslim: Western Women's Conversions to Islam*. New York: Palgrave Macmillan, 2006.

Neville, Robert. *Boston Confucianism: Portable Tradition in the Late-Modern World*. Albany: State University of New York Press, 2000.

Poo, Mu-chou. *In Search of Personal Welfare: A View of Ancient Chinese Religion*. Albany: State University of New York Press, 1998.

Rambo, Lewis R. *Understanding Religious Conversion*. New Haven: Yale University Press, 1993.

Sun, Anna. *Confucianism as a World Religion: Contested Histories and Contemporary Realities*. Princeton: Princeton UP, 2013.

——. "Beyond the 'Is Confucianism a Religion?' Debate: Conceptualizing a New Classification of Chinese Religious Practice." Paper presented at the annual meeting of the American Sociological Association, New York, 2007.

——. "Confusions over Confucianism: Controversies over the Religious Nature of Confucianism, 1870–2007." PhD diss., Princeton University, 2008.

——. "The Fate of Confucianism as a Religion in Socialist China: Controversies and Paradoxes." In *State, Market and Religions in Chinese Societies*, ed. Fenggang Yang and Joseph B. Tamney, 229–255. Leiden: Brill, 2005.

Tu, Weiming. *Confucian Thought: Selfhood as Creative Transformation*. Albany: State University of New York Press, 1985.

——. *Humanity and Self-Cultivation*. Berkeley and Los Angeles: University of California Press, 1979.

Von Falkenhausen, Lothar. *Chinese Society in the Age of Confucius (1000–250 BCE): The Archaeological Evidence*. Los Angeles: Cotsen Institute of Archaeology, UCLA, 2006.

Weber, Max. *The Religion of China: Confucianism and Taoism*. New York: Free Press, 1951.

Wilson, Thomas, ed. *On Sacred Grounds: Culture, Society, Politics, and the Formation of the Cult of Confucius*. Cambridge, MA: Harvard University Asia Center, 2002.

Yamane, David, and Sarah MacMillen. *Real Stories of Christian Initiation: Lessons for and from the RCIA*. Collegeville, MN: Liturgical Press, 2006.

Yang, C. K. *Religion in Chinese Society: A Study of Contemporary Social Functions of Religion and Some of Their Historical Factors*. Berkeley and Los Angeles: University of California Press, 1967.

CHAPTER 24

"CONVERSION" AND THE RESURGENCE OF INDIGENOUS RELIGION IN CHINA

LIZHU FAN AND NA CHEN

MANY scholars have observed in recent years that religion and spirituality are resurgent around the world. Contrary to the predictions of sociologists and others that modern society will eventually become completely secularized, it appears that human beings are engaged in a wide range of religious and/or spiritual experiences, disciplines, beliefs, practices, etc. that were virtually unimaginable two decades ago.

In this chapter we seek to provide evidence that traditional (also known as primal, traditional, folk, indigenous, etc.) religions are also involved in this revitalization, not just Christianity, Islam, Buddhism, and other religions. We will focus on the People's Republic of China as an extended case study of the widespread return to religion and spirituality around the world. Some of our discussion will be based on findings from our own research in China in both urban and rural areas.

During the last thirty years many people in mainland China have rediscovered and revitalized their earlier religious and ritual practices. Kenneth Dean estimates that one to two million village temples have been rebuilt or restored across China, and ritual traditions long thought lost are now being reinvented and celebrated in many of these temples.[1] This very rough figure of well over a million village temples does not include the tens of thousands of large-scale Buddhist monasteries and temples, Daoist monasteries and temples, Islamic mosques, and Christian churches (Catholic or Protestant) that have been rebuilt or restored over the past three decades. Recent anthropological and ethnographic research demonstrates that China's common spiritual heritage and devotional beliefs and rituals are gaining vitality in the everyday lives of ordinary Chinese people.

Religious resurgence is a global phenomenon that expresses the enormous social, cultural, and political impacts of religious change. As Peter Berger noted, "What has in fact occurred is that, by and large, religious communities have survived and even flourished to the degree that they have not tried to adapt themselves to the alleged requirements of a secularized world. To put it simply, experiments with secularized religion have generally failed; religious movements with beliefs and practices dripping with reactionary supernaturalism (the kind utterly beyond the pale at self-respecting faculty parties) have widely succeeded."[2] Some scholars are trying to understand the phenomenon of religious resurgence in the globalizing world by observing and analyzing religious identification through religious change and conversion.[3] According to Rodney Stark and Roger Finke, religious conversion is a common phenomenon in religious traditions worldwide. Even in tiny preliterate societies, religious factions are common and new religious movements often arise. According to Stark and Finke's definition, "Conversion refers to shifts across religious traditions, such as from Judaism or Roman paganism to Christianity, from Christianity to Hinduism, or from the religion of the Nuer to Islam," while "Re-affiliation refers to shifts within religious traditions," such as when Baptists become Catholics or Sunni Muslims become Shi'ites.[4] Conversion, like other terms used in the study of religions in the world, is a problematic term when used in the study of Chinese indigenous religious practices and beliefs. In the preface of his splendid book, *Religion in Chinese Society,* C. K. Yang reports, "For many years, I have been perplexed by the problem of the place of religion in traditional Chinese society." He admits that "there was no strong, centrally organized religion in most periods of Chinese history."[5] Yang recognized that many categories adequate for understanding Western society and culture were not useful—and sometimes even misleading—when applied to Chinese social realities. Many problems arise if we attempt to explain Chinese religious questions by relying exclusively on Western concepts. If we insist on this approach, much of the intellectual heritage and worldview that has influenced Chinese culture over thousands of years will be lost to academic studies.[6] Many concepts created in the Western cultural context would lose much of their original meaning once translated into Chinese and read in the Chinese cultural context.

In the following discussion, we draw on current anthropological and ethnographic research for evidence to examine the continuing vitality of China's common spiritual heritage. Our discussion here will be substantially shaped by studies of popular religion based on devotional beliefs and rituals that are alive in the lives and practices of ordinary Chinese people today. We begin with some major research in the study of Chinese religion to identify the characteristics of "diffused religion" in traditional China. We then describe the contemporary revival of popular religion in China. We conclude with an analysis of how, through the revitalization of their spiritual heritage and the practice of popular religion, individuals and communities discover and reconstruct traditional forms of religion and spirituality that creates modes of self-fulfillment and meaning that transcend the traditional, constricted understandings of conversion.

Pervasiveness of Diffused Religion

In the first years of the twentieth century, a Chinese translation of the English term "religion" (宗教) appeared in China. This new term, along with other terms related to the study of religious belief and practice, were "all adopted from Japanese neologisms crafted a few years before, and were used to express Western notions which had not existed in the Chinese discourse until then."[7] One of those terms is "conversion," which is difficult to fit into Chinese discourse and does not have a proper Chinese translation.[8] For instance, the term "conversion" is usually translated into Chinese as "guiyi" (皈依),[9] but this translation does not adequately convey in the Chinese cultural context the equivalent meaning of "conversion" in English. Contrasted with institutional religions such as Christianity or Islam, "diffused religion" in China is a pervasive factor in all major aspects of social life, contributing to the stability of social institutions. Meanwhile, "institutional religion, although important in its own way, lacked organizational strength to make it a powerful structural factor in the over-all Chinese social organization"[10]

C.K. Yang recognized that China's traditional religiousness was deeply imbedded in family life and civic institutions, rather than expressed in a separate organizational structure. In traditional China, therefore, "it was in its diffused form that people made their most intimate contact with religion."[11]

In institutional religions like Christianity, participation customarily depends on membership, which characteristically involves personal choice. The diffused religiousness of the Chinese culture does not require an explicit decision to join an identifiable group; no call to personal conversion stands as prerequisite for participation. For example, reporting on his contemporary study of the Black Dragon Temple in Shaanxi Province, Adam Chau observed: "The average Shaanbei popular religious 'believer' does not own any religious texts to read, does not form a congregation to meet at regular intervals, and does not pray to any particular deity with any frequency."[12] China's religious practices vary from locale to locale, but in each setting, ritual behavior is highly organized by the community. Local people recognize that there is a proper order to be followed and believe that observing this order is necessary for the ritual to be effective. Normally, temples and their gods have acquired symbolic character, with specific functions involved in the everyday life of the local community. The most common social base for religious activities in China is the "natural village";[13] by being born in a particular village, people inherit its traditions and responsibilities, which are naturally and permanently a part of their lives. Neither a baptism nor any other formal membership ceremony is necessary for people to be involved in the community rituals.

The spiritual orientation and moral convictions that arose in traditional China did not coalesce into a fully formed religious institution like that in the Western context. The usual structures of institutional religion did not pertain in China: no organized church or formal doctrines or official clergy were required for transmission or ongoing vitality of religion. Instead, in this culture "the prime criteria for religious participation is not to believe, but to belong to a community, such as a village temple community, the clan, or a pilgrimage association."[14] "Not to believe, but to belong" means that, in their various local gatherings, the Chinese people enacted their beliefs; in these associations they forged, over many centuries, a spiritual orientation with religious practices including prayers, rituals, and expressions of virtue. We identify this enduring cultural orientation as China's "common spiritual heritage." The term "common" in the phrase "common spiritual heritage" refers to the moral and spiritual convictions widely embraced by ordinary Chinese across history and up to the present. The central elements of this heritage include *tian* (天) as the transcendent source of moral meaning; *qi* (气) as the energy that animates the universe; ancestor veneration; and *bao ying* (报应) as moral reciprocity. Despite the intensely local character of Chinese religiousness, these beliefs form, as Daniel Overmyer notes, "the basic values and symbolic culture of the great majority of the population" and are still honored throughout the Chinese diaspora. The term "spiritual" moves the conversation away from thorny questions provoked by the term "religion"—with its many Western (institutional and monotheistic) nuances—in the direction of a moral orientation and worldview that is diffused throughout Chinese culture. This enduring orientation is deeply embedded in Chinese culture, though it has never been organized into an institutional structure such as Buddhism or Christianity. The term "heritage" points to the long tradition of belief and practice (which C. K. Yang and others have designated as China's "indigenous religion") that endures today as a resource of moral capital for China's future. Viewed through an anthropological lens, this heritage is often identified as "popular religion." Historically, Chinese religiousness has drawn upon plural sources of spiritual nourishment. Resources separately identified with China's three great traditions—Confucianism, Daoism, and Buddhism—have been combined freely in local religious practices, without troubling considerations of denominational distinctions or ritual orthodoxies. In Chinese society, "the Three Teachings did not function as separate institutions each with their own believers; rather, they all served the entire society.... Buddhists, Daoists, and Confucianists were all routinely invited by village and neighborhood communities to officiate at their festivals, offering sacrifices, and submitting prayers to the gods on their behalf."[15] The overlays and borrowings of the religiousness of "diffused religion" from the more formal traditions of Confucianism, Buddhism, and Daoism comprise the major part of China's "common spiritual heritage." So, "in principle, the Chinese groups had no ground for a sharp distinction between initiated and uninitiated, ordinary and hidden truth, public and secret ritual."[16] This pattern continues in many areas in China today, in both urban and rural contexts.

There is no strict distinction among different religious traditions, since the religious beliefs and the religious taboos do not commit to any particular doctrine or sect affiliation. Brokaw's research on "The Ledgers of Merit and Demerit (功过格)"[17] provides a very good example in her use of *The Tract of Taishang on Action and Response* (太上感应篇) to illustrate her point. She comments, "The cosmology of retribution defined in the *Tract on Act and Response* is also accessible to a general audience; unlike the Daoist and Buddhist scriptures of the early medieval period, it does not bind the system to the gods of a particular sect. The other retributive spirits of the *Tract*, both earthly and heavenly, are drawn from a vast nonsectarian pantheon of gods dating back to the Han Dynasty (206 BC–220 AD) at the latest. The pantheon of the Tract is certainly not the exclusive property of any one of the Three Teachings of Confucianism, Buddhism and Daoism."[18]

In the Chinese popular religion that penetrated into everyday life, the values covering filial piety, family rituals, and loyalty to the state are applicable widely to all people, regardless of their status or religious belief. But since these values had been incorporated into Confucian ethics and, to a great extent, into Daoist and Buddhist scriptures, it might be best to consider them as China's "common spiritual heritage," expressed in a diffused form.

COMMUNAL ASPECTS OF POPULAR RELIGION

Chinese local religion involves large-scale festivals participated in by members of the whole village or township community on the occasions of what are believed to be the birthdays of the gods, or to seek protection from droughts, epidemics, and other disasters. In all cases, such festivals invoke the power of the gods for practical goals to "summon blessings and drive away harm."[19]

In the vast land of China, temples, shrines, altars, and other places of worship can be seen everywhere. The numbers of temples and the extent of their ritual activities have grown rapidly over the past thirty years. According to Dean, "in the rural sector . . . if one takes a rough figure of 1000 people per village living in 680,000 administrative villages and assume an average of two or three temples per village, one arrives at a figure of over 680 million villagers involved in some way with well over a million temples and their rituals."[20]

Therefore, popular religion is exhibiting a dramatic revival throughout China. Since the mid-1980s, the government has focused primarily on the modernization of large cities; the rural areas have frequently enjoyed considerable autonomy. With the demolition of the people's commune system, the central government moved to a policy of benign neglect or *wuwei* (无为)[21] in regard to rural community life. The local government's new regulatory relationship with local society is characterized by practical mutual dependence, which gives much space for popular religion to develop. Unlike Daoism or Buddhism, which are among the officially recognized legal religions, popular religion is technically illegal and is seen as a superstitious activity.[22] Despite its immense popularity, popular religion still carries with it an aura of illegality and illegitimacy in China today. Viewing the rebuilding of temples and resurgence of religious activities as communal affairs, however, village people have taken the initiative and ignored government restrictions on popular religion. Meanwhile, given the drastic resurgence of religious activities, many local officials take a one-eye-open-and-one-eye-shut attitude or, in some cases, an even more positive and supportive attitude in the name of carrying on cultural heritage.

A good example comes from Mount Qingxu in Hebei Province, where nineteen temples have been rebuilt since the 1980s. One of them is Ge Hong Temple. According to local legend, Ge Hong (葛洪284–364 C.E.) and his wife, Bao Gu (鲍姑), brought healing to many who suffered in a local epidemic and also provided shelter for the poor. In recognition of their power and compassion, a temple was built in their honor and a local mountain ridge was named after them.[23] Local peasants have a long tradition of organizing their own religious activities. "Since at least the early twentieth century most Hebei community rituals have been organized and led by the people themselves. Their leaders are selected from male heads of families or lineages who have good reputations and own land. These leaders at the same time may be village heads playing ritual roles. Some are involved primarily in preparation and organization, others in the performance of rituals, but these roles can overlap."[24] Many local temple buildings were destroyed during the Boxer Uprising in the early twentieth century; others suffered severe damage during the Japanese invasion of China in 1937. The Cultural Revolution between 1966 and 1976 brought a third effort to destroy these centers of popular religious devotion. With the revival of folk religion since the reform, however, many of the temples have been rebuilt and festivals restored. Now no monks or priests are involved in the temple festivals in the Mount Qingxu area. Organizers of festival activities come from local villages, and each village builds a shed to provide food and boiled water for the pilgrims. Local people, peasants and officials alike, feel pride in their festivals and take an active part in the activities.

These festivals attracted worshipers from ten surrounding counties as far away as neighboring Henan and Shanxi provinces. Worshipers go up and down the mountain day and night, an eight-kilometer trip on a narrow, stony path. Some women put on new clothing and stick squares of yellow paper in their hair, on which are written "going to the mountain to offer incense." Many come to repay vows to the gods by contributing incense, oil, and candles, as well as money. People who come from a distance reserve rooms in advance in nineteen surrounding villages, sleeping on mats, cooking their own food on little stoves, and making small contributions to their hosts.[25] Another local tradition is the participation of performance troupes (*huahui*), involving many different kinds of groups of performers such as stilt walkers, lion dancers, musicians, martial arts masters, *yangge*[26] dancers, and storytellers. These groups arrive a few days before the temple festival begins, staying in nearby villages and putting up flags to announce their presence. Typically, the pilgrims to the temples located on Qingxu Mountain make petitions for peace and good fortune, for the birth of sons, for finding good husbands or wives, and for release from physical and mental illnesses. The festival activities at Ge Hong Temple are replicated in many other shrines throughout Hebei Province; these annual gatherings are complemented by regular visits to various temple sites throughout the year by individuals and families.

The overwhelming majority of Shaanbei[27] temples do not have clergy or a set of doctrines that allow for easy identification. And the range of religious activities at any one temple can be quite wide and confusing for anyone who is looking for "pure" Daoist or

Buddhist characteristics. Even historically, Daoist and Buddhist temples have accommodated elements that are "unorthodox."

A very good example comes from Adam Chau's research about the dragon king (*longwang,* 龙王), who is the agrarian deity par excellence, especially in drought-prone northern China. Torn down completely by the villagers themselves during the Cultural Revolution and rebuilt from scratch in 1982, the Heilongdawang temple has been expanding in grandeur ever since. Its fame really took off in the mid- and late 1980s, when stories of Heilongdawang's[28] efficacy spread widely in Shaanbei and when the Heilongdawang Temple began to host opera performances that are by far the longest, most diverse, and most expensive in Shaanbei.

The temple coffers swelled as its fame grew phenomenally. Compared to the throne of village dragon kings, Heilongdawang is considered a much more powerful god because he has an imperially conferred official title, the Marquis of Efficacious Response (*Lingyinghou,* 灵应侯).[29] In the past, as well as today, believers go to Heilongdawang to pray for divine assistance not only for relief from draught but for all kinds of other problems. Over the last decade or so, however, more and more people have come to ask Heilongdawang to help them with their businesses, to bless them so they will get rich. It is now the richest temple in Shaanbei, receiving more than a million *yuan* RMB[30] in donations from worshipers each year, though the temple is hidden away in a long, narrow valley called Longwanggou (literally the Dragon King Valley).

The Longwanggou temple festival in honor of the Heilongdawang's "birthday" is one of the most famous and well attended temple festivals in Shaanbei. A few hundred thousand visitors and pilgrims come to Longwanggou during the six days of the temple festival. The entire valley is jam-packed with people, food stalls, watermelon sheds, game circles, pool tables, circus and performing troupe tents (even some with "freak" shows), incense and firecracker stands, makeshift convenience stores, all kinds of small, mobile peddling devices, and even little gambling dens strewn here and there among the crowds.[31]

There were and are different levels of beliefs and practices regarding the gods, who possess various types of functions.[32] For example, there is a goddess represented by a female medium who lives next to a temple that she herself built. She claims to be a living manifestation of an ancient goddess: "I am the Silkworm Mother; I am coming here to heal people who have disease." People turn to Mrs. Wu for the healing of illnesses that cannot be cured by either Western or Chinese medicine. As more and more people receive help from Mrs. Wu, they believe that the Cult of the Silkworm Mother is *ling* (灵 efficacious). Thus, efficacious divine power makes the Cult of the Silkworm Mother more and more influential. People come to see Mrs. Wu not only from Zhiwuying village and villages that are nearby but also from distant places such as Beijing, Shijiangzhuang, and other cities. Those people in turn testify that they have benefited from worshiping the Silkworm Mother and spread the good news about Mrs. Wu, and this has made the Cult of the Silkworm Mother grow in popularity among many villages. On the ninth day of the ninth lunar month in 2001, about 150 people gathered in Mrs. Wu's house to begin a pilgrimage to the Silkworm Mother Temple located in the Xi'shan (西山, West Mountains) 200 miles away.[33] A new Silkworm Mother Temple has been built in Yang

Village near the birthplace of the Silkworm Mother; another Silkworm Mother Temple has been rebuilt in Xi'shan, and more religious sites are now being constructed. Temple festivals attended by many worshipers also take place for the Cult of the Silkworm Mother, lasting several days and including offerings in temples and the performance of operas or puppet-plays. For local believers, this goddess is not a fictitious figure but a real human being who lived in the area many years ago. People believe that the Silkworm Mother helps to solve various difficulties and problems. She has the ability to possess shamans, perform cures, send sons, and work miracles, which makes her more accessible and appealing than other gods. Above all, the Silkworm Mother is a local god; she is also identified as a neighbor by villagers.

As we have already pointed out, the diffused religiousness of the Chinese culture does not require an explicit decision to join an identifiable group, since the village people were born in this cultural environment and are naturally and permanently part of the inherited traditions and responsibilities. Popular religious activities with lay leaders have long been active in local communities, featuring their own forms of organizations, activities, rituals, and beliefs. The local divine powers who were also once human beings are believed to sympathize with and respond to their worshipers. To the ordinary people, a deeper understanding of religious doctrines and myths is not really necessary.

THE FAMILY, ANCESTOR VENERATION, AND CULTURAL CAPITAL

Many local religions in China are based on family worship of deities and ancestors on home altars, because clans constitute an important unit in society. In December 2007, the Chinese government added three traditional festivals—*Duanwu* (端午), *Qingming* (清明), and Mid-Autumn (中秋)—to the list of official holidays observed in the People's Republic of China. These festivals have both religious and cultural meanings. Serving to express ancestor veneration, *Qingming* festival is the time when people go to family graves of departed ones to pay respects to their ancestors. The persistence of the *Qingming* Festival demonstrates that the authorities have finally come to terms with the religious traditions of the great majority of the people.

The worship of ancestors still plays an important role for the maintenance of unity and continuity of family, since people believe that the spirits of the ancestors as an integrating factor give people inspiration for achieving success in modern times. There is much evidence coming from ethnographic research that supports the resurgence and vitality of ancestor veneration in China. For instance, in Beijiabi Village, Handan, Hebei Province, local people with the family name Lin are descendants of Lin Xiangru (蔺相如) (329–259 B.C.E.), who was a famous minister of Zhao State during the Warring States Period (475–221 B.C.E.). This lineage has been living in the Handan area for at least 2,200 years. The Lins live in six villages in this area and cooperate in important activities related to ancestor veneration. They regularly maintain the practices for mourning the dead and perform ancestor worship in the home and ancestral temple (*citang*祠堂).[34]

C.K. Yang traces a development within ancestor veneration that not only shows the interaction of various belief systems but also addresses the ways that a diffused religious heritage contributes to social order. An example is found in Wenzhou (温州), a coastal area in Zhejiang Province, East China, which has been known as a "regional center of global capitalism" since the 1990s. During the reform era, Wenzhou's economic development was mainly characterized by private or family-owned businesses making small merchandise such as buttons, shoes, clothes, and household appliances. Meanwhile, Wenzhou is also a place where the tradition of family-clan system and ancestor veneration has been widely revived. In Cangnan County alone, for example, there are 123 ancestral temples of Chen lineage that have been rebuilt in recent years, serving 184,260 local people who are of the Chen lineage.[35] In Chenjiabao Village (陈家堡) of this county, the Chen family has been there since 1250 C.E., a total of twenty-six generations, and they have a current population of 8,810. They completed the reconstruction of an ancestral temple in 2004. The ancestral temple is located at the entrance of Chenjiabao Village as a symbol of the religious devotion of the Chens to the spirits of the ancestors. The facade of the building copies the design of the Tiananmen Tower in Beijing. With its impressive size and elaborate decorations, this temple stands out among the more than one hundred Chen ancestral temples in the county and represents the wealth, influence, and achievement of the Chen clan in the area. Furthermore, there are plaques displaying mottos and exhortations left by the forefathers to inspire ambition and moral achievement among their posterity.

Members of the Chen clan gather annually at this village to mourn the dead and venerate their ancestors. For some special occasions, people from other villages and towns, or even Chen descendants from faraway cities and overseas places, gather in the hall for ancestor veneration and festival celebrations. The whole environment of rituals emphasizes a group tradition and symbolizes a moral atmosphere permeated with the sacred character of the ancestral spirits. "The whole series of sacrificial rites helped to perpetuate the memory of the traditions and historical sentiments of the group, sustain its moral beliefs, and vivify group consciousness. Through these rites and the presence of the group in the full numerical strength, the clan periodically renewed its sentiments of pride, loyalty, and unity."[36]

As ancestor veneration developed in Chinese culture, people took note of certain persons who had made exceptional contributions to their clan and the larger community. Because of the moral excellence of these individuals, people began to believe that such persons do not perish after death but instead are transformed into protector deities. C. K. Yang describes this tradition: "Every culture, simple or complex, develops some mechanism to perpetuate the memory of illustrious men who exhibit extra-ordinary moral qualities and perform public duties unusually well."[37]

Yang describes the "ethnico-political" process by which certain persons who have "rendered distinguished public service often receive posthumous divine titles from the government or had a sanctuary built in their memory after death."[38] Such transformations are driven by the conviction that "for such a personality, death might destroy his body, but his spirit would remain undaunted. As people could not forget his unusual qualities, their memory of his spirit continued and inspired the mythological lore to substantiate and perpetuate his memory."[39]

In Qiang Village, Handan, Hebei Province, the historical figure Lin Xiangru (藺相如) is celebrated as such a deity. More than two millennia after his death, his protection and patronage are celebrated in a recently renewed "temple" (*miao*) in this village. In acknowledgment of Lin Xiangru's protective power, a memorial temple was once built many centuries ago at the site of his tomb. Even during the Cultural Revolution, when the temple building was utterly destroyed, village people maintained a small, hidden shrine in his honor.

In the 1990s, people in the area started plans for rebuilding a memorial to Lin Xiangru at the site of his tomb. Renovating this important shrine was seen as part of a larger refurbishing of the area. Mr. Lin's birthday on July 20 in the lunar calendar is the occasion for a large temple festival. People come from many outlying villages to take part in the religious/civic event. A market naturally springs up to meet the needs of the festival and to take advantage of the heavy flow of traffic.

Although this temple and many of its activities are still seen by the government as "feudal superstition" and thus are, technically, illegal, local officials show no objection to what takes place at Mr. Lin's temple. These officials are themselves part of the community that reveres the memory of this historical figure and have come to believe in his power of protection. The expression of devotion exhibited here does not lead to political unrest. In fact, it appears to contribute to the harmony and well-being of the citizens. For these reasons, the government shows little inclination to suppress the activities at the site. As a matter of fact, the authorities have been increasingly tolerant of these "technically illegal" activities, especially since the start of the new century.

In the yard of Lin's temple are many steles and stone carvings, given by entrepreneurs and local scholars; these are considered "capital improvements" that add to the reputation and spiritual "worth" of the site. As Lin Xiangru is a well-known figure[40] in China, the "temple" was built in the name of a cultural site. Both local people and government officials have become accustomed to seeing Mr. Lin's temple as a cultural site; it is no longer associated with superstition. Everyone sees that the temple and its yard has not only enhanced their pride in their heritage but has substantially increased their cultural esteem in the larger locale. The memory of Lin celebrates a historical person who was both a person of high moral quality and a virtuous official. Thus has the *de facto* religious temple of Lin gained legitimacy; thus has his spiritual *ling* (efficacy) multiplied.

COMMON SPIRITUAL HERITAGE: FROM SPIRITUAL HUNGER TO SPIRITUAL NOURISHMENT

With the death of Mao Zedong in 1976, and as the promise of Marxism eroded, people felt both the disorientation and the exhilaration that came with the collapse of the Cultural Revolution. However, the radical transformation of the Chinese socioeconomic structure also seems to have rendered Maoism obsolete. As the once-sacred canopy was in tatters, society-wide disappointment and a "spiritual vacuum" could be felt throughout China in the late 1970s and early 1980s.[41] "Spiritual needs" arise in various domains of human life. Marxist theory suggests that "spiritual needs" are a projection of unmet "basic needs." Religion functions only as compensation, distracting attention from the struggle for a more just distribution of material resources. When the material needs of a human population are met, this illusory distraction will no longer be needed and religion will disappear. However, this may also hold true the other way round; that is, when people have their material needs met they may have even greater hunger for spiritual fulfillment. Based on the ethnographic studies of migrants in the city of Shenzhen, the following discussion drives this point home.

In 1979, as part of his program of Reform and Opening Up, Deng Xiaoping declared Shenzhen (深圳), a small fishing village in Guangdong Province, next to Hong Kong, plus a vast tract of surrounding territory as a Special Economic Zone. By the 1990s, Shenzhen was already a modern city with a population of millions, including many young urbanized Chinese who had grown up during the Cultural Revolution and were embracing elements of traditional beliefs and practices as part of their personal spiritual awakening. Preeminent here are the quest for meaning and purpose in life as well as for the freedom needed to pursue this search. The new residents of Shenzhen found that economic well-being was not enough. As their initial hopes for a better paying job and a higher standard of living were met (or even exceeded), life questions of a different kind emerged. Many Shenzhen respondents commented that before arriving in this new city they asked few questions of their life's purpose. Instead, whatever came in life was accepted as inevitable: "This is my life." But in Shenzhen they became attuned to the more-than-mundane aspects of their daily experience. Amid the changing fortunes of their lives in Shenzhen, the economic migrants moved toward a new level of awareness. The shift was manifested in a new sensitivity to spiritual dynamics that may be at play in human experience and a heightened sense of responsibility for the direction of their own lives.

The most significant finding of Fan Lizhu's research in Shenzhen is that the once latent religiousness of Chinese traditional culture is now resurgent. Western-style capitalism—with its double threat of "blind" market forces and moral relativism—threatened to undermine traditional values, sounding the death knell for spirituality. But today in the city of Shenzhen, economic opportunity coexists with a new and exciting spiritual awakening. Confronted with new questions of meaning and purpose of life, the respondents[42] did not turn to the officially approved religious institutions of Buddhism, Daoism, Christianity, or others. Instead, they found very personal approaches for their spiritual search from the age-old traditions of China's common spiritual heritage, which does not ask for membership or baptism or limit their spiritual freedom. By turning to their ancient cultural heritage, they find a way to solve the problem of making sense of life and finding inner peace.

The people Fan met in Shenzhen recognized themselves as on a very personal search for spiritual meaning. They were eager to speak about activities and practices gaining new significance in their lives. For example, one group formed a loose network and gathered with some regularity at a vegetarian restaurant owned by a Buddhist lay-woman. Here they would meet with other persons on the spiritual journey. Part of the space in the restaurant is dedicated to a small bookstore featuring a wide array of spiritu-ally oriented titles, and a bulletin board lists activities in which people may be interested, such as a lecture in the community, a ritual gathering planned in the near future, or an ecological project asking for volunteers. Sometimes the restaurant owner invites a local monk or a visiting international author to make a brief public presentation. More often the discussion develops informally, as customers linger after their meal to share con-cerns and speak about their spiritual practices.

People share their experience with the practice of meditation and physical exer-cise and prayer. They talk about the impact of the spiritual insights and ritual activi-ties in their own lives. This kind of preference of religious practice and belief should be understood from the broad definition of religion offered by C. K. Yang: "Religion may be viewed as a continuum ranging from nontheistic belief systems with an emo-tional intensity that borders upon ultimacy, to theistic belief systems with ultimate val-ues fully symbolized in supernatural entities and supported by patterns of worship and organization."[43]

A look at Shenzhen suggests that the values and practices of China's common spiritual heritage continue to energize contemporary Chinese caught up in the cultural dynamics of urbanization. These people quite comfortably employ terms such as *karma* to aug-ment their understanding of the chance events that, upon reflection, they do not see as chance at all. Such terms with strong religious connotations are very common in peo-ple's conversation, even though native speakers are hardly aware that some important words and concepts have been borrowed from various religions. This kind of borrow-ing is especially prevalent in the Chinese spiritual heritage, which never worries about whether it is borrowing or even engaging in syncretism.

Fan's research in Shenzhen sheds light on the human impulse to search out "meaning beyond the mundane." And the findings indicate that economic advancement does not necessarily do away with spiritual needs; instead, it appears to create the conditions for people to face deeper spiritual hunger of which they were previously unaware. In this "free market" atmosphere, people are able to choose their own means of satisfying their spiritual hunger. Many of them returned—often self-consciously—to practices that are part of China's old tradition, practices to which Chinese people over the centuries have turned in their search for deeper meaning and a peaceful way to live in the world. The moral freedom in this city—unimaginable in earlier days and other places in China—generates a resurgence of interest in China's cultural heritage of religiousness. In their discussion about their experience in searching for spiritual fulfillment, the respondents in Fan's research often centered on traditional Chinese themes—*ming yun, yuan fen, bao ying*, and *wu*. In this section, we first briefly define these terms and then illustrate them with case examples from the study.

Personal Destiny (*ming yun*, 命运). Chinese have always believed that a person's life (*ming*) is somehow related to the influence of a transcendent force named *tian* (天) or heaven. What had once been seen as the ruler's "divine right" to rule (his "mandate of heaven," or *tian ming*) was interpreted by the philosopher Mencius (372–289 B.C.E.) as part of every person's destiny, that is, *ming yun* (命运) (Mencius, Tsin Sin I). This ancient belief in *ming yun* should be understood in two aspects: *ming* (命) as the given status of personal destiny and *yun* (运) as the changing circumstances and individual choices. The combination of these two aspects into *ming yun* as personal destiny keeps life open-ended. For the Chinese, as for people of many other cultures, a person's destiny is seen as both fixed and flexible.

For some decades during Mao's time, the "fixed" or fated side of life seemed to dominate. One had to accept one's lot in life as a worker, as a farmer, as a wife, or whatever. Imagining an alternate destiny was all but impossible. Profound changes since the post-Mao reform have attuned China's younger generation to more choices and new possibilities. In place of state-sponsored guarantees of lifetime employment—the so-called "iron rice bowl"—young people today can and must choose their own careers. Their livelihood is no longer chained to the *danwei* (单位),[44] the local work unit that had previously exercised near total control over employment as well as many other aspects of people's lives.

In Shenzhen people live in a "free market" for jobs and salaries. "Here I'm free to choose my work," said Ms. Wang. "I can even leave this job if I don't like it, because I know I can find another job in a short time." For many respondents there, this utterly novel experience of employment freedom was linked to a growing awareness of deeper levels of personal decision-making now available to them. And with their expanded consciousness has come a new range of spiritual questions. If this provokes anxiety, it also brings freedom, with a sense that one's destiny is highly flexible. In contemporary Shenzhen, residents frequently speak of "grasping their fate."

Mr. Zhou is a good example of this attempt to grasp one's fate. In the mid-1990s he moved to Shenzhen to start his own small business; now he has met with material success well beyond his earlier hopes. Living in his hometown, he had never entertained the questions, such as meaning and purpose of life, since any decision about his life would be determined by his family. After several years of struggle in Shenzhen, Zhou was suddenly quite successful, now owning a house and even a private automobile. This financial success triggered deeper questions about life. Now, in the giddy freedom of Shenzhen, he found he was not able to simply enjoy his new wealth. His sudden good fortune led him to ask himself: Why is this success mine? While others he knew—equally hard-working—were still struggling, his life and career had quite suddenly begun to flourish. To make sense out of this turn of events, Mr. Zhou found himself unexpectedly returning to traditional convictions in his culture about personal destiny or *ming yun*. As Mr. Zhou well knew, to say "my life (*ming*) is good" was not to brag but expressed surprise and even gratitude for the good fortune that had come to his life. While the ancient concept of *ming yun* did not fully explain Mr. Zhou's recent successes, it did make him more mindful of the good fortune that had been given him—a fortune that he recognized he was now responsible for. This retrieval of an ancient theme made Mr. Zhou more attentive to the meaning of life, and he eventually started to practice what would be called popular religion.

Fateful Coincidences (*yuan fen*缘分). Another element in the Chinese common spiritual heritage that surfaced repeatedly among the respondents was that of chance or fateful coincidence, which in Chinese is *yuan fen* (缘分). This notion is commonplace in Chinese tradition, serving as a rough equivalent to the English phrase "luck" with an emphasis on certain potential relationship. Chinese are likely to describe any happy coincidence—the chance meeting, for example, of a good friend in a supermarket—as *yuan fen*. There is, of course, also bad *yuan fen*, what in English one might name "an unlucky break."

Almost all of Shenzhen's residents had moved to this burgeoning metropolis in the previous one or two decades. Leaving settled lives in their old home towns, they were intent to make a new life in the new environment. Their re-location brought them much more than physical displacement. Ms. Wang, for example, was struggling to understand her own life journey. Her present economic well-being in Shenzhen had come about through circumstances that were mysterious to her. Several crises and painful setbacks had led her to come to this city, where her fortune experienced an about-face. But, after many reversals of fortune, she found herself in Shenzhen with an excellent job that offered quick promotions.

But Ms. Wang wondered how those earlier crises and reversals contributed to her life today. In this realization her sense of *yuan fen* underwent a transformation; for her, *yuan fen* no longer simply referred to superficial chance events but now registered important links between her previous unfortunate experiences and her present well-being. She seemed to take *yuan fen* out of its more everyday and superficial meaning and assign it a richer sense of "fateful coincidence" that was intimately linked to the current direction of her life.

Despite the pain Ms. Wang's misfortunes caused her at the time, many of the misfortunes she suffered along the way seemed to have led to this new and much better life. How to explain this? To help fathom this contemporary mystery, Ms. Wang rediscovered a theme from China's past: *yuan fen* as fateful coincidence. This deeply embedded aspect of Chinese culture became fused many centuries ago with the Buddhist notion of *karma*; in a universe that is thoroughly moral, there are no mere coincidences. The events of our lives, for better or for worse, are related to past behavior—virtuous or otherwise.

K.S. Yang and David Ho have discussed the psychological advantages of this traditional belief. By assigning causality of negative events to *yuan fen* that is beyond personal control, people are able to "soothe relationships, reduce conflict, and promote
social harmony."[45] Similarly, when positive events are seen to result primarily from *yuan
fen*, personal credit is not directly assigned—thus reducing pride on one side of the relationship and envy and resentment on the other.

Ms. Wang's interpretation of *yuan fen* had undergone a transformation through her
own life journey in Shenzhen. Earlier, she had understood *yuan fen* as a simple coincidence or a casual chance event. Now, she sees fateful coincidences as having shaped her
fortune in a favorable way. This insight has made her grateful. And her new appreciation
of *yuan fen* has moral consequences, which have given rise to a heightened sensitivity
to the ethical dimensions of her professional life. She desires to conduct her life according to high moral principles so that her favorable *yuan fen* will continue. For Ms. Wang,
yuan fen has shifted from cultural cliché to a meaningful marker of a moral life. From
this case, we see another important dynamic aspect in the Chinese spiritual heritage.
Personal destiny and fateful coincidence are linked; what had appeared on the surface to
be chance events (for better or for worse) are, in fact, part of some deeper, more spiritual
rhythm that shapes a person's life.

Moral Reciprocity (*bao ying*报应).[46] Traditional Chinese belief in *bao ying* or moral
reciprocity tells us that people dwell in a moral universe. In *The Ledgers of Merit and
Demerit*, Cynthia Brokaw describes *bao ying* as a "belief in a supernatural or cosmic
retribution, a belief that has been a fundamental, at times *the* fundamental, belief of
Chinese religion since the beginning of recorded history."[47]

For many respondents in this fast-changing city of Shenzhen, questions of morality were of greatest concern. Ms. Shen recalled her early experience in the city, when
she was ready to cheat clients in pursuit of greater profits. As she became increasingly
wealthy, she also experienced an increasing sense of guilt. During this period of regret,
Ms. Shen went with a friend to a public lecture offered by a visiting Buddhist monk. One
of his statements struck home: "If you are meant to have something, it will be yours.
Otherwise there would be *bao ying*." Puzzling over this cryptic statement, she began to
question her own acquisitiveness and greediness. Gradually, she came to see her business pursuits as part of a larger life design. She determined to end her deceitful practices
and adopt a pattern of strict honesty in her dealings with others.[48]

This belief in moral reciprocity, woven deep into the fabric of Chinese culture, is
rooted in the conviction that the universe is moral. This view of fate as moral retribution dominates the earliest Zhou (1046–771 B.C.E.) texts, including those later incorporated into the Confucian canon. The *Classic of History* says, "On the doer of good,
heaven sends down all blessings, and on the doer of evil, he sends down all calamities"
(书经·汤诰). Ms. Shen now recognized that living according to higher moral standards
would affect her own future; good would come from this moral discipline. She began to
believe that, even financially, she would have "what she was meant to have."

These moral themes—fateful coincidence, personal destiny, and moral reciprocity—
are closely interrelated. Apparent chance events, small or big, influence the shape and

fortune of each person's destiny. Recognizing this connection has the moral result of making a person more responsible for his or her actions. The recognition of the Chinese common spiritual heritage tells us that the residents of Shenzhen today enjoy a freedom that is not only economic, but spiritual. Now, in the "free-market" atmosphere of Shenzhen, they are able to choose their own means of satisfying their spiritual hunger. Their interest is seldom in the orthodox understanding of these themes or in the institutional religions. Instead they speak of the impact of these spiritual insights and ritual activities in their own lives through ancient Chinese moral categories that are a crucial part of Chinese popular religions.

Awareness (*wu* 悟). The three themes of personal destiny, chance, and moral reciprocity form an interlocking unity within the Chinese common spiritual heritage. Each is related to the others; seemingly chance events profoundly influence one's destiny; yet one's own responsible performance within a moral universe also gives shape to one's life. Doing good for others produces further good for oneself, according to the traditional theme of moral reciprocity (*bao ying*).

These three themes in the common spiritual heritage of Chinese only come alive when a fourth theme is introduced. Many respondents in Fan's study spoke of a "new awareness" (*kai wu* 开悟 or *jue wu* 觉悟) that triggered their new consciousness of the above three themes. A spiritual awareness is the engine or energy that moves these themes from mere ideas to motivating forces in an individual's life. A new and deeper awareness of *ming yun* ignites a more responsible attitude toward life; a richer awareness of *yuan fen* as more than mere coincidence stirs a person to respond to events instead of simply resigning themselves to a response such as, "That's life."

Mrs. Wei is a well-educated person who enjoys a high profile as the host of a popular call-in television show in Shenzhen. She takes satisfaction in giving good advice to those who call her with questions and problems. And she sees this public service as a fruit of her growing spiritual awareness. Impressed by the calm and peacefulness she has observed in the Buddhist monks who have preached in this city, Mrs. Wei says she has determined to live in a more mindful way. She has arranged a small shrine in her home where each morning she sits quietly in front of a statue of Guanyin. She has become more careful and intentional about her diet and consciously links her nutritional habits with her spiritual nourishment.

Awareness, as a dynamic factor in the Chinese spiritual heritage, appears in two guises: it is first a realization that arrives as a gift, seemingly unbidden; then it necessarily becomes a practice that a person intentionally follows. That is, some of the respondents in the study reported becoming aware in a quite sudden fashion and/or in a way that was triggered by external events (hearing a lecture or reading a book). Having received this new awareness about their destiny, what had seemed like chance events, or the need to do good and benefit their own fate, some respondents told how they had developed this sense of awareness. This might be through practices of private devotion, or periodic discussions in vegetarian restaurants, or a more social, ritualized practice of freeing animals in the Buddhist ceremony of *fang sheng*.

Chinese Popular Religion—Thriving in the Midst of Everyday Life

Daniel Overmyer observes, "Chinese local rituals and beliefs are similar to those of ordinary people in many other cultures, whatever their larger political and intellectual contexts; wherever one looks, one sees people praying and sacrificing to their gods or saints for help in dealing with the difficulties of life, appeals that can also involve festivals and processions."[49]

In the twenty-first century, the Chinese common spiritual heritage continues to exist in China's rural and urban areas. This heritage is characterized as a non-institutionalized, non-rationalized (in the Weberian sense) form of religion; diffuseness remains the major characteristic of folk religion in China. Instead of signaling the demise of traditional religiousness, China's economic development seems to have quickened the impulse of spiritual renewal. The worldview of the Chinese common spiritual heritage is distinctive. Its images and practices are shaped by the elaborate codes of Chinese culture, which help Chinese people to face the challenges and puzzles brought about by modernization.

In conclusion, we are convinced that the dramatic revival and development of Chinese popular religion in recent years is not dependent on institutional "shifts across religious traditions." Every single religious tradition developed in the history of China contributes to the common rich spiritual heritage that pervades various aspects of everyday life.

When a Chinese person turns to certain ideas of the popular religion, or takes part in certain ritualistic activities, it is more likely because he or she feels the necessity of some adjustment in his or her way of everyday life. However, there is not much, if any, thinking or talking about being converted or not converted. Even when a Chinese accepts and practices certain religious principles, he or she is likely not to gain membership in that particular religion through what is generally known as "conversion." After all, the folk religion of China is diffused and highly inclusive.

Understanding the resurgence or revitalization of religions/spirituality around the world may be constricted if the term "conversion" (especially as it has been used in Western Christianity) is deployed. We believe, however, that the return to or the rediscovery or discovery of the depth dimension of human experience, both individual and communal, is important in the study of both global and local manifestations of religious/spiritual change in the contemporary world. (This research is sponsored by the Chinese National Social Science Fund [2010, 10BZJ005]).

Notes

1. Kenneth Dean, "Local Ritual Traditions of Southeast China: A Challenge to Definitions of Religion and Theories of Ritual," in *China: Methodology, Theories and Findings*, ed. Fenggang Yang and Graeme Lang (Leiden: Brill, 2011).

2. Peter Berger, "The Desecularization of the World: An Overview," in *The Desecularization of the World: Resurgent Religion and World Politics*, ed. Peter Berger (Grand Rapids, MI: Eerdmans, 1999), 4.

3. Patricia M. Davis and Lewis R. Rambo, "Converting: Toward a Cognitive Theory of Religious Change," in *Soul, Psyche, Brain: New Directions in the Study of Brain-Mind Science*, ed. Kelly Bulkeley (New York: Palgrave Macmillan, 2005), 4.

4. Rodney Stark and Roger Finke, *Acts of Faith: Explaining the Human Side of Religion* (Berkeley and Los Angeles: University of California Press, 2000), 114.

5. C. K. Yang, *Religion in Chinese Society: A Study of Contemporary Social Functions of Religion and Some of Their Historical Factors* (Berkeley and Los Angeles: University of California Press, 1961), 3–4.

6. Lizhu Fan, "The Dilemma of Pursuing Chinese Religious Studies in the Framework of Western Religious Theories," *Fudan Journal of Humanities and Social Sciences* 2, no. 2 (2009): 29–48.

7. Vincent Goossaert, "Religious Traditions, Communities and Institutions," in *Chinese Religious Life*, ed. David A. Palmer, Glenn Shive, and Philip L. Wickeri (Oxford: Oxford University Press, 2011), 172.

8. Fenggang Yang, trans., Chinese version of *Acts of Faith: Explaining the Human Side of Religion* (Beijing: People's University Press, 2004), 142.

9. The Chinese term *guiyi* (皈依) refers to the ceremony that initiates a person as a Buddhist. This procedure of changing a layman into a believer has very strong Buddhist connotations. More importantly, many people in China, if not the majority, practice Buddhism without going through such a ceremony.

10. Yang, *Religion in Chinese Society*, 296.

11. Ibid.

12. Adam Chau, *Mysterious Response: Doing Popular Religion in Contemporary China* (Stanford, CA: Stanford University Press, 2006), 242.

13. The term "village" (Chinese: 村, pinyin: *cun*) in China today may refer to either a natural village or an administrative village. A natural village (Chinese: 自然村, pinyin: *zìráncūn*) is a spontaneously and naturally formed rural community unit, while an administrative village (Chinese: 行政村, pinyin: *xíngzhèngcūn*) is a grassroots-level administrative unit that is the lowest level of the government system. Quite often an administrative village may include more than one natural village. But sometimes, an administrative village may include only one natural village. In the latter case, they just overlap.

14. Goossaert, "Religious Traditions, Communities and Institutions," 187.

15. Lizhu Fan, James Whitehead, and Evelyn Whitehead, *Sociology of Religion: Religion and China* (Beijing: Current Affairs Press, 2010), 290–291.

16. Ibid., 194.

17. The Ledgers of Merit and Demerit (功过格). The ledgers of merit and demerit are a category of morality book (shan-shu, literally, "good books"), a genre of literature that as a whole became very popular in the sixteenth and seventeenth centuries. The ledgers are founded on the belief in supernatural retribution, that is, the heaven and gods will reward men who do good and punish those who do evil.

18. Cynthia Brokaw, *The Ledgers of Merit and Demerit* (Princeton: Princeton University Press, 1991), 40.

19. Daniel L. Overmyer, *Local Religion in North China in the Twentieth Century* (Leiden: Koninklijke Brill, 2009), 56.

20. Dean, "Local Ritual Traditions of Southeast China," 134.

21. The term *wuwei* (无为), literally meaning non-action, is an important concept of Daoist (Taoist) philosophy that involves knowing when to act and when not to act. When the Han Dynasty (206 B.C.E.–220 C.E.) was first established, the emperor Liu Bang immediately initiated the Daoist *Wuwei* governance, which involved making peace with the Xiongnu (a confederation of nomadic tribes from Central Asia) through Heqin intermarriages, rewarding his allies and giving them pseudo-fiefdoms, and allowing the population to take a breath from centuries of warfare. Later on, *Wuwei* governance developed with local autonomy. Far from the capital, local leaders in the villages negotiated with regional officials in what sociologist Fei Xiaotong has described as a "largely self-regulating" environment.

22. Chau, *Mysterious Response*, 13.

23. Daniel L. Overmyer, "Introduction," in *Collection of Temple Festivals and Folk Customs in Baoding Area* (Tianjin: Tianjin Chinese Classics Press, 2007), 80.

24. Daniel L. Overmyer, *Local Religion in North China in the Twentieth Century: The Structure and Organization of Community Rituals and Beliefs* (Leiden: Koninklijke Brill, 2009), 58.

25. Overmyer, "Introduction," 16.

26. Yangge (秧歌), or "Rice Sprout Song," is a form of Chinese folk dance originating from the Song Dynasty. It is very popular in northern China and one of the most representative forms of folk arts.

27. Shaanbei (陕北) refers to the northern part of Shaanxi (陕西) Province, which is located in northwestern China. It is an area that is cold in the winter and very hot in the summer, with dry winter and spring.

28. Heilongdawang (黑龙大王) literally means "the Great Black Dragon King."

29. Chau, *Mysterious Response*, 88.

30. The official exchange rate between the US dollar and Renminbi yuan is about 1:6.38 (1 US dollar = 6.38 yuan RMB), as of Sept. 2011.

31. Chau, *Mysterious Response*, 86.

32. Yang, *Religion in Chinese Society*, 8–10.

33. Lizhu Fan, "The Cult of the Silkworm Mother as a Core of Local Community Religion in a North China Village: Field Study in Zhiwuying, Baoding, Hebei." Special Issue, *Religion in China Today, China Quarterly*, ed. Daniel Overmyer, 53-66. Cambridge: Cambridge University Press, 2003.

34. Daniel L. Overmyer and Lizhu Fan, *Collection of Folk Customs in Handan Area* (Tianjin: Tianjin Chinese Classic Press, 2006), 65–66.

35. Houqiang Chen, *Overview of Chen Clan in Cangnan County* (Hangzhou: Hangzhou Press, 2006); *Cangnan Xian Chen Xing Tong Lan* (Hangzhou: Hangzhou Chuban She, 2006), 157.

36. Yang, *Religion in Chinese Society*, 43.

37. Ibid., 168.

38. Ibid.

39. Ibid.

40. Lin Xiangru (蔺相如) served as the State Premier in the kingdom of Zhao (403–228 B.C.E.), an area in Hebei Province just south of the modern city of Beijing. He is famous for his wisdom and patriotism, and some of his life stories have come down as proverbs in Chinese culture. For example, "Return the intact jade to Zhao" (完璧归赵), "Making up between the general and the premier" (将相和), etc.

41. For more information on the Shenzhen study, see Lizhu Fan, *Religious Transformation in Contemporary China: Field Study in Shenzhen* (Taipei: Weber Culture, 2005); Lizhu Fan,

James Whitehead, and Evelyn Whitehead, "Fate and Fortune: Popular Religion and Moral Capital in Shenzhen," *Journal of Chinese Religion* 32 (Feb. 2005): 83–101; Lizhu Fan, James Whitehead, and Evelyn Whitehead, "The Spiritual Search in Shenzhen: Adopting and Adapting China's Common Spiritual Heritage," *Nova Religio* 9, no. 2 (Nov. 2005): 50–62.

42. Fan Lizhu conducted lengthy interviews with fifty-six persons, both men and women, in Shenzhen from 1998 to 2000. For details, see Fan Lizhu, *Religious Transformation in Contemporary China.*

43. Yang, *Religion in Chinese Society*, 26.

44. The danwei was a special type of organization in China under the planned economy. Centered on the urban workplace, the *danwei* (work unit) was the fundamental social and spatial unit of urban China under socialism. Not only was it the source of employment, wages, and other material benefits for the vast majority of urban residents, it was also the institution through which the urban population was housed, organized, regulated, policed, educated, trained, protected, and surveyed. Furthermore, as the basic unit of urban society, each *danwei* became a community, providing its members with identity and social belonging.

45. On the role of *Yuan*, see K. S. Yang and David Y. F. Ho, "Chinese Social Life: A Conceptual and Empirical Analysis," *Asian Contributions to Psychology*, ed. Anand C. Paranjpe, David Y. F. Ho, and Robert W. Rieber (New York: Praeger Publishers, 1988), 270. Sociologist Rance Lee (Li Peiliang) reports that a survey of 550 persons in Hong Kong in 1974 showed that more than 50 percent believed in the importance of establishing good *yuan fen* with their physician. (Here, *yuan fen* refers to the "chemistry" or friendly feeling between persons; as such, it is both a "fortunate" relationship and one that people have some responsibility to influence.) Lee argues that such an attitude is both positive and rational; having a comfortable relationship with one's doctor will likely lead to better care and a healthier life.

46. Cynthia Brokaw and other scholars prefer to translate *bao ying* as "moral retribution" (though Brokaw does occasionally use the word "reciprocity"; see *The Ledgers of Merit and Demerit*, 28). The term "retribution" carries negative nuances, suggesting that *bao ying* functions more characteristically as punishment than as positive reward. In our judgment, the term reciprocity better expresses the distribution of both reward and punishment.

47. Brokaw defines this belief as "the faith that some force—either a supernatural force like heaven or the gods, or an automatic cosmic reaction—inevitably recompensed human behavior in a rational manner: it rewarded certain 'good' deeds, be they religious sacrifices, acts of good government, or upright personal conduct, and punished evil ones" (*The Ledgers of Merit and Demerit*, 28).

48. This cannot be considered as a case of conversion, at least not in the meaning defined by Stark and Finke. Rather than being "converted" to the Buddhist religion, Ms. Shen only accepted certain ideas from the Buddhist preaching she heard. This is very common in Chinese culture, where folk religion is diffused and highly inclusive.

49. Daniel L. Overmyer, "Chinese Religious Traditions from 1900–2005: An Overview," in *Cambridge Companion to Modern Chinese Culture*, ed. Kam Louie (Cambridge: Cambridge University Press, 2008), 178.

BIBLIOGRAPHY

Berger, Peter. "The Desecularization of the World: A Global Overview." In *The Desecularization of the World: Resurgent Religion and World Politics*, ed. Peter Berger, 1–18. Grand Rapids, MI: Wm. B. Eerdmans Publishing, 1999.

Brokaw, Cynthia. *The Ledgers of Merit and Demerit*. Princeton: Princeton University Press 1991.

Chau, Adam. *Mysterious Response: Doing Popular Religion in Contemporary China*. Stanford, CA: Stanford University Press, 2006.

Chen, Houqiang. *Overview of Chen Clan in Cangnan County*. Hangzhou: Hangzhou Press, 2006.

Classic of History (尚书). Chinese Text Project (Zhuzi Baijia). http://chinese.dsturgeon.net/text.pl?node=21170&if=en.

Davis, Patricia M., and Lewis R. Rambo. "Converting: Toward a Cognitive Theory of Religious Change." In *Soul, Psyche, Brain: New Directions in the Study of Brain-Mind Science*, ed. Kelly Bulkeley, 159–173. New York: Palgrave Macmillan, 2005.

Dean, Kenneth. "Local Ritual Traditions of Southeast China: A Challenge to Definitions of Religion and Theories of Ritual." In *China: Methodology, Theories, and Findings*, ed. Fenggang Yang and Graeme Lang, 133–165. Leiden: Brill, 2011.

Fan, Lizhu. "The Cult of the Silkworm Mother as a Core of Local Community Religion in a North China Village: Field Study in Zhiwuying, Baoding, Hebei." Special Issue, *Religion in China Today, China Quarterly*, ed. Daniel Overmyer, 53–66. Cambridge: Cambridge University Press, 2003.

——. *Religious Transformation in Contemporary China: Field Study in Shenzhen*. Taipei: Weber Culture, 2005.

——. "The Dilemma of Pursuing Chinese Religious Studies in the Framework of Western Religious Theories." *Fudan Journal of Humanities and Social Sciences* 2, no.2 (June 2009): 29–48.

Fan, Lizhu, and James Whitehead. "Spirituality, Morality and Religiousness: Adopting and Adapting China's Spiritual Heritage Today." In *Chinese Religious Life*, ed. David A. Palmer, Glenn Shive, and Philip L. Wickeri, 13–29. Oxford: Oxford University Press, 2011.

Fan, Lizhu, James Whitehead, and Evelyn Whitehead. "Fate and Fortune: Popular Religion and Moral Capital in Shenzhen." *Journal of Chinese Religion* 32 (Feb. 2005): 83–100.

——. "The Spiritual Search in Shenzhen: Adopting and Adapting China's Common Spiritual Heritage." *Nova Religio* 9, no. 2 (Nov. 2005): 50–61.

——. *Sociology of Religion: Religion and China*. Beijing: Current Affairs Press, 2010.

Goossaert, Vincent. "The Social Organization of Religious Communities in the Twentieth Century." In *Chinese Religious Life*, ed. David A. Palmer, Glenn Shive, and Philip L. Wickeri, 172–192. Oxford: Oxford University Press, 2011.

Lee, Rance (Li Peiliang). "Social Sciences and Indigenous Ideas." In *The Ideas and Behaviors of Chinese People*, ed. Qiaojian & Pan Naigu, 240–252. Tianjin: Tianjin People's Press 1995.

Mencius. *The Works of Mencius*(孟子), trans. by James Legge. New York: Dover, 1970.

Overmyer, Daniel L. *Folk Buddhist Religion: Dissenting Sects in Late Traditional China*. Cambridge, MA: Harvard University Press, 1976.

——. *Buddhism in the Trenches: Attitudes Toward Popular Religion in Chinese Scriptures Found at Tun-Huang*. Cambridge, MA: Harvard-Yenching Institute, 1990.

——. "Introduction," In *Collection of Temple Festivals and Folk Customs in Baoding Area*, 65–77. Tianjin: Tianjin Chinese Classics Press, 2007.

——. "Chinese Religious Traditions from 1900–2005: An Overview." In *Cambridge Companion to Modern Chinese Culture*, ed. Kam Louie, 173–197. Cambridge: Cambridge University Press, 2008.

——. *Local Religion in North China in the Twentieth Century: The Structure and Organization of Community Rituals and Beliefs*. Leiden: Koninklijke Brill, 2009.

Overmyer, Daniel L., and Lizhu Fan. *Collection of Folk Customs in Handan Area*. Tianjin: Tianjin Chinese Classic Press, 2006.

Stark, Rodney, and Roger Finke. *Acts of Faith: Explaining the Human Side of Religion*. Berkeley and Los Angeles: University of California Press, 2000. Yang, Fenggang, trans. Chinese version of *Acts of Faith: Explaining the Human Side of Religion*. Beijing: People's University Press, 2004.

Yang, C. K. *Religion in Chinese Society: A Study of Contemporary Social Functions of Religion and Some of their Historical Factors*. Berkeley and Los Angeles: University of California Press, 1961.

Yang, K. S., and David Y. F. Ho. "Chinese Social Life: A Conceptual and Empirical Analysis." In *Asian Contributions to Psychology*, ed. Anand C. Paranjpe, David Y. F. Ho, and Robert W. Rieber, 263–281. New York: Praeger Publishers, 1988.

CHAPTER 25

CONVERSION TO JUDAISM

ALAN F. SEGAL

THE IDEA OF CONVERSION IN BIBLICAL RELIGION

CONVERSION is a post-exilic phenomenon in Judaism. It was born in the Persian period, in response to a whole new style of Israelite life, and it flourished in the culturally plural, cosmopolitan, and individualistic world of the Hellenistic Mediterranean. Religious conversion reached maturity during the Roman period (beginning roughly in 65 B.C.E.), and then it greatly abated within the Christian and Muslim empires of the Middle Ages. Conversion did not return as a significant issue in Judaism until the modern period. This stands to reason, for conversion demands a mobile population who have the right and the ability to make choices, and it also demands a variety of thought available to make those choices. Such a condition only existed in broad form in the Hellenistic world, as we shall see. But there are significant forerunners to the phenomenon in First Temple times.

The word "conversion" and the related noun "convert" and verb "to convert" appear infrequently in English translations of the Bible. When they do, they translate the Hebrew word *šûb* ("to turn or return") or the Greek *epistrephein* ("to turn around or back"). The terms themselves do not express the full range of meanings and significances of the modern term conversion. To explore the biblical understandings of conversion involves not only a study of particular words but of the social institutions that arose in Hellenistic times.

Although the religion of Israel primarily concerned people who were born into Israel, the Bible in the First Temple period also speaks of Gentile strangers or sojourners (*gērı̄'m*) among the people. Indeed, it is this word that is chosen to express "converts" in the post-Second Temple period. They are restrained from participating in some of the formal rituals of Israel's religious life (Exod. 12:43–45),[1] but they may offer sacrifices to God. A Gentile man may participate in the Passover sacrifice, provided that he has been circumcised (Num. 14:13–15; Exod. 12:48–49). The book of Deuteronomy tells us that female war captives are not to be considered slaves or sexual concubines but are to be offered the possibility of marrying the captor (Deut. 21:10–14). She is asked to go through a series of rituals—cutting her hair, paring her nails, changing her clothing, and mourning her previous relations for a month. No statement of conversion accompanies this ruling, so the religious status of the person is moot. But, though the exact status of the woman is unclear, the intentions of the laws are clear that people from without Israel are allowed to participate in the ritual life of the community and even to marry within it.

Another important precedent is the way that the prophets use the motif of the call for Israel to return (*šûb*) to the Lord. Israel will find mercy and pardon (Jer. 3:12–13; Isa. 55:1–9). What is necessary is that the people sincerely repent and return to God in truth and justice (Jer. 4:1–4), a move that itself requires God's strengthening of Israel (Jer. 3:22) and that will in turn lead to a renewed relationship with God.[2]

Of course, the Bible is mostly concerned with the Children of Israel and their biological descendants. But anyone who knows the Bible can think of several exceptions, the most important of which is the story of Ruth that is recounted in its own small and beautiful book. She was a Moabitess, a widow of an Israelite living East of the Jordan, who followed her mother-in-law Naomi back to Judah and, when she found a husband in Boaz, became not just a Judean but an actual ancestor of David:

> But Ruth said,
>
> "Do not press me to leave you
> or to turn back from following you!
> Where you go, I will go;
> where you lodge, I will lodge;
> your people shall be my people,
> and your God my God.
> [17] Where you die, I will die—
> there will I be buried.
> May the Lord do thus and so to me,
> and more as well,
> if even death parts me from you!" (Ruth 1:16–17)

No argument could have done as much as this charming story to attest that the border of the Israelite people was permeable, that interested non-Israelites could join themselves to Israel by choice. The story therefore repays Ruth's piety and loyalty by finding her the perfect husband, the Judahite Boaz.

But the date of the book is quite different from the ostensible date of the story. The story is set in the time of the Judges, the two hundred years of colonization (1200–1000 B.C.E.) that preceded the rise of kingship in Israel. In fact, it follows the book of Judges in the Protestant order of the Bible. But the book itself is written in very mature and quite late Hebrew. There is no doubt that it comes from much later in the history of the country, most likely in the post-exilic Persian period that stretched from 538 B.C.E. to the arrival of the Greeks around 331 B.C.E. It was the effects of the early post-exilic centuries to which the book of Ruth spoke eloquently.

Then, too, there were the people who were added on, after the return from Babylon. The impurity of the land after the conquest was apparently matched by the anomalous nature of some of the people. The covenant-swearing ceremony contained instructions for those who were "separated from the peoples of the lands" or "attached to the Lord":

> [28] The rest of the people, the priests, the Levites, the gatekeepers, the singers, the temple servants, and all who have separated themselves from the peoples of the lands to adhere to the law of God, their wives, their sons, their daughters, all who have knowledge and understanding, [29] join with their kin, their nobles, and enter into a curse and an oath to walk in God's law, which was given by Moses the servant of God, and to observe and do all the commandments of the Lord our Lord and his ordinances and his statutes. [30] We will not give our daughters to the peoples of the land or take their daughters for our sons; [31] and if the peoples of the land bring in merchandise or any grain on the sabbath day to sell, we will not buy it from them on the sabbath or on a holy day; and we will forego the crops of the seventh year and the exaction of every debt. (Neh. 10:28–31)

Nilvim, those who accompanied the returning exiles, as well as the eunuchs among Israel, were enjoined to abide by the Torah of the Lord and so could be said to have crossed over into full Judaic identity, though there is not enough evidence to understand how or when (Isa. 56:3; Ezra 6:21; Neh. 10:29, 13:3; Esther 9:27; Zech. 2:15):

> And the foreigners who join themselves to the Lord,
> to minister to him, to love the name of the Lord,
> and to be his servants,
> all who keep the sabbath, and do not profane it,
> and hold fast my covenant—
> [7] these I will bring to my holy mountain,
> and make them joyful in my house of prayer;
> their burnt offerings and their sacrifices
> will be accepted on my altar;
> for my house shall be called a house of prayer
> for all peoples.
> [8] Thus says the Lord God,
> who gathers the outcasts of Israel,
> I will gather others to them. (Isa. 56:6–8)

There were two contravening forces at work at the same time. New governments under Ezra and later Nehemiah produced a search for the original purity of the people. Foreign women were divorced in what must have been an extremely painful social program. It was, however, a failure as social policy without the developing notion of incorporation into the community of those who were not pure descendants of the original nation but who were willing to practice Israelite religion. The corresponding antithesis is just as present in the Book of Ruth and in the openness of the religious leaders to these who are like Ruth. Women and men could be added to the people of Israel if they desired to be included and decided to observe the Torah. They could be fully socialized into the people and they could marry and flourish within it. Actually, some socially acceptable identity change was already available in First Temple times (1000 B.C.E. to 587 B.C.E.).

HELLENIZATION

In 333 B.C.E., the huge Persian Empire, the largest empire the world had seen, fell into the hands of Alexander, the young conqueror from Macedonia. Alexander had little ambition to change the structure of the empire, but his military achievements set the stage for a long period of cultural interaction. Almost immediately the countries held captive by the Persians began to accept Hellenization, a word which means that they began to adopt a Greek lifestyle and Greek cultural forms but, in Greek, *Hellenizō*, actually means to learn the Greek language. It was the Greek language that served as the medium for business exchange and, even more, for unprecedented cultural exchange between the various states conquered by Alexander.

In a larger economic, social, and political sense, the changes brought about by the Hellenistic age were already under way before Alexander. The empires of the ancient Near East had always been centered in the river valleys. The Persians were the first to form a huge political entity connected by an expansive road system, which ruled from the Danube to the upper Indus. It was an empire whose wealth existed in trade as well as agriculture. All of these forces increased greatly by the conquest of Alexander, even though his empire quickly splintered into several smaller states, each headed by one of Alexander's incessantly feuding generals. It took a long time to find out who was the strongest. But when it was over, the Ptolemaic Dynasty in Egypt and the Seleucid Dynasty in Antioch were the two greatest victors. None of them were native aristocrats in the lands they ruled, and thus they tended to do away with a great many traditions of the indigenous peoples. So it was a time in which old traditions died and in which rulership depended only on the power to rule.

Israel was no exception. The Davidic king had not ruled during the Persian period; the priests ruled instead. They were the first to Hellenize. Their positive attitude toward Greece and Hellenistic institutions continued unabated from the fourth century for the next century and a half, while Judea was ruled peacefully by the Ptolemaic dynasty, descendants of Alexander's general Ptolemy, who had taken Egypt, the largest and richest corner of Alexander's empire.

The culmination of the first stage of contact between Greeks and Jews was the translation of the Bible into Greek. According to legend in the Letter of Aristeas, this volume was the product of Ptolemy's own scholarly benevolence, as he directed and paid for an institute of advanced study composed of seventy well-chosen scholars who were ensconced on a lovely uninhabited island in the middle of the Nile. Each scholar worked individually and, miraculously, produced the exact same translation of the Bible into

Greek. Anyone who knows academia knows that this is a greater miracle than crossing the Red Sea on dry ground. No doubt, the story was meant to underline that the translation had God's blessing. The edition was thus called the Septuagint (abbreviated LXX) because *Septuaginta* means "seventy" in Latin. Although the legend attributes the document to the intellectual curiosity of King Ptolemy, the Septuagint was largely for use by the large and influential Jewish community of Alexandria, most of whose members had lost the ability to read Hebrew.

Hellenization in Israel was also a colonial phenomenon. Like all colonialism, it did not infuse all parts of society equally. The amount of Hellenization absorbed by each class and group set up a series of conflicts in the society along political, economic, and social lines. But the conflict was often expressed in religious terms, as in the case of the famous Maccabean Revolt, which was as much a civil war as a religious revolt. So the community still living in the land of Israel kept a bit more of its native ways than those living elsewhere, but everyone took on a great many Greek values and customs and formed many different ways of expressing Judaism, each of which depended on a different master narrative of the significance of the Bible and yielded a different definition of self and Judaism. Each of the traditional definitions of Jewishness lost some legitimacy and needed to be argued for in a way that had not previously been necessary. Almost all religions of the period needed to begin an outreach program in order to explain themselves to fellow citizens in other cultures. The most important outcome of this cultural enterprise was the rise of cosmopolitanism and individualism. Cosmopolitanism comes from two Greek words that mean a citizen of the universe, implying that people became aware of the great world around them, thus becoming more a citizen of the empire and less a citizen of their own particular city. Along with this cosmopolitanism came individualism, the notion that each person has an individual history that can be compared with another person's experience and history. That meant seriously considering people from many different cultures and languages. Through the Greek language, everyone had the chance to encounter each other and learn about their experience. With the rise of religious justifications for traditional religions in Greek, transformed as they were by Greek society, together with the developing sense of cosmopolitanism and individualism, religious choice became a significant characteristic of Hellenistic life. With religious choice came conversion.

CONVERSION IN HELLENISTIC JUDAISM IN THE LAND OF ISRAEL

Conversion is an appropriate term for discussing change of religious commitment in the Hellenistic world, even though the texts do not always use the term. There were many consequences of changing commitment from one social group within Judaism to another, whether from a Gentile to a Jewish group, a Jewish to a Gentile group, or from one group within the Jewish community to another. Arthur Darby Nock defined the study of conversion in the ancient world by showing that conversion was a distinctly specialized and rare religious experience.[3] According to Nock, most religious rites of the time helped maintain the political order because they were civic ceremonies. Participation involved adherence, a low level of involvement, as an act of civic piety. But missionary religions such as Judaism and Christianity and some of the Mystery Cults (sodalities with a secret initiation ceremony that promised transformation to a higher state of existence) stimulated conversion, raising commitment far above simple adherence. Conversion necessarily involved a radical change of lifestyle, often a move to a socially stigmatized group. Nock showed that the strong personal commitment of conversion was a quintessential characteristic of Judaism and Christianity. He maintained that conversion uniquely enabled Christianity to gain in popularity while conquering opposition by considering it demonic and unchristian. Further, highly personal piety, an effect of the conversion experience, was characteristic of Christianity and a small number of other cohesive religions in the Roman Empire. Conversion provided the dynamic for a true religious revolution in the late Roman Empire and a startling innovation in religious patterns for the West, starting in the Renaissance and continuing into the modern period. According to Nock, the phenomenon of conversion is remarkably important for understanding the popularity and attractiveness of Christianity. Christian communities organized all their resources for the dissemination of the gospel and quickly spread throughout the Roman world.

Nock has recognized and emphasized an important dynamic in the spread of early Christianity. Subsequent scholarship has not disproven his insight but has instead deepened and broadened it. But Nock's understanding of Christianity was already fitted to Christianity because it stressed sudden change and personal spiritual experience. He followed William James in limiting the experience of conversion to a radical emotional experience or a quick turning to a new way of life and a complete reorientation in attitude, thought, and practice. Furthermore, Nock probably underestimated the level of commitment that adherence to a civic form could generate among the local pagan aristocrats, who vied with each other for social prominence through public benefaction— a process in which Judaism and later Christianity participated in the late Hellenistic era, when the church or synagogue achieved regional importance. Since both internal and external factors are important to the history of any group, Nock's work remains significant.

Christianity was characterized by several paradigmatic conversion experiences of the type that Nock describes. In fact, there had been a tradition in Judaism of dreams and visions, in which Christianity certainly participated. Most significant among those who can be said to have undergone conversion is Paul. His religious life actually contained not only what we would call a conversion but also several visionary experiences about which he speaks and which helped direct his mission (2 Cor. 12:1–9, 3:18–4:6). In Galatians 1:12 he speaks of his own conversion as a revelation (*apocalypsis*), while in 2 Corinthians 12:1 he speaks of both revelations (*apocalypseis*) and visions (*optasiai*). Luke also describes his visions as being in ecstasy (Acts 22:17). But because Paul is a liminal hybrid character who stands at the intersection of Judaism and Christianity, a great deal of his experience can help us understand Judaism as well.

There were, of course, several significant types of conversion experiences. But the Christian form of conversion seems completely unsuited to understanding conversion in the other Jewish sects of the first century. The reason for this is that they all demanded study and catechism, sometimes of long duration, and, in fact, discouraged fast conversions. The difference between most Jewish definitions of conversion and the developing Christian ones can be seen toward the end of Luke's narrative in Acts of Paul's life:

> And as he thus made his defense, Festus said with a loud voice, "Paul, you are mad; your great learning is turning you mad." But Paul said, "I am not mad, most excellent Festus, but I am speaking the sober truth. For the king knows about these things, and to him I speak freely; for I am persuaded that none of these things has escaped his notice, for this was not done in a corner. King Agrippa, do you believe the prophets? I know that you believe." And Agrippa said to Paul, "In a short time you think to make a Christian!" And Paul said, "Whether short or long, I would to God that not only you but also all who hear me this day might become such as I am—except for these chains." (Acts 26:24–29)

Luke has fashioned this encounter into a conventional confrontation between the wise man or philosopher and the ruler. Whether the story is true or not, the storyteller is describing a social situation familiar to him, not an actual event in Paul's life. So what is of particular interest to us is that two different definitions of religious change are being debated. King Agrippa apparently feels that one short interview is not enough to secure a significant religious change. Luke's Paul, acknowledging the difference, replies that the length is of no concern, since the important thing is that God move the convert to understand his message. But such an exchange is not possible without understanding that in Luke's day the nascent Christian conversions could be short, while the more normal Jewish ones took a long time.

According to Luke, Paul's conversion experience was rapid and due to a revelation. It made Paul into a prophet (Paul's conversion is related in Acts 9:1–19, 22:1–21, 26:12–23). Paul himself describes his experience as a prophetic calling (Gal. 1; 1 Cor. 9:1, 14:8 ff.), though when it becomes the basis of later Christian conversion experience, prophecy is less important than his leaving his former life (1 Tim. 1:16, see below). But the other lengthy description of a conversion experience from the first century is quite different, although it is also from someone who professed to be a Pharisee. The difference is that Paul left Pharisaism (though not Judaism) while our second example, Josephus, joined it:

> At about the age of sixteen, I determined to gain personal experience of the several sects into which our nation is divided. These, as I have frequently mentioned, are three in number—the first that of the Pharisees, the second that of the Sadducees, and the third that of the Essenes. I thought that, after a thorough investigation,

I should be in a position to select the best. So I submitted myself to hard training and laborious exercises and passed through the three courses. Not content, however, with the experience thus gained, on hearing of one named Bannus, who dwelt in the wilderness, wearing only such clothing as trees provided, feeding on such things as grew of themselves, and using frequent ablutions of cold water, by day and night, for purity's sake, I became his devoted disciple. With him, I lived for three years and, having accomplished my purpose, returned to the city. Being now in my nineteenth year I began to govern my life by the rules of the Pharisees, a sect having points of resemblance to that which the Greeks call the Stoic school. (Josephus, *Life* 7–12)

Josephus is seeking acceptance not as a prophet but as an educated and well-informed Jewish intellectual. The first thing Josephus tells us is that he submitted to hard work and gained a thorough education. Of course, this is not necessarily to be believed at face value. For one thing, the sum total of his time in laborious exercises in the three dominant sects has to have been around six months to a year because he numbers his time with Bannus as three years. Accounting for the fact that the ancients sometimes included the first and last years in their computation of time, that still does not leave a lot of time for his investigation of the other sects. Furthermore, Josephus' account fits the convention for the story of an individualistic education in his day. He is, in a way, displaying his bona fides as an educated Judean when he relates this story. And the end of the story is not clearly a conversion in the Christian sense either. Josephus's report indicates that he grew up as a young priest, most likely a Sadducee, spending three years with Bannus. From Bannus, with whom he did practice special hardships as he lived in eremitical fashion in the desert near the Dead Sea, Josephus moves to a political career with the Pharisees, whom he describes as the dominant and most politically advantageous sect. He clearly did not have the same kind of experience that the Paul of Acts described.

From this we can conclude many things. First, we can conclude that long education is more usual for Jewish conversion experiences of the first century. On the other hand, Christianity seems to be in the process of constructing its own, new form of conversion experience. And, lastly, this means that the sudden, intense conversion experience was hardly the only form of conversion available. In fact, it is safe to say that each group defines what it considers to be its quintessential conversion pattern; the rest of Judaism may have respected ecstasy but it did not require it for conversion.

Conversion in the Hellenistic Diaspora

The division of Judaism into homeland and diaspora versions is conventional in the study of ancient Judaism. Conventional though it might be, it is misleading. Hellenization affected all parts of Jewish society, both in the diaspora and within the land of Israel. First of all, the very small district of Judea was not even as big as the modern state of Israel. It was closer to the limits of modern metropolitan Jerusalem. Surrounded by cities founded on Greek models on the Mediterranean coast (Caesarea, Joppa, etc.) and inland (Sepphoris, Paneas, Tiberius, Beth Shean, and the other heavily Hellenized cities in upper and lower Galilee), there was a good deal of Hellenistic influence within the confines of Jerusalem itself, as evidenced by the amphitheater and gymnasium constructed there in the second century B.C.E. Like all other Hellenized cities, Jerusalem contained an aristocracy who could read and write in Greek and who participated in the trade that the Hellenistic road system made possible.

In the Diaspora, however, different rules applied. Jews probably governed a great deal more of their public lives and livelihoods in Greek; the LXX itself testifies that Jews in the Diaspora needed a Greek translation of their Bible. In the land of Israel, the rules of the resident stranger were dominant. From biblical times, Jews had specified what resident aliens should be expected to do in order to live among Jews. That was only natural. But in the Diaspora different rules applied, for the Jews were mixed in with a much larger population in which they lived as guests. Here, it seems quite clear, the campaign for conversion had to be more sophisticated and was much attenuated. For one thing, an active mission would have disturbed the good relations between Jews and their neighbors. Instead, Jews developed a different kind of mission. They preached the God of the Hebrew Bible and the rules that would make Gentiles righteous according to standards for all humanity. So the issue was not conversion but righteousness. To have moved to a life of righteousness seems to have been called "God-fearing." The semi-proselytes or "God-fearers" appear in Luke as a group, but no one was entirely sure that they existed until recently; some scholars thought that they were a made-up group, produced for smoothing the relationship between Judaism and Christianity.

To examine the evidence for a group of God-fearers, let us look at Luke first. He does not have a single term but uses at least three to refer to God-fearers: *phoboumenos* (a fearer) is for someone who fears God or someone who worships God (Acts 10:2 and 22). Acts also uses *sebomenos* (a worshiper) and *theosebēs* (a god worshiper). Note that the subject of these attributes is the Italian centurion Cornelius. In Perga, Paul addresses a crowd of "the descendants of Abraham's family"—presumably Jews—"and others who fear God"—presumably God-fearers (Acts 13:13 ff.). God-fearer is thus meant by Acts to be a term that can be used to refer to those Gentiles with varying degrees of commitment to Judaism, all of whom have been attracted to the synagogue for one reason or another. There do not seem to be fine distinctions between the terms.

But there is a more fundamental ambiguity. Fearing God is merely the normal Hebrew idiom for describing His worship. As early as First Temple times and throughout the Hebrew text of the Bible, ordinary Jews can be called "those who fear God in Hebrew," and the usage passes into Greek through direct translation as seen, for example, in the LXX.

The term "God-fearer" is used directly in Acts 10, where Cornelius is described as a God-fearer and also as a pious (*eusebēs*) donor to the synagogue. The term is not a Lukan invention, for Josephus uses it as well to describe Gentiles in *Antiquities* 14.110, as does Julia Severa, a cosponsor of the synagogue building in Acmonia.[4]

Two inscriptions from Aphrodisias seem to settle the question of the existence of God-fearers.[5] These consist of two faces of a single dedicatory inscription found on the adjacent sides of a large stone stela or obelisk, possibly serving as a doorpost within a building. The inscription lists the people who contributed towards a *patella* (plate), an unidentified organization that appears to be a soup kitchen or some kind of institution devoted to feeding the poor. The inscriptions were found face down when stone ruins were being removed from the site to construct a museum and tourist services on the site. Since construction went ahead before the inscription was read, the original context can no longer be studied. However difficult this makes the interpretation of the inscription, it is not like the huge number of suspicious inscriptions that show up for sale in the antiquities market with no known provenance. So there has been no serious debate that the inscriptions have been falsified.

On side A of the inscription, the list of names includes three individuals identified as *proselytos* ("convert," ll. 13, 17, 22) and two men who receive the designation *theosebēs* ("god-fearer," ll. 19–20). On side B, there is a list of fifty-five names, some with occupations attached, and then a declaration: "those who are God-fearers" (line 34) followed by another fifty-two entries. The position of Reynold and Tannenbaum is that the unspecified names are Jewish (many are biblical). Both sides explicitly distinguish between others and God-fearers. Side A distinguishes between proselytes and God-fearers while side B distinguishes between Jews and God-fearers in quite an emphatic way. The two inscriptions may have been inscribed at the same time or one may have been inscribed at a later time than the other.

Besides identifying Jewish donors in a long list containing a mixture of Jewish, biblical, and Hellenistic names, the texts identify a social grouping of people with exclusively Greek names as *theosebeis* ("God-fearers"), some with Gentile occupations such as city councilors. Within the A list there is a sprinkling of people with biblical names and some who are described as proselytes. Although the organization of the two plaques differs slightly, it seems unassailable that three different categories of persons are distinguished: Jews, proselytes or converts, and God-fearers.

These lists have garnered a great many speculations and critiques. Since the inscriptions are likely to be from the third century or later, the term "God-fearer" continued to be used in the community until at least this time. It also seems clear that the category exists in a social sense, not just as another description for Jews or converts. If so, we must surmise that whatever success Christians may have had in evangelizing Jews and adherents in the synagogue, both Jews and God-fearers continued to exist, perhaps even containing Christians among them. Of course, on the other hand, in some cases the term may mean no more than that the person gave money to support the charity and had no other interest in Judaism. That is, of course, possible, but it seems equally impossible that all the God-fearers would be either committed or uncommitted. There was obviously a spectrum of commitment to the synagogue and its institutions. And, conversely, it also suggests that the boundaries between Hellenistic culture and Judaism were fluid and complex.

Despite the vociferous objections of scholars who argue that the term "God-fearer" is a literary creation of Luke with only theological meaning, God-fearer was a real title in use within Hellenistic Judaism with the special technical meaning of a semi-proselyte who is distinct from Jews and proselytes. It certainly does describe Gentiles with varying degrees of interest in Judaism, from very little to quite a bit. It may even suggest that some—but certainly not all—may have received the Christian message readily, just as Acts suggests, but also that some may have even continued some kind of informal relationship with Jewish institutions. Clearly, the Hellenistic world was a competitive marketplace in which Judaism did project its message for the acceptance of ordinary people. Christians both accepted converts and encouraged proselytes (people in the process of converting, often those who had converted save for the ritual of circumcision), just as Luke says. This is an interesting aspect of early Christian mission that has been clarified by the new archaeological evidence.

Conversion and God-fearing at the Court of Adiabene

The importance of circumcision also helps illumine a famous event narrated in Josephus, which is the conversion of Izates, the Crown Prince of Adiabene, son of King Monobazes and Queen Helena. The story is narrated by Josephus in book 20 of his *Antiquities*. According to him, while Izates was residing at Charax Spasini, a Jewish merchant named Ananias visited the King's wives and taught them to worship God in the Jewish tradition. The Greek here uses the term "God-fearing" (34). Helena, Izates's mother, is quite taken with the religion, and Izates is also zealous to convert (38). Aware that circumcision is necessary for a male conversion, Izates prepares for the rite. But Helena and Ananias dissuade Izates from the rite because they are fearful that the populace would not accept him as the heir to the king should he convert. Ananias reassures Izates that he could worship God (*theon sebein*) even without being circumcised, if he was otherwise devoted to Judaism. This clearly acknowledges that there were sometimes reasons within the larger community, as well as in the Jewish community, for a person not to progress from proselyte status to full conversion. It also suggests that the God-fearer is otherwise the equal of the convert, as the rabbis later state. This seems to put the dividing line between Jews and Gentiles at circumcision for men, while the women obviously were able to act with a degree of ambiguity. But it also admits that one receives the benefit of worshiping God even if one is not Jewish.

But that is not the end of the story. After an interval, another Jew arrives on the scene, one Eleazar, who persuades Izates to undergo circumcision. Izates undergoes the ceremony secretly, and when the story finally comes out, Helena and Ananias become anxious. But the story ends happily when Izates is accepted as king. Both he and his mother become famous and generous benefactors of Judaism and the city of Jerusalem. From this we learn that there are some Jews, like Eleazar, who because of their piety recommend circumcision and full conversion. This seems to suggest that within the Diaspora Jewish community several different outcomes were possible in any specific case. Izates could have remained a God-fearer (proselyte), but he is clearly aware that this is a lesser category of commitment and therefore continues through with circumcision because the status more agrees with his personal sense of identity. The story illustrates, further, that conversion to Judaism took a great deal of commitment, which was both its strength and its difficulty. The commitment also includes significant others, apparently. Even Queen Helena, who had already herself converted, was not entirely sure that Izates should convert. The story suggests quite strongly that God-fearing was a possible outcome of Gentile interest in Judaism but that conversion was a preferred end for some, though it meant circumcision. The story thus underlines the later rabbinic notion that circumcision is the *sine qua non* for male conversions to Judaism.

Further support for a class of God-fearers and for this gradual form of conversion is also available from the occasional reports of Hellenistic and Roman writers. Dio Cassius, Epictetus, and Suetonius all mention stories of individuals who act Jewish without actually being Jewish. Suetonius identifies those who live as Jews but do not acknowledge it, giving the Jewish tax as the motivation (Dom. 12:2). Dio Cassius explains Domition's death sentence against Flavius Clemens and his wife Flavia Domitilla on the charge of "atheism" because they drifted into Jewish ways, noting that this was the normal way of dealing with the problem (*His.* 67.2.14.2).

None of these writings mentioned in the previous paragraph explicitly use the terminology of God-fearing. Yet Juvenal, writing his satire in Latin in the late first and early second centuries, describes people who worship (*metuens*, "worshiping," the Latin equivalent of *theosebēs*) the Hebrew God. They begin by revering the Sabbath and the divinity of the Heavens, continue by giving up pork, and in time they take to circumcision. Juvenal's summary comment is that they begin by flouting the laws of Rome and learn to practice and revere the Jewish law (*Saturae* 14.96–102). The order and the slow progress of the process seem to confirm Josephus' understanding of Izates's voyage to Judaism as well.

Two Ways to Avoid Conversion: Noahide Commandments vs. Laws of the Resident Alien

One finds a variety of different approaches to the issue of Gentiles observing Jewish law. The status of Gentiles is certainly discussed in rabbinic Judaism, apparently with different assumptions about the purpose and motivation of gentile interest in Judaism. The laws of the resident alien (*ger*) are derived from biblical rules and incumbent upon "the stranger in your gates." Resident aliens were obliged to abstain from offering sacrifices to strange gods (Lev. 17:7–9), from consuming blood in any form (Lev. 17:10 ff.), from incest (Lev. 18:6–26), from work on the Sabbath (Exod. 20:10 f.), and from eating leavened bread during the Passover (Exod. 12:18 f.). A Gentile who wants to eat the Passover sacrifice must be circumcised, which seems to suggest a full conversion. Indeed the word *ger* comes to mean "proselyte or convert" in rabbinic Judaism.

New Testament tradition shows us how these biblical rules could be applied in a new situation. In Luke 15:20, 29, and 21:25, we discover that the Jewish leadership of early Christianity tried to extrapolate from these rules to discover how the Gentiles could be included in their own community. They did not look upon these laws as a conversion, and they did not expect the Gentiles to be circumcised. One can always argue that they hoped Gentiles would eventually undergo this rite:

> Therefore my judgment is that we should not trouble those of the Gentiles who turn to God but should write to them to abstain from the pollutions of idols and from unchastity and from what is strangled and from blood. For from early generations Moses has had in every city those who preach him, for he is read every sabbath in the synagogues. (Acts 15:19–20)

> That you abstain from what has been sacrificed to idols and from blood and from what is strangled, and from unchastity. (Acts 15:29)

> Thus all will know that there is nothing in what they have been told about you but that you yourself live in observance of the law. But as for the Gentiles who have believed, we have sent a letter with our judgment that they should abstain from what has been sacrificed to idols and from blood and from what is strangled and from unchastity. (Acts 21:24–25)

The predicament of the early Christian church is resolved by apostolic decrees, a very early and ultimately abandoned attempt to resolve the issue of how Jews and Gentiles could live together in one community within Christianity. The decrees are based on the rules for the resident alien. These Gentiles had to abstain from idol sacrifices, from blood (from eating blood entirely), and from strangled food (*pnikton*), which is a good translation of the Hebrew word *Terefa*, meaning "throttled prey," but which had come to stand for all non-kosher food. And they had to stay away from unchastity. All of these, including unchastity, are viewed through its ritual, polluting perspective; none of it is designed as a moral code in and of itself. It is assumed that the Ten Commandments serve as that code for the whole community and do not need to be rehearsed in this context. In short, according to apostolic decree, the Gentiles entering Christianity and who wish to worship and eat with the Jewish Christians must meet the requirements for the rules of the resident alien, as reinterpreted by the specific instance of the early Christian church.

Another rubric available to Jews for understanding the status of Gentiles was and is the Noahide Rules, as it is primarily the theological category now available to Jews for understanding the role that Gentiles play in divine providence. Rabbinic Judaism has debated the issue but in the end has decided to argue that God has provided the same ultimate rewards for righteous Gentiles as for Jews, without even conversion to Judaism. So then the question is: What does the Torah tell us is the minimum standard of behavior for Gentiles? Certainly, one cannot expect Gentiles to keep all the complicated rules of the Torah or even to know what they are. The Seven Commandments of the Children of Noah are meant to answer that question. The earliest complete rabbinic version, as stated in the Tosefta to Avodah Zarah, states:

> Seven commandments were commanded of the sons of Noah: (1) concerning adjudication (*dinim*), (2) concerning idolatry (*avodah zarah*), (3) concerning blasphemy (*qilelat ha-shem*), (4) and concerning sexual immorality (*gilui arayot*), (5) and concerning blood-shed (*shefikhut damim*), and (6) concerning robbery (*ha-gezel*) and (7) concerning a limb torn from a living animal (*eber min ha-hayy*).

The last requirement, the limb torn from a living animal, is exegeted from the pre-Abrahamic sections of the Bible, where they all come from. Except for the final requirement, the rules appear to be a version of "natural law," a recognition that every human being exercising reason can agree to a group of laws that ensure righteousness and an orderly society. As opposed to the laws for the resident alien, this formulation contains no ritual requirements at all. It is interesting that the later rabbis add a considerable number of regulations to this, though this passage remains the classic formulation. There is no real legal issue involved in this discussion, only an answer to the question of what is the minimum moral code necessary for God to give Gentiles the rewards that he gives to Jews.

It is interesting that the Noahide Commandments are more what we would call moral requirements, so they do not necessarily look at the issue of Gentiles living together with Jews. This is to be explained by the vagaries of Jewish existence. During the rabbinic period, the nation state was lost and there was no longer any way for Gentiles to live under Jewish aegis. The moral code, apparently, implies the recognition of God in its commandments against idolatry and blasphemy, for example. In any event, the recognition of God is made an explicit requirement in later commentaries. As opposed to the previous formulation of the resident alien, the Noahide Commandments do not imply any missionizing on the part of Jews. One could assume that it is a kind of natural law, something that anyone operating rationally would conclude. But practically speaking it does involve understanding the basic aspects of the Jewish tradition, so one could argue that these laws are a formalization of the rules for God-fearing as well. They just came to replace the former rules because Jews no longer had a political state in which to enforce their laws on others.

RABBINIC CONVERSION

Matthew 23:15 tells us that the scribes and Pharisees "cross sea and land to make one proselyte," a statement that has been much discussed by scholars. It seems to say that the Pharisees and scribes sought out proselytes. But there seems little evidence of an organized mission to Gentiles in rabbinic literature. Possibly the statement is meant to be ironic, as it points out that there is only one proselyte. Can it mean that compared to Christianity the converts of Pharisees are few but they are twice as committed as their teachers? Most scholars say not, but this is a distinct possibility. The Matthean community may well be observing the difference between the numbers attracted by their mission and the few attracted to rabbinic Judaism. It may also be that the Pharisees only converted people to Pharisaic Judaism from within their midst and that they did not seek converts among the Gentiles. In any event, we have no Pharisaic literature at all about seeking converts among the Gentiles. The best we can do is look carefully at two ex-Pharisees, Paul and Josephus, or to extrapolate backwards from rabbinic literature. Most of what we know about the Pharisees has to be read out of Josephus or extrapolated from rabbinic literature, because the rabbis thought of themselves in many ways as the heirs of the Pharisees.

Although there is no evidence of an organized mission, two aspects of the story seem correct: the rabbis, on the whole, valued proselytes and they tried to make very committed ones during the first few centuries. The most famous story illustrating conversion in rabbinic literature contains two different patterns for accepting proselytes: Hillel's attitude and Shammai's attitude (Shab. 31a). According to the story, a proselyte comes to Shammai and asks to be told enough about Judaism to convert while standing on one foot, surely a very short period of time. Shammai treats the request as an impertinent question. But not Hillel, when the proselyte seeks him out. Hillel says, "What is hateful to yourself, do not do unto others," a form of the golden rule. "That is the essence of the Torah and the prophets," he concludes, and then he advises the proselyte to go and study. Hillel is usually the person who gets to speak the most valued lines in rabbinic literature. It is at this moment that tradition reveals the golden rule, forms of which are present in the Bible and the New Testament. But, implicit in this symbolic story is the whole approach to proselytism of the rabbinic movement. While it is possible to be impatient with the impertinence of proselytes, the wise will answer their questions with wit and set them on the road to study. The result of the longer catechism is that the rabbis hoped for more committed proselytes. That attitude appears to remain in place even when converting Gentiles or Christians becomes dangerous—indeed, even more so then, as the safety of the community is endangered by uncommitted proselytes. This no doubt is responsible for the statements that insincere proselytes "impede the arrival of the Messiah" (e.g., Nid. 13b). But it was during the early period of the rabbis, that is, Palestine of the second century and later, that the procedures and detailed laws governing the acceptance of proselytes were discussed and codified:

> In our days, when a proselyte comes to be converted, we say to him: "What is your objective? Is it not known to you that today the people of Israel are wretched, driven about, exiled, and in constant suffering?" If he says: "I know of this and I am not worthy," we accept him immediately and we inform him of some of the lighter precepts and of some of the severer ones ... we inform him of the chastisements for the transgression of these precepts ... and we also inform him of the reward for observing

these precepts…we should not overburden him or be meticulous with him. (Yeb. 47a; cf. Ger. 1)

The rabbis demanded total sincerity and acceptance of Judaism without reservations, as well as study and knowledge of the Jewish tradition (see, e.g., *Shulhan Arukh* Yoreh Deah 268–269). This refers to a person who has converted through conviction. Jewish tradition also allows as acceptable those who convert to marry or advance themselves or out of fear.

The rites of conversion had to take place under the supervision of a court (*beth din*) of three, though there are different opinions about whether all members had to be present for every aspect of the conversion process. In any event, a proselyte had to undergo three specific rites. While the Temple stood, the proselyte had to provide an animal sacrifice, though once the Temple was gone, proselytes were not obliged to sacrifice at all nor keep aside the price of the sacrifice. The second two rites were circumcision for men and total bodily immersion for all. Immersion means full-body complete immersion in a ritually acceptable *mikveh* (baptistry). Men and women used the ritual bath at different times, and if women were interrogated about their knowledge of Judaism, it was done from behind a screen for modesty's sake. In the event that the male was already circumcised, symbolic blood had to be shed. Although the rabbis argued about when specifically one became converted, for example, after the circumcision or after the immersion (the latter is correct, *pace* Rabbi Eliezer), there is no evidence that they allowed conversion without circumcision, with the exception that both circumcision and immersion could be postponed for health reasons. The halakhic conclusion is that one is a convert only after both have taken place, even though there are arguments on the issue. Obviously, the rite of circumcision is required for men and sets a high and sometimes fearsome price for the ritual. As a result of this process, it was hoped that the commitment level for converts would be very high, though rabbinic literature does admit that many were not strongly committed. The issue was not merely converts' desire to observe the rules of Judaism but whether they informed on the community to the Romans (Josephus, *Apion* 123, *Av. Zar* 3b, *Nid.* 13b etc.). It does seem clear, however, that in all these stories the proselyte comes to see the rabbis first; there is no evidence that the rabbis went out to find proselytes themselves. Yet, if the second missionary to Judaism in the story of Izates were a Pharisee, we could say that they did missionize and that they tended to discount the value of God-fearing.

MISSION: CONVERSION AND COMMITMENT

Since history has provided us with an interesting contrast between Christian and Jewish views of conversion, all coming out of the same historical context, we should not ignore the opportunity to talk about the similarities and differences in Jewish conversion and Christian conversion as a way of highlighting both of them and possibly of looking at principles in the study of religion. Although Judaism may have favored slow education while Christianity at first favored the intensely spiritual experience and quick conversion, both sought to train and educate their new flocks and both constantly tried to intensify the experience of conversion and to create more committed converts, just as both hoped to intensify the lives of ordinary participants.[6]

The necessity for conversion arose from the kind of society in which Judaism and Christianity found themselves—the cosmopolitan and individual society of Hellenism. Obviously, a culture that values knowledge of the world with all its differences must also provide different religious choices for its cosmopolitan individuals. The sects that arose in Judaism—with the exception of the Sadducees, who were largely populated by a Hellenized, inherited priesthood—all sought to make committed converts through long periods of training.

Christianity and rabbinic Judaism both started within this context. Both sought to make as committed converts as possible. One way Christianity had for doing this is through intense personal experience, as narrated in Paul's conversion and in a few other writings. Intense personal experience became the new pattern for conversion in Christianity. We can see Paul's experience being reformulated for use within the Christian community. For example, in 1 Tim. 1:16, Paul is made to say: "And I am the foremost of sinners; but I received mercy for this reason, that in me, as the foremost, Jesus Christ might display his perfect patience for an example to those who were to believe in him for eternal life." Paul himself was no sinner. But the tradition in this letter makes him into a model (*hypotypōsin*). This clearly is not Paul but Paul's conversion experience of moving from one Jewish sect to another transposed into a pattern for all Gentile conversions. And what is more important is the content of the conversion faith: "Those who were to believe in him for eternal life." The *kerygma* of the church is the content of conversion. By comparison to Judaism, affirming this statement in faith is a very quick conversion indeed. It is no surprise then that Christianity always had difficulty with the commitment of its converts, perhaps more than rabbinic Judaism did with its much more elaborate process of conversion.

One should also know that implicit within this statement is an eschatology which is almost entirely missing in Pharisaic Judaism. A key issue of the new engine of Christian conversion must surely be the connection between conversion and salvation, a connection that does not exist in rabbinic Judaism or is at best secondary. But the heavy emphasis on apocalyptic images of the end of days helps Christianity in its mission. It is used to even better advantage in Islam. Judaism's lack of interest in connecting the two ideas—indeed its explicit statement that one does not need to be Jewish to be a *ben olam haba'*, worthy of the next world—seems deliberately designed to neutralize the engine of conversion. Indeed, it is just as much a doctrine designed to allow Jews to live among Gentile nations without being seen as threats to the religious life of the community. If Islam and Christianity are missionary religions, with heavy emphasis on avoiding the negative consequences of the end of days, Judaism has done everything possible to defuse the explosive charges of messianism and apocalypticism. Only this has made possible Jewish survival in Christian and Muslim lands through the medieval and modern periods. One might say that the eschatological context in which conversion takes place is one factor in intensifying the commitment of convert and native-born alike.

MEDIEVAL CONVERSION

It stands to reason that conversion to Judaism was greatly attenuated in medieval and early modern times. Both Christianity and Islam passed laws criminalizing conversion to Judaism and penalizing the agent of the crime with death. Often the entire community suffered exile or other penalties. The one great exception to the rule is the legend of the conversion of the Khazars, a Turkic group of Central Asia. Actually, we know relatively little about the historical event behind the legend, but one supposes that the conversion must have taken place in the middle of the eighth century (ca. 740 C.E.); the Khazars eventually ceased to exist because they blocked the stronger Russians from the lands around the Volga.[7] One hardly hears about them after the tenth century. Two major pieces of Jewish literature are devoted to this conversion. The first is the correspondence between Hisdai Ibn Shaprut, of Muslim Spain, and Joseph, King of the Khazars. The historicity of the correspondence has been much disputed and debated. It seems hard to believe that it is historical. The second great document concerning the legend of the much more famous *The Kuzari* by Yehudah Halevi, is an entirely fictionalized philosophical dialogue between the king of the Khazars and his Jewish interlocutor, ending in his conversion. The story is but the background for Yehudah Halevi's philosophical contemplation of sacred peoplehood.

In contemporary times, the legend has been used by Arab nationalists against the legitimacy of the Israeli state, on the grounds that contemporary Jews are only descendants of the Khazars and not the same people who inhabited the land of Israel in ancient times. But this is simply racist propaganda, assuming that the definition of the Jewish people is based entirely on descent, but we have seen that it does not. Furthermore, the continuity of Jewish identity depends on the mother alone, so even without conversion, peoplehood is not strictly dependent on descent. And, of course, if we were to take the legend as truth, we would have to deal with the extremely limited provenance of the Khazars in Eastern Europe and their complete physical dislocation from the majority of Jews who lived in Mediterranean and Arab countries then as now. In fact the population of Israel is approximately equally divided between Jews of European and Mediterranean descent.

JEWS BY CHOICE

The modern world is a place of unprecedented cosmopolitanism and individualism, and so the phenomenon of conversion has appeared again. Although one might notice the more obvious disappearance of Jews by assimilation to modern European life, there is a smaller movement of people who are sufficiently impressed with Jews or Judaism that they choose to become Jewish. A great many choose to become Jews because they wish to marry a Jew. But others wish to improve their spiritual lives. Some touching memoirs of assimilation away from Judaism as well as conversion to Judaism can be found in modern memoirs.[8] This has occasioned a further point of friction between traditional and progressive Jews. Progressive Jews have designed their own conversion ceremonies that may make reference to the rabbinic laws but essentially do not enforce them. Traditional Jews ensure that all conversions are done exactly by ancient standards and so do not accept conversions done by progressive Jews. Many fear that this schism is unbridgeable, while others work to remediate it by trying to convince progressive Jews to undergo Orthodox marriages, divorces, and conversions.[9] Because of the emphasis of modern Judaism on rationality and the respect that Jews have for the modern scientific worldview, and despite Hitler's mistaken racial definition of Judaism, it is possible to say that all Jews are now Jews by choice.

NOTES

1. All quotations from the Bible are from the New Revised Standard Version.
2. The preceding paragraphs are informed by the article of Beverly Roberts Gaventa, "Conversion" in *The Anchor Bible Dictionary* (New York: Doubleday, 1992), Vol. 1, 1131–1133.
3. Arthur Darby Nock, *Conversion: The Old and the New in Religion from Alexander the Great to Augustine of Hippo* (Lanham, MD: University Press of America, 1988).
4. Jean Baptiste Frey, *Corpus Inscriptionum Iudaicarum* (Rome: Pontificio Instituto de Archeologia Christiana, 1936), 2:766. The literature on this group is endless.
5. Joyce Marie Reynolds and Robert Tannenbaum, *Jews and Godfearers at Aphodisias: Greek Inscriptions with Commentary* (Cambridge: Cambridge Philological Society, 1987).
6. Lewis R. Rambo, *Understanding Religious Conversion* (New Haven: Yale University Press, 1995).
7. Dunlop, Douglas Morton. "The Khazars." in *Encyclopedia Judaica,* ed. Michael Berenbaum and Fred Skolnik (Detroit: Macmillan Reference USA, 2007), Vol. 12, 2nd ed. 108–114.
8. Mary Potter Engel, "Love and the End of Reasoning: Conversion as an Act of Trust and Loyalty," *Spiritus* 7 (2007): 143–168.
9. Aharon Lichtenstein, "On Conversion," *The Conversion Crisis: Essays from the Pages of TRADITION,* ed. Emanuel Feldman and Joel B. Wolowelsky (New York: Ktav, 1990), 1–18.

BIBLIOGRAPHY

Bonz, Marianne Palmer. "The Jewish Donor Inscriptions from Aphrodisias: Are They Both Third-Century, and Who Are the 'Theosebeis'?" *Harvard Studies in Classical Philology* 96 (1994): 281–299.
Boyarin, Daniel. *A Radical Jew: Paul and the Politics of Identity.* Berkeley and Los Angeles: University of California Press, 1994.

Chester, Stephen J. *Conversion at Corinth: Perspectives on Conversion in Paul's Theology and the Corinthian Church.* London: T&T Clark, 2003.

Cohen, Shaye J. D. *The Beginnings of Jewishness: Boundaries, Varieties, Uncertainties.* Berkeley and Los Angeles: University of California Press, 1999.

Crook, Zeba A. *Reconceptualising Conversion: Patronage, Loyalty and Conversion in the Religions of the Ancient Mediterranean.* Leiden: Walter de Gruyter, 2004.

Dunlop, Douglas Morton. "The Khazars." In *Encyclopedia Judaica*, ed. Michael Berenbaum and Fred Skolnik. Vol. 12, 2nd ed. 108–114. Detroit: Macmillan Reference USA, 2007.

Engel, Mary Potter. "Love and the End of Reasoning: Conversion as an Act of Trust and Loyalty." *Spiritus* 7 (2007): 143–168.

Feldman, Louis H. " 'Proselytes' and 'Sympathizers' in the Light of the New Inscriptions from Aphrodisias." *Revue des Etudes Juives* 148 (1989): 265–305.

Frey, Jean Baptiste. *Corpus Inscriptionum Iudaicarum.* Rome: Pontificio Instituto di Archeologia Christiana, 1936.

Gaventa, Beverly Roberts. "Conversion." In *The Anchor Bible Dictionary*, ed. David Noel Freedman. Vol. 1, 1131–1133. New York: Doubleday, 1992.

Gilbert, Gary. "Jews in Imperial Administration and Its Significance for Dating the Jewish Donor Inscription from Aphrodisias." *Journal for the Study of Judaism* 35, no. 2 (2004): 165–184.

Goodman, Martin. *Mission and Conversion: Proselytizing in the Religious History of the Roman Empire.* Oxford: Clarendon Press, 1994.

Kraabel, A. Thomas. "The Disappearance of the 'God-Fearers.'" *Numen* 28 (1981): 113–126.

Lichtenstein, Aharon. "On Conversion," trans. Michael Berger. *Tradition* 23 (1988): 1–18.

——. "On Conversion." In *The Conversion Crisis: Essays from the Pages of TRADITION*, ed. Emanuel Feldman and Joel B. Wolowelsky, 1–18. New York: Ktav, 1990.

Lieu, Judith M. "Do God-Fearers Make Good Christians?" In *Crossing the Boundaries: Essays in Biblical Interpretation in Honour of Michael D. Goulder*, ed. Stanley E. Porter, Paul Joyce, and David E. Orton, 329–345. Leiden: Brill, 1994.

Nanos, Mark. *The Irony of Galatians: Paul's Letter in First-Century Context.* Minneapolis: Fortress Press, 2002.

Nasrallah, Laura. *An Ecstasy of Folly: Prophecy and Authority in Early Christianity.* Cambridge, MA: Harvard Theological Studies, 2004.

Nock, Arthur Darby. *Conversion: The Old and the New in Religion from Alexander the Great to Augustine of Hippo.* Lanham, MD: University Press of America 1988.

Rambo, Lewis R. *Understanding Religious Conversion.* New Haven: Yale University Press, 1995.

Reynolds, Joyce Marie, and Robert Tannenbaum. *Jews and God-Fearers at Aphrodisias: Greek Inscriptions with Commentary.* Cambridge: Cambridge Philological Society, 1987.

Schäfer, Peter. *Judeophobia.* Cambridge, MA: Harvard University Press, 1997.

Segal, Alan F. *Rebecca's Children: Judaism and Christianity in the Roman World.* Cambridge, MA: Harvard University Press, 1986.

——. *Paul the Convert: The Apostolate and Apostasy of Saul of Tarsus.* New Haven: Yale, 1988.

Shantz, Colleen. *Paul in Ecstasy: The Neurobiology of the Apostle's Life and Thought.* Cambridge, MA: Cambridge University Press, 2009.

CHAPTER 26

CONVERSION TO CHRISTIANITY

DAVID W. KLING

CONVERSION—both the word and the concept—is central to Christianity. New Testament (NT) writers employ the Greek terms *epistrephein* (to turn back, to return to the source of the way of the life) and *metanoia* (to think again, to change mentality, to repent) to characterize a radical change of perspective or transformation in one's outlook. "New birth," "new creation," and "born from above" (or "born again") also make up the vocabulary of NT conversion. The Acts of the Apostles narrates the early history of Christian conversions, some described in spectacular terms and others in ordinary ways. The writings of the Apostle Paul are filled with references to abandoning old loyalties ("fleeing from idols") for a new life (faith in Christ) signaled by initiation into the Christian community (baptism). The first Gentile converts generally followed this tripartite formula, and throughout early Christian history, conversion comprised these acts of forsaking, embracing, and incorporation. For some, conversion was instantaneous; for others, conversion was gradual. For some, conversion was a solitary intellectual affair; for others, conversion was a visibly emotional event in a communal setting. Whatever the particular circumstances, the phenomenon of turning from former attitudes and loyalties to a new allegiance to God's saving activity in Jesus Christ forms the basic story line in Christian history.

While the concept of conversion is crucial to early Christianity, it is not unique to the world of the NT. Early conceptions drew upon the vocabulary of Hebrew scripture, especially the word *shubh* (to turn back, to repent, to return, to restore) as used repeatedly by the prophets who chided and pled with the people to return to their covenantal obligations. In addition, Greek philosophers (Cynics, Stoics, and Epicureans) demanded conversion—a moral transformation not unlike that urged by Christians but wrought by education and a commitment to the rational life. Theirs was a language of turning and repentance, rejecting the vices and corruptions of the dominant culture and coming to one's senses so as to live a life of virtue. Despite the rather widespread currency of the concept of conversion, however, by the time of Paul, observes Abraham

Malherbe, "*epistrephein* had become a technical Christian term for conversion."[1] As Latin became the language of Western Christianity, both *epistrophe* and *metanoia* were translated into the word *conversio* (a turning over); subsequently, "conversion" became its English derivative.

Conversion is not only a word but a concept, a tool of analysis. It is not only a name but a phenomenon employed by scholars to describe a universal change—here, either an initial embrace of Christianity or a changed commitment to another form of Christianity. Of course, if there is conversion there can also be "deconversion" (or "apostasy" as those within the tradition would express it) and, vice versa, what was rejected can also be reaffirmed. A crisis of faith may lead to deconversion; a crisis of doubt may lead to reconversion.[2] Conversion is movement from something to something. Its process is dynamic and multifaceted and raises a number of questions: Is the change intellectual, social, psychological, moral, or some combination? Is it an event or a process? Examining conversion over two millennia of Christian history complicates matters even more, for the meaning of the word and the concept itself varies from person to person and from setting to setting. This intangible and elusive term (whether invoked or applied) begs for clarity or at least a working definition. As this chapter indicates, the subjects of conversion and those writing about conversion often disagree as to what the phenomenon actually is. Can any more be added to scholars who propose that conversion is what a convert or a faith group says it is?[3] Obviously, in a Christian context, what is "said" must include Christ—a turning, allegiance, or commitment to Christ, in whom salvation is promised. To step beyond this minimal threshold, however, particularly when viewing Christian conversion historically, is either to run the risk of distortion or to impose a form of scholarly or theological omniscience. As we will see, the experience of conversion as mediated by local faith communities in different times and places displays enormous diversity in theological content, ritual expression, and behavioral expectations.

In this chapter I consider issues and themes in Christian conversion through the lens of a single conversion narrative. At times the lens is narrowly focused on the specific aspects of one person's conversion; at others, the lens is widened to examine the larger panorama of conversion in Christian history. This contraction and expansion suggests that Christian conversion is unique to the individual but also connected to an immediate, proximate, and distant context. A reader familiar with Lewis Rambo's seven-stage model of conversion—to date, the most comprehensive in conversion studies—will detect my indebtedness to his general framework. Rambo observed that of the various stages in the conversion process, the initial stage of "context" is "the most comprehensive of all the stages," for it "shapes the nature, structure, and process of conversion" and includes social, cultural, religious, and personal dimensions. It is more than a "stage," for it sets the parameters of the other six stages. Context provides "metaphors, images, expectations, and patterns for conversion." It "encompasses the modes of access and transmission...and also contains sources of resistance." Rambo concluded that one important topic for further research was "a study of the systematic history of conversion in the development of religions."[4] This chapter takes Rambo's suggestion as a point of departure.

The following is an abbreviated account (and edited for the sake of anonymity) of a fairly typical twentieth-century conversion within the American evangelical tradition. The account comes from my father, Gordon Kling. Told many times after the fact as "testimony," recorded in occasional letters, and most recently recounted in autobiography, his narrative provides a lens for viewing Christian conversion from a variety of disciplinary and theoretical angles drawn from the insights of scholars in sociology, psychology, anthropology, history, and theology. My goal is not to privilege one particular kind of conversion over others—indeed, appropriate examples could have been taken from a variety of Christian traditions and settings—but to detect structural and contextual themes applicable to the study of conversion in Christian history.

Written some seventy years after the fact, the autobiographical account of Gordon Kling (hereinafter Gordon) conforms in many ways to the prototypical "born again" experience—the dramatic movement from an "old life" of despair and alienation to a "new life" of exhilaration and wholeness. As will become apparent, his conversion became the fulcrum upon which his life turned.

"My Conversion"

Although I was a "confirmed" member of Bethany Lutheran Church and believed the Bible was from God and that Jesus was His Son Who died on the cross, I did not have a personal relationship with God. As a youth, I did not realize this, but I remember that I was uncomfortable when people, like my Aunt Esther, would talk about the Lord. I recall one evening, as I stood outside looking at the stars, a sense of fear came over me as I realized I was not prepared to meet the Creator of those heavenly bodies.

My friend, Don, was president of the young people's society of the Mission Church. Occasionally he would talk to me about spiritual matters. I resented this to some extent; I had been "confirmed" and was a member of the Lutheran Church which had a large attractive building a few blocks from my home....

One day, Don invited me to the meeting of the young people and I agreed to go. In the course of the meeting, some of the youth gave testimonies of their faith and experiences with the Lord. I realized right then that, even if I had wanted to, I could not do that for I had nothing to say. Don's older friend, Russell, gave a talk and after the meeting closed, both he and Russell approached me and asked if I wanted to receive Jesus into my life as my Savior. I said, "If you can help me, I'm willing." We went into a little room, got on our knees, and they prayed for me. Nothing seemed different to me. As I was leaving to go home, Don said, "Remember, just believe."

When I arrived home I found that my cousin and her husband were visiting my parents. I joined them but was anxious for them to leave because I wanted to be alone to continue with what had begun in my heart at the meeting. After they left, I went to bed and soon began to think of the impressions I had recently received and that I was not ready to meet God. I remembered Don's last words to me and I said to God: "I believe." He graciously responded by giving what some might term a vision. I had the impression that Jesus was facing me, looking into my eyes and putting His hand on my shoulder. A sense of peace came over me and I soon went to sleep. Ever since, I have considered that date, December 11, 1935, as the date of my spiritual birthday.

The next morning, my first impulse was to find the Bible I had received at confirmation six years earlier and to begin reading it. I had tried that a few times before but found nothing that appealed to my interest. I opened it at random to Psalm 147. Now, as I read, it was as though God was clearly speaking to me, and I knew something had changed within. I was especially impressed when I read verse 16, "He gives snow like wool; He scatters the hoarfrost like ashes," because during the night a light snowfall had covered the ground and transformed every twig and branch of the formerly bare, gray trees. It was symbolic to me of the miraculous transformation within my heart and soul. I later learned that "If any man is in Christ, he is a new creature; old things are passed away and behold, all things are become new" (II Corinthians 5:17). When I told my mother what had happened, her response was, "You've always been a good boy." She had seen only my outward appearance, but, unlike God, had not seen my heart which was sinful and devoid of peace with Him, a peace which I now was experiencing, with much joy, for I knew that Christ had died for my sins.

That afternoon, I drove Mother to [a nearby town] to shop for Christmas. As we mingled with the customers and clerks in the stores, I sensed a warm feeling for everyone, another indication that I was "new" inside. In the evening I visited Don and Russell at Russell's home and shared with them what had transpired and we rejoiced together. Don took me to his home nearby to tell his parents of my experience. They were very encouraging and gave me some Christian literature, including the booklet, "The Reason Why," which greatly helped me to understand better what had taken place in me spiritually.

With a new hunger for God's word, I began reading the Gospel of John. Ever since then, each time I read that Gospel, I remember how captivating and satisfying that first feast was....I continued attending Sunday morning services in the Lutheran Church and began going to the Mission Church in the evenings. The believers there had heard of my conversion and welcomed me warmly....

Russell was acquainted with a group of Christian young people who met for fellowship on Saturday nights in the home of a Mrs. P. Don, Roy, Lester, and I joined him in his car to attend the meetings quite regularly for several months. There I was introduced to the singing of choruses, personal testimonies and challenging messages by guest speakers. The informal, yet worshipful atmosphere created as this group of young people obviously enjoyed spiritual fellowship together made a wholesome impression on me and contributed to my growth in the Lord. Later, the group became more organized and formed a Bible fellowship which met in a rented store front building. Several of the young people involved went into "full time" Christian service as pastors and missionaries.

When Don left to join the Civilian Conservation Corps, Russell and I became close friends even though he was five or six years older than I. He was a student of the Bible and we often talked together about spiritual truths....

As I progressed in my spiritual life, I wanted to be better prepared for Christian service, so, in the fall of 1938 I entered a Bible institute. The study of the Bible and related subjects, the influence of godly professors, and the exposure to well-known Christian leaders in the chapel services contributed to my Christian understanding and growth....After finishing the spring term and returning home for the summer, I decided not to return, since I had no specific goal toward which to prepare. It was during this period, the summer of 1939, that I experienced a spiritual crisis. After a time of "backsliding," during which I lost my appetite for the Bible.... I was challenged by my friend, Roy, to consider attending a nearby Christian college, from which two of his brothers had graduated. I realized it was high time for me to confess my spiritual coldness and receive God's forgiveness and get back into a living relationship with Him.[5]

THE HISTORICAL CONTEXT OF "MY CONVERSION"

Gordon's conversion narrative opens with a historical marker—his membership in the Lutheran Church—and throughout the narrative he supplies enough information that enables us to place his conversion within a religious milieu that defined conversion in a particular way. His immigrant Swedish parents were Lutheran, having identified with the faith that had been introduced to Sweden during the sixteenth-century Protestant Reformation under King Gustav Vasa (1521–63) and that eventually became the state-supported church of Sweden when formalized at the Uppsala Assembly of 1593.[6] So it was that for the past several hundred years, previous generations of Gordon's family had been baptized, catechized, and confirmed in the Lutheran Church.

As dutiful Lutherans, Gordon's parents had their son baptized as an infant, and indeed, from their perspective this sacrament initiated him into the Christian community.[7] Following catechetical instruction and then confirmation in the faith in his early teens, Gordon became a member of Bethany Lutheran Church. His joining the church as a confirmed member identified him as a Christian. There was no single moment of decision, no heart-wrenching, emotional experience. Baptism, instruction, and examination—a process, not an instantaneous, datable event—culminated in his confirmation of Christian faith into the community.

Had Gordon been converted? How far does one need to turn to Jesus in order to be converted? What level of commitment is necessary? We are presented with the thorny issue of what "counts" as conversion and who determines what counts: the subject, the group (church officials), the scholar? From the perspective of the teachings of the Lutheran Church, Gordon had "turned to Jesus" and, indeed, was converted. The eponymous founder of the church, Martin Luther, understood conversion in several ways: an unrepeatable mystery of entrance into the Christian life in baptism, a repeatable event of contrition and penitence, and an event of dramatic personal transformation (such as his tower experience which he recorded as being "born again").[8] So too for Gordon: as long as he had been baptized, expressed contrition for sin, and believed that God's righteousness was imputed to him on account of Christ's death, he could take comfort in his conversion. In answer to the question, when were you saved? Gordon could respond in good Lutheran fashion, "When I was baptized." If conversion meant assent to doctrine (within the distinct theological framework of Luther's Shorter Catechism and the

Augsburg Confession) and allegiance to the church, then, in one sense, at his confirmation Gordon had undergone conversion. This is one level of conversion, that which scholars have labeled "affiliation."

However, as Gordon observes, he had not personalized the faith and thus never really had "true belief." He had not experienced an intimacy with God or the radical, life-changing effects of conversion (as in Luther's third way of understanding conversion): a peace of mind, a new commitment, and a new direction of life centered upon following Christ. That would come six years later at age 18 when, after an invitation from a friend to a young people's meeting at the Mission Church, he was "born again." This church, though independent of any denominational affiliation until the 1940s, identified with the "free church" tradition in Scandinavia—a movement of Christian groups that had separated from the state-supported Lutheran Church and envisioned itself free in matters of personal commitment to the faith.

The free church tradition had been influenced by a variety of movements—indirectly by European Pietism and more directly by revival movements in Scandinavia in the second half of the nineteenth century. Pietism originated in seventeenth-century Germany as a protest against what its founders, Philip Jacob Spener (1635–1705) and August Hermann Franke (1663–1727), considered an arid, scholastic, and contentious Lutheranism. What Pietists stressed and what those in the free church tradition emphasized—and what Gordon reiterated in his conversion account—was that formal doctrine (i.e., assent to God's objective saving act in history) was not enough. Critical of "nominal" religion, Pietists located true religion in the heart, that is, in the will and affections (or "dispositions"). Their language of "rebirth," "regeneration," and the "new man" (terms used in the NT) stressed the subjective, experiential, emotional, even mystical side of the faith drawn from the insights of Johann Arndt (1555–1621), Jakob Böhme (1575–1624), and the Spanish Catholic, Miguel de Molinos (1628–1696).[9] Pietists uplifted "the need for, and the possibility of, an authentic and vitally significant experience of God on the part of individual Christians."[10] The church itself was based not on baptism (the outward means of regeneration) as it was for Luther but on the post-baptismal covenant in conversion, on the personal appropriation of salvation. Obviously, this placed Lutheran Pietists in the ambiguous position of both affirming and challenging traditional Lutheran teaching.

A more direct antecedent to the Scandinavian free church tradition in the United States was a series of revivals in the home countries of Sweden, Denmark, and Norway in the latter part of the nineteenth century that also emphasized a personal experience of salvation by faith. Influenced by evangelical movements in Great Britain and America, the "believers church" concept gained a firm, though small, footing in Scandinavia and was transplanted to the United States by immigrants in the later nineteenth century. The dilemma of Lutheran Pietism (infant, regenerative baptism vs. a subsequent rebirth) was resolved by "believer's baptism," meaning that adult or believer baptism was a public confirmation of an inward change of the heart. Many of these immigrant groups retained their theological conservatism and identified with the broad evangelical stream in America and to some extent with the fundamentalist currents of the 1920s and 1930s.[11]

American evangelical views of conversion developed out of the symbiotic relationship between evangelicalism and the modern world. As Martin Marty has observed, "Evangelicalism is the characteristic Protestant way of relating to modernity." Marty correlates several characteristics of the modern world with evangelicalism that may be applied specifically to conversion. Just as the modern world "chopped up" life into pieces (i.e., differentiated home from work, the economy from society, church from state) and uplifted the autonomy of the individual, so evangelicalism tended (although there are notable exceptions) to restrict the meaning of conversion to the private sphere, emphasizing the personal benefits to the exclusion of care for the larger civic community. Just as a byproduct of the modern world was "choice" (e.g., political and economic freedoms created opportunities to choose), so evangelicalism portrayed conversion as a choice or a decision, not as something ascribed or passed on through the nurture of godly parents or initiated by a sovereign God. With myriad choices to be made in the modern world, the "right" choice demanded that it be "hot"—intense, immediate, personal, and unmediated by authority (ecclesiastical authority in the case of evangelicals).[12]

Gordon's conversion, then, was particular to him but by no means peculiar. For at least 250 years, hundreds of thousands of people within the broad Euro-Anglo-American evangelical tradition experienced similar kinds of conversions as a crisis moment of "new birth," often chartable (the Puritans and Pietists made much of this), datable, and memorable.[13] In sum, Gordon's experience and understanding of conversion was of a distinct Christian variety, mediated by the particular environment. Within a broad historical context, it occurred in the mid-1930s Depression-era democratic capitalist West in a predominantly Protestant culture of the United States. Within a more bounded context, it occurred within a religio-ethnic subculture that was evangelical (oriented around the Reformation doctrine that salvation in Christ was received by faith alone and through the grace of God alone), pietistic (deeply personal and affectional), non-sacramental (baptism and the Lord's Supper were "ordinances" having no saving value), and individual (becoming a Christian was primarily if not exclusively about a relationship to Christ).

"MY CONVERSION" AS AUTOBIOGRAPHICAL NARRATIVE

Gordon's conversion narrative fits within a genre of spiritual autobiography that traces its origins to Augustine, whose late fourth-century *Confessions* is recognized as the first of its kind in the West. Indeed, the highly personal and emotional evocations in the *Confessions* became paradigmatic for Christian conversions in the West. Autobiographical narratives such as Augustine's are acts of reconstruction and interpretation (a type of "fiction" or self-representation), reflections on an experience of divine encounter that reorients one's life. Throughout Christian history, thousands of conversion narratives have been written, though nearly all date from the modern period. To provide perspective, we should remind ourselves that they represent a miniscule fraction of Christian conversions throughout history. In the millennium between the fifth and fifteenth centuries, introspective or dramatic conversions are very rare. "The overwhelming majority of persons who accepted Christianity," writes Richard Fletcher,

> were neither literate nor articulate. When they received the faith they did so, for the most part, millions and millions of them, because they were told to do so or because they were born into it. The struggles they experienced in the course of their usually short lives were not spiritual but the harshest of material ones—just how to keep going in a world that was chronically short of food, warmth, and health.... The spectacle of early medieval conversions to Christianity... is generally not one of individuals acting upon conviction.[14]

If not an individual appropriation of faith in Jesus, in what sense can we call these "conversions"? We will address this issue in more detail later, but the point to be made here is that autobiographical accounts are typically the product of a modern, literate culture, of what the New Testament scholar Krister Stendahl termed "the introspective conscience of the West."[15] Historically, then, autobiographical accounts (whether written or oral) are exceptional, and yet they are privileged over other kinds of conversion narratives. Indeed, they routinely constitute the ideal type or classic form of conversion. In conversion studies this exception has often become the rule, as is evident in a recent anthology of Christian conversion where the editors pass over an entire millennium between Augustine (d. 430) and Ignatius of Loyola (d. 1556) in their selection of exemplary converts.[16] Their reasons for doing so reflect the comment by Gustav Bardy that "the only interesting conversions are those which are resolute and deliberate, and which have their origin in personal reflection."[17]

First-person conversion narratives represent a literate (in some cases, such as Augustine's, a highly literary) expression of an experience of a divine encounter. Gordon's and others' accounts, then, are not the experience itself but attempts to explain the experience by answering the fundamental questions of identity: Who am I? To whom do I belong? What does life mean? Gordon structured his whole life around his conversion; it was, for him, the defining moment in his life. To answer the question of identity requires others with whom to identify (and others with whom not to identify). Gordon's choices were clear. In transforming his self-understanding, his conversion redirected his life choices: his education (first at a Bible institute, then at an evangelical college), his career (the ministry), his marriage (to a believer), and his personal relationships (almost exclusively within the orbit of fellow believers).

As typifies first-person conversion accounts, there is a conventional structure or narrative plot—a beginning, middle, and end—a movement from what Gordon was to what he became. Initially, he "did not have a personal relationship with God"; instead, he had "a sense of fear" when he realized he was unprepared to meet God. During the critical middle (or "liminal," as anthropologists call it) stage of transition, he said to God, "I believe." God responded by giving him a confirmatory vision of Jesus who "was facing me, looking into my eyes and putting His hand on my shoulder." Finally, a sense of peace followed. That night of December 11, 1935, was his "spiritual birthday."

During the next three-and-a-half years Gordon read the Bible, attended church, engaged in "spiritual fellowship" with other Christians, and attended a Bible institute. In the summer of 1939, however, he went through a "spiritual crisis" when the excitement of faith wore thin. Those very things that defined him as a Christian he now found unappealing. After several months of "backsliding," he realized it was time to confess his "spiritual coldness," "receive God's forgiveness and get back into a living relationship with him." These fluctuations, with their peaks, valleys, and plains, are the stuff of spiritual pilgrimage. In fact, several peak spiritual experiences punctuated Gordon's half-century career in ministry. And yet the defining moment in his life—the baseline by which he measured all else—was that day in December of 1935.

The words, phrases, metaphors, and images employed in Gordon's narrative reveal an inherited discourse from the Protestant tradition and, more particularly, a pre-set script from the evangelical subculture. Certain idiomatic expressions—including "personal relationship with God," "not ready to meet God," "hunger for God's word," "personal testimonies," "growth in the Lord"—represented the lingua franca of a subculture into which he had been socialized. The testimonies he had heard and now his own narrative expressed an evangelical strategy to fulfill the New Testament "mandate "—the "Great Commission" of Jesus that his followers were to "go and teach all nations" (Matthew 28-19-20). For Gordon and other evangelicals, the "going and teaching" began with those in one's circle of personal relationships and often culminated in full-time Christian service, either as a pastor at home or a missionary abroad. This coded vocabulary and impetus to spread the gospel defined authentic conversion for evangelicals and *ipso facto* raised questions about the kind of church to which the converted should belong. Because this common vocabulary was not shared within the Orthodox and Catholic traditions (or, if used, was not invested with the same meaning), evangelicals often judged these traditions deficient in their understanding of authentic conversion.

Still, there are deep connections to the Christian past in Gordon's narrative. Several events and expressions parallel the conversion narratives of past Christian luminaries and are in fact the staple of autobiographical conversion accounts through the centuries. Like Augustine who, in the midst of his conversion, "read the first passage on which my eyes should fall" (Rom. 13:13), so Gordon opened his Bible "at random" to Psalm 147.[18] Both incidents are examples of perceived divine prompting and guidance at a critical juncture in the conversion process. Gordon's emphasis on an intensely personalized belief that "Christ had died for my sins," accompanied by the "warm feeling" that he was "new inside," are reminiscent of classic Christian conversion accounts. Augustine writes that after reading Romans 13:13, "in an instant, as I came to the end of the sentence, it was as though the light of confidence flooded into my heart and all the darkness of doubt was dispelled."[19]

In addition, the parallel between Gordon's and John Wesley's conversion accounts is unmistakable. While visiting a Pietist Moravian Church on Aldersgate Street in London on May 24, 1738, Wesley heard the reading of Luther's preface to the New Testament book of Romans. "I felt my heart strangely warmed," he wrote. "I felt I did trust in Christ, Christ alone for salvation; and an assurance was given me that He had taken away *my* sins, even *mine*, and saved *me* from the law of sin and death."[20] Gordon's "hunger for God's word" and newfound ability to comprehend its meaning also corresponds to Martin Luther's life-transforming insights into the meaning of Romans 1:17, when "the whole of Scripture took on a new meaning."[21] What had once been a dull, impenetrable book now became alive and understandable.

Was Gordon familiar with the conversion accounts of Augustine, Wesley, and Luther? Probably so, but they were known only after the fact of his own conversion. Perhaps during his seminary studies or through personal reading he encountered these narratives. Did he intentionally pattern his account after these other accounts? Probably not, but his conceptual and imaginative framework, including his language and patterns of thought, provided a mental tool kit for assembling his experience in ways that paralleled the conversion experiences of others. Indeed, there is a generic quality to his conversion account that conforms to a biblical perspective on conversion, namely, a turning to God in Christ. In the words of the New Testament scholar William Barclay, "In real conversion a man is turned round and left permanently facing God. For him the presence of the risen Christ is the very atmosphere of life. He is as much in Christ, in Paul's great phrase, as he is in the air which surrounds him and which gives him the breath of life.... In real conversion life is no longer an oscillation, but a state in which life is permanently turned towards God."[22]

"My Conversion" and William James's "Twice-Born" Form of Conversion

In many ways Gordon's religious experiences—the vision, the warm feelings, the divine promptings, the sense of new life—conform to the "twice-born" conversion type introduced by William James in his landmark study, *Varieties of Religious Experience* (1902). This is not the place for a full explication of James, but because his pioneering study of religious experience has profoundly influenced conversion studies in general and Christian conversion studies in particular, some space must be given to his contribution.

James argued that religious experience is *sui generis*; it should be judged on its own terms. Just as other areas of life are judged by their results—by so-called "empiricist criteria"—so too should religious experience. He thus proposed evaluating religious experiences by the fruits of their results: "Our practice is the only sure evidence, even to ourselves, that we are genuinely Christians."[23] And what condition or practice is found in religious experience that can be found nowhere else? "There is a state of mind," writes James,

> known to religious men, but to no others, in which the will to assert ourselves and hold our own has been displaced by a willingness to close our mouths and be as nothing in the floods and waterspouts of God. In this state of mind, what we most dreaded has become the habitation of our safety, and the hour of our moral death has turned into our spiritual birthday. The time for tension in our soul is over, and that of happy relaxation, of calm deep breathing, of an eternal present, with no discordant future to be anxious about, has arrived.... Religious feeling is thus an absolute addition to the Subject's range of life. It gives him a new sphere of power.... This sort of happiness in the absolute and everlasting is what we find nowhere but in religion.[24]

This religious feeling and happiness may be found superficially, writes James, among the temperamentally "healthy-minded" sort of people—those "once-born" therapeutic and New Age types who deny the reality of evil, sense the goodness of life and humans, and "live habitually on the sunny side of their misery line." However, more often and most authentically, we find true religious feeling and happiness in "sick souls"—those "twice-born" radically converted types who affirm the reality of evil and see in their essential nature "a wrongness or vice."[25] In short, they understand that they must lose one life (the natural) in order to gain the other (the spiritual). James offers the following definition of conversion:

> To be converted, to be regenerated, to receive grace, to experience religion, to gain an assurance, are so many phrases which denote the process, gradual or sudden, by which a self hitherto divided, and consciously wrong inferior and unhappy, becomes unified and consciously right superior and happy, in consequence of its firmer hold upon religious realities.... To say that a man is "converted" means...that *religious ideas, previously peripheral in his consciousness, now take a central place, and that religious aims form the habitual centre of his energy.*[26]

James concludes his discussion by acknowledging that sudden conversions are often accompanied by "backslidings and relapses." Such fluctuations are common, yet the twice-born (quoting a study by Edwin Starbuck), "having once taken a stand for the religious life, tend to feel themselves identified with it, no matter how much their religious enthusiasm declines."[27]

Gordon's conversion account shares much in common with James's analysis. First, his conversion characterized what James views as the general development of Christian inwardness consisting of "little more than the greater and greater emphasis attached to this crisis of self-surrender."[28] Gordon's spiritual condition mirrored the "sick soul" temperament in that he described his "sense of fear" and a sinful heart devoid of peace with God. During this spiritual crisis, he surrendered to God. An instantaneous "twice-born" conversion followed, producing a unified self. Indeed, the hour of his "moral death" turned into a datable "spiritual birthday." Second, the result of Gordon's conversion fits James's empiricist criteria. The authenticity of his conversion was borne out by a sense of peace, happiness, a new view of himself as "a new creation," and a different perspective on those around him ("a warm feeling for everyone"). Third, the results of Gordon's life conform to James's definition of conversion. Religious ideas and goals, previously peripheral to his life concerns, now became "the habitual centre of his energy." Finally, James recognized that the spiritual life subsequent to conversion is not a smooth upward moving trajectory of spiritual perfection, but one of fluctuation and even, as Gordon noted, of "backsliding." Nevertheless, something has happened. A momentous shift has occurred, in James's words, "to higher levels" that redirected the way Gordon thought about and lived out his life.[29]

Varieties of Religious Experience has been criticized on several levels, including its over-attention to the psychological condition of the convert and inattention to social and historical context. James offers a typology of religious experience, convinced that certain types of conversion transcend particular circumstances, that similarities are more interesting than differences. Gordon's conversion experience thus corresponds to the sick soul, twice-born typology. The historical context sketched out earlier—the combination of Scandinavian revivalist piety and Anglo-American evangelical milieu that promoted a certain kind of conversion experience—is of secondary importance to James. Context matters but only in so far as it points to a certain kind of religiosity. What eludes James is that this very historical and social environment provided the specific language by which to describe the experience. Without it we cannot properly identify and describe the experience itself.

In addition, James minimizes the theological content of conversion. This is most apparent in his definition of religion as "*the feelings, acts, and experiences of individual men in their solitude, so far as they apprehend themselves to stand in relation to whatever they may consider the divine.*"[30] On the one hand, James allows the person who experiences religion to define what counts as religious (rather than others imposing their own definition on the subject); yet on the other, he offers his own explanation of conversion as a transformation or alteration of consciousness, thus depriving the narrator herself of attributing the change to a divine source. To suggest to Gordon that what occurred in his conversion could be explained naturally would be to violate his own understanding of how he stood in relation to God. From his perspective, without direct, supernatural intervention there would have been no conversion. James "does not draw the implication," maintains Wayne Proudfoot, "that a person's explanation of her experience might itself be an ingredient in the experience."[31]

Finally, James ignores what some social scientists view as the most critical factor in the process of conversion, namely, the influence of others. The bonds established through interpersonal relations (a factor we will take up in the next section) are either minimized or unmentioned, again because of James's focus on the experience itself rather than the context surrounding the experience.

"My Conversion" as Type and Motif: Definitional and Evidential Challenges

Another approach toward understanding Christian conversion is to identify its place within the sociological categories of type and motif.[32] Although every individual conversion story is unique, when compared and contrasted with other conversion accounts it often corresponds to an identifiable pattern. As characterizes all conversion narratives, Gordon's account is about personal transformation, turning from one way of viewing himself and living his life while turning to God in Christ as the center of his existence. How far did he turn? If asked, he would invoke standard New Testament imagery and metaphors of stark contrasts: "from darkness to light," "old to new," "death to life," and "lost to found." Again, his self-descriptors reflect a mental framework shaped by social and historical variables; the degree of cultural, social, emotional, and religious turning in the conversion process varies from person to person, group to group, and from one historical setting to another.

Lewis Rambo's proposed typology of conversion includes "tradition transition," or the change from a non-Christian religion to Christianity; "institutional transition" or "intra-conversion," or the change from one Christian community to another; "affiliation," or the change from no or little religious commitment to involvement with a Christian community; "intensification," or a revitalized commitment to the Christian faith; and "apostasy," "defection," or "deconversion," or the rejection of one's Christian commitment.[33] These types are not static but may occur, as discussed below in relation to Gordon's conversion, in a single individual's experience. To cite one well-known example, John Henry Newman (1801–1890) underwent several conversions, moving from intensification to several institutional transitions. He was raised in a conventional Anglican household; at age 15 he underwent a profound inward conversion of a Calvinist persuasion, though he remained in the Anglican Church. While studying at Oxford he rejected the specifics of Calvinism, drifted briefly toward theological liberalism, and then moved into the orbit of Anglo-Catholicism. Two decades of soul-searching and deliberation culminated in his conversion to Roman Catholicism in 1845.[34]

Conversion as Type: An Excursus on Tradition Transition

At one end of the conversion spectrum are converts who make a major break from their past. In the history of Christianity, these "traditional transition" converts have been overwhelmingly adherents of basic or primal religions, although there have been converts (often forced) from Judaism and Islam. Tradition transition is most clearly visible in the initial stages of the three great shifts in the center of gravity of Christian history.

The first shift occurred in early Christianity's formative years with the movement of the nascent faith out of its Jewish milieu into the Greek culture. Second, beginning in the fifth century (and extending through the Middle Ages), tradition transition took place among the peoples of northern and western Europe as pagans replaced their pantheon of gods with the Christian God. Third, beginning in the sixteenth century (and continuing into the present), another profound tradition transition took place with the penetration of Christianity into the Americas and Southern continents.[35] In each of these shifts, we repeatedly bump up against the intractable problem of assessing the nature of conversion.

New Testament writers employ the phrase "turned to the Lord" to depict the conversion of Gentiles who abandoned their gods and turned in faith to the one Christian God (see Acts 9:35; 15:19; 26:18, 20; Gal. 4:9; 1 Thess. 1:9). The modern discussion of this change set in the larger historical context of the ancient world was initially offered by A. D. Nock. In his celebrated study (1933), Nock argued that as prophetic, exclusivist, and monotheistic religions, Judaism and Christianity "demanded renunciation and a new start." They demanded not merely acceptance of a rite or the incorporation of another religion, as was the case with the Greco-Roman polytheistic and assimilative religions of the day, but a "deliberate turning... which implies a consciousness that a great change is involved, that the old was wrong and the new is right."[36] Nock's indebtedness to James is evident; he viewed conversion as an intense, all-consuming process of the "twice-born" type.

Christian conversions meeting Nock's criteria may be found among the educated elite such as Justin Martyr, Tatian, Arnobius, and Cyprian, but because educated Christians were so few and illiterate Christians so many, the adequacy of Nock's definition has been challenged. Writing a half century after Nock, Ramsay MacMullen defined Christian conversion as "that change of belief by which a person accepted the reality and supreme power of God and determined to obey Him."[37] MacMullen agreed with Nock that early Christianity demanded forsaking all gods for the one Christian God. However, few turned to the type of "true Christianity" as defined by Nock; rather, they came to faith simply by crying out, "Great is the God of the Christians."[38] MacMullen argued that divine power was the key factor. Christian leaders demonstrated the supremacy of their faith over all supernatural pretenders by displays of divine power. Jesus worked miracles and exorcised demons; so did his first disciples and Christians well into the second century. With hundreds of gods and hundreds of choices, Christianity won ordinary people over by driving out the competition through displays of the supernatural. Such demonstrations, however, signaled the beginning and not the end of the conversion process. As Robin Lane Fox observes, "To believe that Christians were fully won by the sight of a wonder or an exorcism is to shorten a long process and ultimately to misjudge the extreme canniness of Mediterranean men.... Whereas pagan cults won adherents, Christianity aimed, and contrived, to win converts. It won them by conviction and persuasion, long and detailed sequels to the initial proof that faith could work."[39] MacMullen's and Lane Fox's comments suggest that early Christian conversion was both an event (for which there is ample evidence) and a process (for which there is less evidence, but this represents the ideal from the point of view of the Church).

MacMullen's view of conversion applies with equal force to the kinds of "power conversions" experienced during the second gravitational shift of Christianity in the early medieval period. Richard Fletcher has noted that "demonstrations of the power of the Christian God" through "miracles, wonders, exorcisms, temple-torching and shrine-smashing were in themselves acts of evangelization" that produced conversions.[40] At the same time, however effective these miraculous displays may have been in the conversion of Europe (and here we are dependent upon second-hand sources—*Vita Sancti* and histories from Gregory of Tours, Bede, etc.), most people, who were illiterate and impoverished, became Christian because they were told to or they followed their ruler or they were born into the faith. This was the normal and natural response in a society where the group or the tribe, not the individual, defined the basic unit of society. As much as an individual change of heart has come to define modern views of conversion, in the medieval era masses of people "accepted" or "submitted" to the Christian religion. Consequently, their conversions, equated theologically with the rite of baptism, were often superficial. Baptism was the door to eternal life, but what it meant to the new convert, if it carried any religious meaning at all, is uncertain. For those who practiced traditional religions in which animal sacrifice propitiated the spirits or gods of nature, baptism could mean functionally the same thing; it was viewed as protecting people from calamity. This is, of course, very different from the Christian view of baptism as a rite of passage attesting to or leading to a changed heart and a mind centered on Christ. This is not to say that Christianity had no attraction to ordinary folk. The message delivered by missionary monks fell on the receptive ears of many who, in a fragile, capricious, and violent world, found comfort in knowing their eternal destiny was secured by a forgiving, salvation-promising God.

The group or mass conversions which came to typify the expansion of Christianity in medieval Europe raise several questions: How much turning is involved in belief or behavior? How much of the old must be shed for the new? How much resocialization into a Christian community is required? The anthropologist Robert Hefner suggests that "at an analytical minimum, conversion implies the acceptance of a new locus of self-identification, a new, though not exclusive, reference point in one's identity."[41] Is this reference point theological, behavioral, and/or communal? In the interaction between Christianity and other religions, is Christianity submerged into that religion and, if so, to what extent and at what point?

Some scholars are reticent to propose a baseline for judging Christian conversion. Robert Markus, a historian of late antiquity, observes, "There may be a universally valid and unchanging answer to that question; but the historian can only note the uncertainties, the shifts, doubts and debates concerning it. Assumptions determined by some theological, philosophical or other position may yield certainty: if so, they must at least be openly avowed. From a historical point of view, such certainty must appear as arbitrary dogmatism."[42] A very different perspective is offered by James Russell. In *The Germanization of Early Medieval Christianity*, Russell proposes an "objectivist" standard (what Markus called "arbitrary dogmatism") by which to evaluate Christian conversion. At a minimum, Christianity (and the substance of conversion) is "the belief in individual redemption through the suffering and death of Jesus Christ."[43] Rather than viewing conversion as a moving target whose definition is contingent upon historical circumstances, Russell begins with a definition and judges the moving target by that definition. Without this baseline, Russell argues, there is no meaningful way to distinguish between whether an individual or group is Christian, marginally Christian, or non-Christian. He thus concludes that the so-called "conversion" of Germanic peoples (ca. 750) meant little more than the embrace of a magico-religious cult of a powerful deity.[44]

Similar issues surrounding the nature and extent of conversion became even more complicated as Christianity extended beyond European Christendom to the Americas, Asia, and Africa, signaling the third great shift in missionary expansion. Scholars have employed a variety of terms to describe the nature and type of conversion in these distinct environments: enculturation, indigenization, accommodation, absorption, assimilation, and syncretism. Each of these descriptors carries its own specific meaning, but collectively they point to the degree of complex interaction between European Catholic and Protestant views of conversion within which were embedded assumptions about "normal" conversion. In this process of cross-cultural interaction, not only were converts made, but missionaries often readjusted their thinking about what made converts and constituted conversion.

As the first of several examples of these complex interactions, sixteenth-century Jesuit missionaries in China discovered that the Chinese language had no comparable word to signify "conversion." The inward psychological paradigm of Christian conversion and Paul's instructions to "flee from idols" were totally absent among Chinese converts who incorporated their new faith alongside Buddhist and Chinese statues.[45] In Africa, on the other hand, where primal religions predominated, conversions resembled the "power conversions" of the early church. Palpable divine encounters, be they visionary experiences or supernatural displays of healings and exorcisms, became the primary means for the conversion of thousands of Africans. At the same time, many African converts retained traditional practices such as polygamy, divination, animal sacrifice, and veneration of ancestors. And in India, Christian converts identified sin with bad karma in this life and past lives and interpreted Christ's death on the cross as a self-sacrifice that removed the convert's own karmic deficiency in order to end the cycle of death and rebirth.[46]

In each of these settings, missionaries lived on terms set by the foreigners they encountered (i.e., the host language and culture) and hence were driven to rethink what it meant to turn to Christ. Indeed, the recent demographic transformation of the church from the West to the global South (where the majority of Christians now reside) has placed the latter in the position of influencing Western constructs of conversion. Moreover, the issue of conversion itself has become increasingly problematic. On the one hand, non-Christian critics accuse Christians of exclusivity and hegemonic motives; on the other, Christians who remain convinced of the universality of the gospel continue to rethink the relationship of Christ and the meaning of conversion to cultural heritages that have had no Christian past.

From Tradition Transition to Intensification

Let us return to Gordon's conversion account and his Christian lineage, with an eye to previous developments in the medieval period that illustrate the natural movement from tradition transition to intensification. Gordon's parents could trace their spiritual legacy to Scandinavia during the second gravitational shift in Christian history. In the ninth century the Carolingian (Frankish) missionary monk and bishop, Anskar (ca. 801–865), "the apostle to the north," brought the Christian message to the pagan followers of Nordic gods.[47] We know little of the Viking religion but enough to know that the Scandinavians worshipped many gods associated with war and nature (e.g., Wodan and Odin) and had cult-sites. We also know that the conversion of the populace was hardly an abrupt turning from idols to the Christian God, for Christianization was a slow, long, piecemeal, random process. Yet there was what Peter Foote labels the "moment" of conversion, "when men at the apex of society, whom missionaries sought to influence, decided to abandon their sacrificial celebrations and to seek peace and prosperity by Christian rites only."[48] According to the limited extant sources, that "moment" in Sweden came in the early eleventh century when Olof Skötkonung apparently became the first king who converted to Christianity. Yet Olof's influence as a Christian was limited. Paganism remained entrenched in Uppsala, where throughout much of the eleventh century a heathen temple remained the focus of worship and sacrifice by not only pagans but Christians as well. In the 1080s the Christian King Inge I was ejected by his Christian brother-in-law, "Sven the Sacrificer," who got his nickname for permitting pagan worship to continue.[49] Primal religions and Christianity coexisted in Sweden until the twelfth century, and even then there are recorded instances of people deconverting from Christianity and then reconverting to the faith. As Jean Delumeau has demonstrated, such was the case in parts of Europe well into the eighteenth century.[50]

Over time, as Christianity took root among the ruling classes in Europe (geographically, the movement was generally from the south to the north despite the early conversion of the Swedish king) and expanded into society at large and became the dominant, pervasive religion ("Christendom"), other meanings of conversion existed alongside and eventually displaced the tradition transition. As more monks devoted themselves to the spiritual life and as the Catholic Church was challenged from within by the rise of Protestantism—in short, as the Christian society underwent internal spiritual, social, and political fluctuations—both the word itself and the concept of conversion took on a variety of connotations, primarily of the intensification type.

The most precise definition of conversion during the Middle Ages occurred within the context of monastic calling or the monastic life itself. Conversion thus assumed an institutional form, involving not only a change in heart but a change in social and eventually canonical standing. As early as the end of the fourth century, *conversio* became identified with asceticism and monastic living and its stress on *imitatio Christi* (imitation of Christ). By the twelfth century, conversion had become increasingly identified with the lifelong monastic process of renovation, especially the inner spiritual practice of "taking up penance." Bernard of Clairvaux (1090–1153), the heart and soul of the Cistercian movement, defined conversion in this twofold sense. In his *Sermons on Conversion to Clerics* in Paris, he claimed that "there is no true life except in conversion" and went on to urge the clergy to "Flee and save your souls! Flock to the city of refuge [i.e., the monastery], where you can do penance for the past, obtain grace in the present, and confidently wait for future glory."[51] More than mere entry into the monastery, conversion represented the soul's quest for perfection in imitation of Christ—especially the crucified Christ in his suffering and debasement. Bernard identified conversion with the pangs of conscience, remorse, and broken spirit (*conversio morum*)—the kind of divine knowledge acquired only in the monastery.[52]

Toward the end of the twelfth century, the Cistercian model of conversion, defined by withdrawal into a cloistered community, was challenged by friars and lay movements (e.g., beguines and *devotio moderna* in the Low Countries), for whom conversion meant an active pursuit of holiness in the world. With the growth of European cities and the rise of the mercantile class, new mendicant orders (Franciscan and Dominican) revolutionized the religious and social landscape by taking the life and message of conversion to a growing urban populace. They drew from the wellsprings of Cistercian views of conversion in emphasizing the inward change of heart that accompanied the entrance into a religious order, but they diverged from the lifelong commitment to the cloister in pursuit of the *via apostolica* in the world. Self perfection came by converting others. The friars retained the twofold monastic sense of conversion (initial calling to the monastery and the practice of penitence) but, given their concern with service to the community, enforcement of orthodox Catholicism, and mission to the non-Christian world (all indicative of the universalizing trend in the Church), they also viewed conversion in the traditional sense of converting nominal or heterodox Christians to deeper or proper faith and non-Christians (Jews and "infidel" Muslims) to Christianity. Their mission involved a continuous converting of the self and converting others through preaching, instruction, and baptism.[53]

With the flowering of mysticism in late medieval Europe, the words "convert" and "conversion" (or the expression "turning to God") conformed increasingly to the notion of spiritual reformation. In *The Fire of Love*, Richard Rolle of Hampole (ca. 1300–1349) wrote of "the four years and three months that passed from the beginning of my conversion to the moment when, with God's help, I managed to reach the highest degree of the love of Christ."[54] To Margery Kempe (ca. 1373–ca. 1438), conversion meant turning from sinfulness to a deeper love of and service to God. In *The Imitation of Christ* Thomas à Kempis (ca. 1379–1471) wrote of the monastic life as being "first converted" from worldly knowledge and secular learning to a consciousness of sin, repentance, and a humble desire for knowledge of God.[55]

Whether in a monastic, quasi-monastic, or lay setting, devout Christians challenged notions of conversion as merely affiliation, or affirming and identifying with the externals of the Church—its laws, doctrines, rituals, and traditions. To be sure, affili-ation is an aspect in the conversion process but from the perspective of Bernard and others it is incomplete and must be authenticated by a second conversion of the heart "initiated, sustained, and completed, if at all, by God's actions."[56]

Conversion as intensification contains within itself the seeds of subversion. As Karl Morrison has pointed out, Bernard's sermon on conversion "decried rulers of the Church who had been exalted to priesthood and prelacy without conversion of heart. The whole world is Christian, Bernard wrote, but nearly all deny Christ." The Church's leaders grasped after riches, indulged their sexual appetites, and squandered the Church's resources—all viewed by Bernard as evidences of their unconverted state. God's supernatural grace had not taken hold of their lives.[57]

Bernard's views capture a salient theme that runs throughout the history of Christian conversion; conversion subverts and challenges the status quo. Early Christian conversion, with its demands of uncompromising loyalty to the "Lord" Jesus, subverted the author-ity of the Roman Empire. In the Reformation era and well into the seventeenth century, conversion to Protestantism or Catholicism challenged not only theological convictions but subverted the order of the state, upon which ecclesiastical institutions depended.[58] As we have seen, Pietist demands for conversion subverted the established Lutheran Church. During America's mid-eighteenth century Great Awakening, Gilbert Tennant subverted and enraged the Presbyterian establishment with his infamous sermon, "The Danger of an Unconverted Ministry" (1741).[59] Generally, in societies where Christianity is a minority or outlawed religion, or in societies where one form of Christianity is overwhelmingly pre-dominant, conversion often threatens to subvert the social, political, and religious order.

In Gordon's case, in an environment of religious freedom where evangelical Christianity had a historical presence and within a family that adhered to the Lutheran faith, his conversion was neither politically subversive nor a "tradition transition." Rather, it involved more of an incremental change or a second stage of conversion within the Christian tradition (though he certainly did not see it that way) than a dra-matic change to an altogether different religion. To a degree—and his case illustrates the limitations of ideal types—his conversion corresponds to "institutional transition" or "denominational switching." That is, following a profound religious experience, he changed allegiance from one Protestant group to another. And yet that change was nei-ther immediate nor abrupt; on Sunday mornings he continued to attend and even serve in his home church while attending the Mission Church in the evenings. In this respect his conversion was more akin to intensification, the process whereby conversion deep-ens a commitment within an existing faith community though, to be sure, it eventually led him to change denominations.[60]

Conversion Motifs

Conversion narratives emphasize certain thematic elements and key experiences that correspond to what sociologists John Lofland and Norman Skonovd identified in a 1981 article as "conversion motifs."[61] Basing their study primarily on converts to new religious movements since the 1960s, during the so-called "cult craze," they identified six motifs (which may overlap or combine) by which to classify the influences (the how question) brought to bear in a convert's subjective experience: intellectual, mystical, experimental, affectional, revivalist, and coercive. In instructive ways, these motifs are applicable in the history of Christian conversion, although, as was observed earlier with conversion typologies, the experience of an individual seldom fits neatly into a single category. Conversion has different connotations at different moments.

Perhaps the motif that best fits Gordon's account is the mystical. Characterized by a sudden burst of insight, visionary appearance, or illumination, the mystical experience cannot be fully expressed in logical or coherent terms. The vision recounted by Gordon stands out as somewhat extraordinary within the twentieth-century evangelical tradition. Although revelatory visions have been recorded since the early days of Christianity, Protestants have tended to be less open than Catholics to visionary experiences and, in fact, have often viewed those who experience visions as theologically suspect. Perhaps that is why Gordon mentions "what some might term a vision" almost in passing. Although he had recounted his conversion on numerous occasions, I never recall him speaking of a vision. Unlike many recorded Christic visions, Gordon offers no description of what Jesus looked like, no details of whether this was an imaginary or a corporeal vision of Jesus (the mention of Jesus placing his hand on his shoulder would suggest the latter). The vision functioned as an assurance of divine presence, specifically of a new intimacy with Jesus.[62]

Gordon's conversion also conforms to the experimental motif. Here, the prospective convert takes part in various organizational and ritual activities of the group before full commitment. The process is an assimilative one of increasing interaction with the group. Over a period of time, Gordon was exposed to members of the church youth group and found their fellowship and message attractive. Throughout Christian history, the integrative and ritual process varies in form and content. Gordon's conversion lacked formalized, ritualistic behavior, but nonetheless his exposure to the group's Bible studies and devotional activities was a critical factor in his conversion.

In other contexts, ritual is fundamental to the process of conversion. Anthropologists have been especially alert to ritualistic behavior, arguing that, in the words of Anthony Wallace, "the primary phenomenon of religion is ritual."[63] Bennetta Jules-Rosette's exemplary study of Christian conversion among an indigenous culture in Africa supports Wallace's claim,[64] as does a recent study applying ritual studies to conversion in early Christianity. Thomas Finn contends that conversion in the ancient world, whether pagan, Jewish, or Christian, "was an extended ritual process that combined teaching with symbolic enactment—the cognitive and performative—and yielded commitment and transformation."[65]

The instructions of Cyril (c.315), the fourth-century bishop in Jerusalem illustrate this initiation process.[66] By Cyril's time, Christianity had become the favored religion of the empire, thanks to the conversion of the emperor Constantine in 312. In such a hospitable environment, it had become safe, respectable, and advantageous to become a Christian.

Not surprisingly, "conversions" resulted from mixed motives (e.g., curiosity, desire to please a spouse or master, possible financial gain, desire to belong)—of which Cyril was well aware. "I welcome you as one who shall be saved," he announced in his Catechetical Lectures, "in spite of having come with an unsound intention."[67] Whereas baptism in the New Testament functioned as a ritual expression tied to conversion (baptism followed belief; see Acts 2:41; 8:13), by the fourth century "the baptismal process became instead the means of conveying a profound experience to the candidates in the hope of bringing about their conversion."[68] Through an intricate and dramatic ceremony that was derived from initiation rites of the pagan mystery religions, the church's leaders anticipated that such ceremonies would induce conversion, after which *mystagogy* (post-baptismal instruction) would follow.

In Cyril's Jerusalem church, baptismal candidates prepared for this rite through an elaborate and rigorous eight-week period of training involving exorcisms and instruction. This preparatory period led into Holy Week and culminated in baptism, "the soul's regeneration."[69] None of the baptizands knew what was to happen in the ceremony itself. Once led to the baptistery, they renounced Satan, affirmed a simple Christian creed, removed their clothes, were anointed with olive oil, and then immersed in the baptismal waters. Following baptism, they were anointed again, clothed in white garments, and celebrated their first Eucharist. During Easter week, Cyril met with the newly baptized for "Mystagogical Catechesis" in which he explained the meaning of baptism and the common meal. Converts were thus made. According to Finn, "Nowhere in antiquity...do we have a clearer and more dramatic picture of conversion as a ritual process."[70]

Another conversion motif, prevalent throughout Christian history, is the affectional. As described by John Lofland and Rodney Stark, this motif emphasized the role of interpersonal relationships in conversion. In subsequent studies, Stark has argued that the making of converts in early Christianity was largely the result of person to person contacts.[71] The numerical growth of Christianity in its first three centuries had little if anything to do with advertising, mass conversions, evangelistic rallies and campaigns, or efforts to proselytize in worship services. In an era of potential persecution, any highly visible mass evangelism would have invited even greater suppression. As both contemporary defenders and detractors of Christianity observed, the faith spread primarily through personal contact among family members and friends, between slaves, at social events, in the army, in the workplace, through travel and trade, and even in war.[72] Such has been the case throughout Christian history: under similar conditions of harassment and persecution (e.g., in twentieth-century China), the primary influence in Christian conversion has been interpersonal contacts.

The affectional motif applies to Gordon's conversion in striking ways, for his narrative highlights the impact of relatives and friends. He mentions the influence of Aunt Esther, who "would talk about the Lord." A more direct influence was Gordon's personal friends: Don "would talk to me about spiritual matters"; Russell "asked me if I wanted to receive Jesus into my life as my Savior"; and Roy encouraged Gordon to attend an evangelical college. Indeed, Gordon's conversion is inexplicable without these close relationships.

The fifth motif, the revivalist, is characterized by numerous or mass conversions. The early chapters of Acts record that the preaching of the apostles resulted in mass conversions of 3,000 and 5,000 new believers (2:41; 4:4). These impressive additions—and that is all they are, for we know nothing about the converts themselves—have provided a biblical model for revivalist practitioners to the point where, in the minds of many, conversion and revivalism are synonymous. Indeed, this motif is more prevalent in the modern era because the adaptation of the language and strategies of the marketplace enhance the ability of evangelists to reach large audiences. This particular method of eliciting conversions has been theologically controversial and the conversions themselves ambiguous. In some cases, conversions have been more often an intensification of commitment or a "ritualized reaffirmation of existing beliefs and values" than "true" conversions of non-Christians.[73] And yet for those whose commitment was intensified, in their minds true conversion occurred in a Jamesian sense: Christianity, previously peripheral to their consciousness, now took a central place. Although this motif is not present in Gordon's account of conversion, it has characterized the evangelical tradition as a confirmation of the miraculous "outpouring of the Holy Spirit."

The final and most problematic motif, the coercive motif, was not directly related to Gordon's conversion but was a part of his distant Swedish past. Conversion that is forced upon another person or, more often, peoples, either through psychological pressure, financial coercion, or physical intimidation (and there are some scholars who argue that any form of proselytizing is "forced"), has a long history in Christianity and persists not only in Christianity but in many of the world's great religions. During the medieval period, the formula for coerced conversions was the potent combination of exclusive claims to the truth advanced by warrior kings in an already violent society and the Old Testament model of kingship that included wiping out enemies of Yahweh.

In the case of Gordon's ancestors in Sweden, once rulers accepted the Christian faith, coerced conversion was part and parcel of Christianity's advance. This practice, traceable to the fourth century with the rise of imperial Christianity, was most evident during the reign of the Carolingian emperor Charlemagne (ruled 768–814). As one contemporary noted, Charlemagne "preached with an iron tongue" by exacting forced baptisms of the conquered Saxons and Avars in the last quarter of the eighth century.[74] According to Andrew Walls, conversion at the point of the sword in northern Europe "was used with a ferocity and violence beyond anything the conquistadores did in the Americas and far beyond anything that happened in modern Africa or Asia as a result of imperial association with Christianity."[75] The eleventh to the fifteenth centuries witnessed the persecution of Jews and heretics, crusades against Muslims, and the increasing acceptance of forced conversions, especially in the northern region that remained unconverted— Scandinavia and the Baltic. The degree to which a forced conversion is authentic conversion raises again the question of the meaning of conversion. Have a subjected people under threat of death become Christian when a priest sprinkles water over them and says some words in Latin? Charlemagne said yes, but Alcuin, an abbot, scholar, and member of Charlemagne's court, urged pre-baptismal instruction in Christian creeds and morality before declaring anyone a Christian convert.[76]

"My Conversion": An End and a Beginning

From Gordon's perspective, the most profound and lasting consequences of his conversion were primarily theological. To be sure, one could point to psychological repercussions (e.g., that his conversion at age 18 resolved the natural process of identity formation), but Gordon would understand these as mere byproducts of a profound theological reorientation.[77] The immediate consequences were clear: peace of mind, a new self-understanding shaped by a living relationship to God, and the sense of belonging to a new community of fellow converts. Within Gordon's fundamentalist milieu of the 1930s, conversion began and ended with the individual's relationship to God. The only ultimate existential question from the fundamentalist perspective was that posed by the Philippian jailer to Paul and Barnabas in Acts 16:30: "What must I do to be saved?" Unlike the theologically liberal Social Gospel movement that focused on addressing society's ills, the goal of the fundamentalist movement was "largely reduced to winning converts."[78]

Conversion, however, is not just an individual experience or terminal event. Its consequences are lived out over time. Assessing the long-term sociocultural and historical consequences of a proselytizing movement such as fundamentalism is considerably more complicated than determining the personal results of conversion in Gordon's life. There is an intermediate stage, however, that should not be overlooked. Gordon's conversion not only had immediate consequences in his personal life but was "an event that changed the course of my life forever" (as he put it) that virtually determined the kind of woman he would marry and consequently structured and shaped the religious life of his five children and the hundreds of people he served in ministry. A single drop in the ocean of conversions had a profound ripple effect. And yet that effect would produce its own unanticipated consequences among the post–Second World War "baby boom" generation of evangelicals.

During the half-century from approximately 1925 to 1975, evangelical conversion meant largely an intensely felt personal experience with a specific theological content whose consequences were largely limited to individual behavior and expressions of piety. Conversion meant "living for Christ" and "being a good witness." These generally translated into being an admirable person, eschewing a variety of "worldly" behavioral sins, and separating from non-evangelicals but still seeking opportunities to speak to "the lost" about their "need for a Savior." Evangelicals did not generally meddle in politics, decry social injustices, or challenge "the American way of life." Indeed, their lack of engagement in social issues led to their being criticized for a truncated understanding of conversion. A younger generation of evangelicals coming of age in the 1970s expanded the meaning of conversion beyond its personal benefits to argue that authentic conversion included following the example of Jesus and the Hebrew prophets in a concern for the welfare of others and in confronting institutional injustice in the socio-political arena.[79]

Although an older generation of evangelicals remained aloof from direct social engagement, it nevertheless unleashed a singularly focused spiritual energy whose effects remain with us. The spiritual and activist fervor stirred by thousands of conversions in Gordon's generation inspired renewed efforts to evangelize America and the world. The proliferation of missionary agencies and evangelistic enterprises, symbolized by the worldwide "crusades" of Billy Graham and advanced by creative use of media, boosted the globalization of evangelical Christianity, the consequences of which are profoundly remaking the world.

These efforts to win America and the world for Christ eventually spilled into the US political arena. A resurgent evangelical Christianity, responding to the social upheavals of the late 1960s resulted in, among other things, a variety of high-profile conversions as well as the mobilization of a portion of evangelicals to form the religious-political right. The symbolic call to conversion remained the same, but in a very different cultural climate the symbol was invested with new meaning. Writing in the early 1980s, Martin Marty's insights into deriving new meaning from old symbols are prophetically relevant thirty years later. "In the recent surge," he wrote, "prosperous Evangelicalism still uses the language of a call to turn one's back on the world. But now it serves as a means of providing ritual process for applicants to the approved world, in a day when the President of the United States, business leaders, celebrities, athletes and beauty queens, and civic figures attribute their worldly success to the fruits of conversion. The symbols 'world' and 'convert' remain constant but their content has been drastically changed by an improvising set of leaders and respondents."[80] The same may be said about the entire history of Christian conversion.

CONCLUSION: THE WAY AHEAD

Marty's reference above to the changing content of the symbols of "world" and "convert" points to the task ahead in Christian conversion studies. To begin to comprehend the "drastically changed" content of Christian conversion in different times and places is to recognize the complexities of a phenomenon that includes:

Semantics: How is conversion defined or explained? Who is offering the definition or doing the explaining of the word or the concept? From whose vantage point is conversion explained: the subject, the group, the scholar, the partisan, the critic? What aspects of the former life are retained or discarded in conversion? Is the history of Christian conversion, as Karl Morrison suggests, "wrapped up in the meaning of the word"?[81]

History: In what social, political, cultural, and theological context does conversion occur? In what ways do these contextual factors limit and/or define the meaning of conversion? How open or closed is a group or society to Christian conversion? Is Christian conversion more likely to take place in some areas or regions than others or among some social groups than others? In what context does conversion from a tribal or ethnic religion to Christianity take place? What inducements or attractions factor into conversion? Do people convert for utilitarian reasons (i.e., there are things to be "had," be they material or status-related) or does Christianity offer a way of making sense out of life (which may or may not have material or status consequences)?[82]

Theory: How applicable are conversion theories and models in the social sciences (anthropology, sociology, psychology) to a history of Christian conversion? To what extent does historical particularity defy theoretical constructs and efforts to categorize and explain conversion? Over the past several decades, New Testament scholars have drawn from the theoretical insights in the social sciences to explain the conversions of Jews and Gentiles, disciples and followers of Jesus, and the apostle Paul.[83]

Method: In what ways do biographical, rhetorical, ethnographic, gender, ritual, and quantitative approaches—to name a few—illumine the complexities of Christian conversion? Issues I have not addressed in this chapter but have raised elsewhere include: Why in some settings do females convert at a higher rate than males and vice versa? Do males and females, children and adults experience conversion differently and if so, in what ways and why? What are the social characteristics of the converts?[84]

In this chapter I have addressed a number of these definitional, historical, theoretical, and methodological issues. The challenge ahead is to move from a case study such as this (and the many other local and regional studies in the scholarly literature) to a contextually sensitive, historical, and thematic survey of the complex phenomenon we call Christian conversion.

Notes

1. Abraham J. Malherbe, "Conversion to Paul's Gospel," in *The Early Church in Its Context: Essays in Honor of Everett Ferguson*, ed. Abraham J. Malherbe, Frederick W. Norris, and James W. Thompson, Supplements to Novum Testamentum (Leiden: Brill, 1998), 238.
2. For examples, see John Barbour, *Versions of Deconversion: Autobiography and the Loss of Faith* (Charlottesville: University Press of Virginia, 1994); Timothy Larsen, *Crisis of Doubt: Honest Faith in Nineteenth-Century England* (New York: Oxford University Press, 2006); Lian Xi, *The Conversion of Missionaries: Liberalism in American Protestant Missions in China, 1907–1932* (University Park: Pennsylvania State University Press, 1997).
3. Clifford L. Staples and Armand L. Mauss, "Conversion or Commitment? A Reassessment of the Snow and Machalek Approach to the Study of Conversion," *Journal for the Scientific Study of Religion* 26, no. 2 (1987): 138; Lewis R. Rambo, *Understanding Religious Conversion* (New Haven: Yale University Press, 1993), xiv.
4. Rambo, *Understanding Religious Conversion*, 165, 20, 175.
5. Gordon S. Kling, "Confessions of a Late Bloomer: Memoirs of Rev. Gordon S. Kling," unpublished manuscript in author's possession, 2006, 22–25.
6. Ingun Montgomery, "The Institutionalisation of Lutheranism in Sweden and Finland," in *The Scandinavian Reformation: From Evangelical Movement to Institutional Reform*, ed. Ole Peter Grell (Cambridge: Cambridge University Press, 1995), 156–160.
7. Protestant reformer Martin Luther was fond of quoting Mark 16:16, "He that believeth and is baptized shall be saved." Belief or faith is given by God; it is not something exercised by

humans; "the power, work, profit, fruit, and end of Baptism is this, namely, to save." See *Larger Catechism*, "Holy Baptism," nos. 4, 24, http://bookofconcord.org/lc-6-baptism.php.

8. On Luther and conversion, see Marilyn J. Harran, *Luther on Conversion: The Early Years* (Ithaca, NY: Cornell University Press, 1983).

9. See Philip Jacob Spener, *Pia Desideria*, trans. and ed. Theodore G. Tappert (Philadelphia: Fortress Press, 1964); W. R. Ward, *Early Evangelicalism: A Global Intellectual History, 1670–1789* (Cambridge: Cambridge University Press, 2006), chap. 2.

10. F. Ernest Stoeffler, *German Pietism during the Eighteenth Century* (Leiden: Brill, 1973), ix, quoted in *Pietists: Selected Writings*, ed. Peter C. Erb (New York: Paulist Press, 1983), 7.

11. Although the word "evangelical" is derived from the Greek for "gospel," the word was commonly used for the Anglo-American revival movements of the eighteenth and nineteenth centuries, though clearly it extended beyond the English-speaking world into other parts of Europe and beyond. In this context, evangelical refers to a Protestant tradition that emphasized the Reformation doctrine of the divinely inspired Bible as its sole source of authority; the necessity of conversion or the "new birth" made possible by Christ's death on the cross as a substitution for the deserved condemnation of sinful humanity; and an accompanying desire to spread the good news of Christ's salvation to others by evangelism and missions. I use the term "fundamentalist movement" to refer to the militant, separatist wing of evangelicalism that emerged in the 1930s and 1940s in response to attempts by Protestant liberals to substantially modify the basic tenets of the evangelical faith. See George M. Marsden, *Understanding Fundamentalism and Evangelicalism* (Grand Rapids, MI: Eerdmans, 1991), 1–4.

12. Martin E. Marty, "The Revival of Evangelicalism and Southern Religion," in *Varieties of Southern Evangelicalism*, ed. David Edwin Harrell, Jr. (Macon, GA: Mercer University Press, 1981), 9 (quote), 12–15.

13. On evangelical movements, see Ward, *Early Evangelicalism*; W. R. Ward, *The Protestant Evangelical Awakening* (Cambridge: Cambridge University Press, 1992); Mark A. Noll, David W. Bebbington, and George A. Rawlyk, eds., *Evangelicalism: Comparative Studies of Popular Protestantism in North America, the British Isles, and Beyond, 1700–1990* (New York: Oxford University Press, 1994); and Douglas A. Sweeney, *The American Evangelical Story: A History of the Movement* (Grand Rapids, MI: Baker, 2005). On stages of conversion or "morphology of conversion," for Pietists, see Erb, *Pietists: Selected Writings*, 6; for Puritans, see Edmund S. Morgan, *Visible Saints: The History of a Puritan Idea* (Ithaca, NY: Cornell University Press, 1965).

14. Richard Fletcher, *The Barbarian Conversion: From Paganism to Christianity* (New York: Henry Holt, 1997), 514.

15. Krister Stendahl, *Paul among Jews and Gentiles and Other Essays* (Philadelphia: Fortress, 1976), 78–96.

16. Hugh T. Kerr and John M. Mulder, eds., *Conversions: The Christian Experience* (Grand Rapids, MI: Eerdmans, 1983).

17. Quoted in Eugene V. Gallagher, "Conversion and Salvation in the Apocryphal Acts of the Apostles," *The Second Century: A Journal of Early Christian Studies* 8, no.1 (Spring 1991): 13.

18. *Saint Augustine Confessions*, trans. R. S. Pine-Coffin (Middlesex, England: Penguin, 1961), VIII.12 (p. 177).

19. Ibid., VIII.12 (p.178).

20. Kerr and Mulder, *Conversions: The Christian Experience*, 59.

21. Roland H. Bainton, *Here I Stand: A Life of Martin Luther* (New York: New American Library Mentor Books, 1950), 49–50.

22. William Barclay, *Turning to God: A Study of Conversion in the Book of Acts and Today* (Philadelphia: Westminster, 1964), 28.

23. William James, *The Varieties of Religious Experience: A Study in Human Nature*, ed. Martin E. Marty (1902; New York: Viking Penguin Books, 1982), 20.

24. Ibid., 47, 48.

25. Ibid., 135, 134.

26. Ibid., 189, 196, emphasis added.

27. Ibid., 258.

28. Ibid., 210–211.

29. Ibid., 257.

30. Ibid., 31.

31. Wayne Proudfoot, "Introduction," in William James, *The Varieties of Religious Experience: A Study in Human Nature* (New York: Barnes and Noble Classics, 2004), xxix.

32. Rambo, *Understanding Religious Conversion*, 12–16.

33. Ibid., 12–14.

34. See John Henry Newman, *Apologia pro Vita Sua* (Garden City, NY: Doubleday, 1956).

35. Andrew F. Walls, *The Missionary Movement in Christian History: Studies in the Transmission of Faith* (Maryknoll, NY: Orbis, 1996), 68–75.

36. A. D. Nock, *Conversion: The Old and New in Religion from Alexander the Great to Augustine of Hippo* (London: Oxford University Press, 1933), 14, 7.

37. Ramsay MacMullen, *Christianizing the Roman Empire (A.D. 100–400)* (New Haven: Yale University Press, 1984), 5.

38. Ibid., 40.

39. Robin Lane Fox, *Pagans and Christians* (New York: HarperCollins, 1996), 330.

40. Fletcher, *Barbarian Conversion*, 45.

41. Robert W. Hefner, "Introduction: World Building and the Rationality of Conversion," in *Conversion to Christianity: Historical and Anthropological Perspectives on a Great Transformation*, ed. Robert W. Hefner (Berkeley and Los Angeles: University of California Press, 1993), 17.

42. Robert A. Markus, *The End of Ancient Christianity* (Cambridge: Cambridge University Press, 1990), 6.

43. James C. Russell, *The Germanization of Early Medieval Christianity: A Sociohistorical Approach to Religious Transformation* (New York: Oxford University Press, 1994), 35.

44. Ibid., 199.

45. R. Po-Chia Hsia, "Translating Christianity: Counter-Reformation Europe and the Catholic Mission in China, 1580–1780," in *Conversion: Old Worlds and New*, ed. Kenneth Mills and Anthony Grafton (Rochester, NY: University of Rochester Press, 2003), 88.

46. Philip Jenkins, *The Next Christendom: The Coming of Global Christianity* (New York: Oxford University Press, 2002), 120, 121.

47. See Charles H. Robinson, *Anskar: The Apostle of the North, 801–865*, trans. of Bishop Rimbert's *Vita Anskarii*, Lives of Early and Medieval Missionaries Series (London: Society for the Propagation of the Gospel in Foreign Parts, 1921).

48. Peter Foote, "Conversion," in *Medieval Scandinavia: An Encyclopedia*, ed. Phillip Pulsiano (New York: Garland, 1993), 106.

49. P. H. Sawyer, *Kings and Vikings: Scandinavia and Europe, AD 700–1100* (London: Methuen, 1982), 18; Foote, "Conversion," 106.

50. Jean Delumeau, *Catholicism between Luther and Voltaire: A New View of the Counter-Reformation*, trans. Jeremy Moiser (London: Burns & Oates, 1977).

51. Bernard of Clairvaux, *Sermons on Conversion: On Conversion, a Sermon to Clerics and Lenten Sermons on the Psalm 'He Who Dwells,'* trans. Marie-Bernard Saïd, Cistercian Fathers Series 25 (Kalamazoo, MI: Cistercian Publications, 1981), 31, 75.

52. *The Works of Bernard of Clairvaux: On the Song of Songs*, 4 vols., trans. Kilian Walsh and Irene M. Edmonds (Spencer, MA: Cistercian Publications, 1971–80), 1:64, 102.

53. Bert Boest, "Converting the Other and Converting the Self: Double Objectives in Franciscan Educational Writings," in *Christianizing Peoples and Converting Individuals*, ed. Guyda Armstrong and Ian N. Wood, International Medieval Research, vol. 7 (Turnout, Belgium: Brepols, 2000), 295–301; Donald Mowbray, "*Conversio ad bonum commutaile*: Augustinian Language of Conversion in Medieval Theology," in Armstrong and Wood, eds., *Christianizing Peoples and Converting Individuals*, 289–291. For a broader treatment of Franciscan views of conversion, see E. Randolph Daniel, *The Franciscan Concept of Mission in the High Middle Ages* (Lexington: University Press of Kentucky, 1975).

54. Karen Armstrong, *Visions of God: Four Medieval Mystics and Their Writings* (New York: Bantam, 1994), 25–26. On "turning to God," see Walter Hilton's "Ladder of Perfection," in Armstrong, *Visions of God*, 118–119.

55. Thomas à Kempis, *The Imitation of Christ*, trans. Betty I. Knott (London: Collins, 1963), 51, 55, 66, 72.

56. Karl F. Morrison, *Understanding Conversion* (Charlottesville: University Press of Virginia, 1992), xv.

57. Ibid., 6.

58. For example, see Michael C. Questier, *Conversion, Politics and Religion in England, 1580–1625* (Cambridge: Cambridge University Press, 1996).

59. Gilbert Tennent, "The Danger of an Unconverted Ministry," in *The Great Awakening: Documents Illustrating the Crisis and Its Consequences*, ed. Alan Heimert and Perry Miller (Indianapolis: Bobbs-Merrill, 1967), 81.

60. Rambo, *Understanding Religious Conversion*, 12–14, 38–40.

61. John Lofland and Norman Skonovd, "Conversion Motifs," *Journal for the Scientific Study of Religion* 20 (1981): 373–385.

62. On Christian visionary experiences, see Phillip H. Wiebe, *Visions of Jesus: Direct Encounters from the New Testament to Today* (New York: Oxford University Press, 1997).

63. Anthony F. C. Wallace, *Religion: An Anthropological View* (New York: Random House, 1966), 102.

64. Bennetta Jules-Rosette, *African Apostles: Ritual and Conversion in the Church of John Maranke* (Ithaca, NY: Cornell, 1975).

65. Thomas M. Finn, *From Death to Rebirth: Ritual and Conversion in Antiquity* (New York: Paulist Press, 1997), 9.

66. Extant sources include the *Didache* (ca. 50–150), Justin Martyr's *First Apology* (ca. 160), and Hippolytus' *Apostolic Tradition* (ca. 200). For the *Didache* and *First Apology*, see *Early Christian Fathers*, ed. Cyril C. Richardson (New York: Macmillan, 1970); for *Apostolic Tradition*, see *The Treatise on the Apostolic Tradition of St. Hippolytus of Rome* (London: Alban Press, 1992). For a brief informative discussion of early Christian initiation

rituals, see Paul Bradshaw, *Early Christian Worship: A Basic Introduction to Ideas and Practice* (Collegeville, MN: Liturgical Press, 1996), 2–36.

67. Cyril of Jerusalem, "The Catechetical Lectures," in *Cyril of Jerusalem and Nemesius of Emesa*, ed. William Telfer, Library of Christian Classics, vol. 4 (Philadelphia: Westminster Press, 1955), 68.

68. Bradshaw, *Early Christian Worship*, 22.

69. Cyril, "Catechetical Lectures," 75 (see also 89–98).

70. Finn, *From Death to Rebirth*, 204.

71. See John Lofland and Rodney Stark, "Becoming a World-Saver: A Theory of Conversion to a Deviant Perspective," *American Sociological Review* 30 (1965): 862–875; Rodney Stark, *The Rise of Christianity: How the Obscure, Marginal Jesus Movement Became the Dominant Religious Force in the Western World in a Few Centuries* (San Francisco: HarperCollins, 1997), chap. 1; Rodney Stark, *Cities of God: The Real Story of How Christianity became an Urban Movement and Conquered Rome* (San Francisco: HarperSanFrancisco, 2006), 8–13.

72. Nock, *Conversion*, 212; Lane Fox, *Pagans and Christians*, 316.

73. The "many cases" are conversions associated with Billy Graham crusades. See William G. McLoughlin, *Modern Revivalism: Charles Grandison Finney to Billy Graham* (New York: Ronald Press, 1959); William G. McLoughlin, *Billy Graham: Revivalist in a Secular Age* (New York: Ronald Press, 1960); David A. Snow and Richard Machalek, "The Sociology of Conversion," *Annual Review of Sociology* 10 (1984): 172.

74. Quoted in Richard E. Sullivan, *Christian Missionary Activity in the Early Middle Ages* (Brookfield, VT: Variorum, 1994), 277.

75. Walls, *The Missionary Movement in Christian History*, 72.

76. Sullivan, *Christian Missionary Activity in the Early Middle Ages*, 279–283.

77. The consequences of his conversion closely resemble those of about 200 converts interviewed by Rambo who reported a new, living relationship to God; a sense of relief from guilt; a new direction in life; a new understanding of themselves and the world; and a sense of belonging in a new community (*Understanding Religious Conversion*, 160–162).

78. Joel A. Carpenter, *Revive Us Again: The Reawakening of American Fundamentalism* (New York: Oxford University Press, 1997), 78.

79. See Jim Wallis, *The Call to Conversion* (New York: Harper & Row, 1981).

80. Ibid., 11.

81. Morrison, *Understanding Conversion*, xvi.

82. These questions are addressed (along with a review of previous scholarly literature) in Joel Robbins, *Becoming Sinners: Christianity and Moral Torment in a Papua New Guinea Society* (Berkeley: University of California Press, 2004), chaps. 2–3.

83. See Beverly Roberts Gaventa, *From Darkness to Light: Aspects of Conversion in the New Testament* (Philadelphia: Fortress, 1986); Paula Fredriksen, "Paul and Augustine: Conversion Narratives, Orthodox Traditions, and the Retrospective Self," *Journal of Theological Studies* 37 (Apr. 1986): 3–34; Alan Segal, *Paul the Convert: The Apostolate and the Apostasy of Saul the Pharisee* (New Haven: Yale University Press, 1990); Wayne A. Meeks, *The Origins of Christian Morality: The First Two Centuries* (New Haven: Yale University Press, 1993), chap. 2; Richard V. Peace, *Conversion in the New Testament: Paul and the Twelve* (Grand Rapids, MI: Eerdmans, 1999); Scot McKnight, *Turning to Jesus: The Sociology of Conversion in the Gospels* (Louisville, KY: Westminster John Knox, 2002).

84. David W. Kling, *A Field of Divine Wonders: The New Divinity and Village Revivals in Northwestern Connecticut, 1792–1822* (University Park: Pennsylvania State University Press, 1993), chaps. 6–7.

FURTHER READING

Brereton, Virginia Lieson. *From Sin to Salvation: Stories of Women's Conversions, 1800 to the Present.* Bloomington: Indiana University Press, 1984. Explores conversion narratives of American women as a highly formulaic general literary type. An important contribution for understanding women's experiences.

Fletcher, Richard. *The Barbarian Conversion: From Paganism to Christianity.* New York: Henry Holt, 1997. Wide-ranging historical study of conversion in Europe from the third through twelfth centuries. Nuanced study demonstrating the complexities of conversion over time and place.

Gelpi, Donald L. *The Conversion Experience: A Reflective Process for RCIA Participants and Others.* New York: Paulist Press, 1998. Views conversion as a twofold dynamic process ("initial" and "ongoing"). Normative approach described by a well-known Catholic theologian.

Hefner, Robert W., ed. *Conversion to Christianity: Historical and Anthropological Perspectives on a Great Transformation.* Berkeley and Los Angeles: University of California Press, 1993. Wide-ranging, interdisciplinary study. Provides a healthy sampling of anthropological approaches to conversion.

Jules-Rosette, Bennetta. *African Apostles: Ritual and Conversion in the Church of John Maranke.* Ithaca, NY: Cornell University Press, 1975. A classic anthropological study by an observer-participant. Important for understanding conversion in African independent churches.

Kendall, Calvin, et al., ed. *Conversion to Christianity from Late Antiquity to the Modern Age: Considering the Process in Europe, Asia, and the Americas.* Minneapolis: Center for Early Modern History, University of Minnesota, 2009. Wide-ranging coverage with particularly insightful prologue concerning conversion from a global perspective.

Kreider, Alan. *The Change of Conversion and the Origin of Christendom.* Harrisburg, PA: Trinity Press, 1999. Examines Christian conversion from the first thorough sixth centuries as viewed through the categories of "belief," "belonging," and "behavior." An insightful primer on various entry points of conversion.

Mills, Kenneth, and Anthony Grafton, eds. *Conversion: Old Worlds and New.* Rochester, NY: University of Rochester Press, 2003. Collection of essays exploring "conversion to, with, and around forms of Western Christianity." Vital for understanding the contact and interaction between Western Christianity and the non-Christian world.

Morrison, Karl. *Understanding Conversion.* Charlottesville: University Press of Virginia, 1992. Careful study of eleventh- and twelfth-century Europe. Challenges modern scholars' attempt to establish a general morphology of conversion.

Viswanathan, Gauri. *Outside the Fold: Conversion, Modernity, and Belief.* Princeton: Princeton University Press, 1998. Focusing on India, argues that conversion is one of the most destabilizing political events in the life of a society. Critical for viewing conversion in a non-Western context.

BIBLIOGRAPHY

Armstrong, Karen. *Visions of God: Four Medieval Mystics and Their Writings.* New York: Bantam, 1994.

Augustine, Saint. *Saint Augustine Confessions*, trans. R. S. Pine-Coffin. Middlesex, England: Penguin, 1961.

Bainton, Roland H. *Here I Stand: A Life of Martin Luther*. New York: New American Library Mentor Books, 1950.

Barbour, John. *Versions of Deconversion: Autobiography and the Loss of Faith*. Charlottesville: University Press of Virginia, 1994.

Barclay, William. *Turning to God: A Study of Conversion in the Book of Acts and Today*. Philadelphia: Westminster, 1964.

Bernard of Clairvaux. *Sermons on Conversion: On Conversion, a Sermon to Clerics and Lenten Sermons on the Psalm 'He Who Dwells,'* trans. Marie-Bernard Saïd. Cistercian Fathers Series 25. Kalamazoo, MI: Cistercian Publications, 1981.

——. *The Works of Bernard of Clairvaux: On the Song of Songs*, Vol. 1, trans. Kilian Walsh and Irene M. Edmonds. Spencer, MA: Cistercian Publications, 1971–1980.

Boest, Bert. "Converting the Other and Converting the Self: Double Objectives in Franciscan Educational Writings." In *Christianizing Peoples and Converting Individuals*, ed. Guyda Armstrong and Ian N. Wood, 295–301. International Medieval Research, vol. 7. Turnout, Belgium: Brepols, 2000.

Bradshaw, Paul. *Early Christian Worship: A Basic Introduction to Ideas and Practice*. Collegeville, MN: Liturgical Press, 1996.

Carpenter, Joel A. *Revive Us Again: The Reawakening of American Fundamentalism*. New York: Oxford University Press, 1997.

Cyril of Jerusalem. "The Catechetical Lectures." In *Cyril of Jerusalem and Nemesius of Emesa*, ed. William Telfer. Library of Christian Classics, vol. 4. 64–192. Philadelphia: Westminster Press, 1955.

Daniel, E. Randolph. *The Franciscan Concept of Mission in the High Middle Ages*. Lexington: University Press of Kentucky, 1975.

Delumeau, Jean. *Catholicism between Luther and Voltaire: A New View of the Counter-Reformation*, trans. Jeremy Moiser. London: Burns & Oates, 1977.

Finn, Thomas M. *From Death to Rebirth: Ritual and Conversion in Antiquity*. New York: Paulist Press, 1997.

Fletcher, Richard. *The Barbarian Conversion: From Paganism to Christianity*. New York: Henry Holt, 1997.

Foote, Peter. "Conversion." In *Medieval Scandinavia: An Encyclopedia*, ed. Phillip Pulsiano, 106–108. New York: Garland, 1993.

Fredriksen, Paula. "Paul and Augustine: Conversion Narratives, Orthodox Traditions, and the Retrospective Self." *Journal of Theological Studies* 37 (Apr. 1986): 3–34.

Gallagher, Eugene V. "Conversion and Salvation in the Apocryphal Acts of the Apostles." *The Second Century: A Journal of Early Christian Studies* 8, no. 1 (Spring 1991): 13–29.

Gaventa, Beverly Roberts. *From Darkness to Light: Aspects of Conversion in the New Testament*. Philadelphia: Fortress, 1986.

Harran, Marilyn J. *Luther on Conversion: The Early Years*. Ithaca, NY: Cornell University Press, 1983.

Hefner, Robert W. "Introduction: World Building and the Rationality of Conversion." In *Conversion to Christianity: Historical and Anthropological Perspectives on a Great Transformation*, ed. Robert W. Hefner, 3–44. Berkeley and Los Angeles: University of California Press, 1993.

Hippolytus of Rome. *The Treatise on the Apostolic Tradition of St. Hippolytus of Rome.* London: Alban Press, 1992.

Hsia, R. Po-Chia. "Translating Christianity: Counter-Reformation Europe and the Catholic Mission in China, 1580–1780." In *Conversion: Old Worlds and New*, ed. Kenneth Mills and Anthony Grafton, 87–108. Rochester, NY: University of Rochester Press, 2003.

James, William. *The Varieties of Religious Experience: A Study in Human Nature*, ed. Martin E. Marty. New York: Viking Penguin Books, 1982.

Jenkins, Philip. *The Next Christendom: The Coming of Global Christianity.* New York: Oxford University Press, 2002.

Jules-Rosette, Bennetta. *African Apostles: Ritual and Conversion in the Church of John Maranke.* Ithaca, NY: Cornell, 1975.

Kempis, Thomas à. *The Imitation of Christ*, trans. Betty I. Knott. London: Collins, 1963.

Kerr, Hugh T., and John M. Mulder, eds. *Conversions: The Christian Experience.* Grand Rapids, MI: Eerdmans, 1983.

Kling, David W. *A Field of Divine Wonders: The New Divinity and Village Revivals in Northwestern Connecticut, 1792–1822.* University Park: Pennsylvania State University Press, 1993.

Kling, Gordon S. "Confessions of a Late Bloomer: Memoirs of Rev. Gordon S. Kling." 2006. Unpublished manuscript in author's possession.

Lane Fox, Robin. *Pagans and Christians.* New York: HarperCollins, 1996.

Larsen, Timothy. *Crisis of Doubt: Honest Faith in Nineteenth-Century England.* New York: Oxford University Press, 2006.

Lofland, John, and Norman Skonovd. "Conversion Motifs." *Journal for the Scientific Study of Religion* 20 (1981): 373–385.

Lofland, John, and Rodney Stark. "Becoming a World-Saver: A Theory of Conversion to a Deviant Perspective." *American Sociological Review* 30 (1965): 862–875.

Luther, Martin. *Larger Catechism.* http://bookofconcord.org/lc-6-baptism.php.

McKnight, Scot. *Turning to Jesus: The Sociology of Conversion in the Gospels.* Louisville, KY: Westminster John Knox, 2002.

McLoughlin, William G. *Billy Graham: Revivalist in a Secular Age.* New York: Ronald Press, 1960.

——. *Modern Revivalism: Charles Grandison Finney to Billy Graham.* New York: Ronald Press, 1959.

MacMullen, Ramsay. *Christianizing the Roman Empire (A.D. 100–400).* New Haven: Yale University Press, 1984.

Malherbe, Abraham J. "Conversion to Paul's Gospel." In *The Early Church in Its Context: Essays in Honor of Everett Ferguson*, ed. Abraham J. Malherbe, Frederick W. Norris, and James W. Thompson, 230–244. Supplements to Novum Testamentum, Leiden: Brill, 1998.

Markus, Robert A. *The End of Ancient Christianity.* Cambridge: Cambridge University Press, 1990.

Marsden, George M. *Understanding Fundamentalism and Evangelicalism.* Grand Rapids, MI: Eerdmans, 1991.

Marty, Martin E. "The Revival of Evangelicalism and Southern Religion." In *Varieties of Southern Evangelicalism*, ed. David Edwin Harrell, Jr., 7–21. Macon, GA: Mercer University Press, 1981.

Meeks, Wayne A. *The Origins of Christian Morality: The First Two Centuries.* New Haven: Yale University Press, 1993.

Montgomery, Ingun. "The Institutionalisation of Lutheranism in Sweden and Finland." In *The Scandinavian Reformation: From Evangelical Movement to Institutional Reform*, ed. Ole Peter Grell, 156–160. Cambridge: Cambridge University Press, 1995.

Morgan, Edmund S. *Visible Saints: The History of a Puritan Idea*. Ithaca, NY: Cornell University Press, 1965.

Morrison, Karl F. *Understanding Conversion*. Charlottesville: University Press of Virginia, 1992.

Mowbray, Donald. "*Conversio ad bonum commutabile*: Augustinian Language of Conversion in Medieval Theology." In *Christianizing Peoples and Converting Individuals*, ed. Guyda Armstrong and Ian N. Wood, 283–294. International Medieval Research, vol. 7. Turnout, Belgium: Brepols, 2000.

Newman, John Henry. *Apologia pro Vita Sua*. Garden City, NY: Doubleday, 1956.

Nock, A. D. *Conversion: The Old and New in Religion from Alexander the Great to Augustine of Hippo*. London: Oxford University Press, 1933.

Noll, Mark A., David W. Bebbington, and George A. Rawlyk, eds. *Evangelicalism: Comparative Studies of Popular Protestantism in North America, the British Isles, and Beyond, 1700–1990*. New York: Oxford University Press, 1994.

Peace, Richard V. *Conversion in the New Testament: Paul and the Twelve*. Grand Rapids, MI: Eerdmans, 1999.

Pietists: Selected Writings, ed. Peter C. Erb. New York: Paulist Press, 1983.

Proudfoot, Wayne. "Introduction." In William James, *The Varieties of Religious Experience: A Study in Human Nature*, vii–xxix. New York: Barnes and Noble Classics, 2004.

Questier, Michael C. *Conversion, Politics and Religion in England, 1580–1625*. Cambridge: Cambridge University Press, 1996.

Rambo, Lewis R. *Understanding Religious Conversion*. New Haven: Yale University Press, 1993.

Richardson, Cyril C., ed. *Early Christian Fathers*. New York: Macmillan, 1970.

Robbins, Joel. *Becoming Sinners: Christianity and Moral Torment in a Papua New Guinea Society*. Berkeley and Los Angeles: University of California Press, 2004.

Robinson, Charles H. *Anskar: The Apostle of the North, 801–865*. Lives of Early and Medieval Missionaries Series. London: Society for the Propagation of the Gospel in Foreign Parts, 1921.

Russell, James C. *The Germanization of Early Medieval Christianity: A Sociohistorical Approach to Religious Transformation*. New York: Oxford University Press, 1994.

Sawyer, P. H. *Kings and Vikings: Scandinavia and Europe, AD 700–1100*. London: Methuen, 1982.

Segal, Alan. *Paul the Convert: The Apostolate and the Apostasy of Saul the Pharisee*. New Haven: Yale University Press, 1990.

Snow, David A., and Richard Machalek. "The Sociology of Conversion." *Annual Review of Sociology* 10 (1984): 167–190.

Spener, Philip Jacob. *Pia Desideria*, trans. and ed. Theodore G. Tappert. Philadelphia: Fortress Press, 1964.

Staples, Clifford L., and Armand L. Mauss. "Conversion or Commitment? A Reassessment of the Snow and Machalek Approach to the Study of Conversion." *Journal for the Scientific Study of Religion* 26, no. 2 (1987): 133–147.

Stark, Rodney. *Cities of God: The Real Story of How Christianity Became an Urban Movement and Conquered Rome*. San Francisco: HarperSanFrancisco, 2006.

——. *The Rise of Christianity: How the Obscure, Marginal Jesus Movement Became the Dominant Religious Force in the Western World in a Few Centuries*. San Francisco: HarperCollins, 1997.

Stendahl, Krister. *Paul among Jews and Gentiles and Other Essays*. Philadelphia: Fortress, 1976.

Stoeffler, F. Ernest. *German Pietism during the Eighteenth Century*. Leiden: Brill, 1973.

Sullivan, Richard E. *Christian Missionary Activity in the Early Middle Ages*. Brookfield, VT: Variorum, 1994.

Sweeney, Douglas A. *The American Evangelical Story: A History of the Movement*. Grand Rapids, MI: Baker, 2005.

Tennent, Gilbert. "The Danger of an Unconverted Ministry." In *The Great Awakening: Documents Illustrating the Crisis and Its Consequences*, ed. Alan Heimert and Perry Miller, 71–99. Indianapolis: Bobbs-Merrill, 1967.

Wallace, Anthony F. C. *Religion: An Anthropological View*. New York: Random House, 1966.

Wallis, Jim. *The Call to Conversion*. New York: Harper & Row, 1981.

Walls, Andrew F. *The Missionary Movement in Christian History: Studies in the Transmission of Faith*. Maryknoll, NY: Orbis, 1996.

Ward, W. R. *Early Evangelicalism: A Global Intellectual History, 1670–1789*. Cambridge: Cambridge University Press, 2006.

Wiebe, Phillip H. *Visions of Jesus: Direct Encounters from the New Testament to Today*. New York: Oxford University Press, 1997.

Xi, Lian. *The Conversion of Missionaries: Liberalism in American Protestant Missions in China, 1907–1932*. University Park: Pennsylvania State University Press, 1997.

CHAPTER 27

CONVERSION TO ISLAM
IN THEOLOGICAL AND
HISTORICAL PERSPECTIVES

MARCIA HERMANSEN

ISLAM, with its claim to finality, completeness, and universality, is a missionary religion. Like Christianity, Islam has spread all over the world and has been embraced by populations from widely varying regions and racial backgrounds. Muhammad (570–632) was recognized as Prophet and successfully formed and ruled over a community within his lifetime. By the time of his death, most of the Arabian tribes followed his leadership, both religiously and politically. Under his first four successors, known by Sunni Muslims as the "Rightly Guided Caliphs" (632–661), the political domination of Islam rapidly expanded outside of the Arabian Peninsula. Under the second Caliph, Umar (ruled 634–644), Muslim armies seized Jerusalem from Byzantine control (636) and defeated the Persians (637) and the Egyptians (641). The majority of people living in these territories eventually converted to Islam. In more far-flung regions such as sub-Saharan Africa, South Asia, and Southeast Asia, the process of conversion took place in later periods and through various processes that will be discussed later in this chapter.

The process of "Islamization" was a complex and creative fusion of Islamic practices and doctrines with local customs that were considered to be sound from the perspective of developing Islamic jurisprudence. As historian Richard Bulliet has demonstrated based on the evidence of early biographical compendia, in most cases this process took centuries, so that the stereotype of Islam being initially spread by the "sword" and by forced conversions is a false representation of this complex phenomenon.[1]

Although competition during the medieval period between Islamic and Christian power across the Mediterranean led to the polemic that Islam was a religion spread by violence and forced on subject populations, analysis of the historical evidence indicates that the process of Islamization was much more gradual. Large-scale conversions followed the initial conquests in the Middle East by centuries, peaking in Iran, for example, in about 875, some two hundred and thirty years after the initial conquests, according to Bulliet's estimate.[2] As might be intuitively expected based on sociological observations of other new religious movements, conversions to Islam within the Prophet Muhammad's immediate circle and even subsequently seem to have initially taken place at two opposite poles of society. On the one hand, the new faith attracted individuals from the higher levels of society, who would benefit most from maintaining good relations with the conquerors and who may have had the time and resources to consider the existential elements of a new message. Alternatively, conversions occurred among those who were the poorest and most socially disadvantaged, who thereby had the greatest likelihood of advancing through identification with the faith of the new ruling classes and the least to lose by no longer adhering to the status quo.

THEOLOGY AND RITUALS OF CONVERSION

Theologically speaking, inviting (*da'wa*) others to the Islamic faith is supposed to be part of Muslims' religious obligations. The Qur'an commands, "Invite to the way of your Lord with wisdom and beautiful preaching" (16:125). Unlike Christians, however, until recently most Muslims have not seen personal witnessing or systematic missionary activities as something that they need to pursue as individuals or support through donations to specific proselytizing institutions.[3]

In the earliest biographical dictionaries that compiled data on the first Muslim generations, such as the *Tabaqat* of Ibn Sa'd (ca. 845), two distinct terms are usually combined to refer to a person's becoming Muslim—*bay'a* (a person took allegiance to the Prophet) and *aslama* (a person accepted Islam). This demonstrates a recognition that conversion was a socio-political as well as a faith commitment. In fact, the word "Islam" itself is a verbal noun signifying "the act of accepting or submitting to the will of Allah."[4]

Today, many English-speaking converts to Islam prefer the term "revert," since Islamic theology features the idea that all souls have recognized God in pre-eternity in an episode known as the Primordial Covenant (Qur'an 7:131). Important in retrieving this memory of acknowledging Allah are both perceiving and reflecting on the signs of God disclosed both in the natural world and in the revealed messages transmitted through the series of Prophets sent to all nations. Remembrance (*dhikr*), return (*rija*), and repentance (*tawba*) all are important theological concepts in Islam and represent the means for reconnecting with the ultimate truth.

Islam acknowledges the prophetic nature of the messages revealed to Moses and Jesus, and therefore adherents of the other Abrahamic traditions are known as the "People of the Book." A person from a Jewish or Christian background who becomes Muslim could be thought of as completing or perfecting their previous faith, rather than radically departing from it, according to the Muslim perspective of religious supersession. A well-known saying (*hadith*) of the Prophet Muhammad affirms that every child is born according to a sound original nature (*fitra*). Commentaries have equated this original nature with "Islam." From this perspective, every child and, in a broad sense, every created thing in the universe is generically "muslim" in the sense of necessarily submitting to God, whether consciously and voluntarily or involuntarily.[5]

Since there is no "original sin" doctrine in Islam, the ceremony for entry into the religion consists of the simple recitation of the profession of faith (*shahada*), "There is no God but God, and Muhammad is the Prophet of God" in the presence of two witnesses. Once a person becomes a Muslim, he or she is considered to be free from (previous) sin. Since there is no original sin to be washed away, the baptismal motif is not operative. It is, however, recommended that the full ritual bath (*ghusl*) should be performed before conversion, most probably as a ritual preparation for subsequent prayer.

The Qur'an criticizes those who reject Islam after they become Muslims by saying, "If Muhammad dies, are you going to turn on your heels (to leave Islam)?" (3:144). Abu Bakr, the first caliph, struggled against members of Arab tribes who broke their promises and agreements to the Muslim polity and the Prophet after his death in a series of engagements known as the Wars of Apostasy (Ridda Wars). On this basis, the death penalty is prescribed in Islamic law[6] for those Muslims who become apostates, although this is not stipulated in the Qur'an. Many contemporary Muslim scholars hold that these punishments were not concerned with a person adopting another religion due to a change of heart, but that they had arisen in specific historical contexts where apostasy would be considered treasonable.[7] It is therefore argued that in modern times such punishments for apostasy and restrictions of freedom of belief should no longer apply, and, in fact, in most Muslim societies these are not an aspect of contemporary state laws. In the few countries where they continue to be in force, such as Afghanistan and Saudi Arabia, their rare invocation leads to human rights outcries from around the world, including on the part of many Muslims who deem them incompatible with the basic Qur'anic injunction that "There is no compulsion in religion" (2:256).

CONVERSION, IDENTITY, AND THE EXPANSION OF ISLAM

Conversion to Islam has occurred in vastly differing regions and epochs and continues until today, the general claim being that Islam is currently the fastest growing of the world's religions.[8] This is probably due to higher fertility rates and to successes in areas where Christianity and Islam are competing for converts from indigenous religious, for example, in Africa. While conversions to Islam in Europe and America receive attention and scrutiny, the numbers are not so high as to dramatically impact global growth.[9]

Historically, the reasons for conversion span many factors, including social and economic motivations and inducements as well as matters of personal conscience that are difficult to assess from our modern perspective. What is clear is that historical, geographical, and social factors have played major roles in making histories of conversion to Islam distinct and not amenable to any one simple and universal explanatory paradigm.

The gulf between pre-modern and modern elements and the diverse regional histories of conversion are issues that I would like to briefly address at this point. The topic of the history of conversion to Islam is often colored by political and ideological stances because conversion is so closely linked to identity. In an age of nationalism and conflict along ethnic and religious lines in many parts of the world, past conversions may at times be stigmatized in national narratives as having been a betrayal, a collaboration with foreign conquerors, or a contamination of true origins.

In the case of Iran, a movement known as the "shu'ubiyya" arose in the Abbasid period (750–1258) that asserted a Persian identity as opposed to an Arab one. The concept of a "Persian" Islam as distinct from an Arab one continues to the present time, playing into Iran's distinctive Shi'a identity but also influencing reconsideration of whether the glorious Iranian past is obscured by embracing the later Arab Muslim conquest.

An even more anti-conversion tone arises in regions such as India and the Balkans, where some accounts of the process of conversion to Islam may stress violence, coercion, and the foreignness of Muslims. Conversely, Muslim accounts of these conversions may elide aspects of the process that de-emphasize the attractiveness and pull of the new religious identity among local populations.

The history of conversion to Islam has generally been studied in specific and regional contexts.[10] While this study is worthwhile, attempting to synthesize their conclusions is unlikely to provide a seamless and universal account of pre-modern practices and histories. When we move to contemporary instances of conversion to Islam, we likewise encounter great regional disparity. In particular, the conversions that are occurring in Europe and the Americas need to be understood primarily in terms of the social and psychological dimensions of conversion that are studied across religions in the contemporary period[11] and secondarily in the context of patterns in the history of conversion to Islam.[12]

THE HISTORY OF CONVERSION TO ISLAM

An early account of conversion to Islam is that of the close Companion of the Prophet, Umar ibn al-Khattab (ca. 581–644). Umar was a strong and socially respected Meccan who initially rejected Muhammad and his teachings and spoke of silencing the Prophet until he was informed that his own sister had become a Muslim. Umar then rushed to her house in anger but on entering heard her reciting some of the revelations contained in the Qur'an. This is said to have moved Umar's heart to the point that he joined the new movement and became a staunch supporter. This and other narratives that tell conversion stories of individual Companions of the Prophet indicate that individual change of heart and transformation due to the power and impact of the Islamic teachings was definitely recognized by pre-modern Muslims as an element in conversion. A person's being among the earliest to convert was recognized socially and economically during the reign of the Umar (634–644) through an institution known as the *divan* in which payments arising from the wealth derived due to conquests, tribute, and spoils of war were distributed according to the primacy of an individual's having accepted Islam.

In the time of the Prophet Muhammad, once initial political successes had been achieved and the Prophet became the ruler, first in Medina and then in all of Arabia, incentives to conversion were offered. For example, financial payments were given to those Arab tribes and individuals who had newly embraced Islam. According to Islamic tradition, these payments were given in order to "incline their hearts to Islam."[13]

H. A. R. Gibb categorized three degrees of conversion in this early period: "total," "formal," and "enforced."[14] The formal element of Bedouin tribal allegiance to the new faith is alluded to in a Qur'anic passage (49:14) that enjoins the tribal Arabs, "Do not say 'we have accepted faith'; rather say 'we have accepted Islam', for faith has not yet entered your hearts," thereby distinguishing true inner faith, or *iman,* from the formality of "Islam."

Once Muslim empires were in place with substantial non-Muslim *Dhimmi* populations,[15] there were also financial "penalties" for not converting in the form of two special tax structures, the *jizya,* a "head" tax required only of adult non-Muslims, and the *kharaj,* an additional tax on land-holdings of adult non-Muslims. These elements of pre-modern Islamic rule have become polemicized in some recent studies. One contention is that "dhimmitude" was an oppressive and restrictive regime that persecuted non-Muslims.[16] The contrasting position is that living under Islamic rule was relatively benign for pre-modern minority communities since they could own property, secure employment and education, enjoy freedom of movement, and so on. According to this latter view, the tax structure was ultimately equitable since Muslims alone served in the army and paid the *zakat* to support the services of the governing body such as military protection, public works, and security, but the *zakat* was not levied on the non-Muslim population.

In the newly conquered territories in Iraq, Iran, and Egypt, Muslim soldiers and administrators at first lived separately from the local populations in garrison towns that eventually became centers of a new Islamic civilization. Converts in these areas had to initially establish a relationship of being a client (*wali*) of an Arab patron and his tribe. These early client converts to Islam were known as *mawali.* This system lasted into later Umayyad times (661–750), when Umar the Second (717–720) abolished the tax on the *mawali* and put more effort into increasing, rather than deterring, conversion.[17] By the Abbasid period (post-750), the designation of *mawali* no longer applied because by this time a powerful and critical mass of the Muslim population was derived from non-Arab roots.

In other regions where early conversions to Islam occurred, such as Islamic Spain (al-Andalus), the institution of *mawali* was much less common. This is because most of the conquering Muslim armies came from Berber rather than Arab stock, the conquerors did not live in separate garrison towns, and Maliki fiqh[18] (the prevalent legal code) considered converts to be clients of the entire Muslim polity (*umma*) as opposed to specific Arab tribes.[19]

Mass conversion—which occurred when a chief, king, or feudal leader joined the religion—was common in the pre-modern era. As in the history of early Christian expansion in Europe, a charismatic figure, preacher, or saint might be credited with providing convincing evidence through miracles of the superiority of his God and faith. In Central Asia, for example, DeWeese has mined hagiographies to recover the historical elements of conversion behind the legends of charismatic Turkish Babas who brought many tribes into Islam.[20] In the South Asian Punjab, the Sufi saints are likewise credited with conversion of the local tribes en masse.[21] In another South Asian example, the Sufi Muinuddin Chishti (d. 1236), whose shrine in Ajmer, Rajasthan, remains a pilgrimage site for both Muslims and Hindus, is described in one hagiographic narrative as besting the local Hindu court magician, Ajai Pal, in a dual of magical powers, thereby leading to the conversion of much of the local populace. In Southeast Asia, oral epics feature accounts of the nine founding saints (*wali songo*), who are credited with the conversion of the local populace to Islam, often through triumphing in similar duels of supernatural powers.[22]

CONVERSION IN DIVERSE REGIONS

Despite the diversity and complexity of local situations, it may be helpful to consider several broad patterns of conversion across the Muslim world. Conquered early by smaller Arab Muslim armies, Iran, North Africa, and the Middle East witnessed very high rates of conversion over the centuries. Bulliet's mapping of conversion patterns in regions such as Iran, Iraq, Egypt, Syria, and Spain onto graphs so as to make visible the historical periods of maximum growth corresponding to a phenomenon known as an "innovation curve" has been replicated or confirmed by scholars of other geographic areas. For example, it has recently been argued that conversions in Spain as well as the expansion of Islam to the Balkans during the period of Ottoman rule in the fifteenth and sixteenth centuries share some common patterns with Muslim outreach in the central Islamic lands.[23] The expansion of Islam to the further reaches of Indonesia and Malaysia and to the west and east coasts and sub-Saharan region of Africa took place more gradually and later, after the thirteenth century, and during this period the important agents of conversion were traders, scholars, and Sufis.

The largest numerical concentration of Muslim population today is in South Asia (India, Pakistan, and Bangladesh). A central question for students of conversion in this region is the resistance to conversion of much of the population of today's India, even in areas that were under Muslim rule for long periods. These instances where conversion to Islam failed to occur may also shed light on its processes and successes.[24]

India also problematizes the nature of conversion itself. The oscillating interaction of Islam with indigenous Indian elements has been captured by contrasting Mughal royalty such as Akbar (d. 1605) or Dara Shikoh (d. 1659), who respected indigenous customs and attempted to find common ground, to the Mughal king Aurangzeb (d. 1707), who harshly imposed taxes on non-Muslims and rejected and condemned their customs. At the lower ends of South Asian society, many pre-modern groups seem to have practiced in synthetic ways a blend of Islam and Hinduism, observing some Islamic rituals or using Muslim names yet celebrating Hindu festivals and deities or observing Hindu food taboos. It is now argued that colonial practices such as census taking began to raise challenges to these complex and diffuse identities that caused concern among emerging communal nationalisms in the subcontinent during the late nineteenth and early twentieth centuries.[25] These, in turn, inspired movements such as *shuddhi* or purification aimed at bringing lapsed Hindus who were gravitating to Islam back into the fold. In turn, Muslims such as Muhammad Ilyas (d. 1944) and Khwaja Hasan Nizami (d. 1955) engaged in counterinitiatives of *tabligh*—propagation of the faith. *Tabligh* movements attempted to instill basic tenets and practices of Islam and to teach Islam by humble example to the members of tribes and castes who were not particularly firm or clear about their Muslim identity and Islamic norms and practices.

I will now review some of the preeminent theories of conversion to Islam in India. As previously noted, the nature of conversion to Islam in South Asia is a topic hotly contested by historians, in part due to its contemporary relevance for competing Muslim and Hindu nationalist narratives of identity.

Richard Eaton, an American expert on South Asian Islam, describes four main models that have been posited to explain conversion to Islam in South Asian history.[26] These are: immigration theory, Islam as a religion of the sword, a religion of patronage, and a religion of social liberation. Immigration theory constructs Muslims as outsiders who were not part of the original and authentic South Asian region. In this case, it is their diffusion in the region that is the source of today's Muslim population. The epitome of the conversion by the sword theory is associated with Muslim figures such as Sultan Mahmud of Ghazni (d. 1030), who is blamed for the destruction and plunder of the temple at Somnat, thus symbolizing Islam as alien to and dismissive of local Indian traditions.[27] The usual Pakistani Muslim narrative, in contrast, is of Mahmud as a heroic *ghazi* or fighter for the faith. Ironically, among Indian Muslims themselves there is a special respect given to those who are descended from Arab, Afghan, or Iranian stock, embodied in the idea of being from the "noble classes" (*ashraf*) as opposed to being descended from indigenous converts known as the "inferior classes" (*ajlaf*), who are viewed as descendants of local populations whose ancestors had converted. The patronage explanation for conversion to Islam in South Asia construes it as a social process that occurred over time due to monetary and other favors extended by Muslims to those who joined the faith. Finally, the model of Islam as a religion of social liberation highlights the conversion of members of the lower castes who were seeking upward mobility. Eaton doubts that this explanation is valid in earlier historical periods since such results do not seem to have been achieved by converts.

The pull of upward mobility or protest against the Hindu caste order inspired some mass conversions from Hinduism in the twentieth century. For example, there is the well-known conversion of untouchables to Buddhism within the Ambedkar movements, as well as smaller movements among Muslims in South India who embraced Islam in the early 1980s.[28] Peter van der Veer has argued that these conversions were seen as threatening and helped fuel subsequent Hindu fundamentalism (Hindutva).[29]

In his study of the expansion of Islam in Bengal, Eaton presents conversion to Islam as a process of gradual incorporation of the rice-cultivating peasantry into a cultural framework associated with the religion, rather than conversion arising from domination by a foreign regime that was imposed on them by a central empire. Rather, assimilation to Islam occurred gradually and in a manner that "seeped" into the region, as Islamic symbols became identified with local understandings of the sacred and superhuman cosmos.[30]

CENTRAL ASIA

After most of the Muslim lands were conquered, remarkably within a generation, by the Mongol hordes of Genghis Khan (d. 1227) and especially of his grandson, Hulagu Khan (1265), Mongol leaders and the entire culture assimilated toward Islam, the religion of the conquered. In this case the assimilative power of Islam was such that the descendants of the Mongols embraced the religion and contributed to new flourishing of civilizations under rulers such as Tamurlane (ca. 1336–1405) and his descendants the Timurids (1370–1526) in Central Asia and the Mughals (1526–1857) in South Asia.

The spread of Islam by these Turkish-speaking populations was perhaps the most geographically widespread of all; the Turks carried Islam with them from the Balkans to South Asia and China.

TURKEY AND THE BALKANS

The heart of the Byzantine Empire, Constantinople, did not fall to the Muslim Ottomans until 1453. Before that, however, waves of Turkic nomads who had been immigrating into Anatolia since the battle of Manzikert in 1071 gradually displaced the indigenous population, most of whom were Christians. Scholars estimate that Anatolia had become overwhelmingly Muslim by the sixteenth century.[31]

A further observation is that in Anatolia and the Balkans there was more friction between Muslim and Christian populations than elsewhere, and as a result the numbers of "social conversions" were lower. Anatolia was initially settled by Turkish Muslim nomads who were disruptive of the established order. Conversions there that arose through what Nehemia Levtzion terms "colonization by nomads" are perceived as having been less gradual and more socially traumatic than those that occurred within the borders of an established Islamic government.[32] A word invoked for the context of conversions in early Anatolia, but that applies in certain other regions as well, is "frontier." The hypothesis is that the nature of conversions on the frontiers of expanding spheres of Islamic influence is significantly different from those occurring within stable boundaries. After the first centuries, however, Islamic civilization in Anatolia had stabilized and developed institutions that could prove attractive to new converts and provide them with new social networks and support. Examples of these institutions are charitable endowments (*waqf*), mystical orders, and the schools and authority of Muslim scholars (*ulema*).[33] At the same time, official Christian representation and social support institutions were under pressure and receding, making the continuity of Christian life in this region more difficult.

CONQUEST OF THE BALKANS

The Ottoman conquest of the Balkans took place over a century in two main phases, 1352–1402 and 1415–1467.[34] According to Anton Minkov, today's nationalist historians from the region frame their narratives of these events according to two main paradigms. On the one hand, certain Christian histories of the region have described the Ottoman conquests as nationalist "catastrophes" accompanied by oppression and demographic collapse. Others have seen the Ottoman legacy more favorably in terms of its bringing to the region the benefits of stability. Factors such as the "blessing" of a relatively low *jizya*[35] made the pacification and eventual assimilation of the local population to Islam and Ottoman traditions easier. Conversion seems unlikely without contact with Muslims, and it is clear that Turkish immigration into the region occurred as well. Who these immigrants were is also contested—Sufis, craftsmen, and scholars probably presented a favorable or less coercive face of Islam, while unruly Turkish nomads seem likely to have been alienating forces.

Another Ottoman institution that highlights the ambivalent narratives of conversion in these regions is the *devshirme*, a regular levy of (mainly) Christian youths, particularly from the Balkans, who were taken from their birth families, converted to Islam, and trained to become members of the elite Janissary corps surrounding the Sultan. These children were guaranteed the best education and social mobility, but this practice could also be construed as the most oppressive of practices and tantamount to brainwashing and forced conversion to Islam. The levy of as many as eight thousand youths occurred about every seven years and had practically ceased by the middle of the sixteenth century, although the Janissaries were finally abolished in 1648.[36]

LATER CONVERSIONS: SOUTHEAST ASIA AND AFRICA

Southeast Asia

The spread of Islam to Southeast Asia, Malaysia, and Indonesia occurred relatively late but was quite pervasive, especially in the case of Indonesia. The inception of Islamic influences in South East Asia occurred during the thirteenth to fifteenth centuries.[37] In these cases, a primary factor was the trade engaged in by Arab travelers and merchants from Yemen who undertook long voyages across the Indian Ocean. Among reasons given for the success of these conversions are the prestige of literacy, the inclusive nature of Islamic racial categories, and Muslim marriage laws and customs.

Arab traders often maintained two households with wives and families both in Yemen and the East Indies, multiple marriages being allowed in Islam. The cultural capital of knowing the Arabic language and having Arab descent was considered especially presti-gious in South East Asia, and many Malay families still trace their lineages and maintain strong connections to the Hadramaut region of Yemen. In Indonesia, Islam adapted to local practices and traditions, incorporating a synthesis that has been termed "norma-tive mystical piety."[38] Legends and oral epics suggest gradual conversion that involved acceptance by the rulers first and only later assimilation of the local populace.[39] It has also been noted that in later periods, conversion to Islam increased in the face of Dutch colonialism due to the fact that Islam provided grounding for indigenous solidarity and resistance, while the Dutch in some cases were seen as promoting Christianity.[40]

Africa

In sub-Saharan Africa, as in Southeast Asia, Islam was carried to local populations who had been largely animist through the activities of traders and scholars. Patterns of conver-sions along the East and West coasts of Africa varied. Levtzion characterizes conversions in West Africa as usually proceeding peacefully through Africanization and dispersal. The degree of formal Islamization varied, resulting in "uneven" results ranging from rapid conversion and acculturation to Islamic norms in the cities to nominal allegiance and scattered Islamic practice in more remote areas.[41] Even the nineteenth-century reviv-alist jihads were more about reforming Muslims than converting animists. Among expla-nations for Islam's success in Africa are its integrative power and racial inclusiveness. William Byden, an American Christian of Caribbean origin and African descent, was sent to Africa in the late 1800s as part of a Christian missionary society initiative. He devel-oped a great sympathy for the presence and institutions of Islam in Africa and described how the lack of racial barriers in learning and authority incorporated and empowered Africans in a way that was absent from contemporary Christian institutions.[42]

In the eleventh century, significant numbers of inhabitants began converting to Islam on the East Coast of Africa, most intensively in coastal trading areas like Mombassa and Zanzibar. Arab traders intermarried with the local populations and became the elites of a Swahili culture that fused Arab Islamic and African elements. It was only in the nineteenth century that Islamization spread inland. Arab immigrants from Hadramaut and Oman in the eighteenth and nineteenth centuries carried with them literate Islam and *shari'a*-based practices to East Africa. Colonial policies of the Portuguese and the British complicated affairs by respectively discouraging Islamic practice or attempting to regulate them.[43]

Robin Horton, in his essays on African conversions, describes them as arising from a cognitive process by which individuals tend to convert as a result of social developments that promote comparison between the relative coherence of their own beliefs as compared to others. In such cases, the system with greater explanatory force will be preferred.[44] For example, scholars following the theories of Max Weber and Clifford Geertz[45] have analyzed conversions to Christianity as related to the greater "logical coherence" of major literate world religions in comparison with "traditional" local religions. This theory, by extension, could also apply to modern conversions to Islam in Africa.

Horton further refined this line of argument by positing that the difference between the two kinds of religious systems lies not in their relative degrees of rationality but in the narrower focus of the primal religions, which he relates to the "pre-modern social situation [where] most events affecting the life of the individual occur within the microcosm of the local community... [which is] to a considerable extent insulated from the macrocosm of the wider world."[46]

In the specific case of colonial and modern Africa, conversion to a world religion such as Islam or Christianity involves the extension of social, economic, or political relations in the course of colonialism and integration into the world economy. As the boundaries of small tribal societies are weakened (as by integration into larger political systems, the development of broader commercial networks, and dramatic improvements in communications), according to Horton and others, more and more people come to adopt universalist doctrines which provide ready-made answers to the intellectual challenges of the macrocosmic system.[47]

One question raised by this model is at what historical point does this explanation for conversion based on the need for a more integrative religious view become operative, since a similar argument has been suggested for Muhammad's success among the urban Meccans who were no longer satisfied by the haphazard animism of previous Arabian tribal codes. Today, scholarly and popular discussion about unity versus diversity in material and ideational expressions of Islam and the persistence of pre-Islamic indigenous cultures continues, acquiring increased urgency in the face of modern trends toward scripturalism,[48] monocultures, and "identity-Islam" movements.[49]

INTERNAL CONVERSIONS

In addition to conversion across faiths, we must consider "internal conversions"—changes of heart, interpretation, and level of commitment within a single faith tradition. Most of the early conversion literature, the writings of William James, assumed this perspective, in the sense that most of his subjects went from being Protestant to being "reborn" or "revived" within the same Protestant context.

In the case of Islam, a number of internal conversion narratives fit this category. Among Sufis, in particular, the call to leave the world is a significant, if not altogether common, trope. Ibrahim ibn Adham was said to have been a king in Central Asian Balkh. While out hunting one day he heard a call—"Were you made for this?" Rather like the renunciation account of the Buddha, he packed up and left his wealth and family behind to follow the path of ascetic Sufism.[50]

The famous Muslim scholar al-Ghazzali (d. 1111) authored one of the rare autobiographical accounts of internal conversion in Islam. He was a prominent professor of theology who was struck with existential doubt to the point at which he became afflicted with a mysterious ailment that left him unable to speak. He then set out in search of truth, ultimately finding it among the Sufis and their practices.[51]

In contemporary Muslim societies, the return to piety and extent of religious revival is quite remarkable. In fact, revivalist movements began affecting local traditions of Islamic practices in the late eighteenth century and acquired greater reach due to increased facility of travel and communication and a shared resistance to colonialism through the nineteenth century. By the late-twentieth century, vast mobilizations of individuals to support Islamic organizations or parties, or simply to enact changes in their own daily lives in the name of religion, are apparent almost everywhere among Muslims. Some of these changes of heart involve attraction to Sufism,[52] some to pietistic movements such as the Tablighi Jamaat, and others to Islamist movements and parties.[53]

The modernization theorists of the 1950s and 1960s who argued for an inevitable trajectory of secularism in developing Muslim societies were left behind in the wake of the Iranian revolution of 1979. The continued emergence of successful political Islamization movements in the 1980s, some top-down and some popular, indicates the vitality of internal conversion mechanisms in today's Muslim societies.

Evidence of this internal conversion is the large number of Muslim women—many educated and upwardly mobile—who have adopted forms of a global Islamic (*shar'i*) dress. Cultural capital for today's young Muslims is likely to include manifestations of piety and mastery of *fiqh* and other discourses of "authentic" Islamic knowledge that were marginalized or unknown in their parents' and grandparents' cohorts. Explanations for these changes include responses to modernity and postmodernity, resistance to Western neo-imperialism, and the impact of access to mass literacy and university education.[54]

CONVERSIONS TO ISLAM IN THE WEST

Conversions of Europeans and later of Americans to Islam could only happen through actual contact with Muslims in pre-modern times, and this began to occur in the case of England through encounters with the Ottomans, hence the former pejorative expression for conversion to Islam—to "turn Turk."[55] Accounts of these early conversions have been studied by Nabil Matar, especially the captivity narratives of English seamen and others who fell into the hands of pirates around the Mediterranean. Surprisingly, there was a degree of anxiety in seventeenth-century England about Englishmen turning "renegade" in quest of upward mobility, since the Ottomans were seen as potentially more rewarding of enterprise and as being very welcoming to converts.[56]

Other early forms of contact continued during the colonial period (late eighteenth to twentieth centuries) and, although few, a number of notable cases of conversion to Islam took place, often among privileged Europeans who were stationed in the Muslim world or traveled there. These seem to have increased in number in the twentieth century and, based on a handful of conversion narratives from this period, some of the motivations for conversion included becoming disaffected by the nature of colonial rule over Muslim societies combined with the feeling that as Europeans, the converts could influence the direction of Muslim dealings with Western colonial powers more effectively—for the benefit of Muslims.[57]

Muhammad Asad, author of the classic conversion account, *Road to Mecca*, was originally an Austrian Jew who initially lived in Saudi Arabia, later became the first representative of Pakistan to the United States, and mastered Arabic to the extent that his translation of the Qur'an is one of the most respected in English. He comments on the perplexity of other Westerners when they realized that "my activities at the United Nations made it obvious that I identified myself not merely 'functionally' but also emotionally and intellectually with the political and cultural aims of the Muslim world in general."[58] Another example of someone who admired and wanted to help Muslims is the later American convert, Maryam Jameelah, who as a child in the 1940s wrote in her diary, "I am saving the pictures and books which Daddy gave me on my birthday so I can go to Egypt or Palestine and keep the Arabs like they are instead of copying us."[59] Other pulls toward converting that are mentioned include a sense of the beauty of Muslim societies, cultures, and even individuals, along with respect and admiration for the teachings of Islam.[60]

In the colonial period, contact with Muslims occurred because "Europeans went there," and convert narratives of this period convey the sense of "passing" and even "surpassing" due to the converts' more direct access to Western power and knowledge. In more recent postcolonial, accounts, conversions more likely occur because "they (Muslims) come here (to the West)," providing opportunities for relational contacts as friends, teachers, or spouses. A shift occurs in the nature of American and European converts after the colonial period. Western converts' accounts reflect the new mobility of the period, in terms of new resources available to the middle classes that opened the possibility of travel to exotic locations.

In terms of class analysis, it is clear that European converts to Islam in colonial times were usually privileged males. Although they were perhaps considered eccentric for "turning Turk" by their class equals back home, they still had a voice that would be heeded.

Even in postcolonial conversion accounts we find a certain nostalgia for the authentic, traditional Orient. There is no longer an external "elsewhere" for Western Muslim travelers of the late-twentieth century. They are positioned in a world that is both hybridized and politicized along West versus Islam lines, as well as within a Muslim community that is itself increasingly self-aware of its complexities arising through immigration and internal cultural and ideological diversities.

In the later conversion accounts, there is increased emphasis given to the importance of reading Islamic literature that has become available in translation. Other reasons cited for embracing Islam in later convert testimonials of Westerners prominently feature hearing the Qur'an recited in Arabic, the call to prayer, or reading the Qur'an in translation and becoming convinced of its truth.

Researcher Larry Poston characterizes the conversion process to Islam as one of head not heart, a gradual process, in which a person may feel they had always been Muslim. Conversion to Islam often follows a long period of reflection and seeking. According to surveys of converts and convert literature undertaken by Poston, many converts rejected their upbringing or environment in their teens but only formally converted to Islam in their late twenties or thirties.[61]

CONVERSION TO ISLAM IN THE UNITED STATES

According to a survey conducted in the 1990s among a sample of Muslims in Los Angeles, "a significant number of Muslims in the United States are opposed to any aggressive pursuits to convert others to Islam."[62] They may draw support for this from the previously mentioned Qur'anic injunction, "There should be no compulsion in religion" (2:256).

Some reasons for this reluctance to proselytize might be a negative view of earlier Christian missionary activities in Muslim societies, fear of scorn and rejection on the part of Muslims who see that certain Christian missionary groups such as the Jehovah's Witnesses have a negative image in the United States, or Muslim immigrants' feelings of being inadequately informed or inarticulate and hence unable to properly expound Islamic teachings.[63] While the converted American may be perceived by immigrant Muslims as most equipped to further spread the message of Islam, American traditions of freedom of conscience may compete with notions of promoting exclusivistic truth. For example, I am reminded of a speech given at a Muslim youth seminar by a young American Muslim whose father is a Euro-American convert married to a woman from a Muslim society. The daughter spoke with great passion of the inability for her Muslim friends of immigrant background to understand why she did not preach Islam to her American Christian grandparents. She therefore needed to explain to them in Islamic terms how poor manners (adab)[64] and failure to respect elders would be evidenced by such behavior.[65]

In general, African American Muslims are more likely to attempt to teach others about Islam. According to Kambiz GhaneaBassiri, this is due to the fact that most African Americans "converted to Islam at the hand of organizations that actively proselytized; hence their introduction to Islam and their religious education was most influenced by active da'wa."[66]

Significant exceptions to a general lack of systematic Muslim missionary activity in the United States are efforts made by Islamic movements such as the Ahmadiyya and various Sufi orders, which have made greater inroads, proportionate to their size, in the American population. From this we can conclude that organized activities in spreading Islam do have an impact on conversion. From the 1990s until the present, organized *da'wa* activities in the United States have increasingly been engaged in by specific Muslim organizations.

In terms of impact on mainstream American culture, conversion to Islam receives some attention through African American celebrity conversions such as those of Malcolm X, Kareem Abd al-Jabbar, or Muhammad Ali. Such celebrity conversions, combined with the somewhat negative publicity generated by the activities and pronouncements of figures such as Louis Farrakhan, head of the Nation of Islam, who is usually characterized by the media as a "Muslim" leader, led many Americans in the 1970s and 1980s to perceive Islam in America as a religion primarily identified with the black community. On the one hand, this supported an identification of Islam with political protest and minority status. On the other hand, it reflected an indigenization of Islam that made it difficult for American politicians and opinion-makers to impose restrictions on the immigrant or converted Muslim populations within the United States.

In a study focusing on Islam and African Americans, Richard Brent Turner writes, "Islam has become an increasingly significant element of the African American experience. As the commodification process popularizes elements of Islamic culture among non-Muslims, Islam could indeed prevail in black America in the twenty-first century."[67] A prominent African American scholar of Islam, Sherman Jackson, has given voice to the changing role of African Americans and, by extension, of indigenous and convert Muslims, in shaping the practice of Islam in America. Jackson criticizes in particular the actions and attitudes of Middle Eastern and South Asian immigrant Muslims who seek to impose their cultural practices and attitudes on the indigenous community.[68] At present, a lively debate is ongoing among American Muslim intellectuals on this topic.[69]

As far as concerns the immigrant Muslim community in the United States, which is still at this point the majority of American Muslims, the conversion of mainstream America to Islam is an aspiration but not an expectation. In many immigrant Muslim communities across the United States, converts, whether white or African American, are not highly visible participants. British Islamic activist Khurram Murad at one point criticized those immigrant Muslims who are content with preserving their own cultural identity as a minority by asking, "Why should any non-Muslim ever consider becoming part of a minority culture?... Have new Muslims found an appropriate place in Islamic organizations or on any Islamic platforms during the last 25 years?"[70]

However, since 9/11, especially in the United States, this pattern has been changing, with increasingly visible public leadership coming from converts, whether white or African American, including figures such as Hamza Yusuf Hanson, Ingrid Mattson, and Zayd Shakir.

One reason for the lower visibility of converts within the immigrant community is that African Americans tend to constitute their own congregations and to feel less welcomed by mosques dominated by immigrants, where language, cultural practice, and clothing may reflect a specific ethnic identity.[71] In addition, Muslims of American background play a larger role in American-based institutions that interface with Muslim identity, such as by serving as prison chaplains or military chaplains, teaching the new generation of Muslims in Islamic schools, or in some cases teaching Islamic Studies at American Universities. On occasion, American Muslims of both African and Euro-American backgrounds have served as Imams for immigrant-based mosques.[72]

Converts to Islam are generally welcomed by the Muslim community. In terms of the reception of converts, some may feel that Euro-Americans receive an especially positive reception from the immigrant community, and it may be observed that certain immigrant ethnic groups are particularly impressed by converts, for example, traditional Afghans,[73] while others may be more guarded in their enthusiasm. From the perspective of the world Muslim community, conversions to Islam in the West demonstrate the vibrancy of Islam, and there are increasing moves toward an institutionalization of *da'wa* activities, for example, through the founding of *da'wa* centers in Saudi Arabia and in Houston.[74]

An influential piece written in 1988 by Khurram Murad of the Islamic Foundation in England pointed out the need for specific *da'wa* strategies in particular environments. For example, in America, Muslims should not present Islam as new or different but rather as a continuity of the Judeo-Christian heritage. Murad suggests that in terms of criticizing cultural practices, common ground, such as disapproval of drug use, should be stressed rather than divisive issues such as the prohibition of alcoholic beverages.[75] Which issues are "common" is not entirely obvious. As an example, community concerns such as drug use and gangs were suggested to one American Muslim presenter as appropriate for discussion with a mixed Muslim/non-Muslim audience at a *da'wa* dinner. Further suggestions made about common issues, for example, that Muslim should join some evangelical Christian groups in picketing abortion clinics, were perceived by American Muslims to be less judicious. This is due to the fact that the conservative Christians identified with such activities were least likely to be amenable to conversion to Islam or sympathetic to Muslims, while many liberal Americans would find such activities objectionable.

Conversion to Islam in the West has been studied by Larry Poston[76] and Ali Köse,[77] who focus primarily on two dimensions: the activities of Muslim *da'wa* toward this end and the profile of populations that have been attracted to Islam. Considering who might choose to become Muslim is useful for Muslim strategists in terms of where to direct their efforts. From the point of view of the sociology or the psychology of religion, besides joining cults or New Religious Movements, Islam and perhaps Buddhism are the major conversion choices of contemporary Americans. Köse concludes that the profile of converts to Islam through Sufism may be closer to the profiles of those attracted to New Religious Movements (i.e., they will involve more emotive reactions and a sense of spiritual crisis). Both Köse and Poston have seen non-Sufi conversions to Islam as being more intellectually and reflectively based. While Islam as a choice for African Americans has distinctive cultural and political aspects, it also must have an important personal and psychological component. Similarly, it would be wrong to overlook the element of cultural protest in Euro-American conversions to Islam.[78] In African Americans' self-perception, Islam is clearly associated with their historical travail. According to GhaneaBassiri, "Islam is believed to have served throughout African American history as a progressive movement that helped alleviate the conditions of slavery, segregation, and racism in the United States."[79] He continues, "For most African-Americans, Islam is not a matter of personal faith alone but a matter of the social, economic, and political empowerment of African-Americans."[80]

Poston's study, *Islamic Da`wah in the West*, draws on paradigms of conversion such as those of William James and Erik Erikson, as well as studies of the maturation of moral reasoning, finding that in contrast to the sense of an adolescent "snapping" in what were essentially re-conversions to Christianity, particularly in revivalist contexts, most converts to Islam are adults in at least their late twenties who have spent a long period, since experiencing a loss of conventional faith in adolescence, pursuing serious study and reflecting on existential issues.[81]

In my own writings relative to conversion to Islam, I considered American Muslim women,[82] conversion narratives to Islam from the 1920s to the 1990s,[83] American Sufi movements,[84] and the challenges described by convert mothers in America who are raising their children as Muslims.[85] One aspect of my findings was the importance of what might be termed the surrounding generational or cohort influence on conversion, so that, for example, the type of female American becoming Muslim in the 1970s (individualistic, spiritual seeker, Sufi-oriented) would differ from the cohort of the 1980s (young, married to a student from the Middle East, likely to adopt conservative Islamic dress).[86] Thus, the prevailing currents both in the Muslim World and in Western societies play a role in determining attraction to alternatives such as conversion to Islam, together with elements of organized *da'wa* and the individual social and psychological backgrounds of converts.

In the United States, conversion to Islam covers a broad range of populations, and elements of race, class, gender, and cohort come into play. Common to African American and Euro-American conversions would be what I term an element of cultural protest against the dominant American system. For example, African Americans may find through conversion to Islam a means to reject alien values dictated by the white-dominated society, while white Americans may convert in part as a response to secularization, anomie, lack of authenticity, and so on. The political role of the United States in Middle Eastern affairs and negative media portrayals of Islam and Muslims have ironically made Islam appeal to a small segment of the population who identified sympathetically with Iran during the hostage crisis, with the Palestinian uprising, or with Iraq during the first Gulf War.[87] The attacks of 9/11 shifted the paradigm in certain ways. While some sources claim a rise in conversions, presumably due to a greater awareness of Islam after it became a major media focus in the aftermath of the attacks, others predict a decline in conversions due to the stigmatization of Muslim identity in the broader culture.

Aminah McCloud has studied African American converts to Islam.[88] She argues that African Americans have either followed accommodationist or separatist ideologies with regard to the dominant American culture. The separatists are further characterized as either favoring a "Back to Africa" or a "nation within a nation" position, and it is ultimately this latter group that has been most drawn to conversion to Islam.[89] McCloud argues that "conversion to Islam fits within the orientation of the 'nation within a nation' movement.... It is clear that this religion promised a new identity, a feeling of 'somebodiness' denied by the dominant culture, a liberation from Christian domination and from relegation to insignificance. The new adherents shed Christianity, which they perceived as the root of their oppression in its glorification of suffering and promise of redemption in the hereafter."[90]

For the smaller numbers of Euro-Americans, the process of conversion to Islam has been largely mediated though immigrants from the Muslim world and their literature and institutions. While converting to Islam may be understood as a rejection of modernity or mainstream American culture and values, creating a mythology of cultural return is rather more difficult for this group, and for this reason adopting cultural aspects of Islamic identities may be more problematic. For example, changing names is less common among whites, perhaps due to the sense of discomfort with a foreign-sounding name and the repercussions on a person who could otherwise pass as a member of the dominant cultural group defining themselves as otherwise.

In the case of Hispanic Americans, the choice of Islam may be constructed as "returning to the Andalusian heritage." For Hispanics on the East Coast, conversion has often been mediated through the African American community, an example being the Dar al-Islam movement from which a Hispanic group, Alliansa Islamica, separated about thirty years ago. Like the original Dar, the group is both *sharia* and Sufi oriented. Since 9/11, Hispanic Muslims have received a greater share of media attention than previously. Their numbers have been estimated at about 70,000, and they are served by several websites and publications.[91]

MASS CONVERSIONS

Although the spread of the great religions often occurred through mass conversions in which tribes or peoples followed their leaders or authority figures into a new faith, this is rather rare in modern times. Interestingly, I can think of several instances of mass conversions in American Islam. The most famous is the "mainstreaming" or embracing of Sunni theology and practice on the part of the majority of the members of the former Nation of Islam that took place under the leadership of Warith Deen Muhammad (d. 2008) in 1977. Many anticipate that the same will eventually occur in the Farrakhan branch of the movement, and in fact his statements since the 1990s seem to be a preparation for such a movement. One African American movement, the Nubian Islamic Hebrews, converted en masse first to Islam and subsequently to Judaism, suggesting that the mass conversion phenomenon may be a feature of African American movements rather than attributable directly to Islam.[92] In at least one case known to the author, many Euro- and Asian American members of a martial arts "dojo" in the San Francisco Bay Area followed their teacher in converting to Naqshbandi Sufism and Islam in the 1990s.

STYLES OF DA'WA

Khurram Murad cites three levels of *da'wa* activities:

(1) organized macro—supported by governments
(2) organized macro—supported by institutions
(3) micro-*da'wa* carried out by individuals.[93]

Larry Poston characterizes *da'wa* activities as either "lifestyle" or "activist," while Köse uses the categories "introverted" or "extroverted" to clarify similar distinctions. Lifestyle (indirect *da'wa*) is exemplified in a statement quoted in Poston's study: "Let us take Islam to the west not by pulpit preaching and mailing Islamic literature but by doing what Muslims ought to do, living, drinking, eating, sleeping, and behaving as Muslims are enjoined to do."[94]

On the other hand, activist preaching[95] (extroverted *da'wa*), from the perspective of immigrant Muslims, could include almost any Muslim activity, such as the presentation of information about Islam though call-in phone lines, radio and television programming, publications, mosque open-houses, or more formal interfaith dinners or dialogues. Some of these media are directed to both Muslims and non-Muslims; some are specifically designed as outreach to the non-Muslim American community.

Institutionally, there is no one central organization dedicated to *da'wa* work, although some Islamic centers may have special committees designated for this purpose. A number of private individuals and groups have acted to set up their own committees, and some centers have sponsored *da'wa* workshops. For example, the Muslim Community Center of Chicago, an urban and ethnically diverse center, formed a *da'wa* committee in the 1980s that is composed of members from the immigrant community and of American Muslims of Hispanic, Euro-American, and African American backgrounds. The budget had only been $100 per year. This was increased to $1,000 annually in the 1990s.

Activities undertaken include the production of pamphlets and, on one member's initiative, a telephone hotline. This person placed ads in the *Chicago Sun Times* and the *Chicago Tribune* with lines like, "Do you know that Mary is the most revered woman in Islam," with the telephone number "888-yes-Islam." These advertisements generated some 15–20 calls per week in the 1990s. The member had long phone conversations with the callers and classified interlocutors as either inter-faith types, or argumentative, noting that for each type one must have a repertoire of responses. This real estate agent/*da'i* (missionary) claims, "I could close five or six conversions right now," but he prefers for persons to take their time and feel really committed. An interesting aspect of the ongoing activities of the committee is the discussion concerning which of two styles works in drawing persons to Islam, constructed by the maintainer of the phone line as "Ahmed Deedat"[96] vs. a more Americanized interfaith approach. Some Muslims like the idea of quoting chapter and verses in debates in which scripture and its claims are the main ground of convincing the other. However, it is clear that this approach is the least likely to influence large members of people, since Americans who are oriented to Bible study and debate will be more strongly committed to a conservative interpretation of Christianity.

Numerically, most Euro-Americans who accept Islam do so through marriage, usually between female Americans and male Muslims. Stefano Allievi refers to such conversions as "relational."[97] The wife's conversion is not a requirement of the religion, although Muslim husbands naturally are gratified if their wives adopt the Islamic faith. Other modes of *da'wa* in the form of informational and relational outreach take place on college campuses and have come to include Islamic Awareness Week—sponsored nationally by campus chapters of Muslim Student Associations (MSA)—Ramadan dinners, Id dinners,[98] and lectures sponsored by campus MSAs.[99]

Islamic programs have also sponsored cable television programs, ranging from simple public-access talk shows to full-scale production services such as the Los Angeles-based Islam TV, whose weekly programs were syndicated worldwide.[100] Individual Muslims have made efforts such as buying one minute of radio time weekly in order to propagate the faith. Beginning in the 1980s, testimonial video tapes became available by catalogue. Among the titles of such videos are *Islam My Choice* by Yusuf Islam (Cat Stevens), *Nancy Ali—an Ex-Nun, Pathways to Islam*, and *My Life as a Muslim*. With the rise of YouTube, a broader selection of convert testimonials has become available, as have counter-Islamic polemic videos and sites.

RITUALS AND FORMALITIES OF CONVERSION TO ISLAM

In America, Islamic centers provide locations for conversions to take place in the sense that they issue certificates that enable persons to acquire visas in order to perform the Hajj. Sometimes a conversion takes on ceremonial aspects with the entire mosque congregation on a Friday acclaiming a new Muslim. In the case of a female this would be difficult, since she could not come to the front of the male section of the prayer hall. There is some evidence of a ritualization of conversion on the part of African American congregations in the form of "*shahada* rebirth celebrations."[101] One such celebration in Boston was held in order for the community to express gratitude for twelve new conversions.[102] In a Muslim society, the state is likely to become involved in the conversion process. For example, in Egypt, a convert must obtain a conversion certificate from officials at al-Azhar as well as register with the government, since conversion might entail other legal aspects, such as changes in inheritance and personal status law.

Sufi groups of what I have termed the "hybrid" variety—requiring adherence to Islamic ritual while appealing to Americans[103] —may combine conversion with initiation into a Sufi order. One such leader was criticized for inviting primarily non-Muslim audiences at talks given to Americans to join in reciting the profession of faith (*shahada*). The idea was that even if the participants did not realize it, formally they were becoming Muslims.

The role of Islamic ritual is important in the conversion experience, and non-Muslims are often attracted to join in activities such as *dhikr* (chanting pious phrases or names of God) sessions, prayer, and fast-breaking (*iftar*) dinners in Ramadan. One prison chaplain explained that inmates would often initially watch Muslim prisoners at prayer, then join the rituals, and finally ask to formally make the profession of faith.

SUFI MOVEMENTS

There are a number of Sufi movements operating in the United States, and these provide one source of conversions to Islam. Sufism has had an ambivalent reception in mainstream Islamic institutions, such as the Islamic Society of North America, due to its disparagement by supporters of more austere and literalist interpretations of the religion, and due to what is perceived as less rigorous enforcement of *shari'a* behaviors on the part of Sufi followers. In fact, some New Age Sufi movements are not even nominally Islamic.[104] Sufi activities might be thought of as broadly contributing to conversions to Islam through their greater interface with mainstream American culture. For example, in what I term "the sphere of translation" (i.e., arts and intellectual life) activities of Sufi groups include psychology, holistic health, dance, music, literature, poetry, and publishing. In what I have termed "the sphere of sites and ceremonies" (which take place in Muslim spaces, including mosques, Sufi centers, and shrines) there is broader outreach to the non-Muslim American population.

Within the sphere of translation, the influence of the universalist or "perennialist" Sufi movements, that is, those advocating a transcendent unity of religion rather than exclusively Islamic identity, is broader in mainstream Western culture, although a visit to any "metaphysical" or New Age bookstore will reveal the increasing volume of works by Islamic Sufis and their disciples. The Islamic-oriented Sufi movements favor translations and commentaries on classical Sufi texts,[105] while the perennialist Sufi movements favor quest narratives,[106] teaching stories, and transpersonal psychology.[107]

POST-CONVERSION SUPPORT GROUPS

Convert support groups have been one of the neglected areas of Islamic *da'wa*. It should be noted that, unlike in Judaism and most Christian denominations, Muslims have required little pre-conversion instruction. Thus, the follow-up is even more crucial. For example, every six months the Islamic Foundation in Villa Park, a Chicago suburb, holds instructional classes in the Islamic prayers oriented to converted adults. This center has sponsored a Qur'an study group for new Muslims for thirty years in which the scripture is read and discussed in English in an open way, promoting questions about both belief and practice. Examples of such questions could be the permissibility of deducting *zakat* on income tax. This more critical and open style of religious study is clearly in contrast to more traditional Islamic educational styles of rote memorization in Arabic and reading from classical interpretations. Issues of authority, whether related to the authority of the Arabic language or of particular classical or modern commentators, arise as members proceed past the initial level of new convert and become more aware of the interpretive diversity within contemporary Islam. Support groups seem to work best when run by converts themselves, assuming that the city or Islamic center is large enough to support such a group. In one such group observed at the Islamic Foundation, Villa Park, Illinois, many of the participants were inter-married couples where the spouse had accepted or was considering accepting Islam.

It should be noted that the Muslim community with which converts associate immediately after conversion may be crucial in shaping their attitudes to practice and doctrine. For example, a female convert who is surrounded by more liberal or "cultural" Muslims may feel comfortable about her identity as a Muslim despite not wearing a head scarf. If, soon after conversion, she is surrounded by a community emphasizing that strict forms of Islamic dress are essential, she will assume that this form of dress is a requirement.

Integration into the Muslim community in America may be difficult for single converts, perhaps more difficult for women than for males. The single convert is not likely to find marriage facilitated by becoming Muslim. One member of Chicago's Muslim Community Center *da'wa* group emphasized the importance of social as well as religious support and encouraged activities such as pizza parties and inviting new Muslims to share Id celebrations with Muslim families. On the other hand, inducements to convert, such as providing jobs or financial support, were frowned upon.

As the Muslim community in the United States becomes larger and more well-established, the varieties of *da'wa* may come to compete with each other. Studies in the sociology of religion[108] have described denominations as competing for market shares of the population, and even if that characterization seems rather instrumental, one does have to recognize that there are bound to be affinities between certain groups of Muslims, their ethnicity, class, and ideological perspectives, and the groups of Americans most likely to respond to their style of presenting and practicing Islam.

Beginning in 2005, the Islamic Circle of North America, an offshoot of the conservative Jamaat-i Islamic movement, took on the project of reaching out to potential converts and facing the challenges of "retention."[109] As part of this initiative, a phone hotline for potential converts was set up, a continuing series of "Revert Workshops" were held in the Chicago area, and, most prominently, a series of billboard and bus advertisements were mounted beginning in 2007.

The phone line strategy (1-877-why-Islam) was said to have resulted in twenty conversions in 2006. In order to answer inquiries on the telephone line, personnel are taught organized response strategies. For example, the ideal qualities of a respondent are said to include: the person should be married, be a "revert" themselves, speak good English, and have good pronunciation of the requisite Arabic terms. Once contact is made, the person in charge of *da'wa* follow-up should ideally be the same sex and age as the inquirer, have more or less the same educational level, and live in the same area.[110] Instructions for *da'wa* interactions are sprinkled with the insights of social psychology that enjoin efforts to make the prospective revert "comfortable," "build confidence," "bond," and provide "effective mentoring." Once "face to face contact" is made, the respondent should look the person in the eye, have a friendly smile, say "as-salam alaikum,"[111] and be their usual self—affect should be neither too flat nor overly emotional. They are also advised to not come across as being "too opinionated." Sociable acts, such as taking the person out for samosas (Indian snacks), are recommended.[112]

Another initiative on the part of the Islamic Circle of North America is a periodic "Revert Conference" convened to discuss issues faced by new Muslims. A workshop that I observed, held at a local mosque, included an interactive session focusing on problems that the mentored revert might face. Predictably, females who wanted to wear modest dress (*hijab*), despite family objections, were instructed in a set of rationales. Scriptural proofs included citing Paul's injunctions in Corinthians as proof that female veiling is universally enjoined by religion. An interesting discussion ensued over whether cultural comparison as a proof for the value of the practice could be a risky strategy. There are indeed fewer rapes in Saudi Arabia—Is this a convincing argument that gender segregation protects women, or does it present an apology for restrictions imposed on women in the name of religion?

In general, reverts' relations with the non-Muslim family are to be based on Islamic norms of respect, and a low-key lifestyle *da'wa* is advocated. For example, a revert should aspire to demonstrate that conversion has made one a better person and that one can still participate in normal activities such as joining in laughter, caring about baseball, and so on. An outspoken African American revert suggested that "one should never miss a *da'wa* moment"; for example, avoiding shaking hands with a member of the opposite sex would provide an opportunity to explain how respectful Muslim men are of women. In terms of asserting that Islamic values are universal, he suggested that all good basic values, even ones learned before conversion, could be "connected to the Deen."[113]

The issue of whether to offer material support to converts is complex. The negative perceptions of Christian missionaries offering inducements have made people leery of the stigma of "bribing" for conversions. At the same time, converting to Islam may have real material costs to persons who might lose their jobs and circle of friends or even family as a result of their conversion. The scenario for this seemed primarily to be those employed in a family business, since normally an individual could sue the employer if such religious discrimination could be proven. "Motivating" converts to get on their feet and help themselves was ultimately deemed preferable to providing extended support and charity.

By far the most visible ICNA *da'wa* initiative is one that began in 2007 in Chicago, with the sponsorship of billboards next to major highways and signs on city buses that stimulated interest in the religion and directed the public to the website, "Why Islam." Newspaper articles cited the group as claiming seven to eight conversions a month as a result of this campaign. Chapters in other American cities such as New York and San Francisco joined in the initiative, and other Muslim organizations joined in co-sponsoring the campaign.[114]

FINDING COMMUNITY AND RETENTION

I would generalize that for the first generation of children of convert Euro-American Muslims, retaining Islam has been challenging. Their parents often veer between the extremes of either being so rigid that the children rebel and leave home or being so tolerant that the children decide to reassimilate to an American lifestyle, perhaps not changing religion but not practicing Islam. My research indicated that for females among the early cohort of Euro-American reverts, being married to a man from a Muslim society made inculcating Islamic faith and practice in the next generation much easier. This is due to some of the following factors: the presence of an extended Muslim family, the passing on of faith in conjunction with traditions, and simple acts of every-day life. Two American converts married to each other, especially in the early period of the 1960s or 1970s, would have difficulty in finding an organized Muslim community at all. In cases where one existed, the other members might be ethnically homogeneous and not perceived as supportive or in sync with the values and interests of the convert family. Children of such marriages often drifted away from the religion or rejected it dramatically.[115] It remains to be seen whether children of mixed marriages of immigrant and American Muslims fare better than children from the union of two converted Americans in terms of retaining a commitment to Islam due to the fact that the former often have Muslim family and socializing networks. For example, I suggest that children of cross-cultural marriages are more comfortable with American-born children of immigrants and therefore more likely to be able to find marriage partners within the Muslim community.

In response to the threat of reassimilation, one group of Sufi-oriented American Muslims on the West Coast engaged their children to each other in order to discourage the adolescent fever of dating and romance. In the African American community, Clara

Muhammad schools, following in a tradition founded by the wife of Elijah Muhammad, and strong family orientations to practicing Islam are effective in retention, when they are available.

FUTURE NUMBERS AND TRENDS

In my opinion, the overall numbers of conversions to Islam in America are stable. As Islam becomes more familiar to Americans, through being taught as part of internationalizing the high school and college curriculum, the inclusion in public holiday calendars of holidays such as "Muslim Day" commemorated in December in New York or the Muslim World Day Parade,[116] one may speculate as to whether such cultural inclusion and familiarity will, in fact, reduce the number of conversions or increase it. GhaneaBassiri observed that second and third generation American-born Muslims of the African American community "do not share in their parents' enthusiasm for the proselytization of a new and unique divine message. They tend to concern themselves more with the significance and implications of their faith for their personal lives and surroundings."[117]

Muslims involved with da'wa assert that "only God can change a person's heart." At the same time, Muslim organizations that take an interest in conversion increasingly understand that having materials and support systems available to meet the needs of new Muslims will play a strong role in influencing the success of further conversion efforts.

NOTES

1. Richard W. Bulliet, *Conversion to Islam in the Middle Period: An Essay in Quantitative History* (Cambridge, MA: Harvard University Press, 1979). A very accessible summary of Bulliet's argument is available as "Religious Conversion and the Spread of Innovation," Fathom: The Source for Online Learning, http://www.fathom.com/feature/2199/index.html.
2. Bulliet, *Conversion to Islam*, 73.
3. Some would contest whether organized missionary activity was at all a part of classical Islamic expansion, asserting that those few contemporary movements that are organized for *da'wa* have modeled themselves on Christian missionary activities. On conversion to Islam in the classical period, see Nehemia Levtzion, ed., *Conversion to Islam* (New York: Holmes & Meier, 1979).
4. Wilfred Cantwell Smith, *The Meaning and End of Religion* (New York: Mentor Books, 1962), 103.
5. This is discussed in William Chittick and Sachiko Murata, *The Vision of Islam* (New York: Paragon Press, 1994), 291.

6. There are, however, certain *hadith* that present the Prophet as declaring the death penalty upon apostates. W. Heffening, "Murtadd," in *Encyclopaedia of Islam* (Leiden: E. J. Brill, 1992), 7:736.

7. Among contemporary scholars who have discussed this are Abdulaziz Sachedina, Mahmoud Ayoub, and Khaled Abou El Fadl. See Abdullah Saeed, *Freedom of Religion, Apostasy and Islam* (Aldershot: Ashgate, 2005).

8. See, for example. "The List: The World's Fastest-Growing Religions," in *Foreign Policy Magazine* (May 2007), http://www.foreignpolicy.com/story/cms.php?story_id=3835. Claims of which religions are the "fastest" growing are contested.

9. The article by Jodi Wilgoren, "Islam Attracts Converts by the Thousands," *New York Times,* Oct. 22, 2001, claimed an "expert" source as estimating 25,000 conversions a year in the United States, a number that I believe is somewhat unrealistic. A 2007 survey by the Pew Research Center found that the population of Muslim Americans, in comparison to the rest of the world, is unique in incorporating a relatively large number of converts to the religion—nearly a quarter. Almost all converts to Islam were native-born American (91 percent), and almost three-fifths (59 percent) of converts to Islam were African American. "Muslim Americans: Middle Class and Mostly Mainstream" (Pew Research, 2007), 21, http://pewresearch.org/assets/pdf/muslim-americans.pdf.

10. Exceptions in this regard are the preface to Levtzion's edited volume, *Conversion to Islam,* and attempts to apply Bulliet's statistical methodology in diverse regions.

11. See Karin van Nieuwkerk's chapter in this volume.

12. Lewis Rambo, "Theories of Conversion: Understanding and Interpreting Religious Change," *Social Compass* 46, no. 3 (1999): 259–271.

13. Qur'an 8:63, 9:60.

14. H. A. R. Gibb, *Studies in the Civilization of Islam,* ed. S. J. Shaw and W. R. Polk (Boston: Beacon Press, 1962), 5.

15. The term *dhimmi* referred to the non-Muslim subjects with whom Muslims were understood to be in a contract of responsibility or *dhimma*, entailing obligations on both sides, generally respect and cooperation on the part of the *dhimmi* and protection from the Muslim rulers on the part of the Muslims. Levtzion suggests that measures that discriminated more strongly against *dhimmi*, such as enforcement of distinctive dress codes and behavioral restrictions, were imposed under the Abbasis rule al-Mutawakkil (847–861) and might have increased conversion rates in the central lands as a consequence. Nehemia Levtzion, "Conversion under Muslim Domination: A Comparative Study," in *Islam in Africa and the Middle East: Studies on Conversion and Renewal,* ed. Michel Abitol and Amos Nadan (Aldershot: Ashgate, 2007), 2:23.

16. For example, Bat Ye'or, *Islam and Dhimmitude: Where Civilizations Collide* (Teaneck, NJ: Associated University Presses, 2003).

17. Arthur Goldschmidt, *A Concise History of the Middle East,* 8th ed. (Boulder, CO: Westview Press, 2006), 75.

18. There are four legal schools (*madhahib*) in Sunni Islam. The Maliki school follows the juristic methodology of the scholar Malik ibn Anas (ca. 711–795) and is more prominent in the Maghreb and adjacent African regions.

19. Maribel Fierro, "Mawali and Muwalladun in al-Andalus," in *Patronage and Patronage in Early and Classical Islam,* ed. Monique Bernards and John Nawas (Leiden: E. J. Brill, 1995), 195–235.

20. Devin DeWeese, *Islamization and Native Religion in the Golden Horde* (University Park: Pennsylvania State University Press, 1994).

21. David Gilmartin, *Empire and Islam: Punjab and the Making of Pakistan* (Berkeley and Los Angeles: University of California Press, 1988), 45.

22. Such stories, for example, are found in the Sejarah Malayu, ca. 1615. Accounts from some of these epics are summarized in Karel A. Steenbrink, *Dutch Colonialism and Indonesia Islam: Contacts and Conflict 1596–1950* (New York: Rodopi, 2006), 124–128. See also Russell Jones, "Ten Conversion Motifs from Indonesia," in Levtzion, *Conversion to Islam*, 129–158.

23. For example, on Spain, see Fierro, "Mawali and Muwalladun in al-Andalus," 195–245; on the Balkans, see Anton Minkov, *Conversion to Islam in the Balkans: Kisve Bahas Petitions and Ottoman Social Life, 1670–1730* (Leiden: E. J. Brill, 2004).

24. Richard Eaton notes the importance of this fact in rebutting claims that Islam was forced upon India, since areas under Muslim control were not the ones with the highest conversion rates. *Rise of Islam and the Bengal Frontier, 1204–1760* (Berkeley and Los Angeles: University of California, 1997), 155.

25. Gyanendra Pandey, *The Construction of Communalism in Colonial India* (Delhi: Oxford University Press, 1990).

26. Richard Eaton, "Approaches to the Study of Conversion to Islam in India," in *Approaches to Islam in Religious Studies*, ed. Richard M. Martin (Tucson: University of Arizona Press, 1985), 107 ff. See also Eaton, *Rise of Islam*, 113–123; Peter Hardy, "Modern European and Muslim Explanations of Conversion to Islam in South Asia: A Preliminary Study of the Literature," in *Conversion to Islam*, ed. Nehemia Levtzion (New York: Holmes & Meier, 1979), 68–99.

27. Eaton, "Approaches to the Study of Conversion," 113–119.

28. Abdul Malik Mujahid, *Conversion to Islam: Untouchables Strategy for Protest in India* (Chambersburg, PA: Anima Books, 1989).

29. Peter Van der Veer, "Introduction" to *Conversion to Modernities* (London: Routledge, 1995), 13.

30. Eaton, *Rise of Islam*, 305 ff.

31. Anton Minkov, *Conversion to Islam in the Balkans: Kisve Bahas Petitions and Ottoman Social Life, 1670–1730* (Leiden: E. J. Brill, 2004), 3. Bulliet's theory of populists vs. conservative elitists in Iran is applied to generational shifts in convert mentalities in Anatolia by Minkov, 16. Conversions in Anatolia are also discussed in Cemal Kafadar *Between Two Worlds: The Construction of the Ottoman State* (Berkeley and Los Angeles: University of California Press, 1995), 23.

32. Levtzion, *Conversion to Islam*, 8.

33. Minkov, *Conversion to Islam*, 26.

34. Ibid., 28.

35. Ibid., 33 ff.

36. Godfrey Goodwin, *The Janissaries* (London: Saqi Books, 1994), 35–36.

37. Ira Lapidus, *A History of Islamic Societies*, 2nd ed. (Cambridge: Cambridge University Press, 2002), 203.

38. Mark Woodward, *Islam in Java: Normative Piety and Mysticism in the Sultanate of Yogyakarta* (Tucson: University of Arizona Press, 1989).

39. Russell Jones, "Ten Conversion Myths from Indonesia," in *Conversion to Islam*, ed. Levtzion, 153.

40. Robert W. Hefner, "Social Legacies and Possible Futures," in *Indonesia: The Great Transition*, ed. John Bresnan (Lanham, MD: Rowman and Littlefield, 2005), 91–92.

41. Rex O'Fahey, "Islam, Society and State in Dar Fur," in *Conversion to Islam*, ed. Levtzion, 202.

42. Edward E. Curtis, IV, *Islam in Black America* (Albany: State University of New York Press, 2002), 33.

43. Randall L. Pouwels, "Islam in East Africa," in *Encyclopedia of African History*, ed. Kevin Shillington (New York: CRC Books, 2005), 710–711; Robert Launey, "New Frontiers of Conversion," in *The New Cambridge History of Islam*, ed. Robert W. Hefner (Cambridge: Cambridge University Press, 2010), 6:258–261.

44. This discussion of Horton's theoretical contribution has been largely adapted from Wolfgang Gabbert, "Social and Cultural Conditions of Religious Conversion in Colonial Southwest Tanzania, 1891–1939," *Ethnology* 40, no. 4 (2001): 291–308. See Robin Horton, "African Conversion," *Africa* 41 (1971): 85–108; Robin Horton, "On the Rationality of Conversion," in *Africa* 45 (1975): 219–235, 373–399; Robin Horton, *Patterns of Thought in Africa and the West* (Cambridge: Cambridge University Press, 1993).

45. Clifford Geertz, "Internal Conversion in Contemporary Bali," in *The Interpretation of Cultures* (New York: Basic Books, 1973), 170–189, especially p. 171.

46. Horton, "African Conversion," 101; Horton, *Patterns of Thought*, 175; R. W. Hefner, "Introduction: World-Building and the Rationality of Conversion," in *Conversion to Christianity*, ed. Robert W. Hefner (Berkeley and Los Angeles: University of California Press, 1993), 20–21.

47. Horton, "African Conversion," 102–103; Horton, "On the Rationality of Conversion," 220, 234, 381, 392–393; M. Wilson, *Religion and the Transformation of Society* (Cambridge: Cambridge University Press, 1971), 26–51; I. M. Lewis, *Islam in Tropical Africa* (London: Hutchinson, 1980), vii–viii, 59, 80–81.

48. Clifford Geertz, *Islam Observed: Religious Development in Morocco and Indonesia* (Chicago: University of Chicago Press, 1971).

49. Marcia Hermansen, "How to Put the Genie Back in the Bottle: 'Identity Islam' and Muslim Youth Cultures in America," in *Progressive Muslims: On Pluralism, Gender, and Justice*, ed. Omid Safi (Oxford: Oneworld Publications, 2003), 303–319.

50. Reynold Nicholson, *The Mystics of Islam* (London: Kegan Paul, 1914), 16.

51. al-Ghazzali, *The Faith and Practice of Al-Ghazzali: Al-Munqidh Min Ad-Dalal*, trans. Montgomery Watt (Oxford: Oneworld, 2007).

52. Fedwa Malti-Douglas, *Medicines of the Soul: Female Bodies and Sacred Geographies in a Transnational Islam* (Berkeley and Los Angeles: University of California, 2001) is a work about accounts by modern Egyptian women who rediscover Islamic piety, especially with Sufi influences.

53. Saba Mahmood, *Politics of Piety. The Islamic Revival and the Feminist Subject* (Princeton: Princeton University Press, 2004). The struggle between adherents of Sufi-oriented local Islamic practice and more literalist Wahhabi/Salafi interpretations has been ongoing around the Muslim world since the 1980s.

54. Dale F. Eickelman and Jon W. Anderson, eds., *New Media in the Muslim World* (Bloomington: Indiana University Press, 1999).

55. For this expression and the early history of European conversions to Islam, see Nabil I. Matar, "The Renegade in English Seventeenth Century Imagination," *Studies in English Literature 1500–1900* 33 (1993): 489–505; Nabil I. Matar, "Turning Turk: Conversion

to Islam in English Renaissance Thought," *Durham University Journal* 86, no. 1 (1994): 33–41.

56. Nabil Matar, "Introduction," in *Piracy, Slavery, and Redemption: Barbary Captivity Narratives from Early Modern England*, ed. Daniel J. Vitkus (New York: Columbia University Press, 2001), 2.

57. These elements and some of the following examples are discussed in Marcia Hermansen, "Roads to Mecca: Conversion Narratives of European and Euro-American Muslims," *Muslim World* 89, no. 1 (1999): 56–89.

58. Muhammad Asad, *Road to Mecca* (New York: Simon and Schuster, 1954), 1.

59. Maryam Jameelah, *Memoirs of Childhood and Youth in America (1945–1962): The Story of One Western Convert's Quest for Truth* (Lahore: Muhammad Yusuf Khan and Sons, 1989), 9.

60. Owen Rutter, *Triumphant Pilgrimage: An English Muslim's Journey from Sarawak to Mecca* (London: J. B. Lippincott, 1937), 116–117.

61. Larry Poston, *Islamic Da'wah in the West Muslim Missionary Activity and the Dynamics of Conversion to Islam* (London: Oxford, 1992), 166–168.

62. Kambiz GhaneaBassiri, *Competing Visions of Islam in the United States: A Study of Los Angeles* (Westport, CT: Greenwood Press, 1997), 89. However, many more Muslims in the survey felt that active efforts should be made to convert others.

63. In the results of a survey of Muslims conducted by Kambiz GhaneaBassiri, Muslims who always tried to teach others about Islam were the ones who reported most frequently experiencing prejudice. GhaneaBassiri, *Competing Visions*, 92–93.

64. *Adab* is proper behavior. On *adab*, see Barbara D. Metcalf, *Moral Conduct and Authority: The Case of Adab in South Asian Islam* (Princeton: Princeton University Press, 1984).

65. Participant, Youth Seminar, Chicago Milad Conference. July 27, 1997.

66. GhaneaBassiri, *Competing Visions*, 94.

67. Richard Brent Turner, *Islam in the African American Experience* (Bloomington: Indiana University Press, 1997), 241.

68. Sherman Jackson, *Islam and the Blackamerican: Looking Toward the Third Resurrection* (New York: Oxford University Press, 2005).

69. See, for example, Umar Faruq Abd-Allah, "Islam and the Cultural Imperative," http://www.nawawi.org/downloads/article3.pdf.

70. Khurram Murad, *Da'wah among Non-Muslims in the West: Some Conceptual and Methodological Aspects* (Leicester: Islamic Foundation, 1988), 15.

71. Jackson, *Islam and the Blackamerican*.

72. For example, Bilal Hyde and Hamza Yusuf Hanson in San Jose, California.

73. Some years ago I personally observed elderly Afghan refugee women in the United States requesting an American convert female to pray for them, thereby demonstrating great respect for a person who had voluntarily chosen the religion and was in a state of having previous sin wiped away.

74. The Saudi government associates a number of organizations and official organs as "*da'wa*" centers. http://www.al-islam.com/articles/articles-e.asp?fname=INFO_R3_E. The Houston organization may be viewed at the following site: http://www.islamicdawahcenter.org/html/about_us.html.

75. Murad, *Da'wah among Non-Muslims*, 33.

76. Poston, *Islamic Da'wah in the West*.

77. Ali Köse, *Conversion to Islam: A Study of Native British Converts* (London: Kegan Paul, 1996).

78. On the element of culture in conversion to Islam, see Hermansen, "Roads to Mecca," 56–89.

79. GhaneaBassiri, *Competing Visions*, 170.

80. Ibid., 171.

81. Poston, *Islamic Da'wah in the West*, chs. 9 and 10.

82. Marcia Hermansen, "Two-Way Acculturation: Muslim Women in America," in *The Muslims of America*, ed. Yvonne Haddad (New York: Oxford University Press, 1991), 188–201.

83. Hermansen, "Roads to Mecca."

84. Marcia Hermansen, "In the Garden of American Sufi Movements: Hybrids and Perennials," in *New Trends and Developments in the World of Islam*, ed. Peter Clarke (London: Luzac Oriental Press, 1997), 155–178.

85. Hermansen, "Keeping the Faith."

86. Hermansen, "Two-Way Acculturation."

87. Stefano Allievi, who primarily studies European converts, also noted the dimension of "political" conversions as a sub-category of what he terms "rational" conversions. Stefano Allievi, "Conversions to Islam in Europe," *Social Compass* 46, no. 3 (1999): 243–362; Stefano Allievi, "Converts and the Making of European Islam," *ISIM Newsletter* 11 (2002): 1.

88. Aminah Beverly McCloud, "African-American Muslim Women," in *The Muslims of America*, ed. Yvonne Y. Haddad and Jane I. Smith (New York: Oxford University Press, 1991), 177–187.

89. Ibid., 178.

90. Ibid.

91. http://www.latinodawah.org/; http://hispanicmuslims.com. Other estimates of this population range from 40,000 to 200,000.

92. Kathleen Malone O'Connor, "The Nubian Islamic Hebrews/Ansaaru Allah Community: Jewish Teachings of an African American Muslim Community," in *Black Zion: African American Religious Encounters with Judaism*, ed. Yvonne Chireau and Nathaniel Deutsch, (New York: Oxford University Press, 2000), 118–150.

93. Murad, *Da'wah among Non-Muslims*, 9.

94. Poston, *Islamic Da'wah in the West*, 117, quoting Imran Muhammad.

95. Ibid., 122 ff.

96. Ahmed Deedat (d. 2005) was a popular Muslim preacher and aggressive debater of South African origin who founded the Islamic Propagation Centre International in 1957, which disseminated many books and tapes. He is most well-known in the world Muslim community as the victor in a widely circulated debate over their respective scriptures with the Christian evangelist, Jimmy Swaggart. This took place before Swaggart was publicly discredited for sexual improprieties.

97. Stefano Allievi, *Les Convertis à l'Islam : Les nouveaux musulmans d'Europe* (Paris: L'Harmattan, 1998).

98. Id (Eid) refers to either of the two major Muslim religious festivals—one at the end of the month of Ramadan and the other at the culmination of the Hajj.

99. I discuss the role of "convert panels" during MSA Islamic Awareness weeks in "Muslims in the Performative Mode: A Reflection on Muslim-Christian Dialogue," *Muslim World* 94, no. 3 (2004): 387–396.

100. Islam TV ceased operating in the 1990s. A full-time US-based channel, "Bridges TV," founded in 2004, was available only by subscription and therefore unlikely to have a *da'wa* outreach.

101. The *shahada* is the profession of faith in Islam by declaring that "There is no God but God and Muhammad is the Prophet of God."

102. "A Shahada Rebirth celebration," *American Muslim Journal* 4 (July 17, 1992): 1.

103. Hermansen, "In the Garden of American Sufi Movements."

104. Conversion to Islam is not expected or required in movements such as the Sufi Order International (Inayat Khan) and groups inspired by the teachings of Idreis or Omar Ali Shah.

105. Marcia Hermansen reviews Sufi literatures in more detail in "Western Sufis and Sufi Literatures in the West," in *Sufism in the West*, ed. John Hinnells and J. Malik (London: Routledge, 2006), 28–48. A recent (1990s) trend in the literary production of Western Islamically inclined Sufi movements are spiritual autobiographies such as Muhyiuddin Shakor, *The Writing on the Water: Chronicles of a Seeker on the Islamic Sufi Path* (Shaftesbury, England: Element Books, 1994); and Noorudeen Durkee, *Embracing Islam*, (Charlottesville, VA: Green Mountain School, 1999). An Australian example of this genre is Amatullah Armstrong, *And the Sky Is Not the Limit: An Australian Woman's Spiritual Journey within the Traditions* (Kuala Lumpur: A. S. Noordeen, 1993); see also Maryam Kabeer Faye, *Journey through Ten Thousand Veils: The Alchemy of Transformation on the Sufi Path* (Somerset, NJ: Tughra Books, 2008).

106. See, for example, those produced by the Idries Shah circle, including many fictitious narratives of esoteric schools in the East, such as Rafael Lafort, *Teachers of Gurdjieff* (London: V. Gollancz, 1968); Omar S. Burke, *Among the Dervishes* (London: Octagon, 1973). Also representative would be Ian Dallas, *The Book of Strangers* (New York: Pantheon Books 1972); and Reshad Feild, *The Last Barrier* (New York: Harper & Row, 1976).

107. Among Sufi presses and distributors are Octagon Press, Pir Press, Threshold Books, the Sufi Book Club, and Omega Press.

108. Rodney Stark and William Sims Bainbridge, *A Theory of Religion* (New York: Peter Lang, 1987).

109. On ICNA in the United States, see Aminah Mohammed-Arif, *Salaam America: A Study of Indian Islam in the United States* (New York: Anthem Press, 2002), 171–190.

110. Revert Workshop PowerPoint, Islamic Foundation, Villa Park, IL, Mar. 10, 2007.

111. "Peace be upon you," the traditional Islamic greeting.

112. Revert Workshop, Mar. 10, 2007.

113. *Deen* or *Din* is an Arabic term meaning "religion."

114. Some of these initiatives in New York, San Francisco, and Seattle generated extensive media coverage and some controversy. By 2010 a message of "dispelling negativity about Islam" supplemented the mission of *da'wa* in the bus and train ad campaign. http://www.icna.org/awareness-campaign-attempts-to-dispel-negativity-about-islam/.

115. Marcia Hermansen, "Keeping the Faith: Convert Muslim Mothers in America and the Transmission of Islamic Identity," in *Women Embracing Islam: Gender and Conversion in the West*, ed. Karin van Nieuwkerk (Austin: University of Texas Press, 2006), 250–276.

116. The parade has been studied by Susan Slymovics, "The Muslim World Day Parade and 'Storefront' Mosques of New York City," in *Making Muslim Space*, ed. Barbara D. Metcalf (Berkeley and Los Angeles: University of California Press, 1996), 204–216.

117. GhaneaBassiri, *Competing Visions*, 94.

BIBLIOGRAPHY

"A Shahada Rebirth Celebration." *American Muslim Journal* 4 (July 17, 1992): 1.

Abd-Allah, Umar Faruq. "Islam and the Cultural Imperative." Nawawi Foundation, http://www.nawawi.org/downloads/article3.pdf.

Allievi, Stefano. *Les Convertis à l'Islam: Les Nouveaux Musulmans d'Europe.* Paris: L'Harmattan, 1998.

——. "Conversions to Islam in Europe." *Social Compass* 46, no. 3 (1999): 243–362.

——. "Converts and the Making of European Islam." *ISIM Newsletter* 11 (2002): 1.

Armstrong, Amatullah. *And the Sky Is Not the Limit: An Australian Woman's Spiritual Journey within the Traditions.* Kuala Lumpur: A. S. Noordeen, 1993.

Asad, Muhammad. *Road to Mecca.* New York: Simon and Schuster, 1954.

Bulliet, Richard W. *Conversion to Islam in the Middle Period: An Essay in Quantitative History.* Cambridge, MA: Harvard University Press, 1979.

Burke, Omar S. *Among the Dervishes.* London: Octagon, 1973.

Chittick, William, and Sachiko Murata. *The Vision of Islam.* New York: Paragon Press, 1994.

Curtis, Edward E., IV. *Islam in Black America.* Albany: State University of New York Press, 2002.

Dallas, Ian. *The Book of Strangers.* New York: Pantheon Books, 1972.

Da'wah and Guidance, Ministry of Islamic Affairs. "Al Islam: Islamic Organizations Guide." Kingdom of Saudi Arabia. http://www.al-islam.com/articles/articles-e.asp?fname=INFO_R3_E.

DeWeese, Devin. *Islamization and Native Religion in the Golden Horde.* University Park: Pennsylvania State University Press, 1994.

Durkee, Noorudeen. *Embracing Islam.* Charlottesville, VA: Green Mountain School, 1999.

Eaton, Richard. "Approaches to the Study of Conversion to Islam in India." In *Approaches to Islam in Religious Studies*, ed. Richard M. Martin, 106–123. Tucson: University of Arizona Press, 1985.

——. *Rise of Islam and the Bengal Frontier, 1204–1760.* Berkeley and Los Angeles: University of California, 1997.

Eickelman, Dale F., and Jon W. Anderson, eds. *New Media in the Muslim World.* Bloomington: Indiana University Press, 1999.

Faye, Maryam Kabeer. *Journey through Ten Thousand Veils: The Alchemy of Transformation on the Sufi Path.* Somerset, NJ: Tughra Books, 2008.

Feild, Reshad. *The Last Barrier.* New York: Harper & Row, 1976.

Fierro, Maribel. "Mawali and Muwalladun in al-Andalus." In *Patronage and Patronage in Early and Classical Islam*, ed. Monique Bernards and John Nawas, 195–245. Leiden: E. J. Brill, 1995.

Gabbert, Wolfgang. "Social and Cultural Conditions of Religious Conversion in Colonial Southwest Tanzania, 1891–1939." *Ethnology* 40, no. 4 (2001): 291–308.

Galvan, Juan, and Samantha Sanchez. "Latinos Journey to Islam: A Rebirth of an Experience." HispanicMuslims.com. http://hispanicmuslims.com/index.html.

Geertz, Clifford. "Internal Conversion in Contemporary Bali." In *The Interpretation of Cultures*, 170–189. New York: Basic Books, 1973.

——. *Islam Observed: Religious Development in Morocco and Indonesia.* Chicago: University of Chicago Press, 1971.

GhaneaBassiri, Kambiz. *Competing Visions of Islam in the United States: A Study of Los Angeles.* Westport, CT: Greenwood Press, 1997.

al-Ghazzali. *The Faith and Practice of Al-Ghazali: Al-Munqidh Min Ad-Dalal*, trans. Montgomery Watt. Oxford: Oneworld, 2007.

Gibb, H. A. R. *Studies in the Civilization of Islam*. ed. S. J. Shaw and W. R. Polk. Boston: Beacon Press, 1962.

Gilmartin, David. *Empire and Islam: Punjab and the Making of Pakistan*. Berkeley and Los Angeles: University of California Press, 1988.

Goldschmidt, Arthur. *A Concise History of the Middle East*. 8th ed. Boulder, CO: Westview Press, 2006.

Goodwin, Godfrey. *The Janissaries*. London: Saqi Books, 1994.

Hardy, Peter. "Modern European and Muslim Explanations of Conversion to Islam in South Asia: A Preliminary Study of the Literature." In *Conversion to Islam*, ed. Nehemia Levtzion, 68–99. New York: Holmes & Meier, 1979.

Heffening, W. "Murtadd." In *Encyclopaedia of Islam*, ed. H. A. R. Gibb et al., 7:365–366. Leiden: E. J. Brill, 1992.

Hefner, Robert W. "Introduction: World-Building and the Rationality of Conversion." In *Conversion to Christianity*, ed. Robert W. Hefner, 3–44. Berkeley and Los Angeles: University of California Press, 1993.

——. "Social Legacies and Possible Futures." In *Indonesia: The Great Transition*, ed. John Bresnan, 75–136. Lanham, MD: Rowman and Littlefield, 2005.

Hermansen, Marcia. "How to Put the Genie Back in the Bottle: 'Identity Islam' and Muslim Youth Cultures in America." In *Progressive Muslims: On Pluralism, Gender, and Justice*, ed. Omid Safi, 303–319. Oxford: Oneworld Publications, 2003.

——. "In the Garden of American Sufi Movements: Hybrids and Perennials." In *New Trends and Developments in the World of Islam*, ed. Peter Clarke, 155–178. London: Luzac Oriental Press, 1997.

——. "Keeping the Faith: Convert Muslim Mothers in America and the Transmission of Islamic Identity." In *Women Embracing Islam: Gender and Conversion in the West*, ed. Karin van Nieuwkerk, 250–276. Austin: University of Texas Press, 2006.

——. "Roads to Mecca Conversion Narratives of European and Euro-American Muslims." *Muslim World* 89, no. 1 (1999): 56–89.

——. "Two-Way Acculturation: Muslim Women in America." In *The Muslims of America*, ed. Yvonne Haddad, 188–201. New York: Oxford University Press, 1991.

——. "Western Sufis and Sufi Literatures in the West." In *Sufism in the West*, ed. John Hinnells and J. Malik, 28–48. London: Routledge, 2006.

Horton, Robin. "African Conversion." *Africa* 41 (1971): 85–108.

——. "On the Rationality of Conversion." *Africa* 45 (1975): 219–235, 373–399.

——. *Patterns of Thought in Africa and the West*. Cambridge: Cambridge University Press, 1993.

Islamic Dawah Center. http://www.islamicdawahcenter.org/html/about_us.html.

Islamic Foundation. "Revert Workshop PowerPoint." Presented at the Reverts' Workshop, Villa Park, IL, Mar. 10, 2007.

Jackson, Sherman. *Islam and the Blackamerican: Looking Toward the Third Resurrection*. New York: Oxford University Press, 2005.

Jameelah, Maryam. *Memoirs of Childhood and Youth in America (1945–1962): The Story of One Western Convert's Quest for Truth*. Lahore: Muhammad Yusuf Khan and Sons, 1989.

Joesoef, Harry. "Snouck Hurgronje: Moslim of Niet." *Tirade* 296, no. 29 (Jan.–Feb. 1985): 98–128.

Jones, Russell. "Ten Conversion Myths from Indonesia." In *Conversion to Islam*, ed. Nehemia Levtzion, 129–158. New York: Holmes & Meier, 1979.

Kafadar, Cemal. *Between Two Worlds: The Construction of the Ottoman State*. Berkeley and Los Angeles: University of California Press, 1995.

Köse, Ali. *Conversion to Islam: A Study of Native British Converts*. London: Kegan Paul, 1996.

Lafort, Rafael. *Teachers of Gurdjieff*. London: V. Gollancz, 1968.

Lapidus, Ira. *A History of Islamic Societies*. 2nd ed. Cambridge: Cambridge University Press, 2002.

Latino American Dawah Organization (LADO). http://www.latinodawah.org.

Lawrence, Bruce, ed. *The Rose and the Rock: Mystical and Rational Elements in the Intellectual History of South Asian Islam*. Durham, NC: Duke University Press, 1979.

Levtzion, Nehemia, ed. *Conversion to Islam*. New York: Holmes & Meier, 1979.

——. "Conversion under Muslim Domination: A Comparative Study." In *Islam in Africa and the Middle East: Studies on Conversion and Renewal*, ed. Michel Abitol and Amos Nadan, 19–38. Aldershot: Ashgate, 2007.

Lewis, I. M. *Islam in Tropical Africa*. London: Hutchinson, 1980.

"The List: The World's Fastest-Growing Religions." *Foreign Policy Magazine* (May 2007), http://www.foreignpolicy.com/story/cms.php?story_id=3835.

Mahmood, Saba. *Politics of Piety: The Islamic Revival and the Feminist Subject*. Princeton: Princeton University Press, 2004.

Malti-Douglas, Fedwa. *Medicines of the Soul: Female Bodies and Sacred Geographies in a Transnational Islam*. Berkeley and Los Angeles: University of California, 2001.

Matar, Nabil I. "Introduction: England and Mediterranean Captivity, 1577–1704." In *Piracy, Slavery, and Redemption: Barbary Captivity Narratives from Early Modern England*, ed. Daniel J. Vitkus, 1–54. New York: Columbia University Press, 2001.

——. "The Renegade in English Seventeenth Century Imagination." *Studies in English Literature 1500–1900* 33 (1993): 489–505.

——. "Turning Turk: Conversion to Islam in English Renaissance Thought." *Durham University Journal* 86, no. 1 (1994): 33–41.

McCloud, Aminah Beverly. "African-American Muslim Women." In *The Muslims of America*, ed. Yvonne Y. Haddad, 177–187. New York: Oxford University Press, 1991.

Metcalf, Barbara D. *Moral Conduct and Authority: The Case of Adab in South Asian Islam*. Princeton: Princeton University Press, 1984.

Minkov, Anton. *Conversion to Islam in the Balkans: Kisve Bahas Petitions and Ottoman Social Life, 1670–1730*. Leiden: E. J. Brill, 2004.

Mohammed-Arif, Aminah. *Salaam America: A Study of Indian Islam in the United States*. New York: Anthem Press, 2002.

Mujahid, Abdul Malik. *Conversion to Islam: Untouchables Strategy for Protest in India*. Chambersburg, PA: Anima Books, 1989.

Murad, Khurram. *Da'wah among Non-Muslims in the West: Some Conceptual and Methodological Aspects*. Leicester: Islamic Foundation, 1988.

Nicholson, Reynold. *The Mystics of Islam*. London: Kegan Paul, 1914.

O'Connor, Kathleen Malone. "The Nubian Islamic Hebrews/Ansaaru Allah Community: Jewish Teachings of an African American Muslim Community." In *Black Zion: African American Religious Encounters with Judaism*, ed. Yvonne Chireau and Nathaniel Deutsch, 118–150. New York: Oxford University Press, 2000.

O'Fahey, Rex. "Islam, Society and State in Dar Fur." In *Conversion to Islam*, ed. Nehemia Levtzion, 189–206. New York: Holmes & Meier, 1979.

Pandey, Gyanendra. *The Construction of Communalism in Colonial India.* Delhi: Oxford University Press, 1990.

Pew Research Center. "Muslim Americans: Middle Class and Mostly Mainstream." Pew Research (2007), http://pewresearch.org/assets/pdf/muslim-americans.pdf.

Poston, Larry. *Islamic Da'wah in the West: Muslim Missionary Activity and the Dynamics of Conversion to Islam.* London: Oxford University Press, 1992.

Pouwels, Randall L. "Islam in East Africa." In *Encyclopedia of African History*, ed. Kevin Shillington, 2:710–715. New York: Taylor and Francis (CRC), 2004.

Rambo, Lewis. "Theories of Conversion: Understanding and Interpreting Religious Change." *Social Compass* 46, no. 3 (1999): 259–271.

"Religious Conversion and the Spread of Innovation." Fathom: The Source for Online Learning. http://www.fathom.com/feature/2199/index.html.

Rutter, Owen. *Triumphant Pilgrimage: An English Muslim's Journey from Sarawak to Mecca.* London: J. B. Lippincott, 1937.

Saeed, Abdullah. *Freedom of Religion, Apostasy and Islam.* Aldershot: Ashgate, 2005.

Shakoor, Muhyiuddin. *The Writing on the Water: Chronicles of a Seeker on the Islamic Sufi Path.* Shaftesbury, England: Element Books, 1994.

Slymovics, Susan. "The Muslim World Day Parade and 'Storefront' Mosques of New York City." In *Making Muslim Space in North America and Europe*, ed. Barbara D. Metcalf, 204–216. Berkeley and Los Angeles: University of California Press, 1996.

Smith, Wilfred Cantwell. *The Meaning and End of Religion.* New York: Mentor Books, 1962.

Stark, Rodney, and William Sims Bainbridge. *A Theory of Religion.* New York: Peter Lang, 1987.

Steenbrink, Karel A. *Dutch Colonialism and Indonesia Islam: Contacts and Conflict 1596–1950.* New York: Rodopi, 2006.

Turner, Richard Brent. *Islam in the African American Experience.* Bloomington: Indiana University Press, 1997.

Veer, Peter Van der. "Introduction." In *Conversion to Modernities*, ed. Peter Van der Veer, 1–23. London: Routledge, 1995.

Weber, Max. *Sociology of Religion.* Boston: Beacon Press, 1963.

Wilgoren, Jodi. "Islam Attracts Converts by the Thousands." *New York Times*, Oct. 22, 2001.

Wilson, M. *Religion and the Transformation of Society.* Cambridge: Cambridge University Press, 1971.

Woodward, Mark. *Islam in Java: Normative Piety and Mysticism in the Sultanate of Yogyakarta.* Tucson: University of Arizona Press, 1989.

Ye'or, Bat. *Islam and Dhimmitude: Where Civilizations Collide.* Teaneck, NJ: Associated University Presses, 2003.

CHAPTER 28

"CONVERSION" TO ISLAM AND THE CONSTRUCTION OF A PIOUS SELF

KARIN VAN NIEUWKERK

INTRODUCTION

CONVERSION to Islam is an intriguing phenomenon that has attracted increasing media attention. Particularly after 9/11, the number of converts is assumed to be growing fast and to include mounting numbers of radicalized individuals who turn against their own societies. Media attention is focused on these few radicalized converts, who are also closely followed by security services. Within this politicized context, it is difficult to get reliable statistics on conversion. Politicians and media fearing the phenomenon, as well as Muslim missionaries, might overestimate the case; scholars are left without statistics to make a fair guess. In most statistics, nationalized born Muslims are not distinguished from native converts. Besides, not all converts register after expressing the *shahadah*, the declaration of faith. Some converts say the *shahadah* in front of Muslim friends and feel no need to have their conversion recorded on paper.

This one-sided attention to radicalization and the politicized climate with regard to Islam and conversion foreclose studies of "ordinary converts." They greatly outnumber the radicalized few and are interesting to study because they represent the "mainstream." They are ordinary men and women—not some strange species—making choices not immediately intelligible to most of us. In order to understand their choices, we need an insider's perspective. Why do individuals convert, and why do they turn to Islam? What are their backgrounds, motives, and life stories? How does their conversion process unfold? What kind of Islam appeals to them? Why are more women than men attracted to Islam?

I will use the growing number of studies on conversion to Islam, Internet narratives, and my own fieldwork among Dutch converts to answer these questions. These sources consist mainly of conversion narratives. Narratives, whether testimonies from the Internet or life-story interviews, yield an insider's perspective. But we should keep in mind that conversion testimonies are a specific genre with a particular narrative structure.[1] Conversion narratives are created retrospectively, that is, they are told after the conversion. Past events are reinterpreted in the light of current convictions. Converts also include elements of the new religion into their narratives about conversion. This reconstructing process takes place not only at the individual level but also at the group level. Converts come together to discuss their experiences, and they include common narrative elements in their stories. In the process of telling and retelling their conversion experiences, a common model is created. Particularly with regard to such delicate issues as gender, a shared narrative is constructed. Many conversion stories also function as a form of *da'wah*, or calling to the faith. This means that the narratives are an important source for studying the way conversion is understood and expressed by converts but do not always give direct access to original motives and reasons to convert.

In this chapter I use the story of a Dutch convert to give flesh and bones to the choice of many men and women to become Muslim, without suggesting that this person is in one way or another exemplary for conversion in general. There is no general conversion pattern; I use this story to discuss the many variations. I draw on theories developed within different disciplines—history, sociology, psychology, religious studies, Islamic studies, gender studies, and anthropology—to make sense of the life story. I use Lewis Rambo's stage model as a tool to structure this chapter, employing the stages of context, quest, crisis, advocates, interaction, commitments, and consequences to frame the different approaches towards conversion.[2]

"CONVERSION," REVERSION, AND BECOMING MUSLIM

Before embarking on this project, a closer look at the term "conversion" is helpful.

Many converts seem to dislike the word "convert." They are very careful in the way they describe their experiences and the words they use for their "conversion."[3] Converts prefer to speak about "becoming Muslim," "taking *shahadah*" (that is, pronouncing the declaration of faith), or "embracing Islam," and some opt for the ambiguous term "reversion" to Islam.[4] There is no word for conversion in Arabic, but the verb *aslama* conveys the idea of becoming a Muslim and literally means to submit.[5]

The wide variety of concepts is related to several factors. First, converts posting on the Internet indicate a difference in wording between Muslims and non-Muslims: "Non-Muslims always ask me, "Why did you convert?" and Muslims always ask, "How did you come to embrace Islam?" The concept "convert" is thus considered an outsider's perspective, whereas embracing Islam or becoming Muslim is an insider's view. Second, conversion has the connotation of a radical change, a change to something new. From the narratives of many converts on the Internet, it becomes clear that they already feel Muslim but did not know that their ideas were Islamic. Many of these converts who were raised Christians question central religious ideas about the Trinity and Jesus as Son of God. These "enlightened Christians" can perhaps be considered "anonymous Muslims."[6] When they come into contact with Muslims, they suddenly realize that these notions are in line with Islamic theology. Several converts describe Islam as "the religion of common sense" or describe themselves as "dormant Muslims." An American convert comments: "So it was almost natural to become Muslim. I guess you really couldn't call it converting to Islam, it is what always made sense anyway." They thus avoid the concept of conversion because it does not capture their sense of a gradual realization that their ideas were already Islamic. Lastly, the choice of a concept such as "reversion" is related to a certain missionary ideology. In several testimonies, the idea of "being already Muslim" is taken a step further. "I was a Muslim but just wasn't aware of it" fades into the ideology of "all people are born Muslim." Turning to Islam is thus re-turning. Therefore, conversion is not a correct notion and should be replaced by "reversion."

There are several interrelated arguments given for this notion of reversion. First, the message of Islam is argued to be the universal and original message of the oneness of God, *tawheed*. Muhammad, as the last prophet, sought the reversion of all humanity to this message of *tawheed*. Second, Islam is considered the natural religion. Lady Cecilia Mahmuda Canolly writes in her testimony: "It seems that I have always been a Muslim. This is not so strange when one remembers that Islam is the natural religion that a child, left to itself, would develop. That is, everyone is born as a Muslim and left to itself would become Muslim but many are socialised into being Christian, Jew or atheist." Finally, everyone is born sinless and, by becoming Muslim, the revert returns to this original natural condition at birth. The moderators of the website The True Religion, for instance, explain: "'Revert' is actually a more appropriate term than 'convert', since all human beings are born pure. By embracing Islam, one returns to the original and sinless state in which God created him or her".[7]

The conceptualization of conversion as a form of reversion is also the underlying religious logic for the lack of ritual elaboration of the declaration of faith. Since human beings are born in state of natural purity, there is no need for a divine transformation of their nature.[8] Becoming a Muslim entails public expression in front of two witnesses of the declaration of faith, the *shahadah*, which is the first pillar of Islam.[9] They declare in Arabic that there is no God but God and that Muhammad is God's messenger. There are discussions among scholars about whether not only the nominal conversion but also the required changes must be made in order to be entitled to be called a Muslim. Debates concern whether the new Muslim should also perform the ritual prayer five times a day, pay the annual alms tax of *zakat*, and fast during the month of Ramadan. As is the case for people born and raised as Muslim, another issue in the debate about whether one can or cannot be considered Muslim is whether one consumes alcohol and eats pork and non-*halal* meat. Although not obligatory, most new Muslims tend to take on Islamic names.[10] In practice, converts—as well as born Muslims—diverge widely in the actual level of commitment.

CONTEXT

Anneke—or Sakina, her new Muslim name—converted in 1991. She had been a convert for seven years when I interviewed her in her home town near Amsterdam, the Netherlands. She was raised as a Roman Catholic but was not practicing. Although there was a vague feeling of "something being out there," she was not much concerned with religion. After secondary school she started working for an international company as an assistant controller. She went on holiday to Tunisia and met a young man whom she liked. He studied mathematics in Paris, and she decided to visit him there. He was a Muslim, and she was astonished that "such an intelligent person" could be a believer. One of her Dutch friends was spiritual and triggered her curiosity toward religion as well. Her friend turned to reincarnation and New Age. She decided to look into Islam and Christianity.

Historically, Islam spread as a result of both militant and peaceful activities. Muslim traders paved the way for men of religion, such as Sufi scholars, and once Muslim institutions were organized, an Islamic ambience was created that became conducive to conversion. This model of conversion from "top to bottom" is not common in the West. In the West, conversion to Islam usually has the character of "bottom to top," which means that witnessing through word and lifestyle induces people to convert, after which an Islamic ambiance is created.[11]

The role of Sufism in spreading Islam to the West is large.[12] A considerable number of Westerners are first attracted to Sufism and then to Islam. While during the 1960s Sufism was part of the "hippie" movement and divorced from its Islamic roots, in the 1990s it became increasingly known as Islamic mysticism.[13] Several *da'wah* or missionary organizations are active in diverse countries and on the Internet. Missionary activism, including the *da'wah* movement of the Tablighi Jama'at, is an important factor in the conversion process.[14] As do most *da'wah* movements, the Tablighi Jama'at calls Muslims to become or remain good Muslims as well as calling non-Muslims to the faith.

Despite the importance of organizational *da'wah*, meeting Muslims in daily life is probably more important for present-day conversions. At present, most conversions take place in relation to the immigrant community in the West. Living in a multicultural environment, meeting Muslims, and particularly finding a Muslim partner trigger interest in Islam that eventually can lead to conversion. This was also the case with Anneke.

It is not only the context of globalization, mobility, and migration that influences the phenomenon of conversion but also historical developments noted by sociologists of religion such as pluralism, secularization, and privatization of religion.[15] As is true for most converts in Europe, but less so in the United States, Anneke was secularized and intended to talk her friend out of religion. Many American converts mention in their testimonies that they intended to talk their friends or fellow students out of Islam. In order to do so, they had to study Islam. They intended to replace Islam by Christianity, but in the course of their missionary activism the reverse happened.

In addition, the general process of modernization and individualization, which makes the individual agent the center of his or her biography, has a direct bearing on conversion.[16] The changed place of religion and the process of individualization have transformed religion and religious goods into matters of individual choice. Actors choose from among several religious options the worldview that suits them best. Ideas of religion as a commodity in the expanding market of religious goods, picked and chosen by religious agents, are particularly applied to New Religious Movements.[17] These theories of the religious market and rational choice can also be applied to Islam.[18] Islam has become one of the players in the religious market in the West, and its messages can make sense to individual converts, as is elaborated below.[19] Whereas Anneke's friend chose New Age, Anneke decided to compare Islam and Christianity.

QUEST AND PROCESS

The Muslim guy from Tunisia whom she visited in Paris did not push religion on Anneke. She started reading and searching and decided to convert. She was convinced by the logic and scientific nature of Islam. Anneke describes her conversion as the outcome of an intellectual search and a rational decision. She married the mathematics student. He was unemployed, refused to help her in household chores, and was not that much of a practicing Muslim either. Anneke was eager to study Islam but had no time for reading. They eventually divorced.

Her parents expected her to leave Islam, but she told her father that you cannot convert just for the sake of a husband. If she would remarry, it should be to a Muslim again. Two years later she considered remarrying her former husband. She decided to consult an imam on the matter, who advised her to do *istikhara* (prayer), a prayer in which she asks God to show her the right way. She had a dream about going to Tunisia, but her ex was not there in her dream. She woke up and thought everything would be all right. She phoned him but he became angry and insulted the imam. She decided it was over. The imam, however, phoned her two weeks later about the results and asked her to come over again. The imam then asked her to marry him. She felt attracted to him but wanted to know him first. She planned regular meetings with the imam and asked him about her rights as a woman, could she work, would he help with the household, what about veiling. Every day, she prepared another list of questions. Finally, she married the imam.

It is clear that in Anneke's case friendship, love, and marriage are important facilitating factors in the conversion process. Yet there are also so-called "cold" conversions. Stefano Allievi distinguishes two main forms of conversion: relational conversions and rational conversions.[20] The rational conversion is not induced by people but by an intellectual search. It can be subdivided into an intellectual, a political, and a mystically oriented route. The relational conversion can be either instrumental or non-instrumental. Non-instrumental relational conversion is induced by relationships with Muslims. Instrumental conversion is usually related to marriage of a man to a Muslim woman—who is not allowed to marry a non-Muslim—and does not necessarily entail a religious transformation. The relational type of conversion seems to be more common among women and the intellectual type among men. Yet, many female converts stress the intellectual character of their search and deny the importance of marriage as a crucial factor. So, usually it is a combination of both intellectual search and meeting Muslims that triggers the desire for conversion.

It is also interesting to note that most converts stress the intellectual route and do not often report mystical or spiritual experiences. Whereas born-again Christians[21] or born-again Muslims[22] detail visions and dreams, Western converts more often detail their intellectual search. This is partly due to the discourse to which they are attracted that emphasizes the logical and scientific character of Islam (see below). This discourse is appealing in light of the rationalized and secularized perspectives with which they are familiar. Yet for some converts, dreams and visions do play a part, mostly for those attracted to mystical forms of Islam. Anneke also had a dream and did *istikhara* prayer after being Muslim for some years. So even if reading and rationality were initially the dominant narrative, visions and dreams might become more prominent later on. We should thus understand conversion as a long-term process.

Conversion may develop through the following stages: "love," "disappointment," and "maturity."[23] At first, many converts are emotionally obsessed with the new religion and want to practice every detail of the Islamic precepts. The second stage is strongly linked to a disappointment with the behaviors and ideas of persons who have been Muslims from birth; some converts tend to turn away from Islam during this stage. During the third stage, many converts search for new understandings of Islamic ideas and attitudes according to the particular cultural context they live in. This can lead to European, Western, or Scandinavian forms of Islam.[24] In Anneke's case, her disappointment was more with her husband, and her husband's lack of commitment to Islam, than with Islam itself. She fell in love again with a devoted Muslim man.

BIOGRAPHY AND CRISIS

Anneke did not have any crises before her conversion but only after becoming acquainted with Islam. After being convinced of "the truth" she decided to become Muslim. But she became very confused and unhappy. She said, "I was just a normal Dutch girl, believing there was something but not knowing what. By reading I realized it was true but I did not like it...because what about the headscarf, what about my family! I did not see the beauty of Islam yet. My brains accepted Islam through reading but I did not like it."

After taking *shahadah*, Anneke was in crisis for some time, not knowing how to give this new conviction a practical place in her life: in her work, in her family, and in her choice of clothing. She was overwhelmed by doubt and did the *shahadah* twice to confirm her sincere wish to continue on the road of Islam.

In many conversion theories, psychological factors and biographical crises make up a major part of the explanation for conversion. Ali Köse studied native British Muslims and applied several psychological and religious theories to his sample of seventy converts.[25] He critically assessed crisis theories with regard to the pre-conversion life histories. In his view, common ideas on conversion as being induced by the moral and religious crises of adolescents or by failed socialization do not hold for Islam.

The most important crisis theory with regard to conversion to Islam is the one developed by Monika Wohlrab-Sahr.[26] She connects conversion to biographical experiences. She defines conversion as the symbolic transformation of experiences of crises. In her research, she found three different realms of problems that were transformed by conversion to Islam. The first type of conversion is related to issues of sexuality and gender relations. Converts experience feelings of personal devaluation with regard to sexuality and gender norms. Female converts mention such problems as broken marriages, promiscuity, and sexual relationships with men from marginal groups. Male converts experience problems with regard to transgression of the male gender identity, like loss of the dominant position in the family and shame inflicted by the sexual conduct of female members of the family. Converts seek new boundaries, rules, and interpretations. Islam offers a clear model that articulates and solves the problem of transgressed sexual norms and uncertain relationships between the sexes. The second scope of problems Wohlrab-Sahr distinguishes is related to social mobility. In the case of a failed attempt at upward social mobility, for example, due to drug addiction and criminal behavior, conversion to Islam can provide an alternative and a new career. Third, she mentions problems related to nationality and ethnicity or problems of "belonging." By converting to Islam, a new kind of belonging and community comes into existence. Islam thus offers converts the possibility to transform experiences of devaluation, degradation, and disintegration.

In Anneke's case, I did not come across such a crisis per se, although in many cases of other Dutch converts I recognize forms of crisis as outlined by Wohlrab-Sahr. We should keep in mind that converts are a heterogeneous group with various trajectories and life experiences. Crisis was important to Anneke but as a stage after conversion, and it led her toward more extensive commitment. Generally, the convert's biography is an important factor not only for understanding the motives for conversion but also for grasping the themes and style of the conversion narrative. In my study of Dutch female converts, it became clear that converts' biographies and their Islamic discourse were intimately connected. Whereas for some women a psychological crisis and medicine addiction made them receptive to the message that Islam is a natural and healthy belief system, for others sexual harassment or divorced parents made them realize the importance of a certain distance between the sexes. What Islam meant to them, and the discourse they constructed, was directly connected to their life stories.

ADVOCATES AND ISLAMIC DISCOURSE

Anneke briefly looked into Christianity, but when she compared the way Jesus is perceived in Christianity with Islam she quickly realized Christianity is not logical. Her first husband occasionally mentioned certain verses of Qu'ran in which scientific discoveries of recent times were already mentioned, such as the development of the embryo. She was very much intrigued by this. He told her that he could not discuss Islam with her because she lacked knowledge. So she started reading and studying and was intellectually convinced. "There is so much wisdom in the Qur'an, its scientific character and they also say that the Qur'an is such a masterpiece of poetry that it cannot be imitated. It must be from God." Despite his initial importance in her conversion process, Anneke's first husband did not become her intellectual and religious guide. Her desire for a teacher was fully realized with her imam husband.

The "push factors" of conversion have been reasonably well studied, but the "pull factors" have received less attention. In regard to the question of why people turn to Islam, that is, what is the specific appeal of Islam, less material is available. This immediately raises the question of "which Islam?" Sufism, which stresses spirituality, has different "religious goods" to offer than modernist Islam, with its emphasis on rationality. Also, the large differences within the group of converts with regard to gender and ethnicity make it difficult to assume that there is a single appeal of Islam.

Like many converts, Anneke is attracted to the discourse on Islam as a scientific and logical system of beliefs. This modernist interpretation of Islam as a rational religion is prevalent on the Internet.[27] This discourse shows recurrent patterns. First, Islam is perceived as the ideal social and moral religion, providing a stable family life and regulating the relationships between the sexes. Second, Islam is perceived as a pervasive, practical religion that is embedded in daily life. Third, Islam is perceived as a rational, scientific, and logical religion. This last discourse contrasts Islam and Christianity, using such examples as the concept of the Trinity versus unity of God; Jesus as the son of God versus Jesus as a prophet; the Bible as written and changed by human hand versus the unchanged perfect state of the Qur'an; and the presence versus absence of the idea of original sin. Last but not least, the Bible is in contradiction with modern science whereas the Qur'an is held to be in correspondence with science. Also, the direct accessibility of God without mediators makes Islam a rational and undeniable truth, for instance, for some former Roman Catholics who disagreed with Catholic tenets about the need for a priest to mediate.[28]

A considerable number of people are attracted to Sufism. For example, some "hippies" of the 1960s and 1970s, disillusioned with the Western material way of life, decided to convert.[29] Sufism can fill a spiritual vacuum created by such ideologies as secularism, socialism, and modernism. Also, a significant number of Western intellectuals converted to Sufism, including the late French philosopher Rene Guenon. His teachings on Sufism have become a model for Europeans who are interested in the spiritual dimension of Islam.[30] Currently there are many Sufi groups in Europe and America that attract converts to Islam.

Robert Dannin investigated the appeal of Islam for a specific group of converts, incarcerated African Americans in a New York prison.[31] Islam offers the prisoners an activity structure such as prayers and lessons and an alternative social space within the confinement of the prison walls. The new Islamic identity also means a fresh start. The Islamic counterculture is attractive because, according to Dannin, it has the power to transcend the material and often brutally inhuman conditions of the prison.[32] Aminah McCloud understands the conversion of African Americans to Islam as a response to American racism.[33] Islam promises a new identity, a feeling of "somebodiness," denied by the dominant culture. Conversion brings liberation from Christian domination, perceived as the root of their oppression because of its glorification of suffering and promise of redemption in the hereafter.

Allievi distinguishes different "attractions" for the various conversion itineraries.[34] Whereas "relational converts" are attracted to general aspects such as belonging to a different culture and having a sense of community, "rational converts" have a more specific Islamic discourse. Islam is perceived as clear, simple, and rational. For politically inclined converts, Islam provides a "spiritualization" of politics. For the mystically inclined, Islam has a wide appeal as well. It is precisely Islam's broad spectrum of offerings, religiously, ideologically, and in terms of orthopraxis, that constitutes its appeal to many converts. This is a good reminder that scholars should not essentialize Islam; they should systematically analyze what Islam has to offer diverse groups of converts at different times.

Despite the various Islamic "offerings," a common observation is that Islam appeals because it gives converts the greatest possible contrast with the culture they come from.[35] In particular, converts who are critical of Western society are fascinated by and attracted to the otherness of Islam. It becomes an ideological and political framework from which they criticize Western society. According to Wohlrab-Sahr, conversion becomes "a means of articulating within one's own social context—one's distance from this context and one's conflictive relationship towards it."[36] This conflictive relationship can be the result of a (politically) critical stance or the result of a sense of marginalization. Gabrielle Hofmann also relates Islam's attraction to the convert's possibility to provoke society at large.[37] On the other hand, Hofmann[38] as well as Allievi[39] observes that many of Islam's offerings, particularly relating to gender issues, are close to what former generations in the West found self-evident. Islam can also appeal because it restores familiar notions of gender and the family.

GENDER

Anneke was much disappointed by her first husband's refusal to do any household chores and admires her present husband for his cooking abilities. Most questions she asked her second husband before marriage were related to gender issues: Was she allowed to work? Did she have to veil? Would he help in the household? He convinced her of his idea that women are crucial in Islam. They are not considered less than men. Her husband explained that women are equal but different. She had always felt that way. She hesitated to answer my question about the compatibility of Islam and emancipation. Knowing the common feminist interpretation of emancipation, she eventually answered that women's first task is to stay at home with the children. "Maybe this is against feminist ideas, but I think it is better."

Many female converts eventually find Islamic ideas related to sexuality, the construction of gender, and motherhood appealing. Many female converts feel that the freedom in the West is exaggerated, particularly regarding sexual freedom. Islamic rules, if applied properly, contribute to clarity and stability in familial and marital life. Besides, several converts feel that in Islam they are less perceived as sex objects than in the West. Second, with regard to the construction of gender, converts are convinced of the equality of men and women in Islam. Whereas they hold that the sexes are of equal value, most converts do not consider them of equal nature. They adhere to the concepts of "equal but different" or of "gender equity."[40]

Hofmann focuses on female converts and issues of gender in Germany. She understands female conversion against the background of the process of individualization.[41] Hofmann argues that the process of female individualization shows ruptures and contradictions. Women are strongly connected to the family, which is associated with such values as belonging and connectedness. These values contrast with dominant "modern" values such as rationality, individual performance, and personal perseverance. Women in the West are confronted with conflicting expectations at different stages of their lives. They are brought up with ideals of individual autonomy but are expected to put these ideals aside once they begin raising a family. If they decide to stay at home when they have small children, they experience the lack of esteem for this decision in society at large and as a result of their own socialization. According to Hofmann, the German-Islamic discourse, which is the hybrid discourse of German Muslims, particularly of converts, offers a solution to these conflicting demands. It not only offers clear concepts of marriage and motherhood but also greatly values these states.

Gender equity is not only part of the Islamic discourse but is also plausible in light of German "cultural knowledge." This cultural knowledge about essential manhood and womanhood, however, is no longer uncontested. German-Islamic discourse restores these ideas back to their original position of "truth." Women regain the possibility to live according to their "feminine nature." German-Islamic discourse has a critical stance toward German society. It partly uses a feminist discourse and criticizes the prevalence of "male" norms and the devaluation of "female" qualities. It also attacks the "Western exploitation of female sexuality and the marketing of the female body." These critiques are close to radical feminist ideas. Yet, whereas radical feminism tries to change patriarchal relationships, the German-Islamic discourse tries to restore the original "natural" order. These critical yet familiar views of gender and sexuality make the Islamic discourse attractive and plausible to German female converts.

Hofmann's ideas are valuable for understanding Anneke's ambivalence toward feminist ideas that she partly embraces. Whereas she assertively questions her rights as a
woman and insists on being assisted by her husband and having the right to work outside the home, she embraces the concept of equity and feels women's primary tasks are at
home. The ideas of women being complementary but of equal value are strongly held by
many Dutch, German, and Scandinavian converts.[42] Yet an Islamic feminist discourses is
also gaining ground among converts that differs from this essentialist gender discourse
in which men and women are regarded as having innate qualities. Feminist interpretations of the Qur'an by Asma Barlas and Amina Wadud[43] have inspired other converted
intellectuals to reformulate gender issues. Some converts move over time from an equity
approach to a feminist understanding and critical reading of the Qur`an.[44] For exam-
ple, one of the Dutch converts I interviewed started as an "equal rights" feminist. After
becoming a Muslim, she was inspired by ideas about the innate complementary nature
of the sexes. Presently she is scrutinizing the Qur'an and formulating Islamic notions of
gender that are close to her initial concept of equality.

COMMITMENT AND CONSEQUENCES

Anneke initially found it difficult to pray five times a day, but now it has become an
important habit and she cannot imagine her life without this daily ritual. She tries
to overcome the biggest obstacle of all: veiling. "I used to wear very short clothes,
leather trousers....Even my mother used to be ashamed of my miniskirts. Now
she is ashamed again by my appearance." She is intellectually convinced that veiling is a commandment of God. She exchanged her very short skirts for a wide and
long outfit, but it took her a long time to adapt to an appearance that she herself
considers Islamically correct. It has been one of her main struggles in embodying
Islam. Because she herself found veiling the most terrible consequence of becoming Muslim, she understands her relatives' disgust. She tries to work out fashionable ways of veiling and dressing. Her imam husband did not push veiling, although
he heard comments from his community. They went to Mecca, and Anneke slowly
got used to veiling during her stay of almost a month. She decided not to uncover
anymore. Her parents were scared to death during the first marriage but even more
with this bearded imam and her veiling. Her parents were ashamed to walk beside
their veiled daughter. At work she eventually managed by careful maneuvering to get
the veil accepted. She also had to face the Christmas holidays, parties, drinking or
serving alcohol, and all the other familiar problems with non-Muslim relatives and
colleagues.

Conversion to Islam is a process of embodying religious practices and rituals. It
involves taking up new bodily and ritual practices pertaining to praying, fasting, and
food.[45] In addition, important markers of identity are often changed such as one's name
and appearance, including *hijaab*, the veil, or occasionally *niqaab*, the veil fully covering

the body and the face. Moreover, converting frequently leads to changing social and cultural practices, for example, in relation to celebrations or contact with the opposite sex. Whereas for some new Muslims conversion is radical, others slowly transform aspects of their identity and practice. Converts often say they are like newborns who slowly get used to learning to practice Islamic rituals and behavior. It takes time to adapt and develop a Muslim habitus. Yet many converts do not give themselves much time to embody Muslim lifestyles and are eager to practice all at once. Anneke quickly picked up the habits of fasting and praying, but it took her many years to adapt to veiling. She is still not happy with the way she dresses and feels it should be "more conservative."

Veiling is a condensed symbol of embodying Islam. It means taking on a visible marker of Islam and publicly declaring the new identity. Male converts often trim their beard, but this is a less visible marker of Islam. For female converts, donning the veil often marks a stage of "coming out." Not all converts decide to veil; not all are convinced it is necessary to do so. If converts are convinced they should veil, it can be a difficult struggle, as Anneke's story makes clear. Veiling can be a sacrifice and an enormous source of conflict with people in one's environment. Relatives often indicate their acceptance of conversion and veiling by saying, "I don't mind walking beside her." For most relatives, it takes a while before they dare to walk beside a veiled person. Anneke's relatives were not yet in this stage of acceptance. After starting to wear the veil, converts relate two major changes in the way they are treated: they are considered less intelligent, and they are perceived as foreigners. People react to them as if the veil "is squeezing our brains so that they no longer receive oxygen," as a Dutch convert expressed. Female converts also relate several incidents in which they are treated as foreigners because, by definition, "Islam is the belief of foreigners." Particularly in the labor market, several Dutch women have faced discrimination as a result of wearing the veil.[46]

This strong reaction is related to several factors. First, the veil is perceived as the most visible symbol of female degradation, a condition that marks the "World of Islam" but is alien to the West. Second, the veil is a symbol of foreignness. Parents are rightly concerned that their daughters might face discrimination. Third, the veil is considered "so ugly." Here, ideas on showing and hiding beauty strongly diverge: Muslim converts' concepts of concealment radically oppose Western notions of marketing female beauty. Western male relatives, in particular, express a feeling of affront. Veiling by female relatives is interpreted by male relatives as an accusation of their being sexually aggressive. An uncle had assumed a large part of the upbringing of his niece after her father's death. He no longer visits his niece since she started veiling in front of him. From the role of caretaker, he felt he was put at the level of a sexually aggressive outsider, and he stated, "I am not going to assault her!" The interaction between the sexes generally constitutes a crucial difference between Western and Muslim cultural practice. The introduction of Muslim forms of segregation, whether in space or in veiling, are not only considered conservative but also forms by which male–female relationships are "sexualized."

For most converts, becoming Muslim eventually entails changing many aspects of daily comportment and cultural practices that might conflict with their social environment. Many converts take on new Muslim names. Some use the new name along with their old name, while others reject their original name and only use their Muslim name. Changing this important marker of identity shocks the family, which feels like they are losing their daughter or son. Practices related to food may become sensitive issues, depending on the strictness of the converts and the acceptance of the parents. Refusing to eat pork is not a problem in most families. Insisting on ritually slaughtered *halal* meat is more disturbing. Refusing all products containing animal fat is troublesome. A related issue concerns alcohol. Converts differ in their attitude toward alcohol. Some simply abstain but do not mind others drinking alcohol. Others do not buy and offer alcohol at their parties but allow guests to bring their own drinks. Some refuse to be present at any party where alcohol is consumed. Celebrations such as Christmas, Easter, and birthday parties can be sensitive matters as well. Converts also have to develop their own style of celebrating Muslim festive occasions such as the Feast of Sacrifice (Id al-Adha) or Id al-Fitr.

DISCOURSES, IDENTITIES AND EMBODIED PIETY

Anneke stressed that the longer she is Muslim, the more relaxation and peace of mind she has found. With regard to veiling, she says, "You have to ask and search but on the other hand you should also be able to accept. I can tell you many reasons why the veil is obligatory but all the reasons I will give you I could counter with arguments. In the end you simply have to accept, 'this is the way God wants it to be.' Islam is the most important thing in my life. I am engaged with it the whole day. As a Muslim you are never bored." After years of struggle Anneke is calm and at ease with her new lifestyle and identity. This feeling of rest, which is expressed in her Muslim name, Sakina, was the most important experience gained from becoming Muslim.

To most non-Muslim observers, Anneke's choice and long-term struggle to veil, her eventual peace of mind, and her "submission" might be unintelligible. They might interpret these acts as contrary to her own interests as a well-educated modern woman. In order not to fall prey to arguments such as "false consciousness," "lack of intelligence," and "curbed agency," however, Anneke's own views and discourse on "active engagement," as well as her sense of "feeling at rest," need to be taken seriously.

In order to comprehend conversion as a meaningful process—combining the insider's and outsider's perspectives—I propose combining three sources of inspiration: the well-established research within conversion theories on identity and the equally important work on conversion discourse, in addition to the more recent anthropological work on piety and embodied agency.[47] Several conversion theories concentrate on functions of conversion in solving biographical problems. Others focus on the plausibility of Islamic discourse for individual converts and the important functions of *da'wah* in the conversion process. Both approaches are important and need to be combined. In addition, a more experience-near focus on piety and embodying Islam is necessary. For many converts, the pious construction of self is the most rewarding aspect of conversion. Yet, the gratifying nature of the pursuit of pious perfection is not well theorized within conversion studies, particularly in the case of women and Islam. Anthropological approaches toward piety and agency can be helpful in understanding the enduring importance of converting.

The first approach (that of religious scholars, psychologists, and sociologists) deals with conversion as creating or gaining a new identity. It analyzes biographies, the factors that can explain people's propensities to convert and the crisis experiences they have had. It focuses on the problems converts have encountered and on how conversion has given them a new sense of self and helped them to create a new identity or a new form of belonging. It analyzes motives, routes, and themes in converts' life stories that make them susceptible to conversion. Although this approach does highlight the fact that conversion can become meaningful in a person's life, the reason why individuals have opted for this particular solution, conversion to Islam, is not always clear. What is meaningful in the message of Islam? Why Islam and which Islam? Which discourses are the individuals themselves creating? This approach thus leaves aside the different kinds of Islamic discourses that converts are attracted to.

The second approach of scholars of Islamic studies, historians, and anthropologists deals with the diverse discourses and narratives produced in the communities of converts. This approach urges a strategy to critically deconstruct the discourse and not to confuse conversion narratives with conversion motives. The approach focuses on how discourses and stories are created and recreated in converts' communities and how they become meaningful in communicating conversion experiences. It analyzes the message of Islam and how this can be meaningful for individuals or groups. Although this approach does analyze how Islamic discourses are created, spread, and become meaningful, the biographical aspects of the receivers are not clearly included in the perspective. How an individual comes to be attracted to these discourses, how it makes sense in their unfolding life stories, and how the discourses are turned into lived experiences are questions beyond the scope of this approach.

Both approaches are important and valid in themselves. Yet, the combination of insights from both identity studies and discourse analyses generates a more complex understanding. We need to understand both the receivers and the messages. Conversion is a multilayered, continuous process in which new identities and discourses are produced and reproduced. Some individuals may become receptive to conversion through personal trajectories and biographical experiences. Yet, the new message must be plausible. Islam and Islamic discourse may be plausible to individuals for different reasons. Individuals can be addressed by Islamic discourse in manifold aspects of their identities. People convert to Islam as persons with specific professional, religious, gender, racial, and ethnic identities. Various aspects of a person's identity inform discourse, and discourse appeals to different aspects of their identity.[48]

Theories on Muslim piety[49] can help to bridge and enrich the approaches to identity and discourses. Theories on piety can enlighten the process by which receivers make sense of the messages and turn them into lived experiences and practices. First, these theories on piety analyze the continuous effort to embody Islam in everyday life. Second, Saba Mahmood's work provides a framework to deconstruct binary opposition between agency and submission. And third, the work on piety provides an insider's understanding of the rewarding nature of religious devotion.

As Bryan Turner argues, piety is about the construction of distinctive lifestyles of new religious tastes and preferences.[50] The "pietization" of everyday life is a continuous effort on the part of believers. Piety is not a matter of fact or end result of practicing and being committed but a learned practice or training that needs to be regenerated daily. Fasting, praying, and veiling are not only outwards signs of piety but become important means to cultivate devotion. By praying and veiling, devotees not only express their new conviction but by doing so they become pious Muslims. Piety is a technology of the self designed to produce religious excellence.[51] Anneke's struggle to veil is thus a striving toward greater religious perfection. It is not solely a symbol of her new religious identity or an act corresponding to a certain discourse but also a way to create a pious self. She does not merely veil because she has become a Muslim, but veiling, praying, and other religious rituals constitute her daily engagements and techniques to embody Islam.

By looking into the pious "techniques of the body"[52] and modes of self-fashioning, the dichotomy between agency and submission can be mediated, if not removed. Particularly within the study of women and Islam or conversion by women to Islam, agency is narrowed down to forms of resistance. Yet, as Mahmood has analyzed for the adherents of the Egyptian piety movement, agency is the capacity for action, and people's ability to craft a moral, virtuous self is such an act of agency.[53] Piety is an active engagement in which sacrifice, submission, and agency can come together. It entails a measure of self-control and active commitment, and the outcome can be formulated as the wish to submit to God's will. The struggle to veil or to submit can be an act of self-fulfillment.

The constitution of a pious self is an important and rewarding practice for many devout Muslims. It is a self-controlled form of sacrifice and a spiritual remaking. The religious devotion and spiritual reward of being committed is often expressed as "peace of mind," "calmness," or "finally feeling at ease." For many converts, this is what conversion is all about. The active construction of a pious self yields enormous satisfaction and peace of mind. It is not passive obedience or submission but an active struggle to form a pious disposition, a fuller development of self by devotional practices.

Conversion does not stop at the moment of embracing Islam and is not solely a mental activity of accepting a new belief. It requires the embodiment of new social and religious practices. Within this process of embodiment and learning or ingraining new practices, a new habitus—ideas, insights, tastes, and preferences—is developing. The budding preferences can generate receptivity toward new voices within Islamic discourse or invite the converts to formulate new insights themselves. In different periods of converts' lives, diverse discourses and practices may make sense. The approach to conversion as an active process of embodying pious practices brings to the fore the idea that identities and discourses are implicated in each other. Converts engage in religious practices related to discourses that are meaningful to them. Embodying the new practices can lead to renewed experiences, interpretations, and negotiations of existing discourses. It is a continuous interplay. In their unfolding biographies, converts remake and negotiate discourses which in turn inform the process of identity construction and pious remaking.

This approach understands conversion as a complex contextual experience and long-term process that involves the construction of identities, discourses, and pious embodiment. The approach sensitizes us to the different ways in which converts make sensible choices—choices that can change over time. In addition, the combined insights of identity constructions, discourse formations, and pious subjectivities help us to escape essentializing approaches toward Islam and gender. Moreover, the proposed approach gives a more experience-near understanding of the rewards of active submission to God, the literal meaning of becoming Muslim.

NOTES

1. James A. Beckford, "Accounting for Conversion," *British Journal of Sociology* 29, no. 2 (1978): 249–262; Peter Stromberg, *Language and Self-Transformation: A Study of the Christian Conversion Narrative* (Cambridge: Cambridge University Press, 1993).
2. Lewis R. Rambo, *Understanding Religious Conversion* (New Haven: Yale University Press, 1993).
3. The word "conversion" should be read as "conversion" throughout the text. In order to be in line with the terminology of the other authors of this Handbook, I choose to use the concept of conversion. Yet, with an eye to the discussion outlined in this paragraph, the term is problematic and preferably should be placed between quotation marks.
4. Karin van Nieuwkerk, "'Islam is your birthright': Conversion, Reversion and Alternation: The Case of New Muslims in the West," in *Conversion in Antiquity and Middle Ages*, ed. W. J. van Bekkum, J. N. Bremmer, and A. L. Molendijk (Leuven: Peeters, 2006), 151–165.
5. Yasin Dutton, "Conversion to Islam: Quranic Paradigm," in *Religious Conversion, Contemporary Practices and Controversies*, ed. C. Lamb and M. Bryant (London: Cassell, 1999), 151–153.
6. Bernard Uhde, "Enlightened Christians or Anonymous Muslims: Some Remarks on Unnoticed Conversion," a paper presented at the Comparing Religious Conversion and Crypto-Religion in Christian and Muslim Societies Conference, Freiburg, June 28, 2008.
7. See also Van Nieuwkerk, "Islam is your birthright," 151–165. The website The True Religion no longer exists.
8. Dudley J. Woodberry, "Conversion in Islam," in *Handbook of Religious Conversion*, ed. H. Newton Malony and S. Southard (Birmingham AL: Religious Education Press, 1992), 23, 35.
9. The other pillars are prayer, almsgiving, fasting, and pilgrimage to Mecca.
10. Dutton, "Conversion to Islam," 153–156.
11. Woodberry, "Conversion in Islam."
12. Dutton, "Conversion to Islam."

13. Haifaa Jawad, "Female Conversion to Islam: The Sufi Paradigm," in *Women Embracing Islam: Gender and Conversion in the West*, ed. Karin van Nieuwkerk (Austin: University of Texas Press, 2006).

14. Larry Poston, *Islamic Da`wah in the West: Muslim Missionary Activity and the Dynamics of Conversion to Islam* (Oxford: Oxford University Press, 1992); Yvonne Yazbeck Haddad, "The Quest for Peace in Submission: Reflections on the Journey of American Women Converts to Islam," in *Women Embracing Islam: Gender and Conversion in the West*, ed. Karin van Nieuwkerk (Austin: University of Texas Press, 2006).

15. Thomas Luckmann, "The Religious Situation in Europe: The Background to Contemporary Conversions," *Social Compass* 46, no. 3 (1999): 251–258; Stefano Allievi, *Les Convertis à l'Islam: Les nouveaux musulmans d'Europe* (Paris: L'Harmattan, 1998).

16. Gabrielle Hofmann, *Muslimin werden: Frauen in Deutschland konvertieren zum Islam* (Frankfurt: Universität Frankfurt, 1997).

17. Steve Bruce, *Choice and Religion: A Critique of Rational Choice Theory* (Oxford: Oxford University Press, 1999); Steve Bruce, *God is Dead: Secularization in the West* (Oxford: Blackwell Publishing, 2002); Rodney Stark and R. Finke, *Acts of Faith: Explaining the Human Side of Religion* (Berkeley and Los Angeles: University of California Press, 2000).

18. Allievi, *Les Convertis à l'Islam*; Monika Wohlrab-Sahr, "Symbolizing Distance: Conversion to Islam in Germany and the United States," in *Gender and Conversion to Islam in the West*, ed. Karin van Nieuwkerk (Austin: University of Texas Press, 2006).

19. Karin van Nieuwkerk, "Biography and Choice: Female Converts to Islam in the Netherlands," *Islam and Christian-Muslim Relations* 19, no. 4 (2008): 429–445.

20. Allievi, *Les Convertis à l'Islam*.

21. Stromberg, *Language and Self-Transformation*; Susan F. Harding, "Convicted by the Holy Spirit: The Rhetoric of Fundamental Baptist Conversion," *American Ethnologist* 14, no. 1 (1987): 167–181.

22. Karin van Nieuwkerk, "Piety, Penitence and Gender: The Case of Repentant Artists in Egypt," *Journal for Islamic Studies* 28 (2008): 37–65.

23. Anne Sofie Roald, "The Shaping of a Scandinavian 'Islam': Converts and Gender Equal Opportunity," in *Women Embracing Islam: Gender and Conversion in the West*, ed. Karin van Nieuwkerk (Austin: University of Texas Press, 2006).

24. Stefano Allievi, "Converts and the Making of European Islam," *ISIM Newsletter* 11 (2002): 1, 26; Anne Sofie Roald, *New Muslims in the European Context: The Experiences of Scandinavian Converts* (Leiden: Brill, 2004).

25. Ali Köse, *Conversion to Islam: A Study of Native British Converts* (London: Kegan Paul International, 1996).

26. Monika Wohlrab-Sahr, *Konversion zum Islam in Deutschland und den USA* (Frankfurt: Campus Verlag, 1998).

27. Karin van Nieuwkerk, "Gender, Conversion and Islam: A Comparison of Online and Off-line Conversion Narratives," in *Women Embracing Islam: Gender and Conversion in the West*, ed. Karin van Nieuwkerk (Austin: University of Texas Press, 2006).

28. Allievi, *Les Convertis à l'Islam*; Hofmann, *Muslimin werden*. Van Nieuwkerk, "Gender, Conversion and Islam"; Haddad, "The Quest for Peace in Submission"; Köse, *Conversion to Islam*.

29. Jawad, "Female Conversion to Islam."

30. Köse, *Conversion to Islam*.

31. Robert Dannin, "Island in a Sea of Ignorance: Dimensions of the Prison Mosque," in *Making Muslim Space in North America and Europe*, ed. B. Daly Metcalf (Berkeley and Los Angeles: University of California Press, 1996).
32. Ibid., 144.
33. Aminah Beverley McCloud, "African-American Muslim Women," in *The Muslims of America*, ed. Y. Yazbeck Haddad (Oxford: Oxford University Press, 1991).
34. Allievi, *Les Convertis à l'Islam*.
35. Ibid.; Hofmann, *Muslimin werden*.
36. Monika Wohlrab-Sahr, "Conversion to Islam: Between Syncretism and Symbolic Battle," *Social Compass* 46, no. 3 (1999): 351–362, at 352.
37. Hofmann, *Muslimin werden*, 121.
38. Ibid.
39. Allievi, *Les Convertis à l'Islam*.
40. Madeleine Sultán, "Choosing Islam: A Study of Swedish Converts," *Social Compass* 46 no. 3 (1999): 325–337; Karin van Nieuwkerk, "Veils and Wooden Clogs Do Not Go Together," *Ethnos* 69, no. 2 (2004): 229–247; Roald, "The Shaping of a Scandinavian 'Islam.'"
41. Hofmann, *Muslimin werden*.
42. Van Nieuwkerk, "Veils and Wooden Clogs"; Roald, "The Shaping of a Scandinavian 'Islam.'"
43. Amina Wadud, *Qur'an and Woman* (New York: Oxford University Press, 1999).
44. Margot Badran, "Feminism and Conversion: Comparing British, Dutch and South African Life Stories," in *Women Embracing Islam: Gender and Conversion in the West*, ed. Karin van Nieuwkerk (Austin: University of Texas Press, 2006).
45. Nicole Bourque, "How Deborah Became Aisha: The Conversion Process and the Creation of Female Muslim Identity," in *Women Embracing Islam: Gender and Conversion in the West*, ed. Karin van Nieuwkerk (Austin: University of Texas Press, 2006).
46. Van Nieuwkerk, "Veils and Wooden Clogs."
47. Saba Mahmood, *Politics of Piety: The Islamic Revival and the Feminist Subject* (Princeton: Princeton University Press, 2005).
48. Karin van Nieuwkerk, "Introduction: Gender and Conversion to Islam," in *Women Embracing Islam: Gender and Conversion in the West*, ed. Karin van Nieuwkerk (Austin: University of Texas Press, 2006).
49. Mahmood, *Politics of Piety*; Saba Mahmood, "Feminist Theory, Embodiment, and the Docile Agent: Some Reflections on the Egyptian Islamic Revival," *Cultural Anthropology* 6, no. 2 (2001): 202–236; Bryan Turner, "Introduction: The Price of Piety," *Contemporary Islam* 2, no. 1 (2008): 1–7.
50. Turner, "Introduction: The Price of Piety," 2.
51. Ibid., 3.
52. See also Julius Bautista, "The Meta-Theory of Piety: Reflections on the Work of Saba Mahmood," *Contemporary Islam* 2, no. 1 (2008): 75–85.
53. Mahmood, *Politics of Piety*; Mahmood, "Feminist Theory."

BIBLIOGRAPHY

Allievi, Stefano. *Les Convertis à l'Islam: Les nouveaux musulmans d'Europe.* Paris: L'Harmattan, 1998.

——. "Converts and the Making of European Islam." *ISIM Newsletter* 11 (2002): 1, 26.

——. "The Shifting Significance of the *Halal/Haram* Frontier: Narratives on the *Hijab* and Other Issues." In *Women Embracing Islam: Gender and Conversion in the West*, ed. Karin van Nieuwkerk, 120–150. Austin: University of Texas Press, 2006.

Badran, Margot. "Feminism and Conversion: Comparing British, Dutch and South African Life Stories." In *Women Embracing Islam: Gender and Conversion in the West*, ed. Karin van Nieuwkerk, 192–230. Austin: University of Texas Press, 2006.

Bautista, Julius. "The Meta-Theory of Piety: Reflections on the Work of Saba Mahmood." *Contemporary Islam* 2, no. 1 (2008): 75–85.

Beckford, James A. "Accounting for Conversion." *British Journal of Sociology* 29, no. 2 (1978): 249–262.

Bourque, Nicole. "How Deborah Became Aisha: The Conversion Process and the Creation of Female Muslim Identity." In *Women Embracing Islam: Gender and Conversion in the West*, ed. Karin van Nieuwkerk, 223–250. Austin: University of Texas Press, 2006.

Bruce, Steve. *"Choice and Religion" A Critique of Rational Choice Theory*. Oxford: Oxford University Press, 1999.

——. *God is Dead: Secularization in the West*. Oxford: Blackwell Publishing, 2002.

Dannin, Robert. "Island in a Sea of Ignorance: Dimensions of the Prison Mosque." In *Making Muslim Space in North America and Europe*, ed. B. Daly Metcalf, 131–147. Berkeley and Los Angeles: University of California Press, 1996.

Dutton, Yasin. "Conversion to Islam: Quranic Paradigm." In *Religious Conversion, Contemporary Practices and Controversies*, ed. C. Lamb and M. Bryant, 151–166. London: Cassell, 1999.

Haddad, Yvonne Yazbeck. "The Quest for Peace in Submission: Reflections on the Journey of American Women Converts to Islam." In *Women Embracing Islam: Gender and Conversion in the West*, ed. Karin van Nieuwkerk, 19–48. Austin: University of Texas Press, 2006.

Harding, Susan. F. "Convicted by the Holy Spirit: The Rhetoric of Fundamental Baptist Conversion." *American Ethnologist* 14, no. 1 (1987): 167–181.

Hofmann, Gabrielle. *Muslimin werden: Frauen in Deutschland konvertieren zum Islam*. Frankfurt: Universität Frankfurt, 1997.

Jawad, Haifaa. "Female Conversion to Islam: The Sufi Paradigm." In *Women Embracing Islam: Gender and Conversion in the West*, ed. Karin van Nieuwkerk, 153–172. Austin: University of Texas Press, 2006.

Köse, Ali. *Conversion to Islam: A Study of Native British Converts*. London: Kegan Paul International, 1996.

Luckmann, Thomas. "The Religious Situation in Europe: The Background to Contemporary Conversions." *Social Compass* 46, no. 3 (1999): 251–258.

Mahmood, Saba. "Feminist Theory, Embodiment, and the Docile Agent: Some Reflections on the Egyptian Islamic Revival." *Cultural Anthropology* 6, no. 2 (2001): 202–236.

——. *Politics of Piety: The Islamic Revival and the Feminist Subject*. Princeton: Princeton University Press, 2005.

McCloud, Aminah Beverley. "African-American Muslim Women." In *The Muslims of America*, ed. Y. Yazbeck Haddad, 177–188. Oxford: Oxford University Press, 1991.

Poston, Larry. *Islamic Da'wah in the West: Muslim Missionary Activity and the Dynamics of Conversion to Islam*. Oxford: Oxford University Press, 1992.

Rambo, Lewis R. *Understanding Religious Conversion*. New Haven: Yale University Press, 1993.

Roald, Anne. S. *New Muslims in the European Context: The Experiences of Scandinavian Converts*. Leiden: Brill, 2004.

——. "The Shaping of a Scandinavian 'Islam': Converts and Gender Equal Opportunity." In *Women Embracing Islam: Gender and Conversion in the West*, ed. Karin van Nieuwkerk, 48–71. Austin: University of Texas Press, 2006.

Stark, Rodney, and R. Finke. *Acts of Faith: Explaining the Human Side of Religion*. Berkeley and Los Angeles: University of California Press, 2000.

Stromberg, Peter. *Language and Self-Transformation: A Study of the Christian Conversion Narrative*. Cambridge: Cambridge University Press, 1993.

Sultán, Madeleine. "Choosing Islam: A Study of Swedish Converts." *Social Compass* 46 no. 3 (1999): 325–337.

Turner, Bryan. "Introduction: The Price of Piety." *Contemporary Islam* 2, no. 1 (2008): 1–7.

Uhde, Bernard. "Enlightened Christians or Anonymous Muslims: Some Remarks on Unnoticed Conversion." Paper presented at the Comparing Religious Conversion and Crypto-Religion in Christian and Muslim Societies conference, Freiburg, June 26–28, 2008.

Van Nieuwkerk, Karin. "Biography and Choice: Female Converts to Islam in the Netherlands." *Islam and Christian-Muslim Relations* 19, no. 4 (2008): 429–445.

——. "Gender, Conversion and Islam: A Comparison of Online and Off-line Conversion Narratives." In *Women Embracing Islam: Gender and Conversion in the West*, ed. Karin van Nieuwkerk, 95–120. Austin: University of Texas Press, 2006.

——. "Introduction: Gender and Conversion to Islam." In *Women Embracing Islam: Gender and Conversion in the West*, ed. Karin van Nieuwkerk, 1–18. Austin: University of Texas Press, 2006.

——. "'Islam is your birthright': Conversion, Reversion and Alternation: The Case of New Muslims in the West." In *Conversion in Antiquity and Middle Ages*, ed. W. J. van Bekkum, J. N. Bremmer, and A. L. Molendijk, 151–167. Leuven: Peeters, 2006.

——. "Piety, Penitence and Gender: The Case of Repentant Artists in Egypt." *Journal for Islamic Studies* 28 (2008): 37–65.

——. "Veils and Wooden Clogs Do Not Go Together." *Ethnos* 69, no. 2 (2004): 229–247.

Wadud, Amina. *Qur'an and Woman*. New York: Oxford University Press, 1999.

Wohlrab-Sahr, Monika. "Conversion to Islam: Between Syncretism and Symbolic Battle." *Social Compass* 46, no. 3 (1999): 351–362.

——. *Konversion zum Islam in Deutschland und den USA*. Frankfurt: Campus Verlag, 1998.

——. "Symbolizing Distance: Conversion to Islam in Germany and the United States." In *Gender and Conversion to Islam in the West*, ed. Karin van Nieuwkerk, 71–93. Austin: University of Texas Press, 2006.

Woodberry J. Dudley. "Conversion in Islam." In *Handbook of Religious Conversion*, ed. H. Newton Malony and S. Southard, 22–41. Birmingham AL: Religious Education Press, 1992.

CHAPTER 29

···

CONVERSION TO NEW RELIGIOUS MOVEMENTS

···

DOUGLAS E. COWAN

CONVERSION FRAMED AND REFRAMED: THREE VIGNETTES

···

ELAINE first met members of the Church of Jesus Christ of Latter-day Saints when she was 13. Although she had seen some negative media coverage of Mormon missionaries and knew that her father disapproved of the Mormon Church, Elaine accepted a friend's invitation to learn more about them. Risking her parents' further disapproval, she began going to Latter-day Saint meetings, then held in a rented community hall. "There were about ten or fifteen members that attended at this time," she writes in her testimony. "I couldn't believe that a church could be so small. The members were so warm and friendly that I felt that I'd gone there every Sunday."[1] As her interest in the church grew, she realized that "these people were different and I wanted to be different with them."[2] Despite her parents' skepticism, she continued to attend until one night, as she had been encouraged to do by her Mormon friends, she prayed to understand the deeper meaning of her experience. Waking from a particularly vivid dream, she remembers, "I had this wonderful feeling that this Church had to be true. I got down on my knees and asked Heavenly Father if this could be true and that feeling just intensified."[3] Since that time, she has been a devout member of the Church of Jesus Christ of Latter-day Saints.

Sarah was a twenty-something student at a large American university when she first encountered modern Paganism. Raised in a nominally Catholic home, her dominant religious memories are of catechism classes at a large urban congregation, confirmation at age 13 and occasional church attendance on holy days of obligation for a few years after that. Unsatisfied with the church's position on a variety of issues, she stopped attending in her late teens and began to describe herself as "spiritual, but not religious." A few years later, while browsing a used bookshop near her campus, she found copies of Starhawk's

The Spiral Dance (1989) and Marion Zimmer Bradley's *The Mists of Avalon* (1982), two of the most important texts in the modern revival of goddess worship. Reading them late into the evening, she felt a connection to the beliefs and practices of contemporary Paganism—carefully described by Starhawk's handbook and lyrically evoked in Bradley's novel—that she had never experienced in the Christian church. Seeking out more and more books on Wicca and Witchcraft, she eventually joined a study group organized through a local occult shop and realized that she was not alone, neither in her feelings of disenchantment with the dominant religion nor her excitement at this new religious discovery. Now, many years later, she is the High Priestess of her own coven, which practices a Gardnerian form of Wicca. When asked, she denies that she ever converted to Paganism. "I'd always been a Pagan," she recounts. "I just needed to wake up to that fact. I didn't convert. I came home."

Geoffrey met members of the Unification Church (Moonies) in Toronto while traveling across the country after graduating from university. Although he had not been raised with any particular religion, his parents had always known he was interested in spirituality. They never imagined, however, that he would join a group as controversial as the Unification Church. At this time, the mid-1970s, the Moonies were well known for their high-pressure recruiting tactics: "love bombing," the constant positive reinforcement given to potential new members; endless indoctrination sessions as Sun Myung Moon preached his unique brand of Christianity and family values; the unrelenting push to commit quickly and completely to Moon's vision for the world. When his parents tried to talk to Geoffrey—on the increasingly rare occasions when he called home—he insisted he was fine, but he sounded so different that they began to worry. One night at a church near Geoffrey's parents' home, a former Moonie talked about her experience in the group. She, too, believed she was doing what she wanted, but in reality she had been brainwashed by the cult. Fortunately, her parents had cared enough about her to hire a deprogrammer to help her see the truth. Geoffrey's parents contacted the man she recommended. It was expensive, risky, and illegal—but, to them, worth everything if they could get their son back. Inviting Geoffrey home for his father's fiftieth birthday, they locked him in the basement while a deprogrammer sought to break the hold of the cult. After three weeks, Geoffrey finally realized how the Moonies had brainwashed him, how Moon was not the new Messiah, and how he had made a terrible mistake. Although he has had significant psychological trouble integrating his experiences, he, too, is grateful to his parents for getting him out.

These three vignettes, one taken from a compendium of Latter-day Saint conversion accounts, the other two composites drawn from the voluminous new religions literature, indicate something of the range of conversion motifs in the new religious world. Some adherents are encouraged to participate through social networks and others through literature that speaks to particular issues in their lives, while still others find that their spiritual search has led them places they ultimately wish they had not gone. Each of these examples, however, also demonstrates how conversion to a new religious movement can be both framed and reframed by adherents. Together, they highlight that affiliation, commitment, and disaffiliation are interrelated, ongoing processes rather than points in conceptual or behavioral space, that they describe different personal and social pathways, and that they do not necessarily end when commitment deepens or leave-taking occurs. Complex reinterpretations of the conversion process, which are often intended to conform either to new religious conventions or to post-exit social norms, are an important part of the experience.

Although Elaine's initial encounter with and excitement over the Latter-day Saints clearly occurred as a result of social networking, her conversion story draws on an important Mormon belief called the "burning in the bosom," a personal moment of gnostic insight into the value and verity of the beliefs of the Latter-day Saints church. In terms of understanding the Mormon conversion process, neither aspect should be privileged over the other. Wiccans, on the other hand, do not proselytize, and there are no Wiccan churches that one can simply begin attending. Modern paganism, however, is a tremendously literary religious subculture, and many practitioners come to the Craft as the composite example Sarah did. Although modern Pagans like her deny converting, in the conventional sense this is exactly what happened.[4] One religious worldview is exchanged for another; the former is rejected as the new adherent takes on the latter. Many modern Pagans believe that our spiritual path is an inner constant of which we need only become aware, so as their commitment to the Pagan path deepens, this reframing of the reaffiliation process reinforces modern Pagan ontology.[5] Although the textual initiation of the conversion process is relatively common among modern Pagans, it is not unheard of in other new religious movements in North America.[6] Finally, if Geoffrey was aware that he was being brainwashed by the members of the Unification Church and submitted to it willingly, then we might have cause to question his mental and emotional competence. It is reasonable to assume, however, that this was not the case—that he chose his involvement, perhaps for many of the same reasons Elaine and Sarah chose their new religious affiliation: a welcoming social network created a congenial environment within which to explore new religious options, and the experience of that exploration met felt needs in their lives. Only after he was kidnapped and forcibly deprogrammed, a process Anson Shupe and his colleagues refer to as "the new exorcism,"[7] was his affiliation with the Moonies reframed as brainwashing, a coercive change of personality and perspective. While social scientists have for many years challenged the notion that new religious adherents are little more than passive actors in a play over which they have no control,[8] for decades reductionist explanations such as this have commanded the attention of popular media,[9] the secular anticult movement,[10] and the academy.[11] Indeed, no other explanation of new religious conversion has shaped the debates to the same degree as the brainwashing hypothesis.

THE BRAINWASHING DEBATE

Since the North American efflorescence of new religious movements beginning in the early 1960s and continuing into the present, no issue has dominated both popular and scholarly discourse more than conversion. Why do people join new religions at all? Much of that attention has focused on the relative validity of the brainwashing hypothesis. Also known (among other things) as "mind control," "thought reform," or "coercive persuasion," the argument for brainwashing is relatively simple: using a variety of devious techniques, unscrupulous new religious leaders so completely manipulate recruitment and indoctrination processes that potential adherents lose the ability to make rational, autonomous choices. Their free will effectively suppressed or suspended, group members become deployable agents ready and willing to carry out the commands of the leader. Because friends and family were often at a loss to explain what they regarded as the alarming religious choices made by their loved ones, the idea of brainwashing assumed an explanatory mystique and an ideological power that both described the problem in ways people outside the new religious movements could understand and allowed for the emergence of an organized anticult movement to facilitate the rescue of brainwashed new religionists. Although largely debunked now for lack of solid empirical evidence, the idea of brainwashing still has considerable popular cachet in North America. Some scholars contend that the hypothesis does retain analytic value, while others insist that its usefulness was always more political than theoretical and that conversion processes are always far more complex than can be explained by such a reductionist approach.

Although the brainwashing metaphor was significantly modified by the anticult movement and deployed to address a far wider range of phenomena than originally conceived, such as a rationalization for radical personality change, the metaphor originated in research carried out among American prisoners of war returning from Korea and inmates released after internment in Communist Chinese re-education camps.[12] Nearly two decades after these events, and aided both by sensationalized media coverage of new religious movements (NRMs) and by grossly exaggerated membership claims from many of the groups themselves, members of the nascent anticult movement—which began as a loose coalition of ad hoc oppositional groups—resurrected the concept as a metanarrative for explaining the rising interest in NRMs such as the Unification Church, the Hare Krishna movement, the Children of God, and the Divine Light Mission.

What, then, was this explanation?

In an early entry into the "cult wars" largely fomented by the anticult movement, anthropologist Willa Appel wrote, "combined with mind-altering techniques—chanting, hypnotic training routines, talking in tongues—and in the context of group pressure, [these brainwashing processes] constitute a form of conditioning to break down the individual."[13] That is, these processes undermined the dominant personality of a recruit, gradually conditioning and altering it until new members come to regard the movement's worldview as their own. Individual choice and rationality are sublimated to group beliefs and imperatives. The same year Appel's book was published, psychologist Margaret Singer, who would become one of the most influential anticult intellectuals, testified in a British High Court to the reality of brainwashing. Responding to the simple question, "What is it?" Singer replied, "Well, it is a very well shaped social and psychological manipulation of the people coming into the organization without them being aware that they are being manipulated, and that is why what the Moon organization [i.e., the Unification Church] does as their induction process fits the definition of brainwashing."[14]

More than a decade later, in her best-known work, *Cults in Our Midst*, Singer expanded her definition, arguing that "leaders of cults and groups using thought-reform processes have taken in and controlled millions of persons to the detriment of their welfare."[15] According to Singer, "the tactics of a thought reform program are organized to: destabilize a person's sense of self; get the person to drastically reinterpret his or her life's history and radically alter his or her worldview and accept a new version of reality and causality; develop in the person a dependence on the organization, and thereby turn the person into a deployable agent of the organization."[16] This is not a haphazard process, according to Singer, but a coordinated program designed to change fundamentally the way persons think about, relate to, and behave within the world around them. For Singer, six conditions characterize the thought reform or brainwashing process:

1. Keep the person unaware of what is going on and the changes taking place.
2. Control the person's time and, if possible, physical environment.
3. Create a sense of powerlessness, covert fear, and dependency.
4. Suppress much of the person's old behavior and attitudes.
5. Instill new behavior and attitudes.
6. Put forth a closed system of logic; allow no real input or criticism.[17]

The brainwashing hypothesis provided three principal advantages for late modern opponents of new religious movements: a controlling metaphor for what many saw as the alarming emergence of new religions; a series of explanatory mechanisms for the social problem of new religious conversion; and a raison d'être for the organizational consolidation of anticult groups such as FREECOG (Free the Children of God), COMA (Council on Mind Abuse), CAN (Cult Awareness Network[18]), and the AFF (American Family Foundation, which now does business as the International Cultic Studies Association).

The Brilliance of Brainwashing: Creating the New Religious Problem

It is axiomatic, if somewhat paradoxical, that new religions are not really new. They may be new individual groups, but the processes of religious revitalization, sectarian division, and cultic innovation—and the almost inevitable social tensions these generate—are thousands of years old, and examples can be found in most major faith traditions. Sensationalized media coverage of new religious emergence in the late 1960s and 1970s (and beyond), however, treated the phenomenon as though it was unique in history, as though there was something sinister and singular on the religious horizon.

"They crouch in dark basements in New York and San Francisco, worshiping the Devil," began a sidebar to *Newsweek*'s 1978 special report on "The Worlds of Cults," written to accompany front-page coverage of the Jonestown murder-suicides. "They wait patiently for the Second Coming or scan the skies for the spaceship that will bring the New Age. A few practice polygamy in isolated mountain communes. Tens of thousands have abandoned their families, friends, educations, and careers to follow the teachings of a leader they will never meet."[19] A year later, in their widely read book *Snapping*, journalists Flo Conway and Jim Siegelman sought to divorce the trend from brainwashing as psychologists such as Robert Jay Lifton had used it, rendering it even more mysterious and potent and opining that "our culture has never witnessed transformation of precisely this kind before."[20] Despite the fact that many scholars now regard the "cult wars" as something of a footnote in new religious history, the brainwashing metaphor continues to wield considerable popular power. Two decades after Jonestown, for example, the otherwise persistently cheerful *Homemaker's Magazine* quoted Singer in a lengthy article on "Cults, The Next Wave," and warned readers that the cult danger was not past, that everyone is at risk, and that "anyone could be in a cult without knowing it."[21]

The underlying brilliance of the brainwashing metaphor was its ambiguity and its malleability. Divorced by media hype and popular fear from any real need to demonstrate the validity of its claims, it could be applied to any group—religious, political, or cultural—with which those who deployed it disagreed. Thus, Baptists who joined the Children of God, essentially moving from one fundamentalist form of Christianity to another, were considered brainwashed; Presbyterians who converted to Roman Catholicism, exchanging their family's Protestantism for communion with Rome, were under the influence of mind control; young adults who to that point had shown little interest in religion at all but who were suddenly reading the *Divine Principle* or chanting *sankirtana* were victims of thought reform. Each time a new religious movement emerged that did not fit the brainwashing profile, the profile itself was adjusted to incorporate it.[22] Relatively quickly, anticult use of the metaphor became an extended exercise in confirmation bias, tapping into our propensity to filter and retain information according to our agreement with it. Those data that supported the hypothesis were integrated into it; those that did not were either ignored or explained away. Not unlike the notorious medieval witch-hunting manual, *Malleus Maleficarum*, which advised that a denial of participation in witchcraft was tantamount to an admission of guilt on the part of the accused, the fundamental principle on which the brainwashing hypothesis rests— that victims do not know they are victims—permitted the anticult activists to sweep aside all objections. Proponents of the hypothesis simply obviated the claims of adherents that they made their new religious choices freely and that they were happy in their new religious lives. However flawed, the anticult logic was devastatingly simple: since members of the suspect group had been brainwashed, they were not in a position to know whether they had made the choice to join voluntarily or not.

The Purpose of Brainwashing: Proaction, Retroaction, and Proscription

As an explanation for new religious commitment, the brainwashing metaphor served three principal constituencies: parents and friends of new religious adherents; ex-members struggling to reconcile what they now regard as foolish religious choices; and anticult activists who sought to use the metaphor to expand the social control of new religions. As a comfort, a consolation, and a control measure, parents could explain the inexplicable when it happened, ex-members could resolve the uncomfortable when it was over, and the anticult movement could define new religious adherence without reference to the complex processes of conversion and the numerous personal and social pathways it can take.

The first half of Randall Heller's *Deprogramming for Do-It-Yourselfers: A Cure for the Common Cult!* (1982), for example, tells the story of Debbie, a young woman who joins the Guru Maharaj Ji's Divine Light Mission, breaking her engagement and giving up alcohol, cigarettes, and marijuana along the way. As the tale of her kidnapping, forcible confinement, and deprogramming at the hands of Ted Patrick, the infamous "Black Lightning,"[23] unfolds, much of the narrative relates how profoundly disturbed her parents were by the sudden change in their daughter. Despite the fact that a number of these changes could be seen as demonstrably positive, they agonize over her choice, wondering where they went wrong. Every doubt they raise, however, is answered by the brainwashing hypothesis, either by anticult activists or former group members. The message is clear: the parents did nothing wrong and the fault lies entirely with the group. It takes little reading between the lines to realize that the brainwashing metaphor had at least as much to do with making Debbie's parents feel better about her decision as it did with the decision itself.

By locating the conversion process in an external mechanism, the brainwashing metaphor also effectively removes any responsibility for the conversion decision from the convert. It becomes, as it were, a secular version of the old chestnut, "The devil made me do it." "If, back in 1974," writes sociologist and anticult activist Janja Lalich in an issue of *The Jonestown Report*, "anyone had ever told me that smart, independent, wise-cracking, hard-headed me would one day be under someone's thumb, I would have surely laughed and said, 'No, not me!' But yes, me—and I give this background in part to shatter the enduring myth that only the weak-willed and stupid could ever be in a cult."[24] Put differently, and echoing the warning from *Homemaker's Magazine*, if they can get someone like me, they can get anyone. Following a litany of the "usual suspects" in anticult rhetoric—most prominently Peoples Temple, but including the Branch Davidians, the Order of the Solar Temple, Heaven's Gate, the International Society for Krishna Consciousness, the Manson Family, and the Symbionese Liberation Army—Lalich concludes with a line from a poem she wrote shortly after leaving the group in which she was involved for a decade: "They took my brain and made me something other than I wanted to be."[25] Although in her academic work she has theorized new religious involvement as a "bounded choice,"[26] what seems clear is that the personal responsibility inherent in the concept of choice is obviated before the metaphorical power of bondage on which the concept of brainwashing rests.

The brainwashing metaphor not only generated both proactive and retroactive explanations for new religious involvement, it was key to the emergence of the professional anticult movement and the proscriptive measures it sought to enact. Indeed, without the overarching brainwashing narrative, there would have been no rationale for the anticult movement's engagement in forcible deprogramming, which many commentators consider far more like brainwashing than the alleged problem itself,[27] or to push for judicial reforms and conservatorships, the so-called "anti-cult laws" that would allow parents to take control of their adult children and submit them to coercive deconversion.[28] Even though, at the height of the "cult scare" in North America, anticult activists themselves recognized that there were, at most, no more than several thousand members of any one target group in the United States[29] —a tiny fraction of the religious population— efforts were made to enact legislation restricting freedom of religious choice, belief, and practice, essentially abrogating the "free exercise" clause of the First Amendment.[30] Although these attempts were largely unsuccessful, that they were even proposed as an appropriate response to new religious conversion indicates something of the power of the brainwashing metaphor and the fear it provoked.

The Problem of Brainwashing: Ignoring New Religious Choice

If the power of the brainwashing metaphor was its malleability and its purpose the explanation of new religious choice for those opposed to that choice, its underlying problems are manifold and include: lack of credibility of the process; a paucity of empirical evidence for the effects; disregard for comparative cases that are not considered the result of brainwashing; and a steadfast refusal to recognize other explanations for new religious conversion.

Within a few years of the initial research on brainwashing in Korea and the People's Republic of China, it was evident that the communist experiments in permanent behavior modification were largely a failure.[31] Those few instances in which success might be claimed were clearly attributable to the horrific conditions under which the process was carried out. As Bromley and I note elsewhere, "Only a handful of the thousands of American servicemen who faced extreme cruelty, torture, and death in Korea defected, and the Chinese re-education programs did not produce any results attributable to the re-education process itself."[32] Moreover, well-established behavioral reform programs, from penal systems to established therapeutic regimes, have relatively low success rates overall, many of which operate with the sanction of society at large and either the coercive power of the state or the willing cooperation of the participant. Since these programs often involve highly trained professionals using a wide range of sophisticated techniques, an appropriate question is: how could junior members of socially marginalized new religious movements, with access to none of these resources and with little or no training, effect the kind of dramatic, permanent, and widespread personality change the brainwashing metaphor demands?

In reality, they could not, and this is arguably the most damning indictment of the brainwashing model: new religious movement recruitment efforts have had uniformly poor success. Indeed, despite their most aggressive strategies and their most ardent promises, new religions attract and retain comparatively few adherents. One of the earliest research programs to put this to the test was conducted by sociologist Eileen Barker in the mid-1970s, at the height of popular hysteria over the so-called brainwashing techniques of the Unification Church. Granted unprecedented access to church records, meetings, and prospective members, over a six-year period Barker used a variety of means to probe the simple, all-important question: was it a choice or was it brainwashing? She found that the retention rate of potential Unification Church members was abysmally low. Only 30 percent of those who attended an introductory, two-day workshop chose to continue their involvement at a more intensive week-long seminar, while only a third of those joined the church and remained for more than one week. Two years later, only 5 percent were involved in any way with the Church.[33] A decade later, psychologist Marc Galanter replicated the study, with similar results: four months after their initial contact, only 6 percent of new members remained in the church.[34] Indeed, during the 1970s and 1980s, the "high growth periods" of the new religions in North America, sociologist David Bromley estimates that "the rate of defections varied between 50 and 100 percent annually."[35] Put bluntly, if the brainwashing process is as devastatingly effective as its proponents claim, why then are the retention rates among new religions so low?

Next, there is the issue of when brainwashing is not brainwashing, when the process of indoctrination concerns socially dominant groups that require a high-control environment to function effectively. This is the all-important issue of comparative analysis. If the central concern addressed by the anticult movement is that the brainwashing process removes the ability of a person to exercise free will based on a rational appraisal of options, what about those social organizations in which free will is voluntarily suspended and there is no option but to comply with organizational directives or mandates? Communes and intentional communities, monasteries and convents, and military units, to name just a few, all require that the will of the individual be sublimated to the demands of the group. Yet, as Margaret Singer famously remarked, "I have had to point out why the United States Marine Corps is not a cult so many times that I carry a list to lectures and court appearances."[36] This seems far more a problem with the definition Singer used than the audiences to which she spoke. The anticult response, however, is that participants in these organizations know ahead of time what they are getting into, that there is no deception—intentional or otherwise—involved in recruitment, and that participants are free to leave when they choose. Rather than an answer to the problem, though, these statements reveal a willing ignorance of the social, psychological, and organizational dynamics of these groups. What separates them from "cults" is not process but convention. Indeed, it could be argued that it is considerably easier to leave the

Unification Church than the United States Marines and considerably less traumatic to renounce one's brief flirtation with the Children of God than one's novitiate in the Poor Clares.[37]

Finally, because the anticult movement, both in its ideology and its methodology, is firmly anchored to the brainwashing metaphor, it is forced to ignore voluminous research into the variegated, often mysterious, but always complex social and personal pathways to religious conversion. If, for example, new religious conversion requires a certain amount of environmental control—as Singer, for example, claims—how then does one explain the kind of literary conversion we see evident among modern Pagans? If the process is as singularly deleterious as anticult activists warn, why do the social and psychological effects of new religious involvement seem comparatively rare among ex-members? Indeed, those who have been forcibly removed from new religious environments and coercively deprogrammed often suffer considerably more post-exit trauma than those who leave voluntarily at whatever stage of affiliation.[38]

Choosing New Religions: Beyond Brainwashing

In many ways the field of new religions study has been crisis-driven: watershed events such as the murder-suicides at Jonestown, the confrontation and conflagration at Waco, and the Aum Shinrikyô attack on the Tokyo subway system have raised important issues about new religions and violence, the nature of the charismatic bond, and the relationship between new religions and the state. Although some of the earliest research into new religious conversion identified the social network as a crucial element in the affiliation process[39] and later work refined the concept of the "conversion career,"[40] social panic over brainwashing and media repetition of the anticult trope that no one is immune from the brainwashing effect quickly took attention away from many of the more mundane—and significant—processes of new religious exploration, attachment, and conversion. While recognizing that some work has been done in these areas, three aspects remain in particular need of closer investigation: (1) alternative pathways to new religious choice; (2) new communications technology and new religious recruitment; and (3) the daily maintenance of new religious conversion.

Among the most interesting of the alternative pathways to new religious seekership, and among the least explored, is that presented by popular culture. Consider this one personal example. In the spring of 2005, during the promotional run-up for Steven Spielberg's *War of the Worlds*, the film's star, celebrity Scientologist Tom Cruise, went spectacularly off-message, and I was subsequently contacted by a major metropolitan daily newspaper and asked about Scientology. "Why are so many people interested in Scientology?" the young reporter asked earnestly. "They're not," I responded, to her obvious surprise. "They're interested in Tom Cruise. If Tom Cruise was a Druid, do you think you'd be asking me about Scientology?" Unfortunately, for a variety of reasons, the question of how many people have become interested in the Church of Scientology because of high-profile members such as Cruise, John Travolta and Kelly Preston, Lisa Marie Presley, Anne Archer, Isaac Hayes, and many others remains unanswered.[41]

The case is different for modern Paganism. Although many modern Pagans are loathe to admit it, such pop culture fare as the television series *Charmed* (about three beautiful and talented Witches) and *Buffy the Vampire Slayer* (whose Witch character, Willow, remains a fan favorite), cinematic treatments such as *The Craft* (which both fans and foes have labeled a recruiting film for Wicca), and the staggeringly successful *Harry Potter* series of books and films all provide modern Paganism with a measure of social support and approbation that no other family of new religions has been able to match. Over forty years ago, one of the first modern Pagan organizations to be officially incorporated in North America, the Church of All Worlds, was conceived after its founders read Robert Heinlein's *Stranger in a Strange Land*, and since its publication in 1982 thousands of Pagans have looked to Bradley's *The Mists of Avalon* as a wellspring of inspiration for belief, ritual, and even mythistory. It seems likely that few of those who investigate Paganism as a result of these cultural products pursue their interest past the preliminary stages, and that those who remain involved quickly move beyond the elementary fantasies portrayed on screen and page. That said, though, this pathway is important and cannot be ignored in conversion research.

Other examples of this phenomenon are many but remain similarly underexplored. Although Beat poets such as Gary Snyder and Philip Whalen did enter into traditional Zen training—Whalen eventually received dharma transmission and served as abbot of the Hartford Street Zen Center in San Francisco—Jack Kerouac's "dharma walk" was literary in both entrée and effect. Due to the publication of his writings beginning in 1953, hundreds of thousands of Beat fans were introduced to the (off-)Beat Buddhism of Kerouac and his friends, principally through his largely autobiographical novels, *The Dharma Bums* and *On the Road*. In the welter of swamis, gurus, mystical teachers, human potential facilitators, and outright religious hucksters that populated the new religious renaissance of the 1960s and 1970s, which groups survived the competition for followers was often a function of who could attract high-profile converts—and, by extension, their fans. In the late 1960s, pictures of the Maharishi Mahesh Yogi with the Beatles arguably did more to promote Transcendental Meditation in the West than all other recruiting tactics combined (see Lapham 2005). George Harrison's later involvement with the Hare Krishna movement, including his haunting ballad "My Sweet Lord," with its *mahamantra* refrain; the promotion of Tibetan Buddhism by celebrities such as Richard Gere and the Beastie Boys; Madonna's interest in Kabbalah—all affect the fan pathways of new religious affiliation. Although these remain to be analyzed in more depth and their dynamics and longitudinal effects mapped with more precision, we could posit at least the existence of an "emulative conversion," an exploration of new religious affiliation that is initially marked by fan imitation of celebrity religious practice. Once again, it is likely that many who investigate this or that new religion based on an emulative process abandon their explorations fairly quickly, and there is no reason to believe the demonstrably low rates of new religious retention are altered by the celebrity factor. This, however, is no reason to ignore celebrity emulation as a potential pathway to new religious seekership.

Since its popular emergence in the mid-1990s, Internet communication has attracted bouquets and brickbats alike. Computer enthusiasts see in the growing popularity of electronic communication a bright new dawn of religious tolerance and understanding, while its opponents view it with emotions ranging from nagging suspicion to outright alarm. In 1997, when thirty-nine members of Heaven's Gate chose to end their material existence through ritual suicide, media and countermovement groups were quick to lay a portion of the blame on the Internet. Like the brainwashing hypothesis, the argument was simple: since the Heaven's Gate group operated a moderately successful Web design company and had posted their message in numerous online forums, the Internet was guilty by association in their suicides. Although the *New York Times* reported in its front-page coverage of the event, "there is little evidence that the Net itself is acting as an instigator for cult behavior,"[42] this disclaimer was followed immediately by a quote of alleged cult expert Rick Ross, who declared, "the Internet has proven [to be a] recruitment tool for cults."[43] Quoted in *Newsweek*, evangelical countercult activist Tal Brooke opined, "I think the Net can be an effective cult recruiting tool. It's like fishing with a lure."[44] Largely ignoring both the history of the movement and the sociology of new religious conversion, scholar Hugh Urban erroneously declared Heaven's Gate a "technological, on-line religion" and stated that "the Net is an ideal means of mass proselytization and rapid conversion, a missionary device which operates instantly, globally, and anonymously,"[45] despite the fact that, even then, this was far from empirically demonstrable. It is certainly the case that both new and "old" religions have sought to use the Internet to their advantage, but, so far, research indicates that online recruitment is no more successful in the long term than offline and suffers from a host of problems particular to the medium.[46]

Finally, there is the issue of reality maintenance, the daily process of maintaining and reinforcing one's commitment to a new religion in the face of family disapproval, social disapprobation, burnout, diminishing interest, and personal dissatisfaction, either with oneself or one's new co-religionists. Put differently, what has not been closely studied are the mechanisms by which converts themselves maintain their conversion. What distinguishes those who stay in a movement from those who leave? Despite its pop cultural cachet, for example, contemporary Paganism remains a marginal and often marginalized new religion in North America, and those who choose to affiliate must often endure the hostility of friends and family, the ridicule of society at large, proactive attempts by educational authorities to limit their free exercise of religion, and the personal angst of finding that the religious grass is not necessarily greener on the modern Pagan side.[47] All of these dynamics cluster along a continuum of what we might call low-intensity cognitive dissonance, moments when one's beliefs are challenged, but not to the degree of high-intensity events such as a catastrophic failure of prophecy or the sudden death of a religious leader. It seems axiomatic that these low-intensity moments of dissonance— How could you believe *that*? You're becoming a *what*? You've decided to worship *who?*—occur far more regularly and more frequently than high-intensity events, and thus deserve closer attention. One possible approach to this problem is implicit in the framing and reframing with which we began this chapter. Those who are able to reframe their conversion experiences in manners consonant with the social, ritual, theological, and/or practical expectations of the religious movement will be better able to maintain their affiliation over the long term.

Summary

Debates over new religious conversion, whether popular or scholarly, oppositional or analytic, have largely been defined and constrained by the brainwashing hypothesis. Although it became clear relatively quickly that there is little empirical evidence to support the brainwashing hypothesis and much that argues against it, the concept of coercive thought control retains considerable power in popular discourse about new religions and seems unlikely to disappear any time soon. Conversion to new religions, however, is a far more complex process than the brainwashing hypothesis allows and occurs across a much broader spectrum of affiliation pathways than the hypothesis recognizes.[48] Men and women investigate, affiliate with, convert to, and leave new religions for a wide variety of reasons—personal, theological, ritual, ludic, social, and psychological—and all of these processes warrant ongoing study.

Glossary

Gardnerian Wicca: A form of traditional British Witchcraft that traces its origins to Gerald Brosseau Gardner (1884–1964) in the mid-twentieth century and has been extremely influential in the development of modern Paganism.
mythistory: This term recognizes that there is rarely a strict delineation possible between "myth" and "history" and that the social processes of meaning-making often conflate the two.
Sankirtana: Street chanting, singing, drumming, and dancing through which Hare Krishna devotees express their love of Krishna.

Notes

1. Elaine Price Hall, "Elaine Julie Price Hall," in *Wise Men Still Seek Him: Personal Accounts of the Conversion of Some Members of the Calgary Fifth Ward*, compiled by Carl H. Swendson

and Clark T. Leavitt (Calgary: Church of Jesus Christ of Latter-day Saints, Calgary Fifth Ward, self-published, 1990), n. p.

2. Ibid.

3. Ibid.

4. See Helen M. Berger and Douglas Ezzy, *Teenage Witches: Magical Youth and the Search for the Self* (New Brunswick, NJ: Rutgers University Press, 2007); Eugene V. Gallagher, "A Religion without Converts? Becoming a Neo-Pagan," *Journal of the American Academy of Religion* 62, no. 3 (1994): 851–867.

5. See T. M. Luhrmann, *Persuasions of the Witch's Craft: Ritual Magic in Contemporary England* (Cambridge, MA: Harvard University Press, 1989).

6. See Douglas E. Cowan, "Jack's Buddhism: A Dharma Walk with Jack Kerouac," *Journal of Buddhist and Tibetan Studies* 2 (1996): 38–91.

7. Anson D. Shupe, Jr., Roger Spielmann, and Sam Stigall, "Deprogramming: The New Exorcism," *American Behavioral Scientist* 20, no. 6 (1977): 941–956.

8. See, for example, James T. Richardson, "The Active vs. Passive Convert: Paradigm Conflict in Conversion/Recruitment Research," *Journal for the Scientific Study of Religion* 24, no. 2 (1985): 163–179.

9. See, for example, Flo Conway and Joe Siegelman, *Snapping: America's Epidemic of Sudden Personality Change* (Philadelphia: Lippincott, 1979).

10. See David G. Bromley and Douglas E. Cowan, "The Invention of a Counter-tradition: The Case of the North American Anti-cult Movement," in *The Invention of Sacred Tradition*, ed. James R. Lewis and Olav Hammer (Cambridge: Cambridge University Press, 2007), 96–117; Geri-Ann Galanti, "Reflections on 'Brainwashing,'" in *Recovery from Cults: Help for Victims of Psychological and Spiritual Abuse*, ed. Michael D. Langone (New York: W. W. Norton, 1993), 85–103; Anson D. Shupe and David G. Bromley, *The New Vigilantes: Deprogrammers, Anti-Cultists, and the New Religions* (Beverly Hills, CA: Sage Publications, 1980).

11. See David G. Bromley, "Listing (in Black and White) Some Observations on (Sociological) Thought Reform," *Nova Religio* 1, no. 2 (1998): 250–266; David G. Bromley, "A Tale of Two Theories: Brainwashing and Conversion as Competing Political Narratives," in *Misunderstanding Cults: Searching for Objectivity in a Controversial Field*, ed. Benjamin Zablocki and Thomas Robbins (Toronto: University of Toronto Press, 2001), 318–348; Benjamin D. Zablocki, "The Blacklisting of a Concept: The Strange History of the Brainwashing Conjecture in the Sociology of Religion," *Nova Religio* 1, no. 1 (1997): 96–121; Benjamin D. Zablocki, "Exit Cost Analysis: A New Approach to the Scientific Study of Brainwashing," *Nova Religio* 1, no. 2 (1998): 216–249.

12. Cf. Edward Hunter, *Brainwashing in Red China: The Calculated Destruction of Men's Minds.* (New York: Vanguard, 1953); Robert Jay Lifton, *Thought Reform and the Psychology of Totalism* (New York: W. W. Norton, 1963); William W. Sargent, *Battle for the Mind: A Physiology of Conversion and Brainwashing* (New York: Doubleday, 1957).

13. Willa Appel, *Cults in America: Programmed for Paradise* (New York: Holt, Rinehart & Winston, 1981), 20.

14. Margaret Singer, Transcript of court proceedings, Orme v. Associated Newspapers Group Ltd., Royal Courts of Justice (Mar. 9, 1981): 15, quoted in Eileen Barker, *The Making of a Moonie: Choice or Brainwashing?* (Oxford: Basil Blackwell, 1984), 122.

15. Margaret Thaler Singer with Janja Lalich, *Cults in Our Midst: The Continuing Fight against Their Hidden Menace* (San Francisco: Jossey-Bass, 1995), 52.

16. Ibid., 62.

17. Ibid., 64–69.
18. See Anson D. Shupe and Susan E. Darnell, *Agents of Discord: Deprogramming, Pseudo-Science, and the American Anticult Movement* (New Brunswick, NJ: Transaction Publishers, 2006) regarding this organization.
19. Melinda Beck and Susan Frakar, "The World of Cults," *Newsweek* (Dec. 4, 1978): 78.
20. Conway and Siegelman, *Snapping*, 37.
21. Robert Hoshowsky, "Cults, The Next Wave: Almost Everyone is Vulnerable," *Homemaker's Magazine* (Mar. 1998): 55.
22. See, for example, Bromley and Cowan, "The Invention of a Counter-tradition"; David G. Bromley, Anson D. Shupe, Jr., and J. C. Ventimiglia, "The Role of Anecdotal Atrocities in the Social Construction of Evil," in *The Brainwashing/Deprogramming Controversy: Sociological, Psychological, Legal, and Historical Perspectives*, ed. David G. Bromley and James T. Richardson (New York: Edwin Mellen Press, 1983), 139–160; Philip Zimbardo and Susan Andersen, "Understanding Mind Control: Exotic and Mundane Mental Manipulations," in *Recovery from Cults: Help for Victims of Psychological and Spiritual Abuse*, ed. Michael D. Langone (New York: W. W. Norton, 1993), 104–125.
23. See Ted Patrick and Tom Dulack, *Let Our Children Go!* (New York: Dutton, 1976).
24. Janja Lalich, "The Violent Outcomes of Ideological Extremism: What Have We Learned since Jonestown?" *The Jonestown Report* 10 (Nov. 2008).
25. Ibid.
26. Janja Lalich, *Bounded Choice: True Believers and Charismatic Cults* (Berkeley and Los Angeles: University of California Press, 2004).
27. See, for example, John E. LeMoult, "Deprogramming Members of Religious Sects," in *The Brainwashing/Deprogramming Controversy: Sociological, Psychological, Historical, and Legal Perspectives*, ed. David G. Bromley and James T. Richardson (New York: Edwin Mellen Press, 1983), 234–257.
28. Shupe and Bromley, *The New Vigilantes*, 130–134.
29. Marcia R. Rudin, "The New Religious Cults and the Jewish Community," *Religious Education* 73, no. 3 (1973): 350–360.
30. For examples, see Herbert Richardson, *New Religions and Mental Health: Understanding the Issues* (New York: Edwin Mellen Press, 1980), 20–36.
31. Edgar Schein, "The Chinese Indoctrination Program for Prisoners of War: A Study of Attempted Brainwashing," in *Readings in Social Psychology*, ed. Eleanor Maccoby et al. (New York: Holt, Rinehart & Winston, 1958), 311–334.
32. Bromley and Cowan, "The Invention of a Counter-tradition," 106.
33. Barker, *The Making of a Moonie*, 121–148.
34. Marc Galanter, *Cults: Faith, Healing, and Coercion* (New York: Oxford University Press, 1989), 141.
35. David G. Bromley, "Affiliation and Disaffiliation Careers in New Religious Movements," in *Introduction to New and Alternative Religions in America*, Vol. 1, ed. Eugene V. Gallagher and W. Michael Aschcraft (Westport, CT: Greenwood Press, 2006), 51.
36. Singer and Lalich, *Cults in Our Midst*, 98.
37. Cf. Anson D. Shupe and David G. Bromley, "The Tnevnoc Cult," *Sociological Analysis* 40, no. 4 (1979): 361–366.
38. See, for example, James R. Lewis and David G. Bromley, "The Cult Withdrawal Syndrome: A Case of Misattribution of Cause?" *Journal for the Scientific Study of Religion*

26, no. 4 (1987): 508–522; Trudy Solomon, "Integrating the 'Moonie' Experience: Social Psychology Applied," in *The Brainwashing/Deprogramming Controversy: Sociological, Psychological, Historical, and Legal Perspectives*, ed. David G. Bromley and James T. Richardson (New York: Edwin Mellen Press, 1983), 163–182; Stuart A. Wright, *Leaving Cults: The Dynamics of Defection* (Washington, DC: Society for the Scientific Study of Religion, 1987).

39. John Lofland and Rodney Stark, "Becoming a World-Saver: A Theory of Conversion to a Deviant Perspective," *American Sociological Review* 30 (1965): 862–875.

40. James T. Richardson, *Conversion Careers: In and Out of the New Religions* (Beverly Hills, CA: Sage, 1978).

41. See Douglas E. Cowan, "Researching Scientology: Perceptions, Premises, Promises, and Problematics," in *Scientology*, ed. James R. Lewis (Oxford: Oxford University Press, 2009), 53–79.

42. John Markoff, "Death in a Cult: The Technology," *New York Times*, Mar. 28, 1997.

43. Quoted in Markoff, "Death in a Cult."

44. Quoted in Steven Levy, "Blaming the Web," *Newsweek* (Apr. 7, 1997): 7.

45. Hugh T. Urban, "The Devil at Heaven's Gate: Rethinking the Study of Religion in the Age of Cyber-Space," *Nova Religio* 3, no. 2 (2000): 283.

46. Cf. Douglas E. Cowan, *Cyberhenge: Modern Pagans on the Internet* (New York: Routledge, 2005); Lorne L. Dawson and Jennifer Hennebry, "New Religions and the Internet: Recruiting in a New Public Space," *Journal of Contemporary Religion* 14, no. 1 (1999): 17–39.

47. See Carol Barner-Barry, *Contemporary Paganism: Minority Faith in a Majoritarian America* (New York: Palgrave Macmillan, 2005).

48. See Henri Gooren, "Reassessing Conventional Approaches to Conversion: Toward a New Synthesis," *Journal for the Scientific Study of Religion* 46, no. 3 (2007): 337–353.

Further Reading

Barker, Eileen. *The Making of a Moonie: Choice or Brainwashing?* Oxford: Basil Blackwell, 1984. A now-classic study that was among the first to investigate—and debunk—anticult claims of Unification Church brainwashing.

Bromley, David G., and James T. Richardson, eds. *The Brainwashing/Deprogramming Controversy: Sociological, Psychological, Historical, and Legal Perspectives.* New York: Edwin Mellen Press, 1983. An excellent collection of essays that examines the issue from a variety of analytic viewpoints.

Lifton, Robert Jay. *Thought Reform and the Psychology of Totalism.* New York: W. W. Norton, 1963. One of the early works on which the brainwashing hypothesis was built.

Lofland, John, and Rodney Stark. "Becoming a World-Saver: A Theory of Conversion to a Deviant Perspective." *American Sociological Review* 30 (1965): 862–875. Classic article outlining the importance of social networks in new religious conversion.

Singer, Margaret Thaler, with Janja Lalich. *Cults in Our Midst: The Continuing Fight against Their Hidden Menace.* San Francisco: Jossey-Bass, 1995. Arguably the most well-known anticult statement of the brainwashing theory.

Zablocki, Benjamin, and Thomas Robbins, eds. *Misunderstanding Cults: Searching for Objectivity in a Controversial Field*. Toronto: University of Toronto Press, 2001. Contains some very good essays on the ongoing question of conversion, thought reform, and the reliability of apostate testimony.

BIBLIOGRAPHY

Appel, Willa. *Cults in America: Programmed for Paradise*. New York: Holt, Rinehart & Winston, 1981.

Barner-Barry, Carol. *Contemporary Paganism: Minority Faith in a Majoritarian America*. New York: Palgrave Macmillan, 2005.

Beck, Melinda, and Susan Frakar. "The World of Cults." *Newsweek* (Dec. 4, 1978): 78.

Berger, Helen M., and Douglas Ezzy. *Teenage Witches: Magical Youth and the Search for the Self*. New Brunswick, NJ: Rutgers University Press, 2007.

Bradley, Marion Zimmer. *The Mists of Avalon*. New York: Ballantine Books, 1982.

Bromley, David G. "Affiliation and Disaffiliation Careers in New Religious Movements." In *Introduction to New and Alternative Religions in America*, Vol. 1, ed. Eugene V. Gallagher and W. Michael Aschcraft, 42–64. Westport, CT: Greenwood Press, 2006.

———. "Listing (in Black and White) Some Observations on (Sociological) Thought Reform." *Nova Religio* 1, no. 2 (1998): 250–266.

———. "A Tale of Two Theories: Brainwashing and Conversion as Competing Political Narratives." In *Misunderstanding Cults: Searching for Objectivity in a Controversial Field*, ed. Benjamin Zablocki and Thomas Robbins, 318–348. Toronto: University of Toronto Press, 2001.

Bromley, David G., and Douglas E. Cowan. "The Invention of a Counter-tradition: The Case of the North American Anti-cult Movement." In *The Invention of Sacred Tradition*, ed. James R. Lewis and Olav Hammer, 96–117. Cambridge: Cambridge University Press, 2007.

Bromley, David G., Anson D. Shupe, Jr., and J. C. Ventimiglia. "The Role of Anecdotal Atrocities in the Social Construction of Evil." In *The Brainwashing/Deprogramming Controversy: Sociological, Psychological, Legal, and Historical Perspectives*, ed. David G. Bromley and James T. Richardson, 139–160. New York: Edwin Mellen Press, 1983.

Conway, Flo, and Joe Siegelman. *Snapping: America's Epidemic of Sudden Personality Change*. Philadelphia: Lippincott, 1979.

Cowan, Douglas E. *Cyberhenge: Modern Pagans on the Internet*. New York: Routledge, 2005.

———. "Jack's Buddhism: A Dharma Walk with Jack Kerouac." *Journal of Buddhist and Tibetan Studies* 2 (1996): 38–91.

———. "Researching Scientology: Perceptions, Premises, Promises, and Problematics." In *Scientology*, ed. James R. Lewis, 53–79. Oxford: Oxford University Press, 2009.

Dawson, Lorne L., and Jennifer Hennebry. "New Religions and the Internet: Recruiting in a New Public Space." *Journal of Contemporary Religion* 14, no. 1 (1999): 17–39.

Galanter, Marc. *Cults: Faith, Healing, and Coercion*. New York: Oxford University Press, 1989.

Galanti, Geri-Ann. "Reflections on 'Brainwashing.'" In *Recovery from Cults: Help for Victims of Psychological and Spiritual Abuse*, ed. Michael D. Langone, 85–103. New York: W. W. Norton, 1993.

Gallagher, Eugene V. "A Religion without Converts? Becoming a Neo-Pagan." *Journal of the American Academy of Religion* 62, no. 3 (1994): 851–867.

Gooren, Henri. "Reassessing Conventional Approaches to Conversion: Toward a New Synthesis." *Journal for the Scientific Study of Religion* 46, no. 3 (2007): 337–353.

Hall, Elaine Price. "Elaine Julie Price Hall." In *Wise Men Still Seek Him: Personal Accounts of the Conversion of Some Members of the Calgary Fifth Ward*, compiled by Carl H. Swendson and Clark T. Leavitt. Calgary: Church of Jesus Christ of Latter-day Saints, Calgary Fifth Ward, self-published, 1990.

Heinlein, Robert A. *Stranger in a Strange Land*. New York: Putnam, 1961.

Heller, Randall K. *Deprogramming for Do-It-Yourselfers: A Cure for the Common Cult!* Medina, OH: The Gentle Press, 1982.

Hoshowsky, Robert. "Cults, The Next Wave: Almost Everyone is Vulnerable." *Homemaker's Magazine* (March 1998): 54–60.

Hunter, Edward. *Brainwashing in Red China: The Calculated Destruction of Men's Minds*. New York: Vanguard, 1953.

Kerouac, Jack. *The Dharma Bums*. New York: New American Library, 1958.

——. *On the Road*. New York: Viking, 1965.

Lalich, Janja. *Bounded Choice: True Believers and Charismatic Cults*. Berkeley and Los Angeles: University of California Press, 2004.

——. "The Violent Outcomes of Ideological Extremism: What Have We Learned Since Jonestown?" *The Jonestown Report* 10 (Nov. 2008). http://jonestown.sdsu.edu/AboutJonestown/JonestownReport/Volume10/ Lalich.htm.

Lapham, Lewis. *With the Beatles*. Hoboken, NJ: Melville House, 2005.

LeMoult, John E. "Deprogramming Members of Religious Sects." In *The Brainwashing/Deprogramming Controversy: Sociological, Psychological, Historical, and Legal Perspectives*, ed. David G. Bromley and James T. Richardson, 234–257. New York: Edwin Mellen Press, 1983.

Levy, Steven. "Blaming the Web." *Newsweek* (Apr. 7, 1997): 7.

Lewis, James R., and David G. Bromley. "The Cult Withdrawal Syndrome: A Case of Misattribution of Cause?" *Journal for the Scientific Study of Religion* 26, no. 4 (1987): 508–522.

Lifton, Robert Jay. *Thought Reform and the Psychology of Totalism*. New York: W. W. Norton, 1963.

Lofland, John, and Rodney Stark. "Becoming a World-Saver: A Theory of Conversion to a Deviant Perspective." *American Sociological Review* 30 (1965): 862–875.

Luhrmann, T. M. *Persuasions of the Witch's Craft: Ritual Magic in Contemporary England*. Cambridge, MA: Harvard University Press, 1989.

Markoff, John. "Death in a Cult: The Technology." *New York Times*, Mar. 28, 1997.

Patrick, Ted, and Tom Dulack. *Let Our Children Go!* New York: Dutton, 1976.

Richardson, Herbert, ed. *New Religions and Mental Health: Understanding the Issues*. New York: Edwin Mellen Press, 1980.

Richardson, James T. "The Active vs. Passive Convert: Paradigm Conflict in Conversion/Recruitment Research." *Journal for the Scientific Study of Religion* 24, no. 2 (1985): 163–179.

——. *Conversion Careers: In and Out of the New Religions*. Beverly Hills, CA: Sage, 1978.

Rudin, Marcia R. "The New Religious Cults and the Jewish Community." *Religious Education* 73, no. 3 (1973): 350–360.

Sargent, William W. *Battle for the Mind: A Physiology of Conversion and Brainwashing*. New York: Doubleday, 1957.

Schein, Edgar. "The Chinese Indoctrination Program for Prisoners of War: A Study of Attempted Brainwashing." In *Readings in Social Psychology*, ed. Eleanor Maccoby et al., 311–334. New York: Holt, Rinehart & Winston, 1958.

Shupe, Anson D., and David G. Bromley. *The New Vigilantes: Deprogrammers, Anti-Cultists, and the New Religions*. Beverly Hills, CA: Sage Publications, 1980.

——. "The Tnevnoc Cult." *Sociological Analysis* 40, no. 4 (1979): 361–366.

Shupe, Anson D., and Susan E. Darnell. *Agents of Discord: Deprogramming, Pseudo-Science, and the American Anticult Movement*. New Brunswick, NJ: Transaction Publishers, 2006.

Shupe, Anson D., Jr., Roger Spielmann, and Sam Stigall. "Deprogramming: The New Exorcism." *American Behavioral Scientist* 20, no. 6 (1977): 941–956.

Singer, Margaret. Transcript of court proceedings, Orme v. Associated Newspapers Group Ltd., Royal Courts of Justice (March 9, 1981): 15. Quoted in Eileen Barker, *The Making of a Moonie: Choice or Brainwashing?* Oxford: Basil Blackwell, 1984, 122.

Singer, Margaret Thaler, with Janja Lalich. *Cults in Our Midst: The Continuing Fight against Their Hidden Menace*. San Francisco: Jossey-Bass, 1995.

Solomon, Trudy. "Integrating the 'Moonie' Experience: Social Psychology Applied." In *The Brainwashing/Deprogramming Controversy: Sociological, Psychological, Historical, and Legal Perspectives*, ed. David G. Bromley and James T. Richardson, 163–182. New York: Edwin Mellen Press, 1983.

Starhawk. *The Spiral Dance: A Rebirth of the Ancient Religion of the Great Goddess*. 2nd ed. San Francisco: Harper & Row, 1989.

Urban, Hugh T. "The Devil at Heaven's Gate: Rethinking the Study of Religion in the Age of Cyber-Space." *Nova Religio* 3, no. 2 (2000): 269–302.

Wright, Stuart A. *Leaving Cults: The Dynamics of Defection*. Washington, DC: Society for the Scientific Study of Religion, 1987.

Zablocki, Benjamin D. "The Blacklisting of a Concept: The Strange History of the Brainwashing Conjecture in the Sociology of Religion." *Nova Religio* 1, no. 1 (1997): 96–121.

——. "Exit Cost Analysis: A New Approach to the Scientific Study of Brainwashing." *Nova Religio* 1, no. 2 (1998): 216–249.

Zimbardo, Philip, and Susan Andersen. "Understanding Mind Control: Exotic and Mundane Mental Manipulations." In *Recovery from Cults: Help for Victims of Psychological and Spiritual Abuse*, ed. Michael D. Langone, 104–125. New York: W. W. Norton, 1993.

CHAPTER 30

DISENGAGEMENT AND APOSTASY IN NEW RELIGIOUS MOVEMENTS

STUART A. WRIGHT

TWENTY years ago I was asked by a colleague to write a chapter in an edited volume on religious disaffiliation. My contribution to the volume focused on leaving new or unconventional religious movements.[1] By the late 1980s, there was a small but growing body of research on disengagement from new religious movements (NRMs) and the editor wanted a comprehensive overview of the literature. Since that time we have witnessed an impressive expansion of scholarship in this field. A generation of new scholars has helped to broaden the body of knowledge, and we have also seen an increasing international focus of NRM studies. This chapter reprises my earlier contribution and incorporates additional studies and research from the intervening twenty years.

It now seems obvious that knowing how and why people leave new or unconventional religious movements is just as important as knowing why they join. Some of the same issues and debates that characterize joining pertain to leaving. Processes of attachment, group identification, and commitment building are inherently dynamic and must be sustained perpetually by the group in order to retain members and deter attrition. To the extent that these processes fail, dissolve, or lose their meaning for adherents, leaving becomes more likely. Disillusionment, disaffection, or apostasy can only be understood with reference to the processes or mechanisms that sustain group affectivity, commitment, and belief. Or put another way, how commitment is gained is closely tied to how commitment is lost.

Important insights may be culled from those adherents who find continuation untenable. Locating sources of disillusionment or disaffection can tell us as much about attachment and commitment-building as studying consecrated devotees. By exploring how commitment is weakened or destroyed we advance our understanding of the factors and processes that sustain commitment. In sociological terms, attachment/commitment processes and mechanisms are often mirror images of detachment and withdrawal. The study of "deconversion" in many ways turns the conversion process on its head. Acquiring a new belief system often accompanies the relinquishment or surrender of an old belief system. The acquisition of new affective ties or bonds may well entail the severing of old attachments. Entrance into a new religious role may involve exiting another.[2] Joiners may be leavers before they can become joiners. Studies of NRM converts have shown that some at least are sequential joiners who have "conversion careers" resulting from spiritual journeys that involve an experimental mode of seeking or searching.[3]

The Social and Cultural Context of New Religious Movement Disengagement

We must also consider the cultural context in which leaving (and joining) new religious movements is viewed, framed, or socially constructed. In this respect, our subject matter is distinctive, embedded in and reflective of larger social dynamics and conflicts.[4] Unlike mainline religious institutions which are sustained primarily by the intergenerational transmission of faith, new religious movements must start from scratch in building a viable membership base. New religious movements are challengers to established religions; they must confront and contest traditional dogma and practices, compete for converts, and offer an alternative path of spirituality if they are to succeed. As entrepreneurs and competitors in the spiritual marketplace, NRMs present a threat to institutional religions in an already crowded market. Not surprisingly, traditional religious institutions resist this uninvited competition because they are unwilling to concede hegemony or give up market share. Many mainline churches already have experienced declining memberships in recent decades, especially among younger age groups. The prospect of facing new or additional fronts in the battle for souls only exacerbates the difficulties for the historically entrenched religions. These institutional organizations or actors may respond to the new challenges over contested terrain by fueling antipathy and laying claim to charges of heresy, deception, or even brainwashing.

The most effective strategy deployed by institutional actors and organized NRM opponents involves the attribution of *threat*. New religions are labeled and denounced as "cults" (or "destructive cults") and strategically framed as a threat to the social order. This fundamental dynamic defines the principal relationship of a new religion to mainstream churches and the host society.

It is in this context that any scholarly examination of leave-taking or disengagement from new religious movements must be made. NRMs face a higher degree of tension with their host cultures than traditional religions which, in turn, exposes them to different pressures and conditions. They are likely to have few, if any, institutional allies, making them more vulnerable to the derisive claims of detractors and opponents.[5] Under these circumstances, the ability of NRMs to defend themselves even in the face of weak or baseless charges is severely impaired. Consequently, joining a new religion is more likely to be perceived by others as precarious, risky, or worrisome than merely joining an institutional church. Moreover, these external social pressures and conditions are likely to increase after the individual has joined a new religion.

Distraught family members may be compelled to contact (or be contacted by) anticult movement (ACM) organizations that promote themselves as "educational" or informational services. Confronted by anticult claims of brainwashing, sexual abuse, or other atrocity tales, family and friends may join forces as organized opponents to press authorities to take action.[6] The social networks of organized opponents—anticult organizations, social workers, psychologists, counselors, news reporters, and sometimes law enforcement or regulatory agencies (child and family protection services)—are alerted and possibly mobilized. Investigations can be launched, scandalous news stories may be run in local newspapers or shown on television (including interviews with anticult counselors or mental health professionals), regulatory officials may make site visits, elected officials may feel compelled to get involved (especially during election years), and law enforcement may be pressured to "take action."

It may seem disingenuous to assert that the allegations against NRMs by opponents that lead to official actions are often weak or unsupported. But research suggests that the incident rate of sexual abuse or child abuse among NRMs is certainly no higher, and may be lower, than the general population.[7] Allegations of brainwashing have been rejected by scholars and scholarly professional organizations (American Psychological Associations, American Sociological Association) as empirically unsupportable.[8] While abuse or criminal activity may arise in NRMs, the accusations and claims by detractors are disproportionate to actual incidents. Rather, it is the very characteristics that set NRMs apart from institutional religions that become the grounds for suspicion in a socially inhospitable context. Without institutional allies, groups labeled as "cults" are more vulnerable to attacks by opponents and less likely to be believed in the first place.

As disadvantaged competitors and entrepreneurs in a market oligopoly, new religious movements tend to make greater demands on their members and foster a greater sense of urgency about the new message that must be spread to unbelievers than do established religious institutions. The greater demands of NRMs can translate into more exclusive and extensive commitments of members' time and resources. Members are asked to "invest" more of their human capital in these groups to be a part of the new revelation or mission. This deep and inexplicable commitment to the NRM is strategically framed by opponents as brainwashing to the media and the larger public. At the same time, the greater socio-emotional, psychological, or other types of investments in the religious group also make leaving more difficult, because the "cost" of leaving is higher. However, as we shall see, leave-taking is quite common among new religions, and in fact, they face high attrition rates, despite claims by opponents to the contrary.

As previously stated, the purpose of this chapter is to provide an updated overview of the research on leaving new religious movements, reprising an earlier effort now twenty years old. The chapter is organized around three fundamental aspects of NRM disengagement research: (1) conceptualization, (2) theory, and (3) methodological issues.

CONCEPTUAL ISSUES

A variety of definitional and conceptual issues of disengagement must first be clarified. The numerous terms one finds in the study of NRM disengagement suggests there are multiple dimensions to this process: e.g., *disillusionment, disaffection, disaffiliation, apostasy, defection, withdrawal, expulsion, removal,* and so on. These terms convey different aspects of disengagement, and we cannot assume they are equivalent or interchangeable. Conceptually, important distinctions can be made to better understand how the process of disengagement occurs.

We can refer to the term *disillusionment* as a process of cognitive disengagement wherein belief is disrupted, seriously challenged, or destroyed. Belief is an important part of religious commitment. When core beliefs or central tenets of the faith come to be perceived as faulty or discredited, we may say that the individual is experiencing disillusionment. Of course, disillusionment may be temporal and the individual may find ways to cope with this kind of cognitive dissonance. Festinger, Riecken, and Schacter and others have shown that even in the face of failed prophecy, religious groups survive and, in some cases, thrive.[9] A number of studies have found that religious movements survive prophetic failure and even "serial disconfirmation" of prophecy.[10] Disillusionment does not necessarily lead to leaving, but the individual must successfully steer a corrective course of "dissonance management." The group must also provide incentives and resources to challenged believers, including containing the dissonance within a strong support structure and well-developed belief-system,[11] offering a reinterpretation of the event by the leader,[12] constructing "rituals of apocalypse" that help cultivate an emotional catharsis among devotees,[13] or employing a strategy of "goal displacement."[14] Festinger et al.'s original work claimed that survival of prophetic failure was due largely to intense proselytization efforts following the disconfirmation, but subsequent studies have not supported this argument.

The term *disaffection* denotes affective disengagement from the religious group. Many NRM studies have shown the importance of a nurturing community wherein members feel accepted and embrace "expressive" values, roles, and relationships. These studies suggest an NRM appeal to potential converts as a type of extended or "surrogate" family.[15] Other studies suggest that NRMs may function as therapeutic communities or sanctuaries amidst an impersonal world driven by utilitarian and instrumental values.[16] For some, being part of a conscientious, emotionally supportive community may trump belief as the most important factor in forming attachment and commitment. If and when the individual experiences an event or episode that betrays the emotionally warm or altruistic spirit of the religious community, however, he or she may begin to withdraw emotionally from the group.

The term *disaffiliation* refers to the severance of organizational ties and membership. It makes no assumptions about cognitive or affective aspects of detachment, though they may certainly accompany acts of disaffiliation.

The term *apostasy* is defined in a distinct manner that connotes more than mere leaving. The apostate may be distinguished from the leave-taker in that the former becomes aligned with an oppositional coalition in an effort to broaden a personal dispute and embraces a posture of confrontation through public claims making activities.[17] Unlike the typical leave-taker who departs in a non-public act of personal reflection and deed, the apostate actively seeks a public venue to express grievances. Indeed, the apostate's identity is constructed principally in relation to his or her former group, frequently leading to what we may call a "professional ex" or career apostate:

> The apostate carves out a moral or professional career as an ex, capitalizing on opportunities of status enhancement afforded the individual through organizational affiliation with the oppositional group(s). The post-involvement identity of the apostate is negotiated within an interactional context of a countermovement coalition and packaged as the "wronged" person. The new identity serves to launch the new career of the moral entrepreneur who becomes engaged in a mission to expose the evils of the suspect group—one which features the characteristics of a "subversive" organization.[18]

With regard to new religious movements, apostates often develop a professional role within the anticult network as a counselor, exit therapist, conference speaker, administrative officer, or some combination of these,[19] engendering an "institutionalization of apostasy."[20]

The terms *defection* and *withdrawal* are largely used as generic descriptions of leaving. However, it might be argued that defection seems to imply a greater level of risk or "cost" in leaving. For example, the term was often used to describe individuals hailing from communist countries seeking political asylum during the Cold War. This nuanced distinction is not insignificant considering the Cold War origins of brainwashing and the prolonged attempt by anticult actors to frame conversion to new religions as a form of coercive persuasion or thought reform.

The term *expulsion* raises the issue that leaving may be imposed on the member by the group rather than a decision made by the individual. Members may be expelled or excommunicated for at least three types of behavior: (1) dissidence, insubordination, and/or challenges to authority, (2) rule violations, and (3) incapacity to care for themselves, acts that embarrass the group, or inability to enhance the movement's resources.[21]

Finally, *removal* refers to acts of extraction by external agents—deprogrammers, child protection services, law enforcement. There is a substantial literature on deprogramming and the controversies surrounding deprogrammers.[22] By the end of the 1980s, deprogramming faced serious legal challenges and the practice waned, replaced by softer approaches such as exit counseling or exit therapy. The post-deprogramming methods are less coercive, denouncing kidnapping or abduction of unwilling participants. Other forms of removal might include state raids in which child protection workers, joined by police and even paramilitary SWAT teams, descend on a religious community and take children into state custody based on allegations of abuse. The 2008 Texas raid on the Yearning for Zion ranch in Eldorado, a Mormon polygamist community, is the most recent example of this type of removal effort. Four hundred and thirty-nine children were taken into state custody and then released a few weeks later when the appellate court and the Texas Supreme Court rejected the wholesale taking of children based on evidence of only a few children.[23]

THEORETICAL PERSPECTIVES AND MODELS

Several key theoretical perspectives and models characterize NRM disengagement and apostasy. Since exiting involves an assortment of possible conditions and variables, we must acknowledge that the research is limited to generalizations drawn from case studies, some of which involve very different kinds of new or unconventional religious movements. We will take up the methodological issues in the next section, but it should be noted that there is probably as much variation in belief systems and organization among unconventional religions as there are differences with conventional religions.

Because conversion research has focused disproportionately on social psychological aspects of attachment and commitment, disengagement research has tended to follow suit. This will be reflected in our review. Three analytical frameworks emerge from the research literature on NRM disengagement: (1) causal process models, (2) role theory, and (3) social movement theory.

Causal Process Models: Disengagement as Sequential Withdrawal

A substantial portion of conversion research in the social sciences has involved attempts to model the sequence of causal relations that culminate in conversion. The weight of empirical research has supported a gradual process of conversion involving a series of decisions, incremental commitments, and progressive stages of psychological identification and affective attachment.[24] It is not surprising, then, that causal process models of deconversion or disengagement have developed attempts to identify and describe a sequence of stages of withdrawal.

Skonovd was among the first to develop a causal process model of disengagement.[25] He posited six stages of defection in the following order: (1) crisis, (2) review and reflection, (3) disaffection, (4) withdrawal, (5) cognitive transition, and (6) cognitive reorganization. At the crisis stage, Skonovd identified a set of possible sources of dissonance deriving from both internal and external conditions. The internal sources of crisis included isolation (separation of devotee from the group), interpersonal conflict, and physical and emotional depletion. External sources included career or educational pulls, affectional pulls, and legal or illegal removal. Skonovd argued that most new religions share characteristics of a "totalistic" environment wherein the construction of reality is largely self-contained. Because NRMs stress "the absolute nature of the posited reality" more strenuously than conventional religions, the crisis event is more likely to produce cognitive dissonance.[26]

The crisis stage is followed by a critical reevaluation of identity, group affiliation, and worldview. Initial responses to the crisis may include repression and avoidance, rationalization, redefinition of the problem, withdrawal, or escape. Skonovd says that devotees faced with cognitive dissonance must effectively navigate and assimilate disturbing inconsistencies or start down the path of defection.

The third stage is disaffection. Ideational disruptions are developed into rationales for leaving. Here, the group's dominance over the individual is said to be broken. Affective detachment is accomplished as the believer experiences a distancing from the sacred canopy of solidarity and community. Skonovd does not provide an explanation for why the cognitive stage of disengagement must precede the affective. It seems equally plausible to assert that disaffection may precede cognitive dissonance in some cases, particularly in communities with a strong emphasis on emotional catharsis and solidarity.

The withdrawal stage is marked by a decision to leave and the development of a strategy for leave-taking. The devotee weighs his or her options regarding how and when the departure would best be accomplished.

Following the act of departure, the devotee is officially a defector. He/she enters the cognitive transition stage where one is still "between worlds" and the dismantling one's previous identity is accompanied by the attempt to carve out a new self-concept and worldview.

The final stage is cognitive reorganization. Here, the individual more or less successfully reintegrates into mainstream culture and achieves some degree of philosophical resolution.

While this exploratory work makes some important contributions to a causal process model of disengagement, it also has some decisive limitations. First, Skonovd's model asserts a precedence of cognitive over socio-emotional factors in catalyzing the disengagement process. But why must we assume that belief necessarily trumps affectivity in the initial crisis stage? Could the crisis involve jealousy? What about unrequited love, spurned affection, or other forms of insensitive behavior?

Second, there is a failure to distinguish voluntary leavers and those who were deprogrammed in his sample. Skonovd commingles these two groups, but subsequent research has shown different responses linked to the mode of exit. Voluntary leavers—those who leave without the assistance or intervention of external opposition groups or actors—are much more likely to view their experiences as members favorably and reflexively.[27] On the other hand, involuntary leavers—those who leave through forcible intervention—are much more likely to express unfavorable attitudes toward their former groups and adopt a "brainwashing" narrative to explain their involvement.

Finally, exiting a new religion does not necessarily involve a transition to mainstream society. The leaver may transition into another new or unconventional religion. Leaving may simply entail entry into a religious community that represents a different tradition or lineage but is still not mainstream.

My own work on NRM defection began with an effort to focus on the social psychological and processual aspects of withdrawal.[28] I collected a sample of purely voluntary leavers because I was primarily interested in how members navigated disengagement and departure on their own. Voluntary leavers comprise the overwhelming majority of defectors, and it is this population that I wanted to target. The research design involved matched samples of leavers and stayers from three NRMs (Unification Church, Children of God/The Family, and International Society for Krishna Consciousness). The matched sample of stayers served as a control group. I wanted to identify and separate the factors that were present only in the experimental group (leavers) in order to isolate the variables correlated with disengagement.

I found that a set of triggering factors or conditions set into motion the process of disengagement. These included (1) a breakdown of social insulation, (2) unregulated dyadic relationships, (3) perceived failure in achieving change, and (4) sharp contradictions between the ideal and real actions of leaders. These factors or episodes introduced a crisis.

At a second stage of disengagement, individuals began actively searching for supplementary rationales or justifications for leaving. These are identified as ancillary factors and include the pulls of family, returning to school, and exploring alternative religious belief systems. Similar to studies of divorce, I found people began to prepare for leaving psychologically and emotionally by making contacts and developing relationships outside the religious group.[29]

The third stage entailed members developing "strategies of leave-taking." Three modes of leave-taking were identified: (1) covert, (2) overt, and (3) declarative. Covert exits are stealth departures by night or without notice to others. Overt exits are negotiated without fanfare after unsuccessful attempts to get grievances met. Declarative exits are dramatic departures often involving displays of frustration or anger.

A fourth stage posits a negotiated social relocation whereby a new identity and network of roles and relationships are acquired. Approximately three-fourths (78 percent) of my sample joined another religious community.

Jacobs's study of forty ex-members of sixteen NRMs examines disengagement from a process framework, building on the work of Downton.[30] However, she also adopts a quasi-psychoanalytical perspective in which new religions are analyzed as a family construct. This perspective is described as follows:

> The overall framework for analysis presents a view in which alternative religious movements represent a religious form of family life. Within this perspective, the religious community is created and maintained through the development of surrogate family ties which are characterized by sibling-like relationships with the charismatic leader.[31]

Jacobs notes that this perspective marries two theoretical approaches, the sociological "quest for community" view and the "ego psychology and object relations theory" of

Freud, Kohut, and Pollock.[32] She goes on to say that this merging of perspectives views conversion and disaffection "within a familial context that has as its goal the adoption of the charismatic leader as the symbol of the divine father."[33] This may help to explain Jacobs's disproportionate focus on emotional and psychological abuse.

Unlike previous studies, Jacobs sees the first stage of defection as social exit from the movement, representing a "partial deconversion" that lays the groundwork for the task of psychological disengagement from the charismatic leader. She identifies four sources of initial disillusionment that trigger social exiting: (1) conflict over regulation of intimacy and social life, (2) conflict over time, commitment, doctrine, and practice, (3) conflict over power and status positions, and (4) conflict over sex roles.

The second stage of disengagement is analyzed in the context of how attachment and commitment to the group is first achieved. According to Jacobs, "the first stage of merging is expressed through the child/parent metaphor, while the second stage involves the projection of an ego ideal onto the leader. The final stage of unification is the experience of mystical union with the charismatic figure."[34] At each progressive stage, the ego boundaries between devotee and leader are blurred and less distinct. Hence, the triggering event leading to *psychological* withdrawal is always a form of rejection, betrayal, or abuse, or some combination of these. Jacobs reports that the sources of disaffection from the charismatic leader stem from emotional rejection (unrealized love), physical or psychological abuse, and/or spiritual betrayal (inconsistency between the ideal of godliness and the reality of the pastor/guru's actions and lifestyle). Most respondents experienced more than one source of disaffection.

Total deconversion, the third stage, occurs when the individual achieves the "destruction of the idealized father image." In some cases, destruction of the idealized god image is facilitated by a "replacement object" through reconversion. Following disengagement and deconversion, approximately half of Jacobs's respondents joined another religious group.[35]

Role Theory: Disengagement as Role Exiting/Passage

Role theory posits that needs and behavior are shaped by normative expectations that are part of the social structure of groups. From a role theory perspective, disengagement involves a process of role exiting and passage in which the social actor rejects the social "script" or expectations associated with being a member of the religious group. Successful passage involves the adoption of an identity predicated on the disavowal of the former identity and role. As Ebaugh has shown, being an ex is quite different from never having been a member.[36] For example, ex-members often struggle with "role residual," or the aspects of group identification and role performance the defector maintains after leaving.[37] This kind of "hangover identity" can make it difficult to chart the passage to a new role.[38] But, it may instead facilitate passage to a new role and group, as in the case of the "apostate role" that I examine shortly.

Sociological research on role exiting has built on earlier models of "status passage" or "emergent role passage."[39] The latter focused on women leaving religious convents after Vatican II. The extension of these studies to NRMs was predictable given the comparably rigid organizational features and strict requirements of both.

Jacobs culled a subsample of women from her study to examine how exiting was affected by sex roles. She found that women reported facing demeaning subordinate roles that contributed to disaffection and deconversion.[40] Unlike male devotees, women were expected to perform subordinate traditional sex role duties in order to obtain higher levels of spirituality and demonstrate loyalty to the male god figure. In the "emotional economy" of the religious community, attachments between female devotees and male leaders often developed and became romantically idealized. When male leaders betrayed these intimate ties or failed to realize the idealized images of the god figure, disappointment and disillusionment followed.

Beckford's study of defection from the Unification Church offers important insights into the "role residual" of ex-members. He observes that defectors in his study exhibited ambivalence about former involvement and commitment. Ex-members did not disown entirely their former attachments to fellow Unificationists or to the movement as a whole. However, ex-members often faced situations where they were forced to confront audiences who wanted to hear a testimonial. Since testimonials are constructed around narratives that repudiate one's former group identification, defectors felt pressured to perform a role. Efforts to avoid conflicts or save face engendered role playing in order to appease others. Beckford details several accounts of ex-members who faced family pressure to disavow any continued sympathy or concern toward the Unification Church. Some ex-members were persuaded to take part in carefully orchestrated, highly public testimonies but later admitted to playing the role to satisfy their parents or significant others.[41]

Bromley and Shupe adopt a role theory approach to disengagement from NRMs, stating that "role theory is able to account for data that anti-cultists argue require more exotic [read: brainwashing] theoretical models."[42] Performing the member role may not involve total conversion or commitment. Some members may become involved in an NRM while hedging their bet in case the experiment does not work out. Routine role performance in the group can camouflage doubt and discontent from other members. If and when the devotee does decide to leave, the exit is not as emotionally difficult as is often portrayed; it is simply "the shedding of a social role."

Apostasy is also a learned as function of role-taking. In keeping with the conceptualization of apostasy previously outlined, the apostate role is constructed as part of the social structure of the anticult movement network. Those leavers who endeavor to make their personal grievances a public issue or seek to frame their plight as part of a larger societal concern can find allies and a support system in the ACM. One particularly effective dramatization of apostate identity promoted by the ACM and embraced by defectors is the "survivor/victim role."[43] The survivor/victim role shares similarities with the "sick role" analyzed by social scientists and can best be understood in the context of a "medicalization of deviance" approach.[44] Anticult therapists and counselors contribute significantly to the apostate role by playing to the theme of victimization, often comparing "ex-cultists" to POWs, rape victims, war crime victims, and others who suffer serious traumas.[45] Apostates and ACM supporters routinely use the language of "rehabilitation," "recovery," and "healing" to describe the role passage of NRM defectors. Some apostates become "professional ex-members" who proceed to build a professional counseling career on their prior experiences in a NRM. While entry into a professional counseling career usually requires specialized knowledge acquired at institutions of higher learning, the moral and experiential qualifications of the "ex" permit the apostate to make legitimate claims to the "entitlements of their stigma."[46]

Social Movement Theory: Disengagement as Organizational Transformation, Decline, or Failure

New religions are social movements that fluctuate in their development, variously experiencing growth, change, and decline. Disengagement can occur as a result of movement organization transformation or crisis. By focusing on movement organizations as a unit of analysis, we can gain important insights into structural sources of NRM disengagement.

Studies of the International Society for Krishna Consciousness (ISKCON) reveal a link between attrition and movement organizational change. As the organization shifted goals in the 1980s in response to internal changes in leadership and changing social conditions, ISKCON lost many full-time devotees or *sannyasin*.[47] After the death of ISKCON's leader, Swami Prabhupada, in 1977, the eleven appointed *ritvik-gurus* assumed leadership of the movement. But factionalism and scandal among the gurus threatened to destroy the movement. The failure of organizational leadership in ISKCON contributed significantly to increased attrition rates and movement decline.[48] During this period of transition, ISKCON leaders were also forced to make adjustments to changes both internally and in the surrounding culture, moving away from the previous objective of building a legion of monastic priests and toward establishing a congregational membership among middle-class Indian Hindu immigrants. ISKCON's appeal to the increasing population of Indian Hindu immigrant families in the United States who wanted to educate their children in the faith climbed. The significant organizational shift toward an "ethnic church" eventually stabilized ISKCON and halted the decline of the group, but not without significant losses in membership.

Another example linking movement organization change with membership loss can be found in the Children of God. Several studies have found that a critical organizational change instituted by the movement's founder, Moses David Berg, in 1978 resulted in a wave of attrition.[49] Responding to complaints by members that some of the leaders or shepherds were becoming abusive and authoritarian and living in a style considerably more luxurious than the rank and file, Berg abolished the extant organizational structure. He issued a letter proclaiming the "Re-organization Nationalization Revolution" (RNR) dismantling the previous Chain of Cooperation. Approximately three hundred leaders were dismissed and demoted to ordinary disciples. Movement colonies or "homes" became more independent and were allowed to elect their own leaders democratically. The movement change was signified by renaming it "The Family of Love." A number of key leaders left the movement, including members of Berg's extended family, Deborah, Rachel, Emmanuel, and Timothy Concerned (Michael Sweeney). Between December 1977 and May 1979, The Family of Love dropped from 5,191 full-time members to 4,958 full-time members, a net loss of 233 devotees.[50]

The Family's antinomian sexual mores and infamous recruitment technique of using sex to bring in converts ("flirty fishing"), which had expanded during the early 1980s, also backfired. Chancellor reports that the total number of full-time disciples stagnated at around ten thousand, despite an average of over seven hundred births per year. "Many of the new disciples proved to be short term, and The Family began to lose more people than were joining through evangelism and recruitment."[51] In the late 1980s and early 1990s, The Family also began to see an exodus of teens who had been born into the movement.[52] After the death of Berg in 1994, the leadership acknowledged mistakes and practices that had led to sexual abuse of young members. The introduction of another organizational shift, published in "The Charter of Rights and Responsibilities" in 1995, began to curb the attrition rates of second-generation members and afford older teens more participation in decision making.

Disengagement and attrition are also a result of organizational demise or failure. Balch and Cohig conducted a study of the collapse of the Love Family/Church of Armageddon in Seattle. They found that the dissolution of the church was precipitated by organizational changes requiring socially insulated devotees to work outside the community in secular jobs. As devotees became financially independent they demanded more input into decisions and policies, creating conflicts between the charismatic leader (Love Israel) and the contingent of disgruntled followers. Love Israel resisted any concessions to power, and eventually the conflict became insurmountable. By the end of 1983, according to Balch and Cohig's estimate, 85 percent of the membership had defected.[53]

Carter has described the collapse of Rajneeshpuram in Oregon after the deportation of the group's leader, Bhagwan Shree (or Osho) Rajneesh.[54] Second-tier leaders became embroiled in an escalating power struggle with the local townspeople in Antelope. The Bhagwan's top assistant, Ma Anand Sheela, and a small group of zealots placed salmonella in salad bars in almost a dozen restaurants in the county. The incident was designed to immobilize anti-Rajneesh voters in an approaching key election. Their actions led to criminal charges and intense investigations of the commune. Sheela and other leaders fled Rajneeshpuram for Europe. The Bhagwan agreed to deportation to avoid federal criminal prosecution. Carter observes that the "commune maintained it would continue, but frozen bank accounts and the absence of the Bhagwan soon made it apparent that the commune would be closed."[55] Most of the residents "returned to the world" and sought occupations through Rajneesh networks. Although the Oregon commune collapsed, the Osho Rajneesh movement survived this tumultuous period by reorganizing and "reframing the movement's central doctrines to make them less controversial to outsiders."[56]

Palmer and Finn document the demise of a Canadian NRM, La Mission de l'Esprit Saint (MES). They found that the leader, Emmanuel Robitaille, responded to a failed apocalyptic prophecy in 1975 by exposing his own doubts to the members and then converting to another religious group, Jehovah's Witnesses. Robitaille visited the Witnesses in an attempt to convert them and ended up being converted himself. He soon began to contact MES members and invite them to Jehovah's Witness meetings. A year later, over 1,200 MES members converted to the Witnesses, causing the MES to collapse.[57]

Goldman chronicles the collapse of the Shiloh Youth Revival Centers, the largest of the Jesus People movement organizations, in 1978.[58] She describes how the organizational collapse forced the de facto withdrawal of several thousand members after a coalition of governing board members demanded the resignation of the founder, John Higgins. Rank-and-file members were not disillusioned with Higgins, but board members believed Higgins had become too high-handed in leading the movement and too extravagant in the use of its funds. Thus the dismissal of Higgins came as a complete surprise to Shiloh devotees. Goldman notes that "Shiloh might have survived had the board been able to agree on a new leader or had Higgins resisted his ouster by appealing to membership."[59] However, neither of these things occurred; Higgins left quietly, and the board was unable to agree on a new leader. In the aftermath, "Shiloh's centers began disaffiliating or closing, its financial base crumbled, and its operation ground to a halt. The vast majority of its members had no choice but to leave and support themselves on the outside as best they could."[60]

Whitsel studied the failed apocalyptic prediction of Elizabeth Clare Prophet and its effect on the Church Universal and Triumphant (CUT).[61] In 1986 Ms. Prophet received a Thanksgiving "dictation" from the Ascended Master, Saint Germain, which warned the Montana ranch community to begin preparing underground shelters in anticipation of a nuclear attack by the Soviets. Prophet and church leaders developed a plan to build a large underground complex to house staff and core devotees for at least six months after the nuclear attack, in addition to the dozens in adjacent communities. The underground bunker was designed by a defense contractor and, according to Prophet's daughter, Erin, the total cost for the shelters was at least $20 million.[62] It had its own air and water filtration systems, a decontamination room, living quarters for approximately six hundred people, stockpiles of canned and dry food, a weapons arsenal, and an arrangement of turrets where armed guards could monitor any attempts by locals to break into the shelter. After the failed prophecy in March 1990, disillusioned CUT members left the church in large numbers. Whitsel observes that "half of the three to four thousand CUT adherents who had come to Montana from 1986 until the time of the emergency call suddenly left the area once expectations for a massive Soviet strike dissipated."[63] The true believers were disappointed, confused, and even angry because many "who came to Montana in late 1989 and early 1990 had left jobs, family and friends to prepare for survival in the High Rockies."[64] Whitsel concludes that CUT lost about one-third of its total membership worldwide in the aftermath of the failed prophecy.[65]

Wright and Greil document the collapse of the Taiwanese UFO sect, Chen Tao.[66] The group's leader, Hon Ming Chen, predicted (among other things) the return of Christ in a spaceship in 1998. Approximately 140 members of Chen Tao settled in Garland, Texas, to await the event, but after the failure of several related prophecies, over two-thirds of the group left and returned to Taiwan. Master Chen attempted to minimize the prophetic disconfirmation and declared that God had pushed the apocalyptic date back to 1999. The group reorganized, and Chen led a remnant of the faithful to Lockport, New York. Within a few years, however, the group again experienced serial disconfirmation when the postponed predictions failed a second time. The collective disillusionment in the aftermath of the failed prophecies, combined with financial troubles and other external challenges faced by members, eventually resulted in the collapse of Chen Tao.

METHODOLOGICAL ISSUES

As stated earlier, the principle dynamic defining the relation between NRMs and their host cultures is one of tension and conflict. To the extent that new or alternative religions (1) exist in contested spaces within society, (2) have few institutional allies, and (3) come under frequent scrutiny triggered by claims of apostates and opponents, the viability of ex-member accounts becomes a central issue in the study of disengagement. Here, I outline three major concerns that affect the validity of ex-member (and sometimes member) accounts. These include: (1) retrospective reporting, (2) temporal variability, and (3) assessing conflicting claims.

Retrospective Reporting

Conversion and disengagement both represent significant shifts in personal identity and situated meanings. As such, biographies are defined and redefined in light of ongoing experience and narrative in an effort to make sense of past decisions and provide legitimacy for current ones.[67] Retrospective accounts must be understood in this context and interpreted accordingly. For example, ex-members may need to justify their departures by finding fault with, or attributing blame to, their former groups. Presentation of the emergent self after NRM disengagement often requires a defense against a "spoiled identity" in the face of stigmatizing efforts by significant others.[68] To save face, the ex-member is compelled to negotiate a new identity (apostate, whistle-blower, penitent ex-member) that plays to a new audience and is calculated to defend the self. The new associates in an external or oppositional group may be slow to fully accept the defector until he/she participates in appropriate *rituals of denunciation* (testimonials, confessions). After all, the newly exited person has a lot to live down from his or her "unsavory" past involvements.

Johnson observes that defectors search for "narrative anchors" in constructing retrospective accounts, and this leads to distortions and embellishments. "Every apostate account—even the tamest among them—strives to slacken the lines that tie it to its moorings in 'real' biographical history."[69] In the process of "deanchoring" the biographical narrative from the individual's former group, the defector selectively culls facts or details that shape the biography as "narrative achievement." There is no such thing as "life itself"; only the telling of a story in which the narrator seeks to validate his or her own decisions. "When social actors deal in apostate narrative," Johnson states, "they are dealing in powerful shapers of past and present identities. For it is the stories that these people tell that confirm them in the role of apostate, and this is the role that defines them for who they are—sometimes for the rest of their lives."[70] The authenticity of the apostate's new identity and narrative requires the negation of the former identity and affiliation.

But even these observations may be too simplistic, because disengagement entails a range of pathways and transitional destinations for ex-members. Research indicates that defectors utilize diverse strategies of leave-taking and experience a variety of exiting modes. Exiting modes often correlate with the type of post-involvement attitudes that ex-members form.[71] Defectors who leave of their own volition tend to have more favorable attitudes toward their former groups. They may express some mixed emotions, but they are more likely to see their involvement as a learning experience and identify aspects of personal growth. On the other hand, those who leave through involuntary intervention are more likely than others to see their involvement as a result of psychological manipulation or brainwashing. Deprogrammed members are more likely to adopt the framing of anticult movement organizations and actors. There is also a population of ex-members who voluntarily have sought post-involvement counseling. We know much less about these individuals as a group, but any data we examine must be able to distinguish between those who are counseled by neutral therapists and those counseled by anticult therapists, who frequently have an agenda.[72]

One must also consider the different levels of commitment to the religious movement in assessing retrospective accounts. Most NRMs have categories for both core and peripheral (or associate) members. The latter is usually an accommodation by the organization to those who cannot or will not make the degree of commitment expected of core members.[73] Even the most intensely demanding groups such as ISKCON, The Family International, and the Unification Church have created membership categories for non-core groups. Peripheral members can still provide a useful service to the movement. They may be a source of financial support; serve as a bridge to the larger society, or exhibit the less "fanatical" type of member to a suspicious public, reducing tensions with the host society. Barker observes that peripheral members are often older devotees with job and familial responsibilities. For example, she found that 80 percent of "Home-Church members" of the Unification Church were over 30 years of age.[74] Barker's thesis is advanced to challenge the myth of clear-cut boundaries of NRM membership, constructing an exaggerated insider-outsider mentality. She contends that peripheral and marginal members "blur the strong boundaries" of membership and undermine perceptions and claims about the nature of such groups. Barker does not attempt to make this case, but I would argue that the psychological difficulty of disengagement among peripheral or marginal members would not be the same as for core members. It stands to reason that fully committed or full-time devotees are more psychologically and emotionally invested in the group than peripheral members and thus have more to lose in leaving the religious community.

Temporal Variability

Accounts of defectors vary over time with regard to moral evaluation and psychological affect. The further removed from the exiting experience, the more defectors reconstruct their biographies in light of what has happened to them in the interim. A number of studies have shown that ex-members who experience success in their post-exit roles and relationships are less likely to regret leaving and less likely to see their former involvement as negative.[75] San Giovanni studied the exodus of nuns from convents and reported that as they gained confidence in their ability to move into secular life and adopt new roles; their accounts became less negative and emotionally charged.[76] Ebaugh reports a similar finding; the longer ex-nuns and other ex-members were out of their former groups, the less they felt compelled to reveal or justify their previous involvement.[77]

Another way of looking at this problem is to consider that accounts may be influenced by the timing of the interview or data collection. Accounts given by "fresh defectors" are likely to yield different results than accounts from those who have had time to reflect carefully about their experiences and acquire some emotional distance. As Rothbaum astutely observes, "The middle of a messy divorce is not the time to inquire about the raptures of the honeymoon, and the leavetaking transition is not the time to try to recapture the former member's early sense of gratitude and hope."[78] The analogy of divorce is an appropriate one, as others have shown, given the intimacy and emotional bonds, not to mention sexual unions, that individuals may leave behind in the process of disengagement.[79]

Assessing Conflicting Accounts or Claims

Carter addresses the dilemma posed for researchers in assessing conflicting claims among believers, apostates, and opponents. Carter points out that each source of information, including those of ethnographers, has different strengths and weaknesses. Active members are well positioned in terms of firsthand knowledge but face the pressure to emphasize the positive aspects of the group. Apostates may be well positioned to recount firsthand knowledge "but their perceptions are more likely to be equivocal or negative."[80] Opponents may know more about some limited aspects of the group than low-level members, but they have a vested interest in opposing the group. To resolve the dilemma, Carter suggests implementing a method of triangulation among insider and outsider claims, using logs, letters, official records, and personal biographical accounts to assist in assessing the credibility of the claims of ex-members, believers, and third parties, especially opponents of NRMs.[81]

Since I am addressing disengagement and apostasy in this chapter, I will focus on the claims of ex-members and apostates. To be sure, true believers are certainly not dispassionate observers whose accounts are to be taken at face value. But neither are ex-members, apostates, or opponents of NRMs. So the credibility and accuracy of accounts must fall to the skillful use of independent and verifiable documents and records. The burden rests on the researcher or ethnographer to gather these materials, analyze them, and offer them in compelling fashion as the instruments of assessment. Ideally, this should be supplemented by direct observation and subjected to skeptical inquiry. The following basic questions may help guide the researcher in navigating conflicting accounts: "Does the claimant have the knowledge implied in the account?" "What is the claimant's motive for the account?" "How may the claimant's relationships with others shape or distort the account?"[82]

The more intemperate or extreme the claims by apostates, the more likely the claims are inflated or exaggerated. Zablocki studied ex-member accounts and found that reporting errors were fewer for respondents with "moderate" rather than "extreme" attitudes toward their former groups, irrespective of their current beliefs.[83] The inclination to inflate claims may be explained in part by the "contextualization" in which the account is constructed. Since "apostasy [is] a thoroughly social phenomenon," one must consider for whom the story is told.[84] Apostates speak to opponents of their former groups and those who would become opponents. Ultimately, the purpose of the apostate narrative is to convey a contextual history that must resonate with the intended audience. "Given the apostatic urge to portray the targeted religious group in the worst of lights," Johnson argues, "it is to be expected that most apostate narratives will venture pretty far out into the fictional waters when constructing their contextual histories."[85]

This argument comports with the discussion earlier of the role theory application to apostates and the social interactional dynamics of role passage. By embracing the "victim" role and/or constructing the resonant "captivity narrative," apostates can make legitimate claims to the "entitlements of their stigma" through a kind of status enhancement among the cultural opponents of NRMs. The captivity narrative emphasizes "the alleged manipulation, entrapment and capture of the idealistic and unsuspecting target" by the predatory operatives of the insidious cult.[86] As such, personal accountability is excused since the convert is presumed to be a mental captive trapped in a state of alternate consciousness. Defection, then, is framed as a form of "escape" or, in the case of deprogramming or other type of intervention, "rescue." Indeed, studies show that these are central themes or motifs in ACM ideology. Converts are defined as psychological captives or "hostages" to cultist mind-control techniques which inherently call for a "rescue" strategy.[87]

Sociologists of religion have found similar patterns of narrative distortion in what they call "rhetorics of conversion." McGuire describes rhetorics as attempts by individuals "to construct the story of conversion drawing on a socially available set of plausible explanations."[88] McGuire identifies three rhetorics; choice, continuity, and change. The last type is especially relevant to our discussion. *Rhetorics of change* emphasize the dramatic nature of personal transformation in the narrative, contrasting the evil or unhappiness of the convert's previous life with the enlightenment or liberation of the new life. The darkness-to-light transition is a familiar rhetorical motif that finds deep resonance in religious culture. In this regard, scholars point out that there exists a hidden incentive for converts to exaggerate their former evil ways; the exaggeration is a kind of "negative boasting."[89] The more depraved the sinner was before being saved, the more miraculous the salvation and the more titillating the testimony. The principle holds for apostate narratives as well; the greater the depravity of one's former group, the greater the drama of the "escape" and the more accolades offered the apostate for his or her heroism and moral courage.

Of course, this is not to say there are not Damascus Road conversions or harrowing escapes from oppressive religions. Rather, it is a reminder that scholars must exercise critical judgment and employ refined analytical filters in assessing such claims, knowing that these rhetorical and normative patterns are deeply embedded in our culture.

CONCLUSION

The subjects of disengagement and apostasy will be a continuing focus in future studies of new or alternative religious movements. As the scope of NRM scholarship grows and many of these movements age generationally, prophets and founders die, and the movements undergo organizational changes and culturally accommodate to host societies, the long-term goals of stability and institutionalization are likely to replace those of the first generation (e.g., preparing for an impending apocalypse or ushering in the new age). When these changes occur, they shape organizational identity and management. In terms of attrition and the inevitable mistakes made by the exuberant first generation, NRMs eventually have to adjust to the pools of ex-members, find ways to negotiate less rigid or exclusive claims, and make modifications in beliefs to coexist with other competitors in the pluralistic religious marketplace, if they are to succeed. Defectors and apostates have a significant role in defining the public image of the religious group and, hence, its ability to endure. Indeed, ex-members continue to exercise an influence on how the group is seen by the larger society, and they affect changes in the group long after they have left.

In addition to the obvious part that defectors play in helping scholars understand how belief, commitment, and attachment are lost or relinquished, they tell us something about the culture, organization, and practices of the group in ways that believers cannot. The complex interplay between and among believers, supporters, ex-members, apostates, opponents, and the larger public encompasses a struggle over contested space and identities. The motives and interests of each certainly have to be considered in assessing validity and reliability. But former members do provide a unique narrative and perspective of the insider-turned-outsider. As such, ex-members provide a rich source of information about religious groups, tempered but often empathetic, reflective, and insightful. Religious organizations are judged and evaluated, at least in part, by the narratives and accounts of ex-members; those whose stories they cannot control or edit. Thus it is critically important for scholars studying new or alternative religious movements (about which we may know little) to include the accounts of ex-members in their research. If for no other reason, ex-members are likely to raise issues and questions that group members will not address or perhaps hope to avoid.

NOTES

1. Stuart A. Wright, "Leaving New Religious Movements: Issues, Theory and Research," in *Falling from the Faith*, ed. David G. Bromley (Newbury Park, CA: Sage Press, 1988), 143–165.
2. Helen Rose Ebaugh, *Becoming an Ex: The Process of Role Exit* (Chicago: University of Chicago Press, 1988); Stuart A. Wright and Helen Rose Ebaugh, "Leaving New Religions," in *The Handbook on Cults and Sects in America*, ed. David G. Bromley and Jeffrey K. Hadden (Westport, CT: JAI Press, 1993), Vol. 3, part B, 117–138.
3. James T. Richardson, *Conversion Careers: In and Out of the New Religions* (Beverly Hills, CA: Sage, 1978); James A. Beckford, *Cult Controversies: The Societal Response to New Religious Movements* (London: Tavistock, 1985); James V. Downton, *Sacred Journeys: The Conversion of Young Americans to Divine Light Mission* (New York: Columbia University Press, 1980); Henri Gooren, "Towards a New Model of Conversion Careers: The Impact of Personality and Contingency Factors," *Exchange* 34, no. 2 (2005): 149–166.
4. Stuart A. Wright, "The Dynamics of Movement Membership: Joining and Leaving NRMs," in *Teaching New Religious Movements*, ed. David G. Bromley (New York: Oxford University Press, 2007), 187–210.
5. David G. Bromley, *The Politics of Religious Apostasy* (Westport, CT: Praeger, 1998).
6. John R. Hall, "Public Narratives and the Apocalyptic Sect: From Jonestown to Mt. Carmel," in *Armageddon in Waco*, ed. Stuart A. Wright (Chicago: University of Chicago, 1995), 205–235; John R. Hall and Philip Schuyler, "Apostasy, Apocalypse and Religious Violence: An Explanatory Comparison of People's Temple, the Branch Davidians and the Solar Temple," in Bromley, *The Politics of Religious Apostasy*, 141–170; Stuart A. Wright, "Construction and Escalation of a Cult Threat: Dissecting Moral Panic and Official Reaction to the Branch Davidians," in *Armageddon in Waco*, ed. Stuart A. Wright (Chicago: University of Chicago, 1995), 75–94; Stuart A. Wright, "Public Agency Involvement in Movement-State Confrontations," in *Cults, Religion and Violence*, ed. David G. Bromley and J. Gordon Melton (New York: Cambridge University, 2002).
7. James T. Richardson, "Apostates, Whistleblowers, Law and Social Control," in Bromley, *The Politics of Religious Apostasy*, 171–190; James T. Richardson, "Social Control of New Religions: From Brainwashing Claims to Child Sex Abuse Accusations," in *Children in New Religions*, ed. Susan J. Palmer and Charlotte E. Hardman (New Brunswick, NJ: Rutgers University, 1999), 172–186.
8. Dick Anthony, "Religious Movements and Brainwashing Litigation: Evaluating Key Testimony," in *Gods We Trust*, 2nd ed., ed. Thomas Robbins and Dick Anthony (New Brunswick, NJ: Transaction, 1990), 295–344; Anson D. Shupe and Susan Darnell, *Agents of Discord: Deprogrammers, Pseudo-Science and the American Anticult Movement* (New Brunswick, NJ: Transaction, 2006).

9. Leon Festinger, H. W. Riecken, and Stanley Schacter, *When Prophecy Fails* (New York: Harper & Row, 1956).

10. Robert J. Balch, John Domitrovitch, Barbara Lynn Mahnke, and Vanessa Morrison, "Fifteen Years of Failed Prophecy: Coping with Cognitive Dissonance in a Baha'i Sect," in *Millennium, Messiahs, and Mayhem: Contemporary Apocalyptic Movements*, ed. Thomas Robbins and Susan J. Palmer (London: Routledge, 1997), 73–92.

11. Simon Dein, "Lubavitch: A Contemporary Messianic Movement," *Journal of Contemporary Religion* 12 (1997): 191–204; William Shaffir, "When Prophecy Is Not Validated: Explaining the Unexpected in a Messianic Campaign," *Jewish Journal of Sociology* 37 (1995): 119–136; Richard Singelenberg, "It Separated the Wheat from the Chaff: The '1975' Prophecy and Its Impact among Dutch Jehovah's Witnesses," *Sociological Analysis* 50 (1989): 23–40; Rodney Stark and Laurence R. Iannaccone, "Why the Jehovah's Witnesses Grow So Rapidly: A Theoretical Application," *Journal of Contemporary Religion* 12 (1997): 133–157.

12. J. Gordon Melton, "Spiritualization and Reaffirmation: What Really Happens When Prophecy Fails," *American Studies* 26 (1985): 17–29; Lorne Dawson, "When Prophecy Fails and Faith Persists: A Theoretical Overview," *Nova Religio* 3 (1999): 60–82; Joseph F. Zygmunt, "Prophetic Failure and Chiliastic Identity: The Case of Jehovah's Witnesses," *American Journal of Sociology* 75 (1970): 926–948; Joseph F. Zygmunt, "When Prophecies Fail," *American Behavioral Scientist* 16 (1972): 245–268; Diane G. Tumminia, *When Prophecy Never Fails: Myth and Reality in a Flying-Saucer Group* (Berkeley and Los Angeles: University of California Press, 2005); Jon R. Stone, *Expecting Armageddon: Essential Readings in Failed Prophecy* (New York: Routledge, 2000).

13. Susan J. Palmer and Natalie Finn, "Coping with Apocalypse in Canada: Experiences of Endtime in La Mission de l'Esprit Saint and the Institute of Applied Metaphysics," *Sociological Analysis* 53 (1992): 397–415.

14. Balch et al., "Fifteen Years of Failed Prophecy." According to Balch et al., "goal displacement occurs when an organization's original goals are supplanted by more achievable ends" (88).

15. Dick Anthony and Thomas Robbins, "Cultural Crisis and Contemporary Religion," in *In Gods We Trust*, ed. Thomas Robbins and Dick Anthony (New Brunswick, NJ: Transaction, 1990), 9–31; Arthur Parsons, "Messianic Personalism: A Role Analysis of the Unification Church," *Journal for the Scientific Study of Religion* 25, no. 2 (1986): 141–161; Stuart A. Wright and William V. D'Antonio, "Families and New Religions," in *The Handbook on Cults and Sects in America*, ed. David G. Bromley and Jeffrey K. Hadden (Westport, CT: JAI Press, 1993), Vol. 3, part A, 219–240.

16. Marc Galanter, *Cults: Faith, Healing and Coercion* (New York: Oxford University Press, 1989); Paul Heelas, *The New Age Movement: The Celebration of Self and the Sacralization of Modernity* (Cambridge, MA: Blackwell, 1996); Jeffrey J. Kripal and Glenn W. Shuck, *On the Edge of the Future: Esalen and the Evolution of American Culture* (Bloomington: Indiana University Press, 2005).

17. Bromley, *The Politics of Religious Apostasy*; Massimo Introvigne, "Defectors, Ordinary Leave-Takers and Apostates: A Quantitative Study of Former Members of New Acropolis in France," *Nova Religio* 3, no. 1 (1999): 83–99.

18. Wright, "Exploring Factors that Shape the Apostate Role," 97.

19. Carol Giambalvo, *Exit Counseling: A Family Intervention* (Bonita Springs, FL: American Family Foundation, 1992); Steve Hassan, *Combating Cult Mind Control* (Rochester, VT: Park Street Press, 1988); Joan Carol Ross and Michael D. Langone, *Cults: What Parents Should Know* (Weston, MA: American Family Foundation, 1988); Madeleine Tobias and

Janja Lalich, *Captive Hearts, Captive Minds* (Alameda, CA: Hunter House, 1994); Shupe and Darnell, *Agents of Discord*.

20. Wright, "Exploring Factors that Shape the Apostate Role," 97.
21. Thomas Robbins, *Cults, Converts and Charisma* (Newbury Park, CA: Sage, 1988).
22. David G. Bromley, "Deprogramming as a Mode of Exit from New Religious Movements: The Case of the Unificationist Movement," in Bromley, *Falling from the Faith*, 185–204; David G. Bromley and James T. Richardson, *The Brainwashing/Deprogramming Controversy* (New York: Edwin Mellen, 1983); Shupe and Darnell, *Agents of Discord*.
23. Stuart A. Wright and James T. Richardson, eds., *Saints under Siege: The Texas State Raid on the Fundamentalist Latter Day Saints* (New York: New York University Press, 2011). See especially chapter 10, Tamatha L. Schreinert and James T. Richardson, "Pyrrhic Victory? An Analysis of the Appeal Court Opinions Concerning the FLDS Children," 242–264.
24. Robert W. Balch and David Taylor, "Seekers and Saucers: The Role of the Cultic Milieu in Joining a UFO Cult," *American Behavioral Scientist* 20 (1977): 839–860; Eileen Barker, *The Making of a Moonie: Choice or Brainwashing?* (Oxford: Blackwell, 1984); James V. Downton, "An Evolutionary Theory of Spiritual Conversion and Commitment: The Case of the Divine Light Mission," *Journal for the Scientific Study of Religion* 19, no. 4 (1980): 381–396; Arthur L. Greil and David R. Rudy, "What Have We Learned from Process Models of Conversion? An Examination of Ten Studies," *Sociological Focus* 14, no. 4 (1984): 306–323; John Lofland and Rodney Stark, "Becoming a World-Saver: A Theory of Conversion to a Deviant Perspective," *American Sociological Review* 30, no. 6 (1965): 863–874; Lewis R. Rambo, *Understanding Religious Conversion* (New Haven: Yale University Press, 1993); James T. Richardson and Mary H. Stewart, "Conversion Process Models and the Jesus Movement," in Richardson, *Conversion Careers*, 22–42; David A. Snow and Richard Machalek, "The Sociology of Conversion," *Annual Review of Sociology* 10 (1993): 167–190.
25. L. Norman Skonovd, "Apostasy: The Process of Defection from Religious Totalism," PhD diss., University of California, Davis (Ann Arbor, MI: University Microfilms International, 1981); L. Norman Skonovd, "Leaving the Cultic Religious Milieu," in Bromley and Richardson, *The Brainwashing/Deprogramming Controversy*, 91–105.
26. Skonovd, "Leaving the Cultic Religious Milieu," 63.
27. Stuart A. Wright, *Leaving Cults: The Dynamics of Defection* (Washington, DC: Society for the Scientific Study of Religion, 1987).
28. By "processual" I am referring to the dynamic aspects of identity transformation rather than the structural. See Stuart A. Wright, "Defection from New Religious Movements: A Test of Some Theoretical Propositions," in Bromley and Richardson, *The Brainwashing/Deprogramming Controversy*, 106–121; Stuart A. Wright, "Post-Involvement Attitudes of Voluntary Defectors from New Religious Movements," *Journal for the Scientific Study of Religion* 23, no. 2 (1984): 172–182; Wright, *Leaving Cults*.
29. See also Stuart A. Wright, "Reconceptualizing Cult Coercion: A Comparative Analysis of Divorce and Apostasy," *Social Forces* 70 (1991): 125–145.
30. Janet Jacobs, "The Economy of Love in Religious Commitment: The Deconversion of Women from Nontraditional Religious Movements," *Journal for the Scientific Study of Religion* 23, no. 2 (1984): 155–171; Janet Jacobs, *Divine Disenchantment: Deconverting from New Religions* (Bloomington: Indiana University Press, 1989).
31. Jacobs, *Divine Disenchantment*, 13.

32. Sigmund Freud, *Totem and Taboo* (New York: W. W. Norton, 1950); Heinz Kohut, *The Analysis of the Self* (New York: International University Press, 1971); Griselda Pollock, "Beyond Oedipus: Feminist Thought, Psychoanalysis, and Mythical Figurations of the Feminine," in *Laughing with Medusa*, ed. Vanda Zajko and Miriam Leonard (New York: Oxford University Press, 2006), 67–120.

33. Jacobs, *Divine Disenchantment*, 13.

34. Ibid., 77.

35. Ibid., 104.

36. Ebaugh, *Becoming an Ex.*

37. Cheryl Rowe Taslimi, Ralph W. Hood, Jr., and P. J. Watson, "Assessment of Former Members of Shiloh: The Adjective Check List 17 Years Later," *Journal for the Scientific Study of Religion* 30, no. 3 (1991): 306–311.

38. Wright and Ebaugh, "Leaving New Religions," 124–125.

39. Lucinda San Giovanni, *Ex-Nuns: A Study of Emergent Role Passage* (Norwood, NJ: Ablex, 1978); Helen Rose Ebaugh, "Leaving Catholic Convents: Toward a Theory of Disengagement," in Bromley, *Falling from the Faith*, 100–121.

40. Jacobs, "The Economy of Love in Religious Commitment."

41. Beckford, *Cult Controversies*, 175.

42. David G. Bromley and Anson D. Shupe. "Affiliation and Disaffiliation: A Role Theory Interpretation of Joining and Leaving New Religious Movements," paper presented at the annual meeting of the Association for the Sociology of Religion, San Antonio, TX, 1986, 12.

43. Wright, "Exploring Factors that Shape the Apostate Role," 100.

44. Peter Conrad and Joseph W. Schneider, *Deviance and Medicalization: From Badness to Sickness* (Philadelphia, PA: Temple University Press, 1992).

45. Wright, "Exploring Factors that Shape the Apostate Role," 101.

46. David J. Brown, "The Professional Ex-: An Alternative for Exiting the Deviant Career," in *Deviance: The Interactionist Perspective*, ed. Earl Rubington and Martin Weinberg (Boston: Allyn & Bacon, 1992), 445.

47. Steven J. Gelberg, "The Future of Krishna Consciousness in the West: An Insider's Perspective," in *The Future of New Religious Movements*, ed. David G. Bromley and Philip E. Hammond (Macon, GA: Mercer University, 1987), 187–209; E. Burke Rochford, Jr., *Hare Krishna Transformed* (New York: New York University Press, 2007).

48. E. Burke Rochford, Jr., "Family Formation, Culture, and Change in the Hare Krishna Movement," *ISKCON Communications Journal* 5, no. 2 (1997): 1–14; E. Burke Rochford, Jr., "The Changing Face of ISKCON: Family, Congregationalism and Privatization," *ISKCON Communications Journal* 9, no. 1 (2001): 1–12.

49. James D. Chancellor, *Life in the Family: An Oral History of the Children of God* (Syracuse, NY: Syracuse University Press, 2000); David E. Van Zandt, *Living in the Children of God* (Princeton: Princeton University Press, 1991); Roy A Wallis, "Charisma, Commitment and Control in a New Religious Movement," in *Millennialism and Charisma*, ed. Roy Wallis (Belfast: Queens University Press, 1982), 73–140; Roy A. Wallis, "Hostages to Fortune: Thoughts on the Future of Scientology and the Children of God," in *The Future of New Religious Movements*, ed. David G. Bromley and Phillip E. Hammond (Macon, GA: Mercer University Press, 1987), 80–90.

50. Van Zandt, *Living in the Children of God*, 49.

51. Chancellor, *Life in the Family*, 15.

52. Ibid., 30.

53. Robert Balch and Janine Cohig, "The Magic Kingdom: A Story of Armageddon in Utopia," paper presented at the annual meeting of the Society for the Scientific Study of Religion, Savannah, GA, 1985. According to Charles Lewarne, about one hundred members left and resettled on a ranch the Family retained near the town of Arlington, Washington, north of Seattle, for another twenty years. See Charles P. Lewarne, *The Love Israel Family* (Seattle: University of Washington Press, 2008).

54. Lewis F. Carter, *Charisma and Control at Rajneeshpuram: The Role of Shared Values in the Creation of a Community* (New York: Cambridge University Press, 1990).

55. Ibid., 162

56. Miriam Goldman, "When Leaders Dissolve: Considering Controversy and Stagnation in the Osho Rajneesh Movement," in *Controversial New Religions*, ed. James R. Lewis and Jesper A. Peterson (New York: Oxford University Press, 2005), 119–139.

57. Susan J. Palmer and Natalie Finn, "Coping with Apocalypse in Canada: Experiences of Endtime in La Mission de l'Esprit Saint and the Institute of Applied Metaphysics," *Sociological Analysis* 53 (1992): 397–415.

58. Miriam Goldman, "Continuity in Collapse: Departures from Shiloh," *Journal for the Scientific Study of Religion* 34, no. 3 (199): 342–353.

59. Ibid., 344.

60. Ibid.

61. Bradley C. Whitsel, *The Church Universal and Triumphant: Elizabeth Clare Prophet's Apocalyptic Movement* (Syracuse, NY: Syracuse University Press, 2003).

62. Erin Prophet, *Prophet's Daughter: My Life with Elizabeth Clare Prophet: Inside the Church Universal and Triumphant* (Guilford, CT: Lyons, 2009), 238.

63. Whitsel, *The Church Universal and Triumphant*, 115.

64. Ibid.

65. Ibid., 131.

66. Stuart A. Wright and Arthur L. Greil, "Failed Prophecy and Group Demise: The Case of Chen Tao," in *The Failure of Prophecy: Fifty Years after Festinger*, ed. Diana Tumminia and William Swatos (London: Brill, 2011), 153–172.

67. Jerome Bruner, "Life as Narrative," *Social Research* 54 (1987): 11–32; Lewis F. Carter, "Carriers of Tales: On Assessing the Credibility of Apostate and Other Outsider Accounts of Religious Practices," in Bromley, *The Politics of Religious Apostasy*, 221–237; Daniel Carson Johnson, "Apostates Who Never Were: The Social Construction of *Absque Facto* Apostate Narratives," in Bromley, *The Politics of Religious Apostasy*, 115–138; Anabelle Mooney, *The Rhetoric of Religious "Cults": Terms of Use and Misuse* (New York: Palgrave Macmillan, 2005); Wright and Ebaugh, "Leaving New Religions."

68. Armand L. Mauss, "Apostasy and the Management of Spoiled Identity," in Bromley, *The Politics of Religious Apostasy*, 51–74.

69. Johnson, "Apostates Who Never Were," 118.

70. Ibid., 119.

71. Wright, *Leaving Cults*.

72. Shupe and Darnell, *Agents of Discord*; Wright, "Exploring Factors that Shape the Apostate Role."

73. Eileen Barker, "Standing at the Cross-Roads: The Politics of Marginality in 'Subversive Organizations,'" in Bromley, *The Politics of Religious Apostasy*, 75–95.

74. Ibid., 78.

75. Beckford, *Cult Controversies*; Ebaugh, *Becoming an Ex*; Susan Rothbaum, "Between Two Worlds: Issues of Separation and Identity after Leaving a Religious Community," in Bromley, *Falling from the Faith*, 205–228.
76. San Giovanni, *Ex-Nuns: A Study of Emergent Role Passage*.
77. Helen Rose Ebaugh, *Out of the Cloister* (Austin: University of Texas Press, 1977); Ebaugh, *Becoming an Ex*.
78. Rothbaum, "Between Two Worlds," 208.
79. Wright, "Reconceptualizing Cult Coercion"; Jacobs, *Divine Disenchantment*.
80. Carter, "Carriers of Tales," 222–223.
81. David G. Bromley, "Methodological Issues in the Study of NRMs," in *Teaching New Religious Movements*, ed. David G. Bromley (New York: AAR/Oxford University Press, 2007), 65–89; Robert Balch and Stephan Langdon, "How the Problem of Malfeasance Gets Overlooked in Studies of New Religions: An Examination of the AWARE Study of the Church Universal and Triumphant," in *Wolves within the Fold*, ed. Anson D. Shupe (New Brunswick, NJ: Rutgers University Press, 1998), 24–39; Benjamin Zablocki and Thomas Robbins, *Misunderstanding Cults: Searching for Objectivity in a Controversial Field* (Toronto: University of Toronto, 2001).
82. Carter, "Carriers of Tales," 233.
83. Benjamin Zablocki, "Reliability and Validity of Apostate Accounts in the Study of Religious Communities," paper presented at the annual meeting of the Association for the Sociology of Religion, New York, 1996.
84. Johnson, "Apostates Who Never Were," 120.
85. Ibid., 121.
86. Wright, "Exploring Factors that Shape the Apostate Role," 98.
87. Ibid.
88. Meredith B. McGuire, *Religion: The Social Context*, 4th ed. (Belmont, CA: Wadsworth, 1997), 74.
89. James T. Richardson, Jan van der Lans, and Frans Derks, "Leaving and Labeling: Voluntary and Coerced Disaffiliation from Religious Social Movements," in *Social Movements, Conflict and Change*, ed. Kurt Lang and Gladys Lang (Greenwich, CT: JAI Press, 1986), 97–126.

BIBLIOGRAPHY

Anthony, Dick. "Religious Movements and Brainwashing Litigation: Evaluating Key Testimony." In *In Gods We Trust*, 2nd ed., ed. Thomas Robbins and Dick Anthony, 295–344. New Brunswick, NJ: Transaction, 1990.

Anthony, Dick, and Thomas Robbins. "Cultural Crisis and Contemporary Religion." In *In Gods We Trust*, 1st ed., ed. Thomas Robbins and Dick Anthony, 9–31. New Brunswick, NJ: Transaction, 1981.

Balch, Robert W., and David Taylor. "Seekers and Saucers: The Role of the Cultic Milieu in Joining a UFO Cult." *American Behavioral Scientist* 20 (1977): 839–860.

Balch, Robert W., and Janine Cohig. "The Magic Kingdom: A Story of Armageddon in Utopia." Paper presented at the annual meeting of the Society for the Scientific Study of Religion, Savannah, GA, 1985.

Balch, Robert W., and Stephan Langdon. "How the Problem of Malfeasance Gets Overlooked in Studies of New Religions: An Examination of the AWARE Study of the Church Universal and Triumphant." In *Wolves within the Fold*, ed. Anson D. Shupe, 24–39. New Brunswick, NJ: Rutgers University Press, 1998.

Balch, Robert W., John Domitrovitch, Barbara Lynn Mahnke, and Vanessa Morrison. "Fifteen Years of Failed Prophecy: Coping with Cognitive Dissonance in a Baha'i Sect." In *Millennium, Messiahs, and Mayhem: Contemporary Apocalyptic Movements*, ed. Thomas Robbins and Susan J. Palmer, 73–92. London: Routledge, 1997.

Barker, Eileen. "Defection from the Unification Church: Some Statistics and Distinctions." In *Falling from the Faith*, ed. David G. Bromley, 166–184. Newbury Park, CA: Sage, 1988.

——. *The Making of a Moonie: Choice or Brainwashing?* Oxford: Blackwell, 1984.

——. "Standing at the Cross-Roads: The Politics of Marginality in 'Subversive Organizations.'" In *The Politics of Religious Apostasy*, ed. David G. Bromley, 51–74. Westport, CT: Praeger, 1998.

Beckford, James A. *Cult Controversies: The Societal Response to New Religious Movements.* London: Tavistock, 1985.

Bromley, David G. "Deprogramming as a Mode of Exit from New Religious Movements: The Case of the Unificationist Movement." In *Falling from the Faith: The Causes and Consequences of Religious Apostasy*, ed. David G. Bromley, 185–204. Newbury Park, CA: Sage, 1988.

——. "Methodological Issues in the Study of NRMs." In *Teaching New Religious Movements*, ed. David G. Bromley, 65–89. New York: AAR/Oxford University Press, 2007.

——. *The Politics of Religious Apostasy*, ed. David G. Bromley. Westport, CT: Praeger, 1998.

Bromley, David G., and Anson D. Shupe. "Affiliation and Disaffiliation: A Role Theory Interpretation of Joining and Leaving New Religious Movements." Paper presented at the annual meeting of the Association for the Sociology of Religion, San Antonio, TX, 1986.

Brown, J. David. "The Professional Ex-: An Alternative for Exiting the Deviant Career." In *Deviance: The Interactionist Perspective*, ed. Earl Rubington and Martin Weinberg, 439–447. Boston: Allyn & Bacon, 1996.

Bruner, Jerome. "Life as Narrative." *Social Research* 54 (1987): 11–32.

Carter, Lewis F. "Carriers of Tales: On Assessing the Credibility of Apostate and Other Outsider Accounts of Religious Practices." In *The Politics of Religious Apostasy*, ed. David G. Bromley, 221–237. Westport, CT: Praeger, 1998.

——. *Charisma and Control at Rajneeshpuram: The Role of Shared Values in the Creation of a Community.* New York: Cambridge University Press, 1990.

Chancellor, James D. *Life in the Family: An Oral History of the Children of God.* Syracuse, NY: Syracuse University Press, 2000.

Conrad, Peter, and Joseph W. Schneider. *Deviance and Medicalization: From Badness to Sickness.* Philadelphia, PA: Temple University Press, 1992.

Dawson, Lorne. "When Prophecy Fails and Faith Persists: A Theoretical Overview." *Nova Religio* 3 (1999): 60–82.

Dein, Simon. "Lubavitch: A Contemporary Messianic Movement." *Journal of Contemporary Religion* 12 (1997): 191–204.

Downton, James V. "An Evolutionary Theory of Spiritual Conversion and Commitment: The Case of the Divine Light Mission." *Journal for the Scientific Study of Religion* 19, no. 4 (1980): 381–396.

——. *Sacred Journeys: The Conversion of Young Americans to Divine Light Mission.* New York: Columbia University Press, 1979.

Ebaugh, Helen Rose. *Becoming an Ex: The Process of Role Exit*. Chicago: University of Chicago Press, 1988.

———. "Leaving Catholic Convents: Toward a Theory of Disengagement." In *Falling from the Faith*, ed. David G. Bromley, 100–121. Newbury Park, CA: Sage, 1988.

———. *Out of the Cloister*. Austin: University of Texas Press, 1977.

Festinger, Leon, H. W. Riecken, and Stanley Schacter. *When Prophecy Fails*. New York: Harper & Row, 1956.

Freud, Sigmund. *Totem and Taboo*. New York: W. W. Norton, 1950.

Galanter, Marc. *Cults: Faith, Healing and Coercion*. New York: Oxford University Press, 1989.

Gelberg, Steven J. "The Future of Krishna Consciousness in the West: An Insider's Perspective." In *The Future of New Religious Movements*, ed. David G. Bromley and Philip E. Hammond, 187–209. Macon, GA: Mercer University, 1987.

Giambalvo, Carol. *Exit Counseling: A Family Intervention*. Bonita Springs, FL: American Family Foundation, 1992.

Goldman, Miriam. "Continuity in Collapse: Departures from Shiloh." *Journal for the Scientific Study of Religion* 34, no. 3 (1995): 342–353.

———. "When Leaders Dissolve: Considering Controversy and Stagnation in the Osho Rajneesh Movement." In *Controversial New Religions*, ed. James R. Lewis and Jesper A. Peterson, 119–139. New York: Oxford University Press, 2005.

Gooren, Henri. "Towards a New Model of Conversion Careers: The Impact of Personality and Contingency Factors." *Exchange* 34, no. 2 (2005): 149–166.

Greil, Arthur L., and David R. Rudy. "What Have We Learned from Process Models of Conversion? An Examination of Ten Studies." *Sociological Focus* 17, no. 4 (1984): 306–323.

Hall, John R. "Public Narratives and the Apocalyptic Sect: From Jonestown to Mt. Carmel." In *Armageddon in Waco*, ed. Stuart A. Wright, 205–235. Chicago: University of Chicago Press, 1995.

Hall, John R., and Philip Schuyler. "Apostasy, Apocalypse and Religious Violence: An Explanatory Comparison of People's Temple, the Branch Davidians and the Solar Temple." In *The Politics of Religious Apostasy*, ed. David G. Bromley, 141–170. Westport, CT: Praeger, 1998.

Hassan, Steve. *Combating Cult Mind Control*. Rochester, VT: Park Street Press, 1988.

Heelas, Paul. *The New Age Movement: The Celebration of Self and the Sacralization of Modernity*. Cambridge, MA: Blackwell, 1996.

Introvigne, Massimo. "Defectors, Ordinary Leave-Takers and Apostates: A Quantitative Study of Former Members of New Acropolis in France." *Nova Religio* 3, no. 1 (1999): 83–99.

Jacobs, Janet. *Divine Disenchantment: Deconverting from New Religions*. Bloomington: Indiana University Press, 1989.

———. "The Economy of Love in Religious Commitment: The Deconversion of Women from Nontraditional Religion Movements." *Journal for the Scientific Study of Religion* 23, no. 2 (1984): 155–171.

Johnson, Daniel Carson. "Apostates Who Never Were: The Social Construction of *Absque Facto* Apostate Narratives." In *The Politics of Religious Apostasy*, ed. David G. Bromley, 115–138. Westport, CT: Praeger, 1998.

Kohut, Heinz. *The Analysis of the Self*. New York: International University Press, 1971.

Kripal, Jeffrey J., and Glenn W. Shuck. *On the Edge of the Future: Esalen and the Evolution of American Culture*. Bloomington: Indiana University Press, 2005.

Langone, Michael D. *Recovery from Cults: Help for Victims of Psychological and Spiritual Abuse*. New York: W. W. Norton, 1993.

Levine, Saul. *Radical Departures: Desperate Detours to Growing Up*. New York: Harcourt, Brace & Jovanovich, 1984.

Lewarne, Charles P. *The Love Israel Family*. Seattle: University of Washington, 2008.

Lewis, James R. "Reconstructing the 'Cult' Experience." *Sociological Analysis* 47, no. 2 (1986): 151–159.

Lifton, Robert J. "Cult Processes, Religious Totalism and Civil Liberties." In *Cults, Culture and the Law*, ed. Thomas Robbins, William Shepherd, and James McBride, 59–70. Chico, CA: Scholars Press, 1985.

——. *Thought Reform and the Psychology of Totalism*. New York: W. W. Norton, 1961.

Lofland, John, and Rodney Stark. "Becoming a World-Saver: A Theory of Conversion to a Deviant Perspective." *American Sociological Review* 30, no. 6 (1965): 863–874.

Machelek, Richard, and David A. Snow. "Conversion to New Religious Movements." In *The Handbook on Cults and Sects in America*, ed. David G. Bromley and Jeffrey K. Hadden, Vol. 3, part B, 53–74. Greenwich, CT: JAI Press, 1993.

Mauss, Armand L. "Apostasy and the Management of Spoiled Identity." In *The Politics of Religious Apostasy*, ed. David G. Bromley, 51–74. Westport, CT: Praeger, 1998.

McGuire, Meredith B. *Religion: The Social Context*. 4th ed. Belmont, CA: Wadsworth, 1997.

Melton, J. Gordon. "Spiritualization and Reaffirmation: What Really Happens When Prophecy Fails." *American Studies* 26 (1985): 17–29.

Mooney, Anabelle. *The Rhetoric of Religious "Cults": Terms of Use and Misuse*. New York: Palgrave Macmillan, 2005.

Palmer, Susan J., and Natalie Finn. "Coping with Apocalypse in Canada: Experiences of Endtime in La Mission de l'Esprit Saint and the Institute of Applied Metaphysics." *Sociological Analysis* 53 (1992): 397–415.

Palmer, Susan J., and Charlotte E. Hardman. *Children in New Religions*. New Brunswick, NJ: Rutgers, 1999.

Parsons, Arthur. "Messianic Personalism: A Role Analysis of the Unification Church." *Journal for the Scientific Study of Religion* 25, no. 2 (1986): 141–161.

Pollock, Griselda. "Beyond Oedipus: Feminist Thought, Psychoanalysis, and Mythical Figurations of the Feminine." In *Laughing with Medusa*, ed. Vanda Zajko and Miriam Leonard, 67–120. New York: Oxford University Press, 2006.

Prophet, Erin. *Prophet's Daughter: My Life with Elizabeth Clare Prophet: Inside the Church Universal and Triumphant*. Guilford, CT: Lyons, 2009.

Rambo, Lewis R. *Understanding Religious Conversion*. New Haven: Yale University Press, 1993.

Richardson, James T. "Apostates, Whistleblowers, Law and Social Control." In *The Politics of Religious Apostasy*, ed. David G. Bromley, 171–190. Westport, CT: Praeger, 1998.

——. *Conversion Careers: In and Out of the New Religions*. Beverly Hills, CA: Sage, 1978.

——. "Social Control of New Religions: From Brainwashing Claims to Child Sex Abuse Accusations." In *Children in New Religions*, ed. Susan J. Palmer and Charlotte E. Hardman, 172–186. New Brunswick, NJ: Rutgers University, 1999.

——. "A Social Psychological Critique of 'Brainwashing' Claims about Recruitment to New Religions." In *Handbook on Cults and Sects in America*, ed. David G. Bromley and Jeffrey K. Hadden, Vol. 3, part B, 75–98. Greenwich, CT: JAI Press, 1993.

Richardson, James T., and Mary H. Stewart. "Conversion Process Models and the Jesus Movement." In *Conversion Careers*, ed. James T. Richardson, 24–42. Beverly Hills, CA: Sage, 1978.

Richardson, James T., Mary H. Stewart, and Robert B. Simmonds. *Organized Miracles: A Study of a Contemporary, Youth, Communal, Fundamentalist Organization*. New Brunswick, NJ: Transaction, 1978.

Richardson, James T., Jan van der Lans, and Frans Derks. "Leaving and Labeling: Voluntary and Coerced Disaffiliation from Religious Social Movements." In *Social Movements, Conflict and Change*, ed. Kurt Lang and Gladys Lang, 97–126. Greenwich, CT: JAI Press, 1986.

Robbins, Thomas. *Cults, Converts and Charisma*. Newbury Park, CA: Sage, 1988.

Robbins, Thomas, and Susan J. Palmer. *Millennium, Messiahs, and Mayhem: Contemporary Apocalyptic Movements*. London: Routledge, 1997.

Rochford, E. Burke, Jr. "The Changing Face of ISKCON: Family, Congregationalism and Privatization." *ISKCON Communications Journal* 9, no. 1 (2001): 1–12.

——. "Family Formation, Culture, and Change in the Hare Krishna Movement." *ISKCON Communications Journal* 5, no. 2 (1997): 1–14.

——. "Family Structure, Commitment and Involvement in the Hare Krishna Movement." *Sociology of Religion* 56, no. 2 (1995): 153–176.

——. *Hare Krishna in America*. New Brunswick, NJ: Rutgers University Press, 1985.

——. *Hare Krishna Transformed*. New York: New York University Press, 2007.

Ross, Joan Carol, and Michael D. Langone. *Cults: What Parents Should Know*. Weston. MA: American Family Foundation, 1988.

Ryan, Patrick. "A Personal Account: Eastern Mediation Group." In *Recovery from Cults*, ed. Michael D. Langone, 129–139. New York: W. W. Norton, 1993.

San Giovanni, Lucinda. *Ex-Nuns: A Study of Emergent Role Passage*. Norwood, NJ: Ablex, 1978.

Schein, Edwin, Inge Schneier, and Curtis H. Barker. *Coercive Persuasion*. New York: W. W. Norton, 1961.

Schmalz, Matthew N. "When Festinger Fails: Prophecy and the Watchtower." *Religion* 24 (1994): 298–308.

Schreinert, Tamatha, and James T. Richardson. "Pyrrhic Victory? An Analysis of the Appeal Court Opinions Concerning the FLDS Children." In *Saints under Siege: The Texas State Raid on the Fundamentalist Latter Day Saints*, ed. Stuart A. Wright and James T. Richardson, 242–264. New York: New York University Press, 2011.

Shaffir, William. "When Prophecy Is Not Validated: Explaining the Unexpected in a Messianic Campaign." *Jewish Journal of Sociology* 37 (1995): 119–136.

Shupe, Anson D., and Susan Darnell. *Agents of Discord: Deprogrammers, Pseudo-Science and the American Anticult Movement*. New Brunswick, NJ: Transaction, 2006.

Singelenberg, Richard. "It Separated the Wheat from the Chaff: The '1975' Prophecy and Its Impact among Dutch Jehovah's Witnesses." *Sociological Analysis* 50 (1989): 23–40.

Skonovd, L. Norman. "Apostasy: The Process of Defection from Religious Totalism." PhD diss., University of California, Davis. Ann Arbor, MI: University Microfilms International, 1981.

——. "Leaving the Cultic Religious Milieu." In *The Brainwashing/Deprogramming Controversy*, ed. David G. Bromley and James T. Richardson, 91–105. New York: Edwin Mellen, 1983.

Snow, David A., and Richard Machalek. "The Sociology of Conversion." *Annual Review of Sociology* 10 (1984): 167–190.

Stark, Rodney, and Laurence R. Iannaccone. "Why the Jehovah's Witnesses Grow So Rapidly: A Theoretical Application." *Journal of Contemporary Religion* 12 (1997): 133–157.

Stone, Jon. R. *Expecting Armageddon: Essential Readings in Failed Prophecy*. New York: Routledge, 2000.

Taslimi, Cheryl Rowe, Ralph W. Hood, Jr., and P. J. Watson. "Assessment of Former Members of Shiloh: The Adjective Check List 17 Years Later." *Journal for the Scientific Study of Religion* 30, no. 3 (1991): 306–311.

Tobias, Madeleine Landau, and Janja Lalich. *Captive Hearts, Captive Minds*. Alameda, CA: Hunter House, 1994.

Tumminia, Diana. G. *When Prophecy Never Fails: Myth and Reality in a Flying-Saucer Group*. Berkeley and Los Angeles: University of California Press, 2005.

Van Zandt, David E. *Living in the Children of God*. Princeton: Princeton University Press, 1991.

Whitsel, Bradley C. *The Church Universal and Triumphant: Elizabeth Clare Prophet's Apocalyptic Movement*. Syracuse, NY: Syracuse University Press, 2003.

Wright, Stuart A. "Construction and Escalation of a Cult Threat: Dissecting Moral Panic and Official Reaction to the Branch Davidians." In *Armageddon in Waco: Critical Perspectives on the Branch Davidian Conflict*, ed. Stuart A. Wright, 75–94. Chicago: University of Chicago Press, 1995.

——. "Defection from New Religious Movements: A Test of Some Theoretical Propositions." In *The Brainwashing/ Deprogramming Controversy*, ed. David G. Bromley and James T. Richardson, 106–121. New York: Edwin Mellen, 1983.

——. "The Dynamics of Movement Membership: Joining and Leaving NRMs." In *Teaching New Religious Movements*, ed. David G. Bromley, 187–210. New York: Oxford University Press, 2007.

——. "Exploring Factors that Shape the Apostate Role." In *The Politics of Religious Apostasy*, ed. David G. Bromley, 95–114. Westport, CT: Praeger, 1998.

——. "From Children of God to The Family: Movement Adaptation and Survival." In *Sex, Slander and Salvation*, ed. James R. Lewis and J. Gordon Melton, 121–128. Stanford, CA: Center for Academic Publishing, 1994.

——. *Leaving Cults: The Dynamics of Defection*. Washington, DC: Society for the Scientific Study of Religion, 1987.

——. "Leaving New Religious Movements: Issues, Theory and Research." In *Falling from the Faith*, ed. David G. Bromley, 143–165. Newbury Park, CA: Sage, 1988.

——. "Post-Involvement Attitudes of Voluntary Defectors from New Religious Movements." *Journal for the Scientific Study of Religion* 23, no. 2 (1984): 172–182.

——. "Public Agency Involvement in Movement-State Confrontations." In *Cults, Religion and Violence*, ed. David G. Bromley and J. Gordon Melton, 102–122. New York: Cambridge University Press, 2002.

——. "Reconceptualizing Cult Coercion: A Comparative Analysis of Divorce and Apostasy." *Social Forces* 70 (1991): 125–145.

Wright, Stuart A., and William V. D'Antonio. 1993. "Families and New Religions." In *The Handbook on Cults and Sects in America*, ed. David G. Bromley and Jeffrey K. Hadden, Vol. 3, part A, 219–240. Westport, CT: JAI Press, 1993.

Wright, Stuart A., and Helen Rose Ebaugh. "Leaving New Religions." In *The Handbook on Cults and Sects in America*, ed. David G. Bromley and Jeffrey K. Hadden, Vol. 3, part B, 117–138. Westport, CT: JAI Press, 1993.

Wright, Stuart A., and Arthur L. Greil. "Failed Prophecy and Group Demise: The Case of Chen Tao." In *The Failure of Prophecy: Fifty Years after Festinger*, ed. Diana Tumminia and William Swatos, 153–172. London: Brill, 2011.

Wright, Stuart A., and James T. Richardson, eds. *Saints under Siege: The Texas State Raid on the Fundamentalist Latter Day Saints*. New York: New York University Press, 2011.

Zablocki, Benjamin. "Reliability and Validity of Apostate Accounts in the Study of Religious Communities." Paper presented at the annual meeting of the Association for the Sociology of Religion, New York, 1996.

Zablocki, Benjamin, and Thomas Robbins. *Misunderstanding Cults: Searching for Objectivity in a Controversial Field*. Toronto: University of Toronto, 2001.

Zimbardo, Phillip, and Susan Anderson. "Understanding Mind Control: Exotic and Mundane Mental Manipulations." In *Recovery from Cults*, ed. Michael D. Langone, 104–128. New York: W. W. Norton, 1993.

Zygmunt, Joseph. F. "Prophetic Failure and Chiliastic Identity: The Case of Jehovah's Witnesses." *American Journal of Sociology* 75 (1970): 926–948.

——. "When Prophecies Fail." *American Behavioral Scientist* 16 (1972): 245–268.

CHAPTER 31

....

LEGAL AND POLITICAL ISSUES AND RELIGIOUS CONVERSION

....

JAMES T. RICHARDSON

INTRODUCTION

....

CONVERSION is usually treated in the scholarly literature as an individual behavior engaged in by a person who decides to change his or her religion, or to become religious if they were not.[1] Thus, a study of conversion usually focuses on the convert and is individual and specific in its approach. Proselytizing is usually thought of as more organizational; study of this topic focuses on what religious groups do to recruit and convert new members.[2] Both the individual act of converting and the more organized process of proselytizing have come under scrutiny by government authorities in many nations, and both have had social control efforts focused on them.[3] In some regions it is considered a criminal offense for a person to change his or her religion, and in many others there may be considerable moral approbation associated with the decision to change religion or to become more or less religious.[4] The right to explain one's religion to others, that is, to proselytize, which is integral to efforts to recruit and to activities required or expected in some religions, is often impinged upon by governments. The impingements vary greatly, from outright banning of such activities on pain of death, to subtle normative pressures brought to bear in various ways, as well as everything in between these two extremes.

This chapter discusses and illustrates some legal restrictions and controls on conversion and proselytizing as practiced around the world in various countries and regions and also examines whether some religious traditions seem to foster more restrictive approaches to proselytizing. I begin with a discussion of the situation in the United States, then move to an examination of the European scene, and finally close with some coverage of other nations and regions of the world.

Conversion, Proselytizing, and the Law in the United States

The United States has always been a pluralistic nation, even if that pluralism has some-times been marked with conflict and controversy. Indeed, the establishment of the new nation was steeped in religious conflict, leading to the famous historical compro-mise concerning religion in the First Amendment.[5] Since no one religious group had the numbers and power to have itself designated the state religion for the new nation, an agreement was reached that allowed different religions to be practiced but also pre-cluded the government from selecting one faith as the state religion. Thus the much mimicked "lively experiment" was underway in America, leading to the development of some quite conversionistic religions within this context of open competition. Religious groups were forced to seek new converts in order to survive, and this need has con-tributed to a general, even if sometimes contested, acceptance of religious proselytizing efforts within American culture.

The American experiment of religious competition and conversion has taken many twists and turns over the nearly two and a half centuries since the new nation was formed, and not all of those can be recounted here. However, two major developments will be discussed to demonstrate the development and contours of contemporary legal theories about conversion to and proselytizing by religious groups in America. First, the extremely important line of US Supreme Court cases involving Jehovah's Witnesses that began in the 1940s will be briefly summarized, as they laid the groundwork for modern approaches to religious proselytizing. Then, the more recent controversy over recruit-ment activities of New Religious Movements (NRMs) will be discussed.

Before moving to these two areas, it should be noted that within the American con-text the individual act of conversion generally is legally protected, even if sometimes quite controversial, as will be shown in the discussion of NRM recruitment. The con-stitutional guarantee of freedom of religion has usually been interpreted as meaning that anyone can believe anything they want, and that right includes the right to change one's religion. Indeed, changing one's religion in the United States is something of an art form for some, as sociological studies of denominational switching and the relation-ship of religious affiliation to social class demonstrate.[6] There are, however, limitations on behavior that might be associated with beliefs; thus, handling of poisonous snakes, polygamy, and use of LSD as a religious sacrament are not legally allowed, even if sanc-tioned by certain religious beliefs. What has been controversial in America, and sub-ject to many efforts at social control, both governmental and private self-help, are the organized efforts at proselytizing developed by some of the religious groups operating within American society.

Jehovah's Witnesses and Legalization of Proselytizing

Between 1938 and 1960, more than fifty cases involving the Jehovah's Witnesses[7] reached the US Supreme Court, and the Witnesses won about two-thirds of those cases, many of which involved controversies over Witness proselytizing methods. The methods used, which involved going through neighborhoods knocking on doors, handing out Witness literature, and talking to anyone who answered, were deemed aggressive and intrusive by many. This led to efforts to control such intrusions, with a common tactic being a requirement for a government-issued permit before engaging in such activities.

The Witnesses took severe umbrage at such limitations and refused in droves to abide by them around the country, leading to many confrontations and arrests. Witness attorneys fought these arrests, and eventually cases involving the right to distribute literature and proselytize made their way to the Supreme Court. A number of those cases were won on freedom of speech and freedom of religion grounds, establishing clearly that the right to talk to others in a public space was constitutional. In this way, the sociological fact of a structure of competitiveness established with the First Amendment's religion clauses referred to earlier was finally given overt sanction in law. Anyone in America could talk to others about joining their particular religious faith, within certain bounds set by the Supreme Court decisions. Thus, the motif of proselytizing activities became more acceptable, and more religious groups engaged in such endeavors as they tried to spread their faith.[8]

Legal Strategies Used against NRM Proselytizing

In more recent years, the advent of New Religious Movements (NRMs) has tested the limits of religious freedom, including the right to practice the religion of one's choice and to change religions, both of which typically involve proselytizing activities. When new NRM groups developed in the 1960s and early 1970s, they began getting attention from mass media almost immediately. To most people NRMs were quite strange, and it was not easy to understand why a significant number of young people from America's best-educated and most affluent generation ever would choose to affiliate with such groups. But join they did, even if temporarily,[9] and thus considerable attention was focused on Jesus Movement groups, especially the controversial Children of God, Reverend Moon's Unification Church, the Hare Krishna, the Divine Light Mission, The Way International, The Family of Love, and Scientology, to name a few of the more controversial ones. To see this outpouring of interest in religion among youth in an age that was assumed to be increasingly secular was disquieting to many, including political leaders and the media but also some parents of converts, leading to efforts to exert social control over the new groups and their activities.[10]

Many of the NRMs were quite conversionistic and spent considerable time and resources attempting to disseminate their literature and to recruit others. The groups also had to raise money to support themselves, leading to a confluence of proselytizing and fundraising in some of the more controversial groups such as the Unification Church (UC) and the Hare Krishna (HK), a development that made them more vulnerable to social control efforts.[11] This also led to some limitations on the kinds of activities that had been sanctioned by the line of cases involving Jehovah's Witnesses. Severe "time, place, and manner" restrictions were placed on some activities in particular public locations, such as the quite prevalent for a time fundraising endeavors of the Hare Krishna in airports and in other public places. However, the UC won many legal actions against regulations designed to keep them from raising funds on the streets of America. The UC fought against the same sort of regulatory efforts that the Witnesses had battled in earlier decades, and they usually won, maintaining the concept of public streets being public forums open to religious and politically motivated actions and speech.

Two major and related legal issues related directly to NRM conversion and proselytizing endeavors deserve some discussion. One, which involved a focus on individual converts, was a significant effort to expand what are called conservatorship laws to cover young people who had joined an NRM.[12] This expansion was built upon claims that those involved in NRMs had been "brainwashed" and were under some sort of "mind control." These terms derived from politically charged claims and research associated with the Communist takeover in China and the treatment of Korean War prisoners of war, some of whom chose to stay in Korea after the war was over.[13]

Some were willing to claim that these young people would not be participating in such groups without psychological techniques that could overcome their "free will." Therefore, as the logic went, it should be acceptable to apply conservatorship laws to such cases, since the young people were defined as incapacitated by virtue of their involvement with NRMs. Conservatorship statutes were originally designed to make it possible for adult children to manage the financial affairs and other aspects of the life of aged parents who were incapacitated. Court orders could be sought that would allow the adult children to take over all or part of the affairs of elderly parents who could not function well because of age-related infirmities.

When sons and daughters of relatively high-status Americans started joining strange NRMs, a number of parents sought ways to regain control over their children, even if the children were legally of age (which in the United States is age 18). The tactic of claiming that the children were incapacitated, and thus eligible for application of conservatorship laws by virtue of their having joined an NRM, was tried in a number of states, and for a number of years was sometimes successful. If a conservatorship was granted by the court, then it could be enforced by local law enforcement officials. This occurred a number of times, with the local sheriff serving the order and taking the NRM member into custody in order to return them to their parents. The parents in turn often placed their offspring in the custody of what came to be called "deprogrammers" who attempted to "deconvert" the person using rigorous resocialization techniques. However, the courts finally stated that young adults who were of legal age could not be controlled under such laws just because of their religious preference. The innovative use of conservatorship laws with NRM participants lasted a few years in the mid-1970s and clearly demonstrated the extent to which some parents would go to secure control of their adult children who had converted to an NRM.

Organizations to deprogram members of NRMs were developed in several areas of the country, and a number of individual deprogramming entrepreneurs also offered their services to parents desiring to extract their sons and daughters from NRMs through legal means (conservatorships) if possible, but some offered extra-legal methods if needed.[14] A number of former NRM members, along with a few professional psychologists and others, helped establish the new pseudo-profession of deprogramming, which had as its goal the resocialization of NRM members back into normal society. These organizations sometimes cooperated with those seeking conservatorships and also with some former NRM members who were kidnapped by deprogrammers and "successfully" put through a quite coercive process, both physically and psychologically, that was designed to encourage NRM members to forego allegiance to the NRM.[15]

It is quite noteworthy that although there were thousands of deprogrammings taking place in America, very few deprogrammers were ever charged with violating kidnapping laws, and those who were charged usually were not found guilty. Civil actions against deprogrammers (and those who had hired them, usually parents) also were seldom successful. Thus, it seemed for a time in America that the usual more casual approach to individual conversions was being set aside in favor of a more rigorous limitation on what some young people could do in terms of religious affiliation.

Deprogramming was allowed to flourish for a number of years with impunity in American society because of the widespread, even hegemonic, belief that anyone who participated in a NRM must have been "brainwashed" to do so and must be under "mind control" in order to remain a member. Many NRMs were simply not allowed to self-define themselves as religions, and, as noted, it was assumed that some powerful psychological techniques must have been used to "force" participation. This interpretation of the meaning of participation led to the second major legal issue to be considered with regard to NRM conversion, that being the use of "brainwashing"-based claims in legal actions against NRMs. These claims focused directly on alleged proselytizing methods used by some NRMs, about which there was a widespread belief among the general public that the methods used were unacceptable.[16]

A related effort that did not make much headway legally was that by law professor Richard Delgado, who proposed that religious proselytizing should adhere to strict "informed consent" guidelines.[17] Delgado argued in a major law review article that those doing proselytizing should immediately disclose that they were a member of a religious group and that they were attempting to recruit the person being talked to by the recruiter. Delgado, who implicitly accepted a "brainwashing"-based view of what was happening with NRM recruitment, claimed that when people were first approached by an NRM they were most able to exercise their critical faculties, but that the NRM's deceptive tactics kept them from knowing enough to do so. Later, after the person being recruited knew more about the group, Delgado claimed that their critical faculties had been overcome, thus leaving them in a vulnerable position. Although this proposal did not gain favor and was never enacted into law anywhere in America, its publication in a major law review does demonstrate the strength of concern about NRMs and their recruitment methods.

For decades, a few former members and others involved (such as their parents) relied on civil actions in the courts for a remedy against proselytizing NRMs who had recruited them. This was done in part because governments—local, state, and federal—were precluded by the First Amendment's protection of religious freedom from direct intervention in decisions to join a religious group by people who were legally adults. However, self-help civil actions were filed against a number of NRMs claiming any one or more of several alleged abuses, including intentional affliction of emotional distress, fraud, and false imprisonment. For years these civil suits, though few in number, were successful at least at the trial court level, garnering a tremendous amount of publicity and helping establish the idea that NRM members were indeed "brainwashed."

It took several years and much concerted effort by scholars involved in NRM research and others to get the courts to reject tort actions based on "brainwashing"-based claims.[18] This was finally accomplished with a series of cases in federal courts where judges agreed that such claims were inadmissible because they did not meet basic criteria established for admission of scientific evidence.[19] Although the legal picture has changed as a result of the rulings, it should be understood that the general public and many opinion and political leaders still hold to the "brainwashing" and "mind control" view of proselytizing by NRMs.[20] Also, it should be noted that this idea has been diffused around the world and is still alive and well in some judicial systems and in governmental policymaking in some nations.[21]

THE EUROPEAN WAY OF LIMITATION

Conversion and Proselytizing in Europe

European nations, with some exceptions, tend to be more paternalistic toward their citizens than has typically been the case in the United States, and this certainly includes the area of religion. The reasons for this are many and varied but include the long history of religious conflict and the historical fact of state-sanctioned churches in many European countries. European tendencies toward paternalism concerning the religious preferences of citizens have been exacerbated in recent decades by the affiliation of a number of formerly Soviet-dominated nations from Eastern and Central Europe with Western European nations in the Council of Europe and the European Union. As some of those nations have been relieved of Soviet domination, their long-suppressed traditional state-sanctioned churches have exerted themselves quite strongly, and that exertion has sometimes included efforts to limit the operations of other religious groups, especially proselytizing ones from the West.[22]

The European context for conversion and proselytizing usually translates into much more governmental involvement and official interest in things religious than is the case in the United States.[23] There is not a history of First Amendment jurisprudence in most European countries, even if most do demonstrate considerable tolerance for other "normal" religions, and some, such as The Netherlands, Denmark, and Italy, allow controversial minority faiths to operate with relative impunity.[24] There is no "anti-establishment clause" precluding a state-sanctioned religion in the governing documents of most European countries, which is a reflection of the long history of close church-state relations in Europe. However, there is a general acceptance of the concept of religious freedom, even though there are apparent normative limitations in many European nations on which religious groups are or are not acceptable.

Many legal and political battles have been fought in European countries over minority religions, and a number of these battles focus on recruitment methods. The diffusion from the United States of "brainwashing"-based ideas about how minority religions recruit has undergirded efforts at social control exerted by some nations within the European region. France even attempted to criminalize proselytizing efforts by some religious groups as part of a new, quite punitive law passed in 2001 outlawing "mental manipulation" by representatives of religious "sects and cults." The term "mental manipulation" was defined similarly to the term "brainwashing" within the American context. France has also furnished government funding for anti-sect and -cult groups and has allowed them to have standing to file legal actions against unpopular religious groups.[25] Germany has had a decades-long battle over Scientology and still engages in government surveillance of this organization and its members. Germany also has recently lost another long battle over official recognition of the Jehovah's Witnesses, with major court decisions forcing official recognition of the organization at least in some German states. Several European countries, including Germany and the United Kingdom, have disallowed until very recently any visit by Reverend Moon, leader of the Unification Church, to those countries. And converts to unpopular religions such as Scientology and the Witnesses have been punished in France, Belgium, Germany, and other countries by losing jobs and other negative sanctions, including even custody of children in divorce disputes between former members and spouses who remained in a minority religion. In some (but not all) former Soviet-dominated nations the situation is even worse, with minority religions, especially those engaged in overt proselytizing, being treated in a discriminatory fashion within the legal systems of those countries.

It would be remiss not to discuss the situation with regard to Islam in Europe, as this has become an issue of considerable controversy.[26] European nations made heavy use of "guest workers" after the Second World War as the societies sought to rebuild their economies. Many of those workers came from Turkey and were Muslim, and many of those guests decided to stay in the host country instead of returning home. Also, nations such as France, the United Kingdom, and The Netherlands found themselves being forced by virtue of their colonial history to accept large numbers of people from various colonies and former colonies, and many of them were practitioners of Islam. This influx of people from very different cultural backgrounds into the relatively homogeneous Western European context has led to considerable conflict and controversy. Activities of the Muslim communities designed to promote and develop Islam in Western Europe have tested the normal levels of tolerance in these societies and will continue to do so as Western Europe tries to find a way to deal with the new pluralism that includes a some-times quite aggressively proselytizing Islam.

The European Court of Human Rights

The European Court of Human Rights (ECHR), located in Strasbourg, France, is per-haps the most influential judicial institution in the contemporary world. The Court, established in 1950 to promote and protect human rights in the nations ravaged by the Second World War, is the court of last resort for nearly 900 million people in some forty-six nations that are members of the Council of Europe. The Court is charged with enforcing provisions of the European Convention on Human Rights and Fundamental Freedoms, including its famous Article 9, which reads as follows:

- Everyone has the right to freedom of thought, conscience and religion; this right includes freedom to change his religion or belief, and freedom, either alone or in community with others and in public or private, to manifest his religion or belief, in worship, teaching, practice and observance.
- Freedom to manifest one's religion or beliefs shall be subject only to such limita-tions as are prescribed by law and are necessary in a democratic society in the interests of public safety, for the protection of public order, health or morals, or the protection of the rights and freedoms of others.

On reading the two provisions of Article 9, it is clear that considerable ambiguity exists in reconciling the two provisions, thus allowing considerable discretion in inter-preting and applying Article 9 to specific cases. Indeed it was only in 1993, forty-three years after the establishment of the ECHR, that the Court, in a case involving prosely-tizing by the Jehovah's Witnesses in Greece, finally found a violation of Article 9. Even then it was with a badly divided court and a vote of six to three, and one of the dissent-ing judges used the term "brainwashing" to refer to the proselytizing practices of the Witnesses, suggesting that some on the Court thought the proselytizing tactics of the Witnesses were excessive and even unlawful.[27]

The case, *Kokkinakis v. Greece*, involved a claim by a Witness who had been found guilty of violating a criminal statute in Greece against proselytizing that his rights under Article 9 of the Convention had been violated. Kokkinakis had been arrested a num-ber of previous times for proselytizing, as had thousands of other practitioners of the Witness faith. Indeed, the court record evidenced the fact that the only people ever charged under the criminal statute (several thousand of them) were members of the Jehovah's Witnesses. Kokkinakis and his wife had attempted to recruit the wife of the local Greek Orthodox Kantor to their faith, resulting in both being charged with violat-ing the statute against such activities. Although charges against the wife were eventually dropped, Kokkinakis was fined and sentenced to a term of imprisonment, leading to his appeal to the ECHR.

Why the Court chose this time and this case to finally find, even on a split vote, a violation of Article 9 is subject to some debate. For over forty years a doctrine that is referred to as the "margin of appreciation" had prevailed in ECHR decisions concerning religion. This doctrine meant that nations were free to regulate religion as they saw fit, following the laws and traditions of a given society. Richardson and Garay have suggested that the timing of the *Kokkinakis* decision may have been related to the fall of the Soviet Union and the press of many former Soviet-dominated countries to join the Council of Europe.[28] Given the historical context of Soviet oppression of religion and religious groups, perhaps the ECHR decided to change its long-running posture of ignoring possible violations of Article 9 that favored national autonomy in matters of religion. The Court may have decided to break new ground and establish a precedent concerning religious freedom in order to better deal with the issue of religious freedom in former Soviet-dominated nations. Greece was the only member of the Council of Europe with a law criminalizing proselytizing. Therefore, perhaps Greece was a convenient example to show the nations no longer dominated by the Soviet Union what was to be expected in terms of religious freedom, if they chose to join the Council of Europe.

Whatever the reason, the ECHR, after *Kokkinakis*, started issuing a number of rulings that developed a jurisprudence based on Article 9 claims. The pattern of these cases is fascinating in that Greece has continued to be the "bad example," with many cases resulting in rulings against this long-time member of the Council of Europe. Most of these Greece cases also involve the Jehovah's Witnesses, as this group seems to be establishing a pattern somewhat similar to what happened a few decades ago in the United States and Canada in jurisprudence concerning religious freedom and freedom of speech. Most ECHR cases finding a violation of Article 9 involve countries formerly dominated by the Soviet Union, lending some support to a "double-standard" hypothesis offered by Richardson and Garay. They suggest that the ECHR treats original members of the Council of Europe (except Greece, with it odd criminalization of proselytizing) with deference, leaving the "margin of appreciation" doctrine in place for them but enforcing Article 9 more vigorously with newer members of the COE, a conclusion supported by analysis of more recent ECHR cases.[29]

Even though the ECHR finally did decide to enforce Article 9, its pattern of decisions has been roundly criticized by scholars such as Paul Taylor and Carolyn Evans.[30] They both focus on the issue of protection of the right of individuals to change their religious affiliation, a right they claim is being ignored by the ECHR but which, according to Taylor, has been offered much more protection by the United Nations than in the European context with the ECHR. The United Nations and its Human Rights Committee has over the years always taken a strong position protecting the right to change one's religion and resisting pressures from some states to make such actions illegal, a posture in sharp contrast to the jurisprudence being developed by the ECHR.

Implied in the right to change religions is, of course, the right to proselytize. Although it is theoretically possible to have people change religions without any contact with members of the newly chosen faith, this does not occur with great frequency, even in the Internet age. What usually happens, according to considerable sociological research on conversion and recruitment, is that someone who is a member of the new faith approaches the potential convert and talks to them about joining. A reading of Article 9(1) certainly suggests that this kind of activity would be accepted and perhaps even expected in increasingly pluralistic societies. However, a line of decisions, starting with *Kokkinakis* but continuing with several other key ECHR decisions, has established a "right to be left alone" that is not articulated in the specific wording of Article 9(1). This right to be left alone in matters concerning religion, or "respect" for the beliefs and feelings of others, is not explicitly included in Article 9, but this right has been established by a generous reading of the limitations clause in Article 9(2) by the ECHR, as noted by both Evans and Taylor, which will be discussed below.

In *Kokkinakis* the Court did not explicitly rule that the criminal statute was in violation of Article 9, and the written decision, especially the strongly worded dissent, indicated that some types of proselytizing are unacceptable in that they do not show adequate respect for the religious beliefs of others. This line of thinking was carried forward in some other decisions of the Court, including some that allowed governments in Austria and the United Kingdom to ban the showing of certain films with religious themes that the Court agreed would offend the majority of the general public. In one of these cases, *Otto-Preminger v. Austria*, the Court, according to Taylor, "went so far as to equate 'respect for the religious feelings of believers' with the guarantees in Article 9 even though it is not easy to find anything comparable to such a right within the traditionally recognized realm of Article 9."[31] Taylor adds, "It is paradoxical that rights of doubtful origin may easily be invoked within limitations provisions, while certain rights more traditionally accepted as falling within the protections of Article 9 find limited recognition within European jurisprudence."[32]

In summary, the Court that is most often looked to around the world as a defender of human and civil rights has compromised religious freedom rights, especially the right to proselytize, quite significantly. It has indicated in several rulings that certain forms of proselytizing might be beyond the bounds of civilized society and that minority faiths should be respectful of the religious beliefs and feelings of others as they go about their efforts to recruit new members. The ECHR has established a recent jurisprudence that seems more supportive of religious freedom, with a growing line of cases with findings that seem to establish some authority over at least some Member States in matters concerning religion and religious groups. However, those rights have limitations, as is clearly indicated by the reticence of the Court to rule against most original members of the Council of Europe and its willingness to indicate that some proselytizing does not deserve protections under the European Convention of Human Rights.

PROSELYTIZING AND CONVERSION AROUND THE WORLD

There is a tremendous variation in how nations around the globe view proselytizing and conversion. Some, such as Australia and New Zealand, seem more Western European (and somewhat tolerant) in their approach, while others, particular Muslim-dominated nations, are often very rigorous in their efforts to limit proselytizing by non-Muslin religions and individual conversion to other faiths. Several recent volumes have described this variegated pattern that exists around the world with reference to social control of minority religions, including recruitment methods used by the groups. These include a quite recent article edited by religious studies scholar Rosalind Hackett and two that were produced in 2004 by Philip Lucas and Tom Robbins and by James Richardson, all three of whom are sociologists.[33]

All these volumes and other relevant writings call attention to the ironic fact that religious freedom in the modern age has led to much controversy about efforts to recruit. Much, but not all, of that controversy involves various Western or Christian religious organizations attempting to convert citizens of non-Western, non-Christian societies. Those efforts are frequently viewed within the targeted societies as more ideological and political than religious. Thus, Huntington's "clash of civilizations" seems to be occurring, particularly as Western Christian groups seek to promote their brand of religion to other cultures that are Muslim, Hindu, or officially atheistic and as Muslin groups attempt to spread their religion aggressively into areas typically defined as Western Christian societies.

In a number of nations, laws have been passed making proselytization a criminal offense, and people have been jailed for attempting to propagate their faith. This is the case in some parts of India, in Uzbekistan, and in China, the latter of which has experienced massive suppressions of religions not approved by the State. And in some countries, being a member of an unapproved faith can carry with it severe penalties, including even a death sentence. Iran exemplifies this quite punitive approach to conversion, especially in its treatment of members of the Baha'i faith. China also has visited very harsh treatment on large numbers of participants in the Falun Gong movement; nearly three thousand are estimated to have died in Chinese prisons.[34]

POLITICS AND SCHOLARSHIP OF CONVERSION

Conversion and proselytizing have been controversial in a number of societies, as discussed above. The controversy has also engulfed scholars, as battles have been

fought in legislatures, parliaments, and in court systems around the world. A number of scholars, including this author, have been involved in such activities over the
years, serving as consultants and sources of information to religious groups and to
others concerned about recruitment issues, serving as an expert witness in legal cases
in a number of countries, and testifying in state legislatures and parliaments.[35] A few
scholars, including Gordon Melton, Eileen Barker, and Massimo Introvigne, have
established organizations that often focus on issues related to proselytizing, conversion, and recruitment to New Religious Movements and minority faiths, mainly in
Western countries.[36]

Scholars have become embroiled in these arenas for several reasons. One major
impetus concerns the failure by policymakers to attend to results of considerable
sound research on new and minority faiths. The casual and very problematic adoption of the "brainwashing" and "mind control" myths by policymakers around the
world offends scholars who have done the field work repudiating such ideologically grounded concepts. Some of those scholars have decided to enter the fray to
attempt a corrective and to point out that sometimes those in power use minority
faiths as pawns in larger political games, adopting and promoting the myths cyni-
cally to achieve certain aims. Such policymakers choose to ignore research results
that clearly demonstrate that their citizens have acted on their own volition to seek
an ethic and set of beliefs that they believe will serve them better than those offered
by traditional religious groups.[37]

Other scholars are motivated by more theoretically grounded concerns about the
impact of a failure by policymakers to recognize growing diversity and pluralism
in our contemporary world. Religious and cultural pluralism are here to stay and
suppressing them seems futile and potentially very destructive. Minority religious
groups represent cauldrons of social experimentation and evolution.[38] Attempting
to stop such expected activities can be very costly and defeatist for regimes seeking
to maintain the status quo. The status quo may not serve well in times of rapid social
change, and stifling efforts to find new ways of life that offer some solace in trying
times can undermine political structures. Fostering social experimentation may be
the better course in such situations, and some scholars argue that such an approach
should not be discarded out of hand.

Yet another motivation for some scholars is a personal subscription to a set of values that includes human and civil rights, including religious freedom.[39] The exertion of
social control over new and minority faiths offends such values, leading some scholars
to speak out and become involved in political and cultural battles over the right of citizens to practice the faith of their choice and to change their religion if they desire. Such
action-oriented scholarship raises questions about objectivity of scholars, to be sure,
but a few have been motivated to grapple openly with political leaders, judges, media,
and others who would limit the religious choices of citizens. Their speaking out has not
always been effective, but sometimes it has been possible to discern impacts of such
value-oriented efforts.

CONCLUSION

Ironically, conversion and its organizational counterpart, proselytizing, have become very controversial in the contemporary global society, even as there is an understanding that religious pluralism is a fact of modern life. It seems that in some ways globalization of religious beliefs and practices often has resulted in more of a local or even tribal society, with more carefully defended boundaries of belief and behavior. Cultural and personal identity is often bound up with one's religion, and efforts to change one's religion, or to attempt to get others to change theirs, have become flashpoints of controversy and conflict. This situation has certainly put the lie to most versions of secularization theory, and it has also resulted in governments being forced to attempt to regulate religion even more than has traditionally been the case. Thus, we are seeing more and more efforts to manage religion by governments, even as they espouse notions of religious freedom.[40] Indeed, there are those who would claim that the only way to maintain any semblance of religious freedom is for governments to manage the inter-religious conflicts that regrettably have come to characterize many societies. And this means, of course, that the legal and judicial apparati of many governments are passing and enforcing laws and policies that regulate conversion and proselytizing.

NOTES

1. For examples of the individualized approach, see Lewis Rambo, *Understanding Religious Conversion* (New Haven: Yale University Press, 1993); James T. Richardson, *Conversion Careers: In and Out of the New Religions* (Beverly Hills, CA: Sage, 1979); Heinz Streib, Ralph Hood, Barbara Keller, Rosina-Martha Csoff, and Christopher Silver, *Deconversion: Qualitative and Quantitative Results from Cross-Cultural Research in Germany and the United States of America* (Gottingen: Vandenhoeck & Ruprecht, 2009); Henri Gooren, *Religious Conversion and Disaffiliation* (New York: Palgrave MacMillan, 2010.); Raymond Paloutzian, James Richardson, and Lewis Rambo, "Religious Conversion and Personality Change," *Journal of Personality* 67 (1999): 1047–1079; James T. Richardson, "Clinical and Personality Assessment of Participants in New Religions," *International Journal for the Psychology of Religion* 5 (1995): 145–170.
2. See Rosalind Hackett, *Proselytization* (London: Equinox, 2008); Tad Stahnke, "The Right to Engage in Religious Persuasion," in *Facilitating Freedom of Religion or Belief: A Deskbook*, ed. Tore Lindholm, Cole Durham, and Bahia Tahzib-Lie (Provo, UT: BYU International Center for Law and Religious Studies, 2004), 619–649.
3. See James T. Richardson, *Regulating Religion: Case Studies from around the Globe* (New York: Kluwer, 2004); Phillip Lucas and Thomas Robbins, *New Religious Movements in the 21st Century* (New York: Routledge, 2004).
4. For examples of pressures to maintain certain religious perspectives and involvement, see David Washburn, "State Suspicion of Religious Minorities in Russia as Viewed from the Perspective of a Religious Minority," in *State-Church Relations in Europe* (Bratislava: Institute of Church-State Relations, 2008), 269–277; Marek Smid, "Islam in

Great Britain and Northern Ireland: Accepted or Refused?" in *State-Church Relations in Europe* (Bratislava: Institute of Church-State Relations, 2008), 296–328; Marc Gaborieau, "Proselytism and the State: The Historical Case of Nepal," in *Religion and Law in the Global Village*, ed. David Guinn, Christopher Barrigar, and Katherine Young (Atlanta, GA: Scholars Press, 1999), 203–220; many of the chapters in Hackett, *Proselytization Revisited*; Richardson, *Regulating Religion*.

5. See Sidney Mead, *Lively Experiment* (New York: Harper and Row, 1963); James T. Richardson, "The Sociology of Religious Freedom," *Sociology of Religion* 67 (2006): 271–294.

6. See the classic study by Reinhold Niebuhr, *The Social Sources of Denominationalism* (New York: New American Library, 1957), which has been followed by innumerable studies of development of denominations in America and the propensity of Americans to change denominations as they move within the class structure.

7. On the Jehovah's Witnesses and their controversial beliefs and practices and consequences of same, see James Beckford, *The Trumpet of Prophecy: A Sociological Study of the Jehovah's Witnesses* (New York: Halstead Press, 1975); James Beckford, "Accounting for Conversion," *British Journal of Sociology* 29 (1978): 249–262. For a discussion of legal considerations brought to the fore by the Witnesses, see Pauline Cote and James Richardson, "Disciplined Litigation, Vigilante Litigation, and Deformation," *Journal for the Scientific Study of Religion* 40 (2001): 11–25; Phillip E. Hammond, David W. Machacek, and Eric Michael Mazur, *Religion on Trial: How Supreme Court Trends Threaten Freedom of Conscience in America*. Walnut Creek, CA: Alta Mira Press, 1994.

8. The Witnesses have engaged in a similar effort in Europe over the past few decades and have won about two-thirds of several dozen cases before the European Court of Human Rights. See James T. Richardson, "Minority Religions, Religious Freedom, and Pan-European Political and Judicial Institutions," *Journal of Church and State* 37 (1995): 39–60; Cote and Richardson, "Disciplined Litigation"; James Richardson and Alain Garay, "The European Court of Human Rights and Former Communist Countries," in *Religion and Patterns of Social Transformation*, ed. Dinka Marinović Jerolimov, Siniša Zrinščak, and Irena Borowik (Zagreb: Institute for Social Research, 2004), 223–234; and James T. Richardson and Jennifer Shoemaker, "The European Court of Human Rights: Minority Religions, and the Social Construction of Religious Freedom," in *The Centrality of Religion in Social Life*, ed. Eileen Barker (Aldershot, England: Ashgate, 2008), 103–116.

9. See Richardson, *Conversion Careers*; James T. Richardson, Jan van der Lans, and Franz Derks, "Leaving and Labeling," in *Research in Social Movements, Conflict and Change* (Greenwich, CT: JAI Press, 1986), 97–126; James Richardson, "The Active versus Passive Convert," *Journal for the Scientific Study of Religion* 24 (1985): 163–179; and Stuart Wright, *Leaving the Cults: The Dynamics of Defection* (Washington, DC: Society for the Scientific Study of Religion, 1987).

10. See Anson Shupe and David Bromley, *The New Vigilantes* (Beverley Hills, CA: Sage, 1980); James Richardson, "Law, Social Control, and Minority Religions," in *Frontier Religions in Public Space*, ed. Pauline Cote (Ottawa: University of Ottawa Press, 2001), 139–168; and James T. Richardson, "Social Control of New Religions: From 'Brainwashing' Claims to Child Sex Abuse Allegations," in *Children in New Religions*, ed. Susan Palmer and Charlotte Hardman (New Brunswick, NJ: Rutgers University Press, 1999), 172–186.

11. See James T. Richardson, *Money and Power in the New Religions* (New York: Edwin Mellen, 1988).

12. See David Bromley, "Conservatorships and Deprogramming," in *The Brainwashing/ Deprogramming Controversy*, ed. David Bromley and James T. Richardson (New York: Edwin Mellen, 1983), 267–293; John LeMoult, "Deprogramming Members of Religious Sects," in *The Brainwashing/Deprogramming Controversy*, ed. David Bromley and James T. Richardson (New York: Edwin Mellen, 1983), 234–257; James T. Richardson, "Mental Health of Cult Consumers," in *Religion and Mental Health*, ed. John F. Schumacher (Oxford: Oxford University Press, 1992), 233–244.

13. For more information, see Joel Fort, "What is 'Brainwashing' and Who Says So?" in *Scientific Research and New Religions: Divergent Perspectives*, ed. Brock Kilbourne (San Francisco: AAAS, 1985), 57–63; Dick Anthony, "Religious Movements and Brainwashing Litigation," in *In Gods We Trust*, ed. Tom Robbins and Dick Anthony (New Brunswick, NJ: Transaction Books, 1990), 295–344; David Bromley and James Richardson, *The Brainwashing/Deprogramming Controversy* (New York: Edwin Mellen, 1983).

14. See Shupe and Bromley, *The New Vigilantes*.

15. See Bromley and Richardson, *The Brainwashing/Deprogramming Controversy*.

16. For a sample of sociologically informed writings on "brainwashing," see Bromley and Richardson, *Brainwashing/Deprogramming Controversy*; James T. Richardson, "A Social Psychological Critique of Brainwashing Claims about Recruitment to New Religious Movements," in *Handbook of Cults and Sects in America*, ed. Jeffrey K. Hadden and David Bromley (Greenwich, CT: JAI Press, 1993), 75–97; Anthony, "Religious Movements and Brainwashing Litigation"; James T. Richardson, "Cult Brainwashing Cases and the Freedom of Religion," *Journal of Church and State* 33 (1991): 55–74; Eileen Barker, *The Making of a Moonie: Brainwashing or Choice?* (Oxford: Basil Blackwell, 1984).

17. Richard Delgado, "Religious Totalism as Slavery," *New York University Review of Law and Social Change* 9 (1980): 51–68; Richard Delgado, "Religious Totalism," *Southern California Law Review* 51 (1977): 1–100.

18. See James Richardson, "The Accidental Expert," *Nova Religio* 2 (1998): 31–43; James T. Richardson, "Sociology and the New Religions: 'Brainwashing,' the Courts, and Religious Freedom," in *Witnessing for Sociology*, ed. Pamela J. Jenkins and Steve Kroll-Smith (New York: Praeger, 1997), 115–137; Dick Anthony and Thomas Robbins, "Negligence, Coercion, and the Protection of Religious Belief," *Journal of Church and State* 37 (1998): 509–527.

19. See Gerald Ginsburg and James Richardson, "'Brainwashing' Evidence in Light of *Daubert*," in *Law and Science*, ed. Helen Reece (Oxford: Oxford University Press, 1998), 265–288.

20. See David Bromley and Edward Breschel, "General Population and Institutional Elite Support for Control of New Religious Movements," *Behavioral Sciences & the Law* 10 (1992): 39–52; James T. Richardson, "Public Opinion and the Tax Evasion Trial of Reverend Moon," *Behavioral Sciences & the Law* 10 (1992): 53–65.

21. See James Richardson and Massimo Introvigne, "Brainwashing Theories in European Parliamentary and Administrative Reports on Cults and Sects," *Journal for the Scientific Study of Religion* 40 (2001): 143–168; Dick Anthony and Thomas Robbins, "Pseudoscience versus New Religions," in *Regulating Religion*, ed. James T. Richardson (New York: Kluwer, 2004), 127–149; James T. Richardson, "'Brainwashing' Claims and Minority Religions outside the United States," *Brigham Young University Law Review* 1996 (1996): 873–904.

22. Marat Shterin and James Richardson, "Effects of the Western Anti-Cult Movement on Development of Laws Concerning Religion in Post-communist Russia," *Journal of Church and State* 42 (2000): 247–272.
23. See James Beckford, *Cult Controversies* (London: Tavistock, 1985); Richardson and Introvigne, "Brainwashing Theories in European Parliamentary and Administrative Reports"; James Richardson and Barend van Driel, "New Religions in Europe," in *Anti-Cult Movements in Cross-Cultural Perspective*, ed. Anson D. Shupe and D. Bromley (New York: Garland, 1994), 129–170.
24. See Richardson, *Regulating Religion*, for chapters dealing with how minority religions are treated in various European and former Soviet-dominated nations.
25. See Cyrille Duvert, "Anti-Cultism in the French Parliament," in *Regulating Religion*, ed. James T. Richardson (New York: Kluwer, 2004), 41–52.
26. See chapters on The Netherlands, Denmark, and Germany in Richardson, *Regulating Religion*, for discussions of the problems that have arisen in even these relatively open societies.
27. See James T. Richardson, "Minority Religions, Religious Freedom, and the Pan-European Political and Judicial Institutions," *Journal of Church and State* 37 (1995): 39–60.
28. Richardson and Garay, "European Court of Human Rights."
29. Richardson and Shoemaker, "European Court of Human Rights." Greece was the only country of the original members of the Council of Europe that had a criminal statute making proselytizing a criminal offense, so it apparently became an exemplar for cases coming from the newer COE members who had been part of the Soviet Union or under its domination for decades.
30. Carolyn Evans, *Freedom of Religion under the European Court of Human Rights* (Oxford: Oxford University Press, 2001); Paul Taylor, *Freedom of Religion: UN and European Human Rights Law and Practice* (Cambridge: Cambridge University Press, 2005).
31. Taylor, *Freedom of Religion*, 343.
32. Ibid., 343–347.
33. Hackett, *Proselytization Revisited*; Lucas and Robbins, *New Religious Movements in the 21st Century*; Richardson, *Regulating Religion*.
34. For information on China, India, and Uzbekistan, see Richardson, *Regulating Religion*; for information on Iran, see Said Arjomand, "Law, Political Reconstruction and Constitutional Politics," *International Sociology* 18 (2003): 17–32. On the tragic Falun Gong treatment in China, see James Tong, *Revenge of the Forbidden City: The Suppression of the Falungong in China, 1999–2005* (Oxford: Oxford University Press, 2009).
35. See Richardson, "Sociology and the New Religions"; Richardson, "Accidental Expert"; Massimo Introvigne, "Blacklisting or Greenlisting: A European Perspective on the Cult Wars," *Nova Religio* 4 (1998): 16–23; Thomas Robbins, "Objectivity, Advocacy, and Animosity," *Nova Religio* 4 (1998): 24–30.
36. See Eileen Barker, *New Religious Movements: A Practical Introduction* (London: HMSO, 1995), for information on INFORM, the organization she organized several decades ago; see http://www.CESNUR.org for information on Massimo Introvigne's Center for the Study of New Religions. Gordon Melton's Institute for the Study of American Religion has been located in Santa Barbara, California, but has recently moved to Baylor University.
37. See Richardson, "The Active versus Passive Convert"; Roger Straus, "Changing Oneself: Seekers and the Creative Transformation of Life Experience," in *Doing Social Life*,

ed. John Lofland (New York: Wiley, 1976), 252–272; Roger Straus, "Religious Conversion as a Personal and Collective Accomplishment," *Sociological Analysis* 40 (1979): 18–165.

38. Thomas Robbins and David Bromley, "Social Experimentation and the Significance of American New Religions," in *Research in the Social Scientific Study of Religion* 4, ed. Monty L. Lynn and David O. Moberg, 1–28 (Greenwich, CT: JAI Press, 1999).

39. James Richardson, "Religion, Law, and Human Rights," in *Religion, Globalization, and Culture*, ed. Peter Beyer and Lori Beaman (Boston: Brill, 2007), 407–428; Richardson, "Accidental Expert."

40. See Richardson, *Regulating Religion*, for examples from many countries about how religion is regulated. See James T. Richardson, "Religion in Public Space: A Theoretical Perspective and Comparison of Russia, Japan, and the United States," *Religion, Staat, Gesellschaft* 7 (2006): 45–61; Hackett, *Proselytization Revisited*, for examples of regulating religion in a number of modern societies. Note that many of these efforts at regulation speak directly to conversion and proselytizing.

Bibliography

Anthony, Dick. "Religious Movements and Brainwashing Litigation." In *In Gods We Trust*, ed. Tom Robbins and Dick Anthony, 295–344. New Brunswick, NJ: Transaction Books, 1990.

Anthony, Dick, and Thomas Robbins. "Negligence, Coercion, and the Protection of Religious Belief." *Journal of Church and State* 37 (1998): 509–527.

——. "Pseudoscience versus New Religions." In *Regulating Religion*, ed. James T. Richardson, 127–149. New York: Kluwer, 2004.

Arjomand, Said. "Law, Political Reconstruction and Constitutional Politics." *International Sociology* 18 (2003): 17–32.

Barker, Eileen. *The Making of a Moonie: Brainwashing or Choice?* Oxford: Basil Blackwell, 1984.

——. *New Religious Movements: A Practical Introduction*. London: HMSO, 1995.

Beckford, James. "Accounting for Conversion." *British Journal of Sociology* 29 (1978): 249–262.

——. *Cult Controversies*. London: Tavistock, 1985.

——. *The Trumpet of Prophecy: A Sociological Study of the Jehovah's Witnesses*. New York: Halstead Press, 1975.

Bromley, David. "Conservatorships and Deprogramming." In *The Brainwashing/ Deprogramming Controversy*, ed. David Bromley and James T. Richardson, 267–293. New York: Edwin Mellen, 1983.

Bromley, David, and Edward Breschel. "General Population and Institutional Elite Support for Control of New Religious Movements." *Behavioral Sciences & the Law* 10 (1992): 39–52.

Bromley, David, and James T. Richardson. *The Brainwashing/Deprogramming Controversy*. New York: Edwin Mellen, 1983.

Cote, Pauline, and James Richardson. "Disciplined Litigation, Vigilante Litigation, and Deformation." *Journal for the Scientific Study of Religion* 40 (2001): 11–25.

Delgado, Richard. "Religious Totalism." *Southern California Law Review* 51 (1977): 1–100.

——. "Religious Totalism as Slavery." *New York University Review of Law and Social Change* 9 (1980): 51–68.

Duvert, Cyrille. "Anti-cultism in the French Parliament." In *Regulating Religion*, ed. James T. Richardson, 41–52. New York: Kluwer, 2004.

Evans, Carolyn. *Freedom of Religion under the European Court of Human Rights*. Oxford: Oxford University Press, 2001.

Fort, Joel. "What is 'Brainwashing' and Who Says So?" In *Scientific Research and New Religions: Divergent Perspectives*, ed. Brock Kilbourne, 57–63. San Francisco: AAAS, 1985.

Gaborieau, Marc. "Proselytism and the State: The Historical Case of Nepal." In *Religion and Law in the Global Village*, ed. David Guinn, Christopher Barrigar, and Katherine Young, 203–220. Atlanta, GA: Scholars Press, 1999.

Ginsburg, Gerald, and James Richardson. "'Brainwashing' Evidence in Light of Daubert." In *Law and Science*, ed. Helen Reece, 265–288. Oxford: Oxford University Press, 1998.

Gooren, Henri. *Religious Conversion and Disaffiliation*. New York: Palgrave MacMillan, 2010.

Hackett, Rosalind. *Proselytization Revisited*. London: Equinox, 2008.

Hammond, Phillip E., David W. Machacek, and Eric Michael Mazur. *Religion on Trial: How Supreme Court Trends Threaten Freedom of Conscience in America*. Walnut Creek, CA: Alta Mira Press, 1994.

Introvigne, Massimo. "Blacklisting or Greenlisting: A European Perspective on the Cult Wars." *Nova Religio* 4 (1998): 16–23.

LeMoult, John. "Deprogramming Members of Religious Sects." In *The Brainwashing/ Deprogramming Controversy*, ed. David Bromley and James T. Richardson, 234–257. New York: Edwin Mellen, 1983.

Lucas, Phillip, and Thomas Robbins. *New Religious Movements in the 21st Century*. New York: Routledge, 2004.

Mazur, Eric. *The Americanization of Religious Minorities*. Baltimore: Johns Hopkins University Press, 1999.

Mead, Sydney. *The Lively Experiment*. New York: Harper and Row, 1963.

Niebuhr, Richard. *The Social Sources of Denominationalism*. New York: New American Library, 1957.

Paloutzian, Raymond, James Richardson, and Lewis Rambo. "Religious Conversion and Personality Change." *Journal of Personality* 67 (1999): 1047–1079.

Rambo, Lewis R. *Understanding Religious Conversion*. New Haven: Yale University Press, 1993.

Richardson, James T. "The Accidental Expert." *Nova Religio* 2 (1998): 31–43.

——. "The Active versus Passive Convert." *Journal for the Scientific Study of Religion* 24 (1985): 163–179.

——. "'Brainwashing' Claims and Minority Religions outside the United States," *Brigham Young University Law Review* 1996 (1996): 873–904.

——. "Clinical and Personality Assessment of Participants in New Religions." *International Journal for the Psychology of Religion* 5 (1995): 145–170.

——. *Conversion Careers: In and Out of the New Religions*. Beverly Hills, CA: Sage, 1979.

——. "Cult Brainwashing Cases and the Freedom of Religion." *Journal of Church and State* 33 (1991): 55–74.

——. "Law, Social Control, and Minority Religions." In *Frontier Religions in Public Space*, ed. Pauline Cote, 139–168. Ottawa: University of Ottawa Press, 2001.

——. "Mental Health of Cult Consumers." In *Religion and Mental Health*, ed. John F. Schumacher, 233–244. Oxford: Oxford University Press, 1992.

——. "Minority Religions, Religious Freedom, and Pan-European Political and Judicial Institutions." *Journal of Church and State* 37 (1995): 39–60.

——. *Money and Power in the New Religions*. New York: Edwin Mellen, 1988.

——. "Public Opinion and the Tax Evasion Trial of Reverend Moon." *Behavioral Sciences & the Law* 10 (1992): 53–65.

——. *Regulating Religion: Case Studies from Around the Globe.* New York: Kluwer, 2004.

——. "Religion in Public Space: A Theoretical Perspective and Comparison of Russia, Japan, and the United States." *Religion, Staat, Gesellschaft* 7 (2006): 45–61.

——. "Religion, Law, and Human Rights." In *Religion, Globalization, and Culture*, ed. Peter Beyer and Lori Beaman, 407–428. Boston: Brill, 2007.

——. "Social Control of New Religions: From 'Brainwashing' Claims to Child Sex Abuse Allegations." In *Children in New Religions*, ed. Susan Palmer and Charlotte Hardman, 172–186. New Brunswick, NJ: Rutgers University Press, 1999.

——. "A Social Psychological Critique of Brainwashing Claims about Recruitment to New Religious Movements." In *Handbook of Cults and Sects in America*, ed. Jeffrey K. Hadden and David Bromley, 75–97. Greenwich, CT: JAI Press, 1993.

——. "Sociology and New Religions: 'Brainwashing', the Courts, and Religious Freedom." In *Witnessing for Sociology*, ed. Pamela J. Jenkins and Steve Kroll-Smith, 115–137. New York: Praeger, 1997.

——. "The Sociology of Religious Freedom." *Sociology of Religion* 67 (2006): 271–294.

Richardson, James T., and Alain Garay. "The European Court of Human Rights and Former Communist Countries." In *Religion and Patterns of Social Transformation*, ed. Dinka Marinović Jerolimov, Siniša Zrinščak, and Irena Borowik, 223–234. Zagreb: Institute for Social Research, 2004.

Richardson, James T., and Massimo Introvigne. "Brainwashing Theories in European Parliamentary and Administrative Reports on Cults and Sects." *Journal for the Scientific Study of Religion* 40 (2001): 143–168.

Richardson, James T., and Jennifer Shoemaker. "The European Court of Human Rights, Minority Religions, and the Social Construction of Religious Freedom." In *The Centrality of Religion in Social Life*, ed. Eileen Barker, 103–116. Aldershot, England: Ashgate, 2008.

Richardson, James T., and Barend van Driel. "New Religions in Europe." In *Anti-Cult Movements in Cross-Cultural Perspective*, ed. Anson D. Shupe and D. Bromley, 129–170. New York: Garland, 1994.

Richardson, James T., Jan van der Lans, and Franz Derks. "Leaving and Labeling." In *Research in Social Movements, Conflict and Change*, ed. Kurt and Gladys Lang, 97–126. Greenwich, CT: JAI Press, 1986.

Robbins, Thomas. "Objectivity, Advocacy, and Animosity." *Nova Religio* 4 (1998): 24–30.

Robbins, Thomas, and David Bromley. "Social Experimentation and the Significance of American New Religions." In *Research in the Social Scientific Study of Religion* 4, ed. Monty L. Lynn and David O. Moberg, 1–28. Greenwich, CT: JAI Press, 1999.

Shterin, Marat, and James T. Richardson. "Effects of the Western Anti-Cult Movement on Development of Laws Concerning Religion in Post-Communist Russia." *Journal of Church and State* 42 (2000): 247–272.

Shupe, Anson, and David Bromley. *The New Vigilantes.* Beverley Hills, CA: Sage, 1980.

Smid, Marek. "Islam in the United Kingdom and Northern Ireland: Accepted or Refused?" In *State–Church Relations in Europe*, 296–328. Bratislava: Institute of Church-State Relations, 2008.

Stahnke, Tad. "The Right to Engage in Religious Persuasion." In *Facilitating Freedom of Religion or Belief: A Deskbook*, ed. Tore Lindholm, Cole Durham, and Bahia Tahzib-Lie, 619–649. Provo UT: BYU International Center for Law and Religious Studies, 2004.

Straus, Roger. "Changing Oneself: Seekers and the Creative Transformation of Life Experience." In *Doing Social Life*, ed. John Lofland, 252–272. New York: Wiley, 1976.

——. "Religious Conversion as a Personal and Collective Accomplishment." *Sociological Analysis* 40 (1979): 18–165.

Streib, Heinz, Ralph Hood, Barbara Keller, Rosina-Martha Csoff, and Christopher Silver. *Deconversion: Qualitative and Quantitative Results from Cross-Cultural Research in Germany and the United States of America*. Gottingen: Vandenhoeck & Ruprecht, 2009.

Taylor, Paul. *Freedom of Religion: UN and European Human Rights Law and Practice*. Cambridge: Cambridge University Press, 2005.

Tong, James. *Revenge of the Forbidden City: The Suppression of the Falungong in China, 1999–2005*. Oxford: Oxford University Press, 2009.

Washburn, David. "State Suspicion of Religious Minorities in Russia as Viewed from the Perspective of a Religious Minority." In *State–Church Relations in Europe*, ed. Monty Lynn and David Moberg, 269–277. Bratislava: Institute of Church-State Relations, 2008.

Wright, Stuart. *Leaving the Cults: The Dynamics of Defection*. Washington, DC: Society for the Scientific Study of Religion, 1987.

CHAPTER 32

CONVERSION AND RETENTION IN MORMONISM

SETH L. BRYANT, HENRI GOOREN, RICK PHILLIPS, AND DAVID G. STEWART, JR.[1]

THE Church of Jesus Christ of Latter-day Saints—the official name of the Mormon or LDS Church—has grown from six members in 1830 to about 13.5 million by the end of 2008[2] and is part of a larger Latter Day Saint movement which includes over 100 smaller churches. The largest is the Community of Christ (former Reorganized Church, RLDS) with around 250,000 members, followed by the Church of Jesus Christ (Bickertonite) with about 12,000 members, and the Fundamentalist LDS Church (FLDS) with around 10,000.[3] The LDS Church's self-proclaimed goal is to sound what it calls the "restored Gospel of Jesus Christ" in every ear, gathering God's elect among every land and people. To accomplish this ambitious goal, the LDS Church has the largest full-time missionary force in the world, consisting of over 52,000 missionaries, comprised mostly of young men (75 percent), as well as young women (18 percent) and elderly couples (7 percent).[4] In order to adequately understand the contemporary LDS Church's extraordinary commitment to global proselytizing, it is necessary to review the historical context in which Mormonism emerged and the early doctrinal basis for its enduring missionary ethos.

FRAMEWORK OF CONVERSION IN THE EARLY MORMON CHURCH

Along with several other nineteenth-century American religions, Mormonism grew out of a Christian Primitivist[5] movement to restore "pure" Christian religion unhampered by creeds and sectarian arguments. According to historian Val Rust, "Mormon doctrines reflect almost every facet of the Second Great Awakening," drawing on strains of evangelism, adventism, dispensationalism, millennialism, spiritualism, and folk magic.[6] Mormonism advertised itself as the restoration of ancient lost truths, authority, and practices that were necessary precursors to the second advent of Jesus Christ. Claiming all other forms of Christianity were apostate, the religion presented itself as the restoration of Christ's true church in the last days of human history.

Mormonism drew from the American propositions that tradition is not reason enough to continue or even legitimate an institution and that radicalism is proper when institutions become ends unto themselves. Whereas early American political discourse had drawn from religious ideas for legitimacy, Mormonism further sacralized and exalted the American experience, mapping all things holy onto the American continent. It boldly asserted that the American and Christian covenants had failed and that Mormonism was the fresh start needed to establish the City on the Hill, recreating Americans as Israelites and America as the New Jerusalem.

Converts were empowered through surrendering their will to the voice of God as contained in Mormon prophecy.[7] But other Americans cried foul, for the "revelations...created hostility to acceptable modes of discourse and challenged assumed wisdom."[8] The Mormon reversal, however, made sense to those who found existing social orders lacking and insufficiently attuned to their ultimate concerns. For seekers of all classes, Mormonism provided transcendent meaning and purpose, challenge and demands for both prosperous and poor, socially dislocated and established.

Some studies of early Mormon conversion have tended to emphasize a particular set of doctrinal orientations that attracted converts, such as millennialism, primitivism, mysticism, and so on. But it is likely that Mormonism's varied and malleable message resonated with various groups of converts for different reasons, as evidenced by its historical staying power and its transcendence of cultural boundaries. Central to its religious durability and expansion, Mormonism made (and continues to make) appeals both to common-sense rationality and to peoples' religious feelings or spiritual aspirations.[9] For nineteenth-century converts in an increasingly rational world, it offered membership in a seemingly rational community that embraced biblical supernaturalism.[10] A common denominator for Mormon converts from all backgrounds is a longing for and "expectation of the active presence of the divine in everyday life."[11]

To discover the divine, Mormonism's prophet-founder Joseph Smith (1805–1844) both embraced and struggled against the Bible—the bedrock of American religious legitimacy—by reopening the canon.[12] In so doing, he brought forth new scriptures, including the Book of Mormon, a purported record of ancient Israelites who had migrated to the Americas. Smith's new scriptures both expanded and competed with traditional understandings of the Bible, reclaiming the Christian and Hebrew scriptures' central privilege: "the capacity to know God."[13] Considered equal to the Bible as the word of God but more correctly translated,[14] this new scripture legitimated Smith's calling as a prophet and served as an instrument of conversion for hundreds of thousands of religious seekers in the nineteenth century and millions today.

Parley P. Pratt (1807–1857), an early Mormon church leader and intellectual, said this of his first experience with the Book of Mormon: "As I read, the spirit of the Lord was upon me, and I knew and comprehended that the book was true, as plainly and manifestly as a man comprehends and knows that he exists." From its inception as a new religious movement, this dual experience with reason and spirituality has been the hallmark of and framework to Mormon conversion.[15]

Through their new scriptures, the early Mormons claimed to have more light and knowledge from God than did other Christian sects or denominations. But contemporary religious leader Alexander Campbell dismissed the Book of Mormon as containing "every error and almost every truth discussed in N[ew] York for the last ten years."[16] Campbell, in company with most other Christian clergy, believed that those who converted to Mormonism had been duped. Many historians and other scholars have "assumed Campbell's argument, and, as Jan Shipps has noted, they have written histories that depict Mormonism as pandering 'to the superstitious, the gullible, and the fearful, at least in the beginning.'"[17] But converts like Pratt, who became "the chief Mormon apologist and theologian of the early period,"[18] speak to the depth of intellect that Mormonism attracted. Early Mormon converts were not necessarily on the fringes of society, but virtually all were seekers of a religious quintessence that brought meaning to everything else, resonating with both their intellectual and spiritual longings.

RESTORATION PRIMITIVISM IN KIRTLAND, OHIO

The Mormon Church was founded in upstate New York in 1830, following what Smith described as a restoration of priesthood authority to himself through the laying on of hands of the resurrected New Testament prophet John the Baptist and then a bestowal of authority by Christ's apostles Peter, James, and John. The conversion model of the new church required believers to repent and be baptized by immersion for the remission of their sins. New members also received a "baptism of fire," by the laying on of hands, in which they received the gift of the Holy Ghost as a source of personal guidance and inspiration. Joining a community of "saints" (or members), all were to fast, pray, and serve one another. Meetings were conducted by church elders as led by the spirit, with preaching, praying, singing, and exhortation of one another.[19]

The conversion experience of Sidney Rigdon (1793–1876), an early and influential convert, is typical. A former Campbellite preacher in Kirtland, Ohio, Rigdon differed with Alexander Campbell over the need for charismatic experience, eventually falling away from the Campbellites' rational Restoration. Within Mormonism, Rigdon found not just a rational approach to primitivism, but prophecy, revelation, and the heavens reopened. Atypical of other early Mormons, Rigdon converted hundreds of his former congregation, drawing Smith's Church of Christ from New York to Ohio in 1830; Rigdon would go on to become "second elder," influencing the early organization more than any person save Joseph Smith.

As seekers of miraculous experience, Mormon congregations in the 1830s were much more charismatic than their current counterparts, embracing prophecy, speaking in tongues, and experiencing other ecstatic "gifts of the spirit." Predicated on a conversion model that was "revelatory and empirical,"[20] Mormons believed that the ability to preach convincingly and draw persons to salvation was not based on reason alone but required the power of the Holy Spirit. To this end, a sacramental "endowment" was instituted in Kirtland in 1831 to endow Mormon missionary elders with "power from on high."[21] Endowment practices were continued and expanded upon in the following years, especially in conjunction with emerging temple rituals first enacted in Kirtland, Ohio, and later in Nauvoo, Illinois.[22]

Through the efforts of these missionaries, the church grew from six members at its inception on April 6, 1830, to 300 by January 6, 1831; then to 1,500 in 1835, and 2,500 two years later.[23] In response to this growth, Joseph Smith's revelations institutionalized his authority through expansions in the areas of theology and priesthood organization. While charismatic expressions among the rank-and-file did not cease, it was restrained within ecclesiastical parameters, Smith alone serving as "prophet, seer, revelator, and translator" to the entire church.[24]

Mormonism's founding prophet was preoccupied with restoring the practices of all previous biblical dispensations,[25] not just those of the primitive Christian church.[26] His amalgamation of Christian and Jewish doctrinal practices led to the uniquely Latter Day Saint expression found in temple worship, including "ordinances" such as baptism for the dead, washings and anointings, endowments, and marriage for eternity.

Temples became sacred places for endowing the priesthood in preparation for preaching the gospel and eventually as repositories of rites and knowledge (or "keys") necessary for exaltation in the afterlife. Fusing elements of Christianity and Judaism, Mormons believed themselves to be both Christ's latter-day church and a literal latter-day Israel—God's covenant people preparing for the Millennium. Central to this vision was the building of a literal Zion on earth.

BUILDING ZION AND ADOPTION INTO ISRAEL

Zion became the hope of the Mormon Israel. Smith taught that the original Eden and the site of the future Zion was in Missouri, transfiguring America into the Promised Land. The task of building this New Jerusalem was one of gathering Israel back to Eden, reflecting the Edenic and Utopian characteristics of his "new and everlasting" covenant. This was not just a return to New Testament Christianity but a restoration of ancient Israel and practices of the Hebrew Scriptures. Missionary work meant gathering Israel, for the lost ten tribes were thought to be of European and Native American ancestries.

Early missionaries were sent across the American frontier to preach to whites as well as Indians or "Lamanites" (a name from the Book of Mormon),[27] and Mormon apostles were sent across the Atlantic to England in 1837. By 1844, the apostles' missionary successes had resulted in 8,000 English Mormons compared to 7,000 American members.[28]

Europeans, Americans, and Native Americans who heard Mormonism's message were told that they were a royal and "chosen seed," preserved to build the latter-day Kingdom of God; as with ancient Israel, the blessings of the priesthood were theirs by right of their lineage and promises to their fathers. Expanding upon Paul's teachings on adoption,[29] Smith taught that when "Gentiles"[30] were baptized, they were transformed into the family of Israel.[31] The Mormon Prophet stated that the Holy Ghost has a greater effect in "expanding the mind" of a descendent of Abraham than of a Gentile, but that the effect upon the Gentile would be more apparent, conversion and adoption being literally "visible to the eye" as the person's "old blood" was purged out, transforming him into a "new creation by the Holy Ghost" that "make[s] him actually of the seed of Abraham."[32]

With conversion and salvation involving the necessary gathering of and adoption into Israel, Smith's soteriology and missiology centered upon the yet-to-be-built New Jerusalem in Independence, Missouri. Due to intense conflict with the "old settlers" already in the region, however, the "Saints"[33] were forced to leave Independence behind and postpone their efforts to build Zion in Missouri. After a difficult period, the Saints eventually gathered to Nauvoo, Illinois, where, from 1840 to 1844, they built a city on the banks of the Mississippi that rivaled Chicago as the largest settlement in Illinois.

In Nauvoo, the endowments practiced at Kirtland took on "Old Testament" proportions, involving complex rituals and practices deemed necessary for salvation. Plural marriage (polygyny)—a practice associated with the dispensations involving "Abraham, Isaac, and Jacob, as also Moses, David and Solomon"[34] —was seen as a necessary extension of the restoration of all things. Because of their controversial nature in contemporary society, those initiated into these esoteric rituals swore oaths of secrecy. Involvement in plural marriage was denied publicly, and its theology was not taught to new converts.

Two levels to Mormonism resulted: a public version known to the uninitiated that followed Christian Primitivism more closely, and the esoteric version of Smith's latest and most radical revelations which focused on *Israel* more than *church*. This latter group embraced the attending expansion of theology, which included the arcane rituals of the Nauvoo Temple, polygamy, and human exaltation (entering the kind of existence that God enjoys). With growing tensions between these two modes or expressions of belief, Mormonism's greatest schism occurred following the murder of Joseph Smith and his brother Hyrum by a mob in 1844. For those Saints who did not travel west and who tended not to participate in temple rites, Mormonism "ever afterward took on the character of primitive Christianity that it had had in the very beginning"; but, for Utah Saints, Mormonism tended to model ancient Israel.[35]

GATHERING TO DESERET UNDER BRIGHAM YOUNG

After Smith's death a leadership crisis ensued, for Smith had not clearly outlined procedures for succession upon his death. Smith had presided over the church with two counselors, known as the First Presidency; but different priesthood quorums[36] were said to be of equal authority under the First Presidency: the Nauvoo High Council, and the Twelve Apostles. Sidney Rigdon, a counselor in the First Presidency, made his case, and eventually secured a small following.[37] But it was Brigham Young (1801–1877), the presiding apostle who embraced polygamy, who secured the blessing of the majority of the Saints to be Smith's successor, many of whom were English and had converted and immigrated under his direction. At the same time, because Young intended to continue the new theology, thousands of Latter Day Saints[38] refused to follow him west.[39] Many of these Saints found their way into the RLDS Church.

Young was less concerned with prophecy and more concerned with stabilizing Mormonism as a religious organization. Whereas Smith had produced hundreds of revelations, Young canonized only one. But what Young lacked in prophetic charisma, he made up for in vision and drive. Because of his ability to mobilize and organize people, the city-building efforts of Smith's day mushroomed into vast networks of communities spanning a western corridor of North America from Canada to Mexico. Smith's ambitious missionary efforts were eventually dwarfed by Young's, who needed converts to colonize the settlements of the new Mormon kingdom. For this purpose, the Mormon missionary enterprise expanded throughout North America and Europe, while also being introduced in Australia, Africa, the Middle East, the Pacific Islands, and elsewhere. Relocating Zion to the Great Basin of the United States, the Mormon kingdom was known as "Deseret," the Book of Mormon name for honeybee. Envisioning Deseret like a well-ordered hive of workers, Young gathered in the Latter-day Israel and put its members to work building Zion.

CONVERSION MODELS UP TO AND AFTER THE MANIFESTO OF 1890

Upon arrival in Utah, converts realized that they had not simply joined a church, but had actually assumed citizenship in a new society. Young served not only as the president of the church but also as the governor of Deseret. There was little or no distinction made between ecclesiastical and secular matters. Early meeting houses hosted church services as well as civic functions and town meetings. Church courts were presided over by local bishops, who routinely ruled on secular matters and had the power to levy fines. This conflation of church and state also blurred the distinction between religious and secular behavior in the minds of the Mormon settlers. Damming a stream or building a fence were viewed as religious activities in much the same way as attending church or paying tithes—all designed to build the kingdom of God. Mormons continued to be called on proselytizing missions to seek new converts, but they could also be called on "missions" to establish a new settlement in an uninhabited valley or build a sawmill for a new community.

Conversion meant supporting the theology of plural marriage from the time that it was made public in 1852 until its discontinuation from 1890 to 1904. Baptism only began the entrance into the sacred world of Mormon temple rituals, where families were sealed eternally and became candidates for exaltation. Converts were expected to embrace polygamy, whether they first heard of it in their homeland or upon entering Deseret.

Mormon leaders stirred up revivalistic fervor from 1856 to 1858 to (re)convert the Latter-day Saints to plural marriage, many being lukewarm toward it. Internal issues aside, outside tensions over polygamy eventually reached a breaking point for the Mormon Church. Influenced by US government pressure—including disenfranchising the church, seizing its assets, and imprisoning its leaders—President Wilford Woodruff (Brigham Young had died in 1877) issued the famous Manifesto of 1890, which ended the practice of polygamy in the LDS Church.[40] (Tens of thousands of "fundamentalist" Latter-day Saints, however, refused to acknowledge the Manifesto, forming schismatic groups not authorized by the LDS Church, the best-known being the Fundamentalist Church of Jesus Christ of Latter-day Saints or FLDS Church.)

With polygamy renounced, converts and members were entering new sociological territory. Whereas Mormonism had once been peculiar and persecuted as an alien presence, it was now increasingly tolerated at some level by the American mainstream. With Mormon identity reinforced by persecution, but its survival requiring social legitimacy, the religion of the Latter-day Saints began oscillating between retrenchment from and assimilation toward society.[41]

THE DECENTRALIZATION OF ZION

Before the 1890 Manifesto, Mormons were more lax in their observance of meetings and in their practice of the "Word of Wisdom," the Mormon dietary code forbidding the use of alcohol, coffee, tea, and tobacco.[42] Identity as a Mormon was deeply rooted in polygamy, creating ideological walls of separation from the outside world, aided by the geographic separation of Mormon towns from other American communities. With the coming of the transcontinental railroad and the discontinuance of polygamy, however, these walls were eroding. The Manifesto had placed the Mormons on a path of assimilation and accommodation to the American cultural mainstream and transformed Mormonism from an incipient government into a religious denomination. Community business was no longer conducted during ward meetings ("wards" are local congregations similar to parishes). Church courts were relegated to adjudicating ecclesiastical matters. Religious services, which had once been held throughout the week, were increasingly relegated to Sundays. Now that work and civic life were distinct from religious activity, church leaders began to stress the importance of worship services, the Word of Wisdom, and paying tithes. Mormonism as a regional subculture, with its informal norms and local control, was being supplanted by the rule of a rapidly centralizing ecclesiastical organization concerned less with governing the new state of Utah and more with the spiritual welfare of its members.

In a single generation the Mormons went from being seen as members of a subversive, licentious cult to exemplars of the American values of industry and chastity. The impulse to gather together in Utah persisted, but hard economic times began to change this. High unemployment rates in 1890s Utah made it hard for newly arriving converts to find work. The high birthrates of the previous generation exacerbated this problem, and by the turn of the century most of Utah's arable land was already taken.

Converts had initially been encouraged to build Zion in Utah, the site of all Mormon temples from 1855 until 1919, when the Laie Hawaii Temple was completed. In 1911, a First Presidency letter urged converts to stay where they were and live according to the ideals of Zion in their own homelands. This transformed Zion in the hearts and minds of the Latter-day Saints from a literal place to an ideal. The building of the kingdom was to be done within the walls of homes, local churches, and temples; converts were to be gathered, not to a location, but to a way of life. Latter-day Saints began to see Zion not as a nation with one faith but rather as a people with "one heart and one mind."[43] This rearrangement of the concept of Zion and of building the literal Kingdom of God in preparation for Christ's coming deemphasized an eventual return to Missouri for this purpose and emphasized the family, ward, and temple as the loci of work and salvation.

Converts, as well as children, who had not experienced the earlier days of Mormonism, were in need of instruction in the sacred story and expectations of their religion. The rising importance of local lay leaders and congregations filled this need, reordering the Mormon universe around individual families and wards where Mormons could come together and remind themselves of their uniqueness and separate calling from out of the world as God's covenant people.

By the 1920s, church leaders realized that a literal gathering was no longer feasible, especially with a depressed local economy in Utah.[44] The end of the gathering allowed a new generation of Latter-day Saints to leave Utah to seek employment or higher education. By the end of the Great Depression, the church began to spread eastward. With each foray into new territory, the church added new converts, and the Mormon movement began to grow rapidly again.

This dispersion of the Latter-day Saints, however, also posed threats to Mormon identity and lifestyle. In the past, dense concentrations of Mormons provided the kind of informal social control that helped keep church members on the straight and narrow. Now, many Mormons lived far from the dense enclaves that characterized the gathering, in settings where the church had no control over secular affairs. The LDS Church eventually responded to this situation by standardizing church policy and governance. The "Correlation" movement was a series of bureaucratic reforms designed to bring all of the auxiliaries and programs of the church under the purview of the central hierarchy. One goal of Correlation was to ensure that all church members experienced the restored gospel in much the same way, regardless of where they lived.

CORRELATION AND THE MISSIONARY PROGRAM

Unlike much of Christianity in the United States that is tending toward "de facto [if not outright] congregationalism," and contrary to the notion that "local autonomy fuels church vitality," the LDS Church has a highly centralized authority and standardized message and organizational experience for church members.[45] The Correlation Department was established at LDS headquarters in 1972, under the direction of the First Presidency. Having general officers over the auxiliary programs (Primary, Sunday school, etc.) ensured consistency and oversight by the General Authorities, allowing them to establish orthodox models for the entire church. This standardization pervades the Mormon experience, to the degree that lessons taught on any given Sunday are typically the same for each target audience (based on age and sex) anywhere in the world. Thus, 12-year-old boys in Utah hear the same lesson as their counterparts all across the globe.

The correlation movement not only affected Mormon congregational experience; it also had a major impact on the LDS missionary enterprise. In the early 1960s, missionaries, who once had received little training before entering the mission field, began spending several weeks in language training at church-owned universities in Utah, Idaho, and Hawaii, and in 1978 the Missionary Training Center (MTC) was established in Provo, Utah, near Brigham Young University. The MTC provides a uniform training experience for all missionaries, whether they learn a new language or not, in which "military efficiency of early hours and dedicated study" late into the evening continue for several weeks before entrance into the mission field.[46]

As with LDS auxiliary programs, proselytizing materials had also varied from mission to mission. However, beginning in 1952 all LDS missionaries worldwide began instructing potential converts from "A Systematic Program for Teaching the Gospel," the first official missionary manual which contained seven brief lessons and selected "reasoning principles" and teaching points. This was superseded in 1961 by a "Uniform System for Teaching Investigators" and updated in 1973 with "The Uniform System for Teaching Families."[47] Subsequently, the missionary lesson plan was changed again in 1985 to "The Uniform System for Teaching the Gospel."[48] The 1988 *Missionary Guide* provided further instruction for missionaries based on scriptural teachings, marketing research, and academic psychology. Although the more recent version of the missionary lesson plan lacks reference to uniformity in its title, the purpose is the same, with all potential converts worldwide hearing uniform messages or "discussions" of basic Mormon principles in preparation for baptism, confirmation, and entrance into a local ward.

Although the LDS Church has achieved high rates of missionary mobilization, rates of member participation in missionary work are lower than in many other outreach-oriented faiths. George Barna found that only 26 percent of Latter-day Saints reported initiating a single gospel conversation with a non-member over the past year,[49] whereas LDS apostle Ballard observed that only 3 to 5 percent of active Latter-day Saints in North America regularly participate in missionary work.[50] The repeated transition from one member-missionary model to another over the past fifty years suggests that none has adequately vitalized member-missionary participation, at least to the satisfaction of LDS authorities.

These efforts to provide a uniform teaching experience speak also to the expectations of homogeneity required for new members in order to successfully convert and be integrated into a Mormon ward, with large percentages of converts failing to do so for a variety of reasons that likely include the rigors of membership and Mormon lifestyle.[51] To address the difficulties of convert retention, local church units in developing areas receive a curriculum tailored to newer members; instead of wards, these Latter-day Saints are often found in smaller congregations known as branches and may come under the direct supervision of the mission president (a high priest who oversees a mission focused on proselytizing and staffed by missionaries) instead of a stake president (who oversees several wards that are focused more on congregational matters).

CONTEMPORARY ISSUES IN CONVERSION AND RETENTION

Entrance into the Mormon world includes the expectation that converts will attend church regularly, refrain from alcohol, tobacco, tea, and coffee, refrain from sexual relations outside of marriage, and serve in lay church callings. Adult converts are expected to enter temples to be endowed (to receive a special temple covenant) and, if married, to be ritually sealed to their spouse and any children for eternity (an ordinance that promises that family relationships will remain intact in the afterlife for faithful Mormons). Converted children, if males, are expected to serve missions, and both sexes are expected to marry for eternity in temples and raise a Mormon family. Further, Mormons anticipate that missionary work continues on "both sides of the veil" and that their dead relatives are taught the gospel in the Spirit World beyond this life. To this end, Mormons perform proxy baptisms and other rites for deceased ancestors within their temples in order to provide all of humanity with an opportunity to accept or reject the "true gospel" of Jesus Christ.

The increasing internationalization of the LDS Church as well as challenges in retaining converts, especially outside of North America, has led to considerable study and discussion regarding the missionary program.[52] The primary focus of LDS missions had been on achieving arbitrary monthly baptismal quotas rather than on building the church with active members. Abundant research demonstrates that only a fraction of international converts became participating members.[53]

Most converts come from backgrounds where they had not previously been regularly participating believers in any religious tradition. The transition from little to no religious activity to the intense levels of participation demanded by the Mormon faith is a challenge for many, especially in view of missionary practices that seek to baptize prospective converts within a period of several weeks, often before positive habits of church attendance have been firmly established and before prohibited behaviors have been fully overcome. Convert attrition is particularly high in the first two months following baptism,[54] suggesting that many of those who leave never made the necessary life changes to become committed life-long Mormons.[55]

In 2002, two LDS apostles were stationed overseas to supervise international missionary work. Dallin Oaks in the Philippines and Jeffery Holland in Chile both addressed the challenges of low member retention. Their direct observations led to some tightening of standards. The First Presidency issued a letter on December 11, 2002, requiring that all prospective converts must attend church several times and be keeping all commitments regularly before baptism, although such standards are not consistently implemented in many missions.

This renewed focus on the missionary program culminated in the 2004 *Preach My Gospel* manual, which introduced a four-discussion lesson plan and increased missionary focus on preparing converts not merely to accept baptism, but to become active and participating Mormons. The new program also eliminated many Western cultural trappings of the *Missionary Guide*, focusing on universal principles and scriptural teachings while encouraging missionaries to develop their own cultural insights. The primary focus on baptismal goals remained, but was moderated. Recent initiatives of the *Preach My Gospel* program have encouraged an increased focus on the development of consistent "gospel habits" and the integration of prospective converts with active members before baptism. This hybrid approach has led to some improvements in LDS convert retention, although difficulties have persisted.

As Kosmin and Lachman observed, "The church has a good knowledge of those entering, but knows much less about those leaving the fold."[56] The cumulative effect of the LDS growth policy has led to rising disparities between the number of members claimed by the church and the number of people who identify themselves as Mormons on censuses or surveys.

CONTEMPORARY CONVERSION AND RETENTION IN THE UNITED STATES

Although more than half of nominal LDS members live outside of the United States, the LDS Church still draws its primary strength from the United States. The United States is home to less than 5 percent of the world's population but nearly 50 percent of LDS members. Unique contributors to North American LDS growth include family sizes slightly above the national average and the concentration of nearly one-third of all LDS missions in the United States.

The 1990–2000 Glenmary Survey reported that the LDS Church ranked first in growth among US denominations reporting over one million adherents.[57] Recent growth rates, however, have trended downwards from 1.76 percent annually in the 1990s to 1.71 percent in 2003[58] and 1.63 percent in 2005.[59] This trend reflects primarily the decreasing size of Mormon families.

In the late 1980s, approximately 40 to 50 percent of US LDS converts remained active;[60] some indicators suggest that the number has declined into the high 30th percentile since that time. Dynamics among members born in the faith are somewhat different. One study found that only 22 percent of US members born to active LDS families remain active lifelong, whereas 44 percent returned to the Church after inactivity of at least a year or more.[61] Nineteen percent were disengaged but expressed nominal belief in church doctrines, and 14 percent were disengaged non-believers.

The City University of New York (CUNY) American Religious Identification Survey (ARIS) found that just fewer than 2.8 million American adults identified themselves as Latter-day Saints[62] compared to 5.3 million on official membership rolls at the time, although the latter figure also included children and disaffiliated members. The study found that the LDS Church had one of the highest turnover rates of any US faith. The CUNY authors observed: "Some groups such as Mormons…appear to attract a large number of converts ('in-switchers'), but also nearly as large a number of apostates ('out-switchers')." A USA Today survey conducted in March 2002 also found that the percentage of individuals identifying themselves as Latter-day Saints fell well below official church membership rates in almost every state.[63]

The 2007 Pew Forum American Religious Landscape Study reported that 70 percent of American LDS converts reported being previously unaffiliated with any religious group. Only 23.5 percent of self-identified Latter-day Saints were converts, demonstrating that American LDS growth reflects high Mormon birth rates more than missionary success. The Pew study also found that 83 percent of US Mormons marry within the faith and that at least 70 percent of members born in the faith continued to identify themselves as members.[64] However, by inquiring only about birth religious affiliation and current affiliation but not about prior transient affiliations, the Pew survey missed the considerable Mormon turnover that occurs when baptized converts become disengaged.

CONVERSION AND RETENTION IN EUROPE, ASIA, AND AFRICA

Although the LDS Church has grown internationally, it has experienced difficulty in leveraging its affluent, high-missionary-sending US population into committed international members on a level comparable with other outreach-oriented faiths. In 1996, Bennion and Young wrote: "Only on the Christianized or Westernized edges of the eastern hemisphere has the church established significant beachheads."[65] This is still largely true today. Most LDS members in the eastern hemisphere are concentrated in island nations, including the Philippines, the United Kingdom, and Japan; only 5 percent of all LDS members live in the contiguous continental landmass of Europe, Asia, and Africa that is home to 80 percent of the world's population.

The LDS Church does not officially report church attendance or convert retention rates, but trends can be ascertained from statements of church leaders, national censuses, and other sociological data. It is estimated that 20 to 25 percent of Latter-day Saints in Europe[66] and Asia[67] attend church regularly, although significant regional differences exist.[68] An estimated 20 to 30 percent of the LDS members in Southern Africa and 50–55 percent of those in West Africa[69] attend church weekly. Forty percent of nominal LDS members in the Philippines identified the LDS Church as their faith of preference on the 2000 Philippines census,[70] and Apostle Dallin H. Oaks observed that "about 100,000 Filipinos attend the three hour Sunday meetings at least once each month,"[71] or slightly less than 20 percent of total membership.

Current LDS converts join for a variety of reasons. The sense of purpose and meaning in life, spiritual feelings of confirmation of God's will, and socialization and fellowship are among the top reasons cited. But prospective converts face numerous challenges. The LDS faith prohibits tea, the most widely consumed beverage in Europe, Asia, and Africa, which has cultural significance for many native peoples. Many individuals face strong pressure from family members and acquaintances to remain in national or traditional faiths. Because of the relatively small number of LDS members in Europe, Asia, and Africa, finding suitable marriage partners for young people in these nations, in spite of expansive youth programs promoting socialization, is a constant problem. Refraining from sexual relations outside of marriage is also a challenge for many, especially for young people in societies where such relations are the norm.

Whereas opposition to the LDS Church in North America comes primarily from other Christian groups, especially Protestant Evangelicals, skeptics and atheists are most prominent among European critics. In European cultures that highly value intellectual achievements, the lack of a strong literary and intellectual tradition among local Mormons has been a barrier to the attraction and the cohesiveness of the LDS faith.[72] The limited resources in languages other than English has made it difficult for the Church to attain the immersive element dominating not only spirituality but also cultural and social life, which has been a key feature in promoting high levels of member activity in the Mountain West. For more than a decade, the majority of LDS converts in Western European nations have been immigrants from Eastern Europe, Africa, Southeast Asia, and the Middle East, rather than native-born peoples. As a result, ethnic, cultural, and linguistic differences produce challenges for convert integration.[73]

Eighty percent of the world LDS missionary force comes from North America and thus faces cultural and linguistic barriers, although some areas, such as West Africa, have a higher proportion of native missionaries. The Latter-day Saint faith is seen as a foreign, American church; although missionaries do not discuss politics nor advocate a political agenda, the unpopularity of US foreign policy is often an obstacle to missionary efforts. Challenges of convert integration also arise from differences of agenda between local LDS congregations and the Salt Lake City-administered mission organization, as well as the lack of a lasting link between itinerant, predominantly foreign, missionaries and the local congregation.

In recent years the rate of opening new congregations and areas for missionary work has slowed considerably as the missionary force has leveled off due to declining LDS birth rates and low convert retention as well as increased standards for prospective missionaries. There has been some reallocation of missionaries from low-receptivity areas like Europe and Japan toward more receptive areas, yet many potentially receptive areas, especially in Africa and Asia, remain unreached or under-reached due to lack of mission resources. Nations without any known LDS congregations that allow proselytism include Burkina Faso (15.7 million), Niger (15.3 million), Senegal (13.7 million), Chad (10.3 million), Guinea (10.1 million), the Gambia (1.78 million), Guinea-Bissau (1.53 million), Gabon (1.51 million), Timor-Leste [East Timor] (1.13 million), Equatorial Guinea (0.63 million), Sao Tome and Principe (0.21 million), and Seychelles (0.09 million).[74]

CONVERSION AND RETENTION IN LATIN AMERICA

Latin America is currently the main growth area for Mormonism. Its contribution to worldwide membership increased from 2 percent in 1960 to 38 percent in 2007, while the US proportion declined from 90 percent in 1960 to 45 percent by 2007.[75] If current growth rates continue, the majority of Mormons will be Latin American by 2020.[76]

However, LDS growth in most Latin American countries slowed down after 2000. Membership growth stagnated at 2 to 3 percent annually—comparable to population growth—in Chile, Uruguay, Colombia, Puerto Rico, and five countries in Central America.[77] In these countries, convert growth is slowing, as most people have already heard of the Mormon message. But LDS membership growth is still strong in many other Latin American countries: Brazil, Venezuela, the Dominican Republic, Paraguay, and Nicaragua. The average annual growth rates for these countries ranged from 3.5 (Brazil) to almost 9 percent (Nicaragua).[78] Nevertheless LDS retention rates are low all over Latin America—and elsewhere.[79]

The typical Mormon convert in Latin America is a young urban woman of upper lower class or lower middle-class origins.[80] Many people are attracted to Mormonism because of its organization radiating middle-class values, its strict code of conduct, its practical teachings (e.g., on raising children and household budgeting), its doctrines and spirituality, its style of worship and hymns, and its lay priesthood for men.[81] Most people are recruited through their own social networks (LDS friends and relatives) or through the missionaries.[82] When asked about main attraction factors, Guatemalan Mormons mentioned the strict code of conduct, learning new things in church, feeling the joy of God's love, being blessed with miracles, and receiving support from fellow members.[83]

Henri Gooren's 1993–95 fieldwork in Guatemala provides a microcosm of LDS conversion patterns in Latin America. The average age for conversion among Gooren's informants in La Florida, a typical low-income *barrio* of Guatemala City, was 25. Almost all had gone through periods of inactivity. Many converts were adolescent religious seekers who visited various churches to see which they liked best. Other converts joined the LDS Church (or reactivated their prior church membership) after going through a turning point in their lives, such as starting a family or struggling with alcohol abuse. Finally, some people converted under the influence of their spouses or children.[84] The following case study conversion story in Guatemala City illustrates the *conversion careers*[85] of Mormons in Latin America.

Guillermo, an adolescent seeker, was kicked out of the family home in La Florida by his father at age 13. At 18, Guillermo first learned about the Mormon Church:

> I wanted to change my life, because I used a lot of alcohol, drugs; I hang out with youth gangs. The Sisters [missionaries]...presented a Christ of Love, someone who had mercy and that he could save my life....I got baptized, but I didn't have the strength—or the support, I think—to stay in church. After two months I backslided....I started drinking again and I didn't have anything to do with the church for seven years.[86]

Alcoholics Anonymous (AA) eventually helped Guillermo to overcome his severe alcohol problem, but he still needed marijuana to make it through the day:

> I was fed up with the life I had and there were only two solutions for me: either I changed my life, or I would kill myself. That night I went to bed...and awoke around five in the morning....I saw all the scenes from my life: the bad things I had done, what I was doing to my body, the suffering and pain I was causing in my family....I knelt on the bed and asked God for forgiveness. And I said: God, if you really exist, if you have a purpose for my life, manifest yourself. I put my life into your hands and do what you want with me because *I* could never do anything with it. Take me to a place where I will stop using drugs, where I can change my life, where I can be happy and make my family happy....So I got up, bathed myself, changed clothes, and I didn't know where I was going....And when I noticed, I was again in the church where I had been baptized seven years ago. Since that moment my life began to change....I did have a lot of support from all the brothers and sisters of the church....They took care of me like a baby and taught me really how to live the gospel. After two months in church they conferred the Aaronic priesthood on me. After three months in church they conferred the Melchizedek priesthood on me...and so they... [later] called me as president of the young men of the ward.[87]

Based on Gooren's research, the typical LDS conversion career in Central America may be summarized as follows:

> After the first contact with Mormon members or missionaries, the investigator received the Discussions. She or he was invited to study the Study Guides and the Book of Mormon—the rational elements of conversion—and to ask the Holy Spirit for a confirmation of its veracity. In about half of the cases, a testimony of the truthfulness of the Book of Mormon and hence Joseph Smith and the Mormon Church was gradually built up. With the testimony came acceptance of the church organization and its hierarchical lay priesthood for men. If new members built up a good relationship with the leaders and members, they were more likely to accept a calling and thus became more integrated in the local church community: the ward and stake. In turn, this integration strengthened their commitment.[88]

Approximately half of all new LDS converts, however, become inactive within a year.[89] The typical LDS dropout in Latin America is an urban man of upper lower class or lower middle-class origins.[90] In 2000–2002, the correlation between official LDS membership figures and self-identified religious affiliation on national censuses was 20 percent in Chile, 24 percent in Mexico, and 27 percent in Brazil.[91] Receiving a calling helped some new members, like Guillermo in Guatemala, become integrated in the ward organization. For others, however, performing in a calling was a pressure they were unable to deal with, so they dropped out.[92] If the testimony of the new members was (still) relatively weak, if outside pressure from nonmember relatives was strong, or if good rapport was not established with local LDS leaders, people most likely dropped out. Other important retention problems included the time and money demands (tithes and offerings) made by the church[93] and backsliding into alcohol problems.[94] Inactivity was often related to bad experiences with leaders[95] and members, who rarely devoted time to recent converts.[96]

Another informant in Gooren's study—Miguel from La Florida—was a typical inactive member. Baptized in 1978 at 36, he received a calling to work with the US missionaries, which made him happy. But local officials changed his calling a few years later, and some fellow members ridiculed him because he was illiterate. Miguel soon became inactive, because he felt that leaders and members did not take him seriously. Miguel never attended church thereafter, although he still obeyed the Word of Wisdom by refraining from smoking or drinking alcohol, coffee, and tea.[97]

CONCLUSION

In 1984 sociologist of religion Rodney Stark theorized on the basis of LDS membership statistics that Mormonism was poised to become the first American-made world religion.[98] Stark projected past and present Mormon growth rates into the future and predicted that by 2080 the LDS Church could have as many as 265 million members. In

2005, Stark used these same statistics to demonstrate that his predictions have remained on track.[99] The LDS Church's Public Affairs Department has widely disseminated Stark's calculations. Mormon missionizing efforts have been impressive, but some of the attendant integration and retention problems cited above lead to several caveats in regard to Stark's predictions and the future prospects of international Mormonism.

First, in spite of recent reforms, the LDS Church remains a fairly easy religion to join. The missionary discussions that culminate in baptism take far less time to complete than something like the Rite of Christian Initiation for Adults, which admits new Catholics into the faith just once a year. In addition, conflating baptism with conversion, as Mormons often do, is problematic. While joining the LDS Church is fairly easy, maintaining one's commitment to the faith requires substantial dedication. Mormon lifestyle mandates are often at odds with current fashions and fads, and paying tithes and offerings is essential to retain membership in good standing. Hence, despite large numbers of convert baptisms, there are also large numbers of attritional losses and defections, most of which occur within the first year. This leads to large disparities between the number of members claimed by the church and the number of self-identified members.

Second, the LDS Church and its membership finance the labor of over 50,000 missionaries, most of whom serve for two years. No other denomination has such a large, full-time proselytizing force, and studies show that the size of the missionary cadre is a significant predictor of the number of new convert baptisms.[100] In 2009, these missionaries baptized an average of 5.4 converts each, or a total of almost 280,000 new Mormons.[101] Given the massive expenditures of member-contributed dollars on missionary work, it is useful to think about how many converts the church gets per proselytizing dollar; or, how many converts per hour of mission labor. Moreover, given that, according to recent research, at least half of these new converts will defect from the faith within a year, it is useful to think about how many dollars or how many hours are spent per *retained* convert. In spite of these high costs, LDS authorities remain resolutely committed to the church's core missionary ethos and are highly unlikely to cut back or withdraw institutional resources from its high-maintenance missionary enterprise.

Third, the worldwide LDS membership on record actually consists of at least four different categories.[102] About one-quarter of US Mormons and up to two-thirds of international members are *disaffiliated members*, who no longer consider themselves Mormons and often have joined another church. Between 10 and 25 percent are *inactive believers*, who self-identify as Mormons although they rarely go to church anymore. (Many in this category still obey the Word of Wisdom and refrain from drinking coffee, tea, or alcohol.) *Affiliated members* regularly go to church but do not comply with all membership requirements, such as accepting callings or paying tithes. This category of Mormons makes up 25 to 30 percent of the official membership in the United States and 10 to 12 percent internationally. Finally, the *core members* meet all the expectations of LDS membership and are eligible for a temple recommend. This last group constitutes between 20 and 25 percent of the membership on record—and somewhat less in Latin America, Europe, and Asia.

Difficulties with member retention reflect in part Mormonism's persistent charismatic impulse and rational proselytizing framework. After even a single spiritual experience[103] —often occasioned by reading the Book of Mormon—missionaries rationally explain the validity of LDS doctrine and the need for baptism into Christ's one true Church. While many prospective investigators experience Mormonism's charisma and religious appeal, only a disproportionate few follow the rational path to baptism, and fewer still are retained due to the demands of membership which are in direct contrast to the ease of entrance. Often, true conversion—if it takes place at all among new members—is one of fits and starts following baptism and usually only successful if the person is surrounded by supportive networks of family and friends and/or has a need or desire to radically redefine their worldview. In this way, contemporary conversion careers are not all that unlike early Mormon converts, including its most famous convert, Brigham Young.[104]

Current Mormon officials interpret church growth as an indicator of divine sanction. The LDS Church's self-proclaimed goal has always been (and still is) to propagate its beliefs and ordinances of salvation to the entire world. Within the Mormon worldview, no other option exists but to make salvation available to everyone who has ever lived— both to the living through missionary work and to the dead through vicarious baptism and other temple ordinances—with the expectation that "the elect" will respond positively to the message of the restored gospel. Thus, Mormon leaders and members are not unconcerned about low levels of retention—they are concerned about it—but, in fact, they also expect that even within the church only a portion of church members will achieve exaltation in the celestial kingdom.[105]

For *core members*, maintaining their faith and commitment in the face of criticism and rejection by many outside groups—both religious and secular—is empowering, providing meaning, purpose, and a cohesive identity. The tremendous sacrifices required to sustain active membership (with hopes of eternal exaltation) reinforce Mormons' feelings of exceptionalism and explains—within the faith's worldview—the failure of many newly baptized members to be retained, let alone converted. Because believers consider themselves to be God's chosen instruments in the last days to restore Christ's true gospel to the earth, Mormonism thrives against opposition and is reinforced through rejection. This fosters a corporate perception that "the world" and Zion are inevitably in tension. As with other religious sects historically, this kind of dichotomous theodicy empowers potential converts who reject conventional belief systems and seek greater contact with the Divine. With its continued appeal to both the rational and the supernatural, contemporary Mormon conversion efforts (although much better funded, organized, and institutionally regulated in modern times than in the past) have remained remarkably consistent with their nineteenth-century beginnings.

Mormonism constitutes a religious way of life, creating a new covenant community that sacralizes everyday experience, converting human existence and especially the nuclear family into elements of eternal significance. For those seeking something more to life than secular institutions have to offer, Mormonism can be very fulfilling spiritually; although only a portion of seekers who have heard its message have undergone ultimately successful conversions, millions more will continue to explore its promises through baptism and membership, as Latter-day Saints seek undeterred to build God's literal kingdom on earth and prepare for Christ's Second Coming.

NOTES

1. Our sincere thanks go to Ryan Cragun, Charles E. Farhadian, Armand L. Mauss, Benjamin E. Park, Lewis R. Rambo, Gary Shepherd, Gordon Shepherd, and Richard Stamps for their critical comments and detailed editing suggestions that substantially improved the text.
2. *Deseret News 2009 Church Almanac* (Salt Lake City, UT: Deseret News, 2008), 4.
3. For membership statistics on the Community of Christ, see "Worldwide Membership," http://cofchrist.org/news/GeneralInfo.asp; for the Church of Jesus Christ, see *The Church of Jesus Christ General Business and Organization Conference Minutes* (Bridgewater, MI: Church of Jesus Christ, 2007), 4399; for the FLDS, see p. 17 of "The Primer," Utah and Arizona Attorney Generals Primer on Polygamy, http://attorneygeneral.utah.gov/cms-documents/The_Primer.pdf.
4. *Deseret News 2009 Church Almanac*, 4; Spencer J. Condie, "Missionary," "Missionary Life," in *Encyclopedia of Mormonism*, ed. Daniel H. Ludlow (New York: Macmillan, 1992), 910.
5. Also known as "Restorationism," Christian Primitivism is an attempt to return to the beliefs and practices of the church in the days of the New Testament. Such presupposes an apostasy and the necessity of a restoration of pristine Christianity. The Christian Primitivist movement includes the Latter Day Saints movement, which has produced over 100 different churches (LDS Church, Reorganized LDS/Community of Christ, Fundamental LDS, etc.); other Restorationists within the larger Christian Primitivist movement include the Stone-Campbell movement (Church of Christ, Disciples of Christ) and the Adventist movement (Millerites, Seventh-day Adventists), and Jehovah's Witnesses.
6. Val D. Rust, *Radical Origins: Early Mormon Converts and Their Colonial Ancestors* (Urbana: University of Illinois Press, 2004), 2–3. For a treatment of Mormon millennialism, see Grant Underwood, *The Millenarian World of Early Mormonism* (Champaign: University of Illinois Press, 1999); for Mormonism and occultism, see D. Michael Quinn, *Early Mormonism and the Magic World View* (Salt Lake City, UT: Signature Books, 1987).
7. Steven C. Harper, "'Dictated by Christ': Joseph Smith and the Politics of Revelation," *Journal of the Early Republic* 26, no. 2 (2006): 275–304. See also Stephen J. Fleming, "The Religious Heritage of the British Northwest and the Rise of Mormonism," *Church History* 77, no. 1 (2008): 74; and Stephen J. Fleming, "'Congenial to Almost Every Shade of Radicalism': The Delaware Valley and the Success of Early Mormonism," *Religion and American Culture* 17, no. 2 (2007): 129–165.
8. Harper, "Joseph Smith and the Politics of Revelation," 277.
9. An early Mormon revelation specified this dual appeal by emphasizing that God will speak to "you in your mind and in your heart, by the Holy Ghost" (*Doctrine and Covenants* 8:2 [Salt Lake City: The Church of Jesus Christ of Latter-day Saints, 1989]).
10. E. Brooks Holifield, *Theology in America: Christian Thought from the Age of the Puritans to the Civil War* (New Haven: Yale University Press, 2005), 175, states that "never had the issue of rationality assumed as much importance as it did in the early decades of the nineteenth century," giving rise to a post-Enlightenment school of "evidential Christianity" within a framework of Scottish commonsense rationality. Holifield states further that "Scottish

philosophy seemed tailor-made for a theology that would show the rationality of faith while preserving the necessity for revelation" (178). Mormonism, like the more rational restoration of Alexander Campbell, has deep roots in evidential Christianity. For further treatment on this topic, see Benjamin E. Park, "Rational Supernaturalism: Early Mormonism and Enlightened-Romantic Rhetoric," (Lecture, Mormon History Association, Springfield, IL, May 22, 2009).

11. Fleming, "Religious Heritage of the British Northwest," 75.

12. Philip Barlow, "Before Mormonism: Joseph Smith's Use of the Bible, 1820–1829," *Journal of the American Academy of Religion* 57, no. 4 (1989): 741.

13. Kathleen Flake, "Translating Time: The Nature and Function of Joseph Smith's Narrative Canon," *Journal of Religion* 87 (2007): 500.

14. Of the Book of Mormon, Joseph Smith stated that it "was the most correct of any book on earth," including the Bible. Reflecting his views that Christianity had gone apostate, so too had the Bible been mistranslated and corrupted. In *The Articles of Faith*, a statement of belief embraced by the LDS Church, Smith writes, "We believe the Bible to be the word of God as far as it is translated correctly; we also believe the Book of Mormon to be the word of God." To address biblical inaccuracies, as he saw them, Smith sought to restore the Bible to its original condition, retranslating it prophetically to discern lost or changed passages, but he never completed this work before his death. His son and successor in the Reorganized LDS Church (now Community of Christ), Joseph Smith III, published his father's "restored" Bible in 1867. Known as the "Inspired Version" in the Reorganized branch of the Restoration, portions of this "translation" are used by the LDS Church under the name of the "Joseph Smith Translation," which the church publishes alongside the LDS King James Version of the Bible.

15. Steven C. Harper, "Infallible Proofs, Both Human and Divine: The Persuasiveness of Mormonism for Early Converts," *Religion and American Culture* 10, no. 1 (2000): 101.

16. Alexander Campbell, "Delusions," *Millennial Harbinger* 2, no. 2 (February 7, 1831): 85–96 (quote on p. 93), http://www.mun.ca/rels/restmov/texts/acampbell/tmh/MH0202.HTM.

17. Harper, "Infallible Proofs," 99.

18. *The Encyclopedia of the Stone-Campbell Movement*, ed. Douglas A. Foster, Paul M. Blowers, Anthony L. Dunnavant, D. Newell Williams (Grand Rapids, MI: Wm. B. Eerdmans 2004), 305.

19. See *The Book of Mormon*, 3 Nephi 11:23–28, Moroni 6; see also *Doctrine and Covenants* 20:37–84.

20. Harper, "Infallible Proofs," 101, quoting Gordon S. Wood, "Evangelical America and Early Mormonism," *New York History* 61, no. 4 (Oct. 1980): 359–386 (quote on p. 380).

21. Luke 24:39; see also *Doctrine and Covenants* 38:32, 38.

22. See Gregory A. Prince, *Power from on High: The Development of Mormon Priesthood* (Salt Lake City, UT: Signature Books, 1995), 115–116. Drawing from Christ's instructions before his Ascension (see Luke 24:46–49), Mormon missionaries initiated in this endowment were thought of as being spiritually prepared to take the restored gospel to the world and were considered to possess a higher priesthood authority than the uninitiated. This led to the development of two lay priesthood organizations as understood by Mormonism today, the Aaronic and Melchizedek, with the higher (Melchizedek) priesthood in charge of conducting missionary work.

23. Rust, *Radical Origins*, 7.

24. This set-apart position would eventually develop into the "First Presidency," the quorum or group of high priests that presides over the entire church and is composed of the Church President and his two counselors.

25. Dispensations are construed as historical periods when the truths of the gospel have been present on earth. Dispensations are begun by a prophet who speaks for God and end with apostasy or falling away from the truth. Apostasy requires a restoration of truth in a new dispensation which, according to Mormon belief, occurred periodically through prophets and patriarchs such as Adam, Noah, Abraham, Moses, etc. Smith represented himself as God's appointed latter-day Prophet of the "Dispensation of the Fullness of Times," a dispensation that would end not in apostasy but with the Second Coming of Jesus Christ.

26. This theological fusion of multiple dispensations appealed to converts for a variety of reasons. Many Christians experienced some tension with the Hebrew Scriptures; the Book of Mormon bridged the gap between the Old and New Testaments, connecting ancient Israelites with Christian worship. Mormonism created continuity between biblical prophets and the modern world, reestablishing and expanding a community of covenant people. Living prophets authoritatively conveyed directions for unique, modern challenges through contemporary revelation rather than the mere interpretation of ancient texts.

27. Steve Pavlik, "Of Saints and Lamanites: An Analysis of Navajo Mormonism," *Wicazo Sa Review* 8, no. 1 (1992): 23.

28. Rust, *Radical Origins*, 8.

29. Romans 9:3–8.

30. Gentiles, in Mormon terminology, are non-descendants of Abraham.

31. To this day, an important Mormon ordinance is the Patriarchal Blessing, first established in 1833. The recipient of this blessing has their lineage (among the Twelve Tribes of Israel) declared by revelation in a special blessing given by a church elder ordained specifically for that purpose.

32. Joseph Smith, Jr., *Teachings of the Prophet Joseph Smith*, ed. Joseph Fielding Smith (Salt Lake City, UT: Shadow Mountain, 1977), 149–150.

33. Members of the Latter Day Saint movement commonly refer to themselves as "Saints," believing the same title was used by the early Christian church to refer to its members. They believe their church to be the same church that Christ established during His mortal ministry, but to distinguish themselves from the New Testament Saints in the dispensation of the "meridian of time" (during Christ's life and up unto the Great Apostasy between the first and second centuries C.E.), they are the "Latter-day Saints" or members of Christ's church during the final dispensation of time before Christ's Second Coming.

34. Doctrine and Covenants 132:1.

35. Jan Shipps, *Mormonism: The Story of a New Religious Tradition* (Urbana: University of Illinois Press, 1987), 59.

36. Quorums are groupings of priesthood members holding the same priesthood office and/or responsibilities. The term "quorum" comes into play particularly when business is to be conducted, requiring a certain number of members to be present. In some cases, revelations recorded in the *Doctrine and Covenants* dictate the number of members in each quorum (12 deacons, 24 teachers, 48 priests, 70 seventies, 12 apostles); the revelations also dictate some of the functions and responsibilities of each office and include a structure of general church leadership, beginning with the First Presidency at the top, followed by the two Presiding High Councils—one "traveling" outside of Zion, known as the Quorum of Twelve Apostles, and one "standing" within Zion, known as the Presiding High Council,

which is now defunct in the LDS Church (see *Doctrine & Covenants*, section 107). Other quorums under the First Presidency and Twelve with general church leadership include groupings of Seventies and a Presiding Bishopric. In local jurisdictions known as wards and stakes, other quorums with local authority and responsibilities are organized: deacons, teachers, priests, elders, high priests, bishoprics, stake high councils, and stake presidencies.

37. Today, this group is known as The Church of Jesus Christ, headquartered in Monongahela, Pennsylvania, and known colloquially as "the Bickertonite Church."

38. The unhyphenated version of "Latter Day Saint" refers to all of the Latter Day Saint movement, which contains over 100 churches and 400 expressions (including but not limited to the LDS or "Mormon" Church headquartered in Salt Lake City, Utah). When speaking of individual churches or groups, "Latter Day Saint" refers to members of the Restoration not affiliated with the LDS Church. "LDS" and the hyphenated "Latter-day Saint" refer exclusively to members of the LDS Church.

39. Some followed the charismatic prophets James Strang, who drew away a large faction following the death of Joseph Smith (Vickie C. Speek, *"God Has Made Us a Kingdom": James Strang and the Midwest Mormons* [Salt Lake City, UT: Signature Books, 2006]), and Joseph Morris, who attracted hundreds of followers from immigrant converts in Utah, some of whom knew nothing of polygamy before immigrating (C. Leroy Anderson, *Joseph Morris and the Saga of the Morrisites* [Logan: Utah State University Press, 1988]); another potential successor, who attracted thousands of Latter Day Saints after his father's death, was Joseph Smith III—prophet-president of the Reorganized LDS Church (now Community of Christ). Many Latter Day Saints first followed Strang, but later found their way into the RLDS Church. A small group of Strangites still exist, many near their gathering place of Voree (Burlington), Wisconsin.

40. Omri Elisha, "Sustaining Charisma: Mormon Sectarian Culture and the Struggle for Plural Marriage, 1852–1890," *Nova Religio: The Journal of Alternative and Emergent Religions* 6, no. 1 (2002): 57; Shipps, *Mormonism*, 125–126.

41. Armand L. Mauss, *The Angel and the Beehive: The Mormon Struggle with Assimilation* (Champaign: University of Illinois Press, 1994), 5, states: "Movements which, like Mormonism, survive and prosper are those that succeed in maintaining indefinitely an optimum tension (Stark and Bainbridge, 1985; Stark, 1987) between the two opposing strains: the strain towards greater assimilation and respectability, on the one hand, and that toward greater separateness, peculiarity, and militancy, on the other. Along this continuum between total assimilation and total repression or destruction is a narrow segment on either side of the center; and it is within this narrower range of socially tolerable variation that movements must maintain themselves, pendulum like, to survive."

42. The Word of Wisdom is a crucial doctrine calling for the abstinence from hot drinks interpreted as coffee and tea, as well as liquor, wine, and tobacco (*Doctrine and Covenants* 89:1–21).

43. Moses 7:18.

44. Rick Phillips, "'De Facto Congregationalism' and Mormon Missionary Outreach: An Ethnographic Case Study," *Journal for the Scientific Study of Religion* 47, no. 4 (2008): 628–643.

45. Ibid., 629.

46. Claudia L. Bushman, *Contemporary Mormonism: Latter-day Saints in Modern America* (Westport, CT: Greenwood Publishing Group, 2006, 63). In more recent years, Missionary

Training Centers have been established all over the world; instead of beginning training in Utah, some foreign missionaries begin in these local centers.

47. Richard O. Cowan, *Every Man Shall Hear the Gospel in His Own Language* (Provo, UT: Missionary Training Center, 1984).

48. Bushman, *Contemporary Mormonism*, 63–64.

49. George Barna, "Protestants, Catholics, and Mormons Reflect Diverse Levels of Religious Activity," *Barna Research Update*, July 9, 2001.

50. M. Russell Ballard, "Members are the Key," *Ensign*, Sept. 2000. The 3 to 5 percent figure cited in the Aug. 1999 Conversion and Retention broadcast is correct; the 35 percent figure cited in the Sept. 2000 *Ensign* is an error.

51. Rick Phillips, "Rethinking the International Expansion of Mormonism," *Nova Religio: The Journal of Alternative and Emergent Religions* 10, no. 1 (2006): 58.

52. See, for instance, the Oct. 1997 conference speech by then Church President Gordon B. Hinckley. "Some Thoughts on Temples, Retention of Converts, and Missionary Service," http://www.lds.org/conference/talk/display/0,5232,49-1-32-20,00.html.

53. For detailed data and discussion on convert retention, see David G. Stewart, Jr., *The Law of the Harvest: Practical Principles of Effective Missionary Work* (Henderson, NV: Cumorah Foundation, 2007).

54. Dallin H. Oaks, "The Role of Members in Conversion," *Ensign*, Mar. 2003.

55. A Brigham Young University study concluded that LDS conversion is a process of acculturation during which converts struggle "to learn a new culture, doctrine, and terminology." See Kristy Kuhn, "LDS Conversion is a Process, Study Indicates," *Deseret News*, Apr. 5, 2009, http://www.deseretnews.com/article/705295080/Study-LDS-conversion-is-a-process.html.

56. Barry A. Kosmin and Seymour Lachman, *One Nation under God: Religion in Contemporary American Society* (New York: Harmony Books, 1993), 298.

57. Glenmary Research Center, *Religious Congregations and Membership: 2000*, http://www.glenmary.org.

58. Chris Herlinger, "U.S. Catholic, Episcopal, Mormon, Orthodox, Pentecostal Churches Grow," *Episcopal News Service*, Apr. 5, 2005.

59. Eileen W. Lindner, ed., *Yearbook of American and Canadian Churches 2007* (Nashville, TN: Abingdon Press, 2007).

60. Tim Heaton, "Vital Statistics," *Encyclopedia of Mormonism*, ed. Daniel H. Ludlow (New York: Macmillan, 1992), 1518–1537.

61. Stan L. Albrecht, "The Consequential Dimension of Mormon Religiosity," *Latter-day Saint Social Life: Social Research on the LDS Church and Its Members*, ed. James T. Duke (Provo, UT: Brigham Young University Press, 1998), 253–292.

62. Egon Mayer, Barry A. Kosmin, and Ariela Keysar, *American Religious Identification Survey* (New York: City University of New York, 2008), http://www.americanreligionsurvey-aris.org/reports/ARIS_Report_2008.pdf.

63. Cathy Lynn Grossman, "Charting the Unchurched in America," *USA Today*, Mar. 7, 2002.

64. Pew Forum Study, *2007 Report Religious Landscape Study*, http://religions.pewforum.org/pdf/report-religious-landscape-study-chapter-2.pdf.

65. Lowell C. Bennion and Lawrence Young, "The Uncertain Dynamics of LDS Expansion, 1950–2020," *Dialogue: A Journal of Mormon Thought* 29, no. 1 (1996): 8–32 (quote on p. 16).

66. Wilfried Decoo, "Issues in Writing European History and in Building the Church in Europe," *Journal of Mormon History* 23, no. 1 (1997): 164; Gary C. Lobb, "Mormon

Membership Trends in Europe among People of Color: Present and Future Assessment," *Dialogue: A Journal of Mormon Thought* 33, no. 4 (2000): 55–68; Stewart, *Law of the Harvest*, 43–48.

67. Heaton, "Vital Statistics"; Jiro Numano, "Mormonism in Modern Japan," *Dialogue: A Journal of Mormon Thought* 29, no. 1 (1996): 223–235.

68. Reports that include data and analysis of LDS member activity by country are available on the Cumorah Foundation website at http://cumorah.com/index.php?target=missiology_articles.

69. E. Dale LeBaron, "The Inspiring Story of the Gospel Going to Black Africa," Ricks College Devotional, Apr. 3, 2001, http://www.byui.edu/Presentations/Transcripts/Devotionals/2001_04_03_LeBaron.htm.

70. Aggregate national census data is available at Integrated Public Use Microdata Series International: https://international.ipums.org/international.

71. Dallin H. Oaks, "The Worlds of Joseph Smith," International Academic Conference at the Library of Congress, Washington DC, May 6, 2005.

72. Wilfried Decoo, "Feeding the Fleeing Flock: Reflections on the Struggle to Retain Church Members in Europe," *Dialogue: A Journal of Mormon Thought* 29, no. 1 (1996): 97–113.

73. Lobb, "Mormon Membership Trends."

74. David G. Stewart, Jr., and Matthew Martinich, "Taking the Gospel to the Nations: Challenges and Opportunities for LDS Growth," http://cumorah.com/index.php?target=missiology_articles.

75. Heaton, "Vital Statistics," 1520–1521; *Deseret News 2009 Church Almanac*, 193–195.

76. Mark L. Grover, "The Maturing of the Oak: The Dynamics of LDS Growth in Latin America," *Dialogue: A Journal of Mormon Thought* 38, no. 2 (2005): 79–104.

77. Henri Gooren, "Latter-day Saints under Siege: The Unique Experience of Nicaraguan Mormons," *Dialogue: A Journal of Mormon Thought* 40, no. 3 (2007): 136; Grover, "Maturing of the Oak," 88.

78. Henri Gooren, "The Mormons of the World: The Meaning of LDS Membership in Central America," in *Revisiting Thomas F. O'Dea's "The Mormons": Contemporary Perspectives*, ed. Cardell K. Jacobson, John P. Hoffman, and Tim B. Heaton (Salt Lake City: University of Utah Press, 2008), 369–378.

79. David G. Stewart, Jr., "Growth, Retention, and Internationalization," in *Revisiting Thomas F. O'Dea's "The Mormons": Contemporary Perspectives*, ed. Cardell K. Jacobson, John P. Hoffman, and Tim B. Heaton (Salt Lake City: University of Utah Press, 2008), 333–338; Phillips, "Rethinking the International Expansion of Mormonism," 54–56.

80. The following sources all confirm that the LDS Church in Latin America is predominantly urban: Henri Gooren, *Rich among the Poor: Church, Firm, and Household among Small-scale Entrepreneurs in Guatemala City* (Amsterdam: Thela, 1999), 78; Gooren, "Mormons of the World," 363–365; Heaton, "Vital Statistics," 1528–1529, 1534–1535; David C. Knowlton, "Mormonism in Latin America: Towards the Twenty-first Century," *Dialogue: A Journal of Mormon Thought* 29, no. 1 (1996): 169; Gary Shepherd and Gordon Shepherd, *Mormon Passage: A Missionary Chronicle* (Urbana: University of Illinois Press, 1998), 112, 238; Stewart, "Growth, Retention, and Internationalization," 343.

81. Gooren, "Mormons of the World," 366; Mark L. Grover, "Mormonism in Brazil: Religion and Dependency in Latin America," PhD diss. Indiana University, 1985; Grover, "Maturing of the Oak"; Knowlton, "Mormonism in Latin America"; David C. Knowlton, "How Many Members Are There Really? Two Censuses and the Meaning of LDS Membership

in Chile and Mexico," *Dialogue: A Journal of Mormon Thought* 38, no. 2 (2005), 53–78; Rodney Stark, "The Basis of Mormon Success: A Theoretical Application," in *Latter-day Saint Social Life: Social Research on the LDS Church and its Members*, ed. James T. Duke (Provo, UT: Religious Studies Center, Brigham Young University, 1998), 29–70. Gooren (*Rich among the Poor*, 154) and Shepherd and Shepherd (*Mormon Passage*, 110–111) also reported dissatisfaction with Catholicism.

82. Shepherd and Shepherd, *Mormon Passage*, 111; Stewart, "Growth, Retention, and Internationalization," 347.

83. Gooren, *Rich among the Poor*, 2, 153, 155–156, 160–162, 166–169, 186.

84. Ibid., 153–154; Henri Gooren, "Conversion Careers in Latin America: Entering and Leaving Church among Pentecostals, Catholics, and Mormons," in *Conversion of a Continent: Contemporary Religious Change in Latin America*, ed. Timothy J. Steigenga and Edward L. Cleary (New Brunswick, NJ: Rutgers University Press, 2007), 61. There are obvious parallels between conversion to Mormonism and conversion to Pentecostalism in Latin America (see Gooren, "Mormons of the World," 367–369).

85. See Gooren, this volume; Gooren, "Conversion Careers in Latin America."

86. Gooren, *Rich among the Poor*, 155.

87. Gooren, "Conversion Careers in Latin America," 61–62.

88. Gooren, "Mormons of the World," 367.

89. Gooren, *Rich among the Poor*, 66; Grover, "Mormonism in Brazil," 137–139; Knowlton, "How Many Members Are There Really?" 54. Albrecht ("Consequential Dimension of Mormon Religiosity," 266) and Stewart (*Law of the Harvest*, 37) both report a similar percentage of LDS drop-outs for the United States.

90. Gooren, Mormons of the World," 371–372.

91. Stewart, "Growth, Retention, and Internationalization," 334–335.

92. Gooren, *Rich among the Poor*, 170.

93. Gooren, "Latter-day Saints under Siege," 134–155; Armand L. Mauss, "Mormonism in the Twenty-first Century: Marketing for Miracles," *Dialogue: A Journal of Mormon Thought* 29, no. 1 (1996): 236–249.

94. Gooren, *Rich among the Poor*, 163–165.

95. Gooren *Rich among the Poor*, 85; Gooren, "Mormons of the World," 372–373; F. LaMond Tullis, "The Church Moves outside the United States: Some Observations from Latin America," *Dialogue: A Journal of Mormon Thought* 13, no. 1 (1980): 72.

96. Gooren, "Mormons of the World," 377. See also Phillips, "De Facto Congregationalism," 638–639.

97. Gooren, *Rich among the Poor*, 164.

98. Rodney Stark, "The Rise of a New World Faith," *Review of Religious Research* 26, no. 1 (1984): 118–127.

99. Stark, "Basis of Mormon Success"; Rodney Stark, *The Rise of Mormonism*, ed. Reid L. Neilson (New York: Columbia University Press, 2005).

100. Joseph T. Hepworth, "A Causal Analysis of Missionary and Membership Growth in the Church of Jesus Christ of Latter-day Saints (1830–1995)," *Journal for the Scientific Study of Religion* 38, no. 1 (1999): 59–71; Shepherd and Shepherd, *Mormon Passage*.

101. *Deseret News 2009 Church Almanac*, 4.

102. Gooren, "Mormons of the World," 379–381; Heaton, "Vital Statistics," 1530. Cf. Grover, "Maturing of the Oak," and Knowlton, "How Many Members Are There Really?" 53–78.

103. The spiritual side of Mormon conversion is explored in a 2001 speech by Mark L. Grover, "One Convert at a Time," *BYU Speeches*, http://speeches.byu.edu/reader/reader.php?id=713.
104. Brigham Young took two years to convert, not a few weeks or even months as many Mormon missionaries would prefer. Rationally weighing the evidence, Young's conversion took place during a charismatic experience as an "unpolished" elder witnessed to the truth of Mormonism by "the power of the Spirit."
105. This anticipation of failure from within the church hearkens to the Parable of the Ten Virgins, where only half of Christ's followers are wise and are received into his presence (see Matthew 25:1–13).

FURTHER READING

Harper, Steven C. "Infallible Proofs, Both Human and Divine: The Persuasiveness of Mormonism for Early Converts." *Religion and American Culture* 10, no. 1 (2000): 99–118. Provides a study of nineteenth-century Mormon conversion narratives. Without discounting early Mormonism's place in American and Atlantic discourses, this article examines the intellectual framework informing conversion that set it apart from other nineteenth-century religious movements.

Jacobson, Cardell, John P. Hoffman, and Tim B. Heaton, eds. *Revisiting Thomas F. O'Dea's "The Mormons": Contemporary Perspectives*. Salt Lake City: University of Utah Press, 2008. Various articles analyze both the historical framework of conversion and contemporary issues of recruitment and retention worldwide (e.g., Gooren, Mauss, Spencer, Stewart).

Phillips, Rick. "'De Facto Congregationalism' and Mormon Missionary Outreach: An Ethnographic Case Study." *Journal for the Scientific Study of Religion* 47, no. 4 (2008): 628–643. Combines an excellent ethnographic study of a New Jersey ward with theories contrasting the advantages and disadvantages of congregationalism and centralization.

Shepherd, Gary, and Gordon Shepherd. *Mormon Passage: A Missionary Chronicle*. Urbana: University of Illinois Press, 1998. Authoritative study of the functioning of the LDS missionary system, based on literature review and the personal mission diaries of the authors in 1960s Mexico.

Stewart, David G., Jr. *The Law of the Harvest: Practical Principles of Effective Missionary Work*. Henderson, NV: Cumorah Foundation, 2007. Practical guide for LDS missionaries with an extensive review of data on LDS member activity, convert retention, and other indicators. Also includes historical reviews and some evidence-based constructive criticisms of the current missionary program.

Taber, Susan Buhler. *Mormon Lives: A Year in the Elkton Ward*. Urbana: University of Illinois Press, 1993. Probably the best ethnography of an LDS ward in the United States.

BIBLIOGRAPHY

Albrecht, Stan L. "The Consequential Dimension of Mormon Religiosity." In *Latter-day Saint Social Life: Social Research on the LDS Church and Its Members*, ed. James T. Duke, 253–292. Provo, UT: Brigham Young University Press, 1998.
Ballard, M. Russell. "Members Are the Key." *Ensign* (Sept. 2000).

Barlow, Philip. "Before Mormonism: Joseph Smith's Use of the Bible, 1820–1829." *Journal of the American Academy of Religion* 57, no. 4 (1989): 739–771.

Barna, George. "Protestants, Catholics, and Mormons Reflect Diverse Levels of Religious Activity." *Barna Research Update* (July 9, 2001).

Bennion, Lowell C., and Lawrence Young. "The Uncertain Dynamics of LDS Expansion, 1950–2020." *Dialogue: A Journal of Mormon Thought* 29, no. 1 (1996): 8–32.

Bigler, David. *Forgotten Kingdom: The Mormon Theocracy in the American West, 1847–1896.* Logan: Utah State University Press, 1998.

Bushman, Claudia L. *Contemporary Mormonism: Latter-day Saints in Modern America.* Westport, CT: Greenwood Publishing Group, 2006.

Charney, Linda Ann. "Religious Conversion: A Longitudinal Study." PhD diss., University of Utah, 1986.

Church of Jesus Christ. *The Church of Jesus Christ General Business and Organization Conference Minutes.* Bridgewater, MI: Church of Jesus Christ, 2007.

Church of Jesus Christ of Latter-day Saints. *The Book of Mormon.* Salt Lake City, UT: Church of Jesus Christ of Latter-day Saints, 1989.

——. *Doctrine and Covenants; Pearl of Great Price.* Salt Lake City, UT: Church of Jesus Christ of Latter-day Saints, 1989.

Condie, Spencer J. "Missionary," "Missionary Life." In *Encyclopedia of Mormonism*, ed. Daniel H. Ludlow, 910–913. New York: Macmillan, 1992.

Cowan, Richard O. *Every Man Shall Hear the Gospel in his own Language.* Provo, UT: Missionary Training Center, 1984.

Cunningham, Perry H. "Activity in the Church." In *Encyclopedia of Mormonism*, ed. Daniel H. Ludlow, 13–15. New York: Macmillan, 1992.

Davies, Douglas J. *The Mormon Culture of Salvation: Force, Grace, and Glory.* London: Ashgate, 2000.

Davis, Troy, Richard Nelson, and David Salmons, eds. *Our Miraculous Heritage: Amazing Conversion Stories from the Early Church.* Orem, UT: Cedar Fort, 1991.

Decoo, Wilfried. "Feeding the Fleeing Flock: Reflections on the Struggle to Retain Church Members in Europe." *Dialogue: A Journal of Mormon Thought* 29, no. 1 (1996): 97–113.

——. "Issues in Writing European History and in Building the Church in Europe." *Journal of Mormon History* 23, no. 1 (1997): 140–176.

Deseret News. *2008 Church Almanac.* Salt Lake City, UT: Deseret News, 2007.

——. *2009 Church Almanac.* Salt Lake City, UT: Deseret News, 2008.

Elisha, Omri. "Sustaining Charisma: Mormon Sectarian Culture and the Struggle for Plural Marriage, 1852–1890." *Nova Religio: The Journal of Alternative and Emergent Religions* 6, no. 1 (2002): 45–63.

Flake, Kathleen. "Translating Time: The Nature and Function of Joseph Smith's Narrative Canon." *Journal of Religion* 87 (2007): 497–527.

Fleming, Stephen J. " 'Congenial to Almost Every Shade of Radicalism': The Delaware Valley and the Success of Early Mormonism." *Religion and American Culture* 17, no. 2 (2007): 129–165.

——. "The Religious Heritage of the British Northwest and the Rise of Mormonism." *Church History* 77, no. 1 (2008): 73–104.

Foster, Douglas et al., eds. *The Encyclopedia of the Stone-Campbell Movement.* Grand Rapids, MI: William B. Eerdmans Publishing Co., 2004.

Glenmary Research Center. *Religious Congregations & Membership: 2000.* http://www.glenmary.org.

Gooren, Henri. "Conversion Careers in Latin America: Entering and Leaving Church among Pentecostals, Catholics, and Mormons." In *Conversion of a Continent: Contemporary Religious Change in Latin America*, ed. Timothy J. Steigenga and Edward L. Cleary, 52–71. New Brunswick, NJ: Rutgers University Press, 2007.

———. "Latter-day Saints under Siege: The Unique Experience of Nicaraguan Mormons." *Dialogue: A Journal of Mormon Thought* 40, no. 3 (2007): 134–155.

———. "The Mormons of the World: The Meaning of LDS Membership in Central America." In *Revisiting Thomas F. O'Dea's "The Mormons": Contemporary Perspectives*, ed. Cardell K. Jacobson, John P. Hoffman, and Tim B. Heaton, 362–388. Salt Lake City, UT: University of Utah Press, 2008.

———. *Rich among the Poor: Church, Firm, and Household among Small-scale Entrepreneurs in Guatemala City*. Amsterdam: Thela, 1999.

Grossman, Cathy Lynn. "Charting the Unchurched in America." *USA Today*, Mar. 7, 2002.

Grover, Mark L. "The Maturing of the Oak: The Dynamics of LDS Growth in Latin America." *Dialogue: A Journal of Mormon Thought* 38, no. 2 (2005): 79–104.

———. "Mormonism in Brazil: Religion and Dependency in Latin America." PhD Diss., Indiana University, 1985.

———. "One Convert at a Time." *BYU Speeches*, 2001. http://speeches.byu.edu/reader/reader.php?id=713.

Harper, Steven C. "'Dictated by Christ': Joseph Smith and the Politics of Revelation." *Journal of the Early Republic* 26, no. 2 (2006): 275–304.

———. "Infallible Proofs, Both Human and Divine: The Persuasiveness of Mormonism for Early Converts." *Religion and American Culture* 10, no. 1 (2000): 99–118.

Heaton, Tim. "Vital Statistics." In *Encyclopedia of Mormonism*, ed. Daniel H. Ludlow, 1518–1537. New York: Macmillan, 1992.

Hepworth, Joseph T. "A Causal Analysis of Missionary and Membership Growth in the Church of Jesus Christ of Latter-day Saints (1830–1995)." *Journal for the Scientific Study of Religion* 38, no. 1 (1999): 59–71.

Herlinger, Chris. "U.S. Catholic, Episcopal, Mormon, Orthodox, Pentecostal, Churches Grow." *Episcopal News Service*, Apr. 5, 2005.

Hinckley, Gordon B. "Some Thoughts on Temples, Retention of Converts, and Missionary Service," 1997. http://www.lds.org/conference/talk/display/0,5232,49-1-32-20,00.html.

Holifield, E. Brooks. *Theology in America: Christian Thought from the Age of the Puritans to the Civil War*. New Haven: Yale University Press, 2005.

Knowlton, David C. "How Many Members Are There Really? Two Censuses and the Meaning of LDS Membership in Chile and Mexico." *Dialogue: A Journal of Mormon Thought* 38, no. 2 (2005): 53–78.

———. "Mormonism in Latin America: Towards the Twenty-first Century." *Dialogue: A Journal of Mormon Thought* 29, no. 1 (1996): 159–176.

Kosmin, Barry A., and Seymour Lachman. *One Nation under God: Religion in Contemporary American Society*. New York: Harmony Books, 1993.

Kuhn, Kristy. "LDS Conversion is a Process, Study Indicates." *Deseret News*. April 5, 2009. http://www.deseretnews.com/article/705295080/Study-LDS-conversion-is-a-process.html.

LeBaron, Dale E. Cited in *Ricks College News Release*, Apr. 5, 2001.

Lindner, Eileen W., ed. *Yearbook of American and Canadian Churches 2007*. Nashville, TN: Abingdon Press, 2007.

Lobb, Gary C. "Mormon Membership Trends in Europe among People of Color: Present and Future Assessment." *Dialogue: A Journal of Mormon Thought* 33, no. 4 (2000): 55–68.

Mauss, Armand L. *The Angel and the Beehive: The Mormon Struggle with Assimilation.* Champaign: University of Illinois Press, 1994.

——. "Mormonism in the Twenty-first Century: Marketing for Miracles." *Dialogue: A Journal of Mormon Thought* 29, no. 1 (1996): 236–249.

Mayer, Egon, Barry A. Kosmin, and Ariela Keysar. *American Religious Identification Survey.* New York: City University of New York, 2008. http://www.gc.cuny.edu.

Numano, Jiro. "Mormonism in Modern Japan." *Dialogue: A Journal of Mormon Thought* 29, no. 1 (1996): 223–235.

Oaks, Dallin H. "The Role of Members in Conversion." *Ensign* (Mar. 2003).

——. "The Worlds of Joseph Smith." International Academic Conference at the Library of Congress, Washington, DC, May 2005.

Park, Benjamin E. "Rational Supernaturalism: Early Mormonism and Enlightened-Romantic Rhetoric." Paper presented at the Mormon History Association, Springfield, IL, May 22, 2009.

Pavlik, Steve. "Of Saints and Lamanites: An Analysis of Navajo Mormonism." *Wicazo Sa Review* 8, no. 1 (1992): 21–30.

Pew Forum Study. *Report Religious Landscape Study,* 2007. http://religions.pewforum.org/pdf/report-religious-landscape-study-chapter-2.pdf.

Phillips, Rick. "'De Facto Congregationalism' and Mormon Missionary Outreach: An Ethnographic Case Study." *Journal for the Scientific Study of Religion* 47, no. 4 (2008): 628–643.

——. "Rethinking the International Expansion of Mormonism." *Nova Religio: The Journal of Alternative and Emergent Religions* 10, no. 1 (2006): 52–68.

——. "The 'Secularization' of Utah and Religious Competition." *Journal for the Scientific Study of Religion* 38, no. 1 (1999): 72–82.

Prince, Gregory A. *Power from On High: The Development of Mormon Priesthood.* Salt Lake City, UT: Signature Books, 1995.

Quinn, D. Michael. *Early Mormonism and the Magic World View.* Salt Lake City, UT: Signature Books, 1987.

——. *The Mormon Hierarchy: Origins of Power.* Salt Lake City, UT: Signature Books, 1994.

Rust, Val D. *Radical Origins: Early Mormon Converts and Their Colonial Ancestors.* Urbana: University of Illinois Press, 2004.

Shepherd, Gary, and Gordon Shepherd. *Mormon Passage: A Missionary Chronicle.* Urbana: University of Illinois Press, 1998.

Shepherd, Gordon, and Gary Shepherd. *A Kingdom Transformed: Themes in the Development of Mormonism.* Salt Lake City: University of Utah Press, 1984.

——. "Membership Growth, Church Activity, and Missionary Recruitment." *Dialogue: A Journal of Mormon Thought* 29, no. 1 (1996): 33–57.

Shipps, Jan. *Mormonism: The Story of a New Religious Tradition.* Urbana: University of Illinois Press, 1987.

Smith, Joseph, Jr. *Teachings of the Prophet Joseph Smith,* ed. Joseph Fielding Smith. Salt Lake City, UT: Shadow Mountain, 1977.

Stark, Rodney. "The Basis of Mormon Success: A Theoretical Application." In *Latter-day Saint Social Life: Social Research on the LDS Church and its Members,* ed. James T. Duke, 29–70. Provo, UT: Religious Studies Center, Brigham Young University, 1998.

——. "The Rise of a New World Faith." *Review of Religious Research* 26, no. 1 (1984): 118–127.

——. *The Rise of Mormonism,* ed. Reid L. Neilson. New York: Columbia University Press, 2005.

Statcan. *Selected Protestant Denominations in Canada, 2001 and 1991.* Statcan Press Release, May 2003. http://www.statcan.ca.

Stewart David G., Jr. "Growth, Retention, and Internationalization." In *Revisiting Thomas F. O'Dea's "The Mormons": Contemporary Perspectives,* ed. Cardell K. Jacobson, John P. Hoffman, and Tim B. Heaton, 328–361. Salt Lake City: University of Utah Press, 2008.

——. *The Law of the Harvest: Practical Principles of Effective Missionary Work.* Henderson, NV: Cumorah Foundation, 2007.

Taber, Susan Buhler. *Mormon Lives: A Year in the Elkton Ward.* Urbana: University of Illinois Press, 1993.

Tullis, F. LaMond. "The Church Moves outside the United States: Some Observations from Latin America." *Dialogue: A Journal of Mormon Thought* 13, no. 1 (1980): 63–73.

Underwood, Grant. *The Millenarian World of Early Mormonism.* Champaign: University of Illinois Press, 1999.

Van Wagoner, Richard S. *Mormon Polygamy: A History.* Salt Lake City, UT: Signature Books, 1986.

INDEX

Abbasid period, 635–636
Abu Bakr (Caliph), 63
Acculturation, conversion as, 24, 26–28
Adler, Joseph, 540
Adorno, Theodor, 475
adventism, 757
Afghanistan, 498, 634, 638, 647
Africa, 53–54, 59, 61, 63, 613, 617, 619, 634, 641–642, 646, 647
African Methodist Episcopal Zion Church, 73
agency, 7
ahimsa, 446–447, 450, 452–453, 456
ajiva, 446
ajlaf, 638
Akbar (Emperor), 495, 637
Alcoholics Anonymous, 770
Allah, 3, 6, 17, 31–32, 308, 310, 371, 633
à Kempis, Thomas, 615
al-Azhar (University), 652
al-Ghazzali, 643
al-Jabbar, Kareem Abd, 646
Ali, M. Mahomed, 434
Ali, Muhammad, 646
Allievi, Stefano, 671, 675
Amardas (Guru), 494–495
American Zen Teachers Association, 478
Analects, 541, 546, 548–550
Anandpur, 497
Anatolia, 27, 31, 35–36, 639
Anathapindika, 468
Anthropology of Christianity, 84, 100–101
Antiquities, 588
Ambedkar, B. R., 436, 638
Amritsar, 494–495
ancestral worship (veneration), 542, 544, 546, 550, 552n24, 559, 563–564, 613
Andrews, C. F. 434
Angad (Guru), 493. *See* Lehina Trehan
animal rights, 456

apocalypticism, 583, 594
apostasy (apostate), 8, 96, 148, 170, 179, 271, 274, 412, 467, 510, 599, 610, 634, 706–707, 709–711, 714–715, 722–723. *See* deconversion and disengagement
Appel, Willa, 690
Arabs, 27, 30, 31, 55, 415, 437, 595, 634–637, 638, 641–642, 644, 647, 653–654
Arjan (Guru), 494–495
Arndt, Johann, 603
Archetype, 214
Arnobius, 611f
Arnold, Thomas Walker, 6, 165
Aristotle, 345
art, 327–342, 331 (as spiritual communication)
Arya Samaj, 431, 434
Asad, Muhammad, 344, 357, 361, 644
Asad, Talal, 103
asceticism (ascetics), 444–447, 454–455, 459n11, 472
ashraf, 638
Asia, 27, 54, 59, 61–63, 70, 72–73, 167–168, 175, 192–194, 200–201, 313, 334, 380, 403, 408, 411, 465, 468–469, 471–482, 511, 514, 523–524, 528, 551, 613, 619, 632, 637–638, 640, 641, 643, 646, 650, 767–769, 772
Asian American, 190–191, 200, 472, 650
aslama, 633, 688
Asoka (King), 2, 468
Association of Confucian Learning, 543
atheists, 51–52, 54, 56–57, 470
Attachment theory, 216–217
attachments, 150, 142, 176, 180, 216, 225, 286, 305, 315, 696, 706–709, 711, 714–715, 723
Augustine (Saint), 28, 120, 127–128, 131, 329–330, 345, 347, 353–357, 360–361, 370, 373–374, 379, 381, 604–607
Aurengzeb (Emperor), 495, 637
Austin-Broos, Diane, 84, 99, 104, 538

Austin, Margaret, 358
Australia, 69, 90, 95, 99, 101, 335, 468–469, 472, 499, 527, 746, 761
Australian Aborigines, 90, 335
autobiography, 119, 344–345, 347–348, 352–359, 361, 372, 600, 604
    theory and criticism, 353–354
    history, 354–356
    self-identity, 356–357
    ideology, 357–358
Axial Age, 2

Baba, 488
Babb, Lawrence A., 449
Babur, 491
Badal, Parkash Singh, 500–501
Baer, Marc David, 11, 15, 24–47
Baha'i, 746
Bainbridge, William Sims, 49, 142
Baker, Richard, 480
Bakhtin, Mikhail, 349, 373
Bali, 70, 71, 430, 432
bao ying, 559, 568, 570–571, 575n46
Balkans, 635, 637, 639–640
baptism, 25, 28–29, 71, 87, 90, 92, 95, 171, 180, 265, 303, 357, 434, 540, 558, 567, 598, 602–604, 612, 615, 618–619, 758–759, 762, 764–766, 772–774
Barbour, John D., 271, 282, 289
Barclay, William, 607
Barker, Eileen, 143, 695, 720, 747
Barker, Irwin R., 143
bay'a, 633
Beatles (The Beatles), 456
Beckford, James, 715
Bede, 612
Bedi, Khem Singh, 500–501
Beecher, Henry Ward, 330
Beijing, 562, 564
Beit-Hallahmi, Benjamin, 216, 225
Belgium, 742
Belgium Taoist Association, 526
Benedict XIV (Pope), 513
Benedict XVI (Pope), 469
Berber, 636
Berkeley Buddhist Monastery, 474
Berkeley Buddhist Studies Group, 474

Berger, John, 329–330
Berger, Peter L., 312, 383, 407, 451, 465, 557
Berkhofer, Robert, 86
Bernard of Clairvaux, 615–616
Bernini, Gian Lorenzo, 337
Bernhardt, Sarah, 1
Berthrong, John, 551
Bhagavad Gita, 431
bhakti, 445, 447–448
Bharata, 331
Bhāratī Swami, Śrī Chandraśehara, 431
bhas khana, 490
Bhasour, Teja Singh, 500–501
bhikkhus, 468
Bhindrawale, Jarnail Singh, 500–501
Bible, 96, 99, 111, 121, 131, 146, 149, 197, 263, 299, 315, 334, 338, 347, 370, 435, 578, 579, 581–582, 586, 591, 600–602, 605, 617, 674, 757
Bielefeld-based Study on Deconversion, 281–287
Black Christian Methodist Episcopal Church, 73
Blake, William, 328
Blavatsky, H. P. (Madam) 473
Böhme, Jakob, 603
Book of Mormon, 757–758, 760–761, 771, 773, 775n14
Book of Three-Character Verse, 546
Booth, Wayne, 352, 363n26
born again, 91, 97, 118, 166, 171, 225, 313, 598, 600, 602–604, 607–609, 611, 672
Bourdieu, Pierre, 272–273
Boxer Uprising, 561
brahmans, 446, 494
brainwashing, 17, 250, 692–696, 698–699, 715, 720, 739–741, 743, 747
Brazil, 56, 59–61, 71, 74, 93, 149, 410–411, 469, 526, 769, 771
Brekke, Torkel, 539
Brereton, Virginia, 305, 327
British, 641, 646, 673
British Raj, 439
British Taoist Association, 526
Brockey, Liam Matthew, 542
Brokaw, Cynthia, 559, 570
Bromley, David, 695, 715

Brown, Jerry, 480

Bruce, Steve, 171

Brunn, Stanley, 71

Brusco, Elizabeth, 312, 315, 317

Buddha (Lord), 2, 3, 164, 167–168, 178,
    265–266, 330, 448, 465–469, 471–474,
    476–477, 479–482, 493, 513–514, 643

Buddha's Light International Association
    (BLIA), 471
  in America, 472
  in Australia, 472

Buddhism, 48, 51, 57–58, 429–430, 432, 436,
    445, 455–457, 478, 490, 549
  in America, 468, 469, 472, 474, 477, 479
  in Australia, 468–469
  in Brazil, 469
  in China, 469, 511, 517, 559–560, 613
  in India, 539
  in South Africa, 469, 472
  in Tibet, 523
  interdependence, 478
  Japanese, 469, 477
  "modern," 475, 478–482
  New Vehicle, 478–479
  socially engaged, 478, 481
  "white," 479, 482

Buddhist Peace Fellowship (BPF), 478

Bulliet, Richard, 6, 632–633, 637

Burke, Kenneth, 117, 120, 127–128, 132

Burma, 474

Byden, William, 641

Byzantine Empire, 27, 173, 332, 639

Cabezón, José, 473

Caldwell, Patricia, 120, 128–129

Campbell, Alexander, 758

Cantón Delgado, Manuela, 98

Caravaggio, 336–337

Caribbean, 70, 74

Calvin, John, 74

Cannel, Fenella, 84, 102, 104

Canolly, Cecilia Mahmuda, 669

Carrithers, Michael, 445

Carpenter, Joel, 149

Carter, Lewis, 717, 721

caste system, 433, 439, 490, 638

Catechism of the Catholic Church, 540

Catholic Bishops' Conference of India
    (CBCI), 438

Celestial Masters, 514, 516–519

Central Asia, 31, 173, 511, 574n21, 595,
    637, 639

Ceylon, 432

Ch'an, 467. *See Zen*, 467

Chau, Adam, 558, 562

Chand (Sri), 493

Chapple, Christopher Key, 448

Charlemagne (Emperor), 619

charisma, 6, 72, 85, 87, 94, 446, 453, 457, 471,
    478, 522, 528, 637, 696, 713–714, 717,
    758–759, 761, 773, 781n104

Chaudhuri, Mohuya, 439

Chen, Carolyn, 146, 151

Chesnut, Andrew, 408, 410

China, 2, 17, 29, 31, 33, 52, 56, 59–61, 73, 70, 87,
    90, 141, 147–150, 173–175, 266–267, 270,
    300, 320, 325, 347, 354, 470, 471–472, 482,
    509, 511–515, 517, 520, 523–524, 526–528,
    538–539, 540, 542–545, 547, 549, 550–551,
    555, 556–578, 613, 618, 639, 694, 716,
    739, 746

Chaves, Mark, 144

Children of God (a.k.a. The Family), 690, 692,
    696, 713–716, 738

Ching Chung Taoist Association, 527

Chishti, Muinuddin, 637

Chitrabhanu, 453

Chodorow, Nancy, 305–306

Coleman, James W., 481

Coleman, Simon, 84, 99

Chong, Kelly, 312, 316–317

Christianity (Christian), 2, 4, 7, 10–12,
    14, 17, 26–30, 33–34, 49–50, 53–54, 56,
    59, 61–62, 69–71, 73–76, 84, 86, 88–92,
    95–96, 100–103, 122, 126–127, 130, 132,
    141–142, 144, 146–148, 164–175, 178–180,
    182–185, 193, 195, 200, 212, 251, 261–262,
    267, 298–299, 301, 303–304, 307, 313,
    315, 318–319, 329, 331, 333–337, 344–345,
    347, 374, 406–407, 429, 433–434, 436–437,
    557–559, 567, 572, 578, 583–586, 588,
    590, 592, 594–596, 632–634, 636,
    639, 640–645, 647–649, 651, 653–654,
    670

Christian Missionary Activities Inquiry
    Committee, 437. *See* Niyogi Committee
Christianization, 26–29, 33, 35, 92,
    509, 614
Christiano, Kevin J., 150
church, 31, 33, 35, 51, 55, 69, 72–74, 86, 90–92,
    94–96, 98–100, 102, 118, 129, 141–148, 168,
    171–174, 179–180, 182, 190–202, 264–265,
    273–275, 287, 300, 302–304, 312, 315–317,
    332, 334, 337–338, 360, 389n33, 401,
    405–406, 408–410, 412, 414, 438–439,
    469, 471, 481, 510, 513, 540, 543, 556, 558,
    583, 590, 594, 603, 606–607, 612–618
Church Universal and Triumphant (CTU)
    (New Religious Movement), 718
circumcision, 25, 383, 490, 579, 588–590, 593
City of Ten Thousand Buddhas, 471
Classics of Filial Piety, 546
Clement XI (Pope), 513
Coe, Albert, 213
cognitive neuropsychology, 15, 240–255
    neurogenesis in adolescence, 246–247
    plasticity, 247
    temporal lobe epilepsy, 247–248
    vision, meditation, contemplation, 248–250
Coleman, James W., 481
Collins, Randall, 144–145, 184
colonialism, 89–90, 174–175, 300, 349, 434, 455,
    511, 582, 641–643
Columbia University, 473
Comaroff, Jean, 101, 126–127, 301–302
Comaroff, John L., 101, 126–127, 301–302
Communitas, 99
Community of Christ (Reorganized Church,
    RLDS), 756, 761
Confucianism, 429, 471, 523–524, 559–560
    Boston Confucianism, 551
    civil examination, 542–545
    Political Confucianism, 547
Confucius, 2, 3
Congregation of the Holy Spirit
    (a.k.a. Spiritans), 303
Constantine (Emperor), 28, 170, 173, 261–262,
    336–337, 339, 617
Constantinople, 639
Constitution (India), 437, 439
conversion, 430

and adaptation, 454
and authenticity, 436
and blogs, 453
and choice/volition, 141, 164–167, 169,
    170–171, 174–175, 177, 179–180
and cognitive neuroscience, 240–255
and community, 433
and conflict, 439
and dreams, 256–270, 583, 672
and economic conditions, 436, 446, 508
and elites, 446, 465, 468, 473
and ethical movements, 452, 453, 456
and ethnicity, 53, 439, 519–520
and exorcism, 612–613
and healing, 449–450, 613
and heroes, 449
and Hinduism, 430
and imperialism, 436
and law, 437, 440
and marketing strategies, 452
and miracles, 449, 612–613, 637
and monastics, 449
and morality, 434, 453, 598
and peace, 434
and religious freedom, 440
and religious markets, China (red, black,
    and gray), 149–150, 444
and social conditions, 436, 450
and socioeconomic factors, 450–451
and speaking in tongues (glossolalia), 759
and spread of religions, 164–189
and technology, 451
and transnationalism, 451–453, 455–456,
    468–469, 471, 474–476, 481, 509, 511–512,
    523, 526, 528, 621
and visions, 583, 617
as active/passive, 7, 412–413,
as acculturation, 25–28
as adhesion and syncretism, 5, 24, 28–32
as awakening, 466
as comparative category, 509
as continuous conversion, 84, 99–100, 102
as event, 24–25
as gradual, 467
as homecoming, 466–467
as intensification, 24, 545, 610, 614–616, 619
as process, 25, 95–96

as stages, 87, 95–97, 103, 142, 185, 225–226, 391n57, 412, 415, 467, 479, 599, 610, 668, 672, 711
as sudden, 466
as theoretical category, 361
as Tradition Transition, 24–25, 610–614, 624
as Transformation and turn to piety, conversion category, 32–34
by force, 438, 450, 511, 514, 610, 619, 632, 638, 670
globally, 451
horizontal, 440
mapping of conversion, 67, 69,
mass (conversions), 449, 515, 519, 612, 619, 632, 636, 638, 649–650
models of conversion, 15, 93, 103, 245, 353, 391n57), 395n104), 402, 409, 412, 416, 622, 638, 711, 715, 761, 764
motifs of conversion, 616–619
motivations for conversion, 7–8, 14, 17, 98, 177–178, 181, 183–184, 355
opposition to, 151, 434
politics of, 437
precariousness of, 102
resistance to, 438
vernacular language, 492
vertical, 440
conversion, definitions of
    Apostolos-Cappadona, 328–330
    Austin-Broos, 99
    Baer, 9–11
    Cantón Delgado, 98
    Chaves, 144
    Coleman, 99
    Cucchiari, 100
    Falla, 92–93
    Harding, 97
    Hefner, 89
    Hiebert, 96–97
    James, 5
    Komjathy, 528
    Kraft, 95
    Leone, 170
    Long and Hadden, 146, 155n45
    Montgomery, 166
    Nock, 5
    Snow and Machalek, 122–134

Steigenga, 402, 412, 414, 416–417
Stromberg, 118–119
conversion careers, 8, 100, 313, 412, 414, 707, 770, 773
conversion, categories of
    Acculturation, 26–28
    Adhesion and Syncretism, 28–32
    Transformation and Turn to Piety, 32–34
    Conversion of Sacred Space, 34–36
conversion studies, 5–9
converts
    Anneke/Sakina, 670–681
    Asad, Muhammad, 344
    Augustine, 373–374. See Augustine (Saint)
    Austin, Margaret, (Methodist), 358
    Baxter, Richard, 348
    Beecher, Henry Ward, 330
    Bunyan, John, 347
    Constantine, 261–262, 336–337
    Jackson, Chris, 34
    Jerome, 262–263
    Kling, Gordon, 600–602
    Lady Sarafina, 265–266
    Ruth (Bible), 579–581
    Saul/Paul of Tarsus, 336, 371
    Shabbati Tzevi, 37 (Aziz Mehmed Effendi)
    Staniforth, Sampson, 343–345, 350, 361
    Te-ch'ing, 344, 347
    Therese of Avila, 377
    Tissot, James Jacques, 337–338
    Victoria, 264–265
cosmopolitanism (cosmopolitan), 445, 448, 578, 582, 594, 595
Cowper, William, 348
Cucchiari, Salvatore, 100, 312
Cult of the Silkworm Mother, 562–563
Cultural Revolution (China), 561–562, 565–566
cultural geography, 65–66
Currie, Raymond, 143
Cyprian, 611
Cyril, 617–618

Dakshin Bharat Jain Sabha, 453
Dalai Lama, 469–470, 473–474, 478
Dalits, 436, 438–439
Damasio, Antonio, 259
dana (ritual giving to monastics), 444

Dannin, Robert, 675

Dante, 333

Daode jing, 514, 524

Daoism, 508–537, 549, 559–560

Darbar Sahib, 494, 500

Davidman, Lynn, 151, 311–312, 314

David-Neel, Alexandra, 473

Davis, Patricia M., 257, 268–269

da'wa (or da'wah), 71, 633, 645–648, 650–651,
   653–656, 679

Dean, Kenneth, 556

deconversion, 8, 223–226, 251, 271–296, 599,
   610, 614, 694, 707, 711, 714–715

   as migration within and out of religious
      field, 272

   avenues (paths) of, 272

   definition of, 272–274

   motives for, 276,

   narratives of, 286–287

Deedat, Ahmed, 651, 661n96

Defoe, Daniel, 351

Delgado, Richard, 740

Delumeau, Jean, 614

demography, 15, 49–64

   Brazil and China, case studies, 60–61

   positive factors: births, 52;

   converts, 53;

   immigrants, 54

   negative factors: deaths, 53;

   defectors, 54;

   emigrants, 54

   rates of change: births/deaths; converts/
      defectors; immigrants/emigrants, 52–55

   trends affecting growth and decline of
      religions, 63

   United Nations Continental Areas,
      comparisons, 61–63

de Molinos, Miguel, 603

Deng, Xiaoping, 566

Denmark, 603

deprogramming, 17, 693, 694, 710, 712, 720,
   722, 739–740

de Saussure, Ferdinand, 374–382

deversion, 476. *See* deconversion

development, 439

Devi (also Shakta), 490

devshirme, 640

Digambara, 449

Dharamsala, 470, 473–474

Dharma, 465–466, 469, 471–473, 479

Dharma Masters, 469, 474, 481

   Vietnam, 470

   Taiwan, 471

Dharma Wheel, 466

dhikr, 633, 652

dhimmi, 636, 657n15

diaspora, 68, 70, 452, 489, 559, 585–586, 589

Dilthey, Wilhelm, 354

din, 491

disciplines (academic), 8, 10, 12–13

disengagement, 706–724. *See* apostasy,
      deconversion

   definition, 709

   process of, 711–714

   role exit, 713–716

   social movement theory, 716–719

Dominicans, 513, 542, 615

Domhoff, G. William, 259

Dönme, 37

Douglas, William G. T., 238

Dow, James, 94

dreams, 9, 14, 85, 94, 102, 256–270, 521–522,
   583, 672

Droogers, André, 100

duality, 466

Duara, Prasenjit, 547

dukkha, 467

Dundas, Paul, 447

dunia, 491

Durkheim, Emile, 93, 114, 245, 356,
   410, 444

East Asia, 511, 549, 551

Eaton, Richard, 638

Ebrey, Patricia, 549

ecology, 456

education, 439

Egypt, 51, 581, 632, 636–637, 644, 652

Eliade, Mircea, 245, 327, 330–333

Elijah, 2

Eliot, Sir Charles, 432

Elman, Benjamin, 542

epistrephein, 578, 598–599

Erikson, Erik, 648

eschatological (eschatology), 48, 515, 528,
   594–595

ethnicity, 508, 514

Europe, 54, 59, 61–63, 432, 453, 455–456, 634, 670, 672, 674–675

European Court of Human Rights (ECHR), 743–745

Eusebius, 336

evangelical, 2, 11, 72, 84, 95, 97-98, 103, 121–123, 127, 129–130, 132, 141, 147, 171, 175–176, 179, 199–200, 202, 263, 302, 305, 313, 315–317, 344, 403, 406, 416, 465, 474, 510, 600, 603–604, 606, 609, 612, 617–621, 623n11

Evans, Carolyn, 744–745

Falla, Ricardo, 92–93, 103

Fan, Lizhu, 566

Falun Gong, 746

Family of Love (New Religious Movement), 717

Farhadian, Charles E., 467, 474, 509

Farrakhan, Louis, 646, 649

feminism, 297-326, 474, 479, 676

Fenesh, Louis E., 489

Fields, Rick, 479

filial piety, 546, 550

films

By the Dawn's Early Light: Chris Jackson's Journey to Islam, 47

Gospel According to the Papuans, The, 47

King of Kings, The, 328, 338

Malcolm X, 47

Mission, The, 47

Finland, 74, 76

Finke, Roger, 171, 183, 557

Finn, Thomas, 617–618

fiqh, 636, 643

Fish, Stanley, 350

Fisher, Humphrey, 88–89

fitra, 633

Fletcher, Richard, 605, 612

Fo Guang Shan, 471. *See* Buddha's Light International Association

Foote, Peter, 614

Four Noble Truths, 467

Fox, Robin Lane, 611

Francis of Assisi, 337

Franciscans, 542, 615

Franke, August Hermann, 603

Freedberg, David, 334

French Taoist Association, 526

Freud, Sigmund, 97, 212–214, 219, 242, 245, 256–257, 259, 269, 350, 714

Frye, Northrop, 347

Fuller Theological Seminary, 195

fundamentalism, 48–49, 439

Fundamentalist Latter Day Saints (FLDS), 756, 762

ganadharas, 446, 449

Gannon, Shane P., 11

Gandhi, Mahatma, 434, 436, 440

Garma, Carlos, 94

Gautama, Shakyamuni Siddhartha, 3

Geertz, Clifford, 642

gender, 297–326, 478, 497, 508, 529n2, 561–562, 579, 648, 654, 667, 673, 675, 682

definition of, 298, 301

Gentiles, 262, 578, 582, 586–592, 594, 598, 611, 622

Gerlach, Luther, 84, 87–88, 103

Germany, 33, 35, 54, 225–226, 276–286, 288–289, 310, 317, 455, 603, 676, 742

Gerstel, Naomi, 150

GhaneaBassiri, Kambriz, 645, 648, 656

ghazi, 638

Ghosal, Sarela, 2

Ghost Dance, 85. *See* revitalization movements

Gibb, H. A. R., 636

Gifford Lectures, 213

Gilligan, Carol, 305–306

globalization, 9, 11, 85, 103–104, 141, 147, 408, 413, 416, 451, 465, 469, 481–482, 509–510, 621, 670, 748

Glock, Charles Y., 272

Gobind Singh (Guru), 496–499

God, 1, 3, 13, 15–16, 31–32, 35, 37, 72, 76, 91, 95–98, 103, 118, 120–121, 128, 130, 167–169, 178, 181–182, 214, 216, 219, 223, 251, 261–268, 276–277, 279–280, 299, 304–306, 311, 316, 328-330, 332–333, 336–337, 343–344, 346, 348, 355, 360–361, 377, 432, 435, 440, 466, 496, 509–510, 578–580, 582, 584, 586–591, 593, 598, 600–612, 614–616, 620, 633, 634, 637, 652, 656, 669, 671, 674, 677, 679, 681–682, 719, 756–760, 762–763, 768, 770, 773–774 goddess, 31–32, 448, 491–492, 562–563, 688

Godin, André, 467

gods, 27, 29–31, 33, 91–92, 96, 168, 181–182,
    214, 216, 226, 241, 331, 445, 448, 468, 470,
    491, 527, 541, 558–562, 572, 590, 611, 614,
    714–715

Goffman, Erving, 130, 132

Gombrich, Ernst, 333

Gooren, Henri, 8, 94, 100, 184, 412, 756,
    770–771

Gore, Al, 472

Gospel, 583, 913

Graduate Theological Union, Berkeley
    (GTU), 474

Graham, Billy (Reverend), 621

Granoff, Phyllis, 445, 448

Granqvist, Pehr, 216–217

Great Awakening, 616

Great Britain, 50, 470

Greece, 581, 743

Gregory of Tours, 612

Greil, Arthur L., 151, 718

Greimas, Algirdas J., 375–382

Griffith, R. Marie, 312, 317

Guanyin, 571

Guenon, Rene, 674

Guatemala, 92–95, 98, 104, 412, 770–771

gurdwara, 488, 498, 501

Gujarat (India), 437, 449–450

Guru Granth, 491, 494, 497–499

ghusl, 634

Habermas, Jürgen, 3–4

Hackett, Rosalind, 746

Hacking, Ian, 550

hadith, 633

Hadot, Pierre, 548

Hadramaut, 641

hagiography, 516, 522, 637

Halevi, Yehudah, 595

Hall, Brian, 148

Hall, G. Stanley, 6, 212–213, 241, 246

Handsome Lake, 85–86

Hanson, Hamza Yusuf, 646

Harding, Susan F., 97, 103, 121, 124–125

Hargobind (Guru), 494–495

Haribhadra, 448

Hart-Cellar Act of 1965, 193. *See* migration

Harrison, George, 1

Haughton, Rosemary, 466

health, 439, 525, 527–528

Hefner, Robert W., 3, 85, 89–90, 99, 103, 612

Hellenism (Hellenistic), 578, 581, 583,
    585–589, 594

Hellenization, 581–583, 585

Hesse, Herman, 476

Hiebert, Paul, 96–97

hijab, 654, 677

Hill, Jane 132

Hill, Patricia, 300–301

Hillel, 592

Hindmarsh, Bruce, 13–15, 121–122, 132, 343–368

Hinduism (Hindu), 50, 429, 434, 436, 440, 445,
    450, 456, 489–496, 498–500, 637–638
  and conversion, 429
  Hinduization, 432

Hindustan Times, 438

Hindutva, 438, 638

Hine, Virginia, 84, 87–88, 103

history, 14

Ho, David, 570

Hodgson, Dorothy, 303–304, 317

Hofmann, Gabrielle, 675–677

Homer, 2

Hong Kong, 472, 509, 523–524, 526–527, 543

Horton, Robin, 7, 84, 88–89, 91, 101, 103, 642

Hsi-Lai, 471–472

huahu, 513–514

Huahu jing, 514

Huang, Chin-shing, 543

Hui Neng, 467

hukam, 491

Hungary, 73–74

Huntington, Samuel, 401, 404, 411, 476

Huxley, Aldous, 1

Iannaccone, Lawrence, 409

ibn Adham, Ibrahim, 643

ibn Sa'd, 633

icon, 332–333

Id (Eid), 651, 653, 661n98, 679

identity, 165–166, 168–170, 174–175, 177, 179,
    181–184, 177–178, 181, 183–184, 190, 195,
    197–199, 220, 223, 225, 263, 267–269,

290, 317, 319, 328–330, 344–345, 349–350,
    352–353, 356–357, 359–361, 384, 402, 406,
    413, 444–445, 448, 540, 557, 612
  and modernity, 451, 480
  Buddhist, 480
  Christian, 605, 612, 620
  Confucian, 539–540, 543, 545, 550
  Daoist, 509, 512, 516
  Hindu, 450
  Jain, 450
  Mormonism, 760
  Muslim, 635, 678–680
iftar, 652
Ignatius of Loyola, 605
Ilyas, Muhammad, 638
images (power of), 334–335
iman, 636
immersion, 95, 593, 758
Immigration Act 1924 (a.k.a. Oriental
    Exclusion Act), 192
immigration, 54, 638, 640, 644
India, 1, 2, 27, 49, 71, 75–76, 149, 174, 298–299,
    302–303, 332, 380, 404, 407, 412, 430, 434,
    447, 455, 457, 474, 488, 500, 539, 613, 635,
    637–638, 654, 746
India Today International, 438
indigenization, 451, 476, 520, 556–557, 637, 641
  of Chinese religions, 557–563, 569, 571–572
  of Christianity, 613
  of Buddhism, 476–477, 482
  of Daoism, 511–514, 517, 526, 528
  of Hinduism, 432
  of Islam, 646
individualism, 89–91, 118, 122, 175–176, 179,
    271, 313, 475, 480, 582, 595, 612, 671, 676
Indonesia, 32–33, 50, 71, 174, 408, 430, 637,
    640–641
indri vaddani, 490
initiation, 432, 434, 450, 490, 494–495, 497, 508,
    516, 528, 540, 583, 598, 617–618, 652, 689, 772
Insight Meditation Society, 474
Intellectualist theory of conversion, 88. *See*
    Horton
inter-faith relations, 439–440, 457
International Society for Krishna
    Consciousness (a.k.a. "Hare
    Krishnas"), 149, 697, 713, 716, 738–739
International Social Survey Programme,
    276–279
internet, 667–670, 674, 698, 745
Introvigne, Massimo, 747
introspection, 244, 258
Iran, 74, 403, 407, 498, 632, 635–638, 643, 648
Iraq, 27, 408, 636–637, 648
Irvine, Judith, 132
Isaiah, 2
Isherwood, Christopher, 1
Islam, 4, 6, 7, 10–12, 17, 27, 33–34, 37, 429,
    433–434, 437, 489, 491, 557–558, 594–595,
    610, 742
Islamic Circle of North America, 654
Islamic Society of North America, 652
Islamization, 6, 26–28, 33, 35, 509, 632, 641, 643
Israel, 31, 55, 181–182, 225, 403, 407, 578–582,
    585–586, 592, 595
istikhara, 671–672
Italy, 54, 355, 742
Ivanhoe, P. J., 541
Ivy, Marilyn, 476

Jackson, Sherman, 646
Jacobs, Janet, 713–715
Jakobsh, Doris R., 489
Jain, 3
Jain Association in North America (JAINA),
    451, 453
Jain, Karuna, 455–456
Jain, Aparigraha, 455
Jain Meditation Center, 454
Jainism, 444–464
Jains, 444, 490–491
Jamaica, 75
James, William, 1, 5, 120, 212–213, 245, 297, 538,
    583, 607–609, 611–612, 619, 642, 648
Janam Sikhi, 491–494. See *Puratan Janam
    Sakhi*
Jameelah, Maryam, 644
Japan (Japanese), 172, 174, 182, 191–192, 196,
    265, 335, 354, 370, 380, 404, 407, 469, 477,
    482, 509, 512, 520, 523–526, 528, 551, 558,
    561, 768–769
Jaspers, Karl, 2
Jats, 490–493, 495, 497–500
Jehangir, 495

Jehovah's Witnesses, 225, 510, 645, 718, 737, 739, 742–744

Jeremiah (Book of), 2

Jerome, 262–263

Jesuits (Society of Jesus), 29, 511, 513, 542, 613

Jesus (Christ), 3, 30, 35, 96, 165, 176, 178, 184, 223, 287, 299, 328, 333, 338, 343, 355, 381, 433, 466, 510, 539, 594, 598, 600, 602, 605–606, 611, 613, 616–618, 620, 622, 633, 669, 674, 757

Jesus (People) Movement, 718, 738

Jews (Jewish), 582–584, 619, 633, 644

Jews, 30–31, 36–37, 55, 57, 65, 151, 170, 224–225, 313, 370, 581, 586–591, 594–596, 615, 622

jie-yuan, 472

jihad, 34, 641

jina, 445, 448, 450

Jindra, Ines W., 151, 225

jiva, 446

jizya, 636, 640

Jodhpur, 449

Josephus, 584–586, 588–589, 592–593

joti, 494

Judaism, 420, 430, 510, 514, 557, 610–611, 649

Judaism, 4, 10, 12, 17, 37, 143, 153, 167, 169, 173, 225, 311, 313–314, 318–319, 355, 383, 407, 429, 582–594, 596, 610–611, 649, 653, 659

Judge, William Quan, 473

Juergensmeyer, Mark, 404, 411

Jules-Rosette, Bennetta, 617

Jung, Carl G., 213–214, 219, 256–257, 260–261

junzi, 548

Juster, Susan, 305–306

Justin Martyr, 611

Kang, You-wei, 543

Kang, Xiaoguang, 547

Kaufman, Deborah, 312–314, 319

Kean, Webb, 132

Kempe, Margery, 615

Kennedy, Andrew, 480

karma, 432–433, 446, 459n17, 517, 567, 569, 613

Kartarpur, 488–495, 497

Kashmir, 493, 498

kerygma, 594

kevalajnana, 446

Khadur, 493–495

khalsa, 494, 496, 499

Khalsa Panth, 494, 496–497

Khalsa Raj, 497–500

Khan, Genghis, 639

Khan, Hulagu, 639

khande di pahul, 496–497, 501

kharaj, 636

Khazars, 595

King, Jr., Martin Luther, 470

Kipp, Rita Smith, 98

Kirkpatrick, Lee A., 216–217, 227

kirtan, 491

Kleeman, Terry, 517

Knaus, John Kenneth, 470

Knight, David A., 151

Korea, 175, 190–208, 509, 512, 520, 523–526, 528, 551, 690, 694

Korean-Americans, 190–208

Kornfield, Jack, 474, 480

Köse, Ali, 647, 650, 673, 675

Kōshin, 525

Kraft, Charles H., 95–96, 103

Krishna, 431, 447

Kumar, Sushil, 454

Lancaster, Lewis, 471

langar, 491, 494, 496

Laos, 520

Latin America, 49, 61–63, 69–70, 84, 92–94, 104, 141, 175, 177, 200, 403–404, 407–409, 411, 769–772

Laozi (Lao-tzu), 2–3, 513–515, 517

Learman, Linda, 468

Leuba, James, 212–213

levels of analysis
    macro, 141–142, 147–150
    meso, 140–141, 143–146
    micro, 142–143

Lévi-Strauss, Claude, 129, 375

Levine, Gregory J., 78

Levtzion, Nehemia, 6, 639, 641

li, 548

Liberation theology, 404

lifeways, 3

Lifton, Robert J., 692

Lin, Xiangru, 563, 565, 574n40

Lodhi, Sikandar, 488
Lofland, John, 6–7, 142, 147–148, 150, 177,
    616, 618
Longmen (Dragon Gate), 517, 524
Longwanggou temple, 562
Los Angeles, 645
Lotman, Iurij Michajlovich, 382–384
Lotus Sutra, 468
Lotz, Anne Graham, 328
Lucas, Philip, 746
Luther, Martin, 602–603, 607
Lutheran Church (Lutherans), 73–74, 76, 600,
    602–603, 616

Maasai, 303–304
Machalek, Richard, 122–124
Mack, Phyllis, 350
MacMullen, Ramsay, 611–612
Madeley, John, 69
Mahaprajna, 455
Mahabharata, 447
Mahavira, Vardhamana (Lord), 3, 446,
    449, 453
Mahayana (Buddhism), 466, 468, 472, 474, 511
Mahmud of Ghazni (Sultan), 638
Malherbe, Abraham, 599
Malaysia, 637, 640
Malcolm X, 34, 646
manjis, 492, 494
Mao, Zedong, 566, 568
Maoists, 438
marga, 467
market/marketplace (religion as, supply and
    demand), 140, 146, 148–150, 177, 201, 312,
    402, 408–411, 414–416, 444, 446, 449,
    451–454, 458, 475, 588, 619, 653, 671, 707,
    723, 764
Markus, Robert, 612–613
Marshall-Fratani, Ruth, 91, 104
Marti, Gerardo, 145
Martin, Bernice, 312
Marty, Martin, 604, 621
Marx, Karl, 350
Marxism, 66, 566
masand, 494, 496
Master Xingyun, 471–472
Mata Khivi, 494

Matar, Nabil, 643
Matthiessen, Peter, 477
Mattson, Ingrid, 646
Mauryan Empire, 447
Mauss, Armand L., 123–124
mawali, 636
Mazeway, 85. *See* Wallace and revitalization
    movements
McCarran Walter Act 1952, 192. *See* migration
McCloud, Aminah, 649
McGuire, Meredith B., 722
McNeill, William H., 144
meaning, 220–222
Meaning-System Model, 217–220
    Conversion Research Directions, 224–227
    definition of, 221
    Transformation of a Meaning System,
        221–223
Mecca, 3, 31–32, 34, 344, 357, 635, 642, 644, 677
Mead, George Herbert, 123
Mehmed IV, Sultan, 37
Mehta, P. J., 440
meditation, 454–455
Melton, Gordon, 747
Mencius, 546, 549
Mencius, 568
messianism, 515–516, 592, 594
metanoia, 598–599
Methodist Church (Methodism), 73
Michelangelo, 336
Middle East, 49, 632, 637, 646, 648
migration, 68–71, 88, 94, 164, 190–208,
    272–275, 280, 288, 430, 465, 469
millennialism, 757
Min, Pyong Gap, 194
ming, 568
ming yun, 568
Minkov, Anton, 640
Misch, Georg, 354
missionary (religion), 69, 72, 429, 510
    Buddhism, 468, 472, 474–475. See *bhikkhus*
    Christianity, 70–71, 73, 76, 438, 440, 499,
        588, 594, 606, 612–614, 621, 641, 645, 654
    Daoism, 509, 514, 520–524, 526, 528
    Islam, 594, 632–633, 646, 663, 651, 654,
        656n3, 667, 669–670
    Jainism, 451

missionary (religion) (*Cont.*)
  Judaism, 583, 586, 591–593
  Mormonism, 756, 759–762, 764–765,
    767–773, 775
  Nestorian, 173
Mithras, 432
modernization (modernity), 84–85, 88, 90–94,
    96, 102-104, 122, 140, 148–149, 271, 313,
    356, 380, 401, 451, 455, 475, 476–477, 542,
    560, 572, 604, 643, 649
  and Buddhism, 475
  and Christianity, 604
  and Confucianism, 543
  and Islam, 643, 671, 674
Moharpatra, Satyen, 438
Mombassa, 641
monasticism (monks), 444–445
  Buddhist, 470–471, 473, 480–481, 571
  Christianity, 612, 614–615
  Daoist, 509, 517, 521–523, 556
  Jain, 448–450, 453–455
Mongolian, 172
Mongols, 639
Moon, Sun Myung (Rev.), 688, 738, 742
Mormon Church (LDS), 16, 510, 687–689, 711,
    756–785
Morrison, Karl, 616, 621
Moses, 633
mosque, 490, 540, 556, 647, 650–652, 654
Mount Qingxu, 561
Mu-ch'i (Zen artist), 330–331. *See* Six
    Persimmons
Mughals, 494–498
Muhammad, Clara, 655
Muhammad, Elijah, 307, 656
Muhammad (Prophet), 3, 17, 30–31, 34, 165, 178,
    223, 311, 433, 632–633, 635–636, 644, 669
Muhammad, Warith Deen, 307–308, 649
Müller, Max, 429, 473
Murad, Khurram, 647, 650
Muslims, 3, 6, 26–27, 31–37, 48–54, 56–58, 62,
    70–74, 114, 144, 149, 167, 171, 173–174, 182,
    217, 219, 224, 267–268, 307–310, 313, 357,
    361, 404, 407–408, 415, 436–437, 493–496,
    498, 500, 578, 594–595, 619, 633–656
Muslim Community Center of Chicago, 650
Muslim Student Association, 651

Myer, Birgit, 90–91, 104
mysticism, 37, 213, 245, 445, 508, 521–522,
    527–528, 615, 698, 757

Nanak (Guru), 3, 488, 490–496
Naqshbandi Sufism, 650
narrative, 8, 343–352
  ethical rhetoric, 351–352
  formal system, 346–349
  theory and criticism, 345–346
  political ideology, 349–351
Nash, Manning, 93
Nash, June, 93
Nation of Islam, 34, 307, 309, 646, 649
Native American religions, 515
nativism, 513
Nattier, Jan, 469, 523
Navayana, 478. *See* New Vehicle
nectar, 491
Nestorian, 173
Netherlands, 310, 317, 670, 742
Neville, Robert, 551
neidan, 525
Neo-Confucianism, 549
Nepal, 432
Nevo, Baruch, 216, 225
Northern Ireland, 49, 53
New Age (religions), 48, 477, 608, 652,
    670–671, 692
Newman, John Henry, 610
Newton, John, 348
New Religious Movements (NRM), 633, 647,
    671, 687–706, 737–741
New Vehicle, 478–479. *See* Buddhism
New York, 454
New York Times, 454
Nichiren Shoshu Buddhism, 122–123
Niebuhr, Reinhold, 466
Nietzche, Frederick, 350
Nigeria, 50
Niyogi Committee, 437
Niyogi, M. B., 437
Nizami, Khawaja Hasan, 638
Noahide Rules, 589–591
Nock, Arthur Darby, 5, 89, 583, 611
non-missionary (religion), 429
non-proselytizing (religion), 71, 429–430, 435

North Africa, 637
Norway, 603
Nubian Islamic Hebrews, 649

Oceania, 59, 62–63
Olcott, Henry Steel, 473
Old Path White Clouds, 476
Oman, 641
Orissa (India), 437–439
Orissa Freedom of Religion Act, 439
Orthodox, 606
Ostrowski, Ally, 480
Ottoman Empire, 11, 27–37, 637, 639–640,
    643–644
Overmyer, Daniel L., 559, 572
Oxford University, 473

Pacific Islands, 175
paganism, 614, 618
pahul, 491, 494–495
Pakistan, 432, 488, 500, 638, 644
Palestine, 644, 648
Pali (district), 449
Papua New Guinea, 30, 90, 101, 103
Panth, 488, 494
para-Church, 439
Paramahamsa, Ramakṛṣṇa, 434
passover, 578, 590
Patanjali, 448
Paul (Saint), 3, 466, 539, 583–586, 592, 594, 598,
    607, 613, 620, 622
Pentecostals, 87, 100, 183, 410, 414
People of the Book, 633
People's Republic of China, 543, 556, 563, 694
Parameswaran, Ashvin, 151
Peirce, Charles S., 382–384
Persian, 578–579, 581, 632, 635
Peterson, Linda, 348
Pew Religious Landscape Survey, 274–276,
    279–280, 288, 468, 767
Peyote, 85. *See* revitalization movements
phenomenology, 14, 319, 383, 509–510
Philippines, 175, 766, 768
Pietists, 33, 118, 603–604, 607, 616
piety, 5, 25–26, 30, 32–34, 304, 308, 546, 550,
    560, 579, 583, 589, 609, 620, 641, 643,
    659n53, 679, 680n49, 681

Plato, 2, 349, 360–361
Platonism, 2
Popular Western Taoism (PWT), 526
Portugal, 74, 641
Posten, Larry, 645, 647, 650
postmodernity, 643
Pratt, James B., 213
Pratt, Parley P., 758
preksha, 455–456
Presbyterian, 143, 183, 194, 616, 692
primal (tribal) religions, 12, 429, 432, 556, 610,
    613–614, 621
proselytize, 71, 429, 439–440, 444, 449, 451,
    457, 510, 586–591, 618, 689, 736–748, 756,
    762, 764–765, 772–773
Protestantism (Protestants), 53, 69–70, 73,
    75–76, 439, 476, 579, 602–604, 606,
    612–614, 616–617
Proudfoot, Wayne, 609
psychoanalysis, 216, 257, 479
Priest, Robert J., 126
Punjab, 488–490, 492, 494–501
Puratan Janam Sakhi, 491. See *Janam Sikhi*
Puri, Harbhajan Singh, 501

qi, 559
Qigong (Ch'i-kung), 527
Qing, Jiang, 547
Qing Ming Festival (*Qingming*), 544, 563–564
Quanzhen, 516–517, 520–522, 524
Qur'an, 30–32, 262, 267, 308, 633–636, 644–645,
    653, 674, 677

Rababai, Pandita, 1–2
rabbi (rabbinic), 588–594, 596
Radhakrishnan, Sarvepalli, 430
Raika (people), 449
Rahit Maryada, 488, 501
Rajasthan (India), 437, 449, 450
Ramadan, 651–652, 669
Ramakrishna, 1, 433
Ramayana, 447
Rambo, Lewis, R., 444, 466–467, 474–475, 479,
    509, 545, 599, 610, 668
Rastafarianism, 75
rational choice, 141, 183, 285, 477, 539, 571, 578,
    582, 594–596, 604–605, 611, 671, 674

Ratzinger, Cardinal Joseph, 469. *See* Pope
    Benedict XVI
reconversion, 287, 434, 438–439, 599, 714
Reformation, 69, 73, 75
Reina, Rubin, 93
Reinders, Eric, 149
religion, definition of, 241
    as *sui generis* or ascriptive, 245
    as universal or plural, 245
    as insider or outsider perspectives, 245
    as ordinary or extraordinary
        perspectives, 245
Restorationism, 756, 758–760, 774n5
resurgence (of religion), 51–52, 557, 560,
        563–564, 568, 572, 621
revelation, 495, 508, 515–518, 528
reversion (as homecoming), 431, 668–670
revert, 633, 654–655, 669
revitalization, 4, 17, 84–85, 100, 103–104, 482,
        556–557, 572, 691–692
revitalization movements, 84–85
Ricci, Matteo, 266–267
Richardson, James T., 6–8, 290, 539, 746
Ricoeur, Paul, 350, 359–360, 368
Rigdon, Sydney, 758, 761
Rightly Guided Caliphs, 632
rija, 633
Rinpoche, Sogyal, 482
Rites Controversy (China), 513, 542
Rite of Christian Initiation for Adults
        (RCIA), 540
ritual, 8, 71, 77, 509, 622, 709, 719
    Buddhism, 571
    Chinese indigenous religions, 556–564,
        567, 572
    Christian, 598–599, 612, 616–618, 621
    Confucianism, 538, 540–551
    Daoism, 508, 516, 520, 522, 524–525
    Hindu, 638
    Islam, 634, 651, 669, 677–678, 681
    Jain, 444–445, 448, 450
    Judaism, 578–579, 588, 590–591, 593
    Mormonism, 759–760, 762, 765
    Sikh, 489, 494–497, 501
Robbins, Joel, 84, 100, 414
Robbins, Tom, 746
Robertson, Roland, 465

Rolle, Richard, 615
Roman Catholics, 53, 69, 70–71, 73–76, 439,
        511–513, 517, 606, 613–617, 670, 674, 688
Roman Empire, 73–74, 583
Romanization, 26–28, 35
Rouse, Carolyn Moxley, 307–310
Russell, James, 612–613
Rust, Val, 756

Sacred Books of the East, 473
sacred space, conversion of, 34–36
samanis, 455–456, 462n65
samudaya, 467
San Francisco Zen Center, 480
Saler, Benson, 93
Salinger, J. D., 1
sangha, 471
San Giovanni, Lucinda, 721
Sangh Parivar, 439
saomu, 544
Sarapis, 432
Saraswati, Lakshmanananda (Swami), 438
Sarkisian, Natalia, 150
Saudi Arabia, 33, 634, 644, 647, 654
Sauer, Carl, 65
Saul of Tarsus (Paul the Apostle), 3, 18n7, 211,
        336-337, 371, 379, 381, 583–586, 592, 594
Scandinavia, 603, 609, 614, 619, 672
School of Youth for Social Services, 470
Scientology (Church of), 696–697, 738, 742
Scroggs, James R., 215
Sebastian, Rodney, 151
Second Great Awakening, 757
Second Vatican Council, 469
secularization (secular), 49, 52, 55, 479, 491,
        523, 526, 540–541, 556–557, 643, 648
self-cultivation, 508, 521, 538, 545, 548–549
Semiotics, definition of, 374
Seneca, 85–86
Sermons on Conversion to Clerics, 615
Sexton, James, 94
Shaanbei temple, 561–562
Shah, Atul, 453
Shakir, Zayd, 646
Shakta, 403, 493
shahada, 371, 490, 634, 651–652, 662n101,
        667–669, 672

Shambhala Center, 480
Shandong, 521–522
shari'a, 641
Sharpe, Eric J., 433
Shenzhen, 566–571
Shia (Muslims), 490, 635
Shikoh, Dara, 637
Shinto, 432, 514, 525
Shupe, Anson, 715
Shipps, Jan, 758
Shiva (Shaivism), 448–449, 490, 493
Shvetambara, 449, 453–454
Siddhartha, 476
Sikh, 488–507
sikhia, 491
Sindh, 402
Singapore Taoist Mission, 526
Singer, Margaret, 690–692, 695–696
Singh, Fateh, 501
Singh, Gobind (Guru), 494
Singh, Manmohan, 500
Singh, Rajit, 498
Singh, Rana P. B., 76
Singing, 144, 491, 601, 699, 758
Sinicization, 528
Six Persimmons (Zen art), 331
Skonovd, Norman L., 711–712
Skötkonung, Olof, 614
Smilde, David, 151, 412–413, 416
Smith, Christian, 14, 171, 180, 184
Smith, Donald Eugene, 436–437, 440
Smith, John E., 466
Smith, Joseph (Prophet), 3, 757–761, 771
Socrates, 2
soteriology, 467, 529n6
    Buddhist, 467
    Daoist, 514–515, 528
    Hindu, 433–434
    Jain, 457–458n1
    Mormonism, 760
South Africa, 126, 469, 472
South Asia, 29, 32, 308, 445, 457–458n1, 501,
    637–639, 646
Southeast Asia, 31–32, 172–174, 182, 432, 471,
    637, 640–641, 768
Spain, 74, 636–637
Spener, Philip Jacob, 603

Spirit Rock Meditation Center, 474
Sri Lanka, 474
Staples, Clifford L., 123–124
Starbuck, Edwin, 212–213, 216, 608
Stark, Rodney, 6–7, 49, 142–148, 150, 166, 171,
    177, 183, 557, 618, 771–772
Stendahl, Krister, 605
Strickmann, Michel, 517, 520
Stromberg, Peter, 8, 10, 13, 15, 97, 117–139
Stump, Roger B., 71–72
šûb, 578–579, 598
submission, 445
suffering, 472, 481
Sufi (Sufism), 31, 35, 37, 171, 179, 309, 314, 367,
    637, 640, 642–643, 646–650, 652, 655, 670,
    674–675
Sumatra, 98
Sunni (Muslims), 11, 34, 307, 309, 557,
    632, 649
Sure, Heng (Rev.), 474
Suri, Shanti, 450
Suri, Vijay Indradinna, 450
Sweden, 74, 602–603, 614, 619
Swiss Taoist Association, 526
synagogue, 583, 586, 590
syncretization (syncretism), 28–32, 477–478

tabligh, 638
Tablighi Jamaat, 643, 670
Tagore, Rabindranth, 1–2
Taiji quan (T'ai-chi ch'üan), 527
Taiping, 515–516, 518
Taiwan, 469, 471–472, 543
Tajfel, Henri, 165, 183
Tamils, 29–30, 448
Tamilnadu, 448
Tannen, Deborah, 305
tantra, 448, 466
tathagatagarbha, 466
Taoism, 429
Tatian, 611
tawba, 633
tawheed, 669
Taylor, Charles, 359, 361
Taylor, Paul, 744–745
technology, 53, 72, 258, 451, 477, 681
Tegh Bahadur (Guru), 495–497, 504n33

temples, 29, 35, 445, 490, 540, 556
  Buddhist, 469, 479, 562
  Chinese indigenous religions, 556, 558–565
  Confucian, 543, 550
  Daoist, 523–526, 556, 562
  heathen, 614
  Hindu, 438, 445
  Jain, 446–448, 450–451
  Mormon, 759–760, 762–763, 765, 772–773
Tendzin, Osel, 480
Tennant, Gilbert, 616
Testimony (witnessing), 87, 95, 98, 103, 287,
    297, 301, 317, 600, 669, 687, 723, 771
Thailand, 520
Theological Studies, 13
theosebeis, 587
Theosophical Society, 473
Theravada, 466, 474
Thich Nhat Hanh, 466, 469–470, 476,
    478, 482
Thomas (Saint), 437
Thomas, Pradip Nina, 439
Thrift, Nigel, 77
Thurman, Robert, 473–474
tian, 541, 559, 568
tian ming, 568
Tianshi dao, 517
Tibet, 172, 470, 473, 523
Tibetan Book of the Living and the Dead, 482
Tibetan Book of the Dead, 473
Tillich, Paul, 338–339
Tippett, Alan R., 95, 103
Tissot, James Jacques, 337–339
toleration, 169, 173, 435, 477
Tolstoy, Leo, 1
Torah, 580–581, 591–592
Traditional Chinese Medicine (TCM), 527
transference, 478, 481
translation, 479, 578, 581–582, 586, 590
Trehan, Lehina, 493–494. *See* Guru Angad
tribes (tribal), 53, 71, 75–76, 112, 445, 451, 519,
    612, 638, 649
  Arab, 632–634, 636
  Babas (Turkish), 637
  Christian, 439
  Daoist, 519–520
  Ewe of Ghana, 112

Jain, 446, 449–450
  Tswana, 101, 126–127, 302
Trinity, 669, 674
Trungpa, Chögyam, 480
Tswana, 101, 126–127, 302
Tu, Weiming, 551
Turkey, 36–37, 54, 415, 639, 742
Turks, 27, 37, 173–174, 636, 639–640, 643–644
Turner, Bryan, 681
Turner, Richard Brent, 646
Turner, Victor, 99, 330
Twain, Mark, 351
Tweed, Thomas A., 526

ulema, 640
Ullman, Chana, 216
ummah, 636
Umar (Caliph), 635
Umayyad period, 636
Unification Church (a.k.a. "Moonies"), 6, 142,
    688–691, 713, 715, 720, 738–739, 742
Unitarian Universalist, 225
United Kingdom, 267, 300, 742, 745, 768
United Nations, 50, 56, 58, 644
United States of America, 54, 56–57, 60, 68,
    71, 73, 75–76, 454–455, 457, 470, 526, 600,
    603–604, 609, 611, 613, 619–622, 634–644,
    646, 648, 652–653, 670, 737, 739, 741–742,
    744, 766–767
Universal Declaration of Human Rights,
    50, 440
University of California (Berkeley), 66,
    471, 474
University of California (Santa Barbara), 473
University of Edinburgh, 213
University of Washington (Seattle), 471
Upanishads, 2
Uppsala, 614
Urapmin, 30, 101–102
urbanization, 27, 94, 148, 404, 411, 567
Uzbekistan, 746

Vanavasi Kalyan Ashrams, 438
van der Veer, Peter, 90, 104, 638
van Nieuwkerk, Karen, 309–310, 318, 667–686
Varieties of Religious Experience, 5, 297–298,
    607, 609

Vecsey, Christopher, 92
Vedanta, 1
vegetarianism, 444, 449–450, 454, 456
Venerable Xuanhua, 469, 471, 474
Vietnam, 466, 469–471, 478, 482, 520,
    523–524, 551
Vietnam War, 470
Vincent, Peter, 67
vipassana, 474
Vishnu (Vishnava), 448, 490, 493
Viswa Hindu Parishad (VHP), 438–439
Viswanathan, Gauri, 434
Vivekananda (Swami), 1–2

waqf, 640
wali, 636
Wallace, Anthony F. C., 85–87, 103–104, 617
Wallace, B. Allan, 474
Walls, Andrew, 619
Wang, Chongyang, 515–516, 521
Warf, Barney, 67
Warner, R. Stephen, 141, 144, 200
Warring States Period, 563
Wars of Apostasy, 634
Watkins, Owen, 120
Weber, Max, 85, 89–90, 93, 103, 118, 273,
    572, 642
Wesley, John, 607
Wiccans, 689
Witnessing, 97–98, 103, 670
Willems, Emilio, 93
Wilson, Pete, 471
Wilson, Thomas, 541
Wohlrab-Sahr, Monika, 310, 673, 675
women, 2, 27, 30, 53, 73, 99, 101, 126, 146, 151,
    177, 192, 225, 297–319, 355, 357–358, 360,
    431, 471, 501, 518, 544, 561, 580–581, 588,
    593, 643, 648, 653–654, 667–668, 672–673,
    676–678, 680–681, 699, 715, 756
Wood, Peter, 90
Woodhead, Linda, 151

Woodruff, Wilford (Mormon President), 762
Woods, Robert H., 151
World Parliament of Religions (Chicago), 1
worldview, 7, 16, 96–97, 143, 199, 312, 413–414,
    477, 510, 517, 538, 548
worship, 76, 432, 469, 588
    Chinese indigenous religions, 560–564, 567
    Christianity, 586, 590
    Confucianism, 541–547, 550
    Hinduism, 431
    Jain, 444–445, 447–448, 450
    Jewish, 586, 588–590
    pagan, 614
    Sikh, 488–490, 493, 495, 498, 504n33
wu, 571

Xavier, Francis, 380

yakshas, 448
Yang, C. K., 540, 557–559, 564, 567
Yang, Fenggang, 149–150
Yang, K. S., 570
Yemen, 641
Yijing (Classic of Changes), 527
yin-yang, 527
yoga, 1, 249, 328, 448, 453–456, 458, 501
Young, Brigham, 761–762, 764, 768, 773, 781n104
yuan fen, 568–571, 575n45

Zablocki, Benjamin, 722
zakat, 636, 653, 669
Zanzibar, 641
Zenana missions, 298–299
Zen, 330–331, 335, 467, 477, 479, 510, 527,
    549. *See* Ch'an
Zhang, Daoling, 517
Zhejiang Province, 564
Zhongguo, 512
Zhu, Xi, 549
Zion, 759–763
Zoroastrianism, 74, 429–430